JEHANE BENOIT'S
ENCYCLOPEDIA OF COOKING

JEHANE BENOIT'S ENCYCLOPEDIA OF COOKING

BRIMAR

ERPI

Editorial coordination
Jonathan Paterson

Editing
Jane Broderick
Robyn Bryant
George Ferzoco
Jeanine Floyd
Liliana Melillo
Carolyn Muessig

Proofreading
Joan Irving

Index
Christine Jacobs
Christina Richards

Graphic design
Dufour & Fille

Production
André Thérien
Philippe Morin

Photos
Paul Martin Studio

Films
Pré impression Trans-continentale inc.

Printing
Métropole Litho inc.

Acknowledgment

The table of wine suggestions on page 701 is adapted with permission from *Pour mieux apprécier les vins et les fromages*, published by Les fabricants de fromages fins du Québec, le ministère de l'Agriculture, des Pêcheries et de l'Alimentation du Québec, Les producteurs de lait du Québec and la Société des alcools du Québec.

The publishers wish to thank the following businesses for their assistance in arranging the cover photograph.

Arthur Quentin
Appareils ménagers M.L.
Boutiquatou
Ébénisterie Réal Moore

Registration of copyright: 3rd quarter 1991
Bibliothèque nationale du Québec
National Library of Canada

ISBN 2-7613-0665-1   1234567890 ML 987654321
                                                    2099
PRINTED IN CANADA

TABLE OF CONTENTS

PREFACE

In the fall of 1989, I went horseback riding in the Rockies. There is no better way to see their legendary beauty. A day of riding the rugged trails, even with a hearty breakfast and a sandwich at lunchtime, was enough to sharpen the weakest appetite. When we reached our campsite in the late afternoon, there was a general rush to the cook's tent.

The cook was ready for us, smiling behind his steaming pots. And his kitchen was well equipped: a gas oven, saucepans, skillets, measuring cups, ladles, knives, chopping boards and, on a long shelf, jars of dried herbs, glasses and four or five books. One of them, I saw with a twinge of pride, was *Jehane Benoit's Encyclopedia of Cooking*. In spite of its size and weight, it had earned a place among the essentials carried on a pack-horse. And when asked, the cook admitted that without it he would feel ill-equipped.

Since my wife's death, I have come to realize the daily value of her work. In addition, her methods, her advice and her recipes reflect her personality, which goes to explain why so many people seem to know her, not just her *Encyclopedia*. While thousands actually met her, the *Encyclopedia* has been a constant comfort and companion to many more. All of them credit her with classifying and enlarging our culinary heritage, and with inspiring both professional chefs and those who use her *Encyclopedia* to improve their daily fare.

I take great pleasure in seeing her work take on new life with this edition, and I am sure that my pleasure will be widely shared.

BERNARD BENOIT

Québec, New Brunswick and British Columbia all claim the best salmon. Which you prefer is a matter of taste. Québec's comes from the Gaspé Peninsula and reaches the markets in May.

Fishing guides, who have a well-deserved reputation for fish cookery, broil small trout over an open fire of well-dried maple or brown them in a large cast-iron skillet with a little salt pork.

This traditional cuisine is inherited from the French settlers and adapted to a North American environment. This is what makes it a regional cuisine imbued with intuition and common sense, a cuisine for grand family occasions. At Christmas, for example, and on New Year's Day, the fare is invariably traditional: the Christmas Yule log, garnished with butter cream and surrounded with pine branches and holly; tourtière, served piping hot after Christmas Eve mass; steaming, aromatic oyster soup, made with oysters from the Gulf of St. Lawrence; roast turkey stuffed with potatoes; cranberry sauce; and plum pudding, another contribution from the English, served hot with butter sauce.

In this *Encyclopedia* you will find hundreds of these traditional recipes as well as recipes from other countries and culinary traditions. I hope that they will encourage you to develop your own personality as a cook—everyone can make their own inimitable dishes. Dexterity is important, but the knack also depends on personality and character. Nervous types can ruin steaks by being too impatient to wait for the pan or the butter to reach the right temperature. The absent-minded serve hard-cooked eggs that they meant to be soft. Flavor depends on the quantities of ingredients that all cooks vary according to taste and availability. A recipe, in fact, is a theme on which everyone can improvise.

My greatest desire in writing this book was to enable each of you to cook within your means and aptitudes. Rather than eating "failed" recipes at every meal, it is better to make one successful dish a day.

In China, a chef is called "Dai See Fooh," which means "grand master of culinary arts." Chefs are treated with great reverence and with the deference due to their high standing and vast culture.

The settlers found game to delight any gourmet: fat, tasty partridge, redolent of the berries they eat and of fir trees; wild geese finer and tenderer than any duck; deer, moose and even beaver, whose tail makes excellent stew. Hare is best just after the first snows—then its meat is firmer and tastes of the pine buds it eats. Game and venison were served with apples, with cabbage, in pies and stews, or with brown gravy.

In colonial times, the English ate a "sea pie" made of six layers of pastry filled with fish, potatoes and sliced onions, sprinkled generously with salted water and baked for several hours. It has kept its name but not its spelling or its ingredients: "cipaille" is now a Christmas dish, a traditional Québec feast with layers of pork, chicken, hare and partridge, flavored with thyme, savory, parsley and onion. The bottom layer is filled with a thick stock which steams and scents the other layers of pastry and meat as the cipaille is baked for eight to twelve hours.

French-Canadian pea soup is known and liked throughout North America. In winter, the "habitants" used to make large quantities at a time. They would then freeze it, simply by putting it outside. When some was needed, they broke off a piece and melted it slowly over low heat, filling the kitchen with the aroma of onions, pork, dried peas and savory.

Baked beans have a double origin, both French and English. The French colonists simmered dried beans with onions and wild thyme, to eat as a meal by itself or with a leg of lamb on special occasions. The English cooked their beans with molasses and rum. Rum is no longer used, but molasses is, and the beans are preferably cooked in an earthenware pot, which originally was fired in the bread oven.

Chicken pie is traditionally served at the New Year and for the family supper on Sundays. It is prepared with a fat, tender hen, simmered with herbs and a few vegetables. When the meat comes easily off the bone, it is immersed in a light, creamy white sauce made from the reduced stock. Potatoes, green peas and onions are then added, and the filling is poured in a terrine dish lined with pastry. Topped with another layer of pastry, it is browned in a moderate oven as the sauce gives off its appetizing aroma.

Pumpkin pie, made in the fall, is almost unknown in France and came to Québec from New England.

Building on your knowledge, your artistic sense will help you observe, plan and give free rein to your imagination. And it will constantly suggest new ideas to try.

Eating is one of the few pleasures that we can enjoy at any age. And the lore of cooking, in days of famine and abundance, has enriched itself to become an art reflected in poetry, in literature and in music. Charming legends and beliefs about cookery are transmitted from generation to generation.

A country's cuisine bears witness to its geography and history, to the ingenuity of its people and to their traditions. To this are added long periods of trial and experience.

The cuisine of Québec, which forms the basis of this book, is no exception. And its people are proud, as are peoples everywhere, of the regional variations that provide richness and variety to a cuisine marked by simplicity and originality.

The early French settlers brought culinary traditions with them from France, adapted them to their needs, then transmitted and transformed them from generation to generation. Using the resources of the forests and plains, of the lakes and rivers and of the sea, Québec cuisine is French in origin but North American in inspiration.

The Indians taught the settlers to smoke meat, to broil fish wrapped around stakes of maple and to find parsley, thyme, savory, blueberries and healing herbs in the woods.

The Jesuits noticed a sugary residue on game, boiled by the Indians in maple sap. This observation was the origin of maple syrup and maple sugar, used in many delicious desserts.

From Brittany the settlers brought a taste for buckwheat crêpes and cakes, sometimes eaten with butter and sugar, as in France, but more often with molasses. Brown sugar and molasses were introduced from the West Indies by the English, who also brought various spices.

Also from Brittany came the wood-burning ovens, built outside but next to the house (a few of these ovens still survive). Large round loaves, made with potato yeast, were baked on the stone floor of the oven. What could be better than a thick slice of home-made bread toasted on a wood stove and spread with creamed butter?

Other regions of France made other contributions: cretons, doughnuts and various kinds of crêpes from Poitou, for example, and partridge with cabbage, apple crêpes, duck with apple stuffing and various soups from Normandy.

THE IMPORTANCE
OF BASIC PRINCIPLES

Cooking may be an art, but knowing how to cook requires, besides talent, an understanding of the important role that a healthy, balanced diet plays in maintaining health.

Diet has a great influence on the development of the human body and thus on the well-being of our children.

Just as there are different ways of cultivating various fruits and vegetables, different ways of raising various animals, in cooking there are basic rules that are the foundations on which everything is built. Learning and understanding these rules helps simplify daily life and brings health and vitality to one's family.

A knowledge of these basic rules is also the surest way to learn to eat healthily—by cooking healthy foods well and by organizing varied menus that avoid monotony. In this *Encyclopedia of Cooking*, you will find these basic rules in the appropriate chapters.

I firmly believe that it is useless to collect hundreds of recipes if you do not know when it is better to roast than to braise or broil, in other words if you do not know the fundamental principles of cooking. Many times I have seen people with vast collections of recipes make elementary errors, such as leaving scrambled eggs on the heat until they are done: they keep on cooking for several seconds after they are removed from the heat.

I sincerely hope that you will read and apply these rules carefully—they will make your life easier. For example, when you know how to cook one kind of roast, you know how to cook any roast: the same principles apply. Your knowledge will quickly enlarge your horizons and will be a source of new ideas.

Creative, original cooking becomes easy once you have mastered all the principles that are the foundation of the art. From that moment on, you can let your imagination fly and improvise with culinary flair and finesse.

Here is an example of what I mean by "flair and finesse." If you add puréed spinach or a little tomato paste to mashed potatoes, you will have green or pink potatoes, each with its own special flavor. The result is agreeable to the eye and to the palate. But if you know the basic principles, you know that adding spinach will make the mashed potatoes thinner; because of this, you will reduce the quantity of liquid.

Remember that you can earn a reputation as an inimitable first-rate cook if you have a thorough knowledge of the elementary rules of cooking and if you add variations suggested by your imagination, culture and artistic sense. That is culinary flair and finesse. Perhaps you will become a "Dai See Fooh" to your family or friends and will receive the esteem that goes with the title.

Jehane Benoît

GENERAL
INFORMATION

EQUIPPING YOUR KITCHEN

Equipping your kitchen to suit both your needs and your tastes makes cooking a pleasure rather than a chore.

❧ An efficient kitchen is equipped so that everything is within easy reach. Your cooking implements should not be hidden from view; on the contrary, their visibility is an indication of your experience and skill as a cook. The following list of dishes and implements will help you equip your kitchen.

ESSENTIAL

Dinner plates, 8 to 16
Cups and saucers, 8 to 16
Soup bowls, 8 to 16
Water glasses, 8 to 16
Wine glasses, 8 to 16
Juice glasses, 8 to 16
Teaspoons, 8 to 16
Dessert spoons, 8 to 16
Soup spoons, 8 to 16
Dinner forks, 8 to 16
Dessert forks, 8 to 16
Dinner knives, 8 to 16
Measuring cups, 2
Measuring spoons, set
Mixing bowls, set
Grater
Wooden spoons, 3 assorted
Whisk, stainless steel
Ladle
Skimmer
Rubber spatulas, 2
Egg beater
Sifter
Bread board
Rolling pin
Muffin pan

Square cake pan
Bread pan
Round layer-cake pans, 2
Baking sheets, 2
Pie plates, 2
Cake rack
Potato peeler
Potato masher
Vegetable brush
Sieves, 1 small, 1 large
Funnel, medium-size
Skillets, small, 2
Skillet with cover
Saucepans, 1 large, 2 small
Casserole dish with cover
Stewing pot
Double boiler
Kettle
Roasting pan, large
Dripping pan
Teapot
Coffeepot
Bread knife
Paring knife
Utility knife
Chef's knife
Kitchen scissors
Can opener
Bottle opener
Corkscrew

USEFUL

Side plates, 8 to 16
Dessert dishes, 8 to 16
Platters
Vegetable dishes
Gravy boat
Salad bowl
Cake plate
Creamer and sugar basin
Salt and pepper shakers
Butter dish
Coffee mugs
Demitasses for espresso
Ramekins
Iced tea glasses, 8
Whiskey glasses, 6 to 8

Cocktail glasses
Bowls for dessert, soup or fruit, or as finger bowls, 6 to 8
Liqueur glasses, 6 to 8
Brandy snifters, 6 to 8
Champagne flutes (more practical than goblets)
Beer mugs
Punch set
Seafood cocktail set
Steak knives, 6 to 8
Butter knife
Iced-tea spoons
Demitasse spoons
Seafood forks
Fish knives and forks
Fruit knives and forks
Grape scissors
Nutcracker
Tea strainer
Dessert knife
Cheese knife
Lobster cutters
Blender
Electric mixer
Electric coffee grinder
Coffee maker (espresso, steam, filter, etc.)
Electric kettle
Waffle iron
Pressure cooker
Fine teapot
Glass or porcelain pitchers for milk or water
Ice bucket
Decanters for wine, sherry, liquor
Cocktail shaker
Cheese board
Soufflé dishes
Cutting board
Assorted saucepans
Soup tureen
Hors d'oeuvre tray
Bread basket
Wine basket
Pepper grinder
Fondue set

KITCHEN ARITHMETIC

EQUIVALENT WEIGHTS AND MEASURES

INGREDIENT	WEIGHT	MEASURE
Almonds, whole	1 oz (30 g)	18 almonds
Bacon	1 lb (500 g)	22 to 26 strips
Butter	¼ lb (125 g)	½ cup (125 mL)
Butter	½ lb (250 g)	1 cup (250 mL)
Butter	1 lb (500 g)	2 cups (500 mL)
Butter, margarine or lard	1 oz (30 g)	2 tbsp (30 mL)
Carrots	1 lb (500 g)	5 to 10 carrots
Cocoa	1 lb (500 g)	4 cups (1 L)
Cheese, Canadian	¼ lb (125 g)	1 cup (250 mL) grated
Cheese, cottage	½ lb (250 g)	1 cup (250 mL)
Cheese, grated	1 lb (500 g)	4 cups (1 L)
Cherries	1 lb (500 g)	2¾ cups (675 mL) pits removed
Chicken, boned	5 lbs (2.3 kg)	4½ cups (1.1 L)
Chocolate, unsweetened	1 oz (30 g)	1 block
Dates, pits removed	1 lb (500 g)	2 cups (500 mL)
Dates, pits removed	1 lb (500 g)	2½ cups (625 mL) chopped
Fat, vegetable	1 lb (500 g)	2½ cups (625 mL)
Flour	1 oz (30 g)	1 tbsp (15 mL)
Flour	1 lb (500 g)	4 cups (1 L)
Flour, corn	1 lb (500 g)	3 cups (750 mL)
Flour, rice	1 oz (30 g)	1 tbsp (15 mL)
Flour, sifted	1 lb (500 g)	4½ cups (1.1 L)
Flour, whole-wheat	1 lb (500 g)	3½ cups (875 mL) unsifted
Legumes	1 lb (500 g)	2 cups (500 mL)
Macaroni	1 lb (500 g)	8 cups (2 L) cooked
Marshmallows	½ lb (125 g)	15 marshmallows
Molasses	1 lb (500 g)	1⅓ cups (325 mL)
Onions	1 lb (500 g)	4 to 8 onions
Peaches	1 lb (500 g)	2½ cups (625 mL) sliced
Pears	1 lb (500 g)	2½ cups (625 mL) cooked
Peas, green	1 lb (500 g)	1 cup (250 mL) unshelled
Plums	1 lb (500 g)	4 cups (1 L) cooked
Raisins	1 oz (30 g)	1 tbsp (15 mL)
Rhubarb	1 lb (500 g)	2 cups (500 mL) cooked
Rice	1 lb (500 g)	2 cups (500 mL)
Rice	1 lb (500 g)	6 cups (1.5 L) cooked
Semolina	1 oz (30 g)	1 tbsp (15 mL)
Spaghetti	1 lb (500 g)	8 cups (2 L) cooked
Sugar	1 oz (30 g)	1 heaping tbsp (15 mL)
Sugar	1 lb (500 g)	2¼ cups (550 mL)
Sugar, brown	1 oz (30 g)	1 tbsp (15 mL) well packed
Sugar, brown	1 lb (500 g)	2¾ cups (675 mL) well packed
Sugar, icing	1 oz (30 g)	1 tbsp (15 mL)
Sugar, icing	1 lb (500 g)	4 cups (1 L)
Tomatoes	1 lb (500 g)	3 medium
Walnuts, chopped	¼ lb (125 g)	1 cup (250 mL)
Walnuts, shelled	1 lb (500 g)	3 to 4 cups (750 mL to 1 L) chopped
Walnuts, unshelled	1 lb (500 g)	2 cups (500 mL)

EQUIVALENT QUANTITIES AND MEASURES

QUANTITY	MEASURE
Apples, 3 medium, sliced	3 cups (750 mL)
Bananas, 3 medium, sliced	2½ cups (625 mL)
Crackers, dry, 30 small, crumbled	1 cup (250 mL)
Crackers, Graham, 11, crumbled	1 cup (250 mL)
Crackers, soda, 7, crumbled	1 cup (250 mL)
Cream, whipping, 1 cup (250 mL)	2 cups (500 mL) whipped
Eggs, 5 whole	1 cup (250 mL)
Egg whites, 8 to 10	1 cup (250 mL)
Egg yolks, 12 to 14	1 cup (250 mL)
Lemon, juice of 1	3 to 4 tbsp (45 to 60 mL)
Lemon, zest of 1	1½ tsp (7 mL)
Orange, juice of 1	6 to 8 tbsp (90 to 120 mL)
Orange, zest of 1	1 tbsp (15 mL)
Pineapple, 1	2½ to 3 cups (625 to 750 mL) diced
Potatoes, 3 medium, sliced	3 cups (750 mL)
Raisins, 1 15-oz (450-g) box	2½ cups (625 mL)

IMPERIAL TO METRIC CONVERSION TABLE

IMPERIAL	METRIC
1 tsp	5 mL
1 tbsp	15 mL
2 tsp	15 mL
2 tbsp	30 mL
3 tbsp	45 mL
4 tbsp	60 mL
¼ cup	50 mL
⅓ cup	75 mL
½ cup	125 mL
⅔ cup	150 mL
¾ cup	175 mL
⅘ cup	200 mL
1 cup	250 mL
2 cups	500 mL
3 cups	750 mL
4 cups	1 L
1 oz	30 g
¼ lb	125 g
⅓ lb	150 g
½ lb	250 g
¾ lb	375 g
1 lb	500 g

FAHRENHEIT TO CELSIUS CONVERSION TABLE

FAHRENHEIT	CELSIUS
150°F	70°C
200°F	100°C
250°F	120°C
275°F	140°C
300°F	150°C
325°F	160°C
350°F	180°C
365°F	185°C
375°F	190°C
400°F	200°C
425°F	220°C
450°F	230°C
475°F	240°C
500°F	260°C
525°F	270°C
550°F	290°C

PANS AND DISHES IN STANDARDIZED METRIC VOLUME

	METRIC VOLUME
Cake pans	2 L
	2.5 L
	3 L
	3.5 L
	4 L
	5 L
Round layer-cake pans	1.2 L
	1.5 L
Spring-form pans	1.5 L
	3 L
	4.5 L
Tube pans (sponge, angel food cake)	2 L
	3 L
Jelly-roll sheets	1 L
	2 L
Dishes	500 mL
	750 mL
	1 L
	1.5 L
	2 L
	2.5 L
	3 L
	4 L
Ramekins	150 mL
	200 mL
	250 mL
	300 mL
	500 mL
	750 mL
Loaf pans	1.5 L
	2 L
	3 L
Pie plate	1 L

SIZES OF BAKING PANS AND DISHES USED IN THIS BOOK

ROUND LAYER-CAKE PANS

8 x 1¼ in. (20 x 3 cm)
8 x 1½ in. (20 x 4 cm)
9 x 1½ in. (23 x 4 cm)

SQUARE CAKE PANS

8 x 8 x 2 in. (20 x 20 x 5 cm)
9 x 9 x 2 in. (23 x 23 x 5 cm)

LOAF PANS

9 x 5 x 3 in. (23 x 13 x 8 cm)
10 x 5 x 3 in. (25 x 13 x 8 cm)
10 x 6 x 2 in. (25 x 15 x 5 cm)
11 x 7 x 1½ in. (27.5 x 18 x 4 cm)
12 x 8 x 2 in. (30 x 20 x 5 cm)
13 x 9 x 2 in. (32.5 x 23 x 5 cm)

JELLY-ROLL SHEET

15½ x 10 x 1 in. (39 x 25 x 2.5 cm)

TUBE PANS
(sponge, angel food cake)

9 x 3½ in. (23 x 9 cm)
10 x 4 in. (25 x 10 cm)

CUPCAKES OR MUFFIN PANS

2½ x 1¼ in. (6 x 3 cm)
3 x 1½ in. (8 x 4 cm)

SPRING-FORM PAN

9 x 3 in. (23 x 8 cm)

PIE PLATES

4 in. (10 cm)
5 in. (13 cm)
6 in. (15 cm)
7 in. (18 cm)
8 in. (20 cm)
9 in. (23 cm)

RING MOLDS
(aspics, jellies)

3 cups to 11 cups (750 mL à 2.75 L)
5 cups to 12 cups (1.2 L à 3 L)

EATING NUTRITIOUSLY

Eating well does not mean resorting only to natural foods or taking all kinds of food supplements. You need to eat a regular daily diet of nutritious food, but you do not need to give up all the little treats that you enjoy. It is useless to eat a fresh fruit salad instead of birthday cake if you are then going to revert back to your bad eating habits.

❧The basic principles of a healthful diet are simple ones. Every individual has his or her own personal nutritional and energy needs, but it is essential that everyone's daily intake include foods from each of these four food groups:

❧ milk and dairy products
❧ meat, fish and poultry and their substitutes
❧ breads and cereals
❧ fruits and vegetables

❧ Under milk and dairy products, the suggested servings will vary with age as well as with calcium, vitamin D and protein requirements. Generally, children under 11 should have two or three servings a day; adolescents, pregnant women and nursing mothers require three to four servings per day; and all other adults should have two servings a day.

❧A typical serving of milk or dairy products would be 1 cup (250 mL) milk; 3/4 cup (175 mL) yogurt; or 1½ oz (45 g) cheese.

❧The average person requires two daily servings of meat, fish or poultry or their substitutes.

❧A sample serving would be 2 to 3 oz (60 to 90 g) lean meat, fish, poultry or liver (cooked); 2 eggs; or 1 cup (250 mL) cooked lentils. Amino acids are the main component of protein. Unlike animal protein, vegetable protein—such as that found in legumes—does not contain all the amino acids that are essential to the body. The human body can manufacture most of the amino acids that it requires, but only by eating certain foods can we supply those that are lacking.

❧Your body will get all the amino acids it requires if you have at least two servings of carefully selected protein foods every day: for example, you could eat animal protein and vegetable protein together (macaroni and salmon, chili con carne); or one meal could include two types of vegetable protein that together supply the essential amino acids (baked beans with bread, lima bean salad and almonds).

❧From the breads and cereals food group, everyone should have between three and five servings a day, depending on the energy level required. For example, an office worker who sits all day from Monday to Friday would need three servings a day during the week, but five servings a day on the weekend when he or she goes cross-country skiing.

❧A serving in the bread and cereal food group could be 1 slice of bread; a roll; or ½ to ¾ cup (125 to 175 mL) pasta or cooked rice.

❧From the last essential food group, fruits and vegetables, you should eat four to five servings a day, making sure that at least two of these are vegetables.

❧A typical serving would be ½ cup (125 mL) vegetables or fruit (fresh, frozen or canned); ½ cup (125 mL) vegetable or fruit juice; 1 potato; 1 tomato; or 1 peach.

❧Fruit juice, by the way, must be the real thing and not punch, a fruit-flavored drink or crystals.

❧A great number of the recipes in this book combine foods from the different food groups. They offer excellent suggestions for interesting and healthy eating.

FOOD ENERGY VALUES

All foods supply energy. The energy value of each food is expressed in the form of calories or kilojoules. A surplus of food energy in relation to its expenditure in physical activity will lead to obesity in either the short or the long term.

❧ Research in this area appears to indicate that obese persons are more susceptible to diabetes, hypertension and cardiovascular disease.

❧ To maintain good body weight, you should ensure that there is an equilibrium between the supply and the expenditure of energy. As a general reference, the energy intake recommended for a woman between 25 and 49 years old would be around 1900 calories (8000 kilojoules). A man in the same age group would require about 2700 calories (11,300 kilojoules). The energy needs of a younger, more active person would be higher, while those of an older, less active person would be lower.

❧ "Calorie counters" should be aware that foods contain not only calories, but also ingredients that are essential to the body, such as proteins, sugars, dietary fiber, fat, vitamins and minerals. It is therefore extremely important that as you watch your calories, you make sure that you are getting all the nutrients that are essential to good health.

❧ The following table lists the energy values of a carefully selected range of foods.

Food	Calories	Kilojoules
Almonds, chopped, 1 cup (250 mL)	650	2720
Almonds, shelled, 12	85	360
Apple, 1 medium	80	330
Applesauce, sweetened, ½ cup (125 mL)	100	430
Applesauce, unsweetened, ½ cup (125 mL)	55	230
Apricot, fresh, 1	15	70
Apricots, cooked, 3 halves with 2 tbsp (30 mL) juice	40	170
Apricots, dehydrated, 8 halves	70	280
Artichoke, 1 medium	55	220
Asparagus, cream of, ½ cup (125 mL)	85	360
Asparagus spears, 8	30	130
Avocado, ½	160	670
Bacon, grilled, 4 small strips	100	420
Banana, 1 medium	105	440
Beans, green or wax, cooked, ½ cup (125 mL)	20	80
Beans, lima, cooked, ½ cup (125 mL)	110	460
Beef, ground lean, grilled, 3¼ in. (8 cm) in diameter, ½ in. (1.2 cm) thick	210	880
Beef, meat loaf, 1 slice 4 x 6 x ⅛ in. (10 x 15 x 0.4 cm)	70	300
Beef, rib, roasted, lean only, 1 slice 4¼ x 2½ x ½ in. (11 x 6 x 1.2 cm)	195	820
Beef, salt, lean, boiled, 3½ oz (100 g)	190	800
Beef, steak, bottom round, grilled, lean only, 4½ x 2½ x ½ in. (11 x 6 x 1.2 cm)	155	650
Beef stew, lean, 1 cup (250 mL)	330	1380
Beet greens, ½ cup (125 mL)	40	170
Beets, 2.2 in. (5 cm) in diameter	50	200
Biscuits, baking powder, 2.2 x 1¼ in. (5 x 3 cm)	205	860
Blueberries, fresh, ½ cup (125 mL)	45	180

FOOD	CALORIES	KILOJOULES
Bologna, 1 slice, 4¼ in. (11 cm) in diameter, ⅛ in. (0.3 cm) thick	60	260
Bouillon, 1 cup (250 mL)	15	70
Brazil nuts, 2	45	190
Bread, French, 4-in. (10-cm) baguette	70	300
Bread, pita, 1.6 in. (15 cm) in diameter	165	690
Bread, white, 1 slice	75	310
Bread, whole-wheat, 1 slice	70	300
Breadcrumbs, dry, 1 cup (250 mL)	415	1740
Broccoli, 1 cup (250 mL)	50	200
Brussels sprouts, 6	50	200
Butter, 1 tbsp (15 mL)	100	420
Buttermilk, 1 cup (250 mL)	105	440
Cabbage, cooked, ½ cup (125 mL)	25	100
Cabbage, raw, chopped, ½ cup (125 mL)	20	80
Cabbage salad, ½ cup (125 mL)	45	180
Cake, chocolate, iced, ¹⁄₁₆ of a cake 8 in. (20 cm) in diameter	215	900
Cake, fruit, 1 slice ¼ x 2 x 1½ in. (0.6 x 5 x 4 cm)	60	250
Cake, homemade, sponge, ¹⁄₁₆ of a cake 8¾ in. (22 cm) in diameter	95	400
Cake, homemade, white, without icing, 1 piece 3¼ x 3¼ x 2 in. (8 x 8 x 5 cm)	315	1310
Cake, strawberry shortcake	450	1880
Cake, strawberry shortcake with whipped cream	550	2300
Cantaloupe, ½, 5 in. (13 cm) in diameter	95	400
Carrots, ½ cup (125 mL)	35	160
Cauliflower, ½ cup (125 mL)	20	80
Celery, ½ cup (125 mL)	10	40
Celery, cream of, 1 cup (250 mL)	175	730
Cheese, Cheddar, 1-in. (2.5-cm) cube	70	280
Cheese, Cheddar, grated, 1 tbsp (15 mL)	30	120

Food	Calories	Kilojoules
Cheese, cottage, creamed, ¼ cup (50 mL)	55	210
Cheese, cream, 2 tbsp (30 mL)	100	430
Cheese soufflé, ½ cup (125 mL)	110	460
Cherries, 10 large	50	200
Chicken, roast, without skin, 3½ oz (100 g)	190	790
Chicken salad, ½ cup (125 mL)	220	920
Chocolate, bitter, 1 oz (30 g)	140	590
Chocolate éclair	240	1000
Chocolate, milk chocolate, 1 oz (30 g)	160	660
Chocolate milk, whipped, 2 cups (500 mL)	365	1520
Clams, 6 medium	70	300
Cocoa powder, 1 tbsp (15 mL)	35	140
Coconut, grated, sweetened, 1 tbsp (15 mL)	210	870
Cod, grilled, 1 filet, 5¼ x 2½ x 1¾ in. (13 x 6 x 2 cm)	110	460
Cola, 1 cup (250 mL)	100	420
Consommé, 1 cup (250 mL)	15	70
Cookie, chocolate drop, 2¾ in (7 cm) in diameter	40	170
Corn, 1 ear, 6 in. (15 cm)	95	390
Corn, creamed, canned, ½ cup (125 mL)	100	420
Cornflakes, 1 cup (250 mL)	90	370
Crackers, Graham, 2	55	220
Crackers, soda, 4	50	200
Cream, 15%, 1 tbsp (15 mL)	25	100
Cream, 35%, 1 tbsp (15 mL)	55	210
Cream, cereal, 1 tbsp (15 mL)	25	80
Cream, whipped, 1 tbsp (15 mL)	25	100
Croissant, 1 medium	235	990
Cucumber, 1, 8½ x 2¼ in. (21 x 5.4 cm)	40	170
Currants, fresh, ½ cup (125 mL)	35	140

FOOD	CALORIES	KILOJOULES
Custard, ½ cup (125 mL)	160	670
Dates, 4	90	400
Doughnut, 1 plain, 3½ in. (9 cm) in diameter	50	200
Dressing, Italian, 1 tbsp (15 mL)	95	390
Duck, roasted, meat only, 3½ oz (100 g)	200	840
Egg, 1	80	330
Eggs, scrambled, ¼ cup (50 mL)	100	420
Figs, 1 dried	50	200
Filberts, ¼ cup (50 mL)	160	670
Frankfurter, 1	180	760
Fudge, chocolate, 1-in. (2.5-cm) square	80	340
Grapefruit, ½ medium	40	170
Grapes, 14 large	45	180
Halibut, grilled, 1 filet, 4 oz (125 g)	215	900
Ham, lean only, 4 oz (125 g)	190	750
Honey, 1 tsp (5 mL)	25	100
Ice cream, vanilla, ½ cup (125 mL)	145	600
Icing, chocolate (for cake), ¼ cup (50 mL)	250	1040
Juice, grape, sweetened, ½ cup (125 mL)	70	280
Juice, lemon, 1 tbsp (15 mL)	5	20
Juice, orange, unsweetened, 1 cup (250 mL)	120	500
Juice, pineapple, unsweetened, 1 cup (250 mL)	150	620
Juice, tomato, 1 cup (250 mL)	20	90
Kiwi, 1 medium	45	190
Lamb, chop, 1, grilled, lean only, 3 oz (90 g)	160	680
Lamb, roasted, lean only, 3 oz (90 g)	170	710
Leek, 1	40	170
Lemon, 1 medium	15	70

Food	Calories	Kilojoules
Lettuce, iceberg, ¼ head	15	70
Liver, braised, 3½ oz (100 g)	170	700
Macaroni and cheese, ⅔ cup (150 mL)	270	1140
Macaroni, cooked, ½ cup (125 mL)	85	350
Mackerel, grilled, with butter, 3½ oz (100 g)	235	990
Mayonnaise, 1 tbsp (15 mL)	100	420
Milk, condensed, unsweetened, ½ cup (125 mL)	180	750
Milk, ice, vanilla, firm, ½ cup (125 mL)	100	420
Milk, skim, 1 cup (250 mL)	90	380
Milk, whole, 1 cup (250 mL)	160	660
Muffin, bran, 1	105	440
Oats, plain, cooked, ½ cup (125 mL)	115	480
Olives, 4 small	15	70
Onions, cooked, 3 to 4 small	60	250
Orange, 1 medium	60	250
Oysters, 5 medium	65	270
Parsnip, ½ cup (125 mL)	70	300
Peaches, canned, unsweetened, 2 large halves with ¼ cup (50 mL) juice	70	300
Peach, fresh, 1 medium	35	160
Peanut butter, 1 tbsp (15 mL)	100	420
Peanuts, shelled, ½ cup (125 mL)	440	1830
Pear, fresh, 1 large	100	420
Pears, canned, unsweetened, 2 halves with 2 tbsp (30 mL) juice	80	330
Peas, dried, raw, ½ cup (125 mL)	400	1670
Peas, green, canned, ½ cup (125 mL)	60	250
Pea soup, 1 cup (250 mL)	200	840
Pecans, 6	155	650
Pepper, green, 1 medium	15	60
Pie, apple, ⅙ of 9-in. (23-cm) pie	405	1690

Food	Calories	Kilojoules
Pie, lemon meringue, ⅙ of 9-in. (23-cm) pie	355	1490
Pie, mincemeat, ⅙ of 9-in. (23-cm) pie	430	1790
Pie, pumpkin, ⅙ of 9-in. (23-cm) pie	320	1340
Pie, raisin, ⅙ of 9-in. (23-cm) pie	425	1780
Pie, rhubarb, ⅙ of 9-in. (23-cm) pie	355	1490
Pineapple, canned, crushed, in heavy syrup, ¼ cup (50 mL)	40	170
Pineapple, canned, unsweetened, 1 slice with 2 tbsp (30 mL) juice	55	220
Pineapple, fresh, 1 slice ¾ in. (2 cm)	45	190
Popcorn, plain, 1½ cups (375 mL)	35	150
Pork, 1 chop, grilled, lean only	150	620
Pork sausage, cooked, 1 oz (30 g)	55	230
Potatoes, boiled, 1 medium	115	480
Potatoes, French-fried, 10	110	460
Potato salad, ½ cup (125 mL)	190	790
Prunes, 3 medium	60	250
Pumpkin, baked, mashed, ½ cup (125 mL)	25	100
Radishes, 4 medium	5	20
Raisins, dried, ¼ cup (50 mL)	85	360
Raspberries, fresh, ½ cup (125 mL)	30	130
Rhubarb, cooked, sweetened, ½ cup (125 mL)	150	620
Rice pudding with raisins, ½ cup (125 mL)	205	860
Rice, steamed, ½ cup (125 mL)	100	420
Salmon, pink, canned, ½ cup (125 mL)	130	550
Sardines, canned, 2.3 in. (7 cm)	20	80
Sauce, Hollandaise, 1 tbsp (15 mL)	15	60
Sauce, white, thick, 1 tbsp (15 mL)	30	130
Semolina, cooked, ¾ cup (175 mL)	320	1340

Food	Calories	Kilojoules
Squash, cooked, ½ cup (125 mL)	45	180
Strawberries, fresh, ½ cup (125 mL)	25	100
Sugar, 1 tsp (5 mL)	15	70
Syrup, corn, 1 tbsp (15 mL)	60	260
Syrup, maple, 1 tbsp (15 mL)	55	230
Tapioca, ½ cup (125 mL)	120	490
Tapioca, apple, ½ cup (125 mL)	155	650
Tofu, 1 piece 2½ x 2¾ x 1 in. (6 x 7 x 2.5 cm)	85	360
Tomatoes, canned, ½ cup (125 mL)	25	100
Tomato, cream of, 1 cup (250 mL)	170	710
Tomato, fresh, 1 medium	25	100
Tuna, canned, in oil, ½ cup (125 mL)	170	700
Tuna, canned, in water, ½ cup (125 mL)	100	450
Turnip, ½ cup (125 mL)	15	60
Veal, roasted, fat and lean, 3½ oz (100 g)	270	1130
Waffle, 1.6 in. (15 cm) in diameter	205	860
Watercress, chopped, 1 cup (250 mL)	5	20
Watermelon, 1 slice 10 in. (25 cm) in diameter, 1 in. (2.5 cm) thick	145	600
Yogurt, plain, 1.5% M.F., ½ cup (125 mL)	80	330
Yogurt, with fruit, 1.5% M.F., ½ cup (125 mL)	135	570

ESSENTIAL NUTRITIONAL ELEMENTS

PROTEINS

Proteins are composed of amino acid chains that serve in the production and regeneration of body tissue (skin, nerves, bone, etc.). They are found in many different foods: milk and dairy products, meat, poultry, fish, legumes, eggs, nuts and grains.

SUGARS

Sugars are present in many foods. Certain sugars are digestible (simple sugars, complex sugars), while others are not (dietary fiber).

☙ Simple sugars, which are digested easily and absorbed rapidly, include white sugar, molasses, honey, maple syrup, and jellies and candy. Although these foods do supply energy, they contain few if any vitamins or minerals and are therefore of little nutritive value. This is not the case with simple sugars in the form of fruit, fruit juice, vegetables, milk and yogurt. These foods not only supply energy, but they are also a good source of vitamins and minerals.

☙ Complex sugars are formed by the joining together of many simple sugars. Foods that contain complex sugars include bread, corn, potatoes, cereals, rice, pasta and legumes. As well as being rich in complex sugars, these foods are also a good source of protein, vitamins and minerals. Some are high in dietary fiber as well.

Dietary fiber is found only in vegetables. Its principal characteristic is that it cannot be digested by the body. Dietary fibers fall into two groups: soluble fibers and insoluble fibers.

☙ Examples of soluble fiber are the gums that are found in oat bran and legumes and the pectin in fruits and vegetables. Soluble fibers help reduce blood cholesterol levels, and they also help stabilize glycemia (blood sugar levels) in diabetics.

☙ Insoluble fiber is present in breads and whole-grain cereals. If it is ingested with water, it acts as a natural laxative to help prevent or correct constipation problems. When soaked in water, insoluble fiber facilitates the formation of soft stools, resulting in regular elimination.

☙ People with hearty appetites should note that all soluble and insoluble fibers produce a sensation of fullness very rapidly.

☙ At present, there is a great deal of research being carried out on fiber. The results appear to indicate that regular fiber intake, together with a low-fat diet, may help diminish the risk of certain cancers.

LIPIDS

Fatty matter, or lipids, supplies twice as much energy as sugars or protein. If you want to lose weight, you should certainly reduce your intake of lipids, but not eliminate them entirely. Lipids play an essential role in the transport and absorption of vitamins A, D, E and K. They also help maintain body temperature and produce a feeling of fullness.

☙ Lipids are found in oil, butter, vegetable fat, lard, margarine, meat (even lean meat), poultry, fish, eggs, milk and dairy products. Certain foods, such as nuts, cold cuts, gravies, salad dressings, pies, pastries and cakes, contain much more fatty matter than one might expect.

☙ There has been much talk these past few years about the problems associated with cholesterol.

☙ Cholesterol is a fatty substance produced by the liver and circulated in the blood. It is essential in the synthesis of vitamin D and hormones, and it enters into the cellular membrane structure. Problems arise when blood cholesterol levels become elevated, causing the development of cardiovascular disease.

☙ Cholesterol is found in egg yolk, liver, giblets, seafood, butter and other animal fats. But, as we have seen, cholesterol that originates in food is not necessarily the only cause of high cholesterol levels, since it is produced by the liver as well.

❧ When trying to decrease blood cholesterol levels, it is a good idea not to eliminate all foods that contain cholesterol. It is better to reduce your total intake of fats and saturated fats—coconut oil, palm oil, butter, cream, whole milk, cheese made from whole milk and other animal fats—and to eat more complex sugars and dietary fibers.

VITAMINS AND MINERALS

Vitamins and minerals are essential in very small amounts for the growth and functioning of the body.

VITAMINS AND MINERALS	FUNCTION	MAIN SOURCES	CHARACTERISTICS	REMARKS
Vitamin A	Helps form teeth and bones. Maintains healthy mucous membrane and skin. Assures good vision in the dark.	Liver, kidney Eggs Milk Fruits and vegetables	Sensitive to light	Excessive amounts of vitamin A will turn the skin orange and could even be toxic.
Vitamin B (thiamine, riboflavin, niacin)	Helps make the most of food energy. Helps the functioning of the nervous system. Contributes to normal growth. Stimulates the appetite.	Meat, fish and poultry and their substitutes Breads and cereals	Thiamine content is modified by cooking; riboflavin is sensitive to light.	There are many kinds of vitamin B, all of which have similar functions. These are called the B complex vitamins.
Vitamin C	Helps maintain healthy teeth and gums. Contributes to the healing process. Keeps the blood vessels in good order.	Fruits and vegetables (particularly broccoli, Brussels sprouts, cauliflower, oranges, grapefruit, tomato and vegetable juice, cantaloupe, kiwis, vitamin-enriched apple juice)	Can be destroyed by heat and by exposure to air or light	It is important to take vitamin C every day, since it does not accumulate in the body.

Continued on page 16

[15]

Vitamins and Minerals	Functions	Main sources	Characteristics	Remarks
Vitamin D	Helps form and maintain healthy bones and teeth.	Exposure of the skin to the sun (the sun's rays activate the vitamin D under the skin) Enriched margarine Milk	Sensitive to light	Essential to calcium absorption
Iron	Conveys oxygen in the blood. Component of red blood cells.	Meats (particularly giblets) Egg yolk Legumes Nuts and grains		Iron absorption will be augmented by eating a food rich in vitamin C in the same meal.
Calcium	Plays a role in blood coagulation. Contributes to normal functioning of the nervous system. Helps form and maintain healthy teeth and bones. Aids the growth process.	Milk Cheese Yogurt		Excessive quantities of phosphorus, obtained through the over-consumption of carbonated drinks or caffeine, for example, will hinder calcium absorption.

COOKING WITH A PRESSURE-COOKER

Cooking with a pressure-cooker has a number of advantages. It is very quick, saving both time and cooking fuel. Food cooked in the pressure-cooker usually looks attractive, for the color of the food is preserved. It also retains its flavor. Furthermore, pressure cooking conserves precious vitamins and minerals.

🍃 Most important, however, is that the tougher, less expensive cuts of meat can be cooked until deliciously tender in a fraction of the time that conventional cooking takes.

🍃 Much of the vitamin content of food, particularly vitamin C, is lost when food is cooked for a long time, which is often required by regular cooking methods. The small amount of water required in pressure cooking keeps vitamin and mineral loss down to the very minimum. The fact that pressure cooking takes place virtually without air also eliminates the problems of nutritional loss associated with oxidation.

🍃 It is very important that the food is cooked as quickly as possible. It is therefore essential to respect the cooking times and the instructions given for cooling the pressure-cooker.

🍃 Using a pressure-cooker is so simple that anyone can do it. Following the instructions and the recommended cooking times carefully ensures that every recipe is a success. A pressure-cooker is useful for preparing desserts and baby food. Because it maintains a constant temperature, food is cooked evenly in very little time.

🍃 By using the basic recipes that follow, you will soon be concocting your own recipes for pressure-cooked meals.

KNOWING YOUR PRESSURE-COOKER

Pressure-cookers come in various sizes and are made of either aluminum or stainless steel. Make sure you know the capacity and particular features of the model you have, and always follow the manufacturer's instructions very carefully.

🍃 It is important to keep the cover and inside edges of your pressure-cooker clean to ensure a tight fit. Remove the sealing ring often to wash it, especially after cooking meat or fatty foods.

🍃 After the cooker has been in use for a long period, the sealing ring may shrink slightly. If this happens, change the ring as soon as possible, following the manufacturer's instructions.

🍃 To ensure optimum performance from the pressure-cooker, replace the valve on the air vent when the sealing ring is replaced. It is useful to keep a new sealing ring and valve at hand; they can be bought at large stores or directly from the manufacturer.

USING AND CARING FOR YOUR PRESSURE-COOKER

Before using your cooker for the first time, remove the sealing ring. Wash the ring, the groove and the automatic air vent to remove manufacturing oils and grease.

🍃 Scour the inside of an aluminum cooker carefully with a good non-alkaline aluminum cleanser or a steel wool cleaning pad. Gently wash a stainless steel one with a mild cleaner or fine steel wool. After the cooker and the rack have been washed and rinsed with warm water, the cooker is ready for use. It is not necessary to wash the pressure regulator.

🍃 Never store your cooker with the cover locked on as it may retain cooking odors. The cover may be turned upside down on the cooker; this will allow circulation of air and reduce the risk of odors. Always keep the cooker in a dry place.

🍃 A little unsalted cooking fat or salad oil may be applied to the sealing ring occasionally if the cover becomes hard to close. Make sure the vent pipe is open and clean before each use.

🍃 When removing the cover to open the cooker, make sure the pressure regulator is removed first. If the cover seems to stick or is hard to turn, it means that there is still pressure in the cooker, and further cooling is necessary. After the cooker has cooled, but before you attempt to open it, tilt the pressure regulator and check the automatic air vent to determine whether the pressure has been reduced in the cooker.

🍃 It is important to place the cooker in a pan of cold water or under running water whenever a recipe requires you to. Do this immediately after the cooking time has elapsed. Do not run water on the safety valve as water may be drawn into the cooker when the pressure is completely reduced.

❧ Different foods require different procedures. When braising or frying meats, heat the pressure-cooker, place a spoonful of fat in the bottom and sear the meat in the open cooker. Allow the cooker to cool slightly, then pour in a small amount of water while the meat remains in the pan. Place the cover on the cooker and close it securely. Then follow the cooking time as given in the specific recipe.

❧ To cook vegetables, place them on the rack in the bottom of the pot and add a little water. (Fresh vegetables require very little liquid.) In 2½- and 3½-qt (2½- and 3½-L) cookers, use ½ cup (125 mL) water; in 5-qt (5-L) cookers, use 1 full cup (250 mL). Legumes and dehydrated vegetables or fruits should be covered with water.

❧ It is extremely important to remember that the cooker should never be filled to more than ⅔ of its capacity.

❧ Soups, stews and most cereals are cooked in the bottom of the cooker without the rack.

COOKING MEAT IN A PRESSURE-COOKER

MEAT	COOKING TIME IN MINUTES UNDER 15 LBS (6.8 KG) PRESSURE	AMOUNT OF LIQUID TO BE ADDED AFTER SEARING ON ALL SIDES
Beef, corned	12 to 15 per lb (500 g)	2 cups (500 mL) water
Beef heart, stuffed	45	1 cup (250 mL) water
Beef, pot roast	8 to 10 per lb (500 g)	½ cup (125 mL) water
Beef, short ribs	25	½ cup (125 mL) water
Ham loaf	20	½ cup (125 mL) water
Ham, picnic, plain cut 4 lbs (1.8 kg)	30	1 cup (250 mL) water
Ham shank	35	1 cup (250 mL) water
Ham, slice 3 to 4 lbs (1.4 to 1.8 kg)	30	½ cup (125 mL) water
Hamburger patties	5	¼ cup (50 mL) water
Lamb, leg of	12 to 14 per lb (500 g)	½ cup (125 mL) water
Meatballs	10	½ cup (125 mL) water
Meat loaf	15	½ cup (125 mL) water
Pork loin roast	12 to 15 per lb (500 g)	½ cup (125 mL) water
Spareribs with barbecue sauce	15	¼ cup (50 mL) water
Steak, Swiss	15	½ cup (125 mL) water
Steak, Swiss, deluxe	15	1 cup (250 mL) tomato soup
Tongue, fresh	45	2 cups (500 mL) water

COOKING MEAT IN A PRESSURE-COOKER

MEAT	COOKING TIME IN MINUTES UNDER 15 LBS (6.8 KG) PRESSURE	AMOUNT OF LIQUID TO BE ADDED AFTER SEARING ON ALL SIDES
Tongue, smoked	55	3 cups (750 mL) water
Veal, braised	15 per lb (500 g)	½ cup (125 mL) water
Veal, sliced	10	1 cup (250 mL) water
Veal, spicy	15	1 cup (250 mL) cream
Veal steak, breaded	10	1 cup (250 mL) cream

COOKING POULTRY IN A PRESSURE-COOKER

POULTRY	COOKING TIME IN MINUTES UNDER 15 LBS (6.8 KG) PRESSURE	AMOUNT OF LIQUID TO BE ADDED AFTER SEARING ON ALL SIDES
Chicken fricassée	15 to 25	½ cup (125 mL) water, + 1 cup (250 mL) milk
Chicken, fried 2 lbs (1 kg)	10	½ cup (125 mL) water
Chicken, fried 2 to 4 lbs (1 to 2 kg)	15 to 20	½ cup (125 mL) water
Chicken paprika	15	1 cup (250 mL) cream
Chicken, pressed	15	3 cups (750 mL) water
Chicken, savory	15	1 cup (250 mL) water
Chicken stew	20	2 cups (500 mL) water
Chicken, whole 2 to 4 lb (1 to 2 kg)	20 to 30	½ cup (125 mL) water

COOKING VEGETABLES IN A PRESSURE-COOKER

VEGETABLES	PREPARATION	WATER REQUIRED	COOKING TIME IN MINUTES
Asparagus	Wash and snap off tough parts; large ends may be used in soup	½ cup (125 mL)	1 to 2
Beans (green, lima)	Shell and wash	½ cup (125 mL)	2 to 3

COOKING VEGETABLES IN A PRESSURE-COOKER

VEGETABLES	PREPARATION	WATER REQUIRED	COOKING TIME IN MINUTES
Beans (green or wax)	Wash; remove ends and strings; cut in 1-in. (2.5-cm) pieces	½ cup (125 mL)	3 to 4
Beets (whole)	Wash thoroughly; remove all but 3 in. (7.5 cm) of top and do not remove roots; after cooking, slip skins off	½ cup (125 mL)	10 to 18
Beet greens	Always select young, tender leaves; remove wilted leaves; wash thoroughly several times, lifting from water after each washing	½ cup (125 mL)	3
Broccoli	Wash; score stems; remove leaves and tough parts of stalk	½ cup (125 mL)	2 to 3
Brussels sprouts	Wash; remove wilted leaves; leave whole	½ cup (125 mL)	3
Cabbage	Remove wilted outside leaves; wash and quarter	½ cup (125 mL)	3 to 4
Carrots	Wash and scrape or peel; or leave whole sliced;	½ cup (125 mL)	3 if sliced; 4 to 8 if whole
Cauliflower	Wash; hollow out core or florets;	½ cup (125 mL)	2 if separated into florets; 5 if whole
Celery	Separate stalks; remove tough, stringy fibers; wash and scrape well; cut into ½-in. (1-cm) pieces	½ cup (125 mL)	2 to 3
Corn on the cob	Remove husk and silk; wash	1 cup (250 mL)	3 to 5
Onions (whole) or Bermuda onions	Wash and peel	½ cup (125 mL)	5 to 7
Parsnips	Wash, peel or scrape; leave whole or cut in half lengthwise	½ cup (125 mL)	7 if halved; 10 if whole

COOKING VEGETABLES IN A PRESSURE-COOKER

Vegetables	Preparation	Water required	Cooking time in minutes
Peas (green)	Wash and shell	½ cup (125 mL)	1 if small; 2 if large
Potatoes in jackets	Wash and scrub thoroughly	1 cup (250 mL)	15
Potatoes (for mashing)	Wash and peel; leave small potatoes whole; cut large potatoes in half	1 cup (250 mL)	10
Potatoes (small)	Wash and scrub new potatoes thoroughly	1 cup (250 mL)	10
Rutabagas	Wash, peel and dice	½ cup (125 mL)	3 to 5
Spinach	Always select young, tender leaves; remove wilted leaves; wash thoroughly several times, lifting from water after each washing	½ cup (125 mL)	1 to 3
Sweet potatoes (whole)	Wash and scrub thoroughly	½ cup (125 mL)	10
Turnips	Follow instructions for rutabagas	½ cup (125 mL)	3 to 5
Zucchini	Wash, peel and cut into small pieces	½ cup (125 mL)	10 to 12

🍃 Pour the water required into the cooker. Place the vegetables on the rack. Season before or after cooking. Never fill the cooker more than ⅔ full. Once the cooking time is up, cool the cooker rapidly in cold water to reduce the pressure.

🍃 Different vegetables can be cooked at the same time without losing their flavor or color, provided that they take the same cooking time. Larger vegetables, or those that are less fresh, will take longer to cook.

FREEZING FOODS

Having a freezer and using it intelligently is like having an expandable food budget, or an extra day in the week. A freezer can mean real dividends for the busy homemaker, but only if you learn to use it to best advantage.

Thanks to the freezer, you can store vegetables, fruits, meat, desserts and all kinds of prepared dishes. Your freezer will let you take advantage of market specials by buying large quantities at low prices. It is an excellent way to make substantial savings.

Freezing also saves you time. When cooking regular meals, you can easily double or triple many recipes and freeze the extra. This is particularly useful when you are cooking dishes that take a long time, such as stew, beans or pea soup. And you need never be caught unprepared: if an unexpected guest arrives at mealtime, something from the freezer can be served up at a moment's notice.

It is important to take the time to learn about freezing—how to prepare, package, freeze and store food—and how to cook frozen foods properly.

USING AND CARING FOR YOUR FREEZER

Freezers, like work schedules and budgets, must be used efficiently if you are to make the most of the freezer space you have. Good freezer management starts with a plan. Every household has different needs, but the following questions should help you work out your own plan.

Do you have children? What are their ages and dietary needs?

Is there anyone in the family who needs a special diet?

What does your family like and dislike?

What fresh produce can you get easily?

What do you like to serve when you entertain?

How much time do you have? What kind of cooking do you enjoy?

What is the capacity of your freezer?

What savings can you make by freezing various foods?

By freezing your family's favorite dishes, using them when required and replacing them with other produce, you will ensure an efficient turnover. The freezer works best when it is kept full.

Get into the habit of keeping an accurate inventory. Knowing what is on hand will help you plan more interesting meals, and it will ensure that foods get used within their maximum storage limits. A glance at the inventory will tell you what you need to replace.

The more you use the freezer, the more you will save.

Choose high quality foods. The frozen product will be no better than the food in its original state; freezing will never improve flavor or quality. You cannot freeze food for a lengthy period of time without its flavor and nutritive value deteriorating.

Choose those varieties of fruit and vegetables that freeze well. Fruit should be ripe but firm. Vegetables should be fresh or recently picked. Freeze fruit and vegetables as soon as possible after picking or buying them.

It is important to keep the freezer and its contents clean to reduce the risk of contamination. Some freezers need to be defrosted once a year. Follow the manufacturer's instructions for your model.

FREEZING MEAT

Always keep about 5 percent of your freezer capacity for storing fresh meat. Cut the meat into serving-size portions. Bone it and remove the excess fat. Place the bones in a bag in order to make more efficient use of your freezer space. The fat will freeze well if it is melted first. Wrap the meat in small packages; this way, it will thaw more quickly when the time comes to cook it. Be sure to use proper containers or good freezer paper so that the meat will not absorb unpleasant odors.

When wrapping meat pies, filets or slices of liver, separate them with a double layer of freezer paper. They will then be easier to separate when you are ready to use them.

❧ Cover ham and bacon in two or three layers of freezer paper. Do not freeze for more than two months.

❧ Melted pork fat will keep longer and will retain its flavor better if it is combined with a small amount of vegetable fat. For 50 parts pork fat, use 3 parts vegetable fat.

❧ Do not freeze game for more than six months.

❧ When it comes to freezing an extra large quantity of meat, it may be preferable to ask your butcher or a commercial outfit to cut and freeze it for you. Keep it frozen while transferring it to your freezer.

❧ Buying and freezing a quarter carcass of meat can mean tremendous savings, but it is not suitable for everyone. You should take into account your household's particular tastes. If you are not lovers of stews, soups and braised meats, it may be impractical to buy a side of beef; you would end up wasting too much. You might be better off just buying certain cuts of meat when they are reduced in price.

THAWING MEAT

Allow meat to thaw slowly in its wrappings. It is preferable to thaw it in the refrigerator, but this takes a long time.

❧ Meat will thaw in 2½ hours at room temperature or in 5 to 8 hours in the refrigerator. Well-wrapped frozen meat can also be thawed by placing it under cold running water.

❧ Use meat as soon as it is thawed.

COOKING FROZEN MEATS

It is not really necessary to thaw meat before cooking it; thawed, frozen or partially frozen, it can be juicy and delicious when cooked. Roasts and steaks more than 1½ in. (4 cm) thick, however, will cook more quickly and more uniformly if they are partly thawed. Frozen meat tends to cook much more rapidly on the outside than the inside.

❧ To cook frozen meat, add 10 to 15 minutes per pound (500 g) to the required cooking time.

❧ A 1-in. (2.5-cm) frozen steak will take 13 to 23 minutes to broil.

❧ It is better to thaw poultry in the refrigerator before you cook it. Consult the chart below to see how long this should take.

FREEZING FISH

Most kind of fish freeze well if they are frozen within 24 hours of having been caught and have been kept cold until freezing.

Freeze small fish whole, and large ones as steaks or filets. Place a double layer of wrap between the steaks or filets so that they can easily be separated for cooking. Put only enough fish for one meal in a package, wrap tightly in freezer wrap, seal and label.

❧ Shellfish such as oysters and clams may toughen if they are cooked before freezing, so shuck them and freeze them in containers with their liquid. Crab and lobster, however, should be cooked and the meat removed from the shell before freezing.

❧ Frozen fish and shellfish must never be thawed and refrozen.

FREEZING MAIN DISHES

Always choose ingredients of the highest quality.

❧ Use butter, vegetable oil or peanut oil to brown food used in the preparation of stews or other dishes. Vegetable oils keep better than lard, which tends to spoil after four months.

THAWING POULTRY (in the refrigerator)

CHICKEN

Less than 4 lbs (2 kg)	12 to 16 hours
4 lbs (2 kg) and over	1 to 1½ days

DUCK

3 to 5 lbs (1.5 to 2.5 kg)	1 to 1½ days

GOOSE

4 to 14 lbs (2 to 7 kg)	1 to 2 days

TURKEY

Less than 12 to 18 lbs (5 to 8 kg)	2 to 3 days
18 lbs (8 kg) and over	3 to 4 days

❧ Do not overcook vegetables used in stews and soups. Add them near the end of the cooking period. Meat should be tender, but firm. Macaroni, spaghetti, noodles and rice should also be firm; if they are overcooked before they are frozen, they will be soft and mushy when served.

❧ To freeze stews, spoon the meat and vegetables into the freezer container first and cover with the gravy.

❧ Cool cooked foods quickly before freezing them. To hasten cooling, place the saucepan of cooked food in a large pan of cold water (iced water is best). Stir the food occasionally with a rubber spatula, taking care not to break up or mash it. Main courses can be kept three to four months in the freezer.

❧ Thaw main dishes or sauces in the refrigerator; if you have to thaw them at room temperature, thaw them only partially and then place them in the refrigerator to thaw completely. There is a danger of spoilage if you leave food at room temperature, especially in warm weather. Most main dishes can be heated in a double boiler or a 400°F (200°C) oven without being thawed first.

❧ Take into account the different ingredients that go into a recipe, for freezing affects the taste of different things in different ways. Onion and salt lose much of their flavor once frozen, but garlic, cloves, pepper, green pepper and celery become stronger in flavor. This is why these ingredients are used sparingly.

❧ Add breadcrumbs and grated cheese when the dish is reheated.

❧ If pasta or rice dishes appear dry when they are heated, add about ⅓ cup (75 mL) milk.

❧ Once cooked, ground meat should be frozen in a sauce to prevent drying.

FREEZING VARIOUS FOODS

BEETS
Cook and dice the beets. Freeze in small packets. To serve, place the frozen beets in the top of a double boiler. Add butter, salt and a pinch of sugar. Heat for 15 to 20 minutes.

BROWN SUGAR
Store brown sugar in the freezer so that it will not harden.

CAKES, COOKIES AND BREAD
These all freeze very well.

CAKE FROSTINGS
Butter and icing-sugar frostings freeze well. However, frostings containing egg white should not be frozen.

CELERY
Only the leaves of celery can be frozen. Wash them well, chop, and freeze in plastic bags. Use to flavor stews, soups, mashed potatoes, stuffing, etc.

CUCUMBERS
Peel and grate the cucumbers. Place the pulp in ice-cube trays and freeze. Remove from trays, wrap and freeze. To use in a salad, allow cubes to thaw a little and then crush at the last minute and

toss with the salad. To use for cooking, add the frozen cubes to hot liquids and allow to melt.

EGGS
Eggs can be frozen whole or with the white and yolk separated. Stir whole eggs with a fork to mix them lightly, but do not beat. To 1 cup (250 mL) of egg, add 1 tbsp (15 mL) sugar or 1 tsp (5 mL) salt, depending on how you plan to use the eggs. To use them, thaw them in the refrigerator and use within 24 hours.

❧ Freeze and package egg whites in convenient recipe quantities. The yolks should be stirred with a fork, but not beaten, before freezing.

FRESH HERBS
Freeze fresh herbs in small, labeled individual bags. To use, chop with a sharp knife while still frozen and crisp, or cut with kitchen scissors.

GOOSEBERRIES AND MULBERRIES
Combine these half and half and freeze them, unsweetened, in 4-cup (1 L) containers. Tarts made with this combination are absolutely delicious.

GREEN TOMATOES
Wash and slice. Dip each slice in corn meal. Place the slices side by side on a cookie tray and freeze. Place the frozen slices in small bags. To serve, brown over low heat in oil or other shortening.

LARD AND OTHER SHORTENINGS
Melt the lard (or other shortening) over low heat. Pour through a

strainer over a square cake pan. Allow to cool. Cut into 2-in. (5-cm) squares. Wrap each block separately. This is convenient when you need an exact amount of lard.

LEFTOVER MEAT
Save and freeze small leftover scraps of meat until you have enough to make a fricassée or shepherd's pie.

LEMON JUICE
To have fresh lemon juice at hand whenever you need it, squeeze the juice from very fresh lemons and freeze it in an ice-cube tray. When frozen, remove from the tray and place in a plastic bag.

▪ Lemon juice can also be frozen as follows: mix 1 cup (250 mL) sugar and 1 cup (250 mL) lemon juice. Heat until the sugar dissolves. Freeze in the same way as for fresh lemon juice. Use to sweeten and flavor fruit salads and to make lemonade.

MARSHMALLOWS
Freeze them in their original wrapping; this reduces their tendency to dry out. Frozen marshmallows are easy to cut and will not stick to scissors.

ONIONS
To freeze whole onions, peel them and place in a glass jar. Use them as needed. Freeze grated onion in small quantities in individual plastic bags. Add to stews and soups without thawing.

PEAS AND BEANS
Clean and blanch the peas and beans, spread them on cookie trays and freeze them. Then pour the frozen vegetables into plastic bags or other containers, in individual or family-sized helpings, seal and return to the freezer.

PIES
Pies can be frozen baked or unbaked, although fruit pies taste fresher and have a crisper crust if they are frozen unbaked and then cooked. Baked pies are cooked but not browned, then cooled and frozen; to serve, partially thaw the pie and warm it for ½ hour in a 350°F (180°C) oven. Or you may want to freeze pie fillings in quantities to fill 1 pie; to use, place the unthawed filling in a pastry-lined pie plate and bake in a 425°F (220°) oven.

PIE AND TART SHELLS
Baked pie and tart shells freeze very well, but they must be packaged so that they are not jostled and broken in the freezer.

RHUBARB
Clean the rhubarb stocks. Wrap them in a double layer of freezer paper and freeze. Chop while still frozen and cook.

SWEET PEPPERS
Freeze the peppers whole, diced or cut into strips. Chop the whole peppers while they are still frozen.

PACKAGING FOOD FOR THE FREEZER
It is false economy not to use special freezer paper or proper containers when freezing food. Freezer packaging is specially designed to prevent foods from drying out and hence losing their flavor.

▪ There are two kinds of freezer packaging:

FREEZER WRAP AND BAGS
Some freezer paper is brown or pink on one side and waxed on the other. This type of paper is perfect for foods that you won't be keeping in the freezer for more than two months. But never use ordinary wax paper; use the special freezer kind. And never use the plastic wrapping that bread comes in, as it will not protect the food properly.

▪ Laminated or waterproof paper or polyethylene wrapping is fine for most foods.

▪ Heavy-duty aluminum foil, plastic wrap and sealable plastic bags are ideal for foods that will be frozen for several months, since they are waterproof and air-tight.

CONTAINERS
There are many excellent types of plastic and wax containers made especially for freezing. You should keep in mind that plastic containers and wax cartons won't break, while glass dishes might. Avoid using ice cream cartons, however, as they are too thin and are not waterproof or airtight.

▪ It is wise to use only top quality freezer containers. These may cost a little more, but they'll last longer. You should also consider the shape when shopping for containers: square or rectangular

TIME LIMITS ON FREEZING FOODS

Beef ....6 to 12 months

Bread ....3 months

Bread loaves, wrapped, bought...................................2 weeks

Bread rolls ....3 months

Butter ....6 months

Cake, fruit ....1 year

Cake, frosted..2 to 3 months

Cake, unfrosted ....1 to 2 months

Cookies, baked...9 months

Cookies, unbaked...9 months

Doughnuts ....2 months

Fish...2 to 3 months

Ice cream..1 to 2 months

Lamb...6 to 9 months

Main dishes, cooked, prepared ....3 to 4 months

Meat loaf, cooked..4 to 6 months

Meat patties, cooked...4 to 6 months

Meat, minced ....1 to 3 months

Muffins ....3 months

Pies ....2 months

Pie shells ....2 months

Pork ....3 to 6 months

Poultry ....6 to 12 months

Sandwiches ....2 weeks

Sausages ....1 to 3 months

Soup ....4 months

Stew ....4 months

Veal ....6 to 9 months

packages will take up less freezer space than round ones.

ᨠ When wrapping food for the freezer, you must remove the air. Packages should be hermetically sealed. Make sure you leave a free space of ½ to 1 in. (1 to 2.5 cm) at the top to let the food expand during freezing.

ᨠ Label all packages, indicating clearly the name of the food contained in each as well as the date of freezing. You could also note the number of servings or pieces that you are placing in each package.

ᨠ If you're freezing many different foods at once, place them all in the coldest part of the freezer until they're partly frozen. Then you can move them to whatever part of the freezer you wish to store them in.

ᨠ When freezing several packages of food, place them so that the air can circulate between them. And do not overload the freezer with unfrozen food; freeze only as much food at one time as will not raise the temperature of the foods already stored there. Overloading also keeps new items from freezing quickly enough for optimum quality.

CHAFING-DISH COOKING, FONDUES AND BARBECUES

COOKING
IN A CHAFING DISH

There are three kinds of burners used for chafing dishes. One uses liquid alcohol, the second burns solid fuel (solidified alcohol), and the third has a wick. You can also use an electric skillet to cook food at the table.

❧ Because they are designed to intensify heat, burners fueled with wood alcohol get hot quickly. This type of burner is highly versatile, though, and may be adjusted to a slow, lazy flame. Wood alcohol is comparatively inexpensive and will last longer than solid fuel.

❧ Burners that use solid fuel produce a lazy flame and are especially suitable for slow cooking. They can be used for almost any purpose, such as keeping cooked food warm. Because solid fuel is relatively expensive, it can be costly if used on a regular basis.

❧ A third type of heating unit is the wick alcohol burner, which is similar in principle to the old kerosene lantern. Its flame is rather small and gives off little heat. It is therefore best suited to chafing dishes used solely as food warmers. This type of burner goes back to the old days in England, when sumptuous feasts were the rule. Chafing dishes (then called warming pans) played an important part in keeping a large number of dishes warm on the sideboard until serving time.

❧ An electric skillet can be used to cook food at the table. It is both easy to use and practical.

❧ It is extremely important that the heat given off by the burner is easy to regulate. Open the holes completely for maximum heat. Close them partially with the cover to reduce the temperature.

❧ Another way to control the heat is to place the food in a dish of hot water. (This only applies to certain recipes.) This ensures that the food heats slowly and evenly.

❧ If you're just beginning to prepare food in this way, you can arrange an attractive tray with all the ingredients and utensils you will need for the recipe. Ideally this tray should be rectangular; it will lend itself to all kinds of uses.

❧ If the ingredients are arranged attractively (which will take a few minutes), the display will not only be pleasing to the eye but it will also be mouth watering. It is important to arrange the ingredients in the order in which they are used in the recipe.

❧ Here are some tips to make this kind of cooking easier.

❧ It is a good idea to coat meatballs with bread or cracker crumbs rather than flour. The coating will be firmer and crunchier.

❧ Soy sauce and piquant sauces enhance the appearance of meat cooked in a chafing dish. If brushed on meat before it is cooked, the meat assumes a nice golden color.

❧ Use the chafing dish as a double boiler to keep food warm until it is ready to serve.

❧ Cut the ingredients into evenly shaped portions and arrange them attractively.

❧ Place all the ingredients in the order required by the recipe.

❧ To decorate dishes served in a sauce, keep back some of the ingredients and chop them finely. Use them to garnish the dish when it is ready to serve.

❧ To give a recipe a special look, garnish with spirals of sour cream when it is ready. Serve immediately.

❧ Dishes flavored with garlic are always delicious. Here are some tricks to ensure that the dish has all the flavor of garlic without using large amounts in its preparation.

❧ Stick a clove of garlic with a toothpick so that you can remove it easily when the dish is cooked.

❧ Mince the garlic and crush with coarse salt to make a paste.

❧ Crush the garlic without salt.

❧ Browned flour enhances the flavor of side dishes prepared in the chafing dish. Sauces made with wine or spices are particularly improved if browned flour is used (see page 46).

FONDUES

All around the world, people love to get together over a delicious fondue. Whether Swiss, French or Oriental, fondues all originate from the same peasant custom in which everyone happily ate out of the same pot. However, geographical, climatic and cultural factors have resulted in the creation of fondues that differ from one country to another.

❧ Although technically "fondue" means "melted," the word has taken on a broader significance, since it implies not only the dish itself, but the entire ritual that surrounds it. As an example, Fondue Bourguignonne does not actually involve melting a food, but plunging it in simmering oil. In a sense, meat fondue is closest to the first known fondues—the Peking Fire Kettle, the Japanese Shabu-Shabu and the Mongolian Fire Pot.

❧ When serving a fondue, it is extremely important to observe a few safety rules.

❧ Before using your fondue pot for the first time, carefully read the manufacturer's instructions.

❧ Use a ceramic or pottery fondue pot for cheese fondue. To prevent the cheese becoming tough, keep the burner flame very low.

❧ For Fondue Bourguignonne, or fondues that require very hot oil, always use a metal fondue pot. Other kinds cannot withstand the temperature of the oil and may crack. To prevent accidents, fill the fondue pot only halfway with oil. Heat the oil in the fondue pot on your conventional stove before moving it to the table stand. Light the burner and set the flame at high to keep the oil boiling.

BARBECUING

Line the base of the barbecue with a layer of aluminum foil, for easy cleaning later.

❧ Arrange a small amount of charcoal in the firebox of the barbecue. To obtain optimum performance from your barbecue, it is important to use the best quality charcoal. Here is a little tip that will ensure an excellent barbecue every time: decide how much fuel to use depending on the cooking time required. Use 1 in. (2.5 cm) charcoal for every 15 minutes of cooking.

❧ Light the fire 40 to 80 minutes before starting to cook the food. Wait until the coals are glowing hot and covered with a fine layer of gray or white ash.

❧ Cooking times and temperatures are always difficult to assess when barbecuing. This guide should make the task easier.

❧ For a rare steak, place the meat on a grill 3 to 4 in. (8 to 10 cm) above the coals.

❧ For a medium or well-cooked steak, place the meat 5 to 6 in. (13 to 15 cm) from the heat.

❧ For pork or lamb, the temperature should be lower but more even: place the meat 6 in. (15 cm) from the coals.

❧ Place portions of food that cook quickly, such as fish, 2 in. (5 cm) from the heat.

BARBECUE EQUIPMENT

Long-handled fork

Large spoon

Spatula

Tongs for turning the food—1 wide, 1 narrow

Iron or enameled cast-iron skillet with long handle

Heatproof gloves

Hinged wire broiler for fish

Large carving board

Sharp knives—1 large, 1 small

Small brush for basting

Roll of paper towels

Roll of aluminum foil

Heat-resistant tray to hold food or pans

Tray to hold seasonings, herbs and sauces

Scissors

Skewers (12 to 24) for shish kebab, 6 to 24 in. (15 to 60 cm) long

BARBECUING GUIDE

			Meat Temperature			
Meat/Fish	Size	Recommended heat	Rare 130°F–140°F (55°C–60°C)	Medium rare 140°F–145°F (60°C–65°C)	Medium 145°F–155°F (65°C–70°C)	Well done 155°F–180°F (70°C–85°C)
Beef						
Steak	1 in. (2.5 cm)	high	5 to 6 min.	7 min.	7 to 8 min.	10 min. or more
Steak	1½ in. (4 cm)	high	6 to 7 min.	8 to 9 min.	10 min.	12 to 15 min.
Steak	2 in. (5 cm)	medium-high	8 to 10 min.	10 to 15 min.	15 to 18 min.	20 min. or more
Steak	2½ in. (6.5 cm)	medium-high	12 to 15 min.	15 to 17 min.	18 to 23 min.	25 min. or more
Flank steak	whole	high	4 to 5 min.	5 to 6 min.	—	—
Hamburger	1 in. (2.5 cm)	medium-high	4 min.	5 min.	6 min.	7 min. or more
Sirloin	whole	moyen	12 to 15 min.	15 to 17 min.	18 to 23 min.	—
Lamb						
Chops	1 in. (2.5 cm)	medium	4 to 5 min.	6 min.	6 to 7 min.	8 min. or more
Chops	1½ in. (4 cm)	medium	5 to 6 min.	7 min.	8 to 9 min.	10 min. or more
Chops	2 in. (5 cm)	medium	6 to 7 min.	8 min.	9 to 10 min.	12 min. or more
Pork						
Chops	1 in. (2.5 cm)	medium-low	—	—	—	13 to 18 min.
Chops	1½ in. (4 cm)	medium-low	—	—	—	15 to 23 min.
Chops	2 in. (5 cm)	medium-low	—	—	—	20 to 30 min.
Ham, slice	1 in. (2.5 cm)	medium-low	—	—	—	15 to 18 min.
Ham, slice	1½ in. (4 cm)	medium-low	—	—	—	18 to 23 min.
Spareribs	whole	very low	—	—	—	1 hour
Poultry						
Chicken	1½ to 2 lb (750 g to 1 kg)	medium	—	—	—	20 to 30 min.
Chicken	split in 2	medium	—	—	—	15 to 30 min.
Duck	split in 2	medium-low	4 to 6 min.	6 to 8 min.	9 to 15 min.	15 to 25 min.
Squab	split in 2	medium	—	—	—	12 to 18 min.
Fish						
Steak	1 in. (2.5 cm)	Do not overcook or the fish will be dry; it is cooked when easily flaked with a fork.			3 to 5 min.	
Steak	1½ in. (4 cm)				4 to 6 min.	
Filets or half	small				3 to 6 min.	
Filets or half	large				6 to 9 min.	
Lobster						
Open	1 to 1½ lb (500 to 750 g)	medium-high	—	—	—	12 to 16 min.

DIFFERENT WAYS OF COOKING MEAT

The many ways of cooking meat vary with type and cut. If the meat to be cooked is less tender, it is preferable to braise or boil it, but the more tender cuts are better broiled or roasted.

❧ All meat should be cooked at low or medium heat, as high temperatures will toughen the meat. Temperature plays an important role in cooking meat; it is even more important than cooking time.

BOILING

Meat can be gently boiled, with or without vegetables, in a large quantity of water. This method of cooking is recommended for cuts of meat that are less tender, such as shin, chuck and brisket. The meat can be cooked in one piece or cut into small chunks.

❧ Remove excess fat and coat the meat in a mixture of flour, salt and pepper. Alternatively, seal the meat in the heated fat. Meat can also be boiled without having been sealed. Season to taste using the following suggestions.

❧ **Beef:** celery leaves, chili powder, thyme, bay leaf, savory, mixed spices, whole cloves, mace, catsup

❧ **Pork:** sage, parsley, basil, bay leaf, whole cloves, nutmeg, cinnamon, paprika

❧ **Veal:** curry, thyme, basil, rosemary, cardamom, mint, savory

❧ Add salt at the beginning so that all the savory juices from the meat enrich the gravy.

❧ Add 3 cups (750 mL) liquid to every pound (500 g) meat. You can use the water from cooking vegetables, tea, tomato juice, apple juice, red or white wine, regular or sour cream, consommé or cold coffee.

❧ Bring to the boiling point but do not allow to boil. Cover and allow to simmer over low heat.

❧ Meat can also be boiled with vegetables. Wash and roughly chop vegetables such as onions, celery leaves, carrots, parsnip and garlic. It isn't necessary to peel them.

❧ Seal the meat and put to one side on a warm platter. Place the vegetables in the saucepan. Don't add any liquid. Cover and allow the vegetables to simmer over very low heat in their own juice for about 10 minutes. This process, known as "letting the vegetables sweat," extracts all the flavor from the vegetables. Place the meat on the vegetables. Season with herbs rather than salt, and add the liquid. Cover and simmer over a low heat.

BRAISING

To braise meat, you must start by browning it. To do this, coat it with flour seasoned with salt, pepper, paprika, herbs and sugar. Brown in hot fat. It does not matter what kind of fat you use; choose the type of fat, and the amount, according to your own individual diet. The fat will not only brown the meat, it will penetrate to the inside as well, even if the meat doesn't lie flat in the pan.

❧ For the meat to be perfectly cooked, it is important not to try to speed up the process by increasing the temperature. Braised meat should cook slowly, at low or medium heat. The crust that forms on the surface will retain all the internal juices, preventing the meat from drying out, becoming tough and losing its color.

❧ To braise meat even more simply, brown the meat, then add the herbs, seasoning and the other ingredients called for in a particular recipe. Do not add any liquid. Cover and cook.

❧ Another way of braising is to brown the meat and then add the liquid and whatever other ingredients your recipe requires. Cover and cook over low heat. To make the gravy, thicken the pan drippings with flour and reduce until thick and smooth.

BROILING

Meat can be broiled in the oven, in a skillet or on a barbecue.

❧ Meat broiled in the oven is as delicious as meat cooked over a barbecue. The basic principle applies to both: one side of the meat is cooked at a time. During the cooking process, the air circulates over the side that is not directly exposed to the heat, preventing the meat from drying out. To broil meat in the oven it is important not to let the meat dry out and toughen; the following rules will help. (Steak cooked this way will be comparable to barbecued meat.)

&♣ Preheat the oven.

&♣ Do not keep the heat high during broiling. If it gets too hot, place the meat 4 to 5 in. (10 to 13 cm) from the grill or turn the oven off for a few minutes until the temperature drops.

&♣ Do not close the oven door completely while broiling. (Open it completely if you cannot keep it open part way.)

&♣ To broil meat in a gas oven, place it on an oven rack as close to the source of the heat as possible. The flames will brown the meat slowly without toughening it. Once the oven reaches the desired temperature, it isn't necessary to watch the meat constantly except when it is time to turn it.

&♣ Meat grilled in a skillet also resembles meat cooked over a barbecue. Use a skillet with a thick bottom. Don't grease the pan—its only function is to catch the juices from the meat. Remember that the temperature should be kept low. Warm the skillet and place the meat in it. Don't cover it as this will raise the temperature and toughen the meat. Baste with the fat that runs off the meat.

&♣ If the stove burner gets too hot, remove the skillet and reduce the heat. Because of the heat of the skillet, the meat will continue to cook even when it is removed from the stove. When the burner has cooled down, return the skillet and continue.

&♣ Season the meat with paprika before cooking, if you wish, but don't add salt and pepper until it is ready to serve. Use a meat thermometer to ensure that the meat is cooked, if desired.

FRYING

Frying involves cooking food fast in a small quantity of oil or fat. Temperature plays an important part in this kind of cooking. Basically, when the heat source is too intense, the temperature of the fatty portions increases and the meat burns. This is what happens when bacon is cooked on too high a heat: the fat becomes too hot and the bacon burns. To fry food perfectly, it is best to cook it over medium heat.

Fatty meats such as lamb, pork and ham, and oily fish like salmon and trout, are best suited to frying.

&♣ It is better to sauté lean, tender cuts of meat. This is done by cooking it in a very small amount of fat, just enough to prevent the food from sticking. Place the food in a warm skillet and let it cook over high heat, stirring constantly, until it browns.

&♣ Use a heavy-bottomed skillet 2 to 4 in. (5 to 10 cm) deep. A cast-iron, enameled or thick aluminum skillet is the best. It should have a lid that fits well.

&♣ To fry meat in a skillet, you will need more fat than is used to sauté.

&♣ Use oil or butter. Be careful, though, as butter tends to burn at quite a moderate temperature. This is why it is necessary to keep a close eye on frying food. Mixing the butter with a little oil reduces the chance of its burning, but in general, melted animal fat is best for frying.

&♣ Heat the fat well before adding the food. Turn the food during the cooking process so that both sides are well cooked.

&♣ Serve immediately. If this is not possible, place the food on a hot plate and cover it with a dry cloth or paper towel. Keep warm in a hot oven for 15 minutes at the most.

&♣ Some foods can be cooked by deep frying. Use an electric fryer or a deep saucepan with a frying basket, which allows you to handle the food more easily. Heat the oil to boiling point and drop the food into it. The fat or oil should not be overheated as this contaminates the fryer.

&♣ Cook a little food at a time. Avoid overloading the fryer.

&♣ Check the temperature of the oil before adding new food.

&♣ Because the oil from deep frying can be used again, this is quite an economical way of cooking. After you use the oil, allow it to cool slightly and drain it through a sieve lined with cheesecloth. Allow to cool and then store in the refrigerator in a covered container. The next time you deep fry something, top the used oil up with some fresh oil if necessary.

&♣ Drain fried food well on paper towels.

ROASTING

Temperature plays an essential role in every type of cooking. Meat that is cooked at too high a temperature will be tough. This is particularly true of roasted meat.

⁂ How many good roasts have been spoiled needlessly and how many butchers blamed unfairly because the meat wasn't tender enough? If you follow these simple tips, you will always be sure of a tender, juicy roast.

⁂ Use a roasting pan large enough to hold the meat. It should have a heavy bottom, preferably of enameled cast iron, and should measure 12 x 16 in. (30 x 40 cm). It should be 2 to 4 in. (5 to 10 cm) deep.

⁂ Place the meat in the pan with the bones underneath and the fat on top. To cook a boneless roast, place it lean side down on two or three flat bones (ask your butcher for some). If the roast is rolled, place the leanest part on the bones. It is important to place the meat that is not covered in fat on the bones. If it is exposed, the lean meat will first cook in the steam and then fry in the fat in the bottom of the roasting pan, becoming dry and tough.

⁂ Brush the meat with the following mustard butter made from dry mustard and shortening. This seals the meat, ensuring that the roast retains its juices and con-

MEAT ROASTING CHART

Meat	Approximate Cooking Time in Minutes per 1 lb (500 g)	Oven Temperature	Degree of Doneness	Internal Temperature (Meat Thermometer)
Beef, less tender cuts	45	250°F (120°C)	rare	135°F (75°C)
	55	250°F (120°C)	medium	150°F (66°C)
	60	250°F (120°C)	well done	160°F (71°C)
Beef, tender cuts	18	325°F (160°C)	rare	140°F (60°C)
	20	325°F (160°C)	medium	155°F (68°C)
	27	325°F (160°C)	well done	165°F (74°C)
Chicken, roasting	35	325°F (160°C)	well done	185°F (85°C)
Duck, young	25	325°F (160°C)	well done	185°F (85°C)
Goose, young	25	325°F (160°C)	well done	185°F (85°C)
Ham, cooked	20	325°F (160°C)	well done	150°F (66°C)
Ham, smoked	25	325°F (160°C)	well done	170°F (77°C)
Lamb, leg	25	325°F (160°C)	medium	150°F (66°C)
Lamb, shoulder	40	275°F (160°C)	medium	150°F (66°C)
Mutton, leg or shoulder	60	225°F (105°C)	well done	180°F (82°C)
Pork roast	40	325°F (160°C)	well done	165°F (74°C)
Spareribs	30	325°F (160°C)	well done	180°F (82°C)
Turkey, large	15	325°F (160°C)	well done	180°F (82°C)
Turkey, small	20	325°F (160°C)	well done	180°F (82°C)
Veal, standing roast	40	275°F (140°C)	well done	180°F (82°C)
Veal, rolled	45	275°F (140°C)	well done	180°F (82°C)

serves its flavor. If you do not like the taste of dry mustard, don't worry—it changes considerably during cooking.

3 tbsp (45 mL) shortening: roast dripping, vegetable fat, lard, bacon fat, butter or oil
1 tbsp (15 mL) dry mustard

❧ Cream the fat and add the dry mustard. (Don't replace the dry mustard with prepared mustard.) Mix well. Spread the butter over the meat, but be careful not to put it on the fat or bones. To make spreading easy, make sure the butter is at room temperature.

❧ Make incisions in the roast with the point of a sharp knife and stick cloves of garlic or slices of onion here and there. If desired, season with herbs as well.

❧ To monitor the cooking process precisely, insert a meat thermometer in the thickest part of the meat, taking care that the end of the thermometer does not touch any bone or fat. If you want to be doubly sure, place an oven thermometer beside the roasting pan. Using both thermometers allows you to check how the roast is doing without removing it from the oven.

❧ Preheat the oven to the required temperature. Place the roast in the oven and cook until it is ready. Consult the *Meat Roasting Chart* opposite to find out how long this will take.

❧ Do not cover the pan. If you do, the roast will cook in the steam rather than in dry heat. It will take too long to brown and will probably be overcooked.

❧ Do not salt any meat before roasting. Like steak and chops, roast meat should not be salted until it is ready to serve. Salt tends to absorb the natural juices from the meat, drying it out. You should also not dredge it with flour. The flour will form a thick crust over the meat and the gravy is likely to be grey and lumpy.

❧ Do not add water or any other liquid. Steam will dry out the meat and make it shrink.

❧ Do not sear the meat. In the days when meat was cooked over an open fire, it was seared to seal in its juices. Modern ovens are not powerful enough to sear meat adequately, which is why it is a good idea to cover the roast in mustard butter to prevent it from losing its juices.

❧ Do not baste at any time during the cooking period. As the meat cooks, the fat accumulating in the bottom of the roasting pan will be hotter than the temperature of the oven. If you baste the meat with this fat, the meat will shrink, the surface will split and the juices will run out. Opening the oven door to baste the roast will make the meat shrink even more, because the colder air rushing in from outside contrasts with the hot air in the oven.

❧ When the meat is done, put it on a hot platter, cover with a cloth and let stand 5 to 15 minutes before carving. By letting the roast stand, you allow all the juices that were concentrated in the center during the cooking period to disperse throughout the meat. The meat will be easier to carve and it will taste even better.

❧ Since the meat will continue to cook for about 30 minutes after it is taken from the oven, it is best to take it out when the meat thermometer indicates 5°F (3°C) lower than the temperature given on the cooking table.

❧ For perfect gravy, always pour very cold liquid over very hot fat. This ensures a smooth, tasty sauce.

MAKING A STEW

For 6 servings, use 1 lb (500 g) boned meat or 1½ lb (750 g) with bones. Remove all the fat and melt it slowly in a heavy saucepan or cast-iron pot.

❧ Cut the meat into cubes, coat it in seasoned flour and then brown it in the melted fat. Add just enough water to cover the meat. Cover the pot and let the meat simmer until it is tender. Do not let it boil. Veal, pork and lamb should take 1½ to 2 hours to cook; beef will take 2½ to 3 hours.

❧ About 30 to 45 minutes before the end of the cooking period, add your choice of onions, potatoes, celery, carrots or rutabaga. Dice the vegetables or cut them into sticks. Season according to taste, taking into account the meat you have selected for your stew:

🍂 **Beef:** celery leaves, garlic, paprika, chili powder, catsup, vinegar, cloves, basil

🍂 **Lamb:** dried mint, curry, thyme, savory, catsup

🍂 **Pork:** paprika, chili powder, sage, parsley, celery leaves, bay leaves, cloves

🍂 **Veal:** green pepper, bay leaves, celery leaves, paprika, nutmeg, marjoram, savory

🍂 To thicken the stew: mix 2 tbsp (30 mL) browned flour in 3 tbsp (45 mL) water for 1 cup (250 mL) of stock. Add this to the stew. Bring to the boil and stir until the stew has thickened.

🍂 If you have decided on beef as the meat for your stew, the best cuts to buy are shoulder, flank, short ribs, top round or brisket. If you are making pork stew, you should use shoulder or any lean cut.

🍂 For an interesting variation, you could make a stew pie. Turn the stew into an earthenware dish and cover with mashed potatoes or pie crust. Brush the top with a little melted fat, and bake until golden in a very hot oven.

🍂 Stew can also be served with dumplings. Make dumplings using either flour or potato (see pages 296 and 459), and put them in the stew 15 minutes before the end of the cooking period.

🍂 Your stew can be served with carrots, rutabagas or any other vegetable, but do not cook the vegetables in the pot with the stew.

🍂 Boiled, baked or mashed potatoes can also be used as an accompaniment. Sweet potatoes are delicious with pork or lamb stew.

🍂 Pasta and rice go very well with stew. Either cook the pasta in the stew or boil it separately and serve mixed with sliced mushrooms, celery leaves or chopped parsley.

VARIETY MEATS

Kidney, liver, sweetbreads and brains are strongly recommended by nutritionists because they are high in food value. Liver stores the body's excess protein, vitamins and mineral salts, which makes it a highly nutritive food. Kidneys lag only slightly behind liver in nutritional value. Here are some hints for getting the most out of variety meats.

🍂 As they are rich in B complex vitamins, which are readily dissolved in cold water, they should never be soaked in cold water.

🍂 Variety meats are perishable and should be kept refrigerated until ready for cooking.

🍂 Cook over low heat for a very short period. Use high heat to sear only, as quickly as possible.

🍂 Because variety meats are cooked for so short a time, season them before cooking. However, add salt only when ready to serve.

SOUFFLÉS

SOUFFLÉ DISHES

Soufflé dishes come in a wide variety of shapes and sizes. The size chosen depends on the number of eggs used.

🍂 Bake a 4-egg soufflé in a 6-cup (1.5-L) dish.

🍂 Bake a 6-egg soufflé in an 8-cup (2-L) dish.

🍂 If you don't know the capacity of a dish, measure it by filling it with water. For example, a 6-cup (1.5-L) dish will hold 6 cups (1.5 L) water.

🍂 Never use a dish larger than 8-cup (2-L) capacity or the soufflé will not bake properly.

🍂 The dish should be filled to about ¾ of its capacity, never more.

🍂 If you don't have a dish that is large enough, make what the French call a collar: place a length of wax paper or foil around the outside edge of the dish so that it sticks 1 to 2 in. (2 to 5 cm) above the dish. Secure it with string and hold the top edge in place with a pin. Butter the side of the paper that will come into contact with the soufflé. Remove when ready to serve. This will hold the soufflé even if it rises 3 to 4 in. (8 to 10 cm) above the top of the dish.

🍂 The dish should be made of ovenproof earthenware or glass; earthenware is preferable. The sides should be straight so that the soufflé can rise to its maximum height; if the dish has sloping sides, the soufflé will rise somewhat rounded, like a cake.

A soufflé dish is not normally greased at all, because if the sides of the dish are slippery the soufflé is more likely to fall when removed from the oven. Occasionally, however, a soufflé dish must be buttered, in which case it is always sprinkled with flour, sugar or breadcrumbs.

PREPARING A SOUFFLÉ

Soufflés can be served on any occasion, as an appetizer (cheese soufflé), a main dish (lobster soufflé) or a dessert (an airy concoction flavored with chocolate, honey or liqueur).

Here is the basic method for preparing most soufflés.

Prepare a thick white sauce. The sauce should be smooth and creamy. If it is at all lumpy, the soufflé won't rise evenly).

Allow the sauce to cool slightly and then add the egg yolks. The egg yolks, cheese and any other ingredients are added to thicken and flavor the sauce.

Beat the egg whites and fold them into the sauce mixture. The egg whites should be prepared with great care, for the success or failure of the soufflé depends largely on them.

Make sure the egg whites are at room temperature when you use them. Beat them in a large bowl, preferably with a metal fork.

The only way to tell how long to beat the whites is to watch closely as you beat. You'll first notice a gradual thickening, then a foaminess, with tiny bubbles starting to form. At this point, be very cautious, for the next moment the whites will be stiff but not dry, which is how they must be for a perfect soufflé. If you keep on beating at this stage, the whites will become dry, which means they've lost their air bubbles. The soufflé will be less light and won't rise as well.

Pay particular attention to the way in which you fold the egg whites into the sauce base. Basically, if they are not added correctly, the whole soufflé can fail, even if the whites are beaten to perfection.

Turn the sauce base into a large bowl and fold the egg whites into the cooled mixture. Use a rubber spatula; this is less likely to break down the air cells in the egg whites. Take about ½ the whites and spoon them onto the sauce mixture. Stir thoroughly but slowly and lightly for no longer than 1 minute. Gently add the remaining ½ of the whites to the mixture, again folding carefully—for no more than 20 seconds. It is important to use a slow, continuous movement, turning the mixture over from top to bottom, rather than stirring round and round. There may be patches of egg white showing at the end but this will not affect the final result. You may wish to experiment by adding one or two more egg whites than called for by the recipe. The soufflé is invariably lighter.

Cognac or any other liquor can be used to flavor the soufflé. They all help the soufflé rise more.

Cognac can be added to all types of soufflé without affecting their flavor. Add 2 tbsp (30 mL) to the basic sauce mixture along with any other ingredients.

If you want the soufflé to rise with a little peak at the center, proceed as follows: once the mixture is in the dish, place an upright knife into the mixture, 1 or 2 in. (2 to 5 cm) deep and 1½ in. (4 cm) from the edge of the dish.

Making sure that the knife stays upright, describe a circle in the mixture, using an up and down movement.

Put the soufflé in the oven immediately. The center will rise higher than the rest and the soufflé will appear to be wearing a hat.

BAKING A SOUFFLÉ

Never open the oven door until 5 minutes before the end of baking, as this will let in cool air and the soufflé could then fall. Always open the door slowly and close it gently.

To see if the soufflé is done, pull the dish out slightly on the oven rack and move it carefully back and forth once or twice to see if the mixture is set.

Never test the soufflé with a knife or cake tester as this will let the hot air in the soufflé escape and it will sink.

The soufflé is cooked when the top is golden brown with a very light crust and the mixture does not shake when moved back and forth.

There are two schools of thought as to how long you should bake a soufflé. The French prefer a soufflé that is quite moist inside, and they then serve the partially cooked center as a sauce. To achieve this, increase the temperature by 50°F (20°C) and reduce the cooking time. For example, if the recipe indicates that the oven temperature should be 350°F (180°C), increase the heat to 400°F (200°C) and reduce the cooking time by 10 minutes.

HERBS AND SPICES

HERBS, AROMATIC SEEDS AND SPICES

Herbs, aromatic seeds and spices are indispensable to good cooking. They enhance flavor and sharpen the appetite—they are the good fairies of truly fine cuisine.

ᥤ The amounts of herbs and spices to use in a dish are up to you. But remember that the flavor of the herb, seed or spice should not smother the natural flavor of a dish. Its role is not to hide the flavor of food but to enhance it.

ᥤ It is important to draw a distinction between herbs, seeds and spices. Herbs, which can be bought fresh or dried, are more subtly flavored than seeds and spices. Owing to their medicinal value, most herbs are easily digested, even by a delicate stomach.

ᥤ Aromatic seeds, which usually have a stronger scent, enhance the flavor of a dish. They are used whole, ground or powdered. Whole seeds are perfect in sauces, stews and decoctions (see page 717 for infusion and decoction recipes). Since ground seeds sometimes have a more concentrated flavor than whole or powdered seeds, remember to measure accordingly.

ᥤ Spices such as pepper season a dish and also enhance its flavor. Since spices have a more pronounced flavor than that of herbs or seeds, they should be used sparingly. Don't hesitate to alter your recipe. For example, reduce the quantity of cinnamon in a given recipe if you prefer a less spicy taste. You can also add less salt or replace it with an herb of your choice if you are on a low-sodium diet. Changing the quantities of herbs, seeds and spices in a recipe can only improve it as it will then suit your personal taste. Learning how to use this culinary trio well will give your cooking a truly distinctive and personal touch.

HERBS

Let's take a quick survey of the herbs and spices that are usually found in the kitchen.

MARJORAM
Marjoram is the "grande dame" of the herb family. It can be added to a variety of recipes, but because of its piquancy it should be used with a light hand. Marjoram goes well with thyme.

ᥤ Wild marjoram, also known as oregano, has a marvelous taste that is a favorite among lovers of savory and marjoram.

ᥤ Use marjoram to flavor egg sauce, beef and tomato soups, the stuffing for goose, duck or other game birds, mashed potatoes, puréed spinach, squash, mushrooms and green salad.

ᥤ When preparing fried fish, add a pinch to the batter.

ᥤ Sprinkle marjoram on roast pork or lamb.

SAGE
Sage has a strong, sharp flavor and should be used sparingly.

ᥤ Use it to flavor meat stew, salt-water fish, cold meat salads, vegetable dishes, oxtail soup, mashed potatoes and creamed corn.

ᥤ When you make cranberry sauce, add ½ tsp (2 mL) sage for every 1 lb (500 g) sauce.

ᥤ Add ½ tsp (2 mL) to baking-powder biscuits (see page 648) and serve them hot with jam.

ᥤ Sprinkle on roast pork.

ROSEMARY
Rosemary has a very strong, dis-

Rosemary

tinctive flavor and should be used with discretion.

ᥤ Use to flavor boiled or roasted lamb.

ᥤ Add ½ tsp (2 mL) to the bread stuffing you make for roasted poultry.

ᥤ Add a pinch of rosemary to 1 tbsp (15 mL) browned butter and pour over roasted chicken or boiled cabbage just before serving.

ᥤ Cut a garlic clove in 3 pieces. Rub the garlic in rosemary and stick each piece in a pork roast.

ᥤ Add some sprigs of rosemary to the sauce covering fruit pudding.

ᥤ Add a pinch of rosemary, with a little basil and marjoram, to oxtail soup.

🌿 Use a pinch of rosemary whenever a recipe calls for thyme or shallots.

BASIL

Basil livens up everything it touches. Most people like it in salads and recipes that have a tomato base, but it goes well with all cooked foods.

🌿 Basil has a very aromatic taste and can be used generously. It adds life to even the blandest of dishes.

🌿 Use it when you prepare egg dishes. Sprinkle a pinch over a half-cooked omelet: it's delicious!

🌿 Sprinkle basil and salt over potatoes and onions. Cover and simmer in 1 cup (250 mL) water.

🌿 Before roasting a leg of lamb, sprinkle ½ tsp (2 mL) over it.

🌿 Use basil with marjoram and oregano to enhance the flavor of spaghetti sauce.

🌿 Flavor curried lamb stew (see *Bengal Lamb Curry*, page 228) by adding ¼ tsp (1 mL) basil to every 1 tsp (5 mL) curry.

🌿 Add basil to vegetable soup, with a pinch of savory and marjoram.

TARRAGON

Because tarragon can turn the most uninteresting dish into an exciting culinary experience, it will always be a gourmet's favorite herb. It is particularly indispensable in the preparation of sautéed chicken.

🌿 Tarragon vinegar adds a touch of elegance to tomato juice, scrambled eggs, fish fillets, steak, creamed mushrooms, tomato soup and consommés.

BAY LEAF

Bay leaves are strongly flavored and must be used sparingly. Keep

Bay leaf, thyme and tarragon

this in mind when you are preparing a recipe with any sort of liquid, as the flavor of the bay leaf is released throughout the cooking period.

🌿 For a flavorful bouquet garni, place 1 bay leaf, 1 tbsp (15 mL) parsley, ½ tsp (2 mL) marjoram and ½ tsp (2 mL) thyme in a cheesecloth bag. Use the bouquet garni to flavor cooked dishes such as stew, sauce, soup and vegetables.

🌿 Soak minute steaks for 1 hour in a marinade of 3 tbsp (45 mL) wine or lemon juice and 2 ground bay leaves. Drain the steaks and broil them. When the steaks are cooked, serve them with a sauce made of the pan drippings to which the rest of the marinade has been added.

🌿 Flavor chicken fricassée with 1 bay leaf, 1 tsp (5 mL) savory and a generous amount of parsley.

🌿 Add 1 bay leaf to beets before marinating them in hot vinegar.

🌿 Soak a whole or broken bay leaf

for 5 to 6 hours in tomato soup or tomato juice.

🌿 Add a bay leaf to the cooking water of vegetables, especially beets, onions and potatoes.

🌿 Always add a bay leaf to any soup that contains cabbage, ham or tongue: it's delicious.

THYME

Thyme is simple but elegant. Like the bay leaf, it is quite versatile and mixes well with other herbs to enhance the taste of many dishes.

🌿 Use thyme to accentuate the flavor of soups, sauces, tomatoes, stuffing and meat or fish salads.

🌿 Add ¼ tsp (1 mL) thyme to lamb gravy, the minced pork or beef to be used for meatballs, mashed or diced potatoes and tomato-based cocktails.

DILL

Dill is normally associated with pickles. It has a strong, pungent taste. The feathery bright green leaves of fresh dill, as well as the seeds of the plant, are used.

🌿 Dill leaves give a delicious piquant taste to mashed potatoes and cabbage or salmon salad.

🌿 Add dill to green beans, wax beans, cauliflower and boiled cabbage. If you are using dill leaves, chop them and add at the same time as you add the butter. If you are using dill seeds, add them to the cooking water.

SAVORY

Savory, which I like to call the first herb of Québec cuisine, is found in everything. The taste of this herb, a member of the mint family, is reminiscent of that of thyme, though slightly more subtle.

🍃 You can use savory to season many dishes, especially cabbage, sauerkraut, peas, meatloaf, roast pork, beef stew, pork chops and scrambled eggs.

🍃 Savory is a must for excellent pea soup.

CHERVIL

This annual herb loses its subtle flavor if it is not fresh. The lacy chervil leaf is an appropriate indication of its delicate taste. Because chervil leaves are so fine, never chop them with a knife but instead cut them with scissors.

🍃 Chervil can replace parsley in any recipe.

🍃 Use chervil to flavor green salads, potato or vegetable soup, poultry stuffing and delicate fish such as trout and halibut.

Dill

🍃 It also makes a delicious seasoning for fresh tomatoes.

CHIVES

Surely everyone is familiar with the mildly onion-like taste of fresh chives. Like chervil, chives should be used only when fresh and should not be cut with a knife but with scissors.

🍃 Chives enhance the flavor of green salads and omelets.

🍃 Use chives anywhere you think their piquant, young onion taste is appropriate.

MINT

Mint has a distinctive taste and is best known as a flavoring for the sauce or gravy served with lamb. But this refreshing herb also enhances the flavor of fruit salads, grapefruit, salads, tomatoes, French dressing and even the mayonnaise used to garnish cold fish dishes.

🍃 Its virtues don't stop there! A mint infusion is a delicious pick-me-up and tastes great hot or cold, with or without sugar. Try it with a slice of lemon.

🍃 Mint, lemon and honey create a wonderful blend of flavors. Try this trio in a fruit salad: sweeten a fruit of your choice with honey, add a little lemon juice and sprinkle with finely chopped mint.

AROMATIC SEEDS

ANISE

Anise, a member of the parsley family, is acknowledged as one of the oldest of the aromatic seeds used in cuisine. Today, we use it especially for flavoring licorice. Whenever a recipe calls for anise, be very careful not to use too much of it; it has a very pronounced taste.

🍃 Use anise to flavor cookies, cakes and breads.

🍃 Also try it in vegetable soup, with roast pork or pork chops, in mashed potatoes and in stuffing for duck or partridge.

🍃 Anise also makes a delicious and refreshing infusion that tastes great hot or cold.

CARAWAY SEEDS

Caraway is a plant belonging to the parsley family. Its seeds are small and almost black. Their flavor is similar to that of anise, but they have a more pronounced and peppery taste. Caraway seeds are most commonly used to sprinkle on rye bread or sugar and spice cookies.

🍃 Use caraway seeds to flavor roast pork, tuna salad or sauce, pork or veal stew, cabbage salad, turnips, pickled beets and fresh cheese.

CARDAMOM

Cardamom is the dried seed pod of a plant from the ginger family and is about the size of a pea. Each small ivory-colored pod contains about 5 to 8 small black seeds which are used to flavor various dishes. Cardamom can be bought as a seed or as a powder. The seeds keep for a long time. Before using them, crush them with the back of a wooden spoon to release their flavor, which is delicate, lightly aromatic and subtly peppery. Cardamom's special taste is successful in sweet as well as savory dishes—and even in coffee! The Scandinavians love cardamom and often add a seed to a cup of coffee. The French call these seeds the "seeds of paradise."

❧ Use cardamom in cakes, cookies, apple or rhubarb pie, rice pudding, custards and Danish pastries.

❧ Try it also in split pea soup or with sweet potatoes and roast leg of lamb.

❧ Add some to boiled tongue or stuffed beef heart as well as to marinades.

CELERY SEEDS

Despite the name, celery seeds do not come from the celery plant that we buy in the supermarket; although both plants belong to the parsley family, they taste quite different.

❧ The flavor of celery seeds is hot and mildly aromatic. The seeds contain an essential oil that gives food the flavor of fresh celery.

❧ Use celery seeds to flavor sauces, soups, vegetable salads, marinades, fish, vegetables and rolls. Indeed, use it whenever you wish to capture the taste of fresh celery.

CUMIN

Cumin seeds have a rather strong flavor which gives food an exotic, eastern taste. It is used in certain Dutch cheeses and when preparing curry. Cumin is also found in many Mexican dishes such as chili con carne and tamales.

❧ Sprinkle cumin lightly on sweet rolls and on apple or cherry pies.

❧ Cumin also goes well with tomato sauce, all savory rice dishes, stuffed eggs and baked beans.

CORIANDER

Coriander is an annual herb which comes originally from Greece and Italy, but I have grown it very easily in my own garden. Its grayish seeds, which look a little like lead shot, have an unpleasant odor when they are fresh but develop a taste like a blend of lemon and sage as they dry. Most people enjoy the taste of coriander, but, like cumin, it should be used sparingly. It is used mainly in the preparation of smoked sausage.

❧ Use coriander in marinades, especially those used for making pickles.

❧ Add it to pastries, fruit tarts, cookies, spiced cakes, lentils, cream cheese, rice and meat cooked in brown or tomato sauce.

JUNIPER BERRIES

The juniper berry, the smokey-blue fruit of the juniper bush, is small and round. To get an idea of its flavor, remember that it is one of the main ingredients of gin.

❧ Use juniper berries when preparing game and sauerkraut.

❧ Toss some crushed juniper berries in the butter used to sauté veal or lamb kidneys.

SESAME SEEDS

Sesame seeds are tiny ivory-colored seeds which are smooth and shiny. They are crunchy, like small nuts, and have a very delicate, sweet taste. To bring out their flavor, spread the seeds on a cookie sheet and place them in the oven until golden brown. Let them cool and store them in a glass container.

❧ Sprinkle sesame seeds on cooked vegetables and pasta for added flavor and an interesting texture.

Cardamom, celery seeds, cumin and coriander

❧ Sprinkle them on cookies, bread and pie crusts.

SPICES

CINNAMON

Cinnamon is the dried bark of the cinnamon tree. It has a long tradition of use—it is mentioned in the *Song of Songs*—and is probably the best known of all the spices. Cinnamon sticks or cinnamon powder may be used, depending on the recipe and the flavor required.

❧ Use cinnamon to flavor chocolate, cakes, puréed fruit, poached pears, apple pie and desserts made with rice or semolina.

❧ Sprinkle cinnamon on stews and pork dishes before cooking them.

❧ Cinnamon also goes well with stewed prunes, sweet yogurt and marinades.

CLOVES

The clove is the dried flower bud of the clove tree. The finest of these trees grow in Java, Madagascar and the American tropics. Cloves can be bought whole, powdered or as an extract. Whole cloves are most commonly used to stud the outside of baked ham. Clove powder is delicious with fruit and in cakes, as well as in meat loaves, stews and game dishes. Clove extract is used in the preparation of candy. It also eases toothache.

🍃 Flavor stock or stew by adding a garlic clove or an onion studded with cloves.

🍃 Add a few cloves to court bouillon for fish or to the sauce served with any game dish.

NUTMEG

Nutmeg is the seed of a tree that grows in certain tropical regions. The tree produces two spices: the shiny brown kernel, the nutmeg, is surrounded by a pale beige fibrous covering which, when dried, gives mace. Mace is similar to nutmeg but is less fragrant and not as sweet. It is used with meats and dishes where a lighter taste is desired. Ideally, nutmeg should be round rather than long and emit a fresh, subtle, but lasting perfume. It is preferable to use fresh nutmeg, which you can easily grate yourself with a nutmeg grater or any kind of sharp grater. However, nutmeg can be bought as a powder.

🍃 Use nutmeg in white sauce and with Brussels sprouts, cauliflower, roast chicken and veal.

🍃 Also use it to season mashed potatoes, pears and pastries.

Ginger, nutmeg, cloves and cinnamon

ALLSPICE

Allspice, often wrongly called "four-spice powder," is not a mixture of pepper, nutmeg, cinnamon and cloves although its aroma evokes these four spices. The distinctive and powerful flavor of allspice can work wonders in a recipe, but this spice should be used judiciously.

GINGER

Whether it comes from the West or the East Indies, ginger is an excellent digestive aid. As a powder, it gives a piquant flavor to cookies and cakes. As a dried root, it can be used to spice up marinades and jams and to flavor fruit purées. Ginger is at its best when fresh. Fresh roots are found in Asian grocery stores and in many supermarkets. Peel the root and grate it very finely, as you will need only a tiny amount to flavor an entire dish. Frozen in a sealed container, ginger root keeps indefinitely; you can even peel and grate it without defrosting it.

SAFFRON

Saffron is made from the dried stigmas of a species of crocus grown in Spain, Italy and the Gatinais region of France. It contains an essential orange-colored oil which both flavors and colors food. Saffron is the world's most expensive spice, but fortunately a little goes a very long way. It is worth taking time to experiment with this spice as you will soon come to love its special flavor.

🍃 Saffron is indispensable when you are making Spanish or Italian rice, paella and bouillabaisse.

🍃 Use saffron when preparing fish, all kinds of meat cooked in a sauce and certain dried vegetables.

🍃 Add saffron to cakes and rolls to give them a pleasing color and flavor.

🍃 Saffron is also excellent in French dressing, to which it gives an unexpected lift.

CURRY

Curry is a yellow powder broadly composed of several ground spices such as ginger, coriander, cumin and saffron or turmeric, the proportions of which vary according to the recipe. This is why different brands of curry differ considerably. Curry is the basis of many fine Indian dishes, which often have a beautiful vibrant yellow color. It is best to use curry judiciously as it can be quite strong.

🍃 Use with rice, fish, meats, stews and poultry.

TURMERIC

Turmeric powder is the ground

root of an East Indian plant from the ginger family. It has a slightly bitter taste. Turmeric is the principal ingredient in Indian curries and prepared mustard.

❧ For many years I have added a little turmeric to French dressing. One Christmas I added a pinch to my cookie dough to give the cookies a beautiful golden color. From Persian cuisine, I learned to add turmeric to the seasoned flour used in the preparation of fried chicken. I also add ¼ to ½ tsp (1 to 2 mL) to the butter or oil in which I cook onions. An old French chef taught me to add a pinch to scrambled eggs to give them a lovely color. Try turmeric in egg sauces and in rice dishes.

PAPRIKA

Paprika, a vibrant red powder with a sweet, mild flavor, is made from small red peppers which have been dried and ground. Paprika is appreciated for its color, but it plays a more important role when added to sauces and meat in small quantities mixed with a little soft butter or sour cream. It is the spice most used in Hungarian cuisine; in fact, the best paprika comes from Hungary.

❧ Just before barbecuing, roasting or frying meat, sprinkle it with paprika to give it a beautiful golden color.

PEPPER

Pepper comes mainly from India and Indochina. No matter what its color, pepper stimulates and aids digestion. When using pepper, remember the saying, "Entrust salt to the wise man and pepper to the miser"—a warning that neither salt nor pepper should be used excessively.

❧ White pepper is obtained by soaking peppercorns in salt water before removing the outer covering. It is therefore milder than black pepper, but more aromatic. Both black and white pepper have their uses in the kitchen. Black pepper is used to accentuate the flavor of soup stocks, which are cooked over a low heat for a long time, and white pepper is used to flavor salads and fine sauces.

❧ It is far better to buy peppercorns and crush them in a small mill when needed. Fresh pepper has an exquisite flavor and is tastier than ready ground pepper.

SALT

Salt, coarse or fine, is surely the

Curry, paprika, salt and pepper

most widely used and the most needed spice. Coarse salt is used in cooking and fine salt at the table. In general, use ½ tsp (2 mL) salt for every 4 cups (1 L) liquid or 3 to 4 cups (750 mL to 1 L) food. You can even use salt in cakes and all sorts of sweets since it brings out the flavor of sugar.

CAYENNE PEPPER

Cayenne pepper comes from a small crushed berry that is extremely hot. It should be used sparingly. A pinch added to fish, sauces or stocks brings out the flavor of the dish. Tabasco sauce is cayenne liquid; it must be used with discretion as it is very hot.

HORSERADISH

This dark yellowish root is the size of parsnip and is covered with a brown skin. It tastes similar to mustard. If you buy it fresh, you have to grate and salt it and add vinegar; this is a complicated and somewhat unpleasant undertaking. Fortunately, you can buy prepared horseradish that is just as good as fresh horseradish.

❧ Use horseradish with pot roast, roast beef and game dishes and to season certain sauces.

❧ Add a little dry horseradish to sauces and soup stocks.

MUSTARD

The mustard seed comes from the family of plants known as Cruciferae. Mustard is recognized as one of the oldest seasonings and is made by husking and crushing the seeds and mixing them with sour wine, the juice from green grapes, vinegar, and so on. Learning how to make different sorts of mustard, seasoned with various fresh herbs, is very satisfying. It is impossible to list the innumerable uses of this well known condiment.

SALTED HERBS

In order to prepare salted herbs for the winter, be sure to start with very fresh herbs. Choose from a variety of herbs: parsley, chervil, savory, marjoram, basil, thyme, tarragon, rosemary and sage, among others. Once you have chosen your herbs, remove the leaves and wash and chop one variety at a time. Sterilize the container in which you will store the herbs.

🌿 Choose your first herb and place a 1-in. (2-cm) layer in the container. Sprinkle generously with coarse salt. Cover the first layer with another variety in a 1-in. (2-cm) layer and sprinkle with coarse salt. Repeat this process until the pot is full. Seal tightly and keep in the refrigerator. When cooking, use these herbs as required. Salted herbs will keep from 1 month to 1 year.

DRY SALTED HERBS

To prepare dry salted herbs, cut the stems of the chosen herbs. Put the leaves in an earthenware or a glass bowl in 1-in. (2-cm) layers, covering each layer with salt to taste. Do not cover, or cover with cheesecloth to keep the dust out. Leave to dry for 1 month in a dark, well-ventilated place. When the herbs are dry, pass them through a sieve. Place the powdered herbs in small jars and seal.

🌿 Use dry salted herbs as a substitute for salt, sprinkling them on food. Add to stews or sauces 20 to 30 minutes before the end of the cooking period.

AROMATIC SALT

🌿 Prepare this salt with fresh or commercially dried herbs.

¼ cup (50 mL) savory
¼ cup (50 mL) parsley
2 tbsp (30 mL) thyme
1 tbsp (15 mL) sage
½ cup (125 mL) celery leaves

zest ½ lemon
1 cup (250 mL) fine salt

🌿 Place all the ingredients in a bowl. Blend by crushing with a wooden mortar or spoon. Pass through a sieve and keep in small, well-sealed jars.

BUTTER WITH HERBS

¼ cup (50 mL) sweet butter
1 tsp (5 mL) lemon juice
1 tbsp (15 mL) herbs taken from vinegar or 1 tsp (5 mL) dried herbs or 2 to 3 tbsp (30 to 45 mL) fresh chopped herbs

🌿 Mix the ingredients together well. Cover tightly and keep refrigerated.

🌿 Add herb butter to cooked fish or vegetables.

🌿 Add a generous serving to soups and sauces.

🌿 Use to butter slices of bread. Reassemble the loaf and heat in a 350°F (180°C) oven for 15 to 20 minutes. Serve hot.

GRAVIES, SAUCES AND SALAD DRESSINGS

GRAVIES

Three types of gravy can be made from the pan juices of a roast:

🍂 a pan gravy, made of the pan juices thickened with flour

🍂 a clear gravy, made with the pan juices and a liquid

🍂 a perfect quick gravy made with a consommé base.

PAN GRAVY

A good pan gravy should have an appetizing brown color, no matter what type of meat or poultry juices you begin with. This means that you must heat the drippings and fat until they begin to boil, then add the flour and cook it, stirring, for 5 to 8 minutes or until the flour is well browned.

🍂 To make an even darker and more savory gravy, use whole-wheat flour. If you brown ordinary white flour beforehand, it will enhance the flavor and color of the gravy. I like to keep some browned flour on hand all the time.

🍂 The best proportions for a pan gravy are 2 tbsp (30 mL) flour for every 2 tbsp (30 mL) of fat. Avoid using more fat than necessary, since it will not blend in well and will give the gravy a greasy taste. When the flour is well combined with the fat, stir in ½ cup (125 mL) liquid for every 1 tbsp (15 mL) of flour. (If using whole-wheat or highly browned flour, add an additional 1 tbsp (15 mL) of flour, as these have less thickening power.)

🍂 You can use any number of liquids in pan gravy—for example, cold water, tomato juice, leftover tea or coffee, milk, cream or wine—to create a variety of flavors and colors.

HOW TO BROWN FLOUR

To brown flour, simply spread it evenly in a flat baking pan and heat slowly in a 300°F (150°C) oven. Stir it occasionally and continue cooking until light brown. Pass it through a sieve and store in a glass jar in a cool place.

CLEAR GRAVY

To make clear gravy, you should remove about half the fat that has accumulated in the bottom of the roasting pan, then stir in the liquid of your choice. To be sure of success, first heat the fat in the roasting pan and then add the cold liquid. Bring the mixture to a boil, stirring constantly and incorporating the scrapings from the bottom and sides of the roasting pan. The gravy is ready as soon as it begins to boil.

PERFECT QUICK GRAVY

This is the easiest gravy to prepare and quite possibly the most delicious. To make it, simply remove the roast from the pan and place the pan over a burner. Heat the pan drippings until they start to boil, then add a can of cold, undiluted consommé. Mix well, scraping the bottom and sides of the pan. Remove from

the heat as soon as the gravy starts to boil. For extra flavor, add 1 tbsp (15 mL) brandy or lemon juice to the consommé mixture.

SEASONINGS FOR GRAVY

🍂 For beef gravy: select from marjoram, oregano, finely chopped leeks, parsley, catsup or mustard.

🍂 For chicken: try sage, tarragon, chives or paprika.

🍂 For lamb: rosemary, basil, dill seeds, capers or Tabasco sauce.

🍂 For pork: sage, thyme, parsley, garlic, mustard or anise seed.

🍂 For turkey: basil, thyme or marjoram, mixed with lemon zest and nutmeg.

🍂 For veal: use any of the seasonings suggested for beef or chicken.

WHITE SAUCES

White sauce is the base for many different sauces and for creamed dishes.

EASY WHITE SAUCE

THIN WHITE SAUCE:
1 tbsp (15 mL) butter or fat
1 tbsp (15 mL) flour
1 cup (250 mL) liquid

MEDIUM WHITE SAUCE:
2 tbsp (30 mL) butter or fat
2 tbsp (30 mL) flour
1 cup (250 mL) liquid

THICK WHITE SAUCE:
3 tbsp (45 mL) butter or fat
4 tbsp (60 mL) flour
1 cup (250 mL) liquid

❧ Melt the butter in a skillet or saucepan. Remove the pan from the heat, add the flour and blend it in well. Add the liquid and cook over medium heat, stirring constantly, until the sauce reaches the desired consistency. Season to taste.

❧ White sauce prepared this way is never lumpy.

MORNAY SAUCE

2 egg yolks
½ cup (125 mL) cream
1 cup (250 mL) medium white sauce
½ cup (125 mL) cheese, grated

❧ Beat the egg yolks together with the cream.

❧ Add the white sauce and the grated cheese, stirring briskly. Simmer for a few minutes over low heat.

SOUBISE SAUCE

3 onions, finely chopped
1 tbsp (15 mL) butter
3 tbsp (45 mL) water
2 cups (500 mL) medium white sauce
salt, pepper and nutmeg

❧ Cook the onions in the butter and water until soft, but do not allow them to change color.

❧ Stir the onions along with their cooking liquid into the white sauce. Season to taste with salt, pepper and nutmeg. Boil gently for 5 minutes.

Mornay Sauce

❧ If you want a very smooth sauce, strain the mixture through a sieve, pressing firmly on the onions to extract all their flavor.

CAPER SAUCE

¼ cup (50 mL) capers
1 green onion, finely chopped
pinch of curry powder
1 tsp (5 mL) butter
1 cup (250 mL) medium white sauce

❧ Stir all the ingredients into the white sauce. Let simmer for 3 or 4 minutes over low heat.

ITALIAN SAUCE

2 tbsp (30 mL) butter
6 sprigs parsley, finely chopped
2 green onions, finely chopped

¼ lb (125 g) mushrooms, sliced
½ cup (125 mL) white wine
1 cup (250 mL) medium white sauce

❧ Melt the butter and add the parsley, onions and mushrooms. Sauté for about 10 minutes.

❧ Add the white wine and cook over high heat until the liquid is reduced by half. Stir this mixture into the white sauce and simmer for 3 to 4 minutes.

HUNGARIAN SAUCE

2 green onions, finely chopped
1 tbsp (15 mL) tomato paste
1 tsp (5 mL) paprika
¼ tsp (1 mL) nutmeg
1 cup (250 mL) medium white sauce

❧ Stir all the other ingredients into the white sauce. Simmer over medium heat for 5 minutes.

PROVENÇALE SAUCE

3 tbsp (45 mL) olive oil
1 medium onion, finely chopped
2 tomatoes, chopped
1 handful parsley, finely chopped
2 cloves garlic, crushed
1 cup (250 mL) medium white sauce

🖜 Heat the olive oil and add the onion, tomatoes, parsley and garlic. Sauté for 20 minutes.

🖜 Prepare a white sauce, using either consommé or cream for the liquid, and add it to the tomato mixture. Simmer for 10 minutes.

OLIVE SAUCE

¾ cup (175 mL) grated mild cheese
½ cup (125 mL) green or black olives, finely sliced
1 cup (250 mL) medium white sauce

🖜 Stir the cheese and olives into the white sauce. Simmer for 5 minutes.

AURORE SAUCE

3 tbsp (45 mL) butter
4 tbsp (60 mL) flour
2 cups (500 mL) milk
or chicken stock
½ cup (125 mL) whipping cream
salt and pepper to taste
3 tbsp (45 mL) tomato paste
1 tsp (5 mL) basil
3 tbsp (45 mL) finely chopped parsley
1 tbsp (15 mL) soft butter

🖜 Make a white sauce with the 3 tbsp (45 mL) butter, the flour and the milk. When the sauce is smooth and creamy, gradually add the cream, stirring constantly. Season to taste.

🖜 Place over low heat and add the tomato paste, basil and parsley. Stir well and remove from the heat.

🖜 Add the soft butter and stir until melted. Do not reheat the sauce after adding the butter.

MUSHROOM SAUCE

½ lb (250 g) mushrooms
3 tbsp (45 mL) butter
1 small clove garlic, minced
6 green onions, finely chopped
pinch of tarragon
salt and pepper
2 cups (500 mL) medium white sauce

🖜 Clean and slice the mushrooms. Melt the butter in a skillet until nutty brown in color. Add the mushrooms, garlic and onions. Cook over high heat for 3 minutes, stirring constantly. Remove from the heat. Add the tarragon and season to taste with salt and pepper.

🖜 Pour the white sauce over the mushroom mixture. Mix well and simmer for 5 minutes, stirring often. Taste for seasoning.

🖜 To make a mushroom sauce flavored with sherry or port, add 3 tbsp (45 mL) of either liquid to the mushrooms and green onions just before removing from the heat.

Provençale Sauce

❧ TECHNIQUE ❧

PROVENÇALE SAUCE

1 Prepare a white sauce.

2 Sauté the onion, tomatoes, parsley and garlic in the hot olive oil.

3 Let simmer for 20 minutes.

4 Add the tomato mixture to the white sauce. Simmer for another 10 minutes.

WHITE OR BROWN ROUX

Melt some butter in a heavy skillet or saucepan until it turns a nutty brown color. Stir in the flour. Stir constantly over medium heat until the mixture reaches the desired color.

❧ The cooking time determines the color of the roux. Use a white roux to give body to a very pale sauce, a blonde roux for an ivory-colored sauce and a brown roux for a darker sauce.

WHITE OR BROWN STOCK

Many sauces are prepared by mixing white or brown stock with a roux. Rather than making your own stock, you can use canned consommé or bouillon, a bouillon cube dissolved in water, or liquid beef or chicken concentrate.

❧ If your recipe calls for white stock, use a can of consommé or a chicken bouillon cube; if you need brown stock, use beef bouillon, beef bouillon cubes or beef concentrate. You can always dilute the consommé or concentrate to produce a lighter stock.

❧ Homemade stocks are easy to make, and they are a good way to use leftover bones. Here are my own recipes for both white and brown stock. They enhance the flavor of sauces and are delicious on their own, served either hot or cold. Both versions will keep in the refrigerator for 10 to 12 days.

CLASSIC WHITE STOCK FOR SAUCES

2 to 3 lbs (1 kg) veal shank, cut in 6 pieces
1½ lbs (750 g) chicken giblets
6 chicken backs or 1 chicken or turkey carcass
4 large carrots, peeled and sliced
3 large onions, peeled and sliced
3 stalks celery with leaves, chopped
1 tsp (5 mL) dry mustard
1 tbsp (15 mL) coarse salt
½ tsp (2 mL) thyme
1 bay leaf
28 cups (7 L) hot water

❧ Place all the ingredients in a large stock pot and bring to a boil. Skim off any foam. Cover and simmer for 3½ hours. At the end of the cooking period, there should be about 20 cups (5 L) of stock left. If you have more than that, boil the liquid a little longer, uncovered, until it is reduced to 20 cups (5 L). Cool and strain.

❧ To make a chicken stock, replace the veal shank with a stewing fowl.

CLASSIC BROWN STOCK FOR SAUCES

2 to 4 lbs (1 to 2 kg) beef bone, cut in small pieces
1 meatless ham bone (optional)
4 lbs (1.8 kg) lean brisket or beef shoulder, diced
1 cup (250 mL) beef fat, diced
2 tbsp (30 mL) butter
3 large carrots, sliced
3 large onions, chopped
1 leek, sliced
1 bay leaf
1 clove garlic, crushed
1½ tbsp (25 mL) thyme
1 tbsp (15 mL) coarse salt
¼ tbsp (4 mL) pepper
28 cups (7 L) hot water

❧ Ask the butcher to cut the bones into small pieces. Cut the meat into large cubes. Melt the beef fat with the butter. Add all the ingredients except the water and cook over fairly high heat, stirring often, until lightly browned. (This operation brings color and flavor to the stock.) Add the water, bring to a boil, then cover and simmer for 4 to 6 hours, or until reduced to 20 cups or 5 L. Cool and strain.

❧ To keep either white or brown stock, let the stock cool and then strain through a fine sieve lined with a double thickness of cheesecloth. Do not stir but let the stock drain slowly. Pour the clarified stock into glass jars, cover and place in the refrigerator. The fat will rise to the top and harden, creating a natural lid. When you wish to use the stock, remove the fat and take what you need. Then melt the fat and pour it back on top. Kept this way, stock will last for 10 to 15 days.

❧ To make a tomato stock, simply add a 6-oz (175-mL) can of tomato paste to either white or brown stock.

❧ Use these stocks in all types of sauce or as a replacement for the water called for when heating canned soups. Or serve these stocks cold as a consommé.

Béchamel Sauce

Béchamel sauce used to be made using a reduced velouté sauce as the base. Nowadays, Béchamel is prepared more like a white sauce, that is, with an equal quantity of butter and flour. But it is quite a bit richer and more flavorful than an ordinary white sauce. A white sauce does not use vegetables for flavoring, and it uses water or a mixture of milk and water as the liquid. Béchamel, on the other hand, contains milk, beaten eggs, lemon juice and a pinch of nutmeg, and is sometimes flavored with vegetables.

❧ If you like, you can substitute chicken, fish or vegetable stock for the milk. To add even more flavor, cook onion and diced vegetables in the butter before adding the flour. (In this case, strain the sauce before serving.) Add the rest of the ingredients, cover the mixture and simmer over low heat.

English Béchamel Sauce

Quick Béchamel Sauce

1 tbsp (15 mL) carrot, grated
1 tbsp (15 mL) onion, grated
1 tbsp (15 mL) butter
½ bay leaf
pinch of thyme
¼ cup (50 mL) consommé
1 cup (250 mL) medium white sauce

❧ Cook the carrot and onion in the butter over low heat until soft but not browned. Add the bay leaf, thyme and consommé. Boil for 3 minutes over high heat, stirring constantly.

❧ Stir in the white sauce and simmer for another 10 minutes. Strain through a sieve before serving.

English Béchamel Sauce

1 cup (250 mL) milk, cream, or chicken, fish or vegetable stock
1 small onion, finely chopped
½ stalk celery
½ carrot
6 peppercorns
½ bay leaf
2 tbsp (30 mL) butter
2 tbsp (30 mL) flour
1 egg yolk
1 tbsp (15 mL) lemon juice
salt and nutmeg

❧ Pour the milk or stock into a saucepan. Add the onion, celery, carrot, peppercorns and bay leaf. Simmer for 15 minutes. Strain through a fine sieve.

❧ Melt the butter in a skillet and stir in the flour. Mix well and add the prepared milk or stock. Cook over medium heat, stirring constantly, until the sauce is thick and creamy. Remove from the heat.

❧ Beat together the egg yolk and lemon juice and beat the mixture into the sauce. Season to taste with salt and nutmeg.

Basic Brown Sauce

¼ cup (50 mL) boiling water
2 slices of bacon
3 tbsp (45 mL) butter
3 tbsp (45 mL) fat
⅓ cup (75 mL) thinly

❦ TECHNIQUE ❦

ENGLISH BÉCHAMEL SAUCE

1 Pour the milk into a saucepan. Add the onion, celery, carrot, peppercorns and bay leaf.

2 Strain through a fine sieve.

3 Melt the butter and stir in the flour.

4 Fold the egg yolk into the sauce.

sliced carrots
⅓ (75 mL) cup diced celery
1 onion, finely chopped
4 tbsp (60 mL) flour
6 cups (1.5 L) consommé
2 tbsp (30 mL) tomato paste
1 bay leaf
¼ tsp (1 mL) thyme
3 sprigs parsley
salt and pepper

❧ Pour the boiling water over the bacon slices. Let stand for 10 minutes. Drain well and cut the bacon into four pieces.

❧ Combine the butter, fat, bacon, carrots, celery and onion in a saucepan. Cook for 10 minutes over medium heat.

❧ Stir in the flour. Continue cooking the mixture over high heat, stirring constantly, until the flour turns light brown. Remove the pan from the heat.

❧ Add the consommé, tomato paste, bay leaf, thyme and parsley. Bring to a boil, stirring constantly. Partially cover the pot and cook over very low heat for about 2 hours or until the sauce is reduced to 4 cups (1 L). It may be necessary to cook the mixture a little longer to reduce it sufficiently.

❧ Strain the sauce through a fine sieve. Season to taste with salt and pepper. This sauce will keep in the refrigerator for 2 to 3 weeks, or can be frozen for 3 to 4 months. Since it requires such a long cooking period, I find it convenient to prepare a large quantity.

❧ Brown sauce is handy for making gravy. All you have to do is remove some of the fat from the roasting pan and stir a little brown sauce into the remaining pan juices.

Devil Sauce

1 tbsp (15 mL) butter
4 French shallots, finely chopped
1 cup (250 mL) white wine
or ⅔ cup (150 mL) vermouth
2 cups (500 mL) basic brown sauce
freshly ground pepper

❧ Melt the butter in a skillet over low heat. Add the shallots and sauté them over low heat for 2 minutes, without allowing them to change color.

❧ Add the wine or vermouth and boil until the liquid is reduced to 3 or 4 tbsp (45 to 60 mL).

❧ Heat the brown sauce and stir it into the reduced wine mixture. Simmer gently over low heat for a few minutes. Add pepper to taste and serve.

Sauce Robert

1 tbsp (15 mL) butter
1 tbsp (15 mL) vegetable oil
1 onion, finely chopped
1 cup (250 mL) white wine
2 cups (500 mL) basic brown sauce
3 to 4 tsp (15 to 20 mL) Dijon mustard
3 tbsp (45 mL) finely chopped parsley
3 tbsp (45 mL) soft butter

❧ Melt the butter and oil in a saucepan. Brown the onion in the heated fat. Add the white wine and boil over high heat until the liquid is reduced to only 3 or 4 tbsp (45 to 60 mL).

❧ Heat the brown sauce and add it to the reduced wine mixture. Simmer for a few minutes, stirring constantly.

❧ Combine the mustard and the

Sauce Robert

chopped parsley with the soft butter. Remove the sauce from the heat and add the mustard mixture. Stir until the butter has melted. Season to taste and serve.

MADEIRA SAUCE

½ cup (125 mL) Madeira wine or port
2 cups (500 mL) basic brown sauce
2 tbsp (30 mL) butter

🍃 Boil the Madeira or the port until it is reduced to 3 tbsp (45 mL).

🍃 Add the brown sauce to the wine. Cover and simmer for 5 minutes. Remove the pan from the heat, add the butter and stir until it is melted. Serve.

CHASSEUR SAUCE

2 tbsp (30 mL) butter
4 French shallots, finely chopped
1 cup (250 mL) fresh tomatoes
1 small clove garlic
½ tsp (2 mL) basil
½ tsp (2 mL) sugar
¼ tsp (1 mL) salt
½ cup (125 mL) white wine
1 cup (250 mL) basic brown sauce
2 tbsp (30 mL) butter
¼ lb (125 g) mushrooms, thinly sliced

🍃 Melt 2 tbsp (30 mL) of butter in a saucepan. Add the shallots and cook for 5 minutes over low heat.

🍃 Peel the tomatoes and cut them into dice. Add them to the shallots along with the garlic,

basil, sugar and salt. Cover and let simmer for 5 minutes.

🍃 Add the wine and the brown sauce. Boil over medium heat for 5 to 6 minutes, stirring 3 or 4 times.

🍃 In the meantime, melt the second 2 tbsp (30 mL) of butter in a skillet until it turns a nutty brown color. Add the mushrooms and cook them over high heat for 1 minute, stirring constantly. Add them to the sauce and simmer for 1 minute. Adjust the seasonings.

🍃 To prepare *Chicken Chasseur* or a *Veal Chop Chasseur*, brown the meat on both sides in butter. Cover and cook for 15 to 20 minutes over low heat. Add the chasseur sauce and simmer over low heat until the chicken or meat is tender.

LIGHT HOLLANDAISE SAUCE

2 eggs
½ tsp (2 mL) salt
2 tbsp (30 mL) lemon juice
½ cup (125 mL) soft butter
pinch of pepper
½ cup (125 mL) hot water

🍃 Place the eggs, salt, lemon juice, soft butter and pepper in the jar of a blender. Cover and blend at high speed for 1 second. Without turning off the blender, remove the stopper from the lid and add the hot water a little at a time.

🍃 Pour the mixture into a saucepan and cook it over very low heat, stirring constantly, until the Hollandaise is thick and creamy. Serve immediately.

HOLLANDAISE SAUCE

¼ to ½ cup (50 to 125 mL) very cold butter
2 egg yolks, beaten with a fork
juice of ½ lemon (or to taste)

🍃 There is no magic to making an excellent Hollandaise sauce. In fact, it is one of the easiest sauces to make. All you need to remember is that you must use a minimum of heat, so that the butter and egg yolks combine in an emulsion. Here is the simplest and quickest way to make Hollandaise sauce without a double boiler or bain-marie.

🍃 Place the cold butter, lightly beaten egg yolks and lemon juice in a small saucepan over low heat. Stir continuously until the mixture resembles creamed butter. If the pan becomes too hot, remove it from the burner and continue to stir. Often, the heat retained in the pan will be sufficient to finish cooking the sauce.

🍃 If the sauce separates or curdles, quickly add 1 tbsp (15 mL) of ice water or an ice cube and remove the pan from the heat. Beat vigorously until the mixture becomes smooth again. If this does not work, beat another fresh egg yolk and add it to the separated sauce, beating continuously over very low heat.

MOUSSELINE SAUCE

🍃 Add 2 stiffly beaten egg whites to a batch of Hollandaise sauce. Fold in the egg whites just before serving, to make sure the sauce is as fluffy as possible.

DE LUXE MUSTARD SAUCE

❧ Dissolve 1 tbsp (15 mL) Dijon mustard in 2 tbsp (30 mL) cold water. Replace the lemon juice in the Hollandaise recipe with this mixture.

MALTAISE SAUCE

❧ Replace the lemon juice in the Hollandaise recipe with 4 tbsp (60 mL) orange juice and the grated zest of an orange. This is an excellent sauce to serve with asparagus.

CHANTILLY HOLLANDAISE SAUCE

1 recipe Hollandaise sauce
½ cup (125 mL) whipping cream

❧ Prepare a Hollandaise sauce according to the basic recipe. Just before serving, whip the cream and fold it into the sauce.
❧ This sauce should be served lukewarm, as reheating usually causes it to collapse or separate. It is an ideal sauce to serve with cold fish, chicken or asparagus.

BÉARNAISE SAUCE

¼ cup (50 mL) cider vinegar or wine vinegar
1 French shallot, finely chopped

Béarnaise Sauce

1 tsp (5 mL) tarragon
4 freshly ground peppercorns

❧ Heat the vinegar, green onion, tarragon and pepper over medium heat.
❧ Cook until the liquid is reduced to 3 tbsp (45 mL). Strain through a fine sieve. Substitute this liquid for the lemon juice in the Hollandaise sauce recipe.

CHORON SAUCE

1 recipe Béarnaise sauce
2 tbsp (30 mL) tomato paste

❧ Prepare the Béarnaise sauce according to the recipe; then stir in the tomato paste, 1 tsp (5 mL) at a time, stirring constantly.
❧ Serve with steak, fried fish, chicken or eggs.

COLBERT SAUCE

2 tbsp (30 mL) meat glaze
1 tbsp (15 mL) white wine or lemon juice
1 recipe Béarnaise sauce

❧ Melt the meat glaze (the brown jellied residue left in the bottom of the pan after cooking a roast) in the white wine or lemon juice, without letting it boil.
❧ Prepare the Béarnaise sauce and gradually add the meat glaze mixture, stirring constantly. Serve Colbert sauce with any type of broiled or roasted meat.

SAUCES TO SERVE WITH BROILED FISH

CUCUMBER SAUCE

❧ Combine ¼ cup (50 mL) sour cream with 1 cup (250 mL) finely diced cucumber and ¼ tsp (1 mL) celery seeds. Salt and pepper to taste.

LEMON SAUCE

❧ Combine ⅓ cup (75 mL) mayonnaise with 1 tsp (5 mL) of prepared horseradish, 1 tsp (5 mL) prepared mustard and 2 tbsp (30 mL) of lemon juice.

SHERRY SAUCE

❧ Combine 1 cup (250 mL) mayonnaise with ¼ cup (50 mL) of sherry and 2 tbsp (30 mL) finely chopped chives or green onion.

CHUTNEY SAUCE

❧ Combine 1 tsp (5 mL) curry powder with 2 tbsp (30 mL) cognac. Stir in ½ cup (125 mL) mayonnaise and 2 tbsp (30 mL) of chutney.

BASTING SAUCE FOR ROASTS AND FISH

It is important to baste roasted or broiled meat and fish while they are cooking. A little melted butter is sufficient, but a specially prepared sauce will improve the taste and keep the meat or fish juicy.

❧ All the following basting sauces keep very well. Put any leftover sauce in a clean jar, seal it well, and refrigerate.

PIQUANT SAUCE

(for beef)

½ cup (125 mL) catsup
1 tsp (5 mL) dry mustard
1 tbsp (15 mL) Worcestershire sauce
1 tbsp (15 mL) vegetable oil

❧ Combine all the ingredients. Baste a roast beef or meatballs with this sauce as they cook.

❧ Yields ½ cup (125 mL) of basting sauce.

ENGLISH SAUCE

(for beef)

½ cup (125 mL) finely chopped onions
¼ cup (50 mL) butter
1⅓ cups (325 mL) chili sauce
⅓ cup (75 mL) soy sauce

❧ Brown the onions in the butter. Remove the pan from the heat. Add the chili sauce and soy sauce and mix well.

❧ Yields 1¾ cups (425 mL) of basting sauce.

BASTING SAUCE

1 cup (250 mL) finely chopped mushrooms
¼ cup (50 mL) vegetable oil
6 anchovies, finely chopped
½ cup (125 mL) finely chopped parsley
6-oz can (175 mL) tomato paste
4 cloves garlic, crushed
¾ cup (175 mL) vegetable oil
3 cups (750 mL) red wine

¼ cup (50 mL) cognac
½ tsp (2 mL) salt
¼ tsp (1 mL) pepper

❧ Sauté the mushrooms in ¼ cup (50 mL) oil over high heat for 1 minute.

❧ Place the remaining ingredients in a heavy saucepan. Add the mushrooms. Let simmer over medium heat for 15 minutes, stirring often.

❧ Let the sauce cool and pour it into a clean jar. Cover well and store in the refrigerator.

❧ Use this sauce to baste steaks, roasts or chicken (whole or in pieces) before cooking them. You can also stir a few spoonfuls into scrambled eggs or into ground beef when making meat balls or meat loaf. A few spoonfuls will enhance the flavor of almost any sauce or stew.

WHITE WINE SAUCE

(for chicken and veal)

¼ cup (50 mL) vegetable oil
½ cup (125 mL) white wine
1 clove garlic, minced
1 onion, minced
½ tsp (2 mL) salt
½ tsp (2 mL) celery salt
¼ tsp (1 mL) pepper
¼ tsp (1 mL) thyme
¼ tsp (1 mL) marjoram

❧ Place all the ingredients in a jar with a tight-fitting lid and shake well. Allow to stand for 4 to 6 hours before using.

GREEK SAUCE

(for lamb)

½ cup (125 mL) vegetable oil
2 tbsp (30 mL) lemon juice
zest of 1 lemon, grated
½ tsp (2 mL) freshly ground pepper
1 tsp (5 mL) salt
¼ tsp (1 mL) thyme
1 clove garlic, minced (optional)

❧ Place all the ingredients in a jar with a tight-fitting lid. Shake well and allow to stand for 1 hour. Use to baste lamb during roasting or broiling.
❧ Yields ½ cup (125 mL).

HERB SAUCE

(for fish and sausages)

¼ cup (50 mL) finely chopped onion
¼ cup (50 mL) vegetable oil
2 tbsp (30 mL) brown sugar
½ tsp (2 mL) salt
½ tsp (2 mL) paprika
½ cup (125 mL) lemon juice
½ cup (125 mL) water
1 cup (250 mL) chili sauce
¼ tsp (1 mL) rosemary
¼ tsp (1 mL) basil

❧ Sauté the onion in the oil over low heat, without letting it brown.
❧ Add the remaining ingredients and let simmer for 15 minutes, stirring from time to time. This sauce can be used hot or cold.
❧ Yields 2 cups (500 mL).

PINK SAUCE

(for turkey, chicken or rabbit)

2 tsp (10 mL) salt
¼ tsp (1 mL) pepper
1½ cups (375 mL) tomato juice or white wine
¼ tsp (1 mL) dry mustard
2 tsp (10 mL) Worcestershire sauce
1 bay leaf
½ tsp (2 mL) savory
pinch of thyme
½ cup (125 mL) cider vinegar
1 tbsp (15 mL) sugar
2 or 3 cloves garlic, minced
3 tbsp (45 mL) butter

❧ Place all the ingredients in a saucepan. Bring to a boil and let simmer, uncovered, for 10 minutes over low heat. This sauce can be used hot or cold.
❧ Yields 2 cups (500 mL).

CREAM SAUCE

4 tbsp (60 mL) butter
1 French shallot, finely chopped
4½ cups (1.1 L) flour
1½ cups (375 mL) cream

½ cup (125 mL) milk
salt and pepper
¼ cup (50 mL) finely chopped parsley

❧ Melt the butter in a saucepan and add the chopped shallot. Simmer over low heat for 5 minutes. Remove the pan from the heat.
❧ Add the flour and blend it in well, then add the cream and milk. Stir until well blended, then return the pan to the heat. Beat with a wire whisk or stir with a wooden spoon until the sauce is smooth and creamy. Salt and pepper to taste. Add the parsley and simmer over very low heat for a few seconds.

CURRY SAUCE

4 tbsp (60 mL) butter
½ cup (125 mL) finely chopped onions

Curry Sauce

❦ TECHNIQUE ❦

CURRY SAUCE

1 Melt the butter and add the onions. Cook over low heat for 10 minutes.

2 Sprinkle the curry over the onions and mix well.

3 Add the flour and blend it in.

4 Stir in the consommé or milk.

2 to 4 tbsp (30 to 60 mL) curry
powder
4 tbsp (60 mL) flour
2 cups (500 mL) consommé
or milk
¼ cup (50 mL) cream
juice of ½ lemon
salt and pepper

🌢 Melt the butter and add the
chopped onions. Cover and cook
over low heat for 10 minutes, stirring occasionally. Do not allow
the onions to brown.
🌢 Sprinkle the curry powder over
the onions and stir until completely blended. Add the flour
and mix well. Add the consommé
or milk. Continue to cook, stirring constantly, until the sauce is
smooth and creamy.
🌢 Stir in the cream and lemon
juice. Salt and pepper to taste.

CHEESE SAUCE

2 tbsp (30 mL) butter
1 tbsp (15 mL) flour
1½ cups (375 mL) milk
½ lb (250 g) Cheddar cheese,
grated
2 tbsp (30 mL) sherry
salt and pepper

🌢 Heat the butter and flour in a
saucepan until the flour browns
slightly. Remove the pan from the
heat.
🌢 Add the milk, then stir over
low heat until the sauce is
smooth and creamy.
🌢 Add the cheese and sherry. Stir
over very low heat until the
cheese is thoroughly melted. Salt
and pepper to taste.

ENGLISH MUSTARD SAUCE

4 egg yolks, lightly beaten
1 tbsp (15 mL) flour
juice of 1 lemon
¼ tsp (1 mL) sugar
½ cup (125 mL) butter, melted
2 cups (500 mL) consommé
1 tbsp (15 mL) dry mustard
salt and pepper

🌢 Combine the egg yolks, flour
and lemon juice in the top of a
double boiler.
🌢 Add the sugar, melted butter
and consommé. Cook over boiling water until the sauce is
creamy and smooth, stirring frequently. Add the mustard, salt
and pepper to taste. Avoid boiling
this sauce once it is thickened.

CANNED TOMATO SAUCE

1 large can tomatoes
2 onions, finely chopped
1 sprig parsley
1 bay leaf
pinch of thyme
2 cloves
1 tbsp (15 mL) sugar
1 tbsp (15 mL) butter mixed
with 1 tbsp (15 mL) flour
or ½ cup (125 mL) breadcrumbs
or soda cracker crumbs

🌢 Place the canned tomatoes,
onions, parsley, bay leaf, thyme,
cloves and sugar in a skillet.
Simmer for 1 hour. Season to
taste.
🌢 If desired, strain the sauce. A
few minutes before serving, thick-
en the sauce with the butter and
flour mixture, or with the bread
or cracker crumbs.

Canned Tomato Sauce

RAISIN SAUCE

½ cup (125 mL) brown sugar
1 tsp (5 mL) dry mustard
1 tbsp (15 mL) flour
2 tbsp (30 mL) vinegar
2 tbsp (30 mL) lemon juice
1½ cups (375 mL) water
zest of ½ lemon
⅓ cup (75 mL) raisins

🍃 Mix together the brown sugar, dry mustard and flour. Add the remaining ingredients and blend well.

🍃 Cook over low heat, stirring constantly, until the mixture thickens. Let simmer for 5 minutes.

VARIATION

Soak the raisins in ½ cup (125 mL) cognac or whisky for 24 hours. Prepare the sauce as described above, and then stir in the alcohol gradually as the sauce simmers.

🍃 Serve with boiled or braised beef tongue or with game.

FRESH TOMATO SAUCE

2 lbs (1 kg) fresh tomatoes, chopped
2 medium onions, minced
2 cloves
1 tbsp (15 mL) sugar
parsley, thyme and bay leaf, to taste
1 tbsp (15 mL) tomato paste
1 tbsp (15 mL) butter

🍃 In a large saucepan, cook the tomatoes with the onions, cloves, sugar, parsley, thyme and bay leaf

for 25 minutes. Season to taste.

🍃 As soon as the sauce is thick, add the tomato paste and the butter. Remove from the heat and stir until the butter has melted.

TOMATO SAUCE WITH MUSHROOMS

This is a good way to use up mushroom stems and trimmings. Of course you can also use sliced whole mushrooms.

4 tbsp (60 mL) butter
½ to 1 lb (250 to 500 g) fresh mushroom stems or sliced mushrooms
2 leeks, thinly sliced
1 large can tomatoes
1 tsp (5 mL) sugar
½ tsp (2 mL) basil
1 bay leaf
salt and pepper

🍃 Heat the butter in a saucepan and add the mushroom stems or sliced mushrooms and the leeks. Stir well, then cover and simmer over low heat for 5 minutes.

🍃 Add the tomatoes, sugar, basil and bay leaf. Bring to a boil and simmer uncovered for 40 to 60 minutes. Salt and pepper to taste and serve.

VELOUTÉ SAUCE FOR FISH

STOCK:
1½ lbs (750 g) fish bones and heads
1 tbsp (15 mL) butter

8 cups (2 L) water
½ tsp (2 mL) thyme
1 clove garlic, unpeeled
1 onion, chopped
5 peppercorns
2 carrots, quartered
1 small bunch leeks (the green part)
1 small bunch celery leaves
1 tsp (5 mL) salt

VELOUTÉ:
¾ cup (175 mL) butter
1½ cups (375 mL) flour
5 cups (1.2 L) fish stock

🍃 To prepare the stock, put the fish bones, butter and water in a stock pot and cook over high heat for 5 minutes.

🍃 Add the thyme, garlic, onion, peppercorns, carrots, green part of leeks, celery leaves and salt. Bring to a boil. Boil over high heat for 30 minutes.

🍃 Strain through a fine sieve. This will yield about 5 to 5½ cups (1.25 L) of fish stock.

🍃 To prepare the velouté, melt the butter in a saucepan, add the flour and blend it in well. Remove the pan from the heat and add the fish stock. Beat with an electric mixer or wire whisk. Return the pan to the burner. Cover and simmer over low heat for 1 hour. Stir 3 or 4 times during the cooking period. Season to taste and serve.

🍃 This sauce can be frozen or stored in the refrigerator for up to 2 weeks. It is delicious with all kinds of fish. Vary it by adding mushrooms, tomato paste, white wine or other flavorings.

CAPER SAUCE FOR FISH

2 tbsp (30 mL) butter
3 tbsp (45 mL) flour
2 cups (500 mL) fish stock
or water
1 egg yolk
2 tbsp (30 mL) cream
2 tbsp (30 mL) lemon juice
2 to 3 tbsp (30 to 45 mL) capers
salt and pepper
3 tbsp (45 mL) soft butter

❧ Make a white sauce with the 2 tbsp (30 mL) of butter, the flour and the fish stock or water. When the sauce is smooth and creamy, remove the pan from the heat.

❧ Beat the egg yolk with the cream. Pour the egg mixture into the sauce, stirring constantly. Add the lemon juice and capers. Salt and pepper to taste.

❧ Simmer the sauce for 1 or 2 minutes more, stirring constantly. Remove the pan from the heat, add the soft butter and stir until it is melted. Pour the sauce over the fish and serve.

❧ Caper sauce for boiled lamb: use stock from the lamb instead of the fish stock or water in the above recipe.

❧ Thinly sliced gherkins may be substituted for capers.

NORMANDY OYSTER SAUCE

(for fish)

1 hard-cooked egg
8 to 10 raw oysters
4 mushrooms, finely chopped

1 tbsp (15 mL) butter
1 tbsp (15 mL) flour
2 tbsp (30 mL) lemon juice
or 1 tbsp (15 mL) white wine
¼ cup (50 mL) cream
pinch of nutmeg
salt and pepper to taste

❧ Chop the white and yolk of the egg separately. Cut each oyster in 4 pieces. Melt the butter and cook the chopped mushrooms in it for about ½ minute. Add the flour and mix well.

❧ Take 1 cup (250 mL) of the liquid used to cook the fish. (Add enough water to make 1 cup (250 mL), if necessary.) Add to this liquid the chopped yolk of the hard-cooked egg and pour over the mushrooms. Stir until the sauce is creamy.

❧ Add the chopped egg white and the lemon juice or white wine. Mix well, then add the oysters, cream and nutmeg. Salt and pepper to taste. Pour the sauce over the cooked fish.

❧ The heat of the sauce is enough to cook the oysters.

COLD SAUCE

1¼ cups (300 mL) cream
1½ cups (375 mL) chicken stock
pinch of tarragon
salt and pepper
1 tbsp (15 mL) unflavored gelatin
3 tbsp (45 mL) white wine
or lemon juice

❧ In a saucepan, simmer the cream with the chicken stock and tarragon until reduced to 2 cups (500 mL). Salt and pepper to taste. Strain through a very fine sieve.

❧ Dissolve the gelatin in the white wine or lemon juice and let stand for 5 minutes. Stir the gelatin into the cream sauce and stir over low heat until the gelatin is completely melted.

❧ Spread a layer of this sauce over well-chilled cooked chicken breasts or cooked salmon. Chill in refrigerator to set the first coat, then repeat the process until glazed to the desired thickness.

ALMOND SAUCE

¼ lb (125 g) butter
¼ to ½ cup (50 to 125 mL) almonds, blanched and slivered
juice of ½ lemon
salt and pepper

❧ Heat the butter in a skillet until well browned. Add the almonds and stir quickly until lightly browned.

❧ Add the lemon juice and remove the sauce from the heat. Season lightly with salt and pepper. Serve this sauce with baked fish, green beans, cauliflower or other vegetable.

BREAD SAUCE FOR PARTRIDGE

2 cloves
1 small onion
1 cup (250 mL) milk
1¼ cups (300 mL) fresh breadcrumbs
salt and pepper
1 tbsp (15 mL) butter
1 tbsp (15 mL) cream

Sauce Diablo

• Place the milk in a saucepan. Stick the cloves in the onion and add it to the milk. Bring to a boil over low heat.

• Add the breadcrumbs and simmer, covered, for 20 minutes. Remove the onion. Salt and pepper to taste.

• When ready to serve, stir the butter and cream into the very hot sauce. Beat for a few minutes with a wire whisk. Serve in a gravy boat.

PLUM SAUCE

for beef and chicken)

2 white onions, chopped
16 to 18 small fresh blue plums
1½ cups (375 mL) red wine
or apple juice
4 cloves
3 tbsp (45 mL) butter
1 tbsp (15 mL) sugar
½ tsp (2 mL) salt
¼ tsp (1 mL) pepper

• Peel and chop the onions. Wash the plums, split them in half and pit them. Place the plums and cloves in a saucepan with the red wine or apple juice. Bring to a boil. Let simmer for 10 minutes.

• Melt the butter and add the onions, sugar, salt and pepper. Cover and simmer for 10 minutes. Add the butter mixture to the plums and let simmer over low heat for about 40 minutes or until the sauce has the desired consistency.

• To freeze this sauce: when the sauce has cooled, freeze it in freezer containers. To serve, place a containerful of frozen sauce in the top part of a double boiler and heat. If the frozen sauce is difficult to remove from the container, place it in hot water for 1 minute.

VIMOT SAUCE

This sauce can be prepared ahead of time and refrigerated. When ready to serve, warm it without letting it boil.

1½ lbs (750 g) fresh tomatoes, unpeeled
4 thin slices fat salt pork
3 medium onions, finely chopped
⅓ cup (75 mL) finely chopped parsley
1 tsp (5 mL) sugar
½ tsp (2 mL) basil

• Wash and dice the tomatoes. In a saucepan, simmer the tomatoes over medium heat until thick and creamy, stirring occasionally. This cooking brings out the full taste of the tomatoes.

• In the meantime, cut the salt pork into small cubes and fry them in a heavy skillet until the fat is melted and the pork is crisp and golden. Add the onions, parsley, sugar and basil. Stir over medium heat until the onion starts to change color. Add the tomatoes and let simmer for a few moments, stirring. Season to taste with salt and pepper and serve.

GRIBICHE SAUCE

This is a classic of the French sauce repertoire. Serve it on a green salad or with a lobster salad. It's delicious!

3 hard-cooked eggs
3 green onions, finely chopped
3 tbsp (45 mL) finely chopped parsley
½ tsp (2 mL) tarragon

1 tbsp (15 mL) Dijon
or German mustard
1 cup (250 mL) vegetable oil
1 tsp (5 mL) wine vinegar
or lemon juice
salt and pepper

🍃 Chop the egg whites. Cover them and set aside.

🍃 Mash the egg yolks and add the chopped green onions, parsley, tarragon and mustard. Mash until thoroughly blended.

🍃 Add the oil a little at a time, beating continuously with an electric mixer. Stir in the vinegar or lemon juice and season to taste with salt and pepper. Fold in the chopped egg whites. Store in a tightly sealed container in the refrigerator. This sauce will keep for 3 to 4 days. Beat thoroughly before serving.

SAUCE DIABLO

This sauce is not only delicious with Fondue Bourguignonne but can also be served with grilled fish or chicken.

1 cup (250 mL) white wine
2 green onions, chopped
½ clove garlic, crushed
½ cube beef stock
pinch of cayenne pepper
½ tsp (2 mL) Dijon
or German mustard
2 tbsp (30 mL) catsup

🍃 Place the wine, green onions and garlic in a saucepan. Boil, uncovered, until the liquid is reduced by half.

🍃 Add the beef cube and cayenne pepper. Stir until dissolved.

Remove from the heat and add the mustard and catsup. Stir until well blended and serve.

🍃 This sauce can be made in advance, but it is at its best when freshly prepared.

RAVIGOTE SAUCE

It's the combination of fresh parsley, fresh chives and, when possible, fresh chervil or tarragon that makes this sauce so delicious. Serve chilled.

3 to 4 tbsp (40 to 60 mL) vegetable oil
1 tbsp (15 mL) wine
or cider vinegar
salt and pepper
1 green onion, finely chopped
1 tsp (5 mL) capers
2 tbsp (30 mL) fresh parsley
2 tbsp (30 mL) fresh chives
½ tsp (2 mL) fresh chervil
or tarragon

🍃 Mix the oil and wine or vinegar. Salt and pepper to taste. Add the green onion and capers. Finely chop the parsley, chives and chervil or tarragon (or whatever combination you prefer). Stir into the sauce and serve.

🍃 This sauce can be prepared ahead of time. Although it does not have to be refrigerated, it is better chilled.

PIQUANT SWISS SAUCE

This unusual sauce is very tasty and easy to prepare.

🍃 Blend together ⅓ cup (75 mL) sour cream, ⅓ cup (75 mL) French dressing of your choice and 3 tbsp (45 mL) of chutney. Serve.

Ravigote Sauce

TOMATO SAUCE

3 slices bacon, diced small
1 onion, finely chopped
1 tbsp (15 ml) flour
4 large fresh tomatoes, unpeeled
1 tbsp (15 mL) finely chopped
parsley
½ tsp (2 mL) thyme
½ tsp (2 mL) salt
pepper to taste
pinch of nutmeg
½ cup (125 mL) tomato paste
¼ tsp (1 mL) sugar

🍂 Fry the bacon until lightly browned. Add the onion and sauté until it turns a pale golden color. Sprinkle the flour on top and blend thoroughly.

🍂 Chop the unpeeled tomatoes in small pieces and add to the onions and bacon. Add the parsley, thyme, salt, pepper and nutmeg. Stir until the mixture is smooth.

🍂 Stir in the tomato paste and the sugar. Cook over low heat for 15 to 25 minutes or until the sauce is creamy. If you wish to remove the seeds from the sauce, strain before serving.

COCKTAIL SAUCE

½ cup (125 mL) catsup
2 tbsp (30 mL) lemon juice
1 tbsp (15 mL) horseradish,
drained
½ tsp (2 mL) dry mustard
1 tbsp (15 mL) onion juice
¼ tsp (1 mL) celery seeds
¼ cup (50 mL) tomato juice

🍂 Thoroughly mix all the ingredients. Refrigerate the sauce for 1 to 2 hours before serving.

BARBECUE SAUCE

This sauce is perfect for barbecued chicken. You'll want to broil 2 or 3 chickens to serve 4 to 6 people, or 5 chickens for 10 people (half a chicken per person).

4 TO 6 PORTIONS:
½ cup (125 mL) butter
1 cup (250 mL) cider vinegar
1 tsp (5 mL) salt
½ tsp (2 mL) paprika
¼ tsp (1 mL) thyme
¼ to ½ cup (50 to 125 mL) water

10 PORTIONS:
½ lb (250 g) butter
2 cups (500 mL) cider vinegar
1 oz (30 g) salt
½ oz (15 g) paprika
2 tsp (10 mL) thyme
2 cups (500 mL) water

🍂 Place all the ingredients in a skillet. Bring to a boil and simmer over low heat for 5 minutes.

🍂 Brush the chicken with the sauce each time you turn it. Always heat the sauce before using it.

BARBECUE SAUCE FOR CHICKEN

2 tbsp (30 mL) chicken fat
or other meat fat
2 tbsp (30 mL) flour
1 cup (250 mL) water
or consommé
1 tbsp (15 mL) beef extract
1 tsp (5 mL) soy sauce
pinch of allspice
salt, pepper and cayenne pepper

🍂 Heat the fat until it turns a pale nut brown in color. Add the flour and cook over low heat, stirring constantly, until golden. Remove the pan from the heat.

🍂 Add the consommé, beef extract and soy sauce. Return the pan to the heat. Cook, stirring constantly, until the sauce is smooth and creamy.

🍂 Add the allspice, salt, pepper and cayenne pepper. Simmer for a few seconds before serving.

SMOKY BARBECUE SAUCE

(for lamb, spareribs and chicken)

¼ cup (50 mL) cider vinegar
½ cup (125 mL) water
2 tbsp (30 mL) sugar
1 tbsp (15 mL) mustard
¼ tsp (1 mL) pepper
½ lemon, sliced and unpeeled
1 onion, thinly sliced
¼ cup (50 mL) butter
½ cup (125 mL) catsup
1 tsp (5 mL) smoke flavoring
or smoke salt

🍂 In a saucepan, combine the cider vinegar, water, sugar, mustard, pepper, lemon slices, onion slices and butter. Simmer for 20 minutes.

🍂 Add the catsup and the smoke flavoring. Boil for 1 minute. This sauce can be served hot or cold.

LEMON BARBECUE SAUCE

(for chicken and fish)

1 clove garlic, minced
½ tsp (2 mL) salt

¼ cup (50 mL) vegetable oil
½ cup (125 mL) lemon juice
1 green onion, finely chopped
¼ tsp (1 mL) pepper
¼ tsp (1 mL) thyme

🍂 Mix together all the ingredients. Stir well and place the sauce in a jar with a tight-fitting lid. Close tightly and refrigerate for 24 hours before using.

TOMATO BARBECUE SAUCE

(for steak, pork and duck)

1½ tsp (7 mL) salt
¼ tsp (1 mL) pepper
1½ cups (375 mL) tomato juice
¼ tsp (1 mL) dry mustard
4 tsp (20 mL) Worcestershire sauce
1 bay leaf
½ cup (125 mL) malt vinegar
1 tsp (5 mL) sugar
2 cloves garlic, minced
3 tbsp vegetable oil

🍂 Place all the ingredients in a bowl and blend well. Pour into a glass jar and close tightly. Refrigerate for at least 1 hour before using.

WINE BARBECUE SAUCE

(for chicken, duck and ground beef)

¼ cup (50 mL) oil
½ cup (125 mL) red wine
1 clove garlic, crushed
1 small onion, grated
½ tsp (2 mL) salt
½ tsp (2 mL) celery salt
¼ tsp (1 mL) pepper

Tomato Barbecue Sauce

¼ tsp (1 mL) marjoram
¼ tsp (1 mL) rosemary

🍂 Place all the ingredients in a bowl in the order given and stir until well blended.
🍂 Pour over the chicken, duck or meatballs. Cover and let marinate in the refrigerator for 3 hours.
🍂 Broil the meat, basting 2 or 3 times with the sauce.

BARBECUE SAUCE FOR SAUSAGES

¼ cup (50 mL) vegetable oil
1 onion, finely chopped
1 tbsp (15 mL) Worcestershire sauce
2 tbsp (30 mL) brown sugar
½ tsp (2 mL) salt
½ tsp (2 mL) paprika
¼ cup (50 mL) lemon juice
½ cup (125 mL) water
1 cup (250 mL) chili sauce

🍂 Place the oil and onion in a saucepan. Let simmer over low heat for 10 minutes.
🍂 Add the remaining ingredients. Bring to a boil, then simmer over very low heat for 15 minutes, stirring frequently.
🍂 You can baste sausages with this sauce as they cook or use it as a dipping sauce for cooked sausages.

VERMONT BARBECUE SAUCE

⅔ cup (150 mL) chili sauce
⅔ cup (150 mL) catsup
1 small onion, finely chopped
1 tbsp (15 mL) cider vinegar
juice of 1 lemon
½ tsp (2 mL) salt
pinch of pepper
1 clove garlic, minced
1 tsp (5 mL) Worcestershire sauce

Place the ingredients in the order given in a jar with a tight-fitting lid. Cover and shake well. Refrigerate for a few hours.

Use this sauce on sausages, ground beef, etc. It keeps very well in the refrigerator.

FAST AND EASY BARBECUE SAUCE

1 or 2 cloves garlic, crushed
1½ tsp (7 mL) salt
¼ cup (50 mL) finely chopped green onion
2 tsp (10 mL) mustard
1 tsp (5 mL) dry mustard
¼ cup (50 mL) brown sugar
juice of 1 lemon
3 tbsp (45 mL) Worcestershire sauce
1 can tomato soup, undiluted

Place all the ingredients in a bowl. Using an electric mixer, thoroughly blend the ingredients. Pour the sauce into a jar, seal tightly and refrigerate.

Serve this sauce with meatballs, sausages or broiled chicken.

HERB MUSTARD

5 tbsp (75 mL) dry mustard
½ cup (125 mL) brown sugar
¼ tsp (1 mL) marjoram
¼ tsp (1 mL) pepper
1 tsp (5 mL) coarse salt
½ cup (125 mL) lemon juice
few drops Tabasco sauce (optional)
½ cup (125 mL) olive oil

Place all the ingredients in a blender jar. Cover and blend for 1 minute at high speed. Pour the

mustard into small jars with tight-fitting lids. Cover and let stand for 8 to 10 days before using.

FINNISH MUSTARD

This mustard, which is very popular in Finland, is delicious as an accompaniment for ham. It is easy to make and has a terrific sweet and sour taste. My Finnish friend Peter taught me how to make it.

4 tbsp (60 mL) dry mustard
3 tbsp (45 mL) sugar
½ tsp (2 mL) salt
1 tbsp (15 mL) cider vinegar or malt vinegar
4 tbsp (60 mL) boiling water

In the top part of a double boiler, combine the dry mustard, the sugar and the salt. Combine the boiling water and vinegar and stir it into the mustard mixture. Place the mixture over boiling water and stir very slowly until the mixture resembles a smooth paste. As soon as the mustard mixture is smooth and slightly thickened, remove it from the heat. The mixture will thicken as it cools. Pour it into small jars, cover and let the mustard sit for at least a few days before using. It does not have to be refrigerated.

Serve with ham loaf.

WHITE BUTTER

¼ cup (50 mL) cider vinegar or lemon juice
¼ cup (50 mL) dry white wine
1 tbsp (15 mL) finely chopped French shallots

¼ tsp (1 mL) salt
pinch of pepper
1½ cups (375 g) butter, diced and very cold

Place the vinegar or lemon juice, white wine, onion, salt and pepper in a small saucepan. Boil uncovered until the liquid is reduced to 1½ tbsp (25 mL). Strain to remove the shallot pieces. Place the strained juice back in the saucepan and heat it to the boiling point.

Remove the pan from the heat and start adding the cold butter. As soon as 1 cube of butter melts and becomes creamy, add another. Place the saucepan over very low heat and continue adding 1 cube of butter at a time, beating constantly with a wire whisk. Always wait until the cube of butter has melted before adding another. Avoid over-beating and do not boil, as the sauce will separate. Serve as soon as it turns an ivory color.

This is the classic sauce to serve with poached pike. It is also delicious with asparagus, broccoli, cauliflower and poached eggs.

BLACK BUTTER

(Beurre Noir)

4 tbsp (60 mL) butter
3 tbsp (45 mL) finely chopped parsley
4 tbsp (60 mL) lemon juice
salt and pepper

The first step when preparing black butter is to clarify the butter. Cut the butter into pieces and place them in a saucepan over medium heat. As soon as the butter has melted, skim the foam from the top and carefully pour the clear yellow part (clarified butter) into a skillet. Wipe away the whitish residue from the bottom of the saucepan.

🍃 Heat the clarified butter over medium heat until it is dark nutty brown in color. Immediately remove it from the heat and return it to the saucepan.

🍃 Place the parsley, lemon juice and salt and pepper in the skillet. Boil over high heat until the liquid is reduced to 1 tbsp (15 mL). Add the lemon juice mixture to the blackened butter. Serve with boiled fish, poached brains or vegetables.

BROWN BUTTER

🍃 Follow the directions for black butter, but do not allow the clarified butter to become as dark.

MUSTARD BUTTER

¼ cup (50 mL) butter
1 tbsp (15 mL) Dijon mustard
salt and pepper
chives or parsley, finely chopped

🍃 Cream the butter, then add the mustard and blend well.

🍃 Add salt and pepper to taste. Stir in the chives or parsley.

🍃 This butter is delicious dotted on broiled calves' liver, steak or broiled fish. You can also use it to add extra richness to sauces.

Garlic Butter

GARLIC BUTTER

4 cloves garlic, unpeeled
4 cups (1 L) boiling water
½ cup (125 mL) butter
salt and pepper

🍃 Place the garlic cloves in the boiling water. Return to a boil. As soon as the water is boiling, drain it off and peel the garlic cloves. Rinse them in cold water. Repeat the process with the peeled garlic.

🍃 Crush the garlic to a paste. Add the butter and cream together well. Salt and pepper to taste. Serve with broiled or poached fish, lamb chops, boiled potatoes or even on toasted bread. You can also use this mixture to flavor soups and sauces.

WINE BUTTER

¼ cup (50 mL) red wine
1 tbsp (15 mL) finely chopped green onion
1 tbsp (15 mL) meat glaze or ½ cup (125 mL) consommé
½ cup (125 mL) butter
2 tbsp (30 mL) finely chopped parsley
salt and pepper

🍃 In a saucepan, combine the wine, onion and the meat glaze (the gelatinous part left in the pan after cooking a roast) or consommé. Boil until reduced to 1½ tbsp (25 mL). Let cool.

🍃 Cream the butter and add it, 1 tsp (5 mL) at a time, to the reduced cooled wine, beating thoroughly after each addition. Add the parsley and season to taste with salt and pepper. Serve with steak or calf's liver or use the butter to add extra richness to sauces.

BERCY BUTTER

❧ Prepare Bercy butter the same way as wine butter, but replace the red wine with dry white wine. Serve with chicken or veal or use to add richness to white sauces.

SNAIL BUTTER

½ cup (125 mL) butter
2 tbsp (30 mL) finely chopped green onion
2 cloves garlic, minced
2 tbsp (30 mL) finely chopped parsley
salt and pepper

❧ Cream the butter. Add the onion and garlic. Mash together thoroughly until the onion and garlic can barely be detected.
❧ Add the parsley, salt and pepper and continue to stir until the butter turns pale green. This butter is delicious served with broiled meats and fish, mushrooms, mussels, hot oysters and, of course, snails.

TARRAGON BUTTER

½ cup (125 mL) butter
1 tbsp (15 mL) lemon juice
2 tbsp (30 mL) fresh tarragon or 1 tbsp (15 mL) dried tarragon
2 tbsp (30 mL) finely chopped parsley
salt and pepper

❧ Cream the butter. Add the lemon juice, a drop at a time, beating vigorously after each addition.
❧ Stir in the chopped tarragon and parsley. Continue to mix until the herbs are well blended. Season to taste with salt and pepper.
❧ Serve with broiled meat or poached or broiled fish or use to enrich soups and sauces.

STEAK BUTTER

1 clove garlic
½ cup (125 mL) butter
1 tsp (5 mL) finely chopped green onion
1 tsp (5 mL) basil
½ tsp (2 mL) marjoram
1 tsp (5 mL) lemon juice
½ tsp (2 mL) smoke flavoring
1 tsp (5 mL) paprika

❧ Cut the garlic in half and rub it over the interior of a bowl. Cream the butter in the bowl.
❧ Add the onion, basil, marjoram, lemon juice, smoke flavoring and paprika. Stir until well blended and very smooth.
❧ Spread this tasty butter over steak or fish fresh from the grill or barbecue.

SALAD DRESSINGS

The classic salad dressing, or vinaigrette, is prepared with oil, vinegar, salt and pepper. As a rule, 1 part vinegar is combined with 2 to 3 parts oil, and salt and pepper are added to taste.
❧ In spite of its great simplicity, the flavor and even the color of this dressing can be varied considerably depending on the type of

Snail Butter

vinegar and oil you use. Try French, Italian, Spanish or Greek olive oils or even corn oil. You can also experiment with flavored vinegars—tarragon, basil, cider, malt or wine vinegar as well as good old reliable white vinegar.

🍂 A change in any of the ingredients alters the flavor of the dressing: you could replace the vinegar with lemon juice or use freshly ground white pepper instead of black. Vary the ingredients depending on whether you want an everyday dressing or one for a special dish. Experiment with different combinations and discover what pleases you the most. I have my own favorites.

🍂 For a tomato salad, I like a dressing of Italian or Greek olive oil combined with white wine vinegar flavored with basil.

🍂 With cold salmon, I prefer lemon juice and a French oil.

🍂 With rice or fresh vegetables, I use cider vinegar and corn oil.

🍂 Finally, when making a classic green salad, I first crush a little coarse salt in the bottom of the salad bowl. I then sprinkle fresh lemon juice mixed with French or Spanish oil over the salad and grind a little black pepper over it all. Nothing enhances the flavor of a salad better than this simple mixture.

🍂 Use your imagination and try different combinations. There's always a tasty new dressing waiting to be discovered.

Dijon Dressing

FRENCH DRESSING

(Classic Vinaigrette)

1 tsp (5 mL) Dijon mustard
1 tbsp (15 mL) salt
½ tsp (2 mL) pepper
4 tbsp (60 mL) cider
or wine vinegar
½ cup (125 mL) olive oil

🍂 Place all the ingredients in a bowl. Beat until thoroughly blended.

ENGLISH DRESSING

½ cup (125 mL) malt or tarragon vinegar
1 cup (250 mL) olive oil
1 tsp (5 mL) dry mustard
½ tsp (2 mL) Worcestershire sauce
½ tsp (2 mL) salt
½ tsp (2 mL) pepper
¼ tsp (1 mL) celery seeds
2 ice cubes

🍂 Place the vinegar in a bowl and add the oil a little at a time, beating constantly.

🍂 Add the mustard, Worcestershire sauce, salt, pepper and celery seeds 1 ingredient at a time, beating well after each addition.

🍂 Add the ice cubes and beat for 3 or 4 seconds. Refrigerate for 30 minutes. Stir well before using.

DIJON DRESSING

1½ tsp (7 mL) salt
½ tsp (2 mL) pepper
1 tsp (5 mL) Dijon mustard
1 tbsp (15 mL) tarragon vinegar
1 tbsp (15 mL) red wine
1 cup (250 mL) olive oil
1 tbsp (15 mL) finely chopped onion
1 clove garlic, crushed

Roquefort Dressing

☙ Combine all the ingredients in a jar with a tight-fitting lid. Cover and shake vigorously. Remove the garlic before serving.

VEGETABLE OIL VINAIGRETTE

1 cup (250 mL) vegetable oil
⅓ cup (75 mL) vinegar
1 tsp (5 mL) sugar
1½ tsp (7 mL) salt
½ tsp (2 mL) paprika
½ tsp (2 mL) dry mustard
1 clove garlic

☙ Measure all the ingredients into a jar with a tight-fitting lid. Cover and shake vigorously. Refrigerate for several hours. Remove the garlic and shake well before serving.
☙ Yields 1⅓ cups (325 mL).

CHIFFONADE DRESSING

☙ To the basic recipe for vegetable oil vinaigrette, add 2 tbsp (30 mL) chopped hard-cooked egg, 1 tbsp (15 mL) finely chopped green pepper, 1 tbsp (15 mL) chopped red pepper, 1 tsp (5 mL) chopped parsley and ¼ tsp (1 mL) onion juice. Shake well to combine.

CHUTNEY DRESSING

☙ Add 2 tbsp (30 mL) chutney to ¾ cup (175 mL) of the basic recipe for vegetable oil vinaigrette.

3 tbsp (45 mL) finely chopped parsley

☙ Mix together the salt, the pepper and the mustard.
☙ Stir in the tarragon vinegar and red wine. Add the olive oil a little at a time, beating constantly. Add the onion, garlic and parsley. Beat for a few seconds longer.

ROQUEFORT DRESSING

4 oz (125 g) Roquefort cheese
¼ tsp (1 mL) salt
½ tsp (2 mL) paprika
6 tbsp (90 mL) cider vinegar
or port wine
6 to 8 tbsp (90 to 120 mL) olive oil

☙ Place the cheese in a bowl and crush it with a fork. Add the salt, paprika, vinegar or wine and olive oil. Beat with a wire whisk until the mixture is smooth and creamy.
☙ If you want a smoother consistency, force this dressing through a sieve. Store it in a closed container in the refrigerator.

HERBES DRESSING

1 cup (250 mL) vegetable or olive oil
¼ cup (50 mL) cider or tarragon vinegar
1 tsp (5 mL) salt
½ tsp (2 mL) sugar
1 tsp (5 mL) paprika
½ tsp (2 mL) mustard
1 tbsp (15 mL) grated onion
1 tsp (5 mL) Worcestershire sauce
1 tsp (5 mL) basil
1 clove garlic

❦ TECHNIQUE ❦
ROQUEFORT DRESSING

1 Place the cheese in a bowl and mash it with a fork.

2 Add the salt, paprika and vinegar.

3 Add the olive oil.

4 Beat with a wire whisk until the mixture is smooth and creamy.

PINK VINAIGRETTE

1 cup (250 mL) vegetable oil
¼ cup (50 mL) malt vinegar
1½ tbsp (25 mL) catsup
1 tsp (5 mL) sugar
½ tsp (2 mL) paprika
1 tsp (5 mL) salt
½ tsp (2 mL) dry mustard
1 tsp (5 mL) grated onion
1 egg white

🍃 Place all the ingredients in a bowl and beat until well blended and smooth. Keep refrigerated. Stir before serving.

SOUR CREAM DRESSING

1 egg yolk
4 tbsp (60 mL) sour cream
½ cup (125 mL) classic vinaigrette (French dressing)
lemon juice to taste
2 tbsp (30 mL) finely chopped parsley or dill

🍃 Beat the egg yolk and the sour cream until they are well blended.
🍃 Gradually add the vinaigrette, beating constantly.

🍃 Season with salt and pepper and add lemon juice to taste. Just before serving, stir in the herbs.
🍃 Use this dressing with egg or fish salads.

MAYONNAISE

Mayonnaise is an emulsion of egg yolk and oil which becomes thick and creamy not with cooking but with beating. Mayonnaise can be beaten with 2 forks held in one hand, with a wire whisk, or with a rotary or electric mixer. With a little practice, you can make 3 to 4 cups (750 mL to 1 L) of mayonnaise by hand in less than 15 minutes. Mayonnaise can also be made in an electric blender.

🍃 Mayonnaise is easier to make when all the ingredients and utensils are at room temperature or you can rinse the bowl in hot water, making sure to dry it thoroughly before placing the egg yolks in it.
🍃 Always beat the egg yolks for 1 or 2 minutes before adding another ingredient. As soon as the yolks start to thicken, they are ready to absorb the oil.
🍃 The first ¼ cup (50 mL) of oil must be added almost a drop at a time until the mixture begins to thicken. The rest of the oil can then be added more rapidly.
🍃 The yolk of a large egg will usually absorb ¾ cup (175 mL) of oil. If you go beyond this limit there is a risk of the mayonnaise separating. It is safer, if you are not too experienced, to use only about ½ cup (125 mL) of oil per egg yolk.
🍃 For a 3-egg mayonnaise, you will need to use a 12-cup (3-L) stainless steel or glass bowl. Set the bowl on a damp cloth to prevent it from slipping.
🍃 As a rule, you should stir in the vinegar or lemon juice, salt, pepper and mustard before adding the oil.

WHAT TO DO IF MAYONNAISE SEPARATES

Warm a bowl with boiling water and dry it well. Place in it 1 tbsp (5 mL) of the separated mayonnaise with 1 tsp (15 mL) prepared mustard. Beat a few seconds with a wire whisk until the mixture thickens and becomes creamy. Add the rest of the mayonnaise, 1 tsp (5 mL) at a time, beating hard after each addition.

MAYONNAISE CHART

EGG YOLKS	OIL	VINEGAR OR LEMON JUICE	YIELD
2	1 to 1½ cups (250 to 375 mL)	2 to 3 tbsp (30 to 45 mL)	1¼ to 1¾ cups (315 to 425 mL)
3	1½ to 2¼ cups (375 to 550 mL)	3 to 5 tbsp (45 to 75 mL)	2 to 2¾ cups (500 to 675 mL)
4	2 to 3 cups (500 to 750 mL)	4 to 6 tbsp (60 to 90 mL)	2½ to 3⅔ cups (625 to 900 mL)
6	3 to 4½ cups (750 mL to 1.1 L)	6 to 10 tbsp (90 to 150 mL)	3¾ to 5½ cups (925 mL to 1.3 L)

TO AVOID THE RISK OF SALMONELLA POISONING
Uncooked eggs may carry salmonella bacteria. To cut down on the risk of salmonella poisoning, never make mayonnaise from cracked or damaged eggs. Always keep mayonnaise, or any food containing it, well refrigerated.

BLENDER MAYONNAISE

For perfect results, make sure the eggs and oil are at room temperature.

1 whole egg or 2 egg yolks
½ tsp (2 mL) salt
¼ tsp (1 mL) pepper
½ tsp (2 mL) dry mustard
or 1 tsp (2 mL) mustard
2 tbsp (30 mL) cider vinegar
or lemon juice
1 cup (250 mL) vegetable oil

❧ Place the egg, salt, pepper, mustard, vinegar and ¼ cup (50 mL) of the oil in the blender jar. Cover and blend for 1 minute at high speed. Without turning off the blender, remove the stopper and add the remaining oil a little at a time. Blend until firm and creamy.

GREEN MAYONNAISE

❧ Add 4 sprigs parsley, 3 raw spinach leaves and 3 or 4 sprigs of watercress to the basic mayonnaise recipe. Blend for 1 minute. This dressing is an attractive green and has a distinctive flavor. Serve with fish or veal.

Blender Mayonnaise

PINK MAYONNAISE

❧ Add 1 fresh tomato, peeled and quartered, 1 tbsp (15 mL) chili sauce, 1 small clove garlic and 3 sprigs parsley to the prepared basic mayonnaise. Cover and blend for 1 minute. This mayonnaise is simply delicious.

MAYONNAISE WITH OLIVE OIL

2 egg yolks
1 tsp (5 mL) salt
¼ tsp (1 mL) pepper
1 tsp (5 mL) dry mustard
1 tbsp (15 mL) vinegar
1 cup (250 mL) olive oil
1 tbsp (15 mL) boiling water

❧ Place the egg yolks, salt, pepper, dry mustard and vinegar in a bowl. Stir for a few seconds to blend well. Cover and let stand for 20 minutes.

❧ Add the olive oil slowly, beating vigorously, until the mixture becomes thick and creamy. The first 4 or 5 tbsp (60 to 75 mL) of oil should be added in a thin stream; the mayonnaise may separate if the oil is added too quickly.

❧ Stir in the boiling water. Use this mayonnaise immediately. It does not improve with refrigeration.

GARLIC MAYONNAISE

1 clove garlic, cut in half
½ tsp (2 mL) sugar
1 tsp (5 mL) dry mustard
1 tsp (5 mL) salt
2 egg yolks
3 to 4 tbsp (45 to 60 mL) lemon juice
1½ to 2 cups (375 to 500 mL) olive oil

Thousand Island Dressing

½ cup (125 mL) horseradish mayonnaise and ¼ cup (50 mL) black currant jelly. Beat until the mixture is smooth. Fold in the whipped cream and refrigerate until ready to serve. This mayonnaise is delicious with fruit salad.

HERB MAYONNAISE

&To 1 cup (250 mL) basic mayonnaise, add 1 tsp (5 mL) chopped parsley, 1½ tsp (7 mL) chopped chives, ¼ tsp (1 mL) chopped fresh basil and a few drops of lemon juice. Blend well.

CREAMY HERB SAUCE

This is a perfect dressing for fresh shrimp, poached salmon, asparagus or roast veal, served hot or cold.

1 cup (250 mL) mayonnaise
1 cup (250 mL) sour cream
½ cup (125 mL) fresh parsley
1 bunch fresh chives
3 tbsp (45 mL) fresh dill
6 anchovies

&Place all the ingredients in a blender jar. Cover and blend until smooth. This recipe produces a lovely green sauce with a wonderful flavor.

TARTAR SAUCE

&Add 2 tbsp (30 mL) chopped stuffed olives, 2 tbsp (30 mL) chopped sweet pickles, 1 tbsp

&Rub a mixing bowl with the garlic. Add the sugar, mustard and salt.

&Add the egg yolks and beat thoroughly. Add 2 tbsp (30 mL) lemon juice and mix well.

&Slowly add the olive oil, a little at a time, beating constantly. Add the remaining lemon juice and continue to beat until the mayonnaise has the desired consistency.

MAYONNAISE WITH LEMON JUICE

2 egg yolks
1 tsp (5 mL) salt
1 tsp (5 mL) sugar
¼ tsp (1 mL) paprika
1 tsp (5 mL) dry mustard
pinch of pepper
4 tbsp (60 mL) lemon juice
1¾ cups (425 mL) vegetable oil

&Place the egg yolks, salt, sugar, paprika, mustard, pepper and

2 tbsp (30 mL) lemon juice in a mixing bowl. Beat well. Add 1 cup (250 mL) of the oil, 1 tbsp (15 mL) at a time, beating well after each addition.

&Gradually add 1 tbsp (15 mL) lemon juice, then add the remaining oil, a little at a time. Continue to beat the mixture and add the remaining lemon juice.

HORSERADISH MAYONNAISE

&Add 2 to 4 tbsp (30 to 60 mL) horseradish to 1 cup (250 mL) mayonnaise. Mix well.

CREAMY HORSERADISH MAYONNAISE

&Whip ¼ cup (50 mL) whipping cream. In a second bowl, combine

(15 mL) minced parsley and 1 tbsp (15 mL) grated onion to 1½ cups (375) of mayonnaise.

COOKED SALAD DRESSING

¼ cup (50 mL) butter
¼ cup (50 mL) sugar
4 tbsp (60 mL) flour
½ tsp (2 mL) dry mustard
1 tsp (5 mL) salt
2 eggs, beaten
1¼ cups (300 mL) milk
or sour cream
½ to ¾ cups (125 to 175 mL) cider vinegar

🍃 Melt the butter in the top of a double boiler. Remove from the heat and stir in the sugar, flour, mustard, salt, eggs and milk or sour cream.

🍃 Cook over boiling water until the mixture becomes thick and creamy. Slowly add the cider vinegar and stir until smooth. Keep in a covered jar in the refrigerator.

THOUSAND ISLAND DRESSING

1 tsp (5 mL) dry mustard
½ tsp (2 mL) paprika
1 hard-cooked egg, chopped
½ cup (125 mL) celery, chopped
4 green onions, finely chopped
4 gherkins, chopped

4 tbsp (60 mL) tomato paste
1 cup (250 mL) mayonnaise

🍃 Mix all the ingredients together.

ANDALUSIAN MAYONNAISE

🍃 Add 4 tbsp (60 mL) tomato paste and 2 green peppers cut in julienne to 1 cup (250 mL) mayonnaise.

RUSSIAN MAYONNAISE

(European style)

2 tbsp (30 mL) sugar
4 tbsp (60 mL) water
½ tsp (2 mL) salt
½ tsp (2 mL) paprika
1½ tsp (7 mL) celery seeds
juice of 1 lemon
4 tbsp (60 mL) vinegar
3 tbsp (45 mL) tomato paste
¼ cup (50 mL) grated onions
1 cup (250 mL) vegetable oil

🍃 Heat the sugar and water until the mixture reaches the consistency of a thick syrup. Let cool.
🍃 Mix together the remaining ingredients.
🍃 Add the cooled syrup and beat for 3 minutes.

RUSSIAN MAYONNAISE

(American style)

🍃 Add ½ cup (125 mL) chili sauce to 1 cup (250 mL) mayonnaise. Blend well.

GELATIN MAYONNAISE

(Mayonnaise Chaud-Froid)

1 tbsp (15 mL) unflavored gelatin
2 tbsp (30 mL) cold water
2 cups (500 mL) mayonnaise

🍃 Soak the gelatin in the cold water for 5 minutes. Heat gently over hot water until the gelatin is completely dissolved.
🍃 Pour the gelatin mixture into the mayonnaise, stirring vigorously. Use this chaud-froid to coat vegetables, fish or meat. You can also mix it with vegetables, fish or meat and pour into small oiled molds. Refrigerate until set.

CUCUMBER MAYONNAISE

1 large cucumber or 2 small cucumbers
2 tbsp (30 mL) finely chopped green onions
¼ tsp (1 mL) dried dill
1 tbsp (15 mL) mustard
1 tbsp (15 mL) lemon juice
1 cup (250 mL) mayonnaise

🍃 Peel the cucumber, remove the seeds and grate the flesh.
🍃 Add the remaining ingredients. Mix together and refrigerate until ready to use. This mayonnaise is perfect with fish.

MINT SAUCE

3 tbsp (45 mL) cider vinegar
⅔ cup (150 mL) water
½ to ¾ cup (125 to 175 mL)
finely chopped fresh mint leaves
or ¼ cup (50 mL) dried mint
1 tbsp (15 mL) lemon juice
(optional)

1 to 2 tbsp (15 to 30 mL) sugar
¼ tsp (1 mL) salt

🔊 In a saucepan, combine the vinegar, ⅓ cup (75 mL) of the water and 2 tbsp (30 mL) of the mint. Let simmer for 5 minutes. Strain through a fine sieve, reserving the liquid.

🔊 Add the rest of the water and mint, as well as the lemon juice, sugar and salt, to the mint-flavored liquid. Heat just until it starts to boil. Pour into a container, cover and refrigerate. When ready to serve, heat the mixture again without letting it boil. You can also serve this sauce cold.

🔊 This sauce can be kept in the refrigerator for several weeks.

HORS D'OEUVRES AND CANAPÉS

Like many people, you probably enjoy entertaining and take pride in planning the perfect party. Because of a busy schedule, however, you may not feel that you have the time for a formal or complicated affair. Here, then, are a few tips for planning a successful party the easy way.

A cup of punch, a cocktail, a special blend of tea, or rich, dark coffee may be all you need to accompany an assortment of hors d'oeuvres and canapés. It's a quick and easy way to arrange a delightful party. Almost everything can be prepared and set up ahead of time. All your guests have to do is help themselves and enjoy. You'll be amazed at how simple it can be!

Hors d'oeuvres and canapés can be served as an appetizer to a meal or as a snack after the theater or a concert. Of course, the recipes included here are not exhaustive. Use them as a source of inspiration . . . and don't be afraid to improve or modify. All you need is a little imagination.

What exactly is a canapé? During the Victorian era, these bite-size morsels were served before dinner with a glass of sherry. With time, they were adopted by the French, who transformed them into more elaborate fare. Today, although they have regained some of their original simplicity, canapés are as attractive and mouth-watering as ever.

Hors d'oeuvres are small por- tions of hot or cold foods that are generally served before a meal and that turn lunch or dinner into a special occasion. They are made from any combination of savory foods such as eggs, pâtés and delicatessen meats, as well as fish, seafood and vegetables. Very much a herald to a meal, hors d'oeuvres should always be chosen to complement what follows. Their flavor should be distinctive and appetizing but not so overpowering as to spoil the flavor of the main course.

Hors d'oeuvres come in such an infinite variety they can easily become a meal in themselves. You may, however, want to serve only a few and arrange them attractively on a plate. When selecting hors d'oeuvres, take care not to include foods that will be served again during the meal (avoid serving a tomato salad when stuffed tomatoes are on the menu or a potato salad when French fries or mashed potatoes accompany the meat). Hot or spicy foods such as certain kinds of sausages or anchovies should not be served before a delicate meat dish. And keep the hors d'oeuvres light and simple if you are planning a rich, substantial dinner. Let common sense, taste and experience guide you in your selection.

If you serve hors d'oeuvres in individual portions, place them on the table before your guests sit down. Have a small plate, fork and knife at each place. Should you wish to serve wine with hors d'oeuvres, choose a dry white wine such as a Graves, a Meursault or an Alsatian wine.

When serving hors d'oeuvres and canapés, remember to contrast colors, textures, seasoning and presentation. And make a memorable impression.

VEGETABLE HORS D'OEUVRES

Celery and carrot sticks, radishes and marinated fresh mushrooms are the classics of a vegetable hors d'oeuvres platter.

MARINATED MUSHROOM CAPS
Remove the stems from ½ lb (250 g) of fresh mushrooms (saving them for another use) and clean and dry the caps. Mix the caps with 1 tbsp (15 mL) lemon juice, 2 tbsp (30 mL) olive oil, ¼ tsp (1 mL) marjoram and 1 chopped green onion. Add ½ tsp (2 mL) salt and ¼ tsp (1 mL) pepper. Do not cook the mixture.

Prepare the mushrooms a few hours in advance so that they have ample time to marinate. Just before serving, sprinkle them with finely chopped parsley.

SLICED TOMATOES
Arrange sliced tomatoes in a fan shape on a platter. Grate some raw carrots and season with a little lemon juice, pepper and salt and a drop of oil. Place the carrots in a mound at the base of the tomato fan. Garnish with mixed black and green olives.

SALAD MEDLEY
Line the bottom of a dish with finely shredded lettuce leaves. Garnish with potato salad, green

peas and diced beets, each lightly tossed with a French dressing of your choice or with mayonnaise thinned with a touch of cream. Use the dressing sparingly to prevent the hors d'oeuvres from becoming too heavy or oily.

VEGETABLE BOUQUETS
Arrange florets of cooked cauliflower, cooked green beans and tomato wedges separately on a platter. Season each vegetable with French dressing and garnish with finely chopped black olives and parsley.

EGG HORS D'OEUVRES

Hard-cooked eggs are a popular hors d'oeuvre because of their lovely color and their elegant shape. They can be halved, quartered, sliced, chopped or crumbled, and will always be very attractive.

MASKED EGGS
This recipe is simple and tasty. Cut hard-cooked eggs in half lengthwise. Brush the surface of each half with a coating of mayonnaise and garnish with capers, a few sprigs of parsley, a rolled anchovy filet or finely chopped pickles.

EGGS MIMOSA
For a more elegant hors d'oeuvre, the following recipe gives the appearance of a mimosa, that lovely flower from the South of France.
❧ Cut hard-cooked eggs in half lengthwise. Remove the yolk and fill the hollow egg white with a spoonful of mayonnaise. Place on

Shrimp Cocktail

a platter of meat and sprinkle with watercress. The overall appearance should be that of light greenery. Crumble the yolks over the watercress.
❧ The following ingredients can be served either combined with the yolk as stuffing for deviled eggs or simply arranged on a platter with hard-cooked eggs and assorted delicatessen meats: tomatoes, watercress, parsley, chopped green onion, green pepper, shrimp, tuna, black olives, rice, lettuce, or that perfect accompaniment to hard-cooked eggs—mayonnaise.

FISH AND SEAFOOD HORS D'OEUVRES

Canned fish such as anchovies, sardines, tuna, salmon, herring filets, lobster or crab make ideal hors d'oeuvres.

ANCHOVIES
Serve anchovies straight out of the tin, lightly sprinkled with their oil and accompanied by a potato salad seasoned with a little onion and lots of fresh parsley. Garnish with a few black olives, tomato slices, wedges of hard-cooked egg and butter.

SARDINES
The easiest and best way to serve sardines as an hors d'oeuvre is on individual plates. Place a few lettuce leaves on each plate and top with 4 to 6 small sardines. Pour a little of the sardine oil over the lettuce, sprinkle with paprika and garnish with one or two lemon wedges.

CANNED SALMON
Mix the salmon with mayonnaise or a French dressing of your choice. Surround it with cold rice salad or homemade or canned

macédoine (cooked diced carrots, turnips, onions, peas and beans).

SMOKED SALMON
Place thin slices of smoked salmon on individual plates and sprinkle with a few drops of olive oil. Garnish with a lemon wedge and finely chopped parsley or watercress.

CANNED TUNA
Tuna can be served following the instructions for preparing canned salmon.

FRESH OYSTERS
Fresh oysters make elegant hors d'oeuvres and have a loyal following. This light food is rich in vitamins and minerals. Oysters can be eaten plain, with a few drops of lemon juice, or with a Mignonette Sauce prepared from ¼ cup (50 mL) wine vinegar, 3 chopped green onions and 1 tbsp (15 mL) ground pepper.

☙ Serve oysters with thin slices of buttered brown or rye bread and celery hearts. In certain parts of France, piping hot cocktail sausages are alternated with cold oysters—a very pleasant experience for the palate, provided the oysters are very cold and the sausages very hot.

SHRIMP
Shrimp cocktail is perhaps one of the most popular hors d'oeuvres today. Arrange fresh-cooked or canned shrimp on a lettuce leaf, a bed of watercress or a mound of crushed ice. Garnish with mayon-

naise and lemon wedges or one of the following sauces.

COCKTAIL SAUCE:
⅔ cup (150 mL) tomato catsup
3 tbsp (45 mL) chili sauce
2 tbsp (30 mL) prepared horseradish
3 tbsp lemon juice
pinch of pepper
or dash of Tabasco sauce

☙ Combine the ingredients in a bowl. To vary, add finely chopped onion, diced celery, grated cucumber or pickles. Chill before serving. Makes 6 to 8 servings.

CATSUP SAUCE
☙ Combine 4 tbsp (60 mL) catsup or chili sauce with 4 drops Tabasco sauce, 4 tbsp (60 mL) horseradish and a pinch of salt.

LEMON CATSUP SAUCE
☙ Combine ¼ cup (50 mL) catsup or chili sauce with 6 tbsp (90 mL) fresh lemon juice, 1 tbsp (15 mL) horseradish, 3 drops Tabasco sauce and ¼ tsp (1 mL) celery salt.

CREAMY HORSERADISH SAUCE
☙ Combine ¼ cup (50 mL) horseradish with ¾ tsp (3 mL) salt, ¼ tsp (1 mL) pepper and 1 tsp (5 mL) vinegar. Whip ½ cup (125 mL) whipping cream until stiff and fold into horseradish mixture.

CAPER SAUCE
☙ Combine 3 tbsp (45 mL) mayonnaise with 1 tbsp (15 mL) chopped capers.

SEAFOOD PLATTER

Serve with a glass of chilled white wine or with a cup of hot Ceylon tea. These delightful seafood hors d'oeuvres are sure to be a hit with party guests.

6 to 12 fresh oysters
1 small jar red or black caviar
1 tbsp (15 mL) prepared horseradish
2 lemons or limes
4 cups (1 L) water
½ tsp (2 mL) salt
2 lbs (1 kg) raw shrimp
1 to 2 lbs (500 g to 1 kg) fresh or frozen lobster
1 avocado
4 green onions, chopped
4 tbsp (60 mL) chopped fresh parsley
½ tsp (2 mL) fresh-ground pepper
6 tbsp (90 mL) vegetable oil
2 tbsp (30 mL) wine or cider vinegar
½ tsp (2 mL) HP sauce
dash of Tabasco sauce
¼ tsp (1 mL) curry powder or tarragon
1 tbsp (15 mL) cognac or whiskey

☙ Fill a large tray with crushed ice and place in the freezer, or prepare just before serving.

☙ In the center of the tray, arrange the oysters on the half shell. Mix the caviar with the horseradish and spread carefully on the oysters. Cut the lemons or limes in wedges and arrange on the crushed ice around the oysters. Wrap each wedge in a small piece of cheesecloth to prevent the juice from squirting when the fruit is squeezed.

🍃 Bring to a boil 4 cups (1 L) water. Add 2 slices unpeeled lemon, ½ tsp (2 mL) salt and the raw shrimp. Reduce the heat and let simmer for 5 minutes. Remove from the heat. Allow to cool, drain and shell. Place the shelled shrimp in a bowl, cover and refrigerate until ready to serve.

🍃 Allow frozen lobster to thaw overnight in the refrigerator. Open the container and dry the pieces of lobster with a paper towel.

🍃 Halve the avocado lengthwise. Remove the pit and scoop out the pulp, keeping the shell intact. Place a half shell at each end of the tray.

🍃 Combine the onions, parsley, pepper, avocado pulp, vegetable oil, vinegar, HP sauce, Tabasco, salt, curry powder or tarragon, and cognac or whiskey in a bowl. Fill the avocado shells with the mixture, making sure you keep enough for a refill. This will be the dip for the shrimp and lobster.

🍃 To serve, arrange the shrimp between the wedges of lemon or lime and skewer with colored toothpicks. Arrange the lobster on either side of the tray. Tuna, crab, clams or small pieces of cooked halibut may also be used.

🍃 Although this recipe may appear complicated, it is really quite simple. Everything can be prepared ahead and kept in the refrigerator until serving time.

Then arrange the various ingredients attractively on a tray of crushed ice and serve.

MARINATED MUSHROOMS

1 lb (500 g) mushrooms
juice of ½ lemon
½ tsp (2 mL) salt
¼ tsp (1 mL) pepper
2 green onions, finely chopped
2 to 3 tbsp (30 to 45 mL) olive oil
1 loaf French bread, thinly sliced

🍃 Clean the mushrooms and slice as thinly as possible. Add the lemon juice, salt, pepper, green onions and olive oil. Stir until well blended. Refrigerate 2 to 3 hours.

🍃 Arrange the mushrooms evenly on each slice of bread and place on a large platter.

CHOPPED CHICKEN LIVERS

6 chicken livers
2 tbsp (30 mL) butter
1 small onion, chopped
2 hard-cooked eggs
salt and pepper to taste

🍃 Clean the chicken livers and sauté them lightly in butter over medium heat. Add the onion and cook 2 to 3 minutes. Remove from the heat and cool.

🍃 Mince the livers and the eggs. Mix well. Season with salt and pepper.

🍃 Serve as an hors d'oeuvre on toasted bread or use as a filling for sandwiches.

Marinated Mushrooms

Eggs and Artichokes Italian Style

EGGS AND ARTICHOKES ITALIAN STYLE

Here is an attractive hors d'oeuvre that is easily prepared using ingredients available at your local supermarket.

1 14-oz (400-mL) can artichoke hearts
juice and grated zest of 1 lemon
3 tbsp (45 mL) vegetable oil
½ tsp (2 mL) salt
¼ tsp (1 mL) pepper
1 small garlic clove
6 hard-cooked eggs
1 can rolled anchovy filets
1 head lettuce
chopped parsley

🍃 Drain the artichoke hearts. Combine the lemon juice and zest, vegetable oil, salt, pepper and crushed garlic. Add the artichokes. Cover and set aside for 2 to 6 hours. Do not refrigerate.

🍃 Chop the eggs coarsely. Place them in a bowl, cover and refrigerate. Remove the anchovies from the can and drain.

🍃 Wash the lettuce, cut it into small pieces and refrigerate in a damp towel in order to keep it crisp.

🍃 Arrange a base of lettuce on a platter. Place the artichoke mixture and the marinade in the center. Arrange the eggs around the artichokes in a ring. Garnish with the anchovy filets and sprinkle with parsley.

CHICKEN LIVER PÂTÉ

½ lb (250 g) chicken livers
1 cup (250 mL) hot water
1 hard-cooked egg, finely chopped
2 green onions, finely chopped
½ tsp (2 mL) basil
2 tbsp (30 mL) mayonnaise
¼ tsp (1 mL) salt
pinch of pepper

🍃 Simmer the chicken livers in the hot water for 5 minutes. Drain and chop fine.

🍃 Combine the egg, chopped liver, green onions, basil, mayonnaise, salt and pepper. Blend well, using a food processor or electric blender if possible.

🍃 This pâté can be used as a filling for sandwiches or canapés, or it can be shaped into small balls, rolled in chopped nuts and served on Melba toast.

COLMAR PÂTÉ

1 lb (500 g) liverwurst or liver pâté
½ lb (250 g) sweet butter
½ cup (125 mL) whipping cream
¼ tsp (1 mL) nutmeg
¼ tsp (1 mL) pepper
½ cup (125 mL) port wine
⅓ cup (75 mL) chopped pistachio nuts or pine nuts
1 small can truffles (optional)

🍃 Place all the ingredients in an electric blender or food processor and blend until light and creamy. Cover and refrigerate until ready to serve.

FRESH TOMATO MOUSSE

4 tbsp (60 mL) butter
2 lbs (1 kg) peeled tomatoes

1 tbsp (15 mL) sugar
1 tsp (5 mL) basil
1 cup (250 mL) thick white sauce
2 tbsp (30 mL) unflavored gelatin
4 tbsp (60 mL) cold water
1½ cups (375 mL) whipping cream

🎝Melt the butter in a skillet. Add the peeled tomatoes, sugar and basil. Simmer, uncovered, for 30 minutes.

🎝Add the cup of thick white sauce (see page 46). Soften the gelatin in the cold water. Add to the sauce and beat for 5 minutes until the gelatin is dissolved. Force the mixture through a sieve.

🎝Let cool. Whip the cream and fold into the cooled mixture.

🎝Turn into a mold and chill until set.

INDIAN MOUSSE

½ lb (250 g) cream cheese
1 tsp (5 mL) curry powder
¼ cup (50 mL) capers or relish
2 tbsp (30 mL) sour cream
1 tbsp (15 mL) butter
2 tbsp (30 mL) sherry or port wine

🎝Combine all the ingredients and blend until creamy.

CRUDITÉS AMANDINES

🎝Six to 12 hours before serving, prepare any of the following raw vegetables: carrot strips, cauliflower florets, turnip strips, radish slices or celery sticks. Place in a bowl and cover with as much ice

as possible. Cover and refrigerate.

🎝To serve, dry the vegetables thoroughly. Arrange attractively on a large platter and garnish with salted almonds.

MUSHROOMS SMETANA

1 lb (500 g) mushrooms
3 tbsp (45 mL) butter
¼ tsp (1 mL) marjoram
pinch of nutmeg
juice of ½ lemon
salt and pepper to taste
1¼ cups (300 mL) sour cream
6 slices bread, toasted

🎝Clean and slice the mushrooms. Sauté in hot butter for 2 minutes over high heat, stirring constantly.

🎝Remove from heat, add the marjoram, nutmeg, lemon juice, salt and pepper. Place over low heat, add the sour cream and stir

until the mixture is hot but not boiling.

🎝Top the slices of toast with the mixture and serve.

STUFFED TOMATOES

6 small tomatoes
2 potatoes, cooked
1 tbsp (15 mL) vinegar
¼ tsp (1 mL) tarragon or basil
2 green onions, chopped
salt and pepper to taste
¼ cup (50 mL) black olives
1 small cucumber
mayonnaise

🎝Scald and peel the tomatoes. Cut off the tops and discard. Refrigerate for 1 hour. Carefully scoop out the pulp and set aside.

🎝Peel and dice the potatoes. Add the vinegar, the tarragon or basil and the green onions. Salt and pepper to taste. Mix thoroughly.

🎝Mince the olives and peel and

Stuffed Tomatoes

❧ TECHNIQUE ❧

STUFFED TOMATOES

1   Scald the tomatoes.

2   Combine the potatoes, the tarragon or basil and the green onions in a bowl. Add the vinegar. Salt and pepper to taste.

3   Add the chopped olives and the cucumbers. Combine all the ingredients and season with mayonnaise.

4   Fill the tomatoes with the mixture.

Spanish Hors d'Oeuvres

dice the cucumber. Add to the potatoes. Combine all the ingredients, adding mayonnaise to taste. Fill the tomatoes with the mixture. Serve on a bed of lettuce.

SPANISH HORS D'OEUVRES

2 tbsp (30 mL) vegetable oil
1 tbsp (15 mL) vinegar
or lemon juice
¼ tbsp (4 mL) salt
¼ tsp (1 mL) dry mustard
¼ tsp (1 mL) pepper
1 cucumber
2 tomatoes
1 tsp (5 mL) minced chives
or 1 tsp (5 mL) chopped green onion

❧ Blend thoroughly the vegetable oil, vinegar or lemon juice, salt, mustard and pepper to make a French dressing.

❧ Peel the cucumber and the tomatoes. Slice them very thin and marinate in the French dressing for approximately ½ hour. Add the chives or green onion. Keep refrigerated until ready to serve.

SPICED WALNUTS

6 tbsp (90 mL) vegetable oil
2 tbsp (30 mL) curry powder
1 tbsp (15 mL) ground ginger
2 tbsp (30 mL) brown sugar
2 cups (500 mL) walnuts
3 tsp (15 mL) chutney
salt to taste

❧ Heat the oil slowly, add the curry powder, ginger and brown sugar. Mix well. Remove from the heat and add the nuts. Stir until the mixture is completely absorbed. Add the chutney.

❧ Spread the nuts on a cookie sheet lined with brown paper.

Place in a 350°F (180°C) oven. Turn off the heat and allow the nuts to dry for 20 to 30 minutes.

❧ Sprinkle lightly with salt. Store in an airtight jar in a cool, dry place.

SEVILLIAN OLIVES

2 cups (500 mL) black olives
¼ cup (50 mL) sherry
2 whole cloves of garlic
parsley to taste
8 to 12 slices pepperoni

❧ Drain the olives and place them in a soup bowl. Add the sherry and garlic. Mix, cover and let stand 24 hours.

❧ To serve, place the olives in the center of a serving dish, surround with thin slices of pepperoni and garnish with finely chopped parsley. Serve with buttered Melba toast.

ANCHOVY CANAPÉS

6 anchovies in oil
2 tbsp (30 mL) grated Swiss cheese
rounds of small pickles
small pastry shells, baked

❧ Mash the anchovies with the grated cheese. Fill the pastry shells with the mixture. Garnish with one or two rounds of pickle.

ANCHOVY ÉCLAIRS

4 hard-cooked eggs, grated
2 tbsp (30 mL) anchovy paste
2 tsp (10 mL) capers
12 small éclairs, 2 in. (5 cm) long

🔹Combine the grated eggs, anchovy paste and capers in a small bowl. Blend well.

🔹Open the éclairs and fill with the anchovy mixture. Serve.

SWEDISH CANAPÉS

2 tbsp (30 mL) butter
1 tsp (5 mL) horseradish
rounds of black bread
smoked salmon, thinly sliced
lemon juice

🔹Cream the butter with the horseradish. Spread generously on the rounds of black bread.

🔹Top each bread round with a piece of smoked salmon and sprinkle with a few drops of lemon juice.

RUSSIAN CANAPÉS

liver pâté
small rounds of toast

rolled anchovy filets
caviar
hard-cooked egg white

🔹Spread the liver pâté on small rounds of toast. Top each round with a rolled anchovy filet and surround the anchovy with a little caviar. Garnish with a piece of diced hard-cooked egg white.

FRENCH SARDINE CANAPÉS

strips of bread
butter
sardines
1 tsp (5 mL) chopped parsley
¼ cup (50 mL) mayonnaise
pinch of tarragon
1 chopped green onion
½ tsp (2 mL) prepared mustard

🔹Sauté the strips of bread in butter over low heat, until golden brown. Remove from the heat,

drain on a paper towel and let cool.

🔹Top each strip with a small sardine and sprinkle with the chopped parsley. Mix the mayonnaise with the tarragon, green onion and prepared mustard, and pipe around the edge of each strip of bread.

INDIAN CANAPÉS

1 tbsp (15 mL) butter
1 tsp (5 mL) curry powder
½ cup (125 mL) crab meat
2 or 3 eggs
salt and pepper
Melba toast
chopped parsley

🔹Melt the butter in a skillet, add the curry powder and mix well. Add the crab meat and heat for a few minutes, stirring constantly.

🔹Beat the eggs with salt and pepper. Add to the crab meat and cook according to the directions for scrambled eggs (see page 354). Cool. Spoon some of the mixture onto each canapé and sprinkle with parsley.

EPICUREAN CANAPÉS

Roquefort cheese
butter
chopped walnuts
rounds of toast

🔹Combine an equal quantity of cheese, butter and walnuts in a bowl. Beat until creamy. Spread the mixture on the rounds of toast.

Swedish Canapés

CRAB MEAT CANAPÉS

butter
small rounds of white bread
cucumber
mayonnaise
crab meat
capers

🍤 Melt the butter in a skillet and sauté the bread until golden brown. Set aside on paper towels and let cool.

🍤 Place a thin slice of cucumber on each round of bread and dot with mayonnaise. Place a little crab meat over the mayonnaise and garnish with a caper.

Crab Meat Canapés

NEW ENGLAND CLAM DIP

1 clove garlic, halved
1 can minced clams
or baby clams
8-oz (250-g) package of cream cheese
juice of 1 lemon or lime
1 tsp (5 mL) Worcestershire sauce
salt and pepper to taste

🍤 Rub the inside of a bowl with the cut garlic and set aside. Drain the clams and reserve the liquid.

🍤 Place the clams in the prepared bowl and add the cream cheese, lemon or lime juice and Worcestershire sauce. Mix well. Season with salt and pepper. Thin the dip as needed with the reserved clam broth, adding a spoonful at a time.

PINK LADY DIP

1 cup (250 mL) mayonnaise
½ cup (125 mL) chili sauce
½ cup (125 mL) finely chopped celery
2 or 3 green onions, chopped
juice of 1 lemon
salt and pepper to taste
2 hard-cooked eggs, chopped

🍤 Combine the mayonnaise, chili sauce, celery, green onions and lemon juice in a bowl. Season with salt and pepper. Cover the mixture completely with the chopped eggs and refrigerate until needed.

🍤 To serve, put the dip in three small bowls. Arrange the bowls on a large platter and surround with small slices of crusty bread or with corn or oat muffins divided into two or three pieces. For variety, add an assortment of crackers and chips.

CURRIED DIP

¼ cup (50 mL) sour cream
¼ cup (50 mL) puréed peas (baby food)
1 tsp (5 mL) curry powder
¼ cup (50 mL) chopped cooked chicken or ham
salt to taste

🍤 Combine all the ingredients and beat until creamy. Turn into a serving bowl, cover and refrigerate. To serve, surround with endive leaves or potato chips.

ZIPPY EGG DIP

4 hard-cooked eggs, chopped
3 strips crumbled cooked bacon, crumbled

Lobster Cream Dip

1 tsp (5 mL) chopped onion
1 tsp (5 mL) Worcestershire sauce
1 tsp (5 mL) horseradish, well drained
mayonnaise, if needed for consistency

🥄 Combine the ingredients and beat until well blended.

VEGETABLE CHEESE DIP

2 cups (500 mL) cottage cheese
¼ cup (50 mL) heavy cream
¼ cup (50 mL) grated raw carrot
½ cup (125 mL) finely chopped onion
¼ cup (50 mL) chopped green pepper

🥄 Combine the ingredients and beat until well blended.

LOBSTER CREAM DIP

4 oz (125 g) cream cheese
¼ cup (50 mL) softened butter
1 tsp (5 mL) tarragon
1 3-oz (90-g) can lobster paste
1 tbsp (15 mL) cognac

🥄 Beat the ingredients with an electric mixer. Blend thoroughly until smooth and creamy. Cover and refrigerate until ready to serve.

BASIC ASPIC

4 cups (1 L) stock or 2 cans undiluted consommé and 1 can water
2 tbsp (30 mL) each of diced carrots, chopped onion and chopped celery
1 tsp (5 mL) pickling spices

2 envelopes unflavored gelatin
½ cup (125 mL) cold water
2 to 4 tbsp (30 to 60 mL) lemon juice
2 egg whites, unbeaten
4 tbsp (60 mL) sherry
or few drops Tabasco sauce
salt and pepper to taste

🥄 Heat the stock or the undiluted consommé and water and add the vegetables and the pickling spices. Bring to a boil, cover and simmer for 25 minutes. Pour through a fine sieve or cheesecloth.

🥄 Soften the gelatin in cold water for 5 minutes; add the hot consommé and stir until the gelatin is dissolved.

🥄 Blend the lemon juice and egg whites, add to the consommé and bring to a boil. Cover and simmer over low heat for 20 minutes. Pass through a cheesecloth that has been rinsed in cold water and then wrung out.

🥄 Add the sherry or Tabasco. Salt and pepper to taste. Pour into a greased mold and chill until set.

TOMATO ASPIC
Use 2 8-oz (250-g) cans of tomato sauce instead of 1 can of water or 1½ cups (375 mL) stock.

CUCUMBER ASPIC
Substitute 1 unpeeled grated cucumber for the carrots.

FISH OR SEAFOOD ASPIC
Follow the master recipe for *Basic Aspic*. Refrigerate until partially set, then add 2 cups (500 mL) cooked or canned shredded fish or seafood.

MEAT ASPIC

Follow the recipe for *Basic Aspic*. Refrigerate until partially set, then add 2 cups (500 mL) of cooked diced chicken, duck, sweetbreads or ham.

EGG ASPIC

Prepare hard-cooked eggs or stuffed eggs. Follow the master recipe for *Basic Aspic*. Pour a thin layer of aspic into a mold and refrigerate until set. Place the hard-cooked or stuffed eggs on top. Cover with the rest of the aspic. Put back in the refrigerator until firm.

❧ All aspics are served unmolded on a bed of lettuce and are accompanied by mayonnaise.

ASPIC CANAPÉS

2 envelopes unflavored gelatin
2 10-oz (284-mL) cans undiluted beef bouillon
1 cup (250 mL) wine, sherry or apple juice
¼ tsp (1 mL) Tabasco sauce
24 sliced of hard-cooked egg
24 rounds of toast

❧ Sprinkle the gelatin over the beef broth and allow to soften. Place over low heat and stir until the gelatin is dissolved. Remove from the heat and stir in the wine, sherry or apple juice and the Tabasco sauce. Turn half of the mixture into a greased 15- x 10- x 1-in. (40- x 25- x 2-cm) pan or into two 8-in. (20-cm) square pans. Chill until the mixture is almost firm.

❧ Arrange egg slices 1 in. (2 cm) apart in the jelly. Carefully spoon in the remaining jelly, making sure each egg slice is well covered. Chill until firm.

❧ Slice the aspic, leaving a thin edge of jelly around each egg slice. Place on rounds of toast and serve.

❧ For added flavor, spread the rounds of toast with anchovy, sardine, shrimp, ham or lobster paste before garnishing with aspic.

TOMATO ASPIC

1 envelope unflavored gelatin
1¾ cups (425 mL) tomato juice
¼ tsp (1 mL) salt
1 tsp (5 mL) sugar
½ tsp (2 mL) Worcestershire sauce
½ tsp (2 mL) basil
2 tbsp (30 mL) lemon juice

❧ Sprinkle the gelatin over ½ cup (125 mL) tomato juice and allow to soften. Place over low heat and stir until the gelatin is dissolved. Remove from the heat and stir in the remaining 1¼ cups (300 mL) tomato juice and seasonings.

❧ Pour into a 2-cup (500-mL) mold or into individual molds. Refrigerate until firm. To serve, unmold on a serving plate and garnish with salad greens, cucumber slices and black olives. Serve with mayonnaise.

VARIATIONS

❧ Follow the master recipe for *Tomato Aspic* but do not turn into

a mold. Instead, chill the mixture until it has the consistency of unbeaten egg whites. Fold in 1 cup (250 mL) shredded cabbage, ½ cup (250 mL) chopped celery and 1 cup (250 mL) finely chopped green pepper. Turn into a 3-cup (750-mL) greased mold.

❧ Or substitute one of the following for the raw vegetables in the tomato-vegetable aspic above: 1½ cups (375 mL) cooked vegetables; 1 cup (250 mL) diced cooked chicken and ¼ cup (50 mL) sliced olives; 1 cup (250 mL) cooked shrimp; or 1 cup (250 mL) strips of cooked ham and ¼ cup (50 mL) pickle relish.

ANGELS ON HORSEBACK

6 strips smoked bacon
12 oysters

❧ Cut the bacon strips in 2 to make 12 servings and arrange on a plate. Top each strip with an oyster and secure with wooden or metal picks. Or, if you prefer, wrap the oysters in bacon and fasten them so that they are ready for cooking. Place the plate of oysters on a tray along with a chafing dish and a bottle of chutney and a bottle of tomato catsup.

❧ When it is time to serve, place the chafing dish on the table and brown the oysters and bacon at high heat. Season to taste.

STEAK BITES

2 tbsp (30 mL) soy sauce
2 tbsp (30 mL) lemon juice
2 tbsp (30 mL) sherry
2 tbsp (30 mL) honey
1 small clove garlic, crushed
3 tbsp (45 mL) butter
1 lb (500 g) top round steak

🍃 Combine all the ingredients, except the steak, in an attractive bowl. Slice the steak in thin strips and marinate in the sauce for 1 hour. In the meantime, prepare a basket of small, hot crusty rolls.

🍃 When ready to serve, place the marinated beef and the basket of bread on a tray along with bamboo sticks and a small bowl of minced chives, green onions or parsley.

🍃 At the table, light the chafing dish in front of your guests. Heat the butter until brown. Let each guest spear a strip of steak with a bamboo stick, wrap it around the tip and then sauté it in the butter for 1 or 2 seconds. The cooked steak can be eaten as is on rooled in parsley, chives or green onions.

DEVILED COCKTAIL SAUSAGES

small cocktail sausages
1 cup (250 mL) tomato catsup
¼ cup (50 mL) sherry
1 garlic clove, finely chopped

🍃 Brown the sausages in a skillet. Combine the tomato catsup, sherry and garlic in a bowl.

🍃 Once the sausages are well browned, cover them with the sauce and let stand overnight, if possible, as this will enhance their flavor.

🍃 Before serving, place the sausages and the sauce in a serving dish and warm at 350°F (180°C) for 30 minutes. Serve hot on picks.

SAUSAGES IN A BLANKET

1 lb (500 g) cocktail sausages
½ cup (125 mL) sifted flour
⅓ cup (75 mL) beer
1 egg
1 tsp (5 mL) grated onion
oil (for frying)

🍃 Cook the sausages in boiling water for 2 minutes. Drain and pat dry.

🍃 Combine the flour, beer, egg and onion, and beat until smooth. Dip each sausage in the batter and fry in hot oil at 365°F (185°C) for 3 to 4 minutes or until brown and puffy. Drain on brown paper. Serve with a bowl of cocktail sauce.

WALNUTS HÉLOISE

1 lb (500 g) walnuts
zest of 1 orange, grated
1 tsp (5 mL) cinnamon
½ tsp (2 mL) cardamom
¼ tsp (1 mL) freshly grated nutmeg

🍃 Crack open the walnut shells but do not remove the nutmeats. Place them on a cookie sheet.

🍃 Mix together the orange zest, cinnamon, cardamom and nutmeg. Blend thoroughly, preferably in a mortar. Sprinkle the mixture over the walnuts. When ready to serve, bake at 450°F (230°C) for 20 minutes. Serve hot in an attractive basket.

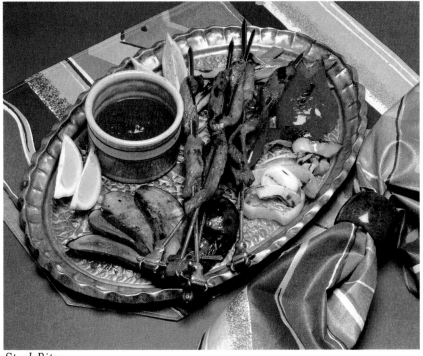

Steak Bites

SMOKED OYSTERS CANCALE

1 can smoked oysters
¼ tsp (1 mL) curry powder
1 tbsp (15 mL) cognac
1 tbsp (15 mL) butter
Melba toast

🍤 Place the contents of 1 can of smoked oysters in a small baking dish.

🍤 Mix the curry with the cognac and pour over the oysters. Dot the oysters with butter. Bake for 10 minutes at 400°F (200°C). Serve with Melba toast.

TURKISH BUREK

Burek are little crêpes filled with a mixture of spinach and soft white cheese flavored with mint. The Turks use a flaky pastry dough called phyllo, but you can use any good flaky pastry rolled very thin.

🍤 Cut the pastry into 2-in. (5-cm) squares.

🍤 On each square, place 1 tbsp (15 mL) whole or finely chopped creamed spinach. Top with 1 tsp (5 mL) heavy cream or cottage cheese, and sprinkle with fresh or dried mint. Fold the pastry over to make a triangle. Seal the edges

🍤 Heat a small amount of oil in a large skillet. Fry the burek for about 3 minutes on each side or until golden brown. Drain on brown paper. Serve hot or cold.

Sausages in a Blanket

FLAVORED BUTTERS FOR FLAVORFUL CANAPÉS

🍤 Take 1 lb (500 g) sweet or salted butter out of the refrigerator 1 hour ahead of time. Place the softened butter in a bowl and beat with an electric mixer until light and fluffy. Gradually add the juice of 1 lemon.

🍤 Place the whipped butter in a dish, cover and refrigerate as you would ordinary butter. This tasty butter will add extra flavor to hors d'oeuvres and canapés.

🍤 To prepare any of the following savory butters, mix the ingredients with ¼ cup (50 mL) whipped butter.

ANCHOVY BUTTER
Add 1 tbsp (15 mL) anchory paste or 3 mashed anchovy filets.

CAPER BUTTER
Add 1 tbsp (15 mL) capers.

CAVIAR BUTTER
Add 2 tsp (10 mL) caviar and ¼ tsp (1 mL) grated onion. (The onion will help preserve the caviar.)

BLUE CHEESE BUTTER
Add ¼ cup (50 mL) grated blue cheese, French Roquefort, English Stilton or Italian Gorgonzola.

INDIAN BUTTER
Add 1 tbsp (15 mL) chutney, ½ tsp (2 mL) curry powder and 2 tbsp (30 mL) brandy.

EGG BUTTER

Add 2 grated hard-cooked eggs, a dash of Tabasco sauce and onion juice. Salt to taste.

GARLIC BUTTER

Add 1 small clove garlic, minced or crushed.

HORSERADISH BUTTER

Add 2 tbsp (30 mL) drained horseradish.

LOBSTER BUTTER

Add 2 tbsp (30 mL) lobster paste and a dash of paprika and dry mustard.

OLIVE BUTTER

Add ¼ cup (50 mL) finely chopped green or black olives and a few drops of onion juice.

HERB BUTTER

Add ½ tsp (2 mL) dried fines herbes: tarragon, basil, fennel, savory, sage or marjoram.

MINT BUTTER

Add 2 tbsp (30 mL) finely chopped fresh mint leaves.

SOUPS

Jellied Tomato Broth

CHICKEN BROTH

1 cooked chicken or turkey carcass
1 to 2 lbs (500 to 900 g) chicken
backs (as needed)
8 cups (2 L) water
4 or 5 celery stalks with leaves
1 onion, quartered
1 sliced carrot
2 tbsp (30 mL) coarse salt
½ tsp (2 mL) pepper
1 tsp (5 mL) thyme
1 bay leaf
¼ cup (50 mL) rice or ½ cup
(125 mL) oatmeal
or 1 cup (250 mL) diced potatoes
2 tbsp (30 mL) chopped parsley
or chervil

🍃 Place the chicken or turkey carcass in a large saucepan. Add the
chicken backs and cover with
water. Add the celery, onion, carrot, salt, pepper, thyme and bay

leaf. Cover. Bring to a boil and
simmer for 2 hours. Strain and
add your choice of rice, oatmeal
or diced potatoes. Simmer 15
minutes longer.

🍃 To serve, garnish with chopped
parsley or chervil.

JELLIED TOMATO BROTH

2 envelopes (2 tbsp or 30 mL)
unflavored gelatin
½ cup (125 mL) cold water
2 cups (500 mL) tomato juice
2 cups (500 mL) consommé or
broth
1 small onion, grated
½ cup (125 mL) finely chopped
celery leaves
½ tsp (2 mL) basil
1 tsp (5 mL) sugar
1 tsp (5 mL) coarse salt
1 tbsp (15 mL) lemon juice

🍃 Soak the gelatin in cold water
for 5 minutes. Place the remaining ingredients in a large
saucepan and bring to a boil. Boil
for 2 minutes. Remove from the
heat and add the gelatin while
stirring to dissolve it completely.
Strain through a damp cheesecloth. (See the instructions for
Basic Consommé, below.) Refrigerate until the broth begins to
jell.

🍃 To serve, break up the jelly
with a fork and serve it in cups.
Garnish with a slice of lemon and
a dusting of paprika.

VEAL BROTH

2 lbs (900 g) veal shank
½ lb (250 g) veal shoulder
or the bone from a veal roast
2 leeks, sliced
1 large onion, whole
2 cloves, stuck in the onion
½ tsp (2 mL) pepper
½ tsp (2 mL) thyme
1 bay leaf
1 tbsp (15 mL) coarse salt
8 cups (2 L) water

🍃 Place all the ingredients in a
saucepan. Bring to a boil. Cover
and simmer for 3 hours. Strain
through a cheesecloth. (See the
instructions for *Basic Consommé*,
below.)

BASIC CONSOMMÉ

2 tbsp (30 mL) beef fat or butter
2 lbs (900 g) beef plate or shoulder
1 to 2 lbs (500 to 900 g) veal
shank

12 cups (3 L) lukewarm water
4 medium onions, quartered
2 whole carrots
3 whole cloves
1 tbsp (15 mL) coarse salt
½ tsp (2 mL) dry mustard
½ tsp (2 mL) thyme
1 cup (250 mL) chopped celery leaves

🎝 Melt the beef fat or butter in a saucepan and brown the piece of beef lightly. Add the remaining ingredients. Bring to a boil. Skim off the scum, cover and simmer gently over low heat for 2½ hours.

🎝 To strain the consommé, line the bottom of a large colander with a double layer of clean cheesecloth. Place the colander over a large bowl. Pour the stock through the colander and let the liquid drain, without pressing (it takes only a few seconds). Refrigerate. As the consommé cools, the fat will rise to the top and harden. This will prevent air from altering the flavor of the consommé. You can refrigerate the jellied consommé for 2 to 3 weeks.

Irish Consommé

Long, slow cooking is the secret behind this delicious consommé. The Irish say it is as clear as whiskey, as stimulating as champagne and as nourishing as stout. Although it is made from many ingredients, it requires little preparation.

2 to 3 lbs (1 to 1.5 kg) beef shank
1 pig's foot or 2-lb (1-kg) veal shank
12 cups (3 L) cold water
2 Spanish or large onions, unpeeled
2 large carrots, well scrubbed
4 celery stalks
1 leek
6 whole cloves
2 bay leaves
½ tsp (2 mL) thyme
8 peppercorns
1 bunch parsley, tied
2 tsp (10 mL) salt
2 to 4 tbsp (30 to 60 mL) Irish whiskey

🎝 Ask the butcher to cut the beef shank and the pig's foot, or veal shank, in 2-in. (5-cm) pieces. Place in a large kettle. Pour the cold water on top. Slowly bring to a boil.

🎝 In the meantime, wash the onions and cut them in two (the peel is left to give an amber color to the consommé). Leave the carrots whole and unpeeled. Cut the celery stalks in two. Slice open the leek (lengthwise) and wash the inside of the leaves under cold running water. When the water comes to a boil, add the vegetables one by one so that the water does not stop boiling. Wrap the whole cloves, bay leaves, thyme, peppercorns, salt and parsley, in clean cheesecloth and tie the bunch well, so that it does not come undone while cooking. The vegetables are uncut to prevent the consommé from clouding.

🎝 Cover and simmer for 7 to 8 hours over low heat. Remember, slow cooking is the secret. If scum forms around the edges during cooking, skim it off carefully.

🎝 When the consommé is done, strain it through a large sieve or colander lined with a double layer of cheesecloth. Let the consommé drain, without pressing it. (For the vegetables, see the note below.)

🎝 Pour the consommé into a large bowl. Refrigerate at least 12 hours. The fat will rise to the top and act as a cover.

🎝 To serve, remove the fat. Heat the consommé and add the whiskey. Garnish the soup with a sprig of watercress or with finely chopped parsley.

Note: In Ireland, the vegetables are often used in another dish. The following day, they are mashed with an equal quantity of butter and served as *Irish Colcannon.*

Wine Consommé

🎝 To each cup of boiling consommé, add 1 tbsp (15 mL) sherry or port wine, or 2 tbsp (30 mL) red wine.

CURRIED CONSOMMÉ

2 slices bacon
2 tbsp (30 mL) butter
1 chopped onion
1 tsp (5 mL) curry powder
1 tbsp (15 mL) flour
5 to 6 cups (1.2 to 1.5 L) consommé
⅓ cup (75 mL) uncooked rice
chopped parsley

🍃 Fry the bacon over low heat. Remove the bacon from the pan, leaving the drippings. Add the butter to the drippings and brown the onion.

🍃 Add the curry and mix well. Stir in the flour. Pour the mixture into the hot consommé. Stir in the rice and simmer over low heat for 25 minutes. To serve, sprinkle with chopped parsley.

JELLIED CONSOMMÉ MADRILENE

2 lbs (900 g) veal shank
½ lb (250 g) lean ground beef
1 large onion, sliced
1 clove garlic, chopped
1 bay leaf
½ tsp (2 mL) thyme
salt and pepper to taste
1 tbsp (15 mL) sugar
1 20-oz (575-mL) can tomatoes
6 cups (1.5 L) water

🍃 Place all the ingredients in a large saucepan and bring to a boil. Cover and simmer for 3 hours. Once the stock is cooked, strain it according to the recipe for basic consommé (see *Basic Consommé*, page 94). Pour the consommé into a bowl, cover and refrigerate. Once cooled, it turns into a lovely pink jelly.

CROÛTE-AU-POT CONSOMMÉ

🍃 Cut a loaf of French bread in two, lengthwise. Hollow out the bread and cut the crust into 2- to 3-in. (5- to 8-cm) pieces. Butter the crusts and brown them in a 375°F (190°C) oven. Serve the consommé piping hot with a basket of these croûtes (crusts) and a platter of the vegetables that were used to prepare the consommé. Let everyone dig in and enjoy.

CHICKEN SOUP

1 3-lb (1.5-kg) chicken
1 tsp (5 mL) salt
1 celery stalk, diced
1 medium carrot, diced
1 chopped onion
pinch of thyme
6 cups (1.5 L) water

🍃 Cut the chicken into individual portions. Place the chicken in a pressure-cooker. Add the salt, celery, carrot, onion, thyme and water.

🍃 Close the lid securely. Cap the vent, making sure the valve is closed, and cook for 15 minutes. Remove from the heat, lift the valve lever and let off the steam completely.

🍃 Chicken wings, necks and backs also make excellent soup. Combine them with the ingredients listed above. If you use chicken breast or legs, you will have enough meat to prepare another delicious dish. See the chapter on poultry.

Curried Consommé

Vegetable Soup

1 lb (500 g) soup meat
1 small soup bone
4 cups (1 L) water
2 tsp (10 mL) salt
¼ cup (50 mL) rice
2 cups (500 mL) tomatoes
1 onion, chopped
1 clove garlic, minced
¼ tsp (1 mL) savory
¼ tsp (1 mL) marjoram
¼ cup (50 mL) diced potatoes
¼ cup (50 mL) diced carrots
¼ cup (50 mL) diced green beans
¼ cup (50 mL) diced celery
1 tbsp (15 mL) chopped parsley

🍲 Place the soup meat, bone, water, salt, rice, tomatoes, onion, garlic, savory and marjoram in a pressure-cooker. Secure the lid and cook for 17 minutes. Remove from the heat, lift the valve lever and let the steam off completely.

🍲 Remove the lid, add the potatoes, carrots, green beans, celery and parsley. Secure the lid and continue cooking for another 3 minutes. Let the steam off completely.

Québec Vegetable Soup

1½ to 2 lbs (750 to 900 g) beef plate or shoulder
1 meatless beef bone or 1 roast-beef bone
2 cups (500 mL) diced carrots
½ cup (125 mL) diced parsnip
3 large onions, thinly sliced

1 cup (250 mL) finely chopped celery stalks and leaves
1 large leek, sliced (as needed)
1 tsp (5 mL) savory
½ tsp (2 mL) marjoram
¼ tsp (1 mL) anise
1 tsp (5 mL) dry mustard
½ tsp (2 mL) peppercorns
2 tbsp (30 mL) coarse salt
1 tbsp (15 mL) sugar
1 20-oz (575-mL) can tomatoes
12 cups (3 L) water
½ cup (125 mL) whole barley

🍲 Place all the ingredients in a large saucepan. Bring to a boil. Cover and simmer over low heat for 4 hours. Stir 2 or 3 times during the first hour of cooking. The barley may be replaced with macaroni, spaghetti, vermicelli, noodles or rice, whatever your preference; add to the soup 15 to 20 minutes before the soup is done. Remove the beef from the pot and serve it as a pot-au-feu (see page 105.

Family Soup

🍲 To make a delicious broth and fresh-tasting soup, there are five steps to follow:

🍲 Use beef bones, ham bones, bones from a roast and chicken bones and giblets, as well as chops and steak bones. Mix the bones in whatever combination and quantity you choose. If you don't have any of these on hand, you may substitute ½ cup leftover gravy or roast drippings.

🍲 Place all the bones in a saucepan and cover with water. Then add as much water again. Bring to a boil. If using ½ cup (125 mL) of gravy or drippings, use 4 cups (1 L) of water.

🍲 Flavor with thyme, bay leaves, savory, marjoram or basil, or a combination of aromatic herbs such as savory and marjoram with a little dill. When the water begins to boil, season with coarse salt, peppercorns, celery leaves or parsley stems. Add onion and garlic to taste. (Each combination gives a slightly different flavor.) Then cover the soup and cook it for 4 to 6 hours over very low heat. Do not let it boil.

🍲 Remove the bones or strain the stock. before adding the vegetables to the stock. Prepare the vegetables. Choose any combination you wish, but keep in mind that the taste of the soup will change depending on the vegetables used. Peel and cut the vegetables. Melt 1 tbsp (15 mL) butter for every 4 to 6 cups (1 to 1.5 L) of vegetables. Add the vegetables to the butter, cover and cook for 20 minutes over low heat. This softens the vegetables and brings out their full flavor.

🍲 Place the vegetables in the stock. Add your choice of vermicelli, tapioca, rice or noodles. Simmer, covered, just long enough to cook the pasta or rice. Don't be afraid to experiment with the ingredients—you'll be amazed at the delicious soups you'll invent.

Vegetarian Soup

VEGETARIAN SOUP

6 cups (1.5 L) water
4 tbsp (60 mL) pearl barley
½ tsp (2 mL) basil or savory
4 carrots
2 onions
4 celery stalks
1 large potato
½ lb (250 g) fresh mushrooms
butter

🥄 Bring the water to a boil. Add the barley and the basil or savory. Cover and simmer for 1 hour.
🥄 Grate the carrots, onions, celery and potato or put them through a food chopper. Cut the mushrooms into very thin slices.
🥄 Add the prepared vegetables to the barley broth. Season with salt and pepper and simmer for 20 minutes. Place ½ tsp (2 mL) butter in each bowl, pour the soup over the butter and serve.

VENETIAN SOUP

1 tbsp (15 mL) butter
1 tbsp (15 mL) flour
½ cup (125 mL) water
1 cup (250 g) canned tomatoes
¼ tsp (1 mL) basil or thyme
½ tsp (2 mL) celery salt
1 tsp (5 mL) chopped parsley
1 tsp (5 mL) sugar
salt and pepper
1 can consommé
1½ cups (375 mL) water
1 hard-cooked egg, chopped

🥄 Melt the butter. Add the flour and mix well. Add the water, tomatoes, basil or thyme, celery salt, chopped parsley, sugar, salt and pepper. Boil for 15 minutes, and then add the consommé, water and chopped hard-cooked egg. Return to a boil and simmer for another 5 minutes. Serve with croutons and a bowl of grated cheese.

CHEESE AND CELERY SOUP

This hearty soup is a meal in itself. To serve cold, put through a blender and refrigerate until needed. Garnish with chives or parsley.

1 can cream of celery soup
1 cup (250 mL) milk
1 small onion, finely chopped
½ cup (125 mL) finely diced celery
1 tbsp (15 mL) butter
½ tsp (2 mL) paprika
pinch of nutmeg or basil
pinch of cayenne pepper
1 to 1½ cups (250 to 375 mL) cottage cheese
1 small hot pepper, finely chopped (optional)

🥄 Combine the soup and the milk in a saucepan. Brown the onion and the celery lightly in butter in a separate saucepan and add to the soup. Stir in the rest of the ingredients. Continue cooking over low heat until thoroughly blended.

CABBAGE SOUP

3 tbsp (45 mL) butter or fat
2 medium carrots, grated
3 onions, thinly sliced
4 to 6 cups (1 to 1.5 L) finely chopped cabbage
celery leaves, minced
1 tsp (5 mL) salt
½ tsp (2 mL) pepper
½ tsp (2 mL) sugar

4 cups (1 L) water or consommé
2 cups (500 mL) milk
slices of bread, browned in butter
grated cheese

🍃Melt the butter or fat in a saucepan. Add the carrots, onions, cabbage, celery leaves, salt, pepper and sugar. Mix well, cover and simmer for 25 minutes over low heat. Add the water, or consommé, bring to a boil and simmer for another 15 minutes. Add the milk, heat and adjust the seasoning. When ready to serve, brown the slices of bread in butter. Place one slice in each bowl and sprinkle with cheese. Pour the soup over the bread slices.

MONDAY'S ONION SOUP

4 tbsp (60 mL) bacon or pork fat
4 tbsp (60 mL) butter
8 large onions, peeled and thinly sliced
6 tbsp (90 mL) concentrated beef extract
8 cups (2 L) water
¼ tsp (1 mL) thyme
salt and pepper

🍃Melt the fat and butter in a saucepan. Add the onions. Cook the onions, without frying them, until tender.

🍃Pour the beef extract over the cooked onions and stir so that the onions are well coated with the extract. Add the water, thyme, salt and pepper to taste. Bring to a boil. Cover and simmer for 40 minutes.

🍃To serve, simply sprinkle with grated cheese.

LES HALLES FRENCH ONION SOUP

4 or 5 large onions
4 tbsp (60 mL) butter
2 tbsp (30 mL) flour
6 cups (1.5 L) lukewarm water or consommé
1 tsp (5 mL) coarse salt
4 to 6 slices bread
¼ tsp (1 mL) pepper
2 cups (500 mL) boiling milk (as needed)

🍃Peel and halve the onions. Place each half cut-side down on a chopping board and, using a very sharp knife, cut it into thin, regular slices; this will ensure that the onion slices cook evenly.

🍃Heat the butter in a heavy metal saucepan, preferably an enameled cast-iron one. Add the onions and stir almost constantly with a wooden spoon until the onions are golden. (Take care not to let them become too brown as this can give an acrid taste to the soup.) Once the onions are golden brown, add the flour and continue cooking over low heat, stirring often, until the flour takes on a light golden color.

🍃Add the water or consommé and the salt. Bring to a boil, stirring constantly, and then simmer over low heat for 8 to 10 minutes.

🍃In the meantime, toast the bread. Place one slice in each bowl and dust lightly with pepper.

🍃Add the boiling milk to the soup. Adjust the seasoning and pour over the bread slices. Serve with a bowl of grated cheese.

🍃To serve with Gruyère cheese: grate ½ lb (250 g) cheese or cut it into very thin slices. Place one-third of the toasted bread slices at the bottom of a soup tureen or an

Les Halles French Onion Soup

❧ TECHNIQUE ❧

LES HALLES FRENCH ONION SOUP

1 Melt the butter, add the onions and cook until golden brown.

2 Add the flour, stir and continue cooking over low heat.

3 Add the water or consommé and the salt.

4 Add the milk.

ovenproof glass dish. Season with pepper and sprinkle or cover with one-third of the cheese. Make 3 such layers. Pour in the onion soup (with or without milk). Cover and place in a 400°F (200°C) oven for 10 minutes.

❧ To prepare gratinéed onion soup: for a good gratin, use a bowl that is wider than it is high, so that the heat spreads evenly over the surface. A few minutes before serving, pour the onion soup into the bowl. Top with the toasted bread and sprinkle generously with the grated or sliced cheese. Pour 1 tbsp (15 mL) melted butter seasoned with pepper over the cheese. Place in a 500°F (260°C) oven until the crust turns golden (about 10 to 20 minutes). Serve immediately.

White Wine Onion Soup

8 large onions
1/3 cup (75 mL) butter
1/2 cup (125 mL) flour
12 cups (3 L) water
1 bottle dry white wine
salt and pepper
French bread
grated Parmesan cheese

❧ Mince the onions and brown in half the butter, according to the recipe for *Les Halles French Onion Soup*, page 99.

❧ Melt the remaining butter in a saucepan, add the flour and cook over medium heat, stirring often, until the mixture is a light golden color. Add the water and wine and mix. Add the sautéed onions and season with salt and pepper to taste. Boil over medium heat until the broth is reduced to 12 cups (3 L).

❧ Cut 24 thin slices of French bread. Butter each slice and sprinkle it with pepper and Parmesan cheese. Place on a cookie sheet and bake in a 400°F (200°C) oven until golden brown. Set the slices in a soup tureen or in individual soup bowls. Pour the soup over the bread 5 minutes before serving. Keep warm. This soup is never served au gratin.

French Onion Velouté

3 tbsp (45 mL) butter
2 tbsp (30 mL) bacon drippings
1 1/2 cups (375 mL) thinly sliced onions
3 tbsp (45 mL) flour
2 cups (500 mL) light cream
1 egg, well beaten
pinch of thyme
salt and pepper to taste

❧ Heat the butter and bacon drippings in a saucepan and add the onions. Mix well, cover and simmer 20 minutes over low heat. Beat the flour, cream, egg and thyme until thoroughly blended. Stir the egg mixture into the onions and cook until slightly thickened. Season to taste. Serve as is. If you prefer a cream soup, put through a food mill or blend for 1 minute in an electric blender. Garnish each bowl with 1 tbsp (15 mL) finely chopped raw celery.

Parmentier Soup

This nutritious and tasty soup can be prepared in 10 minutes. It also freezes well, so it can be kept for emergencies.

4 slices bacon
1 large onion, finely chopped
1/4 cup (50 mL) celery, diced
1 1/2 cups (375 mL) boiling water
3 cups (750 mL) milk
1 tsp (5 mL) salt
1/2 tsp (2 mL) pepper
1/4 tsp (1 mL) savory
1 1/2 to 2 cups (375 to 500 mL) instant potato flakes

❧ Fry the bacon and drain on paper towels. To the fat in the pan add the onion and celery and cook over medium heat until golden brown. Stir in the water, milk, salt, pepper and savory. Simmer 5 minutes and add the potato flakes, beating vigorously. Add as many potato flakes as needed to obtain the desired consistency or flavor. Simmer 2 to 3 minutes and serve.

Meatless Pea Soup

2 cups (500 mL) dried peas
8 cups (2 L) cold water
4 tbsp (60 mL) fat, of your choice
1 large onion, thinly sliced
1 tbsp (15 mL) coarse salt
small piece lemon zest
1 tsp (5 mL) savory

❧ Sort and wash the peas, cover with cold water and soak for 12 hours.

❧ Melt the fat in a saucepan, add the onion and sauté lightly but do

Classic Pea Soup

not brown. Add the peas, the water and the remaining ingredients. Bring to a boil, cover and simmer for 2 hours or until the peas are tender.

🍂 For a cream soup, put the cooked soup through a food mill or blend in an electric blender.

CLASSIC PEA SOUP

1 lb (500 g) dried yellow peas
½ lb (250 g) salt pork
12 cups (3 L) water
3 medium onions, minced
2 diced carrots
2 or 3 bay leaves
handful of celery leaves, chopped
few sprigs parsley, chopped
1 tsp (5 mL) savory

🍂 Wash and drain the peas. Place them in a large saucepan with all the other ingredients. Boil for 2 minutes. Remove from the heat and let the soup stand for 1 hour.

🍂 Return the soup to the heat and bring to a boil once again. Lower the heat and simmer, covered, for 1 hour or until the peas are cooked. Season with salt and pepper.

🍂 Serve as is, or put through a food mill, chopper or electric blender and serve as a purée.

VARIATIONS
🍂 For a leaner soup, replace the salt pork with 8 cubes of vegetable broth and 10 cups (2½ L) of water.

🍂 Heat the soup and stir in cooked corn and pieces of cooked sausage.

🍂 Add cheese and bacon. When ready to serve, sprinkle each soup bowl with a little grated cheese and bits of crisp bacon.

🍂 Top each serving with a dollop of sour cream and sprinkle with chopped chives.

🍂 Combine 4 cups (1 L) pea soup, 1 can tomato soup and 1 can water in a saucepan and heat for a few minutes.

🍂 For American-style pea soup, substitute a ham bone for the salt pork

TOMATO VERMICELLI SOUP

2 tbsp (30 mL) butter
2 onions, peeled and chopped
3 ripe tomatoes, sliced
5 cups (1.2 L) consommé
or potato cooking water
¼ tsp (1 mL) thyme
1 bay leaf
1 sprig parsley
1 tsp (5 mL) sugar
¼ cup (50 mL) vermicelli

🍂 Melt the butter in a saucepan. Add the onion and brown over low heat, uncovered, for 10 minutes, stirring frequently with a wooden spoon. Add the tomatoes and cook for 10 to 15 minutes over medium heat.

🍂 Add the liquid, thyme, bay leaf, parsley and sugar. Cover and boil over medium heat for 15 to 20 minutes.

Force through a fine sieve, pressing with the back of a wooden spoon to mash the vegetables. Put the purée back in the saucepan and bring to a boil. Add the vermicelli and season with salt and pepper. Simmer 10 minutes longer and serve.

GREEN TOMATO SOUP

3 cups (750 mL) green tomatoes, unpeeled and chopped
1 onion, minced
¼ tsp (1 mL) cinnamon
pinch of ground cloves
1 tsp (5 mL) sugar
¼ tsp (1 mL) pepper
4 cups (1 L) water
¼ tsp (1 mL) baking soda
3 tbsp (45 mL) butter
3 tbsp (45 mL) flour
4 cups (1 L) milk

Place the tomatoes, onion, cinnamon, ground cloves, sugar, pepper and water in a saucepan. Bring to a boil and simmer for 20 minutes. Add the baking soda.

Melt the butter, stir in the flour and blend well. Add the milk and cook, stirring constantly, until creamy. Add the green tomato mixture. Mix thoroughly. Salt to taste and serve immediately.

QUÉBEC TOMATO SOUP

1 20-oz (575-mL) can tomatoes
1 finely chopped onion
few chopped celery leaves

1 tbsp (15 mL) sugar
pinch of savory
1 tbsp (15 mL) cornstarch
½ cup (125 mL) cold milk
2 cups (500 mL) milk

Pour the tomatoes into a saucepan. Add the finely chopped onion, chopped celery leaves, sugar and savory and simmer for 20 minutes.

In a separate saucepan, combine the cornstarch with the ½ cup (125 mL) of cold milk. Add the remaining 2 cups (500 mL) of milk. Bring to a boil and cook over low heat until the liquid thickens slightly. When ready to serve, pour the hot milk mixture over the hot tomatoes all at once and stir quickly. Do not boil once the milk has been added. Cooked rice (½ cup or 125 mL) may also be added. It is not necessary to salt this soup before serving it.

BROAD BEAN SOUP

1 lb (500 g) fresh broad beans
4 cups (1 L) boiling water
1 tsp (5 mL) coarse salt
½ tsp (2 mL) sugar
½ tsp (2 mL) savory
½ lb (250 g) fat salt pork
2 large onions, chopped
1 tbsp (15 mL) cider vinegar
1 tbsp (15 mL) butter

Shell the fresh broad beans and remove a thin layer of peel from each one. In a large saucepan, bring the water to a boil and add the beans, salt, sugar and savory. Cover and simmer from 1 to 1 1/2 hours or until the beans are tender.

Dice the salt pork and sauté until the cracklings are crisp and golden. Add the onions and sauté until golden brown. Add this mixture to the soup and continue

Québec Tomato Soup

cooking. When ready to serve, add the cider vinegar and butter.

SORREL SOUP

3 tbsp (45 mL) butter
2 cups (500 mL) chopped sorrel
8 cups (2 L) hot water
6 potatoes, peeled and sliced
1 tbsp (15 mL) coarse salt
½ tsp (2 mL) pepper
1 egg
2 tbsp (30 mL) cream

🍃 In a saucepan, melt the butter, add the sorrel and simmer over low heat for 5 minutes. Add the water, potatoes, salt and pepper. Cover and simmer for 1 hour. Force through a fine sieve or put through a food mill to purée. Beat together the egg and the cream and stir in a spoonful of hot soup. Then pour the egg mixture into the hot soup, stirring constantly.

Do not boil after adding the egg as this will ruin the soup.

MAJORCAN SOUP

4 to 5 cloves garlic
2 Spanish onions
1 leek
2 canned hot peppers
1 green pepper
3 tomatoes
4 tbsp (60 mL) olive oil
6 cups (1.5 L) boiling water
1 cup (250 mL) chopped cabbage
½ tsp (2 mL) thyme
1 bay leaf
2 whole cloves
1 tsp (5 mL) coarse salt

🍃 Peel and mince the garlic. Peel the onions and cut into rings. Wash and slice the leek. Drain the hot peppers and dice. Wash, seed and dice the green pepper. Peel and slice the tomatoes.

🍃 Heat the olive oil in a saucepan and stir in the garlic, onion and leek. Mix well. Cover and simmer for 10 minutes over low heat, stirring occasionally. Add the tomatoes, hot peppers and green pepper and simmer 15 minutes longer. Pour in the hot water, bring to a boil, and add the chopped cabbage, thyme, bay leaf, cloves and coarse salt. Cover and simmer over low heat for 1½ to 2 hours. To serve, place a bottle of olive oil and a pepper mill on the table and let your guests season their soup to taste.

CORN SOUP

2 slices salt pork
1 chopped onion
1 can corn
1 cup (250 mL) diced cooked potatoes
2 cups (500 mL) milk
¼ tsp (1 mL) savory
1 tsp (5 mL) salt
½ tsp (2 mL) pepper

🍃 Dice the salt pork and sauté until the cracklings are crisp and golden. Add the onion and brown over high heat. Add the remaining ingredients. Bring to a boil, reduce the heat and simmer for 10 minutes. To serve, garnish with parsley or dried celery leaves.

CANADIAN CHEDDAR SOUP

3 tbsp (45 mL) butter
2 grated carrots
1 minced onion

Canadian Cheddar Soup

½ cup (125 mL) finely chopped celery
¼ cup (50 mL) flour
4 cups (1 L) consommé
½ lb (250 g) mild or sharp Canadian Cheddar cheese
2 cups (500 mL) hot milk
2 tbsp (30 mL) parsley or chervil

🍃Melt the butter, add the carrots, onion and celery. Sauté over medium heat until golden brown. Add the flour and blend well. Pour in the consommé (you may also use 4 cups (1 L) of hot water and 4 cubes of chicken broth) and mix well until smooth and creamy. Add the cheese and hot milk. Remove from the heat. Salt and pepper to taste. Stir for a few minutes and serve with a sprinkling of parsley or chervil.

OLD-FASHIONED BARLEY SOUP

1 cup (250 mL) hulled barley
12 cups (3 L) cold water
2 lbs (900 g) beef plate or 1 roast-beef bone
1 tbsp (15 mL) coarse salt
2 carrots, sliced
1 large onion, minced
2 celery stalks, diced
2 leeks, thinly sliced (as needed)
½ tsp (2 mL) thyme
½ tsp (2 mL) savory
1 lemon
3 tbsp (45 mL) butter

🍃Place the barley in a bowl, cover with lukewarm water and soak for 1 hour. (Do not use pearl barley for this soup.)

🍃Place the cold water, the beef plate or roast-beef bone and the coarse salt in a saucepan. Drain the barley and add it. Bring to a boil and cook over low heat. Skim using the method given for pot-au-feu (see below). Add ½ cup (125 mL) of cold water and continue to skim. This step is important, as it will prevent the barley soup from turning gray.

🍃When all the scum has been removed, add the carrots, onion, celery, leeks, thyme and savory. Bring to a boil. Reduce the heat and simmer, partially covered, for 3 hours. Remove the meat. Add the 3 tbsp (45 mL) of butter as well as the lemon juice and zest. Do not boil once the butter has been added. Serve garnished with chopped parsley or chervil.

CLASSIC POT-AU-FEU

This recipe produces both a delicious vegetable soup and an appetizing meat dish.

3 lbs (1.5 kg) flat beef ribs
12 cups (3 L) cold water
1 tbsp (15 mL) coarse salt
3 whole carrots, peeled
1 small turnip, peeled and halved
2 large leeks, cleaned and tied
3 peeled onions, one clove stuck in each
1 medium parsnip, peeled
2 celery stalks
1 clove garlic, finely chopped
3 sprigs chervil (optional)

🍃Place the meat at the bottom of a large saucepan. Add the water and coarse salt. Place the saucepan over medium heat, uncovered. Slowly bring to a boil. This is important for the flavor and the clarity of the pot-au-feu. As the heat slowly penetrates the meat, both foam and fat will escape (this may take up to 30 minutes). Remove this first scum with a skimmer. When the water begins to boil rapidly, add another ½ cup (125 mL) of cold water to slow down the boiling and allow the remainder of the scum to rise to the surface where it can be removed.

🍃Add the remaining ingredients. Bring to a boil once again, then partially cover the saucepan. As the stock cooks, it will become clear. Simmer over low heat for 2 to 3 hours or until the meat is tender.

🍃When the meat is cooked, remove it at once, if you wish to serve it hot. To serve the meat cold, let it cool in the stock and then drain and place on a platter. Cover with wax paper and refrigerate.

🍃Hot, the meat is served surrounded with the pot-au-feu vegetables as well as with boiled potatoes sprinkled with chervil or parsley.

🍃Cold, the boiled beef is sliced very thin, sprinkled with French dressing and garnished with chopped parsley and small chopped onions.

SERI NO OYNYN

(Pork and Watercress Soup)

Now that watercress is readily available all year round, try this nutritious soup. It is very light and delicious and can be easily prepared right at the table in a chafing dish or fondue pot. All you need to do is arrange the prepared ingredients on a tray. Serve with crackers.

1 lb (500 g) lean pork
⅔ cup (150 mL) mild, unsalted soy sauce
6 cups (1.5 L) boiling water
2 bunches watercress, washed and drained
2 eggs or ½ cup (125 mL) diced shrimp

🍃 Dice the pork and place in a saucepan along with the soy sauce. Stir until the meat is well coated.

🍃 Add the boiling water and slowly return to a boil. Simmer 5 minutes.

🍃 Chop the watercress, add to the broth and simmer 2 minutes. Beat the egg with a little salt and pour the egg on top of the soup.

🍃 Do not touch or stir for 2 minutes. Then beat with a fork and serve.

🍃 If shrimp is used, omit the egg and add the shrimp when you add the watercress. Simmer for 2 minutes.

OXTAIL SOUP

1 or 2 oxtails, cut into chunks
3 carrots, diced
1 bay leaf

½ tsp (2 mL) thyme
1 thick slice lemon
3 cloves, stuck in the lemon slice
1 chopped onion
2 celery stalks, diced, with leaves
8 peppercorns
1 15-oz (425-mL) can tomatoes
1 tbsp (15 mL) salt
8 cups (2 L) boiling water
½ cup (125 mL) sherry

🍃 Place all of the ingredients, except the sherry, in a soup kettle.

🍃 Bring to a boil. Cover and simmer until the meat is tender and is easily removed from the bone, approximately 3 hours.

🍃 When ready to serve, add the sherry, to taste. Garnish each bowl of soup with sprig of parsley.

OYSTER SOUP

3 cups (750 mL) milk
2 celery stalks
1 small onion, halved
1 bay leaf
salt and pepper
¼ cup (50 mL) cream or white wine
1 cup (250 mL) oysters, with juice
1 tbsp (15 mL) butter
paprika

🍃 Combine the milk, celery, onion, bay leaf, salt and pepper in a saucepan and simmer for 30 minutes over low heat. Do not let the mixture boil. Strain it and return it to the saucepan.

🍃 Heat the cream or white wine to the boiling point; pour in the oysters. Cover, remove from the heat and let stand for 10 minutes.

🍃 When ready to serve, pour the oysters into the hot milk. Add the butter and sprinkle the soup with paprika. Serve immediately.

FRESH COD SOUP

3 slices salt pork
2 lbs (900 g) fresh cod
1 large onion, thinly sliced
2 cups (500 mL) sliced potatoes
1½ cups (375 mL) hot water
2 cups (500 mL) hot milk
1 tsp (5 mL) salt
¼ tsp (1 mL) savory
2 tbsp (30 mL) butter

🍃 Cut the salt pork into 1½-in. (4-cm) cubes. Sauté in a large saucepan over medium heat until translucent. Cut the cod filets, or slices, into 1-in. (2.5-cm) pieces.

🍃 Arrange the potatoes, onions and fish in alternate layers in the saucepan. Add the hot water. Cover and bring to a boil. Reduce the heat and simmer 10 to 15 minutes, or until the potatoes are tender. Add the milk, salt, savory and butter. Do not mix; simply keep the soup warm until ready to serve it.

NEW ENGLAND CLAM CHOWDER

4 tbsp (60 mL) butter or 3 slices salt pork
2 medium onions, minced
1½ cups (375 mL) fresh or canned clams

1 cup (250 mL) clam juice
1 tbsp (15 mL) salt
½ tsp (2 mL) pepper
8 cups (2 L) boiling water
1 large potato, diced
2 cups (500 mL) cream
2 cups (500 mL) milk
paprika

🍂 Melt the butter in a saucepan, or dice the salt pork and sauté it until golden brown. Add the onions to the fat and sauté lightly. Stir in the clams, simmer for 5 minutes and remove from the pan.

🍂 Add the clam juice, salt, pepper, boiling water and diced potato to the fat. Cover and simmer for 30 minutes. Add the cream and milk. Simmer, but do not boil as this will ruin the soup. Add the clams to the chowder and heat for 5 minutes over very low heat. Serve immediately. Sprinkle each serving with paprika.

New England Clam Chowder

NEW YORK CLAM CHOWDER

2 cans clams or 24 fresh clams
2 slices salt pork
1 leek, thinly sliced
½ cup (125 mL) chopped onion
1 clove garlic, pressed
½ cup (125 mL) chopped green pepper
½ cup (125 mL) diced carrots
¼ cup (50 mL) chopped celery
3 cups (750 mL) diced potatoes
6 cups (1.5 L) water
1 cup (250 mL) canned tomatoes
¼ cup (50 mL) tomato paste
1 tbsp (15 mL) sugar
¼ cup (50 mL) minced parsley
½ tsp (2 mL) thyme
1 bay leaf
4 cloves
1 tsp (5 mL) salt
pepper, to taste

🍂 Drain the canned clams and reserve the juice. If using fresh clams, scrub them with a brush, place in a saucepan and cover with water. Bring to a boil and simmer, covered, until the shells open slightly (10 to 15 minutes). Remove the clams from their shells and reserve the clam broth.

🍂 Dice the salt pork and sauté in a saucepan until translucent. Add the leek, onion and garlic and brown for about 5 minutes. Add the clams, green pepper, carrots, celery, potatoes and the 6 cups (1.5 L) water. Bring to a boil, cover and simmer for 10 minutes. Add the clam broth together with the tomatoes, tomato paste, sugar, parsley, thyme, bay leaf, cloves, salt and pepper. Simmer 20 minutes longer and serve.

POITOU PANADE SOUP

2 to 3 cups (500 to 750 mL) dry bread
6 to 8 cups (1.5 to 2 L) lukewarm water
3 onions, thinly sliced
4 tbsp (60 mL) melted lard or bacon drippings
½ tsp (2 mL) savory
1 egg
½ cup (125 mL) milk

1 tbsp (15 mL) butter
salt and pepper, to taste

🍀 Crumble the bread and place it in a bowl. Pour the lukewarm water over it and soak for 30 minutes.

🍀 In the meantime, sauté the onions in the melted lard or bacon drippings. Add the savory, mix well and pour over the bread. Season with salt and pepper. Bring to a boil over low heat, stirring constantly. Cover and simmer 10 to 20 minutes over very low heat. Beat together the egg and the milk. Remove the soup from the heat and stir in the egg mixture and the butter. Keep the soup hot until serving, but do not let it boil.

GREEN HERB SOUP

🍀 Lettuce, watercress, spinach, leek, celery leaves, parsley and sorrel can all be used to prepare herb soup. Use only one of these herbs or leafy vegetables, or a combination of them.

🍀 The basic method consists of melting butter or other fat, adding the greens and then cooking them over low heat. Cover and simmer until they have lost their rawness and are "wilted". The greens will have released their juices and absorbed the fat. Personally, I find these soups particularly tasty when I replace the butter with thin slices of very fat salt pork, sautéed over low heat.

🍀 Once the greens are "wilted", the liquid is added. Here also the variations are endless: you may use the water in which the vegetables or herbs were cooked, the water from boiled potatoes, ordinary water, a combination of milk and water, or veal or chicken stock.

🍀 Egg yolks are used to thicken the cooked soup. Beat the egg yolk and stir in a hefty spoonful of the hot soup. Remove the soup from the heat and fold the egg yolks into the soup, stirring quickly. To warm the soup, place it over very low heat. Do not let it boil. Green herb soup is served as is or garnished with ¼ cup (50 mL) semolina, very fine vermicelli or cooked rice, simmered in the soup 5 minutes before the soup is thickened with the egg yolks.

2 tbsp (30 mL) butter
1 large leek, thinly sliced
1 cup (250 mL) finely chopped spinach
1 cup (250 mL) chopped lettuce
½ cup (125 mL) chopped sorrel (as needed)
5 cups (1.2 L) boiling water
4 tbsp (60 mL) cooked rice
or 3 tbsp (45 mL) semolina
or 3 tbsp (45 mL) fine vermicelli
½ cup (125 mL) light cream
1 tsp (5 mL) salt
3 egg yolks

🍀 Melt the butter in a saucepan. Add the leek, spinach, lettuce and sorrel and mix well. Cover and simmer over low heat until just wilted, as explained above. Add the boiling water. Cover and simmer for 20 minutes. Force through a large sieve, squeezing hard, or put through a food mill. Place this green purée back into the saucepan and slowly bring it to a boil. Add the cooked rice, semolina or vermicelli. Blend the cream and salt with the egg yolks. Add a few spoonfuls of the hot

Celery Soup

soup to the egg mixture, stirring quickly. Remove the soup from the heat and slowly add the egg mixture to the hot soup, stirring constantly. Adjust the seasoning and serve.

COUNTRY-STYLE SOUP

4 potatoes
2 leeks or 3 onions
or 1 cup (250 mL) chives
1 to 3 tbsp (15 to 45 mL) butter
4 cups (1 L) hot water
or consommé
1 tsp (5 mL) salt
1 cup (250 mL) milk
or light cream
2 tbsp (30 mL) fresh parsley
small croutons, browned in butter

🍃 Potatoes are the main ingredient of this delicious meatless soup. Leek is included for flavor but in small quantity so that its flavor does not overpower that of the other ingredients. You may replace the leeks with onion or with chives, when they are available in sufficient quantity (you'll need at least 1 cup or 250 mL).

🍃 Peel and dice the potatoes. Wash the leeks and cut both the green and white parts into very thin slices.

🍃 Melt the butter in a saucepan and add either the leeks, onions or chives. Cover the saucepan and simmer over low heat for 10 minutes. Add the water or consommé and the salt. Cover and boil for 20 minutes. When ready to serve, add the milk, fresh pars-

Potage Saint Germain

ley and buttered croutons. This soup may be puréed by forcing it through a sieve or putting it through a food mill.

CELERY SOUP

4 cups (1 L) water or consommé
3 cups (750 mL) finely diced celery stalks and leaves
2 medium potatoes, grated
¼ tsp (1 mL) pepper
1 tsp (5 mL) salt
¼ cup (50 mL) finely chopped parsley
3 tbsp (45 mL) butter
1 cup (250 mL) hot milk

🍃 Pour the water or consommé into a saucepan and bring to a boil. Add the celery, potatoes, pepper, salt, parsley and butter. Cover and simmer for 1 hour over medium heat.

🍃 Just before serving, add the hot milk.

POTAGE SAINT GERMAIN

10 lettuce leaves
10 fresh spinach leaves
2 packages frozen green peas
1 medium leek
¼ cup (50 mL) butter
1 tsp (5 mL) coarse salt
½ tsp (2 mL) sugar
1 cup (250 mL) water
4 cups (1 L) veal or chicken broth
1 lb (500 g) fresh green peas (as needed)
½ cup (125 mL) cream
chopped parsley or chervil

🍃 Wash the lettuce and spinach leaves and cut into thin strips. In

❦ TECHNIQUE ❦

POTAGE SAINT GERMAIN

1 Place the frozen peas, sliced leek, shredded lettuce and spinach leaves, butter, coarse salt, sugar and water in a saucepan.

2 Put through a food mill to make a purée.

3 Add the chicken broth and simmer.

4 Add the fresh peas and the cream.

Cream of Pea Soup

an enameled cast-iron saucepan, place the frozen green peas, sliced leek, shredded lettuce and spinach leaves, butter, coarse salt, sugar and water. Bring to a boil.

❧ Cover and simmer over low heat for 25 to 30 minutes. Force through a fine sieve or put through a food mill to make a purée. Return to the saucepan and gradually add the veal or chicken broth, stirring constantly. Simmer 10 to 15 minutes. Cook the fresh green peas and add them to the soup together with the cream. Serve piping hot, garnished with chervil or parsley.

CREAM OF PUMPKIN SOUP

2 lbs (900 g) pumpkin, peeled and coarsely chopped
2 to 3 tbsp (30 to 45 mL) butter
¼ tsp (1 mL) nutmeg
1 cup (250 mL) water
1 cup (250 mL) milk
½ cup (125 mL) cream
½ cup (125 mL) small croutons

❧ Peel and chop the pumpkin. Melt the butter in a saucepan and add the pumpkin and nutmeg. Cover tightly and simmer over low heat for 20 minutes. Add the water and the milk. Continue cooking for 10 minutes. Force through a sieve or put through a food mill. Add the ½ cup (125 mL) of cream and the croutons. Season to taste and serve immediately.

CREAM OF PARSLEY SOUP

1 cup (250 mL) parsley (leaves and stems)
3 cups (750 mL) consommé
1 tbsp (15 mL) flour
1 tbsp (15 mL) butter
2 cups (500 mL) milk
salt and pepper

❧ Chop the parsley very fine. Simmer for 20 minutes in the consommé.
❧ Make a white sauce with the flour, butter and milk. When the sauce begins to thicken, add the parsley broth. Add salt and pepper to taste. Serve with a bowl of grated cheese.

CREAM OF PEA SOUP

3 tbsp (45 mL) butter
½ lb (250 g) fresh mushrooms, finely chopped
2 cups (500 mL) milk
1 can small green peas

❧ Melt the butter in a saucepan. Sauté the mushrooms over high heat for 2 to 3 minutes. Add the milk, cover and simmer for 20 minutes.
❧ Drain the peas and reserve the liquid. Put through a food mill to make a purée. Add this purée to the mushrooms and simmer 10 minutes longer. If you prefer a lighter cream, dilute the soup with some of the water drained from the peas.

BLENDER GREEN PEA SOUP

1 cup (250 mL) green peas, fresh or frozen
1 tsp (5 mL) salt
¼ (1 mL) tsp sugar
pinch of basil
2 tbsp (30 mL) flour

My Favorite Cream of Mushroom Soup

2 cups (500 mL) milk
1 green onion, quartered
2 sprigs parsley

• Combine all the ingredients in the jar of a blender. Cover and blend approximately 1 minute, long enough to chop the vegetables.

• Pour the mixture into a saucepan, cook over medium heat, stirring constantly, until light and creamy. Add 1 tbsp (15 mL) butter and serve.

• You can replace the green peas with asparagus, carrots, lima beans or any other vegetable.

• To partially thaw frozen vegetables, place the unwrapped package in a bowl of hot water for 20 minutes. The vegetables need not be completely thawed.

• Fresh vegetables need only to be washed; they require no previous cooking.

CREAM OF ASPARAGUS SOUP

2 cups (500 mL) fresh asparagus or 1 package frozen asparagus
2 celery stalks
1 sprig parsley
pinch of tarragon or thyme
1 tsp (5 mL) salt
2 cups (500 mL) boiling consommé or 2 cups (500 mL) cream or 2 cups (500 mL) water
1 cube chicken bouillon

• Wash the fresh asparagus and cut into 1-in. (2.5-cm) pieces or thaw the frozen asparagus.

• Combine all the ingredients in the bowl of a food processor or the jar of an electric blender. Cover and blend 1 minute.

• Pour into a saucepan and heat but do not boil. Serve the soup immediately.

• All fresh or frozen vegetables may be prepared this way. In the space of a few minutes, you can serve piping hot soup. Vary the vegetables, using only one or combining two or three at a time. By using different seasonings and varying the broth, you can create a different soup every time.

MY FAVORITE CREAM OF MUSHROOM SOUP

½ lb (250 g) fresh mushrooms
3 cups (750 mL) boiling water
½ tsp (2 mL) salt
1 small onion
2 tbsp (30 mL) butter
3 tbsp (45 mL) butter
3 tbsp (45 mL) flour
1 cup (250 mL) cream
salt and pepper

• Peel the mushrooms and remove the stems. Place the peels and stems in a saucepan. Cover with boiling water. Season with salt and simmer for ½ hour. Drain and set the mushroom broth aside. Discard the peels.

• Cut the peeled mushroom caps into thin slices. Chop the onion and sauté slowly in 2 tbsp (30 mL) butter until the mushrooms are brown and tender, about 3 or 4 minutes.

• Melt 3 tbsp (45 mL) butter in a separate saucepan. Stir in the flour, blend thoroughly and add the mushroom broth together with the cream. Cook, stirring constantly, until the mixture is smooth and creamy. Salt and pepper to taste. Add the onion and the mushrooms. Simmer for 5 minutes and serve.

❦ TECHNIQUE ❦

My Favorite Cream of Mushroom Soup

1 Place the mushroom peels and stems in a saucepan. Cover with boiling water. Season with salt and simmer.

2 Sauté the mushroom caps and onion in butter.

3 Add the flour to the hot butter.

4 Add the mushroom broth.

Fresh Tomato Velouté

2 tbsp (30 mL) softened butter
3 tbsp (45 mL) flour
½ cup (125 mL) boiling water
1½ cups (375 mL) milk
3 to 4 fresh tomatoes, quartered
1 small onion, peeled and quartered
1 tsp (5 mL) sugar
½ tsp (2 mL) salt
pinch or two of basil or thyme

❧ Place the softened butter and flour in the jar of an electric blender. Cover and blend 3 seconds. With the motor still running, remove the stopper and pour in the boiling water. Then gradually add, in the following order, the milk, fresh tomatoes (seeded), onion, sugar, salt and basil or thyme. Cover and blend another 30 seconds. Stop the motor and pour the soup into a saucepan. Heat 15 to 20 minutes over low heat. Do not let the soup boil. Serve immediately.

Curry Soup

¼ cup (50 mL) butter
1 large onion, sliced
¼ cup (50 mL) chutney
2½ cups (625 mL) consommé
1 to 2 tsp (5 to 10 mL) curry powder
¼ tsp (1 mL) ginger
2 tbsp (30 mL) flour
1 egg
1 cup (250 mL) cream or yogurt
3 tbsp (45 mL) sherry

❧ Melt the butter and add the onion. Sauté until tender and translucent but do not brown. Place in the jar of an electric blender and add the chutney, consommé, curry powder, ginger, flour and egg. Cover and blend 1 minute.

❧ Pour the blended mixture into a saucepan and heat until smooth and golden. Add the cream or yogurt and the sherry. Heat the soup well and serve at once.

Polish Egg Soup

2 cups (500 mL) consommé
2 cups (500 mL) milk
4 tbsp (60 mL) butter
½ cup (125 mL) chopped mushrooms
4 tbsp (60 mL) flour
1 tbsp (15 mL) chopped cooked ham (optional)
1 tbsp (15 mL) capers
3 hard-cooked eggs
2 tbsp (30 mL) fresh lemon juice

❧ Heat together the consommé and the milk. In a separate saucepan, melt the butter and sauté the mushrooms lightly. Stir in the flour and blend well; then incorporate the mushrooms into the hot milk. Bring to boil, stirring constantly. Season to taste. Add the ham, capers and thinly sliced egg whites. When ready to serve, grate the egg yolks and sprinkle them over each bowl. Add a dash of lemon juice.

Cream of Oyster Soup

1 cup (250 mL) milk
1½ cups (375 mL) light cream
3 tbsp (45 mL) butter
½ tsp (2 mL) salt
freshly ground pepper, if possible
1 tsp (5 mL) Worcestershire sauce
2 cups (500 mL) bulk oysters
paprika

❧ Place a chafing dish on the table. Pour the milk and cream into a pitcher. Put the butter on a plate and the oysters into a glass bowl. Place everything on a large serving tray along with a salt shaker, a pepper mill, Worcestershire sauce and paprika.

❧ Warm up the soup bowls. When ready to serve the soup, place the bowls on the serving tray.

❧ Prepare a small basket of crackers to serve with the oyster soup.

❧ At the table, heat the chafing dish. Pour in the milk and cream and bring to a boil. Add the butter, salt, pepper and Worcestershire sauce. Simmer a few seconds.

❧ Add the oysters and their juice. Heat without boiling and serve. Garnish each bowl with a dusting of paprika.

Lobster Bisque

1 lb (500 g) lobster or shrimp
3 tsp (15 mL) olive oil
1 tsp (5 mL) vinegar
salt and pepper
2 tbsp (30 mL) butter
1 to 2 tbsp (15 to 30 mL) tomato paste
⅓ cup (75 mL) rice flour
5 cups (1.2 L) broth
½ cup (125 mL) cream, heated
2 egg yolks
1 tbsp (15 mL) butter

❧ A bisque is always tastier when prepared with live lobster. If shrimp are used, wash and shell them and reserve the shells for the broth.

ϡ The lobster to be cooked alive is immersed head first into boiling water and boiled about 10 minutes. Drain, crack open and remove the meat. Place the broken shell in a large bowl. If using shrimp, cook the tails only and follow the procedure above. Then, using a wooden pestle, break up the shells as much as possible.

ϡ Cut the meat into small pieces and combine with the oil, vinegar, salt and pepper. Marinate for 2 hours.

ϡ Melt the butter in a saucepan. Stir in the tomato paste, blending it thoroughly with the butter, and add the rice flour. When well mixed, pour in the broth as well as the broken shells and simmer over medium heat, stirring constantly until light and creamy, about 15 minutes. Force through a sieve. Return to the saucepan. Add the lobster or shrimp meat. Beat the egg yolks with the lukewarm cream. Add to the bisque, stirring quickly. Add the butter. Adjust the seasoning. Do not let the soup boil after the eggs and cream have been added.

CREAM OF SHRIMP SOUP

½ lb (250 g) haddock or fish heads
1½ lbs (750 g) uncooked shrimp
1 medium onion, quartered
zest of a large lemon
¼ tsp (1 mL) basil

Vichyssoise

pinch of fennel seed
¼ tsp (1 mL) thyme
6 cups (1.5 L) cold water
3 tbsp (45 mL) fresh breadcrumbs
4 tbsp (60 mL) butter
juice of 1 lemon
pinch of nutmeg
½ cup (125 mL) cream or milk
1 egg yolk
salt and pepper, to taste

ϡ Place the fish heads or haddock in a large saucepan. Shell the shrimp and add the shells to the fish heads. Add the onion, lemon zest, basil, fennel, thyme and cold water. Bring to a boil and boil for 20 minutes. Force through a fine sieve. Add the breadcrumbs to the stock and mix thoroughly.

ϡ Cover the shrimp with the cold water, bring to a boil and simmer until the shrimp turn pink. Drain and place the shrimp in a wooden bowl with the butter. With a pestle, mash the buttered shrimp while adding the lemon juice and nutmeg. Add the shrimp paste to the fish stock and beat with a hand beater.

ϡ Beat the egg yolk with the cream or milk. Add a little of the hot stock to the egg mixture, blend thoroughly and pour this into the hot stock in the saucepan. Do not allow the soup to boil after the egg has been added. Adjust the seasoning and serve.

VICHYSSOISE

¼ cup (50 mL) melted butter
½ cup (125 mL) chopped onions
2 cups (500 mL) sliced leeks
2 cups (500 mL) diced potatoes

4 cups (1 L) chicken broth
or consommé
salt and pepper
1 cup (250 mL) milk or cream
2 tbsp (30 mL) chives

🍃 Melt the butter in a saucepan and add the onions and the leeks (use both green and white parts). Cover and simmer over very low heat for 15 to 20 minutes. Do not brown the vegetables, simply cook them until slightly wilted.

🍃 Add the raw potatoes, the broth or consommé and the salt and pepper. Simmer until the potatoes are tender. Put through a food mill or force through a fine sieve, making sure the vegetables are finely mashed. Add the milk or cream. Heat slowly, stirring vigorously. Pour into a bowl and refrigerate until ready to serve. Garnish with chives.

CHILLED CREAM OF TOMATO SOUP

12 large, very ripe tomatoes
2 grated onions
1 tbsp (15 mL) salt
1 tsp (5 mL) pepper
1 tbsp (15 mL) sugar
1 tsp (5 mL) basil
sour cream or whipping cream

🍃 Peel the tomatoes and cut into small pieces. Add the remaining ingredients and beat with a hand beater. Refrigerate. Adjust the seasoning. To serve, garnish with the cream of your choice.

CREAM OF CUCUMBER SOUP

4 cups (1 L) chicken broth
2 or 3 cucumbers
1 onion
2 tsp (10 mL) butter

1 cup (250 mL) cream
4 or 5 fresh mushrooms (as needed)
¼ tsp (1 mL) garlic powder
chives

🍃 Pour the chicken broth into a saucepan and bring to a boil. Peel and grate 1 or 2 cucumbers (set aside a half cucumber for garnish), taking care to reserve the juice. Add the pulp and juice to the hot broth. Simmer 10 minutes.

🍃 Brown the onion in 1 tsp (5 mL) butter. Add to the soup, together with the cream. Simmer 5 minutes.

🍃 Slice the mushrooms and sauté quickly in the remaining butter. Add to the soup along with the garlic powder. Heat for a few minutes. Refrigerate.

🍃 Serve cold, garnished with chives and diced cucumber (use the half cucumber that was set aside).

MY FAVORITE GAZPACHO

½ cup (125 mL) chopped chives
1 cup (250 mL) chopped parsley
½ cup (125 mL) chopped chervil
1 clove garlic, crushed
1 green pepper, diced
2 large tomatoes, peeled and seeded
1 cup (250 mL) olive oil
¾ cup (175 mL) fresh lemon juice
1 large Spanish onion, thinly sliced
1 diced cucumber
salt and pepper
3 slices dry bread
ice cubes

My Favorite Gazpacho

☙ TECHNIQUE ☙

MY FAVORITE GAZPACHO

1 Using a food processor, chop the chives, parsley, chervil and garlic.

2 Add the green pepper and tomatoes.

3 Pour in the olive oil while blending.

4 Add the lemon juice, onion and cucumber.

Chilled Crème Crécy

❧ Place the chives, parsley, chervil and garlic in the bowl of a food processor and chop.
❧ Add the green pepper and tomatoes, and blend. With the motor running, gradually pour in the olive oil.
❧ Add the lemon juice, onion and cucumber. Salt and pepper to taste. Crumble the dry bread and add to the soup.
❧ Refrigerate 3 to 4 hours. Adjust the seasoning. To serve, place a cube of ice in each bowl and ladle the chilled soup over the ice.

Cucumber and Beer Soup

1 12-oz (340-mL) bottle of light beer
½ cup (125 mL) sour cream
2 medium cucumbers
1 tsp (5 mL) salt
¼ tsp (1 mL) garlic powder
½ tsp (2 mL) sugar

❧ Beat the beer gradually into the sour cream using a hand beater. Peel and grate the cucumbers and add to the beer mixture. Stir in the remaining ingredients. Refrigerate until ready to serve.

Chilled Crème Crécy

(Cream of Carrot Soup)

8 medium carrots, thinly sliced
2 celery stalks with leaves, chopped
1 onion, chopped
1 bay leaf
2 cloves
4 cups (1 L) chicken broth
¼ cup (50 mL) chopped parsley
½ cup (125 mL) cream

❧ Place the carrots, celery, onion, bay leaf, cloves and chicken broth in a large saucepan. Bring to a boil, cover and simmer until the carrots are tender. Put through a food mill or purée using a food processor. Add the parsley. Refrigerate. When ready to serve, adjust the seasoning and stir in the cream.

Thatched-Cottage Soup

This traditional Welsh recipe has been adapted to modern cooking methods. Using a blender, it takes only minutes to prepare. It's ideal for summertime entertaining—try it as a first course while the steaks are grilling.

1 can cream of tomato soup
2 cups (500 mL) milk or 1 cup (250 mL) milk and 1 cup (250 mL) cream
1 tbsp (15 mL) lemon juice
1 tsp (5 mL) prepared horseradish, well drained
½ tsp (2 mL) curry powder
½ cup (125 mL) cottage cheese
2 chopped green onions or 1 tbsp (15 mL) chopped chives
½ cucumber, peeled and grated

❧ In the jar of an electric blender, place the tomato soup, the milk (or milk and cream), lemon juice, horseradish and curry powder. Cover and blend 1 minute at high speed. Pour into a bowl, cover and refrigerate until needed.
❧ Just before serving, stir in the cottage cheese and onions or chives. Prepare a small bowl of grated cucumber and pass it around the table.

❦ TECHNIQUE ❦
CHILLED CRÈME CRÉCY

1 Place the carrots, celery and onion in a saucepan.

2 Season the mixture and add the chicken broth.

3 Put through a food mill, or purée using a food processor.

4 When ready to serve, add the cream.

Senegalese Cream Soup

2 leeks
2 onions
4 celery stalks
4 tbsp (60 mL) butter
1 tbsp (15 mL) curry powder
3 tbsp (45 mL) flour
8 cups (2 L) chicken broth
1 cup (250 mL) cream
2 chicken breasts (as needed)

❧ Cut the leeks, onions and celery into thin slices. Melt the butter, add the vegetables and cook over moderately high heat for 3 to 4 minutes, stirring almost constantly. Add the curry powder and the flour. Blend thoroughly. Pour into the chicken broth. Bring to a boil, while stirring. Cover and simmer for about 30 to 40 minutes. Force through a sieve to mash the vegetables. Refrigerate until ready to serve. Then add the chilled cream and beat 1 minute with a hand beater.

❧ The classic garnish for this cream soup is cooked and thinly sliced breast of chicken. Garnish each serving generously with the slivers of chicken. This delicious chilled cream soup can be served in winter as well as summer.

FISH AND SEAFOOD

FISH

FRESH FISH

Truly fresh fish has no fishy smell and the flesh is firm and elastic. But fish doesn't stay fresh for long, so, if at all possible, serve it the day you buy it. To keep it at its freshest right up to the moment of cooking, wrap the fish in clean waterproof wrapping and seal it in a tightly covered container. Store the fish in the coldest part of the refrigerator.

❧ Fresh fish can be bought whole or cleaned or cut into sections, filets or steaks. Filets and steaks will, of course, cook faster than whole fish or large pieces.

FROZEN FISH

Frozen fish compares favorably with fresh fish in flavor, appearance and food value, and it is generally cheaper. To preserve its quality, though, you should keep it frozen right up to the last moment.

❧ In most cases, it is not necessary to thaw the fish before you cook it, although you will have to adjust the cooking time. If you do defrost it first, it is a good idea to let it thaw in the refrigerator and then cook it immediately. Never refreeze fish once it has thawed.

CANNED FISH

By far the most common canned fish are tuna, salmon and sardines. However, you can buy a wide variety of fish and shellfish in cans, including herring, mackerel, clams, crab and lobster.

❧ For those occasions when we're pressed for time or when inspiration eludes us, it's handy to have a selection of canned fish or fish soups on hand. They can be used to prepare some excellent dishes in almost no time.

SMOKED FISH

The art of smoking fish is an ancient one. Originally, fish was smoked in order to dry and preserve it, but now we appreciate smoked fish for its special flavor. Today, most smoked fish is nearly as perishable as fresh fish, which is why it is often sold frozen or canned.

❧ Fish is smoked using one of two basic methods—cold smoking or hot smoking. Fish that is hot smoked is completely cooked when you buy it, while cold smoked fish may require some additional cooking. Salmon, whitefish and eel are usually prepared by the hot smoke method; herring, cod and Winnipeg goldeye are more often cold smoked.

CLEANING
AND PREPARING FISH

The first step in preparing a fish is removing the scales. Hold the tail end firmly with a towel. Using a fish scaler (available at sports or hardware stores) or a sharp knife, scrape off the scales, beginning at the tail and working toward the head. End each stroke just behind the gills. When all the scales are loosened, rinse the fish under running water.

❧ Next, cut off the fins. At this point you may want to skin the fish, although it will have a better flavor if you cook it with the skin on. To skin it, place the fish on a flat surface and run a sharp knife down the backbone. Loosen the skin near the head and strip it off toward the tail. Skin the second side the same way.

❧ To clean the fish, make an incision down the length of the abdomen. Remove the entrails and wash the fish thoroughly inside and out in very cold water. It should be completely clean.

❧ To remove the bones, slit the fish open along the length of its abdomen so that it can be spread open and laid flat. Use the tip of the knife to loosen the backbone near the neck; then lift it out, along with the bones connected to it, cutting it free from the flesh as you work toward the tail. Go over the fish to remove any remaining small bones.

❧ Use the fish whole or cut it into two filets.

COOKING FISH

Every good cook knows there are several important rules for cooking fish of any type.

❧ Fish should be handled gently and as little as possible, both before and after cooking, so that it will keep its attractive appearance.

❧ Fish should never be cooked longer than necessary, so that it will retain its full flavor.

❧ The flesh of fish is not particularly firm; it is not necessary to cook fish for long to make it tender or to bring out its full flavor. Fish can be delicious baked, steamed, barbecued, poached or fried. Whatever method you choose, however, it is important that you pay close attention to the cooking time; in general, the thickness of the fish is a more important indicator of required cooking time than the weight.

❧ Raw fish, whether pink, white or cream-colored, is always translucent in appearance. During cooking, the flesh becomes opaque, and this is an indicator that never fails—as soon as the flesh is opaque in the center, it is perfectly cooked. The fish is also properly cooked when the flesh flakes when prodded with a fork or when the bones separate easily from the flesh. If you keep cooking the fish beyond this point, it will lose its juiciness and become dry, tough and flavorless.

COOKING
IN COURT-BOUILLON

Court-bouillon is the name given to any liquid in which fish is poached or simmered, but the exact ingredients of court-bouillon can be as varied as your imagination permits.

❧ A court-bouillon can be nothing more than salted water or wine. Often, however, it is made of salted water flavored with vinegar, lemon juice or red or white wine as well as small quantities of carrots, onions, garlic, parsley and herbs.

❧ Whatever the components of the court-bouillon, the cooking method is always the same—the fish is poached, covered, over low heat in the court-bouillon, which should simmer but never reach a boil. This technique ensures that

the poaching liquid penetrates the tissues gradually, so that the flesh will have less tendency to fall apart or to dry out.

❧ To poach fish, first simmer the court-bouillon for 30 to 40 minutes and then allow it to cool. Wrap the fish in a piece of cheesecloth and immerse it in the court-bouillon. (Or you can lay the fish on the rack of a fish-poaching pan.) Bring the court-bouillon slowly to a boil over low heat. Heating the liquid too rapidly can cause the flesh to fall apart, and cooking at high heat can also toughen the exterior and prevent the inner flesh from cooking. As soon as the court-bouillon starts to bubble, reduce the heat, cover, and simmer slowly. Start calculating the cooking time from the moment the liquid reaches the boil. The cooking time will vary somewhat, depending on the type and size of fish.

❧ For best results, no matter what the recipe, follow this basic cooking guide. It applies to all types of fish and all cooking methods.

Large fish
10 minutes per lb (500 g)

Small fish
10 to 12 minutes in total

Fish slices
12 to 15 minutes in total

Flatfish (plaice, sole, etc.)
8 to 9 minutes per lb (500 g)

BAKED STUFFED FISH

An oven-baked stuffed fish makes a dramatic first course. Choose a 2- to 3-lb (1-kg to 1.5-kg) fish or piece of fish; possible choices are salmon, trout, fresh tuna, bass or pike. Prepare a bread or rice stuffing. You can either stuff a whole fish or layer the stuffing between 2 fish filets or steaks. Nothing is more delicious!

❧ For whole fish, stuff the cavity loosely, so that there is room for the stuffing to absorb the juices and to swell. Sew or skewer the cavity shut. Place the fish in a baking pan and baste with oil or melted butter. Measure the fish at its thickest point, and bake it in a preheated oven at 450°F (230°C) for 10 minutes per in. (2.5 cm) of thickness.

❧ Baked fish reaches the height of perfection when the flavors of the stuffing marry the unique flavor of the type of fish you are cooking.

FISH BAKED IN FOIL

This method of cooking will ensure that all the flavor and natural juices of the fish are retained. It is similar to the steaming method.

❧ You can use this technique to cook whole fish, slices, filets or even frozen fish. (It is not necessary to thaw frozen fish before cooking.)

❧ Measure the thickness and length of the fish. Cut pieces of heavy-duty aluminum foil large enough to completely envelop the whole fish or each piece of fish.

Fumet or Fish Stock

You can use Soyer's method to cook almost any kind of fish. If you use aluminum foil, grease the side that will touch the fish with butter or bacon grease and seal the fish tightly in the foil. If you would rather use a paper bag, grease the inside lightly. Place the fish inside and fold the bag tightly to form a package, fastening it with paper clips. Then barbecue for the length of time recommended in the appropriate recipe for barbecued fish.

COOKING SMOKED FISH

2 lbs (900 g) smoked fish filets
2 cups (500 mL) milk
1 tbsp (15 mL) butter
1 thick slice of onion
pinch of pepper

Cut the filets into individual serving portions. Heat the milk with the butter, onion and pepper. Add the fish pieces. Cover and let simmer for 10 to 20 minutes over medium heat. Or bake in a 450°F (230°C) oven for 20 minutes. Remove the fish from the milk and serve it with a sauce.

You can prepare a sauce from the leftover milk by stirring in 2 tbsp (30 mL) flour or cornstarch dissolved in ¼ cup (50 mL) cold milk. Garnish the sauce with chopped fresh parsley.

Grease the side of the foil that will touch the fish.

Place the fish on the greased surface. Fold the foil and seal it tightly, to form a package or papillote.

Place the packages on a baking sheet. Bake in a preheated 500°F (260°C) oven, allowing 10 minutes per in. (2.5 cm) of thickness for fresh fish or 20 minutes per in. (2.5 cm) thickness for frozen fish.

BARBECUING FISH

Any fisherman will tell you there's nothing quite as delicious as fresh-caught speckled trout cooked in a pan right over the campfire. But the truth is that fish is even better wrapped in foil or a paper bag and cooked on the barbecue.

Simply season the fish with a little salt and pepper and baste it with butter or oil. If you want to create a real epicurean delight, add some fresh herbs such as tarragon, rosemary or sage. Then wrap the fish in heavy-duty aluminum foil, folding the ends in to create a leak-proof package. Place the package on the grill over very hot coals and cook for 8 to 10 minutes, turning once midway through the cooking period.

This foil method is a variation of a technique invented by Nicolas Soyer. In 1912, his method of cooking fish inside a paper bag created a sensation in England.

FUMET OR FISH STOCK

Fish fumet is a very concentrated court-bouillon. It is often used in haute cuisine in the preparation of sauces for fish dishes, as well as for poaching fish.

1½ to 2 lbs (750 to 900 g) fish trimmings
2 cups (500 mL) water
1 bay leaf
1 onion, sliced
2 cups (500 mL) white wine
1 carrot, scrubbed and sliced
2 celery stalks cut in 1-in. (2.5-cm) pieces
2 tbsp (30 mL) parsley
¼ tsp (1 mL) pepper
¼ tsp (1 mL) salt

🥄 Suitable fish trimmings include fish tails, larger bones and the heads of firm-fleshed fish such as cod and haddock.
🥄 Place all the ingredients in a large stainless steel or enamel saucepan. Bring to a boil. Cover and simmer for 1 hour or until the liquid is reduced by half.
🥄 Line a strainer or colander with cheesecloth and pour in the fumet. Let it drip, without stirring or touching it, for about 30 minutes. It is then ready to use.
🥄 Fish can be cooked in a number of ways. Any of the following 11 basic preparation methods is appropriate for any type of fish.

Fish Boiled in Milk

BOILED FISH

whole fish or pieces of fish
lemon juice
salt
boiling water

🥄 Wash and dry the fish. Sprinkle with a little lemon juice and salt.
🥄 Enclose the fish in a piece of cooking parchment or in cheesecloth and tie with string. Plunge the package into boiling water.
🥄 Return the water to the boil and then simmer for 8 to 10 minutes per lb (500 g).

FISH BOILED IN MILK

fish
chilled salted water—2 tbsp salt per cup (30 mL per 250 mL)
boiling milk
flour
butter

🥄 Cut the fish into individual portions and soak for 5 minutes in chilled salted water. Drain.
🥄 Place the fish pieces in enough boiling milk to cover them. Simmer for 8 to 10 minutes per lb (500 g).
🥄 The cooking milk can be made into a sauce once the fish is cooked. Knead together 2 tbsp (30 mL) each of flour and butter for each cup (250 mL) of milk and add to the pan. Stir until thickened.

FISH POACHED IN COURT-BOUILLON

12 cups (3 L) water
2 tbsp (30 mL) coarse salt
½ cup (125 mL) vinegar
2 large carrots, sliced

[125]

6 sprigs parsley
1 bay leaf
pinch of thyme
½ tsp (2 mL) whole peppercorns
2 large onions, quartered

❧ Place all the ingredients in a saucepan. Bring to a boil. Then simmer, uncovered, for 30 minutes.

❧ Let the court-bouillon cool before adding the fish.

❧ Make sure that the fish is completely covered by the court-bouillon. Simmer for 8 to 10 minutes per lb (500 g).

❧ If preparing a court-bouillon for salmon, use lemon instead of vinegar.

BROILED FISH

whole fish or fish pieces
salt
lemon juice

❧ Small fish can be broiled whole; larger fish should be cut into pieces. Season each fish or piece of fish with lemon juice and salt. If you are using a type of fish with relatively dry flesh, sprinkle with a little oil.

❧ Preheat the broiler to 450°F (230°C). Broil whole fish for 8 to 10 minutes per lb (500 g). Fish cut into serving pieces will cook in 10 to 12 minutes in total.

WHOLE BAKED FISH

whole fish
salt
fine breadcrumbs
dry mustard
olive oil or melted butter

❧ Cut off the tail and fins. Slit the fish open along the whole length of its belly. Cut through the flesh along the backbone so that the fish can be spread open and laid flat.

❧ Grease a baking dish and arrange the fish in it, skin-side down. Sprinkle the flesh side with salt and with a thin layer of breadcrumbs mixed with a little dry mustard. Sprinkle with olive oil.

❧ Bake the fish in a preheated 500°F (260°C) oven for 10 minutes per in. (2.5 cm) of thickness. The breadcrumb topping should be lightly browned. For large fish, reduce the temperature toward the end of the cooking period so that the topping does not burn.

FISH FILETS MEUNIÈRE

flour
fish filets or slices
salt and pepper
oil or butter
lemon juice
chopped parsley
butter

❧ Fish is composed of 75% water and 18% albumin. That's why you should cook it as gently as you would eggs, as quickly as possible and over moderate heat. To retain all the natural juices of a delicate type of fish, it is best to cook it in smaller pieces; if the pieces are too large, the exterior tends to dry out before the interior is completely cooked. For frying, vegetable oil is a better choice than butter; butter has a tendency to burn and will mask the flavor of the fish.

Fish Filets Meunière

🐦 Dredge the fish filets or pieces of fish lightly in flour. Sprinkle with salt and pepper. Put just enough oil in a skillet to cover the bottom. Fry the fish over moderate heat for 3 minutes on each side, turning only once.

🐦 It can be served as is or Meunière-style: sprinkle with a little lemon juice and chopped parsley; just before serving, melt some butter until it is lightly browned and pour it over the fish.

POACHED FILETS OF FISH

fish filets
¼ cup (50 mL) cream, milk, white wine or water
salt, pepper, nutmeg

🐦 Butter a baking dish well and arrange the fish filets in one layer over the bottom. Cover with the cream or whatever poaching liquid you have chosen. Sprinkle with salt, pepper and nutmeg. Cover with a greased piece of aluminum foil.

🐦 Bake in a preheated 450°F (230°C) oven for 10 to 20 minutes. (Calculate the cooking time at about 10 minutes per in. (2.5 cm) of thickness.)

FISH FILETS GRATINÉ

2 lbs (900 g) fish filets
2 cups (500 mL) milk
½ tsp (2 mL) salt

½ tsp (2 mL) dry mustard
1 bay leaf
¼ tsp (1 mL) thyme
breadcrumbs
melted butter
lemon juice

🐦 Cut the fish into individual portions. In a glass bowl, combine the milk, salt, dry mustard, bay leaf and thyme. Marinate the fish in this mixture for 2 hours. Remove the fish from the marinade and dredge in fine breadcrumbs. Arrange the pieces in a shallow baking dish. Pour on equal quantities of melted butter and lemon juice and top with the leftover marinade.

🐦 Place the pan in a preheated 400°F (200°C) oven and cook the fish 20 to 30 minutes or until the top is crusty and golden brown.

FISH FILETS PÊCHEUR

2 onions, sliced and lightly sautéed
2 to 3 lbs (1 to 1.5 kg) fish filets
salt, pepper and nutmeg
lemon juice
½ tsp (2 mL) thyme
2 tbsp (30 mL) butter

🐦 Grease a baking dish and cover the bottom with sliced sautéed onions. Cut the fish filets into individual portions and arrange them in the dish. Sprinkle with salt, pepper, nutmeg, thyme and lemon juice. Dot with pieces of butter. Cover the dish with greased aluminum foil.

🐦 Bake in a preheated 375°F (190°C) oven for 10 to 15 minutes per lb (500 g).

Fish Filets Gratiné

[127]

STUFFED FILETS OF FISH

2 filets of fish of your choice
¼ cup (50 mL) water
1 tbsp (15 mL) butter

STUFFING:
butter
4 slices bread
1 egg
2 small gherkins, minced
½ tsp (2 mL) paprika
pinch of curry powder
pinch of thyme
4 tbsp (60 mL) milk
salt and pepper

🍂 To prepare the stuffing, butter the slices of bread on both sides and cut into small cubes. In a bowl, combine the bread cubes with the egg, gherkins, paprika, curry powder, thyme, milk, salt and pepper.

🍂 Butter a baking dish and place one filet in it. Spread the stuffing over the fish and then top with the second filet. Add the butter and water and bake in a preheated 375°F (190°C) oven for about 30 minutes.

STEAMED FISH

🍂 Put ½ cup (125 mL) water in the bottom of a fish steamer (or a fish-poaching pan with the rack raised above the level of the water). Bring the water to a boil. Put the fish on the rack, cover the pan and lower the heat.

🍂 Cook for 3 to 4 minutes per in. (2.5 cm) of thickness. Fish that is more than 2 in. (5 cm) thick should be cut into thinner pieces. If the fish is chilled from the refrigerator, add 2 to 3 minutes to the cooking time.

FISH SOUFFLÉ

1 cup (250 mL) cooked or canned fish, shredded
3 tbsp (45 mL) finely shredded raw carrots
1 tbsp (15 mL) chopped parsley
3 tbsp (45 mL) butter
3 tbsp (45 mL) flour
1 tsp (5 mL) salt
1 cup (250 mL) milk
3 eggs, separated
1 tsp (5 mL) lemon juice

🍂 Combine the fish, carrots and parsley. Prepare a white sauce with the butter, flour, salt and milk (see page 46).

🍂 Stir in the fish mixture. Beat the egg yolks until light and foamy and stir in the lemon juice. Combine with the fish mixture.

🍂 Beat the egg whites until stiff and fold them gently into the fish mixture. Turn the mixture into an ungreased 6-cup (1.5-L) soufflé dish. Place the dish in a pan with 1 in. (2.5 cm) hot water.

🍂 Set the pan in a preheated 350°F (180°C) oven and bake for 45 minutes or until the soufflé is set and golden brown. Serve immediately. If you like, serve with a warm sauce made of equal portions of butter and lemon juice.

GALANTINE OF SALMON

STUFFING:
4 slices buttered bread, diced small
1 egg
2 gherkins, minced
½ tsp (2 mL) paprika
pinch of curry powder
pinch of thyme
4 tbsp 60 mL) milk
salt and pepper
1 4-lb (1.8-kg) salmon

GELATIN MIXTURE:
2 cups (500 mL) court-bouillon
1 lb (500 g) spinach, cleaned
1 tbsp (15 mL) gelatin
2 tbsp (30 mL) cold water
1 medium cucumber, peeled and grated
½ cup (125 mL) whipping cream, whipped

🍂 To prepare the stuffing, combine the bread cubes, egg, gherkins, paprika, curry, thyme and milk. Salt and pepper to taste.

🍂 Stuff the salmon with this mixture and wrap it in a piece of cheesecloth. Cook the salmon in a court-bouillon. (Follow the instructions for *Fish Poached in Court-Bouillon* on page 125.)

🍂 Place the cooked salmon on a platter and remove the skin. Refrigerate until chilled.

🍂 To prepare the gelatin mixture, strain the court-bouillon and cook the spinach in it for 10 minutes. Pour the spinach mixture through a strainer into a saucepan, pressing with a spoon to remove all the liquid. Discard the spinach leaves.

Soak the gelatin in the cold water for 5 minutes. Stir it into the green court-bouillon and cook over low heat, stirring constantly, until the gelatin is completely dissolved. Add the grated cucumber and season to taste. Refrigerate until the gelatin mixture has the consistency of egg white. Fold in the whipped cream, combining well.

Spoon some of the mixture over the salmon to cover it. Refrigerate until the gelatin is set and then repeat the procedure until the gelatin mixture is all used.

Serve the salmon chilled, decorated with thinly sliced cucumber and sprigs of watercress.

Baked Salmon

BAKED SALMON

1 whole 4-lb (2-kg) salmon
salt and pepper
flour
5 tbsp (75 mL) butter
1 tsp (5mL) sugar
1 onion, grated
1 clove garlic, crushed and minced
1½ tbsp (25 mL) Worcestershire sauce
1 cup (250 mL) canned tomatoes, drained

Rub the salmon with salt and pepper and sprinkle with flour. Grease a baking pan and lay the salmon in it. Bake for 10 minutes in a preheated 450°F (230°C) oven.

Remove the pan from the oven and add the butter, sugar, onion, garlic, Worcestershire sauce and tomatoes. Return the pan to the oven and cook another 30 min-

utes, basting from time to time.

Place the salmon on a hot platter and serve with the sauce. If you prefer, thicken the sauce with a little flour combined with butter.

MARY'S BOILED SALMON

COURT-BOUILLON:
8 cups (2 L) water
2 bay leaves
1 tbsp (15 mL) salt
1 tsp (5 mL) paprika
10 peppercorns
1 tbsp (15 mL) pickling spices
½ lemon, unpeeled, thinly sliced
1 whole salmon, 3 to 5 lbs (1.5 to 2.5 kg)

To prepare the court-bouillon, combine the water, bay leaves, salt, paprika, peppercorns, pickling spices and lemon in a saucepan and boil for 25 minutes.

Wrap the salmon in a piece of cheesecloth and add it to the court-bouillon. Bring to a boil and then cover and simmer for 10 minutes per lb (500 g).

Unwrap the salmon and serve hot with an egg sauce.

This dish is also delicious served cold. Place the salmon, still wrapped in cheesecloth, in a bowl and cover with the court-bouillon. Refrigerate for 12 to 24 hours. Remove the cheesecloth and peel off the skin. Serve garnished with *Andalousian Mayonnaise* (see page 75).

STEAMED SALMON STEAKS

fresh salmon steaks
salt and pepper
paprika
lemon juice
chives

☙ Place each salmon steak on a square of aluminum foil. Sprinkle each steak with salt, pepper, paprika, a little lemon juice and some minced chives. Seal the steaks in the foil to make individual packages (papillotes).

☙ Set the packages side by side in a large, heavy skillet. Cook over low heat for 20 minutes. (It is not necessary to add liquid to the pan.) Unwrap the steaks and arrange on a heated platter. Top each steak with a pat of butter and serve.

BROILED SALMON STEAKS

salmon steaks, 1 steak per person
1 in. (2.5 cm) thick
milk
fine cracker-crumbs
pinch of savory or basil
salt and pepper
paprika
oil or butter

☙ Soak the salmon steaks 1 hour in enough milk to cover. Drain.

☙ Combine the cracker-crumbs, savory or basil, salt and pepper, and paprika. Dredge the salmon steaks in the seasoned crumbs and brush them with melted butter or oil.

☙ Broil the salmon steaks 2 in. (5 cm) from the source of heat, about 7 minutes on each side, turning only once. Serve immediately, as cooked salmon toughens when it stands.

COLD SALMON ALI BABA

1 2-lb (900-g) piece of salmon
⅓ cup (75 mL) melted butter
⅓ cup (75 mL) dry vermouth or lemon juice
salt and pepper

☙ Place the salmon on a large piece of heavy-duty aluminum foil. Fold the sides to create a pan. Set the foil on a dripping pan.

☙ Pour the melted butter and the vermouth or lemon juice over the salmon. Salt and pepper to taste.

☙ Bake in a preheated 350°F (180°C) oven for 40 minutes. Remove from the oven and let cool. Close the foil to cover the fish and refrigerate for 12 hours. The pan juices will set into a delicious jelly. Serve with parsleyed mayonnaise.

SALMON CROQUETTES

1 7½-oz (200-g) can salmon
1 cup (250 mL) hot mashed potatoes
1 egg, beaten
1 tbsp (15 mL) lemon juice
1 tsp (5 mL) grated onion
¼ tsp (1 mL) salt
pinch of pepper
½ tsp (2 mL) celery salt
breadcrumbs
1 egg, lightly beaten
½ cup (125 mL) breadcrumbs

☙ Drain the salmon and mash it. Stir in the hot mashed potatoes,

beaten egg, lemon juice, onion, salt, pepper and celery salt. Add enough breadcrumbs (no more than 2 tbsp or 30 mL) to make the mixture rather stiff, so that it can be easily handled.

☙ Shape the mixture into small balls or cigar shapes. Dip each croquette into the second beaten egg and then dredge in breadcrumbs. Refrigerate for 1 hour.

☙ Brown the croquettes in 2 in. (5 cm) hot oil (375°F or 190°C) for about 5 minutes. Drain on paper towels. Serve with a sauce of your choice.

☙ If you prefer to bake the croquettes, place them on a well-greased cookie sheet. Bake in a preheated 450°F (230°C) oven for about 15 minutes.

SALMON PIE

1 15-oz (425-g) can salmon
4 tbsp (60 mL) butter
4 tbsp (60 mL) flour
½ tsp (2 mL) salt
pinch of pepper
2 cups (500 mL) liquid (juice from salmon mixed with milk)
¾ cup (175 mL) grated Cheddar cheese
½ cup (125 mL) diced celery
1 raw carrot, grated
2 cups (500 mL) mashed potatoes

☙ Drain the liquid from the salmon and reserve. Break up the salmon.

☙ Make a white sauce: melt the butter and stir in the flour, salt and pepper. Gradually add the 2 cups (500 mL) of liquid and cook over low heat, stirring constantly, until thick and creamy. Stir in the grated cheese until the cheese is melted.

🐦 Add the salmon, celery and grated carrot. Stir gently and season to taste. Turn into a 6-cup (1.5-L) baking dish and top with the mashed potatoes.

🐦 Bake in a preheated 450°F (230°C) oven for 10 to 15 minutes or until the potatoes are golden brown.

CHINESE-STYLE FISH

1½ to 2 lbs (750 to 900 g) fish filets, fresh or frozen
2 tbsp (30 mL) cornstarch
5 tbsp (75 mL) peanut or vegetable oil
3 green onions, cut on the bias
1 clove garlic, minced
1 tsp (5 mL) fresh ginger, grated
8 to 10 mushrooms, sliced thin
¼ cup (50 mL) bamboo shoots, cut in matchsticks
¼ cup (50 mL) soy sauce
1 tbsp (15 mL) brown sugar
½ tsp (2 mL) salt
2 tbsp (30 mL) sherry
¾ cup (175 mL) consommé

🐦 Cut the filets into individual portions and dredge them in cornstarch. Heat the oil in a wok or large skillet and fry the fish for 2 minutes on each side, turning only once. Keep the fish in a warm dish while you prepare the vegetables.

🐦 Add the green onions, garlic and grated fresh ginger to the pan. Stir quickly, over medium heat, for 1 minute. Add the mushrooms and bamboo shoots and continue cooking, stirring constantly, for 30 seconds.

🐦 Combine the soy sauce, brown sugar, salt, sherry and consommé and pour the mixture into the pan with the vegetables. Stir until the mixture comes to a boil and then remove from the heat.

🐦 Place the fish in the sauce. Cover and let sit for 10 minutes before serving. Serve with boiled rice.

🐦 To prepare Chinese stir-fried shrimp: instead of fish filets use 1½ lbs (750 g) raw shrimp, peeled and cut into 3 pieces. Dredge the shrimp in cornstarch and cook according to the directions for fish.

🐦 Fresh ginger root has a distinctive flavor. If you cannot find it, it is better to omit it completely than to replace it with dried ground ginger.

FISH CROQUETTES

1 cup (250 mL) cooked cream of wheat or farina
1 7-oz (200-g) can salmon or tuna
1 onion, minced
pinch of thyme or savory
salt and pepper
1 egg, beaten
3 tbsp (45 mL) water
uncooked cream of wheat or farina

🐦 Prepare the 1 cup of cream of wheat according to the directions on the package (or use leftovers). Combine 1 cup (250 mL) of the cereal with the salmon or tuna, onion, thyme or savory, salt and pepper. Refrigerate 2 to 3 hours.

🐦 Shape the mixture into small patties. Dip the croquettes in the egg and dredge them in the uncooked cream of wheat. Brown in hot fat or oil, over medium-low heat, turning once. Serve plain or with an egg sauce.

Chinese-Style Fish

[131]

BARBECUED FISH STEAKS

juice of 1 lemon
¼ cup (50 mL) vegetable oil
¼ tsp (1 mL) curry
1 tsp (5 mL) paprika
salmon or halibut steaks, about
¾ in. (2 cm) thick

❧ Combine the lemon juice, oil, curry and paprika. Marinate the fish steaks in this mixture for 1 hour.

❧ Place the steaks on a well-oiled barbecue rack positioned close to the coals. Or place the steaks inside a hinged fish griller and place directly on the coals. The fish should cook rapidly over high heat so that it does not become dry.

❧ Barbecue 4 to 5 minutes, basting frequently with the marinade.

SALMON LOAF

1 cup (250 mL) cooked salmon or 1 7½-oz (200-g) can salmon
2 eggs
2 tbsp (30 mL) butter
1 small onion, quartered
¼ cup (50 mL) celery leaves
1 sprig parsley
½ tsp (2 mL) salt
¼ tsp (1 mL) dry mustard
1½ cups (375 mL) breadcrumbs

❧ Place the salmon, eggs, butter, onion, celery leaves, parsley, salt and mustard in the jar of a blender or in a food processor. Cover and blend at high speed for 30 to 40 seconds.

❧ Combine this mixture well with the breadcrumbs. Pour into a buttered loaf pan or a 5-in. (13-cm) square mold. Bake in a 375°F (190°C) oven for 45 minutes or until the top is golden brown.

❧ Serve with *White Sauce* or *Hollandaise Sauce* (see pages 46 and 54). This dish is also delicious served cold with mayonnaise.

SALMON VOL-AU-VENT

1 7½-oz (200-g) can salmon
3 tbsp (45 mL) butter
2 tbsp (30 mL) flour
2 cups (500 mL) milk
1 can cream of celery soup
salt and pepper
puff-pastry shells or toast

❧ Break up the salmon and remove the skin. Reserve the juice.

❧ Prepare a white sauce with the butter, flour and milk. When smooth and creamy, add the undiluted cream of celery soup. Cook until thick.

❧ Stir in the salmon and the juice and cook for 5 minutes. Salt and pepper to taste.

❧ Serve in warm puff-pastry shells or over hot toast.

❧ If you prefer, the sauce may be prepared in advance and reheated in the top of a double boiler just prior to serving time. Do not let it boil.

DÉLICE DE MER

Not only is this dish good, but it improves if prepared in advance. Leftover cold salmon can be used instead of canned salmon.

½ cup (125 mL) mayonnaise
3 tbsp (45 mL) chili sauce or catsup
1 green onion, chopped fine
1 tsp (5 mL) Worcestershire sauce
1 tbsp (15 mL) lemon juice
1 sour or sweet pickle, chopped
1 tbsp (15 mL) cream
1 7½-oz (200-g) can salmon

❧ Blend the mayonnaise with the chili sauce or catsup, the green onion, Worcestershire sauce, lemon juice, pickle and cream. Drain the salmon and break it into pieces, removing the skin. Combine with the mayonnaise mixture, mixing well.

❧ Serve with crackers, potato chips or dry toast.

BAKED FRESH TUNA

2 thick slices fresh tuna
salt, pepper and marjoram
onion slices
tomato slices
1 tsp (5 mL) vinegar
1 tsp (5 mL) olive oil
juice of 1 lemon

❧ Cover the tuna with water and simmer it 10 minutes. Drain.

❧ Place the tuna in a baking pan and sprinkle with salt, pepper and marjoram. Cover the fish with slices of onions and tomatoes. Sprinkle with the vinegar, oil and lemon juice.

⁊ Bake in a preheated 350°F (180°C) oven for 25 minutes.

MOLDED TUNA SALAD

1 cup (250 mL) canned or left-over tuna
2 hard-cooked eggs, grated
½ cup (125 mL) chopped olives
2 green onions, chopped
salt and pepper
1 tbsp (15 mL) gelatin
¼ cup (50 mL) cold water
2 cups (500 mL) mayonnaise

⁊ Break up the tuna and combine it with the boiled eggs, olives and green onions. Salt and pepper to taste.
⁊ Soak the gelatin in the cold water for 5 minutes. Add just enough hot water to melt the gelatin. Pour slowly into the mayonnaise, stirring.
⁊ Stir in the tuna mixture. Turn the mixture into an oiled mold. Refrigerate until set. Serve, unmolded, on lettuce leaves.
⁊ Any type of leftover cooked fish can be used instead of tuna.

SEAFOOD SALAD

1 cup (250 mL) mayonnaise
2 tbsp (30 mL) lemon juice
1 tbsp (15 mL) prepared mustard
2 cups (500 mL) canned tuna or salmon

Halibut à la Russe

2 cups (500 mL) diced unpeeled apples
½ cup (125 mL) diced celery

⁊ Combine the mayonnaise, lemon juice and mustard.
⁊ Drain and break up the fish. Add the diced apples and celery. Using a fork, gently fold in the mayonnaise mixture.
⁊ Arrange on crisp greens of your choice. Garnish with ripe olives and tomato wedges.

HALIBUT À LA RUSSE

2 halibut steaks, 1 in. (2.5 cm) thick
salt, pepper and sugar
thinly sliced onion
thinly sliced lemon
1 tbsp (15 mL) melted butter
1 tbsp (15 mL) catsup

⁊ Cut each steak in half and place in a buttered baking dish. Season with salt, pepper and sugar to taste. Arrange several slices of onion and one slice of lemon on each piece of fish. Top with the melted butter and the catsup.
⁊ Bake in a 350°F (180°C) oven for 30 minutes. Add a little water if the fish starts to look dry.

HALIBUT CASSEROLE

1 lb (500 g) halibut steaks
salt and pepper
¼ tsp (1 mL) curry powder
2 tbsp (30 mL) vegetable oil
1 large onion, chopped fine
6 to 8 small potatoes, cooked
3 tomatoes, peeled and sliced
pinch of sugar
1 cup (250 mL) sour cream

½ tsp (2 mL) dry mustard
pinch of sage
1 tbsp (15 mL) lemon juice
salt and pepper
paprika

🐚 Sprinkle the halibut steaks with salt, pepper and curry powder. Heat the oil in a skillet and sear the steaks on both sides. Arrange the steaks in an 8- x 12-in. (20- x 30-cm) baking dish.

🐚 Add the onions and potatoes to the remaining fat in the skillet and sauté over high heat until lightly browned. Spread the onions and potatoes over the halibut. Cover with the sliced tomatoes and sprinkle lightly with sugar.

🐚 Combine the sour cream with the dry mustard, sage and lemon juice and pour the mixture over the tomatoes. Sprinkle with salt, pepper and paprika to taste. Bake for 20 minutes in a 350°F (180°C) oven.

MARINATED SMOKED HERRING

12 small salt-smoked herring
milk
1 tbsp (15 mL) whole peppercorns
3 bay leaves
1 onion, finely chopped
4 whole cloves
3 thin slices lemon
2 tsp (10 mL) mustard seed
½ cup (125 mL) vinegar
½ cup (125 mL) water
1 tbsp (15 mL) sugar

🐚 Soak the herring in enough milk to cover for 12 to 24 hours in order to remove the excess salt. Rinse well.

🐚 Layer the herring in a glass jar or bowl with the peppercorns, bay leaves, onion, cloves, lemon and mustard seed. Combine the vinegar, water and sugar and pour this over the herring. Cover and let marinate for 24 hours in the refrigerator. Serve as an appetizer.

HERRING IN SOUR CREAM

6 to 8 fresh filets of herring
juice of 4 lemons
24 peppercorns
1¼ cups (300 mL) sour cream
1 onion, thinly sliced in rings

🐚 Place the herring filets in a glass container. Pour the lemon juice over the filets. Cover and refrigerate for 24 hours. (The lemon juice will "cook" the fish.)

🐚 Remove the herring from the lemon juice. Combine the herring with the peppercorns, sour cream and onion rings. Refrigerate several hours. Serve garnished with sliced hard-cooked eggs and tomatoes.

BRANDADE OF COD

2 lbs (1 kg) fresh cod
juice of 1 lemon
½ cup (125 mL) olive oil
light cream
1 clove garlic, crushed and minced
toasted bread

🐚 Remove the skin and the bones from the fish and place the cod in a heavy saucepan with the lemon juice and the olive oil. Cook the fish over moderate heat, breaking it up with a fork as it cooks.

🐚 As soon as the fish becomes hot, add the cream, a few table-

Brandade of Cod

spoons at a time, until the mixture is thick and creamy. The mixture should never boil. Remove it from the heat just before it starts to boil but keep stirring until the mixture is smooth. Add the garlic. Season to taste. Serve very hot over buttered hot toast.

MARINATED HERRING

5 to 7 fresh herring filets
2 large onions, thinly sliced in rings
½ cup (125 mL) water
2 carrots, peeled and thinly sliced
½ cup (125 mL) cider or malt vinegar
10 peppercorns
¼ tsp (1 mL) thyme
3 bay leaves
½ cup (125 mL) olive oil

🐟 Arrange the herring and the onions in alternate layers in an earthenware or glass dish.

🐟 Place the carrots and the water in a saucepan and bring to a boil. Simmer, covered, for 10 minutes. Add the vinegar, peppercorns, thyme and bay leaves. Simmer another 10 minutes. Let cool.

🐟 Pour the carrot mixture and the olive oil over the herring. Let stand, covered, in a cool place for 3 to 4 days. Herring prepared in this manner will keep for 8 to 10 days. It is delicious served with potato salad.

Scalloped Cod

FRESH COD WITH HOLLANDAISE

Winter is by far the best time to buy fresh cod. Since the fish is quite large, it is usually sold fileted. If you can, though, buy filets cut from the tail end.

🐟 Cook the cod in a court-bouillon. (See the instructions for *Fish Poached in Court-bouillon*, page 125.)

🐟 Serve the cooked cod topped with a little melted butter and surround with parsleyed boiled potatoes. Accompany with *Hollandaise Sauce* (see recipe on page 54).

SCALLOPED COD

1 clove garlic
medium white sauce
cooked or leftover cod, fresh or salt
cooked potatoes, thinly sliced
breadcrumbs
melted butter

🐟 Rub the inside of an ovenproof dish with the cut clove of garlic.

🐟 Fill the dish with alternating layers of white sauce (see page 46), cooked cod and thinly sliced cooked potatoes. Top with a layer of the white sauce. Sprinkle with breadcrumbs and melted butter. Bake in a preheated 500°F (260°C) oven until the top is golden brown.

FRESH COD CREOLE

¼ cup (50 mL) olive oil
¾ cup (175 mL) finely chopped celery with leaves
1 large onion, thinly sliced
2½ cups (625 mL) canned tomatoes, drained
1 tsp (5 mL) salt
1 tsp (5 mL) sugar

3 lbs (1.5 kg) fresh cod, in thick slices
6 small potatoes, peeled

☙ Heat the olive oil and sauté the celery and the onion. When soft, add the tomatoes, salt and sugar. Bring to a boil. Add the cod and the potatoes.

☙ Cover and simmer over low heat for about 30 minutes, stirring occasionally.

MARINATED FRESH COD

3 lbs (1.5 kg) fresh cod steaks (or halibut steaks)
pepper
flour
1 cup (250 mL) olive oil or vegetable oil
2 medium onions, sliced
10 peppercorns
3 bay leaves
1 cup (250 mL) pitted olives (green or black)
½ cup (125 mL) cider or ½ cup (125 mL) wine vinegar
1 tsp (5 mL) salt

☙ Rub the fish steaks on both sides with pepper and dredge them with flour. Heat the oil in a large skillet and fry the fish in it. Arrange the cooked fish in a glass dish.

☙ Add the onions, peppercorns, bay leaves, pitted olives, cider or vinegar, and salt to the oil remaining in the pan. Simmer for 3 minutes and then pour over the fish steaks. Cover and refrigerate at least 24 hours.

☙ Garnish the cod steaks with parsley and wedges of tomato, lime or lemon. Serve with mayonnaise.

ATLANTIC FISH CAKES

The best fish cakes are made the old-fashioned way using flaked salt cod.

1 lb (500 g) salt cod
5 medium potatoes, peeled and sliced
2 tbsp (30 mL) butter
¼ tsp (1 mL) Worcestershire sauce
¼ tsp (1 mL) dry mustard
¼ tsp (1 mL) pepper
3 egg yolks, lightly beaten
flour

☙ Soak the cod overnight in cold water.

☙ Cook the potatoes in boiling salted water until tender. Drain and mash. (Put them through a fine sieve to achieve a perfectly smooth consistency.) Keep the potatoes warm.

☙ Drain the fish and simmer for 5 minutes in fresh water. (Do not boil, or the fish will toughen.) Drain and dry the fish on a towel; it is important to dry the fish well.

☙ Flake the cod and add it to the potatoes. Do not let the mixture get cold or soggy.

☙ Add the butter, Worcestershire sauce, dry mustard, pepper and egg yolks. Stir until well blended.

☙ Shape the mixture into balls and dredge them in flour. Fry the fish cakes in 3 in. (8 cm) of fat at 370°F (190°C). Or shape the mixture into round, flat cakes and

pan-fry them in butter or in pork or bacon fat. Serve with lemon wedges and a green salad.

FRIED COD TONGUES

cod tongues
milk
1 egg, beaten
flour
butter or fat

☙ If the tongues are salted, soak them in milk to remove the salt. Dip the fresh or desalted tongues in the beaten egg and then in flour. Fry in butter or fat until done. Serve with a cream sauce.

TOMCOD

Tomcod (called poissons des chenaux in Québec) are baby cod, 3 to 5 in. (8 to 13 cm) long. These delicious little fish are sometimes available frozen and uncleaned.

☙ Soak the fish in cold water at least 1 hour or until thawed. Slit them open along the belly and gut them. Wash the tomcod well, dry them and then dredge them in flour seasoned with salt, pepper and paprika. Fry the fish in hot oil or fat for about 5 minutes on each side, turning once. Serve hot.

SMELT

One of the most delicious fish available is the smelt, a tiny member of the salmon family measuring about 4 to 9 in. (10 to 23 cm) in length.

🍂 Many varieties of smelt can be found in Canadian waters. They are fished along the eastern seaboard from New Jersey to Labrador, but are particularly plentiful in the Gulf of St. Lawrence. Every fall, the smelt swim from the sea to the estuaries of numerous rivers. After the spring thaw, they head up the rivers to spawn. Fishermen along the coast usually fish for smelt during the winter, using nets anchored under the ice.

🍂 Smelt are sold by the pound, either fresh or frozen. Their flesh and flavor are delicate, and many people find them most delicious pan-fried. When they are well prepared, smelt can create a sensation.

PAN-FRIED FRESH SMELT

2 lbs (900 g) smelt
½ cup (125 mL) flour
½ tsp (2 mL) salt
pinch of pepper
1 egg
1 tbsp (15 mL) lemon juice
½ cup (125 mL) fine bread-crumbs
⅓ cup (75 mL) shortening or vegetable oil

🍂 Use kitchen shears to snip off the heads, tails and fins of the smelt. Slit open the belly of each smelt and remove the innards. Wash under cold water. If the fish are relatively large, remove the

backbone: insert the tip of a knife under the backbone near the neck and then grip the backbone with your fingers and pull free.

🍂 Combine the flour, salt and pepper in a shallow dish. Beat the egg and lemon juice together in a second dish. Place the bread-crumbs in a third dish. Dredge the fish first in the seasoned flour, then dip it in the egg mixture and finally coat with bread-crumbs.

🍂 Fry in shortening or oil over medium heat, keeping the cooked smelt hot in the oven until all are cooked. Serve with lemon wedges.

SMELT AU GRATIN

2 lbs (900 g) smelt
½ cup (125 mL) milk
½ tsp (2 mL) salt
breadcrumbs
4 tbsp (60 mL) melted butter
¼ tsp (1 mL) dried mint or 1 tbsp (15 mL) grated lemon rind

🍂 Wash and clean the smelt. Soak the fish in a mixture of the milk and the salt. Then coat with the breadcrumbs and place in a buttered baking dish. Pour the melted butter on top and sprinkle with the mint or grated lemon rind.

🍂 Bake in a 450°F (230°C) oven for about 10 minutes or until the flesh flakes and can easily be pulled off the backbone.

SMELT IN CREAM SAUCE

2 lbs (900 g) smelt
3 tbsp (45 mL) butter
3 tbsp (45 mL) flour
1 tsp (5 mL) salt
¼ tsp (1 mL) pepper
¼ tsp (1 mL) nutmeg
1 cup (250 mL) milk
1 cup (250 mL) light cream
½ cup (125 mL) breadcrumbs

🍂 Remove the heads and tails from the smelts, then gut and wash them. Arrange them in a buttered ovenproof dish.

🍂 Prepare a white sauce with the butter, flour, salt, pepper, nut-meg, milk and light cream. Cover the smelt with the cream sauce and top with breadcrumbs.

🍂 Bake in a 450°F (230°C) oven for 15 minutes.

CASSEROLE OF FROZEN FISH FILETS

1 lb (500 g) frozen filets of haddock, cod or halibut
1 tsp (5 mL) flour
1 can cream of celery soup
¼ cup (50 mL) milk
3 tbsp (45 mL) finely chopped parsley
1 small onion, minced
¼ cup (50 mL) chopped olives

🍂 The fish does not need to defrost before cooking.

🍂 Arrange the fish in a baking dish and sprinkle with the flour.

Haddock à la Grecque

🍂 Heat the cream of celery soup gently with the milk, parsley, onion and olives, stirring constantly.

🍂 Pour the sauce over the fish. Bake in a preheated 375°F (190°C) oven for 25 to 35 minutes. Serve with mashed potatoes.

HADDOCK À LA GRECQUE

1 can tomatoes
1 tsp (5 mL) sugar
¼ tsp (1 mL) basil
¼ tsp (1 mL) pepper
½ tsp (2 mL) salt
1 to 2 lbs (500 to 900 g) fresh or frozen haddock filets
3 green onions, finely chopped
¼ cup (50 mL) finely chopped parsley
¼ cup (50 mL) vegetable oil
2 tbsp (30 mL) flour
1 tsp (5 mL) paprika
½ tsp (2 mL) salt

🍂 Drain the liquid from the tomatoes (reserve for soups, sauces, etc.). Place the tomato pulp in a buttered baking dish. Sprinkle with the sugar, basil, pepper and salt. Arrange the fish filets on the tomatoes. (Frozen filets do not need to be defrosted.)

🍂 Combine the green onions, parsley, oil, flour, paprika and remaining salt. Spread over the fish.

🍂 Bake in a 500°F (260°C) oven for 15 to 18 minutes. For a quick meal, serve with peas and boiled potatoes.

FINNAN HADDIE MARITIME STYLE

3 tbsp (45 mL) butter
1 tbsp (15 mL) green pepper, chopped
1 tbsp (15 mL) onion, finely chopped
3 tbsp (45 mL) flour
2 cups (500 mL) milk
smoked haddock (finnan haddie)
breadcrumbs
butter

🍂 Simmer the smoked haddock in fresh water for 20 minutes and then drain.

🍂 Sauté the green pepper and onion in the butter until they are soft but not browned. Stir in the flour and the milk. Cook until smooth and creamy.

🍂 Stir in the smoked haddock and then pour the mixture into a buttered baking dish. Top with breadcrumbs and dot with butter. Bake for 20 minutes in a 375°F (190°C) oven.

STUFFED HADDOCK FILETS

butter
4 slices bread
1 egg
2 small gherkins, finely chopped
½ tsp (2 mL) paprika
pinch of curry
pinch of thyme
4 tbsp (60 mL) milk
salt and pepper, to taste
2 fresh haddock filets
¼ cup (50 mL) water
1 tbsp (15 mL) butter

🍂 To make the stuffing, butter the bread on both sides and dice. In a bowl, combine the egg, gherkins, paprika, curry, thyme, milk, salt and pepper. Add the bread cubes and mix well.

🍂 Butter a shallow baking dish and place one filet in the bottom.

🍂 Cover with a thick layer of stuffing and top with the second filet. Add the water and butter.

🍂 Bake in a preheated 375°F (190°C) oven for 30 minutes or until the fish is tender.

NEW BRUNSWICK HADDOCK HASH

This is an unusual but delicious brunch dish. Serve with hot corn-bread and gooseberry jam for a perfect meal.

1 lb (500 g) haddock
2 slices lemon
1 bay leaf
3 cups (750 mL) diced cooked potatoes
1 cup (250 mL) diced cooked beets
2 slices salt pork or 4 strips bacon
¼ cup (50 mL) cream or milk

🍂 Place the haddock in a saucepan with the lemon and bay leaf and enough cold water to cover. Bring to a boil and then simmer for 10 minutes. Drain and flake the fish. Add the diced cooked potatoes and beets and combine.

🍂 Dice the salt pork or bacon and brown in an electric skillet at 375°F (190°C). Combine the cream and the fish mixture and stir it into the browned pork. Reduce the heat to 300°F (150°C), cover and cook for 40 minutes, until the bottom becomes golden brown and crispy.

🍂 Or bake the mixture in the oven at 225°F (110°C) for about 15 minutes. Serve with sweet pickles or homemade chili.

OCEAN PERCH

For some years, a small flame-colored fish caught in the deep waters of the North Atlantic has been gaining increasing popularity in North America. Fishermen call it rosefish, but it is more often marketed as ocean perch or redfish.

🍂 Ocean perch looks something like freshwater perch, but its head is disproportionately large for its body, which is short and has a spiny dorsal fin. This fish is not very big—its average weight is about ¾ lb (375 g). Its length from end to end does not exceed 1 foot (33 cm).

🍂 The color of ocean perch, which ranges from orange to fiery red, serves as a protective device. It seems that many deepwater ocean fish are red because the light that manages to penetrate into the depths is green, making the fish a neutral gray and therefore invisible.

🍂 This fish is usually sold frozen in filets. It is easily recognized by its speckled skin.

🍂 Ocean perch can be cooked using any of the standard cooking methods, and it is delicious served either plain or with a sauce.

BAKED OCEAN PERCH

1 lb (500 g) frozen ocean perch filets
salt and pepper
3 tbsp (45 mL) chopped green onions
¼ tsp (1 mL) basil
½ tsp (2 mL) sugar
2 tomatoes, quartered
¼ cup (50 mL) melted butter

🍂 Thaw the fish and separate the filets. Remove the skin and arrange the filets in a single layer in a buttered ovenproof dish. Salt and pepper to taste and sprinkle with the green onions, the basil and the sugar. Arrange the tomatoes around the fish. Top with the melted butter.

🍂 Bake in a 450°F (230°C) oven for 10 minutes.

OCEAN PERCH SOUFFLÉ

1 lb (500 g) ocean perch filets
salt and pepper
1 tbsp (15 mL) butter
1 egg white
3 tbsp (45 mL) mayonnaise
2 tbsp (30 mL) toasted chopped almonds

🍂 Thaw the filets and separate them. Place in a shallow baking dish. Salt and pepper to taste. Dot with butter and bake in a preheated 450°F (230°C) oven for 10 minutes.

Sole Amandine

1 bay leaf
1 whole clove
1 cup (250 mL) water
12 raw shrimp
6 sole filets
12 oysters
salt
½ cup (125 mL) butter
½ cup (125 mL) white wine
5 egg yolks
2 tbsp (30 mL) white wine
salt and pepper
2 tbsp (30 mL) whipping cream

🍃 Remove the stems from the mushrooms and cut the tops in two. Cook the mushrooms in the 2 tbsp (30 mL) butter over high heat for 1 minute, stirring constantly. Remove from the heat and add salt, pepper and lemon juice. Reserve the mushrooms.

🍃 In the same pan, put the onion, parsley, salt, peppercorns, thyme, bay leaf, whole clove and water. Bring to a boil and add the shrimp. Cover and simmer over low heat for 3 minutes. Remove the shrimp and peel them, reserving the cooking liquid.

🍃 Arrange 3 sole filets in a 14- x 9- x 2-in. (35- x 23- x 5-cm) baking dish. Salt lightly and top with the remaining 3 filets. Arrange the oysters around the filets. Strain the reserved cooking liquid through a fine strainer onto the fish. Cover the dish with aluminum foil and bake in a 325°F (160°C) oven for 10 to 12 minutes.

🍃 Remove the filets and oysters from the dish and keep the filets warm on an ovenproof platter. Pour the liquid into a saucepan and cook over high heat until it is

🍃 Meanwhile, beat the egg white until stiff and fold into the mayonnaise. Spread this mixture over the filets 2 or 3 minutes before the 10 minutes are up, then sprinkle on the toasted almonds. Return to the oven until the top is golden-brown and puffy. Serve immediately.

SOLE AMANDINE

1 whole sole or 2 to 4 sole filets
flour
4 tbsp (60 mL) butter
salt and pepper
¼ lb (125 g) slivered almonds
1 tsp (5 mL) wine vinegar

🍃 Dry the filets and dredge them in flour.
🍃 Melt the butter in a skillet until it is a nutty brown color. Pan-fry the fish. (See *Fish Filets Meunière*, page 126.) Cook whole fish about

8 minutes on each side, filets 3 minutes on each side.
🍃 Arrange the cooked fish on a warm platter. Salt and pepper to taste. Add the almonds to the butter remaining in the pan and brown them for a few seconds. Blend in the vinegar, stirring vigorously. Pour over the fish and serve immediately.

SOLE MARGUERY

¼ lb (125 g) button mushrooms
2 tbsp (30 mL) butter
salt and pepper
2 tsp (10 mL) lemon juice
6 very thin slices onion
4 sprigs parsley
½ tsp (2 mL) salt
10 peppercorns
pinch of thyme

reduced to ⅔ of the original amount. Add the butter and the ½ cup (125 mL) white wine and cook over low heat for 2 to 3 minutes, stirring with a whisk.

𝓫 In the top of a double boiler, combine the egg yolks and the 2 tbsp (30 mL) wine. Add salt and pepper to taste. Little by little, beat the baking liquid into the egg yolk mixture, stirring constantly. Continue cooking and stirring in the double boiler over low heat until the sauce is thick and creamy. (Make sure the water in the bottom of the double boiler does not boil or touch the bottom of the upper pot, or the sauce may curdle.) Pour the sauce over the sole filets. Garnish with the mushrooms, oysters and shrimp.

𝓫 Whip the cream and spoon it in an even pattern on top of the sauce, swirling it lightly into the sauce with the tip of the spoon. Place under the broiler for a few seconds, until the top is slightly golden, and then serve immediately.

Rolled
Filets of Sole

1 lb (500 g) fresh sole filets
salt and pepper to taste
a few gherkins or slivers of dill pickle
½ cup (125 mL) minced onion
2 tbsp (30 mL) butter
1 cup (250 mL) tomato sauce
¼ tsp (1 mL) salt

𝓫 Sprinkle each filet with salt and pepper. Place a gherkin or a piece of dill pickle on the thick end of each filet. Roll up the filets and place them side by side in a buttered baking dish, with the ends tucked under.

𝓫 Sauté the onions in the butter for 5 minutes, without browning. Stir in the tomato sauce and the salt. Bring to a boil and then pour over the fish.

𝓫 Bake in a preheated 450°F (230°C) oven for 15 to 20 minutes or until the fish is opaque and flakes easily when prodded with a fork.

Filet of
Sole Beaufort

1 sole filet
1 large slice of bread, toasted
creamed spinach
cheese sauce

𝓫 Cook the sole filet meunière-style (see *Fish Filets Meunière*, page 126).

𝓫 Place the cooked filet on the crouton. Cover with the creamed spinach and then with *Cheese Sauce* (see page 59). Bake in a preheated 500°F (260°C) oven for about 5 minutes.

Broiled Swordfish

Swordfish is popular among sport fishermen because it is such a combative fish. Many are caught off the coast of Nova Scotia, and in the summertime it is often found fresh in fish markets. The flesh is free of small bones; it is most tender and delicious when simply broiled.

2 lbs (900 g) swordfish, sliced 1½ in. (4 cm) thick
juice of 2 lemons
1 tsp (5 mL) fresh chopped mint
¼ cup (50 mL) olive or vegetable oil

Filet of Sole Beaufort

1 tbsp (15 mL) oregano
salt and pepper to taste

🍃 Wash and dry the swordfish slices.

🍃 Combine the lemon juice, mint, oil, oregano, salt and pepper. Baste one side of the fish with this mixture. Broil in the oven. (See *Broiled Fish*, page 126.) Turn the fish over midway through the cooking time and baste the second side with the lemon juice mixture. When the fish is cooked, baste it once more with the lemon mixture.

🍃 Serve with buttered rice mixed with peas.

SQUID

The squid is a relative of the octopus but its body is narrower, almost pen-shaped. The squid that are sold for consumption measure about 12 in. (30 cm) in length. Squid are delicious simply grilled with butter and a touch of rosemary, but they are particularly tasty prepared with a tart or wine sauce, as is done in the South of France.

SQUID SAUTÉED IN WINE SAUCE

2 lb (900 g) squid
¼ lb (125 g) butter
1 clove garlic, minced
2 tbsp (30 mL) mint or dill, minced
1 tbsp (15 mL) parsley, chopped
¼ tsp (1 mL) salt
pinch of pepper
¼ cup (50 mL) white wine

🍃 Wash the squid thoroughly. Remove the inkbag, if it has not already been removed, as well as the head and the innards. Cut the tentacles into bite-size lengths and the body into 2-in. (5-cm) cubes. Wipe with a damp cloth.

🍃 Melt the butter in a saucepan over medium heat. Sauté the tentacle sections just until they change color. Add the garlic, mint or dill, parsley, salt and pepper. Sauté for 3 minutes, stirring frequently. Add the cubed squid and sauté for another 3 minutes. Add the wine. Cover and simmer 10 minutes or until the squid is tender but not mushy.

🍃 Serve very hot with buttered toast.

TROUT

For the purposes of cooking and eating, trout may be divided into two categories: small ones, such as speckled and brook trout; and large trout, which include rainbow, lake trout and steelhead. All varieties deserve to be well prepared because they are all delicious. Here are my favorite recipes, passed down to me by avid fishermen.

POACHED SPECKLED TROUT

speckled, brook or any other small trout
clam juice (optional)
onion
celery seed

🍃 This technique is good for small trout such as brook or speckled trout. Clean and wash the fish and place them in a shallow pan with just enough water to cover. (You can use clam juice instead of water if it is available.) Add a piece of onion and a pinch of celery seed. Bring to a boil, then cover, reduce the heat and simmer 5 minutes for each 2 lbs (1 kg) of fish. Drain. Serve on a folded napkin with bowls of chopped parsley, melted butter and lemon wedges.

🍃 Trout steamed in clam juice makes a treat fit for a gourmet. A Nova Scotia fishing guide taught me this method years ago, and it has been my favorite ever since.

BAKED TROUT

1 trout, 2 to 4 lbs (1 kg to 2 kg)
3 slices unpeeled lemon
salt and pepper
hot sauce or chutney
3 strips bacon
2 cups (500 mL) shredded lettuce (use coarse outer leaves)
4 slices unpeeled lemon
1 tbsp (15 mL) sherry or cognac

🍃 Wash and dry the trout. Place the 3 slices of lemon in the cavity. Rub the skin with salt, pepper and hot sauce or chutney. Arrange the strips of bacon on top.

🍃 Put the shredded lettuce and the 4 slices of lemon in a baking dish and lay the fish on top. Bake in a 425°F (220°C) oven 5 minutes for each lb (500 g). Add the sherry or cognac 5 minutes before the cooking time is up. It will impart a delicate but distinctive flavor to the fish.

Trout Barbecued in Bacon

whole trout
lemon, cut in half
pepper
bacon

🍂 Clean the trout and rub them all over with the lemon halves. Sprinkle the insides with pepper. Wrap each fish in strips of bacon so that it is well covered. Fasten the bacon with toothpicks.

🍂 Place the fish on the barbecue grill. Grill 6 to 10 minutes, according to size, turning once during the cooking period.

Pickerel Bonne Femme

Marinated Trout or Salmon

½ cup (125 mL) cider vinegar
2 cups (500 mL) white wine
1 large onion, thinly sliced
1 carrot, thinly sliced
1 tbsp (15 mL) salt
3 whole cloves
¼ tsp (1 mL) thyme
6 peppercorns
½ tsp (2 mL) celery salt
10 to 12 small trout or 4 to 5 lbs (2 to 2.5 kg) salmon, sliced

🍂 In a saucepan, combine the cider vinegar, white wine, onion, carrot, salt, whole cloves, thyme, peppercorns and celery salt. Bring to a boil and simmer, uncovered, 20 minutes.

🍂 Clean the trout and place them whole (or, alternatively, the salmon slices) in the boiling liquid. Simmer gently for 20 minutes; do not let the fish boil or the

flesh will fall apart.

🍂 Gently arrange the fish in a dish and cover with the cooking liquid. Serve very cold in the liquid. If it is well covered, this fish dish will keep for 15 to 20 days in the refrigerator.

Cold Trout with Tomato Mayonnaise

6 brook or speckled trout
⅓ cup (75 mL) cider vinegar or white wine
4 cups (1 L) cold water
1 tsp (5 mL) salt
1 small carrot, thinly sliced
1 medium-size onion, thinly sliced
6 peppercorns
1 whole clove
1 bay leaf
¼ tsp (1 mL) thyme
5 celery leaves

TOMATO MAYONNAISE:

1 6-oz (175-mL) can tomato paste
⅓ cup (75 mL) mayonnaise
juice of 1 lemon
1 tsp (5 mL) grated lemon rind
salt and pepper to taste

🍂 Clean the trout and wash quickly under cold water. Arrange them on a greased rack in a shallow saucepan. (This will make it easier to handle the fish during cooking.)

🍂 In a second saucepan, combine the white wine or cider vinegar, cold water, salt, carrot, onion, peppercorns, clove, bay leaf, thyme and celery leaves. Bring to a boil and then simmer for 20 minutes. Pour the liquid through a sieve over the fish. Cover and let the trout simmer for 15 minutes. Place the cooked trout on a platter, cover and refrigerate.

🍂 To serve, garnish the platter

[143]

with fresh parsley and quartered hard-cooked eggs. Serve with *Tomato Mayonnaise*.

🐛 To prepare the tomato mayonnaise, combine the tomato paste, mayonnaise, lemon juice, lemon rind and salt and pepper to taste. Drizzle a little of this sauce over each fish and serve the remainder in a bowl.

PIKE, PICKEREL AND MUSKELLUNGE

Pike, pickerel (walleye) and muskellunge are all popular with sport fishermen, and all are good eating. My personal favorite is the muskellunge, or "muskie," but as its flesh is a little on the dry side it is best served with some kind of sauce. Because the muskellunge is such a large fish, you will probably want to cut it into steaks.

🐛 I prefer small pike and pickerel cooked whole. You can treat the two fish the same way.

PICKEREL BONNE FEMME

mushrooms, finely chopped
parsley, finely chopped
green onions, finely chopped
salt and pepper
pickerel or walleye filets
½ cup (125 mL) white wine or
consommé

🐛 Butter a shallow baking dish. Cover the bottom with the chopped mushrooms, parsley and green onions. Season with salt and pepper. Arrange the fish filets on top. Pour on the white wine or consommé and cover with a piece of buttered aluminum foil.

🐛 Poach in a preheated 400°F (200°C) oven for 25 minutes. Serve hot.

MY MOTHER'S BAKED PIKE

🐛 Clean the fish and split it open, so that the two halves are held together only by the skin along the back. If you wish, you can remove the backbone and other visible bones. Wipe dry with a towel. Rub the fish with salt and butter and place it, skin-side up, in an oiled pan. Brush the skin with an egg beaten with 2 tbsp (30 mL) cold water and sprinkle with fine breadcrumbs. Bake in a 400°F (200°C) oven for 10 minutes.

🐛 Meanwhile, mix until smooth 3 tbsp (45 mL) flour and 1½ cups (375 mL) sour cream. Sauté 1 large chopped onion in 2 tbsp (30 mL) butter.

🐛 Remove the fish from the oven and top with the sour cream mixture, the fried onions, 1 bay leaf and ¼ tsp (1 mL) thyme. Bake for another 10 minutes or until the fish is tender. Slide the fish onto a hot serving platter. Stir the sauce remaining in the baking dish until it is well blended. Season the sauce to taste and pour it over the fish. This dish is equally superb made with pickerel.

PIKE BAKED IN CREAM

1 pike
salt and pepper
1 egg
water

Pike Baked in Cream

breadcrumbs
1 cup (250 mL) cream or
top milk

🍂Cut the pike into serving
pieces and salt and pepper them.
Beat the egg with a little water
and dip the pieces of pike in it.
Dredge each piece in the breadcrumbs.

🍂 Place the fish in a greased baking dish and bake in a preheated
400°F (200°C) oven for 30 minutes, basting from time to time
with the cream or top milk.

🍂 Serve with an egg sauce flavored with savory or rosemary.

NORTH SHORE MUSKELLUNGE

*This is an old fish recipe that is
still very popular. It's also my personal favorite.*

🍂 Dredge 5 or 6 muskellunge
steaks in flour. Brown the steaks
in melted butter in a heavy skillet, turning once. Remove the
steaks to a hot platter.

🍂 Add some sliced onions to the
pan and cook until golden. Stir in
3 tbsp (45 mL) flour and cook
1 minute. Add 2 cups (500 mL)
milk and cook, stirring constantly,
until the sauce is creamy. Add salt
and pepper to taste, as well as a
pinch of thyme or summer savory.
Place the muskellunge steaks in
the sauce. Cover and simmer over
very low heat for 25 minutes.
Serve with mashed potatoes.

BASS

Many varieties of bass inhabit our
lakes and rivers. When cooking
bass, treat all varieties as lean but
not dry fish. Bass weighing up to
2 or 2½ lbs (1 kg) are best simply
broiled or fried.

🍂 The following recipe, which
dates from the early 1900s, makes
a superb bass casserole that you
can serve at a buffet. In some
parts of Québec, this dish is
called "gibelotte" or bass fricassée.

🍂 Grate 3 medium unpeeled
potatoes and 3 medium unpeeled
carrots. Melt 3 tbsp (45 mL) butter in a casserole dish and add the
grated potatoes and carrots, 1 celery stalk chopped fine and 1 or 2
cloves of garlic chopped fine.
Cover and cook over low heat for
10 minutes or until the flavors are
blended. Add salt, pepper and
chopped parsley to taste.

🍂 Butter a shallow baking dish
and spread the vegetables over
the bottom. Arrange small
cleaned bass on top, each one
topped with a strip of bacon. Bake
for 20 minutes in a 400°F (200°C)
oven. Sprinkle with the juice of
1 lemon and bake another 10
minutes. Serve.

STUFFED BASS

1 4-lb (1.8-kg) bass
salt and pepper
2 cups (500 mL) coarse breadcrumbs
2 tbsp (30 mL) finely chopped
onion

1 tbsp (15 mL) capers
I tsp (5 mL) parsley
2 tbsp (30 mL) melted butter
4 tbsp (60 mL) cream or wine
salt, pepper, paprika
hot water
melted butter

🍂 Salt and pepper the bass both
inside and outside.

🍂 Combine the breadcrumbs,
onion, capers, parsley, butter, and
cream or wine. Add salt, pepper
and paprika to taste. Work this
mixture with your hands until it
has the consistency of dough and
then stuff the fish with it. Tie or
sew the fish closed and place it in
a buttered shallow pan. Bake 45
minutes in a 400°F (200°C) oven.

🍂 Baste every 10 minutes with an
equal mixture of hot water and
butter. When the fish is done,
make a sauce from the juices left
in the baking pan by blending in a
little cream.

PERCH

🍂 In my opinion, perch is one of
the best fish available. It is easy to
cook and delicious to eat, even
though it has all kinds of little
bones.

🍂 I like mine fried or broiled and
served with French dressing prepared with olive oil, lemon juice,
salt and pepper, sliced hard-
cooked eggs and watercress.

🍂 When I have too many perch
on hand, I pickle the extra ones.
This way, they will keep about 10
days in the refrigerator. They are

a treat eaten cold with sour cream and a potato salad or green salad.

☙ To marinate perch: clean, skin and remove the tails from 8 or 10 small perch. Put them in a saucepan with 1 sliced onion, 5 whole peppercorns, 4 whole cloves, 1 bay leaf, 1 tsp (5 mL) salt and just enough water to cover the fish. Bring to a boil, cover and simmer for 3 minutes. Carefully remove the fish and put them in a glass or ceramic dish.

☙ Add to the cooking liquid 4 tbsp (60 mL) butter creamed together with 2 tbsp (30 mL) flour. Bring to a boil, stirring constantly. Add 1 cup (250 mL) cider vinegar and pour over the fish while it is piping hot. Cover and refrigerate.

WINNIPEG GOLDEYE

This delicious fish is found in only one region of Canada, in the lakes of Manitoba near Winnipeg. Although there are similar species in other areas, real Winnipeg goldeye is in a class by itself. Usually sold smoked, its skin is reddish-brown, its flesh is white and succulent. Smoked Winnipeg goldeye can be eaten cold, without additional cooking, simply sprinkled with a good lemony French dressing and accompanied with sliced tomatoes or boiled potatoes.

☙ It is also delicious lightly broiled or poached and served hot.

BROILED WINNIPEG GOLDEYE

1 Winnipeg goldeye
2 tbsp (30 mL) soft butter

Broiled Winnipeg Goldeye

☙ Broil the fish 2 to 3 in. (5 to 8 cm) from the heat source, 4 to 5 minutes on each side, turning only once.

☙ To serve, place the fish on a hot platter and baste with butter. Remove the head and the skin. Serve with coleslaw and French-fried potatoes.

WHITEFISH

As far as I'm concerned, fresh-water whitefish—especially the 2- to 5-lb ones (1 to 2.5 kg) fished in the Great Lakes—are even tastier than speckled trout because of their nutty flavor. Fried, boiled or baked, they are always a treat. But smoked whitefish is a truly regal dish.

☙ When I serve whitefish broiled or pan-fried, I like to accompany it with cucumber sauce. Here's my simple recipe: wash a medium-size cucumber and leave the skin on. Quarter it and remove the seeds, then grate it. Mix with 1 cup (250 mL) sour cream and a little grated onion. Salt and pepper to taste. Serve very cold with the hot fish.

☙ Many of the most interesting recipes for North American fish were adapted by immigrants from the traditional recipes of their native lands. This one, which was given to me by a Polish-born friend, is delicious, and I enjoy it often.

☙ Fry 2 lbs (1 kg) of whitefish filets in bacon fat or oil, along with sliced onions, thyme and parsley. Salt and pepper to taste. Add 1 cup (250 mL) white wine and simmer 10 minutes over low heat. Add 1 onion, very thinly sliced, ½ cup (125 mL) blanched and slivered almonds and ½ cup (125 mL) currants. Let simmer for another 8 to 10 minutes. Serve the fish in the sauce in a deep serving dish. Accompany with boiled potatoes or noodles.

WHITEFISH RAGOUT

3 tbsp (45 mL) oil or bacon fat
3 onions, thinly sliced
3 medium potatoes, peeled and thinly sliced
1 cup (250 mL) celery with leaves, chopped
4 cups (1 L) water
1 tsp (5 mL) salt
¼ tsp (1 mL) pepper
pinch of basil
1 bay leaf
1½ to 2 lbs (750 to 900 g) white-fish
¼ cup (50 mL) tomato paste
1 tsp (5 mL) paprika

❧ Heat the oil or bacon fat in a saucepan and add the onions, potatoes and celery. Stir until the vegetables are coated with oil. Cover and simmer 20 minutes, stirring occasionally.

❧ Add the water, salt, pepper, basil and bay leaf. Bring to a boil and boil gently, uncovered, for 20 minutes.

❧ Cut the fish into individual portions and add them to the vegetables, along with the tomato paste and the paprika. Stir gently until mixed. Cover and simmer for another 20 minutes. The sauce should be relatively thick. Serve in soup bowls.

SHELLFISH

The delicate flavors of shellfish are highly esteemed by gourmets the world over. Here are the varieties of shellfish you are most likely to find at your local market.

LOBSTER

Lobster is trapped all along the Atlantic Coast. The market weight of a lobster can range from 1 to 3 lbs (900 g to 1.5 kg). A small 1-lb (500-g) lobster produces about ¼ lb (125 g) of cooked meat. In season, during the summer, lobster can be purchased at markets throughout North America. Lobster is also sold cooked, frozen and canned.

CRAB

Some of the best crab on the market comes from the Gulf of St. Lawrence and from Alaska (called snow crab and king crab, respectively). It can be purchased fresh in season, and it is also available frozen and canned.

SHRIMP

Shrimp is harvested in many parts of the world, but some of the most highly regarded shrimp comes from the Gulf of St. Lawrence. The fresh shrimp purchased in North American markets is likely to come from northern waters. It can also be bought cooked, canned and frozen. Most of the canned salad and cocktail shrimp comes from Southeast Asia.

CLAMS

Clams are harvested along both the Atlantic and Pacific coasts and can be bought fresh year-round. They are also available shucked and canned.

OYSTERS

❧ The best oysters come from the cold waters off the coast of Nova Scotia and New Brunswick. They can be purchased fresh in season (in the fall) and are available in different sizes. Cultivated and canned oysters are also available.

SCALLOPS

❧ Scallops are harvested in the Gulf of St. Lawrence and around the Magdalen Islands, as well as along the entire eastern seaboard. They are sold already shucked; the shells are discarded, leaving only the muscle. Scallops can be purchased fresh or frozen.

BROILED LOBSTER

❧ Sever the vein at the base of the neck of a live lobster. Split the lobster in half with a sharp knife, working from the head down through the abdomen. Place the halves on the barbecue grill or under the broiler, shell side down. Baste generously with melted butter. Grill 3 in. (8 cm) from the coals or broiler element for 15 to 20 minutes. Turn the halves over midway through cooking.

Authentic Lobster Newburg

Remove the flesh and cut it into small pieces. Reserve the shell. Sauté the mushrooms in melted butter. Add the paprika, mustard, tarragon, parsley, white sauce (see page 46) and sherry. Cook the sauce for a few minutes and then spread some in the bottom of each lobster shell. Fill with the lobster pieces and top with the rest of the sauce. Dot with butter and sprinkle with grated cheese.

Bake in a 450°F (230°C) oven for 10 minutes.

AUTHENTIC LOBSTER NEWBURG

2 live lobsters, 1½ lbs (750 g) each
¼ cup (50 mL) butter
2 egg yolks
½ cup (125 mL) heavy cream
2 tbsp (30 mL) sherry
salt and pepper
pinch of cayenne
pinch of nutmeg

Cook the live lobsters for 15 minutes in boiling water. Remove from the water and let cool. Remove the meat from the shells and dice large.

Melt the butter in a skillet. Add the lobster meat and cook 2 minutes. Remove the lobster meat and set aside.

Beat the egg yolks and stir in the cream. Pour this mixture into the same skillet. Cook over low heat, stirring constantly, until smooth and creamy.

Stir in the sherry and the lobster pieces. Mix well. Season with

FRESH BOILED LOBSTER

live lobsters
salt and pepper
melted butter

Plunge the lobsters, head first, into a large pot of boiling salted water. Make sure there is enough water to cover all the lobsters and add 1 tbsp (15 mL) salt for each 5 cups (1.2 L) of water. Boil briskly for 5 minutes. Reduce heat and simmer for another 20 minutes.

Plunge the hot lobsters into cold water for a few seconds to stop the cooking process. Before serving, split the lobsters in half lengthwise and remove the coral and tomalley (reserve for sauces). Discard the stomach and intestinal vein. Crack the large claws.

Salt and pepper the flesh. Serve with a sauceboat of melted butter.

LOBSTER THERMIDOR

1 lobster
¼ lb (125 g) mushrooms
melted butter
½ tsp (2 mL) paprika
1 tsp (5 mL) mustard
¼ tsp (1 mL) tarragon
1 tbsp (15 mL) parsley
1 cup (250 mL) medium white sauce
½ cup (125 mL) sherry
butter
grated Parmesan or Gruyère cheese

Boil or broil the lobster. (See *Broiled Lobster* and *Fresh Boiled Lobster*, above.)

❧ TECHNIQUE ❧

AUTHENTIC LOBSTER NEWBURG

1 Live lobster.

2 Cook the lobsters for 15 minutes in boiling water.

3 Add the lobster meat to the melted butter and cook 2 minutes.

4 Remove the lobster and set aside.

salt, pepper, cayenne and nutmeg. Heat just until the sauce starts to boil and then serve at once.

LOBSTER SALAD

2 cups (500 mL) lobster meat
1 tbsp (15 mL) chopped chives
1 tbsp (15 mL) capers
salt and pepper to taste
½ cup (125 mL) lemon mayonnaise
2 tbsp (30 mL) finely chopped chives or green onions
pinch of tarragon
lettuce

❧ Although fresh-cooked lobster is tastier, use canned lobster if you wish. Cut the lobster meat into large pieces. Toss with chives and capers, using a fork. Salt and pepper to taste. (Avoid adding too much salt to canned lobster.)
❧ Mix the lemon mayonnaise (see *Lemon Sauce* on page 56) with the chives or green onion and tarragon. Stir half the mayonnaise into the lobster, mixing gently with a fork. Serve on a bed of lettuce, garnished with the remaining mayonnaise.
❧ Crab or shrimp can be used instead of lobster.

LOBSTER DELIGHT

1 lb (500 g) canned lobster or crab meat
1 cup (250 mL) finely diced celery
1 small onion, finely chopped
½ tsp (2 mL) curry powder

½ cup (125 mL) mayonnaise
1 tbsp (15 mL) prepared mustard
6 slices white or whole wheat bread
6 thin slices Swiss cheese
4 eggs
2 cups (500 mL) hot milk
½ tsp (2 mL) salt
¼ tsp (1 mL) pepper

❧ Drain the lobster or crab meat and shred it. Add the celery, onion, curry, mayonnaise and mustard, and mix well. Adjust the seasoning to taste. Spread equal amounts of this mixture on 3 slices of the bread and top with the other 3 slices. Cut in half on the diagonal.
❧ Butter a shallow baking dish and arrange the sandwiches in it, topping each with a slice of cheese.
❧ Beat the eggs and stir in the hot milk, salt and pepper. Pour over the bread and cheese.
❧ Let stand 30 minutes. Then place the dish in a larger pan, filled with hot water to halfway up the sides of the smaller dish. Bake in a 325°F (160°C) oven for 40 or 50 minutes or until puffy and golden brown.

CRAB ROYAL

1 lb (500 g) crab meat, fresh or frozen
2 tbsp (30 mL) sherry
4 tbsp (60 mL) butter
1 clove garlic, minced
1 onion, finely chopped
1 cup (250 mL) fresh breadcrumbs
1 tbsp (15 mL) lemon juice

½ tsp (2 mL) dry mustard
1 tbsp (15 mL) capers
⅓ cup (75 mL) mayonnaise
salt and pepper
grated cheese
butter

❧ Cover the fresh or defrosted crab meat with the sherry and let stand for 30 minutes.
❧ Melt the butter in a large skillet. Add the garlic and onion and sauté until golden. Add the breadcrumbs. Cook and stir until lightly browned.
❧ Add the lemon juice, dry mustard, capers and mayonnaise. Salt and pepper to taste. Stir in the crab meat and sherry and remove from the heat. Mix well.
❧ Place this mixture in 4 to 6 vol-au-vent shells or small baking dishes. Sprinkle with grated cheese and dot with butter. Bake in a 400°F (200°C) oven for 10 to 15 minutes. Serve immediately.

STUFFED CRAB NEW ORLEANS

2 tbsp (30 mL) butter or bacon fat
2 onions, finely chopped
6 stalks celery, diced
1 clove garlic, minced
1 tbsp (15 mL) minced parsley
½ green pepper, diced
3 slices bread, crusts removed
milk
1 to 2 lbs (500 to 900 g) crab meat, fresh or canned
salt and pepper

❧ Melt the butter or bacon fat in a skillet. Add the onions, celery, garlic, parsley and green pepper.

Cook over low heat for 15 to 20 minutes, stirring frequently. The vegetables should not be allowed to brown.

🍃 Meanwhile, soak the slices of bread (crusts removed) for 2 minutes in a little milk. Squeeze out the excess milk and crumble the bread into the vegetables. Stir in the crab meat. Add salt and pepper to taste. Cook for a few minutes over very low heat, stirring constantly.

🍃 Serve in small individual dishes. If you prefer, you can prepare the crab-meat mixture in advance. Then spoon the mixture in individual baking dishes and top with crumbs and melted butter. Bake in a 350°F (180°C) oven for 15 to 20 minutes.

CRAB FRICASSEE

3 tbsp (45 mL) butter
1 onion, finely chopped
1 clove garlic, minced
1 tsp (5 mL) curry powder
or ¼ tsp (1 mL) basil
1 tsp (5 mL) flour
1 small can tomatoes
½ tsp (2 mL) sugar
salt and pepper
1 can crab meat
1 to 2 cups (250 to 500 mL) rice
chopped parsley
butter

🍃 Melt the butter in a skillet. Add the onion and garlic and brown lightly. Add the curry powder or basil and the flour and mix well.

🍃 Add the tomatoes and the sugar. Bring to a boil and let sim-

mer for 15 to 20 minutes. Salt and pepper to taste.

🍃 Add the crab meat. Simmer for 5 minutes.

🍃 Boil the rice according to the basic recipe. With a fork, stir in parsley and butter to taste. Make a ring of rice on a hot platter and fill the center with the hot crab fricassee.

Note: Crab is also delicious served in white sauces, salads and sandwiches. Consider substituting it for shrimp in recipes that call for shrimp.

CRAB QUICHE COVEY COVE

I learned how to prepare this dish in Covey Cove, tucked away in a rugged, wonderful corner of Nova Scotia. I was lucky enough to spend a few days at a fisherman's cottage; it sat on a high rock surrounded by big waves. His wife was a marvelous cook—a master at making bread and an artist when it came to creating dishes with the fresh lobster that abounded. This recipe is an adaptation of her lobster pie.

pie pastry of your choice
1 cup (250 mL) canned sliced mushrooms
2 tbsp (30 mL) cognac or lemon juice
1 cup (250 mL) canned crab
¼ pound grated Swiss or mild Cheddar cheese
3 eggs
1 tbsp (15 mL) all-purpose flour
pinch of nutmeg
½ tsp (2 mL) salt
1 cup (250 mL) cream

🍃 Line 8 small tart pans with thinly rolled pastry.

🍃 Thoroughly drain the sliced mushrooms and mix with the cognac or lemon juice. Shred the crab, removing any hard parts. Fill each tart shell with a layer of sliced mushrooms, crab and grated cheese.

🍃 Beat the eggs with the flour, nutmeg, salt and cream. Pour an equal amount into each tart shell. Place the tarts on a baking sheet and bake in a preheated 375°F (190°C) oven for 20 to 30 minutes or until the custard is set and the top is golden brown. Serve warm.

🍃 To freeze, wrap the cooled tarts individually in squares of foil and then freeze. To reheat, unwrap and heat in a 375°F (190°C) oven for 10 to 15 minutes or until hot.

SEAFOOD AVOCADO

1 avocado, unpeeled
juice of ½ lemon
3 tbsp (45 mL) olive oil
1 tsp (5 mL) capers
¼ tsp (1 mL) curry
1 cup (250 mL) crab meat or shrimp
salt and pepper
parsley
lettuce

🍃 Cut the avocado in half and remove the pit.

🍃 Combine the lemon juice, olive oil, capers and curry. Pour over the crab meat or shrimp. Mix well. Salt and pepper to taste.

🍃 Fill the avocado halves with the seafood. Sprinkle with parsley and serve on a lettuce leaf.

Shrimp-stuffed Avocado

SHRIMP

The slender tapering shell of the fresh uncooked shrimp is a translucent greenish gray. Like the lobster, the shrimp does not turn a brilliant color until it is cooked; then it becomes bright pink. You can buy shrimp fresh, cooked, frozen or canned.

To prepare shrimp cocktail, you will need:

6 large shrimp per serving
or
10 small shrimp per serving
or
⅓ to ½ lb (150 to 250 g) raw shrimp per serving

1 lb (500 g) raw shrimp yields about ½ lb (250 g) cooked shrimp.

PREPARING SHRIMP

Fresh shrimp should be washed in cold water. They can be shelled and deveined before or after they are cooked. However, if you plan to use shrimp in a sauce or in a cooked dish, they will be juicier and tastier if you peel and devein them before cooking.

It is not necessary to peel shrimp that are to be used in shrimp cocktail or salad.

TO COOK SHRIMP

Bring to a boil 5 cups (1.2 L) water with 1 tsp (5 mL) coarse salt and 2 slices of unpeeled lemon for each 1 lb (500 g) of shrimp.

Add the shrimp as soon as the water starts to boil. Reduce the heat and cook, uncovered, for 5 minutes. Drain.

Peel, if desired, working from the underside of each shrimp. Slit open along the back and remove the vein.

The uncooked shells can be used to prepare a shrimp broth: boil the shells for 20 minutes in 1 cup (250 mL) salted water flavored with a slice of lemon. Pour through a strainer, pressing down on the shrimp shells to remove the juices. This broth will give a very fine flavor to sauces.

CANNED SHRIMP

Canned shrimp should be rinsed well before being used in any recipe. Drain on a paper towel or a dish towel.

FROZEN SHRIMP

Frozen shrimp are sold both raw and cooked. If the shrimp are already cooked, simply thaw before using. Raw frozen shrimp should be cooked without defrosting.

SHRIMP-STUFFED AVOCADO

Cut an avocado in half lengthwise and remove the pit. Rub the avocado flesh with some lemon juice mixed with salt.

Combine ½ lb (250 g) chopped cooked shrimp with 3 finely chopped celery stalks and 1 finely chopped green onion. Sprinkle with lemon juice or vinegar. Stuff the avocado halves with the shrimp mixture and garnish with watercress or parsley.

Shrimp Sandwich

❧ Combine 6 to 8 oz (175 to 225 g) chopped cooked shrimp with 3 tbsp (45 mL) mayonnaise, 1 tsp (5 mL) lemon juice, ½ cucumber, finely chopped, and 1 chopped green onion or some chopped chives. Spread between slices of bread. This will make 4 good-sized sandwiches.

Seafood Salad

18 to 24 raw shrimp
3 eggs
2 cups (500 mL) cockles or winkles
2 green onions
1 small clove garlic, crushed
3 sprigs parsley
1 cup (250 mL) mayonnaise
½ lb (250 g) crab meat

❧ Boil the shrimp for 10 minutes in enough boiling water to cover, with 1 slice of lemon, ½ tsp (2 mL) salt and a pinch of pepper. Drain and peel. Refrigerate, covered, until ready to use.

❧ Cook the eggs until hard, about 20 minutes. Shell and refrigerate.

❧ Wash the cockles under cold running water. Place in a saucepan with 1 tsp (5 mL) coarse salt, ½ tsp pepper and enough cold water to cover. Bring to a boil, cover and boil for 10 minutes. Drain and refrigerate, covered, until ready to serve.

❧ Finely chop the green onions, garlic and parsley; stir into the mayonnaise. Add the crab meat and mix well.

❧ At serving time, prepare each salad as follows: place half a hard-cooked egg in the middle of each plate. Surround with 3 or 4 shrimp, a few cockles and several spoonfuls of crab in mayonnaise. Top each egg half with a small cockle.

❧ Escargot forks are used to dig the cockles out of their shells. To eat, dip the seafood in crab mayonnaise.

❧ Serve with bread and butter.

Shrimp Salad à la Française

French dressing or tarragon vinegar
lettuce
shrimp

❧ To prepare the French dressing, combine 4 tbsp (60 mL) olive oil with 1 tbsp (15 mL) wine vinegar or cider vinegar. Salt and pepper to taste.

❧ Line a plate with lettuce. Mound the shrimp in the middle and sprinkle with 1 tbsp (15 mL) of the French dressing. Garnish with a lemon wedge. Serve with toasted French bread and sweet butter.

Deep-Fried Shrimp

❧ Shell and devein 1½ lbs (750 g) raw shrimp. Dip each shrimp in batter.

❧ To make the batter, combine 1 cup (250 mL) flour, 2 beaten eggs and 1 cup (250 mL) milk in a bowl. Beat until light and smooth.

❧ Heat 2 cups (500 mL) peanut oil or vegetable oil to 375°F (190°C). Fry the battered shrimp for 3 minutes. Serve hot with chutney.

Butterflied Shrimp

1½ lbs (750 g) fresh or frozen raw shrimp, peeled and deveined
1 egg
1 tbsp (15 mL) water
2 tbsp (30 mL) vegetable oil
1 large onion, sliced into thin rings
¼ cup (50 mL) consommé
1 tbsp (15 mL) cornstarch
1 tsp (5 mL) soy sauce

❧ If possible, buy large shrimp for this recipe.

❧ Slit each shrimp open along the back so that it can be spread flat to resemble a butterfly.

❧ Beat the egg with the water and dip each shrimp in it. Heat the oil, add the shrimp in a single layer and fry until the shrimp have become pink in color, turning once. Repeat until all the shrimp have been fried, adding more oil if necessary.

❧ Drain the shrimp on paper towels and keep them in a warm place. Pour off all but 2 tbsp (30 mL) of the oil from the skillet and add the onion rings. Sauté until tender and golden.

❧ Stir the cold consommé into the cornstarch, a little at a time, and then add the soy sauce. Stir this mixture into the onions in the skillet. Cook and stir until the sauce is thickened and glossy. Arrange the shrimp in a warmed bowl and place the onions and sauce over them. Serve at once with fluffy white rice.

SHRIMP VICTORIA

1 lb (500 g) shrimp, fresh or cooked
¼ cup (50 mL) butter
2 tbsp (30 mL) chopped chives
1 lb (500 g) fresh mushrooms, quartered
2 tbsp (30 mL) flour
½ tsp (2 mL) salt
pinch of pepper
3 tbsp (45 mL) sherry (optional)
¼ tsp (1 mL) curry or sage
1¼ cups (300 mL) sour cream

❧ Shell and clean the shrimp. Melt the butter in a large skillet and add the chives and the shrimp. Cook, stirring, over moderate heat for 5 minutes (10 minutes if you are using raw shrimp).

❧ Add the mushrooms and cook another 2 minutes, stirring constantly. Sprinkle on the flour, salt, pepper, sherry, curry or sage and sour cream.

❧ Simmer gently until hot, stirring constantly. Do not let the mixture come to a boil.

SHRIMP CASSEROLE

1 lb (500 g) shrimp, raw or cooked
3 tbsp (45 mL) butter
1 large onion, finely chopped
1 green pepper, diced
1½ cups (375 mL) long-grain rice, uncooked
1 tsp (5 mL) curry powder
¼ tsp (1 mL) tarragon
1 tsp (5 mL) sugar

1 tsp (5 mL) salt
3 cups (750 mL) tomato juice

❧ Shell the shrimp.

❧ Heat the butter in a skillet and add the onion and green pepper. Cook until limp and lightly browned. Add the uncooked rice and stir over medium heat until the rice is lightly browned. Add the curry, tarragon, sugar and salt. Mix well. Add the tomato juice and bring to a boil.

❧ Remove the rice mixture from the heat and stir in the shrimp. Turn into a buttered casserole. Cover and bake in a 350°F (180°C) oven for 30 to 40 minutes or until the rice is tender and the tomato juice is all absorbed.

CURRIED SHRIMP SOUFFLÉ

2 tbsp (30 mL) olive oil
1½ cups (375 mL) beaten yogurt
2 tsp (10 mL) brown sugar
½ cup (125 mL) shredded coconut
2 tbsp (30 mL) butter
2 onions, finely chopped
1 clove garlic, minced
2 tsp (10 mL) curry powder
3 tbsp (45 mL) flour
2 tbsp (30 mL) milk
4 egg yolks, lightly beaten
¾ cup (175 mL) puréed peas
1 lb (500 g) shrimp, peeled and chopped
salt to taste
6 egg whites
chives or parsley

❧ Brush an 8-in. (20-cm) soufflé dish with olive oil and let stand in a warm place.

Shrimp Casserole

In a bowl, combine the yogurt, brown sugar and coconut. Let stand for 1 hour.

Heat the remaining olive oil and the butter in a skillet. Sauté the onions and garlic for 2 to 3 minutes. Stir in the curry powder and cook another 3 minutes. Fold in the yogurt mixture and simmer for 10 minutes, stirring frequently.

Combine the flour and the milk into a paste and add this to the yogurt mixture. Cook, stirring constantly, until thick.

Remove the mixture from the heat and fold in the beaten egg yolks and green pea purée. Add the shrimp. Salt to taste.

Preheat oven to 375°F (190°C). Beat the egg whites until they are stiff and fold them into the shrimp mixture. Spoon the mixture into the oiled soufflé dish. Bake 40 to 45 minutes, until the soufflé is set and golden.

Serve sprinkled with minced chives or parsley.

Lobster, crab meat or tuna can be substituted for the shrimp.

SHRIMP TEMPURA

1 lb (500 g) fresh shrimp
1 cup (250 mL) flour
2 tbsp (30 mL) soy sauce
2 eggs
⅔ cup (150 mL) milk
peanut oil for deep frying

Shell and clean the shrimp, leaving the tails intact. Slit them down the back without cutting through so that each shrimp can be spread flat to resemble a butterfly.

Prepare a batter with the flour, soy sauce, eggs and milk. Beat together until the batter is smooth. Dip the butterflied shrimp in the batter and deep-fry in hot (375°F or 190°C) oil until golden.

If you wish, you can prepare tempura vegetables the same way. Thinly slice sweet potatoes, green or red peppers, turnips, celery and green beans. Pour boiling water over the sliced vegetables and let stand 5 minutes. Drain the vegetables and rinse them under cold water, then refrigerate them until it is time to cook them. Dip each vegetable piece in tempura batter and fry the same way as the shrimp.

Serve *Shrimp Tempura* and vegetables with the following sauce: combine ½ cup (125 mL) sherry, ¼ cup (50 mL) soy sauce, 1 tsp (5 mL) grated fresh ginger and 1 tsp (5 mL) sugar.

SPANISH PAELLA

1 whole chicken, 4 to 5 lbs (2 kg)
4 cups (1 L) water
celery leaves
salt and pepper
2 large onions, finely chopped
2 cloves garlic, minced
½ cup (125 mL) olive oil
4 tomatoes, peeled and sliced
2 cups (500 mL) long-grain rice
¼ tsp (1 mL) marjoram
½ tsp (2 mL) tarragon
1 tsp (5 mL) paprika
salt and pepper to taste
1 good pinch saffron
1 small package frozen peas
1 lb (500 g) fresh shrimp
12 mussels
12 slices salami

Put the chicken in a large saucepan with the water, celery leaves and some salt and pepper. Cover and simmer until the chicken is tender. Remove the chicken from the broth, let it cool and remove the meat from the bones. Cut the meat into serving pieces and set it aside in a warm place. Reserve the broth for later.

Sauté the onions and garlic in the olive oil. Add 4 cups (1 L) of the chicken broth and the tomatoes. Bring to a boil, then add the rice, marjoram, tarragon and paprika. Simmer 15 to 20 minutes or until the rice is tender and has absorbed all the broth. Remove from the heat and add salt and pepper to taste. Add the saffron and mix well.

Cook the frozen green peas and drain well. Cook the shrimp and peel them. Cook the mussels until the shells open up.

In a large serving dish, combine the hot rice, the chicken pieces, the salami slices, the green peas and the shrimp. Top with the mussels. Serve hot.

MUSSELS MARINIÈRE

green onions, chopped
parsley sprigs

American Fried Oysters

pinch of thyme
½ bay leaf
8 cups (2 L) mussels, scrubbed
1 tbsp (15 mL) butter
1 cup (250 mL) white wine
chopped parsley

🥄 Grease a large saucepan and add some chopped green onions, parsley sprigs, thyme and bay leaf. Top with the mussels and add the butter and white wine.

🥄 Cover and cook over high heat for 15 to 20 minutes or until the mussels are open. Serve the mussels in a warm serving dish, sprinkled with chopped fresh parsley.

CLAM CAKES

2 cups (500 mL) clams, shucked or canned, drained and chopped

2 eggs, lightly beaten
1 cup (250 mL) fine bread-crumbs
¼ tsp (1 mL) salt
¼ tsp (1 mL) thyme
2 tbsp (30 mL) finely chopped onion
breadcrumbs
vegetable oil
butter

🥄 In a large bowl, combine the clams, eggs, breadcrumbs, salt, thyme and onion. Let stand one hour.

🥄 Shape the mixture into 24 small cakes or croquettes. Dredge in the breadcrumbs and fry quickly in a mixture of half butter, half oil for about 3 minutes.

🥄 Serve with hot chili sauce, a curried white sauce or a curried mayonnaise.

AMERICAN FRIED OYSTERS

½ cup (125 mL) vegetable oil
1 cup (250 mL) all-purpose flour
1 egg
1½ cups (375 mL) milk
2 cups (500 mL) fresh shucked oysters
flour
peanut oil for deep frying

🥄 Combine the vegetable oil and the flour until smooth. Add the egg and the milk and beat with an electric mixer until the batter is light and smooth.

🥄 Dry the oysters in a clean cloth. Dust them lightly with flour. Using a fork, dip each oyster in the batter, making sure it is completely covered. Fry in 3 to 4 in. (8 to 10 cm) of peanut oil heated to 375°F (190°C) for 3 to 4 minutes or until golden brown. Drain on paper towels and serve immediately.

PAN-FRIED OYSTERS

🥄 In order for this recipe to be successful, you will have to make sure the oysters are well chilled. Drain the oysters and let them sit between two pieces of clean toweling for 20 minutes to dry.

🥄 Before frying the oysters, dredge them in flour seasoned with paprika, salt and pepper. Or you can dip them in 1 egg beaten with 2 tbsp (30 mL) water and then roll them in a mixture of half fine breadcrumbs, half seasoned flour.

🐟 Heat 2 in. (5 cm) vegetable oil in a skillet. When the oil is hot, add the oysters, one at a time. Cook for 2 minutes, turning them over once midway through. Serve piping hot.

DEEP-FRIED OYSTERS

2 eggs
½ tsp (2 mL) salt
pinch of pepper
2 tbsp (30 mL) cold water
oysters
breadcrumbs

🐟 Beat the eggs with the salt, pepper and cold water. Dip the oysters in this mixture and roll them in breadcrumbs. Let stand for 5 minutes and then deep-fry until golden brown.

ANGELS ON HORSEBACK

🐟 Roll each fresh oyster in a ½ strip of bacon. Secure with a toothpick. Cook in a skillet with a little butter until golden on all sides. Serve on squares of toasted bread.

COQUILLES SAINT JACQUES

2 cups (500 mL) dry white wine
1 cup (250 mL) water
1 tsp (5 mL) salt
few celery leaves
few parsley sprigs

1 bay leaf
2 lbs (900 g) scallops
2 tbsp (30 mL) butter
1 onion, minced
½ lb (250 g) mushrooms, thinly sliced
1 tsp (5 mL) lemon juice
4 tbsp (60 mL) butter
¼ cup (50 mL) flour
2 egg yolks, lightly beaten
¼ cup (50 mL) cream
4 tbsp (60 mL) fine breadcrumbs
butter

🐟 Bring to a boil the white wine, water, salt, celery leaves, parsley and bay leaf. Add the scallops. Cover and simmer for 3 minutes. Remove the scallops and strain the broth. Reserve.

🐟 Melt the 2 tbsp (60 mL) butter and add the onion, mushrooms and lemon juice. Simmer over very low heat for 10 minutes. Add the scallops and simmer for another 2 minutes.

🐟 Make a white sauce with the remaining 4 tbsp (60 mL) butter, the flour and the strained liquid from the scallops. When the sauce is smooth and creamy, stir in the beaten egg yolks and the cream. Stir vigorously over low heat for 2 minutes. Stir in the scallop mixture.

🐟 Divide the mixture into 6 to 8 buttered coquille Saint Jacques shells or small ovenproof dishes. Sprinkle with breadcrumbs and dot with butter. Bake for 5 minutes in a 500°F (260°C) oven.

🐟 *Coquilles Saint Jacques* can be prepared in advance and refrigerated until ready to serve. In this case, bake for 15 minutes in a 450°F (230°C) oven.

Coquilles Saint Jacques

❦ TECHNIQUE ❦

COQUILLES SAINT JACQUES

1 Bring to a boil the white wine, water, salt, celery leaves, parsley and bay leaf.

2 Add the scallops. Cover and simmer.

3 Add the onion, mushrooms and lemon juice to the melted butter. Simmer over very low heat.

4 Add the scallops and simmer.

SCALLOP CASSEROLE

1 lb (500 g) frozen scallops
salt
2 tbsp (30 mL) butter
½ cup (125 mL) chopped onion
1½ cups (375 mL) chopped celery
1 cup (250 mL) sliced fresh
mushrooms
¼ cup (50 mL) melted butter
¼ cup (50 mL) flour
1 tsp (5 mL) salt
2 cups (500 mL) milk
1 to 2 cups (250 to 500 mL)
breadcrumbs
¼ cup (50 mL) finely grated
cheese

🍴 Thaw the scallops. Separate them and sprinkle them with salt. Heat the 2 tbsp (30 mL) butter and sauté the onions, celery and mushrooms over low heat for about 12 minutes or until partially cooked but still crisp. Set the vegetables aside.

🍴 Mix the ¼ cup (50 mL) melted butter with the flour and salt over low heat. Gradually stir in the milk and cook, stirring constantly, until thickened. Add the vegetables and scallops and mix gently.

🍴 Turn the mixture into a greased 6-cup (1.5-L) ovenproof dish.

🍴 Top with buttered breadcrumbs (1 tbsp or 15 mL of butter for each cup or 250 mL of breadcrumbs). Sprinkle with the grated cheese.

🍴 Bake in a 350°F (180°C) oven for about 20 minutes or until the sauce starts to bubble and the breadcrumbs turn golden brown.

SCALLOPS AMANDINE

1 lb (500 g) scallops
flour
butter
¼ lb (125 g) slivered almonds
1 tsp (5 mL) vinegar

🍴 Dry the scallops thoroughly in a clean cloth and dredge them in flour. Melt some butter until browned and add the scallops. Cook for 5 to 8 minutes, depending on the size of the scallops. Remove from the pan.

🍴 Add the almonds to the butter remaining in the pan and stir until golden brown. Stir in the vinegar, then pour the almond sauce over the scallops. Serve.

TEMPURA

Tempura is a marvelous dish of fish or seafood and vegetables fried in oil. There are actually two versions—tempura and kara-age—both using the same ingredients. For tempura, the ingredients are coated with batter and then deep-fried. For kara-age, the same ingredients are simply coated with cornstarch and fried in a small amount of oil.

1½ to 2 lbs (750 to 900 g) fresh
fish or shellfish
assorted vegetables

TEMPURA BATTER:
1 egg
1½ cups (375 mL) water
1½ cups (375 mL) cornstarch
pinch of salt
1¼ cups (300 mL) flour

TEMPURA SAUCE:
⅓ cup (75 mL) sake or dry sherry
⅓ cup (75 mL) soy sauce
1 cup (250 mL) Dashi broth or
clam juice
3 cups (750 mL) peanut oil for
frying

Select 2 kinds of fish or 3 kinds of shellfish from among the following:

white fleshed fish, such as perch, sole, flounder or halibut, cut into 1-in. (2.5-cm) cubes
small whole fish such as smelt
shelled deveined shrimp, tail on
lobster, cut in cubes
whole oysters or clams, cooked

Then choose three or four types of vegetables from among the following:
eggplant, peeled, cubed and dipped in lemon juice
zucchini, cut into 1-in. (2.5-cm) slices
green peppers, cut in rings or strips
whole green onions with part of the green left on
onions, sliced and separated into rings
mushroom caps
bamboo shoots, cut into strips
broccoli, broken into flowerets

TO PREPARE THE BATTER
🍴 Do not prepare the batter until you're ready to proceed with the cooking. Beat the egg with the water, cornstarch and salt. Beat in the flour, bit by bit, and continue beating until smooth.

TO MAKE THE SAUCE

🍃 Combine the sake or sherry, the soy sauce and the Dashi or clam juice. Simmer for 5 minutes, and then refrigerate and serve cold.

TO COOK

🍃 Heat the peanut oil to 350°F (180°C) or until a crust of bread browns in 60 seconds. Coat the fish and vegetables with batter just before you fry them. Fry 3 to 5 pieces at a time until they are golden brown. Drain on paper towels and serve as soon as each portion is ready.

🍃 Serve the dipping sauce in individual bowls.

CLASSIC BOUILLABAISSE

Bouillabaisse, a specialty of Provence in the South of France, contains a variety of seafood. Although purists would say you have to be near a fishing port to make this dish, you can prepare it as long as you have access to a variety of fresh fish. It is time-consuming and somewhat expensive to make, but it is a meal in itself. You will need only a simple salad and a light dessert to make a feast fit for a king.

2 fresh lobsters, 2 lbs (1 kg) each
1½ lbs (750 g) perch or striped bass
3 lbs (1.4 kg) mackerel
24 shrimp
24 mussels
24 clams
¼ cup (50 mL) olive oil
½ cup (125 mL) diced carrots
2 leeks, cleaned and sliced
¾ cup (175 mL) onion, finely chopped
4 cups (1 L) canned tomatoes, drained and chopped
4 cloves garlic, crushed
2 tbsp (30 mL) fresh parsley, finely chopped
1 tsp (5 mL) fennel seed
¼ tsp (1 mL) saffron
1 bay leaf
½ tsp (2 mL) thyme
1 tbsp (15 mL) coarse salt
1 cup (250 mL) dry white wine
¼ cup (50 mL) melted butter
12 thick slices French bread
freshly ground pepper

🍃 Split the lobsters in two, lengthwise. Remove the stomach and intestinal vein. Cut the lobster halves so as to have at least one piece for every guest. Do not remove the shell. Cut the perch and the mackerel into slices 1½ in. (4 cm) thick. Scrub the mussels and the clams to remove any sand.

🍃 Heat 2 tbsp (30 ml) of the olive oil and add the carrots, leeks and onions. Cover and simmer over low heat for 10 minutes. Add the tomatoes, 3 crushed garlic cloves, the parsley, fennel seed, saffron, bay leaf, thyme, salt and pepper. Mix thoroughly and cook over low heat for 20 minutes. Reserve the mixture for later.

🍃 Heat the rest of the oil in a skillet. Add the pieces of lobster, perch and mackerel. Cook 4 minutes over high heat.

🍃 Add the shrimp, the mussels and the clams (without removing the shells). Add the white wine, bring to a boil and cook over low heat for 4 to 5 minutes.

🍃 Add the tomato mixture, season and let simmer for 8 to 10 minutes over very low heat. Serve with garlic bread.

GARLIC BREAD

🍃 Combine the butter with one crushed garlic clove and brush this on one side of each slice of bread. Brown the buttered sides quickly over high heat and then butter the second side and brown. Serve the garlic bread in a basket.

BEEF

BEEF

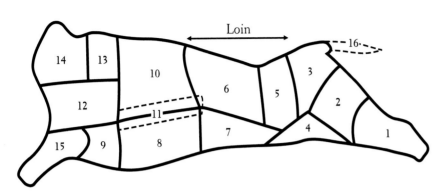

1. Shank
2. Round
3. Rump
4. Sirloin tip
5. Sirloin
6. Shortloin
7. Flank
8. Short plate

9. Brisket
10. Rib
11. Short ribs
12. Shoulder
13. Chuck
14. Neck
15. Foreshank
16. Tail

FILET OF BEEF (TENDERLOIN)

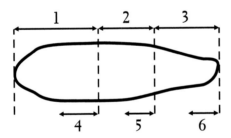

1. Sirloin steak section
2. Porterhouse steak section
3. T-bone steak section
4. Châteaubriand (filet)
5. Tournedos
6. Filet mignon

Châteaubriand is traditionally cut from the sirloin or butt end of a filet. Filet mignon steaks and tournedos are cut from the area closer to the tail end of the filet. The ends of the filet are also used cut up for Fondue Bourguignonne, brochettes, steak tartare, and so on.

Note: Any steak cut from the whole filet is called a filet steak.

Depending on where you buy your meat, you may find that some of the cuts of beef described in this chapter are unfamiliar. That is because French and American butchers cut up beef carcasses in different ways.

&❧ For example, French butchers remove the filet, which runs from the thirteenth rib through to the rump, in one piece. The filet is then cut up into Châteaubriand, tournedos and filets mignon. The loin strip, which lies above the filet, is boned and used for roasts or boneless steaks.

&❧ In most of North America, butchers treat the loin strip and the filet as one unit, from which they cut T-bone, Porterhouse and sirloin steaks. Because most American butchers reserve their best carcasses for these cuts, it may be hard to find a good-size filet of beef.

&❧ If you cannot find a butcher who supplies French-style cuts of beef, you can substitute American-style cuts, as described in the following section.

&❧ How to select a steak: the meat should be firm, velvety and fine-grained with streaks of fat through it. It should be a uniform, rich red color but may vary from light red to dark red. The outside fat should be white or creamy white and firm.

SHANK

The muscles found in the shank are relatively tough. The shank is an excellent choice for making beef stocks and gelatin, as well as for stewing. Like flank, neck and the trimmings from other cuts, the shank is often sold cubed as stewing beef for making stews and fricassées.

ROUND
The round, which is the section just under the rump, is a relatively tender section that can be cut into either roasts or steaks.

෯ Round steak is an oval-shaped cut that is boneless and contains very little fat. It contains two sections—top round and bottom round. Bottom round is generally the more tender cut and is suitable for grilling or pan-broiling. Top round is somewhat tougher, and benefits from braising, roasting or stewing techniques.

RUMP
The rump is usually sold as boneless rump, a lean cut that is fairly tender. Standing rump contains bone.

෯ Rump steaks have excellent flavor but are not really tender; they are better treated with a moist heat method such as braising.

SIRLOIN TIP
The sirloin tip is a triangle-shaped piece of meat cut from beneath the round. Also called Silvertip, the meat is lean and boneless. It is sold whole for roasting or cut into tip steaks.

SIRLOIN
Sirloin is part of the loin and is located next to the shortloin section. It is used most commonly as steak.

෯ It is similar to the French cut entrecôte. Sirloin goes under a variety of names, depending on how it is cut and whether or not it contains bone. Boneless sirloin is often called Boston steak. The eye of the sirloin, called sirloin strip, is the tenderest part and is often cut into strip steaks.

SHORTLOIN
Found next to the ribs, this section is the tenderest part of the loin. It also contains most of the filet. This section is usually cut into steaks. Club steaks, cut from the front end of the shortloin, are a good size for an individual serving. The larger T-bone steak and Porterhouse steak are also cut from the shortloin.

෯ The boneless tender section under these cuts, the loin section, may be cut into loin strip steak or strip steak. French butchers label this cut the contre-filet.

FLANK
The flank is not considered a choice cut, because the muscles are very short and become tough if dry-cooked to medium or well-done. It is more commonly ground or cut into stewing beef, but flank steak can also be braised or broiled.

SHORT PLATE
The short plate is located between the flank and the brisket. Relatively tough, it works best when ground or stewed. It can also be boned and rolled for braising.

BRISKET
The brisket is right next to the front leg. Boned, it is often sold for braising or stewing. However, it also makes excellent pot roast. Butchers use this cut to make corned beef and smoked meat.

RIBS
The rib section is sold both bone-in and boneless, for roasts or for steaks. Bone-in cuts include prime rib, standing rib roast, rolled rib roast and rib steaks. The undercut or filet section is called faux-filet or Spencer, and is excellent roasted or cut into steaks.

SHORT RIBS
The short ribs contain the lower tips of the ribs as well as layers of meat and fat. Excellent boiled or stewed, they are also delicious marinated and braised using the same methods as for pork spareribs.

SHOULDER
The shoulder is located above the brisket, and it is quite thick and meaty. One of the less tender cuts, shoulder roast is appropriate for pot roasts and other moist heat cooking methods. It is also ground and cut up for stewing beef.

CHUCK
The chuck section lies forward of the ribs and is ideal for preparing braised roasts. It is sold as boneless chuck roast as well as blade pot roast and blade steak.

NECK
The neck section is usually cut up for use in stews and fricassées.

FORESHANK
See Shank.

OXTAIL
The oxtail contains lots of bones but is rich in flavor and delicious in soups and stews.

Roast of Beef

weight and quality that only a meat thermometer can ensure perfect results.)

❧ Roast for 12 minutes per lb (500 g) or until the meat thermometer registers 140°F (60°C) for a rare roast.

❧ To make roast filet with red wine: baste the roast throughout cooking with ½ to 1 cup (125 to 250 mL) of warmed (not boiling) red wine.

❧ To serve cold: remove the filet from the oven while rare or medium; let cool in the pan, covered with a cloth or aluminum foil. This roast will be tastier and more juicy if served at room temperature rather than chilled.

SPIT-ROASTED BEEF

❧ For maximum flavor, select a rib roast, faux-filet (Spencer roast) or sirloin.

❧ Take the roast out of the refrigerator an hour before you start to cook it. Trim excess fat to a uniform thickness.

❧ If you like the taste of garlic, marinate the roast in a mixture of ⅓ cups (75 mL) vegetable oil and 2 minced garlic cloves for 1 hour.

❧ Secure the roast on the spit, making sure it is well-balanced. Cook for 15 to 18 minutes per lb (500 g). Do not add salt until the roast is done.

❧ Let the meat stand for 10 to 15 minutes after removing from the spit.

ROAST OF BEEF

1 thin slice pork fat (lard)
1 4- to 8-lb (2- to 3.5-kg) beef filet
salt and pepper
3 tbsp (45 mL) butter
1 tsp (5 mL) dry mustard
½ cup (125 mL) beef suet

❧ Lay the slice of lard on the bottom of a roasting pan and arrange the beef filet on top so that it does not touch the bottom of the pan. Salt and pepper to taste.

❧ Cream together the butter and the mustard. Spread the top and sides of the beef filet with this mixture. Dice the suet and place on top of the filet.

❧ Preheat the oven to 450°F (230°C) for 15 minutes. If you have a meat thermometer, insert it in the thickest part of the filet. (Filets can vary so much in

STEAK

HOW TO COOK STEAK
There are 3 basic methods of cooking steak:

❧ Broiling over hot coals or in the oven under direct heat.

❧ Pan-broiling without any fat.

❧ Pan-frying in butter or other fat.

❧ These three methods are described in the section on meat cookery (see page 30).

❧ Whichever method you choose, observe the following basic rules:

❧ If a steak is more than 1½ in. (4 cm) thick and is to be served rare, it should be removed from the refrigerator at least 1 hour before cooking, to ensure that the interior does not remain cold after the steak is cooked.

❧ Remove excess fat from around

a steak before cooking it, leaving a maximum thickness of ⅓ in. (0.8 cm).

🍃 If you like the taste of garlic, rub the steak with a clove of garlic 1 hour before cooking.

🍃 Do not add salt or pepper until after the steak is cooked, unless you are preparing pepper steak.

🍃 You can tell that a steak is cooked to medium doneness when interior juices rise to the surface of the meat. The steak is well done when the juices withdraw to the inside of the steak.

🍃 Rub the grill or broiler pan with oil or a piece of beef fat before placing the steak on it, to help prevent the meat from sticking.

🍃 Steaks more than 1 in. (2.5 cm) thick should be broiled rather than pan-fried.

STEAK BORDELAISE

🍃 Steak Bordelaise can be made with a boneless rib steak, rib eye steak or club steak. It is broiled and garnished with Bordelaise sauce and poached slices of beef marrow.

🍃 Bordelaise sauce is brown sauce flavored with green onions and Bordeaux wine.

🍃 To make Bordelaise sauce: melt 2 tbsp (30 mL) butter, add 1 small carrot, sliced, 1 small onion, sliced thin, a sprig of parsley, a pinch of thyme and a ½ bay leaf. (This preparation is called a mirepoix.) Cook over medium heat, stirring often, until it reaches a light golden color. Then stir in 3 tbsp (45 mL) flour and con-

tinue cooking until you have a thick brown roux. Add 2 to 3 cups (500 to 750 mL) diluted consommé (either canned or made from cubes) or veal stock. Cook, stirring, over medium heat until the sauce is smooth. Cover and simmer over low heat 20 to 30 minutes. Put through a sieve to strain the vegetables.

🍃 Meanwhile, combine in a saucepan 3 chopped green onions, 1 cup (250 mL) Bordeaux or any other wine of your choice, a pinch of pepper and a very small pinch of thyme. Boil, uncovered, until reduced to ⅓ cup (75 mL) liquid. Strain and add to the brown sauce. Stir in 1 to 3 tsp (5 to 15 mL) butter. Keep warm in a bain-marie or the top of a double boiler.

🍃 To prepare the beef marrow, remove the marrow from the bones and dice with a sharp knife

dipped in hot water; drop into boiling water, cover and simmer over very low heat for 6 to 8 minutes. Meanwhile, broil the steak.

🍃 To serve, garnish the steak with diced marrow and cover with Bordelaise sauce.

BARBECUED STEAK

🍃 Prepare the barbecue to cook at high heat. Slash the fat around the edge of the steaks at 1½-in. (4-cm) intervals, being careful not to cut the meat.

🍃 Rub the grill with vegetable oil or a piece of beef fat. Place 2 or 3 garlic cloves on the coals. Put the steak on the grill set close to the coals and sear for 2 or 3 minutes on each side. Move the grill to 3 in. (8 cm) from the coals and continue cooking until meat juices start to appear on the surface.

Barbecued Steak

🌰 Turn the steak over and continue cooking until the steak reaches the required degree of doneness. A 1-in. (2.5-cm) steak will require about 5 minutes per side to be cooked rare. Adjust the cooking time for thicker cuts.

OVEN-BROILED STEAK

🌰 Choose steaks cut approximately 1 in. (2.5 cm) thick. You can select from club steaks, T-bone, Porterhouse, rib, sirloin or filet mignon. (If you choose filet mignon, wrap with a strip of bacon.)

🌰 Remove the steak from the refrigerator about half an hour before cooking so that it will be at room temperature. Trim excess fat so that it is no more than ⅓ in. (0.8 cm) thick. If you plan to use a meat thermometer, insert it in the thickest part of the steak, making sure it doesn't touch the bone.

🌰 Brush the meat on both sides with olive oil or vegetable oil and sprinkle generously with paprika. If you like the taste of garlic, rub the steak with a garlic clove before you baste with the oil. Do not add salt and pepper before cooking.

🌰 If you use a gas range, place the steaks on the broiler rack about 2 in. (5 cm) from the flame, and reduce the flame.

🌰 If you use an electric range, set the rack 5 or 6 in. (13 to 15 cm) from the heat. (If you use a meat thermometer, insert it in the meat horizontally.)

🌰 Cook until desired degree of doneness, turning the steaks midway through.

BROILED BOTTOM ROUND

MARINADE:
⅓ cup (75 mL) lemon juice or vinegar
½ cup (125 mL) vegetable oil
2 tsp (10 mL) onion juice*
1 tbsp (15 mL) Worcestershire sauce

ROUND STEAK (bottom round)
🌰 Combine in a bowl the lemon juice or vinegar, oil, onion juice and Worcestershire sauce.

🌰 Pour this marinade over the beef and let marinate at room temperature for 12 hours, turning the meat from time to time.

🌰 Drain the steak and place it on the grill about 3 in. (8 cm) from the source of heat. Broil 4 to 5 minutes on each side.

🌰 Serve with a piece of butter on each steak. Salt and pepper to taste.

🌰 The marinade mixture will keep several weeks when refrigerated in a covered glass jar.

*To make onion juice, rub half an onion on a fine grater and collect the pulp with the blade of a knife.

LONDON BROIL

½ cup (125 mL) sherry or ¼ cup (50 mL) lemon juice
½ cup (125 mL) soy sauce
2 cloves garlic, minced
1 tsp (5 mL) ground ginger
1 flank steak

London Broil

🍃 Combine the sherry, soy sauce, garlic and ginger. Add the steak and marinate 4 to 5 hours in the refrigerator.

🍃 Drain the steak well and brush on both sides with vegetable oil. Broil on the barbecue or under the broiler for 3 to 5 minutes on each side. To serve, slice the meat very thin on the bias.

STEAK DIANE

2 tbsp (30 mL) butter
chives, parsley and
green onion, to taste
salt and pepper
1 boneless rib steak, ½ in. (1 cm) thick
1 tbsp (15 mL) brandy
2 tbsp (30 mL) sherry
1½ tsp (7 mL) Worcestershire sauce

🍃 Cream 1 tbsp (15 mL) of the butter with chives, parsley, green onion, salt and pepper, to taste.

🍃 Melt the remaining 1 tbsp (15 mL) butter in a heavy skillet and brown a few chopped green onions in it. Sear the steak 30 seconds to 1 minute on each side, over high heat. Keep warm.

🍃 Pour the brandy into the skillet and set it alight. Stir in the creamed butter, the sherry and the Worcestershire sauce. As soon as the butter is melted, pour over the steak and serve.

Steak Diane

ITALIAN STEAK

½ cup (125 mL) olive oil
2 medium onions, chopped
4 filet steaks,* 1 in. (2.5 cm) thick
⅓ cup (75 mL) lemon juice
3 tbsp (45 mL) capers
salt and pepper

🍃 Heat the oil in a heavy skillet and brown the onions in it. Push the onions to the sides of the pan and add the steaks, cooking to the desired degree of doneness. Remove the steaks and keep them warm.

🍃 Add the lemon juice to the onions and stir over high heat, scraping the bottom of the pan. Add the capers, salt and pepper. Pour over the steaks and serve.

*Any steak cut from the filet section.

PEPPER STEAK

½ tsp (2 mL) peppercorns
1 steak, 1 to 1½ in. (2.5 to 4 cm) thick
salt
2 tbsp (30 mL) butter
2 tbsp (30 mL) vegetable oil
3 tbsp (45 mL) cold tea or consommé
3 tbsp (45 mL) white wine or lemon juice
2 tbsp (30 mL) brandy (or to taste)

🍃 Crush the peppercorns with the back of a wooden spoon. Coat both sides of the steak with the crushed pepper, pressing well into the meat. Salt each side.

🍃 Heat the butter and oil in a heavy skillet and sear the steak quickly on both sides. Then pan-broil for 3 to 4 minutes on each side, or until done to taste. Move

Pan-fried Filet Mignon

the steak from the pan to a warm platter.

🍃 Add the tea and wine (or consommé and lemon juice) to the pan. Bring to a boil, scraping the bottom of the pan. Stir in the brandy. Pour the sauce over the steak and serve immediately.

PAN-FRIED FILET MIGNON

salt, pepper and paprika
filets mignons
olive oil or soft butter

🍃 Sprinkle one side of each filet with salt, pepper and paprika. Baste the other side with olive oil.

🍃 Heat a heavy skillet over high heat. Remove from the burner and add the filets, oiled side down. Cook for 4 to 6 minutes over moderate heat. Turn the filets and cook another 1 to 3

minutes, depending on the desired degree of doneness.

OLD-FASHIONED BEEF ROLL

1 whole round steak
2 large onions, finely chopped
1 cup (250 mL) dry bread, coarsely crushed
3 carrots, grated
½ cup (125 mL) melted butter
1 tsp (5 mL) coarse salt
½ tsp (2 mL) celery seed
¼ tsp (1 mL) pepper
½ tsp (2 mL) dry mustard
pinch of ground cloves
1 tsp (5 mL) cinnamon
1 tbsp (15 mL) coarse salt

🍃 Have the butcher cut the steak into one long slice ⅛ to ¼ in. thick (about 0.5 cm). Remove any fat and bones.

🍃 Render the fat trimmings and sauté the chopped onions in it. Combine the onions with the bread, grated carrots, melted butter, 1 tsp (5 mL) of salt, celery seed, pepper, dry mustard, cloves and cinnamon to make a stuffing. When well blended, spread the mixture on the meat.

🍃 Roll the steak jelly-roll fashion. Then carefully wrap the roll in a square of clean white cotton and sew tightly shut with heavy thread, so that it resembles a giant sausage.

🍃 Place the roll in a heavy pot of boiling water (the water should cover the meat). Cover and simmer about 4 hours, adding the final 1 tbsp (15 mL) of coarse salt midway through the cooking period.

🍃 When the meat is done (it should be tender when pierced with a sharp knife), remove it from the water and place it in a serving dish. Put a heavy weight on top of the roll (you can use a chopping board weighed down with a large can, for example). Once the roll has cooled, refrigerate until ready to serve.

🍃 To serve, remove the cloth wrapping and cut into thin slices.

BEEF ROULADES

6 minute or cubed steaks
3 cups (750 mL) diced stale bread
1 cup (250 mL) hot chicken stock
½ tsp (2 mL) sage
2 tbsp (30 mL) parsley
¼ tsp (1 mL) thyme
1 tsp (5 mL) salt

3 tbsp (45 mL) melted butter
grated zest of 1 orange
1 cup (250 mL) chopped raw
cranberries or 1 cup (250 mL)
diced orange pulp
¼ cup (50 mL) flour
1 tsp (5 mL) salt
¼ tsp (1 mL) pepper
4 tbsp (60 mL) melted beef suet
¼ cup (50 mL) consommé
or water

🥄 Make sure the steaks have been well tenderized, as this cut tends to be tough.

🥄 To make the stuffing, combine in a large bowl the diced bread with the chicken stock, herbs, 1 tsp (5 mL) salt, butter, orange zest and the cranberries or orange pulp. Spread an equal quantity of stuffing mixture on each steak and roll it up. Fasten each closed roulade with a skewer (I use kitchen string).

🥄 Combine the flour, the second quantity of salt and the pepper and roll each roulade well in the mixture.

🥄 Heat the beef suet in a heavy skillet until melted, and then add the roulades and brown them on all sides. Arrange the roulades in an ovenproof dish and add the consommé. Roast for 35 minutes in a 275°F (140°C) oven.

🥄 Serve each roulade napped with some of the cooking sauce. Potatoes and mushrooms make good accompaniments.

🥄 These roulades freeze well if you cool them first, then wrap

well. To reheat, put the unthawed roulades in a 275°F (140°C) oven for 45 to 50 minutes.

Braised Beef French Style

¼ lb (125 g) salt pork, sliced thin
4 onions, sliced into rings
4 carrots, cut in 1-in. (2.5-cm) pieces
2 cloves
1 clove garlic, chopped fine
½ tsp (2 mL) thyme
¼ tsp (1 mL) sage
grated zest of ½ orange
3 to 6 lbs (1.5 to 2.5 kg) top or bottom round

🥄 Place all the ingredients in a heavy enameled pot and cook over high heat until the pork starts to brown. Stir to sear the meat on all sides. Cover and cook over low heat for 2 to 3 hours or until the beef is tender. Add no

liquid as the beef will provide its own juices.

Pot-au-Feu

1 tbsp (15 mL) fat
4 lbs (2 kg) beef shoulder, chuck, brisket or any other less tender cut
salt and pepper to taste
1 carrot, diced
1 onion, chopped
1 bay leaf
¼ tsp (1 mL) thyme
½ cup (125 mL) water

🥄 Melt the fat in the bottom of a pressure-cooker. Add the meat and brown it on all sides. Salt and pepper to taste and add the carrot, onion, bay leaf, thyme and water.

🥄 Cover and cook 35 minutes at 15 lbs pressure. Let the pressure drop by itself before opening the pot. If you wish, make a gravy from the cooking juices.

Braised Beef French Style

AMERICAN BRAISED BEEF

¼ cup (50 mL) all-purpose flour
1 tsp (5 mL) salt
¼ tsp (1 mL) pepper
½ tsp (2 mL) marjoram or savory
4 lbs (2 kg) short ribs, rump
or ribs, cubed
4 tbsp (60 mL) fat
4 whole onions
4 whole carrots
½ cup (125 mL) tomato juice
⅓ cup (75 mL) vinegar
1 tbsp (15 mL) sugar
¼ tsp (1 mL) ground cloves

🍃 Combine the flour with the salt, pepper and marjoram or savory and dredge the meat in it. Brown the cubes in the fat in a large heavy pot.

🍃 When the meat is well browned, add the remaining ingredients. Cover and simmer for 2½ to 3 hours or until the meat is very tender. Mash the vegetables into the gravy before serving.

BRAISED POT ROAST

This recipe freezes well and is handy to have on hand for emergencies.

½ cup (125 mL) chopped suet
6 to 8 lbs (3 to 3.5 kg) boneless
shoulder, plate or brisket
6 onions, sliced
1 tsp (5 mL) salt
1 bay leaf
1 tsp (5 mL) curry powder
or ½ tsp (2 mL) ground cinnamon
3 whole cloves
1 slice orange zest

🍃 Melt the fat in a heavy pot or Dutch oven. Brown the meat over medium heat. Add the onions, salt, bay leaf, curry powder or cinnamon, whole cloves and orange zest. You don't need to add any liquid because the meat will provide its own juices as it cooks. Simmer over low heat for 3 to 3½ hours or until the meat is tender. The secret to success in braising meat is to avoid high temperatures.

🍃 To freeze, remove the meat from the pot and store the cooking liquid in a separate container. Cool the meat and the liquid in the refrigerator. Cut the meat into meal-sized portions and cover with some of the cooking liquid. Wrap and freeze.

🍃 Makes 16 portions

🍃 Freezer storage limit: 2 to 3 months

🍃 To serve: defrost in the refrigerator or at room temperature, counting on about 8 hours in the refrigerator, 2 hours at room temperature.

🍃 Heat, in a covered container, for about 1 hour in a 350°F (180°C) oven, basting as necessary.

BELGIAN BEEF CARBONNADE

1½ lbs (750 g) top or bottom round
salt and pepper
2 tbsp (30 mL) fat or oil
1 cup (250 mL) chopped onions
2 tbsp (30 mL) flour
1 tbsp (15 mL) brown sugar
2 cups (500 mL) beer
1 cup (250 mL) consommé
½ tsp (2 mL) anise seed (optional)

🍃 Cut the meat in 2-in. (5-cm) cubes, and salt and pepper each

Belgian Beef Carbonnade

piece. In a heavy pot, brown the cubes on all sides in the fat.

🍴 Remove the beef from the pot and add the onions. Cook until golden; then add the remaining ingredients. Stir until the mixture boils. Add the meat.

🍴 Cover and cook over medium heat for 1½ hours, stirring occasionally. Serve with noodles or mashed potatoes.

🍴 To make this recipe in a pressure cooker, follow the same procedure but reduce the liquids to 1 cup (250 mL) beer and ½ cup (125 mL) consommé. Cook for 20 minutes.

Beef Bourguignonne

BEEF À LA MODE

4- to 5-lb (2- to 2.5-kg) piece of braising beef (such as top round)
1 tsp (5 mL) salt
¼ tsp (1 mL) pepper
¼ tsp (1 mL) nutmeg or ground cloves
2 bay leaves
¼ tsp (1 mL) thyme
few celery leaves
1 cup (250 mL) red or white wine
1 cup (250 mL) consommé
3 tbsp (45 mL) beef or bacon fat
½ lb (250 g) pork fatback, sliced thin
1 large onion, sliced
5 carrots

🍴 In a large bowl, combine the beef with the salt, pepper, nutmeg or cloves, bay leaves, thyme, celery, wine and consommé. Cover and allow to marinate for

12 to 24 hours in the refrigerator. Drain the meat, reserving the marinade.

🍴 Melt the beef or bacon fat in a large, heavy pot and brown the meat in it on all sides over low heat. In a second pan, brown the fatback. Drain and add to the beef. Add the onion, carrots and reserved marinade. Bring to a boil, cover and simmer over low heat for 3 to 5 hours or until the meat is tender. Turn the meat 2 or 3 times during cooking.

🍴 This dish is delicious served hot or cold. However, if you plan to serve it cold, add a bony veal knuckle to the pot for the entire cooking period. When the dish is cooled, the cooking liquid will gel. Serve with the sliced meat.

BEEF BOURGUIGNONNE

3 to 4 lbs (1.5 to 2 kg) beef shoulder or round
4 slices salt pork, more fat than lean
all-purpose flour
1 tsp (5 mL) salt
½ tsp (2 mL) pepper
1 leek, sliced thin
¼ tsp (1 mL) thyme
¼ cup (50 mL) parsley, chopped
2 cloves garlic, minced
red wine
2 tbsp (30 mL) butter
½ lb (250 g) mushrooms, whole or sliced

🍴 Cut the beef into cubes about 1½ to 2 in. (4 to 5 cm) square. Trim off excess fat and remove any bones. Dice the salt pork small. Dredge the meat in flour.

❦ TECHNIQUE ❦

BEEF BOURGUIGNONNE

1 Dredge the beef cubes in flour.

2 Render the salt pork and brown the beef cubes in the fat. Add the salt, pepper, leeks, thyme, parsley and garlic.

3 Add the red wine.

4 Sauté the mushrooms in hot butter.

In a large, heavy pot, render the salt pork and brown the beef cubes in the fat over high heat.

Add the salt, pepper, sliced leek, thyme, parsley and garlic. Stir to combine and add enough red wine to cover the meat. Bring to a boil. Cover and cook over very low heat until the meat is tender.

In a separate pan, melt the butter until a brown nutty color and add the whole or sliced mushrooms. Cook over high heat for 2 minutes, stirring constantly. Add the mushrooms to the beef.

If you wish, thicken the sauce with 2 tbsp (30 mL) flour blended with cold water. Adjust the seasonings. Serve with boiled potatoes and small boiled onions sautéed in butter.

BEEF EN DAUBE

1 cup (250 mL) diced salt pork
3 lbs (1.5 kg) beef rump
or shoulder
2 tbsp (30 mL) flour
1 cup (250 mL) water
½ cup (125 mL) red wine
1 tbsp (15 mL) brandy (or to taste)
1 tbsp (15 mL) beef extract
2 carrots, peeled and sliced
6 medium-size onions, whole
1 small rutabaga, peeled, cut in eighths
salt and pepper to taste
1 clove garlic, crushed
3 sprigs parsley, chopped
chives or chervil to taste

Melt the diced salt pork in a large casserole and brown the beef on all sides in the melted fat. Remove the meat.

Stir in the flour and cook a few minutes until browned. Add the water, red wine, brandy and beef extract. Bring to a boil, stirring constantly. Return the beef to the pot. Add the carrots, onions and rutabaga. Salt and pepper to taste. Cover and simmer over very low heat, or bake in a 325°F (160°C) oven 1½ to 2 hours or until the meat is tender.

Again, remove the meat from the casserole. Stir in the crushed garlic, minced parsley and chives or chervil. Return the mixture just to a boil and then remove from the heat.

To serve, set the meat on a serving platter and arrange the hot vegetables around it. Put the sauce into a gravy boat.

SAUERBRATEN

1½ cups (375 mL) wine vinegar
½ cup (125 mL) red wine
2 onions, thinly sliced
2 carrots, peeled and sliced
1 bay leaf
3 whole cloves
1 tbsp (15 mL) peppercorns
1 tbsp (15 mL) salt
4 lbs (2 kg) beef shoulder, round or rump
4 tbsp (60 mL) butter
1 tbsp (15 mL) vegetable oil
5 tbsp (75 mL) flour
1 tbsp (15 mL) sugar
⅔ cup (150 mL) gingersnap cookies, crushed

To prepare the marinade: in a large bowl, combine the vinegar, wine, onions, carrots, bay leaf, cloves, pepper and salt.

Place the meat in the mixture. Cover and marinate for at least

Beef en Daube

[173]

24 hours (up to 3 days) in the refrigerator, turning the meat from time to time. Drain the meat, reserving the marinade.

✖ Heat the butter and oil in a large heavy casserole or pot and brown the meat on all sides over moderate heat. Turn the meat often, sprinkling the top with a little of the flour each time.

✖ Heat the marinade and pour it over the meat. Cover and simmer over low heat for about 3 hours or until the meat is tender.

✖ Remove the meat from the casserole and keep it warm. Meanwhile, skim off the excess fat from the top of the cooking liquid and reserve. Add the remaining flour and the sugar to a few tablespoons of the skimmed-off fat and blend well. Stir this paste into the cooking liquid, and simmer, stirring, until the sauce is smooth and creamy. Stir in the cookie crumbs. Return the meat to the sauce and simmer over low heat for 30 minutes.

✖ Serve with dumplings or noodles.

BEEF AND RED CABBAGE

2 lbs (1 kg) stewing beef
2 large onions, thinly sliced
3 tbsp (45 mL) fat
1 tsp (5 mL) salt
½ tsp (2 mL) pepper
1 tsp (5 mL) anise seeds
1 bay leaf
3 cups (750 mL) boiling water
3 tbsp (45 mL) cider vinegar
1 small red cabbage, cut in 8 wedges
3 slices whole-wheat bread, toasted and crumbled

✖ Brown the meat and thinly sliced onions in hot fat in a deep heavy pan. Add the salt, pepper, anise and bay leaf.

✖ Pour the boiling water over the meat and add the vinegar. Place the cabbage wedges on top of the meat. Cover and simmer 2 hours over low heat. Add the toasted breadcrumbs and simmer an additional 15 minutes, stirring often.

✖ Serve with mashed potatoes.

HUNGARIAN BEEF GOULASH

¼ lb (125 g) bacon or salt pork, diced
2 lbs (1 kg) stewing beef
4 onions, sliced thin
¼ tsp (1 mL) marjoram
1 tsp (5 mL) salt
½ tsp (2 mL) pepper
1 clove garlic, minced
1 tsp (5 mL) paprika
¾ cup (175 mL) red wine or apple juice
1 cup (250 mL) sour cream

✖ Brown the bacon or salt pork in a heavy pan or casserole. Add the meat and brown on all sides. Remove the meat and add to the pan the onions, marjoram, salt, pepper and minced garlic. Stir over high heat until the onions are golden. Return the meat to the pan, sprinkle with paprika and add the red wine or apple juice. Bring to a boil. Cover and simmer over very low heat for 1 to 1½ hours, or until the meat is tender. Just before serving, stir in the sour cream and heat, but do not boil the sauce.

Hungarian Beef Goulash

❦ TECHNIQUE ❦

HUNGARIAN BEEF GOULASH

1 Brown the beef with the bacon or salt pork.

2 Remove the meat. Add the onions, marjoram, salt, pepper and garlic.

3 Return the beef to the casserole and sprinkle with paprika.

4 Add the red wine.

BEEF AND TOMATO STEW

1½ lbs (750 g) beef shoulder
⅓ cup (75 mL) browned flour
1 tsp (5 mL) salt
¼ tsp (1 mL) pepper
1 tsp (5 mL) savory
½ tsp (2 mL) ground cloves
2 tbsp (30 mL) fat
1 clove garlic
2 onions, sliced thin
1 can tomatoes
1 tbsp (15 mL) sugar

☙ Cut the meat in 10 to 14 pieces. Dredge each piece in a mixture of the flour, salt, pepper, savory and cloves and brown in the fat. Add the remaining ingredients.
☙ Cover and simmer for 1½ hours. If you wish, you can add sliced carrots and rutabaga for the final ½ hour of cooking.

CHILI CON CARNE

1 lb (500 g) dried kidney beans
¼ lb (125 g) salt pork, diced
1 large onion, chopped fine
2 cloves garlic, minced
2 tbsp (30 mL) chili powder
1 tsp (5 mL) salt
¼ tsp (1 mL) cumin
1 tsp (5 mL) oregano
2 5½-oz (160-mL) cans tomato paste
1 cup (250 mL) tomato sauce
1½ lbs (750 g) pork shoulder
1½ lbs (750 g) stewing beef

Swiss Steak with Sour Cream

4 tbsp (60 mL) butter
1 tbsp (15 mL) salt
½ tsp (2 mL) pepper

☙ Simmer the beans in 8 cups (2 L) water for 2 to 3 hours or until tender. Do not overcook. Drain the beans, reserving 1 cup (250 mL) of the cooking liquid.
☙ Brown the salt pork until crisp and golden brown. Add the onion and garlic and cook until golden. Add the chili powder, salt, cumin, oregano, tomato paste and tomato sauce. Simmer the mixture for 15 to 20 minutes, stirring often.
☙ Add the beans and the 1 cup (250 mL) cooking liquid. Cover and simmer for 2 hours.
☙ Meanwhile, cut the beef and pork into 1-in. (2.5-cm) cubes. Melt the butter in a heavy pan. Add the meat and brown over

moderate heat, stirring frequently. Add salt and pepper.
☙ Add the meat to the bean mixture for the last ½ hour of cooking. Serve.

SWISS STEAK WITH SOUR CREAM

3 tbsp (45 mL) flour
½ tsp (2 mL) salt
¼ tsp (1 mL) pepper
½ tsp (2 mL) paprika
1½ to 2 lbs (750 to 900 g) round steak or shoulder, cut in 1-in. (2.5-cm) cubes
3 tbsp (45 mL) fat
3 onions, sliced thin
½ cup (125 mL) water
½ cup (125 mL) sour cream

In a bowl, combine the flour, salt, pepper and paprika. Dredge the meat cubes in the mixture and brown the meat on all sides in hot fat in a heavy skillet. When the meat is browned, add the onions. Once the onions have turned golden, stir in the water and sour cream. Cover and simmer 1 hour or until the meat is very tender. (The liquid should never boil.)

BOILED BEEF

8 to 10 cups (2 to 2.5 L) water
1 unpeeled carrot, scrubbed
1 large onion, quartered
½ tsp (2 mL) thyme
4 cloves
1 bay leaf
1 tbsp (15 mL) coarse salt
¼ tsp (1 mL) pepper
5 lbs (2.5 kg) stewing beef

Bring the water to a boil and add the rest of the ingredients. Cover and simmer slowly 3 to 4 hours or until the meat is tender. To turn out well, boiled beef should never actually boil but only simmer.

You can, if you wish, cook vegetables along with the beef. Prepare vegetables such as carrots, parsnips, fresh green peas or green beans and wrap them in a piece of cheesecloth. Add to the stock for the last 25 to 30 minutes of cooking.

When the beef is cooked, set it on a serving platter and sprinkle with about 1 tbsp (15 mL) coarse salt. Arrange the vegetables around the meat, along with some boiled potatoes. (The potatoes should be cooked separately.)

To serve cold, let the beef cool in the stock until just warm. Then drain and sprinkle with coarse salt. Refrigerate, covered with wax paper, until ready to serve.

To make *Beef Vinaigrette*, serve the boiled beef and vegetables with a plain French dressing flavored with finely chopped chives and parsley.

OVEN-BOILED BRISKET OF BEEF

This is a simple and delicious recipe for preparing brisket.

3 to 4 lbs (1.5 kg) beef brisket
4 tbsp (60 mL) chicken fat
or butter
1 large onion, sliced thin
1 tbsp (15 mL) coarse salt
3 tbsp (45 mL) soy sauce
6 to 8 cups (1.5 to 2 L) hot water
(or enough to cover meat)

Brown the brisket on all sides in the butter or chicken fat. Put it in a 12-cup (3-L) casserole. Add the thinly sliced onion, coarse salt, soy sauce and enough water to cover the meat. Cover and cook 3 to 4 hours in a preheated 350°F (180°) oven. Check liquid occasionally, as the water must always cover the meat.

When done, you can make a simple tasty sauce by stirring 1 tbsp (15 mL) cornstarch blended with 3 tbsp (45 mL) water into 2 cups (500 mL) of the cooking liquid. Simmer until thickened.

CORNED BEEF AND CABBAGE

4 lbs (2 kg) corned beef
1 onion, stuck with whole cloves
1 bay leaf
2 cloves garlic
1 sprig parsley
1 stalk celery
1 green cabbage, cut in 6 wedges

Place the meat in a large casserole, cover with cold water and bring to a boil. Simmer over medium heat 10 minutes. Pour off the water.

Cover again with cold water and add the onion, bay leaf, garlic, parsley and celery. Bring to a boil. Cover and simmer over low heat for 3 to 4 hours, or until the meat is tender.

Add the cabbage 30 or 40 minutes before the end of the cooking period.

Serve the beef, sliced thinly, with mustard and boiled potatoes.

To serve corned beef cold, place the hot meat in a bowl rubbed with a clove of garlic. Cover with wax paper and place a heavy weight on top. (This will make it easier to slice when cold.) Serve with mustard and potato salad.

FONDUE BOURGUIGNONNE

You can vary its ingredients and even change its name, but the dish classically known as Fondue Bourguignonne is the perfect meal to make when you want to

Beef Stroganoff

entertain a group of 6 to 8. Of course, you can double the quantities to serve 16, but in that case you will need two fondue pots, arranged at either end of a large table or on two smaller tables.

❧ To add a really elegant note to your meal, use a copper fondue set. But it's possible to set an equally attractive table by improvising with utensils you already have in your kitchen. First, you need a deep heavy pot, tall and narrow, 6 to 8 in. (15 to 20 cm) in diameter, which will fit on a chafing-dish stand or something similar. Second, you need a good fuel. Sterno and alcohol are the best, as they provide a steady source of heat. A candle simply cannot provide enough heat to cook meat.

❧ You can even make an excellent Fondue Bourguignonne in an electric skillet. You may need to use more oil, but it's easy to keep

the oil at the optimum temperature of 400°F (200°C).

❧ To complete the equipment, you need long-handled fondue forks or wooden skewers soaked in water.

❧ To make your fondue complete, you absolutely must provide your guests with a selection of sauces in which they can dip their cooked tidbits of meat. Simple, ready-made sauces such as catsup, hot mustard or chili sauce are perfectly acceptable, especially if you jazz them up a bit with the addition of lemon juice, capers or chopped sour pickles. The traditional bottled English sauces, such as Worcestershire and HP Sauce, are also delicious. If you want to add a more original sauce or two, try one of the recipes in this book, such as *Béarnaise* (page 55), *Vimot, Gribiche, Ravigote or Sauce Diablo* (page 62

and 63). The choice is up to you, but make sure you have at least three or four different sauces.

❧ You can serve your fondue with French-fried potatoes or potato chips, if you wish, or simply accompany it with a green salad. But because a fondue meal involves a relatively long period sitting at the table, it's a nice opportunity to wrap up the meal with a particularly rich and delicious dessert.

❧ Try serving a fondue the next time you entertain. It's sure to lead to a relaxed and convivial meal, even if your guests begin the evening as strangers.

❧ Fondue Bourguignonne can be made with beef tenderloin or even Polish sausage. Tenderized round of beef is very successful, and well-seasoned meatballs are delicious.

1½ to 2 lbs (750 g to 1 kg) lean ground beef, shaped into balls
or 1 lb (500 g) Polish sausage, cut in 1-in. (2.5-cm) slices
or 2 lbs (1 kg) beef filet, thinly sliced
peanut oil
thick slice of raw potato

❧ Arrange the meat attractively on individual serving dishes and let stand at room temperature for ½ hour.

❧ Set the fondue pot on the stand and fill with 1½ to 2 in. (4 to 5 cm) peanut oil. Light the fuel and bring the oil to a boil. Add the slice of raw potato to keep the fat from spattering.

❧ Place the fondue set in the center of the table within easy reach of each person. Each place setting should be equipped with a dinner plate or fondue plate as well as a fondue fork (or skewer) and a platter of meat. Bowls of sauces, relishes, etc., should be placed on the table so that all the guests can serve themselves.

❧ I also like to lay out a tossed green salad and crusty bread or, as is my preference, large puffy hot popovers. I make them in the morning and warm them up when I'm ready to serve them.

❧ To eat the fondue: spear a piece of meat on a long-handled fork and dip it in the bubbling oil until cooked to taste. Then dip it into one of the sauces.

BEEF STROGANOFF

1½ lbs (750 g) beef filet or sirloin
5 tbsp (75 mL) butter
2 tbsp (30 mL) olive oil
2 green onions, finely chopped
¼ cup (50 mL) white wine
1½ cups (375 mL) sour cream
1 tbsp (15 mL) lemon juice
salt and pepper
parsley or chervil, finely chopped

❧ Slice the beef in strips as thin as possible. Melt 4 tbsp (60 mL) butter in a cast-iron skillet and add 1 tbsp (15 mL) oil. When the fat is hot, add the beef strips and sear on both sides over high heat, as quickly as possible. One minute should be enough. Place the meat in a warm dish.

❧ Add the remaining butter and oil to the skillet, along with the chopped onions, and cook for 1 minute, stirring constantly. Add the wine, sour cream and lemon

juice and simmer, without boiling, for another minute, stirring constantly. (The cream will curdle if you let it boil.)

❧ Pour the hot sauce over the beef strips. Salt and pepper to taste. Sprinkle with minced parsley or chervil. Serve with egg noodles or boiled rice.

SUKIYAKI

This is the ideal fondue variation for people who are watching their fat intake. A pleasant mixture of sweet and tart, this beef and vegetable dish is a real winner.

1 to 1½ lbs (500 to 750 g) eye of round or sirloin steak
2 medium onions, thinly sliced
1 cup (250 mL) carrots, cut in fine julienne strips
¾ lb (375 g) fresh spinach
1 cup (250 mL) bamboo shoots, thinly sliced
1½ cups (375 mL) celery, sliced on the bias
6 green onions, sliced on the bias
½ lb (250 g) fresh mushrooms, thinly sliced
½ cup (125 mL) water chestnuts, sliced
1½ cups (375 mL) bean sprouts
2 tofu cakes, diced (optional)
1 piece beef suet
2 cups (500 mL) Dashi* or 3 cups (750 mL) beef consommé
⅓ cup (75 mL) sake or dry sherry
3 tbsp (45 mL) sugar
6 bowls cooked long-grain rice

*Preparation of Dashi: use "Dashi no moto," which is sold in packages (like our dehydrated soups) in stores that stock Japanese foods. Just add the contents to 4 cups (1 L) of boiling

water. Simmer, covered, 30 minutes. Alternatively, you can combine 1 tbsp (15 mL) dried katsuobushi or borato with 1 tbsp (15 mL) kombu or seaweed in 4 cups (1 L) boiling water.

❧ Use a very sharp knife to cut the meat, on the bias, in thin strips. Arrange the meat attractively on a large platter, alongside the onions, carrots, spinach (whole leaves only), bamboo shoots, celery, green onions, mushrooms, water chestnuts, bean sprouts and the tofu cut in small cubes. Add the piece of suet to the platter. Cover the platter with foil and refrigerate until ready to use.

❧ Combine the Dashi or beef consommé, the sake or dry sherry, and the sugar in an attractive pitcher.

❧ Sukiyaki can be prepared in the kitchen or right at the table. To prepare it at the table, heat an electric skillet to 400°F (200°C). You can also use a heavy metal pan set over a butane heater. Rub the inside of the pan with the piece of suet until well greased.

❧ This dish is best cooked in batches just large enough to provide one small serving per person, rather than all at once. Fry 6 pieces of meat (or 1 per person), stirring with a fork to prevent sticking. When the strips are lightly browned (which should take about 1 minute), start adding the vegetables, one type at a time, starting with the ones that require the longest cooking time (onions and carrots). With each addition, add 1 tsp (5 mL) of the Dashi mixture for each portion of each vegetable. Cook, stirring, for about ½ minute before adding the next vegetable. Stir in the tofu and then add the meat and 1 tsp (5 mL) of Dashi per serving.

🍢 Provide each guest with a bowl of hot rice, and let the guests help themselves to the Sukiyaki.

🍢 Continue making batches until all the ingredients are used up.

🍢 Sukiyaki is often served with a raw egg yolk in a small bowl and a second small bowl of horseradish for each person. Bits of food are dipped in the yolk, and the meat is dipped in horseradish. You might also provide some soy sauce for the rice.

TERIYAKI

In Japan, adults as well as school children carry lunch boxes. But instead of a peanut butter sandwich, their lunch boxes are likely to contain rice and some Teriyaki made with fish or vegetables. The Teriyaki recipe here is made with beef, but you could also make it with pork, chicken, lamb, or even fish.

½ cup (125 mL) soy sauce
¼ cup (50 mL) sugar
1 clove garlic, crushed
1 tbsp (15 mL) sake or dry sherry
2 tbsp (30 mL) fresh ginger root, minced, or 2 tsp (10 mL) ground ginger
2 lbs (1 kg) eye of round, filet or sirloin

🍢 In a saucepan, combine the soy sauce, sugar, garlic, sake or dry sherry and ginger. Heat, stirring, until the sugar is dissolved. When cooled, pour this mixture over the beef and marinate 2 to 12 hours, turning the meat a few times to make sure that all sides are well soaked with the marinade.

🍢 Drain the meat and place on a grill or under the broiler about 5 in. (13 cm) from the flame. Cook until it has reached the desired degree of doneness, turning only once.

SHABU SHABU

Shabu Shabu (Japanese fondue) is similar to Chinese fondue but a little different from other types of fondue because it involves two separate courses. It falls into the category the Japanese call "nabe-mono," to signify dishes that you cook as you go along. You'll find this a delightful and very healthy fondue variation.

6 to 8 cups (1.5 to 2 L) chicken bouillon
1 lb (500 g) beef, sliced thin
6 squares tofu
4 green onions
6 leaves Chinese cabbage

🍢 To prepare homemade chicken bouillon: put 6 to 8 cups (1.5 to 2 L) water in a large pot; add one celery stalk, a pinch of salt and the skin, neck, heart, liver and gizzard of 2 chickens. Simmer for 1 hour.

🍢 Or, dissolve 2 to 3 chicken bouillon cubes in 6 to 8 cups (1.5 to 2 L) of water.

🍢 For the meat, choose bottom round, sirloin point or Spencer steak (faux-filet). The meat should be sliced no more than ⅛ in. (0.3 cm) thick.

🍢 Arrange the meat slices on a platter. Cut the tofu into cubes and slice the green onions on the bias. Cut the Chinese cabbage into bite-size pieces. Arrange everything on the platter with the meat.

🍢 Strain the bouillon into a fondue pot or casserole that can be set on top of a burner. Bring the bouillon to a boil. It must continue to boil throughout the meal.

🍢 Each person will use a fondue fork or bamboo stick to plunge a piece of meat into the bouillon. Be careful not to drop the meat into the pot as it may overcook. The meat will be at its most tender and flavorful when it is still slightly rosy-colored. Each piece should then be dunked in dipping sauce (see recipe below) before it is eaten.

🍢 Once all the meat has been cooked and eaten, add the green onions and tofu cubes all at once to the boiling bouillon and cook for a few minutes. Add salt and pepper and serve the bouillon in small bowls that your guests can sip from.

🍢 To make the dipping sauce: toast 4 tbsp (60 mL) sesame seeds in a heavy skillet or in a 325°F (160°C) oven until golden. Combine the sesame seeds with the juice of 1 lemon or lime, 2 tbsp (30 mL) rice vinegar or cider vinegar, 3 tbsp (4 mL) soy sauce and 2 green onions, finely chopped.

GROUND BEEF

1 lb (500 g) of ground beef will make 4 ¼-lb (125-g) patties or 4 average servings.

🍴 You can buy meat already ground or have it ground for you from your preferred cut, such as top round or shoulder. Ask the butcher to put it through the grinder only once to make perfect burgers.

🍴 Ground meat does not store well in the refrigerator. Never buy it more than 2 days in advance. To store, remove it from its package and wrap loosely in wax paper.

🍴 Ground meat can be stored for up to 3 months in the freezer. To make thawing easier, shape the meat into patties and place a piece of wax paper between each patty. Wrap packages of 4 or 8 burgers in two layers of wax paper and seal in aluminum foil or in a freezer bag. For best results, thaw the meat before you cook it.

BASIC BEEF PATTIES

1 lb (500) ground beef
1 tsp (5 mL) salt
¼ tsp (1 mL) pepper
2 tbsp (30 mL) chopped onion
¼ tsp (1 mL) thyme
1 tbsp (15 mL) oil
paprika

🍴 Put all the ingredients into a bowl (omit the onion or thyme, if you wish) and combine them gently with a fork.

🍴 Shape the mixture into patties, handling the meat as little as possible. One pound (500 g) of ground beef will make 4 patties 3½ in. across and ¾ in. thick (9 x 2 cm) or 8 patties 3 in. across and ¼ in. thick (8 x 0.6 cm).

🍴 To pan-fry: heat the fat in a skillet. Sprinkle the patties with paprika. Place in the hot fat. Cook over medium heat, turning only once. Cook large patties 4 to 8 minutes, smaller ones 2 to 6 minutes.

🍴 To pan-broil: rub the inside of a warm skillet with a small piece of suet and sprinkle with salt. Cook the patties over medium heat. Cook large patties 4 to 8 minutes, smaller ones 2 to 6 minutes.

VARIATIONS
🍴 Wrap each patty in a slice of bacon.

🍴 Use only ¾ lb (375 g) meat, and add 1 cup (250 mL) chopped baked beans.
🍴 Add 1 cup (250 mL) grated cheese and ¼ cup (50 mL) water.
🍴 Add ¼ cup (50 mL) cream or evaporated milk.
🍴 Add 1¾ cups (425 mL) fresh breadcrumbs, 1 beaten egg and ¼ cup (50 mL) milk. (Yield: 6 large patties or 10 small ones.)
🍴 Thyme, marjoram, savory, celery leaves, parsley, onion and garlic are all appropriate seasonings for ground meat.

GROUND BEEF CASSEROLE

1 onion, chopped fine
2 tbsp (30 mL) fat
1 lb (500 g) ground beef
1 to 2 cups (250 to 500 mL) vegetables, cooked or canned
1 can tomato soup, undiluted

Basic Beef Patties

1 cup (250 mL) brown sauce
1 tsp (5 mL) salt
½ tsp (2 mL) French mustard
½ tsp (2 mL) thyme or savory

❧ Brown the chopped onion in hot fat. Add the ground beef and cook over high heat, stirring often, until the meat loses its pink tinge. Remove from the burner and stir in the vegetables, tomato soup, brown sauce, salt, mustard and thyme or savory. Mix well and turn into an ovenproof baking dish.

❧ Cover with mashed potatoes to which a whole egg has been added. (The egg is not essential but it improves the texture of the potatoes). Bake in a 375°F (190°C) oven for 15 to 20 minutes or until the sauce bubbles up around the potatoes.

❧ You can replace the ground beef with 2 cups (500 mL) of cooked meat, finely chopped.

BEEF AND CABBAGE CASSEROLE

½ medium cabbage, finely shredded
3 tbsp (45 mL) bacon or beef fat
1½ lbs (750 g) ground beef
2 onions, chopped fine
2 cups (500 mL) tomato sauce
½ tsp (2 mL) savory
1 clove garlic, minced
1 tsp (5 mL) salt
¼ tsp (1 mL) pepper
3 cups (750 mL) cooked rice

❧ Spread half the cabbage in a well-buttered baking dish.

❧ In a large skillet, heat the fat and add the ground beef. Cook, stirring from time to time, until the meat loses its pink tinge. Add the onions, ½ cup (125 mL) tomato sauce, savory, garlic, salt, pepper and rice. Stir to blend thoroughly.

❧ Pour another ½ cup (125 mL) of the tomato sauce over the cabbage in the baking dish. Spread the beef and rice mixture over the cabbage and top with the remaining shredded cabbage. Pour the second cup of tomato sauce over the top layer of cabbage. Bake 1 hour in a 350°F (180°C) oven.

FREEZER MEATBALLS AND SPAGHETTI SAUCE

I like to make large quantities of meatballs and spaghetti sauce and freeze them separately in meal-size containers. The following recipes produce enough sauce and meatballs to provide 4 4-cup (1-L) containers of each. The sauce and meatballs can be used together or separately in a variety of dishes, and it takes only 15 to 20 minutes to reheat a container. You can even keep precooked spaghetti on hand in your freezer.

MEATBALLS:
3 lbs (1.5 kg) ground beef
1 cup (250 mL) fine bread-crumbs
½ cup (125 mL) soda cracker crumbs
4 tbsp (60 mL) chopped parsley
½ tsp (2 mL) celery seed
2 cloves garlic, crushed
½ tsp (2 mL) nutmeg or allspice

½ tsp (2 mL) thyme
½ cup (125 mL) milk
6 eggs, beaten
2 tsp (10 mL) salt
½ tsp (2 mL) pepper
1 cup (250 mL) beef suet or oil

SPAGHETTI SAUCE:
2 large onions, sliced thin
6 cups (1.5 L) fresh or canned tomatoes
6 cups (1.5 L) water
3 chicken bouillon cubes
3 beef bouillon cubes
3 5½-oz (160 mL) cans tomato paste
2 tbsp (30 mL) sugar
3 tsp (15 mL) salt
1 tsp (5 mL) pepper
2 tsp (10 mL) basil
1 tsp (5 mL) oregano or marjoram
3 bay leaves

SPAGHETTI:
4 8-oz (250-g) packages spaghetti
olive oil
4 cups (1 L) grated cheese

❧ To prepare meatballs: combine the beef, breadcrumbs, cracker crumbs, parsley, celery seed, garlic, nutmeg, thyme, milk, eggs, salt and pepper. Shape into small balls. Heat the suet or oil in a skillet and brown the meatballs on all sides over medium heat. Cook the meatballs in batches rather than overfilling the pan. Let the meatballs cool before placing them in freezer containers.

❧ To use without sauce, warm up in a double boiler for 15 to 20 minutes.

To prepare spaghetti sauce: brown the onions in the fat leftover from frying the meatballs. Add more oil, if necessary, and the rest of the ingredients. Bring to a boil, stirring frequently. Simmer, uncovered, for about 2 hours. Let cool before ladling into freezer containers.

To serve: heat the spaghetti sauce slowly in a saucepan; it is not necessary to thaw it first. Add the meatballs and heat the meat and sauce together to serving temperature.

To prepare spaghetti: cook one package of spaghetti at a time according to package directions. Drain and stir in 2 to 3 tbsp (30 to 45 mL) olive oil. Wrap one serving-size amount of spaghetti around your hand and drop it onto a double thickness of freezer foil. Use the same procedure to make 5 more portions. Seal and freeze.

To reheat spaghetti: unwrap single portions, put one at a time in a strainer and plunge into boiling water for a few moments until hot. Drain and top with sauce and cheese.

Plan on 4 cups (1 L) sauce and 4 cups (1 L) meatballs for each 8-oz (250 g) package of spaghetti.

PORCUPINE BALLS

1½ lbs (750 g) ground beef
½ cup (125 mL) uncooked rice
1 tsp (5 mL) salt
½ tsp (2 mL) pepper
1 tbsp (15 mL) chopped onion

Family-size Meat Loaf

1 10½-oz (300 mL) can tomato soup
½ cup (125 mL) water
1 tsp (5 mL) sugar
½ tsp (2 mL) basil

Combine the meat, rice, salt, pepper and onion. Shape into small balls.

In a pressure-cooker, combine the tomato soup with the water, sugar and basil. Add the meat balls. Close cover securely. Cook 10 minutes at 15 lbs pressure. Let pressure drop of its own accord and serve.

FAMILY-SIZE MEAT LOAF

3 lbs (1.5 kg) ground beef or veal
2 eggs, lightly beaten
1 tbsp (15 mL) salt

1 onion, chopped fine
½ tsp (2 mL) ground mace or nutmeg
¼ tsp (1 mL) ground cloves
1 tsp (5 mL) savory
½ lb (250 g) ground ham or salt pork
1 cup (250 mL) breadcrumbs or soda cracker crumbs
juice of ½ lemon
½ cup (125 mL) tomato juice, heated

In a bowl, combine the ground beef, beaten eggs, salt, onion, spices, savory, ham or pork, breadcrumbs and lemon juice. Mix with the hands until blended. Press into a loaf pan.

Bake for 2 hours in a 350°F (180°C) oven, basting several times with the hot tomato juice. Makes 10 servings.

PERFECT MEAT LOAF DINNER

This meat loaf is simply delicious. I like to double the recipe, serving half hot for dinner and freezing the other loaf to have on hand for those occasions when there's no time to prepare dinner from scratch.

2 potatoes, peeled and diced
3 slices dry bread
1½ lbs (750 g) ground beef
½ lb (250 g) ground pork
or sausage meat
2 eggs, beaten
1 tsp (5 mL) salt
½ tsp (2 mL) pepper
1 onion, chopped fine
½ tsp (2 mL) celery seed
¼ tsp (1 mL) marjoram
or oregano
parsley to taste
6 portions instant mashed
potatoes

¼ cup (50 mL) sour cream
4 carrots, diced
2 stalks celery, diced
2 green onions, chopped
pinch of thyme
pinch of sugar
1 tsp (5 mL) butter
juice of 1 lemon
salt and pepper

❧ Cook the potatoes until soft in just enough water to cover. Drain and mash, reserving the cooking liquid.

❧ Crumble the bread slices into a large bowl and pour on ¼ cup (50 mL) of the hot potato water. Add the potatoes, mix well and add the ground beef, ground pork or sausage meat, eggs, salt, pepper, onion, celery seed, marjoram or oregano and parsley. Mix thoroughly. Pat into a loaf pan. Bake 1½ hours at 275°F (140°C).

❧ Prepare instant mashed potatoes according to the package directions for 6 portions, but using ½ cup (125 mL) less liquid. When mixed, stir in the ¼ cup (50 mL) sour cream.

❧ Put the carrots, celery, green onions, thyme and sugar in a saucepan. Barely cover with boiling water, cover the pan, and boil 5 minutes. Drain. Add the butter, lemon juice, and salt and pepper to taste.

❧ Serve the meat loaf with the potatoes and vegetables.

❧ To make individual servings for the freezer: cut 2 to 3 slices of meat loaf for each ovenproof plate and top with 1 tsp (5 mL) chili sauce or catsup. Put a serving of mashed potatoes and of vegetables on each plate. Cover with foil and freeze.

❧ To serve: without removing the foil, place the frozen servings in a 400°F (200°C) oven for 25 minutes.

DEVILED MEAT LOAF

⅔ cup (150 mL) breadcrumbs
1 cup (250 mL) milk
1½ lbs (750 g) ground beef
2 eggs, well beaten
½ cup (125 mL) grated onions
1 tsp (5 mL) salt
¼ tsp (1 mL) pepper
½ tsp (2 mL) sage or marjoram

DEVILED SAUCE:
3 tbsp (45 mL) brown sugar
¼ cup (50 mL) catsup

Deviled Meat Loaf

¼ tsp (1 mL) nutmeg
1 tsp (5 mL) dry mustard

❧ Soak the breadcrumbs in the milk for 20 minutes. Add the remaining ingredients and mix well. Turn into a greased loaf pan. Cover with the sauce and cook in a 350°F (180°C) oven for 1 hour.
❧ To prepare the sauce: mix the brown sugar, catsup, nutmeg and dry mustard until smooth.

BEEF AND RICE LOAF

1 egg, lightly beaten
1 lb (500 g) ground beef
1 tsp (5 mL) salt
½ tsp (2 mL) dry mustard
pinch of pepper
¼ tsp (1 mL) sage
½ cup (125 mL) milk
1 onion, grated
1 cup (250 mL) cooked rice

❧ Combine all the ingredients in a bowl.
❧ Pat the mixture into a greased loaf pan. Bake in a 350°F (180°C) oven for 45 minutes. Refrigerate at least 12 hours before serving.

INDIVIDUAL MEAT LOAVES

I like to make these little loaves for the freezer because they thaw and cook far more rapidly than ordinary meat loaves. The recipe came to me from a reader who had many good ideas about freezing foods.

2 eggs
1 cup (250 mL) milk

2 cups (500 mL) soft white breadcrumbs
2 tsp (10 mL) salt
1 tsp (5 mL) dry mustard
1 tsp (5 mL) turmeric
1 tsp (5 mL) celery seed or celery salt
¼ tsp (1 mL) pepper
1 large onion, chopped fine
2 lbs (1 kg) ground beef
paprika

❧ Beat the eggs in a bowl, stir in the milk and add the breadcrumbs. Let soak for a few minutes. Add the salt, dry mustard, turmeric, celery seed and pepper. Beat well. Add the onions and ground beef. Mix thoroughly.
❧ Shape the mixture into 12 small round loaves. Sprinkle each with paprika. Wrap individually in aluminum foil and freeze.
❧ Makes 12 single-serving loaves.
❧ Freezer storage limit: 2 to 3 months.
❧ To serve: remove the foil and place on an ovenproof dish. Bake in a preheated oven for 45 minutes at 375°F (190°C).

IRISH BURGERS

1½ lbs (750 g) ground beef
½ cup (125 mL) raw, finely chopped potatoes
½ cup (125 mL) raw, finely chopped carrots
½ cup (125 mL) chopped green onion
¼ tsp (1 mL) ground pepper
1½ tsp (7 mL) salt

1 tbsp (15 mL) Worcestershire sauce
1 egg
8 hamburger buns

❧ Combine the beef, potatoes, carrots, onion, pepper, salt, Worcestershire sauce and egg. Mix well. Shape into 8 patties. Grill about 8 minutes per side in a lightly oiled skillet.

BEEF EXPRESS

You can serve this mixture over spaghetti, on top of toasted hamburger buns or with sausages. It is also good combined with pasta in a casserole. You can even use it to stretch leftover meats or whatever else you have on hand. Because this recipe is so flexible, I like to make it in large quantities.

¼ cup (50 ml) drippings, fat or oil
4 onions, chopped
3 cloves garlic, chopped or 1 tsp (5 mL) garlic flakes
3 cups (750 mL) celery, chopped
4 lbs (2 kg) ground beef
4 tsp (20 mL) salt
½ tsp (2 mL) pepper
1 tsp (5 mL) savory
2 bay leaves
3 tbsp (45 mL) Worcestershire sauce
2 14-oz (400 mL) bottles catsup
1 tbsp (15 mL) brown sugar

❧ In a large pan, heat the drippings or oil and add the onions, garlic and celery. Stir over high

Stuffed Cabbage Leaves

heat until soft and lightly browned. Add the ground beef and cook, stirring, until the pink tinge disappears. Add the salt, pepper, savory, bay leaves, Worcestershire sauce, catsup and brown sugar. Bring to a boil and simmer over low heat for 40 to 50 minutes. The mixture can be served at this point.

❧ To freeze: pour into a bowl and cool in refrigerator. Skim off excess fat, if necessary. (Save the fat for cooking purposes; it adds flavor.)

❧ Pack into 2-cup (500-mL) containers. Seal, label, date and freeze.

❧ Makes 12 cups (3 L).

❧ Freezer storage limit: 3 to 6 months.

❧ To use: partially thaw in the covered container, overnight in the refrigerator, or under cold running water for 20 to 30 minutes or until the mixture slips out of the container. Heat and serve.

BEEF EXPRESS CASSEROLE

❧ Cook 1½ cups (500 mL) elbow macaroni or other pasta in plenty of boiling water. Heat 2 cups (500 mL) of partially thawed express hamburger mix. Stir in the pasta and 1 cup (250 mL) freshly cooked or leftover vegetables. Pour into a casserole dish. Sprinkle with ½ cup (125 mL) grated cheese. Cover and heat until cheese melts.

EXPRESS CASSEROLE WITH MEAT

❧ Dice 2 cups (500 mL) of any leftover meat. Heat 2 cups (500 mL) express mix. Cook 4 oz macaroni or 1 cup (250 mL) rice. Spread the rice or macaroni in the bottom of a casserole dish and cover with the diced meat. Pour the express mix on top. Sprinkle top with buttered crumbs. Bake 20 minutes in a 375°F (190°C) oven.

STUFFED CABBAGE LEAVES

1 medium cabbage, core removed
2 onions, finely chopped
⅔ cup (150 mL) oil
¾ cup (175 mL) cooked rice
2 tbsp (30 mL) tomato paste
1 tsp (5 mL) paprika
1 tsp (5 mL) mint
1 tbsp (15 mL) grated lemon zest
juice of ½ lemon
1½ lbs (750 g) ground beef
or pork
salt and pepper
2 slices bacon
1 cup (250 mL) tomato juice
1 tsp (5 mL) sugar

❧ Place the whole cabbage, cored, in a large pot of boiling salted water. Cook, uncovered, for 10 minutes. Drain and let cool.

❧ Fry the chopped onions in the oil. Add the rice and cook until golden. Add the tomato paste, paprika, mint and lemon zest and juice. Mix well and add the meat. Stir over high heat until the meat loses its pink tinge. Let cool slightly. Salt and pepper to taste.

STUFFED CABBAGE LEAVES

1 Blanch the cabbage leaves.

2 Fry the onions in the oil.

3 Add the rice and cook until golden.

4 Add the tomato paste.

🎗 Remove the blanched cabbage leaves, setting aside the larger ones for later. Place a large spoonful of the meat mixture on each of the more tender leaves and roll up into a fat cigar shape.

🎗 Oil or butter a casserole and cover the bottom with a few of the reserved, large cabbage leaves. Arrange the cabbage rolls on top. Lay the bacon slices on top. Add the tomato juice and sugar. Put a plate on top to keep the cabbage rolls in place. Cover and cook over very low heat for 2 to 3 hours.

OLD-FASHIONED MINCEMEAT

1½ lbs (750 g) lean beef
or venison
1½ lbs (750 g) ground pork
½ lb (250 g) lard or ground suet
4 cups (1 L) water
2 lbs (1 kg) raisins
2 lbs (1 kg) currants
2 whole oranges
2 whole lemons
8 cups (2 L) peeled apples, grated
2 lbs (1 kg) sugar
1 lb (500 g) dark brown sugar
½ lb (250 g) mixed candied peel
1 cup (250 mL) molasses
2 tsp (10 mL) ground cloves
3 tsp (15 mL) cinnamon
3 tsp (15 mL) ground ginger
1 tsp (5 mL) fresh grated nutmeg
1 cup (250 mL) apple juice, sherry, orange juice or rum

🎗 Place the beef or venison, pork, and suet or lard in a saucepan

with the water. Bring to a boil. Cover and simmer until the meat is tender. Drain and reserve the juice. Cool the meats and chop fine or put through a grinder.

🎗 Cook the raisins and currants for 20 minutes in the reserved juice, adding a little water if necessary to make a total of 3 cups (750 mL) liquid.

🎗 Grind the unpeeled oranges and lemons. Add the raisins and currants, the grated apples, the meat, suet and remaining ingredients. Simmer for 12 minutes, stirring often. Pour into sterilized jars and seal. The mincemeat will keep in the refrigerator for 4 to 6 months. This recipe is sufficient for 6 large pies.

POLISH MEATBALLS

4 slices rye or brown bread
½ cup (125 mL) water
1½ lbs (750 g) ground beef
1 onion, grated
1 tsp (5 mL) salt
¼ tsp (1 mL) pepper
1 tsp (5 mL) caraway seeds
1 cup (250 mL) sour cream
breadcrumbs
2 tbsp (30 mL) butter
½ beef bouillon cube
2 tbsp (30 mL) lemon juice
2 tbsp (30 mL) white wine
1 10½-oz (300 mL) can condensed cream-of-mushroom soup
chopped fresh parsley

🎗 Remove the crusts and tear the bread into small pieces. You should have 1½ cups (375 mL) of

bread. Add the water to the bread and let sit for 5 minutes. Squeeze out the excess liquid with your hands.

🎗 Put the bread into a mixing bowl and add the ground beef, grated onion, salt, pepper, caraway seeds and 2 tbsp (30 mL) of the sour cream. Blend thoroughly and shape into 1-in. (2.5-cm) balls. Roll in the breadcrumbs and fry in the hot butter in a large, deep skillet until browned on all sides.

🎗 Remove the meatballs from the pan and pour off any excess fat. Dissolve the ½ bouillon cube in ½ cup (125 mL) water and add to the pan with the lemon juice and white wine. Bring to a boil, blending the pan scrapings into the liquid with a wooden spoon. Gradually stir in the mushroom soup, undiluted, and the remainder of the sour cream. Blend well. Add the meatballs and heat gently until heated through, making sure the sour cream doesn't boil. Garnish with chopped fresh parsley.

HOME-STYLE BEEF FRICASSÉE

½ cup (125 mL) meat fat
or leftover gravy
2 to 3 cups (750 mL) cooked meat, diced
2 cups (500 mL) onions, chopped
4 cups (1 L) raw potatoes, diced

1 tsp (5 mL) savory
salt and pepper

🌿 Melt the fat, add the diced meat and onions and fry for a few minutes. Add the raw potato and savory. Salt and pepper to taste. Cover with water and cook over medium heat for 30 to 40 minutes, preferably covered.

🌿 This recipe seems simple, but it makes a delicious family supper. Here are a few tips that will make your fricassée even more tasty.

🌿 Chicken or turkey fat will make this dish taste even better.

🌿 If you have any leftover gravy, remove the fat from the top and add the brown jelly to the recipe.

🌿 The meat must always be diced finely.

🌿 If possible, use starchy "winter" potatoes rather than new potatoes; the starch helps thicken the sauce.

🌿 To give this dish a truly French-Canadian flavor, you must not forget the savory.

SHEPHERD'S PIE

3 tbsp (45 mL) meat fat
2 large onions, finely chopped
1 to 2 cups (500 mL) chopped, cooked leftover beef
or 1 lb (500 g) ground beef
½ tsp (2 mL) savory
salt and pepper to taste
1 can creamed corn
4 cups (1 L) mashed potatoes

Home-Style Beef Fricassée

🌿 In a large skillet, melt the fat and brown the onions in it over high heat. Add the leftover or ground meat, savory, salt and pepper. Stir over medium heat 3 to 4 minutes.

🌿 Spoon the meat mixture into a baking dish. Pour the corn over the meat and top with mashed potatoes. (Do not put milk in the potatoes, but add a little butter if you like.) Smooth the surface with a knife and dot with butter. Bake in a 375°F (190°C) oven for 15 to 20 minutes.

BEEF ROBERT

3 tbsp (45 mL) roast beef drippings
2 large onions, sliced
1 small clove garlic, minced

1½ tbsp (25 mL) mushrooms, cleaned and chopped
½ tsp (2 mL) paprika
½ tsp (2 mL) basil
pinch of ground cloves
jelly from roast beef gravy
2 tbsp (30 mL) brandy (optional)
1 can onion soup, undiluted
leftover roast beef

🌿 Melt the beef drippings and add the onions, garlic and mushrooms. When they are browned, add the remaining ingredients except for the onion soup and the beef. Cook, uncovered, over high heat, until the liquid is absorbed.

🌿 Add the onion soup and mix well. Pour this sauce over the leftover roast beef in an ovenproof dish. Bake in a 400°F (200°C) oven for 25 minutes.

🍃 This dish can also be made in a pressure-cooker but use only ½ the can of soup. Cook for 10 minutes.

BEEF CROQUETTES

2 cups (500 mL) cooked beef, ground
1 small onion, finely chopped
¼ cup (50 mL) parsley, minced
½ tsp (2 mL) salt
½ cup (125 mL) chili sauce
1 egg, lightly beaten
2 tbsp (30 mL) cold water
1 cup (250 mL) fine breadcrumbs
3 tbsp (45 mL) butter or oil

🍃 In a large bowl, combine the beef, onion, parsley, salt and chili sauce. Shape the mixture into small sausage-shaped or round croquettes.

🍃 Beat together the egg and cold water. Roll each croquette in the egg and then in the breadcrumbs.
🍃 Brown the croquettes in the hot oil or butter, over low heat. Serve with tomato sauce or on a bed of buttered spinach with white sauce.

GOURMET ROAST BEEF HASH

4 tbsp (60 mL) fat or butter
2 large onions, chopped
2 to 3 cups (500 to 750 mL) left-over roast beef, diced
2 cups (500 mL) boiled potatoes, diced
¼ cup (50 mL) fresh parsley, chopped
2 tsp (10 mL) soy sauce or A-1 sauce
1 tsp (5 mL) salt
¼ tsp (1 mL) pepper
¼ tsp (1 mL) thyme

Beef Croquettes

3 tbsp (45 mL) cream
1 egg per person

🍃 Melt the beef fat or butter in an electric skillet set at 300°F (150°C). Add the chopped onions and fry until golden.
🍃 In a bowl, combine the diced roast beef, fried onions, potatoes, parsley, soy sauce (or A-1 sauce), salt, pepper, thyme and cream. Add the mixture to the remaining fat in the skillet and pack it down lightly. Continue cooking at 300°F (150°C), turning from time to time, for 20 to 30 minutes or until bubbly. Break one egg per person on top of the hot hash and cover the skillet. Continue cooking until the eggs are set. Serve with chili sauce.
🍃 This is a soft hash, not the usual crisp-bottomed kind. I find it easier to make with the controlled heat of an electric skillet, but it can also be made on the stove top.

BOILED BEEF SALAD

2 to 3 cups (500 to 750 mL) left-over boiled beef
3 potatoes, chopped fine
1 small onion, minced
2 pickles, chopped fine
salt and pepper, to taste
¼ cup (50 mL) vegetable oil
3 tbsp (45 mL) cider vinegar or lemon juice
¼ cup (50 mL) mayonnaise
capers, to taste

🍃 Dice the boiled beef, trimming off all fat and gristle. Peel and dice the potatoes. Combine both with the diced onion. Add the chopped pickles and salt and pepper.

☙Combine the oil, vinegar or lemon juice and mayonnaise. Pour the mixture over the beef salad and mix well. Taste and adjust the seasonings. Serve on a nest of shredded cabbage. Garnish to taste with capers.

OXTAIL STEW DIJONNAISE

3 tbsp (45 mL) butter
2 oxtails cut in 2-in. (5-cm) pieces
2 10½-oz (300 mL) cans consommé, undiluted
1 large onion, sliced thin
1 clove garlic, minced
1 green pepper, diced
1 small can tomatoes
3 small carrots, sliced thin
1 tsp (5 mL) salt
6 peppercorns
1 tsp (5 mL) brown sugar
¼ tsp (1 mL) basil
pinch of marjoram
pinch of thyme
1 cup (250 mL) red wine
1 tsp (5 mL) lemon juice

☙ In a large pan, brown the oxtail in the butter over high heat. Place the meat in an earthenware casserole and cover it with the consommé. Brown the onion and garlic in the butter remaining in the pan. Spread over the oxtails. Add the rest of the ingredients. Cover the casserole and cook in a 325°F (160°C) oven 3 to 4 hours or until the oxtails are tender.

☙ To serve, arrange the oxtails in the center of a serving platter and surround with 6 to 8 small boiled potatoes rolled in finely chopped parsley. This casserole can be made two or three days before serving. It reheats very well.

BRAISED BEEF HEART

1 beef heart
¼ cup (50 mL) vinegar
½ cup (125 mL) dry breadcrumbs
2 strips bacon, diced small
parsley and basil, to taste
juice and grated zest of ½ lemon
1 tsp (5 mL) salt
½ tsp (2 mL) pepper
1 egg, lightly beaten
1 cup (250 ml browned flour
5 tbsp (75 mL) fat or oil
1 cup (250 mL) milk
1 cup (250 mL) water

☙ Put the heart in a large bowl and cover with cold water. Add the vinegar and soak for 4 hours. Drain and cut out the inside membranes with scissors.

☙ Combine the breadcrumbs, chopped bacon, parsley, basil, lemon juice, zest, salt and pepper. Add the egg. Stuff the heart with this mixture. Sew the openings shut so the stuffing does not escape.

☙ Dredge the heart in the browned flour and brown on all sides in the fat of your choice. Add the milk and the cup of water. Cover and simmer 2 to 4 hours or bake in a 350°F (180°C) oven 5 to 7 hours.

☙ This dish can be served hot with tomato sauce. If you want to serve it cold, let it cool in its own juices and serve it with mustard and pickled beets.

BEEF LIVER JULIENNE

1 lb (500 g) beef liver
2 tbsp (30 mL) flour
1 tsp (5 mL) salt
¼ tsp (1 mL) pepper
pinch of thyme
1 tsp (5 mL) paprika
2 tbsp (30 mL) butter
2 tbsp (30 mL) vegetable oil
2 onions, chopped fine
½ cup (125 mL) parsley, chopped fine
½ cup (125 mL) consommé
or sherry
1 cup (250 mL) sour cream

☙ Cut the liver in narrow strips (julienne). Combine the flour with the salt, pepper, thyme and paprika. Dredge the liver in the seasoned flour. Fry in the hot butter and oil, over high heat, for 2 minutes, stirring constantly. Remove the liver from the pan.

☙ Add the onions and parsley to the remaining fat in the pan. Stir over medium heat 2 or 3 minutes. Add the consommé or sherry and the beef liver. Cover and simmer over very low heat for 30 to 40 minutes.

☙ Just before serving time, stir in the sour cream and taste for seasoning. Stir constantly over medium heat for a few minutes but do not allow to boil or the cream will curdle. Serve with boiled rice.

LIVER AND BACON LOAF

½ lb (250 g) beef liver
8 strips bacon
1 large onion, chopped fine
2 shredded wheat biscuits, crumbled
3 eggs, beaten
1 cup (250 mL) milk
2 tbsp (30 mL) molasses
¾ cup (175 mL) cornmeal
2 tsp (10 mL) salt
½ tsp (2 mL) pepper
½ tsp (2 mL) marjoram
½ cup (125 mL) catsup

❧ Grind the liver and 4 of the bacon strips in a food chopper, using the medium blade. Put into a bowl and stir in the onion, shredded wheat, eggs, milk, molasses, cornmeal, salt, pepper and marjoram. Blend thoroughly.

❧ Line a loaf pan with the remaining bacon. Pour in the liver mixture. Spread the top with the catsup (and place a few more strips of bacon on top, if you like). Bake 1½ hours in a 350°F (180°C) oven.

❧ Serve hot with a white sauce flavored with parsley. Or serve cold with potato salad. This loaf also makes excellent sandwiches.

BEEF TONGUE CUMBERLAND

1 fresh 3- to 4-lb (1.5-kg) beef tongue
2 onions, sliced
2 bay leaves
few celery leaves
½ unpeeled lemon, sliced thin
6 peppercorns
or ½ tsp (2 mL) ground pepper
1 tbsp (15 mL) coarse salt

CUMBERLAND SAUCE:
1 tbsp (15 mL) butter
1 tbsp (15 mL) flour
½ cup (125 mL) cider vinegar
¼ cup (50 mL) red wine
or apple juice
½ cup (125 mL) brown sugar
ground cloves, cinnamon and nutmeg to taste
½ cup (125 mL) raisins
1 cup (250 mL) pitted prunes (optional)

❧ Cover the tongue with cold water and soak for 1 hour. Drain and place in a large casserole or heavy pot. Cover with cold water. Add the onions, bay leaves, celery leaves, lemon slices, peppercorns and salt. Bring to a boil, cover and simmer 2 to 3 hours or until the tongue is tender. (You can tell that the tongue is cooked if the skin pulls off easily.) Remove from the broth and peel off the skin. Serve hot or let it cool in the cooking broth.

❧ To prepare *Cumberland Sauce:* melt the butter, add the flour and mix well. Add the vinegar and wine and stir over medium heat until the sauce is smooth and creamy. Stir in the brown sugar and spices. Add the raisins and pitted prunes. (Unless the prunes are very soft, they should be soaked in apple juice for several hours before adding to the sauce.)

❧ Pour the sauce over the drained tongue in the casserole dish and simmer for ½ hour, turning the tongue several times.

Beef Tongue Cumberland

BEEF TONGUE STEW

1 fresh, smoked or salted
beef tongue
1 bay leaf
6 peppercorns
¼ tsp (1 mL) pepper
2 cloves
1 onion, quartered
celery leaves
1 leek

🍂 Soak the fresh tongue 3 hours in cold water. Salted or smoked tongue must be soaked at least overnight. Drain the tongue.

🍂 Put the tongue in a large heavy pot with the remaining ingredients and enough fresh water to cover. Bring to a boil, cover and simmer for 2 to 3 hours or until the tongue is tender. (The tongue is cooked when the skin can be peeled off easily.) When cooked, remove from the broth and peel off the skin. Serve hot or let it cool in the broth.

BEEF AND KIDNEY PIE

1 cup (250 mL) kidney fat, diced
1 beef kidney, diced
1 lb (500 g) stewing beef, diced
3 onions, chopped
3 cups (750 mL) hot water
1 tsp (5 mL) salt
½ tsp (2 mL) pepper
1 tsp (5 mL) dry mustard
½ cup (125 mL) browned flour
½ cup (125 mL) cold water

🍂 Render the kidney fat until crisp. Add the diced kidney and

Beef Tongue Stew

stewing beef and brown over high heat for 2 minutes. Add the onions and continue to brown. Add the hot water, salt, pepper and mustard. Bring to a boil. Cover and cook over low heat for 2 hours or until the kidney is tender. When cooked, thicken the broth by adding the browned flour blended with the cold water.

🍂 Line a casserole dish or deep pie plate with pastry. (I suggest *Hot Water Pie Crust*, page 520.) Fill the dish with the beef and kidney mixture and cover with a top crust. Seal the edges. Bake in a 400°F (200°C) oven until the crust is golden brown. Serve with mashed potatoes.

🍂 If you don't have time to make pie crust, this recipe can also be served on crispy toast triangles.

QUICK KIDNEY DELIGHT

1 beef kidney
4 tbsp (60 mL) butter
½ tsp (2 mL) mustard
pinch of tarragon
juice of 1 lemon
salt and pepper to taste

🍂 This recipe can be prepared in a skillet on the stove top, but it is so simple that it can also be prepared right at the table in a chafing dish or electric skillet.

🍂 In advance, slice the kidney as thin as possible. Arrange the slices on a platter in an overlapping pattern. Place the butter in a small earthenware bowl. In a second bowl, combine the mustard, tarragon, lemon juice and salt and pepper. Keep refrigerated until ready to serve.

🍃 To prepare at the table, arrange all ingredients on a tray. Melt the butter in the pan or chafing dish until brown. Add the kidney, one slice at a time, arranging the pieces side by side. Cook for ½ minute on each side, turning only once. Add the mustard mixture and stir just until the mixture starts to boil. Serve with parsleyed buttered rice.

🍃 The secret to success with this dish is to slice the kidney as thin as possible and to cook it over high heat as quickly as possible, otherwise the kidney will be tough.

KIDNEY CASSEROLE À LA FRANÇAISE

3 tbsp (45 mL) butter
2 beef kidneys, diced
1 large can tomatoes
1 tbsp (15 mL) sugar
2 cloves garlic, minced
4 onions, sliced
¼ tsp (1 mL) marjoram
pinch of thyme
1 bay leaf
2 whole cloves
1 cup (250 mL) red wine
salt and pepper to taste

🍃 Heat the butter until brown. Add the diced kidneys and stir over high heat until they lose their pink tinge.

🍃 Pour in the tomatoes and sprinkle in the sugar. Stir in the garlic, onions, marjoram, thyme, bay leaf and cloves. Cover and simmer over low heat, or cook in a 325°F (160°C) oven for 2 hours.

🍃 Add the red wine, salt and pepper to taste, and cook uncovered until the sauce has a rich consistency. Serve with boiled noodles or over toasted English muffins.

TRIPE À LA MODE DE CAEN

3 lbs (1.5 kg) tripe
2 to 3 lbs (1 to 1.5 kg) veal knuckle
¼ lb (125 g) beef fat
4 medium onions, sliced
1 bay leaf
½ tsp (2 mL) thyme
1 tbsp (15 mL) coarse salt
½ tsp (2 mL) pepper
¼ cup (50 mL) cognac
or red wine

🍃 Ask the butcher to cut the veal knuckle into 1-in. (2.5-cm) pieces. Cut the tripe into 4- x 2-in. (10- x 5-cm) strips. Dice the beef fat.

🍃 Cover the bottom of a casserole or deep ovenproof dish with a layer of beef fat and top with successive layers of tripe and veal knuckle. Add the rest of the ingredients and enough red wine to cover the meat.

🍃 Cover and cook for 3 hours in a 350°F (180°C) oven. Reduce the heat to 250°F (120°C) and cook for a further 5 hours. Remove from the oven and allow to cool. Skim off the grease and reheat. Serve hot, with baked potatoes.

VEAL

VEAL

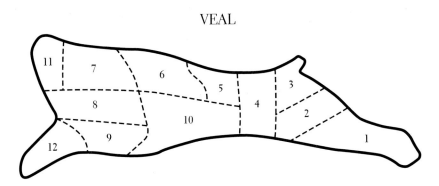

1. Hind shank
2. Round
3. Rump
4. Sirloin
5. Loin (filet end)
6. Loin (rib end)
7. Shoulder (blade)
8. Shoulder (arm section)
9. Breast
10. Flank
11. Neck
12. Fore shank

VEAL

HIND SHANK
Hind shank of veal is cut from the lower part of the leg. It is a meaty cut, with little fat, and is often boned and stuffed for roasting.

ROUND
Round of veal is cut from the mid-section of the leg and contains the small round bone. It can be purchased whole, boned and rolled, or cut in thin slices for cutlets.

RUMP
The rump of veal is a lean, triangular-shaped cut from the top of the leg. This cut is more tender than the shank section, but the bone formation makes it more difficult to carve.

SIRLOIN
The sirloin is a meaty section next to the rump. This part is good for roasting and can also be boned and stuffed. You can also buy sirloin sliced into steaks.

LOIN (FILET END)
The leg end of the loin, next to the sirloin butt, contains the T-shape bones and tenderloin and is very meaty. It is also the most tender cut of veal and is served as roasts or as chops.

LOIN (RIB END)
The rib section of the loin is less meaty than the leg end. It contains rib bones and none of the tenderloin. When you buy it, have the butcher partially cut through the backbone to make carving easier. Roasted, this cut has more flavor than the leg section but is less economical. The chops cut from this section are triangular in shape; they are cheaper than loin chops and very tasty.

SHOULDER (BLADE)
The shoulder roast contains the thin blade bone, which can be removed if you plan to stuff the roast or simply to make carving easier. This cut is excellent for roasting, but can also be sliced and braised, sautéed or cooked in a sauce.

SHOULDER (ARM SECTION)
This section, cut from next to the blade, is finer in texture. It contains the small, round shoulder bone and rib bones. This section is the source of the arm roast and arm steak. Roasts may be partly or completely boned.

✿ Rolled shoulder roast is made from the whole shoulder, both blade and arm section. It is often sold with a thin layer of fat tied on. This roast is handy to keep in the freezer, but should be thawed before roasting.

BREAST
The breast section, next to the round shoulder, contains layers of lean meat, fat and bone. Use this cut for stews, fricassees and braising.

FLANK
Like the breast, the flank contains layers of lean meat, fat and bone, but the flank is less meaty. It may be left whole for braising or boned, sliced or ground.

NECK
This section contains considerable bone. It can be purchased whole or cut up, and is used most often for stews and stocks.

FORE SHANK
This cut, from the front leg, contains coarse meat with bone and gristle. The less meaty lower section is often used to make gelatin.

The meatier upper section is used for soups, stews and fricassees.

TIPS FOR PREPARING VEAL

PURCHASE AND PREPARATION

Veal is most plentiful and at its best in the spring and early summer months, but is usually available year round. It comes from young animals 3 to 12 weeks old, but is not as tasty when the animal is less than 8 weeks old. Look for pearly white and firm flesh; the fat should be matte white.

☙ The loin, the leg and the shoulder roast can be oven-roasted or pot-roasted.

☙ Chops cut from the loin are best for pan-frying.

☙ To prepare stews, soups or the famous blanquette de veau, use meat from the shank, flank or shoulder.

☙ Calf's liver, brains and sweetbreads are the most popular variety meats from veal.

SEASONINGS

The flavorings and seasonings that work best with veal include thyme, chives, parsley, tarragon, bay leaf, savory, garlic, onions, celery leaves, nutmeg and tomatoes.

ACCOMPANIMENTS

The best vegetables to serve with veal are green peas, boiled onions, mushrooms, Brussels sprouts, green beans, spinach, asparagus, cucumber, carrots and corn.

☙ For condiments, choose from: cranberry sauce, chili sauce, currant jelly and sweet pickles.

ROASTING CHART FOR VEAL

Cut	Oven Temperature	Cooking time (minutes per lb/500 g)
Rump	325°F (160°C)	25 to 30 minutes
Leg	325°F (160°C)	20 to 25 minutes
Shoulder (blade)	325°F (160°C)	25 to 30 minutes
Loin (rib)	325°F (160°C)	25 to 30 minutes

☙ Leftover veal is easy to use in salads, white or tomato sauce, croquettes, pâté or simply as a delicious cold cut.

ROAST VEAL

☙ Veal must always be roasted slowly, so that the meat doesn't toughen.

veal roast
salt and pepper to taste
garlic cloves
2 tbsp (30 mL) butter
3 tbsp (45 mL) fat
1 tsp (5 mL) dry mustard
1 onion, thinly sliced
1 tsp (5 mL) thyme, tarragon
or bay leaf

☙ Season the roast generously with salt and pepper and stud with slivers of garlic, if desired. Cream the butter and the fat together with the dry mustard. Spread this mixture over the veal. Cover the roast with the sliced onion. Sprinkle with the herb of your choice. Do not add any liquid to the roasting pan and do not cover.

☙ Put the roast in a preheated 350°F (180°C) oven and cook for the time indicated on the roasting chart above. Baste 2 to 3 times during the roasting period.

☙ To give a rich, rosy hue to the finished roast and pan drippings, add 2 tbsp (30 mL) catsup or tomato paste and 1 tbsp (15 mL) paprika to the creamed fat and mustard mixture.

PRESSURE-COOKER VEAL ROAST

☙ Cooking veal in a pressure-cooker requires more care and attention than other types of meat.

☙ Wash the leg of veal with vinegar first, then make incisions and insert small slivers of garlic in them, or flavor the veal with a little thyme or tarragon. Sprinkle the meat with 1 tbsp (15 mL) paprika.

1 tbsp (15 mL) vegetable oil
2 tbsp (30 mL) bacon fat
or butter
leg of veal, 4 to 5 lbs (2 kg)
1 tsp (5 mL) salt
½ tsp (2 mL) pepper
1 onion, minced

☙ Heat the oil and the bacon fat in the pressure-cooker. When hot, brown the meat lightly on all sides. Season and cover with the onion.

eal the lid and cook the leg ... 30 minutes. (A rolled veal shoulder roast will take about 50 minutes.) Remove from heat and release the pressure. The veal is ready to serve.

❧ Even without the addition of liquid, a 4- to 5-lb (2-kg) roast will produce 1½ to 2 cups (375 to 500 mL) delicious pan juices, which you can serve as is with the veal.

Veal Marengo

3 lbs (1.5 kg) veal shoulder
or breast
2 tbsp (30 mL) olive oil
1 cup (250 mL) onions, minced
2 tbsp (30 mL) flour
1 tsp (5 mL) salt
¼ tsp (1 mL) pepper
2 cups (500 mL) white wine
1 lb (500 g) fresh tomatoes
or 1½ cups (375 mL) drained
canned tomatoes

½ tsp (2 mL) basil
½ tsp (2 mL) thyme
1 piece orange zest
about 3 x 1 in. (7.5 x 2.5 cm)
2 cloves garlic, crushed
½ lb (250 g) mushrooms
1½ tbsp (25 mL) cornstarch
1 tbsp (15 mL) water
3 tbsp (45 mL) chopped parsley

❧ Cut the veal into 2-in. (5-cm) cubes. Heat the oil in a large skillet and brown the meat cubes over high heat. Remove the meat from the oil.

❧ Lower the heat. Brown the onions in the same fat for 5 to 6 minutes. While the onions are cooking, dredge the meat with the flour seasoned with the salt and pepper. Add the meat to the onions and brown over medium heat for 3 to 4 minutes. Remove the meat from the pan.

❧ Add the wine to the onions. Boil for 1 minute, scraping the bottom of the skillet well. Add the meat and return to a boil, stirring constantly.

❧ Peel and seed the tomatoes and cut them in small pieces. Add them to the meat, along with the basil, thyme, orange zest and garlic. Salt and pepper to taste. Cover and simmer for 1 to 1½ hours or until the meat is tender.

❧ Add the mushrooms. Simmer for 15 minutes more. Skim off the excess fat and thicken the gravy with the cornstarch dissolved in the cold water.

❧ Turn the veal mixture into a heated serving dish and sprinkle with chopped fresh parsley. Serve with boiled noodles.

Viennese Veal

2 veal steaks cut ½ in. (1 cm)
thick
4 tbsp (60 mL) flour
salt and pepper
2 tbsp (30 mL) butter
2 large onions, sliced
1 tsp (5 mL) paprika
½ lemon, unpeeled, thinly sliced
1 cup (250 mL) sour cream
parsley

❧ Cut the veal into individual portions. Dredge the veal in the flour seasoned with salt and pepper.

❧ Melt the butter in the bottom of a pressure-cooker until golden. Brown the veal on both sides. Add the onions and paprika to the fat and stir over medium heat until limp.

❧ Arrange the veal pieces in a layer on the bottom of the pot,

Veal Marengo

❧ TECHNIQUE ❧
VEAL MARENGO

1 Brown the cubes of veal in the oil.

2 Remove the meat. Brown the onions in the same pan.

3 Add the white wine.

4 Dredge the cubes of veal in the flour.

cover with the onions and top each veal piece with a slice of lemon. Pour the sour cream over all.

❧ Close the lid of the pressure-cooker and cook for 10 to 12 minutes. Let the pressure drop of its own accord. Garnish the meat with parsley.

BRAISED VEAL

3 to 4 lbs (1.5 kg) leg of veal
or 3 to 5 lbs (1.5 to 2.5 kg) rolled veal shoulder
2 cloves garlic
3 tbsp (45 mL) fat
1 tsp (5 mL) salt
½ tsp (2 mL) pepper
¼ tsp (1 mL) thyme or savory
6 medium onions
6 potatoes

❧ Make a few incisions in the meat with a sharp knife and insert slivers of the garlic cloves.

❧ Melt the fat in a large cast-iron or enamelled saucepan or casserole and brown the meat on all sides over medium heat. It is important to brown the meat slowly and thoroughly. Sprinkle with the salt and pepper and the thyme or savory. Arrange the peeled whole onions and potatoes around the meat. Do not add any liquid.

❧ Cover and cook over low heat for 1½ to 2 hours or until the meat is tender.

❧ Move the meat from the pan to a heated platter. Roll the onions and potatoes in the pan juices to coat (there should be 1 to 1½ cups or nearly 375 mL of pan juices left).

❧ Surround the meat with the vegetables and serve the gravy separately in a gravy boat.

FRENCH-STYLE BRAISED LOIN OF VEAL

4 tbsp (60 mL) butter
4 medium onions, sliced
1 loin of veal, 3 to 4 lbs (1.5 kg)
2 tbsp (30 mL) flour
salt and pepper
basil or thyme, to taste
1 cup (250 mL) consommé
8 oyster plants, diced
¼ cup (50 mL) cream

❧ Melt the butter in a skillet. Fry the onions in the butter, then remove them from the pan. Place the veal in the pan and brown it on all sides. Sprinkle on the flour and blend it in well. Season to taste with the salt, pepper and herb of your choice. Add the consommé.

❧ Cover and simmer for 25 minutes per lb (500 g) of meat.

❧ A half hour before the end of the cooking period, add the oyster plants (or other vegetables). Just before serving, skim off the fat and stir the cream into the gravy.

STUFFED BREAST OF VEAL

1 clove garlic
1 egg
3 tbsp (45 mL) sherry
or lemon juice
1 tsp (5 mL) salt
½ tsp (2 mL) pepper
¼ tsp (1 mL) nutmeg
¼ cup (50 mL) chopped fresh parsley
½ lb (250 g) ground pork (optional)
2 cups (500 mL) fine breadcrumbs
1 boned breast of veal, 3 to 4 lbs (1.5 kg)

❧ To make the stuffing: rub a bowl with the garlic, break the egg into it and add the sherry or lemon juice, salt, pepper, nutmeg and parsley. Beat together well, then add the ground pork and breadcrumbs. Mix well.

❧ Stuff the cavity of the veal breast with the breadcrumb stuffing. Sew the cavity closed with heavy white thread, just as you would a turkey.

❧ Cook the stuffed veal following the directions for *Braised Veal* (see above). Serve.

❧ This variation of braised veal is economical because you can serve it hot for one meal, then refrigerate the leftovers and serve them as a delicious stuffed cold meat, quite similar to stuffed turkey.

❧ If any pan juices remain along with the leftover veal, pour them over the veal before it cools; this will form a delicious brown jelly.

BLANQUETTE DE VEAU

A fine veal blanquette is delicious, a dish you can serve your guests with pride. The following recipe applies equally well to other white meats such as poultry, rabbit and lamb.

❧ A blanquette may be served as is or with a garnish, the most common being small white onions and mushrooms (two onions and a mushroom on each plate).

🍃 For a starchy dish, serve with boiled noodles or steamed rice, flavored with parsleyed butter.

🍃 Whichever meat you choose to use, the preparation of a blanquette is always the same, the only difference being cooking time. For example, veal should cook for at least 1½ hours, whereas lamb needs only 60 minutes.

🍃 For a veal blanquette, use veal breast or shoulder. You can also combine various cuts. Choose quality veal that is pinkish-white in color. You will need about ¼ to ½ lb (125 to 250 g) of meat per person.

🍃 Use a deep saucepan that is just large enough to hold the meat cubes in several layers; this limits the amount of liquid required to cover the meat, thus producing a far richer and more successful gravy. If too much liquid is used, the broth will be less concentrated and the gravy will be less tasty. Use a heavy stainless-steel or enameled cast-iron saucepan, but avoid plain cast-iron, which will give a grayish tinge to the dish.

🍃 This recipe takes about 2½ hours to prepare and serves 6 to 8 people .

Blanquette de Veau

MEAT:

2 lbs (1 kg) veal breast
or shoulder
4 cups (1 L) cold water
1 tsp (5 mL) salt
1 large onion
1 whole clove
2 medium carrots
1 stalk celery
¼ tsp (1 mL) thyme
1 bay leaf

¼ tsp (1 mL) pepper

GARNISH:

12 to 15 small onions
1 tbsp (15 mL) butter
2 tbsp (30 mL) juice from
cooking the veal
pinch of sugar
8 fresh mushrooms
½ cup (125 mL) water
pinch of salt
1 tbsp (15 mL) lemon juice
1 tsp (5 mL) butter

SAUCE:

3 tbsp (45 mL) butter
3 tbsp (45 mL) flour
4 cups (1 L) cooking broth
from the veal
stems of 8 mushrooms, chopped
pinch of nutmeg
2 egg yolks
½ cup (125 mL) cream
1 tbsp (15 mL) lemon juice
1 tbsp (15 mL) chopped fresh
parsley

🍃 Cut the meat into 1-in. (2.5-cm) cubes. Place in the pot with the cold water and the salt. Slowly bring to a boil, being careful not to sear the meat. Once the liquid comes to a gentle boil, add the onion stuck with the clove, the thinly sliced carrots, the diced celery, thyme, bay leaf and pepper.

🍃 Bring the mixture to a boil, cover and simmer over low heat for about 1 hour or until the meat is cooked but still firm.

🍃 In the meantime, prepare the garnish. Peel and cook the small onions separately, to ensure that they keep not only their shape but also their full flavor. (A hint for peeling onions: place them in a sieve and dip them in boiling water for 1 minute; this will loosen the skin and you will be able to peel them easily, without tears.) Once the onions are peeled, make a crosswise incision

❦ TECHNIQUE ❦

BLANQUETTE DE VEAU

1 Put the meat in a saucepan with the cold water and salt. Bring slowly to a boil.

2 Add the vegetables and seasonings.

3 Add the cooking juices to the flour and butter mixture.

4 Beat the egg yolks with the cream and lemon juice. Add to the sauce mixture.

at the root with the point of a small knife.

❧ Melt the 1 tbsp (15 mL) butter and add the 2 tbsp (30 mL) juice from the cooked veal, the cooked onions and the pinch of sugar. Cover and simmer over very low heat, stirring from time to time, until the onions are white and slightly glazed but not browned. This should take 20 to 30 minutes. Keep warm until ready to use.

❧ Clean the 8 mushrooms and remove the stems, reserving these for the sauce. Bring to a boil the ½ cup (125 mL) water, the salt and the 1 tbsp (15 mL) lemon juice. When the water comes to a boil, add the mushrooms and the 1 tsp (5 mL) butter. Bring to a rolling boil, then cover and remove from the heat. Let stand 5 minutes.

❧ Drain the mushrooms, reserving the cooking liquid for use in the sauce.

❧ To make the sauce, melt the 3 tbsp (45 mL) butter in a saucepan and stir in the 3 tbsp (45 mL) flour. Cook over very low heat for 1 minute. Strain the 4 cups (1 L) cooking broth from the veal and slowly add it. Bring to a boil, stirring constantly. Add the 8 chopped mushroom stems and the pinch of nutmeg. Simmer for 10 minutes, stirring often. Gradually add the cooking liquid from the mushrooms.

❧ Beat the 2 egg yolks with the ½ cup (125 mL) cream and 1 tbsp (15 mL) lemon juice.

❧ Remove the sauce from the heat and stir in the egg-yolk mixture.

❧ Add the cooked meat, onions,

mushrooms and chopped fresh parsley to the sauce. Taste for seasoning.

❧ Reheat, if necessary, and serve.

VEAL PRINTANIER

2 lbs (1 kg) veal shoulder,
cut in large cubes
2 tbsp (30 mL) butter or veal fat
3 cups (750 mL) thin white sauce
(see page 46)
pinch of thyme
1 bay leaf
pinch of marjoram
¼ lb (125 g) mushrooms, sliced
¼ cup (50 mL) diced turnip
12 small whole onions
2 carrots, diced
1 cup (250 mL) green peas

❧ Brown the cubes of veal in the melted butter or fat. Add the white sauce and the herbs.

❧ Cover and simmer for 1 hour,

stirring occasionally. Add the vegetables and cook for another ½ hour or until the vegetables are tender.

ABOUT VEAL CHOPS

Veal chops can be prepared in many ways, but by far the most popular method is to brown them in a skillet, nap them with a sauce and garnish them with vegetables.

❧ They should always be cooked over medium-low heat, for about 10 to 15 minutes on each side, and turned only once.

❧ Veal chops are tastiest when cooked in butter or olive oil; you will need 1 tsp (5 mL) of butter or oil for each chop.

❧ The best accompaniments for veal chops are puréed spinach, creamed or buttered carrots, potato croquettes, green peas, green beans, noodles with butter or

Veal Printanier

Sautéed Veal Chop

until the sauce comes to a boil. Pour it over the chop.

ABOUT VEAL CUTLETS

The thin, boneless pieces of meat called cutlets are the basis for collops or "escalopes," scallopine or schnitzels, and the method of cooking is pretty well always the same. Although these well-known dishes are usually prepared with veal, pork can also be used.

ı Cutlets are cut from the leg or from the boned loin, the latter being more expensive. (Pork cutlets are also taken from the leg or the tenderloin.)

ı A leg of veal has three distinct sections. The best one to use for cutlets is the round, referred to in French as the "noix." Ask the butcher to cut it on a slight diagonal in slices ¼ to ⅜ in. (0.65 to 1 cm) thick, carefully trimmed of all fat and sinew.

ı To prepare the cutlets for cooking, place a single slice between 2 squares of wax paper and pound it with a wooden mallet or the flat side of a cleaver or large knife until it is ¹⁄₁₆ in. (0.15 cm) thick. The meat should be flattened evenly, and it should retain its original shape.

ı I prefer to cut my own cutlets, so I buy a 2-to 2½-lb (1-kg) piece of top round of veal. With a sharp knife, I cut the piece into thin steaks and then I pound them. This is not only cheaper, I get my cutlets exactly the way I like them. (The meat will slice easily if it is first chilled overnight or

Parmesan cheese, rice cooked with tomatoes, stuffed tomatoes or mashed potatoes.

VEAL CHOPS AU JUS

veal chops
1 tsp (5 mL) butter for each chop
salt and pepper
4 tbsp (60 mL) white wine

ı Melt the butter in a skillet. Add the chops, seasoned with salt and pepper, and cover. Brown over medium heat; turn the chops and brown the other side.

ı Add the white wine, cover and simmer over low heat for 4 to 6 minutes.

SAUTÉED VEAL CHOP

1 veal chop
salt and pepper

paprika
1 tsp (5 mL) butter or oil
4 to 5 tbsp (60 to 75 mL) cold tea, coffee, water, white wine, orange juice or tomato juice

ı With a sharp knife, remove the membrane around the chop as well as the bone. (The bone will prevent the chop from browning evenly.)

ı Flatten the chop by hammering it lightly on both sides with the flat of a large knife. Salt and pepper the chop and sprinkle with paprika. Melt the butter or oil in a skillet, add the chop and cook until golden brown, uncovered, over medium heat for 15 to 20 minutes on each side, turning only once.

ı To make the gravy, remove the meat from the skillet and add the liquid of your choice, stirring and scraping the bottom of the pan placed in the freezer for 1 hour.)

&❧ Always remember that veal cutlets need very little cooking; 3 to 4 minutes on each side is enough, because the pounding breaks down the muscle fibers. A cast-iron skillet is ideal for cooking cutlets, but do not crowd them in the pan.

&❧ To serve 6 to 8, you will need 2 lbs (1 kg) of cutlets.

VEAL CUTLETS PARISIENNE

2 lbs (1 kg) veal cutlets
1 tsp (5 mL) salt
¼ tsp (1 mL) freshly ground pepper
¼ tsp (1 mL) thyme
¼ tsp (1 mL) paprika
4 tbsp (60 mL) butter
4 tbsp (60 mL) cognac
1 cup (250 mL) heavy cream
mushrooms

&❧ Prepare the cutlets according to the directions on the opposite page. Combine the salt, pepper, thyme and paprika and sprinkle this on the veal.

&❧ Sauté the cutlets in the browned butter over medium heat for about 3 minutes on each side. Remove them to a heated platter.

&❧ Pour the cognac over the cutlets and set it aflame; let the flame die down. Pour the cream into the skillet and stir, scraping the bottom of the pan thoroughly so the drippings are well combined with the cream. Bring to a boil, then simmer for 2 to 3 minutes, stirring constantly, until the cream thickens slightly

and changes texture.

&❧ Pour over the veal and serve with mushrooms sautéed in butter.

VEAL CORDON BLEU

6 small slices veal steak
6 thin slices Mozzarella cheese
6 thin slices cooked ham
Dijon mustard
2 eggs
2 tbsp (30 mL) water
1½ cups (375 mL) fine dry breadcrumbs
1 tsp (5 mL) salt
¼ tsp (1 mL) pepper
¼ tsp (1 mL) thyme
¼ tsp (1 mL) garlic powder
¼ cup (50 mL) vegetable oil
¼ cup (50 mL) butter
1 cup (250 mL) dry white wine or dry vermouth

&❧ Pound each slice of veal until paper thin. On each slice, lay a

slice of cheese and a slice of ham. Baste the ham with a little Dijon mustard. Roll up the three layers like a jelly roll and fasten with wooden toothpicks. Dip each veal roll in the eggs beaten lightly with the cold water. Combine the breadcrumbs with the salt, pepper, thyme and garlic powder and coat the rolls in this mixture.

&❧ Set the veal rolls on a plate and refrigerate, uncovered, until ready to cook. These rolls can be prepared 6 to 8 hours ahead of time, if you wish.

&❧ To cook, heat the oil and butter in a skillet or an electric skillet set at 375°F (190°C). When hot, add the veal rolls and brown them over medium heat for 6 to 8 minutes on each side. Add the white wine or vermouth and simmer for 10 minutes, uncovered, turning the rolls once or twice. Serve.

Veal Cutlets Parisienne

SWISS VEAL

8 very thin slices veal
8 small, thin slices ham
8 small, thin slices Swiss cheese
2 tbsp (30 mL) flour
½ tsp (2 mL) salt
¼ tsp (1 mL) pepper
pinch of nutmeg
1 egg
1 tbsp (15 mL) water
1 cup (250 mL) breadcrumbs
3 tbsp (45 mL) butter
½ cup (125 mL) white wine

❧ Top each veal cutlet with a smaller slice of ham and of Swiss cheese. Fold the veal over the ham and cheese and fasten with wooden toothpicks.

❧ Combine the flour, salt, pepper and nutmeg. Beat the egg with the water. Place the breadcrumbs on a large plate. Dredge the veal packages in the flour mixture, then in the egg and finally in the breadcrumbs.

❧ Heat the butter in a skillet until it is a nutty brown color. Brown the veal on all sides in the butter, for approximately 10 minutes in all. Then add the white wine and simmer for 3 minutes, scraping the bottom of the pan well.

❧ Serve with a green salad.

VEAL SCALLOPINE

1 lb (500 g) thinly sliced veal (leg, shank end)
4 tbsp (60 mL) flour
salt and pepper
3 tbsp (45 mL) butter
4 tbsp (60 mL) white wine
juice of 1 lemon
2 tbsp (30 mL) chopped parsley

❧ Dredge the veal in the flour. Salt and pepper.

❧ Heat the butter in a skillet until it is a nutty brown color.

Brown the slices of meat over medium heat, 2 at a time, for approximately 1 minute on each side.

❧ When they are all browned, move the slices to a heated platter and add the white wine to the pan. Cook for 1 minute over high heat, then add the lemon juice and parsley and cook another 30 seconds.

❧ Pour the pan juices over the scallopine and serve at once.

WIENER SCHNITZEL

1½ lbs (750 g) small veal cutlets
juice of 1 lemon
½ tsp (2 mL) salt
¼ tsp (1 mL) pepper
¼ cup (50 mL) flour
1 egg
1 tbsp (15 mL) cold water
1 cup (250 mL) fine dry breadcrumbs
6 tbsp (90 mL) butter
sprigs of fresh parsley or dill

❧ Prepare the cutlets according to the basic directions (see page 204).

❧ Baste the cutlets on both sides with some of the lemon juice. Sprinkle with the salt and pepper. Dredge in flour, shaking off the excess. Then dip the cutlets in the egg beaten with the cold water and, finally, in the breadcrumbs.

❧ Sauté the cutlets, without crowding them, in 4 tbsp (60 mL) of the butter over medium heat until brown on both sides. As they are cooked, arrange them on a heated platter.

Veal Scallopine

☙ Add the remaining lemon juice and butter to the pan juices, scraping the bottom well. When the sauce foams up, pour it over the schnitzel. Garnish with the sprigs of fresh parsley or dill.

VEAL ROULADES

1¼ lbs (625 g) round veal steak, ¼ in. (0.5 cm) thick
2 garlic cloves
seasoned flour
1 tbsp (15 mL) oil
1 cup (250 mL) heated consommé

STUFFING:
3 cups (750 mL) fresh breadcrumbs
¾ tsp (3 mL) salt
½ tsp (2 mL) thyme
1 stalk celery, chopped
2 tbsp (30 mL) chopped fresh parsley
1 onion, minced
4 tbsp (60 mL) butter

☙ Have the butcher flatten the steak. Cut the steak into 4 serving pieces and rub each with a clove of garlic.

☙ To make the stuffing, combine the breadcrumbs, salt, thyme, celery and parsley. Brown the onion lightly in the butter and add to the breadcrumb mixture. Adjust the seasoning to taste.

☙ Spread a portion of the stuffing on each piece of veal and roll up the pieces. Tie the rolls closed with kitchen string.

☙ Dredge each roll in seasoned flour to coat completely.

☙ Brown the rolls on all sides in

Osso Bucco

the hot oil, and then add the consommé. Cover the skillet and simmer over low heat for 30 to 40 minutes or until the veal is tender.

☙ Serve with the pan gravy.

OSSO BUCCO

1 veal shank
flour
2 tbsp (30 mL) vegetable oil
2 tbsp (30 mL) butter
1 tsp (5 mL) salt
¼ tsp (1 mL) pepper
2 onions, chopped
¼ cup (50 mL) grated carrots
1 tsp (5 mL) basil
2 tbsp (30 mL) tomato paste
1 cup (250 mL) white wine
½ cup (125 mL) water
2 tsp (10 mL) lemon zest
1 clove garlic
2 tbsp (30 mL) chopped parsley

☙ Ask the butcher to cut the veal shank in round slices 3 in. (8 cm) thick. Each piece will have a small round bone in the middle—the marrow bone. Dredge each slice in flour.

☙ Brown the veal in the oil and butter heated together. Add the salt, pepper, onions, carrots and basil. Cover and cook over low heat for 10 minutes.

☙ Mix together the tomato paste and the white wine and add to the meat, along with the water. Cover and simmer over low heat for 1¾ hours, or until the meat is tender.

☙ When the meat is cooked, add the lemon zest, garlic and chopped parsley. Cook for 5 minutes. Season to taste and serve with boiled rice or an Italian risotto.

❧ TECHNIQUE ❧

OSSO BUCCO

1   Dredge each piece of veal in flour.

2   Brown the veal in the oil and butter heated together.

3   Add the salt, pepper, onions, carrots and basil. Cover and cook.

4   Add the mixture of tomato paste and white wine.

CLASSIC ITALIAN MEAT LOAF

Italian cooking is as diversified as it is traditional, and each region has its own style. This recipe is typical of the northern region. This loaf is tasty and attractive when sliced.

3 slices bread, crusts removed
½ cup (125 mL) milk
2 lbs (1 kg) ground veal
or 1 lb (500 g) ground lamb
and 1 lb (500 g) ground pork
1 onion, finely chopped
½ cup (125 mL) grated Parmesan
or mild Cheddar cheese
¼ cup (50 mL) chopped parsley
2 eggs
1½ tsp (7 mL) salt
½ tsp (2 mL) pepper

STUFFING:
⅔ cup (150 mL) breadcrumbs
1½ lbs (750 g) cottage cheese
¼ cup (50 mL) grated Cheddar cheese
½ lb (250 g) cooked ham, chopped
2 egg yolks
½ tsp (2 mL) marjoram or basil

🍃 Soak the bread slices in the milk. Drain and squeeze out the excess milk.

🍃 Mix the meat well with the remaining ingredients and the soaked bread, crumbled. Place the meat on a board, cover with a sheet of wax paper, and flatten out into a rectangle 1 in. (2.5 cm) thick.

🍃 To make the stuffing, combine all the stuffing ingredients, mixing well. If the stuffing seems too stiff, add about 1 tbsp (15 mL) milk.

🍃 Arrange the stuffing down the center of the veal mixture, lengthwise. Roll into a large sausage shape. Wrap in foil and twist the ends tightly shut.

🍃 Place the loaf on a baking sheet and bake in a 350°F (180°C) oven for 1½ to 2 hours.

🍃 To serve hot, unwrap and slice. To serve cold, cool in its foil wrapping and refrigerate; unwrap when ready to serve.

VEAL CROQUETTES

3 tbsp (45 mL) butter
3 tbsp (45 mL) flour
1 cup (250 mL) water
or consommé
juice of ½ lemon
½ cup (125 mL) cream
salt and pepper
2 egg yolks
2 cups (500 mL) cooked veal, ground
¼ tsp (1 mL) basil

🍃 Melt half the butter saucepan. Add the flour, co mé, lemon juice, cream, salt and pepper. Boil the mixture until it is the consistency of heavy cream. Fold in the egg yolks and the cooked ground veal. Stir a few moments. Season with basil.

🍃 Let cool and then cut into squares or form into short cigar shapes.

🍃 Roll the croquettes in flour and brown in butter or bacon fat.

MUSHROOM VEAL LOAF

1 lb (500 g) ground veal
1 lb (500 g) fresh ham, ground
4 tbsp (60 mL) catsup
3 tbsp (45 mL) chopped green pepper
1 medium onion, grated
2 eggs
1 tsp (5 mL) salt

Mushroom Veal Loaf

Calf's Brains with Black Butter

¼ cup (50 mL) breadcrumbs
1 cup (250 mL) mushroom soup, undiluted
1 cup (250 mL) fried mushrooms (fresh or canned)

🙚 Combine the veal, ham, catsup, green pepper, grated onion, eggs, salt, breadcrumbs and mushroom soup. Mix thoroughly. Turn half the mixture into a loaf pan. Cover with the fried mushrooms and top with the remaining mixture.
🙚 Bake for 1 hour in a 350°F (180°C) oven. Serve hot or cold.

VEAL SALAD

2 cups (500 mL) diced cooked veal
¼ cup (50 mL) chopped onion
¼ cup (50 mL) diced celery
¼ cup (50 mL) walnuts
⅔ cup (150 mL) mayonnaise

1 tsp (5 mL) tarragon
1 tbsp (15 mL) lemon juice
lettuce
tomatoes
olives

🙚 Mix together the diced veal, onion, celery and walnuts.
🙚 Blend the mayonnaise with the tarragon and the lemon juice. Add enough mayonnaise mixture to the veal mixture to coat it well.
🙚 Line a salad bowl with lettuce leaves. Place the veal salad in the middle. Surround with quartered tomatoes garnished with more seasoned mayonnaise. Decorate with olives.

POACHED CALF'S BRAINS

1 lb (500 g) calf's brains
2 cups (500 mL) cold water

1 tbsp (15 mL) vinegar
1 onion, cut in half
1 bay leaf
¼ tsp (1 mL) dry mustard
1 tsp (5 mL) salt
¼ tsp (1 mL) pepper

🙚 Soak the brains in the cold water for 30 minutes. Remove the thin membrane covering.
🙚 Add 1 tbsp (15 mL) vinegar to the water and soak the brains for another 10 minutes, or until well blanched.
🙚 Make a court-bouillon of the remaining ingredients (see page 123). Add the brains and cook for 15 to 20 minutes. Drain and serve plain or with melted butter or mayonnaise.

CALF'S BRAINS WITH BLACK BUTTER

calf's brains, poached
salt and pepper
4 tbsp (60 mL) butter
1 handful parsley, finely chopped
½ tsp (2 mL) wine vinegar

🙚 Poach the calf's brains in court-bouillon (see page 123). Arrange them on a platter and season well with salt and pepper.
🙚 Heat the butter in a skillet until dark brown. Add the finely chopped parsley. Pour over the calf's brains.
🙚 Quickly heat the vinegar in the same pan and pour it over the poached brains.

LIVER

In any sophisticated cuisine, liver is one of the choicest dishes. On the whole, however, liver is far from being appreciated as it should be. Perhaps this is because it is referred to as a variety meat or an organ meat, which makes many people shrink at the thought of eating it. But I think the real reason is that most of the time liver is badly cooked, even though it is really one of the easiest meats to prepare.

• There are many good reasons for including liver in your diet. It contains an abundance of iron in the right form for use by the body, and it is a good source of copper as well as vitamins A, B and C.

• Liver is also a very tender meat, although it can be made tough by overcooking.

• Beef, calf, lamb and pork liver vary widely in price, but all are good and can be prepared into many tasty dishes. Calf's liver is by far the most tender and delicate in flavor. Beef liver is similar in flavor, but not as tender or delicate in texture. Pork liver has a more pronounced flavor, but it also contains more iron. Liver from older animals is stronger in flavor than liver from younger ones.

• One sure way to obtain tender liver without a strong flavor is to cover the slices with milk and place them in the refrigerator for 12 hours.

• Liver is versatile. It can be baked in one piece, or liver slices can be broiled, braised or fried. You can use ground liver in a variety of ways.

• To prepare sliced liver for cooking, use scissors to cut out the large blood vessels, if any, then peel off the paper-thin membrane using a sharp knife.

• Always cook liver quickly, over high heat if the slices are thin, or over medium heat if they are thick. Remove from the heat as soon as it changes color.

BROILED LIVER

• This method is appropriate only for fresh calf's liver sliced ½ in. (1 cm) thick, or for lamb liver, sliced and soaked in milk for 12 to 24 hours. Properly done, this is a superb dish.

calf's liver, sliced ½ in. (1 cm) thick
peanut or olive oil
fresh lemon juice
paprika

• If the liver has been soaked in milk, drain and dry it with paper towels.

• Baste each slice of liver generously on both sides with the oil, then with lemon juice. Place on an oiled rack of a broiler pan and sprinkle lightly with paprika.

• Preheat the broiler element. Broil 3 in. (8 cm) from the element for 3 minutes. Turn and broil another 2 to 4 minutes.

• Serve immediately.

LIVER IN CREAM SAUCE

4 to 6 small slices calf's liver, ½ in. (1 cm) thick
1 cup (250 mL) milk
2 tbsp (30 mL) flour
½ tsp (2 mL) salt
¼ tsp (1 mL) pepper
¼ tsp (1 mL) curry
½ tsp (2 mL) paprika
3 tbsp (45 mL) butter
1 cup (250 mL) light cream
¼ cup (50 mL) chopped parsley

• Soak the liver in the milk for 4 to 8 hours in the refrigerator.

• Combine the flour, salt, pepper, curry and paprika. Drain the meat and dredge each slice in the flour mixture until well coated.

• Melt the butter in a large skillet until nutty brown and sauté the liver over medium heat for 5 minutes on each side, turning only once. Lower the heat if the liver seems to be browning too fast. Move the meat to a heated platter.

• Pour the cream into the hot skillet. Add the parsley. Stir over medium heat until hot. Pour over the liver.

• Serve with boiled potatoes.

PAN-FRIED LIVER

After many years of experimenting, I have learned a never-fail way to pan-fry any kind of liver so that it is always tender and tasty. It's best to use very thinly sliced liver, but the same method can be used for thicker slices.

3 tbsp (45 mL) butter
juice of 1 small lemon
3 tbsp (45 mL) fresh chopped parsley
¼ tsp (1 mL) seasoned pepper
salt to taste
3 tbsp (45 mL) cold water

1 to 1½ lbs (500 to 750 g) thinly sliced liver
flour

ᶏ Heat the butter in a large cast-iron skillet until light brown.

ᶏ Meanwhile, combine in a small bowl the lemon juice, parsley, seasoned pepper, salt and water.

ᶏ Dredge the sliced liver lightly in the flour.

ᶏ When the butter is ready, raise the heat and add the liver, being careful not to crowd the pieces. As soon as the last piece is in the pan, start turning the other pieces, beginning with the first in the pan. When the pieces have cooked for ½ minute over high heat, move them from the pan to a heated platter. Repeat until all the liver is cooked.

ᶏ Turn the lemon-juice mixture into the skillet and stir with a wooden spoon, scraping the bottom of the pan, for about 30 seconds. Pour this over the liver and serve.

VARIATIONS

ᶏ You can alter the recipe for pan-fried liver by substituting the following steps:

ᶏ Add ½ to 1 tsp (2 to 5 mL) curry powder to the flour before dredging the liver slices.

ᶏ Replace the parsley in the lemon-juice mixture with an equal quantity of minced chives.

ᶏ Add 1 large clove of crushed garlic to the lemon-juice mixture.

ᶏ Replace the lemon-juice mixture with a wine mixture made with the following ingredients:

1 cup (250 mL) port or dry sherry
¼ tsp (1 mL) tarragon
¼ tsp (1 mL) fresh ground black pepper
1 tsp (5 mL) honey

Broiled Calf's Liver

BROILED CALF'S LIVER

4 tbsp (60 mL) butter or margarine
2 tbsp (30 mL) chopped onion
2 tbsp (30 mL) lemon juice
pinch of thyme or marjoram
flour
salt and pepper
paprika
1 lb (500 g) calf's liver, sliced ⅓ in. (0.8 cm) thick

ᶏ Melt the butter. Add the onion and simmer over low heat for 5 to 10 minutes, stirring often. Remove from heat and add the lemon juice and the thyme or marjoram.

ᶏ Combine the flour with the salt, pepper and paprika. Roll the liver in the flour mixture, then in the butter mixture.

ᶏ Place the liver slices side by side in the broiler tray (without the grill). Top with the rest of the butter mixture.

ᶏ Broil 3 to 4 in. (8 to 10 cm) from the element for 4 to 8 minutes in total, turning at the halfway point. Baste from time to time.

ᶏ Serve immediately, sprinkled with parsley and accompanied with sautéed potatoes.

FRENCH-STYLE CALF'S LIVER

2 tbsp (30 mL) sugar
2 tbsp (30 mL) cold water
½ tsp (2 mL) dried sage or marjoram

2 tbsp (30 mL) flour
½ tsp (2 mL) salt
½ tsp (2 mL) pepper
1½ to 2 lbs (750 to 900 g) calf
liver, sliced ½ in (1 cm) thick
3 tbsp (45 mL) butter
3 tbsp (45 mL) dry vermouth
or port
3 tbsp (45 mL) heavy cream
¼ cup (50 mL) chopped fresh
parsley

🍃 Melt the sugar in a small skillet over medium heat until it is syrupy, then add the cold water all at once. It will splatter, and the sugar will harden. Let it simmer for a few seconds until it caramelizes. Set aside.

🍃 Combine the sage or marjoram, flour, salt and pepper in a bowl. Dredge the liver slices in this mixture.

🍃 Heat the butter in a cast-iron skillet and add 2 tbsp (30 mL) of the caramel. When very hot, add the liver and brown it well over high heat, about 1 to 1½ minutes on each side. Lower the heat and simmer for 3 minutes.

🍃 Remove the liver from the pan and put it on a hot platter.

🍃 Add the vermouth or port and the cream to the pan. Stir until hot. Pour over the liver.

🍃 Sprinkle with the parsley and serve.

LIVER KUGEL

This recipe from Jewish cuisine is a perfect way to use leftover cooked liver. I like it so much I sometimes cook some liver just to make kugel.

8 oz (250 g) fine noodles
3 tbsp (45 mL) butter
1 large onion, chopped
2 to 3 cups (500 to 740 mL)
chopped cooked liver
½ tsp (2 mL) celery salt
salt and pepper to taste
2 eggs, well beaten

🍃 Boil and drain the noodles.

🍃 Melt the butter, add the onion and fry until golden brown. Combine the cooked noodles, chopped liver, fried onion, celery salt, salt and pepper and beaten eggs.

🍃 Pour into a well-greased baking dish and bake in a 350°F (180°C) oven for about 35 minutes or until the top is brown.

LIVER AND ONION CASSEROLE

1½ lbs (750 g) calf's, beef or lamb's liver
¼ cup (50 mL) sweet pickles
1½ cups (375 mL) mashed potatoes
½ tsp (2 mL) salt
2 tsp (10 mL) Worcestershire sauce
1 egg
4 tbsp (60 mL) cream
4 tbsp (60 mL) bacon fat
creamed onions
2 or 3 strips bacon

🍃 Pour boiling water over the liver and boil for 5 minutes. Drain and put through a meat chopper with the pickles.

🍃 To this mixture, add the mashed potatoes, salt, Worcestershire sauce, egg and cream. Mix well and shape into small patties.

Brown lightly in the fat.

🍃 Cover the bottom of a baking dish with the creamed onions. Place the meat patties over the onions and top with the strips of bacon.

🍃 Bake, uncovered, in a 400°F (200°C) oven for 20 minutes.

LIVER PATTIES

This recipe can also be baked in a loaf pan and served as a meat loaf.

1 tbsp (15 mL) bacon fat
½ cup (125 mL) uncooked rice
1 cup (250 mL) water
1½ lbs (750 g) ground liver
2 tbsp (30 mL) vegetable oil
1 onion, grated or chopped fine
2 eggs, beaten
1 tsp (5 mL) salt
¼ tsp (1 mL) thyme
¼ tsp (1 mL) marjoram
3 tbsp (45 mL) wheat germ
(optional)
3 tbsp (45 mL) molasses
6 strips bacon

🍃 Melt the bacon fat in a saucepan and add the uncooked rice. Stir over low heat until the rice is coated with fat. Add the water and bring to a boil. Stir again, cover and cook for 15 minutes over low heat.

🍃 Put the ground liver in a bowl with the cooked rice and the remaining ingredients, except for the strips of bacon. Mix thoroughly and shape into 6 large patties.

🍃 Wrap a strip of bacon around each pattie and fasten with a wooden toothpick. Place the patties in an oiled shallow baking pan.

Ris de Veau with Mushrooms

🍃 Bake in a preheated 400°F (200°C) oven for 30 to 40 minutes or until the bacon is crisp.

🍃 As a variation, serve with a tomato sauce.

DANISH LIVER PÂTÉ

1 lb (500 g) ground calf's or beef liver
¼ cup (50 mL) fried onion
½ lb (250 g) ground pork
2 eggs
2 cups (500 mL) light cream
1 tsp (5 mL) pepper
1 tbsp (15 mL) salt
1¼ cup (300 mL) bread flour
3 bay leaves

🍃 Place all the ingredients in a bowl and beat together until creamy.

🍃 Pour into a well-buttered mold. Cover.

🍃 Place the mold in a pan of hot water and bake in a 350°F (180°C) oven for 2 hours. Remove the cover after 1 hour.

JELLIED VEAL TONGUE

4 veal tongues
3 carrots, diced
2 onions, minced
1 clove garlic
handful celery leaves
2 tbsp (30 mL) parsley
¼ tsp (1 mL) marjoram
1 bay leaf
salt and pepper
4 cups (1 L) water
1 envelope gelatin

🍃 Soak the veal tongues for 1 hour in salted water.

🍃 Put the tongues in a large saucepan or casserole with all the remaining ingredients, except the gelatin. Cover and simmer for 2 hours (or cook in a pressure-cooker for 40 minutes).

🍃 Peel the tongues when they are cool enough to handle.

🍃 Dissolve the gelatin in a little cold water and stir it into the cooking broth.

🍃 Pour the broth and the vegetables over the tongues (diced, if desired) and refrigerate until set.

RIS DE VEAU WITH MUSHROOMS

4 to 6 calf's sweetbreads
1 tsp (5 mL) salt
1 tbsp (15 mL) vinegar
pinch of thyme
1 bay leaf

SAUCE:
2 tbsp (30 mL) fat
3 shallots, finely chopped
½ lb (250 g) mushrooms, sliced
2 tbsp (30 mL) cognac or sherry

🍃 No matter how you plan to cook sweetbreads, you should always blanch them first by soaking them for 1 hour in cold water.

🍃 Drain the sweetbreads, then place them in a large saucepan and cover with water. Add the salt and the vinegar, along with the thyme and the bay leaf. Bring slowly to a boil and simmer, uncovered, for 2 to 5 minutes, depending on the size.

🍃 Drain the sweetbreads and place them in cold water. When cool, trim away any connective tissue, cartilage, tubes and membranes. Lay the sweetbreads on a clean cloth, cover with a second

❦ TECHNIQUE ❦

RIS DE VEAU WITH MUSHROOM

1 Blanch the sweetbreads.

2 Drain and rinse well under cold water. Clean the sweetbreads and remove the tendons.

3 Cover the sweetbreads with a clean cloth.

4 Place a weight on the sweetbreads and let cool.

cloth, and weight them, refrigerated, for several hours. The sweetbreads are then ready to use.

🍂 Leave the prepared sweetbreads whole or cube them.

🍂 To make the sauce, heat the fat and add the chopped shallots and the sweetbreads. When the sweetbreads are brown, add the sliced mushrooms. Stir over high heat for about 2 minutes. Add the cognac or sherry to taste.

🍂 Serve in small pastry or vol-au-vent (puff-pastry) shells, on toast or on a bed of boiled rice garnished with fresh parsley.

VEAL KIDNEYS BERCY

1 or 2 veal kidneys
or 4 to 6 lamb kidneys
1 tbsp (15 mL) flour
1 tbsp (15 mL) butter
3 or 4 green onions, chopped
½ cup (125 mL) sherry
or consommé
½ cup (125 mL) brown sauce
3 to 4 tbsp (45 to 60 mL) parsley
salt and pepper

🍂 Remove the fat and the outer

Veal Kidneys Bercy

membrane from the kidneys. Slice the kidneys thin, removing the white part in the middle. Dredge the slices in the flour.

🍂 Heat the butter until nutty brown. Add the kidneys and sear them over high heat, no more than 4 or 5 seconds, stirring constantly. Reduce the heat and simmer for 3 minutes. Remove the kidneys from the skillet and keep warm.

🍂 Add the chopped green onions to the fat in the skillet and brown them over medium heat for a few minutes, stirring. Add the sherry or consommé and simmer for 5 minutes. Add the brown sauce along with the parsley, salt and pepper.

🍂 Pour the sauce over the kidneys and serve immediately.

LAMB

LAMB

1. Leg
2. Loin
3. Rib or Rack
4. Breast
5. Shank
6. Shoulder
7. Neck

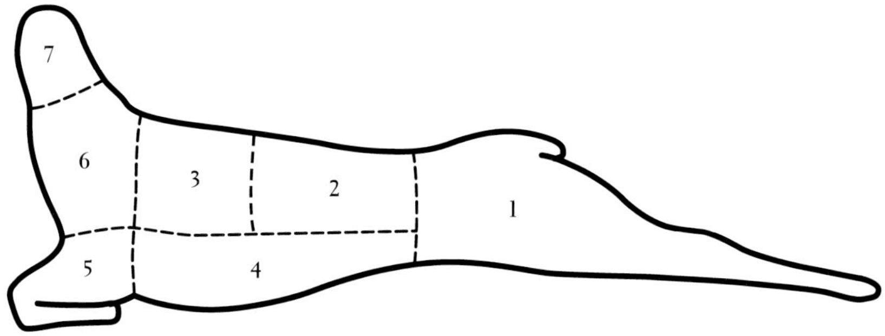

(Diagram of lamb with numbered cuts: 7, 6, 5, 3, 4, 2, 1)

LAMB

Lamb is the meat of the animal when it is less than 14 months old. Over that age, the meat is referred to as mutton. Spring lamb, also known as milk-finished lamb or baby lamb, is from an animal 3 to 5 months old.

Good quality lamb is firm and has a smooth, velvety texture. The lean meat is pinkish; mutton is a darker red.

Lamb fat is firm and tender; it is creamy white or slightly pink in color. Mutton fat is drier and whiter.

The bones of a young lamb are small, porous and pinkish. They can easily be cut or sawed. As the animal matures, the bones become larger, harder and whiter, and more difficult to cut.

Lamb kidneys, liver, heart and tongue have a delicious, delicate flavor.

To refrigerate lamb, cover it with wax paper and keep it in the coldest part of the refrigerator. Steaks and chops should be eaten within 2 or 3 days of purchase, while roasts can be kept a little longer. Ground lamb must be eaten within 24 hours of purchase.

LEG

Almost every part of the animal may be eaten, but by far the most popular cut is the leg of lamb.

The leg is often sold as a whole leg of lamb, but it may also be cut horizontally into 2 sections. The shank end is the lower part of the leg. Usually the shank bone is cut through and removed from the bottom end, and the remaining flap of flesh is folded under the leg. The butt is the upper half or thicker part of the leg. Since it contains the large rump knuckle bone, it is not as easy to carve as the shank end.

The large cut made up of the 2 rear legs and a portion of the loin is called a baron of lamb and is generally roasted for particularly grand occasions. You must have an especially large oven in order to roast this cut at home.

LOIN

The leg end of the loin, which contains the T-bone and filet, is the meatiest part. It can be purchased whole, rolled or cut into loin chops. However, for very special occasions you can ask the butcher for the 2 whole loins still attached but with some of the smaller bones removed. This whole piece can be rolled and the cavity stuffed with lamb kidneys. This is a smaller cut than the baron of lamb, but it is equally good for large dinners.

RIB OR RACK

The rib or rack section of lamb contains the rib bones and no tenderloin, and is less meaty than the loin section. It is sold either whole as a rack of lamb or cut into rib chops. An elegant cut, known as crown roast, is made from 2 racks of lamb.

BREAST

The breast of lamb next to the round bone shoulder contains the end of the round bone and shank bone but is fairly meaty. It is sold whole for braising and is often cubed into stewing meat. This cut is also often made into ground lamb.

Lamb riblets, cut from the flank section behind the breast and under the loin and ribs, are delicious barbecued or braised. The flank contains layers of fat, lean meat and bone; it may be left whole, boned and rolled or minced.

SHANK
Lamb shank must be cooked longer than the breast, but it is excellent braised, and it produces lots of gelatin.

SHOULDER
The shoulder section, just forward of the rib section, contains the thin blade bone, the small round shoulder bone and some ribs. It is sold as a whole roast or divided in 2 and sold as palette roast or square cut shoulder. The shoulder is also sometimes boned and sold as rolled shoulder.

❧ Various chops cut from the shoulder section, including blade chop and arm chop, are cheaper than the various rib and loin chops, but they contain more bone and so may not be as good value. However, this cut has very good flavor.

NECK
The neck section contains lots of bone, but when braised whole it is considered a delicacy by many. It is also cut in pieces for stews and fricassees.

TIPS FOR PREPARING LAMB

To add a special flavor to lamb, no matter how you plan to cook it, first sprinkle the meat with your choice of basil, rosemary, thyme, oregano, ground ginger or curry powder.

❧ Or make slits in the flesh with a sharp knife before roasting and insert into each slit a slice of garlic, some fresh mint, shreds of lemon zest, fresh parsley or fresh dill.

❧ Or sprinkle the roast or chops as soon as they're cooked with a little lemon juice, cognac or crème de menthe.

❧ Lamb should always be cooked at a moderate temperature, whether roasted, broiled or braised. Never overcook it. Lamb is at its best when served with a rosy tinge, rather than well done.

ACCOMPANIMENTS
The best vegetables to serve with lamb are green peas, asparagus, broccoli, carrots, green beans, fried onions and squash. I think lamb teams up much better with rice than with potatoes.

❧ Lamb should always be served on well-heated plates. Otherwise, the lamb fat may congeal as soon as it comes into contact with the cold plate, which is very unappetizing.

GLAZE
Roast leg of lamb may be glazed just as a ham is glazed. Here's an excellent mixture.

❧ Combine ½ cup (125 mL) mint jelly with ½ tsp (2 mL) dry mustard, 2 tbsp (30 mL) lemon juice or cider vinegar and a pinch of basil or rosemary. Spread this mixture on the roast 30 minutes before the end of the cooking period and baste several times.

SPIT-ROASTED LEG OF LAMB

❧ Do not remove the leg bone from the leg of lamb. It is important that the leg be well skewered on the spit. Before you start cooking, give the spit handle a few test turns to make sure the leg is well balanced and stable in every roasting position.

❧ Use a *Greek Sauce* (see page 57) to baste the leg of lamb during roasting. Or rub the leg vigorously before cooking with a garlic clove and then half a lemon; once it is secured to the spit, sprinkle the lamb with oil and a little thyme. Salt and pepper only at the end of cooking.

❧ Roast 20 to 25 minutes per lb (500 g).

❧ If desired, glaze the leg of lamb by basting it during the last 10 minutes of spit-roasting with 1 cup (250 mL) black currant jelly

ROASTING CHART FOR LAMB

Cut	Oven Temperature	Cooking time (minutes per lb/500 g)
Rack	400°F (200°C)	10 to 12 minutes
Crown	350°F (180°C)	15 minutes
Shoulder	325°F (160°C)	20 to 25 minutes
Leg	350°F (180°C)	15 minutes
Loin	350°F (180°C)	15 minutes

If you use a meat thermometer, the lamb is done when the internal temperature reads 145°F (65°C).

Barbecued Leg of Lamb

and 4 tbsp (60 mL) prepared mustard blended with a rotary beater.

COLD LEG OF LAMB

🖐 Remove the leg of lamb from the refrigerator at least 30 minutes before serving. Slice as thinly as possible and remove all visible fat.

🖐 Serve with a mustard-spiked mayonnaise, made by combining ½ cup (125 mL) mayonnaise with 2 tbsp (30 mL) mustard, and a rice salad made with cold cooked rice, chopped sweet peppers and green onions, and seasoned with French dressing.

LEG OF LAMB À LA BRETONNE

2 cups (500 mL) dried white beans
2 garlic cloves
leg of lamb
¾ cup (175 mL) consommé
salt and pepper
¼ cup (50 mL) tomato paste
2 tbsp (30 mL) butter
½ cup (125 mL) chopped fresh parsley

🖐 If possible, use white kidney beans or Great Northern beans for this recipe. Soak the beans for 12 hours before starting the rest of the dish. Boil the beans until tender but still whole. They will be tastier if cooked in the water in which they were soaked. Keep the beans warm.

🖐 Meanwhile, quarter 1 of the garlic cloves and insert the pieces in incisions in the leg of lamb.

🖐 Roast the lamb according to the lamb roasting chart (see previous page). Baste 3 times with the consommé during the cooking period.

🖐 Drain the cooked beans and add salt and pepper to taste. Mince the remaining garlic clove and add to the beans together with the tomato paste. Stir in the butter and some of the cooking juices from the roast.

🖐 When the roast is cooked, place it on a warm platter.

🖐 Reheat the beans if necessary and sprinkle them with the parsley. Serve with the lamb.

BARBECUED LEG OF LAMB

1 small leg of lamb
1 clove garlic
¼ cup (50 mL) bacon fat
¼ cup (50 mL) vegetable oil
pinch of cayenne pepper
juice of 1 lemon
1 tsp (5 mL) basil
8 to 10 cloves

🖐 Have your butcher bone the leg, but do not have it rolled.

🖐 Sliver the garlic and insert the slivers into incisions in the meat.

🖐 Beat the bacon fat until creamy and gradually beat in the vegetable oil, cayenne, lemon juice and basil. Pepper the roast generously and tie it up. Use the bacon-fat mixture to baste one side of the roast.

🖐 Place the lamb on the grill basted side down about 5 or 6 in. (15 cm) from the coals. Stick the roast with the whole cloves and broil for 40 minutes without turning.

🖐 Baste the top of the roast with the remaining bacon-fat mixture, then turn and barbecue another 40 minutes or more, depending

❧ TECHNIQUE ❧

BARBECUED LEG OF LAMB

1 Boned leg of lamb.

2 Make incisions in the meat and insert garlic slivers.

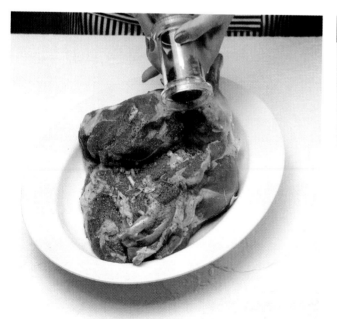

3 Pepper generously.

4 Baste with the bacon-fat and oil mixture.

on the degree of doneness desired. A medium-cooked roast will require about 40 minutes cooking on each side.

SCOTTISH BOILED LEG OF LAMB

1 leg of lamb, 4 to 6 lbs (2 to 2.5 kg)
¼ cup (50 mL) peppercorns or ground cloves (this is not a mistake, it should really be this much!)
1 tbsp (15 mL) coarse salt
10 whole cloves garlic
12 juniper berries

🦐 With a sharp knife, trim the excess fat from the leg of lamb. Carefully wrap the leg in a cheesecloth and sew the cloth tightly closed.

🦐 Place the leg in a large kettle and add enough boiling water to cover.

🦐 Add the remaining ingredients. Cover and simmer over low heat, calculating 15 minutes per lb (500 g) of meat.

🦐 When the meat is cooked, remove it from the pot, unwrap the cheesecloth and place the leg of lamb on a heated platter.

🦐 Serve hot or cold.

🦐 To serve hot, garnish with chopped fresh parsley and surround with boiled potatoes. Accompany with a *Caper Sauce* (see page 61) or a *Hollandaise Sauce* (see page 54) with capers. Mint sauce is not really suitable for this dish.

🦐 To serve cold (or to reheat later), leave the leg of lamb wrapped in the cheesecloth and place it in the refrigerator. Reheat, if desired, in its own juices. Garnish at serving time with chopped fresh parsley.

FRENCH-STYLE BOILED LEG OF LAMB

1 leg of lamb, 4 to 6 lbs
(2 to 2.5 kg)
8 cups (2 L) boiling water
12 small onions
12 small carrots
1 small turnip, quartered
1 tbsp (15 mL) salt
10 peppercorns or 1 tsp (5 mL) ground pepper
3 tbsp (45 mL) flour
3 tbsp (45 mL) butter
1 tbsp (15 mL) vinegar or lemon juice
2 tbsp (30 mL) chopped pickles or capers

🦐 Wrap the leg of lamb in cheesecloth. Place in a large kettle and cover with the boiling water. Add the prepared vegetables and seasonings. Cover and simmer until done, calculating 12 to 15 minutes per lb (500 g).

🦐 Unwrap the leg of lamb and set it on a heated platter.

🦐 Make a gravy using 3 cups (750 mL) of the cooking broth thickened with the butter and the flour. When smooth and creamy, add the vinegar or lemon juice and the chopped pickles or the capers. Serve in a gravy boat.

🦐 Accompany the lamb and boiled vegetables with boiled potatoes.

BARBECUED KEBABS

🦐 To barbecue kebabs, you will need metal skewers 6 to 24 in. (15 to 60 cm) long, depending on how much food you intend to serve on each.

🦐 Alternate the cubes of meat on the skewer with a selection of garnishes or vegetables. Salt and pepper to taste.

🦐 Broil the kebabs 2 to 3 in. (5 cm) from the coals, basting frequently with an equal quantity of butter and lemon juice heated together, or with the barbecue sauce of your choice.

KEBAB COOKING

🦐 Although shish kebab usually comes to mind when we think of kebabs, this method of cooking works for many types of ingredients, and can take inspiration from different parts of the world.

🦐 Below are some of my favorite combinations, but you can experiment. Just choose ingredients that will require the same cooking time and alternate them on the skewer. Baste during cooking with a sauce of your choice, or with an equal amount of lemon juice and melted butter blended together.

🦐 Broiling time will vary depending on ingredients and preference. As a general rule, the kebab is cooked when the meat is browned.

ENGLISH KEBABS
🦐 Lamb kidneys, halved; tiny white onions, parboiled; whole mushrooms

ITALIAN KEBABS

🍃 Cubed veal or chicken liver; rolled bacon strips; whole mushrooms. Sprinkle with a little thyme before cooking.

SPICY KEBABS

🍃 Alternate on the skewer 1-in. (2.5-cm) cubes of lamb with salami sliced ½-in. (1-cm) thick. Brush with oil before cooking.

NEW ENGLAND KEBABS

🍃 Shelled large shrimp; scallops; diced salt pork or bacon. Baste with herb sauce during cooking.

TURKISH KEBABS

🍃 Flavor minced lamb with minced garlic, a little chopped onion, a pinch of thyme, salt and pepper to taste, 2 tbsp (30 mL) olive oil and 1 tbsp (15 mL) lemon juice for each 1¼ lbs (625 mL) ground lamb. Shape into balls and skewer alternately with tomato halves and onion wedges.

Lamb Kebabs

LAMB KEBABS

2 to 3 lbs (1 to 1.5 kg) lamb shoulder
½ cup (125 mL) vegetable oil
¼ cup (50 mL) lemon juice
2 cloves garlic, crushed
½ cup (125 mL) chopped fresh parsley

🍃 Cut the meat into 1½-in. (4-cm) cubes.

🍃 Combine the remaining ingredients in a large bowl. Add the meat and marinate 2 to 6 hours.

🍃 Remove the meat from the marinade. Place 4 to 6 cubes of meat on each skewer and broil in the oven or on the barbecue until the meat is browned. Serve with sliced French bread or toast.

SHISH KEBABS

1 leg of lamb, 4 to 5 lbs
(2 to 2.5 kg)
1 clove garlic, minced
3 onions, sliced thin
2 tbsp (30 mL) olive oil
⅓ cup (75 mL) sherry
or lemon juice
½ tsp (2 mL) pepper
½ tsp (2 mL) basil or marjoram
¼ tsp (1 mL) thyme
1 tsp (5 mL) salt
6 green peppers, cored
6 tomatoes, very firm, stems removed

🍃 Bone the leg of lamb and cut it into 1½-in. (4-cm) cubes. Trim the excess fat.

🍃 In a large bowl, combine the garlic, onions, olive oil, sherry or lemon juice, pepper, basil or marjoram, thyme and salt. Add the lamb cubes and mix well. Cover and refrigerate for 24 hours.

🍃 Place the washed and cored green peppers on a 24-in. (60-cm) skewer. Put the tomatoes on a second skewer and the marinated lamb on a third. Broil 2 in. (5 cm) from the coals of a barbecue.

🍃 Pour the marinade into a cast-iron skillet and heat on top of the grill while the meat is cooking.

🍃 As soon as the tomatoes and peppers are cooked, remove them from the skewers and put them in the heated marinade until the meat is finished cooking.

🍃 Cut the peppers and tomatoes in wedges. Add the cooked meat cubes and stir to mix.

🍃 Serve with a large bowl of well-seasoned hot rice.

🍃 This is an easy way to make an outdoor barbecue for 4 to 6 people.

BARBECUED GROUND-LAMB KEBABS

જી Substitute 2 lbs (1 kg) ground lamb shoulder for the leg of lamb in the recipe for *Shish Kebabs* (see previous page).

જી Combine the ground lamb with the remaining ingredients, except the green peppers and tomatoes.

જી Shape the meat into meatballs and skewer or simply cook the meatballs on the grill.

જી Serve with hot crusty bread.

PERSIAN KEBABS

2 lbs (1 kg) ground lamb
½ cup (125 mL) walnuts
½ cup (125 mL) chopped fresh parsley
1 tsp (5 mL) salt
¼ tsp (1 mL) pepper
1 clove garlic, minced
1 egg
1 tbsp (15 mL) olive oil

જી Put the ground lamb in a bowl. Chop the walnuts fine and add them to the lamb, along with the remaining ingredients. Mix together for 5 minutes, preferably using an electric mixer set at medium speed. Refrigerate for 1 hour.

જી Form into long sausage shapes molded onto each skewer. Brush with oil and broil in the oven or on the barbecue until browned.

જી Serve on a bed of steamed rice.

PEKING FONDUE

જી Use a Mongolian fire pot (available at Oriental groceries), or an electric wok or deep-fryer, or a soup pot or casserole placed over a burner or hot plate. The heat should be high enough to keep the stock at a rolling boil. This is a delicious dish when made with lamb, but beef is a good substitute.

10 cups (2.5 L) consommé or bouillon
2-lb (1-kg) leg of lamb, sliced paper-thin
2 lamb kidneys, thinly sliced
1 lb (500 g) fresh spinach
12 to 14 fresh mushrooms
1 bamboo shoot, thinly sliced
2 slices fresh ginger root (optional)
3 green onions
8 oz (250 g) vermicelli

જી For the consommé, use canned beef consommé twice diluted (1 can consommé, 2 cans water), or make your own bouillon by simmering 3 lbs (1.5 kg) meatless beef bones in 12 cups (3 L) water. Season to taste and strain before using.

જી Arrange the sliced lamb and kidneys attractively around a large platter, with the spinach (washed, dried and stalks removed) in the center. Remove the stems from the mushrooms and arrange the cleaned mushroom caps and bamboo shoots around the meat. Grate the ginger and sprinkle it on the kidneys. Sprinkle short lengths of green onions over the lamb.

જી Place the vermicelli in boiling water and boil until cooked to taste. Drain and stir in 2 tbsp (30 mL) vegetable oil. Mound the vermicelli on a platter.

જી To prepare a Peking dipping sauce, combine in a bowl 3 tbsp (45 mL) dry sherry, ¼ cup (50 mL) soy sauce (not the salty type), 3 tbsp (45 mL) peanut oil, 1 tbsp (15 mL) cider vinegar, 3 tbsp (45 mL) chopped parsley, ¼ tsp (1 mL) ground fennel or anise seeds and 1 crushed clove of garlic. Stir and let sit until ready to serve.

જી To serve, set each place with bamboo sticks, skewers or fondue forks and a small dish of the dipping sauce. Put the platters of prepared food on the table. Each person skewers a piece of meat or vegetable, or rolls a few vermicelli around the stick, and dips it in the boiling broth. The meat will cook very rapidly. Dip the tidbits in the sauce and eat.

ROAST RACK OF LAMB

1 rack of lamb
1 clove garlic, minced
¼ tsp (1 mL) basil or rosemary
2 tbsp (30 mL) butter
salt and pepper to taste

જી A rack of lamb is the perfect cut for 2 or 3 people. It is cut from the rib section of the loin and usually contains 6 to 8 ribs. The tips of the bones are usually trimmed off.

જી Combine the garlic and the basil or rosemary with the butter and rub this mixture over the roast. Salt and pepper to taste.

જી Roast in a 400°F (200°C) oven

for 10 minutes per lb (500 g), basting every 15 minutes with the pan dripping.

ᕕ Serve very hot with potatoes and buttered green peas.

CROWN ROAST OF LAMB

2 racks of lamb
½ lb (250 g) salt pork, all fat
½ lb (250 g) fresh spinach
1 can green peas
3 tbsp (45 mL) butter
¼ tsp (1 mL) basil
1 lb (500 g) mushrooms

ᕕ Ask the butcher to tie together the 2 rib sections to make a crown roast. Protect the ends of the bones from burning by covering them with cubes of salt pork. Roast in a 350°F (180°C) oven for 1 hour. This cut should be served rare rather than well done.

ᕕ To serve, remove the cubes of salt pork, place the roast on a very hot platter and decorate each rib end with a paper frill.

ᕕ Fill the center of the roast with buttered spinach (see page < >).

ᕕ Drain the green peas, put them through a food mill and add the butter and basil. Heat. Surround the spinach with this purée.

ᕕ Fry the mushrooms quickly in 2 tbsp (30 mL) butter and arrange them around the crown roast.

BROILED LAMB CHOPS

ᕕ Sprinkle the chops with paprika. Make incisions in each and stuff with bits of lemon zest or chopped garlic. Brush with olive oil.

ᕕ Place the chops on a broiler pan 4 in. (10 cm) from the element. Broil with the oven door slightly ajar.

ᕕ Broiling time for chops 1½ in. (4 cm) thick:

ᕕ Rare: 4 minutes each side
ᕕ Medium: 6 minutes each side

BROILED GREEK-STYLE
ᕕ Make incisions in the chops and stuff in a little lemon zest; salt and pepper and sprinkle with fresh lemon juice.

BROILED ITALIAN-STYLE
ᕕ Make incisions in the chops and stuff with basil or minced garlic; brush generously with olive oil and sprinkle with lemon juice; salt and pepper.

PAN-FRIED
ᕕ In a cast-iron skillet, melt 1 tbsp (15 mL) of vegetable oil, butter or lamb fat. Cook the chops over high heat for about 4 minutes for a 1½-in. (4-cm) chop. Adjust the time for thicker or thinner chops. Reduce the heat, if necessary, to prevent the chops from browning too much, but make sure it is high enough for the meat to broil rather than stew. Turn and cook another 4 minutes on the other side. Salt and pepper to taste.

LAMB CHOPS BARMAN

6 thick lamb chops
3 tomatoes
6 large mushrooms
6 strips bacon

ᕕ Pan-fry or pan-broil the chops.
ᕕ When cooked, remove the chops and fry the remaining

Broiled Lamb Chops

[225]

ingredients in the pan drippings.
🏵 Garnish each chop with ½ tomato and 1 mushroom and top with a strip of bacon.

SHERRIED ORANGE LAMB CHOPS

¼ cup (50 mL) sherry
½ tsp (2 mL) salt
½ tsp (2 mL) dry mustard
¼ tsp (1 mL) pepper
½ clove garlic, minced
4 lamb chops
1 large orange
3 tbsp (45 mL) brown sugar
2 tsp (10 mL) sherry

🏵 A day in advance, combine the ¼ cup (50 mL) sherry, salt, mustard, pepper and garlic. Use to marinate the lamb chops overnight in the refrigerator.
🏵 About 30 minutes before serving time, preheat the broiler for 10 minutes. Cut the unpeeled orange into ½-in. (1.2-cm) slices and sprinkle with the brown sugar and the sherry; set aside.
🏵 Drain the lamb chops, reserving the marinade.
🏵 Arrange the chops on a broiler rack and broil 3 in. (8 cm) from the element for about 6 minutes. Turn the chops and pour the reserved marinade over them; arrange the orange slices around the chops. Broil another 6 minutes, or until the meat is done to taste and the oranges are golden.
🏵 Serves 2.

BARBECUED LAMB CHOPS

lamb chops, 1 to 1½ in.
(2.5 to 4 cm) thick or lamb steak,
1 in. (2.5 cm) thick
barbecue sauce of your choice
or 1 cup (250 mL) grape jelly and
2 tbsp (30 mL) prepared mustard

🏵 Remove excess fat from the chops or steak.
🏵 Place the lamb on the barbecue grill 2 to 3 in. (5 to 8 cm) from the coals.
🏵 Baste 5 to 6 times during cooking with the barbecue sauce or with the grape jelly mixed with the mustard. Cook 2 to 5 minutes on each side, depending on the degree of doneness desired.

STUFFED PEACHES WITH LAMB CHOPS

4 ripe peaches
chutney
2 tbsp (30 mL) butter
juice of 1 large lemon
lamb chops

🏵 Butter a shallow baking dish. Peel and halve the peaches, discarding the pits. Arrange them in the dish, hollow side up, and fill each cavity with a spoonful of chutney; dot with butter. Squeeze the lemon juice over all.
🏵 Bake 35 minutes in a 375°F (190°C) oven.
🏵 Serve hot with broiled lamb chops.

LAMB STEAK BIGARADE

2 lamb steaks cut from the leg
½ tsp (2 mL) salt
2 unpeeled oranges, sliced
2 tbsp (30 mL) brown sugar
1 tbsp (15 mL) orange zest
½ tsp (2 mL) ginger
¼ tsp (1 mL) ground cloves
1 tsp (5 mL) dried mint
¼ cup (50 mL) melted butter

🏵 Place the steaks in a baking dish 1½ to 2 in. (4 to 5 cm) deep. Salt and cover with the orange slices.
🏵 Combine the remaining ingredients and pour the sauce over the steaks.
🏵 Bake 40 minutes in a 325°F (170°C) oven, basting several times with the juice.
🏵 Serve with steamed rice.

TURKISH BROILED LAMB STEAK

🏵 Oven-broil or pan-broil a lamb steak of your choice. Do not marinate.
🏵 Five minutes before the end of the cooking period, brush with the following mixture:

1 tsp (5 mL) prepared mustard
1 tsp (5 mL) honey
pinch of thyme

🏵 Serve with puréed lentils.

Breast of Lamb à la Bretonne

4 lbs (2 kg) breast of lamb
1 onion
2 whole cloves
1 bay leaf
1 clove garlic
1 stalk celery
1 carrot
1 tsp (5 mL) salt
prepared mustard
salt and pepper
breadcrumbs
melted butter

❧ Place the first 8 ingredients in a Dutch oven or large casserole. Cover with cold water and bring to a boil. Cover and simmer until the meat is tender, approximately 1 hour.

❧ Remove the meat from the broth and place on a large platter. Remove the bones, cover with a second platter set directly on the meat and place a weight on top. Let sit until the meat is cooled.

❧ Cut the meat into serving pieces. Baste with mustard, salt and pepper, to taste, and roll in breadcrumbs.

❧ Place in a broiler pan, baste with melted butter and broil 4 in. (10 cm) from the element until lightly browned on both sides. Baste with melted butter 2 or 3 times during broiling.

❧ Serve with a tomato sauce and noodles.

Sardinian Shoulder of Lamb

❧ With the sharp point of a

Braised Lamb

knife, make incisions in a shoulder of lamb and stud it with 2 to 4 cloves of garlic, slivered. Make 8 or 10 more incisions in the roast and stuff each with a few sprigs of rosemary.

❧ Heat ½ cup (125 mL) sherry together with the juice of ½ lemon, ¼ tsp (1 mL) pepper and 1 tsp (5 mL) salt.

❧ Secure the lamb on a rotisserie spit or over a barbecue and cook 1 to 1½ hours or until the meat is tender. Baste every 10 minutes with the heated sherry mixture.

Braised Lamb

1 tsp (5 mL) salt
½ tsp (2 mL) pepper
1½ tbsp (25 mL) paprika
¼ tsp (1 mL) nutmeg
½ tsp (2 mL) sugar
1 lamb shoulder, 4 to 6 lbs (2 to 2.5 kg)

3 tbsp (45 mL) melted fat
2 onions, sliced

❧ Combine the salt, pepper, paprika, nutmeg and sugar and dredge the meat in the mixture.

❧ Brown the lamb in the melted fat and add the onions. Cover and cook over low heat for about 1 hour or until the meat is tender.

❧ To make the gravy, remove the lamb and bring the drippings to a boil, stirring constantly.

❧ Serve with boiled rice or parsleyed noodles.

Marinated Braised Shoulder of Lamb

1 cup (250 mL) tomato juice
1 tbsp (15 mL) cider vinegar
1 onion, chopped fine
1 clove garlic, halved
1 bay leaf
¼ tsp (1 mL) basil

leaf. Sprinkle the diced green pepper evenly over the 6 portions.

ta Combine the salt, pepper and thyme. Sprinkle evenly over each portion. Close the foil as tightly as possible.

ta Line a baking pan with aluminum foil and place the parcels, known as papillotes, side by side. Cover with another sheet of foil and barbecue on the grill for 1½ to 2 hours.

ta To serve, let the 6 guests open their own papillotes.

Bengal Lamb Curry

¼ tsp (1 mL) salt
4 to 6 lbs (2 to 2.5 kg) shoulder of lamb
3 tbsp (45 mL) lamb fat
1 tbsp (15 mL) sugar

ta In a large bowl, combine the tomato juice, vinegar, onion, garlic, bay leaf, basil and salt. Place the lamb shoulder in the mixture and marinate for 12 hours.

ta Melt the lamb fat (cut from the shoulder) in a heavy saucepan and brown the lamb in it. Add the marinade and the sugar. Cover and simmer for 2 hours or until the lamb is tender.

ta This dish can also be cooked in a pressure-cooker, but in this case add only ¼ cup (50 mL) of the marinade. Cook for 30 minutes.

ta Serve the meat with boiled and parsleyed macaroni shells. Serve the cooking liquid in a gravy boat.

BARBECUED SHOULDER OF LAMB EN PAPILLOTE

4 lbs (2 kg) lamb shoulder
⅓ cup (75 mL) flour
1 tbsp (15 mL) vegetable oil
6 small potatoes, peeled
6 small onions, peeled
6 small tomatoes, whole
3 bay leaves
¼ cup (50 mL) diced green pepper
1 tsp (5 mL) salt
½ tsp (2 mL) pepper
1 tsp (5 mL) thyme

ta Cut 6 pieces of aluminum foil 15 x 15 in. (40 x 40 cm) square. Divide the lamb into 6 serving pieces, trim off the excess fat and dredge in the flour.

ta Place a piece of meat on each square of foil, along with 1 potato, 1 onion, 1 tomato and a half bay

BENGAL LAMB CURRY

2 tbsp (30 mL) flour
1½ tsp (7 mL) salt
2 tbsp (30 mL) curry powder
2 lbs (1 kg) lamb shoulder
½ cup (125 mL) margarine
2 large onions, sliced
2 small apples, peeled and grated
1 lemon, peeled and sliced
1 clove garlic, minced
2 tbsp (30 mL) brown sugar
2 tbsp (30 mL) currants
2 tbsp (30 mL) coconut, grated*
½ cup (125 mL) cashews
2 cups (500 mL) water

ta Combine the flour, salt and curry powder. Cube the lamb and dredge it in the flour mixture.

ta Melt the margarine in a large heavy saucepan and brown the onions in it. Push the onions to the side of the pan and add the meat cubes. Stir over high heat until the lamb is seared on all sides.

ta Add the remaining ingredients. Bring to a boil, cover and cook over low heat for 1 hour or until the meat is tender.

🍃 Serve with steamed rice.

*If possible, use fresh coconut and substitute the coconut milk for part of the water called for.

ARMENIAN LAMB CASSEROLE

3 lbs (1.5 kg) lamb shoulder
½ cup (125 mL) vegetable oil
2 large onions, chopped
1 green pepper, diced
1 cup (250 mL) rice, uncooked
2 medium eggplants
2½ cups (625 mL) canned tomatoes
1 cup (250 mL) red wine
½ cup (125 mL) grated cheese
pinch of cinnamon
salt and pepper
1 clove garlic, minced

🍃 Cut the lamb shoulder in small cubes and brown in hot oil in a large skillet. Add the onions and green pepper and continue cooking for 5 minutes, stirring constantly.

🍃 Cook the rice. Peel and dice the eggplants. Place the eggplant cubes in a saucepan, cover with boiling water and boil 5 minutes. Drain the eggplant thoroughly.

🍃 Combine the cooked lamb with the cooked rice and drained eggplant. Stir in the tomatoes, wine, grated cheese and cinnamon. Add salt and pepper to taste, then the garlic, and blend thoroughly.

🍃 Turn the mixture into an 8-cup (2-L) casserole. Cover and bake 1 hour in a 350°F (180°C) oven.

🍃 Serves 8 to 10.

HUNGARIAN LAMB AND BARLEY STEW

2 lbs (1 kg) lamb shoulder
all-purpose flour
salt and pepper
2 tbsp (30 mL) vegetable oil
1 cup (250 mL) chopped onions
4 tomatoes, quartered
2 bay leaves
2 tbsp (30 mL) pearl barley
6 prunes, pitted
1 clove garlic, minced
1 tsp (5 mL) paprika
1 cup (250 mL) water
2 tbsp (30 mL) sour cream

🍃 Cut the lamb into serving pieces. Dredge in flour; salt and pepper to taste.

🍃 Brown the meat in the oil over high heat.

🍃 Add the onions, cover and simmer for 10 minutes. Add the remaining ingredients, except the sour cream.

🍃 Cover and simmer over low heat for about 2 hours or bake covered in a 350°F (180°C) oven for 2 hours.

🍃 When ready to serve, add the sour cream and mix thoroughly.

ARMENIAN LAMB STEW

2 lbs (1 kg) lamb shoulder
2 tbsp (30 mL) vegetable oil
1 cup (250 mL) sliced onions
2 lbs (1 kg) fresh spinach
1 cup (250 mL) tomato juice
1 tsp (5 mL) salt
¼ tsp (1 mL) pepper
1 tsp (5 mL) sugar
1 cup (250 mL) water

🍃 Cut up the lamb and trim off the excess fat.

Armenian Lamb Stew

❦ TECHNIQUE ❦

ARMENIAN LAMB STEW

1   Brown the lamb in the fat.

2   Add the onions, cover and cook over medium heat.

3   Add the spinach.

4   Add the tomato juice.

꘡ Brown in the oil over high heat. Add the onions, cover and cook over medium heat for 10 minutes.

꘡ Chop the spinach coarsely and add it to the lamb, together with the remaining ingredients.

꘡ Cover and simmer until the meat is tender, about 40 to 60 minutes.

IRISH STEW

2 to 4 lbs (1 to 2 kg) stewing lamb (shoulder or breast)
2 onions, quartered
½ cup (125 mL) chopped celery leaves
2 carrots, cut in 3 pieces
½ tsp (2 mL) dry mustard
½ tsp (2 mL) thyme
1 tbsp (15 mL) coarse salt
¼ tsp (1 mL) pepper
12 cups (3 L) lukewarm water
3 or 4 whole potatoes
3 or 4 whole carrots
3 or 4 whole onions

꘡ Place all the ingredients except the whole potatoes, carrots and onions in a large saucepan and bring to a rolling boil. Cover and simmer for 1½ to 2 hours or until the meat is tender.

꘡ Halfway through the cooking period, add the peeled whole potatoes, carrots and onions.

꘡ To serve, place the meat in the middle of a heated serving dish and surround with the vegetables.

꘡ Use the broth to make a delicious soup by adding 1 can tomatoes, 1 tbsp (15 mL) sugar and ½ cup (125 mL) barley. Simmer for about 1 hour.

Lamb with Sauerkraut

LAMB WITH SAUERKRAUT

4 slices bacon
1 onion, minced
3 to 4 cups (750 mL to 1 L) sauerkraut
salt and pepper
1 tsp (5 mL) anise seed
2 to 3 cups (500 to 750 mL) diced cooked lamb

꘡ Fry the bacon, then add the onion and brown it in the bacon grease. Add the sauerkraut, salt, pepper and anise seed. Cover and simmer for 1 hour.

꘡ Add the lamb, cover and simmer for another 15 minutes. Serve with boiled potatoes.

LAMB STEW WITH RICE

2½ lbs (1.2 kg) lamb shoulder
3 tbsp (45 mL) butter or vegetable oil
1¼ cups (300 mL) chopped onions
2 tbsp (30 mL) flour
salt and pepper, to taste
2 cups (500 mL) canned tomatoes
1 cup (250 mL) water
1 clove garlic, minced
1 tsp (5 mL) turmeric or a pinch of saffron
1 bay leaf
½ tsp (2 mL) thyme
1 tsp (5 mL) sugar
1 cup (250 mL) long-grain rice

꘡ Cut the meat into pieces of equal size. Brown in the butter or oil.

🖎 Add the onions and continue cooking until the onions are lightly browned. Add the flour and mix well.

🖎 Salt and pepper to taste. Add the tomatoes, water, garlic, turmeric or saffron, bay leaf, thyme and sugar. Bring to a boil. Cover and simmer for 1 hour.

🖎 Stir in the rice and transfer the mixture to an ovenproof casserole dish suitable for the table.

🖎 Cover and bake for about 35 minutes in a 350°F (180°C) oven.

LAMB MEATBALLS

2 thick slices stale bread
2 tbsp (30 mL) milk
1 lb (500 g) cooked lamb, finely chopped
2 fresh tomatoes, diced
1 small onion, chopped fine
1 beaten egg
salt and pepper
nutmeg, to taste
breadcrumbs
oil or fat

🖎 Soak the bread in the milk, and then mash it to a paste with a fork.

🖎 Add the cooked lamb, tomatoes, onion and beaten egg. Add salt, pepper and nutmeg to taste.

🖎 Shape into patties, roll in the breadcrumbs and brown in the oil or fat over medium heat for 2 or 3 minutes on each side.

LAMB FRICASSÉE

1 onion, minced
2 tbsp (30 mL) butter or lamb fat

1 tbsp (15 mL) parsley
or celery leaves
1 cup (250 mL) tomato sauce
1 cup (250 mL) leftover lamb gravy or ½ cup (125 mL) water
salt and pepper
pinch of thyme
2 to 3 cups (500 to 750 mL) cooked lamb, chopped

🖎 Fry the onion in the butter or lamb fat. Add the minced parsley or celery leaves, tomato sauce, gravy or water, salt and pepper and thyme. Simmer for 10 minutes.

🖎 Add the lamb. Cover and simmer for 1 hour or bake for 45 minutes in a 350°F (180°C) oven.

🖎 To serve, cover with mashed potatoes or accompany with rice.

LAMB HASH

1 onion, minced
2 tbsp (30 mL) butter or lamb fat
3 cups (750 mL) diced cooked lamb
1 cup (250 mL) diced cooked potatoes
½ cup (125 mL) diced celery
1 cup (250 mL) lamb stock
2 egg yolks, slightly beaten
1 cup (250 mL) light cream or milk
¼ tsp (1 mL) basil
salt and pepper to taste
chutney

🖎 Brown the onion lightly in the butter or fat. Add the meat, potatoes, celery and stock. Bring to a boil and simmer for 15 minutes.

🖎 Beat together the egg yolks,

cream or milk, basil, salt and pepper. Stir into the hash mixture and simmer a few minutes, but do not let boil.

🖎 Serve with chutney.

MOUSSAKA

1 large eggplant
¼ cup (50 mL) flour
6 tbsp (90 mL) butter
or margarine
½ cup (125 mL) chopped onion
1 lb (500 g) lean lamb shoulder, ground
¼ cup (50 mL) chopped parsley
¼ tsp (1 mL) pepper
2 tsp (10 mL) salt
½ tsp (2 mL) paprika
1 cup (250 mL) tomato sauce
½ cup (125 mL) dry white wine
1 medium tomato, sliced
1 tbsp (15 mL) flour
2 eggs, beaten
½ tsp (2 ml) salt
½ cup (125 mL) yogurt

🖎 Peel the eggplant and cut it into slices ¼ to ½ in. (0.6 to 1 cm) thick. Dredge lightly in flour.

🖎 Melt 2 tbsp (30 mL) of the butter or margarine in a large skillet and brown a single layer of eggplant slices on both sides over high heat; drain on paper towels. Cook the remaining eggplant the same way and set aside.

🖎 In the same skillet, brown the onion until tender. Add the lamb and sauté 5 minutes or until the meat loses its pink tinge. Add the parsley, pepper, the 2 tsp (10 mL) salt and the paprika, together with the tomato sauce and the white wine. Mix well and simmer a few minutes.

🦃 Arrange a third of the eggplant slices in the bottom of an 8-cup (2-L) casserole; cover with half the lamb mixture and top with another third of the eggplant slices. Place the remaining lamb mixture over all. Arrange the rest of the eggplant slices and the tomato slices on top, overlapping them in a decorative pattern.

🦃 Beat together 1 tbsp (15 mL) flour with the eggs until the mixture is smooth; mix in the ½ tsp (2 mL) salt and the yogurt. Use this to cover the lamb and eggplant.

🦃 Bake for 30 minutes in a preheated 375°F (190C) oven or until the top is well browned.

🦃 Serve with a green salad and garlic bread. This recipe yields 4 to 6 servings.

Lamb Pilaf

1 small onion, chopped
1 tbsp (15 mL) fat
2 cups (500 mL) diced cooked lamb
1 cup (250 mL) rice, uncooked
2 cups (500 mL) hot water
½ cup (125 mL) chili sauce
1 clove garlic, crushed
salt and pepper
¼ lb (125 g) fresh mushrooms, sliced, or ½ cup (125 mL) diced celery

🦃 Fry the onion in the fat. Add the lamb, rice, hot water, chili sauce, garlic, salt and pepper.

Cover and simmer 35 to 45 minutes or until the rice is tender.

🦃 Add the sliced mushrooms or diced celery and cook for 5 minutes more.

Spanish Rice with Lamb

1 large onion, finely chopped
1 green pepper, finely chopped, or 1 cup (250 mL) chopped celery
2 tbsp (30 mL) olive oil
1½ cups (375 mL) canned tomatoes
1 to 2 cups (250 to 500 mL) diced cooked lamb
2 cups (500 mL) cooked rice
½ tsp (2 mL) basil
salt and pepper, to taste

🦃 Fry the onion and the green pepper or celery in the olive oil.

🦃 Add the tomatoes and bring to

a boil. Add the remaining ingredients and stir well. Cook until piping hot.

🦃 Serve with grated cheese.

Navarin of Lamb

2 to 4 lb (1 to 2 kg) lamb shoulder, in 1-in. (2.5-cm) cubes
3 tbsp (45 mL) all-purpose flour
1 tsp (5 mL) salt
½ tsp (2 mL) pepper
¼ tsp (1 mL) nutmeg
4 tbsp (60 mL) butter or fat
2 large onions, minced
3 cups (750 mL) water
½ cup (125 mL) carrots, diced
½ cup (125 mL) turnips, diced
½ cup (125 mL) potatoes, diced

🦃 Dredge the cubed lamb in a mixture of the flour, salt, pepper and nutmeg.

🦃 Brown the meat cubes in the hot butter or fat over medium heat. Add the minced onions and

Navarin of Lamb

❦ TECHNIQUE ❦

NAVARIN OF LAMB

1 Dredge the cubes of lamb in a mixture of flour, salt, pepper and nutmeg.

2 Brown the meat in the butter or fat.

3 Add the onions and continue cooking.

4 Add the vegetables.

continue cooking for 1 minute.

❧ Add the water and stir until the mixture comes to a boil. Cover and simmer for 1 hour.

❧ Add the vegetables and simmer for another 1½ hours.

❧ Navarin is an excellent dish to make in advance and reheat, but in this case you should leave out the potatoes.

Lamb-Stuffed Green Peppers

4 green peppers
1 small onion, chopped
1 tbsp (15 mL) oil or fat
¼ cup (50 mL) water
2 fresh tomatoes, diced
pinch of basil
salt and pepper
1 cup (250 mL) cooked lamb
½ cup (125 mL) cooked rice
½ cup (125 mL) water
1 tsp (5 mL) sugar
1 tbsp (15 mL) fat

❧ Slice off the top of each pepper and scoop out the seeds and ribs. Blanch the peppers in boiling water for 5 minutes. Drain on paper towels.

❧ Fry the onion in the oil or fat until golden. Add the ¼ cup (50 mL) water, diced tomatoes, basil, salt, pepper and lamb (finely chopped); simmer for 10 minutes. Add the rice.

❧ Stuff the peppers with the lamb mixture. Place in a baking dish and pour the ½ cup (125 mL) water in the bottom of the dish with the sugar and the 1 tbsp (15 mL) fat.

❧ Bake in a 350°F (180°C) oven for 35 to 40 minutes.

Lamb Paté

¾ cup (175 mL) water
1 tsp (5 mL) salt
½ lb (250 g) diced lard or leftover ham fat
½ lb (250 g) lamb or calf's liver
1 bay leaf
1 clove garlic

❧ Place all the ingredients in a saucepan. Bring to a boil, then cover and simmer 15 minutes. Cool.

❧ Remove the bay leaf. Put the mixture into a blender or food processor, cover and blend 1 minute at high speed or until smooth.

❧ Turn into a dish. Cover and refrigerate.

Lamb Kidney Canapés

2 tbsp (30 mL) butter
8 lamb kidneys
4 tsp (20 mL) flour
2 tbsp (30 mL) parsley, minced
1 small onion, minced
½ cup (125 mL) consommé or water
¼ cup (50 mL) tomato juice
salt to taste
1 tsp (5 mL) Worcestershire sauce or chutney
4 slices buttered toast

❧ Trim off the outer membrane of the kidneys. Slice the kidneys in half, lengthwise. Remove any visible fat and trim off the white core and veins with scissors.

❧ Melt the butter in a large skillet until nutty brown. Add the kidneys and cook over medium heat for 6 to 8 minutes, turning frequently. Sprinkle on the flour and stir until it is well blended with the fat.

❧ Add the parsley, onion, consommé or water, tomato juice, salt and Worcestershire sauce or chutney. Cook over low heat, stirring constantly, for 2 or 3 minutes, or until the sauce thickens.

❧ Place the cooked kidneys on the 4 slices of buttered toast and sprinkle with parsley.

Kidneys in Mustard Sauce

4 lamb kidneys or 2 veal kidneys
3 tbsp (45 mL) butter or fat
1 tbsp (15 mL) butter
1 medium onion, sliced thin
4 mushrooms, sliced
1 tsp (5 mL) dry mustard
1 can consommé
3 tbsp (45 mL) flour
¼ tsp (1 mL) tarragon
salt to taste
3 tbsp (45 mL) sour cream (optional)
2 tbsp (30 mL) wine (optional)

❧ Slice the kidneys thin. Brown them in the 3 tbsp (45 mL) butter or fat over high heat for 2 minutes on each side. Remove the kidneys and any juice from the pan and set aside. Note that some kidneys will not brown in 2 minutes, but do not cook them any longer than the specified time or they will toughen.

❧ Put the 1 tbsp (15 mL) butter in the pan. Add the onion and the mushrooms and cook until lightly browned, then stir in the dry mustard and 1 tbsp (15 mL) of the consommé. Stir over medium heat for a few seconds. Stir in the flour, then the rest of the consommé, the tarragon and salt. Mix well. Cook over medium heat until the sauce is thick and creamy.

❧ Remove the sauce from the heat and stir in the kidneys with their juice, the sour cream and the wine. Simmer for another 5 minutes without boiling.

❧ Serve with steamed rice.

PAN-FRIED LAMB KIDNEYS

4 to 6 lamb kidneys
vinegar
prepared mustard or chutney
1 tbsp (15 mL) butter
or bacon fat
salt and pepper, to taste
1 tsp (5 mL) water

❧ Trim off the outer membrane covering the kidneys. Leave them whole or cut them in half, lengthwise.

❧ Rub the kidneys with vinegar, then baste them with prepared mustard or chutney.

❧ Melt the butter or fat in a skillet and brown the kidneys. Cook over high heat for 3 minutes on each side. You may have to regulate the heat so that the kidneys don't scorch, but make sure the heat is high enough to keep them from stewing in the pan juices.

❧ Salt and pepper to taste. Add the water and stew for several seconds before serving.

LAMB KIDNEY STEW

8 lamb kidneys
½ cup (125 mL) milk
4 tbsp (60 mL) butter
½ lb (250 g) mushrooms, sliced
2 tbsp (30 mL) chopped fresh parsley
1 small onion, minced
¼ cup (50 mL) sherry
¼ cup (50 mL) cream
salt and pepper to taste

❧ Remove the outer membranes covering the kidneys. Cut each kidney in half, lengthwise, and soak for 20 minutes in the milk. Drain and dry the kidneys and cut them into thin slices.

❧ Heat the butter in a skillet until nutty brown in color. Add the kidneys and the sliced mushrooms and sauté over high heat, stirring constantly, for 2 minutes.

❧ Add the parsley and the onion and simmer for 5 minutes.

❧ Add the sherry and the cream. Bring the mixture to a boil. Remove from the heat and add salt and pepper to taste.

❧ Serve plain or in vol-au-vent (puff-pastry) shells.

PORK

PORK

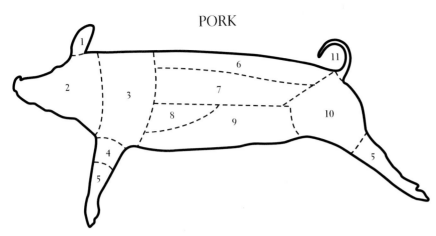

1. Ears
2. Head
3. Shoulder
4. Pork hocks
5. Pigs' feet
6. Fat back
7. Loin
8. Spareribs
9. Flank
10. Ham
11. Tail

PORK

EARS
Boiled, broiled or pickled, the pig's ears are a novelty dish.

HEAD
Everyone appreciates a delicious head cheese.

SHOULDER
The shoulder of the pig is normally divided into two sections:

🍃 The lower part of the shoulder, near the leg, is called picnic shoulder (or shoulder arm) and may be sold as fresh picnic shoulder or as rolled fresh picnic shoulder. The meat is quite lean.

🍃 This cut is also cured and smoked to make smoked picnic shoulder.

🍃 The upper part of the shoulder is called shoulder butt and can be marketed as fresh pork butt, Boston butt (rolled or bone-in) or cottage cut. It is also cured and smoked. The meat is a combination of fat and lean.

🍃 Shoulder may be cut up in 2 ways:

🍃 New York-cut shoulder has had the rind and outside fat removed from the butt end only.

🍃 Montreal-cut shoulder has the skin completely removed and only a thin layer of fat is left on. The shank is removed and the jowl trimmed off but the neck and rib bones are not taken out.

🍃 Shoulder cuts are delicious roasted or braised but are tastier if cooked with the skin still on. Since they are not normally marketed this way, it may be necessary to place an advance order with your butcher.

🍃 Boneless rolled roasts are easier to slice. Shoulder cuts are also good for stews and in sausages.

PORK HOCKS
Pork hocks are cut from the front legs and are very meaty although they contain some shank bone. In Europe, they are especially popular served with sauerkraut, in pot-au-feu, boiled and braised. They are sold fresh, smoked or pickled.

PIGS' FEET
The feet contain lots of bone and tendon but little meat. They are often used instead of pork rind in recipes such as galantine, because they produce lots of natural gelatin and add body to a sauce.

FAT BACK
The fat back is, as the name implies, mostly fat. It is a source of slat pork and lard.

LOIN
The pork loin has 3 sections:

🍃 The loin end, or filet, is the meatiest part of the loin, containing most of the tenderloin and some bones. It is sold as roasts or chops.

🍃 The center cut is less meaty and contains rib bones (T-bone) and little or no tenderloin. Sold as roasts or chops.

🍃 The rib end contains rib bones, a portion of the blade bone and none of the tenderloin. Sold as roasts or chops.

SPARERIBS
Try to purchase spareribs cut from the area near the back (back ribs); they are meatier than the side ribs cut from near the flank or bacon section. Pork spareribs are delicious cooked Chinese-style, boiled with cabbage or sauerkraut or grilled on the barbecue.

FLANK

The pig's flank is very fatty and is usually sold smoked as bacon.

HAM

The ham, or rear leg, may be left whole or divided into shank and butt sections.

🦐 The shank section contains the shank bone and joint.

🦐 The thicker butt end of the ham contains the ham bone. This is by far the meatier part of the full ham.

🦐 Ham slices or ham steaks are cut from the center ham, or butt end, and have a small round bone in the center.

TAIL

In Europe, broiled or boiled pig's tail is considered a real treat. The tail is gelatinous and can be used in place of pigs' feet to give body to dishes.

SEASONINGS FOR ROAST PORK

These seasonings go especially well with fresh roast pork: garlic, sage, ground cloves, bay leaf, marjoram, dry mustard, parsley, savory and paprika.

🦐 The following accompaniments are perfect for roast pork: applesauce, unpeeled apple rings fried in butter, pickled beets, mustard relish, chili sauce, apple or currant jelly, cranberry sauce, mashed potatoes and coleslaw.

ROASTING CHART FOR FRESH PORK

CUT	OVEN TEMPERATURE	COOKING TIME (minutes per lb/500 g)
Ham, leg	325°F (160°C)	35 to 45 minutes
Loin	325°F (160°C)	30 to 35 minutes
Shoulder		
—bone in	325°F (160°C)	35 to 40 minutes
—rolled	325°F (160°C)	35 to 40 minutes

NORMANDY-STYLE ROAST LOIN OF PORK

salt and pepper
5 lb (2 kg) joint of pork
6 to 8 apples, peeled and sliced
1 tbsp (15 mL) sugar
3 tbsp (45 mL) butter
½ cup (125 mL) heavy cream

🦐 Salt and pepper the loin of pork, place it in a roasting pan and roast in a 325°F (160°C) oven for 60 minutes.

🦐 Remove it from the oven and skim off the fat accumulated in the pan.

🦐 Surround the roast with the apple slices sprinkled with sugar and dotted with butter. Return it to the oven to finish cooking (see the roasting chart above). Baste 3 or 4 times during the roasting period with a spoonful of the reserved fat.

Normandy-Style Roast Loin of Pork

❧ To make the gravy, pour the contents of the pan through a sieve, making sure you crush the apple slices well to help thicken the gravy. Stir in the cream. Heat, if necessary, before pouring into a gravy boat.

❧ Serve with mashed potatoes.

ROAST SUCKLING PIG

1 suckling pig

STUFFING:
1 large onion, minced
2 tbsp (30 mL) butter
heart, liver and kidneys of the pig, chopped
2 cups (500 mL) cubed bread or cooked rice or whole buckwheat
cold water
½ tsp (2 mL) sage
¼ tsp (1 mL) marjoram or savory
2 tbsp (30 mL) salt
½ tsp (2 mL) pepper
2 cups (500 mL) diced unpeeled apples

MUSTARD BUTTER:
2 tbsp (30 mL) butter
1 tsp (5 mL) mustard

BASTING SAUCE:
2 cups (500 mL) water
¼ lb (125 g) butter
½ tsp (2 mL) salt
¼ cup (50 mL) sherry, or to taste

GARNISH:
2 small carrots
6 cranberries with cocktail picks
fresh watercress or cooked Brussels sprouts

APPLESAUCE:
2 cups (500 mL) apples, peeled and quartered
4 tbsp (60 mL) water
1 tbsp (15 mL) butter

❧ Fry the onion in the butter and add the giblets, finely chopped or put through a meat chopper. Toast the cubed bread in the oven, then add enough cold water to the bread (or rice or buckwheat) to make a paste. Combine this mixture with the sautéed onion, along with the herbs, seasonings and diced apples. Mix well.

❧ Wash the suckling pig well inside and out with a cloth dipped in vinegar and stuff it with the above mixture. Close the cavity and place the pig, with its legs folded underneath, in a large roasting pan. Brush the surface with the mustard butter. Roast for 20 minutes per lb (500 g) in a 325°F (160°C) oven.

❧ To make the basting sauce, boil the water with the butter and salt for 1 minute. Remove from heat and add the sherry. Baste the pig every 20 minutes during the first 1½ hours of roasting.

❧ At the end of this time, carefully remove the pig from the pan and place on a hot platter. Put a small carrot in each ear and 3 cranberries speared on a cocktail pick in each eye. Surround with watercress or cooked Brussels sprouts.

❧ To make the applesauce, peel and quarter the apples and cook over low heat in the water. When the apples are soft, force them through a sieve and beat them with the butter. Do not add sugar. Serve hot or cold.

ROAST FRESH HAM

½ or 1 whole fresh, unsmoked ham
1 tsp (5 mL) coarse salt
½ tsp (2 mL) thyme
1 clove garlic, crushed
½ tsp (2 mL) pepper

❧ If possible, purchase a fresh ham complete with the rind. Score the fat or rind into a diamond pattern (just as you would do for a glazed ham).

❧ Combine the remaining ingredients thoroughly and rub the mixture generously over the surface of the ham.

❧ Place the ham in a heavy baking pan. Do not add water. Bake in a 325°F (160°C) oven for the time indicated on the roasting chart (see previous page).

❧ Remove the meat from the pan and let stand in a warm place for 20 minutes before carving.

❧ Make a gravy using cold tea, apple juice, tomato juice or red wine as the liquid.

QUÉBEC-STYLE ROAST OF PORK

2 cloves garlic
4 to 5 lb (2 kg) pork loin
1 tsp (5 mL) dry mustard
1 tsp (5 mL) savory
salt and pepper

1 pork rind or pig's foot
1 cup (250 mL) water

🔸 Cut the garlic cloves in half and insert them in incisions in the pork loin. Rub the meat with the dry mustard and the savory, making sure as much as possible sticks to the fat.

🔸 Place the roast in an enamel Dutch oven. (The fat will be whiter if the roast is cooked in an enameled pot, but it will taste just as good prepared in a cast-iron pot). Salt and pepper to taste. Cut up the pork rind or pig's foot and place around the roast. Add the water.

🔸 There are 2 ways to cook this recipe.

🔸 To cook it on the top of the stove, place the pot on the burner and bring to a boil. Cover and simmer for 2 hours, then uncover and cook over high heat until the liquid is evaporated. Turn the roast and continue cooking until the fat is browned. Move the roast to a warm platter. Add 1 cup (250 mL) cold water to the residue in the pan and simmer for 10 minutes, stirring and scraping the bottom well. Strain this liquid through a sieve and serve these delicious pan drippings with the roast.

🔸 Or you can cook the roast, uncovered, in a 325°F (160°C) oven. Roast for 45 minutes per lb (500 g). (See the roasting chart on page 239). When the roast is done, move it to a warm platter. Place the pan on a burner and add 1 cup (250 mL) cold water to the residue in the pan. Simmer for 10 minutes, stirring and scraping the bottom. Strain through a sieve to make the pan drippings.

Loin of Pork Boulangère

LOIN OF PORK BOULANGÈRE

1 4- to 6-lb (2- to 3-kg) loin of pork
2 garlic cloves, slivered
1 large piece raw pork rind
salt and pepper
6 potatoes

🔸 Insert slivers of garlic in the pork loin. Place the pork rind, fat side down, in a roasting pan. Place the tenderloin on top.

🔸 Salt and pepper.

🔸 Roast in a 325°F (160°C) oven for 35 minutes per lb (500 g). (See the roasting chart on page 239.)

🔸 In the meantime, peel the potatoes and scald them for 10 minutes in boiling water. Drain.

🔸 Halfway through the cooking period, arrange the potatoes around the meat. Baste and turn several times during the roasting period.

🔸 To serve, cut the well-browned rind into small squares, using scissors. Return the squares to the pan drippings.

ROAST PORK TENDERLOIN

2 medium pork filets, butterflied lengthwise
1 clove garlic
6 medium potatoes
½ tsp (2 mL) savory
1 fried onion
1 tsp (5 mL) bacon fat
or soft butter
½ tsp (2 mL) mustard
salt and pepper, to taste
¼ cup (50 mL) hot water

🔸 Rub the filets with the garlic.

🔸 Cook and mash the potatoes

and add the savory, fried onion and seasonings. When cooled, shape the potato into a roll the same length as the filets. Sandwich the potato roll between the filets. Tie string loosely around the two ends and the middle to hold together. Brush the top filet with the bacon fat or soft butter. Sprinkle with the mustard. Salt and pepper to taste.

🍂 Place the roll in a small baking pan with ¼ cup (50 mL) hot water.

🍂 Bake 30 to 35 minutes per lb (500 g) in a 350°F (180°C) oven, basting a few times during the cooking period.

🍂 Served hot or cold, this roast is easy to slice and is a meal in itself.

ROAST LOIN OF PORK WITH ROSEMARY

4- to 5-lb (2-kg) loin of pork
1 clove garlic
1 tsp (5 mL) salt
1 tsp (5 mL) rosemary
¼ cup (50 mL) white wine
½ cup (125 mL) heavy cream
roast potatoes
buttered spinach

🍂 Rub the loin of pork thoroughly with the garlic. Place the meat in a roasting pan and sprinkle with salt and rosemary.

🍂 Roast in a 325°F (160°C) oven for the time indicated in the roasting chart (see page 239).

🍂 When the roast is done, remove from the pan and skim off the excess fat. Add the white wine and the cream and stir over low

heat, scraping the bottom, until hot. Avoid boiling.

🍂 Serve with the roast potatoes and buttered spinach.

APPLE-STUFFED LOIN OF PORK

1 cup (250 mL) diced peeled apples
3 cups (750 mL) fresh breadcrumbs
¾ tsp (3 mL) salt
¼ tsp (1 mL) sage or rosemary
¼ tsp (1 mL) pepper
1 tbsp (15 mL) brown sugar
1 onion, sliced
2 tbsp (30 mL) bacon fat or butter
3 tbsp (45 mL) hot water or tomato juice
1 loin of pork, with 6 ribs
½ cup (125 mL) water

🍂 In a bowl, mix the apples, breadcrumbs, salt, sage or rosemary, pepper and brown sugar.

🍂 Brown the onion lightly in the bacon fat or butter and add the hot water or tomato juice. Combine with the apple mixture. Mix well.

🍂 Slice between each rib as if cutting into chops, but do not cut through the chine bone (backbone), as it must hold the roast together. Place in a greased roasting pan. Stuff the space between each chop to capacity with the apple stuffing. Pour the water on top.

🍂 Bake 30 to 35 minutes per lb (500 g) in a 350°F (180°C) oven. If the top starts to brown too much, cover loosely with aluminum foil.

PORK TENDERLOIN ORIENTALE

1 or 2 pork filets
2 eggs, beaten
3 tbsp (45 mL) cornstarch
1 carrot cut in thin strips
1 green pepper cut in thin strips
2 tbsp (30 mL) sugar
2 tbsp (30 mL) vinegar
1 bouillon cube
1 cup (250 mL) hot water
4 tbsp (60 mL) vegetable oil

🍂 Cut the pork into ½-in. (1-cm) cubes. Dip the cubes in the beaten eggs, then dredge in the cornstarch. Set on a piece of wax paper to dry.

🍂 In a bowl, combine the vegetables, sugar, vinegar and the bouillon cube well dissolved in the hot water. Let sit for 30 minutes.

🍂 Heat the oil in a large skillet and add the cubes of tenderloin. Brown quickly over high heat, stirring constantly. After 3 or 4 minutes, add the vegetable mixture. Continue stirring over medium heat another 2 to 3 minutes.

🍂 Serve with steamed or boiled rice.

BRAISED SHOULDER OF PORK

3- to 5-lb (1.5- to 2.5-kg) pork shoulder
3 carrots, peeled and chopped
4 onions, peeled and chopped
2 cloves garlic, minced

1 tsp (5 mL) salt
½ tsp (2 mL) pepper
½ tsp (2 mL) marjoram or thyme
1 cup (250 mL) consommé
3 cups (750 mL) cooked rice
¼ cup (50 mL) parsley

🍃 Trim off ½ cup (125 mL) of fat from the roast and melt it in a heavy pan or Dutch oven. Brown the meat in the fat on all sides over low heat.

🍃 Add the carrots, onions, garlic, salt, pepper, and marjoram or thyme. Cover and cook over low heat for 35 minutes per lb (500 g). (See the roasting chart on page 239.)

🍃 When the roast is done, remove it from the pan and stir the consommé into the pan drippings. Bring to a boil, stirring constantly.

🍃 Serve as is or put through a food mill to mash the vegetables.

🍃 Serve with boiled rice garnished with parsley.

FILET OF PORK WITH MUSHROOMS

1 filet of pork
1 clove garlic
paprika
2 tbsp (30 mL) butter
1 cup (250 mL) fresh mushrooms, sliced thin
3 tbsp (45 mL) white wine or lemon juice
salt and pepper
½ tsp (2 mL) marjoram or savory

1 tbsp (15 mL) flour
½ cup (125 mL) water, consommé or cream

🍃 Rub the filet of pork on both sides with the clove of garlic. Sprinkle with paprika and brown in hot butter over medium heat.

🍃 Add the mushrooms and stir quickly to coat with butter, then add the wine or lemon juice, salt and pepper, and marjoram or savory. Cover and simmer for approximately 40 minutes or until the filet is tender.

🍃 Remove the filet to a warm platter.

🍃 Blend the flour with the water, consommé or cream. Add to the pan drippings and the mushrooms. Stir constantly, scraping the bottom of the pan, until the sauce is creamy. Season to taste. Serve with the filet.

CANTONESE BROILED FILETS OF PORK

¼ cup (50 mL) soy sauce
¼ cup (50 mL) sherry
3 cloves garlic, sliced thin
4 tbsp (60 mL) grated fresh ginger root
4 small filets of pork
½ cup (125 mL) orange juice
1 tsp (5 mL) dry mustard

🍃 In a bowl, combine the soy sauce, sherry, garlic and ginger. Mix well.

🍃 Place the filets in this mixture, making sure they are well covered. Cover and marinate for 3 hours or overnight in the refrigerator.

🍃 Remove the filets from the marinade and broil until browned on both sides (15 to 18 minutes in total).

Cantonese Broiled Filets of Pork

❦ TECHNIQUE ❦

CANTONESE BROILED FILETS OF PORK

1 Put the soy sauce, sherry, garlic and grated ginger in a large bowl.

2 Mix well.

3 Cover the pork filets with the marinade.

4 Combine the orange juice and mustard and use as a basting sauce for the filets.

Combine the orange juice and dry mustard and use the mixture to baste the filets several times during the cooking period.

FILETS OF PORK WITH SAGE STUFFING

This old-fashioned recipe is generally cooked on the stove-top rather than in the oven. This produces a juicy meat and a rich brown gravy.

2 filets of pork
½ lemon

STUFFING:
2 tbsp (30 mL) butter
1 onion, chopped fine
1 cup (250 mL) packed fresh breadcrumbs
1 tsp (5 mL) sage
grated zest of ½ lemon
½ tsp (2 mL) salt
¼ tsp (1 mL) pepper
1 egg
flour
2 slices bacon, diced
1 tbsp (15 mL) butter

Butterfly each filet by slicing in half lengthwise, being careful not to cut all the way through. Spread flat and rub with the ½ lemon.

To prepare the stuffing, melt the 2 tbsp (30 mL) butter. Add the onion and sauté over medium heat until transparent but not browned. Remove from the heat and stir in the breadcrumbs, sage, lemon zest, salt and pepper. Add the raw egg and mix well.

Spread the stuffing mixture over 1 of the butterflied filets. Top with the second filet and tie them together with kitchen string. Dredge both sides with flour.

Melt the diced bacon together with the 1 tbsp (15 mL) butter in a large heavy pan or Dutch oven. Brown the filets on both sides. Cover and cook over low heat for 35 to 40 minutes per lb (500 g).

To serve, arrange the filets on a hot platter.

To prepare the gravy, add 1 tbsp (15 mL) flour to the pan drippings and stir for about 5 minutes or until browned. Then add 2 cups (500 mL) consommé, weak tea or water. Cook, stirring, until creamy and slightly thick.

PORK TENDERLOIN FONDUE

This is inspired by the Japanese Teriyaki, which is usually broiled. It has a lovely flavor and cooks very well in a fondue pot.

2 lbs (1 kg) pork tenderloin
piece of fresh ginger root
1 clove garlic
½ cup (125 mL) soy sauce
1 tsp (5 mL) sugar

Slice the tenderloin 1 in. (2.5 cm) thick. Pound each slice until thin and place in a bowl.

Chop the ginger and garlic fine, or, preferably, crush in a garlic press, and mix with the soy sauce. Add this to the pieces of pork in the bowl. Stir in the sugar. Cover the bowl and marinate in the refrigerator for 24 hours.

Allow the meat to reach room temperature 2 hours before cooking. To cook, follow the procedure for *Fondue Bourguignonne* (see page 177).

Serve with plain boiled rice and a choice of spicy sauce or plum sauce.

CHOP SUEY

3 tbsp (45 mL) vegetable oil
2 tsp (10 mL) salt
½ tsp (2 mL) pepper
1 lb (500 g) pork shoulder, cubed
3 tbsp (45 mL) soy sauce
3 cups (750 mL) celery, in 1-in. (2.5 cm) pieces
2 large onions, each cut into 6 wedges
1 tbsp (15 mL) molasses
2 cups (500 mL) boiling water
2 cups (500 mL) bean sprouts
3 tbsp (45 mL) cornstarch
¼ cup (50 mL) cold water
3 cups (750 mL) hot cooked rice

Heat the oil, salt and pepper in a large skillet. Add the pork and sear over high heat for 2 to 3 minutes, stirring often. Reduce heat and simmer, uncovered, for 5 to 8 minutes.

Add the soy sauce and mix well, then stir in the celery and onions and cook for 3 more minutes. Combine the molasses and boiling water and pour over the mixture. Cover and simmer over very low heat for 10 to 20 minutes.

Milanese-Style Pork Chops

Add the bean sprouts and cook for another 3 minutes.

Blend the cornstarch with the cold water. Add to the chop suey and continue cooking, stirring, for 3 to 4 minutes or until the sauce thickens and becomes transparent.

Serve with hot rice.

Serves 6.

PAN-FRYING PORK CHOPS

Sauté the chop over high heat in a little butter or olive oil. When slightly browned on 1 side, turn and sprinkle with salt, pepper and a little marjoram. Cover the pan and cook over low heat for 20 minutes. Remove the cover and brown quickly over high heat for 2 minutes.

Thick pork chops can be stuffed with a bread or potato stuffing. Slit the fat side of the chop to make a pocket, fill with stuffing, then fasten with string or toothpicks. Cook following the instructions for pan-frying pork chops.

MILANESE-STYLE PORK CHOPS

Dredge the pork chops in flour, then dip in an egg beaten with 3 tbsp (45 mL) cold water. Coat with a mixture of half breadcrumbs, half grated Parmesan cheese.

Cook according to the instructions for pan-fried pork chops.

Serve with lemon wedges and a green salad.

BAKED PORK CHOPS

Rub a cold cast-iron skillet with a clove of garlic or a slice of onion. Heat gently, then rub with a small piece of fat from the chop.

Brown the chops on 1 side over medium heat, then turn and sprinkle with salt, pepper and marjoram to taste. Finish cooking in a 325°F (160°C) oven, calculating the time as follows:

Cooking time for slices 1-in. (2.5-cm) thick:

chop:
10 to 12 minutes each side

shoulder steak:
16 to 18 minutes each side.

round steak:
26 to 28 minutes each side.

DEVILED PORK CHOPS

6 pork chops
1 onion, finely chopped
3 tbsp (45 mL) lemon juice
1 tsp (5 mL) dry mustard
1 tbsp (15 mL) brown sugar
6 tbsp (90 mL) chili sauce
or catsup
2 tsp (10 mL) Worcestershire sauce

Remove most of the fat from the chops. Soak the chops for 1 hour in a marinade made from the remaining ingredients.

🍂 Melt and brown the fat in a skillet. Drain the chops and brown them in the melted fat. When browned on both sides, add the marinating mixture.

🍂 Cover the skillet and simmer for 15 minutes.

🍂 These chops are delicious served with plain spinach and mashed potatoes.

PORK CHOPS NIÇOISE

6 pork chops
4 tomatoes, peeled and sliced
2 cloves garlic, minced
1 green pepper, chopped
1 tsp (5 mL) basil
1 tbsp (15 mL) sugar
½ cup (125 mL) pitted black olives

🍂 Remove some of the fat from the chops and melt it in a cast-iron skillet.

🍂 Add the chops, along with all the other ingredients, except the olives. Cover and cook over medium heat for 15 to 20 minutes, turning the chops once.

🍂 When the chops are cooked, add the olives and continue cooking for another 3 minutes over low heat.

🍂 Serve with boiled rice.

CHINESE SPARERIBS

1½ lbs (750 g) small spareribs
¾ cup (175 mL) soy sauce
2 cloves garlic, minced
½ tsp (2 mL) salt

2 tbsp (30 mL) honey
1 tbsp (15 mL) sherry

🍂 Ask your butcher to cut the spareribs into 1-in. (2.5-cm) pieces.

🍂 Combine all the other ingredients in a bowl and coat the meat with the sauce. Marinate for ½ hour.

🍂 Place the ribs on a rack over a drip pan. Broil 4 in. (10 cm) from the heat source for 40 to 50 minutes or bake for 1 hour in a 400°F (200°C) oven.

PORK CHOPS CHARCUTIÈRE

8 pork chops
2 onions, sliced
salt and pepper, to taste
1½ cups (375 mL) consommé
¼ cup (50 mL) tomato paste
1 tsp (5 mL) dry mustard

1 tsp (5 mL) brown sugar
2 tbsp (30 mL) flour
¼ cup (50 mL) cold water
2 sour pickles, chopped

🍂 Trim some of the fat from the chops and melt it in a cast-iron skillet. Lightly brown the chops on both sides in the melted fat. Add the onions. Cover the pan and simmer for 5 minutes.

🍂 Salt and pepper to taste and keep cooking over low heat until the chops are tender. Move the meat to a hot platter.

🍂 Add to the remaining onions in the pan the consommé, tomato paste, dry mustard and brown sugar. Bring to a boil and simmer for 2 minutes.

🍂 Blend the flour with the water and add to the sauce. Continue cooking, stirring, until the sauce is thick. Stir in the chopped pickles.

Pork Chops Charcutière

[247]

❧ TECHNIQUE ❧

PORK CHOPS CHARCUTIÈRE

1 Trim some of the fat from the pork chops.

2 Brown the chops in the hot fat.

3 Add the onions. Cover and simmer.

4 Remove the chops. Add the consommé, tomato paste, mustard and brown sugar to the onions.

⋙ Pour the sauce over the chops.

⋙ Serve with mashed potatoes.

BARBECUED BABY SPARERIBS

1 clove garlic, minced
3 tbsp (45 mL) bacon fat
3 lbs (1.5 kg) small spareribs
3 onions, sliced thin
1 cup (250 mL) catsup
½ cup (125 mL) cider vinegar
1 tsp (5 mL) curry
1 tsp (5 mL) paprika
¼ tsp (1 mL) chili powder
1 tbsp (15 mL) brown sugar
1 cup (250 mL) consommé
½ tsp (2 mL) salt
pinch of pepper
½ tsp (2 mL) dry mustard
steamed rice

⋙ Brown the garlic in the bacon fat. Cut the spareribs into serving pieces. Remove the garlic from the fat and brown the spareribs over high heat.

⋙ Place the garlic and the meat in an ovenproof dish. Arrange the sliced onions on top of the meat.

⋙ Combine the remaining ingredients and place the mixture over the meat and onions. Cover.

⋙ Bake in a 350°F (180°C) oven for 40 to 50 minutes or until the meat is tender.

⋙ Serve with steamed rice.

PRESSURE-COOKER BARBECUED SPARERIBS

3 lbs (1.5 kg) small spareribs
salt and pepper
paprika
1 tbsp (15 mL) bacon fat
1 large onion, chopped
¼ cup (50 mL) catsup
2 tbsp (30 mL) vinegar
1 tsp (5 mL) Worcestershire sauce
pinch of chili powder
¼ tsp (1 mL) celery seed
3 tbsp (45 mL) brown sugar
¼ cup (50 mL) water

⋙ Cut the sparerib sections into individual ribs. Season with the salt, pepper and paprika.

⋙ Melt the bacon fat in the bottom of the pressure-cooker and brown the ribs in it over high heat. Add the onion, catsup, vinegar, Worcestershire sauce, seasonings, brown sugar and water.

⋙ Close the cover securely and cook 15 minutes. Let the pressure drop of its own accord.

SAUSAGES

There are 4 ways of cooking sausages to perfection:

⋙ To pan-fry: place the sausages in a cold, lightly greased skillet and cook over medium heat for 15 to 20 minutes, turning often so that they will be evenly browned. Remove excess fat as it collects.

⋙ To pan-fry par-boiled sausages: this will result in plumper, leaner sausages. Prick the sausages with a fork and pour boiling water over them; cover and bring to a boil, then drain and pan-fry slowly

Barbecued Baby Spareribs

until evenly browned, as in the first method.

🍂 To bake: arrange the sausages in a lightly greased shallow baking pan and bake 25 to 30 minutes in a 350°F (180°C) oven, turning once halfway through the cooking period. This method is a time-saver if you are baking something else at the same time.

🍂 To broil: place the sausages in a broiler pan 6 in. (15 cm) from direct heat and broil 2 to 3 minutes on each side or until browned.

UPSIDE-DOWN SAUSAGE BREAD

This is a Vermont specialty I once had at a roadside church sale. It was served as a main dish with a choice of hot buttered maple syrup or homemade green chow chow.

1 lb (500 g) pork sausage meat or 1 lb (500 g) link sausages
1½ cups (375 mL) cornmeal
½ cup (125 mL) all-purpose flour
½ tsp (2 mL) salt
2 tsp (10 mL) baking powder
½ tsp (2 mL) baking soda
1 egg
1 cup (250 mL) sour milk or buttermilk
½ tsp (2 mL) sage or savory
2 tbsp (30 mL) sausage drippings

🍂 Break the sausage meat with a fork while browning it thoroughly in a cast-iron skillet. Or brown link sausage using one of the methods above. In either case, drain off and reserve the drippings.

🍂 Stir together in a bowl the cornmeal, flour, salt, baking powder and baking soda.

🍂 Combine the egg, sour milk or buttermilk and sage or savory. Add 2 tbsp (30 mL) of the sausage drippings.

🍂 Pour the liquid mixture over the dry ingredients all at once and stir just enough to mix well.

🍂 Turn the batter over the sausages still in the hot skillet.

🍂 Bake in a 400°F (200°C) oven 30 to 35 minutes or until golden brown. Invert on a warm platter.

SAUSAGE BAKE

The Welsh serve this dish at what they call a "Big Feed," an expression I have heard in New Brunswick to describe a lobster or chicken barbecue party on the beach. The Germans prepare a similar dish using frankfurt sausages.

1 lb (500 g) fresh pork sausages
prepared mustard
nutmeg
salt and pepper
2 cups (500 mL) cooked beets
1 cup (250 mL) beer, preferably ale

🍂 With a sharp knife, split the pork sausages in half, just enough to butterfly them. Spread each with prepared mustard and sprinkle with nutmeg, salt and pepper.

🍂 Arrange the prepared sausages in a single layer in a shallow baking dish. Cover with a thick layer of thinly sliced cooked beets. Pour the beer over all.

🍂 Bake 30 minutes in a 400°F (200°C) oven.

🍂 Serve this casserole with hot crusty bread or toast and buttered green beans.

SAUSAGES AND ONIONS

1 to 2 lbs (500 to 900 g) sausages
cold water to cover
3 onions, sliced thin
2 tbsp (30 mL) water
1 tsp (5 mL) sugar
2 tbsp (30 mL) flour
1 cup (250 mL) consommé, water or tomato juice
¼ tsp (1 mL) savory

🍂 Place the sausages in a cold skillet and cover with cold water. Cover the skillet and bring to a boil. As soon as the water boils, drain the sausages.

🍂 Return the sausages to the skillet and fry over medium heat for 5 to 8 minutes.

🍂 Remove the sausages and add to the fat in the pan the onions, water and sugar. Stir until the onions are golden. Sprinkle on the flour and stir, then add the consommé, water or tomato juice (although consommé will enhance the flavor, the sausages produce such a rich flavor that water will do). Bring to a boil and stir until thick.

🍂 Return the sausages to the pan and heat in the onion sauce. Add the savory to taste.

🍂 Serve with mashed potatoes and coleslaw.

ITALIAN SAUSAGE AND RICE CASSEROLE

1 lb (500 g) sausages
2 onions, finely chopped
1 clove garlic, minced
1 cup (250 mL) celery, diced
½ cup (125 mL) green pepper, diced
2 tbsp (30 mL) vegetable oil
1 cup (250 mL) uncooked rice
1 tsp (5 mL) salt
½ tsp (2 mL) pepper
¼ tsp (1 mL) basil or savory
3 cups (750 mL) water (or half water, half consommé or tomato juice)

🥄 Start browning the sausages over low heat. When they begin to cook, remove the excess fat and raise the heat.

🥄 When the sausages are brown, add the onions, garlic, celery and green pepper. Stir over medium heat for about 2 minutes.

🥄 Turn the sausage mixture into a large heavy pot or casserole. Add the vegetable oil and the uncooked rice. Stir over medium heat until the rice is golden. Add the salt, pepper, basil or savory and the liquid. Cover and cook for 40 to 50 minutes or until all the liquid is absorbed.

YORKSHIRE SAUSAGES

This recipe is proof that sausages can be a truly gourmet dish.

1 lb (500 g) sausages
¾ cup (175 mL) pastry flour
⅓ tsp (1.5 mL) salt

Sausages and Onions

½ tsp (2 mL) baking powder
¾ cup (175 mL) milk
2 eggs

🥄 Preheat the oven to 450°F (230°C).

🥄 Brown the sausages in a lightly greased skillet for 10 minutes, turning so they are golden on all sides.

🥄 Sift together the dry ingredients, add the milk and beat into a smooth batter. Add the eggs and beat well.

🥄 Pour the batter over the sausages and bake for 20 minutes.

🥄 Serve with creamed onions or creamed corn.

BATTER-FRIED SAUSAGES

½ lb (250 g) sausages
½ cup (125 mL) flour, sifted
⅓ cup (75 mL) beer

1 egg
1 tsp (5 mL) onion
fat for frying

🥄 Cook the sausages in boiling water for 2 minutes. Drain and dry. Cut into 1-in. (2.5-cm) lengths.

🥄 Prepare a batter with the flour, beer, egg and onion.

🥄 Heat the fat to 375°F (190°C) in a skillet.

🥄 Dip each piece of sausage in the batter and fry a few pieces at a time for 3 to 4 minutes, or until browned and puffy. Drain on paper towels.

SAUSAGE MEAT LOAF

🥄 In this recipe, 1 lb (500 g) of sausage meat, combined with mashed potatoes and a few other ingredients, will serve 6, and it is equally good hot or cold.

1 lb (500 g) sausage meat
1¼ cups (300 mL) instant potato flakes
⅓ cup (75 mL) milk
2 eggs, lightly beaten
1 tsp (5 mL) salt
¼ tsp (1 mL) pepper
1 tsp (5 mL) sage or savory
1 tsp (5 mL) prepared mustard
¼ cup (50 mL) instant potato flakes
¼ cup (50 mL) oatmeal
2 tbsp (30 mL) melted butter

🖎 Combine in a bowl the sausage meat, the 1¼ cups (300 mL) potato flakes, the milk, beaten eggs, salt, pepper, sage or savory and prepared mustard. Mix thoroughly.
🖎 Combine the ¼ cup (50 mL) of potato flakes with the oatmeal and melted butter.
🖎 Sprinkle half of the oatmeal mixture in the bottom of a loaf pan. Pack in the meat mixture, then top with the rest of the oatmeal mixture.
🖎 Bake 1½ hours in a 350°F (180°C) oven.
🖎 Cool 15 minutes before unmolding.

NEW ENGLAND SAUSAGE STUFFING

Use this stuffing for turkey, chicken, duck or meat loaf. You can even use it to stuff a boned shoulder of pork or veal.

½ lb (250 g) sausage meat
or ½ lb (250 g) sausages
cut in 1-in. (2.5-cm) lengths
2½ cups (625 mL) packed bread cubes
1½ tsp (7 mL) salt
¼ tsp (1 mL) pepper

1 tsp (5 mL) sage
or poultry seasoning
1 small onion, chopped fine
½ tsp (2 mL) baking powder
1¼ cups (300 mL) hot milk
2 tbsp (30 mL) meat drippings

🖎 Fry the sausage meat, or the sausages, in its own fat over low heat until the pink tinge has disappeared.
🖎 Drain off the fat and combine the meat with the bread, salt, pepper, sage or poultry seasoning, onion and baking powder. The baking powder is the secret to making this stuffing light and fluffy. Add the hot milk.
🖎 Melt the meat drippings in a large skillet. Add the stuffing mixture and sauté until the milk is evaporated and the bottom is browned in places.
🖎 Let the stuffing cool until you are ready to use it.
🖎 This will make enough stuffing for a 3- to 4-lb (1.5-kg) chicken or duck. Double the recipe to stuff a turkey.

QUÉBEC TOURTIÈRE

1 lb (500 g) ground pork
1 small onion, chopped
1 small clove garlic, minced
½ tsp (2 mL) salt
½ tsp (2 mL) savory
¼ tsp (1 mL) celery seed
¼ tsp (1 mL) ground cloves
½ cup (125 mL) water
¼ to ½ cup (50 to 125 mL) breadcrumbs

Québec Tourtière

🖈 Place all the ingredients except the breadcrumbs in a saucepan. Bring to a boil and cook over medium heat, uncovered, for 20 minutes, stirring often to break up the meat. Remove from heat.

🖈 Add some of the breadcrumbs and let stand 10 minutes. If the fat is sufficiently absorbed by the breadcrumbs, do not add more. If there is still some visible fat, add enough breadcrumbs to absorb the fat.

🖈 When the mixture is cool, use it to fill a double pie crust. Bake in a 500°F (260°C) oven until the crust is golden.

🖈 Serve hot.

PORK MEAT LOAF

1¾ cups (425 ml) white breadcrumbs
½ cup (125 mL) milk
1 egg, lightly beaten
2 tbsp (30 mL) celery, minced
2 lbs (1 kg) ground pork
1½ tsp (7 ml) salt
pinch of pepper
½ tsp (2 mL) marjoram

🖈 Preheat the oven to 375°F (190°C).

🖈 Mix the breadcrumbs with the milk in a large bowl and let stand for a few minutes. Then add the remaining ingredients and mix well.

🖈 With wet hands, press the mixture into a shallow loaf pan. Bake, uncovered, for 1¼ hours.

🖈 Unmold on a serving platter.

Pork Meat Loaf

QUÉBEC MEATBALL STEW

1 lb (500 g) fresh lean pork
½ lb (250 g) ground beef
¼ lb (125 g) salt pork
1 small onion, minced
2 tbsp (30 mL) parsley
¼ tsp (1 mL) ginger
½ tsp (2 mL) cinnamon
½ tsp (2 mL) ground cloves
½ tsp (2 mL) dry mustard
2 slices bread, diced
½ cup (125 mL) milk
salt and pepper
3 tbsp (45 mL) fat
3 cups (750 mL) water
4 tbsp (60 mL) browned flour
½ cup (125 mL) water

🖈 Grind the fresh pork, ground beef and salt pork 3 times in a meat grinder.

🖈 Add the onion, parsley, ginger, cinnamon, ground cloves and dry mustard. Add the diced bread soaked in the milk and crumbled. Salt and pepper to taste. Shape into small meatballs.

🖈 Fry the meatballs in a fat of your choice. Pour the 3 cups (750 mL) water over the meatballs. Cover and simmer for 30 minutes.

🖈 Shake together in a jar the flour and the ½ cup (125 mL) water. Turn into the broth and continue cooking, stirring, until thick.

SPANISH PORK KIDNEYS

2 to 4 pork kidneys
2 tbsp (30 mL) bacon fat
1 onion, chopped

3 fresh tomatoes, peeled
and diced
½ tsp (2 mL) sugar
1 clove garlic, crushed
pinch of rosemary, sage
or marjoram
salt and pepper
celery seed

❧ Remove the fat and the outer membrane from the kidneys. Halve them lengthwise.

❧ Heat the bacon fat and sear the kidneys for 20 or 30 seconds over high heat. Remove from the skillet and keep warm.

❧ To the remaining fat in the skillet, add the onion, tomatoes, sugar, garlic and herb of your choice. Mix together and bring to a boil over medium heat, then simmer for 15 minutes. Salt and pepper to taste. Add the kidneys, cover and cook over low heat for 15 to 20 minutes. The kidneys must not boil.

❧ Serve immediately with mashed potatoes seasoned with celery seed.

❧ For pork kidneys to be tender, they must be seared very quickly over very high heat, then simmered over low heat for not more than 20 minutes.

❧ Serve with mashed potatoes flavored with celery seeds.

Pickled Pork Tongue

2 pork tongues
hot water to cover
3 peppercorns
6 cloves
2 tsp (10 mL) salt

2 bay leaves
½ cup (125 mL) vinegar
¼ cup (50 mL) sugar

❧ Cover the tongues with hot water and simmer for 1 hour. Add the peppercorns, cloves, salt, bay leaves, vinegar and sugar. Cover and continue simmering until the tongues are tender.

❧ Let the tongues cool in the cooking stock. Peel off the skin and trim away the roots, small bones and gristle. Leave whole or cut in pieces.

❧ Place in sterile jars.

❧ Defat the cooking stock, strain it and bring to a boil. Pour the boiling liquid over the tongue.

❧ Seal the jars and refrigerate.

Québec Pork Hock Stew

2 to 3 lbs (1 to 1.5 kg) pork hocks, cut in pieces
1 tsp (5 mL) coarse salt
¼ tsp (1 mL) pepper
½ tsp (2 mL) cinnamon
¼ tsp (1 mL) ground cloves
pinch of nutmeg
2 tbsp (30 mL) fat
1 cup (250 mL) onions, sliced thin, browned
4 to 6 cups (1 to 1.5 L) lukewarm water
4 tbsp (60 mL) browned flour
½ cup (125 mL) water

❧ Dredge the pork hocks in a mixture of the salt, pepper, cinnamon, cloves and nutmeg.

❧ In a heavy saucepan, melt some of the fat trimmed from the hocks. Brown the hocks until they are dark brown (this is the secret

to a successful stew). When the meat is well browned, add the browned onions and the warm water. Cover and simmer until the meat is tender, approximately 2 hours.

❧ Shake together in a glass jar the flour and the ½ cup (125 mL) water. Pour into the broth and cook, stirring, until the gravy is thick.

Boiled Pork Hocks

3 to 4 lbs (1.5 to 2 kg) pork hocks, cut in pieces
3 onions, sliced thick
1 tbsp (15 mL) coarse salt
1 bay leaf
½ tsp (2 mL) pickling spices
1 cup (250 mL) water
4 to 6 carrots
1 medium-size cabbage, quartered
potatoes

❧ Place the pork hocks in a heavy saucepan and add the thickly sliced onions, salt, bay leaf, spices and water. Cover and boil slowly for 2 hours or until tender.

❧ About 30 minutes before the end of the cooking period, add the carrots, cabbage and as many potatoes as desired. Continue cooking until the vegetables are tender.

Head Cheese

❧ The gelatin part of head cheese will be clearer if the head is sewn into a piece of cloth while it simmers. This will also make it easier to separate the meat from the bones afterwards.

🍃 Use no more than 12 cups (3 L) of water for each head. Part of the water may be replaced with apple juice (Normandy-style), white wine (Poitevine-style) or chicken or beef consommé (Brittany-style).

🍃 Head cheese will keep for 2 to 3 weeks as long as it is not stored in metal and is well wrapped. Frozen, it will keep for 2 to 3 months: the jelly will lose some of its clarity but the flavor will not change.

1 small or ½ a large pig's head or 4 to 6 pork hocks
6 cloves
2 cinnamon sticks or 1 tbsp (15 mL) cinnamon
2 tbsp (30 mL) salt
2 large onions, chopped
1 large carrot, grated
8 cups (2 L) hot water

🍃 Wrap the head or hocks in a cloth. Place in a saucepan with the remaining ingredients and bring to a boil. Cover and simmer for 2 hours.

🍃 Unwrap the head, remove the meat from the bones and chop it, then return it to the hot broth. Boil rapidly for 10 minutes.

🍃 Pour into molds and refrigerate until jelled.

OLD QUÉBEC GALANTINE OF PORK

4 to 5 lbs (2 kg) pork loin or pork shoulder, with rind
1 to 2 lbs (500 g to 1 kg) pigs' feet

2 large onions, sliced
garlic, to taste
1 tbsp (15 mL) coarse salt
¼ tsp (1 mL) ground cloves
½ tsp (2 mL) savory
1 cup (250 mL) hot water
½ cup (125 mL) green or black tea or ½ cup (125 mL) cold water

🍃 Use an enameled or cast-iron casserole with a tight-fitting cover.

🍃 Place the meat in the pot, fat side down. Surround with the pigs' feet, cut in 3 pieces. Add all the remaining ingredients except the liquid. Do not cover.

🍃 Bake in a 325°F (160°C) oven, uncovered, for 2½ hours without opening the oven. Add the hot water, cover and bake 1 more hour.

🍃 Remove from the oven and take the meat out of the pot. Pick out the bones and shred the meat coarsely with 2 forks. Finely dice the skin of the pigs' feet and

place in the bottom of a mold. Add the shredded meat.

🍃 Place the casserole with the cooking juices on the burner and bring the juices to a boil.

🍃 Add the tea or cold water. Stir, scraping the bottom of the pot.

🍃 Strain the sauce and pour it over the meat. Cool, then cover and refrigerate.

🍃 Unmold at serving time.

CRETONS

🍃 Cut a cooked pork rind or pig's foot into small pieces and remove any bones.

🍃 Salt and pepper to taste. Add a pinch of cinnamon, a pinch of cloves and a small clove of garlic, crushed. Crush and mix well, add 1 to 2 tbsp (15 to 30 mL) strained pan drippings.

🍃 Turn into a small bowl and refrigerate.

Boiled Pork Hocks

[255]

OLD-FASHIONED CRETONS

1 lb (500 g) fatty ground pork
1 cup (250 mL) dry breadcrumbs
1 onion, grated
salt, pepper
ground cloves
cinnamon, to taste
1 cup (250 mL) milk

❧ Place all the ingredients in a saucepan. Mix together, cover and cook over low heat for 1 hour. Stir once or twice during the cooking period.
❧ Turn into a bowl and refrigerate.

RILLETTES BONNE FEMME

2 lbs (1 kg) fresh pork shoulder or butt
1 lb (500 g) salt pork, more fat than lean
2 pork kidneys or 1 lb (500 g) calf's liver
1 onion, very finely chopped
2 cloves garlic, chopped
2 tsp (10 mL) salt
1 tsp (5 mL) pepper
2 bay leaves
¼ tsp (1 mL) allspice
1 lb (500 g) pork bones
cold water to cover

❧ Cut the pork shoulder or butt, the salt pork and the kidneys or liver into 1-in. (2.5-cm) cubes.
❧ Place these 3 ingredients in a saucepan and add the onion, garlic, salt, pepper, bay leaves and allspice. Mix together and add the pork bones and enough water to cover.
❧ Simmer for 5 to 6 hours or until the water has evaporated and the meat is cooked. Remove the bones and bay leaves. Cool.
❧ Put the meat through a meat chopper or food processor to make a fine purée.
❧ Spoon into small jars and refrigerate.
❧ Rillettes freeze well and can be frozen for 6 months.

RILLETTES DE TOURS

1½ lbs (750 g) lean pork, ground
2 lbs (1 kg) pork lard, ground or diced
¼ tsp (1 mL) pepper
1½ tsp (7 mL) salt
pinch of thyme
1 bay leaf
1 cup (250 mL) boiling water

❧ Place all the ingredients in an enameled saucepan and simmer, uncovered, for approximately 1 hour or until the water evaporates and the meat and fat start to sizzle.
❧ Empty into a sieve placed over a bowl. Remove the bay leaf. Put the drained meat in a second bowl and beat with a rotary beater or put through a food mill to obtain a heavy purée. Gradually stir in 1 cup (250 mL) of the strained drippings. Mix well.
❧ Turn into small jars. Top each jar with a layer of the remaining fat.
❧ Cover and refrigerate.
❧ Unlike cretons, rillettes should be beaten to a smooth consistency like that of pâté de foie. To do so easily, process the meat and 1 cup (250 mL) fat for 1 or 2 minutes in a blender or food processor.

Old-fashioned Cretons

Pork Liver Pâté

2½ lbs (1.2 kg) pork liver
3½ lbs (1.6 kg) ground pork
2 onions, chopped
3 cloves garlic, crushed
1 tsp (5 mL) thyme
1½ tbsp (25 mL) salt
2 tsp (10 mL) pepper
½ cup (125 mL) cognac
or sherry
4 eggs
½ cup (125 mL) flour
1 lb (500 g) salt pork, mostly fat

☙ Grind the pork liver. Place in a large bowl and add the remaining ingredients, except the salt pork. Beat at high speed with an electric mixer (the more it is beaten, the finer the pâté).

☙ Slice the salt pork as thin as possible and use it to line the bottom and sides of a mold of your choice. Fill the mold with the liver mixture, then cover with a layer of salt pork slices. Cover the mold with a lid or a double thickness of aluminum foil.

☙ Place the mold in a pan half filled with boiling water. Bake 2 hours in a 350°F (180°C) oven.

☙ Remove from the oven and let stand 25 minutes. Weight the top of the pâté (with a can, for instance) and refrigerate for at least 12 hours.

☙ This homemade pâté is absolutely delicious.

HAM

Cured pork, or ham, may be sold under various names, including whole ham, cottage ham, picnic ham, center ham slice and smoked butt.

☙ Whole ham is made from the rump and rear leg of pork, cured and smoked. It is sold as whole ham, divided into shank and butt half hams, cut lengthwise or sliced as ham steak. The skin may be partly or completely removed. Deboned hams are often vacuum packed.

☙ Picnic ham is the lower part of the shoulder, which is cured, smoked and sold bone-in or boneless. It is cured and smoked like whole ham.

☙ Cottage ham is made from the upper or butt end of the shoulder, boned, cured and usually smoked. The curing solution is generally sweeter and spicier than those used for other cuts.

WHAT YOU SHOULD KNOW ABOUT HAM

When buying a half ham, be sure it is a full half, as sometimes the center cut has been removed to be sold as ham steaks. The center cut is the most tender part, and it is more economical to buy it as part of a full half ham.

☙ The shank end of ham is excellent boiled or wrapped in foil and oven-baked. Consider having it cut in 2 when you buy it, so you can prepare it 2 different ways.

☙ The butt end is excellent baked.

☙ Center-cut steaks can be sliced thick or thin according to how you plan to cook them—baked, broiled or pan-fried.

PREPARATION OF HAM

Cured smoked pork cuts are given varying degrees of "tenderizing" during the smoking process. Some may be fully cooked. It is wise to follow the directions on the label to know if further cooking is necessary.

☙ Hams from well-known producers tend to require less cooking than other hams. The terms "precooked," "tenderized," "partially cooked" or "sugar cured" on the label will give you an idea of the degree of cooking already done. These pretreated hams are usually sold with most of the rind removed. They do not require soaking or parboiling, but it is still best to purchase a brand-name one.

☙ Keep ham refrigerated until cooking time. Remove the wrapping. Washing the ham is not necessary.

☙ Ham can easily be done in the oven by wrapping it in aluminum foil or heavy wax paper and placing it in a shallow baking pan, cut side down. Cook for the time indicated on the cooking chart (see following pages).

Baked Ham

☙ Place the ham in a heavy-bottomed roasting pan, fat side up. Do not cover. Do not add liquid.

☙ Bake in a 325°F (160°C) oven for the appropriate cooking time (see chart on the next page), or until the internal temperature registers 170°F (75°C) on a meat thermometer.

🕊 Let stand for 20 minutes before slicing, if it is to be served hot.

🕊 To glaze the ham, remove it from the oven ½ hour before the end of the cooking period and follow the instructions for glazing (see below).

GARNISHING A HAM

🕊 Surround the baked ham with pineapple slices rolled in finely minced fresh mint.

🕊 Surround with small bunches of green and purple grapes.

🕊 Garnish the top of the ham with canned apricot halves held in place with almond halves.

🕊 Surround the ham with orange halves, scooped out and filled with cranberry sauce or applesauce.

🕊 Fill canned pear halves with currant, gooseberry or cranberry jelly and place around the ham.

🕊 Surround the ham with slices of pineapple topped with small mounds of coleslaw.

🕊 Whichever garnish you choose, do not overcrowd the platter. The carver will need room to work!

GLAZES FOR HAM

🕊 The following recipes will make enough glaze for a whole ham. Make half the recipe for a half ham, picnic ham or a cottage ham.

BAKING CHART FOR HAM

Set oven at 325°F (160°C).

CUT	WEIGHT	BAKING TIME	INTERNAL TEMPERATURE
BONE IN			
Whole	8 to 10 lbs (3.6 to 4.5 kg)	3½ hours	150°F to 155°F (65°C to 68°C)
Shank or butt end, whole	5 to 8 lbs (2.3 to 3.6 kg)	3¼ to 3½ hours	150°F to 155°F (65°C to 68°C)
BONELESS			
Whole	10 to 12 lbs (4.5 to 5.4 kg)	3½ to 4 hours	150°F to 155°F (65°C to 68°C)
Half	5 to 8 lbs (2.3 to 3.6 kg)	2½ to 3½ hours	150°F to 155°F (65°C to 68°C)
Picnic	4 to 6 lbs (1.8 to 2.7 kg)	2½ to 3 hours	170°F (75°C)
	6 to 8 lbs (2.7 to 3.6 kg)	3 to 4 hours	170°F (75°C)
	8 to 10 lb (3.6 to 4.5 kg)	4 to 4½ hours	170°F (75°C)

HONEY ORANGE GLAZE

🕊 Heat without boiling ½ cup (125 mL) honey, 1 cup (250 mL) brown sugar and ½ cup (125 mL) fresh or frozen undiluted orange juice.

GRAPE JELLY GLAZE

🕊 Add ½ tsp (2 mL) dry mustard and 3 tbsp (45 mL) prepared horseradish to 1 cup (250 mL) grape jelly. Blend with a fork.

BROWN SUGAR GLAZE

🕊 Combine 2 cups (500 mL) brown sugar with ½ cup (125 mL) flour and about ¼ cup (50 mL) cider vinegar or enough to make a thick paste.

PINEAPPLE GLAZE

🕊 Combine ¾ cup (175 mL) crushed pineapple, ¾ cup (175 mL) brown sugar, ¾ cup (175 mL) fresh breadcrumbs and ¼ cup (50 mL) melted fat from the ham.

CRANBERRY GLAZE

🕊 Combine ½ cup (125 mL) maple syrup or corn syrup with 1 cup (250 mL) cranberry jelly or sauce.

WINE GLAZE

🕊 Combine 1 cup (250 mL) honey, ½ cup (125 mL) port wine and ½ tsp (2 mL) cinnamon. Rub

BAKING CHART FOR PRECOOKED HAM

Set the oven at 325°F (160°C).

Cut	Weight	Baking time	Internal temperature
BONE IN			
Shank or butt end, whole			
	5 to 8 lb (2.3 to 3.6 kg)	1¾ to 2 hours	130°F (55°C)
Whole	8 to 10 lb (3.6 to 4.5 kg)	2 to 2¼ hours	130°F (55°C)
	10 to 12 lb (4.5 to 5.4 kg)	2¼ to 2½ hours	130°F (55°C)
	12 to 15 lb (5.4 to 6.8 kg)	2½ to 3 hours	130°F (55°C)
	15 to 18 lb (6.8 to 8 kg)	3 to 3½ hours	130°F (55°C)
BONELESS			
Half	5 to 8 lb (2.3 to 3.6 kg)	1½ to 2 hours	130°F (55°C)
Whole	10 to 12 lb (4.5 to 5.4 kg)	1½ to 2¾ hours	130°F (55°C)
	12 to 14 lb (5.4 to 6.4 kg)	2 hours	130°F (55°C)
Picnic	4 to 6 lb (1.8 to 2.7 kg)	2 hours	130°F (55°C)
	6 to 8 lb (2.7 to 3.6 kg)	2½ hours	130°F (55°C)
	8 to 10 lb (3.6 to 4.5 kg)	3 hours	130°F (55°C)

the cooked ham with prepared mustard and baste with the wine mixture during baking.

GLAZED HAM CHAUD-FROID

🍂 Bake or boil the ham and refrigerate for 48 hours.

🍂 Make a white sauce by melting 6 tbsp (90 mL) butter or ham drippings and stirring in 6 tbsp (90 mL) flour. Blend well and add 3 cups (750 mL) warm milk, cream or white wine, or a mixture of these. Season with salt and pepper to taste.

🍂 Soak 3 envelopes unflavored gelatin for 5 minutes in ½ cup (125 mL) cold water. Pour into the hot white sauce and stir until the gelatin is completely dissolved.

🍂 Refrigerate until the mixture has the consistency of unbeaten egg whites.

🍂 Spread several layers of the sauce on the ham, refrigerating between each addition, until the ham is well glazed. If desired, at this point decorate the surface of the ham with strips of red and green peppers, sliced black olives or another garnish.

🍂 Refrigerate until set.

GLAZED GARNISHED HAM

Cook the ham 2 days ahead and keep refrigerated. Thinly sliced and garnished with hard-cooked eggs, it will make a beautiful platter.

12- to 14-lb (6-kg) cooked ham

GLAZE:
1 cup (250 mL) apricot jam
3 tbsp (45 mL) cider vinegar
¼ cup (50 mL) maple or corn syrup
1 tsp (5 mL) ground ginger

EGG GARNISH:
20 hard-cooked eggs
1 cup (250 mL) mayonnaise
1 tsp (5 mL) prepared mustard
1 tsp (5 mL) curry powder
¼ tsp (1 mL) garlic salt
thin strips of green pepper

🍂 Preheat the oven to 325°F (160°C). Place the ham in a shallow roasting pan and bake for 20 minutes per lb (500 g). When

Spiced Cottage Roll

Spiced Cottage Roll

2 to 2½ lb (1 kg) cottage roll
1 clove garlic, minced
6 whole cloves
1 bay leaf
4 peppercorns
1 tsp (5 mL) celery seed
½ cup (125 mL) cider vinegar

❧ Remove the wrapper from the ham. Place the ham in a pot with enough boiling water to cover it completely.

❧ Add the remaining ingredients, cover and simmer for 2 hours or until the ham is tender.

❧ Serve hot or cold.

Glazed Half Ham

1 tsp (5 mL) bacon fat
3- to 4-lb (1.5-kg) half leg of ham
whole cloves (optional)
1 tbsp (15 mL) brown sugar
1 small can diced pineapple
½ cup (125 mL) water

❧ Melt the bacon fat in the bottom of a pressure-cooker. Brown the ham quickly in the fat on all sides. Remove from the pan and score the fat into diamond shapes. Stud with whole cloves.

❧ Place the ham on a rack in the pressure-cooker. Pour in the water and add the brown sugar and pineapple.

❧ Close the cover and cook for 30 minutes. Let the pressure drop of its own accord.

done, the ham should register 130°F (55°C) on the meat thermometer.

❧ In a saucepan, combine the apricot jam, cider vinegar, maple or corn syrup and the ground ginger. Simmer for 10 minutes.

❧ Thirty minutes before the ham is cooked, remove it from oven. Peel off the rind, trim the fat to a uniform layer and score the top in a diamond pattern.

❧ Discard the excess fat in the baking pan. Baste the ham all over with the glaze and bake for another 30 to 40 minutes or until nicely glazed, brushing several times with any remaining glaze or the glaze that drips onto the bottom of the pan.

❧ Cool and refrigerate.

❧ Halve the hard-cooked eggs lengthwise. Remove the yolks and sieve them into a bowl. Add the mayonnaise, mustard, curry powder and garlic salt. Blend thoroughly and season to taste with salt and pepper.

❧ For a fancy touch, you can use a pastry bag to pipe the yolk mixture into the egg whites, or simply use a spoon.

❧ Decorate the top of each egg half with a thin strip of green pepper. Arrange the egg halves in a deep pan. Cover the pan with plastic wrap or aluminum foil. Refrigerate. These can be prepared a day ahead.

❧ To serve the ham, slice as thinly as possible, then arrange the slices in their original ham shape in the middle of a large platter. Surround with the stuffed eggs. This dish is very easy to serve and is ideal for a buffet table.

❧ Move the ham to a platter. Remove the rack and boil the juice in the pot over high heat, until syrupy. Pour over the ham.

CANADIAN GLAZED BOILED HAM

1 boiled ham
whole cloves
1 cup (250 mL) brown sugar
2 tbsp (30 mL) molasses
1½ cups (375 mL) breadcrumbs

❧ Peel the rind from the ham. Stud the fat with whole cloves.
❧ Combine the brown sugar and molasses and spread over the fat. Sprinkle with breadcrumbs.
❧ Bake in a 275°F (140°C) oven until the top is golden and crusty.

VIRGINIA HAM

1 whole ham, baked or boiled
20 to 30 whole cloves
6 tbsp (90 mL) pepper
3 cups (750 mL) brown sugar
2 cups (500 mL) cider
or red wine

❧ While the ham is still hot, peel off the rind. Trim the fat to an even thickness and score it in a diamond pattern. Stud with a whole clove in each diamond. Place in a roasting pan.
❧ Sprinkle the pepper over the fat. Cover the ham with the brown sugar, making it stick to the fat as much as possible.
❧ Place in a preheated 400°F (200°C) oven for 40 to 50 min-

utes, basting every 10 minutes with the cider or wine and then with the drippings in the bottom of the pan.
❧ When the ham is well glazed, remove from the pan and serve warm or cold.
❧ Discard the pan drippings.

SUGAR SHACK HAM

5- to 10-lb (2.5- to 5-kg) ham
12 cups (3 L) apple juice
or maple sap
2 cups (500 mL) maple sugar
1 tsp (5 mL) dry mustard
2 tsp (10 mL) ground cloves
¼ cup (50 mL) water
2 cups (500 mL) raisins
browned flour (optional)

❧ Bring the apple juice or maple sap to a boil and place the ham in it. Cover and simmer 2½ to 3 hours or until the ham is tender. Remove from liquid.
❧ Remove the rind and cover the fat with a mixture of the maple sugar, dry mustard, cloves and water.
❧ Place the ham fat side up in a baking pan with 1 cup (250 mL) of the cooking liquid and the raisins. Bake another 30 minutes in a 300°F (150°C) oven.
❧ If desired, thicken the pan juices with a little browned flour blended with cold water.
❧ Serve this delicious raisin sauce with the hot ham.
❧ This ham is equally good served cold.

HAM PERSILLADE

This classic dish from the Burgundy region of France is served, according to tradition, with a white Burgundy wine.

5- to 8-lb (2.5- to 4-kg) ham, boned and rolled
1 can consommé, undiluted
½ bottle white wine
2 cups (500 mL) water
1 veal knuckle bone, meatless
½ cup (125 mL) chopped fresh parsley
1 tbsp (15 mL) tarragon
2 bay leaves
½ tsp (2 mL) thyme
3 small onions, quartered
1 clove garlic, crushed
¼ tsp (1 mL) pepper
2 envelopes gelatin, unflavored
¼ cup (50 mL) cold water
1 cup (250 mL) chopped fresh parsley
2 tbsp (30 mL) cognac
or lemon juice

❧ Place the ham in a large saucepan. Add the consommé, white wine, water, veal knuckle, the ½ cup (125 mL) fresh parsley, tarragon, bay leaves, thyme, onion, garlic and pepper. Bring to a boil, cover and simmer for several hours or until the ham is tender.
❧ When cooked, remove the ham from the broth and trim off the rind.
❧ Cut up the ham and fat as for a galantine (see page 255, but do not chop too finely or slice too thinly. Strain the cooking liquid through a fine sieve and add the

gelatin that has been soaked for 5 minutes in the ¼ cup (50 mL) cold water. Stir until the gelatin is completely dissolved.

🖎 Refrigerate until the fat is sufficiently set on top to be removed.

🖎 In the meantime, pat the shredded ham into a mold or loaf tin. Refrigerate, covered, until the gelatin mixture is ready.

🖎 Skim off the fat from the gelatin broth mixture and pour 2 cups (500 mL) over the ham, shaking to make sure it penetrates well.

🖎 Refrigerate the ham again until the gelatin is set, from 30 to 60 minutes.

🖎 Add the 1 cup (250 mL) chopped fresh parsley and the cognac or lemon juice to the remaining broth gelatin mixture. Pour over the ham.

🖎 Cover the mold carefully and refrigerate again.

🖎 Serve, unmolded, with herb mustard.

🖎 This jellied ham may be prepared up to 6 days in advance and refrigerated until serving time.

MADEIRA HAM

2 tbsp (30 mL) butter
1 tbsp (15 mL) vegetable oil
2 onions, sliced thin
2 carrots, sliced thin
6- to 8-lb (3- to 4-kg) ham
2 cups (500 mL) Madeira wine
3 cups (750 mL) consommé
6 sprigs parsley
1 bay leaf
½ tsp (2 mL) thyme
3 tbsp (45 mL) cornstarch

2 tbsp (30 mL) cold water
½ cup (125 mL) mushrooms, sliced
1 tbsp (15 mL) butter

🖎 Preheat the oven to 325°F (160°C). Heat the butter and oil in the roasting pan. Add the onions and carrots and brown over medium heat, stirring constantly.

🖎 Set the ham on the browned vegetables. Add the wine, consommé, parsley, bay leaf and thyme. Bring to a boil.

🖎 Cover and bake in a preheated oven for 2½ hours or until the ham is tender, basting every 20 minutes.

🖎 Remove the ham from the pan and cut off the rind. Skim the excess fat off the cooking juices and reduce the liquid over high heat to 3 cups (750 mL).

🖎 Combine the cornstarch with the cold water. Add to the reduced cooking juices, stirring constantly, until creamy. Add the mushrooms, sautéed in butter for 3 minutes.

🖎 Serve this gravy with the hot ham. Accompany with a bottle of good red wine.

HAM EN CROUTE

8- to 10-lb (4- to 5-kg) ham
6 cups (1.5 L) all-purpose flour
¼ cup (50 mL) shortening
½ cup (125 mL) butter
1½ tsp (7 mL) salt
¼ tsp (1 mL) sugar
2 eggs
⅔ cup (150 mL) cold water
1 egg
1 tsp (5 mL) cold water

🖎 Cook the ham using your favorite recipe (if you use the preceding *Madeira Ham* recipe, omit the sauce). When cooked, cool for 1 hour, then remove the rind.

🖎 Place the flour, shortening, butter, salt and sugar in a bowl. Knead with the fingertips until the mixture is mealy. Beat the 2 eggs with the ⅔ cup (150 mL) cold water, then add to the flour mixture and mix thoroughly. Pat the dough into a ball.

🖎 Cover and refrigerate for 2 to 6 hours.

🖎 Roll out ⅔ of the dough and lay it on the bottom of a baking pan. Put the cooked ham on top and fold up the sides of the dough.

🖎 Roll out the remaining dough, setting a small piece aside for decoration.

🖎 Beat the other egg with the 1 tsp (5 mL) cold water and use to brush the edges of the bottom crust.

🖎 Cut the top crust in a decorative shape and place it over the ham, sealing the edges well. Baste the top of the crust with the remaining egg.

🖎 With the remaining dough, cut out small rounds with a 1½-in. (4-cm) cookie cutter and decorate the crust using your own imagination.

🖎 Bake in a 400°F (200°C) oven until the crust is well browned.

🖎 Let cool at least 4 to 6 hours before refrigerating, as the crust will soften if refrigerated before the interior is well cooled.

Molasses Ham

4-lb (2-kg) ham
1 cup (250 mL) water
6 cloves
½ cup (125 mL) molasses

🥄 Wash the ham and soak for at least 2 hours in cold water with the cloves and the molasses. Pour the liquid into a pressure-cooker and set the ham in it, on top of a rack, fat side up.

🥄 Seal the cover and pressure-cook for 30 minutes. Let the pressure drop by itself. Remove the rind.

Ham Boiled with Beer

8 cups (2 L) cold water
8 cups (2 L) beer, apple juice or red wine
3 carrots, quartered
4 onions, quartered
1 garlic clove, chopped
4 celery stalks, with leaves
8 peppercorns
1 tbsp (15 mL) dry mustard
½ cup (125 mL) molasses
6 whole cloves
10 to 12 lb (5 kg) ham
chopped fresh parsley

🥄 Put all the ingredients except the ham and the parsley in a large pot. Bring to a boil, cover and simmer for 30 minutes.

🥄 Put the ham in the hot stock. Cover and simmer until tender, calculating 25 minutes per lb (500 g). Cooking slowly over low heat will make for a tender and tasty ham.

🥄 Let the ham cool in the cooking liquid. Remove the rind and cut off the excess layer of fat.

🥄 Serve as is, sprinkled with chopped fresh parsley.

🥄 Serve hot or cold with hot or cold potato salad and buttered cabbage.

Pressure-cooked Ham

3- to 4-lb (1.5-kg) ham
1 cup (250 mL) water
½ cup (125 mL) apple or orange juice
2 cloves
1 celery stalk
1 onion, halved
¼ cup (50 mL) brown sugar
1 tsp (5 mL) dry mustard
1 tbsp (15 mL) apple juice

🥄 Place the ham in a pressure-cooker. Add the water, the ½ cup (125 mL) apple or orange juice, cloves, celery and onion. Seal the pressure-cooker and cook for 40 minutes. Let the pressure drop of its own accord.

🥄 Place the ham on a serving platter and remove the rind.

🥄 In another pot, slowly bring to a boil the brown sugar, dry mustard and the 1 tbsp (15 mL) apple juice. Stir constantly until thick and syrupy.

🥄 Slowly pour the mixture over the ham and keep spooning it over until it cools and sticks to the meat.

🥄 Serve hot or cold.

Ham Boiled with Beer

BOILED HAM AND VEGETABLES

½ ham, shank end
1 clove garlic, minced
¼ tsp (1 mL) celery seed
1 tbsp (15 mL) salt
6 medium potatoes, peeled
6 whole carrots, peeled
6 medium onions, peeled
1 small cabbage, cut into 6 wedges
horseradish
Dijon mustard

🍂 Put the ham in a large pot and add the garlic, celery seed, salt and enough cold water to cover. Bring to a boil, cover and simmer for the same time as if baking (see chart on page 258).

🍂 About 45 minutes before the end of the cooking period, add the potatoes, carrots and onions. Cover and cook for 20 to 25 minutes, then add the cabbage. Cover and cook until the vegetables are tender.

🍂 Serve hot with horseradish and Dijon mustard.

BAKING A HAM STEAK

🍂 Choose a ham steak that is 1½ to 2 in. (4 to 5 cm) thick, cut from the center of the whole ham or the middle of a rolled shoulder (cottage ham).

🍂 Use a scissors or sharp knife to slash the fat around the steak so that the meat will stay flat during cooking. Place in a shallow baking dish.

🍂 Sprinkle the ham with 2 tbsp (30 mL) brown sugar mixed with

BROILING CHART FOR HAM

THICKNESS	BROILING TIME PER SIDE
CURED UNCOOKED HAM	
½ in. (1.2 cm)	5 minutes
¾ in. (2 cm)	7 minutes
1 in. (2.5 cm)	10 minutes
1½ in. (4 cm)	12 to 15 minutes
PRECOOKED HAM	
½ in. (1.2 cm)	2 minutes
¾ in. (2 cm)	3 minutes
1 in. (2.5 cm)	5 minutes

a pinch of ground cloves and a pinch of dry mustard. Or use a half portion of one of the glaze recipes in this chapter (see page 258). Cover with a lid or a piece of aluminum foil.

🍂 Bake in a 325°F (160°C) oven:

🍂 1½-in. (4-cm) steak: 1 to 1¼ hours.

🍂 2-in. (5-cm) steak: 1¾ to 2 hours.

🍂 Uncover the pan for the last 15 to 20 minutes of cooking so that the top can brown.

BAKING A PRECOOKED HAM STEAK

🍂 If the ham steak is precooked or "ready to serve," you can use the technique for uncooked ham steak (see pages 258 and 259), but in this case reduce the cooking time.

🍂 Bake the prepared steak in a 325°F (160°C) oven, covered, for 25 to 30 minutes. Then remove

the cover and bake for another 15 minutes or until browned.

BROILED HAM STEAK

🍂 Select a ham steak ½ in. to 1½ in. (1 to 4 cm) thick, with or without the bone. Slash the fat around the meat to prevent it from curling.

🍂 Adjust the broiler rack to 2 to 3 in. (5 to 8 cm) from the heat source, then preheat for 10 minutes.

🍂 Place the ham on the rack and broil as indicated on the ham broiling chart above. Turn once and broil the other side.

SEASONINGS FOR HAM STEAK

When the first side of the ham is broiled, turn it and cover the other side with your choice of the following mixtures:

🍂 1 tbsp (15 mL) mustard or horseradish mixed with ¼ cup (50 mL) brown sugar.

PAN-FRYING CHART FOR HAM STEAK

THICKNESS	PAN-FRYING TIME PER SIDE
CURED UNCOOKED HAM	
¼ in. (0.6 cm)	2 to 3 minutes
½ in. (1 cm)	4 to 5 minutes
¾ in. (2 cm)	6 minutes
PRECOOKED HAM	
¼ in. (0.6 cm)	1½ minute
½ in. (1 cm)	2 minutes
¾ in. (2 cm)	3 minutes

ða ¼ cup (50 mL) currant jelly mixed with 1 tbsp (15 mL) horseradish.

ða ¼ to ½ cup (50 to 125 mL) honey or marmalade.

ða 3 tbsp (45 mL) melted butter combined with 2 finely chopped green onions.

PAN-FRYING A HAM STEAK

ða Select and prepare the steak following the instructions for baked ham steak (see opposite).

ða Heat a heavy skillet and rub it with a small piece of ham fat. Pan-fry the steak over medium heat for the time indicated on the pan-frying chart above.

ða Pan-fry precooked ham over low heat, turning only once.

SEASONINGS FOR PAN-FRIED HAM STEAK

A few seconds before the ham is fried, sprinkle it with a little sugar, brown sugar or grated maple sugar.

ða To serve with a sauce, remove the steak from the skillet and add to the remaining fat 3 tbsp (45 mL) cider vinegar or lemon juice, 1½ tsp (7 mL) prepared mustard and 1 tbsp (15 mL) grape or currant jelly.

ða Stir well until hot, then pour over the ham.

HAM STEAK WITH PEACHES

2 large peaches
¼ cup (50 mL) sugar
1 ham steak 1 in. (2.5 cm) thick
¼ cup (50 mL) peach jam
1 tsp (5 mL) lemon juice
2 tbsp (30 mL) butter

ða Peel and pit the peaches. Slice them thin and arrange in the bottom of a rectangular baking dish. Sprinkle with the sugar. Arrange the ham slice on top.

ða Combine the peach jam and lemon juice and spread the mixture over the ham.

ða Bake for 1 hour in a 350°F (180°C) oven. After the first 15 minutes of baking, spread the butter over the ham. Baste the ham with pan juices from time to time during the remaining cooking period.

Ham Steak with Peaches

Rolled Ham Steak with Beer

HAM STEAK WITH VEGETABLES

1 ham steak, ½ to 2 in.
(1 to 5 cm) thick
3 tbsp (45 mL) rendered ham fat
2 onions, sliced thin
1 green pepper, sliced in strips
4 to 5 fresh tomatoes
2 garlic cloves, minced
¼ tsp (1 mL) pepper
¼ tsp (1 mL) thyme
1 tsp (5 mL) sugar
3 tbsp (45 mL) chopped fresh parsley

🍂 Trim enough fat from the ham to yield 3 tbsp (45 mL) melted fat.

🍂 Brown the ham steak on both sides in a heavy skillet, then move it to an ovenproof dish.

🍂 Sauté the onion and green pepper in the ham fat for about 5 minutes over medium heat, stirring often.

🍂 Peel and halve the tomatoes and squeeze out the seeds and juice. Chop the flesh coarsely. Add the chopped tomatoes to the onion and green pepper and simmer for 5 minutes. Add the remaining ingredients except the parsley.

🍂 Pour the vegetable sauce over the ham. Cover and bake in a 350°F (180°C) oven for 20 to 30 minutes or until the ham is tender.

🍂 Sprinkle with chopped fresh parsley.

🍂 To prepare this dish for the freezer:

🍂 Combine the fresh peach slices with the lemon juice to prevent browning. Arrange the peaches in an ovenproof freezer container, top with the ham and spread the jam on top. Bake as described above. Cool, then wrap well and freeze. To serve, place the unwrapped frozen container directly in a 475°F (240°C) oven, cover and bake about 35 minutes or until hot.

ROLLED HAM STEAK WITH BEER

1 garlic clove, halved
½ in. (1.2 cm) thick ham steak
pepper
1 cup (250 mL) beer
1 tbsp (15 mL) dry mustard
1 tsp (5 mL) sugar

🍂 Rub a heavy skillet with the garlic clove. Sprinkle the ham with pepper, then roll it like a jelly roll and fasten with kitchen string in several places.

🍂 Melt a piece of ham fat in the skillet, then add the ham and pan-fry on all sides until golden.

🍂 Add the beer to the skillet. Place the garlic clove on top of the meat. Cover the pan and simmer for 25 to 35 minutes.

🍂 Serve the ham roll, well drained, surrounded by French-fried potatoes and tomato wedges.

🍂 Make a mustard sauce by adding enough cooking liquid to the dry mustard and sugar to make a creamy consistency.

Ham Steak with Molasses

1½ lbs (750 g) ham sliced 1 in. (2.5 cm) thick
¼ cup (50 mL) molasses
¼ cup (50 mL) cold water
¼ tsp (1 mL) cinnamon
10 cloves

🙠 Place the ham in a baking dish. Pour the molasses over the ham and let stand 20 minutes.

🙠 Pour the water around the ham, sprinkle with the cinnamon and stud with the cloves. Cover.

🙠 Bake in a 325°F (160°C) oven for 45 to 60 minutes or until the meat is tender.

Ham Steak with Sweet Potatoes

1 tsp (5 mL) prepared mustard
2 tbsp (30 mL) maple syrup or brown sugar
1 ham steak, 1 to 2 in. (2.5 to 5 cm) thick
1 tbsp (15 mL) butter
3 sweet potatoes
salt and pepper
1 tbsp (15 mL) brown sugar
1 cup (250 mL) heavy cream

🙠 Blend the mustard with the 2 tbsp (30 mL) maple syrup or brown sugar.

🙠 Coat the ham with the mixture and brown in the butter over low heat.

🙠 Peel and halve the sweet potatoes and arrange them over the ham. Salt and pepper and sprinkle with the 1 tbsp (15 mL) brown sugar.

🙠 Pour the cream over all.

🙠 Cover and cook over low heat for 40 minutes or until the ham is tender and the sweet potatoes are cooked.

Broiled Ham with Currant Jelly

½ cup (125 mL) currant jelly
¼ cup (50 mL) prepared mustard
1 ham steak ½ to 1 in. (1 to 2.5 cm) thick

🙠 Combine the currant jelly and the prepared mustard. Place the ham steak in a broiler pan and brush the top with some of the mustard mixture.

🙠 Broil 4 in. (10 cm) from the source of heat for 5 to 8 minutes. Brush on more of the mustard mixture and broil for 5 minutes more. Baste with a final coating of the mixture and broil for another 2 minutes, or until the top is browned.

🙠 Place on a hot platter. Surround with scrambled eggs and serve.

Ham Grilled in Sauce

This old-fashioned dish once involved simmering the ham in sauce for a long time in order to tenderize it. With today's precooked ham, just 10 minutes of cooking is required.

1 slice precooked ham, ½ in. (1.2 cm) thick

½ cup (125 mL) whipping cream
2 tbsp (30 mL) water
3 tbsp (45 mL) brown sugar
¼ to ½ tsp (1 to 2 mL) cinnamon or 6 whole cloves

🙠 Place the ham in an ungreased, preheated electric or heavy skillet. Cook over high heat for 3 minutes on each side, turning only once.

🙠 Combine the rest of the ingredients and pour over the ham.

🙠 Simmer for 5 to 8 minutes over low heat. Serve.

Ham Roulade

🙠 This dish takes only 15 minutes to prepare, and the ingredients are easily available. The recipe for the dressing is an excellent one to have on hand since it is goes well with all types of salads.

🙠 For a special lunch, serve the ham roll on a bed of potato salad, surrounded by sliced tomatoes and watercress.

pinch of prepared mustard
⅓ to ½ cup (75 to 125 mL) olive oil
2 hard-cooked eggs
2 tsp (10 mL) lemon juice
1 cup (250 mL) finely diced celery
salt and pepper
6 slices cooked ham
1 tbsp (15 mL) chopped fresh parsley

🙠 To make the dressing, put the mustard (preferably a good

Dijon) in a bowl and gradually add the olive oil, beating vigorously with a wooden spoon. The mixture will thicken gradually as you beat in the oil.

❧ Grate the hard-cooked eggs and add them to the oil mixture, along with the lemon juice and the diced celery. Salt and pepper to taste. Mix well.

❧ Place a spoonful of dressing on each slice of ham. Roll up the slice and put it on a plate. Sprinkle with chopped fresh parsley.

SLICED HAM IN BARBECUE SAUCE

2 lbs (1 kg) cottage roll cut in 1-in. (2.5-cm) slices
1 onion, sliced
1 tbsp (15 mL) vegetable oil
2 tbsp (30 mL) brown sugar
½ tsp (2 mL) salt

¼ tsp (1 mL) ground cloves
¼ cup (50 mL) chili sauce
¾ cup (175 mL) tomato juice
1 tbsp (15 mL) Worcestershire sauce
2 tbsp (30 mL) malt vinegar

❧ Place the ham slices in a large skillet and cover with boiling water. Cover the skillet and simmer for 1 hour.

❧ In the meantime, prepare the sauce: brown the onion in the oil, add the remaining ingredients and simmer for 20 minutes.

❧ Drain the liquid from the ham and pour the sauce over it. Simmer for another 20 minutes.

❧ Serve with boiled rice.

TUSCAN HAM SOUFFLÉ

2 tbsp (30 mL) butter
1 cup (250 mL) chopped cooked spinach
1 tbsp (15 mL) flour
1 tsp (5 mL) salt
½ tsp (2 mL) pepper
½ cup (125 mL) consommé, heated
1 cup (250 mL) diced cooked ham
5 tbsp (75 mL) grated cheese
3 egg yolks
4 egg whites

❧ Melt the butter in a saucepan and add the chopped cooked spinach, well drained. Cook over low heat for 5 minutes.

❧ Sprinkle in the flour, salt and pepper. Stir well.

❧ Add the heated consommé and bring to a boil, stirring constantly. Cover and simmer for 10 minutes. Remove from heat and cool for 15 minutes.

❧ Gradually stir in the diced ham, grated cheese and the 3 egg yolks, stirring after each addition.

❧ Beat the 4 egg whites into stiff peaks and fold them carefully into the spinach mixture.

❧ Turn into a greased 8-in. (20-cm) soufflé dish. Bake in a 350°F (180°C) oven for about 25 minutes or until golden.

❧ Serve immediately.

HAM AND EGG CASSEROLE

This wonderful brunch dish is very easy to make. For a more substantial meal, serve it with creamed corn and a green salad.

6 servings instant mashed potatoes
5 to 6 slices cooked ham

Sliced Ham in Barbecue Sauce

½ cup (125 mL) fine breadcrumbs
6 eggs
salt and pepper
3 tbsp (45 mL) melted butter

🍂 Prepare the mashed potatoes according to the package directions. Cut the ham into fine strips and mix them with the potatoes, along with the breadcrumbs. Stir well.

🍂 Spread the potato mixture in a shallow round baking dish or pie plate. Use the bottom of a glass to make 6 indentations in the mixture. Break an egg into each indentation and salt and pepper each. Pour the melted butter over all.

🍂 Bake in a 400°F (200°C) oven for 10 to 15 minutes or until the eggs are cooked to taste.

🍂 Serve plain, with fried bacon or tomato sauce.

ITALIAN HAM LOAF

Don't let the simplicity of this glazed ham loaf deceive you into thinking it's just another meat loaf. When cooked it will be as pink as baked ham and very tasty and attractive. It slices nicely and is equally good hot or cold.

1½ lbs (750 g) lean cured uncooked ham
1½ lbs (750 g) fresh pork shoulder
2 eggs
1 cup (250 mL) fine breadcrumbs
1 cup (250 mL) milk
¼ cup (50 mL) chopped fresh parsley

¼ cup (50 mL) light brown sugar
2 tsp (10 mL) prepared mustard

🍂 Ask the butcher to grind the ham and the fresh pork shoulder together. (If you do it yourself, put the meat through the meat chopper twice.)

🍂 Combine the ground meat with the eggs, breadcrumbs, milk and parsley. Do not add salt or pepper. Knead until thoroughly blended. You can pack this mixture into a large loaf pan, but for a special dinner mold it into a ham shape; it will be very easy to work with.

🍂 Place in a baking dish. Rub half the brown sugar on top of the meat. Spread the mustard on top, then cover with the remaining sugar.

🍂 Bake in a 325°F (160°C) oven for 1¾ hours, basting 3 or 4 times with the cooking juices.

🍂 Serve hot or cold.

HAM MEAT LOAF

3½ cups (875 mL) ground cooked ham
½ lb (250 g) ground veal
½ lb (250 g) ground beef
2 cups (500 mL) diced bread
¼ tsp (1 mL) savory
½ tsp (2 mL) salt
¼ tsp (1 mL) pepper
1 egg, lightly beaten
¼ cup (50 mL) catsup
2 stalks celery, finely chopped
¾ cup (175 mL) milk
1 medium onion, chopped
2 tbsp (30 mL) parsley
½ cup (125 mL) brown sugar
4 slices pineapple

🍂 You can grind up leftover cooked ham for this recipe, supplementing it with canned ham if necessary, or use canned ground ham only.

🍂 Put the ground ham in a large bowl and add the ground veal and the ground beef. Mix well.

🍂 Add the diced bread (with or without the crusts), the savory, salt, pepper, lightly-beaten egg, catsup, celery, milk, onion and parsley. Mix well.

🍂 Sprinkle the brown sugar into a shallow 9- x 9-in. (23- x 23-cm) baking dish and arrange the pineapple slices over it, then top with the ham mixture. Press to compact the loaf.

🍂 Bake in a preheated 350°F (180°C) oven for 1 hour.

🍂 Drain off the accumulated juices and unmold.

🍂 Serve hot or cold.

MOTHER'S HAM LOAF

1 lb (500 g) uncooked ham, ground
1 lb (500 g) pork loin, ground
1 cup (250 mL) breadcrumbs
2 eggs, lightly beaten
1 cup (250 mL) sour cream
juice of 1 lemon
1 onion, minced
½ tsp (2 mL) curry
1 tsp (5 mL) ground ginger
1 tsp (5 mL) dry mustard
¼ tsp (1 mL) paprika
¼ tsp (1 mL) nutmeg

Mother's Ham Loaf

SAUCE:
½ cup (125 mL) water
1 cup (250 mL) cider vinegar
juice of 1 lemon
1 cup (250 mL) brown sugar
1 tsp (5 mL) dry mustard

🍂 In a bowl, combine the ground ham, ground pork, breadcrumbs, eggs, sour cream, lemon juice and onion. Mix well, then add the curry, ginger, dry mustard, paprika and nutmeg. Mix thoroughly until well blended.

🍂 Shape the meat mixture into a loaf and place in a small roasting pan. Cover.

🍂 Bake in a 325°F (160°C) oven for 25 minutes. Uncover and continue baking for an additional 35 minutes.

🍂 In the meantime, prepare the sauce. Place the water, cider vinegar, lemon juice, brown sugar and dry mustard in a saucepan. Simmer for 10 minutes.

🍂 Ten minutes before the ham loaf is done, increase the temperature to 375°F (190°C) and pour the sauce over the loaf. Continue cooking.

🍂 Serve hot with the sauce and with mashed potatoes.

HAM PÂTÉ

1 cup (250 mL) ground ham
¼ cup (50 mL) mayonnaise
2 tbsp (30 mL) prepared mustard
2 tbsp (30 mL) Worcestershire sauce
½ tsp (2 mL) paprika
1 tbsp (15 mL) chives or small onions, minced

🍂 Mix all the ingredients and refrigerate.

🍂 This pâté is delicious as a sandwich filling or spread on crackers.

ORANGE HAM SALAD

3 tbsp (45 mL) olive oil
2 tbsp (30 mL) cider vinegar
1 tsp (5 mL) prepared mustard
salt and pepper to taste
2 large slices cold ham, chopped
3 small pickles, chopped
3 olives, sliced
1 orange

🍂 Stir together the olive oil, cider vinegar, mustard, salt and pepper. Add the chopped ham, chopped pickle, sliced olives and the orange, peeled and cut up.

🍂 Serve with cottage cheese or toast.

HAM AND MACARONI SALAD

4 oz (125 g) dried macaroni
8 cups (2 L) salted boiling water
1½ to 2 cups (375 to 500 mL) diced cooked ham
2 stalks celery, diced
1 onion, chopped
½ cup (125 mL) mayonnaise
¼ cup (50 mL) milk or light cream
1 tsp (5 mL) horseradish
1 tsp (5 mL) salt
pepper to taste

🍂 Cook the macaroni in the salted boiling water for 15 to 20 minutes or until tender. Drain and rinse under cold water.

🍂 Add the diced ham, celery and onion.

🍂 Mix together the mayonnaise, milk or cream, horseradish and seasonings. Add to the salad and blend well. Refrigerate.

🍴 Serve in tomato cups or on lettuce leaves.

HAM SPREAD

½ cup (125 mL) cooked ham, finely chopped
2 tbsp (30 mL) green pepper, finely chopped
1 tsp (5 mL) prepared mustard
2 tbsp (30 mL) mayonnaise
1 tbsp (15 mL) onion, minced

🍴 Blend all the ingredients thoroughly and refrigerate.

SPIT-ROASTED BACON

2- to 3-lb (1 kg to 1.5-kg) piece of cured bacon

SAUCE:
½ cup (125 mL) orange juice
¼ cup (50 mL) cider vinegar
1 garlic clove, minced
½ cup (125 mL) brown sugar
1 tbsp (15 mL) prepared mustard

🍴 Prepare a sauce by combining all the ingredients and mixing well.
🍴 Spear the bacon lengthwise on a spit and baste with the sauce.
🍴 The bacon will cook in about 1 to 1½ hours, and will be tender and delicious.
🍴 Serve hot or cold.

POTATOES WITH SMOKED PORK

Of course, the smoked pork in this recipe is really bacon. Whenever you have a few cold leftover potatoes, try this quick meal. Or serve it as a salad with cold chicken or veal.

4 strips bacon
1 small onion, chopped
4 to 5 cooked potatoes
2 tsp (10 mL) cider vinegar
salt and pepper to taste

🍴 Fry the bacon until crisp. Remove from the pan and cook the onion in the bacon fat until lightly browned.
🍴 Slice the potatoes into a bowl and sprinkle with the vinegar, salt and pepper. Toss. Crumble the bacon and add it to the mixture.

🍴 Drain the fat from the onions and add them to the potatoes.
🍴 Toss everything together and serve.

USING LEFTOVER HAM

PEA SOUP
Substitute the ham bone or the rind from a baked ham for salt pork in pea soup.

CRACKLINGS
Bake the rind trimmed from the ham for 1 hour in a 350°F (180°C) oven. It will become very crisp and will be easily broken into small pieces that are delicious with bread or in soup.
🍴 Keep the melted fat in the refrigerator to use as a substitute for lard or to use in pie crust.

Ham Spread

LEFTOVER HAM LOAF

Combine 2 cups (500 mL) finely chopped leftover ham with 1 cup (250 mL) dry breadcrumbs. Place in a baking dish.

 Combine 1 cup (250 mL) milk, 1 beaten egg and 1 tbsp (15 mL) prepared mustard and pour this over the ham.

Bake in a 350°F (180°C) oven for 30 minutes.

Serve hot or cold.

POULTRY

POULTRY

The term poultry applies to all domestic fowl raised for their flesh or their eggs. The most popular by far is chicken, ranging from the juicy young bird weighing only 1½ lbs (750 g) to the big 6-lb (2.5-kg) roasting chickens. Stewing chickens normally weigh close to 6 lbs (2.5-kg). Capons can weigh as much as 7 lbs (3 kg).

✿ But other popular poultry choices include turkey, duck, goose and Rock Cornish game hen.

POULTRY TIPS

Stewing hens can be boiled, braised or fricasséed.

✿ A 5-lb (2.5-kg) stewing hen yields about 2 lbs (1 kg) of cooked meat, as well as 8 to 10 cups (2 to 2.5 L) of chicken stock.

✿ Chickens weighing 3 to 5 lb (1.5 to 2.5 kg), as well as the young 1½-lb (750-g) birds usually labeled broiler-fryers, can be oven-roasted, pan-fried or deep-fried.

✿ A 2- to 3-lb (1- to 1.5-kg) chicken will yield 4 servings, usually cut into 2 breast sections and 2 leg sections.

✿ A 4- to 5-lb (2-kg) chicken will yield 6 servings. To serve, remove the legs and separate the leg from the thigh, remove the wings and cut the breast in half or slice off the meat.

✿ Capons, which normally weigh 5 to 8 lbs (2.5 to 3.5 kg), are excellent spit-roasted, oven-roasted or braised, but they lose all their delicate flavor when boiled.

✿ To serve a capon or turkey, remove the wings, the leg and the thigh and slice the breast into thin slices.

✿ Whole poultry is generally sold with the giblets, which include the liver, heart, gizzard and sometimes the neck.

✿ Poultry should never be soaked in water except for defrosting, in which case it should be left in its original wrapping. Wash the chicken under running cold water and dry it well.

✿ It is always better to thaw poultry completely before roasting.

✿ To thaw a turkey in the refrigerator, allow 5 hours per lb (500 g). Leave the turkey in its original packaging.

✿ To defrost a chicken or a capon in the refrigerator, allow 2 hours per lb (500 g). In cold water, allow 20 minutes per lb (500 g).

✿ To broil a chicken in the oven or on the barbecue, split it in half along the backbone (but leave the flesh in one piece); place the bird on a carving board breast side down. Using poultry shears or a sharp knife, cut through the bones along one side of the backbone, starting at the neck end. Push down on the two sides and flatten the bird using a heavy rolling pin.

✿ Before cooking, rub the bird all over with a piece of lemon to keep the flesh white; then rub all over with a piece of whole nutmeg.

✿ To roast poultry, first baste the breast and legs with a mixture of 3 tbsp (45 mL) butter or other fat of your choice and 1 tsp (5 mL) dry mustard. The chicken will be less likely to dry out during roasting retain all its juices and nutritive value.

✿ Never add water to the roasting pan before roasting.

✿ Do not cover the roasting pan.

✿ Salt the inside of the bird before roasting.

✿ Never pack poultry too full of stuffing, because the breadcrumbs or rice will absorb the poultry juices and swell up during the roasting process.

✿ Never reheat leftover poultry in its gravy, as this may toughen the meat. Instead, wrap the meat in aluminum foil and heat it in a 500°F (260°C) oven for about 20 to 30 minutes, depending on the size. If desired, baste the flesh with softened butter before wrapping it. Heat the leftover gravy separately.

✿ Serve boiled chicken in a white sauce prepared with milk and some of the cooking stock, or with an egg sauce flavored with parsley.

✿ Boiled chicken is better served with rice than with potatoes.

SAFETY CONSIDERATIONS

To avoid the risk of salmonella poisoning, it is important to follow a few simple safety tips when preparing poultry, especially chicken.

✿ Chicken should never be served undercooked; it is important always to cook it for the full cooking period recommended in the recipe.

✿ Do not stuff chicken or turkey until just before you put it in the oven; you can store the stuffing mixture in a covered bowl in the refrigerator until you are ready to use it.

✿ Wash all knives, utensils and cutting boards in hot soapy water as soon as you have finished preparing the bird. Never place raw chicken directly on a bread board or any surface that cannot be properly cleaned and sterilized.

🐦 Refrigerate leftover chicken immediately.

CHICKEN À LA CLAMART

1 2-lb (1-kg) broiler-fryer
3 green onions, chopped
salt and pepper
3 tbsp (45 mL) butter
2 lbs (1 kg) green peas, shelled
1 head lettuce, shredded
with scissors
8 baby onions, whole
1 cup (250 mL) light cream
1 tbsp (15 mL) sherry

🐦 Make incisions in the chicken and stuff them with the pieces of green onion. Salt and pepper. Truss the chicken and brown it in the butter.

🐦 Meanwhile, boil the green peas until tender-crisp.

🐦 When the chicken is well browned, place it in a baking dish with the green peas. Add the shredded lettuce, onions and cream. Salt and pepper to taste. Flavor with the sherry.

🐦 Cover and bake in a 375°F (190°C) oven for 1 hour.

CHICKEN BONNE FEMME

1 broiler-fryer, 2 to 4 lbs
(1 to 2 kg)
½ cup (125 mL) salt pork, diced
20 small onions
salt and pepper
½ tsp (2 mL) thyme
raw diced potatoes or baby new potatoes
parsley and chives, minced

Chicken à la Clamart

🐦 Truss the chicken. Melt the salt pork and brown the chicken in the melted fat over medium heat.

🐦 Add the onions, salt and pepper. Flavor with thyme. Cover and bake in a 375°F (190°C) oven for 30 minutes.

🐦 Add the raw potatoes. Cover and cook another 25 minutes or so, depending on the size of the chicken.

🐦 When everything is tender and ready to serve, garnish with the chopped parsley or chives.

AMBASSADOR'S CHICKEN

½ lb (250 g) sweetbreads
3 tbsp (45 mL) butter
½ lb (250 g) mushrooms, thinly sliced
6 green onions, finely chopped
1 good pinch of tarragon
salt and pepper

1 egg, beaten
1 broiler-fryer, 3 to 4 lbs (1.5 kg)

SAUCE:

2 tbsp (30 mL) butter
1 tbsp (15 mL) flour
1 cup (250 mL) consommé
3 tbsp (45 mL) port or cognac

🐦 Prepare the sweetbreads according to the basic method (see page 214) and dice them.

🐦 Sauté the sweetbreads in the butter along with the mushrooms and chopped onion. Flavor with tarragon, salt and pepper. Remove from the heat and stir in the egg.

🐦 Stuff the chicken with the sweetbread mixture. Truss the chicken and brown it in a little butter.

🐦 Prepare a white sauce using the butter, flour and consommé (see page 46).

🐦 Place the chicken in a deep baking dish and pour the sauce over it. Cover and bake in a 375°F

Roast Chicken with Potato Stuffing

(190°C) oven for 1 hour.
❧ When ready to serve, add the port or cognac.

CHICKEN IN THE POT

1 stewing chicken, 3 to 4 lbs
(1.5 kg), with giblets
2 cups (500 mL) dry breadcrumbs
¼ lb (125 g) diced ham
1 clove garlic, minced
2 eggs
salt, pepper, parsley and tarragon, to taste
1 small turnip
4 carrots
3 onions
1 small green cabbage, whole
1 lb (500 g) fresh raw ham or salt
pork (optional)
1 bay leaf

❧ In a food processor, chop the liver, heart and gizzard of the chicken. Add the breadcrumbs, diced ham, garlic, eggs, salt, pepper, parsley and tarragon, to taste. Stuff the chicken with this mixture.
❧ Truss the chicken and place it in a large pot of boiling water, allowing 2 cups (500 mL) water for each lb (500 g) chicken. Add the turnip, carrots, onions, green cabbage, raw ham or salt pork and bay leaf. Bring to a boil.
❧ Partially cover and simmer for 20 minutes per lb (500 g) or until the chicken is tender.
❧ Serve the chicken on a warmed platter with the vegetables arranged attractively around it. Thinly slice the salt pork or fresh ham and arrange over the vegetables. Sprinkle with fresh chopped parsley.

ROAST UNSTUFFED CHICKEN

1 chicken, 4 to 5 lbs (2 kg)
1 small onion, halved
¼ tsp (1 mL) thyme
½ tsp (2 mL) salt
¼ tsp (1 mL) pepper
3 tbsp (45 mL) butter
1 tbsp (15 mL) dry mustard
1 can consommé
½ cup (125 mL) cream

❧ Clean the chicken. Place the onion, thyme, salt and pepper in the cavity and truss the chicken. Place in an open roasting pan.
❧ Cream the butter with the dry mustard and spread this mixture over the chicken.
❧ Roast the chicken in a 375°F (190°C) oven for 18 to 20 minutes per lb (500 g). Chicken roasted this way needs no basting. Do not cover the pan. Do not add water. The chicken will have crispy skin and juicy, tender meat.
❧ To make the gravy, remove the chicken from the pan and keep it warm. Set the baking pan over high heat and bring the pan drippings to a boil. Add a can of undiluted consommé or ½ cup (125 mL) cream. Stir over high heat, scraping the bottom, but do not let boil. Serve in a gravy boat.

ROAST CHICKEN WITH POTATO STUFFING

1 chicken, 5 to 6 lbs (2.5 kg),
with giblets
3 medium onions

1 small clove garlic
4 tbsp (60 mL) butter
or chicken fat
4 cups (1 L) cooked mashed
potatoes
1 tsp (5 mL) savory
salt and pepper

🐦 Grind the heart, gizzard and liver, along with the onions and garlic, in a meat chopper or food processor. Fry in the butter or melted fat for a few minutes.

🐦 Add this mixture to the cooked mashed potatoes. Flavor with the savory. Salt and pepper to taste. Stuff the chicken with this mixture.

🐦 Roast in a 375°F (190°C) oven for 10 to 20 minutes per lb (500 g).

ITALIAN-STYLE ROAST CHICKEN

3 cups (750 mL) cooked noodles
½ lb (250 g) mushrooms,
sliced thin
1 cup (250 mL) grated cheese
¼ cup (50 mL) milk or cream
1 tbsp (15 mL) salt
pepper to taste
1 chicken, 5 to 6 lbs (2.5 kg)

GRAVY:
2 tbsp (30 mL) flour
1 cup (250 mL) cold milk
½ cup (125 mL) grated cheese

🐦 Mix together the cooked noodles, the mushrooms, the 1 cup (250 mL) grated cheese, the milk or cream, salt and pepper. Stuff the chicken with this mixture and set it in a roasting pan.

🐦 Roast the chicken in a 375°F (190°C) oven for 18 to 20 minutes per lb (500 g). Remove the chicken from the roasting pan.

🐦 To make the gravy, add the flour to the drippings in the pan and stir it in well. Add the cold milk. Cook, stirring constantly, until smooth and creamy. Add the ½ cup (125 mL) grated cheese. Continue to cook, while stirring, until the cheese is melted. Serve in a gravy boat.

ROAST CORNISH GAME HENS

3 or 6 Cornish hens
1 lemon, halved
3 medium onions, halved
¼ cup (50 mL) soft butter
½ tsp (2 mL) basil or thyme
salt and pepper

🐦 One Cornish hen will make 1 or 2 servings. If you plan to serve 6 people with 3 Cornish hens, split the hens in half before cooking them. Otherwise leave them whole.

🐦 Rub the hens inside and out with the halved lemon. Arrange in a roasting pan and stuff each bird or half bird with ½ onion. Brush the flesh with soft butter and sprinkle with basil or thyme and salt and pepper.

🐦 Place the hens in a preheated 450°F (230°C) oven. Immediately reduce the oven temperature to 350°F (180°C) and roast for 30 minutes per lb (500 g).

🐦 Serve the Cornish hens on a bed of rice.

COUNTRY ROAST CHICKEN

🐦 Salt and pepper a 5- to 7-lb (2.5- to 3-kg) chicken inside and out. Rub the skin vigorously all over with a lemon half or baste it with cider vinegar.

🐦 Brush the wings and breast with bacon fat or softened butter. Tie the legs together with kitchen string.

🐦 Place the chicken on a large piece of aluminum foil and wrap it well. Put the wrapped chicken in a roasting pan and roast in a 375°F (190°C) oven for 18 to 20 minutes per lb (500 g).

🐦 For lovely golden skin, remove the aluminum foil at the end of the cooking period. Place the chicken back in the roasting pan, along with the juices that have accumulated in the foil, and roast at 450°F (230°C) for another 20 minutes or so, basting 3 or 4 times with the pan juices.

BOILED CHICKEN

1 stewing chicken, 5 to 7 lbs
(2.5 to 3.5 kg), with giblets
¼ cup (50 mL) celery leaves
pinch of nutmeg
1 tbsp (15 mL) coarse salt
10 peppercorns
¼ tsp (1 mL) thyme
½ tsp (2 mL) savory
1 large onion, quartered
2 cloves garlic, minced

🐦 You can cook this chicken whole or cut it into serving pieces.

It will be tastier if cooked whole, however.

🍂 If the chicken is cut up, first place the back in the bottom of a soup kettle surrounded by the gizzard and heart (and feet, if you have them, first removing the tough outer scale). Place the wings, breast and legs on top. If you cook the chicken whole, place it breast side up in the pot.

🍂 In either case, choose a pot just big enough to hold the chicken so that it stays in position during the cooking process.

🍂 Add 1 cup (250 mL) water for each lb (500 g) chicken. The chicken will not be completely covered with water, but the breast will cook perfectly from the steam as long as the pot has a tight-fitting lid.

🍂 Add the remaining ingredients. Bring to a boil. Cover and simmer over low heat for 20 minutes per lb (500 g) or until the chicken is tender. A cut-up chicken will take a little less time than a whole chicken.

🍂 If the chicken is to be served cold in a salad, it is a good idea to let it cool in its broth. It will be tastier and moister.

QUÉBEC-STYLE BOILED CHICKEN DINNER

1 stewing chicken, 4 to 5 lbs (2 kg)
½ tsp (2 mL) nutmeg
1 tbsp (15 mL) lemon juice
salt and pepper
½ tsp (2 mL) thyme
2 lbs (1 kg) salt pork, lean and fat
12 cups (3 L) hot water
1 tsp (5 mL) coarse salt
½ tsp (2 mL) savory
2 onions, minced
½ cup (125 mL) celery leaves

1 small green cabbage, quartered
12 small whole carrots, peeled
12 small whole onions, peeled
2 lbs (1 kg) yellow
or green beans
12 new potatoes, scrubbed

SAUCE:
½ cup (125 mL) butter
½ cup (125 mL) chopped parsley
½ cup (125 mL) chopped chives

🍂 Remove the excess fat from the chicken cavity, cut it in small pieces and melt it over high heat in a pan large enough to hold the chicken.

🍂 Rub the chicken all over with the nutmeg and the lemon juice. Sprinkle the inside of the bird with the salt, pepper and thyme.

🍂 Brown the chicken in the fat over medium heat. Add the salt pork, hot water, coarse salt, savory, minced onions and celery leaves. Bring to a boil, partially cover and simmer over low heat for 15 to 16 minutes per lb (500 g) or until the chicken is nearly done.

🍂 Add the quartered cabbage, whole carrots, onions, yellow or green beans (tied into small bundles with kitchen string) and the new potatoes. Return to a boil, cover and continue to cook another 30 minutes or until everything is cooked to taste.

🍂 To make the sauce, melt the butter and stir in the chopped parsley and chives.

🍂 To serve, place the chicken and the salt pork in the middle of a heated platter, surround with the vegetables and top with the butter sauce.

Chicken with Port

CHICKEN WITH PORT

5- to 6-lb (2.5-kg) chicken
4 tbsp (60 mL) butter
1 clove garlic, crushed
3 green onions, chopped fine
½ cup (125 mL) heavy cream
½ cup (125 mL) port
a few thin slices salt pork
salt

🏵 Clean and truss the chicken and brown it in the butter. When the bird is well-browned, add the crushed garlic, green onions, cream and port.

🏵 Place everything in a baking dish and lay the salt pork slices over the chicken. Sprinkle with salt.

🏵 Bake in a 350°F (180°C) oven for 20 minutes per lb (500 g), basting 2 or 3 times.

🏵 Serve the chicken garnished with sautéed mushrooms.

BARBECUED HALF CHICKEN

🏵 Buy broiler-fryers weighing about 1½ to 2½ lbs (750 g to 1.2 kg). Have the butcher split them in half. You will need a half chicken per serving.

🏵 Wash the chickens and dry them well. Brush with vegetable oil or barbecue sauce. Let stand for 1 hour.

🏵 Place the chicken halves on the barbecue grill close to the coals. Sear the halves for 2 or 3 minutes on each side. Then move the grill to 3 in. (8 cm) from the coals and continue cooking 25 to 30 minutes in total, until the flesh is tender and the skin crisp.

🏵 Baste often with oil or barbecue sauce during the cooking period and turn the pieces frequently.

🏵 The chicken is done when the wings tear off easily.

LEMON BARBECUED CHICKEN

1 broiler-fryer, 2 to 3 lbs (1.5 kg)
2 whole lemons, halved
1 tsp (5 mL) salt
¼ tsp (1 mL) pepper
½ tsp (2 mL) paprika
3 tbsp (45 mL) melted butter
¼ tsp (1 mL) thyme

🏵 Split the chicken in 2. Rub all over with a lemon half. Combine the salt, pepper and paprika and sprinkle it over the chicken halves on both sides.

🏵 Mix the melted butter with the thyme. Spear a lemon half on a fork, dip it in the butter mixture and use it to baste the chicken skin.

🏵 Place the chicken on the barbecue grill 3 in. (8 cm) from the coals and grill for a total of 25 or 30 minutes, turning often, until tender.

🏵 Keep the butter warm. Use the same lemon half to baste the chicken often. This will make the skin crisp and tasty while flavoring the chicken.

TARRAGON BROILED CHICKEN

1 chicken, 2 to 3 lbs (1 to 1.5 kg)
6 tbsp (90 mL) butter
½ cup (125 mL) minced parsley
¼ tsp (1 mL) tarragon
½ tsp (2 mL) salt
2 whole cloves garlic

🏵 Split the chicken along the back and flatten it out, as described on page 274.

🏵 In a small saucepan, combine the butter, parsley, tarragon and salt. Add the peeled whole garlic cloves. Heat for a few minutes.

🏵 Brush the chicken on both sides with the butter mixture.

🏵 Place the chicken on the broiler pan skin side up, 6 to 7 in. (15 to 18 cm) from the broiler element. Turn occasionally during broiling, basting the chicken each time with a generous amount of the butter mixture. Cook until the skin is crispy and browned, about 50 to 60 minutes in all.

🏵 If the skin seems to be browning too much before the flesh is tender, place a piece of aluminum foil loosely over the chicken for the last 10 minutes of cooking.

OVEN BARBECUED CHICKEN

If you have a good broiler, you can make your own delicious barbecued chicken with hardly any effort.

1 chicken, 2 to 4 lbs (1 to 2 kg)
2 tbsp (30 mL) butter or olive oil
1 tsp (5 mL) paprika

Broiled Chicken in Barbecue Sauce

½ tsp (2 mL) tarragon or basil
¼ tsp (1 mL) pepper
1 tsp (5 mL) salt

❧ Use kitchen shears or poultry shears to split the chicken open by cutting along the backbone. You can cook it spread open in a butterfly shape or separate the two halves entirely. I prefer to cut the chicken only after it is cooked, as broiling it in one piece seems to keep it juicier.

❧ Place the chicken on the rack of a broiler pan, skin side down.

❧ Melt the butter or olive oil with the paprika, tarragon or basil, pepper and salt. Brush the chicken all over with this mixture.

❧ Place the broiler pan 6 to 7 in. (15 to 18 cm) from the element. Broil 25 minutes, brushing once with some of the remaining butter. Turn the chicken and brush with the remaining butter. Broil

another 25 to 30 minutes or until the skin is crispy and golden.

❧ If the chicken seems to brown too quickly, cover it with a piece of foil for the last 10 minutes or so of cooking.

❧ Serve immediately with a salad.

BROILED CHICKEN IN BARBECUE SAUCE

1 or 2 broiler-fryers
2 tbsp (30 mL) butter
1 tsp (5 mL) paprika
½ tsp (2 mL) basil or tarragon
1 tsp (5 mL) salt

BARBECUE SAUCE:
1 clove garlic, minced
1½ tsp (7 mL) salt
¼ tsp (1 mL) pepper
3 green onions, finely chopped
2 tsp (10 mL) prepared mustard
1 tsp (5 mL) dry mustard

¼ cup (50 mL) brown sugar
juice of 1 lemon
3 tbsp (45 mL) Worcestershire sauce
1 can tomato soup, undiluted

❧ Split the chicken open along its back so that it can be laid flat. Place in the bottom of a broiler pan, skin side down.

❧ Melt the butter and add the paprika, basil or tarragon and salt. Brush the chicken with the butter mixture.

❧ To prepare the barbecue sauce, combine all the sauce ingredients, beating them together well for a few minutes.

❧ Place the broiler pan in the oven 5 to 6 in. (13 to 15 cm) from the element. Broil for 25 minutes. Turn and broil for another 30 or 35 minutes, or until the chicken is tender and browned. Baste several times with the barbecue sauce during the last 10 minutes of broiling. Pour the remaining sauce into the broiler pan.

CHICKEN À LA MODE DE CAEN

2 broilers-fryers, 2 to 2½ lbs (1 kg) each
salt and pepper
4 tbsp (60 mL) butter
milk and cream (optional)

❧ Cut the broilers in half or split them along the backbone but leave them whole, flattened. Place them in a baking pan and season them. Dot with the butter.

❧ Place the chicken in a 400°F (200°C) oven, uncovered, and

cook for 15 minutes or until it begins to brown. Cover the pan and reduce the heat to 350°F (180°C). Cook for another 30 minutes or until tender.

🐦 It may be necessary to add some liquid to the pan to keep the chicken from burning. In this case add a mixture of half cream, half milk. The liquid must be completely absorbed by the chicken.

🐦 Serve with parsleyed noodles.

STUFFED BROILER HALVES

3 small broiler-fryers
1 tsp (5 mL) salt
¼ tsp (1 mL) pepper
½ tsp (2 mL) ginger
¼ tsp (1 mL) tarragon
6 tbsp (90 mL) melted butter or olive oil

STUFFING:

½ lb (250 g) fresh mushrooms, chopped fine
1 cup (250 mL) breadcrumbs
⅔ cup (150 mL) melted butter
3 egg yolks, well beaten
½ cup (125 mL) chopped fresh parsley
grated zest of 1 lemon
1 strip bacon, chopped fine
1 small garlic clove, crushed
salt and pepper

🐦 Split each broiler in half. Mix together the salt, pepper, ginger and tarragon. Rub the chickens inside and out with this mixture. Set aside.

🐦 To prepare the stuffing, place in a bowl the chopped mushrooms and the breadcrumbs. Add the

melted butter and stir until well mixed. Add the beaten egg yolks, parsley, lemon zest, bacon and crushed garlic. Salt and pepper lightly. Blend thoroughly.

🐦 Cut a piece of aluminum foil larger than the pan and line the pan with the foil. Stuff the chicken halves and arrange them skin side up in the pan. Lift the foil up to make a collar around the sides, but do not cover the top.

🐦 Pour 1 tbsp (15 mL) melted butter or olive oil over each chicken half. Cover the pan. Bake in a preheated 300°F (150°C) oven for 1¼ hours.

🐦 No sauce will be necessary, as the stuffing will keep the chicken moist. However, if you really want a sauce, combine 1 cup (250 mL) table cream with salt, pepper and a few spoonfuls of cognac or whiskey. Stir into the pan drippings and heat.

AMERICAN-STYLE FRIED CHICKEN

1 broiler-fryer, 2 to 2½ lbs (1 kg)
1 cup (250 mL) milk
½ tsp (2 mL) salt
pinch of basil or tarragon
¼ tsp (1 mL) pepper
¼ tsp (1 mL) paprika
1 or 2 green onions, finely chopped
¼ cup (50 mL) vegetable oil or shortening

SAUCE:

2 tbsp (30 mL) flour
½ cup (125 mL) chopped fresh parsley (optional)

🐦 Split the chicken in half, starting at the back; or leave it whole but split it open along the backbone and spread flat. Wash inside and out with a cloth dipped in vinegar or lemon juice.

American-Style Fried Chicken

[281]

Combine the milk, salt, basil or arragon, pepper, paprika and chopped green onion. Place the chicken in this mixture, skin side down, and marinate for 2 hours. This will keep the chicken from drying out during cooking.

ஃ Drain the chicken well and sprinkle with flour. Reserve the marinade.

ஃ Heat the oil or shortening in a skillet large enough for the chicken to be easily turned. Place the chicken in the hot fat and fry over medium heat 5 minutes on each side, starting with the bone side. Lower the heat, cover the skillet and cook for another 20 minutes, turning the chicken after the first 10 minutes. Remove the pan from the heat.

ஃ To prepare the milk gravy, add the flour to the fat remaining in the pan and stir over high heat until the flour is golden brown. Add 1 cup (250 mL) of the milk

marinade and continue cooking and stirring until thick.

ஃ To make a parsley sauce, stir in ½ cup (125 mL) fresh chopped parsley.

CHICKEN COCOTTE

2½- to 3-lb (1.5-kg) broiler-fryer
3 tbsp (45 mL) butter
1 onion, minced
¼ cup (50 mL) white wine
pinch of basil
pinch of thyme
salt and pepper, to taste
½ cup (125 mL) sour cream
or heavy cream

ஃ Quarter the chicken. Melt the butter in an enamelled cast-iron baking dish (cocotte), and brown the chicken and onion in it.

ஃ Add the white wine, basil and thyme. Salt and pepper to taste. Cover and simmer for 40 to 45

minutes, or until the chicken is tender.

ஃ When ready to serve, add the cream and heat the sauce without letting it boil.

HONEY CHICKEN

¼ cup (50 mL) honey
¼ cup (50 mL) butter
2 tsp (10 mL) soy sauce
1 broiler-fryer, 3 lbs (1.5 kg)
salt and pepper

ஃ Heat the honey with the butter and the soy sauce.

ஃ Cut the chicken in half and place in a baking dish, skin side down. Baste with 2 tbsp (30 mL) of the honey mixture. Cover and bake in a 350°F (180°C) oven for 40 minutes.

ஃ Turn the chicken and baste with the rest of the honey mixture. Continue cooking, uncovered, for another 20 to 30 minutes or until the flesh is tender and the skin is crisp and brown.

ஃ Salt and pepper before serving.

MUSHROOM BRAISED CHICKEN

1 3-lb (1.5 kg) chicken
3 tbsp (45 mL) butter
salt and pepper
1 onion, sliced thin
½ lb (250 g) mushrooms, diced
¼ to ½ cup (50 to 125 mL) white wine
¼ tsp (1 mL) tarragon
1 tbsp (15 mL) flour
1 cup (250 mL) light cream

Chicken Cocotte

❦ TECHNIQUE ❦

CHICKEN COCOTTE

1 Put the chicken pieces in the hot butter.

2 Add the onions and brown them.

3 Add the wine, basil and thyme. Cover and let simmer.

4 Add the cream and heat without boiling.

Chicken with White Wine

☙ Cut the chicken into serving pieces. Melt the butter in a large skillet over medium heat and brown the chicken. Salt and pepper to taste.

☙ When the chicken is well browned, add the sliced onion and the mushrooms. Stir a few minutes. Add the white wine and the tarragon. Cover and simmer 35 to 45 minutes or until the chicken is tender. Remove the chicken from the pan.

☙ Blend the flour with the cream and stir this mixture into the juices remaining in the pan. Simmer, stirring and scraping the bottom of the pan well, until the sauce is thick and creamy. Adjust the seasonings to taste. Pour over the chicken.

☙ Serve with buttered and parsleyed noodles.

CHICKEN WITH WHITE WINE

2- to 3-lb (1- to 1.5-kg) chicken
salt and pepper
3 tbsp (45 mL) butter
⅓ cup (75 mL) white wine
¼ tsp (1 mL) tarragon
1 tbsp (15 mL) flour
½ cup (125 mL) water
3 tbsp (45 mL) cognac

☙ Quarter the chicken. Salt and pepper the pieces. Melt the butter in a skillet and brown the chicken in it over medium heat.

☙ Add the wine and the tarragon. Cover and let simmer for about 45 minutes or until the chicken is tender. Remove the cooked chicken from the pan.

☙ Add the flour to the pan juices, mix well and add the water.

Cook, stirring constantly, until the sauce is smooth. Taste for seasoning.

☙ Place the chicken in the sauce and heat for a few minutes, basting occasionally with the sauce. Pour the cognac over all and simmer for 1 minute more. Serve.

BROILER PARISIENNE

2- to 3-lb (1- to 1.5-kg) broiler chicken
1 whole nutmeg
3 tbsp (45 mL) butter
salt and pepper
½ tsp (2 mL) tarragon
¼ cup (50 mL) dry white wine
¼ cup (50 mL) heavy cream
1 cup (250 mL) minced chives or ½ cup (125 mL) chopped green onions

RICE WITH CARROTS:
1 cup (250 mL) long-grain rice
2 cups (500 mL) consommé
3 medium-size carrots, peeled and grated
1 tbsp (15 mL) butter

☙ Clean and quarter the chicken. Rub each piece with the whole nutmeg (grating the nutmeg now and then to bring out the oil).

☙ Melt the butter in a heavy saucepan until a nutty brown color. Brown the chicken pieces in the butter over medium heat. Salt and pepper to taste and sprinkle with tarragon. Add the white wine and the cream. Bring to a boil. Cover and simmer over low heat for 20 minutes.

☙ Add the chives or onions and simmer over low heat, uncovered, for another 20 or 30 minutes, or until the chicken is tender.

🍀 To prepare the rice with carrots, first rinse the rice. Bring the consommé to a boil and add the rice and the peeled and grated carrots. Cook for 15 to 20 minutes over medium heat. When ready to serve, add a little butter and season to taste.

BROILERS WITH MAPLE SYRUP

2 broilers, 2½ lbs (1.5 kg) each
4 tbsp (60 mL) flour
½ tsp (2 mL) salt
¼ tsp (1 mL) pepper
4 tbsp (60 mL) butter
2 onions, sliced thin
pinch of anise seed
pinch of savory
maple syrup
½ cup (125 mL) water

🍀 Quarter the broilers. Combine the flour, salt and pepper, and dredge the chicken in this mixture. Melt the butter in a skillet and brown the chicken over medium heat. Place the pieces in a baking pan.

🍀 Fry the onions in the fat remaining in the pan and place on top of the chicken. Sprinkle with the anise seed and the savory. Dribble 1 tsp (5 mL) maple syrup over each piece of chicken.

🍀 Rinse the skillet with the water and pour it over the chicken. Bake, uncovered, in a 375°F (180°C) oven for 40 minutes.

BROILED CHICKEN BREASTS

It takes only 30 minutes to turn out these crispy, full-flavored chicken breasts. They are just wonderful served in a nest of Chinese fried noodles and accompanied with a crisp green salad.

juice of 1 lemon
2 tbsp (30 mL) chopped fresh parsley
1 clove garlic, chopped
1 tsp (5 mL) basil or oregano
⅓ cup (75 mL) peanut oil
½ tsp (2 mL) salt
¼ tsp (1 mL) pepper
2 whole chicken breasts

🍀 In a shallow bowl, combine the lemon juice with the parsley, garlic, basil or oregano, peanut oil, salt and pepper.

🍀 Brush the chicken breasts on both sides with this mixture and place skin side down on the rack of a broiler pan.

🍀 Broil 6 in. (15 cm) from the element for 15 minutes, basting occasionally with the lemon juice mixture.

🍀 Turn the breasts and broil another 15 minutes, basting again with the mixture.

🍀 The chicken is done when the breasts are brown and crisp. Avoid overcooking, which will dry out the meat. Serve a half chicken breast to each person, with the pan juices spooned on top.

MUSTARD BROILED CHICKEN BREASTS

4 whole chicken breasts
⅓ cup (75 mL) margarine or butter
1 tbsp (15 mL) cider vinegar
½ tsp (2 mL) tarragon (optional)
1 tsp (5 mL) dry or Dijon

Broilers with Maple Syrup

mustard
½ tsp (2 mL) salt
¼ tsp (1 mL) pepper
⅓ cup (75 mL) slivered toasted almonds

🡒 Split the chicken breasts in half. Place them in a deep bowl and cover with boiling water. Soak for 5 minutes, drain and pat dry with paper towels or a clean cloth.

🡒 Melt the butter with the vinegar, tarragon, mustard, salt and pepper.

🡒 Brush each chicken piece all over with the mustard butter. Place skin side down on the rack of a broiler pan.

🡒 Broil 6 in. (15 cm) from the element for 15 minutes, basting with some of the remaining mustard butter. Turn, baste on the skin side and cook for another 10 or 15 minutes, basting once or twice, until the meat is tender.

🡒 Serve on a heated platter, with the pan juices spooned on top.

🡒 Sprinkle with the slivered toasted almonds.

CHICKEN CASINO

Sometimes this dish is called Chicken Monaco, but whatever you call it, it's perfectly delicious. To serve it cold, prepare the day before and refrigerate until 1 hour before serving.

¼ cup (50 mL) fresh lime juice
¼ cup (50 mL) lemon juice
⅓ cup (75 mL) apple juice
or white wine
1 crushed clove garlic (optional)
1 tsp (5 mL) salt
½ tsp (2 mL) tarragon

¼ tsp (1 mL) pepper
3 whole chicken breasts, (6 halves)
3 tbsp (45 mL) butter

🡒 Combine the lime juice, lemon juice and apple juice or white wine with the garlic, salt, tarragon and pepper.

🡒 Arrange the chicken breasts side by side in a shallow dish. Pour the juice mixture on top and refrigerate for 2 hours. Remove the chicken from the marinade and arrange in a shallow casserole or baking pan; the pieces should not overlap. Dot the chicken with the butter. Reserve the marinade.

🡒 Bake the chicken, uncovered, in a preheated 375°F (190°C) oven for 35 to 40 minutes or until the flesh is tender. Baste with the marinade every 10 minutes.

🡒 Serve hot or cold.

CHICKEN BREASTS BORDELAISE

This is a specialty of the Bordeaux district of France—a tender, meaty chicken breast simmered in a delectable sauce of mushrooms, dry white wine and herbs. To add a really elegant touch to this dish, bone the breasts before cooking.

4 whole chicken breasts
juice of 1 lemon
½ tsp (2 mL) salt
¼ tsp (1 mL) pepper
pinch of thyme
3 tbsp (45 mL) peanut oil
3 tbsp (45 mL) butter
½ lb (250 g) fresh mushrooms, thinly sliced
4 tbsp (60 mL) flour
2 cups (500 mL) chicken stock

½ cup (125 mL) dry white wine
1 bay leaf or ⅛ tsp (0.5 mL) tarragon

🡒 Cut each chicken breast in half and baste with the lemon juice. In a shallow dish, combine the salt, pepper and thyme. Roll the breast halves in this mixture. Cover and refrigerate for 2 hours.

🡒 Heat the peanut oil in a skillet. Fry the chicken breasts in it over medium heat to a deep golden color on all sides. Place the chicken in a deep casserole or a covered baking dish.

🡒 Melt the butter in the same skillet and cook the mushrooms over high heat, stirring, for 1 minute. Add the flour and stir it well into the mushrooms. Then add the chicken stock and the wine. Cook, stirring constantly, until creamy. Add the bay leaf or tarragon. Taste for seasoning and pour over the chicken.

🡒 Cover and bake for 1 hour in a 300°F (150°C) oven. Serve with parsleyed rice, buttered green beans and a chilled white wine.

GLAZED CHICKEN BREASTS OSTEND

This classic Belgian dish is equally good hot or cold. You can also use the delicious oyster stuffing for roast whole chicken.

4 whole chicken breasts
salt and pepper
1 cup (250 mL) red currant jelly
juice and grated rind of 1 orange

STUFFING:
2 cups (500 mL) bread cubes

1 tsp (5 mL) salt
½ tsp (2 mL) pepper
¼ tsp (1 mL) mace or nutmeg
½ cup (125 mL) chopped fresh
parsley
1 small onion, diced
½ cup (125 mL) melted
margarine or butter
3 tbsp (45 mL) margarine
or butter
4 tbsp (60 mL) flour
2 cups (500 mL) milk
1 cup (250 mL) fresh oysters

🐚 Split the breasts in half. Salt and pepper both sides.

🐚 To prepare the stuffing, remove the crusts from enough bread to make 2 well-packed cups (500 mL) of small cubes. Place the cubes on a baking sheet and bake in a 325°F (160°C) oven until golden brown. Cool.

🐚 Combine these croutons in a bowl with the salt, pepper, mace or nutmeg, parsley, onion and the ½ cup (125 mL) melted margarine or butter. Stir until well blended.

🐚 Make a white sauce (see page 46) with the 3 tbsp (45 mL) margarine or butter, the flour and the milk. When creamy and smooth, add the well-drained oysters. Cool the sauce, and then pour it over the bread-cube mixture. Toss together lightly with 2 forks.

🐚 Place each ½ chicken breast on a square of aluminum foil, breast side down. Fill each with about ½ cup (125 mL) stuffing. Turn the breast so the stuffing is against the foil, and fold up the sides of the foil to surround the chicken without covering the top.

Chicken Véronique

🐚 Arrange side by side in a shallow roasting pan. Brush the top of each breast with soft butter.

🐚 Bake in a preheated 325°F (160°C) oven, uncovered, for 40 to 50 minutes.

🐚 Meanwhile, beat the red currant jelly with a rotary beater until smooth. When the chicken breasts have cooked for 25 minutes, baste them with the melted jelly. Continue cooking for the remaining 15 to 25 minutes, basting 3 to 4 times with the jelly.

🐚 When done, remove the chicken breasts from the roasting pan and keep warm.

🐚 Scrape the drippings collected in the foil into the pan. Stir the orange juice and grated rind into the pan drippings. Stir until hot, then strain and pour over the chicken breasts.

🐚 Serve with buttered noodles and diced or sliced carrots.

CHICKEN VÉRONIQUE

This is probably the best-known of the classic French chicken dishes. Serve these succulent chicken breasts with rice tossed with chives or finely chopped parsley. Accompany it with fresh asparagus in hollandaise sauce.

4 chicken breasts
salt and pepper
2 tbsp (30 mL) butter
1 tsp (5 mL) olive oil
pinch of basil
1 to 2 cups (250 to 500 mL) fresh
cold seedless grapes
3 tbsp (45 mL) whipped cream

SAUCE:
3 tbsp (45 mL) butter
3 tbsp (45 mL) flour

Chicken de la Vallée d'Auge

⅓ cup (75 mL) chicken broth
1 cup (250 mL) white wine
or vermouth
salt and pepper

🦐 Bone the chicken breasts or leave them as is. Season with salt and pepper.

🦐 Heat the 2 tbsp (30 mL) butter and the olive oil in a large skillet and add the chicken breasts, skin side down. Sprinkle with the basil and cook over low heat until golden brown. The slow cooking is important to prevent drying.

🦐 When nicely browned on the skin side, turn the chicken, cover the skillet and simmer over low heat another 15 minutes.

🦐 Meanwhile, make the sauce, which will take longer to prepare than an ordinary cream sauce as it involves the French process of reducing a liquid. Still, the end result is so good that it is well worth the extra time.

🦐 Melt the 3 tbsp (45 mL) butter in a heavy skillet or enamelled pan. Add the flour and stir until well blended. Add the chicken broth. Stir and cook until the sauce is smooth and creamy, then simmer over low heat until it is reduced to 2½ cups (625 mL); this will take from 25 to 30 minutes. Stir once or twice. Add the white wine or vermouth and simmer again, stirring occasionally, until the sauce is reduced to 2 cups (500 mL), which will take from 15 to 20 minutes. Season to taste with salt and freshly ground white pepper.

🦐 Arrange the chicken breasts on an ovenproof serving platter and surround them with the seedless green grapes. Pour the wine sauce over the chicken, then whip the cream and spread it on top of the chicken and the sauce.

🦐 Bake in a preheated 500°F (260°C) oven for 3 to 4 minutes, or until the top is golden and glazed. Serve.

CHICKEN-LEG SALAD

2 cooked chicken legs or wings
crisp iceberg lettuce
2 tomatoes, chopped
2 tbsp (30 mL) cider vinegar
1 tsp (5 mL) curry powder
or 1 tsp (5 mL) ground cumin
½ cup (125 mL) whipping cream
1 tsp (5 mL) mustard
½ tsp (2 mL) sugar
salt and pepper to taste
hard-cooked eggs (optional)

🦐 Have the chicken legs or wings at room temperature.

🦐 Cut 4 thick slices of lettuce and arrange 2 slices on each plate. Top with the chopped tomatoes. Place the chicken on top.

🦐 Blend the cider vinegar with the curry or cumin.

🦐 Whip the cream and add the mustard, sugar, salt and pepper. Beat in the vinegar. Stir well. Pour on top of the chicken.

🦐 Garnish the salad with slices of hard-cooked eggs.

CHICKEN DE LA VALLÉE D'AUGE

3 tbsp (45 mL) butter
4- to 5-lb (2-kg) chicken
2 medium onions, chopped fine
2 cloves garlic, crushed
6 apples, peeled and sliced
2 cups (500 mL) finely chopped celery
salt and pepper
1 tbsp (15 mL) flour

1 cup (250 mL) white wine
or apple juice
½ tsp (2 mL) basil

🌢 Melt the butter in a skillet and brown the chicken, whole or cut into individual pieces.

🌢 When the chicken is browned, remove it from the pan and add the chopped onions, garlic, apples, celery, salt and pepper. Cover and simmer over medium heat for 10 minutes.

🌢 Stir in the flour, the wine or apple juice and the basil. Return the chicken to the sauce and cook over medium heat until the chicken is tender.

CAPON WITH WHITE WINE

2 to 5 tbsp (30 to 75 mL) butter
4 slices salt pork, diced small
1 large capon
3 carrots, sliced in rounds
24 tiny onions
½ tsp (2 mL) marjoram
2 stalks celery
2 to 5 tbsp (30 to 75 mL) chopped parsley
12 peppercorns
2 cups (500 mL) consommé
1 clove garlic, crushed
1 bay leaf
½ cup (125 mL) white wine
1 tsp (5 mL) salt

🌢 In a large heavy saucepan or casserole, melt the butter and brown the diced salt pork.

🌢 Clean and truss the capon and brown it in the butter and salt-pork fat over low heat. Remove the capon from the pan.

🌢 Add the carrots, onions, marjoram, celery, parsley and pepper to the pan. Cook for a few minutes, stirring constantly.

🌢 Place the capon on top of the vegetables. Add the consommé, the crushed garlic and the bay leaf. Bring to a boil. Add the white wine and the salt. Cover and simmer for 1 to 1½ hours or until the capon is tender.

🌢 To serve, remove the skin and cut the bird into large pieces, or remove the meat from the bones. Arrange the meat on a heated serving platter. Strain the cooking juices through a sieve and pour over the capon.

🌢 Serve this sophisticated dish with parsleyed baby potatoes and asparagus or buttered broccoli.

GARLIC CHICKEN

5- to 6-lb (2.5-kg) chicken
salt
2 onions, quartered
2 cloves
¼ tsp (1 mL) thyme
1 bay leaf

SAUCE:
⅓ cup (75 mL) butter
2 green onions, minced
4 tbsp (60 mL) flour
1 cup (250 mL) cream
2 cups (500 mL) chicken broth
2 cloves garlic, minced
4 egg yolks
salt and pepper

MUSHROOM RICE:
2 cups (500 mL) uncooked rice
½ lb (250 g) mushrooms

2 tbsp (30 mL) butter
½ cup (125 mL) sherry
salt and pepper

GARNISH:
paprika
parsley

🌢 Sprinkle the chicken with salt inside and out.

🌢 Stick the onions with the cloves and place them in a large saucepan, along with the chicken, the thyme and the bay leaf. Add enough hot water to cover the chicken. Simmer over low heat for 1½ to 2 hours or until the chicken is tender.

🌢 To prepare the sauce, melt the butter in a saucepan and add the chopped green onions. Cook over low heat, without browning the onions. Add the flour and stir until well blended. Add the cream and the chicken broth. Cook, stirring, until the sauce is thick and creamy. Add the garlic.

🌢 Remove from the heat and beat the egg yolks into the sauce one by one, beating well after each addition. Taste for seasoning.

🌢 Cut the chicken into serving pieces and place in the sauce.

🌢 To prepare the mushroom rice, cook the 2 cups (500 mL) rice. Meanwhile, sauté the mushrooms in the 2 tbsp (30 mL) butter over high heat for 3 minutes. Add the sherry. Bring to a boil and pour over the cooked rice. Salt and pepper to taste.

🌢 Serve the rice with the boiled chicken. Garnish the platter with paprika and parsley.

SAUTÉED CHICKEN

1 chicken, 2 to 3½ lbs
(1 to 1.5 kg)
flour
salt and pepper
paprika
½ tsp (2 mL) tarragon
1 tbsp (15 mL) butter
1 tbsp (15 mL) bacon fat
½ cup (125 mL) consommé

❧ Cut the chicken into serving-size portions. Wash and dry them well and roll in the flour seasoned with salt, pepper, paprika and tarragon.

❧ Remove the rack from a pressure-cooker. Heat the butter and bacon fat and brown the chicken pieces in it. Add the tarragon and the consommé.

❧ Close the pressure-cooker and cook the chicken for 15 minutes. Let the pressure drop of its own accord.

❧ Serve the chicken in its sauce.

BAKED BREADED CHICKEN

1 3-lb (1.5-kg) chicken
¼ cup (50 mL) flour
1 tsp (5 mL) salt
¼ tsp (1 mL) pepper
½ tsp (2 mL) tarragon, thyme
or curry powder
½ cup (125 mL) melted butter
or margarine

❧ Cut the chicken into serving-size portions.

❧ Put the flour, salt and pepper, along with the tarragon, thyme or curry powder, in a paper bag. Add the chicken pieces. Close the bag and shake well to coat the chicken completely.

❧ Arrange the chicken pieces side by side in a roasting pan. Pour the melted butter or margarine over the chicken.

❧ Cover the pan and bake in a preheated 400°F (200°C) for 30 minutes. Uncover and bake for another 15 to 20 minutes or until the chicken is tender and golden.

FRIED CHICKEN

1 3-lb (1.4-kg) broiler-fryer
1 cup (250 mL) milk
½ cup (125 mL) light cream
½ cup (125 mL) flour
2½ tsp (12 mL) salt
¼ tsp (1 mL) pepper
¼ tsp (1 mL) thyme or savory

❧ Cut the chicken into serving-size serving pieces.

❧ Mix the milk and cream in a bowl. Mix the flour, salt, pepper and thyme or savory.

❧ Dip the chicken pieces in the milk mixture and then roll them in the seasoned flour.

❧ Heat ½ in. (1 cm) oil or shortening in a skillet. Fry the chicken over medium heat for 15 minutes, then turn the pieces and fry for another 15 minutes.

❧ Place the chicken on a heated platter and serve.

COQ AU VIN

1 3- to 4-lb (1.5-kg) chicken,
cut into serving pieces
3 tbsp (45 mL) flour
4 tbsp (60 mL) butter
salt and pepper
3 tbsp (45 mL) cognac
½ tsp (2 mL) thyme
2 bay leaves
red wine, preferably Burgundy
4 slices salt pork, diced

Coq au Vin

❦ TECHNIQUE ❦

COQ AU VIN

1 Dredge the chicken pieces in the flour.

2 Melt the butter and brown the chicken over low heat.

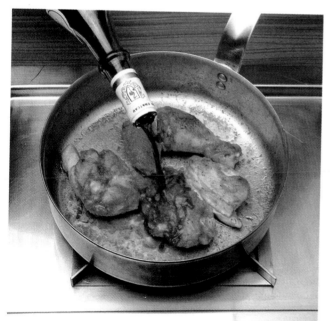

3 Add the cognac and flambé it. Add the seasonings and the wine.

4 Add the mushrooms to the pan with the onions.

Chicken Marengo

12 small onions
12 whole mushrooms

🍂 Roll the chicken pieces in the flour.

🍂 In a skillet, melt the butter and brown the chicken pieces in it over low heat. Salt and pepper.

🍂 Pour the cognac over the chicken, heat it, then flambé it. Add the thyme, bay leaves and enough wine to cover the chicken. Cover the skillet and simmer over low heat for 40 minutes or until the chicken is tender.

🍂 In a second skillet, brown the diced salt pork and add the whole onions. Cover and cook over low heat for approximately 20 to 30 minutes or until the onions are tender. Add the mushrooms and cook for another 2 minutes.

🍂 Arrange the onions, mushrooms and salt pork in a ring on a heated platter. Place the chicken pieces in the middle.

🍂 Boil the wine sauce over high heat for a few minutes to reduce it slightly.

🍂 Pour the sauce over the chicken and garnish with buttered toast points.

CHICKEN MARENGO

4- to 5-lb (2-kg) chicken
salt and pepper
flour
4 tbsp (60 mL) olive oil
1 cup (250 mL) white wine
2 cloves garlic, minced
¼ tsp (1 mL) thyme
1 bay leaf
2 large fresh tomatoes
or 1 cup (250 mL) tomato sauce
12 mushrooms, quartered
chopped fresh parsley
heart-shaped croutons, fried in butter

🍂 Cut the chicken into serving-size pieces. Salt, pepper and flour each piece.

🍂 In a skillet, heat the olive oil and brown the chicken; move the chicken to a heavy saucepan or casserole.

🍂 Pour the wine into the skillet and bring to a boil, scraping the bottom of the pan.

🍂 Pour the wine over the chicken. Add the minced garlic, thyme, bay leaf and the fresh tomatoes, peeled and diced, or the tomato sauce. Cover and simmer over low heat for 30 to 45 minutes or until the chicken is almost cooked, turning the pieces 2 or 3 times during cooking.

🍂 Taste for seasoning. Add the mushrooms and continue to cook until the chicken is tender.

🍂 To serve, place the chicken on a heated platter. Sprinkle with fresh minced parsley. Surround with the croutons.

CHICKEN CURAÇAO

1 broiler, 2½ to 3 lbs (1 kg)
3 tbsp (45 mL) butter
1 cup (250 mL) orange juice
1 piece of orange zest
1 tsp (5 mL) ground ginger
4 green onions, chopped fine
½ tsp (2 mL) garlic powder
1 tsp (5 mL) salt
pinch of pepper
2 tbsp (30 mL) Curaçao

🍂 Cut the chicken into serving-size pieces. Brown in the butter. As the pieces brown, place them in a baking dish.

🍂 Add the remaining ingredients to the chicken. Cover and bake in a 375°F (190°C) oven for approximately 30 minutes or until the chicken is tender.

🌿 If desired, thicken the pan juices with 1 tbsp (15 mL) cornstarch dissolved in 2 tbsp (30 mL) cold water.

CHICKEN VERMOUTH

4-lb (2-kg) stewing chicken
¼ cup (50 mL) flour
1 tsp (5 mL) salt
¼ tsp (1 mL) pepper
pinch of thyme
4 tbsp (60 mL) butter
¾ cup (175 mL) vermouth
1 cup (250 mL) light cream

🌿 Cut the chicken into serving-size pieces.

🌿 Put the flour, salt, pepper and thyme into a paper bag. Add the chicken, close the bag and shake until the chicken is well coated.

🌿 Melt the butter and brown the chicken in it over medium heat.

🌿 Arrange the chicken in a baking dish. Sprinkle with the vermouth and pour on the cream.

🌿 Bake, uncovered, in a 375°F (190°C) oven for 40 to 45 minutes. Turn the pieces occasionally and stir the sauce.

🌿 Serve with rice.

BAKED ONION CHICKEN

1 stewing chicken, 4 to 5 lbs (2 kg)
salt, pepper and paprika
½ tsp (2 mL) ground ginger
½ tsp (2 mL) savory
5 onions, sliced thin
½ cup (125 mL) parsley, minced
1 cup (250 mL) water

🌿 Cut the chicken into individual serving pieces.

🌿 Mix together the salt, pepper, paprika, ginger and savory. Roll the chicken pieces in the mixture.

🌿 Place half the onions in a baking pan and arrange the chicken pieces on top. Cover with the remaining onions. Sprinkle with the parsley, and pour the 1 cup (250 mL) water over all.

🌿 Cover tightly and bake in a 300°F (150°C) oven, or cook on the top of the stove over very low heat, for 1½ hours.

🌿 Serve with mashed potatoes.

OLD-FASHIONED CHICKEN

This is simply chicken baked in a white sauce, but in the early 1900s it was the most elegant dish to order when lunching at Delmonico's. It has lost none of its charm and I like its simplicity.

1 chicken, 3 to 4 lbs (1.5 kg)
1 tsp (5 mL) salt
½ tsp (2 mL) pepper
½ tsp (2 mL) thyme or sage

SAUCE:
2 tbsp (30 mL) butter
3 tbsp (45 mL) all-purpose flour
2 cups (500 mL) milk
2 stalks celery, diced
¼ cup (50 mL) chopped parsley
¼ cup (50 mL) dry sherry

🌿 Cut the chicken into individual serving portions and place them in a large bowl. Cover with ice cubes and add enough water to completely cover the chicken. Soak for 1 hour, then drain and pat each piece as dry as possible. Arrange the chicken in a shallow baking dish, salt and pepper to taste and

Baked Onion Chicken

[293]

Chicken Chasseur à l'Italienne

sprinkle with the thyme or sage.

🦋 To prepare the sauce, melt the butter in a skillet, then add the flour and mix well. Add the milk. Cook, while stirring, until smooth and creamy. Add the celery, parsley and sherry.

🦋 Pour the mixture over the chicken.

🦋 Cover and bake in a 300°F (150°C) oven for 50 to 60 minutes or until the chicken is tender.

CHICKEN ÎLE DE FRANCE

4- to 5-lb (2-kg) chicken
3 tbsp (45 mL) diced salt pork
3 tbsp (45 mL) butter
1 large onion, sliced thin
½ clove garlic, crushed
5 sprigs fresh tarragon
or 1 tsp (5 mL) dried tarragon

SAUCE:
3 tbsp (45 mL) butter
3 tbsp (45 mL) flour
1 cup (250 mL) milk

🦋 Cut the chicken into individual serving pieces. Brown the diced salt pork in the butter and then add the chicken. When the chicken is browned, add the onion, garlic and tarragon. Cover the saucepan and simmer for 45 minutes.

🦋 Prepare a white sauce (see page 46) with the butter, flour, milk and 1 cup (250 mL) of the cooking juices drained from the cooked chicken (add more milk to make up the 1 cup or 250 mL, if necessary). Cook until the sauce is smooth and creamy.

🦋 Pour the sauce over the chicken and simmer for 20 minutes.

🦋 Serve in a ring of parsleyed noodles.

CHICKEN À L'ITALIENNE

1 broiler-fryer, 3 to 4 lbs (1.5 kg)
3 tbsp (45 mL) butter
1 clove garlic, minced
3 French shallots, chopped
½ cup (125 mL) consommé
½ cup (125 mL) white wine
1 tbsp (15 mL) tomato paste
¼ tsp (1 mL) thyme
¼ tsp (1 mL) marjoram
salt and pepper
½ cup (125 mL) parsley, minced
½ lb (250 g) mushrooms

🦋 Cut the chicken into individual serving pieces.

🦋 Heat the butter in a skillet and sauté the garlic and shallots. Remove them when well browned. Brown the chicken in the same butter over medium heat.

🦋 Add the consommé, white wine, tomato paste, thyme and marjoram. Salt and pepper to taste. Cover and simmer over low heat for 40 to 45 minutes. Or you can bake it in a 375°F (190°C) oven for the same period.

🦋 To serve, set the chicken on a heated platter and sprinkle it with minced parsley. Surround it with mushrooms sautéed in butter for 2 or 3 minutes over high heat.

CHICKEN À LA SUISSE

1 chicken, 4 to 6 lbs (2 to 2.5 kg)
3 tbsp (45 mL) butter
½ cup (125 mL) white wine
1 cup (250 mL) consommé
1 bunch parsley, minced
2 green onions, chopped

❧ TECHNIQUE ❧

CHICKEN CHASSEUR À L' ITALIENNE

1 Brown the garlic and shallots in butter.

2 Remove the garlic and shallots. Add the chicken and brown.

3 Add the consommé and white wine.

4 Add the spices and tomato paste.

1 clove garlic, minced
2 cloves
½ bay leaf
¼ tsp (1 mL) basil
salt and pepper
1 tbsp (15 mL) cornstarch
2 tbsp (30 mL) cold water
½ lb (250 g) Gruyère cheese, grated

🍃 Cut the chicken into individual serving pieces. In a heavy casserole, brown the chicken in the butter.

🍃 Pour the white wine and the consommé over the chicken. Flavor with the parsley, green onions, garlic, cloves, bay leaf and basil. Salt and pepper to taste. Cover and simmer over low heat for 1 hour or until the chicken is tender.

🍃 Remove the chicken from the cooking liquid.

🍃 Thicken the cooking liquid with the cornstarch dissolved in the cold water. Cook until slightly thickened, about 2 minutes.

🍃 Place half the sauce in the bottom of a baking dish. Sprinkle with ½ the grated Gruyère cheese. Arrange the chicken in the dish, cover with the remaining sauce and sprinkle with the rest of the grated cheese.

🍃 Brown under the broiler for about 8 minutes or until the top is browned.

CABBAGE BAKED CHICKEN

1 chicken, 4 to 5 lbs (2 kg)
½ lb (250 g) salt pork, diced
1 large green cabbage, coarsely chopped
4 to 6 large onions, thinly sliced

1 tsp (5 mL) salt
¼ tsp (1 mL) pepper
½ tsp (2 mL) thyme
½ cup (125 mL) water

🍃 Cut the chicken into individual serving pieces and dredge in flour.

🍃 Melt the diced salt pork in a cast-iron pot or heavy casserole and brown the chicken in the melted fat. Remove the chicken pieces as they brown.

🍃 Drop the cabbage and onions into the remaining fat in the pan and cook over medium heat, stirring often, for approximately 15 minutes or until the vegetables are soft.

🍃 Then place the chicken pieces back in the pan, cover with the cabbage and add the salt, pepper, thyme and water.

🍃 Cover and bake in a 300°F (150°C) oven for 1½ hours.

CHICKEN KIEV

Chicken lovers adore this dish. But to make it properly, you must make sure the butter is very cold and the chicken is sliced very thin. The oil in which you cook it should not be too hot.

½ lb (250 g) butter
I small clove garlic, chopped fine
2 tbsp (30 mL) chopped chives or onions
2 tbsp (30 mL) chopped fresh parsley
salt and pepper
1 extra-large chicken breast (from a 5-lb or 2.3-kg chicken)
flour
1 egg, beaten
½ cup (125 mL) breadcrumbs
vegetable oil

🍃 Cream the butter and add the minced garlic, chives, parsley, salt and pepper. Mix well. Cover and refrigerate until the butter hardens, then divide it into 6 finger-sized sticks. Wrap and freeze for at least 4 hours.

🍃 Cut the chicken breast into 6 attractive slices. Place each slice between two sheets of wax paper and pound with a wooden mallet or the flat side of a large knife until the meat is quite thin.

🍃 Salt and pepper the slices of chicken. Place a frozen butter stick in the middle of each and roll it. You can tie each roll with white thread, if you wish.

🍃 Sprinkle the chicken rolls lightly with flour. Dip each roll in the beaten egg, then in the breadcrumbs. Sauté in the oil until well browned.

🍃 Serve immediately with mashed potatoes.

CHICKEN FRICASSÉE WITH DUMPLINGS

1 chicken, 4 to 5 lbs (2 kg)
2 tbsp (30 mL) butter
8 cups (2 L) boiling water
2 tsp (10 mL) salt
1 carrot, sliced thin
1 onion, minced
3 sprigs parsley, minced
1 clove
1 bay leaf
pinch of thyme
1 clove garlic, minced

DUMPLINGS:
2 cups (500 mL) all-purpose flour
2 tbsp (30 mL) baking powder

½ tsp (2 mL) salt
2 eggs
1 cup (250 mL) milk

🍃 Cut the chicken into individual serving pieces. Melt the butter and brown the chicken in it over medium heat.

🍃 Add the boiling water, salt, carrot, onion, parsley, clove, bay leaf, thyme and garlic. Bring to a boil. Cover and simmer over low heat for approximately 2 hours or until the chicken is tender.

🍃 To prepare the dumplings, sift together the flour, baking powder and salt. Beat the eggs with the milk. Add the sifted ingredients all at once. Beat until the mixture has the consistency of a light batter.

🍃 When the chicken is cooked, remove it from the broth.

🍃 Drop large spoonfuls of the dumpling batter into the hot broth, cooking 4 to 6 at a time, depending on the size of the pan. Cover and simmer over medium heat for 10 minutes. Continue making dumplings in this way until all the batter is used up.

🍃 Arrange the cooked dumplings around the chicken. Pour the cooking juices over all.

🍃 Sprinkle with parsley and serve.

Chicken Kiev

SUMMER CHICKEN CASSEROLE

1 chicken, 4 to 5 lbs (2 kg)
2 tbsp (30 mL) butter
salt and pepper
1 tsp (5 mL) tarragon
¾ cup (175 mL) water
3 tbsp (45 mL) white wine

or lemon juice
1 bunch radishes
1 bunch green onions
1 medium cucumber
salt and pepper
chives or watercress

🍃 Cut the chicken into individual serving pieces.

🍃 Melt the butter in a skillet and brown the chicken pieces on all sides. Add the salt, pepper, tarragon, water and the white wine or lemon juice. Cover and cook over low heat for 40 to 50 minutes or until the chicken is tender.

🍃 Slice the radishes and green onions into strips. Peel and slice the cucumber.

🍃 Stir the vegetables into the chicken and the sauce. Salt and pepper to taste. Do not let the vegetables cook.

🍃 Top with minced chives or watercress and serve.

ACADIAN STEW

4-lb (2-kg) chicken
or stewing chicken
3 cups (750 mL) water
1 tsp (5 mL) salt
pepper
1 stalk celery, diced fine
1 carrot, thinly sliced
2 onions, minced
1 clove garlic, minced
¼ tsp (1 mL) savory

DUMPLINGS:
½ cup (125 mL) all-purpose flour
4 tsp (20 mL) baking powder
½ tsp (2 mL) salt
½ tsp (2 mL) nutmeg
1 tbsp (15 mL) melted butter
1 egg, beaten
⅔ cup (150 mL) milk

🍃 Cut the chicken into individual serving portions.

🍃 Remove the rack from a pressure-cooker and place the chicken

Chicken Crêpes

in the bottom with the water, salt, pepper, celery, carrot, onion, garlic and savory.

🖎 Close the cover securely and set the pressure regulator. Cook the chicken for 15 minutes (stewing chicken will need an extra 5 minutes). Let the pressure drop of its own accord.

🖎 To prepare the dumplings, sift together the flour, baking powder, salt and nutmeg. Add the melted butter. Beat the egg and the milk together and add all at once to the dry ingredients. Stir just enough to blend.

🖎 Remove the chicken from the pressure cooker.

🖎 Drop the dumpling batter by the spoonful into the cooking liquid. (Make sure there is at least 3 cups or 750 mL of the liquid; add boiling water if necessary.) Close the lid and steam the

dumplings for 10 minutes over medium heat, without pressure.

🖎 Arrange the dumplings around the chicken on a platter. Serve the cooking juices in a gravy boat.

CHICKEN CRÊPES

2 onions, minced
½ green pepper, chopped fine
5 stalks celery, diced small
3 tbsp (45 mL) butter
½ lb (250 g) mushrooms, sliced thin
3-lb (1.5-kg) chicken, cooked

CRÊPE BATTER:
1 cup (250 mL) milk
2 eggs
2 tbsp (30 mL) melted butter
½ cup (125 mL) flour
½ tsp (2 mL) salt

CHEESE SAUCE:
1 tbsp (15 mL) butter
1 tbsp (15 mL) flour
1½ cups (375 mL) milk
1 cup (250 mL) grated cheese
salt and pepper

🖎 Brown the onions, green pepper and celery lightly in the butter. Add the mushrooms and simmer for 3 minutes, stirring constantly.

🖎 Remove the skin from the cooked chicken and cut the meat in ¼-in. (0.6-cm) cubes. Add the chicken to the vegetables.

🖎 To prepare the crêpe batter, beat together the milk, eggs and melted butter. Add the flour sifted with the salt. Beat the batter until smooth.

🖎 To cook the crêpes, butter a small skillet. Pour a little of the crêpe batter into the heated pan. Tilt the pan so that the batter is spread evenly over the bottom, pouring off any excess, if necessary. Brown over medium heat on one side only. Slide the crêpe onto a tea towel. Continue in this way until all the batter is used up.

🖎 Spread some of the chicken mixture down the middle of the browned side of each crêpe. Roll up to enclose the filling. Place the filled crêpes side by side in a shallow casserole or baking dish.

Make a cheese sauce (see page 59) with the butter, flour, milk and grated cheese. Salt and pepper to taste.

🖎 Place the cheese sauce over the crêpes in the baking dish.

🖎 Bake in a 350°F (180°C) oven for 30 minutes. If desired, brown the top under the broiler for a few seconds before serving.

CHICKEN TOSCA

3 cups (750 mL) cooked rice
2½-lb (1.2-kg) cooked chicken
2 cups (500 mL) mushroom
sauce
breadcrumbs
grated cheese
1 tbsp (15 mL) butter

🍂 Place the rice in a well-buttered baking dish. Cover with diced cooked chicken.

🍂 Pour 2 cups (500 mL) mushroom sauce (see page 48) over the chicken. Sprinkle with breadcrumbs and grated cheese. Dot with the butter.

🍂 Bake in a 400°F (200°C) oven for 18 minutes or until the top is browned.

CHICKEN DIVAN

salt and pepper
3-lb (1.5-kg) chicken
2 cups (500 mL) water
1 package frozen broccoli
2 tbsp (30 mL) butter
3 tbsp (45 mL) flour
½ cup (125 mL) chicken broth
½ cup (125 mL) light cream
2 tbsp (30 mL) sherry
Parmesan cheese, grated

🍂 Salt and pepper the chicken. Add the water, cover and simmer for 1 hour. Remove the chicken from the broth, bone the meat and cut it into large pieces.

🍂 Cook the broccoli according to the package directions. Drain it and arrange in the bottom of a baking pan. Arrange the chicken pieces on top.

🍂 Make a white sauce (see page 46) with the butter, flour, chicken broth and cream. When the sauce is quite thick and very smooth, stir in the sherry.

🍂 Pour the sauce over the chicken. Sprinkle the top with grated Parmesan cheese.

🍂 Bake for approximately 15 minutes in a 400°F (200°C) oven.

CHICKEN DIABLO

1 broiler-fryer, 2 to 3 lbs (1.5 kg)
½ cup (125 mL) flour
1 tsp (5 mL) salt
¼ tsp (1 mL) pepper
1 tsp (5 mL) paprika
1 tsp (5 mL) curry powder
½ cup (125 mL) butter
1 cup (250 mL) finely chopped onion

🍂 Cut the chicken in 1-in. (2.5-cm) cubes.

🍂 In a large shallow dish, blend together the flour, salt, pepper, paprika and curry powder. Roll the chicken cubes in this mixture.

🍂 Melt the butter in a baking dish or casserole. Place the chicken cubes side by side, skin side down, in the butter. Cover with a layer of the onions, lightly fried.

🍂 Bake in a 400°F (200°C) oven for about 16 minutes.

🍂 Serve hot or at room temperature.

CHICKEN POT PIE

1 chicken, 5 to 6 lbs (2.5 kg)
1 tbsp (15 mL) salt
¼ tsp (1 mL) pepper
few stalks celery
1 onion, thinly sliced
¼ tsp (1 mL) thyme or savory
1 bay leaf
1 lb (500 g) carrots, sliced in 1-in (2.5-cm) rounds
2 cups (500 mL) celery, cut on the bias
12 to 24 small white onions
2 tbsp (30 mL) butter
½ lb (250 g) mushrooms, quartered
¾ cup (175 mL) butter
¾ cup (175 mL) flour
3 cups (750 mL) milk
1 tbsp (15 mL) lemon juice
2 tbsp (30 mL) chopped fresh parsley

🍂 Place the chicken in a large saucepan with the salt, pepper, celery, onion, thyme or savory and the bay leaf. Cover with hot water. Cover the pot and simmer until the chicken is tender and the meat separates easily from the bones.

🍂 Remove the chicken from the broth and discard the skin. Remove the meat from the bones and cut in cubes of about 1 in. (2.5 cm). Place the chicken in a bowl and cover with the reserved cooking broth. Cover and refrigerate for 12 hours.

🍂 Remove the chicken pieces from the jellied stock and set aside.

🍂 Boil the stock until it is reduced to 3 cups (750 mL). Reserve the stock.

🍂 Cook the carrots and the 2 cups (500 mL) celery in boiling water until tender-crisp. Cook the small onions in salted boiling water for 15 to 20 minutes.

🍂 Meanwhile, heat the 2 tbsp (30 mL) butter in a skillet and brown the mushrooms over high heat for 2 minutes.

🍂 Melt the ¾ cup (175 mL) butter in a large saucepan. Add the flour. Stir to blend well, then add the milk and the 3 cups (750 mL) reduced chicken broth. Cook, stirring constantly, until the sauce is smooth and creamy.

🍂 Add the cooked carrots, celery, mushrooms, chicken, lemon juice and chopped parsley. Heat for a few minutes and taste for seasoning.

🍂 Place the chicken mixture in a baking dish. Cover with a pastry crust of your choice. Bake in a 400°F (200°C) oven for 40 to 50 minutes.

🍂 You can prepare all the elements of this dish a day in advance, but the pie should be assembled only when you are ready to bake it. In this case, you do not need to heat the vegetables or the sauce before putting the pie in the oven.

QUÉBEC CIPAILLE

1 small turkey, 6 to 8 lbs (3 to 3.5 kg) or 1 chicken, 5 to 6 lbs (2.5 kg)
1 partridge or 1 wild or domestic duck
1 pork filet
1 cup (250 mL) flour, seasoned with salt and pepper
10 slices fatty salt pork
4 onions, chopped fine
½ cup (125 mL) chopped fresh parsley
1 tsp (5 mL) savory
¼ cup (50 mL) chopped celery leaves
1 tbsp (15 mL) salt
½ tsp (2 mL) pepper
¼ tsp (1 mL) cinnamon
pastry dough
2 cups (500 mL) breadcrumbs or 2 cups (500 mL) cooked potato, grated
1 cup (250 mL) consommé

🍂 Cut the turkey or chicken and the partridge or duck into individual serving pieces and bone it. Grind the pork filet in a meat chopper or food processor.

🍂 Dredge the poultry in the seasoned flour. Melt the salt pork in a skillet and brown the poultry in it. Remove the pieces of poultry as they brown and place them in a dish.

🍂 Brown the onions, parsley and savory in the remaining fat. Remove and set aside. Then brown in the same pan the ground pork filet, celery leaves, salt, pepper and cinnamon.

🍂 Roll out the pastry dough to a thickness of ½ in. (1 cm). Use it to line a baking dish 4 to 5 in. (10 to 13 cm) deep. Spread the pork and celery mixture in the bottom of the pastry shell. Sprinkle with a layer of breadcrumbs or grated cooked potato. Top with a few slices of the browned salt pork and a few spoonfuls of the onion, parsley and savory mixture. Pour the consommé over all.

🍂 Cover this top layer with a second sheet of dough rolled quite thin. Cover the pastry with the pieces of chicken or turkey. Sprinkle with more of the breadcrumbs or grated potato, then with a layer of salt pork slices and a few spoonfuls of onion.

🍂 Place a third, thin layer of pastry dough over the chicken or turkey. Top with the pieces of par-

Chicken à la King

tridge or duck, a final layer of breadcrumbs or potato, the remaining salt pork slices and the rest of the onion mixture.

🕿 Top everything with another layer of pastry dough rolled ½ in. (1 cm) thick.

🕿 Bake in a 300°F (150°C) oven for 4 hours.

🕿 Serve hot or cold.

CHICKEN VOL-AU-VENT

1 chicken, 4 to 5 lbs (2 kg)
1 onion, quartered
1 carrot, sliced
3 stalks celery
1 tbsp (15 mL) salt
½ tsp (2 mL) pepper
pinch of thyme
½ tsp (2 mL) tarragon
½ cup (125 mL) water per lb (500 g) of chicken

SAUCE:

3 tbsp (45 mL) butter
4 tbsp (60 mL) flour
2 cups (500 mL) reserved chicken broth, strained
2 tbsp (30 mL) heavy cream
1 tsp (5 mL) butter
1 tsp (5 mL) tarragon or basil or ½ tsp (2 mL) thyme

🕿 Place the chicken in a saucepan with the onion, carrot, celery, salt, pepper, thyme, tarragon and water. Cover and simmer until the chicken is tender, about 40 to 60 minutes. Let the chicken cool in its broth. Reserve 2 cups (500 mL) of the broth for the sauce.

🕿 To prepare the sauce, melt the butter and stir in the flour. When well blended add the chicken broth. Stir over medium heat until the sauce is smooth and thick. Add the cream and the butter, a little at a time, stirring constantly. Season with the tarragon, basil or thyme.

🕿 Cut the chicken into medium-size pieces and place in the sauce.

🕿 If desired, stir in ½ lb (250 g) mushrooms, fried quickly in butter. Taste for seasoning.

🕿 Serve in warm puff-pastry shells.

CHICKEN À LA KING

This dish was created in honor of Charles II of England.

2 tbsp (30 mL) butter
¼ cup (50 mL) diced green pepper
1 cup (250 mL) thinly sliced mushrooms
1 small onion, chopped
2 tbsp (30 mL) flour
2 cups (500 mL) light cream
¾ tsp (3 mL) salt
3 cups (750 mL) cooked diced chicken
¼ tsp (1 mL) paprika
1 tbsp (15 mL) lemon juice
2 tbsp (30 mL) sherry

🕿 Melt the butter in a skillet and add the green pepper, mushrooms and onion. Simmer for 5 minutes. Sprinkle on the flour, stir well and then add the cream. Cook, stirring constantly, until the mixture thickens. Salt to taste. Add the chicken and simmer for 3 minutes.

🕿 Add the paprika, lemon juice and sherry. Cook over low heat, stirring almost constantly, for

3 minutes.

🕿 Serve in hot puff-pastry shells.

CHICKEN SOUFFLÉ

1 cup (250 mL) cooked white chicken meat, ground
3 tbsp (45 mL) butter
3 tbsp (45 mL) flour
¾ cup (175 mL) milk
salt to taste
¼ cup (50 mL) cognac or sherry
¼ tsp (1 mL) dry mustard
4 egg yolks
6 egg whites

🕿 Grind the cooked chicken meat in a meat grinder or food processor. Measure when ground.

🕿 Prepare a white sauce with the butter, flour and milk. Cook until the sauce is smooth and creamy. Salt to taste. Remove the sauce from the heat and stir in the sherry or cognac. Stir in the dry mustard.

🕿 Add the egg yolks, one at a time, beating vigorously after each addition. Blend in the ground chicken.

🕿 Beat the egg whites until stiff peaks form, then fold them gently into the chicken mixture.

🕿 Make a collar out of wax paper for an 8-in. (20-cm) soufflé dish. Turn the chicken mixture into the dish.

🕿 Bake in a preheated 350°F (180°C) oven for 40 to 50 minutes.

🕿 Serve with a light white sauce made with half concentrated chicken stock, half cream. Flavor with sherry or cognac.

Chicken Martini

Québec Chicken Galantine

1 fat stewing chicken,
5 to 6 lbs (2.5 kg)
10 cups (2.5 L) hot water
4 tsp (20 mL) salt
½ tsp (2 mL) pepper
1 carrot, grated
1 parsnip, grated
1 onion, grated
1 cup (250 mL) diced celery
½ cup (125 mL) fresh chopped parsley
1 tsp (5 mL) savory or thyme
1 bay leaf

🍃 Remove the fat from the chicken and melt it over low heat in a large heavy saucepan or casserole. Brown the chicken in the fat on all sides over medium heat.

🍃 Add the rest of the ingredients. Bring to a boil, cover and simmer over low heat for 2 to 2½ hours or until the chicken is tender. Remove the chicken from the broth.

🍃 Boil the broth briskly, uncovered, over high heat, until reduced by half. Reserve the broth.

🍃 Remove the meat from the bones before the chicken is completely cooled. Shred the meat into small pieces and place them in an oiled 9- x 5- x 3-in. (23- x 13- x 8-cm) loaf pan.

🍃 Pour the reduced broth over the meat (it is not necessary to strain it). Cover and refrigerate for 12 hours.

🍃 Unmold and serve.

Individual Chicken Molds

1 stewing chicken, 4 lbs (2 kg)
5 cups (1.2 L) water
1 onion
2 stalks celery
1 bay leaf
¼ tsp (1 mL) thyme
½ tsp (2 mL) dry mustard
salt and pepper
½ cup (125 mL) mayonnaise
2 tbsp (30 mL) capers
or chopped gherkins

🍃 Place the chicken in a saucepan with the water, onion, celery stalks, bay leaf, thyme and dry mustard. Bring to a boil and add the salt and pepper. Cover and simmer approximately 2½ hours or until the chicken is tender.

🍃 Remove the skin and bone the chicken. Cut the meat into bite-size pieces.

🍃 Boil the broth briskly, uncovered, until it is reduced to 2 cups (500 mL). Reserve.

🍃 Place the chicken pieces in oiled individual serving molds. Cover with the reduced chicken broth. Refrigerate until the chicken is chilled and the broth is set.

🍃 Meanwhile, beat the mayonnaise with the capers or chopped gherkins.

🍃 To serve, unmold the chicken and garnish with the mayonnaise.

Creamy Chicken Galantine

4-lb (2 kg) chicken
3 tbsp (45 mL) butter
2 onions, sliced thin
1 tsp (5 mL) salt
¼ tsp (1 mL) pepper
1 bay leaf
pinch of thyme
2 cups (500 mL) water
1 cup (250 mL) whipping cream

🍗 Cut the chicken into individual serving pieces.

🍗 Melt the butter in a skillet and brown the chicken pieces over medium heat. Add the onions, salt, pepper, bay leaf and thyme. Pour the water over all. Cover and simmer until the chicken is tender, about 25 to 30 minutes.

🍗 Remove the chicken pieces from the skillet.

🍗 Boil the remaining liquid until it is reduced to 1 cup (250 mL). Add the cream and heat it, without boiling.

🍗 Remove the chicken meat from the bones and cut it up. Add it to the broth and cream mixture. Taste for seasoning.

🍗 Pour into an oiled mold and refrigerate for 24 hours.

🍗 Unmold and serve garnished with watercress and mayonnaise.

CHICKEN MARTINI

You will be surprised and delighted with this Italian way of roasting a broiler chicken.

1 3-lb (1.5-kg) broiler, quartered
¼ cup (50 mL) butter, diced
8 to 10 juniper berries
¼ cup (50 mL) vermouth
2 tbsp (30 mL) dry gin
or juice of ½ lemon
salt and pepper

🍗 Place the 4 pieces of chicken in a shallow baking dish. Dot all over with the butter.

🍗 Crush the juniper berries with the back of a wooden spoon and sprinkle over the chicken.

🍗 Mix together the vermouth and the dry gin or lemon juice and pour this over the chicken. Sprinkle to taste with salt and pepper.

🍗 Bake, uncovered, in a 350°F (180°C) oven for 40 to 45 minutes, or until the chicken is tender and brown. Baste with the pan juices every 15 minutes.

🍗 Serve with rice.

CHICKEN SALAD

4 cups (1 L) diced cooked chicken or 1 stewing chicken, 4 to 5 lbs (2 kg), cooked, diced
2 cups (500 mL) diced celery
½ cup (125 mL) sliced olives
¼ cup (50 mL) French dressing with lemon
lettuce
½ cup (125 mL) mayonnaise
tomatoes, quartered
parsley

🍗 Put the cooked cubed chicken in a bowl. Add the celery, the olives and the French dressing. Marinate for 1 hour.

🍗 To serve, place the salad in a nest of lettuce. Garnish with the mayonnaise and tomato wedges. Sprinkle with chopped fresh parsley.

ROAST CHICKEN SALAD

1 4- to 5-lb (2-kg) chicken, roasted
1 cup (250 mL) diced celery
2 tbsp (30 mL) capers
3 hard-cooked eggs, sliced
3 tomatoes, peeled and quartered
salt and pepper to taste
½ cup (125 mL) mayonnaise
¼ cup (50 mL) whipping cream

🍗 Remove the skin from the chicken while it is still warm. Remove the meat from the bones and dice into fairly large pieces.

🍗 Mix together the chicken, celery, capers, sliced hard-cooked eggs and tomatoes. Salt and pepper to taste.

🍗 Combine the mayonnaise and the cream. Add to the chicken and mix gently with two forks. Taste for seasoning.

🍗 Serve the chicken mixture in a nest of lettuce or watercress.

ENGLISH CHICKEN SALAD

3 cups (750 mL) cooked chicken
2 cups (500 mL) diced celery
⅓ cup (75 mL) salted slivered almonds
juice of 1 lemon
1 small onion, grated
½ cup (125 mL) mayonnaise
2 tsp (10 mL) curry powder
1 tsp (5 mL) salt
pepper to taste
lettuce

🍗 Cut the chicken meat into small cubes. Add the celery and almonds.

🍗 Combine the lemon juice with the grated onion and the mayonnaise. Add the curry powder and the salt. Pepper to taste. Beat well.

🍗 Stir into the chicken mixture, using a fork so that the mixture is not mashed.

🍗 Serve the chicken salad on a bed of lettuce.

CHICKEN AND RICE SALAD

¾ cup (175 mL) rice, uncooked
2 cups (500 mL) diced cooked chicken
1 cup (250 mL) diced celery
2 green onions, chopped fine
½ green pepper, diced
1 tbsp (15 mL) lemon juice
½ to ¾ cup (125 to 175 mL) mayonnaise
lettuce

🎝 Cook the rice according to the instructions on the package. Let cool. Add the diced chicken, celery, onions and green pepper. Mix gently with a fork.

🎝 Mix together the lemon juice and the mayonnaise.

🎝 Add the lemon mayonnaise to the chicken mixture, tossing gently with a fork. Taste for seasoning.

🎝 Serve the chicken salad in a nest of lettuce.

CHICKEN LIVERS FRANCESCA

½ lb (250 g) chicken livers
2 tbsp (30 mL) flour
¼ tsp (1 mL) salt
1 tsp (5 mL) paprika
½ tsp (2 mL) curry powder
3 tbsp (45 mL) butter
4 chopped green onions
½ cup (125 mL) red wine
½ cup (125 mL) consommé
1 cup (250 mL) long-grain rice
½ cup (125 mL) parsley, chopped

🎝 Clean the chicken livers and cut them in small pieces.

🎝 Mix together the flour, salt, paprika and curry powder. Dredge the livers in this mixture.

🎝 Melt the butter. Brown the livers and the green onions for 2 to 3 minutes over high heat. Add the red wine and the consommé. Bring to a boil, stirring constantly,

until the sauce is creamy. Cover and simmer for 10 to 15 minutes.

🎝 Serve the chicken livers with the rice cooked and flavored with the chopped parsley.

CHICKEN LIVER PÂTÉ

1 lb (500 g) chicken livers
½ lb (250 g) sausages
1 tsp (5 mL) salt
1 tsp (5 mL) pepper
½ cup (125 mL) parsley
1 cup (250 mL) chopped celery
2 onions, minced
¼ tsp (1 mL) thyme
pinch of ground cloves
1 beaten egg
¼ cup (50 mL) port, sherry or cognac
6 strips bacon

🎝 Clean and chop the chicken livers and remove the casings from the sausages. Grind both meats in a meat chopper or food processor. Put into a large bowl.

🎝 Add the salt, pepper, parsley, celery, onions, thyme, ground cloves, beaten egg and the port, sherry or cognac. Beat together until the consistency is almost like a mousse.

🎝 Cut the bacon in small pieces and fry it. Add it to the chicken-liver mixture. Mix well.

🎝 Turn the mixture into a pâté mold or loaf pan.

🎝 Cover and bake in a 250°F (120°C) oven for 2 hours. Remove from the oven and cool.

Chicken Liver Pâté

❧ TECHNIQUE ❧

CHICKEN LIVER PÂTÉ

1 Clean the chicken livers and chop them coarsely.

2 Put the chicken livers and sausage meat through a meat grinder.

3 Add the seasonings, beaten egg, onion, celery and port.

4 Add the bacon, mix well and turn into a pâté mold.

❧ Cover and refrigerate for 24 hours before serving.

Creamed Chicken Livers and Vegetables

1 lb (500 g) green peas
¾ cup (175 mL) diced carrots
2 tbsp (30 mL) butter
½ lb (250 g) chicken livers, well cleaned
1½ tbsp (25 mL) flour
⅓ cup (75 mL) vegetable cooking water
⅓ cup (75 mL) light cream
salt and pepper

❧ Cook and drain the peas and carrots, reserving the cooking water. If you are using a pressure-cooker, cook for 2 minutes under 15 lbs (6.8 kg) of pressure. Reduce the pressure quickly.

❧ Mix the drained cooked vegetables and divide into individual bowls.

❧ Melt the butter in a skillet and add the chicken livers. Brown over medium heat for 4 to 5 minutes. Place the livers on top of the vegetables.

❧ Add the flour to the butter remaining in the skillet and mix well. Add the cooking water and the cream, a little at a time, stirring constantly. Salt and pepper to taste.

❧ When the sauce is smooth and slightly thickened, pour it over the meat and vegetables. Serve immediately.

❧ This dish can be prepared in advance. Keep it refrigerated, then, at serving time, reheat it in

ROASTING CHART FOR TURKEY

Weight	Oven Temperature	Cooking time (minutes per lb/500 g)
6 to 12 lb (3 to 6 kg)	350°F (180°C)	18 to 25 minutes
12 lb (6 kg) and over	325°F (160°C)	15 to 18 minutes

a 350°F (180°C) oven until the sauce is hot.

Chicken Liver Salad

romaine or iceberg lettuce
2 tbsp (30 mL) butter
4 chicken livers
1 small garlic clove, minced
salt and pepper, to taste
pinch of tarragon
chives or green onions, finely chopped
French dressing, to taste

❧ Wash the lettuce and separate the leaves. Wrap them in a clean cloth or paper towels and refrigerate until you are ready to assemble the salad.

❧ Heat the butter in a skillet until it is nutty brown. Brown the chicken livers and the minced garlic for 3 or 4 minutes. Remove from the heat and let the livers cool. Salt and pepper to taste. Sprinkle with the tarragon. Cut the livers into small pieces.

❧ Arrange the lettuce leaves in a salad bowl. Add the chopped chives or green onions.

❧ Combine the chopped chicken livers with a few spoonfuls of French dressing. Add to the lettuce.

❧ Toss and serve.

ROASTING A TURKEY

Wipe the turkey inside and outside with a cloth dipped in vinegar. Sprinkle the inside with salt. Rub the exterior with a whole nutmeg and a half lemon. Stuff the neck cavity loosely with the stuffing of your choice. Tie the neck skin to the back of the turkey. Stuff the crop cavity loosely as the stuffing will expand. Close the opening and baste the turkey with butter or fat. Salt and pepper the surface.

❧ Place the turkey in a roasting pan. Do not add any liquid. Do not cover the pan. Roast according to the turkey roasting chart.

❧ To see if the turkey is done, press the thighs with your fingertips. If they seem to be still hard, let the bird cook longer. Do not prick with a fork; this will waste the tasty juices.

❧ Once the turkey is cooked, let it stand in a warm place for 20 minutes to allow the juices to spread throughout the bird.

TURKEY TIPS

A female turkey will always be more tender than a male turkey. The tastiest birds weigh between 8 and 15 lbs (3.5 and 7 kg). The bone at the base of the breast should be very white.

☙ To defrost a frozen turkey in the refrigerator, count on about 3 days. Leave it in its original wrapping.

☙ Fresh cleaned turkey will keep for 3 to 4 days in the refrigerator, as long as the giblets are removed. Leftover cooked turkey will keep for several days in the refrigerator and several weeks in the freezer.

BREAD STUFFING

Using the exact quantities in this recipe is not really important; the stuffing is always tasty and light.

☙ Mix 2 parts diced toasted bread (white or whole wheat) with 1 part finely chopped celery and/or onions. Season with thyme, marjoram, basil or lots of parsley.

☙ Season the inside of the turkey with salt and paprika. Fill the cavity half full with the bread and celery stuffing. Pour in about ¼ cup (50 mL) melted butter. Finish stuffing the cavity, taking care not to stuff it too tightly. Pour in some more melted butter, as well as a few spoonfuls of sherry, brandy or consommé. Close the opening.

☙ To vary this recipe slightly, add one or more of the following ingredients to the stuffing mixture: nuts, oysters, diced apples, chestnuts, chopped liver, minced lean pork, ground turkey giblets or mushrooms.

Dutch Potato and Bread Stuffing

FRENCH STUFFING WITH HAM AND GIBLETS

turkey giblets
1 lb (500 g) fresh ham, uncooked
3 eggs
salt, pepper, nutmeg
1 large onion, finely chopped
1 clove garlic, crushed
¼ cup (50 mL) chopped fresh parsley
½ tsp (2 mL) tarragon
½ cup (125 mL) light cream
6 cups (1.5 L) breadcrumbs

☙ Finely chop the giblets and the ham, including the fat.

☙ Beat the eggs in a large bowl. Add the salt and pepper to taste. Season with grated nutmeg.

☙ Mix together the onion, garlic, parsley and tarragon.

☙ Heat the cream and pour it over the breadcrumbs. Let soak for 10 minutes.

☙ Add the chopped giblets and ham, the beaten eggs and the onion mixture. Knead with your hands until the ingredients are well blended.

☙ This will make enough stuffing for a 10- to 16-lb (4.5- to 7-kg) turkey.

DUTCH POTATO AND BREAD STUFFING

2 beaten eggs
2 cups (500 mL) milk
4 cups (1 L) coarse dry breadcrumbs
1 tbsp (15 mL) salt
½ tsp (2 mL) pepper
2 cups (500 mL) mashed potatoes

½ cup (125 mL) finely chopped celery
¼ cup (50 mL) butter
1 large onion, chopped

🐦 Beat the eggs until very light; stir in the milk. Pour the mixture over the dry breadcrumbs. Add the salt and pepper, potatoes and celery. Mix well.

🐦 Melt the butter in a large saucepan, add the onion and brown it over medium heat for 5 to 6 minutes. Add the bread and potato mixture and cook for approximately 10 minutes, stirring almost constantly.

🐦 This recipe will stuff an 8- to 10-lb (4-kg) turkey.

ENGLISH SAGE STUFFING

1 tbsp (15 mL) sage or savory
1½ tsp (7 mL) salt
¾ tsp (3 mL) pepper
½ cup (125 mL) fresh chopped parsley
¾ cup (175 mL) chopped celery with leaves
3 cups (750 mL) chopped onion
1 cup (250 mL) melted butter
11 to 12 cups (3 L) diced dry bread

🐦 Combine the sage or savory, salt, pepper, parsley, celery and onions with the melted butter. Cook for 10 minutes over medium heat, stirring often.

🐦 Pour the butter mixture over the diced bread. Mix well and taste for seasonings.

🐦 This recipe will stuff a 10- to 14-lb (4.5- to 6.5-kg) turkey.

TURKEY GRAVY

¾ cup (175 mL) flour
1 cup (250 mL) pan drippings
3 cups (750 mL) cold water or giblet stock
3 cups (750 mL) milk
1 tbsp (15 mL) salt
pepper

🐦 Stir the flour into the pan drippings. Cook for 2 minutes over low heat, stirring constantly.

🐦 Add the cold water or giblet stock and the milk all at once. Beat with a wire whisk over high heat until the gravy is smooth and creamy. Add the salt. Pepper to taste.

🐦 Simmer over low heat, uncovered, for 3 to 5 minutes.

VICTORIAN BREAD SAUCE FOR TURKEY

This dish was a must with roast turkey in the early 1900s. Today we use cranberry sauce or gravy, but nothing will ever be better than a plump hen turkey roasted to perfection, beautifully carved and served with clear gravy and a rich, creamy, velvety bread sauce.

1 cup (250 mL) well-packed fresh bread cubes
1 cup (250 mL) hot consommé
pinch of nutmeg
salt and pepper to taste
2 tbsp (30 mL) butter
whipping cream

🐦 Make sure no crusts remain on the bread; cut it into small cubes and pack it tightly to measure the 1 cup (250 mL).

🐦 Put the bread cubes in a saucepan and cover with very hot consommé (undiluted canned consommé will do).

🐦 Add the nutmeg, salt and pepper. When the bread has soaked up all the consommé, simmer over low heat, stirring often, until the liquid has completely disappeared. Add the butter and enough cream to reach the desired consistency.

🐦 If desired, add a thick slice of onion to the bread before adding the boiling consommé. Remove before adding the butter.

TURKEY WITH WHITE WINE

A 6- to 8-lb (2.5- to 3.5-kg) young turkey cut up and prepared as follows will serve up to 10 people. If you plan on serving more people, buy 2 small 6-lb (2.5-kg) birds rather than 1 large one.

1 turkey, 6 to 8 lbs (2.5 to 3.5 kg)
salt and pepper to taste
1 tsp (5 mL) tarragon or ground sage
½ cup (125 mL) white wine
½ cup (125 mL) vegetable oil

🐦 Ask your butcher to cut the turkey into individual serving pieces, or cut it up yourself as follows:

Separate the legs from the bird at the thigh and then separate the drumstick from the thigh at the joint. This will give you 4 pieces of turkey. Remove the wings, which will make 2 more pieces. Split the back all the way down the middle and open the whole breast flat on the table. Then, with poultry shears, cut through the breast bone. Remove the 2 back pieces but leave them whole. Cut each ½ breast into 2 or 3 pieces, depending on the thickness of the breast meat. I usually cut each ½ breast into 3 pieces, because I am careful to select birds with meaty breasts.

You should end up with either 10 or 12 pieces of turkey.

Place the turkey pieces in a glass dish and sprinkle them with salt and pepper, then with the tarragon or sage. Mix together the wine and vegetable oil and pour it over the turkey. Cover and refrigerate overnight to marinate.

The next day, place each piece of turkey on a double thickness of heavy-duty aluminum foil. Pour a few spoonfuls of the marinade on top and fold the foil securely so that no juices can escape.

Place the pieces of turkey side by side on the rack of a broiler pan. Roast in a 350°F (180°C) oven for 1 to 1½ hours, turning each package twice.

When ready to serve, move the turkey packages to a plate. Remove the rack from the pan and unwrap the foil in the pan, so that the juices will empty into the bottom of the pan.

Arrange the turkey on a heated platter.

Add 1 tbsp (15 mL) butter to the juices in the pan and stir over medium heat until just boiling, then pour over the turkey.

Garnish with parsley, watercress or minced pimento.

TURKEY CROQUETTES

½ cup (125 mL) thinly sliced mushrooms
3 tbsp (45 mL) butter
5 tbsp (75 mL) flour
1 cup (250 mL) milk
½ tsp (2 mL) salt
¼ tsp (1 mL) curry powder
1 cup (250 mL) turkey, cooked and minced
1 tsp (5 mL) chopped parsley
1 egg, lightly beaten
2 tbsp (30 mL) cold water
soda-cracker crumbs

Sauté the sliced mushrooms in the butter for 2 minutes. Add the flour and mix well. Add the milk and continue to cook, stirring constantly, until the sauce is creamy and slightly thickened.

Add the salt, curry powder, minced turkey and chopped parsley. Mix well. Turn into a dish and refrigerate for 4 to 5 hours. This step is important as the mixture has to be well chilled to produce light croquettes.

Beat the egg with the cold water. Divide the turkey mixture into 8 portions and shape each into a small ball or flat cake.

Roll the croquettes in the cracker crumbs and then dip them in the beaten egg and water mixture. Dredge them once more in the cracker crumbs.

Heat enough vegetable shortening or oil to cover the croquettes.

Turkey Croquettes

Fry for 3 minutes or until well browned. Drain on paper towels.

TURKEY TETRAZZINI

16 oz (500 g) uncooked spaghetti
¾ cup (175 mL) butter
1½ cups (375 mL) diced celery
1 cup (250 mL) diced
green peppers
1 large onion, minced
½ lb (250 g) mushrooms,
thinly sliced
¼ cup (50 mL) flour
2 cups (500 mL) milk
½ lb (250 g) grated cheese
2 tsp (10 mL) salt
¼ tsp (1 mL) pepper
½ tsp (2 mL) marjoram
1½ to 2 cups (375 to 500 mL)
diced cooked turkey
¼ cup (50 mL) sherry
¾ cup (175 mL) Parmesan cheese

🍃 Cook the spaghetti according to the instructions on the package. Drain.

🍃 Melt the butter and cook the celery, green pepper, onion and mushrooms until tender. Blend in the flour. Add the milk and stir over medium heat until the sauce is smooth and creamy.

🍃 Add the ½ lb (250 g) grated cheese, salt, pepper, marjoram, diced cooked turkey and sherry. Cook over low heat until the cheese has melted.

🍃 Pour the sauce over the cooked spaghetti. Stir to blend. Place in a casserole or baking dish and sprinkle with the ¾ cup (175 mL) Parmesan cheese.

🍃 Bake in a 350°F (180°C) oven for 10 to 12 minutes.

TURKEY SURPRISE

🍃 Make a white sauce with 4 tbsp (60 mL) butter or vegetable shortening, 4 tbsp (60 mL) flour and 2 cups (500 mL) turkey broth or other stock. If desired, season with pressed garlic.

🍃 Add 1 tbsp (15 m) soy sauce and 3 cups (750 mL) cooked turkey.

🍃 Heat and serve on a bed of cooked rice.

TURKEY WITH NOODLES

🍃 Make a white sauce with 4 tbsp (60 mL) shortening, 4 tbsp (60 mL) flour and 3 cups (750 mL) turkey broth or other stock.

🍃 Add 1 cup (250 mL) grated cheese, 8 oz (500 g) noodles, cooked, and 2 to 3 cups (750 mL) cooked turkey. Stir in 1 large onion, chopped, and ½ tsp (2 mL) oregano. If desired, stir in ½ lb (250 g) mushrooms, fried quickly in butter.

🍃 Turn into a buttered casserole and sprinkle with cheese.

🍃 Bake in a 350°F (180°C) oven for 15 to 18 minutes.

DUCK

A good duck has a meaty breast, and the lower part of the beak and the wing tips are flexible. The fat is pale grey or white, depending on the species, and the skin should be supple. Try to select a duck that is plump but not too fat.

🍃 It is best to buy a duck weighing at least 3 lbs (1.5 kg); a smaller duck may be very tender, but the percentage of bone compared to flesh is very high.

🍃 The duck is smaller than the drake, has finer bones and is more tender, but it is also more expensive.

🍃 Buy ½ to ¾ lb (250 to 375 g) of duck per serving.

PREPARING DUCK
Rub the duck inside and out with a lemon or orange half. Truss the duck, folding the rump or "pope's nose" inside. Leave the legs untied.

🍃 Whether the duck is to be roasted or braised, it is preferable to season the inside before you truss it.

🍃 Roast the duck in a 425°F (220°C) oven for 45 minutes to 1 hour, basting with the pan juices 3 or 4 times during roasting.

TASTY STUFFINGS FOR DUCK
You will need about 1½ cups (375 mL) stuffing for an average size duck.

GIBLET STUFFING:
🍃 Grind the liver, heart and gizzard in a food processor; add 2 cups (500 mL) breadcrumbs, 2 eggs, 1 garlic clove and chopped onions or chopped green onions; season with savory or marjoram.

CANADIAN STUFFING:
🍃 Combine salt, pepper, ground cloves, cinnamon, nutmeg and dry mustard; dredge 3 unpeeled

quartered apples with this mixture and use them to stuff the duck.

NORMANDY STUFFING:

🍃 fry ½ lb (250 g) boudin or blood sausage in 2 tbsp (30 mL) butter over low heat; add 2 thinly sliced onions; when the onions are golden, crush them into the crumbled boudin.

ENGLISH STUFFING:

🍃 Boil 3 or 4 red onions, drain them well, and then chop them; add 2 cups (500 mL) breadcrumbs, ¼ cup (50 mL) heated cream, 2 beaten eggs and ¼ tsp (1 mL) sage; combine well.

DUCK GRAVY

To make a clear gravy, do not degrease the cooking juices; simply stir in 1 can undiluted consommé and ¼ cup (50 mL) cognac or lemon juice. Bring to a boil, stirring and scraping the bottom of the pan well to incorporate all the drippings. Strain and serve very hot.

🍃 To make a thick gravy, add to the pan juices ¼ cup (50 mL) flour and stir constantly over medium heat until the flour is somewhat browned. Add 2 cups (500 mL) consommé. Cook, stirring, until creamy and smooth.

QUÉBEC-STYLE ROAST DUCK

3 apples
½ tsp (2 mL) salt
¼ tsp (1 mL) pepper
¼ tsp (1 mL) ground cloves

Duck à l'Orange

¼ tsp (1 mL) cinnamon
¼ tsp (1 mL) nutmeg
¼ tsp (1 mL) dry mustard
1 duck, 4 to 5 lbs (2 kg)
1 cup (250 mL) apple juice
1 onion, thinly sliced
2 slices salt pork
salt and pepper to taste

🍃 Peel and quarter the apples. Combine the salt, pepper, ground cloves, cinnamon, nutmeg and dry mustard. Roll the apple quarters in this mixture.

🍃 Stuff the duck with the prepared apple quarters and place in a heavy casserole with the apple juice and onion. Arrange the salt pork slices over the duck breast. Salt and pepper.

🍃 Roast in a 450°F (230°C) oven for 1½ to 1¾ hours, basting 3 or 4 times. Duck should always cook uncovered in a hot oven.

DUCK À l'ORANGE

1 duck, 4 to 5 lbs (2 kg)
½ tsp (2 mL) salt
½ tsp (2 mL) curry powder
zest of 1 orange
2 apples, peeled and sliced
3 tbsp (45 mL) soft butter
2 unpeeled oranges, sliced thin
½ cup (125 mL) cold water
1 cup (250 mL) orange juice
¼ cup (50 mL) cognac
or Cointreau

🍃 Wash the duck. Combine the salt, curry powder, orange zest and apples. Stuff the duck with this mixture.

🍃 Place the duck in a baking pan, brush with the butter and cover with the orange slices. Add the cold water and roast in a 375°F (190°C) oven for about 1½ hours, depending on the size of the duck.

Duck in Red Wine

½ cup (125 mL) consommé. Stir over medium heat until the gravy is smooth. Strain and serve with the duck.

SPIT-ROASTED WILD DUCK

&- Clean 2 wild ducks and place them in a large bowl. Pour over the ducks ¼ cup (50 mL) cognac, ¼ cup (50 mL) melted butter and 1 cup (250 mL) apple juice. Marinate for 6 to 12 hours, turning the duck 2 or 3 times.

&- To cook, remove the ducks from the marinade, drain them well and secure them on the spit, with a drip pan arranged underneath.

&- Cook 30 to 60 minutes, depending on the size of the ducks. Baste a few times with the remaining marinade combined with ½ cup (125 mL) cream.

&- To make the sauce, add ½ cup (125 mL) apple juice and 1 cup (250 mL) applesauce to the pan drippings. Heat and serve in a gravy boat.

DUCK WITH RED CABBAGE

1 duck
3 cups (750 mL) red wine
1 medium red cabbage
1 large onion, minced
2 unpeeled apples, grated
½ tsp (2 mL) ground cloves
½ tsp (2 mL) cinnamon
1 tsp (5 mL) savory
salt and pepper
6 slices fat salt pork

&- To make the orange sauce, remove the orange slices from the duck and leave them in the roasting pan. Set the duck on a heated platter. Place the baking pan on a burner and add the orange juice and the cognac or Cointreau. Heat over medium heat, scraping the bottom of the pan and crushing the orange slices, until well blended and hot.

&- Strain the liquid into a gravy boat and serve with the duck.

BRAISED DUCK

2 tbsp (30 mL) butter
1 duck, 4 to 5 lbs (2 kg)
salt
1 onion, sliced thin
1 clove garlic, minced
1 slice bacon
1 tsp (5 mL) sugar

6 peppercorns
½ tsp (2 mL) rosemary
1 cup (250 mL) white wine or cider
½ cup (125 mL) water

&- Melt the butter in a heavy casserole or Dutch oven. Place the cleaned and trussed duck in it. Salt the duck and surround with the onion, garlic, bacon, sugar, pepper and rosemary. Mix well.

&- Add the white wine and the water. Bring to a boil. Cover and simmer over very low heat for about 1 to 1½ hours, or until the duck is tender.

&- When the duck is done, remove the skin and carve the meat into slices. Place the slices on a heated platter and keep warm.

&- To the pan drippings, add 1 tbsp (15 mL) flour, 1 tbsp (15 mL) cognac or port and

❦ TECHNIQUE ❦

DUCK IN RED WINE

1 Cut the duck into serving pieces.

2 Marinate 24 hours in the refrigerator.

3 Brown the pieces of duck in the hot oil.

4 Pour the marinade on top.

Clean the duck, place it in a bowl and pour the red wine over it. Marinate for 12 hours in the refrigerator.

Chop the cabbage fine. Add the onion, apples, ground cloves, cinnamon and savory.

Remove the duck from the red wine, reserving the wine. Salt and pepper the bird well inside and outside, and fill it with as much of the cabbage mixture as possible. Close the opening and tie the legs.

Line the bottom of a deep baking dish or casserole with the sliced salt pork. Place the remainder of the cabbage mixture over the salt pork, then set the duck on the cabbage bed and pour the red wine on top.

Cover and bake in a 375°F (190°C) oven for 1½ hours. Uncover the pan during the last 30 minutes of cooking.

Barbecued Duck

1 duck, 4 to 5 lbs (2 kg)
¼ cup (50 mL) honey
2 tsp (10 mL) hot sauce
½ tsp (2 mL) salt
½ tsp (2 mL) ground ginger

Remove the neck, wings and backbone from the duck. Then separate the legs from the duck and split the duck in half.

Mix together the honey, hot sauce, salt and ginger in a small saucepan that can be kept warm on the barbecue grill.

When the coals are ready, place the duck quarters, meat side down, on the grill. Cook for 40 to 50 minutes, turning often. Baste the pieces of duck thoroughly with the hot sauce each time you turn them.

Serve immediately, as broiled duck tends to become greasy if it sits.

Duck in Red Wine

1 duck, 4 to 5 lbs (2 kg)
salt and pepper
1 onion, sliced thin
2 bay leaves
½ tsp (2 mL) basil
¼ tsp (1 mL) sage
2 whole cloves
1 garlic clove, crushed
3 cups (750 mL) red wine
½ cup (125 mL) olive oil

Cut the duck into individual serving pieces. Salt and pepper each piece.

Place the duck in a bowl with the onion, bay leaves, basil, sage, whole cloves, garlic and red wine. Cover and marinate 24 hours in the refrigerator.

Remove the pieces of duck from the marinade, drain and brown them in the hot olive oil. When all the pieces are browned, pour the marinade on top.

Cover and simmer over low heat until the duck is tender, about 40 to 50 minutes.

Serve with rice flavored with chutney and curry.

Duck Morency

1 duck, 4 to 5 lbs (2 kg)
salt and pepper
3 tbsp (45 mL) butter
1 cup (250 mL) port
½ can consommé, undiluted
2 tsp (10 mL) cornstarch
¼ cup (50 mL) cold consommé
1 to 2 lbs (500g to 1 kg) fresh cherries, pitted

Cut the duck into serving pieces. Salt and pepper.

Melt the butter in a skillet or heavy saucepan and brown the pieces of duck over medium heat until the skin is crisp. Remove the duck from the pan.

Skim off the excess fat. Add the port and the ½ can of consommé. Cook over medium heat, scraping the bottom of the pan to stir in the browned-on drippings. Return the duck to the skillet. Cover and simmer approximately 40 to 50 minutes or until tender.

Place the cooked duck on a heated platter.

Blend the cornstarch with the ¼ cup (50 mL) cold consommé. Add to the drippings, stirring constantly, until the sauce is creamy and thickened slightly. Add the cherries. Cover and simmer for 10 minutes.

Pour this sauce over the duck and serve.

CASSOULET

1 duck, domestic or wild
2 lbs (1 kg) white broad beans
½ lb (250 g) salt pork, cut in half
1 lb (500 g) pork rind
1 onion stuck with 4 whole cloves
1 tbsp (15 mL) salt
¼ tsp (1 mL) thyme
1 cup (250 mL) chopped
celery leaves
1½ lbs (750 g) pork shoulder
1½ lbs (750 g) lamb shoulder
2 onions, minced
2 cloves garlic, minced
1 6 oz can (150 mL) tomato
paste
½ lb (250 g) garlic sausage
breadcrumbs
butter
pepper to taste

🐚 Roast the duck in a 325°F (160°C) oven, calculating 20 minutes per lb (500 g). After 40 minutes of cooking, pierce the thigh and drumstick with a fork to let the fat drain out. Baste the duck 4 to 5 times during the rest of the cooking period with the fat in the bottom of the pan.

🐚 Remove the cooked duck from the pan. Cover and refrigerate.

🐚 Scrape the residue from the bottom of the pan, add to the melted fat, cover and refrigerate.

🐚 Soak the beans for 12 hours in 15 cups (3½ L) cold water.

🐚 The next day, place the beans and water in a soup kettle. Add the salt pork cut in 2, the pork rind rolled and tied with a string, the onion stuck with cloves, salt, thyme and celery leaves. Bring to a boil, cover and simmer for 1½ hours. Drain the beans, reserving the cooking liquid.

🐚 Cut the pork shoulder and the lamb shoulder into ½-in. (1-cm) cubes.

🐚 Melt the refrigerated duck fat and brown the pork and lamb cubes in it. Add the minced onions and garlic and brown them. Remove any excess fat. Add the tomato paste and 1 cup (250 mL) of the reserved bean cooking liquid. Cover and simmer for 1 hour or until the meats are tender. If it is necessary to add water during cooking, use some of the reserved cooking liquid.

🐚 When the meat is cooked, skim it out of the pot and reserve the remaining tomato sauce.

🐚 Remove the salt pork and the pork rind from the beans. Cut the salt pork into small cubes.

🐚 Untie the pork rind and spread it flat, fat side down, in the bottom of a large earthenware casserole.

🐚 Remove the casing from the garlic sausage and slice the sausage in thin rounds.

🐚 Cut the duck into individual serving pieces.

🐚 Spread a layer of the cooked beans over the pork rind. Cover with a layer of the duck pieces, a layer of beans, then a layer of sausages, a third layer of beans, and a layer of the pork and lamb mixture. Pour over all the reserved tomato sauce and bean water. Sprinkle with breadcrumbs. Dot with butter and sprinkle with pepper.

🐚 Cover and bake in a 300°F (150°C) oven for 2 hours. Uncover for the last 20 to 30 minutes.

🐚 This recipe makes 12 to 14 servings. Cassoulet will keep for 3 to 4 days in the refrigerator and 2 months in the freezer. It will reheat perfectly.

ROAST GOOSE

1 goose

MARINADE:
juice of 2 lemons
½ cup (125 mL) oil
1 carrot, coarsely grated
1 onion, thickly sliced
1 clove garlic, halved
6 whole cloves
½ tsp (2 mL) thyme
½ tsp (2 mL) basil
handful of parsley

STUFFING:
2 lbs (1 kg) apples, peeled and sliced
¼ lb (125 g) melted butter
1 cup (250 mL) raisins
5 cups (1.2 L) diced toasted bread
½ tsp (2 mL) thyme or marjoram
1 tsp (5 mL) salt
½ tsp (2 mL) pepper

🐚 Wipe the goose with a cloth dipped in vinegar. Do not scald the goose, soak it in cold water or use soap.

🍃Combine the marinade ingredients and marinate the goose for 24 hours, turning from time to time.

🍃Mix together all the stuffing ingredients. Stuff the goose and truss it.

🍃Place the goose in a roasting pan and pour 2 cups (500 mL) boiling water over it. Cover the pan and roast in a 350°F (180°C) oven for 25 to 30 minutes per lb (500 g). After 1 hour of cooking, prick the wings and legs with a fork to let the fat escape. Uncover the pan for the last 20 minutes of cooking. Remove the excess fat.

🍃Make a gravy following the instructions for *Turkey Gravy*; see recipe on page 308).

GOOSE WITH CHESTNUT STUFFING

1 cup (250 mL) ground veal
1 cup (250 mL) ground pork
¼ lb (125 g) salt pork, diced
1 goose
2 lbs (1 kg) chestnuts
3 cups (750 mL) consommé
1 tsp (5 mL) marjoram
salt and pepper

🍃Mix together the veal, pork, diced salt pork and finely chopped goose liver.

🍃Peel the chestnuts (following the instructions for chestnuts on page 512). Cook them for 30 minutes in the consommé and then chop them fairly coarsely. Add the chestnuts to the goose-liver mixture. Add the marjoram, salt and pepper.

🍃Stuff the goose with the chestnut mixture and truss it.

🍃Roast the goose according to the instructions above.

KITCHENER STUFFED GOOSE

10- to 12-lb (5 kg) goose
juice of 1 lemon
1 tsp (5 mL) salt
¼ tsp (1 mL) pepper
¼ tsp (1 mL) nutmeg
½ lb (250 g) chicken livers
1 tbsp (15 mL) chopped fresh parsley
2 onions, minced
1 clove garlic, crushed
½ tsp (2 mL) marjoram
1 bay leaf
1 cup (250 mL) red wine
2 tbsp (30 mL) butter
2 egg yolks
1 cup (250 mL) orange juice
1 tbsp (15 mL) prepared mustard
1½ cups (375 mL) breadcrumbs

GRAVY:
2 tbsp (30 mL) red currant jelly
grated zest of 1 orange
1 tbsp (15 mL) brandy
1 can undiluted consommé

🍃Wash the goose with a cloth dipped in vinegar. Combine the lemon juice with the salt, pepper and nutmeg and use to baste the goose inside and outside.

🍃Put the goose liver, chicken livers, parsley, onion, garlic, marjoram, bay leaf and red wine in a saucepan. Simmer for 30 minutes, turning the livers from time to time. Drain off the wine and reserve it.

🍃Chop the liver and seasonings together, as fine as possible. Add the butter and the egg yolks. Blend together. Taste for seasoning. Stuff the goose cavity with the liver mixture.

🍃Close the goose cavity. Fold the skin back over the neck and prick the skin all over with a fork so that the fat will run out during cooking. Place the goose in a roasting pan, breast side up.

🍃Combine the orange juice and the reserved red wine. Pour into the roasting pan.

🍃Roast the goose, uncovered, in a 350°F (180°C) oven for 15 minutes per lb (500 g). Baste every 25 minutes with the liquid in the pan.

🍃When the goose is cooked, remove it from the roasting pan. Drain off the fat into a bowl and place the goose back in the roasting pan.

🍃Mix 3 tbsp (45 mL) of the reserved fat with the prepared mustard and rub it all over the bird. Sprinkle all over with the breadcrumbs. Return the goose to the oven for another 15 minutes or until the skin is crisp and brown.

🍃To make the gravy, add to the drippings in the pan the red currant jelly, grated orange rind, brandy and consommé. Bring to a boil, stirring. Serve in a gravy boat.

GAME

Rabbit Terrine

RABBIT TERRINE

1 rabbit, 3 to 4 lbs (1.5 kg)
½ lb (250 g) ground pork
¼ lb (125 g) ground fatty salt pork
½ cup (125 mL) milk
½ cup (125 mL) breadcrumbs
2 beaten eggs
¼ tsp (1 mL) thyme
¼ tsp (1 mL) marjoram
¼ tsp (1 mL) savory
¼ tsp (1 mL) nutmeg
pinch of ground cloves
¼ cup (50 mL) chopped parsley
¼ tsp (1 mL) pepper
1 tsp (5 mL) salt
2 tbsp (30 mL) cognac or port
several thin slices of fatty salt pork
1 bay leaf

☙ Bone the rabbit. Put the meat, liver, heart and kidneys of the rabbit through a meat grinder.

Add the ground pork and the ground salt pork. Mix well.

☙ Heat the milk, add the breadcrumbs, mix, then squeeze out the excess milk. Add this mixture to the meat mixture.

☙ Beat the eggs with the thyme, marjoram, savory, nutmeg, cloves, parsley, pepper and salt. Pour this into the meat mixture. Add the cognac or port. Beat until thoroughly blended.

☙ Butter a loaf pan or an terrine mold. Line it with thin slices of very fatty salt pork. Pour the rabbit mixture into the pan, packing it in well. Place the bay leaf on top of the pâté.

☙ Cover the pâté with white cooking parchment, buttered on both sides. Cover the pan and set it in a larger pan of hot water. Bake in a 325°F (160°C) oven for 2½ hours. Let cool without uncovering. Refrigerate for 2 days before serving. This terrine keeps very well in the refrigerator for 8 to 10 days.

RABBIT IN MUSTARD SAUCE

1 rabbit, 3 to 4 lbs (1.5 kg)
2 tbsp (30 mL) Dijon mustard
3 tbsp (45 mL) vegetable oil
½ tsp (2 mL) tarragon
½ cup (125 mL) milk
1 tsp (5 mL) salt
¼ tsp (1 mL) pepper
¼ cup (50 mL) whipping cream

☙ Cut the rabbit into serving-size pieces as you would cut up a chicken, (separating the legs, and cutting the body into 4 pieces). Rub each piece with mustard.

☙ Heat the oil in a large heavy pot and brown the rabbit pieces in it on all sides. Add the remaining ingredients.

☙ Cover and cook over very low heat for 40 to 45 minutes or until the rabbit is tender.

☙ Add the cream only when ready to serve. Heat, but do not boil. Serve with boiled potatoes.

RABBIT WITH BACON

1 rabbit, 3 to 4 lbs (1.5 kg)
½ cup (125 mL) flour
½ tsp (2 mL) salt
¼ tsp (1 mL) pepper
½ tsp (2 mL) curry powder
9 to 10 slices bacon
2 large onions, sliced
¾ cup (175 mL) water
1 cup (250 mL) cold water
1 tbsp (15 mL) chopped parsley

❦ TECHNIQUE ❦

RABBIT TERRINE

1 Bone the rabbit.

2 Put the rabbit meat, liver, heart and kidneys through a meat chopper. Add the ground pork and the ground salt pork. Mix well.

3 Add the breadcrumbs soaked in milk.

4 Add the egg and herb mixture.

❧ Cut the rabbit into serving-size pieces.

❧ Mix together the flour, salt, pepper and curry powder, then dredge the rabbit pieces in this mixture. Reserve the remaining flour mixture for later use.

❧ Cook 3 slices of bacon in a large heavy pot. Add the onion slices and cook them until golden in the bacon fat. Remove the onions with a slotted spoon.

❧ Wrap each piece of floured rabbit in a slice of bacon. Brown the pieces on all sides in the fat remaining in the pan. Remove each piece as soon as it is browned.

❧ Put the browned onions back in the bottom of the pan and top with the rabbit and the ¾ cup (175 mL) water.

❧ Add the rabbit liver and kidney, if you have them, minced with a knife. Cover and simmer for 1½ to 2 hours over low heat or until the rabbit is tender.

❧ To make the sauce, remove the rabbit from the pan and arrange it on a heated platter. Thicken the sauce with the remaining flour mixture dissolved in 1 cup (250 mL) cold water. Bring to a boil, stirring constantly, until the sauce thickens. Stir in the parsley and serve.

RABBIT À LA FRANÇAISE

1 young rabbit
1 cup (250 mL) white wine
or apple juice
1 slice onion
2 cloves garlic
1 bay leaf
pinch of thyme
3 cloves
½ cup (125 mL) salt pork, diced
1 tbsp (15 mL) butter
20 tiny onions
1 tbsp (15 mL) flour

1 tsp (5 mL) savory
1 tbsp (15 mL) chopped parsley
3 chopped leeks

❧ Cut the rabbit into serving-size pieces and marinate it for 6 hours in the white wine or apple juice with the onion slice, garlic, bay leaf, thyme and cloves. Drain well, reserving the marinade for later use.

❧ Brown the diced salt pork in the butter in a large, heavy pan. Add the rabbit and brown the pieces on all sides. Add the small whole peeled onions and sprinkle in the flour. Pour the strained marinade on top. Add the savory, parsley and chopped leeks.

❧ Cover and simmer over low heat for 40 to 45 minutes or until the rabbit is tender.

ROAST SQUAB

4 squabs
4 tbsp (60 mL) butter
½ tsp (2 mL) marjoram
1 tsp (5 mL) butter
the squab livers
1 tsp (5 mL) butter
½ cup (125 mL) cold water
or red wine
salt and pepper

❧ Clean the squabs and rub them with butter. Sprinkle them inside and out with salt and pepper. Sprinkle the inside with marjoram.

❧ Heat the oven to 500°F (260°C) for 10 minutes. Place the squabs in a roasting pan and cook them for 10 to 20 minutes (depending on the age and size of the birds). Reduce the heat to

Rabbit à la Française

375°F (190°C) and roast the squabs another 30 to 50 minutes (depending on the age and size).

⁊ Place the cooked squabs on a warm platter. Lightly brown the livers in 1 tsp (5 mL) butter and add them to the drippings remaining in the roasting pan. Crush the livers with a fork. Add the ½ cup (125 mL) water or wine. Bring to a boil and serve with the roast squab.

SQUAB SAINT GERMAIN

¼ cup (50 mL) salt pork
4 to 6 squabs
12 small onions
1 tbsp (15 mL) flour
1 cup (250 mL) consommé
2 lbs (1 kg) fresh green peas
3 juniper berries
pinch of thyme or basil
salt and pepper
1 cup (250 mL) white wine
or apple juice

⁊ Dice the salt pork and melt it. Brown the squabs and onions in the melted fat, then remove them from the fat. Stir in the flour, then add the consommé and bring to a rapid boil, stirring until the sauce is smooth.

⁊ Place the squabs and the onions in the sauce. Add the green peas, juniper berries, thyme or basil, salt and pepper. Cover and simmer slowly until the squabs are tender (25 to 55 minutes, depending on the age and size of the birds).

⁊ Make the sauce by adding the white wine or apple juice to the pan drippings and stirring until smooth.

BROILED SQUAB

4 plump squabs
bacon fat
salt and pepper
¼ tsp (1 mL) marjoram
3 tbsp (45 mL) butter
½ lb (250 g) mushrooms
4 tbsp (60 mL) brandy

⁊ Split the squabs open along the backbone and flatten them. Rub each bird with bacon fat. Salt and pepper the birds. Sprinkle with a little marjoram. Let stand for 1 or 2 hours at room temperature before cooking.

⁊ Heat the butter to a nutty brown color. Remove the stems from the mushrooms and brown the caps over high heat in the butter, stirring constantly, for 3 or 4 minutes. Add the brandy. Salt and pepper. Set the mushroom mixture aside for later use.

⁊ Place the squabs in the bottom of a broiling pan (without the rack), and set the pan 5 in. (13 cm) from the broiler element. Broil 5 minutes on one side, turn and broil 5 minutes on the other side. Baste the birds with the pan drippings, then broil for another 10 minutes on each side, basting again when you turn them. When done, place the squabs on a heated platter.

⁊ To the pan drippings, add the brandied mushrooms and the finely chopped stems together with ¼ cup (50 mL) cold water.

Stir over medium heat, scraping the bottom of the pan well to incorporate the browned drippings. Salt and pepper the mushroom mixture and pour it over the squabs.

PHEASANT FLAMBÉ

3 tbsp (45 mL) olive oil
1 pheasant
salt and pepper
3 tbsp (45 mL) brandy
2 cups (500 mL) hot consommé
2 tbsp (30 mL) butter
2 tbsp (30 mL) flour
the pheasant liver
1 tsp (5 mL) Dijon mustard
½ cup (125 mL) whipping cream
2 cups (500 mL) well-toasted croutons

⁊ Heat the olive oil in a large heavy pot. Brown the pheasant on all sides for 10 to 15 minutes. Add the salt and pepper. Pour the brandy on top. Heat for a moment and flambé.

⁊ Add 1 cup (250 mL) of the hot consommé. Cover and let simmer for approximately 1 hour or until the pheasant is tender.

⁊ While the pheasant is cooking, cream the butter with the flour. Crush the pheasant liver and add it to the butter. Stir in the Dijon mustard.

⁊ Remove the cooked pheasant from the pan. Add the remaining 1 cup (250 mL) consommé and the liver mixture to the pan drippings. Stir together, scraping the bottom, until slightly thickened. Stir in the cream. Adjust for seasoning and pour into a gravy boat.

Pheasant Normandy

Serve the pheasant surrounded by the toasted croutons.

PHEASANT TERRINE

❧ Clean the pheasant. Remove the skin, being careful not to tear it too much, and set it aside for later. Carve the breast meat into neat slices with a sharp knife. Remove the rest of the meat from the bones and set aside. Put 6 thin slices of veal or pork in a large bowl along with the sliced pheasant breast.

MARINADE:
½ tsp (2 mL) salt
½ tsp (2 mL) tarragon
½ tsp (2 ml) powdered bay leaf
2 tbsp (30 mL) brandy
or lemon juice
¼ cup (50 mL) sherry
or apple juice
3 sprigs parsley
1 clove garlic

1 small onion
1 tbsp (15 mL) olive oil

❧ Mix together all the marinade ingredients, then pour over the sliced meat. Cover and refrigerate for 12 hours.

STUFFING:
the reserved pheasant meat, chopped
¾ lb (375 g) ground fresh pork
or veal
¾ lb (375 g) ground fat salt pork
1 egg
½ tsp (2 mL) salt
pinch of thyme
2 tbsp (30 mL) cognac
or lemon juice
¼ cup (50 mL) white wine, sherry
or apple juice

❧ Mix together the stuffing ingredients. Cover and refrigerate for 12 hours.
❧ To assemble the terrine, line a terrine mold with the reserved

pheasant skin or with thin slices of salt pork.
❧ Pour the marinade over the stuffing and mix well. Place ⅓ of this stuffing in the bottom of the mold. Press it down well, then cover with a layer of ½ the pheasant slices and ½ the veal or pork slices. Cover with another third of the stuffing then a layer of pheasant and veal slices, and top with the remaining stuffing. Press to pack firmly. Cover with thin slices of salt pork, or fold the pheasant skin over top. Cover the mold with its lid, or with aluminum foil.
❧ Place the mold in a pan of hot water. Bake in a 350°F (180°C) oven for 2 hours. The terrine is cooked when the juices around the meat run clear.
❧ Remove the terrine lid and replace it with a piece of foil. Weight the contents with a heavy object. Refrigerate for 12 to 24 hours.

PHEASANT NORMANDY

1 pheasant
6 tbsp (90 mL) butter
8 peeled apples, sliced thin
½ cup (125 mL) whipping cream
salt and pepper
3 tbsp (45 mL) cognac

❧ Clean, truss and brown the pheasant in 3 tbsp (45 mL) butter.
❧ Line the bottom of an earthenware casserole with half the apple slices. Top with 3 tbsp (45 mL) of melted butter. Salt and pepper

❦ TECHNIQUE ❦

PHEASANT NORMANDY

1 Brown the pheasant in butter.

2 Line the bottom of the casserole with half the apples. Add melted butter.

3 Place the pheasant on the bed of apples.

4 When the pheasant is cooked, add the cream and the cognac.

the pheasant and place it on the bed of apples, then surround it with the remaining apples.

☙ Bake in a 375°F (190°C) oven for 1¼ hours or until the pheasant is tender.

☙ When cooked, pour the cream and cognac over all. Heat just until warm and serve.

JUGGED HARE

1 hare
salt, pepper, thyme and bay leaf
1 onion, chopped
4 tbsp (60 mL) vegetable oil
½ cup (125 mL) wine
½ lb (250 g) salt pork, diced
2 onions, quartered
2 tbsp (30 mL) flour
2 cloves garlic, crushed
1 handful celery leaves, chopped
12 small onions
1 lb (500 g) mushrooms
3 to 4 tbsp (45 to 60 mL) heavy cream

☙ Cut the hare into serving-size pieces, reserving the blood and the liver (from which the gall bladder has been removed) in a bowl.

☙ Place the hare pieces in an earthenware dish. Season them with the salt, pepper, thyme and bay leaf. Add the chopped onion and sprinkle with the oil and wine. Let marinate for 12 hours.

☙ Melt the salt pork in a large, heavy pot. When well-browned, add the 2 quartered onions and sprinkle with flour. Cook, stirring constantly, until the flour browns slightly.

☙ Wipe the pieces of hare with a cloth and place them in the pot with the salt pork. Brown them in the melted fat, stirring, until browned on all sides. Add just enough water to cover the hare. Add the garlic and celery leaves. Cover and cook over medium heat for 1 hour.

☙ Sauté the mushrooms quickly in butter. Add the mushrooms, the small onions and the strained marinating mixture to the hare. Cover and simmer over low heat for 30 minutes.

☙ A few minutes before serving, add the chopped hare liver and the blood mixed with the cream to the hare. Serve surrounded by croutons.

LAC SAINT JEAN TOURTIÈRE

1 hare
3 cups (750 mL) water
1 onion, sliced into rings
2 stalks celery
½ tsp (2 mL) savory
1 tsp (5 mL) cinnamon
¼ tsp (1 mL) ground cloves
1 tsp (5 mL) coarse salt
2 eggs
1 lb (500 g) ground pork
1 lb (500 g) ground beef
salt and pepper to taste
pastry dough

☙ Clean the hare and cut it into serving-size pieces.

☙ Bring the water to a boil together with the onion, diced celery, savory, cinnamon, cloves, and coarse salt. Add the pieces of hare. Cover and simmer over low heat for approximately 1 hour or until the hare is tender.

☙ Remove the pieces of hare and boil the broth over high heat until the liquid is reduced to 1 cup (250 mL). Meanwhile, remove the meat from the bones.

☙ Beat the eggs. Slowly add the unstrained broth, stirring the egg mixture constantly. Add the hare meat together with the ground beef and pork. Mix. Season to taste.

☙ Line a deep pie plate with a layer of pastry dough of your choice. Pour the meat mixture into the pie shell. Cover with a pastry top. Bake in a 375°F (190°C) oven until the crust is golden brown.

HARE WITH WHITE WINE

2 cups (500 mL) white wine
1 large red onion, chopped
1 bay leaf
¼ tsp (1 mL) basil
6 whole cloves
¼ tsp (1 mL) ginger
1 tsp (5 mL) salt
¼ tsp (1 mL) pepper
1 large hare or 2 rabbits
1 piece beef suet
12 small white onions, peeled
6 small carrots
½ cup (125 mL) apples, diced
1 clove garlic
pinch of thyme
2 tbsp (30 mL) chopped parsley
¼ tsp (1 mL) rosemary

☙ Bring the white wine to a boil along with the red onion, bay leaf, basil, cloves, ginger, salt and pepper. Boil for 1 minute. Let cool.

☙ Cut the hare or rabbits into serving-size pieces. Arrange the pieces in a bean pot or earthenware casserole. Pour the cooled marinade mixture on top. Cover and marinate for 12 hours in the refrigerator or in a cool place.

❧ To cook, remove the meat and marinade from the container. Layer in the bottom of the casserole the beef suet cut into small dice, the small peeled onions, the carrots cut in 2-in. (5-cm) lengths, the diced unpeeled apples, the garlic, thyme, parsley, and the rosemary. Top with the pieces of hare or rabbit. Pour the marinade through a fine sieve and pour it over the meat. Cover and bake in a 300°F (150°C) oven for 2 hours.

❧ Serve with potato cakes.

Hare with White Wine

HARE
À LA FLAMANDE

1 large hare
2 cups (500 mL) beer or ale
1 clove garlic, minced
1 tsp (5 mL) salt
¼ tsp (1 mL) pepper
1 bay leaf
4 onions, sliced thin
1 carrot, peeled and grated
¼ tsp (1 mL) allspice
¼ tsp (1 mL) nutmeg
½ cup (125 mL) bacon fat
½ cup (125 mL) all-purpose flour
½ tsp (2 mL) salt
1 tsp (5 mL) paprika
6 potatoes

❧ Cut the hare into serving-size pieces. Wash the pieces with a little beer.

❧ Combine the beer, garlic, salt, pepper, bay leaf, onions, carrot, all-spice and nutmeg in a large bowl. Add the pieces of hare. Mix well together, cover and let marinate for 24 hours in the refrigerator.

❧ Heat the bacon fat. Place the flour, salt and paprika in a paper bag. Remove the pieces of hare from the marinade and wipe them with paper towels, then put them in the bag with the seasoned flour. Shake to coat the pieces evenly. Brown the pieces on all sides in the bacon fat, over medium heat. Add the marinade mixture. Cover and simmer for 1½ hours or until the hare is tender.

❧ Peel the potatoes and slice them ¼ in. (0.6 cm) thick. Arrange the potato slices over the hare ½ hour before the end of the cooking period. Cover and simmer until the meat and potatoes are cooked.

HARE
GRANDE CIPAILLE

1 or 2 hares (or rabbits)
3 pork filets, whole
1 clove garlic, halved
2 chickens, 4 to 5 lbs (about 2 kg) each
1 whole nutmeg
3 lbs (1.4 kg) ground beef
salt and pepper
1 piece of veal, 3 to 4 lbs (about 1.5 kg)
2 cloves garlic
2 partridges or squab
½ cup (125 mL) lard or roast pork fat
8 cups (2 L) water
6 large onions, in rings
1 tsp (5 mL) thyme
1 tbsp (15 mL) coarse salt
4 small carrots, peeled
2 leeks, cleaned
10 sprigs parsley, washed

celery leaves
3 bay leaves
4 cloves
2 cinnamon sticks

❧ Clean the hares or rabbits and cut them into serving-size pieces. Rub the pork filets with the halved garlic clove. Debone the chickens, cut them into serving-size pieces and rub each piece with the nutmeg.

❧ Season the ground beef with salt and pepper and shape it into small meatballs. Make incisions in the veal and stuff it with slivers of the 2 garlic cloves.

❧ Clean the partridges and truss them.

❧ Melt the lard or roast pork fat in a large, heavy pot. Brown the meat and bird pieces one at a time in the hot fat over high heat. Remove each piece of meat as soon as it is browned and add another.

❧ Add the onion rings to the fat remaining in the pot and cook them, stirring almost constantly, until soft. Pour the onions over the pieces of meat.

❧ Tie together the carrots, leeks, parsley and celery leaves with a piece of kitchen string to make a bouquet. Stick the cloves into the leeks and insert the bay leaves and cinnamon sticks in the middle of the bouquet.

❧ Bring the water to a boil in the same pot as used for browning the meat. Add the thyme and coarse salt. When the water boils, put the vegetable bouquet in the middle of the pot and surround it with the pieces of the veal and hare. Top this layer with the pork filets. On top of the pork place the chicken pieces, then the partridges. Bring the contents of the pot to a boil. Cover and simmer gently over low heat for 1 to 1½ hours or until the meats are tender.

❧ Meanwhile, brown the ground beef meatballs in a skillet, then cover and refrigerate until ready to prepare the cipaille.

❧ Transfer the cooked meats, birds, and vegetable bouquet to a large bowl and cover with the cooking broth. Cover and refrigerate for 24 hours.

❧ To assemble the cipaille, remove the fat accumulated on top of the chilled meats. Discard the vegetable bouquet. Arrange the meat and fowl in a large cast-iron pot or a large casserole. You can arrange the various types of meats in separate layers, or mix them. If you wish, cut the veal and pork into cubes and quarter the partridges. Over the first layer of meat, pour ¾ cup (175 mL) of the cooking broth. Set the remainder aside for the sauce. (If the cooled broth has jelled, warm it up first.)

❧ Cover the first layer of meat with a layer of pastry (made according to the recipe that follows). Continue layering meat and pastry until there are 5 layers of meat and 6 of pastry dough, finishing with a pastry layer. Make a few incisions in the last layer of dough. Bake in a 375°F (190°C) oven for 1 to 1½ hours or until the top pastry layer is well browned.

❧ To make the sauce, thicken the remaining broth with butter and flour. Just before serving the sauce with the cipaille, stir in ¼ cup (50 mL) heavy cream and chopped chives to taste.

Quail with Grapes

❦ TECHNIQUE ❦

QUAIL WITH GRAPES

1 Pluck and clean the quails.

2 Place the quail livers, bread, cream, seasonings and cognac in a bowl. Mix well.

3 Stuff the quails.

4 Wrap each quail in a grape leaf, then in a thin slice of the pork fat.

PASTRY CRUST FOR CIPAILLE

🍂 Sift together 3 cups (750 mL) all-purpose flour with ¾ tsp (3 mL) baking powder and 1½ tsp (7 mL) salt.

🍂 In a large bowl, place ¼ cup (50 mL) butter. Pour ½ cup (125 mL) boiling water over the butter. Stir vigorously until the butter is creamed, then stir in a lightly beaten egg. Add the sifted flour mixture and mix well. This dough should be quite soft, but it may be necessary to add a little more flour. Cover the dough and refrigerate it for 6 to 8 hours or until it is firm enough to be rolled out.

QUAIL WITH GRAPES

4 quails
4 grape leaves
¼ cup (50 mL) cognac
3 slices bread, crusts removed, diced
¼ cup (50 mL) heavy cream, heated
¼ tsp (1 mL) rosemary
salt and pepper to taste
4 very thin slices fresh pork fat
2 tbsp (30 mL) butter
50 green grapes
4 slices brioche

🍂 Pluck and bleed the quails. Reserve the livers. Soak the grape leaves in the cognac for 1 hour.

🍂 Place in a bowl the chopped quail livers, diced bread slices, warm cream, rosemary, salt and pepper as well as 1 tbsp (15 mL) of the cognac used for soaking the grape leaves. Mix well, mashing everything together to form a paste.

🍂 Stuff each quail with this mixture and wrap each in a grape leaf, then in a slice of pork fat. Heat the butter in a casserole. Place the quails in the casserole and baste them with the melted butter. Salt and pepper lightly.

🍂 Bake in a 400°F (200°C) oven for 10 minutes, then add the grapes and the remaining cognac. Cover the casserole and bake for another 15 minutes.

🍂 To serve, brown the brioche slices in a little butter over low heat. Place a quail on each slice and surround with a little of the grape sauce.

QUAIL WITH WILD RICE

3 tbsp (45 mL) butter
2 French shallots, chopped
1 2-in. (5 cm) piece beef marrow
1 cup (250 mL) wild rice
6 juniper berries
2 cups (500 mL) boiling consommé
4 to 6 quails
salt and pepper
½ cup (125 mL) melted butter
4 tbsp (60 mL) cognac

🍂 Place the butter in a casserole and brown the chopped shallots in it. Add the beef marrow, removed from the bone, and continue cooking over low heat until the marrow is transparent. Remove from the heat and crush everything together. Add the carefully-washed wild rice, the juniper berries and the boiling consommé. Place over low heat, cover and let simmer for 30 to 40 minutes or until the rice is tender.

🍂 In the meantime, clean the quails and split them along the backbone, flatten them out, and salt and pepper them on both sides. Place the quails in a broiler pan, skin-side down, and position the broiler pan 5 in. (12 cm) from the broiler element. Baste every 5 minutes with the melted butter and cognac mixed together. Broil for 10 minutes on one side, then turn and cook for another 10 minutes. When cooked, cut each quail in half along the backbone.

🍂 To serve, place the wild rice on a heated platter. In the middle, set a small silver dish filled with mango chutney. Arrange the broiled quails around the rice. Pour the pan drippings over everything.

PARTRIDGE WITH CABBAGE

½ lb (250 g) fat salt pork
4 tbsp (60 mL) flour
4 partridges
1 large green cabbage, chopped coarsely
4 to 6 large onions, sliced thin
1 tbsp (15 mL) salt
¼ tsp (1 mL) pepper
½ tsp (2 mL) thyme
½ cup (125 mL) liquid (white wine, red Burgundy, cognac, cider or apple juice)

🍂 Dice the salt pork and melt it in a large, heavy pot or casserole.

Split the partridges in half or leave them whole and tie the legs close to the body. Dredge them in flour. Brown the quails on all sides in the melted fat over very low heat for 25 minutes.

&❧ Remove each partridge from the pan as soon it is browned on all sides. Add the cabbage and onions to the remaining fat. Cover and cook over medium heat, stirring often, until the vegetables are tender (approximately 15 minutes).

&❧ Arrange the partridges on top of the cabbage mixture. Add the salt, pepper, thyme and liquid of your choice. Cover and cook over very low heat for about 2 hours, or until the partridges are tender.

&❧ This recipe is also a delicious way to prepare hen, pigeon or squab, and pork filet; simply adjust the cooking time.

ROAST PARTRIDGE

2 tbsp (30 mL) butter
1 tsp (5 mL) dry mustard
2 partridges
2 tsp (10 mL) butter
salt and pepper
4 slices bacon or 3 very thin slices salt pork
1 carrot, diced
3 stalks celery, chopped
4 sprigs parsley
¼ cup (50 mL) water
½ cup (125 mL) red wine
4 tbsp (60 mL) apple
or grape jelly

&❧ Cream together the 2 tbsp (30 mL) butter and the dry mustard. Rub the partridges with this mixture. Place 1 tsp (5 mL) of butter

Roast Partridge

inside each partridge. Salt and pepper the birds, and cover each with the bacon or salt pork slices.

&❧ Combine the carrot, celery and parsley and place the mixture in the bottom of a roasting pan. Arrange the partridges on top of the vegetables. Add the water and red wine.

&❧ Cover and bake in a 525°F (270°C) oven for 20 minutes. Lower the oven temperature to 450°F (230°C) and cook for 1 hour more. Uncover the pan for the final 10 minutes of baking. Do not baste the partridges, except in the last 10 minutes, when they should be basted with the pan juices 3 or 4 times.

&❧ Strain the pan drippings, stir in the apple or grape jelly and serve this sauce in a gravy boat with the roast quails.

TRAPPER'S PARTRIDGE

4 cups (1 L) chopped cabbage
4 cups (1 L) chopped onions
2 eggs, lightly beaten
1 cup (250 mL) heavy cream
salt and pepper to taste
1 or 2 plump partridges
pork fat slices

&❧ Combine the chopped onions and the cabbage in a large bowl.

&❧ Add the beaten eggs, mix well, and add just enough heavy cream to make the mixture creamy. Add salt and pepper. Clean the partridges and stuff them with some of the cabbage and onion mixture. Sew the openings shut. Rub each partridge with butter. Cover the breast with thin salt pork slices.

&❧ Butter generously a cast-iron pot and arrange the partridges in it. Bake in a 400°F (200°C) oven,

Frog Legs Provençale

uncovered, for 30 to 40 minutes. Baste often with melted butter. When the partridges are browned, add the remaining cabbage mixture. Bake for another 30 minutes or until the partridges are tender.

☙ Serve with baked potatoes and garnish with small pieces of salt pork fried very crisp with a little garlic.

WOODCOCK OR SNIPE WITH COGNAC

6 woodcocks
1 truffle
1 chicken liver
pinch each of salt, pepper, nutmeg and cinnamon
1 tsp (5 mL) cognac
6 very thin slices fresh pork fat
½ cup (125 mL) Madeira wine
pinch of thyme

3 slices lemon, unpeeled
½ cup (125 mL) chopped mushrooms
6 slices bread, crusts removed
2 tbsp (30 mL) cognac
½ lemon
1 clove garlic
nutmeg, freshly grated

☙ Pluck and clean the birds. Reserve the giblets, except the gizzard.

☙ Place the giblets in a bowl, together with the chicken liver, the truffle (cut in small pieces), salt, pepper, nutmeg, cinnamon and cognac. Mix well, mashing the ingredients together until the mixture resembles a paste.

☙ Stuff the birds with this mixture, then sew the cavities shut and wrap each bird in a slice of pork fat. Arrange the birds in a baking dish just large enough to hold them. Pour the Madeira wine on top. Add the thyme,

lemon slices and chopped mushrooms. Cover and let marinate for 2 days in the refrigerator, turning them every day.

☙ Remove the birds from the marinade. Place them in a pie plate or shallow baking dish and bake in a 475°F (240°C) oven for 20 minutes or until they are tender. Woodcocks cook very quickly.

☙ In the meantime, pour the leftover marinade into a saucepan and boil it, uncovered, until the liquid is reduced by half. Toast the bread slices and place them on a baking sheet. Over each slice sprinkle 1 tsp (5 mL) heated cognac. Flame the cognac immediately. Then rub each toast slice with a half lemon and a clove of garlic, and sprinkle with a little freshly grated nutmeg.

☙ To serve, place the flambéed toast pieces on a heated platter or directly on plates. Sprinkle some hot reduced marinade over each slice of toast and arrange one of the cooked birds on each.

WOODCOCK OR SNIPE PIE

¼ lb (125 g) lean pork
¼ lb (125 g) veal
½ lb (250 g) salt pork
nutmeg
pepper and salt
½ tsp (2 mL) powdered bay leaf
¼ cup (50 mL) light cream
6 snipe or woodcocks, cut in half
semi-puff pastry

☙ Grind the lean pork, veal and salt pork 3 times through the meat grinder. Sprinkle with nutmeg, pepper and salt to taste. Flavor with the bay leaf. Add the cream and mix well.

🍃 Line the bottom of a well-buttered casserole or deep baking pan with half the meat mixture. Split the birds in half, arrange them on top of the stuffing and cover with the remaining stuffing. Top with a layer of semi-puff pastry (see page 514). Bake in a 350°F (180°C) oven for 35 to 45 minutes.

FROG LEGS PROVENÇALE

½ to 1 lb (250 to 500 g) frog legs, fresh or frozen
salt and pepper
lemon juice
olive oil
parsley, chopped
1 clove garlic crushed
flour or batter or 1 beaten egg and flour
vegetable oil
2 to 4 cloves garlic, minced
3 tbsp (45 mL) butter
lemon wedges

🍃 Thaw frozen frog legs in their wrapping. Marinate the legs for 1 hour in a mixture of salt, pepper, lemon juice, olive oil, chopped parsley and crushed garlic.

🍃 Remove the legs from the marinade and coat each leg in flour, or in a batter for deep-frying, or in a beaten egg and then in flour. (I prefer the last option.) Brown the legs in 3 to 4 in. (8 to 10 cm) of oil over medium heat for 10 to 12 minutes.

🍃 To serve Provençale-style, fry the minced garlic in the butter until golden. Pour immediately over the legs and garnish with the lemon wedges.

VENISON — MOOSE AND DEER

Technically, the term venison can refer to any game meat, but here in Québec we usually mean deer meat.

🍃 However, moose meat is equally delicious. It is tender when it comes from a young animal, but the flesh of adult moose is a little tough and chewy and benefits from marinating. Otherwise, you can cook moose meat the same way as deer.

🍃 Once cleaned and dressed, the average weight of a deer is about 120 lbs (50 kg).

🍃 Deer and moose carcasses can be cut up the same way, and the various cuts can be cooked using the same basic techniques.

🍃 The neck and shank cuts lend themselves to stewing techniques. You can also grind them and use them in meatballs or pâté; in this case you might want to combine 2 parts venison with 1 part ground beef suet for a different flavor.

🍃 You can also make excellent sausages by adding to the moose or deer meat ⅓ of its weight in fresh pork fat. To season 4 lbs (2 kg), add 5 tsp (25 mL) salt, 2 tsp (10 mL) freshly ground pepper and ½ tsp (2 mL) sage or savory.

🍃 The shoulder cut, extending as far as the ribs, can be roasted,

braised or cut into 1-in. (2-cm) cubes for a stew.

🍃 The whole loin section of a deer usually weighs about 22 lbs (10 kg) and actually consists of two sections: the ribs and the loin proper, or saddle, which is near the haunch.

🍃 The rib section can be roasted. The saddle or loin is the choicest cut for roasting and is similar to filet of beef. It is equally delicious cut into steaks or cutlets and seasoned with salt and pepper, then sautéed in very hot oil as quickly as possible. Remember that the less you cut or handle the venison, the more tender it will be.

🍃 The haunch is equivalent to the rump of beef and makes a delicious roast. Oven roast it at 400°F (200°C), calculating 15 minutes for every lb (500 g). Use the same cooking time if you want to spit-roast the haunch.

🍃 The lower part of the haunch is equivalent to the round of beef and is best cut into steaks.

🍃 Venison and moose meat freeze well. Wrap the pieces carefully and tightly in aluminum foil, then in a layer of freezer wrap.

TIPS FOR PREPARING VENISON

The gamey flavor of venison comes predominantly from the fat; so if you don't care for a gamey flavor, you should carefully trim off all visible fat. This is especially important with older animals, and even more so with moose meat. Replace the fat with bacon fat or lard when cooking, if you wish.

🍃 Venison heart can be stuffed with a bread, onion and celery mixture and cooked in exactly the same way as you would cook beef heart.

🍂 Some hunters consider the liver the choicest part of the animal and like to cook it fresh right at the hunting spot. If you are lucky enough to get hold of some fresh venison liver, peel off the thin outer membrane and slice the liver into very thin slices. Dredge the slices in flour and cook the slices quickly in a single layer over high heat in browned butter, for about 1 minute on each side.

🍂 The kidneys can be prepared in a sauce, using one of the recipes for beef kidneys, or simply grilled in butter with onions, tarragon and a dash of cognac.

🍂 Seasonings for venison: salt, freshly ground pepper, sugar, tomatoes, onions, garlic, parsley, celery, rosemary, lemon, chutney, or horseradish.

🍂 The pan drippings can be enriched with butter and flavored with currant jelly or dry vermouth.

🍂 Simple marinade for venison: combine 1 cup (250 mL) of olive oil and ½ cup (125 mL) fresh lemon juice. Pour over the meat and let it soak for 24 hours, turning the meat 4 or 5 times to marinate it evenly. You can alter the flavor of this marinade by adding bay leaves, whole cloves, juniper berries, garlic, dry mustard or onions. You can also replace the lemon juice with 1 cup (250 mL) of red wine. Roast or braise the marinated meat.

🍂 To accompany venison, try red cabbage, chestnut or pumpkin purée, pickled beets, stewed or broiled tomatoes, brown rice or wild rice, mushrooms, Hollandaise sauce, grape jelly, spiced crab apples, chutney, or horseradish.

COOKING VENISON

🍂 Venison is best when it is properly hung for a few days before cooking. Young deer is a tender meat that is at its most flavorful when cooked quite rare, rather than well done. So as a general rule you should cook it like beef, and never like veal or pork. The important point when roasting venison is to retain all the inner juices. It is therefore important to baste it frequently with butter seasoned with dry mustard during the roasting process.

🍂 Moose meat tends to contain more fat and should be cooked like pork, rather than rare.

🍂 Roasted deer is more tender and flavorful when roasted rare or medium rare. To sear in the juices, roast it for 5 minutes at 550°F (290°C). Then turn the oven temperature down to 450°F (230°C) and roast for 15 minutes per lb (500 g), basting every 15 minutes.

🍂 Roasted deer fat tends to be soggy and many people find the flavor objectionable, so you should remove it completely before roasting.

🍂 The best venison steaks are cut from the loin or the leg. The steaks can be broiled or pan-fried exactly as you would cook a beef steak, but only the most tender cuts of venison can be broiled successfully.

🍂 To make an easy venison stew, cut venison into cubes, dredge them in flour seasoned with salt and pepper, and sear the cubes quickly in hot butter. Add onions, garlic, marjoram, fresh tomatoes, sherry and paprika. Let simmer for about 1½ hours or until the meat is tender. If you want to cook the stew in the oven, bake it in a 350°F (180°C) oven for about 1½ hours. You can if you wish add 1 cup (250 mL) of red wine or of sour cream (stirred in during the last few minutes).

BROILED VENISON CHOPS

🍂 Cut chops about ½ in. (1 cm) thick and season them with salt and pepper. Arrange them in a shallow pan. Sprinkle them with olive oil, then cover and let marinate for 12 hours.

🍂 Preheat the oven to 400°F (200°C). Arrange the broiler pan 5 to 6 in. (13 to 15 cm) from the broiler element and broil the chops for 10 to 20 minutes, depending on whether you want the meat rare or well done. Turn the chops only once.

🍂 Serve the chops with a sauce made from half melted butter and half grape jelly seasoned with 1 tbsp (15 mL) Worcestershire sauce.

AUSTRALIAN FILET OF VENISON

1 filet of venison, 6 to 8 lbs
(3 to 3.5 kg)
1 clove garlic
2 cups (500 mL) red wine

1 cup (250 mL) water
4 peppercorns
1 tsp (5 mL) tarragon
1 tsp (5 mL) coarse salt
½ lb (250 g) salt pork, sliced very thin
¼ cup (50 mL) cognac
2 cups (500 mL) sour cream
salt and pepper

🙠 Make incisions in the filet of venison and stuff with a sliver of the garlic. Mix together the red wine, water, freshly ground pepper, tarragon and coarse salt in a large bowl. Add the filet and coat it thoroughly in the marinade. Cover and refrigerate to marinate for 24 hours, turning 3 or 4 times.

🙠 Remove the filet from the marinade and dry it well. Reserve the marinade for later use. Place the meat in a baking pan and cover it with the thin slices of salt pork.

🙠 Preheat the oven to 450°F (230°C) for 10 minutes. Put in the roast and cook it for 1½ hours, reducing the oven temperature to 375°F (190°C) after the first hour of roasting. Baste often with the pan drippings.

🙠 To make the sauce, take the roast out of the pan and place it on a heated platter. Place the roasting pan on a burner over high heat, then add to the drippings 1 cup (250 mL) of the reserved marinade (strained through a fine sieve) and the cognac. Bring to a vigorous boil, stirring and scraping the bottom. Add the sour cream and heat, but do not let boil. Pour the sauce over the filet and serve.

Venison Ragout

CAMP-STYLE VENISON WITH BEANS

2 lbs (1 kg) venison
3 cups (750 mL) dried beans
4 cups (1 L) pale ale
1 bay leaf
½ lb (250 g) salt pork
2 carrots, diced
4 large onions, thinly sliced
1 tsp (5 mL) savory
1 cup (250 mL) molasses
salt and pepper

🙠 Sort the beans and soak them in cold water to cover for 12 hours.

🙠 Drain the beans, reserving the soaking water. Place the beans in a bean pot or large casserole. Add the beer, 3 cups (750 mL) of the bean soaking water, the bay leaf, the salt pork cut into 1-in. (2-cm)

cubes, the diced carrots, sliced onions, savory and molasses, salt and pepper. Cover and bake in a 300°F (150°C) oven for 5 hours. The beans should always be just covered with liquid; if more is required during the cooking process, use some of the reserved water used to soak the beans.

🙠 When the beans are barely tender, but not completely cooked, add the venison cut into 1-in. (2-cm) cubes and cook, covered, for another 2 hours.

🙠 Partridge may be prepared following the same recipe. After the beans have cooked 6 hours, bury the trussed partridge in the middle of the beans and cook for 1 more hour only.

VENISON RAGOUT

3 lbs (1.5 kg) shoulder of venison
2 cups (500 mL) red wine

¼ cup (50 mL) cider
2 large onions, thinly sliced
2 carrots, sliced
6 peppercorns, ground
2 bay leaves
2 cloves
1 clove garlic
1 tsp (5 mL) thyme
1 tbsp (15 mL) salt
3 tbsp (45 mL) bacon fat
3 tbsp (45 mL) flour
2 stalks celery with leaves
4 carrots, sliced
12 to 15 peeled chestnuts
(optional)
salt and pepper

🍃 Remove the excess fat from the meat and cut it into 2-in. (5-cm) pieces. In a large bowl, combine the next 10 ingredients, including the salt. Add the venison and mix well. Cover and let the venison marinate for 2 days in the refrigerator.

🍃 To cook, remove the meat pieces from the marinade, wipe them dry and brown them in the bacon fat. When browned on all sides, sprinkle on the flour. Mix together, then pour the strained marinade over the meat. Stir in the sliced carrots, celery and peeled chestnuts. Salt and pepper to taste. Cover and bake for 2 hours in a 350°F (180°C) oven. Serve with mashed potatoes.

BRAISED VENISON

4 to 6 lbs (2 to 3 kg) venison
shoulder or ribs, boned
¼ lb (125 g) salt pork
¼ cup (50 mL) flour
1 tsp (5 mL) salt
pepper to taste

½ tsp (2 mL) marjoram
½ cup (125 mL) salt pork, melted
½ cup (125 mL) red wine
or ½ cup (125 mL) orange and
apple juice
1 tbsp (15 mL) vinegar
2 unpeeled apples, sliced and
broiled

🍃 Wipe the piece of venison with a cloth dipped in vinegar.

🍃 Cut the salt pork into strips and arrange them on top of the roast. Roll and tie the meat into a compact shape. Blend together the flour, salt, pepper and marjoram and sprinkle the mixture over the venison.

🍃 Brown the roast in the melted salt pork in a heavy pot. Add the wine or orange and apple juice, and the vinegar.

🍃 Cover and cook over medium heat for 2 hours, stirring from time to time. Strain the cooking juices through a sieve and serve in a gravy boat with the braised roast. Garnish with the broiled apple slices.

VENISON CASSEROLE

2 to 3 lbs (1 to 1.5 kg) moose
or deer meat
1 tsp (5 mL) salt
¼ tsp (1 mL) pepper
2 bay leaves
½ tsp (2 mL) rosemary
3 cups (750 mL) milk
½ cup (125 mL) flour
1 tbsp (15 mL) paprika
¼ lb (125 g) salt pork fat
1 tbsp (15 mL) vegetable oil
2 tbsp (30 mL) butter

2 onions, thinly sliced
2 cups (500 mL) consommé
2 cups (500 mL) red wine
½ cup (125 mL) sour cream
juice of ½ lemon

🍃 Cut the meat into ½-in. (1-cm) cubes and place them in a large bowl. Sprinkle with the salt, pepper and rosemary. Add the bay leaves and pour the milk on top. Cover and refrigerate for 24 hours, turning the meat cubes occasionally.

🍃 Remove the meat from the milk marinade and wipe the pieces dry. Place the flour and paprika in a paper bag, add the meat cubes and toss until they are lightly coated. Melt the salt pork in a large, heavy pot with the vegetable oil. Add the butter and, when it is very hot, add the meat cubes. Sear the meat quickly over high heat, stirring, for no longer than 1 minute. Remove the meat from the pot.

🍃 Add the onions to the hot pan and stir until browned. Add the consommé and the wine, bring to a boil, then add the meat. Cover and simmer over low heat for 1 to 2 hours or until the meat is tender.

🍃 Just before serving, mix together the leftover flour and paprika with the sour cream and lemon juice. Add to the meat mixture. Stir until creamy and smooth. Correct the seasonings. Pour into a casserole or deep serving dish to serve.

🍃 This dish can be prepared several days ahead, and refrigerated. When ready to serve, reheat in a 400°F (200°C) oven.

PASTA

PASTA

Pasta comes in various shapes. Macaroni, spaghetti, noodles and vermicelli are the most common, but there are also a number of fancy-shaped pastas such as shells and rigatoni that can be used for variety.

BASIC COOKING METHOD

The amount of pasta you should prepare for each person depends to a degree on the type that you are using. But as a rule of thumb, allow 1 oz (30 g) of dry pasta per serving, if it is going to be combined with other foods, and from 1½ to 2 oz (45 to 60 g) if you are serving it plain or with a simple sauce.

ᴥ To prepare 8 oz (250 g) of pasta, bring to a rolling boil 8 cups (2 L) water combined with 1 tsp (5 mL) salt in a large pot. You can add 1 tsp (5 mL) butter or oil to the water before adding the pasta; this helps prevents it from foaming up. Add the pasta gradually so that the water does not stop boiling. Cook the pasta uncovered, stirring once or twice in the first few minutes to prevent the pasta from sticking together.

ᴥ The cooking time varies widely depending on the type of pasta, the brand, and whether you are using fresh or dry pasta. When it is cooked to your taste, empty it into a strainer. Rinse off the starch under hot or cold running water, depending on whether you are serving the pasta in a hot or cold dish. Toss the pasta gently with a fork while rinsing.

HOW TO REHEAT COLD OR FROZEN COOKED PASTA

If you are not serving the pasta immediately, return it to the cooking pot and add 1 or 2 tbsp (15 to 30 mL) olive oil or butter, stirring gently with a fork so that it is thoroughly coated.

ᴥ If you wish, you can cook pasta ahead of time, drain it well, then refrigerate it in a covered container. To reheat it, simply plunge it into boiling water for 1 minute. To warm up a single serving, place it in a sieve and dip it in a pot of boiling water for 1 minute. Let it drain thoroughly in the sieve before pouring it onto a plate.

ᴥ Cooked pasta freezes well. Simply package it in individual portion sizes in well-sealed containers. When ready to serve, reheat the frozen pasta without preliminary thawing by plunging it in boiling water in a strainer.

PASTA FOR VARIETY

Pasta lends itself to a wonderful variety of economical and nourishing dishes. Instead of always making the same old stand-bys, try experimenting with some of the more unusual recipes.

ᴥ Feel free to substitute the type of pasta called for in recipes to accommodate personal tastes or to use whatever type you have on hand. You may, however, have to adjust the cooking time. Check the cooking chart below.

PASTA COOKING CHART

FRESH PASTA (will keep 2 to 3 days in refrigerator)

Spaghetti, fettucini, linguini, etc.	5 minutes
Ravioli, tortellini, etc.	12 to 15 minutes

FRESH PACKAGED PASTA (sealed to keep 2 to 3 months in refrigerator)

Spaghetti, fettucini, linguini, etc.	7 to 8 minutes
Ravioli, tortellini, etc.	12 to 15 minutes

DRY PASTA

Macaroni (elbow)	8 to 10 minutes
Macaroni (long)	10 minutes
Spaghetti, fettucini, linguini, etc.	10 minutes
Rigatoni	12 minutes
Alphabet noodles	4 to 6 minutes

Pasta Shells au Gratin

4 cups (1 L) consommé
2 cups (500 mL) milk
6 oz (170 g) small pasta shells
5 tbsp (75 mL) butter
1 slice ham, diced fine.
6 tbsp (90 mL) grated cheese
salt and pepper to taste
2 tbsp (30 mL) breadcrumbs
2 tbsp (30 mL) butter, diced
1 tbsp (15 mL) chopped parsley

🍃 In a large pot, bring the consommé and milk to a boil. Add the pasta shells. Boil for approximately 10 minutes, until the pasta is al dente. Drain. (The leftover cooking broth may be thickened and served with croutons as a soup, or used to make a béchamel sauce to serve with pasta.) Add 5 tbsp (75 mL) butter to the shells.

🍃 Dice the ham and add it to the pasta. Mix in the cheese. Salt and pepper to taste. Turn the mixture into a buttered baking dish and sprinkle with breadcrumbs. Brown in a 400°F (200°C) oven for 20 minutes.

🍃 Five minutes before the end of the cooking time, dot the shells with the diced butter and sprinkle with the parsley.

Pasta and Lobster Salad

8 oz (250 g) pasta shells
1 can (8 oz or 200 g) lobster or crabmeat
1 can (4 oz or 100 g) shrimp
1 slice cooked ham, diced

¼ lb (125 g) mushrooms, sliced thin
2 tomatoes, diced
3 tbsp (45 mL) olive oil
1 tbsp (15 mL) cider vinegar
salt and pepper to taste
⅓ cup (75 mL) mayonnaise
grated zest of ½ lemon

🍃 Cook the pasta shells. Drain them, rinse them under cold water and drain again.

🍃 Drain the lobster or crabmeat, pouring the juice into a bowl for later use. Dice the lobster or crabmeat. With two forks, toss together in a large bowl the cooked pasta shells, the lobster or crabmeat, shrimp, ham, mushrooms, tomatoes, olive oil, vinegar and the reserved juice from the lobster or crab. Salt and pepper to taste.

🍃 Mound the mixture in a salad bowl and arrange it attractively. Combine the lemon zest with the mayonnaise and use it to decorate the top of the salad.

Roman Lasagne

Sauce:
1 onion, chopped
1 clove garlic, minced
¼ cup (50 mL) olive oil
1 28-oz (800-mL) can Italian tomatoes
1 tbsp (15 mL) chopped parsley
½ tsp (2 mL) basil
1 5½-oz (150-mL) can tomato paste
1 tbsp (15 mL) sugar
salt and pepper to taste

🍃 Brown the onions and garlic in the olive oil. Add the remaining ingredients. Bring to a boil and let simmer, uncovered, for 15 minutes.

Roman Lasagne

[337]

MEAT MIXTURE:

½ lb (250 g) ground beef
½ lb (250 g) ground pork
2 tbsp (30 mL) chopped parsley
½ tsp (2 mL) oregano
2 eggs, lightly beaten
3 tbsp (45 mL) grated Parmesan cheese
salt and pepper to taste

🍃 Mix all the ingredients together in a bowl. Add the mixture to the tomato sauce after it has simmered for 15 minutes. Stir well and simmer for another 40 minutes.

PASTA:

24 cups (6 L) boiling water
3 tbsp (45 mL) salt
1 tbsp (15 mL) olive oil
1 lb (500 g) lasagne

🍃 Pour the water into a large pot and add the salt and oil. Bring to a rolling boil. Put the lasagne noodles in the water one by one. Boil uncovered over high heat for 12 to 15 minutes. Drain well.

CHEESE:

¼ lb (125 g) mozzarella, thinly sliced
1 lb (500 g) cottage cheese
2 tbsp (30 mL) hot water
½ cup (125 mL) grated Parmesan cheese

🍃 Place 6 or 7 tbsp (100 g) of the sauce in the bottom of a large, oiled baking dish. Cover with a layer of lasagne noodles. Then add a layer of mozzarella. Cover the mozzarella with a layer of cottage cheese thinned a bit with the hot water. Top with ¼ of the tomato sauce. Continue in this manner until all the ingredients have been used. Sprinkle the grat-

ed Parmesan on top. Bake in a 350°F (180°C) oven for 30 to 40 minutes.

CREAMED MACARONI

8 oz (250 g) macaroni
1½ cups (375 mL) table cream
½ tsp (2 mL) each of salt and pepper
pinch of nutmeg
grated cheese to taste

🍃 Cook the macaroni and drain it. Stir in the cream. Simmer, uncovered, over low heat for 10 to 12 minutes.

🍃 When ready to serve, add the salt, pepper, nutmeg and grated cheese. The cheese can also be served in a separate dish and added according to individual taste.

MACARONI AND CHEESE

Here's a familiar dish that's always popular. It can be served in a variety of ways, and it freezes well too. To save time, replace the sauce with canned tomatoes. If you would like a meaty macaroni and cheese, stir in 1 lb (500 g) sautéed ground beef.

2 cups (500 mL) elbow macaroni
1½ tsp (7 mL) salt
2 tbsp (30 mL) margarine
2 tbsp (30 mL) flour
3 cups (750 mL) milk
¼ tsp (1 mL) pepper
2 cups (500 mL) grated strong cheddar
1 onion, minced

1 tbsp (15 mL) Worcestershire sauce or juice of ½ lemon
½ tsp (2 mL) savory
½ cup (125 mL) buttered breadcrumbs

🍃 Bring to a boil 8 to 12 cups (2 to 3 L) of water salted with 1 tsp (5 mL) of salt. Add the elbow macaroni and cook according to the package directions. Drain and rinse with cold water. Prepare a white sauce with the margarine, flour and milk. When it is smooth and creamy, add the remaining salt and the pepper. Stir the cheese into the sauce until the cheese melts. Pour the sauce over the macaroni. Mix together the onion, Worcestershire sauce and the savory and add to the macaroni mixture. Mix well. Cool rapidly in the refrigerator.

🍃 Pour the macaroni mixture into an oiled baking pan. Cover and freeze. Do not add the buttered breadcrumbs until you are ready to reheat it.

🍃 Yields 4 to 8 servings

🍃 Freezer storage limit: 6 to 8 weeks

🍃 To serve, thaw for 18 hours in the refrigerator or for 4 hours at room temperature. Top with buttered crumbs and cover with foil. Bake in a preheated 350°F (180°C) oven for 25 minutes, remove the foil and bake another 15 to 20 minutes.

🍃 Or you can place the frozen casserole directly in the oven. Sprinkle the macaroni and cheese with buttered breadcrumbs and cover with aluminum foil. Bake in a preheated 400°F (200°C) oven for 25 minutes. Uncover and let brown for 15 to 20 minutes until the cheese browns and starts to bubble.

MACARONI AU GRATIN

3 tbsp (45 mL) butter
3 tbsp (45 mL) flour
2 cups (500 mL) milk
1 cup (250 mL) grated cheese
½ cup (125 mL) minced fresh parsley or 1 tbsp (15 mL) dry parsley
1 small onion, chopped
8 oz (250 g) macaroni, cooked
breadcrumbs to taste
butter, diced

Macaroni au Gratin

🍃 Make a white sauce with the butter, flour and milk.
🍃 Layer the cheese, parsley and onion in a buttered dish alternately with the cooked macaroni. Add the white sauce. Cover with breadcrumbs and dot with butter.
🍃 Bake in a 400°F (200°C) oven for 25 to 35 minutes or until the crust is brown.

MILANESE MACARONI

1 cup (250 mL) grated cheese
1 tsp (5 mL) dry mustard
¼ tsp (1 mL) pepper
8 oz (250 g) macaroni, cooked
1½ cups (375 mL) milk

🍃 Mix together the cheese, mustard and pepper. Place in a buttered baking dish in alternate layers with the cooked macaroni. Pour in the milk.

🍃 Bake in a 350°F (180°C) oven for 30 minutes.

MACARONI WITH GREEN PEPPERS

8 oz (250 g) macaroni
1 tbsp (15 mL) olive oil
1 large onion, minced
3 tbsp (45 mL) bacon fat
1 green pepper, diced
1 14-oz (400-mL) can tomatoes
1 tsp (5 mL) sugar
½ tsp (2 mL) oregano
salt and pepper to taste

🍃 Cook the macaroni, rinse it under hot water and drain it well. Return the macaroni to the same pot. Add the olive oil and stir with a fork. Cover.
🍃 Fry the onion in the bacon fat. Add the diced green pepper, tomatoes, sugar, oregano, salt and pepper to taste. Boil for 20 minutes.

🍃 Pour the sauce over the macaroni. Blend well and simmer for 5 minutes. Serve with a dish of grated cheese.

MACARONI WITH TOMATOES

1 28-oz (800-mL) can tomatoes
1 tbsp (15 mL) sugar
1 tsp (5 mL) dry mustard
½ tsp (2 mL) pepper
¼ tsp (1 mL) thyme
or ½ tsp (2 mL) savory
¼ to ½ cup (50 to 125 mL) celery leaves, finely chopped
1 tsp (5 mL) paprika
1 5½-oz (150-mL) can tomato paste
8 oz (250 g) macaroni, cooked
½ lb (250 g) grated strong or mild cheese
breadcrumbs
butter, diced

Macaroni Carbonara

MACARONI CARBONARA

3 cups (750 mL) macaroni
(or rigatoni)
1 lb (500 g) cooked ham, diced
1 cup (250 mL) grated Gruyère
cheese
1 cup (250 mL) grated Parmesan
cheese
⅓ cup (75 mL) butter or olive oil
3 eggs, beaten
1 cup (250 mL) milk or light
cream
1 clove garlic, crushed
½ tsp (2 mL) basil
salt and pepper to taste

🍃 Cook the macaroni in 12 cups
(3 L) of boiling water until tender. Drain.

🍃 Arrange the macaroni in a buttered baking dish in alternate layers with the ham, Gruyère cheese
and Parmesan cheese. Dot with
pieces of butter or sprinkle with
olive oil.

🍃 Beat the eggs together with the
milk or cream, garlic, basil, salt
and pepper. Pour this mixture
over the macaroni. Cover and
bake in a 300°F (150°C) oven for
1 hour. Let cool and refrigerate
for 24 hours. Unmold and serve
cold with a green salad.

🍃 Pour ⅓ of the tomatoes into a
well-buttered casserole or baking
dish.

🍃 To the remaining tomatoes,
add the sugar, dry mustard, pepper, thyme or savory, celery leaves,
paprika and tomato paste. Mix
well.

🍃 Make alternate layers of the
macaroni, tomato mixture and
grated cheese in the baking dish.

🍃 Top with the breadcrumbs and
dot with butter. Bake in a 350°F
(180°C) oven for 35 to 45 minutes.

MACARONI WITH SALMON

4 oz (125 g) macaroni
1 6½-oz (180-mL) can salmon
2 tsp (10 mL) cornstarch
3 eggs
2 cups (500 mL) milk
salt and pepper to taste
1 tbsp (15 mL) parsley
1 onion, chopped
1 tbsp (15 mL) lemon juice
2 tbsp (30 mL) grated cheese

🍃 Cook the macaroni. Rinse it
under cold water and drain it
well. Flake the salmon. Mix
together the macaroni and
salmon and place the mixture in a
buttered baking dish.

🍃 Blend together the cornstarch
and the eggs. Add the milk.
Season to taste and add the
remaining ingredients.

🍃 Pour the egg mixture over the
macaroni. Set the baking dish in a
shallow pan with 1 in. (2 cm) of
water. Bake in a 325°F (160°C)
oven for 35 minutes.

MACARONI PATÉ

8 oz (250 g) macaroni
3½ cups (875 mL) consommé
12 small white onions
3 tbsp (45 mL) olive oil
1 tbsp (15 mL) chopped parsley
1 lb (500 g) fresh tomatoes,
peeled and sliced

❦ TECHNIQUE ❦

MACARONI CARBONARA

1 Place the macaroni in a buttered baking dish in alternate layers with the ham, Gruyère cheese and Parmesan cheese.

2 Sprinkle with olive oil.

3 Beat the eggs with the milk, garlic, basil, salt and pepper.

4 Pour the egg mixture over the macaroni.

Macaroni Salad

salt and pepper to taste
½ lb (250 g) mushrooms, thinly
sliced
¼ cup (50 mL) port or sherry
2 tbsp (30 mL) sliced green
olives
4 tbsp (60 mL) grated cheese
1 recipe for pastry dough
cold milk

❧ Cook the macaroni in boiling water for 5 minutes. Drain. Bring the consommé to a vigorous boil. Add the macaroni and finish cooking until tender. Drain.

❧ Brown the small whole onions in the oil over medium heat. Add the parsley and tomatoes. Salt and pepper to taste. When the tomatoes begin to cook, add the mushrooms. Let simmer for 15 minutes.

❧ Pour the tomato sauce over the cooked macaroni. Add the port or sherry, the chopped olives and the grated cheese. Stir well.

❧ Line a buttered mold or loaf pan with a layer of the pie dough rolled very thin. Pour the macaroni mixture into the mold. Top with a layer of crust and brush with a little cold milk. Bake in a 425°F (220°C) oven for 40 minutes or until the crust is golden brown.

SCALLOPED MACARONI AND HAM

8 oz (250 g) elbow macaroni
1 cup (250 mL) cooked ham,
chopped
½ cup (125 mL) breadcrumbs
2 chives, chopped
2 tbsp (30 mL) butter, diced
salt and pepper to taste
milk

❧ Cook the macaroni in boiling salted water. Drain.

❧ Arrange half the cooked maca-
roni in a buttered baking dish, cover it with half the ham, then with half the breadcrumbs and chives. Dot with 1 tbsp (15 mL) of the butter. Salt and pepper to taste. Repeat with remaining ingredients to make a second layer.

❧ Add milk enough milk to almost cover the macaroni mixture. Bake uncovered in a 375°F (190°C) oven for 20 to 30 minutes.

GRANDMOTHER'S MACARONI AND CHEESE

8 oz (250 g) long macaroni
1¼ cups (300 mL) mild yellow
cheddar
½ cup (125 mL) melted butter
½ cup (125 mL) light cream
½ tsp (2 mL) salt
½ tsp (2 mL) freshly ground
pepper
½ cup (125 mL) chopped fresh
parsley or chives
paprika
milk

❧ Break the macaroni into 1-in. (2-cm) pieces. Cook in boiling salted water until tender. Drain well.

❧ Grate the cheese. Add half of the cheese along with the melted butter and the cream to the macaroni. Stir gently and season to taste with the salt, pepper, and parsley or chives. Pour into a buttered baking dish. Sprinkle the rest of the cheese on top. Dust with paprika.

❧ Add enough milk to almost cover the macaroni mixture. Bake in a 300°F (150°C) oven until golden brown on top.

MACARONI SALAD

6 to 8 oz (200 to 250 g) elbow macaroni
2 tbsp (30 mL) olive oil
4 tbsp (60 mL) mayonnaise
1 6½-oz (180-mL) can tuna, flaked
2 hard-cooked eggs, sliced
2 tomatoes, peeled and sliced
black olives to taste
1 tsp (5 mL) curry powder
3 tbsp (45 mL) grated cheese
salt and pepper to taste

❧ Cook the macaroni then drain it thoroughly. Stir in the olive oil while the pasta is hot. Let cool. Add the mayonnaise and stir again.

❧ Mix the remaining ingredients and add them to the macaroni. Stir well but gently with a fork and serve in a bed of lettuce.

CHEF'S MACARONI SALAD

8 oz (250 g) elbow macaroni
¼ cup (50 mL) French dressing (vinaigrette)
1 cup (250 mL) julienned ham
1 cup (250 mL) julienned chicken
½ cup (125 mL) julienned Swiss cheese
mayonnaise
lemon juice to taste
lettuce

❧ Cook the macaroni in boiling salted water. Drain and refrigerate until cold.

❧ Stir the vinaigrette into the chilled macaroni. Arrange the mixture on an attractive round platter. Garnish with rows of the ham, chicken and cheese.

❧ Thin the mayonnaise to taste with the lemon juice. Brush it on the meats and cheese. Decorate with lettuce wedges.

HOW TO MAKE FRESH PASTA
Making fresh pasta is a skill that requires plenty of practice. Remember that the quantity of flour needed may vary slightly depending on the brand of flour, the amount of moisture it contains, and the size of the eggs. To be on the safe side, add the flour little by little until the dough is smooth and elastic. It is extremely important to combine the flour and eggs very well.

❧ It will also take some practice before you will be able to roll the dough out to a uniform thickness, but this produces the most attractive noodles.

❧ It is difficult even for experts to make pasta successfully in damp weather.

❧ To make bows, cut the dough into ½-in. (0.6-cm) squares and pinch each square in the middle to shape a bow.

HOMEMADE PASTA

3 eggs, lightly beaten
2 cups (500 mL) all-purpose flour
½ tsp (2 mL) salt

❧ Beat the eggs just enough to mix the yolks with the whites but do not beat until foamy. Place the

flour in a large bowl. Add the salt. Make a well in the center and pour in the beaten eggs.

❧ Using your finger tips, start working the flour into the eggs. Continue working them together until the dough is homogenous and quite firm. Then knead the ball of dough until it is elastic, working in a little more flour if the mixture sticks too much to your fingers. Let the dough rest for 10 minutes.

❧ Divide the ball of dough into thirds. On a lightly floured surface, roll out each ball until it is as thin as possible. Let each flattened ball dry for 20 minutes. Roll up each piece like a jelly roll. Cut the roll crosswise into thin sections with a very sharp knife. When you unroll each section, you will have one noodle, its width depending on how close together you have made the slices. Spread the noodles out on a lightly floured clean cloth. Let dry at room temperature.

❧ The noodles may be cooked in salted boiling water after they have dried for 20 minutes. Or you can let them dry very thoroughly, then store them in tightly closed jars, or package and freeze them.

SPINACH FETTUCINI

2 eggs
4 cups (1 L) all-purpose flour
1 tsp (5 mL) salt
¾ cup (175 mL) puréed spinach

❧ Use the same procedure to make these as for regular pasta, adding the spinach purée along with the eggs. However, you will need to let these noodles dry a little longer before you cook them.

🦪 To make the puréed spinach, cook 1 lb (500 g) spinach for 5 minutes over medium heat. Chop the leaves, then force through a sieve or purée in a blender for 30 seconds.

SPINACH FETTUCINI AU GRATIN

8 oz (250 g) spinach noodles
1 cup (250 mL) chopped fresh parsley
2 cups (500 mL) grated mild cheese
salt and pepper to taste
1 cup (250 mL) hot milk or cream
1 cup (250 mL) soft breadcrumbs
¼ cup (50 mL) melted butter

🦪 Cook the noodles in boiling salted water until tender. Drain well.

🦪 In a buttered baking dish, arrange alternate layers of cooked noodles, parsley and cheese. Salt and pepper each layer. Pour the hot milk or cream on top. Then top with the soft breadcrumbs mixed with the melted butter. Bake in a 375°F (190°C) oven until the top is golden brown.

NOODLE RING

8 oz (250 g) fine noodles
3 tbsp (45 mL) butter
2 tbsp (30 mL) flour
½ cup (125 mL) light cream
¼ tsp (1 mL) marjoram
salt and pepper to taste
4 egg yolks
4 egg whites
¼ cup (50 mL) chopped parsley

🦪 Cook the noodles and drain them well.

🦪 Prepare a white sauce with the butter, flour and cream. Flavor with marjoram. Salt and pepper to taste.

🦪 Beat the egg yolks and add them to the noodles. Stir in the white sauce. Blend thoroughly.

🦪 Beat the egg whites until stiff and fold them into the noodles together with the parsley. Pour into a well-buttered ring mold. Place the mold in a shallow pan with 1 in. (2 cm) of water. Bake in a 350°F (180°C) oven for 40 minutes. Unmold and serve as is or garnished with green peas, diced carrots, eggs in white sauce or creamed seafood.

NOODLES AMANDINE

8 oz (250 g) medium noodles
½ cup (125 mL) butter
4 onions, chopped
3 tbsp (45 mL) shortening
½ cup (125 mL) blanched almonds
3 cups (750 mL) small croutons
salt and pepper to taste

🦪 Cook the noodles, then drain them well. Melt ¼ cup (50 mL) of the butter and sauté the cooked noodles in it for a few minutes.

🦪 Fry the onions in the shortening until they are golden. Add them to the noodles.

🦪 Heat the remaining butter, add the almonds and brown them over low heat. Remove the almonds from the butter and stir them into the noodles. Fry the croutons in the remaining butter

Noodles Amandine

and pour over the noodles. Salt and pepper to taste.

NOODLES WITH ONIONS

8 oz (250 g) noodles
1 cup (250 mL) grated cheese
⅓ cup (75 mL) breadcrumbs
2½ cups (625 mL) milk
3 eggs, lightly beaten
½ tsp (2 mL) salt
1 tsp (5 mL) Worcestershire sauce
3 onions, finely chopped
butter or olive oil

❧ Cook the noodles in salted boiling water. Rinse, drain and place the noodles in a buttered baking dish in alternate layers with the cheese and the breadcrumbs.

❧ Mix together the milk, eggs, salt and Worcestershire sauce. Pour over the noodle mixture.

❧ Put the baking dish in a shallow pan containing 1 in. (2 cm) of hot water. Bake in a 350°F (180°C) oven for 45 minutes. Noodles cooked in this manner unmold very well.

❧ Fry the onions in the butter or the oil until they are golden brown. Cover the noodles with the fried onions.

NOODLES WITH COTTAGE CHEESE

8 oz (250 g) medium noodles
1 cup (250 mL) cottage cheese
8 oz (250 g) cream cheese
1 cup (250 mL) sour cream
½ tsp (2 mL) salt
¼ tsp (1 mL) pepper
6 green onions, minced

½ cup (125 mL) grated Parmesan cheese

❧ Cook the noodles, drain them, and place them back in the saucepan to keep warm.

❧ Beat together the cottage cheese, cream cheese and sour cream. Add the salt and pepper. Fold the cheese mixture into the noodles along with the green onions. Adjust the seasonings. Warm the mixture for a few minutes over low heat, stirring gently with a fork.

❧ To serve, place the noodles in a warm dish and sprinkle with grated Parmesan cheese, or serve the Parmesan in a dish on the side.

OYSTERS TETRAZZINI

2 cups (500 mL) oysters
8 oz (250 g) fine noodles
1 cup (250 mL) fresh breadcrumbs
¼ cup (50 mL) grated Parmesan cheese
7 tbsp (105 mL) butter
¼ cup (50 mL) flour
3 cups (750 mL) milk
½ tsp (2 mL) salt
pinch of pepper
2 tsp (10 mL) lemon juice
¼ cup (50 mL) sherry
paprika
salt and pepper to taste

❧ Drain the oysters, reserving ½ cup (125 mL) of the juice.

❧ Cook the noodles. Drain them. Mix the noodles with the breadcrumbs and the grated cheese. Turn the mixture into a 12- x 8- x 2-in. (30- x 20- x 5-cm) baking dish.

❧ Melt the butter in a skillet. Pour 3 tbsp (45 mL) of the melted butter over the noodle mixture. To the remainder of the butter, add the flour. Blend well, then add the milk, salt, pepper, lemon juice, sherry and oyster juice. Cook over medium heat, stirring constantly, until the sauce is smooth and creamy.

❧ Arrange the oysters on top of the noodles. Salt and pepper lightly. Cover with the white sauce. Sprinkle with paprika. Bake in a 400°F (200°C) oven for 40 minutes. Serve hot.

NOODLES WITH SAUSAGE

8 oz (250 g) noodles, large or medium
½ cup (125 mL) olives, green or black
1 lb (500 g) sausages
1 tsp (5 mL) olive oil
3 tbsp (45 mL) vegetable oil
2 tbsp (30 mL) flour
¼ cup (50 mL) tomato paste
½ tsp (2 mL) basil
1 cup (250 mL) milk
3 tbsp (45 mL) grated cheese
salt and pepper to taste

❧ Cook the noodles and drain them. Pit the olives and cut them in quarters.

❧ Brown the sausages in the olive oil over low heat.

❧ Heat the vegetable oil, add the flour and blend it in well. Add the tomato paste, basil and milk. Cook over low heat, stirring, until the sauce is creamy. Add the grated cheese. Remove from the heat.

Noodles with Sausage

Cut the sausages in half and mix them with the noodles, olives and the sauce. Salt and pepper to taste.

🐟 Pour the mixture into a baking dish. Bake in a 375°F (190°C) oven for 20 minutes.

CHINESE FRIED NOODLES

8 oz (250 g) noodles, very fine
8 cups (2 L) water
peanut oil

🐟 Bring the water to a vigorous boil in a large pot and add the noodles. (Add 8 cups or 2 L of water for each additional 8 oz or 250 g of noodles.) Let the noodles boil for 7 or 8 seconds. Drain them, then dry them on a clean cloth to prevent them sticking together.

🐟 When the noodles have cooled, heat enough oil in a deep fryer to fry the quantity of noodles. Place the noodles in a heat-resistant sieve and dip the sieve into the boiling fat for 30 to 60 seconds, or until the noodles are golden. Drain them on paper towelling.

🐟 To store fried noodles, let them cool and place in a tightly closed metal container.

BAKED EGGPLANT SPAGHETTI

8 oz (250 g) spaghetti
3 hard-cooked eggs
1 medium eggplant
3 tbsp (45 mL) vegetable oil
¼ lb (125 g) cooked ham
10 to 15 black olives, pitted
¼ cup (50 mL) grated Parmesan cheese
2 tbsp (30 mL) olive oil

🐟 Cook the spaghetti, drain it and add salt to taste. Cut the eggs into quarters.

🐟 Peel the eggplant and cut it into small pieces. Fry the eggplant in vegetable oil over high heat. Drain and salt to taste.

🐟 Dice the ham and halve the olives.

🐟 In a buttered baking dish, place a layer of eggplant along with half the ham and half the olives. Cover with 6 to 8 egg quarters and half the spaghetti. Sprinkle with half the grated Parmesan cheese. Continue in the same manner with the remaining ingredients. Sprinkle the mixture with olive oil. Bake in a 400°F (200°C) oven for 15 to 20 minutes.

EGGPLANT SPAGHETTI SAUCE

1 medium eggplant
2 tbsp (30 mL) bacon fat
1 clove garlic, chopped
1 green pepper, chopped
½ tsp (2 mL) basil
1 28-oz (800 mL) can tomatoes, drained and chopped
½ tsp (2 mL) salt
¼ tsp (1 mL) pepper
8 oz (250 g) spaghetti or elbow macaroni

🐟 Peel and dice the eggplant. Soak it in cold water for 10 minutes. Drain.

🐟 Heat the bacon fat. Add the chopped garlic, chopped green pepper and basil. Cook over low heat until the vegetables are tender. Add the tomatoes, salt, pepper and the diced eggplant.

❦ TECHNIQUE ❦

NOODLES WITH SAUSAGE

1 Brown the sausages in the olive oil.

2 Add the tomato paste to the flour mixture.

3 Add the basil and milk. Cook, stirring, over low heat.

4 Add the grated cheese.

Simmer for 1 hour.

🍂 Cook the spaghetti in boiling salted water until tender. Drain and mix with the sauce. Serve with grated cheese.

CATALAN SPAGHETTI AU GRATIN

16 oz (500 g) spaghetti
1 28-oz (800-mL) can tomatoes
1 tsp (5 mL) sugar
½ tsp (2 mL) dry mustard
1 tsp (5 mL) salt
½ tsp (2 mL) pepper
1 bay leaf
pinch of thyme
3 cloves garlic, minced
¼ cup (50 mL) butter
1 cup (250 mL) soda crackers, finely crumbled

🍂 Cook the spaghetti and drain it.
🍂 Mix together the tomatoes, sugar, dry mustard, salt, pepper, bay leaf and thyme.

🍂 Butter a baking dish generously. Fill it with alternate layers of spaghetti, the tomato mixture and the minced garlic. Dot each layer with bits of butter. Top with the crushed crackers. Bake in a 375°F (190°C) oven for 45 to 60 minutes.

VEGETABLE SPAGHETTI SAUCE

½ cup (125 mL) olive
or vegetable oil
2 carrots, peeled and grated
2 onions, very thinly sliced
2 leeks, sliced into rings
1 28-oz (800 mL) can tomatoes
1 tbsp (15 mL) sugar
½ tsp (2 mL) salt
1 tsp (5 mL) basil
8 oz (250 g) spaghetti, cooked

🍂 Heat the oil. Add the grated carrots, onions, leeks, tomatoes,

sugar, salt and basil. Cover and simmer for 1 hour. Pour the vegetable sauce over the cooked spaghetti.
🍂 This sauce tastes best when made with olive oil.

NEAPOLITAN SPAGHETTI

6 thin slices salt pork
¼ cup (50 mL) olive oil
2 large onions, chopped
1 green pepper, diced
1 to 3 cloves garlic, minced
½ tsp (2 mL) salt
1 tbsp (15 mL) sugar
3 cups (750 mL) canned tomatoes
1 5½-oz (150-mL) can tomato paste
1 tsp (5 mL) marjoram
½ tsp (2 mL) basil
¼ cup (50 mL) sherry or red wine
2 tbsp (30 mL) capers
½ cup (125 mL) black olives, chopped
8 to 16 oz (250 to 500 g) cooked spaghetti

🍂 Dice the salt pork. Brown it in the olive oil over low heat.
🍂 Add the onions, green pepper and garlic. Stir well. Cover and simmer over low heat for 15 minutes.
🍂 Add the salt, sugar, tomatoes, tomato paste, marjoram and basil. Cover and simmer for 2 hours or until the sauce thickens.
🍂 Add the sherry, capers and olives. Simmer for 5 minutes and serve over the cooked spaghetti.
🍂 This sauce reheats very well.

Baked Eggplant Spaghetti

SICILIAN SPAGHETTI

8 oz (250 g) spaghetti
1 clove garlic, minced
¼ cup (50 mL) vegetable oil
6 anchovy filets, chopped
¼ tsp (1 mL) pepper
½ cup (125 mL) grated Parmesan cheese

❧ Cook the spaghetti in boiling salted water until tender. Drain and arrange it on a heated serving dish.

❧ Fry the garlic lightly in the oil. Remove the garlic from the skillet before it has a chance to burn and add the anchovies. Cook about 2 minutes. Pour over the spaghetti and add the pepper. Serve with the grated cheese.

PARSLEYED SPAGHETTI

½ cup (125 mL) butter
1 clove garlic, minced
8 oz (250 g) spaghetti
½ cup (125 mL) grated cheese
1½ cups (375 mL) parsley, minced

❧ Melt the butter, add the garlic and cook over low heat until the garlic is golden.

❧ Cook the spaghetti. Drain it and return it to the same pot. Pour the garlic butter on top, then sprinkle with the grated cheese and parsley. Toss with two forks over low heat until the cheese and parsley are well mixed with the spaghetti. Serve at once.

Vegetable Spaghetti Sauce

TOMATO PASTE SPAGHETTI SAUCE

4 tbsp (60 mL) vegetable oil
2 cloves garlic, minced
1 5½-oz (150 mL) can tomato paste
1 bay leaf
½ tsp (2 mL) thyme
1 tsp (5 mL) sugar
½ tsp (2 mL) salt
¼ tsp (1 mL) pepper
grated cheese to taste
8 oz (250 g) spaghetti, cooked

❧ Heat the vegetable oil in a large saucepan. Brown the garlic until just golden. Add the tomato paste, bay leaf, thyme, sugar, salt and pepper. Cover and cook for 1 hour over very low heat.

❧ Pour the sauce over cooked spaghetti. Serve with grated cheese.

BOLOGNESE SPAGHETTI

¼ cup (50 mL) olive or vegetable oil
2 onions, chopped
3 cloves garlic
1 green pepper, diced
4 stalks celery and leaves, chopped
½ lb (250 g) calf or beef liver, chopped
1 28-oz (800-mL) can tomatoes
1 5½-oz (150-mL) can tomato paste
½ cup (125 mL) chopped parsley
½ tsp (2 mL) rosemary
½ tsp (2 mL) marjoram
1 tsp (5 mL) basil
½ lb (250 g) mushrooms, thinly sliced
16 oz (500 g) spaghetti, cooked
2 cups (500 mL) grated cheese

Parsleyed Spaghetti

🍴 Heat the olive oil or vegetable oil. Add the onions, garlic, green pepper, celery and liver. Cook over medium heat for 10 minutes, stirring constantly.

🍴 Add the tomatoes, tomato paste, parsley, rosemary, marjoram, basil and the mushrooms. Cover and let simmer for 2 hours or until the sauce has the desired consistency.

🍴 Pour the sauce over the cooked spaghetti. Serve with grated cheese.

SIENESE SPAGHETTI

16 oz (500 g) spaghetti
3 tbsp (45 mL) butter
½ cup (125 mL) olive oil
1 5½-oz (150-mL) can tomato paste
¼ tsp (1 mL) thyme
½ tsp (2 mL) basil
1 tbsp (15 mL) sugar
salt and pepper to taste
1 tbsp (15 mL) butter
½ lb (250 g) ground beef
1 tbsp (15 mL) Worcestershire sauce
4 tbsp (60 mL) grated Parmesan cheese

🍴 Cook the spaghetti. Drain it, rinse it under hot water and return it to its cooking pot. Add the butter and toss with two forks until the butter is melted. Cover.

🍴 In a second saucepan, put the olive oil, tomato paste, thyme, basil, sugar, salt and pepper. Bring the mixture to a boil, then cover and let simmer for 20 to 25 minutes, stirring occasionally.

🍴 Melt 1 tbsp (15 mL) butter in a skillet and add the ground beef. Cook the beef over medium heat, crushing the large pieces with a fork. Add the tomato sauce. Cover and let simmer for 10 minutes. Add the Worcestershire sauce.

🍴 Arrange the spaghetti on a heated serving dish. Sprinkle with grated Parmesan cheese and pour the sauce over the spaghetti. Serve with a dish of grated cheese.

SPAGHETTINI RING

8 oz (250 mL) thin spaghetti (spaghettini)
½ cup (125 mL) coarsely grated cheese
2 tbsp (30 mL) diced green pepper
2 tbsp (30 mL) diced red pepper or pimiento
3 eggs, beaten
1 cup (250 mL) milk
½ tsp (2 mL) salt

🍴 Cook the spaghettini in boiling salted water until tender. Drain it well.

🍴 Butter a ring mold generously and place in it alternating layers of spaghettini, cheese, green pepper and pimiento.

🍴 Beat the eggs, milk and salt together. Pour the egg mixture over the spaghettini ring. Put the ring mold in a shallow pan containing 1 in. (2 cm) of hot water. Bake in a 350°F (180°C) oven for 45 minutes. Unmold and fill the center of the ring with a cream sauce of your choice.

QUICK PASTA SAUCES

BASIC SAUCE:
1 to 2 cloves garlic, minced
3 tbsp (45 mL) vegetable oil
1 tbsp (15 mL) flour

1 5½-oz (150-mL) can tomato paste
1 cup (250 mL) water
½ tsp (2 mL) basil
¼ tsp (1 mL) rosemary
1 tsp (5 mL) sugar
½ tsp (2 mL) salt
¼ tsp (1 mL) pepper

❧ Brown the garlic in the oil over low heat just until golden.

❧ Add the flour and blend well. Add the remaining ingredients. Bring to a boil, stirring constantly. Cover and simmer for 20 to 30 minutes.

VARIATIONS

❧ To make a tasty variation of this sauce, you can add one of the following ingredients before simmering:

½ cup (125 mL) pitted olives
2 tbsp (30 mL) capers
chopped leftover pork, ham or veal
½ lb (250 g) mushrooms, thinly sliced and browned with the garlic
¼ to ½ lb (125 to 250 g) tiny beef or pork meatballs.

Genovese Pesto Sauce

1 cup (250 mL) fresh basil leaves
2 sprigs marjoram
½ tsp (2 mL) salt
4 tbsp (60 mL) grated Parmesan cheese
1 cup (250 mL) olive oil

❧ It is impossible to make this sauce without fresh herbs. On the other hand, it keeps well for 1 month in the refrigerator, and if frozen will keep for 3 to 6 months. Thaw before using.

❧ The easy way to make this sauce is to use a blender. Simply place the ingredients in the blender jar, cover and blend for 1 minute.

❧ To make this sauce by hand, mince the basil and the marjoram, then crush and grind them with the salt, using the back of a wooden spoon, until the mixture becomes a green paste. Stir in the cheese. Mix, then add the olive oil one drop at a time while beating vigorously. At this stage, you can use an electric beater to beat in the oil, if you wish. To serve, simply add a small amount of the pesto sauce to cooked spaghetti or macaroni, to taste. It may also be served over cold pasta or with salads.

Cold Onion Sauce

1 hard-cooked egg yolk
1 tsp (5 mL) lemon juice
½ tsp (2 mL) dry mustard
¾ cup (175 mL) olive oil
1 tsp (15 mL) cider
or tarragon vinegar
salt and pepper to taste
¼ cup (50 mL) light cream
2 tbsp (30 mL) chopped onions

❧ In a bowl, mash together the hard-cooked yolk, the lemon juice and the dry mustard until it forms a paste. Set the bowl in a dish filled with ice. Let chill for 20 minutes.

❧ Slowly pour in the olive oil in a thin stream, while beating constantly with a wire whisk. When the sauce has the consistency of mayonnaise, add the vinegar and the salt and pepper, beating constantly.

Sienese Spaghetti

Tuna Sauce

🍃 When the oil is completely incorporated, stir in the cream and the onions; they will thin the sauce slightly.

🍃 Use this sauce instead of French dressing in pasta and rice salads.

PARSLEYED CREAM SAUCE

3 tbsp (45 mL) butter
3 tbsp (45 mL) flour
1½ cups (375 mL) consommé or cream
¼ cup (50 mL) milk
chopped parsley to taste
salt and pepper to taste

🍃 Make a white sauce with the butter, flour, consommé or cream and milk. Simmer for 5 minutes.

🍃 Stir in the parsley, salt and pepper. Serve over hot pasta.

TUNA SAUCE

3¾ to 6½-oz (100 to 200 g) can tuna in oil
2 tbsp (30 mL) vegetable oil
2 cloves garlic, minced
2 tbsp (30 mL) tomato paste
½ tsp (2 mL) marjoram
1 tsp (5 mL) sugar
salt and pepper to taste
grated cheese

🍃 Drain the oil from the tuna into a saucepan. Add the vegetable oil. Brown the garlic in this oil mixture until golden.

🍃 Flake the tuna. Add the tuna, tomato paste, marjoram, sugar, salt and pepper to the oil mixture. Cover and let simmer over low heat for 15 minutes.

🍃 Pour this sauce over cooked pasta of your choice and sprinkle with grated cheese.

EGGS

EGGS

Eggs can be used in hundreds of ways in the kitchen; indeed, it's almost impossible to cook without having some at hand. You can serve them soft-cooked, hard-cooked, poached, fried, scrambled, as an omelet, etc. And they are used in every kind of dish, from soups to desserts. Clearly, it's important to know how to cook eggs.

BOILED EGGS (Soft-Cooked and Hard-Cooked)
Put eggs in boiling salted water (the salt gives the eggs more flavor). Continue to cook over low heat in simmering water; this prevents the shells from breaking while they cook and keeps the eggs soft. The cooking time varies from 3 to 10 minutes, depending on whether you want a soft-cooked or hard-cooked egg.

🕭 Placing a cold egg into boiling water may crack the shell, so try to use eggs that are at room temperature.

🕭 Peel soft-cooked or hard-cooked eggs as soon as they are cooked; this prevents the shell from sticking to the white. To simplify peeling, put the eggs in a bowl of cold water, then break the shell by tapping it gently on the

Editors' Note:
In 1990, the U.S. Food and Drug Administration classified eggs as a potentially dangerous food because some eggs carry the salmonella bacteria. As a result, many nutritionists recommend that eggs should always be well cooked, as salmonella is killed at 160°F (71°C).
The risk is lowered if cracked eggs are discarded and intact eggs are kept refrigerated, cooked thoroughly and served immediately.

edge of a table. Peel off the shell under running water.

POACHED EGGS
Use a large skillet, and do not poach more than 4 or 5 eggs at a time.

🕭 Add 2 tbsp (30 mL) vinegar for every 4 cups (1 L) of water. Do not salt. Break the eggs into a cup or a small bowl and slide them into boiling water. The water should not be at a high boil since this will prevent the white from setting evenly. Use a spoon to shape the white close to the yolk.

🕭 After 2 or 3 minutes, remove from the water with a slotted spoon and place on a clean, wet cloth to drain.

HELPFUL HINTS
🕭 The vinegar added to the water will help the white to set rapidly. It is best to use cider or white vinegar.

🕭 To slide the eggs easily into the water, wet the edge of the container holding the eggs. Be sure to slide them into the water with care. The white sets very rapidly around the yolk.

🕭 Remove the poached egg from the water with a slotted spoon and slide it gently onto a dish.

🕭 To make it perfectly round, trim the edges of the white with scissors.

🕭 Drain the eggs on a wet cloth; eggs will stick to a dry cloth.

SCRAMBLED EGGS
It is better to prepare scrambled eggs in a heavy-bottomed saucepan than in a skillet.

🕭 Heat the butter. Break the eggs directly onto the butter, add salt

and pepper, and beat continuously with a fork over low heat until creamy. Add 1 to 2 tsp (5 to 10 mL) of milk or cream to stop the cooking, but continue to stir the eggs for a few seconds.

🕭 Serve immediately on toast, on slices of tomato or with sausage, bacon or ham.

OMELETS
Beat the eggs in a soup plate rather than in a bowl in order to allow as much air as possible to enter the mixture (but be careful not to make it too foamy). Add salt and pepper and mix well. Add 1 or 2 tsp (5 or 10 mL) cream, milk or cold water.

🕭 Pour the mixture into an omelet pan or skillet that is just large enough for the number of eggs you are cooking. The pan must be very hot and the butter must be melted. Lift the edges of the mixture with a fork and keep pushing it toward the center of the pan so that it receives as much heat as possible. Continue cooking over high heat until the eggs are set. Serve as soon as done.

FRIED EGGS "SUR LE PLAT"
Fried eggs are at their best when served directly in the pan in which they are cooked. This prevents rapid cooling and allows you to prepare each serving individually. Small pans (earthenware, aluminum or ovenproof glass) are suitable and easily obtainable.

🕭 Generously butter the small pan or the skillet before heating it. Break the egg (or eggs) into it. Place over low heat until the egg is set.

🐦 Serve plain or garnish with grated cheese, minced parsley, green onion or chives.

FRIED EGGS

Since the temperatures of the fat and the skillet are difficult to control, fried eggs are often overcooked and dry, making them almost indigestible.

🐦 For best results, the skillet should be greased, oiled or buttered before it is heated. The eggs should be broken into a bowl, then slipped one at a time into the pan. Add ½ tsp (2 mL) of water.

🐦 Cover the pan and cook the eggs over very low heat until the whites are well set. The small amount of water added to the pan prevents the egg from hardening and its edges from drying up; it also cooks the white with steam, making the egg more digestible.

🐦 To fry eggs in brown butter, put 1 tsp (5 mL) of butter in the pan and brown it over medium heat until it is a nut-brown color. Break the eggs into a bowl, slide them into the hot butter and cook, uncovered, over low heat for 4 to 6 minutes.

MOLDED EGGS (OR EGGS EN COCOTTE)

Generously butter small, individual molds or ramekins. Break an egg into each one and add salt and pepper.

🐦 Immediately put the molds into a saucepan with about 1 in. (2 cm) of boiling water; this will keep the yolk from falling to the bottom of the mold. Cover and cook until the eggs are set.

Poached Eggs Parmentier

Cooking takes anywhere from 5 to 15 minutes, depending on whether you want soft-cooked or hard-cooked eggs. Unmold and serve.

POACHED EGGS PARMENTIER

3 large potatoes
3 tbsp (45 mL) butter
3 tbsp (45 mL) grated cheese
4 slices cooked bacon
6 eggs
salt and pepper to taste
cream

🐦 Bake the potatoes. When cooked, cut them in half lengthwise. Remove some of the pulp to form a small cavity.

🐦 In each cavity, place a little butter, grated cheese and diced bacon. Top with a poached egg. Add salt and pepper.

🐦 Mash the pulp from the potatoes with a little butter and cream. Place around the eggs. Heat in a 450°F (230°C) oven for 5 minutes.

POACHED EGGS FLORENTINE

4 eggs
1 lb (500 g) fresh spinach
2 tbsp (30 mL) butter
2 tbsp (30 mL) flour
1½ cups (375 mL) milk
½ cup (125 mL) grated cheese
salt and pepper to taste

🐦 Poach the eggs and drain on a damp cloth.

🐦 Cook and drain the spinach. Add salt and pepper, then 1 tbsp (15 mL) butter. Place in a baking dish.

🐦 Arrange the poached eggs on the spinach and cover with a

white sauce prepared with 1 tbsp (15 mL) butter, the flour and the milk. Sprinkle grated cheese on top. Bake in a 400°F (200°C) oven for 8 minutes.

POLISH POACHED EGGS

1 tbsp (15 mL) butter
1 lb (500 g) ground beef
1 cup (250 mL) tomato sauce
1 tsp (5 mL) sugar
¼ tsp (1 mL) savory
salt and pepper to taste
buttered toast
6 eggs, poached or molded

🍴 Brown the butter. Crumble the ground beef in the butter with a fork. Cook over medium heat until the beef is cooked.
🍴 Add the tomato sauce, sugar, savory, salt and pepper. Simmer for 10 minutes.
🍴 Pour the meat mixture onto a warm platter. Garnish with poached eggs or molded eggs. Surround the eggs with buttered toast triangles.

RED WINE JELLIED EGGS

6 eggs
1 envelope unflavored gelatin
3 tbsp (45 mL) cold water
juice of ½ lemon
⅓ cup (75 mL) red wine or port
¼ lb (125 g) mushrooms, chopped
2 thin slices cooked ham
½ cup (125 mL) mayonnaise
pinch of nutmeg

1 tsp (5 mL) lemon zest
¼ tsp dry mustard
sweet almond oil*

🍴 Poach the eggs (see page 354) and keep them in a bowl of cold water.
🍴 Soak the gelatin in cold water for 5 minutes and add the lemon juice and the red wine or port. Stir over boiling water in a double boiler until the gelatin is dissolved.
🍴 Brush 6 small oval egg molds, ramekins or medium-size cups with the sweet almond oil. Pour into each mold enough of the gelatin mixture to cover the bottom. Place in the refrigerator to set.
🍴 Blend together the mayonnaise, nutmeg, lemon zest and mustard. Add the mushrooms and ham. Mix together and place 1 tbsp (15 mL) of this mixture over the gelatin in each mold.
🍴 Place a poached egg, shaped with scissors, over the mayonnaise mixture. Top with the remaining gelatin mixture. Refrigerate until firm. Unmold onto a bed of lettuce or watercress. Serve as an appetizer or as a light luncheon dish.

*Sweet almond oil can be purchased in pharmacies or natural food stores. If you use it to oil the molds, the molded gelatin will slide out easily, without the need to dip the molds in hot water. It can be used with any molded gelatin recipe, as it is odorless, colorless and tasteless and gives the surface a glaze. To unmold, simply slide the tip of a knife around the mold.

POACHED EGGS BOURGUIGNONNE

10 to 12 small white onions
4 very thin slices salt pork
1 tbsp (15 mL) flour
½ cup (125 mL) red wine
½ cup (125 mL) water
salt and pepper to taste
6 eggs

🍴 Peel the onions and leave whole. Brown the salt pork slices over low heat until crisp. Add the small onions and brown over low heat.
🍴 Add the flour. Stir well. Add the red wine and water. Bring to a boil, stirring constantly. Cover and simmer until the onions are tender. Salt and pepper to taste.
🍴 Poach the eggs in the wine sauce. Adjust the seasoning to taste. Pour the sauce into a round vegetable dish and top with the eggs.

POACHED EGGS WITH PEA PURÉE

1 can small peas
2 tbsp (30 mL) butter
pinch of basil
salt and pepper to taste
4 slices toasted bread, crusts removed
4 eggs, poached

🍴 Drain the green peas. To purée, use a food mill or force the peas through a sieve with a wooden spoon. Add the butter, basil, salt and pepper. Heat in the top of a double boiler.

Butter the toast. Garnish each slice with a thick layer of hot puréed peas. Set a poached egg on top of the purée. Serve.

SWISS EGGS

Place 1 tbsp (15 mL) cream in a small ramekin or egg mold. Sprinkle with a small spoonful of grated cheese. Break one egg into the cream and add salt and pepper. Dot the egg yolk with butter.

Place the ramekin in a saucepan with just enough boiling water to cover the bottom. Cover the saucepan and poach the egg over low heat 3 to 8 minutes or until it is cooked to taste. Serve without unmolding.

CREAMY SCRAMBLED EGGS

In England, scrambled eggs are appropriately called buttered eggs, since good scrambled eggs require a great deal of butter. They are best if served as soon as they are ready. It is entertaining to cook them in an electric skillet or on a hotplate in front of your guests.

3 tbsp (45 mL) butter
5 eggs
salt and pepper to taste
(or seasoned salt and pepper)
¼ cup (50 mL) cream
2 tbsp (30 mL) chopped chives
or green onions
bacon

Melt the butter in a heavy saucepan or medium-size skillet. Beat the eggs until light but not foamy. Add salt and pepper. Pour into the melted butter and cook over moderate heat. Stir constantly with a wooden spoon, scraping the edges of the pan to prevent the eggs from sticking. When they start to set, add the cream all at once and keep stirring until the consistency is creamy. Serve immediately on a heated dish. Sprinkle with the chives or green onions. Garnish with fried or broiled bacon.

SCRAMBLED EGGS WITH CORN

2 tbsp (30 mL) butter
pinch of curry powder
1 16-oz (450-mL) can corn niblets, well drained
salt and pepper to taste
4 eggs, beaten

Melt the butter in a skillet. Add the curry. Blend well and add the drained corn together with the eggs. Salt and pepper to taste.

Cook following the directions for *Creamy Scrambled Eggs*. Serve on toast rubbed with a garlic clove and buttered.

SCRAMBLED EGGS WITH CROUTONS

2 tbsp (30 mL) butter
1 cup (250 mL) diced bread
3 tbsp (45 mL) parsley, minced
4 eggs, lightly beaten
salt and pepper to taste

Melt 1 tbsp (15 mL) butter. Add the diced bread and brown over low heat. Remove half and mix with the parsley. Set aside.

Add the remaining 1 tbsp (15 mL) of butter and the beaten

Scrambled Eggs with Croutons

Lobster Omelet

eggs to the remaining croutons. Salt and pepper to taste. Cook following the directions for *Creamy Scrambled Eggs*. Place on a heated platter and garnish with parsleyed croutons.

SCRAMBLED EGGS WITH ONIONS

1 onion, chopped
2 tbsp (30 mL) butter
pinch of savory
pinch of sugar
4 eggs, lightly beaten
salt and pepper to taste
rice or buttered toast

🍃 Brown the onion in butter over medium heat. Add the savory and sugar.

🍃 Add the eggs, salt and pepper to taste and cook following the directions for *Creamy Scrambled Eggs*.

Serve on a bed of boiled rice or on buttered toast.

AMERICAN SCRAMBLED EGGS

6 slices bacon
3 tomatoes, halved
salt and pepper to taste
sugar
6 eggs
French-fried potatoes

🍃 Brown the bacon slices over low heat, turning once in the skillet. Remove and set aside.

🍃 Place the halved tomatoes in the remaining bacon grease. Add salt and pepper and sprinkle with a pinch of sugar. Cook 5 minutes over low heat.

🍃 Cook the eggs according to the the directions for *Creamy Scrambled Eggs*. Place in the cen-

ter of a heated platter. Arrange the tomatoes on one side, the bacon on the other. Garnish each end of the platter with the French-fried potatoes. Serve very hot.

LOBSTER OMELET

This makes a very tasty and elegant lunch. Equal quantities of crab or chopped shrimp can be used instead of the lobster. If desired, prepare at the table in an electric skillet set at 375°F (190°C).

2 tbsp (30 mL) butter
6 to 8 green onions, chopped
2 stalks celery, diced
½ cup (125 mL) clam juice or chicken broth
2 tbsp (30 mL) soy sauce
pinch of sugar
1½ to 2 cups (375 to 500 mL) diced cooked lobster
salt to taste
6 eggs, beaten
6 tbsp (90 mL) light cream
pinch of pepper
1 tbsp (15 mL) peanut oil or butter

🍃 Melt 1 tbsp (15 mL) butter in a large skillet. Add the green onions and celery and simmer over low heat until they are softened. Add the clam juice or chicken broth, soy sauce, sugar, lobster and salt to taste.

🍃 Simmer about 10 minutes, uncovered, until the sauce is smooth.

🍃 Beat the eggs with the cream and a pinch of pepper. Heat the peanut oil or the remaining butter in an omelet pan or skillet.

❧ TECHNIQUE ❧

LOBSTER OMELET

1 Melt the butter in a skillet. Add the green onions and celery. Let simmer.

2 Add the clam juice, soy sauce, sugar and lobster. Salt to taste. Simmer uncovered.

3 Put the eggs, cream and a pinch of pepper in a bowl.

4 Beat the eggs.

Pour in the egg mixture and cook according to the general directions for omelets (see page 354).

🍃 As soon as it is ready, place the omelet on a heated dish and surround with the hot lobster sauce.

PIPERADE

This specialty of Basque cuisine is a sort of highly seasoned scrambled egg dish, delicious when served either hot or cold.

1 lb (500 g) tomatoes
2 green peppers
2 tbsp (30 mL) butter
salt and pepper to taste
4 thin slices ham
¾ cup (175 mL) croutons
½ cup (125 mL) milk
6 eggs

🍃 Peel and cube the tomatoes. Remove the cores of two large green peppers and cut the peppers in thin strips. Heat the butter in a skillet. Toss in the vegetables, add salt and pepper and cook over low heat for about 20 minutes. Stir occasionally.

🍃 Fry the ham on a griddle or skillet for 1 minute, then set aside and keep warm until needed. Let the croutons soak in the milk until soft. Squeeze out the excess liquid with your hand.

🍃 Beat the eggs lightly and mix with the soft croutons. Add the vegetables, stir and cook until the mixture begins to set. Serve on a warmed platter with the ham on top.

🍃 This recipe makes enough for four people, even very hungry ones!

CHEESE OMELET "BAVEUSE"

This is the French type of omelet—creamy and light. It is easy to make and always a success.

6 eggs
6 tbsp (90 mL) cold water or milk
3 tbsp (45 mL) butter
salt and pepper to taste
½ cup (125 mL) grated Swiss or mild Cheddar cheese
2 tbsp (30 mL) grated Parmesan cheese
1 tbsp (15 mL) minced parsley

🍃 Beat the eggs along with the water, salt and pepper. Melt the butter in a skillet over high heat. Pour in the eggs. Do not stir. Lift the pan off the burner and tilt it so that the egg mixture covers the entire bottom of the pan. Lift the edge of the egg mixture with a spatula to let some of the egg mixture run underneath the set egg.

🍃 Continue lifting and tilting until most of the egg mixture is set; the center will remain soft.

🍃 Sprinkle the grated cheeses on top. The heat of the eggs will melt the cheese. Fold the omelet and slide it out of the pan onto a warmed serving platter. Sprinkle with the parsley and serve garnished with watercress.

POTATO OMELET

4 eggs
2 large potatoes
1 onion, chopped
salt and pepper to taste
4 slices salt pork
parsley, minced

🍃 Beat the eggs. Peel and grate the potatoes and add them to the eggs together with the onion. Season with salt and pepper.

🍃 Heat the salt pork in a skillet until crisp and golden brown, then pour the egg mixture over it. Cover and cook over low heat for 15 minutes. Flip the omelet with a large spatula and cook the other side for 5 to 8 minutes over low heat. Slide onto a warmed plate, sprinkle with parsley and serve.

COUNTRY-STYLE OMELET

2 tbsp (30 mL) butter
2 tbsp (30 mL) vegetable oil
4 raw potatoes, peeled and diced
5 slices bacon
1 onion, chopped
pinch of savory
½ cup (125 mL) diced cheese or minced parsley
4 to 6 eggs, lightly beaten
2 tbsp (30 mL) cold water
salt and pepper to taste

🍃 Heat the butter and oil in a skillet. Brown the diced potatoes on all sides over medium heat for approximately 20 minutes, or until crisp.

❧ Cut the bacon in 2-in. (5-cm) pieces, then add to the potatoes together with the onion and savory. Stir until the bacon is cooked.

❧ Sprinkle the diced cheese or minced parsley over the potatoes, but do not mix. Cover and heat very slowly for 2 minutes.

❧ Beat the eggs with the cold water. Salt and pepper to taste. Pour over the potatoes. Cook over medium heat according to the general directions for omelets (on page 354). Serve immediately.

MUSHROOM OMELET

½ lb (250 g) mushrooms
4 tbsp (60 mL) butter
1 clove garlic, minced
salt and pepper to taste
5 eggs

❧ Slice the mushrooms and fry in the butter with the garlic. Add salt and pepper.

❧ Beat the eggs. Pour over the mushrooms and cook according to the general directions for omelets (on page 354).

ONION OMELET

2 white onions, thinly sliced
2 tbsp (30 mL) butter
¼ cup (50 mL) cream
salt and pepper to taste
pinch of nutmeg
5 eggs

Mushroom Omelet

❧ Cook the onions in butter until golden brown, stirring often.

❧ Add the cream, salt, pepper and nutmeg. Boil over high heat for 10 minutes or until the cream thickens slightly.

❧ Beat the eggs (without adding cream or milk). Pour them over the onion and cream mixture and cook according to the general directions for omelets (on page 354).

OMELET MAGDA

4 eggs
¼ cup (50 mL) grated cheese
½ tsp (2 mL) prepared mustard
chives or green onions
parsley to taste
croutons

❧ Beat the eggs with the grated cheese, prepared mustard, chives or green onions and parsley.

❧ Cook according to the general directions for omelets (on page 354) and serve surrounded with croutons.

BAKED CHEESE OMELET

4 eggs
3 cups (750 mL) milk
2 cups (500 mL) fresh bread-crumbs
½ lb (250 g) mild cheese, grated
1 tsp (5 mL) salt
1 tbsp (15 mL) Worcestershire sauce
minced parsley to taste

❧ Beat the eggs lightly. Add the milk, cheese, breadcrumbs, salt, Worcestershire sauce and parsley.

❧ Turn into a buttered ovenproof glass dish. Place in a dripping pan

Savoyarde Omelet

containing 1 in. (2 cm) hot water. Bake in a 375°F (190°C) oven for approximately 30 minutes. To test, insert a knife into the center; if it emerges perfectly clean, the omelet is done.

SAVOYARDE OMELET

3 raw potatoes, diced
3 tbsp (45 mL) olive oil
1 cup (250 mL) grated cheese
5 eggs

🍠 Cook the potatoes in the oil over medium heat, stirring often, until well browned and completely cooked (about 25 minutes).
🍠 Sprinkle with grated cheese.
🍠 Beat the eggs. Pour over the potatoes and cook according to the general directions for omelets (see page 354).

SCOTTISH OMELET

½ cup (125 mL) hot milk
½ cup (125 mL) fresh breadcrumbs
4 eggs, separated
½ tsp (2 mL) salt
2 tsp (10 mL) butter
creamed corn

🍠 Pour the hot milk over the breadcrumbs.
🍠 Beat the egg whites and the yolks separately. Add the soaked breadcrumbs and the salt to the yolks. Fold the whites into the mixture.
🍠 Melt the butter in a skillet and pour the egg mixture into it.
🍠 Cover and cook over low heat for 10 to 15 minutes without stirring. Serve with creamed corn.

SPANISH OMELET

1 tbsp (15 mL) vegetable oil
½ green pepper, minced
1 small onion, chopped
¼ cup (50 mL) diced celery
2 fresh tomatoes, diced
1 tsp (5 mL) sugar
½ tsp (2 mL) salt
pinch of thyme
3 to 6 eggs

🍠 Heat the oil. Add the green pepper, onion and celery. Cover and simmer for 5 minutes.
🍠 Add the fresh tomatoes, sugar, salt and thyme. Simmer for 15 minutes.
🍠 In the meantime, prepare a plain omelet with the eggs.
🍠 Pour the vegetable mixture over the cooked omelet and serve.

CHICKEN LIVER OMELET

2 chicken livers
1 tbsp (15 mL) butter
pinch of tarragon
salt and pepper to taste
1 tbsp (15 mL) tomato sauce
½ tsp (2 mL) butter
1 tbsp (15 mL) consommé
4 eggs
2 tbsp (30 mL) parsley, minced

🍠 Brown the chicken livers in 1 tbsp (15 mL) butter over medium heat for 5 minutes. Add the tarragon. Salt and pepper to taste. Cut the livers into small pieces.

Simmer the tomato sauce with the ½ tsp (2 mL) butter and the consommé.

Prepare an omelet with the eggs (see page 354). Garnish with the liver. Fold the omelet and pour the tomato sauce over it. Sprinkle with parsley.

OMELET BONNE FEMME

8 or 9 slices bacon
1 onion, thinly sliced
2 mushrooms (optional)
6 eggs

Dice the bacon and brown over low heat. Remove the bacon bits from the skillet but leave the melted fat. Fry the onion in the remaining fat until brown and tender.

Thinly slice the mushrooms and add to the onion. Cook for 2 minutes.

Beat the eggs and pour over the mixture. Cook over medium heat until the eggs begin to set around the edges. Sprinkle the bacon on the omelet and finish cooking.

OMELET EPICURE AU GRATIN

I think this is the best egg dish of all. It's fancy when made with shrimp, but also delicious when made with leftover chicken or canned lobster.

3 tbsp (45 mL) butter
3 tbsp (45 mL) flour
2 cups (500 mL) milk

1 box frozen peeled shrimp or 1 cup (250 mL) cooked chicken breasts, sliced
1 tsp (5 mL) capers
salt and pepper to taste
½ tsp (2 mL) basil
3 eggs
2 tbsp (30 mL) cream
4 tbsp (60 mL) grated cheese
3 tbsp (45 mL) fine breadcrumbs

Make a white sauce with the butter, flour and milk (see page 46). When smooth and creamy, add the thawed shrimp (or the chicken) and the capers. Salt and pepper to taste. Simmer 15 minutes. Add the basil.

Butter generously a shallow baking dish and heat it in a 400°F (200°C) oven for a few minutes. Beat the eggs with the cream and pour into the heated dish. Bake 10 minutes or until the omelet is puffed up and cooked.

Pour the hot cream sauce over the omelet. Sprinkle with the grated cheese and breadcrumbs. Broil until the cheese is browned.

OMELET SOUFFLÉ

2 tbsp (30 mL) butter
2 tbsp (30 mL) flour
1 cup (250 mL) milk
2 green onions, chopped
½ tsp (2 mL) salt
pinch of pepper
4 egg yolks, beaten
4 egg whites, stiffly beaten

Prepare a white sauce with the butter, flour and milk (see page 46). When smooth and creamy, add the green onions, salt and pepper.

Add the beaten egg yolks to the sauce, stirring vigorously. Carefully fold in the stiffly beaten egg whites.

Omelet Soufflé

❦ TECHNIQUE ❦

OMELET SOUFFLÉ

1 Melt the butter in a saucepan. Add the flour and mix well.

2 Add the milk, then cook until thick. Add the green onions, salt and pepper.

3 Add the yolks and stir vigorously.

4 Beat the whites until stiff.

Pour the mixture into a greased pie dish. Bake in a preheated 325°F (160°C) oven for 20 minutes.

STRAWBERRY OMELET

4 eggs
2 tbsp (30 mL) butter
3 tbsp (45 mL) sugar
1 package fresh or frozen strawberries
whipped cream

Arrange on a tray: eggs, a bowl, a beater, a dish of butter, the sugar, the strawberries in an attractive glass or crystal bowl, and a pitcher of cream.

At the table: break the eggs into the bowl and beat with the sugar. Melt the butter in a chafing dish and pour the eggs into it. Cook, lifting the edges of the omelet and letting the uncooked eggs run underneath. When cooked, roll and serve each person a portion garnished with very cold strawberries and cream.

BACON AND EGGS

Place the required number of bacon strips side by side in a cold skillet. Cook over medium heat approximately 2 minutes on one side, then turn and cook 1 minute more. Remove the bacon fat from the skillet as it accumulates; this makes the bacon crispier and more digestible.

Break the required number of eggs around, between or over the

Strawberry Omelet

bacon. Cover the skillet and cook over very low heat for 2 to 5 minutes, depending on whether you want the eggs soft or well done.

Bacon and eggs cooked in this manner are very easy to digest and the eggs are never dry.

FRIED EGGS BORDELAISE

½ lb (250 g) fresh mushrooms
1 clove garlic
1 small onion
2 fresh tomatoes, cut in small pieces
pinch of sugar
1 tbsp (15 mL) parsley, minced
salt and pepper to taste
2 tbsp (30 mL) butter
1 tsp (5 mL) flour
½ cup (125 mL) red wine
4 eggs, fried in butter

Slice the mushrooms, garlic and onion and mix together with the tomatoes. Add the sugar and some of the parsley, along with salt and pepper to taste. Mix thoroughly.

Make a sauce with the butter, flour and red wine. When thick and creamy, add the vegetable mixture. Cover and simmer for 20 minutes over low heat.

Pour into a warmed dish and top with the fried eggs. Garnish to taste with parsley and serve.

HAM AND EGGS

1 tbsp (15 mL) butter
4 slices ham
pinch of brown sugar
4 eggs
salt and pepper to taste

Fried Eggs des Landes

🌢 Melt the butter in a large skillet. Add the ham slices and cook over low heat for 3 minutes. Turn and sprinkle with brown sugar. Cook for 3 minutes more. Remove from the skillet and place on a warmed platter.

🌢 Break the eggs into the remaining fat in the skillet and cook to taste. When done, place an egg on each slice of ham. Salt and pepper to taste. Serve.

FRIED EGGS DES LANDES

1 onion, chopped
1 tbsp (15 mL) butter
4 sausages
2 tomatoes
pinch of sugar
1 bay leaf

salt and pepper to taste
4 to 6 eggs

🌢 Fry the onion in the butter.
🌢 Slice the sausages thin and cut the tomatoes into pieces. Add these to the onions, along with the sugar and bay leaf. Simmer over low heat for 5 to 10 minutes. Salt and pepper to taste.
🌢 Fry the eggs. Place in a warmed dish and surround with the sauce.

DUCHESS MOLDED EGGS

🌢 Butter ramekins, break an egg into each and cook according to the directions for molded eggs (see page 355).
🌢 Prepare Duchess potatoes (page 458). Unmold the eggs onto the prepared potatoes and serve with tomato sauce or a brown sauce.

CARDINAL MOLDED EGGS

🌢 Prepare a medium white sauce (see page 46). Add lobster to taste, a pinch of tarragon, salt and pepper.
🌢 Heat puff-pastry shells.
🌢 Top each with a molded egg and nap with the sauce.

PORTUGUESE MOLDED EGGS

🌢 Butter ramekins or small molds. Sprinkle with minced parsley or chives. Break an egg into each one. Cook over low heat in a covered saucepan with a little hot water in the bottom.
🌢 Brown tomato halves in butter. Salt and pepper and sprinkle with a pinch of sugar. Unmold each cooked egg onto a tomato half. Garnish with a spoonful of warmed chili sauce.

ALSATIAN EGGS

2 cups (500 mL) water
1 tbsp (15 mL) vinegar
½ cup (125 mL) milk
6 eggs
6 tbsp (90 mL) liver pâté
paprika
1 envelope unflavored gelatin
2 cups (500 mL) consommé
lettuce
1 tbsp (15 mL) mayonnaise

🐟 Heat together the water, vinegar and milk. Break the eggs into a soup bowl and slide them slowly into the hot liquid. Cover and remove from the heat; let the eggs stand in the hot liquid for 15 minutes. Remove the eggs and drain thoroughly on a paper towel.

🐟 Trim each egg neatly and place on an individual plate. Top each egg with 1 tbsp (15 mL) liver pâté. Sprinkle lightly with paprika.

🐟 Soak the unflavored gelatin in ¼ cup (50 mL) cold water for 5 minutes. Heat the consommé. Add the gelatin and stir until it is dissolved. Pour into a dish and refrigerate until set.

🐟 To serve, break the gelatin into small pieces with 2 forks and place around the poached eggs.

🐟 These eggs may also be molded into the gelatin; place each neatly trimmed poached egg in a small individual mold and top with some of the liver paté. Then cover with slightly chilled gelatin mixture. Refrigerate to set. Unmold onto a bed of shredded lettuce and garnish with 1 tbsp (15 mL) mayonnaise.

BAKED EGGS WITH POTATOES

6 small potatoes
6 tsp (30 mL) bacon fat
6 eggs
6 tsp (30 mL) milk or cream
salt and pepper to taste
grated cheese

🐟 Peel the potatoes and slice thin. Heat the fat in a large skillet. Cook the potatoes over medium heat, stirring often, until brown and tender.

🐟 Place in a pie plate. Break the eggs over the top and pour 1 tsp (5 mL) milk or cream over each egg. Salt and pepper to taste and sprinkle lightly with grated cheese.

🐟 Bake in a 500°F (260°C) oven for 5 to 8 minutes.

HARD-COOKED EGGS WITH GRATED CHEESE

4 eggs, hard-cooked
2 tbsp (30 mL) butter
2 large onions, thinly sliced
1 tbsp (15 mL) soft butter
3 tbsp (45 mL) flour
1½ cups (375 mL) milk
1 cup (250 mL) grated cheese

🐟 Slice the hard-cooked eggs and place in the bottom of a baking dish.

🐟 Melt the butter, add the onions, cover and cook over low heat for 20 minutes. Be careful not to burn the onions.

🐟 After 20 minutes, add the soft butter and flour to the onions. Stir well and add the milk. Cook, stirring constantly, until the sauce is creamy. Add the cheese. Stir over low heat until melted.

🐟 Pour this sauce over the egg slices. Cook for 10 minutes in a 350°F (180°C) oven. Or heat the eggs and sauce in a double boiler.

CHEESE AND EGG CASSEROLE

6 hard-cooked eggs, sliced
2 cups (500 mL) fresh breadcrumbs
1 cup (250 mL) grated cheese
salt and pepper to taste
½ cup (125 mL) light cream
2 tbsp (30 mL) butter
pinch of nutmeg

🐟 Place the eggs, breadcrumbs and grated cheese in alternate layers in a baking dish. Salt and pepper each layer.

🐟 Heat the cream, butter and nutmeg together without boiling. Pour over the egg mixture. Bake in a 350°F (180°C) oven for 30 to 35 minutes. Serve hot.

MADEIRA EGGS

1 onion, chopped
½ pound (250 g) mushrooms, chopped
2 tbsp (30 mL) butter
¼ cup (50 mL) Madeira wine or sherry
salt and pepper to taste
12 eggs, hard-cooked

🐟 Fry the onion and mushrooms in butter until the onion is lightly browned.

🐟 Add the Madeira or sherry. Salt and pepper to taste. Cut the eggs in half lengthwise. Place in a warmed serving dish and top with the wine sauce. Serve with buttered toast triangles.

Eggs Benedict

EGGS BENEDICT

1 poached or molded egg
1 round of bread, toasted
1 thin slice ham
Hollandaise sauce

🍃 Place the egg on the round of toast. Top with a slice of ham. Cover with *Hollandaise Sauce* (see page 54). Serve.
🍃 One recipe of *Hollandaise Sauce* will be sufficient for 6 eggs. The toast rounds may be replaced with English muffin halves, toasted and buttered.

EGGS IN WHITE SAUCE

2 tbsp (30 mL) butter
2 tbsp (30 mL) flour
1 cup (250 mL) milk

1 tbsp (15 mL) parsley
pinch of nutmeg
1 tsp (5 mL) vinegar
salt and pepper to taste
4 eggs, hard-cooked

🍃 Melt the butter. Add the flour and blend. Add the milk. Cook over medium heat, stirring constantly, until the sauce is thick and creamy.
🍃 Flavor with the parsley and nutmeg. Add the vinegar. Salt and pepper to taste. Mix together. Add the eggs, sliced or quartered. Serve.

CREAMED EGGS SOUBISE

2 tbsp (30 mL) butter
2 tbsp (30 mL) flour
1 cup (250 mL) milk
salt and pepper to taste

2 onions, thinly sliced
1 tbsp (15 mL) butter
6 hard-cooked eggs, sliced or quartered

🍃 Make a white sauce with 2 tbsp (30 mL) butter, the flour and the milk. Salt and pepper to taste.
🍃 Fry the onions in 1 tbsp (15 mL) butter. Add the onions to the sauce, together with the sliced or quartered hard-cooked eggs.
🍃 If you wish, serve the eggs in hot puff-pastry shells.

LOST EGGS

🍃 Butter a dish. Separate the eggs and place the yolks in the buttered dish. Beat the whites until stiff.
🍃 Pour a spoonful of cream over each yolk. Place the beaten egg whites around the yolks like a crown, pushing the yolks toward the center. Salt and pepper to taste. Bake in a 400°F (200°C) oven for 10 to 15 minutes.

EGGS IN A NEST

Here's a new way of serving eggs, bacon and tomatoes. It's a light, pleasant dish that can be prepared ahead. Simply bake, then sprinkle with chopped chives or parsley and serve with hot rolls or buttered toast.

6 medium tomatoes
salt and pepper to taste
6 eggs
12 slices bacon
3 tbsp (45 mL) chives or parsley,

finely chopped
hot rolls or toast (buttered)

🍃 Wash the tomatoes and hollow them out. Salt and pepper the inside of each. Place them side by side in a baking dish. Break an egg into each tomato and refrigerate until ready to cook.

🍃 When close to mealtime, preheat the oven to 350°F (180°C). Arrange the bacon on the rack of a broiler pan. Bake both the bacon and the tomatoes, uncovered, for 10 minutes. When the tomatoes are ready, the bacon should be crisp and browned. Arrange the bacon around the tomatoes and sprinkle the eggs with the chives or parsley.

SAFFRON EGGS

Saffron Eggs is a Spanish dish. You can prepare this recipe ahead of time and heat it when you're ready to serve it.

8 eggs, hard-cooked
2 tbsp (30 mL) butter
2 tbsp (30 mL) flour
1 cup (250 mL) milk
or light cream
¼ tsp (1 mL) salt
parsley, minced
¼ tsp (1 mL) pepper
½ tsp (2 mL) saffron
1 tbsp (15 mL) breadcrumbs

🍃 Cut 8 hard-cooked eggs in half lengthwise. Remove the yolks and mash them until they are smooth. Put the whites aside. Melt the butter in a skillet, add the flour

while stirring constantly, and add the milk or cream. Cook the sauce, stirring slowly and constantly, until the mixture just starts to boil. Season with ¼ tsp (1 mL) salt.

🍃 Mix half the sauce with the mashed yolks along with the parsley, pepper and ¼ tsp (1 mL) salt. Stuff the mixture into the whites and arrange in a baking dish. Stir the saffron into the remaining sauce and pour it over the top of the eggs. Sprinkle with the breadcrumbs, dot with butter. Bake about 10 minutes in a preheated 425°F (220°C) oven.

🍃 This recipe serves 6 people. Serve with bread, a green salad and a glass of dry sherry.

RED PICKLED EGGS

1½ tsp (7 mL) salt
1 tsp (5 mL) whole cloves
1 tsp (5 mL) peppercorns
½ tsp (2 mL) celery seed
2 cups (500 mL) white vinegar
1 cup (250 mL) pickled beet juice
1½ cups (375 mL) cold water
12 to 24 eggs, hard-cooked

🍃 Place the spices in a cheesecloth bag.

🍃 Bring the white vinegar, beet juice, cold water and the bag of spices to a boil. Let cool.

🍃 Place the hard-cooked eggs in a glass jar. Pour the vinegar mixture on top. Cover and refrigerate for a few days before using.

PICKLED EGGS

🍃 Follow the recipe for *Red Pickled Eggs*, replacing the pickled beet juice with ½ cup (125 mL) water and ½ cup (125 mL) vinegar.

EGGS RÉMOULADE

A classic of French cuisine, and one of my favorite picnic foods. This is a hard-cooked or poached egg dish served with a superb sauce that also goes beautifully with shrimp or salads or with cold boiled salmon.

6 eggs, poached or hard-cooked
6 small tomatoes
salt and pepper to taste
6 slices buttered toast, crusts removed
2 hard-cooked egg yolks
1 raw egg yolk
½ cup (125 mL) vegetable oil
2 tbsp (30 mL) lemon juice
½ tsp (2 mL) prepared mustard
2 small gherkins, minced
2 anchovies, minced (optional)
1 tbsp (15 mL) capers
1 tbsp (15 mL) parsley, minced

🍃 If the eggs are poached, drain on paper towels. If they are hard-cooked, shell. Scoop out the tomatoes and sprinkle the insides with salt and pepper. Turn upside-down on a plate for 25 minutes. Prepare the toast and set aside.

🍃 Now it's time to make the Rémoulade sauce. Press the 2 hard-cooked egg yolks through a sieve, then add the raw egg yolk. Reserve the cooked whites. Beat the yolks until well blended. Add the oil very slowly, beating constantly. When the mixture is as smooth as mayonnaise, gradually add the lemon juice and mustard, while stirring. Then fold in the gherkins, anchovies, capers and parsley. Season to taste.

🍃 To serve, place each tomato on a slice of buttered toast. Fill the tomato with a poached or hard-cooked egg. Spoon as much sauce as you wish on top. Garnish with slivers of the hard-cooked egg whites.

HOT STUFFED EGGS

6 eggs, hard-cooked
6 mushrooms, minced
1 tbsp (15 mL) butter
1 tsp (5 mL) tomato paste
1 tsp (5 mL) light cream
3 tbsp (45 mL) grated cheese
6 tbsp (90 mL) Hollandaise sauce
salt and pepper to taste

🍃 Cut the eggs in two lengthwise. Remove the yolks without damaging the whites. Mash the yolks with a fork. Add the mushrooms after frying them in butter for 1 minute. Then add the tomato paste, cream and grated cheese. Mix well. Salt and pepper to taste. Stuff the whites with this mixture.

🍃 Place the stuffed eggs in a baking dish and heat in a 300°F (150°C) oven for 5 to 10 minutes. Garnish each egg half with a large spoonful of *Hollandaise Sauce* (see page 54). Serve immediately.

SCOTCH EGGS

5 eggs, hard-cooked
2 tbsp (30 mL) bacon fat
1 onion, chopped
1 clove garlic, minced
1 tsp (5 mL) curry or chutney
1½ tbsp (25 mL) flour
1 lb (500 g) ground beef
½ cup (125 mL) water
1 tsp (5 mL) salt
1 egg, beaten
1 tbsp (15 mL) water
¾ cup (175 mL) breadcrumbs

🍃 Shell the hard-cooked eggs and place in a bowl of cold water.

🍃 Heat the bacon fat and fry the onion and garlic. Add the curry or chutney and the flour. Stir just enough to mix, then add the ground beef. Stir, crushing the meat with a fork. Add the water and the salt. Simmer, uncovered, until the meat is well cooked and the liquid is completely evaporated. Season to taste. Let cool.

🍃 When the meat mixture has cooled, take a few spoonfuls and carefully cover each egg. Next, roll each egg in the beaten egg mixed with the water, and then roll it in the breadcrumbs. Fry at low heat in butter or bacon fat until brown on all sides.

BREAD AND CHEESE FONDUE

A nice, creamy brunch dish that is usually served with crisp celery or cucumber sticks. If you like, add fish, lobster or crab meat.

6 slices bread, crusts removed
½ cup (125 mL) soft butter
2 tbsp (30 mL) prepared mustard
2½ cups (625 mL) diced mild Cheddar
3 eggs

Hot Stuffed Eggs

2¾ cups (675 mL) milk
1 tsp (5 mL) salt
¼ tsp (1 mL) pepper
¼ (1 mL) sage or basil

❧ Butter a loaf pan. Spread each slice of bread generously first with butter, then with mustard. Make alternate layers of the bread and the diced cheese, without packing them down.

❧ If using lobster or crab meat, reduce the cheese to 1½ cups (375 mL) and mix it with 16 oz (500 g) of lobster or crab meat, fresh or canned.

❧ Beat the eggs lightly, add the milk, salt, pepper and sage or basil. Pour over the bread. Cover and refrigerate 3 to 5 hours.

❧ Bake in a preheated 350°F (180°C) oven for 30 to 45 minutes or until a knife inserted in the center comes out clean. Serve hot.

JELLIED EGGS À LA GRECQUE

6 eggs
1 can consommé, undiluted
1 tbsp (15 mL) tomato paste
2 tbsp (30 mL) lemon juice
½ tsp (2 mL) sugar
pinch of basil
1 envelope unflavored gelatin
½ cup (125 mL) cold water
6 sprigs parsley
lettuce or watercress
mayonnaise to taste

❧ Cook the eggs according to the directions for molded eggs (see page 355).

❧ Heat the consommé with the tomato paste, lemon juice, sugar and basil.

❧ Soak the gelatin in the cold water for 5 minutes. Add to the hot consommé and stir to dissolve the gelatin. Refrigerate until the gelatin mixture is lukewarm. Also refrigerate the mold.

❧ Pour a little of the gelatin mixture into the well-oiled mold, tilting the mold in order to coat the sides and bottom. Place the parsley sprigs in the bottom, cover with the eggs placed side by side, and pour the remaining gelatin on top. Refrigerate until firm. Serve on a bed of lettuce or watercress. Garnish with mayonnaise to taste.

CONVENT STUFFED EGGS

In my boarding-school days, this dish was served on Fridays as a vegetarian meal. I have never stopped making it. Hot or cold, it makes an excellent picnic dish or a delicious appetizer before a barbecue meal.

4 eggs, hard-cooked
½ lb (250 g) cottage cheese
1 tbsp (15 mL) grated Cheddar cheese
salt and pepper to taste
pinch of nutmeg
1 tbsp (15 mL) minced parsley
1 tbsp (15 mL) flour
1 egg, lightly beaten
2 tbsp (30 mL) water
1 cup (250 mL) fine breadcrumbs
peanut oil

❧ Peel the eggs and cut in half. Put the yolks in a bowl and mix with the cottage cheese, grated cheese, salt and pepper. Beat with a hand beater. Add nutmeg and parsley.

❧ Fill the whites with the mixture and shape so that each half resembles a whole egg. Roll each egg in the flour, dip it in the egg beaten with the water, then roll it in the breadcrumbs. Set on a plate. Refrigerate 20 minutes. Fry in hot oil until golden brown. Serve.

EGG SALAD

6 eggs, hard-cooked
1 cup (250 mL) diced celery
2 tbsp (30 mL) diced green pepper
5 or 6 green onions, chopped
¼ cup (50 mL) mayonnaise
1 tbsp (15 mL) lemon juice
1 tsp (5 mL) salt
pepper to taste
lettuce
6 strips fried bacon

❧ Cut the hard-cooked eggs into large pieces.

❧ Mix together in a large bowl the eggs, celery, green pepper and onions, stirring with a fork.

❧ Blend the mayonnaise, lemon juice, salt and pepper. Add to the eggs and stir delicately with a fork in order to avoid breaking up the eggs too much.

❧ Serve on a bed of lettuce. Garnish with the fried bacon, drained on paper towels and cut into small pieces.

EGGS MIMOSA

This should make you dream of the South of France and its beautiful mimosa. Very nice with a slice of buttered crusty bread.

2 eggs, hard-cooked
few spoonfuls mayonnaise
½ head lettuce

❧ Cut the shelled eggs in half and remove the yolks. Fill the whites with mayonnaise and set on a plate. Finely shred the lettuce and sprinkle over the whites. Grate the egg yolks over the lettuce and serve.

MY MOTHER'S FRENCH TOAST

8 slices bread
3 eggs
pinch of salt
pinch of nutmeg
½ cup (125 mL) maple syrup
1 cup (250 mL) milk
¼ cup (50 mL) light cream
butter

❧ Cut the bread slices in half. Beat the eggs with the salt, nutmeg and maple syrup. Blend well with the milk and cream.

❧ In an electric skillet set at 350°F (180°C), melt enough butter to cover the bottom. Do not let the butter brown. Quickly dip the bread in the egg mixture, one piece at a time. Fry on both sides.

❧ When cooked, the bread is crisp on the outside and creamy on the inside. Serve this French toast with apple jelly or fresh cranberry sauce.

SANDWICHES

THE COMPONENTS OF A GOOD SANDWICH

Sandwiches are part of our everyday life, yet we make them mechanically, using the same ingredients time after time. We forget that a good sandwich does not have to contain ham, cheese or tomato. Here are some simple recipes that will help you prepare your own delicious and original sandwich treats.

THE BREAD
Since bread constitutes ⅔ of a sandwich, it can hardly be ignored. Why not vary it on occasion? Or you could combine breads, for instance, one slice of white bread and one slice of whole-wheat bread. You'll find that a change of bread alters the appearance and taste of the sandwich.

🍂 Use fresh or day-old bread, cutting it to produce slices of equal size. The slices should be neither too thick nor too thin (although tea sandwiches should be sliced very thin). Leave the crust on from time to time; it will lend a different texture to the sandwich and also prevent it from drying out too quickly.

BUTTER AND OTHER SPREADS
For a sandwich spread, you can use butter, margarine or cream cheese or a mixture of ½ butter and ½ margarine or cheese. With certain rich fillings, like peanut butter, it is better not to use a spread.

🍂 Avoid using hard butter; it is difficult to spread and unpleasant to bite into. On the other hand, butter that is too soft becomes oily. Butter that has been whipped spreads easily, so you might want to prepare a large quantity of whipped butter to be used as you need it. Margarine and cream cheese can also be whipped.

🍂 To whip a spread, let the chosen ingredient soften at room temperature. Then, using an electric beater, whip until frothy and light. Place in a plastic container, seal hermetically and refrigerate. Take it out of the refrigerator 30 to 60 minutes before using; it will soften much more quickly than unwhipped butter.

🍂 It is important to spread the entire surface of the bread so that the filling will not soften the bread.

FILLINGS
Preparing sandwiches does take time. If you are rushed, do not throw yourself into making party sandwiches; you will be better off making something simple, like ham and tomato sandwiches. There is nothing to stop you from adding your own personal touch to this simple fare, though. You could mix fresh parsley with mayonnaise as a spread for tomato sandwiches, for example, or flavor ham sandwiches with Dijon mustard or horseradish.

🍂 While certain sandwiches can be prepared in advance, others cannot. Sandwiches made with a filling that might soften the bread or give off a strong odor should not be made more than an hour in advance. In a lunchbox, for instance, the smell of some sandwich ingredients can penetrate and ruin other foods.

🍂 Sandwich meat should be sliced very thin or put through a meat-grinder. It is better to use 2 to 4 thin slices of meat than 1 thick slice; the sandwich will be easier to chew.

🍂 Sandwiches have more flavor if seasoned just to taste. Add a pinch of salt, a dash of pepper, a little mustard, catsup or mayonnaise to the filling to enhance the taste. Adding fresh herbs (parsley, chives, basil, etc.) or grated carrot, chutney or curry will produce a sandwich worthy of even the finest gourmet palate.

PRESENTATION
To make your sandwiches really inviting, serve them on a pretty plate and garnish them with a little parsley, a few lettuce leaves or some olives. You can even garnish a lunchbox sandwich before packing it. The simplest garnish can make any sandwich seem like something special.

MAKING SEVERAL SANDWICHES AT A TIME

Buy sliced bread. For small sandwiches, buy small loaves and slice them yourself.

🍂 Arrange the slices of bread in 2 rows of 4 to 8 slices each. Lay out more bread as required.

Prepare the filling. Using whipped or softened butter, spread it on the bread then add the filling.

If different fillings have been prepared, use only 1 kind at a time. When the sandwiches of a particular filling are made, stack and cut them. Wrap the sandwiches and set them aside before going on to the next filling.

To wrap sandwiches, place them in the middle of a piece of wax paper. Bring the opposite sides to the center, fold the 2 edges, then fold the remaining sides at each corner in parcel fashion and fold under the sandwiches.

To store the sandwiches for several hours, place unwrapped sandwiches on a platter that has been covered with wax paper, separating each type of sandwich with a sheet of wax paper. Cover the whole with aluminum foil or wax paper (in the latter case, top with a damp cloth). Refrigerate until 15 to 20 minutes before serving.

FRIED SANDWICHES

Prepare a meat, cheese or vegetable sandwich of your choice.

To make 4 sandwiches, beat 2 eggs with ¼ cup (50 mL) milk and a pinch of salt. Soak the sandwiches on both sides in this mixture.

Brown the sandwiches on both sides in a little hot butter over medium heat. Serve immediately.

Fried Sandwiches

MEAT SANDWICHES, HOT OR COLD

CHICKEN OR TURKEY
Place thin slices of meat between 2 slices of white bread.

Hot: cover with hot gravy or with cream of mushroom or chicken soup heated with ½ can of milk.

Cold: accompany with cranberry sauce or lettuce and mayonnaise.

BEEF
Place thin slices of meat between 2 slices of rye bread; sprinkle the meat with a few drops Worcestershire sauce, or a little chutney, or spread with mustard or horseradish.

Hot: pour a good, hot gravy or tomato sauce over the sandwich.

Cold: serve with catsup, chili sauce or pickles.

PORK
Hot: place thin slices of meat between 2 slices of white bread. Cover with well-heated barbecue sauce or gravy. Serve with applesauce or sliced apples cooked in butter.

Cold: spread 2 slices of white bread with roast-pork drippings or cretons, if available, and fill with several slices of meat. Serve with dill pickles, pickled beets or a cucumber salad.

❦ TECHNIQUE ❦

FRIED SANDWICHES

1   Beat the eggs, the milk and a pinch of salt.

2   Soak one side of the sandwich in the mixture.

3   Turn the sandwich over and soak the other side.

4   Brown on both sides in a little hot butter.

LAMB

Place thin slices of meat between 2 slices of whole-wheat bread.

🍃 Hot: spread butter on one slice of bread, mustard on the other and cover the sandwich with canned vegetable or celery soup heated with ½ cup (125 mL) milk. Garnish with mint jelly.

🍃 Cold: spread the bread with butter and mayonnaise, sprinkling the mayonnaise with a little curry or a spoonful of chopped nuts. Garnish with tomato wedges and sprinkle with chopped parsley.

BACON, CHICKEN-LIVER, AND MUSHROOM SANDWICH

3 slices bacon
¼ to ½ lb (125 to 250 g) chicken livers
1 small onion, chopped
1 cup (250 mL) mushrooms, sliced thin
pinch of thyme or tarragon
salt and pepper

🍃 Fry the bacon over low heat until crisp. Remove from skillet.

🍃 To the fat in the skillet, add the chicken livers, cut up small, the onion and the mushrooms. Sprinkle with thyme or tarragon and cook over high heat for 2 minutes, stirring constantly. Add salt and pepper to taste. Stir in the crisp bacon.

🍃 Spread the mixture on slices of whole-wheat bread. Makes 4 sandwiches.

🍃 Serve with a salad for a complete, light meal.

HOT HAM AND POTATO SANDWICH

4 slices ham, cooked
prepared mustard
8 slices rye bread
3 potatoes, cooked
1 small onion, minced
1 tbsp (15 mL) butter

🍃 Brush each slice of ham with the mustard and place on a slice of rye bread.

🍃 Dice the potatoes and spread over the ham. Top with a second slice of bread.

🍃 Melt the butter in a large skillet. Brown each sandwich in the melted butter over low heat, for 2 minutes on each side, turning the sandwich only once.

🍃 Cold ham and cold potatoes may be used, as the browning of the sandwich will heat all the ingredients.

🍃 For a complete, light meal, serve with coleslaw.

BEEF AND VEGETABLE SANDWICH

1 lb (500 g) ground beef
1 tbsp (15 mL) butter
1 medium onion, grated
2 tbsp (30 mL) flour
1 can vegetable soup, undiluted

🍃 Place the ground beef in a skillet and cook over high heat until well seared. Add the butter and blend with the meat.

🍃 Add the onion and flour; mix well, then add the vegetable soup. Stirring frequently, cook over

Bacon, Chicken-Liver and Mushroom Sandwich

[377]

Scrambled Egg and Bacon Sandwich

medium heat for 3 or 4 minutes, or until the sauce is creamy.

❧ To serve, spread some filling on a slice of toasted or untoasted bread and top with another slice of bread.

SCRAMBLED EGG AND BACON SANDWICH

4 to 6 strips bacon
4 eggs
1 tbsp (15 mL) parsley
1 green onion, chopped
salt and pepper
8 slices white bread

❧ Place the strips of bacon in a cold skillet. Cook over low heat until crisp. Remove from the skillet and chop lightly.

❧ Break the eggs into the bacon fat. Add the parsley and green onion, salt and pepper. Stir with a fork to scramble the eggs. Cook gently until the eggs are firm but not hard.

❧ Place the eggs on a slice of bread (this recipe yields 4 sandwiches). Sprinkle with a few pieces of bacon and top with the other slice of bread.

❧ Serve as is or brown in butter following the instructions for *Hot Ham and Potato Sandwiches* (see previous page).

3-DECKER SANDWICH

❧ Toast 3 slices of bread for each sandwich. Either remove the crusts or leave them, as you prefer.

❧ Spread each slice on one side with butter, mayonnaise or chili sauce.

❧ Cover the first slice with one or more of the ingredients shown as No. 1 in the following list. Top with the second slice, buttered side up. Cover this slice with the ingredients shown as No. 2 in the list.

❧ To cut, place cocktail picks in the 2 opposite corners and cut the sandwich on the diagonal, in 2 or 4 triangles.

❧ Garnish with potato chips, celery hearts, olives, pickles, etc.

BACON AND TOMATO
1. Bacon strips, fried
2. Tomato slices, lettuce

CHEESE, HAM, TOMATO
1. Thin slice of cheese, slice of ham
2. Tomato slices, lettuce

CHEESE, BACON, TOMATO
1. Swiss cheese, fried bacon
2. Tomato slices, lettuce

CHICKEN, BACON OR SALAMI, ONION, TOMATO
1. Sliced chicken, fried bacon or thinly sliced salami
2. Tomato slices and onion rings

CHICKEN, BACON, TOMATO
1. Thin chicken slices or chicken salad, fried bacon
2. Tomato slices, lettuce

CHICKEN, CHEESE, ROAST PORK
1. Thin chicken slices, Swiss cheese
2. Thin slices of roast pork, lettuce

LOBSTER, TOMATO, EGG
1. Lobster with a little mayonnaise, sliced tomatoes
2. Sliced hard-cooked egg, lettuce

HAM, CHEESE, BACON, TOMATO
1. Thin ham slices, cheese to taste
2. Fried bacon, tomato slices, lettuce

TUNA, EGG, TOMATO, BACON
1. Flaked tuna, sliced hard-cooked egg
2. Tomato slices, fried bacon, lettuce

GROUND BEEF SANDWICH FILLING

½ lb (250 g) ground beef
½ tsp (2 mL) salt
pinch of pepper
2 tbsp (30 mL) chopped dill pickle
1 tbsp (15 mL) chopped parsley
1 tbsp (15 mL) diced celery or onion
¼ cup (50 mL) mayonnaise or French dressing
5 rolls, cut in half

🍃 Brown the ground beef. Add the salt and pepper. Mix with the chopped dill pickle, the parsley, the celery or onion and the mayonnaise or French dressing.
🍃 Serve hot or cold on the rolls.

HAM SALAD SANDWICH FILLING

2 tbsp (30 mL) mayonnaise
¾ tsp (3 mL) prepared mustard
1 cup (250 mL) cooked ham cut in ½-in. (1-cm) cubes

½ cup (125 mL) diced celery
½ cup (125 mL) diced green pepper

🍃 Place mayonnaise and mustard in a blender jar. Cover and blend at maximum speed. Remove the stopper in the lid and add the remaining ingredients, a few pieces at a time, holding the stopper over the opening between each addition. Work quickly; the operation should take about 45 seconds.

FISH SANDWICH FILLINGS

Salmon, cucumber, onion and mayonnaise
Lobster or crab meat, green pepper, celery and mayonnaise
Tuna, grated apple, lemon juice and mayonnaise

Leftover fish, celery, chopped nuts and mayonnaise
Salmon, cream cheese and relish

VEGETABLE SANDWICH FILLINGS

Grated cabbage, chopped nuts, mayonnaise
Grated cabbage, grated carrots, green onion, mayonnaise
Grated carrot, celery, chili sauce, mayonnaise
Thinly sliced radishes, cucumber, green pepper, mayonnaise

MEAT SANDWICH FILLINGS

Bologna, coleslaw
Sliced chicken, grated apple, celery, mayonnaise
Chicken or turkey, chopped nuts, green olives, mayonnaise

3-Decker Sandwich

Ground roast beef, celery, onion, chili sauce, mayonnaise
Ground ham, cheese, pickles, mayonnaise
Ground veal, chives, celery, mayonnaise

ASSORTED SANDWICH FILLINGS

❧ Blend cream cheese with:

Fried bacon and a dash of relish
Minced onions and chili sauce
Chopped dates and peanuts
Diced green pepper, olives and celery
Peanut butter, orange zest, mustard, chopped parsley and a little orange juice
Thinly sliced radishes
Minced chives
Grated carrots and chopped nuts
Sardines and lemon juice

❧ Spread one slice of bread with peanut butter, the other with:

Applesauce and dates
Cream cheese and chopped prunes
Ham and relish
Sliced pork and mustard

❧ Blend together hard-cooked eggs and:

Fried bacon, chives and mayonnaise
Grated raw carrots, black olives and mayonnaise
Chopped chicken, celery, onions and mayonnaise
Minced ham, pickles, mustard and mayonnaise
Salmon, celery, relish and mayonnaise

❧ Blend together grated cheese and:

Minced ham and chili sauce
Fried bacon and catsup
Deviled ham and relish
Cottage cheese and minced peanuts
Strong Cheddar and cream cheese
Salami and olives

RIBBON SANDWICHES

❧ Use fresh or day-old bread. Alternate rows of whole-wheat bread with rows of white bread, 3 slices whole-wheat, 2 slices white. Use the spread of your choice and 1 or 2 different fillings.
❧ Place the 5 filled slices 1 on top of each other and press down firmly. Using a sharp knife, remove the crusts.
❧ Place the sandwiches on a platter and cover with wax paper and a damp cloth.
❧ Refrigerate 3 to 4 hours, then cut into ½-in. (1-cm) strips.

CHECKERED SANDWICHES

❧ Use 2 slices white bread, 2 slices whole-wheat bread. Spread with the filling of your choice.
❧ Place the 4 filled slices on top of each other and press down firmly. Remove the crusts using a sharp knife.
❧ Cut into 3 slices. Butter the slices so they will stick together and place the 3 slices on top of each other, alternating the colors.

Assorted Sandwich Fillings

🍃Place on a platter and cover with wax paper and a damp cloth.
🍃Refrigerate 2 to 3 hours. Then, with a sharp knife, cut into ½-in. (1-cm) strips.

PINWHEEL SANDWICHES

🍃Use unsliced bread. Remove the crust from all but the bottom of the loaf. With the bottom crust to the left, cut the loaf lengthwise into ⅛- to ¼-in. (0.5-cm) slices. Set the crust aside.
🍃Run a rolling pin lightly over each slice, to prevent it from tearing.
🍃Butter each slice with soft butter, then spread with the filling of your choice. If desired, garnish one end of the slice with a sprig of watercress, an asparagus spear, a gherkin or 3 olives. Then roll, beginning at the garnished end, or, if you have not garnished the slice, at either end. It is important that you roll as evenly and as tightly as possible.
🍃Wrap each roll securely in wax paper or aluminum foil. Place the rolls side by side on a platter.
🍃Cover and refrigerate 3 to 4 hours.
🍃Cut each roll into ¼- to ½-in. (0.5- to 1-cm) slices—or leave whole for a larger sandwich.

MOSAIC SANDWICHES

🍃Spread with the filling of your choice on 1 round slice of whole-wheat bread and 1 round slice of white bread.

Croque-Monsieur

🍃Cut small circles from the center of another slice of whole-wheat and another slice of white bread.
🍃Then place the whole-wheat slice, with the circle removed, over the white slice that has been spread with the filling. Place the circle cut from the white slice into the hole left in the whole-wheat. Continue this operation, alternating the whole-wheat and white bread circles.

WRAP-AROUND SANDWICHES

🍃Trim the crusts from a slice of bread; butter and fold the slice into a triangle. Spread with parsley, watercress or the filling of your choice. Hold the points together with a toothpick until chilled.

MAKING A SANDWICH LOAF

🍃Use unsliced bread. Remove the crusts using a serrated knife. Place the loaf on its side and cut 5 long slices of ½ in. (1 cm) each.
🍃Prepare 4 fillings using either ham, eggs, chicken, vegetables or cheese. Make creamy fillings of different colors: a creamy filling will make the loaf easy to cut, and the colors will enhance its appearance.
🍃For example, you could spread the first slice of bread with a pink cheese filling, the second with an ivory-colored chicken or veal filling. Cover this with thin tomato slices and top with a thin layer of chicken to prevent the bread from becoming soaked before serving

time. Spread the third slice with an egg filling containing black or green olives and the fourth slice with a ham filling. Top with the fifth slice. The bread need not be buttered as the fillings will be rich enough. The slices should not be pressed too firmly together or the fillings will ooze out.

❧ To frost the loaf, cream together 12 to 16 oz (375 to 500 g) cream cheese and ⅓ cup (75 mL) cream, or just enough for the mixture to resemble heavy whipped cream. Frost the sides first, holding the loaf on top; then frost the top. Refrigerate 4 to 6 hours.

❧ To serve, garnish with minced parsley or chives, thin slices of radishes or olives, or bunches of watercress. A whole loaf should yield 10 1-in. (2-cm) slices. Slice with a very sharp knife and serve with a cake server.

❧ For a more colorful loaf, alternate 2 slices of white bread with 3 slices of whole-wheat bread, or 2 slices whole-wheat with 3 slices white. Choose fillings that will contrast in color with the bread.

CROQUE-MONSIEUR

This dressed-up version of the grilled-cheese sandwich is a popular snack among the patrons of Parisian sidewalk cafés.

soft butter
2 slices crusty white bread
1 slice ham
2 slices tomato
sprinkling of chives or parsley
1 slice Swiss or Dutch cheese

❧ Butter the 2 slices of bread. On 1 slice, place the ham. Cover with the tomato and sprinkle with the chives or parsley. Top with the cheese and the second slice of bread. Butter the top of the sandwich.

❧ Place on a baking sheet and brown in a preheated 475°F (240°C) oven for about 10 minutes.

FRENCH LOAF

❧ Heat 2 tbsp (30 mL) vegetable oil in a skillet. Add 1 minced onion, 1 thinly sliced green pepper and 1 clove crushed garlic. Fry together until well blended. Remove the pan from the heat.

❧ Add ½ tsp (2 mL) salt, ¼ tsp (1 mL) tarragon or basil and 2 cups (500 mL) ground, cooked meat (any leftover roasted meat will do). Pepper to taste. Mix well.

❧ Slice a loaf of French bread lengthwise into 3 even slices.

❧ Spread the bottom slice with Dijon mustard and the meat mixture. Place the second slice on top and spread with butter and mayonnaise and cover with sliced tomatoes or cucumber, or a mixture of both. Butter the third slice and place it on top of the tomato and/or cucumber.

❧ Place on a tray and garnish with shallots and radishes. To serve, cut into slices.

❧ This loaf can also be served hot. When filled, make gashes in the loaf; it will be easier to slice when hot. Wrap in aluminum foil and heat for 20 minutes in a 375°F (190°C) oven. Unwrap when ready to serve.

VEGETABLES

VEGETABLES

In addition to being essential to a well-balanced diet, fresh vegetables add variety to our meals.

❧ The real pleasure and delight in vegetable cookery is that you are never tied down to one method. Vegetables can be steamed, sautéed, fried, pressure-cooked, cooked without water, broiled or baked. There are also many ways of serving vegetables: English-style (à l'anglaise), French-style (à la française), Italian-style (à l'italienne), Greek-style (à la grecque), Spanish-style (à l'espagnole), with aromatic herbs (aux fines herbes) or just as they are.

❧ One of the main problems, however, is that we tend to overcook vegetables. Not only do they become lifeless and limp, they also lose their vitamins, color and delicate flavor. Always keep in mind that cooked vegetables, like fresh ones, should be crispy, colorful and fragrant. They will be tastier and more nutritious.

STEAMING VEGETABLES

To steam vegetables, it is preferable to use a steamer. This cooking utensil consists of a basket with large holes that fits snugly into a large pot, much like a double boiler. A French steamer has leaves that spread to fit different sizes of saucepan and works just as well.

❧ Place the vegetables in the steamer. Fill the bottom of the pot with water and arrange the steamer so that the basket sits above the water level. Bring the water to a rolling boil and cover the pot. Steam the vegetables until they reach the desired degree of doneness.

❧ Not only does steaming take less time than boiling, but the vegetables will be tastier and they will retain more of their vitamins. In fact, many dietitians and physicians strongly recommend that vegetables be cooked in this way.

SAUTÉING VEGETABLES

Sautéed vegetables are cooked basically in their own juices with a small amount of oil or butter.

❧ Melt 1 to 2 tbsp (15 to 30 mL) butter or oil in a skillet and add the vegetables. Cook over low heat, stirring often, so that all cut surfaces are well coated with the hot fat. Cover the skillet with a tight-fitting lid and continue cooking over low heat.

❧ One important factor to remember when sautéing vegetables is that they must be thoroughly dry so that the fat will seal in the juices.

❧ To sauté vegetables such as spinach, shredded cabbage or chopped celery, it is better to clean and dry the vegetables and then toss them with the melted butter (or hot oil) in a large bowl before cooking. Blend well to coat the vegetables completely. Place in a saucepan, cover and cook over low heat.

❧ To sauté whole vegetables such as onions or large carrots, add 2 tbsp (30 mL) water after coating with the butter or oil.

❧ Sautéing vegetables is easy, and it brings out their natural color and delicate flavor. It is also an excellent way to cook vegetables without using salt. Try it with spinach.

FRYING VEGETABLES

Frying is the French way of cooking vegetables, but not all vegetables lend themselves to this cooking method. It is good for tuberous vegetables, such as potatoes, carrots and onions, but not ideal for green vegetables.

❧ To prepare perfect fried vegetables, make sure you chill the vegetables thoroughly before you begin. Always fry the vegetables in small quantities, and always use moderate heat.

❧ Cut the vegetables the desired way and refrigerate.

❧ Half fill a 3-in. (8-cm) skillet with melted fat or peanut oil. When the fat is hot, add the chilled vegetables and cook 3 to 5 minutes, depending on the vegetable.

❧ Remove from the heat and drain on paper towels.

PRESSURE-COOKING VEGETABLES

I am extremely fond of this method because it cooks vegetables very quickly—in about 1 to 5 minutes.

❧ Since operating instructions are included with each type of cooker, I will not give any directions here. But no matter what type of pressure-cooker you use, one thing is of the utmost importance—watch the cooking time with stopwatch precision. Otherwise the vegetables will overcook, and a mere 30 seconds of over-cooking can ruin them. For the same reason, cool the cooker (under cold, running water until the pressure is completely reduced) as soon as the cooking time has elapsed. Do not let the pressure drop by itself or the vegetables will be overdone.

🍂 Because the vegetables are always on a rack, they are not in contact with the water. The few spoonfuls of water needed to steam them will be full of nutrients and can be served with the vegetables or added to soups.

COOKING VEGETABLES WITHOUT WATER

To cook vegetables without water, you will need a heavy aluminum, stainless-steel or enameled cast-iron saucepan that will distribute the heat evenly. It must have a tight-fitting lid.

🍂 All fresh vegetables contain 70% to 90% water, which will be more than enough to cook them if the heat is controlled and if steam is not allowed to escape.

🍂 In many cases, vegetables can be cooked without adding any water at all. However, in winter, because vegetables are not freshly picked, it is better to add 1 or 2 tbsp (15 to 30 mL) water. Always add this water once the pan begins to heat.

🍂 Keep the heat low so that the steam does not escape; otherwise the vegetables will dry up or burn.

🍂 The cooking period varies from 20 to 35 minutes.

BOILING VEGETABLES

Clean and prepare the vegetables. Leave whole, slice, cut into thin strips (julienne) or dice.

🍂 Cooking time will vary depending on the type of vegetable and how it is cut. For example, allow 10 minutes for a medium-size carrot cooked whole, 4 to 5 minutes if it is diced, 3 minutes if it is thinly sliced and 1 minute if it is grated.

🍂 It is preferable to cook vegetables in an enameled cast-iron or stainless-steel saucepan. Never salt vegetables while they are cooking or they will become tough. Add enough boiling water to cover the vegetables completely, but do not exceed this amount or the vegetables will be bland.

🍂 Cook until tender and crisp.

🍂 Always strain boiled vegetables in a colander to remove excess water.

BAKING VEGETABLES

The only vegetables that lend themselves to baking are root vegetables. These can be cooked whole and unpeeled, or sliced and wrapped in parchment paper or aluminum foil.

🍂 To cook whole, place the unpeeled vegetables in a saucepan and cover with boiling water. Cook over high heat for 1 minute. Drain thoroughly in a colander.

🍂 Place the vegetables on a baking sheet and cook in a 350°F (180°C) oven for 30 to 45 minutes. Remove from the oven, peel and serve.

🍂 Beets and onions are particularly delightful baked this way.

🍂 To bake vegetables in parchment paper, cut the paper to the proper size. Soak it in warm water and then wring out the excess water. Peel the vegetables and place them on the paper. Add butter to taste. Secure with string and bake in a 350°F (180°C) oven for 30 to 50 minutes.

🍂 Baking saves time and energy. In fact, you can prepare an entire meal right in the oven. Potatoes and onions are a snap when baked in the oven along with a roast.

🍂 If your oven is too small to hold three baking sheets, wrap the vegetables in foil or parchment paper and place them directly on the rack.

GRILLING OR BROILING VEGETABLES

Cooking vegetables on the grill is becoming increasingly popular now that we have become fans of the barbecue.

🍂 But you don't have to use the barbecue to grill or broil vegetables; you can just as easily do it in your oven.

🍂 Brush the vegetables lightly with oil. Then place them on the rack about 4 in. (10 cm) from the source of heat and broil for 4 minutes. Turn the vegetables once and reduce the heat.

🍂 Bake 20 to 30 minutes or until tender.

🍂 Broiling is the ideal way of cooking unpeeled beets or medium-size potatoes. New spring potatoes are especially good.

🍂 Grilling or broiling is an excellent way to prepare vegetables, as steam is prevented from condens-

Ratatouille Niçoise

RATATOUILLE NIÇOISE

4 tomatoes
1 medium zucchini
1 medium eggplant
2 green peppers
2 large onions
2 or 3 cloves garlic
½ cup (125 mL) olive oil
¼ tsp (1 mL) thyme
½ tsp (2 mL) basil
1 tsp (5 mL) sugar
salt and pepper to taste

🍃 Blanch, peel and quarter the tomatoes. Peel the zucchini and the eggplant. Seed the green peppers and remove the soft membrane. Cut the zucchini, eggplant and green peppers into medium-size slices.

🍃 Slice the onion and mince the garlic.

🍃 Heat the oil in a heavy saucepan (preferably enameled cast-iron). Add the onion and garlic and brown quickly over high heat. Add the eggplant and tomatoes. Mix thoroughly, crushing the mixture with the back of a wooden spoon. Add the zucchini and green pepper.

🍃 Cook over high heat for a few minutes, stirring almost constantly.

🍃 Add the rest of the ingredients.

🍃 Cover and simmer 1 hour, over low heat, stirring occasionally.

🍃 Ratatouille is served hot or cold, as an hors d'oeuvre, a salad or a vegetable.

🍃 If serving cold, sprinkle with the juice of half a lemon and 3 tbsp (45 mL) olive oil before serving.

ing on the vegetable and the full flavor is sealed in.

COOKING
FROZEN VEGETABLES

Whenever I write about frozen vegetables I could go on for pages about their wonderful quality, color and flavor. They're economical, too: just compare the prices to those for fresh vegetables.

🍃 Frozen vegetables are quite easy to prepare. In fact, there's only one way to do it, no matter what brand you use. Don't follow the instructions on the package too closely. The method described below will yield far better results.

🍃 Never thaw frozen vegetables before cooking them.

🍃 Place the frozen vegetable in a saucepan and add enough water

to half fill the saucepan. (The water may be cold, lukewarm or boiling.) Do not add salt. Cover the pan, place over high heat and boil 5 to 8 minutes, depending on how you like your vegetables. Experiment with each type of vegetable to determine the ideal cooking time.

🍃 When cooking vegetables such as spinach or broccoli, break them into pieces and stir after 3 or 4 minutes.

🍃 To test for doneness, cut off a small piece and taste it. Testing with a fork is not recommended as the vegetables are usually overcooked by the time the fork pierces them easily.

🍃 When the vegetables are cooked, drain and serve.

🍃 Keep the cooking water for soups and sauces.

Vegetable Purée

3 cups (750 mL) diced potatoes
1 cup (250 mL) diced carrots
1 apple, peeled and sliced
½ onion, sliced
1 tsp (5 mL) salt
pinch of pepper
¼ tsp (1 mL) savory
½ cup (125 mL) water
2 tbsp (30 mL) butter
1 tsp (5 mL) minced parsley

❧ Peel the vegetables. Place the potatoes, carrots, apple, onion, salt, pepper, savory and water in a pressure-cooker.
❧ Secure the lid, cap the vent and cook 3 minutes. Cool the cooker under the cold running water until the pressure is completely reduced.
❧ Drain and mash the vegetables. Add the butter and beat vigorously until creamy.
❧ Garnish with the parsley and serve.

TOSSING A SALAD

Although there is more than one way to make a salad, this will help you serve crisp, tasty salads every time.
❧ Choose a large glass, earthenware or wooden salad bowl. Rub the bottom with a clove of garlic.
❧ Fill with an assortment of washed greens, well drained and cut into small pieces. Garnish with finely chopped parsley, chives or onion rings.
❧ Prepare the dressing of your choice and pour a little over the salad. Toss lightly with a fork and spoon until the vegetables are well coated with the dressing. Adjust the seasoning and add more dressing, if necessary.
❧ Serve at once.

Garden Salad

lettuce
juice of ½ lemon
3 to 4 tbsp (45 to 60 mL) sour cream
salt and pepper to taste
2 hard-cooked eggs

❧ Wash enough lettuce to fill a medium-size salad bowl. Wrap the lettuce in a cloth and refrigerate for 2 to 3 hours to make it nice and crisp.
❧ When ready to serve, place the lemon juice, sour cream, salt and pepper at the bottom of the salad bowl. Mix together, then add the lettuce. Toss gently. Garnish with a ring of sliced hard-cooked eggs.
❧ Serve at once.

Garden Salad

1 cucumber, peeled
1 bunch radishes
4 to 5 green onions
2 tomatoes, peeled
2 small carrots, peeled
sour cream
salt and pepper
1 head leaf lettuce

❧ Slice the cucumber as thinly as possible. Clean, wash and slice the radishes. Chop the green onions. Cut the tomatoes into small wedges. Grate the carrots.
❧ Place the prepared vegetables in a large salad bowl.
❧ Add the sour cream, to taste. Season with salt and pepper and mix thoroughly. Arrange the lettuce leaves in a ring around the vegetables.

Spring Salad

❧ On a bed of lettuce, arrange cooked asparagus, cooked green beans, cooked or raw green peas and thin radish slices.
❧ Toss lightly with French dressing.
❧ Sprinkle with minced chives and garnish with wedges of hard-cooked eggs.

Summer Salad

❧ Toss the following ingredients with a French dressing of your choice: sliced tomatoes, thinly sliced cucumber (peeled or unpeeled), thinly sliced cooked new potatoes, Spanish onion (cut into rings) and a heart of celery (diced).
❧ Place on a bed of shredded spinach or Boston lettuce.
❧ Sprinkle with minced celery leaves and garnish with parsley and watercress.

Autumn Salad

❧ Toss each of the following with your favorite French dressing: diced cooked beets, shredded raw carrots, thinly sliced peeled apples, sliced green pepper and diced celery.

❧ Arrange each vegetable in a separate mound on a bed of shredded cabbage.

❧ Sprinkle with minced parsley and onion. Garnish with finely shredded Cheddar cheese.

WINTER SALAD

❧ Toss cooked lima beans with oil and lemon juice.

❧ Arrange the lima beans in a ring and fill the center of the ring with hard-cooked eggs (sliced and tossed with mayonnaise), tomatoes (sliced and sprinkled with basil) and cooked potatoes (sliced and sprinkled with French dressing).

❧ Garnish with minced olives.

❧ Decorate with iceberg lettuce leaves and mayonnaise.

SPANISH SALAD

2 large Spanish onions
1 red apple, unpeeled and finely chopped (or grated)
2 tbsp (30 mL) cider vinegar
½ tsp (2 mL) salt
1 head iceberg lettuce
3 tbsp (45 mL) olive oil

❧ Place the unpeeled onions in a pie plate. Bake in a 350°F (180°C) oven for 1 hour. Make an incision on one side with a pair of scissors and remove the skin. Cool.

❧ Mix together in a bowl the apple, vinegar and salt.

❧ Separate the lettuce leaves and wash them. Wrap in a towel and refrigerate.

❧ To serve, place the lettuce in a large salad bowl and cover with the onions cut into large pieces. Top with the olive oil and the apple-vinegar mixture. Toss lightly using a fork and a spoon.

❧ Adjust the seasoning and serve.

CAESAR SALAD

1 lb (500 g) romaine lettuce
2 medium cloves garlic (halved)
1 tsp (5 mL) salt
6 tbsp (90 mL) oil
2 tbsp (30 mL) wine vinegar
1 tbsp (15 mL) fresh lemon juice
½ tsp (2 mL) Worcestershire sauce
1 tsp (5 mL) dry mustard
½ tsp (2 mL) salt
1 tsp (5 mL) black pepper
4 anchovies cut into small pieces or 3 oz (90 g) blue cheese
1 tbsp (15 mL) Parmesan cheese
1 raw egg
24 small croutons

❧ Cut the lettuce into bite-size pieces and refrigerate.

❧ In a large wooden salad bowl, place the garlic cloves and 1 tsp (5 mL) salt. Crush with a fork and rub the bowl with the garlic for about 2 minutes. Discard the garlic and salt. (If you prefer, leave the garlic and salt in the bowl but do not season with salt later.)

❧ Add the oil and beat with a fork for about 1 minute or until slightly thickened. Add the vinegar and lemon juice and beat until thoroughly blended. Add the Worcestershire sauce, dry mustard, salt, pepper, anchovies, Parmesan cheese and egg; beat until well blended.

❧ Add the chilled romaine lettuce. Toss gently using a fork and a spoon until the leaves are well coated with the dressing. Add the croutons, tossing gently so that they do not become soggy.

❧ Serve at once in individual salad bowls.

AVOCADO SALAD

I like to serve this beautiful green salad in a cut-glass salad bowl topped with a few nasturtiums from the garden. To make sure the vegetables are fresh and crispy, wash, clean and refrigerate them before serving.

1 large avocado
juice of 1 lime or ½ lemon
1 head Boston lettuce
1 head romaine or iceberg lettuce
3 green onions
⅓ cup (75 mL) 10% cream
2 tbsp (30 mL) fresh lime or lemon juice
1 tbsp (15 mL) finely chopped chives
¼ tsp (1 mL) salt
pinch of pepper
pinch of sugar

❧ Peel the avocado but do not remove the seed. Rub with lime or lemon juice, cover with plastic wrap and refrigerate.

❧ Wash the lettuce and shake out the excess water. Fold a paper towel or a cloth in two and place at the bottom of a large plastic bag. Fill the bag with the cleaned lettuce and refrigerate.

❧ Mince the green onions, wrap in foil and refrigerate.

❧ In a bottle, combine the fresh

lime or lemon juice, the chives, salt, pepper and sugar. Shake vigorously until well mixed, then refrigerate. The dressing will thicken. Shake well before using.

🌶 When ready to serve, place the lettuce in a salad bowl and sprinkle with the green onions.

🌶 Halve the peeled avocado, slice it and arrange the slices on top of the lettuce. Pour the dressing over the salad.

🌶 Toss only when ready to serve.

CHIFFONADE SALAD

2 hard-cooked eggs
2 cooked beets
3 sprigs parsley
French dressing
lettuce

🌶 Chop the hard-cooked eggs. Peel and grate the beets. Mince the parsley.

🌶 Mix together the eggs, beets and parsley with your favorite French dressing.

🌶 Wash and thoroughly dry the lettuce. Tear into pieces and place in a salad bowl.

🌶 When ready to serve, place the beet mixture over the lettuce. Toss and serve.

ENDIVES

PREPARATION
Cut the end off each endive and remove the wilted outer leaves. Endives should not soak in water since this will make them bitter. They require little cleaning. Simply rinse the first few leaves under running water and dry at once. They do not have to be wrapped, and will keep for 4 to 5 days in the refrigerator.

🌶 Endives are served raw in salads or cooked with meat, chicken or fish.

BASIC COOKING METHOD
Endives are usually steamed.

🌶 Wash, pat dry and place in a baking dish. For 1 lb (500 g) endives, sprinkle with ¼ tsp (1 mL) sugar and a pinch of pepper.

🌶 Add ½ cup (125 mL) cold water. Dot with 1 tsp (5 mL) butter and add the juice of half a lemon.

🌶 Cover the endives only (not the baking dish) with aluminum foil. Bring to a boil, then bake in a 350°F (180°C) oven for 30 minutes and serve.

CREAMED ENDIVES

1 lb (500 g) endives
2 tbsp (30 mL) flour
1 tbsp (15 mL) soft butter
½ cup (125 mL) cream
pinch of nutmeg
salt and pepper

🌶 Steam the endives. Drain and reserve the cooking liquid.

🌶 Blend together the flour and butter. Add the reserved cooking liquid and the cream and stir over low heat until smooth and creamy. Add the nutmeg, salt and pepper.

🌶 Pour the sauce over the endives and serve.

ENDIVE SALAD

🌶 Clean the endives and separate the leaves. Or quarter them

Creamed Endives

[389]

lengthwise and then slice them crosswise into 1-in. (2-cm) pieces. Toss with your favorite French dressing and serve.

🍃 If desired, garnish with shrimp, avocado or finely chopped hazelnuts.

ENDIVES MEUNIÈRE

1 lb (500 g) endives
1 cup (250 mL) water
or consommé
¼ tsp (1 mL) sugar
pinch of pepper
3 tbsp (45 mL) butter
salt to taste

🍃 Place the endives in a saucepan with the water or consommé, sugar and pepper. Bring to a rolling boil. Cover and simmer for 15 to 20 minutes, depending on the size of the endives. Drain and spread out on a cloth or paper towels to drain.

🍃 Melt the butter in a skillet and heat until browned. Place the endives in the skillet and brown over medium heat, turning only once. Salt to taste and serve.

SPINACH

PREPARATION
Remove the coarse stems from the spinach. Rinse once in lukewarm water, then twice in cold water to remove the sand. Wrap in a clean cloth and refrigerate. The spinach will stay fresh for several days.

BASIC COOKING METHOD
Place the spinach in a saucepan with 1 tbsp (15 mL) butter. Do not add water; the water already clinging to the washed leaves is sufficient. Cover and cook over high heat for 3 minutes. Turn the spinach and cook for another 2 minutes.

🍃 Drain thoroughly, reserving the cooking liquid for use in soups and sauces.

🍃 Return the spinach to the saucepan and season to taste. Heat for a few minutes and serve.

SPINACH SALAD

1 lb (500 g) very fresh spinach
1 tsp (5 mL) minced onion
4 or 5 strips bacon
4 tbsp (60 ml) French dressing

🍃 Remove the stems from the spinach. Rinse the leaves several times. Roll in a cloth and dry thoroughly. Place in a salad bowl. Add the onion.

🍃 Fry the bacon over low heat and drain on paper towels. When cool, cut into small pieces and add to the spinach mixture. Reserve 3 tbsp (45 mL) bacon fat.

🍃 Heat reserved bacon fat with 4 tbsp (60 mL) of your favorite French dressing. Pour over the spinach mixture.

🍃 Toss and serve immediately.

CREAMED SPINACH

🍃 Cook 1 lb (500 g) spinach. Do not drain.

🍃 Sprinkle with 1 tbsp (15 mL) all-purpose flour. Add 2 tbsp (30 mL) cream and 1 tbsp (15 mL) butter. Cook over medium heat, stirring constantly, until thick and creamy.

🍃 Serve hot.

SPINACH AU GRATIN

2 lbs (1 kg) spinach
1 cup (250 mL) bread cubes
1 tbsp (15 mL) butter

SAUCE:
2 tbsp (30 mL) butter
2 tbsp (30 mL) flour
½ tsp (2 mL) salt
1 cup (250 mL) milk
½ tsp (2 mL) dry mustard
5 tbsp (75 mL) grated cheese
3 tbsp (45 mL) cream

🍃 Wash and cook the spinach. Drain. Brown the bread cubes in the 1 tbsp (15 mL) butter. Combine the bread cubes and spinach and place in a baking dish. Set aside.

🍃 To prepare the sauce, melt the 2 tbsp (30 mL) butter in a saucepan. Stir in the flour and the salt. Add the milk all at once and heat until the mixture is thick and creamy, stirring constantly.

🍃 Add the dry mustard, grated cheese and cream. Simmer over low heat for 5 minutes, stirring often.

🍃 Pour the cheese sauce over the spinach.

🍃 Bake in a 475°F (240°C) oven for 10 minutes.

SPINACH LOAF

1 lb (500 g) fresh spinach
or 1 package frozen spinach
¼ cup (50 mL) soft butter

4 egg yolks
3 tbsp (45 mL) finely chopped parsley
3 slices bread
milk
4 egg whites
½ cup (125 mL) sour cream
salt and pepper to taste
1 tsp (5 mL) curry powder
1 cup (250 mL) breadcrumbs

🍂 Cook the spinach and drain. Chop very fine.

🍂 Beat together the butter and the egg yolks. Mix in the spinach and the parsley.

🍂 Soak the slices of bread (with crusts) in just enough milk to make a thick paste. Add to the spinach mixture and stir well.

🍂 Beat the egg whites until stiff and fold into the spinach together with the remaining ingredients. Reserve 1 tbsp (15 mL) of the breadcrumbs.

🍂 Generously butter a mold and sprinkle with the reserved bread-crumbs.

🍂 Turn the spinach mixture into the mold and place the mold in a saucepan of boiling water (the water in the saucepan should come no further than halfway up the mold). Cover the saucepan and steam over low heat for 50 to 60 minutes, or until the mixture is firm.

🍂 To serve, unmold the spinach loaf onto a warm platter.

🍂 Heat together 1 tbsp (15 mL) butter and 1 tbsp (15 mL) lemon juice. Pour over the loaf.

🍂 This loaf is equally delicious cold, served with a salad and may-onnaise.

Spinach Mousseline

SPINACH WITH SOUR CREAM

1 package frozen chopped spinach.
1 tbsp (15 mL) butter
2 tsp (10 mL) flour
½ cup (125 mL) sour cream
½ tsp (2 mL) salt
½ tsp (2 mL) pepper
¼ tsp (1 mL) celery salt
½ tsp (2 mL) nutmeg
1 tsp (5 mL) lemon juice
1 hard-cooked egg, sliced

🍂 Cook the spinach according to the directions on the package. Drain.

🍂 In the same saucepan, melt the butter over medium heat. Blend in the flour. Add the sour cream, salt, pepper, celery salt, nutmeg, lemon juice and spinach, stirring to mix thoroughly.

🍂 Cook over low heat, stirring constantly, for 5 minutes, or until the mixture thickens slightly. Adjust the seasoning.

🍂 Garnish with the slices of hard-cooked egg.

🍂 Serve hot.

SPINACH MOUSSELINE

1 cup (250 mL) whipping cream
½ cup (125 mL) grated cheese
3 cups (750 mL) cooked spinach
½ tsp (2 mL) salt
¼ tsp (1 mL) pepper
1 pinch nutmeg

🍂 Whip the cream. Fold in the cheese and beat the mixture together with the cooked spinach. Add the salt, pepper and nutmeg and stir to blend.

❧ Butter a pie plate and turn the spinach mixture into it. Sprinkle with a little cheese, if desired.

❧ Bake in a 375°F (190°C) oven until the top is browned.

SORREL

PREPARATION

Sorrel resembles spinach and is cleaned in the same manner. Because of its bitter taste, it is seldom eaten alone, but it can be used like lemon to add flavor to dishes. For example, a handful of sorrel will enhance spinach. Adding a few leaves to boiled potatoes before they are mashed will yield interesting results. It can be used in salads, or added to soups. In short, sorrel, like lemon, has its place in the kitchen.

BASIC COOKING METHOD

Cook according to the *Basic Cooking Method* for spinach (see page 390).

USES

In an omelet: blend together 4 tbsp (60 mL) puréed sorrel, 4 eggs, salt, pepper and 1 tbsp (15 mL) milk or cream. Cook as you would any other omelet.

❧ In mashed potatoes: add ½ to 1 cup (125 to 250 mL) puréed sorrel to 4 cups (1 L) mashed potatoes.

❧ In vegetable soup: add 1 cup (250 mL) puréed sorrel 20 minutes before the end of the cooking period.

OLD-FASHIONED DANDELION SALAD

6 slices salt pork or bacon
1 small onion, finely chopped
3 to 4 tbsp (45 to 60 mL) cider vinegar
1 large bowl dandelion greens, cleaned
salt and pepper to taste

❧ In an enameled cast-iron skillet, fry the salt pork over medium heat until crisp and golden. Drain on paper towels. My grandmother's recipe calls for salt pork, but you could use bacon.

❧ Add the onion and vinegar to the remaining fat in the skillet. Bring to a boil. Remove from heat and let stand 1 minute.

❧ Turn the vinegar and onion mixture over the dandelion greens. Season to taste with salt and pepper. Add the salt pork and mix well.

❧ Serve immediately.

FIDDLEHEADS

Fiddleheads are young fern sprouts. They are picked in early spring, before they unfold and when they resemble fiddle or violin heads—hence the name.

❧ For generations, in the Maritimes, fiddleheads were the first fresh green of the year. This explains their popularity. Fiddleheads are difficult to clean but delicious, a cross between spinach and asparagus. They are sold fresh, frozen or canned. Every year, I wait impatiently for them to grow on my farm in Québec.

❧ Wash 3 or 4 times, place in a saucepan and add a little water. Cover and cook for 10 to 15 minutes over medium heat. Tender young fiddleheads take only 5 minutes to cook, so keep a close watch on them. Do not overcook.

❧ Serve fiddleheads the traditional way, with salt, pepper, butter and a dash of vinegar.

CABBAGE

PREPARATION

Before cooking either green or red cabbage, let it soak for 20 minutes in cold water to which 1 tbsp (15 mL) coarse salt has been added. Place the cabbage, head down, in a bowl. Remove the thick and wilted outer leaves.

❧ To cook a cabbage whole, make 6 to 8 incisions in the core so that the core and the leaves will cook at the same rate. The cabbage can also be cut into 4 or 8 wedges without removing the core. For fast cooking, shred the cabbage coarsely and grate the core.

BASIC COOKING METHOD

Bring 6 cups (1.5 L) water and ½ tsp (2 mL) sugar to a boil over high heat. Add the shredded cabbage. Cover and cook over very high heat for 3 to 5 minutes. Cabbage cooked in this manner will remain green and tasty and will not give off a strong, lingering odor.

❧ Cook a whole cabbage for 15 to 35 minutes.

RED AND GREEN CABBAGE SALAD

3 cups (750 mL) green cabbage, shredded

3 cups (750 mL) red cabbage, shredded

1 small onion, finely chopped

1 red apple, unpeeled and thinly sliced

pinch of anise

pinch of pepper

½ cup (125 mL) French dressing

&. In a large salad bowl, mix together the green and red cabbage. Add the onion and the apple and toss well. Sprinkle with the anise and pepper. Refrigerate until 20 minutes before serving time.

&. Add the French dressing and mix well. Refrigerate for 20 minutes before serving.

APPLE AND CABBAGE SALAD

SALAD:

1 medium cabbage

2 to 4 red apples, unpeeled

½ cup (125 mL) celery leaves, finely chopped

FRENCH DRESSING:

½ cup (125 mL) olive oil

¼ cup (50 mL) cider vinegar

½ clove garlic, crushed

or 1 small onion, finely chopped

1 tsp (5 mL) salt

½ tsp (2 mL) pepper

&. Shred the cabbage and drop into a bowl of ice water. Refrigerate for 1 hour. Drain and pat dry thoroughly with a clean cloth.

&. Thinly slice the apples and add to the cabbage with the finely chopped celery leaves.

&. Beat together the oil, vinegar, garlic or onion, salt and pepper.

&. Add ½ cup (125 mL) of this dressing to the apple and cabbage mixture. Mix well. Adjust the seasoning.

&. Let stand for 30 minutes before serving.

GERMAN COLESLAW

1 small cabbage, shredded

1 onion, minced

4 egg yolks

½ tsp (2 mL) dry mustard

1 tbsp (15 mL) sugar

1 tbsp (15 mL) flour

1 tbsp (15 mL) melted butter

¾ cup (175 mL) cider vinegar

1 cup (250 mL) whipping cream

salt and pepper to taste

¼ cup (50 mL) olive oil

&. Mix the cabbage and the onion in a bowl.

&. In the top of a double boiler, mix together the egg yolks, dry mustard, sugar, flour and melted butter. Beat with an electric beater until well blended. Add the cider vinegar, whipping cream, salt and pepper. Beat until smooth.

&. Place the top of the double boiler over simmering water and cook, stirring constantly, until the sauce thickens. Remove from heat and beat in the olive oil. Adjust the seasoning.

&. Pour the hot sauce over the cabbage. Toss well and serve.

SOUR CREAM AND CABBAGE SALAD

3 cups (750 mL) shredded cabbage

1 small onion, finely chopped

½ tsp (2 mL) salt

Sour Cream and Cabbage Salad

[393]

Sweet and Sour Cabbage

1 tbsp (15 mL) sugar
1 tbsp (15 mL) vinegar
¼ tsp (1 mL) salt
¼ tsp (1 mL) pepper
½ cup (125 mL) sour cream

🌱 Mix together in a bowl the cabbage, onion and salt.
🌱 Mix together the remaining ingredients and add to the cabbage mixture. Toss well to blend. Adjust the seasoning.
🌱 Refrigerate for 20 minutes before serving.

OLD-TIME CABBAGE SALAD

4 cups (1 L) shredded cabbage
1 cup (250 mL) sour cream
¼ cup (50 mL) cider vinegar
2 tbsp (30 mL) clear honey
½ tsp (2 mL) salt
2 tsp (10 mL) celery salt

🌱 Cover the cabbage with ice cubes or very cold water. Refrigerate for 1 hour. Drain, wrap in a cloth and refrigerate until ready to serve.
🌱 Beat the sour cream until it thickens. While still beating, slowly add the vinegar, then the honey, salt and celery salt.
🌱 Pour the sour-cream mixture over the cabbage. Toss well and serve.

RED CABBAGE SALAD

1 small red cabbage
1 cup (250 mL) sour cream
2 tbsp (30 mL) honey
1 tsp (5 mL) vinegar
¾ tsp (3 mL) salt
1½ tsp (7 mL) celery salt
pinch of pepper
1 small onion, minced

🌱 Shred the cabbage. Wrap in a damp cloth and refrigerate 4 to 6 hours.
🌱 Blend together the sour cream, honey, vinegar, salt, celery salt, pepper and onion. Stir vigorously.
🌱 To serve, pour the sour-cream mixture over the chilled cabbage. Blend well.
🌱 If desired, garnish with strips of green pepper or sliced hard-cooked eggs.

CREAMED CABBAGE

¾ cup (175 mL) whipping cream
1 tbsp (15 mL) butter
1 tbsp (15 mL) finely chopped parsley
1 onion, grated
2 cloves
5 cups (1.2 L) shredded cabbage
salt and pepper to taste

🌱 Place the cream, butter, parsley, onion and cloves in a saucepan. Bring to a boil.
🌱 Add the cabbage and mix well. Cover and cook over low heat for 35 minutes. Season to taste with salt and pepper and serve.

GREEN CABBAGE WITH APPLES

½ cup (125 mL) salt pork, diced
1 medium cabbage, sliced
4 unpeeled apples, sliced
½ tsp (2 mL) salt
1 tbsp (15 mL) lemon juice or vinegar
2 tbsp (30 mL) brown sugar
2 cloves

🌱 Brown the salt pork in a skillet. Add the remaining ingredients.

🍃 Cover and simmer over low heat for 20 minutes, stirring 3 or 4 times.

🍃 The cabbage will brown somewhat where it touches the bottom of the pan.

OLD-FASHIONED CABBAGE

4 cups (1 L) shredded cabbage
¼ cup (50 mL) butter
½ cup (125 mL) flour
3 cups (750 mL) milk
1 tsp (5 mL) salt
¼ tsp (1 mL) pepper
¼ cup (50 mL) breadcrumbs
2 tbsp (30 mL) melted butter

🍃 Place the shredded cabbage in a buttered baking dish.

🍃 Mix together the butter and the flour. Add the milk and stir over medium heat until the sauce is thick. Season with salt and pepper.

🍃 Pour the warm sauce over the raw cabbage. Blend well.

🍃 Mix the breadcrumbs with the melted butter. Sprinkle over the cabbage.

🍃 Bake in a preheated 400°F (200°C) oven for 20 minutes. Serve immediately.

🍃 It is important that the oven be preheated for this dish. The cabbage must not bake for more than 20 to 25 minutes, and it must be served immediately. The cabbage should be bright green, slightly crisp and very creamy. It will be mushy if overcooked.

DUTCH-STYLE CABBAGE

1 tbsp (15 mL) butter
1 tbsp (15 mL) flour
½ cup (125 mL) water or consommé
1 tbsp (15 mL) brown sugar
½ tsp (2 mL) salt
½ medium cabbage, shredded
3 tbsp (45 mL) cider vinegar
1 egg yolk, beaten

🍃 Heat the butter until melted and slightly browned. Add the flour and blend well. Add the water or consommé and cook until the mixture is creamy. Add the brown sugar, salt and cabbage. Mix well. Cover and simmer over medium heat for 20 minutes. Remove from heat.

🍃 Meanwhile, slowly mix together the vinegar and the egg yolk. Add to the cooked cabbage, beating vigorously.

🍃 Turn the cabbage mixture into a dish and let stand for 1 hour before serving. It should be eaten lukewarm.

🍃 This dish is delicious with game, pork or sausages.

GREEK-STYLE CABBAGE

1 small cabbage
¼ cup (50 mL) currants
¼ cup (50 mL) olive oil
salt, pepper and nutmeg
zest of ½ lemon

🍃 Shred the cabbage and add the currants.

🍃 Heat the oil in a saucepan. Add the cabbage mixture and blend well. Cover and simmer over low heat for 5 minutes.

🍃 Season to taste with salt, pepper and nutmeg. Add the lemon zest. Mix well. Cover and cook over low heat until the cabbage is tender, 5 to 6 minutes. Serve.

SWEET AND SOUR CABBAGE

4 cups (1 L) shredded red or green cabbage
2 cups (500 mL) thinly sliced apples, unpeeled
¼ cup (50 mL) cider vinegar
¼ cup (50 mL) water
½ cup (125 mL) brown sugar
6 cloves
1 tsp (5 mL) salt
3 tbsp (45 mL) butter

🍃 Place the cabbage, apples, vinegar, water, brown sugar, cloves and salt in a saucepan. Cover and cook over low heat for 40 minutes, stirring frequently.

🍃 If necessary, uncover and boil briskly over high heat for a few minutes to reduce the liquid.

🍃 Add the butter and stir until melted. Serve.

BRAISED CABBAGE

1 medium cabbage
6 thin slices fat salt pork
3 carrots, peeled and sliced
1 onion, minced
pinch of thyme
1 bay leaf

¼ tsp (1 mL) salt and pepper
1 cup (250 mL) hot consommé

🐦 Cut the cabbage into 8 wedges. Line a skillet with the slices of salt pork. Top with the cabbage.
🐦 Place the carrots, onion, thyme and bay leaf over the cabbage and around it. Sprinkle with salt and pepper. Pour the consommé over all. Cover and simmer over low heat for 2 hours.
🐦 Serve with game, venison or pork.

Cabbage with Sour Cream

1 medium cabbage
2 tbsp (30 mL) butter
1 onion, minced
1 tbsp (15 mL) flour
2 tsp (10 mL) cider vinegar
1 cup (250 mL) sour cream
1 tsp (5 mL) salt
pepper to taste
½ tsp (2 mL) sugar

🐦 Cut the cabbage into quarters. Cook according to the *Basic Cooking Method*, page 392. Drain well. Arrange on a serving dish.
🐦 Meanwhile, heat the butter in a saucepan. Add the onion and cook until browned. Add the flour and mix well. Stir in the vinegar and the sour cream. Cook, stirring constantly, until the sauce is creamy. Add the salt, pepper and sugar. Simmer for a few more minutes.
🐦 Pour the sauce over the warm cabbage. Serve immediately.

Cabbage Rolls Stuffed with Mushrooms

1 small cabbage
3 tbsp (45 mL) vegetable oil
1 large onion, minced
½ lb (250 g) mushrooms, thinly sliced
½ cup (125 mL) uncooked rice
1 cup (250 mL) boiling water
1½ tsp (7 mL) salt
¼ tsp (1 mL) basil
1 cup (250 mL) tomato sauce

🐦 Remove the core from the cabbage. Place the cabbage in a large bowl and cover with boiling water. Let stand for 20 minutes. Remove 16 leaves.
🐦 Heat 1 tbsp (15 mL) of the vegetable oil in a skillet. Add the minced onion and cook until slightly browned. Add the sliced mushrooms and stir over high heat for 2 minutes. Remove the onions and the mushrooms from the skillet.
🐦 Add the remaining oil and the rice to the skillet. Cook over medium heat until the rice begins to brown. Add the boiling water. Cover and simmer over low heat for 12 to 14 minutes or until the rice is tender and all the water has been absorbed. Add the onions, mushrooms, salt and basil and stir to blend well.
🐦 Place a spoonful of the rice and mushroom mixture in the center of each cabbage leaf. Roll into a cigar shape.
🐦 Shred the remaining cabbage and place in the bottom of a baking dish. Top with the cabbage rolls. Pour the tomato sauce over all.
🐦 Cover and bake in a 350°F (180°C) oven for 1 hour. Uncover during the last 15 minutes of baking.

Red Cabbage

Red cabbage is prepared and cooked exactly the way green cabbage is (see page 392).

Spicy Red Cabbage

1 red cabbage, shredded
6 cups (1.5 L) boiling water
3 tbsp (45 mL) pickling spices
4 tbsp (60 mL) brown sugar
4 tbsp (60 mL) vinegar
3 tbsp (45 mL) butter
salt and pepper to taste

🐦 Place the cabbage in boiling water. Tie up the pickling spices in a small square of cheesecloth. Add to the cabbage. Boil over high heat for 8 to 10 minutes or until the cabbage is tender. Drain well. Remove the spices.
🐦 Place the brown sugar, vinegar and butter in a saucepan. Cook over low heat until the butter is melted. Add the cabbage and mix well. Season to taste with salt and pepper. Serve.

Flemish-Style Red Cabbage

1 medium red cabbage
2 tbsp (30 mL) butter
1 large onion, grated

2 apples, peeled and sliced
¼ cup (50 mL) water
3 cloves
1 tbsp (15 mL) vinegar
1 tsp (5 mL) sugar
salt and pepper to taste

🍂 Shred the cabbage. Melt the butter in a saucepan. Add the cabbage and the remaining ingredients.

🍂 Cover and simmer over low heat, stirring occasionally, until the cabbage is tender and all the liquid has been absorbed.

🍂 Add a little butter. Stir and serve.

VIENNESE RED CABBAGE

1 medium red cabbage
4 tbsp (60 mL) sugar
1 tbsp (15 mL) salt
½ cup (125 mL) cider vinegar
4 tbsp (60 mL) chicken fat
3 tbsp (45 mL) butter
3 apples, peeled and cut into 8 wedges
½ cup (125 mL) red wine
salt to taste

🍂 Shred the cabbage and place in a saucepan. Add the sugar, salt and cider vinegar. Mix well and let stand for 30 minutes.

🍂 Melt the chicken fat with the butter, then add the cabbage. Mix well. Top the cabbage with the apple wedges. Cover and simmer over low heat for 10 minutes.

🍂 Add the red wine. Cover and simmer for 30 minutes more. If

Red cabbage à l'orange

there is still too much liquid, uncover and boil for a few minutes. Salt to taste.

🍂 This dish reheats very well.

RED CABBAGE WITH CHESTNUTS

1 medium red cabbage
1 large onion
4 tbsp (60 mL) bacon fat
salt and pepper to taste
½ cup (125 mL) red wine
1 lb (500 g) chestnuts

🍂 Shred the cabbage coarsely. Brown the onion in the bacon fat. Add the cabbage. Mix well. Season with salt and pepper, then add the wine. Cover and simmer over medium heat.

🍂 Cut a cross into the flat side of each chestnut. Place in a saucepan and cover with boiling water.

Boil for 20 minutes. Drain. Remove the shells and the brown skin (the hotter the chestnuts are, the easier this will be).

🍂 Place the whole chestnuts over the cabbage. Cover and simmer over low heat for 1 hour.

🍂 When ready to serve, adjust the seasoning and add a little butter.

RED CABBAGE À L'ORANGE

1 medium red cabbage
2 cups (500 mL) water
2 tbsp (30 mL) sugar
¼ cup (50 mL) cider vinegar
pinch of nutmeg
½ tsp (2 mL) basil
zest and juice of 1 orange
1 tbsp (15 mL) cornstarch
salt and pepper to taste

❧ Shred the cabbage and place in a saucepan with the water. Cover and simmer for 20 minutes.

❧ Add the sugar, vinegar, nutmeg, basil and orange zest. Cover and simmer for 1 hour or until the cabbage is transparent.

❧ Mix together the cornstarch and orange juice. Add to the cabbage. Stir until the mixture is slightly thickened.

❧ Season to taste with salt and pepper and serve.

BRUSSELS SPROUTS

PREPARATION

Brussels sprouts require careful preparation. Remove the outer leaves and let the Brussels sprouts soak for 1 hour in a mixture of salt water and vinegar (1 tbsp or 15 mL vinegar and 1 tsp or 5 mL salt per 4 cups or 1 L cold water). Drain well.

BASIC COOKING METHOD

Place the soaked Brussels sprouts in a saucepan. Sprinkle with ¼ tsp (1 mL) sugar. Pour in boiling water until the water reaches 3 in. (8 cm) up the side of the saucepan. Cover and boil vigorously for 12 to 20 minutes, depending on the size of the sprouts.

IN A PRESSURE-COOKER

Brussels sprouts are very easy to cook in a pressure-cooker. Place the Brussels sprouts on the rack of the pressure-cooker. Add ½ cup (125 mL) water. Secure the lid

and let the pressure rise. Cook for 1 minute. Reduce the pressure immediately. Serve.

CURRIED BRUSSELS SPROUTS

2 tbsp (30 mL) butter
2 tbsp (30 mL) flour
1 tsp (5 mL) curry powder
1 cup (250 mL) milk
salt and pepper to taste
1 apple, peeled and grated
2 to 3 cups (500 to 750 mL) Brussels sprouts

❧ Make a white sauce with the butter, flour, curry powder and milk. Season to taste with salt and pepper.

❧ Add the grated apple and the cooked Brussels sprouts. Simmer for 4 minutes and serve.

BRUSSELS SPROUTS WITH MUSHROOMS

2 to 4 cups (500 mL to 1 L) Brussels sprouts
4 tbsp (60 mL) butter
¼ to ½ lb (125 to 250 g) mushrooms, thinly sliced
1 small onion, minced
1 tbsp (15 mL) lemon juice
pinch of pepper
salt to taste

❧ Boil the Brussels sprouts. Drain well.

❧ Meanwhile, heat the butter in a skillet until melted and slightly browned. Add the mushrooms and the onion. Cook over high heat for 3 minutes, stirring constantly. Add the lemon juice, salt and pepper.

❧ Cover the sprouts with the mushroom mixture. Serve in a warmed vegetable dish.

BUTTERED BRUSSELS SPROUTS

2 to 3 cups (500 to 750 mL) cooked Brussels sprouts
4 tbsp (60 mL) butter
2 tbsp (30 mL) lemon juice
salt and pepper to taste

❧ Drain the cooked sprouts and place in a warmed serving dish.

❧ Heat the butter over low heat until it is melted and slightly browned. Add the lemon juice, salt and pepper. Pour over the sprouts and serve.

BRUSSELS SPROUT SALAD

❧ Soak Brussels sprouts for 1 hour in a mixture of salt water and vinegar (1 tbsp or 15 mL vinegar and 1 tsp or 5 mL coarse salt per 4 cups or 1 L water). Drain well.

❧ Shred each sprout as you would a small cabbage and place in a salad bowl. Add 1 chopped green onion.

❧ Toss with your favorite French dressing. Sprinkle with slivered almonds and serve.

BROCCOLI

Broccoli belongs to the cabbage family and is sold fresh or frozen. Fresh broccoli should be full and dark green or slightly purple in color. If it is yellow, it is not fresh. The stalks as well as the florets are edible. Keep refrigerated in the vegetable crisper. 1 lb (500 g) fresh broccoli will yield 3 servings; a 10-oz (300-g) package of frozen broccoli will yield 2 or 3 servings.

PREPARATION

With a sharp knife, sever the broccoli florets from the stalks. Remove the tough leaves. For even cooking, quarter the larger stalks. If the head of broccoli is large, peel the stalks; they will be more tender.

❧ Soak in salted water for 20 minutes. Drain well.

BASIC COOKING METHOD

Place the stalks in a saucepan and cover with the florets. Add enough boiling water to cover half the broccoli. Cover the saucepan and boil vigorously for 10 to 18 minutes. Drain and serve.

IN A PRESSURE-COOKER

Place the broccoli on the rack, stalks at the bottom, florets on top. Add ½ cup (125 mL) boiling water and a little salt. Secure the lid and let the pressure rise. Cook for 2 minutes. Reduce the pressure immediately. Serve.

FROZEN BROCCOLI

1 package frozen broccoli
1 cup (250 mL) hot or cold water
½ tsp (2 mL) sugar

❧ Place the frozen broccoli in a saucepan. Add 1 cup (250 mL) water and ½ tsp (2 mL) sugar. Cover and cook over high heat for 12 minutes.

❧ After 5 minutes of cooking, separate the broccoli with a fork and continue to cook for 3 to 4 minutes more. Repeat this procedure if necessary. Drain.

❧ Serve with *Hollandaise Sauce* (see page 54) or a mixture of melted butter and lemon juice, or garnish with grated cheese and melted butter.

BROCCOLI AMANDINE

2 lbs (1 kg) fresh broccoli
¼ tsp (1 mL) butter
2 green onions, minced
¼ cup (50 mL) chopped almonds
2 tsp (10 mL) lemon juice
salt and pepper to taste

❧ Cook the broccoli in boiling water. Drain and keep warm.

❧ Heat the butter until melted and slightly browned. Add the green onions and almonds and stir over medium heat for approximately 2 minutes. Add the lemon juice, salt and pepper.

❧ Pour the sauce over the broccoli and serve.

CHINESE BROCCOLI

1 lb (500 g) broccoli
3 tbsp (45 mL) olive oil
1 small onion, diced
2 tbsp (30 mL) soy sauce
1 tsp (5 mL) sugar
1 tsp (5 mL) cornstarch
½ cup (125 mL) chicken stock

❧ Wash the broccoli and cut into 1-in. (2-cm) pieces.

❧ Heat the olive oil in a skillet and cook the onion until golden.

Broccoli Amandine

[399]

Cauliflower au Gratin

Add the broccoli and cook over medium heat, stirring constantly, for 3 minutes. Add the soy sauce and the sugar.

🎗Blend the cornstarch and the chicken stock. Add to the broccoli mixture.

🎗Cook over high heat for 1 minute, stirring constantly. Serve.

BROCCOLI PARMIGIANA

🎗Heat 4 tbsp (60 mL) butter and 2 tbsp (30 mL) olive oil in a skillet. Add 2 heads of fresh broccoli or 2 packages of frozen broccoli.

🎗Stir-fry over high heat for 2 minutes.

🎗Place in a warm serving dish.

🎗Sprinkle with the juice of ½

lemon and ½ to ¾ cup (125 to 175 mL) grated Parmesan cheese. Serve.

CAULIFLOWER

PREPARATION

Unfortunately, many people are unaware that almost every part of the cauliflower is edible. They cut off the florets and throw away the rest. But the core, the stalks and the leaves, if they are prepared properly, can be as tasty as the florets.

🎗Remove the large outer green leaves, leaving a little ring around the base of the cauliflower. The leaf stems are good boiled. Remove the leaves and cook the stems as you would celery.

🎗The core, stalks and leaves can be used to flavor soups—not only

will using the entire cauliflower save you money, but it will enrich your culinary experience.

BASIC COOKING METHOD

Soak the cauliflower for 20 minutes head down in a mixture of cold salt water to which 1 tbsp (15 mL) vinegar has been added. Drain well.

🎗Place the cauliflower in a saucepan and sprinkle with ¼ tsp (1 mL) salt. Pour enough boiling water over the cauliflower to cover three-quarters of it.

🎗Cook a head of cauliflower cut into florets for 10 to 15 minutes. Cook a whole cauliflower for 25 to 30 minutes.

CAULIFLOWER AU GRATIN

1 head cauliflower
1 tbsp (15 mL) butter
salt and pepper to taste
3 tbsp (45 mL) butter
3 tbsp (45 mL) flour
1¾ cups (425 mL) milk
½ to ¾ cup (125 to 175 mL) grated cheese

🎗Separate the cauliflower into florets and cook (see above). Drain well.

🎗Heat the 1 tbsp (15 mL) butter until melted and slightly browned. Add the cauliflower and toss to coat well.

🎗Place in a baking dish. Season to taste with salt and pepper.

🎗Make a white sauce with the 3 tbsp (45 mL) butter, the flour and the milk. Season to taste with salt and pepper.

&⬥ Pour the white sauce over the hot cauliflower. Sprinkle with the grated cheese. Bake in a 400°F (200°C) oven for 20 minutes.

&⬥ This dish can be prepared ahead of time. Do not refrigerate. Cook for 24 to 26 minutes in a 400°F (200°C) oven.

CAULIFLOWER PROVENÇALE

1 whole cauliflower
3 cloves garlic
salt and pepper to taste
2 tbsp (30 mL) butter
½ lb (250 g) mushrooms, thinly sliced

&⬥ Cook the cauliflower, adding the peeled whole garlic cloves to the cooking liquid. Drain well.

&⬥ Place the cauliflower on a warm serving platter and season to taste with salt and pepper.

&⬥ Heat the butter in a skillet until it is melted and slightly browned. Add the mushrooms and cook over high heat for 2 minutes, stirring constantly. Place on top of the cauliflower and serve.

GREEK-STYLE CAULIFLOWER

1 large cauliflower
¼ cup (50 mL) olive oil
2 onions, finely chopped
2 cloves garlic, minced
2 cups (500 mL) canned tomatoes

1 tsp (5 mL) salt
½ tsp (2 mL) pepper
pinch of thyme
1 tsp (5 mL) sugar
¼ cup (50 mL) finely chopped parsley

&⬥ Wash the cauliflower and separate into florets.

&⬥ Heat the olive oil in a saucepan. Add the onion and the garlic and brown slightly. Add the tomatoes, salt, pepper, thyme and sugar. Bring to a boil and simmer over low heat for 10 minutes.

&⬥ Add the cauliflower. Cover and simmer for approximately 20 minutes or until the cauliflower is cooked. Sprinkle with parsley and serve.

CAULIFLOWER PURÉE

1 medium head cauliflower
3 tbsp (45 mL) butter
1 green onion, finely chopped
salt and pepper to taste
1 tbsp (15 mL) breadcrumbs

&⬥ Separate the cauliflower into florets and cook. Drain well.

&⬥ Return the cauliflower to the same saucepan. Add the butter, chopped green onion, salt, pepper and breadcrumbs. Mash with a fork, mixing well. The purée should not be too smooth.

CAULIFLOWER WITH FRENCH DRESSING

1 small head cauliflower
3 tbsp (45 mL) olive oil

1 tbsp (15 mL) lemon juice or vinegar
¼ tsp (1 mL) salt
1 green onion, minced
pinch of pepper

&⬥ Separate the cauliflower into florets and cook until tender-crisp. Drain well. Turn onto a clean cloth and let cool.

&⬥ Mix together the remaining ingredients and then add the cooled cauliflower. Mix well.

&⬥ Place on a bed of lettuce or in a shallow serving dish. If desired, garnish with strips of green pepper.

CREAMED CAULIFLOWER

This dish is light, golden and perfectly balanced.

1 head cauliflower
2 tbsp (30 mL) butter
2 tbsp (30 mL) flour
1½ cups (375 mL) milk
½ cup (125 mL) cream
½ tsp (2 mL) dry mustard
1 tsp (5 mL) salt
¼ tsp (1 mL) pepper
½ cup (125 mL) grated medium Cheddar cheese
2 egg yolks
2 egg whites

&⬥ Separate the cauliflower into florets. Cover with boiling water and boil, uncovered, over high heat for 15 to 18 minutes or until tender. Drain well.

&⬥ Make a white sauce with the butter, flour, milk and cream.

&⬥ When the sauce is smooth and creamy, add the dry mustard, salt, pepper and all but 2 tbsp (30 mL) of the grated cheese. Remove from heat and stir until well blended. Add the egg yolks, one at a time, beating vigorously after each addition.

🌭 Beat the egg whites until stiff and gently fold them into the sauce.

🌭 Place the cauliflower in a shallow baking dish and top with the sauce. Sprinkle with the reserved cheese.

🌭 Bake for 25 to 30 minutes in a 375°F (190°C) oven.

POLISH-STYLE CAULIFLOWER

1 cauliflower, separated into florets
salt and pepper to taste
2 to 3 tbsp (30 to 45 mL) butter
½ cup (125 mL) bread cubes

1 hard-cooked egg, grated
1 tbsp (15 mL) finely chopped parsley

🌭 Cook the cauliflower (see *Basic Cooking Method*, page 400) and drain well. Place in a warm serving dish and season to taste with salt and pepper.

🌭 Melt the butter in a skillet and brown the bread cubes over low heat.

🌭 Remove from heat and add the egg and the parsley. Blend well and place over the cauliflower.

CHINESE-STYLE CAULIFLOWER

🌭 Remove the leaves and core from a small or medium-size head of cauliflower. With a sharp knife, cut the head into thin slices.

🌭 Place the slices in a skillet with a pinch of sugar and ½ cup

(125 mL) boiling water. Cover and cook over high heat for approximately 7 minutes.

🌭 Serve immediately.

MUSHROOMS

PREPARATION

When mushrooms are very fresh, they are firm, dry to the touch and white. When they're not so fresh, the caps open and the underside turns a darker color; at this stage, though, the mushrooms are still edible.

🌭 Keep mushrooms refrigerated in a paper bag or an open container, covered loosely with a damp paper towel.

🌭 It is not necessary to peel white mushrooms, but they should be washed under cold running water. Do not soak. Drain washed mushrooms on a clean cloth until ready to use.

🌭 Remove approximately ¼ in. (0.5 cm) from the end of the stem. If a recipe calls for the caps only, set aside the stems for soups or sauces. They do not have such a subtle flavor as the caps, but they are still good.

BASIC COOKING METHOD

Mushrooms should be cooked as quickly as possible. To sauté, heat 2 to 3 tbsp (30 to 45 mL) butter per ½ lb (250 g) mushrooms until melted and slightly browned. Add the whole or sliced mushrooms and sauté over very high heat, for 2 to 4 minutes, depending on the size of the mushrooms, stirring constantly. Remove from heat.

🌭 Season to taste with salt and pepper. If desired, add herbs,

Polish-Style Cauliflower

wine or cognac.

🍂 To boil or blanch mushrooms, bring 1 cup (250 mL) water to a boil and add ½ tsp (2 mL) salt, 2 slices unpeeled lemon and ½ lb (250 g) mushrooms. Boil for 5 minutes, uncovered. Drain well and use as needed.

🍂 Blanching is an excellent way to preserve mushrooms. Place the boiled and drained mushrooms in a clean glass jar, cover and refrigerate. They will keep for 1 week.

🍂 The flavor and texture of boiled mushrooms is similar to that of canned mushrooms.

SAUTÉED MUSHROOMS

🍂 In a heavy skillet, heat 3 tbsp (45 mL) of butter for each ½ lb (250 g) mushrooms until melted and lightly browned. Add the mushrooms.

🍂 Sauté over high heat, uncovered, stirring constantly. Cook sliced mushrooms for 2 minutes, whole mushrooms for 4 minutes. Do not overcook as they will become dry.

🍂 A little garlic or green onion added to the mushrooms during cooking will add a pleasant flavor. Basil and tarragon go especially well with mushrooms.

SAUTÉED MUSHROOMS NEAPOLITAN

½ lb (250 g) mushrooms
2 tbsp (30 mL) olive oil
1 clove garlic, thinly sliced
salt and pepper to taste
3 tomatoes, peeled and diced
1 tsp (5 mL) sugar

🍂 Separate the stems from the caps. Chop the stems and quarter the caps.

🍂 Heat the olive oil in a skillet and brown the garlic. Add the stems and caps and stir over high heat for 2 minutes. Remove from heat. Season to taste with salt and pepper.

🍂 Add the tomatoes and the sugar to the mushroom mixture. Simmer over medium heat for 8 to 10 minutes or until well blended. Serve.

MUSHROOMS WITH PEAS

½ lb (250 g) mushrooms
4 tbsp (60 mL) bacon fat
or butter
1 14-oz (400-ml) can green peas, undrained
1 medium onion, grated
¼ tsp (1 mL) dry mustard
salt and pepper to taste
2 tbsp (30 mL) butter
2 tbsp (30 mL) flour
¼ cup (50 mL) sherry or cream
pinch of marjoram

🍂 Thinly slice the mushroom stems and caps.

🍂 In a skillet, melt the bacon fat or butter and sauté the mushrooms over very high heat. Add the green peas, grated onion and dry mustard. Cover and cook for 10 minutes. Season to taste with salt and pepper. Reserve the cooking liquid.

🍂 Blend together the butter and flour. Add the reserved cooking liquid, the sherry or cream and the marjoram. Bring to a boil. Add this mixture to the vegetables, boil for a few minutes and serve.

MUSHROOMS WITH SOUR CREAM

1 large onion, finely chopped
4 tbsp (60 mL) butter
1 to 1½ lbs (500 to 750 g) mushrooms, sliced
1 tsp (5 mL) salt
¼ tsp (1 mL) pepper
2 tsp (10 mL) paprika
1 cup (250 mL) sour cream
¼ cup (50 mL) finely chopped parsley

🍂 Sauté the onion in the butter. Add the sliced mushrooms, salt and pepper. Cook over high heat, stirring constantly, for 3 minutes or until all the liquid has evaporated.

🍂 Add the remaining ingredients. Heat through, but do not boil or the cream will curdle.

🍂 Serve on toast.

MUSHROOMS WITH LEMON

1 lb (500g) mushrooms
1 onion, minced
3 tbsp (45 mL) butter
2 tbsp (30 mL) minced parsley
juice of 1 lemon
1 tbsp (15 mL) flour
½ cup (125 mL) consommé

Mushrooms Toscana

½ cup (125 mL) 10% cream
¼ tsp (1 mL) basil
salt and pepper to taste

𝄢 Thinly slice the mushroom stems and caps.

𝄢 Sauté the onion in the butter and add the mushrooms. Stir over high heat for 2 minutes. Add the parsley and the lemon juice and simmer until the mushrooms have absorbed all the liquid.

𝄢 Sprinkle the mushrooms with the flour. Add the consommé, cream and basil. Cook, stirring, until the mixture is slightly thickened.

𝄢 Season with salt and pepper and serve.

MUSHROOMS TOSCANA

½ lb (250 g) mushrooms
2 tbsp (30 mL) butter
2 tomatoes, peeled and diced

pinch of rosemary
1 tsp (5 mL) sugar
salt and pepper to taste

𝄢 Chop the mushroom stems; leave the caps whole.

𝄢 Melt the butter in a saucepan and add the diced tomatoes, rosemary and sugar. Cook over high heat for 15 minutes, stirring occasionally. Season to taste with salt and pepper. Add the mushroom stems.

𝄢 Turn into a buttered baking dish. Top with the mushroom caps and dot with butter.

𝄢 Bake in a 500°F (260°C) oven for 10 to 15 minutes. Garnish with parsley and serve.

CREAMED MUSHROOMS

1 lb (500 g) mushrooms
4 tbsp (60 mL) butter

1 clove garlic, minced
salt and pepper to taste
½ cup (125 mL) flour
1 cup (250 mL) 10% cream
1 cup (250 mL) sour cream
¼ tsp (1 mL) tarragon
¼ cup (50 mL) sherry (optional)

𝄢 Slice the mushroom stems; leave the caps whole.

𝄢 Melt 3 tbsp (45 mL) of the butter in a skillet. Add the minced garlic and the mushroom caps and cook over high heat, stirring constantly. Remove from heat and add the mushroom stems. Season with salt and pepper.

𝄢 Melt the remaining 1 tbsp (15 mL) butter in a saucepan. Add the flour and the cream. Blend thoroughly and cook over low heat, stirring, until the sauce is creamy. Add the sour cream and the tarragon. Heat through but do not boil.

𝄢 Add the mushrooms and the sherry. Simmer for a few minutes, but do not boil. Adjust the seasoning and serve.

MUSHROOM SOUFFLÉ

2 tbsp (30 mL) chicken fat or bacon fat
3 tbsp (45 mL) flour
½ tsp (2 mL) salt
¾ cup (175 mL) milk
1 tbsp (15 mL) butter
½ cup (125 mL) thinly sliced mushrooms
4 egg yolks
2 tbsp (30 mL) grated Parmesan cheese
5 egg whites

❧ TECHNIQUE ❧
MUSHROOMS TOSCANA

1 Chop the mushroom stems; leave the caps whole.

2 Melt the butter in a saucepan and add the diced tomatoes, rosemary and sugar.

3 Add the mushroom stems.

4 Turn into a buttered baking dish. Top with the mushroom caps.

❧ Prepare a white sauce with the chicken or bacon fat, flour, salt and milk.

❧ Melt the butter and sauté the mushrooms over high heat for 1 minute, stirring constantly.

❧ Add the mushrooms to the white sauce along with the egg yolks and the grated cheese. Mix thoroughly.

❧ Beat the egg whites until stiff and carefully fold into the mushroom mixture.

❧ Line an 8-in. (20-cm) soufflé dish with wax paper. Turn the mushroom mixture into the dish.

❧ Bake for 30 minutes in a preheated 400°F (200°C) oven and serve.

SWISS-STYLE MUSHROOMS

1 lb (500 g) mushrooms
3 tbsp (45 mL) butter
1 tsp (5 mL) salt
¼ tsp (1 mL) pepper
1 tbsp (15 mL) butter
2 tbsp (30 mL) flour
1 cup (250 mL) cream
1 cup (250 mL) grated Swiss cheese

❧ Thinly slice the mushroom stems and caps.

❧ In a saucepan, heat the 3 tbsp (45 mL) butter until melted and slightly browned. Add the mushrooms and cook over high heat for 2 minutes, stirring constantly. Season with salt and pepper.

❧ Melt the 1 tbsp (15 mL) butter and add the flour and the cream. Cook until creamy, stirring constantly.

❧ Add the grated cheese and the mushrooms. Simmer over very low heat for 10 minutes, stirring frequently. Serve.

MUSHROOMS WITH SAUCE

❧ Peel and slice 1 lb (500 g) fresh mushrooms.

❧ Heat together 3 tbsp (45 mL) butter and 2 tbsp (30 mL) consommé or water. Add the mushrooms and simmer for 5 minutes.

❧ Add 1 cup (250 mL) sour cream and season to taste with salt, pepper and nutmeg.

❧ Cook over very low heat until the sauce thickens. Do not allow to boil.

❧ Place over slices of rye or whole-wheat toast. Serve with sliced tomatoes and parsleyed rice.

STUFFED MUSHROOMS

½ lb (250 g) mushrooms
3 tbsp (45 mL) butter
1 tbsp (15 mL) minced parsley
1 clove garlic, minced
½ tsp (2 mL) salt
pinch of pepper

❧ Remove the stems from the mushrooms and finely chop them. Place the caps in a baking dish, round side down.

❧ Cream the butter with the parsley, garlic, salt, pepper and finely chopped stems. Stuff the mushroom caps with this mixture.

❧ Cook over very high heat for 2 to 3 minutes, taking care not to overbrown, or bake in a preheated 500°F (260°C) oven for 5 to 6 minutes.

Swiss-Style Mushrooms

MARINATED MUSHROOMS

½ lb (250 g) mushrooms
4 tbsp (60 mL) olive oil
2 tbsp (30 mL) cider vinegar
or wine vinegar
½ tsp (2 mL) salt
pinch of pepper
2 green onions, minced

🌢 Finely chop the mushroom stems and caps. Add the remaining ingredients. Mix together and let stand for 1 hour to blend flavors.

🌢 Do not cook the mushrooms.

🌢 Serve on a bed of lettuce instead of French dressing or on unbuttered slices of toasted French or white bread. The mushrooms are delicious with cold chicken or lobster, or as an hors d'oeuvre.

ARTICHOKES

PREPARATION
To prepare an artichoke for cooking, hold it against the counter with one hand and with the other hand twist off the stem (the tough fibers will come off at the same time). Remove the coarse outer leaves.

BASIC COOKING METHOD
Place the artichokes in boiling salted water. Cook over high heat for 30 to 40 minutes or until the leaves come out easily when pulled.

🌢 Artichokes are normally served with melted butter, *Hollandaise Sauce* (page 54), *French Dressing*

Stuffed Mushrooms

(page 68) or a mixture of white sauce (see page 46) and egg yolk.

PARISIAN-STYLE ARTICHOKES

6 artichoke bottoms
½ cup (125 mL) fresh mushrooms
¼ lb (125 g) liver pâté
¼ cup (50 mL) sherry
¼ cup (50 mL) consommé
1 tsp (5 mL) butter

🌢 Clean the artichoke bottoms and place in a saucepan of boiling water. Cover and cook over medium heat for 15 to 20 minutes. Place in a buttered baking dish.

🌢 Thinly slice the mushrooms. Cream together with the liver pâté.

🌢 Divide the mushroom mixture evenly among the artichoke bottoms.

🌢 Pour the sherry and the con-

sommé into the baking dish. Dot each artichoke bottom with butter.

🌢 Bake in a 400°F (200°C) oven for 15 minutes.

🌢 Serve hot or cold.

ARTICHOKES FLORENTINE

6 artichoke bottoms
1 lb (500 g) fresh spinach
1½ cups (375 mL) medium white sauce
1 egg, slightly beaten
1 tbsp (15 mL) butter
¼ cup (50 mL) grated Gruyère cheese

🌢 Clean the artichoke bottoms and place them in a saucepan with boiling water. Cover and cook over medium heat for 15 to 20 minutes. Drain and place in a buttered baking dish.

Asparagus au Gratin

🍃 Cook and finely chop the spinach.

🍃 Make a medium white sauce with 2 tbsp (30 mL) butter, 2 tbsp (30 mL) all-purpose flour and 1½ cups (375 mL) milk. Season to taste with salt and pepper.

🍃 Remove the sauce from heat, add the egg and beat for a few seconds. Add the butter and cheese and stir until both are melted.

🍃 Stuff the artichoke bottoms with the spinach. Cover with the cheese sauce.

🍃 Heat in a 400°F (200°C) oven for 15 minutes and serve.

GREEK-STYLE ARTICHOKES

1 can or 1 package frozen artichoke hearts
12 small white onions
1 clove garlic, minced
¼ cup (50 mL) olive oil
½ cup (125 mL) lemon juice
1 tbsp (15 mL) sugar
1½ tsp (7 mL) salt
¼ tsp (1 mL) pepper
¼ cup (50 mL) water

🍃 Allow the artichoke hearts to thaw.

🍃 Place the onions, garlic, olive oil, lemon juice, sugar, salt, pepper and water in a saucepan and bring to a boil. Simmer for 25 minutes.

🍃 Add the artichoke hearts and cook for 5 minutes. Adjust the seasoning. Turn into a serving dish and refrigerate.

🍃 Frozen artichoke hearts prepared in this manner will keep for 2 weeks. They are delicious as an hors d'oeuvre or in a salad.

ASPARAGUS

Nothing can compare with asparagus.

🍃 When fresh, asparagus. is firm and shiny, the stalks are heavy, and the tips are firm and tightly closed, with a lavender tint. One way of determining whether asparagus is fresh is to test the hard part with your fingernail. If your nail easily penetrates the flesh, the asparagus is fresh. Old asparagus is stringy and tastes bitter.

🍃 Asparagus, like corn, is best on the day it is picked. To store fresh asparagus, wrap in a damp cloth (which will prevent contact with air) and refrigerate. Do not clean asparagus until you are ready to prepare it.

PREPARATION

Snap off the ends by gently bending each stalk; the woody end should break off at the right spot. Soak the stalks in cold water to remove any dirt. If they are sandy, rinse in cold running water. With a sharp vegetable peeler, peel the very fat stalks and any that are not so fresh. When the stalks are of different sizes it is best to tie the smaller ones in bunches.

BASIC COOKING METHOD

Place the large stalks in an enameled cast-iron skillet and cover with the bunches of small stalks. Add water to cover. Boil, covered, over high heat for 8 to 12 minutes. Do not overcook, or the asparagus will become waterlogged and tasteless.

Serve immediately. If necessary to keep warm, drain and place in a cloth-lined dish; cover with another cloth. The cloths will absorb the moisture and prevent the asparagus from becoming mushy. Cover the dish and keep it warm.

IN A PRESSURE-COOKER

Wash and prepare the asparagus and set it on the rack of the pressure-cooker. Add ½ cup (125 mL) water. Secure the lid and let the pressure rise. Cook for 1 minute. Reduce the pressure immediately. Serve.

Hot asparagus can be served buttered, English-style, or with a *Hollandaise Sauce* (see page 54), Maltese sauce (orange-flavored Hollandaise) or a bowl of melted butter and lemon.

Cold, it can be served with a mayonnaise mousseline (a mixture of whipped cream and mayonnaise) or with a lemon French dressing.

FLEMISH-STYLE ASPARAGUS

1 lb (500 g) asparagus
1 hard-cooked egg
1 tbsp (15 mL) parsley
3 tbsp (45 mL) melted butter
2 tbsp (30 mL) lemon juice

Cook the asparagus. Drain and place on a warm serving platter.

Finely chop the hard-cooked egg and parsley. Add the melted butter and lemon juice.

Heat and place over the asparagus.

ASPARAGUS AU GRATIN

1 lb (500 g) asparagus
1 cup (250 mL) medium white sauce (see page 46) with cheese
½ cup (125 mL) grated cheese
1 tbsp (15 mL) melted butter

Place the asparagus in a baking dish.

Wrap the stalks in buttered wax paper.

Cover the tips with the white sauce with cheese and sprinkle the tips with the grated cheese. Pour the melted butter over.

Brown in a 400°F (200°C) oven.

Remove the wax paper and serve.

ASPARAGUS MILANAISE

1 lb (500 g) cooked asparagus
½ cup (125 mL) grated cheese
2 tbsp (30 mL) butter

Arrange the cooked asparagus on a serving platter in one layer. Sprinkle the tips with the grated cheese. Heat the butter until it is melted and slightly browned and pour over the asparagus. Serve.

POLISH-STYLE ASPARAGUS

1 lb (500 g) cooked asparagus
2 hard-cooked eggs, chopped
¼ cup (50 mL) minced parsley
½ cup (125 mL) small croutons

Arrange the cooked asparagus on a serving dish in one layer.

Corn

Sprinkle with a mixture of the chopped eggs and the parsley. Sauté the croutons in butter and place them over the asparagus. Serve.

PARISIAN-STYLE ASPARAGUS

❧ Blend ½ cup (125 mL) hot white sauce with 1 cup (250 mL) hot mayonnaise. Add 2 tbsp (30 mL) lemon juice.

❧ Pour over cooked asparagus and serve with fish or seafood.

CORN

PREPARATION
Fresh corn is a nice shade of green, and the husks are tight and even slightly damp. The silk at the top should not be brittle, and the stem should be moist. Break off 1 in. (2 cm) from each end of the ear of corn and remove the outer leaves. Pull the husks down one by one until the corn is exposed, then pull off the silk. Carefully rewrap the corn in its husk and tie it at the top with string.

BASIC COOKING METHOD
For 12 ears of corn, mix 2 cups (500 mL) water, 1 cup (250 mL) milk and 1 tsp (5 mL) sugar in a large saucepan. Bring to a boil. Add the corn, cover and boil vigorously for 12 to 15 minutes, depending on the size of the ears.

❧ Do not add any salt to the corn while it is cooking.

❧ Store leftover corn at room temperature, since it tends to toughen in the refrigerator.

❧ Reheat leftover corn in its husk. Simmer for 10 minutes in 1 cup (250 mL) water.

IN A PRESSURE -COOKER
Place the corn in the bottom of the pressure-cooker (without the rack). Add ¼ cup (50 mL) milk, ¼ cup (50 mL) water and a pinch of sugar and salt. Secure the lid and let the pressure rise. Cook for 5 minutes. Reduce the pressure immediately. Serve.

CHARLESTON CORN

3 cups (750 mL) fresh
or canned corn
3 eggs, beaten
1 tsp (5 mL) salt
2 tbsp (30 mL) sugar
3 tbsp (45 mL) melted butter
1⅛ cup (275 mL) warm milk

❧ Mix all the ingredients and turn into a buttered glass baking dish. Bake in a 325°F (160°C) oven for 30 to 40 minutes or until the blade of a knife inserted in the center comes out clean.

❧ As a variation, add to the mixture 2 tbsp (30 mL) grated onion or ½ cup (125 mL) chopped walnuts.

SCALLOPED CORN

3 cups (750 mL) fresh
or canned corn
2 eggs, well beaten
½ tsp (2 mL) salt
¾ cup (175 mL) cracker-crumbs
2 tbsp (30 mL) melted butter
1 cup (250 mL) milk

❧ Mix together the corn, eggs, salt, cracker-crumbs and butter. Turn into a buttered baking dish.

❧ Pour the milk over and bake in a 325°F (160°C) oven for 30 minutes.

CORN FRITTERS

1 cup (250 mL) fresh
or canned corn
1 egg, separated
¼ tsp (1 mL) salt
½ tsp (2 mL) sugar
⅓ tsp (1.5 mL) baking powder
2 tbsp (30 mL) flour
1 tbsp (15 mL) 10% cream
2 tbsp (30 mL) melted butter

❧ Drain the canned corn.

❧ Beat the egg yolk and the egg white separately.

❧ Mix together the corn, salt, sugar, baking powder, flour, cream and melted butter. Blend in the egg yolk and then the egg white.

❧ Drop by spoonfuls onto a well-greased skillet. Brown for 2 to 3 minutes on each side.

PUFFED CORN FRITTERS

4 eggs, separated
3 tbsp (45 mL) flour
¾ tsp (3 mL) salt
½ tsp (2 mL) sugar
¾ tsp (3 mL) baking powder
¾ cup (175 mL) fresh
or canned corn

❧ Beat the egg whites until stiff. Beat the yolks until foamy and fold into the whites.

❧ Mix together the flour, salt, sugar and baking powder. Sprinkle over the eggs and fold in carefully. Add the corn (if using canned corn, drain first).

❧ Deep-fry spoonfuls of the mixture at 350°F (180°C) until each fritter is golden brown.

ROAST CORN ON THE COB

Soak each ear of corn on the cob in cold salted water for approximately 10 minutes so that the husks will not burn during roasting. Drain well.

❧ Place the corn on the barbecue grill.

❧ Roast over hot coals for approximately 10 minutes, or until the corn is very hot. Turn frequently during cooking to brown all sides. Remove the husks and serve immediately.

FOIL-WRAPPED

Foil wrapped corn will steam in the foil and won't have that grilled flavor. Remove the husks. Spread each ear with soft butter and sprinkle with a pinch of sugar. Place the ear on a square of aluminum foil and seal the foil tightly. Roast directly on hot coals for 10 to 15 minutes, turning 2 or 3 times. Serve immediately.

WITH BACON

Remove the husks and brush each ear with a little peanut butter. Wrap 1 or 2 strips of bacon around each ear and hold in place with toothpicks. Place the corn on the barbecue grill and roast for

French-Style Green Peas

10 minutes, turning 2 or 3 times. Serve immediately.

BARBECUE-BOILED

Corn can be barbecue-boiled with or without the husk. Place a large kettle on the barbecue grill and bring 3 cups (750 mL) water, 3 cups (750 mL) milk and 1 tsp (5 mL) sugar to a boil. Add the corn and cover. Cook in the husk for 10 minutes, shucked for 5 to 6 minutes. Drain. Brush each ear with melted butter. Place on the barbecue grill and cook for another few minutes or until the corn is golden. Serve immediately.

PEAS

PREPARATION

Wash and shell the peas only when you are ready to cook them. If they must be shelled in advance, wrap them in a moist cloth and store them in a cool place. Shelled peas dry out and toughen very quickly.

BASIC COOKING METHOD

Place the shelled green peas in a saucepan. Add boiling water to a depth of 1 in. (2.5 cm). Sprinkle with a pinch of sugar and salt. Cover and boil vigorously for 10 to 20 minutes.

POTTED GREEN PEAS

2 lbs (1 kg) green peas, shelled
1 tbsp (15 mL) butter
½ tsp (2 mL) sugar
6 fresh mint leaves, or to taste

❧ Place the shelled peas in a large glass jar with a tight-fitting lid. Add the remaining ingredients.

❧ Close the jar tightly and place it in a saucepan filled with lukewarm water. Cover and bring to a boil. Boil for 1 hour.

🌲 Turn the peas into a serving dish and serve.

FRENCH-STYLE GREEN PEAS

1 head lettuce, shredded
1 to 2 lbs (500 g to 1 kg) shelled green peas
1 tsp (5 mL) sugar
2 tbsp (30 mL) butter
4 to 6 small onions, peeled

🌲 Place the lettuce in a saucepan. Top with the green peas, sugar, butter and whole onions. Add enough boiling water to cover.

🌲 Cover and cook over high heat for 20 to 30 minutes or until the peas are tender. Drain and serve.

GREEN PEAS WITH BACON

4 strips bacon
4 green onions, minced
2 tbsp (30 mL) flour
½ tsp (2 mL) salt
pinch of pepper
pinch of sugar
1 cup (250 mL) consommé
or 10% cream
2 packages frozen green peas

🌲 In a skillet, fry the bacon and the green onions. Cut the bacon into small pieces.

🌲 Remove all but 2 tbsp (30 mL) fat from the skillet. Add the flour, salt, pepper and sugar. Stir until well blended, then add the consommé or cream. Cook, stirring

constantly, until smooth and creamy.

🌲 Add the unthawed green peas to the sauce. Cover and simmer over medium heat for 10 minutes. Serve.

🌲 Fresh green peas can be used instead of frozen. Simmer fresh peas for 10 minutes longer.

GREEN PEAS PRINTANIERE

2 lbs (1 kg) green peas
6 small new carrots
12 small onions or green onions
1 small head garden lettuce
12 small new potatoes
4 tbsp (60 mL) butter
2 tbsp (30 mL) flour
1 tsp (5 mL) sugar
salt and pepper to taste
1 cup (250 mL) consommé
½ cup (125 mL) 10% cream

🌲 Shell the green peas. Scrape the carrots and cut into thin slices. Peel the onions but leave them whole. Wash the lettuce and separate the leaves. Scrape the potatoes.

🌲 Melt the butter in a saucepan, then add 2 tbsp (30 mL) flour, 1 tsp (5 mL) sugar, salt and pepper. Blend well. Add the consommé and the cream. Stir over medium heat until the sauce is slightly thickened.

🌲 Add the lettuce leaves, onions, potatoes, carrots and peas. Cover and simmer for 30 minutes or until the vegetables are cooked.

GREEN PEAS WITH RICE

¾ cup (175 mL) uncooked rice
1 lb (500 g) green peas, shelled
1 carrot, diced
pinch of thyme
¼ tsp (1 mL) basil
½ tsp (2 mL) sugar
1 tsp (5 mL) salt
2 cups (500 mL) water, consommé or milk
1 tbsp (15 mL) butter, cut into small pieces
2 tbsp (30 mL) minced parsley

🌲 Place the rice, green peas, carrot, thyme, basil, sugar and salt in a saucepan. Add the water, consommé or milk. Bring to a boil. Cover and simmer for 20 minutes or until the green peas are tender and all the liquid has been absorbed.

🌲 Turn into a warm serving dish. Add the butter and sprinkle with the parsley.

GREEN OR WAX BEANS

PREPARATION
Rinse the beans under cold water and cut off the ends. Remove threads as necessary. If you prepare the beans a few hours in advance, wrap them in wax paper and refrigerate until ready to use.

BASIC COOKING METHOD
Place the beans in a medium saucepan. Add enough boiling water to half fill the saucepan. Sprinkle with ½ tsp (2 mL) salt.

🌲 Cover and boil over high heat

for 15 to 20 minutes, depending on the size of the beans.

IN A PRESSURE-COOKER

Place the beans on the rack of the pressure-cooker. Add ¼ cup (50 mL) water. Add salt. Secure the lid and let the pressure rise. Cook for 4 to 5 minutes, depending on the size of the beans. Reduce the pressure immediately and serve.

GREEN BEAN SALAD

1 lb (500 g) green beans
pinch of savory
French dressing
2 hard-cooked eggs
3 tbsp (45 mL) slivered
salted almonds

ᴥ Cook the green beans with the pinch of savory until tender-crisp. Drain the beans and rinse under cold running water until cool. Pat dry with paper towels.

ᴥ To serve, mix the chilled green beans with the French dressing. Place in a salad bowl. Garnish with quartered hard-cooked eggs all around and sprinkle the slivered almonds in the middle.

GREEN BEANS TOURANGELLE

1 lb (500 g) green beans
1 tsp (5 mL) butter
1 tsp (5 mL) flour
½ cup (125 mL) milk
1 clove garlic, minced
½ cup (125 mL) parsley, minced
salt and pepper to taste

ᴥ Clean and cook the green beans (see *Basic Cooking Method*, opposite).

ᴥ Melt the butter in a skillet. Add the flour and the milk. Stir until creamy. Add the garlic and the parsley. Season to taste with salt and pepper. Simmer for a few minutes.

ᴥ Top the green beans with the sauce and serve.

AMERICAN-STYLE GREEN BEANS

3 tbsp (45 mL) butter
or bacon fat
1 medium onion, finely chopped
⅓ cup (75 mL) chili sauce
4 cups (1 L) cooked green beans, cut into 1-in. (2-cm) pieces
salt and pepper to taste

ᴥ Melt the butter or bacon fat in a skillet and brown the onion.

Add the chili sauce and mix well. Add the cooked beans and stir to blend. Simmer for a few minutes.

ᴥ Season to taste with salt and pepper and serve.

FRESH BEAN SALAD

1 lb (500 g) green or wax beans
3 green onions, minced
¼ cup (50 mL) French dressing
1 head lettuce

ᴥ Cut the beans on the diagonal and cook until tender-crisp. Drain well. Add the green onions and the French dressing. Blend well. Serve on a bed of lettuce.

ᴥ If desired, add 1 cup (250 ml) thinly sliced radishes, ½ cup (125 ml) grated cheese or sliced hard-cooked eggs and toss.

American-Style Green Beans

GREEN BEANS NIÇOISE

1 large onion, finely chopped
1 clove garlic, minced
½ green pepper, diced
¼ cup (50 mL) olive oil
1½ cups (375 mL) fresh tomatoes, peeled and diced
1 tsp (5 mL) salt
¼ tsp (1 mL) pepper
1 bay leaf
1½ lbs (750 g) green beans
¼ tsp (1 mL) sugar
2 tbsp (30 mL) finely chopped parsley

🍃 Brown the onion, garlic and green pepper in the olive oil. Add the tomatoes, salt, pepper and bay leaf. Bring to a boil and simmer for 10 minutes.

🍃 Cut the beans into 1-in. (2-cm) pieces. Add them to the tomato mixture, then add the sugar and the parsley. Cover and cook for 25 minutes over low heat.

Green Beans Niçoise

FRESH BEANS GERMAN-STYLE

1 lb (500 g) green or wax beans
pinch of savory
1 tbsp (15 mL) lemon juice
2 tbsp (30 mL) fresh dill, minced
3 tbsp (45 mL) butter
salt and pepper to taste

🍃 Cook the beans with the savory. Drain well. Add the remaining ingredients and simmer for a few minutes.

🍃 Season to taste with salt and pepper. Serve.

ORIENTAL GREEN BEANS

1 lb (500 g) green beans
2 strips bacon, diced
1 onion, minced
2 tbsp (30 mL) cider vinegar
1 tsp (5 mL) sugar
1 tbsp (15 mL) parsley, minced
salt and pepper to taste

🍃 Cook the beans (see *Basic Cooking Method*, page 412). Drain, reserving the cooking liquid.

🍃 Fry the bacon. Add the onion and brown slightly. Add the reserved cooking liquid. Boil over high heat until the liquid is reduced to ¼ cup (50 mL).

🍃 Add the cider vinegar, sugar and parsley. Simmer for 5 minutes. Add the beans and cook until the beans are heated through.

🍃 Season with salt and pepper and serve.

WAX BEANS WITH TOMATOES

1 onion, minced
1 clove garlic, minced
3 tbsp (45 mL) olive oil
1 cup (250 mL) canned tomatoes
½ tsp (2 mL) salt
1 tsp (5 mL) sugar
¼ tsp (1 mL) oregano
1 bay leaf
1 lb (500 g) wax beans
salt and pepper to taste

Brown the onion and garlic in the olive oil. Add the tomatoes, salt, sugar, oregano and bay leaf. Bring to a boil and simmer for 20 minutes.

Wash the beans, remove the ends and cut into 1-in. (2-cm) pieces. Add to the tomato mixture. Cover and simmer for 30 minutes or until the beans are tender. Season to taste with salt and pepper.

You may substitute 1 or 2 packages frozen beans for the fresh beans. Place unthawed in the tomato sauce and cook for approximately 30 minutes.

POLISH-STYLE BEAN SALAD

1½ lbs (750 g) green or wax beans
⅓ cup (75 mL) water
1 tbsp (15 mL) olive oil
pinch of savory
1 green onion, minced
½ tsp (2 mL) sugar
1 hard-cooked egg, grated
½ cup (125 mL) French dressing

Place the beans in a skillet. Add the water, olive oil, savory, green onion and sugar. Bring to a boil. Cover and cook over low heat for 20 minutes or until the beans are tender-crisp and the water has almost completely evaporated. Drain and cool.

Mix the grated hard-cooked egg with the French dressing. Toss with the lukewarm beans. Serve. Do not refrigerate or the oil will congeal and the beans will become tough.

ARMENIAN-STYLE GREEN BEANS

Sauté 1 cup (250 mL) diced onions in ¼ cup (50 mL) olive oil until tender but not brown.

Slice 1 lb (500 g) green beans on the diagonal. Add to the onions along with 1 cup (250 mL) drained canned tomatoes, 1 tsp (5 mL) sugar, 1 tsp (5 mL) salt and ¼ tsp (1 mL) savory or oregano.

Simmer for 30 minutes. Do not boil. The beans should stay green and crisp.

Serve with poached or scrambled eggs.

To bring out the full flavor of the beans, add toasted almonds, chopped parsley or chives; or fresh marjoram, nutmeg and prepared mustard or chili sauce to warm, cooked green beans.

VARIATIONS
Add cooked green peas, julienne carrots, lima beans or sautéed sliced mushrooms to warm, cooked green beans before serving; dab with a little butter.

LIMA BEANS

PREPARATION
Shell fresh lima beans just before cooking. If they are shelled in advance, they tend to be tough when cooked. Rinse in cold water. Rinse dried lima beans several times in cold water to remove any dirt. Soak for 1 hour in cold water before cooking.

BASIC COOKING METHOD
To prepare fresh lima beans, shell the beans and place in a saucepan. Add enough boiling water to half-fill the saucepan. Bring to a boil. Cover and simmer over low heat for 20 to 30 minutes.

To prepare dried lima beans bring 4 cups (1 L) water to a boil for each cup (250 mL) dried lima beans. Do not add salt. Add the prepared lima beans. Simmer for 1½ to 2 hours. Add 1 tsp (5 mL) salt during the last 30 minutes of cooking. Drain.

The cooking liquid can be used in soups and sauces, and is an interesting alternative to water for diluting canned soups.

Frozen lima beans are the easiest and quickest to prepare. Place a package of frozen beans in a saucepan. Add hot or cold water to cover. Add a pinch of sugar. Cover and boil over medium heat for 15 to 20 minutes.

SEASONING TIPS
Savory, marjoram and bay leaves all bring out the natural flavor of lima beans.

Onions, tomatoes, green peppers, chives and parsley are delicious with lima beans.

TOMATOES

To peel tomatoes, place them in a bowl and pour boiling water over them. Let stand for 2 to 3 minutes, then drain and place the tomatoes in a bowl of cold water. The skin will then come off easily. Start peeling from the top.

🍂 Remove the seeds by squeezing the tomato gently, cut side down.

🍂 When cooking tomatoes, always add 1 tsp (5 mL) sugar for every 4 to 6 tomatoes. It will sweeten them and bring out their flavor and color.

🍂 Keep tomatoes refrigerated.

🍂 Serve raw tomatoes at room temperature. They will have more flavor than if served cold.

SALADE NIÇOISE

This salad is delicious as an hors d'oeuvre or a light lunch. Use whole olives. Serve with hot French bread and tea.

4 tomatoes
1 green pepper
3 green onions or 1 small onion
½ cup (125 mL) black olives
½ cup (125 mL) flaked tuna
French dressing
2 hard-cooked eggs

🍂 Slice the tomatoes. Seed the green pepper and cut into strips. Chop the green onions.

🍂 Mix together the tomatoes, green pepper, green onions, the whole black olives and the tuna.

🍂 Add the French dressing and toss gently.

🍂 Place on a serving platter lined with lettuce leaves. Garnish with quartered hard-cooked eggs.

PARISIAN-STYLE TOMATOES

Here's a nutritious snack that's easy to prepare. As a variation, add a bit of diced cucumber. If desired, serve with unbuttered crackers.

1 tomato
1 cooked potato, diced
1 green onion, chopped
black or green olives, chopped
pinch of basil

2 tsp (10 mL) mayonnaise
½ tsp (2 mL) vinegar
or lemon juice
salt and pepper to taste

🍂 Cut a thin slice from the top of the tomato. Remove some of the pulp.

🍂 Mix the tomato pulp, potato, green onion, olives, basil, mayonnaise and vinegar in a bowl. Add salt and pepper to taste and blend well. Spoon into the tomato shell.

🍂 Serve on a bed of lettuce.

TOMATOES STUFFED WITH MUSHROOMS

4 tbsp (60 mL) butter
½ lb (250 g) mushrooms, chopped
1 cup (250 mL) tomato sauce
1 egg yolk, beaten
pinch of thyme
1 tsp (5 mL) salt
pinch of pepper
6 tomato shells
1 tbsp (15 mL) breadcrumbs
1 tbsp (15 mL) butter

🍂 Melt the butter in a skillet and cook the mushrooms until slightly browned.

🍂 Add the tomato sauce, beaten egg yolk, thyme, salt and pepper. Stir to blend well.

🍂 Stuff the tomatoes with the mixture. Sprinkle each tomato with breadcrumbs and dot with butter.

🍂 Bake in a 400°F (200°C) oven for 20 to 30 minutes.

🍂 Serve with roast chicken.

Tomatoes Stuffed with Mushrooms

❧ TECHNIQUE ❧

TOMATOES STUFFED WITH MUSHROOMS

1 Scoop out the tomatoes.

2 Melt the butter in a skillet and cook the mushrooms until slightly browned.

3 Add the tomato sauce, egg yolk, thyme, salt and pepper.

4 Stuff the tomatoes with the mixture.

SAVOY PAN-BROILED TOMATOES

4 to 6 tomatoes
3 tbsp (45 mL) butter
1 tsp (5 mL) dry mustard
sugar
1 egg yolk

❧ Cut the unpeeled tomatoes in two. Sprinkle each half with salt.

❧ Place in a shallow dish, cut side down. Let stand for 20 minutes. Drain, rinse and pat dry.

❧ Cream together the butter, dry mustard and egg yolk.

❧ Rub each tomato half with a little sugar. Spread the cut side with the butter mixture.

❧ Place the tomatoes in a skillet, cut side down. Cook for 20 minutes over low heat, without turning.

❧ Using a spatula, remove the tomato halves from the skillet and serve. The golden butter paste will add an exquisite flavor.

TOMATOES PROVENÇALE

12 tomatoes
3 to 5 tbsp (45 to 75 mL) peanut or olive oil
2 or 3 cloves garlic, finely chopped
2 tbsp (30 mL) finely chopped parsley
¼ tsp (1 mL) thyme
1 tbsp (15 mL) sugar
½ tsp (2 mL) salt
¼ tsp (1 mL) pepper

❧ Peel the tomatoes and squeeze them gently to remove the pulp and seeds. Cut into small pieces.

❧ Place the oil, garlic, parsley, thyme, sugar, salt and pepper in an enameled cast-iron saucepan. Heat for a few minutes. Add the tomatoes. Cover and cook over low heat for 1 hour.

❧ Adjust the seasoning and serve.

BUTTERED TOMATOES

2 lbs (1 kg) very firm tomatoes
4 tbsp (60 mL) butter
1 tbsp (15 mL) sugar
½ tsp (2 mL) pepper
pinch of thyme or marjoram

❧ Peel the tomatoes and squeeze them gently to remove the pulp and seeds. Cut into quarters.

❧ Melt the butter in a skillet and add the tomato quarters in one layer. Add the sugar, pepper and the thyme or marjoram. Cook over medium heat, stirring constantly, for 3 to 4 minutes or until the tomatoes are hot but still firm.

❧ Serve immediately.

CURRIED TOMATOES

2 lbs (1 kg) tomatoes
3 tbsp (45 mL) olive oil or butter
2 tsp (10 mL) curry powder
2 large onions, sliced
1 clove garlic, minced
1 tsp (5 mL) salt
1 tsp (5 mL) sugar
¼ cup (50 mL) water

❧ Wash and quarter the tomatoes.

❧ Heat the oil or butter. Add the curry powder and mix well. Add the onion, garlic, salt, sugar and water. Bring to a boil. Add the tomatoes.

❧ Cover and boil over medium heat for 15 minutes or until the mixture has a sauce-like consistency.

BROILED TOMATOES

4 large, firm tomatoes
1 tsp (5 mL) salt
¼ tsp (1 mL) pepper
1 tbsp (15 mL) sugar
4 tbsp (60 mL) chopped onion
2 tbsp (30 mL) finely chopped parsley
2 tbsp (30 mL) butter

❧ Cut the tomatoes in half crosswise.

❧ Sprinkle each tomato half with salt, pepper, sugar, onion and parsley. Place on a broiler rack or a baking sheet, or in a pie plate.

❧ Dot each tomato half with butter.

❧ Broil 5 to 6 in. (13 to 15 cm) from the heat for approximately 10 minutes or bake in a 450°F (230°C) oven for 10 minutes.

FROZEN TOMATOES

When summer comes around, tomatoes are so plentiful that we're sometimes hard pressed to find ways to eat them all. Freezing some of them will mean you can prepare tomato-based dishes year-round. However, I do not recommend freezing whole tomatoes.

4 lbs (2 kg) ripe tomatoes
4 medium onions, chopped
2 whole cloves
2 tbsp (30 mL) sugar
½ tsp (2 mL) thyme
2 bay leaves
handful of parsley
2 tbsp (30 mL) tomato paste
2 tbsp (30 mL) butter

🍂 Quarter the tomatoes and place them in a saucepan along with the chopped onions, cloves, sugar, thyme, bay leaves and parsley. Bring to a boil, stirring constantly. Boil for 25 minutes over medium heat, uncovered.

🍂 Force the mixture through a sieve.

🍂 Return to the heat. Stir in the tomato paste and the butter. Stir until the mixture starts to boil.

🍂 Pour the mixture into containers. Cool before freezing.

🍂 Use in any recipe that calls for tomato sauce.

VARIATION

🍂 Add ½ cup (125 mL) cracker-crumbs to 2 cups (500 mL) of tomato sauce.

GARDEN TOMATO SALAD

This refreshing salad is at its best at the height of summer, when tomatoes are firm and juicy. For a tastier salad, refrigerate the tomatoes for 8 to 9 hours.

5 or 6 large ripe tomatoes
1 head Boston or garden lettuce
2 tbsp (30 mL) minced chives or 3 green onions, minced
⅓ cup (75 mL) chopped parsley

Stuffed Tomatoes

🍂 Place the tomatoes in a bowl and cover with boiling water. Let stand 5 minutes. Transfer them to a bowl of ice water. Peel and cut into thick slices.

🍂 Wash the lettuce. Line a shallow bowl with lettuce leaves and place the tomatoes in a circle, in 2 or 3 rows.

🍂 Mix together the chives or green onions and the parsley. Sprinkle over the tomatoes.

🍂 Cover and refrigerate until ready to serve.

STUFFED TOMATOES

Tasty, colorful and nutritious, these tomatoes can be served just about any time.

6 medium tomatoes
2 cups (500 mL) cottage cheese
¼ cup (50 mL) mayonnaise
¼ cup (50 mL) diced celery
⅓ cup (75 mL) minced celery

leaves
2 to 3 green onions, finely chopped
¼ cup (50 mL) chopped walnuts or almonds

🍂 Cut a thin slice from the top of each tomato and remove the pulp and seeds. Place the tomatoes on a plate, cut side down.

🍂 Combine the cottage cheese, mayonnaise, celery, celery leaves, green onions and chopped nuts. Toss lightly with a fork. Cover and refrigerate.

🍂 Stuff the tomatoes with the cottage cheese mixture at serving time.

🍂 Serve on a bed of lettuce with a light French dressing.

CREAMED TOMATOES

Here's a dish that's quick and easy to prepare. To ensure perfect

Eggplant Provençale

results, cook the tomatoes slowly over low heat, without stirring. Once prepared, this dish will keep for up to 1 week in the refrigerator.

1 28-oz (800-ml) can whole, peeled tomatoes
2 thick slices bread, crusts removed
1 tbsp (15 mL) butter
1 onion, finely chopped
1 tbsp (15 mL) sugar
1 tsp (5 mL) salt
¼ tsp (1 mL) pepper
1 bay leaf, crushed
¼ tsp (1 mL) thyme
parsley to taste

❧ This recipe works best with Italian or Bulgarian whole, peeled tomatoes. If these are unavailable, use any kind of tomatoes but extend the cooking time by 15 to 20 minutes.

❧ Toast the bread in a 300°F (150°C) oven. Set aside to cool while preparing the tomato mixture.

❧ Melt the butter in a saucepan and add the onion. Stir over low heat until the onion is tender but not browned. Add the tomatoes, sugar, salt and pepper.

❧ Break the toasted bread into small pieces and add to the tomatoes. Simmer, uncovered, for 1 hour.

❧ Add the crushed bay leaf, the thyme and the parsley. Stir well and simmer for another 40 to 60 minutes.

❧ The tomatoes are ready when the mixture is thick and creamy. Serve.

LOW-CALORIE STUFFED TOMATOES

6 medium tomatoes
2 tbsp (30 mL) butter
1 small onion, grated
1 cup (250 mL) soft breadcrumbs
1 tsp (5 mL) sugar
½ tsp (2 mL) salt
¼ tsp (1 mL) pepper
¼ tsp (1 mL) marjoram
2 egg yolks, beaten
1 tbsp (15 mL) minced parsley

❧ Cut a thin slice from the top of each tomato. Hollow out with a small spoon. Force the pulp through a sieve. Set aside.

❧ Melt the butter in a saucepan. Add the onion, breadcrumbs, tomato pulp, sugar, salt, pepper and marjoram. Cook for a few minutes. Remove from the heat and stir in the beaten egg yolks and the parsley.

❧ Stuff the tomatoes with this mixture.

❧ Bake in a 400°F (200°C) oven for 30 to 40 minutes.

SCALLOPED TOMATOES

3 tbsp (45 mL) butter
1 large onion, minced
2 cups (500 mL) soft breadcrumbs
½ tsp (2 mL) sugar
1 tsp (5 mL) salt
¼ tsp (1 mL) pepper
½ tsp (2 mL) basil or thyme
3½ cups (875 mL) canned

tomatoes
1 tbsp (15 mL) melted butter

❧ In a skillet, melt the butter and cook the onion until golden. Add the breadcrumbs, sugar, salt, pepper and the basil or thyme.

❧ In a buttered baking dish, alternate the tomatoes and the breadcrumb mixture in thin layers, ending with the breadcrumb mixture. Pour the melted butter over all.

❧ Bake in a 375°F (190°C) oven for 45 minutes.

OLD-FASHIONED GREEN TOMATOES

4 tbsp (60 mL) butter
5 to 8 green tomatoes, in thick slices
4 onions, in thick slices
3 apples, peeled and sliced
1 tsp (5 mL) salt
½ tsp (2 mL) pepper
1 whole clove
½ tsp (2 mL) ground cinnamon
½ tsp (2 mL) dry mustard
1 tbsp (15 mL) sugar
½ cup (125 mL) water

❧ Melt the butter in a skillet. Add all the remaining ingredients, except the water. Mix well. Cover and simmer for 20 minutes.

❧ Add the water and simmer for about 1 hour or until the mixture is thicke.

EGGPLANT

PREPARATION
Eggplant can be prepared in many different ways, all of them tasty. But whether steamed, fried or prepared au gratin, the eggplant must first have its excess water removed. The result will be a tastier and crisper vegetable.

❧ To rid an eggplant of excess water, peel and cut the eggplant into slices or large cubes. Sprinkle with coarse salt and let stand for 30 minutes. Rinse under cold running water and pat dry.

❧ In addition, salting eggplant before frying will reduce the amount of oil needed by more than half.

EGGPLANT PROVENÇALE

1 medium eggplant
flour
4 tbsp (60 mL) butter
2 tbsp (30 mL) soft breadcrumbs
1 tbsp (15 mL) fresh parsley
1 small clove garlic, finely chopped

❧ Slice the eggplant, salt and let stand for 30 minutes. Coat the slices with flour.

❧ Melt 3 tbsp (45 mL) of the butter and cook the eggplant over medium heat for 4 to 5 minutes on each side. Place in a serving dish.

❧ Melt the remaining 1 tbsp (15 mL) butter and add the breadcrumbs, parsley and garlic. Stir for a few minutes over low heat.

❧ Place over the eggplant and serve.

SAUTÉED EGGPLANT

1 medium eggplant
flour
oil
3 tbsp (45 mL) olive oil
2 to 4 tomatoes
1 green pepper, finely chopped
2 cloves garlic, crushed
¼ tsp (1 mL) basil
parsley to taste
pinch of sugar

❧ Slice the eggplant, salt and let stand for 30 minutes. Coat the slices in flour and sauté in oil.

❧ Heat the olive oil and add the tomatoes, green pepper, garlic, basil, parsley and sugar. Simmer until mixture is of desired consistency.

❧ Add the sautéed eggplant. Blend well and serve.

CREAMED EGGPLANT

1 medium eggplant
2 tbsp (30 mL) butter
1 tbsp (15 mL) olive oil
1 onion, thinly sliced
4 mushrooms, sliced
2 tomatoes, peeled and chopped
2 strips bacon, diced
pinch of sugar
½ tsp (2 mL) salt
¼ tsp (1 mL) pepper
½ tsp (2 mL) marjoram
2 tbsp (30 mL) whipping cream

❧ With a sharp knife, peel the eggplant and cut into ½-in. (1-cm) slices.

❧ In a large skillet, heat the butter and the olive oil. Add the sliced onion and brown. Add the eggplant slices and the mushrooms. Cook over medium heat until the eggplant is almost cooked.

ಶಿ Add the tomatoes, bacon, sugar, salt, pepper and marjoram. Cook until the eggplant is tender. Then cook over high heat until the liquid has evaporated and the mixture is creamy.

ಶಿ Add the cream. Adjust the seasoning and serve.

EGGPLANT PURÉE

1 medium eggplant
1 tsp (5 mL) salt
¼ tsp (1 mL) pepper
2 hard-cooked eggs
¼ cup (50 mL) mayonnaise
juice of ½ lemon

ಶಿ Wipe the eggplant with a damp cloth. Place in a pie plate and bake in a 325°F (160°C) oven

for 1 hour.

ಶಿ Peel the cooked eggplant and mash with a fork. Add the remaining ingredients and blend well.

ಶಿ Serve in a salad or as an hors d'oeuvre.

ಶಿ Eggplant purée does not have to be very smooth.

STUFFED EGGPLANT

1 eggplant
3 tbsp (45 mL) olive oil
¼ lb (125 g) mushrooms, chopped
1 clove garlic
6 green onions, chopped
4 fresh tomatoes, peeled and chopped
3 tbsp (45 mL) finely chopped parsley
thyme and basil to taste
salt and pepper to taste
½ cup (125 mL) breadcrumbs
2 tbsp (30 mL) melted butter

ಶಿ Cut the eggplant in half lengthwise. Remove the pulp with a spoon, being careful not to break the skin. Rid the eggplant of excess water (see opposite page). Chop the pulp and set aside.

ಶಿ Heat the olive oil and sauté the mushrooms, garlic, green onions and eggplant pulp. Mix well, then add the tomatoes, parsley and seasonings. Simmer for 10 to 20 minutes.

ಶಿ Stuff the eggplant halves with the mushroom mixture. Sprinkle with the breadcrumbs and top with melted butter.

ಶಿ Bake in a 400°F (200°C) oven for 20 minutes or until golden.

STUFFED EGGPLANT TURKISH-STYLE

Nothing compares with onions, garlic, tomatoes, thyme and red wine to bring out the natural flavor of the eggplant. This dish combines all of these ingredients.

ಶಿ Heat 3 tbsp (45 mL) olive oil in a skillet and lightly brown 3 thinly-sliced onions. Add 1 lb (500 g) sliced tomatoes. Season to taste with salt, pepper and thyme. Add ⅓ cup (75 mL) sesame seeds and mix well. Simmer until the mixture is smooth and well blended.

ಶಿ Meanwhile, with a sharp knife, cut a medium eggplant in half lengthwise. Place in a saucepan filled with boiling water and cook for 8 minutes. Drain.

ಶಿ Remove the pulp. Sprinkle the interior with salt and lemon juice.

ಶಿ Cook the pulp in 3 tbsp (45 mL) butter. Season with salt

Stuffed Eggplant

❦ TECHNIQUE ❦

STUFFED EGGPLANT

1   Remove the pulp with a spoon.

2   Heat the oil and sauté the mushrooms, garlic, green onions and eggplant pulp.

3   Add the tomatoes, parsley and seasonings.

4   Stuff the eggplant halves with the mushroom mixture. Sprinkle with breadcrumbs and top with melted butter.

Stuffed Green Peppers

and pepper.

🍃 Stuff the eggplant with the pulp mixture and cover with the tomato mixture. Place in a greased baking dish.

🍃 Bake, uncovered, in a 300°F (150°C) oven for 1 hour.

🍃 This dish is delicious with lamb or any barbecued meat.

GREEN PEPPERS

PREPARATION

Whether green, red or yellow, sweet peppers are all prepared in the same manner. They are delicious raw or cooked.

🍃 Wash the peppers, then remove the seeds and the white ribs. Cut in strips or cubes of any size.

🍃 To peel a green pepper, spear the stem end with a fork and hold the pepper over direct heat until the skin turns black and blisters and can be removed easily with a small knife. Or cook the whole pepper in a 500°F (260°C) oven for 20 minutes, then peel.

STUFFED GREEN PEPPERS

4 green peppers
½ lb (250 g) ground beef
½ cup (125 mL) whipping cream
½ cup (125 mL) soft breadcrumbs
1 egg, beaten
pinch of thyme
salt and pepper to taste
1 cup (250 mL) tomato sauce
½ cup (125 mL) water
½ tsp (2 mL) basil

🍃 Peel the green peppers. Cut a 1-in. (2-cm) slice off the top, then remove the seeds and the ribs.

🍃 In a bowl, mix the ground beef, cream, breadcrumbs, beaten egg, thyme, salt and pepper. Stuff the green peppers with this mixture. Place standing up in a baking dish.

🍃 Blend together the tomato sauce, water and basil. Pour over the green peppers.

🍃 Cover and bake in a 400°F (200°C) oven for 1 hour or until the peppers are tender.

VARIATION

🍃 Instead of the ground beef stuffing, use a tuna and celery stuffing, substituting rice for the breadcrumbs. Add onions and garlic.

STEWED GREEN PEPPERS ACADIAN-STYLE

3 tbsp (45 mL) bacon fat
1 onion, sliced
2 green peppers
4 large green tomatoes
1 tbsp (15 mL) brown sugar
¼ tsp (1 mL) cinnamon
2 whole cloves
1 tsp (5 mL) butter

🍃 In a skillet, melt the bacon fat and add the sliced onion. Cook for 3 minutes.

🍃 Wash and core the green peppers and the tomatoes. Cut each of the peppers and tomatoes in 8 lengthwise. Add to the onion and mix well.

🍃 Add the brown sugar, cinnamon and whole cloves. Cover and simmer for 20 minutes or until the peppers are just tender.

🍃 Add the butter, season to taste and serve.

ITALIAN GREEN PEPPERS

4 tbsp (60 mL) olive oil
1 large onion, chopped
4 cups (1 L) chopped
green peppers
1 14-oz (400-ml) can tomatoes
1 tsp (5 mL) sugar
¼ tsp (1 mL) rosemary
salt and pepper to taste
2 tbsp (30 mL) minced parsley

🍃 Heat the oil in a large skillet. Add the onion and brown slightly. Add the green pepper and the remaining ingredients. Cover and simmer for 20 minutes.

🍃 Remove the lid and boil over high heat until the mixture is of the desired consistency. Serve.

HAM-STUFFED GREEN PEPPERS

4 green peppers
2 cups (500 mL) boiling water
1 cup (250 mL) uncooked rice
1 onion, minced
2 tbsp (30 mL) butter
½ tsp (2 mL) sage
¾ cup (175 mL) water
½ lb (250 g) cheese, diced
1 cup (250 mL) diced cooked ham
2 tbsp (30 mL) finely chopped parsley

🍃 Cut the green peppers in half crosswise. Remove the seeds and the ribs. Cook for 5 minutes in boiling water. Drain, reserving the liquid.

🍃 Cook the rice according to the directions on the package.

🍃 Fry the onion in the butter until golden brown. Add the sage and stir for a few minutes. Remove from heat and add the water and the cheese. Stir until well blended. Add the ham, rice and parsley. Season to taste.

🍃 Fill the pepper halves with the ham mixture.

🍃 Place them on a rack in a skillet and add 1½ cups (375 mL) of the reserved cooking liquid. Cover and simmer for 15 to 20 minutes.

CUCUMBERS

Cucumbers are usually eaten raw, so we tend to forget how good they can be when they're cooked. Cucumbers are delicious creamed, with rice, with butter, à la provençale, fried and cooked in many other ways. And, of course, they make wonderful pickles.

PREPARATION

Choose cucumbers that are firm, straight and not too big. They're tastier when they're dark green in color. Yellow cucumbers are too ripe to eat raw; reserve these for pickling.

🍃 Peel the cucumber, if desired. Remove a ½-in. (1-cm) slice from each end. Cut into slices or wedges, or halve lengthwise.

BASIC COOKING METHOD

Peel the cucumbers and quarter them lengthwise. Remove the seeds with a small spoon. Place in a saucepan containing a mixture of salt water and vinegar (½ tsp or 2 mL salt and 2 tbsp or 30 mL vinegar for each 2 cups or 500 mL water). Cover and boil for 10 minutes. Drain well.

🍃 Serve with a white sauce, butter, *Hollandaise Sauce* (see page 54) or any way that suits your fancy.

REMOVING EXCESS LIQUID

Peel and dice the cucumbers, or cut them as indicated in your recipe. Place in a glass dish. Sprinkle with salt (1 tsp or 5 mL per medium cucumber). Let stand for 1 hour and drain. Dry thoroughly and cook.

Proceed with this step if the recipe calls for it.

CUCUMBER SALAD

4 small cucumbers
salt
½ cup (125 mL) sour cream
2 tbsp (30 mL) minced chives
or green onions
pepper
1 tsp (5 mL) cider vinegar

🍃 Peel the cucumbers and slice them as thin as possible. Place in a large dish and salt generously. Place a heavy plate over the cucumbers and let stand for 2 hours.

🍃 Rinse well under cold running water, dry thoroughly and refrigerate until ready to serve.

🍃 To serve, mix the cucumbers with the sour cream, chives, pepper and vinegar. Toss to blend well.

🍃 If desired, use French dressing instead of sour cream.

OLD-FASHIONED CUCUMBER SALAD

This cool, refreshing salad is a real treat on hot summer days.

3 medium cucumbers
5 green onions
3 to 6 radishes
1½ tsp (7 mL) salt
¼ cup (50 mL) cider vinegar
or wine vinegar
1 tsp (5 mL) sugar
1 cup (250 mL) sour cream

ð Peel and thinly slice the cucumbers. Mince the green onions and slice the radishes.
ð Mix together the cucumbers, green onions and radishes. Season with salt. Cover and refrigerate for 4 to 5 hours.
ð About 20 minutes before serving, drain the mixture. Add the vinegar, sugar and sour cream. Stir to blend well and refrigerate until ready to serve.

MOLDED CUCUMBER SALAD

¾ cup (175 mL) boiling water
1 package lime or lemon gelatin
1 cup (250 mL) mayonnaise
2 to 3 oz (60 to 90 g) cream cheese, at room temperature
1 tsp (5 mL) horseradish
2 tbsp (30 mL) lemon juice
¾ cup (175 mL) grated, unpeeled cucumber, drained and squeezed
¼ cup (50 mL) finely chopped green onions

ð Pour the boiling water over the gelatin and dissolve. Let cool slightly.
ð Stir in the mayonnaise, cream cheese, horseradish and lemon juice. Beat with an electric mixer until smooth.
ð Chill until slightly thickened, then stir in the cucumber and green onion.
ð Turn into a mold. Refrigerate for at least 6 hours before serving.

CREAMED CUCUMBER

1 large cucumber
2 tbsp (30 mL) butter
2 tbsp (30 mL) flour
1 cup (250 mL) milk
pinch of marjoram
1 tbsp (15 mL) finely chopped parsley
salt and pepper to taste

ð Peel the cucumber and cut into thick slices. Cook according to the *Basic Cooking Method* on page 425. Drain and place in a warm baking dish.
ð Make a white sauce with the butter, flour and milk. When the sauce is smooth and creamy, add the marjoram, parsley, salt and pepper.
ð Top the cucumbers with the sauce. If desired, sprinkle with ½ cup grated cheese.
ð Bake in a 450°F (230°C) oven for 10 minutes.

CUCUMBERS WITH RICE

2 cucumbers
3 tbsp (45 mL) butter
1 tbsp (15 mL) vegetable oil
2 cups (500 mL) cooked rice
⅔ cup (150 mL) grated cheese

ð Peel the cucumbers and cut into ⅓-in. (1-cm) slices.
ð Sauté the cucumbers in the butter and oil, then add the rice and the grated cheese.
ð Stir with a fork for a few minutes to blend. Serve.

CUCUMBERS À LA PROVENÇALE

2 cucumbers, unpeeled
2 tbsp (30 mL) butter
1 tbsp (15 mL) vegetable oil
4 green onions, finely chopped
2 cloves garlic, minced
3 strips bacon, cut into small pieces
4 slices salami, cut into strips
2 tbsp (30 mL) tomato paste

ð Wash and dice the cucumbers.
ð Heat the butter with the oil and add the green onions and the garlic. Brown.
ð Then add the bacon, salami and cucumbers. Cook over high heat for 10 minutes.
ð Add the tomato paste and continue to cook until the cucumbers are tender.

DEVONSHIRE CUCUMBERS

3 small cucumbers
¾ cup (175 mL) 10% cream
1 tbsp (15 mL) flour
1 clove garlic, minced
1 tsp (5 mL) butter
¼ tsp (1 mL) pepper
3 tbsp (45 mL) parsley

🍃 Peel the cucumbers and cut into 1-in. (2.5-cm) pieces. Salt and let stand for 30 minutes. Rinse under cold running water and drain.

🍃 Place the cucumbers in a saucepan with the remaining ingredients.

🍃 Cook over medium heat, uncovered, for 25 minutes or until the mixture is creamy and the cucumbers are tender.

🍃 Adjust the seasoning and serve.

BREADED CUCUMBERS

3 large cucumbers, unpeeled
3 tbsp (45 mL) flour
3 tbsp (45 mL) breadcrumbs
¾ tsp (3 mL) salt
pepper to taste
pinch of curry powder
¼ tsp (1 mL) garlic powder
¼ cup (50 mL) vegetable oil

🍃 Wash the unpeeled cucumbers and cut into ⅛-in. (0.3-cm) slices. Coat the slices with flour.

🍃 Mix together the breadcrumbs, salt, pepper, curry powder and garlic powder. Coat the cucumber slices with this mixture.

Cucumbers à la Provençale

🍃 In a skillet, heat the oil and brown the cucumbers on both sides over medium heat. Drain on paper towels and serve at once.

CUCUMBER FRITTERS

3 or 4 small cucumbers
few fennel seeds, to taste
salt, pepper, paprika
1¼ cups (300 mL) flour
2 tsp (10 mL) baking powder
1 egg
⅔ cup (150 mL) milk
peanut oil

🍃 Peel the cucumbers. Halve lengthwise, then cut into 2-in. (5-cm) pieces. Remove the seeds.

🍃 Crush the fennel seeds and mix together with the salt, pepper and paprika. Coat the cucumber pieces with this mixture. Let stand 20 minutes.

🍃 Sift the flour and the baking powder.

🍃 Beat the egg with the milk; add the flour and baking powder and continue beating until the batter is light and fluffy.

🍃 Spear the pieces of cucumber with a fork and dip them into the batter.

🍃 Heat the peanut oil and brown the coated cucumbers. Turn the fritters to brown the other sides. Drain on a paper towel.

🍃 Serve hot.

SOUR CREAM CUCUMBERS

3 medium cucumbers
1½ tsp (7 mL) salt
¼ cup (50 mL) sour cream
2 tbsp (30 mL) lemon juice
1 tbsp (15 mL) finely chopped onion

Braised Cucumbers

Adjust the seasoning.
❧ Turn into a greased mold. Refrigerate until set.
❧ Unmold the mousse on a bed of lettuce.
❧ Serve with lobster-flavored mayonnaise made from 1 cup (250 mL) mayonnaise and 1 can lobster paste.

LEMON CUCUMBERS

Lemon cucumbers are delicious with poached salmon or boiled lobster, cold or hot.

❧ Using a fork, streak an unpeeled medium-size cucumber, lengthwise. Remove the ends of the cucumber.
❧ Cut the cucumber into thin slices. Place the slices in a bowl and cover completely with ice cubes. Refrigerate for 2 to 3 hours.
❧ To serve, drain the cucumber slices well. Spread on a cloth and pat dry. Season with salt and pepper and sprinkle with a few drops of lemon juice. Serve in a glass bowl.

CUCUMBER PURÉE

Cucumbers, like tomatoes, abound in the summertime. They cannot be frozen whole, unfortunately, but must first be puréed. Cucumber purée, seasoned with a few drops of lemon juice or with cloves or dill, will enhance the flavor of any salad dressing, soup or sauce. It can also be used to prepare beautiful aspics.

12 cucumbers
2 tsp (10 mL) salt
½ cup (125 mL) boiling water

2 tbsp (30 mL) chopped pickles
¼ tsp (1 mL) sugar
pinch of pepper
1½ tsp (7 mL) finely chopped parsley

❧ Peel the cucumbers and cut into thin slices. Sprinkle with the salt and mix well. Refrigerate for 1 hour. Drain carefully and cover with ice cubes. Refrigerate until ready to serve, then drain again.
❧ Combine the sour cream, lemon juice, onion, pickles, sugar and pepper.
❧ Add the cucumbers and blend thoroughly.
❧ Serve chilled on a bed of lettuce. Garnish with the chopped parsley.

CUCUMBER MOUSSE

1½ envelopes unflavored gelatin
½ cup (125 mL) cold water

½ cup (125 mL) sugar
¼ cup (50 mL) lemon juice
½ cup (125 mL) wine vinegar
½ tsp (2 mL) salt
2 cups (500 mL) hot water
1 large cucumber, unpeeled and grated
1 green pepper, diced
1 onion, finely chopped
3 stalks celery, diced
3 green cabbage leaves, finely chopped

❧ Soak the gelatin in the cold water for 5 minutes.
❧ In a saucepan, combine the sugar, lemon juice, vinegar, salt and hot water and bring to a boil. Continue boiling for 3 minutes.
❧ Dissolve the gelatin in the hot liquid.
❧ Refrigerate until the mixture begins to set (it should have the consistency of egg white).
❧ Add the cucumber, green pepper, onion, celery and cabbage.

❧ Peel the cucumbers and cut lengthwise. Remove the seeds and slice thinly. Sprinkle with the salt.

❧ Place in a heavy metal saucepan, add the boiling water and bring to a boil. Simmer, uncovered, for 10 minutes.

❧ Put through a food mill, or purée in a food processor.

❧ Turn into 1-cup (250-ml) containers and freeze.

BRAISED CUCUMBERS

4 small cucumbers
3 tbsp (45 mL) butter
¼ cup (50 mL) consommé
pinch of pepper
2 tsp (10 mL) parsley or chives

❧ Peel the cucumbers. Cut in half lengthwise and remove the seeds.

❧ Melt the butter in a skillet and brown the cucumbers for 5 minutes.

❧ Add the consommé and the pepper. Cover and cook over low heat for 5 minutes.

❧ To serve, sprinkle with parsley or chives.

SQUASH

Squash is a widely cultivated vegetable that comes in many varieties: pumpkin, acorn squash, butternut squash, zucchini—to name but a few. In my opinion, zucchini, with its delicate pulp, is the best.

AS HORS D'OEUVRES
Peel the squash of your choice

and cut into cubes or strips. Place in a glass jar, sprinkling each layer with cinnamon, cloves, thyme, bay leaf and a little grated nutmeg.

❧ Boil white vinegar with some sugar (1 tbsp or 15 mL sugar for every 2 cups or 500 mL vinegar). Let cool and pour over the squash.

❧ Cover and marinate for 10 to 12 days in the refrigerator.

IN A WHITE SAUCE
Pare and cube the squash. Drop into salted boiling water and simmer for 2 minutes. Drain.

❧ Place in a baking dish, sprinkle with grated cheese and melted butter. Cover with white sauce (see page 46).

❧ Bake in a 375°F (190°C) oven for 20 minutes.

WITH RICE
Pare and cube the squash. Drop into salted boiling water and simmer for 2 minutes. Drain.

❧ Place in a baking dish, making alternate layers of cheese, cooked rice and squash. Cover with white sauce.

❧ Bake in a 375°F (190°C) oven for 20 minutes.

WITH TOMATOES
Prepare a tangy tomato sauce and cook the squash in the sauce.

BAKED SQUASH
Cut the squash in 2 and remove the seeds. Brush the inside with melted butter. Season with salt and pepper.

❧ Bake in a 400°F (200°C) oven for 40 minutes.

SQUASH FRITTERS

4 cups (1 L) squash, peeled and diced
½ tsp (2 mL) fennel seed
½ tsp (2 mL) salt
¼ tsp (1 mL) pepper
1 tsp (5 mL) sugar
½ cup (125 mL) water
1 cup (250 mL) cream or milk
2 eggs, separated
peanut oil

❧ In a saucepan, place the squash, fennel seed, salt, pepper and sugar. Add ½ cup (125 mL) water. Cover and simmer until the squash is tender. Drain.

❧ Mash the squash. Add the milk or cream and the egg yolks. Blend thoroughly. Add enough flour to make a thick batter (the amount will depend on the type of squash used).

❧ Beat the egg whites until stiff and gently fold them into the batter.

❧ Heat at least 2 in. (5 cm) peanut oil in a skillet. Drop the batter into the oil a spoonful at a time and fry until the fritters are golden brown. Drain on paper towels.

❧ Serve at once.

STUFFED SQUASH

1 small squash
1 lb (500 g) spinach
salt and pepper
pinch of nutmeg
1 tbsp (15 mL) butter
1 tbsp (15 mL) grated cheese

1 tbsp (15 mL) finely chopped parsley
1 clove garlic, crushed
¼ cup (50 mL) breadcrumbs
¼ cup (50 mL) vegetable oil

🍂 Wash the squash. Cut off a slice at the top of the squash, lengthwise. Remove the fibers and seeds. Make small incisions in the pulp with the tip of a knife. Steam for 30 minutes.

🍂 Cook the spinach (see page 390. Drain well and season with salt and pepper. Add the nutmeg, butter, grated cheese, parsley and garlic. Mix well.

🍂 Fill the squash with the spinach mixture.

🍂 Blend together the breadcrumbs and the oil. Sprinkle over the spinach.

🍂 Bake in a 375°F (190°C) oven for 30 minutes.

🍂 If desired, add leftover ground meat before filling the squash with the spinach mixture. Baste the meat with a little catsup.

CINNAMON SQUASH

1 small acorn squash
1 tbsp (15 mL) butter
1 tsp (5 mL) sugar
pinch of cinnamon
salt and pepper to taste

🍂 Place the squash in a saucepan containing 2 in. (5 cm) hot water. Cover and cook over very low heat for 1 hour. Add more water if necessary.

🍂 Cut off the top of the squash. Scoop out the pulp and mash with a fork. Add the remaining ingredients and mix well.

🍂 Serve at once.

ZUCCHINI SQUASH

The smaller the zucchini, the tastier it will be.

PREPARATION
Do not peel zucchini. Simply wash and slice off the ends. Cut in half lengthwise or into ¼-in. (0.5-cm) slices.

BOILED ZUCCHINI
Season the zucchini with salt and pepper and place in a saucepan. Add 3 tbsp (45 mL) hot water for every zucchini. Cover and boil over medium heat for 10 minutes. Drain.

🍂 Add 1 tbsp (15 mL) butter or salad dressing and 2 tbsp (30 mL) lemon juice for every 3 zucchini.

FRIED ZUCCHINI
Wash the zucchini and cut into ¼-in. (0.5-cm) slices. Coat with flour seasoned with salt and pepper.

🍂 Fry in butter or oil for 5 to 7 minutes or until golden grown.

BREADED ZUCCHINI
Wash the zucchini and cut into ¼-in. (0.5-cm) slices.

🍂 In a bowl, beat 2 eggs with 1 tsp (5 mL) fresh basil. Season with salt and pepper.

🍂 Dip the zucchini slices into the egg mixture, then coat with ½ cup (125 mL) fine breadcrumbs mixed with 3 tbsp (45 mL) grated Parmesan cheese.

🍂 Fry in hot olive oil until golden brown.

Celery Hearts and Tomatoes

ZUCCHINI ITALIAN STYLE

🍂 Melt a small amount of butter in a saucepan. Add unpeeled zucchini, cut in half lengthwise.

🍂 Cover and simmer for 15 minutes.

🍂 Season with salt and pepper. Sprinkle with a few drops of lemon juice.

CELERY

In general, both the stalk and the root of celery are edible. These can be served raw, in salads or cooked. Celery has diuretic properties, and it also stimulates the appetite.

BASIC COOKING METHOD
Wash the outer stalks of a head of celery, keeping the heart whole. Using a vegetable parer, shave off the strings from the outer stalks.

🍂 Place the stalks at the bottom of a saucepan and the heart on top. Cover with boiling salted water and cook for 15 minutes. Drain.

🍂 Serve as is or in one of the following recipes.

IN A PRESSURE-COOKER
Place the celery stalks and heart on the rack of the pressure-cooker. Add ¼ cup (50 mL) water. Season with salt. Secure the lid of the pressure-cooker and let the pressure rise. Cook for 3 minutes. Reduce the pressure immediately. Serve.

🍂 Celery root can be prepared in the same way.

CRISPY CELERY HEARTS

Celery hearts are easy to prepare and so pleasant to munch on.

🍂 If possible, prepare celery hearts a day in advance so that the celery is chilled and crisp at serving time.

🍂 Select 2 heads of celery with crisp stalks and fresh green leaves.

🍂 Trim the base and remove the leaves. Wash and remove the outer stalks. Cut the inner, tender stalks (the heart) into 4 sections, lengthwise.

🍂 Place in a bowl of ice-cold water with 1 tsp (5 mL) salt, preferably with the celery lying flat in the bowl. Refrigerate overnight.

🍂 To serve, drain and arrange in a serving dish. Garnish with a few olives.

CELERY HEARTS AND TOMATOES

4 celery hearts
1 clove garlic, halved
¾ cup (175 mL) catsup
2 tbsp (30 mL) olive oil
1 tbsp (15 mL) cider vinegar
1 tbsp (15 mL) lemon juice
½ tsp (2 mL) celery salt
pepper to taste

🍂 Wash the celery hearts and remove the leaves. Tie celery each heart loosely with string.

🍂 Place in a saucepan and cover with boiling water. Cover and boil for 20 minutes, or until the celery

hearts are tender. Drain and arrange on a warm serving dish.

🍂 Meanwhile, rub a bowl with the garlic clove. Add the catsup, olive oil, cider vinegar and lemon juice. Season with celery salt and pepper. Mix well.

🍂 Heat the sauce and use it to top the celery hearts.

CELERY AU JUS

1 medium head of celery
2 cups (500 mL) boiling water
1 tsp (5 mL) sugar
¼ tsp (1 mL) celery seed
½ cup (125 mL) brown gravy
or veal drippings
2 tsp (10 mL) cornstarch
2 tbsp (30 mL) water or milk
salt and pepper to taste
1 tbsp (15 mL) butter

🍂 Wash the head of celery under running water, separating the stalks without breaking them off. Drain well. Tie the head loosely with string.

🍂 Place in a saucepan or a skillet. Add the boiling water, sugar and celery seed. Bring to a rolling boil, cover and cook over medium heat for 30 minutes. Drain on a towel and reserve the cooking liquid.

🍂 Return the cooking water to a boil and reduce to 1 cup (250 mL). Add the gravy or veal drippings (leftover gravy from braised or roast veal) and boil for 5 minutes.

🍂 Dissolve the cornstarch in the water or milk and add this to the veal gravy. Cook until the mixture is smooth, stirring constantly. Season with salt and pepper.

🍂 Pour this sauce over the drained celery. If necessary, simmer for a few minutes to warm the celery. Remove from the heat, add the butter and stir until melted.

DEVILED CELERY

4 cups (1 L) celery, cut into 1-in. (2.5-cm) pieces
1 tsp (5 mL) sugar
2 tbsp (30 mL) butter
1 tsp (5 mL) Dijon
or Aurora mustard
salt and pepper
nutmeg

🍂 Place the celery and sugar in a saucepan. Cover with boiling water. Cover and boil 8 to 10 minutes. Drain.
🍂 Melt the butter and then add the mustard. Cook just to heat the mixture.
🍂 Top the celery with the butter sauce. Season to taste with salt, pepper and nutmeg.

FENNEL

Fennel is a very aromatic bulbous plant. It looks like a stubby head of celery but tastes like anise.
🍂 The roots and stalks of the fennel can be eaten raw, in salads or hors d'oeuvres, or cooked in the same way as celery (see Previous page).

ONIONS

PREPARATION
Select clean, hard onions with dry, papery skins.

🍂 For boiling, use small white or yellow onions. The large ones cook better when sliced.
🍂 Peel onions in a bowl of water or under running water.
🍂 Store in a dry place, as onions do not keep well in damp conditions.
🍂 Do not refrigerate.

BASIC COOKING METHOD
Boil 1 cup (250 mL) water in a saucepan. Add the onions and cover tightly. Boil small onions about 20 to 25 minutes, large ones about 28 to 30 minutes and sliced onions about 5 minutes.
🍂 In Spain, onions are simply washed and cooked in boiling water until tender. They are then peeled and served with a tomato sauce or butter.

IN A PRESSURE-COOKER
This is the ideal way to cook onions. Place them, unpeeled, on the rack in the pressure-cooker. Add ½ cup (125 mL) water. Secure the lid and let the pressure rise. Cook 3 to 6 minutes, depending on the size of the onions. Reduce the pressure at once.
🍂 Peel and serve with butter and parsley.

IN THE OVEN
Place the unpeeled onions on a piece of aluminum foil or a pie plate. Bake in a 300°F (150°C) oven for 1 to 1½ hours.
🍂 Peel and dot with butter.

RED ONION SALAD

½ tsp (2 mL) salt
½ cup (125 mL) olive oil
¼ cup (50 mL) vinegar
juice of 1 lemon
3 sprigs fresh savory
or ½ tsp (2 mL) powdered savory
4 large red onions
1 lemon, unpeeled and cut into thin slices

🍂 In a bowl, combine the salt, olive oil, vinegar, lemon juice and savory.
🍂 Cut the onions into very thin slices and separate the slices into rings. Add the onions and the lemon to the salad dressing and mix well.
🍂 Cover and marinate in a cool place for 24 hours.
🍂 These onions will keep 3 to 6 weeks in the refrigerator.

CREAMED ONIONS

16 to 20 cloves
8 to 10 onions
1 tbsp (15 mL) butter
pinch of thyme
1 bay leaf
salt and pepper to taste
2 tbsp (30 mL) butter
2 tbsp (30 mL) flour
1½ cups (375 mL) onion cooking water
breadcrumbs to taste
grated cheese to taste

🍂 Stud each onion with 2 cloves. Place the onions in a saucepan and cover with water. Add the 1 tbsp (15 mL) butter, thyme, bay leaf, salt and pepper.
🍂 Boil for 1 hour or until half the water has evaporated. Remove the onions from the pan and drain.

Prepare a white sauce with the 2 tbsp (30 mL) butter, the flour and the onion cooking water (add milk, if more liquid is needed).

Cover the drained onions with the sauce. Sprinkle with breadcrumbs and grated cheese.

Brown in a 450°F (230°C) oven for 20 to 30 minutes and serve.

FRENCH-FRIED ONION RINGS

1½ lbs (750 g) large white onions
1 egg white
⅓ cup (75 mL) milk
½ cup (125 mL) fine breadcrumbs

Peel the onions and cut them into ⅓-in. (0.3-cm) slices. Separate the slices into rings.

Beat the egg white lightly with the milk. Dip each onion ring in this mixture and coat with the breadcrumbs.

Place the onions in the basket of a deep-fryer and immerse in fat heated to 365°F (190°C). Fry until light brown.

Drain on paper towels and serve at once.

FRENCH-STYLE ONIONS

12 onions
¼ cup (50 mL) butter
1 tsp (5 mL) salt
¼ tsp (1 mL) pepper
½ tsp (2 mL) sugar

Peel the onions and slice ¼ in. (0.5 cm) thick.

Creamed Onions

Melt the butter in a skillet. Add the sliced onions, salt, pepper and sugar. Simmer gently for 25 to 30 minutes, stirring occasionally.

To brown the onions slightly, do not cover the saucepan. Slow cooking will bring out the flavor.

HONEY-GLAZED ONIONS

¼ cup (50 mL) honey
2 tbsp (30 mL) sugar
1 tbsp (15 mL) butter
1 tbsp (15 mL) lemon juice
1 tsp (5 mL) Worcestershire sauce
1 tsp (5 mL) cider vinegar
¼ tsp (1 mL) salt
pinch of pepper
2 lbs (1 kg) onions, peeled, cooked and drained

In a large saucepan, combine the honey, sugar, butter, lemon juice, Worcestershire sauce, cider vinegar, salt and pepper. Bring to a boil. Continue to boil for 1 minute, while stirring.

Add the onions. Stir until the onions are completely coated with the sauce. Then cook over low heat, stirring frequently, until the onions are shiny and glazed.

Turn into a warm dish. Add the remaining sauce and serve.

Vegetables such as carrots, beets and turnips can also be prepared this way. Use cooked, whole vegetables or drained, canned vegetables.

PURÉED ONIONS SOUBISE

2 tbsp (30 mL) butter
4 large onions, thinly sliced
4 tbsp (60 mL) rice, uncooked
½ cup (125 mL) boiling water

Stuffed Onions

½ tsp (2 mL) salt
¼ tsp (1 mL) dry mustard
½ cup (125 mL) thick white sauce

≈ Melt the butter in a saucepan. Add the onions. Cover and cook over low heat, stirring from time to time, until the onions are tender but not brown.

≈ Add the rice, water, salt and mustard. Cover and cook over low heat for 35 minutes or until all the water has been absorbed. Put through a food mill or purée using an electric blender.

≈ Make the white sauce using 2 tbsp (30 mL) butter, 2 tbsp (30 mL) flour and ½ cup (125 mL) milk or cream. Salt and pepper to taste.

≈ Add the white sauce to the onion purée. Heat gently and serve.

STUFFED ONIONS

6 large yellow onions, whole
¼ lb (125 g) mushrooms, cooked and chopped
6 strips bacon, cooked and cut into small pieces
½ cup (125 mL) bread, cubed
1 tsp (5 mL) salt
pinch of pepper
pinch of thyme
1 cup (250 mL) grated cheese
2 tbsp (30 mL) butter

≈ In a pan of salted water, cook the onions, covered, for 30 minutes or until tender. Drain and cool.

≈ Scoop out the onions and chop the center part very fine (you will need about 2 cups or 500 mL).

≈ Combine the chopped onion with the mushrooms, bacon, bread, salt, pepper and thyme.

Add ½ cup (125 mL) of the cheese. Mix well.

≈ Place the onion shells in a baking dish. Stuff each onion with as much of the mixture as possible. Pour ½ cup (125 mL) water into the dish.

≈ Bake in a 400°F (200°C) oven for 20 minutes.

≈ Sprinkle with the rest of the grated cheese. Dot with butter and return to the oven for 10 minutes. Serve.

SHERRIED ONIONS

12 small onions
pinch of ground cloves
¼ cup (50 mL) sherry
¼ cup (50 mL) chopped walnuts
3 tbsp (45 mL) butter

≈ Peel the onions and cook until tender. Drain and place in a baking dish.

≈ Heat the remaining ingredients and spread over the onions.

≈ Bake in a 450°F (230°C) oven for 15 minutes and serve.

FRIED ONIONS

The following recipe will give you crisp, golden-brown onions every time.

≈ Peel the onions and chop, dice or slice them.

≈ Heat 1 tbsp (15 mL) butter and 1 tbsp (15 mL) oil per 6 to 8 onions. Add the onions along with 1 tbsp (15 mL) cold water and ½ tsp (2 mL) sugar.

🐦 Sauté over high heat, stirring frequently.

🐦 When the onions begin to brown, reduce the heat and continue cooking over medium heat until the onions are golden brown.

🐦 Season with salt and pepper and serve.

ONION PIE

🐦 Peel and slice 4 large onions.

🐦 Beat 2 eggs with ½ cup (125 mL) light (10%) cream. Season to taste with salt, pepper and ¼ tsp (1 mL) tarragon. Add the onions.

🐦 Turn the onion mixture into an 8-in. (20-cm) pie shell. Sprinkle with diced bacon. Bake 30 minutes in a 350°F (180°C) oven.

🐦 Cut into wedges and serve with a side dish of cold meat and a green salad.

🐦 Serves 6.

LEEKS

PREPARATION

To clean leeks, remove the outer leaves and make an incision in the green part, lengthwise. Wash under running water, letting the water run through the leaves, where sand is usually lodged.

BASIC COOKING METHOD

Clean the leeks and place them in a saucepan. Pour in enough boiling water to fill half the pan. Add a pinch of salt. Cover and boil over high heat for about 20 to 35 minutes. Drain thoroughly.

IN A PRESSURE-COOKER

Clean the leeks and place them on the rack of the pressure-cooker. Add ½ cup (125 mL) water. Secure the lid and let the pressure rise. Cook for 3 minutes. Reduce the pressure at once. Serve.

LEEKS AND TOMATOES

6 leeks
3 tbsp (45 mL) olive oil
1 large onion, finely chopped
½ cup (125 mL) grated carrots
1 cup (250 mL) fresh tomatoes, diced
1 tsp (5 mL) sugar
½ tsp (2 mL) salt
pinch of pepper
pinch of basil

🐦 Clean the leeks and cut both green and white parts into 1-in. (2-cm) pieces.

🐦 Heat the oil and sauté the onion.

🐦 Add the carrots, tomatoes, sugar, salt, pepper and basil. Stir. Simmer for 5 minutes.

🐦 Add the leeks. Cover and simmer for 20 minutes or until the leeks are tender.

BRAISED LEEKS

6 leeks
4 tbsp (60 mL) butter
½ tsp (2 mL) sugar
½ tsp (2 mL) salt
pepper, to taste
juice of 1 lemon

🐦 Clean the leeks. Lay them flat in a skillet. Cover with boiling water. Cover and boil for 10 minutes. Drain thoroughly.

🐦 Heat the butter until nutty brown. Stir in the leeks, sugar and salt. Season with pepper to taste.

Creamed Leeks

Cook over medium heat, uncovered, for 20 minutes.

☙ Sprinkle with the lemon juice and serve.

☙ Braised leeks are simply divine. They go equally well with beef, chicken, lamb and fish.

CREAMED LEEKS

3 tbsp (45 mL) butter
6 medium leeks
1 cup (250 mL) cream
¼ cup (50 mL) minced parsley

☙ Melt the butter in a skillet. Clean the leeks and add to the butter. Cover and simmer over medium heat for 15 to 20 minutes (no water is required).

☙ Add the cream and simmer for another 30 minutes.

☙ Season to taste, sprinkle with parsley and serve.

LEEKS VINAIGRETTE

☙ Boil the cleaned leeks whole if small and young, or cut in 1-in. (2-cm) pieces if large. Drain on paper towels or a clean cloth and allow to cool.

☙ To serve, place on a flat dish and sprinkle with a dressing of your choice.

☙ Garnish with grated hard-cooked eggs and finely minced parsley.

CARROTS

PREPARATION
Scrub young carrots but do not peel them; remove a very thin peel from the older ones.

☙ To serve raw, scrub the carrots without peeling. Place them whole in a dish of cold water. Keep refrigerated.

BASIC COOKING METHOD
Place the carrots in a saucepan. Add 2 in. (5 cm) boiling water. Sprinkle with sugar. Cover.

☙ Cook young carrots for 8 to 10 minutes, older ones for 12 to 15 minutes and thinly sliced or diced carrots for 2 to 4 minutes.

IN A PRESSURE-COOKER
Place the carrots on the rack of the pressure-cooker. Add ¼ cup (50 mL) water. Secure the lid and let the pressure rise. Cook for 2 to 4 minutes, depending on the size of the carrots.

CARROTS WITH HERBS

5 or 6 carrots
3 tbsp (45 mL) butter
½ tsp (2 mL) sugar
½ tsp (2 mL) salt
1 tbsp (15 mL) parsley
¼ tsp (1 mL) thyme
2 tbsp (30 mL) cream

☙ Scrape the carrots and cut them into strips.

☙ Place in a saucepan and add the butter, sugar, salt, parsley and thyme. Stir until the butter has melted. Cover and cook over very low heat for 20 minutes or until the carrots are tender.

☙ Add the cream, simmer for a few minutes and serve.

GRATED BUTTERED CARROTS

6 to 8 medium carrots
1 tbsp (15 mL) olive oil
1 small clove garlic, minced
½ tsp (2 mL) salt
pinch of pepper
pinch of thyme
2 tbsp (30 mL) water
¼ cup (50 mL) butter

☙ Peel and grate the carrots.

☙ Heat the olive oil in a skillet. Add the garlic, salt, pepper, thyme, water and grated carrots. Cover and cook over medium heat for 6 to 8 minutes, stirring 2 or 3 times. Remove from heat.

☙ Add the butter and stir until the butter is melted and the carrots are well coated.

GLAZED MUSTARD CARROTS

3 lbs (1.5 kg) carrots
¼ cup (50 mL) butter
or margarine
½ cup (125 mL) brown sugar
¼ cup (50 mL) mustard
2 tbsp (30 mL) minced chives, mint and parsley

☙ Wash and peel the carrots. Cut them on the diagonal into 1-in. (2-cm) slices.

☙ Place the carrots in a saucepan. Add 1 in. (2-cm) boiling water. Cover and simmer for 20 minutes. Drain the carrots, if necessary (the water may evaporate completely).

Place the butter or margarine, the brown sugar and the mustard in a separate saucepan. Melt the butter or margarine over low heat, stirring constantly. Continue to heat for another 3 minutes.

Stir in the drained carrots and blend thoroughly. Heat for a few minutes, if necessary.

Add the minced chives, mint and parsley and serve.

CREAMED CARROTS

2 cups (500 mL) sliced or diced carrots
1 tsp (5 mL) chopped parsley or ¼ cup (50 mL) minced celery leaves
1½ cups (375 mL) milk
2 tbsp (30 mL) butter
2 tbsp (30 mL) flour

Place the carrots, parsley or celery leaves and milk at the bottom of the pressure-cooker, without the rack.

Cream together the butter and flour and shape into balls. Place the balls over the carrots.

Secure the lid and let the pressure rise. Cook for 3 minutes. Reduce the pressure at once. Remove the lid and stir the carrots briskly.

The sauce will become smooth and creamy in spite of its curdled appearance when the lid is removed.

Any vegetable can be creamed this way in a pressure-cooker.

Gingered Carrots

GINGERED CARROTS

5 young carrots
1 tbsp (15 mL) butter
1 tbsp (15 mL) sugar
½ tsp (2 mL) ground ginger

Boil and drain the carrots. Place in a cold skillet.

Add the butter, sugar and ground ginger. Cook over medium heat until the carrots are well coated with the mixture.

GOLDEN GLAZED CARROTS

For this recipe I use baby carrots fresh from the garden. I always glaze a batch of them and then freeze them to have on hand for special occasions. But carrots bought at the supermarket will do just as well.

1½ lbs (750 g) whole baby carrots, or regular carrots cut into strips
2 tbsp (30 mL) flour
¼ cup (50 mL) brown sugar or maple sugar
½ tsp (2 mL) salt
¼ tsp (1 mL) thyme
1 tbsp (15 mL) cider vinegar
1 tbsp (15 mL) fresh lemon juice
½ cup (125 mL) orange juice
grated zest of 1 orange

Place the carrots in a saucepan. Add boiling water and boil for 5 minutes. Drain thoroughly.

Blend together the flour, sugar, salt and thyme. Add the cider vinegar, lemon juice, orange juice and orange zest. Bring to a boil, stirring constantly.

Line a baking dish with aluminum foil and add the carrots. Cover with the sauce. Freeze.

❧ When the carrots are frozen, wrap them in another sheet of aluminum foil. Remove from the baking dish and return to the freezer.

❧ To serve, unwrap the carrots and place them in a baking dish. Bake, covered, in a 350°F (180°C) oven for approximately 40 minutes, then uncover for the last 15 minutes of baking.

RED CURRANT GLAZED CARROTS

Dress up your carrots with this bright red, spicy, easy-to-make glaze. Cook the carrots 1 day ahead and then refrigerate. Glaze when ready to serve. This dish is excellent with chicken or any other poultry.

12 carrots
½ tsp (2 mL) sugar
3 tbsp (45 mL) butter
4 tbsp (60 mL) tart red-currant jelly
juice of ½ lemon

❧ Peel the carrots and cut into 2-in. (5-cm) julienne strips. Place in a large saucepan with the sugar. Add enough boiling water to completely cover the carrots. Boil over high heat, uncovered, for 5 minutes. Drain.

❧ Turn into a bowl, cover and refrigerate until ready to serve.

❧ Blend together the butter, red currant jelly and lemon juice in a large skillet.

❧ When ready to serve, add the cold carrots to the cold red currant mixture in the skillet. It is important that all the ingredients

be cold.

❧ Cook over medium heat, stirring gently and constantly with a spatula, for 3 to 5 minutes or until the carrots are well coated with the glaze.

CARROTS LYONNAISE

2 tbsp (30 mL) butter
2 medium onions, thinly sliced
salt and pepper
4 cups (1 L) sliced cooked carrots

❧ Melt the butter and brown the onions. Season with salt and pepper.

❧ Add the cooked carrots. Cover and simmer for 15 minutes.

❧ Sprinkle with parsley and serve.

BEETS

PREPARATION
Scrub the beets well under cold water. With a sharp knife, cut the stems, leaving 1 in. (2 cm). Do not remove the root. Do not peel.

BASIC COOKING METHOD
Place the prepared beets in a large saucepan. Add enough cold water to cover. Bring to a boil. Cover and cook for 25 to 50 minutes, depending on the size of the beets. Drain.

❧ Rinse under cold running water and then peel. (It is very easy to peel well-cooked beets.)

IN A PRESSURE-COOKER
Wash and peel the beets and place them on the rack of the

pressure-cooker with ½ cup (125 mL) water. Cook small and medium-size beets for 10 minutes. Quarter large beets.

BEET SALAD

4 to 6 beets
4 green onions, finely chopped
2 tbsp (30 mL) tarragon vinegar
4 tbsp (60 mL) olive oil
salt, pepper and celery salt
1 hard-cooked egg, grated

❧ Cook the beets. Peel and slice thinly. Arrange in a salad bowl.

❧ Blend together the green onions, tarragon vinegar, olive oil, salt, pepper and celery salt. Pour this over the beets.

❧ Refrigerate until ready to serve.

❧ Garnish with the grated hard-cooked egg.

CANADIAN BEETS

4 beets
1 apple, grated
2 onions, grated
3 tbsp (45 mL) butter

❧ Peel and grate the raw beets.

❧ Place the apple, onion, butter and beets in a saucepan. Cover and cook over low heat for 1 hour, stirring often. Serve.

CREAMED BEET GREENS

2 cups (500 mL) beet greens
¼ cup (50 mL) salted water
½ tsp (2 mL) flour
1 small piece butter or fat

1 tbsp (15 mL) milk or cream
nutmeg or fried garlic

🖛 Beet greens taste like a cross between spinach and beets, and are prepared in much the same way as spinach.

🖛 Choose young beets with very fresh leaves and cook the leaves before they wilt (they will not keep for very long).

🖛 Like spinach, beet greens reduce considerably when cooked.

🖛 Wash the leaves and stems thoroughly and cut into 1-in. (2-cm) pieces using a pair of scissors.

🖛 Place in a saucepan with the salted water. Cover and boil over high heat for 6 to 8 minutes. Drain, return to the saucepan, and sprinkle in the flour. Add the butter and the milk. Stir over high heat until creamy.

🖛 Season with nutmeg or fried garlic.

🖛 Beet greens can be eaten plain, with a little salt, pepper and butter, as long as they are cooked and well drained.

🖛 To serve with cooked beets, arrange the beets in a ring and place the greens in the center.

HARVARD BEETS

2 tsp (10 mL) cornstarch
½ cup (125 mL) sugar
⅓ cup (75 mL) water
⅓ cup (75 mL) vinegar
4 cups (1 L) sliced, cooked beets
3 tbsp (45 mL) butter
salt and pepper

🖛 Mix together the cornstarch and the sugar. Add the water and the vinegar. Boil for 5 minutes.

🖛 Place the mixture over the sliced cooked beets. Cover and simmer for 20 minutes.

🖛 Add the butter and the seasonings and serve.

POLISH-STYLE BEETS

12 small beets
1 tbsp (15 mL) cider vinegar
1 tbsp (15 mL) tarragon vinegar
2 tbsp (30 mL) sugar
2 tbsp (30 mL) olive oil
salt and pepper to taste
1 tbsp (15 mL) butter
1 tbsp (15 mL) flour
½ cup (125 mL) sour cream

🖛 Cook the beets; peel and slice them.

🖛 Mix together the cider vinegar, tarragon vinegar, sugar, olive oil,

salt and pepper. Pour over the sliced beets.

🖛 Melt the butter. Add the flour and blend well. Add the beet mixture and cook over medium heat, stirring constantly, until the sauce is smooth.

🖛 Add the sour cream. Heat but do not boil or the cream will curdle.

FRENCH-STYLE BEETS

6 medium or 12 small beets
2 tbsp (30 mL) butter
½ tsp (2 mL) sugar
4 lettuce leaves
salt to taste
2 tbsp (30 mL) minced chives
1 tbsp (15 mL) minced parsley

Polish-Style Beets

🍃 Peel and thinly slice the raw beets.

🍃 Melt the butter in a large saucepan and add the sugar. Heat until the sugar is melted. Add the beets and toss until well coated.

🍃 Cover with the lettuce leaves (keep the lettuce in cold water).

🍃 Cover and simmer over very low heat for 25 to 30 minutes.

🍃 When the beets are tender, discard the lettuce leaves. Salt to taste. Add the minced chives and the minced parsley and serve.

VARIATION

Instead of the chives and parsley, use 2 tbsp (30 mL) sour cream and ¼ tsp (1 mL) minced dill, or 2 tbsp (30 mL) lemon juice and a pinch of tarragon.

CELERY ROOT

PREPARATION

Celery root (or celeriac) is a root vegetable that tastes like celery and is prepared in the same way. It is delicious raw or cooked, in salads, as an hors d'oeuvre or with a white sauce or a cheese sauce.

🍃 To prepare celery root, wash well, peel and cut into large cubes. Place in a mixture of salt water and vinegar. It is then ready to be cooked or eaten raw.

🍃 To bring out its delicate flavor, and to keep it white, celery root that is to be used in salads can be blanched for 1 to 2 minutes in water spiked with lemon juice.

BASIC COOKING METHOD

Melt 1 tbsp (15 mL) fat in a saucepan and add 1 tbsp (15 mL) flour. Blend well. Add the cubed celery root and enough hot water to cover. Bring to a rolling boil.

🍃 Cover and cook for 20 minutes or until tender-crisp. Avoid overcooking.

CELERY ROOT HORS D'OEUVRES

1 medium celery root
3 tbsp (45 mL) olive oil
1 tbsp (15 mL) vinegar
1 clove garlic, minced
½ tsp (2 mL) salt
¼ tsp (1 mL) pepper
1 tsp (5 mL) prepared mustard
½ cup (125 mL) mayonnaise

🍃 Wash and peel the celery root. Grate with a fine or medium grater. Place in a bowl with a mixture of cold water and vinegar (3 tbsp or 45 mL vinegar per 4 cups or 1 L water).

🍃 In a jar with a tight-fitting lid, blend the olive oil, vinegar, garlic, salt and pepper. Shake vigorously. Pour over the drained celery root. Mix well. Turn onto a serving platter.

🍃 Blend together the prepared mustard and mayonnaise. Spread over the celery root mixture.

🍃 Refrigerate until ready to serve.

MARINATED CELERY ROOT

1 celery root
¼ cup (50 mL) olive oil
¼ cup (50 mL) Dijon mustard
2 tbsp (30 mL) wine vinegar
½ tsp (2 mL) salt
pepper to taste

🍃 Peel and quarter the celery root. Place in a saucepan and cover with boiling water. Boil over high heat for 5 minutes. Drain.

🍃 Refrigerate until chilled. Either cut into strips or grate.

🍃 Beat together the olive oil, mustard, wine vinegar and salt. Season to taste with pepper.

🍃 When ready to serve, add the celery root to the French dressing and mix well.

CELERY ROOT WITH GRUYÈRE CHEESE

1 large celery root
2 slices lemon, unpeeled
⅔ cup (150 mL) grated Gruyère cheese
2 tbsp (30 mL) butter

🍃 Peel and slice the celery root. Place in a saucepan and add enough water to cover. Add the lemon slices. Boil over medium heat for 25 minutes. Drain well.

🍃 On a serving platter, arrange the celery root and grated cheese in alternate layers. Dot with the butter.

🍃 Brown in a 400°F (200°C) oven for 15 minutes.

OYSTER PLANT

PREPARATION

To prepare oyster plant, or salsify, scrape or peel with a potato peeler. With a sharp knife, remove the leaves and cut off a little piece at the pointed end.

🍃 Split the thicker pieces in half lengthwise so that all the pieces will be the same size.

🍃 Place the prepared oyster plant in a mixture of cold water and vinegar (1 tbsp or 15 mL vinegar per 4 cups or 1 L water) so that it remains white. When it comes into contact with air, oyster plant tends to turn brown.

BASIC COOKING METHOD

Oyster plant should be cooked à blanc or boiled in a mixture of water and vinegar. Any vegetable that tends to turn brown on contact with air, such as oyster plant or parsnip, should be cooked à blanc.

🍃 Mix 1 tbsp (15 mL) flour with 4 tbsp (60 mL) water. Add 4 cups (1 L) cold water, salt, the juice of half a lemon and 2 tbsp (30 mL) fat. Boil for a few minutes, then add the oyster plant (or other vegetable to be cooked à blanc). Cook for 8 to 15 minutes, depending on the size of the vegetables. Drain.

🍃 In cooking vegetables à blanc the butter or fat added to the water forms an insulating layer, preventing the vegetable from coming into contact with the air and thus turning color.

Marinated Celery Root

🍃 Serve oyster plant sautéed in butter with parsley, or with a white sauce or tomato sauce.

🍃 Oyster plant is also used in stews or served with braised veal or lamb.

JERUSALEM ARTICHOKES

The Jerusalem artichoke resembles a potato but tastes like an artichoke. In reality, it is the tuber of the sunflower. The name is a corruption of the Italian girasole, or "turn-to-the-sun," as sunflowers are obliged to do.

🍃 The French found it growing in Nova Scotia at the beginning of the 17th century—Indian tribes were well acquainted with this delicious vegetable.

PREPARATION

Wash and peel the Jerusalem artichokes. Like artichokes, contact with air causes discoloration; they should therefore be soaked in a mixture of water and vinegar as soon as they are washed.

BASIC COOKING METHOD

Boil Jerusalem artichokes in water, milk or consommé for 20 minutes. Peel before or after cooking.

🍃 They can also be steamed with butter, fried or puréed.

🍃 In certain recipes Jerusalem artichokes can replace regular artichokes. Shape them into cups and cook in salt water for 5 minutes. Drain.

[441]

Mashed Rutabaga Parmentier

PURÉED JERUSALEM ARTICHOKES

1 lb (500 g) Jerusalem artichokes
1 tbsp (15 mL) butter
2 tbsp (30 mL) sour cream
1 tbsp (15 mL) finely chopped parsley
salt and pepper to taste

🍃 Boil the Jerusalem artichokes. Drain and mash with the butter, sour cream, parsley, salt and pepper. Serve.

BUTTERED STEAMED JERUSALEM ARTICHOKES

1 lb (500 g) Jerusalem artichokes
2 tbsp (30 mL) butter
parsley, finely chopped

green onions, finely chopped
salt and pepper

🍃 Clean and peel the Jerusalem artichokes. Melt the butter in a skillet with a tight-fitting lid. When hot, add the Jerusalem artichokes. Stir to coat well.

🍃 Cook over low heat, covered, for 20 minutes, shaking the pan frequently without removing the lid.

🍃 Uncover and brown lightly over medium heat for a few minutes.

🍃 Garnish with chopped parsley and green onions. Season to taste with salt and pepper.

🍃 Serve with a white sauce.

RUTABAGAS AND TURNIPS

Rutabagas are about the size of a head of cabbage and have orange flesh. Turnips are smaller and have white flesh. Rutabaga is one of the most popular vegetables in Québec.

PREPARATION
Peel the rutabagas only when ready to cook. The peel is rather thick.

BASIC COOKING METHOD
Peel the rutabagas and cut into thick slices.

🍃 Place in a saucepan and add enough boiling water to cover. Add a pinch of sugar and a pinch of pepper. Cook, uncovered, for 20 to 35 minutes. (Prolonged cooking will change the color of the rutabaga and make it harder to digest.)

🍃 Cook grated rutabaga for 5 minutes.

IN A PRESSURE-COOKER
Place the rutabaga on the rack of the pressure-cooker. Add ½ cup (125 mL) water and a pinch of salt. Secure the lid and let the pressure rise. Cook for 4 minutes. (Cook grated rutabaga for only 1 minute.) Reduce the pressure immediately and serve.

RUTABAGA SALAD

½ cup (125 mL) cider vinegar
1 tsp (5 mL) salt
¼ tsp (1 mL) pepper
3 tbsp (45 mL) maple sugar
or brown sugar
2 tbsp (30 mL) freshly grated horseradish (optional)
5 cups (1.2 L) peeled and grated rutabaga

1 large red onion, finely chopped

🍃 Mix together the vinegar, salt, pepper, maple or brown sugar and grated horseradish.

🍃 Top the rutabaga and onion with this mixture. Mix well. Cover and refrigerate for 24 hours before serving.

RUTABAGA COMPOTE

🍃 Peel and dice a medium rutabaga. Cook, drain, mash and add 1 cup (250 mL) unsweetened applesauce. Blend well and add 2 to 3 tbsp (30 to 45 mL) butter. Serve.

FRENCH-STYLE RUTABAGA

2 cups (50 mL) mashed rutabaga
1 egg
2 tbsp (30 mL) butter
pinch of savory
salt and pepper to taste
3 tbsp (45 mL) butter
3 tbsp (45 mL) flour
1 cup (250 mL) milk
½ cup (125 mL) grated cheese

🍃 Blend together the mashed rutabaga, egg, 2 tbsp (30 mL) butter, savory, salt and pepper. Stir well. Place in a buttered baking dish.

🍃 Make a white sauce with the 3 tbsp (45 mL) butter, the flour and the milk. Pour the sauce over the rutabaga and sprinkle with the grated cheese.

🍃 Bake in a 400°F (200°C) oven for 25 minutes or until the cheese is melted.

MASHED RUTABAGA PARMENTIER

1 medium rutabaga (2 to 3 lbs or 1 to 1.5 kg)
5 potatoes
1½ cups (375 mL) consommé or water
1 tsp (5 mL) salt
½ tsp (2 mL) sugar
¼ tsp (1 mL) savory
2 tbsp (30 mL) butter

🍃 Peel the rutabaga and either slice thinly or grate. Peel and slice the potatoes. Place in a saucepan.

🍃 Add the consommé or water, salt, sugar and savory. Bring to a boil over high heat and cook until the rutabagas and the potatoes are tender.

🍃 If using water as the liquid, drain the vegetables; if consommé, uncover and cook over high heat until the consommé has evaporated.

🍃 Add the butter. Mash and serve.

MASHED RUTABAGA

1 rutabaga
½ tsp (2 mL) sugar
1 tbsp (15 mL) sour cream
2 tbsp (30 mL) butter
pinch of pepper
parsley to taste

🍃 Peel the rutabaga and cut into thin strips. Cover with boiling water, add the sugar and boil for

8 to 9 minutes over high heat. Drain. Return to the saucepan.

🍃 Add the sour cream, butter, pepper and parsley. Mash with a fork. Serve.

TURNIP WITH ONION

2 lbs (1 kg) turnips
1 lb (500 g) small white onions
¼ cup (50 mL) butter
1 tsp (5 mL) salt
pinch of pepper

🍃 Peel the turnips and slice ¼ in. (0.5 cm) thick. Cook and drain.

🍃 Peel the onions and cut in thin slices; separate into rings. Brown in the butter and add to the turnips. Season with salt and pepper. Mix well and serve.

TURNIP WITH CONSOMMÉ

8 turnips or 1 medium rutabaga (2 to 3 lbs or 1 to 1.5 kg)
4 tbsp (60 mL) vegetable oil
1 cup (250 mL) stock or consommé
¼ cup (50 mL) finely chopped green onion
1 tbsp (15 mL) soy sauce
pinch of pepper
salt to taste

🍃 Peel and grate the turnips.

🍃 Heat the oil in a large skillet. Add the turnips and cook for 1 minute over medium heat, stirring constantly. Add the consommé and bring to a boil.

🍃 Cover and simmer for 5 minutes.

🐚 Add the green onion, soy sauce and pepper. Season to taste with salt.

🐚 Simmer, uncovered, for 3 minutes and serve.

PARSNIP

PREPARATION

The parsnip is used mostly to flavor stews and soups. It can also be eaten as a vegetable; it substitute, for carrots in any recipe.

🐚 Peel the parsnips. To prevent discoloration, place them in a mixture of cold water and vinegar (1 tbsp or 15 mL vinegar per 2 cups or 500 mL water).

BASIC COOKING METHOD

Place the whole or sliced parsnips in a saucepan with boiling water. For every 6 parsnips, add ½ tsp (2 mL) sugar. Cover and boil for 15 to 18 minutes or until tender, depending on the size of the parsnips.

🐚 Drain and serve with butter, lemon and parsley.

🐚 When parsnips are overcooked, they have an unpleasant flavor and turn yellow.

PARSNIPS PARMIGIANA

6 large parsnips, boiled
4 tbsp (60 mL) butter
¼ to ½ cup (50 to 125 mL) grated Parmesan cheese
salt, pepper and paprika to taste

🐚 Cut off the thin ends of the parsnips and quarter the thick ends lengthwise.

🐚 Heat the butter in a skillet until melted and slightly browned. Add the parsnips and cook over low heat, turning occasionally, until browned on all sides.

🐚 Sprinkle with the cheese and continue cooking over low heat until well blended.

🐚 Turn onto a warm platter and top with the butter from the skillet. Sprinkle lightly with salt, pepper and paprika.

GLAZED PARSNIPS

4 to 8 parsnips, boiled
4 tbsp (60 mL) butter
4 tbsp (60 mL) brown sugar
pinch of cinnamon

🐚 Cut the parsnips into pieces of equal size.

🐚 Place the butter, brown sugar, cinnamon and parsnips in a skillet. Stir over low heat until the parsnips are browned and well-coated. Serve.

SWEET POTATOES

PREPARATION

Sweet potatoes resemble potatoes. They are sweeter, however, and anywhere from pale yellow to dark yellow in color. It is not necessary to peel them, and since they are tastier in their jackets simply scrub well under cold running water. Remove a small piece at each end.

BASIC COOKING METHOD

Bake in a 350°F (180°C) oven for 30 to 40 minutes; or boil, unpeeled, for 20 to 30 minutes.

🐚 Season with salt when cooked.

Sweet Potatoes with Sherry

New Orleans Sweet Potatoes

6 sweet potatoes
1½ cups (375 mL) brown sugar
1½ cups (375 mL) water
2 tbsp (30 mL) butter
¼ tsp (1 mL) salt

❧ Peel the sweet potatoes and cut into ½-in. (1-cm) slices.
❧ Place in a skillet and cover with the remaining ingredients. Cover and bake in a 350°F (180°C) oven for 20 minutes. Uncover and cook for 30 minutes longer.
❧ For a real treat, serve this dish with ham.

Orange-glazed Sweet Potatoes

Sweet Potatoes with Sherry

8 sweet potatoes, well scrubbed
½ cup (125 mL) butter
1 cup (250 mL) orange juice
zest of ½ orange
¼ cup (50 mL) sherry
½ cup (125 mL) chopped walnuts

❧ Boil the sweet potatoes (see opposite). Drain, peel and mash. Add the remaining ingredients, except the walnuts. Purée.
❧ Place in a baking dish and sprinkle with the walnuts. Bake in a 375°F (190°C) oven for 25 minutes.
❧ If using to stuff chicken, duck or pork shoulder, add the walnuts to the purée and refrigerate for 4 to 6 hours before using.

Sweet Potato Loaf

⅔ cup (150 mL) butter
1 cup (250 mL) brown sugar
½ tsp (2 mL) salt
2 eggs
2 cups (500 mL) peeled and grated raw sweet potatoes
zest of 1 orange
½ tsp (2 mL) ground ginger
½ tsp (2 mL) mace
2 tbsp (30 mL) cognac or orange juice

❧ Cream the butter with the brown sugar and the salt. When light and creamy, add the eggs, one at a time, beating after each addition. Add the grated sweet potatoes and the remaining ingredients. Beat vigorously.
❧ Turn the mixture into a well-buttered 8- x 12-in. (20- x 30-cm) pan and bake in a 350°F (180°C)

oven for 1 hour.
❧ Serve hot.
❧ This sweet potato loaf is excellent with turkey.

Orange-glazed Sweet Potatoes

1 can sweet potatoes or 6 boiled sweet potatoes
3 tbsp (45 mL) butter
½ cup (125 mL) orange marmalade
½ tsp (2 mL) cinnamon
pinch of nutmeg
1 tbsp (15 mL) brandy

❧ Drain the sweet potatoes and cut into halves or quarters, depending on their size.
❧ Melt the butter in a large skillet and add the orange mar-

[445]

malade, cinnamon, nutmeg and brandy. Cook until the mixture bubbles.

🍂Add the sweet potatoes and toss to coat well with the marmalade mixture.

🍂Cook over low heat, stirring occasionally, for about 15 minutes.

🍂Serve the sweet potatoes very hot with the marmalade glaze. If desired, sprinkle the sweet potatoes with cinnamon and broil for a few minutes before serving.

PARSLEYED SEMOLINA

2½ cups (625 mL) milk
½ cup (125 mL) wheat semolina
2 tbsp (30 mL) dried parsley
or ½ cup (125 mL) fresh parsley
1 tsp (5 mL) salt
1 tbsp (15 mL) butter
2 well-beaten eggs

🍂In a saucepan, bring the milk to a boil. Blend in the semolina, stirring constantly. When well creamed together, add the parsley and the salt.

🍂Continue to cook over low heat for 5 to 8 minutes, stirring frequently. Remove from heat. Add the butter and the beaten eggs and cook for another 2 minutes, stirring vigorously.

🍂Turn the mixture into a warmed serving dish.

🍂Serve as a vegetable with veal or chicken.

POTATOES

BASIC PREPARATION

For maximum flavor and nutrition, potatoes should be cooked in their skins unless they are particularly old or discolored. Clean them well with a vegetable brush and rinse them two or three times under cold running water.

BASIC BOILED POTATOES

Choose potatoes of more-or-less equal size, or cut larger ones in half. Place the cleaned potatoes in a saucepan. Cover them with boiling water. Add 1 tsp (5 mL) of coarse salt for each 4 cups (1 L) of water used. Cover the potatoes and boil until tender, about 20 to 30 minutes depending on the size of the potatoes. Drain and return the pan to the burner over low heat to remove excess moisture. Peel.

PRESSURE-COOKING POTATOES

With this method, the potatoes are actually steamed, producing a tastier result. Do not peel the potatoes before cooking. At most, peel a narrow band around the middle of each potato. Place the potatoes in the pressure-cooker. (Choose potatoes of equal size or cut larger ones in half.) Add just enough boiling water to cover the pressure-cooker rack. Close the cover. Heat over high heat to bring up the pressure. Cook small potatoes for 8 minutes, medium ones for 10 minutes and large ones for 12 to 15 minutes. Reduce the pressure quickly. Open the cover and drain off the water. Remove the rack and return the uncovered pot of potatoes to the burner for a few seconds to dry out any remaining water. Peel, if desired.

TIPS FOR PREPARING POTATOES

If at all possible, avoid peeling potatoes before cooking. Potatoes cooked in their skin have much more flavor than those that are peeled first.

⬥ Once potatoes are washed, they should not be allowed to soak in water before cooking. The exception is old or winter potatoes which have lost some of their natural moisture in storage.

⬥ To restore the crispness to winter potatoes that have softened in storage, soak them for 12 hours in cold salted water: these will also make the very best French fries.

⬥ Always use mature or winter potatoes in recipes that call for grated potatoes; new potatoes will not produce the desired results.

⬥ As the cooking period of potatoes depends on their size, you should either choose potatoes of roughly equal size, or cut them into pieces of more or less equal size.

⬥ Boiled potatoes are cooked when they can be pierced easily with a fork. They should be drained immediately; do not let them soak in the cooking water.

⬥ New potatoes have fine-grained skins and firm centers. Cooking them at a rolling boil in an uncovered pot allows the heat to penetrate them fully.

⬥ On the other hand, older potatoes have coarse-grained skin. If boiled too quickly, the cellulose will break down and the flesh will turn mushy. Old potatoes should be cooked, covered, over medium heat.

⬥ Boiled unpeeled potatoes will keep in the refrigerator for 2 to 3 days. They can be reheated by plunging them in salted boiling water and leaving them in for 2 or 3 minutes. When reheated, pour off the water and dry the potatoes over low heat for a few seconds.

⬥ Never peel cooked potatoes if you plan to store them in the refrigerator, or they will develop an unpleasant flavor.

FRENCH-FRIED POTATOES

⬥ Wash and peel 6 medium-size mature potatoes. Cut into sticks ½ in. (1 cm) thick. Soak the potatoes for 30 minutes in cold salted water.

⬥ Heat 6 cups (1.5 L) of peanut oil in a 12-cup (3-L) pot or deep fryer until it reaches 390°F (200°C) or until a 1-in. (2 cm) square piece of bread takes 25 seconds to turn golden-brown.

⬥ Meanwhile, drain the potatoes and dry them thoroughly on paper towels or clean dish towels.

⬥ Place some of the potatoes in a wire basket; (do not try to fry too many pieces at one time). Immerse the potatoes in the hot fat for about 7 minutes or until they are tender and golden brown. Drain on paper towels.

⬥ Keep the cooked potatoes warm in the oven while you cook the remaining fries. Salt before serving.

Potato Chips

❧ Peel large mature potatoes and slice them as thinly as possible with a very sharp knife, vegetable slicer or special slicing attachment. Each inch of potato should produce about 20 slices. (10 slices per cm.)

❧ Cover the potato slices completely with ice water and let them soak for 1 hour. Add about 2 tbsp (30 mL) white vinegar to the water. Drain the slices and dry them thoroughly with paper towels or clean dish towels.

❧ Fill a large pot about ⅓ full with 4 cups (1 L) peanut oil and very slowly heat it to 360°F (180°C) on the thermometer.

❧ Put some of the separated potato slices in a frying basket and immerse them in the hot fat. Cook until golden, lifting and moving the chips once or twice with a slotted spoon.

❧ Let the chips drain on paper toweling. Salt them to taste.

❧ To keep the chips fresh and crisp, let them cool completely, then place them in a metal container lined with wax paper. Cover and keep in a cool place.

Fried Boiled Potatoes

4 potatoes, unpeeled
2 cups (500 mL) peanut oil
salt to taste
1 onion, chopped
1 tsp (5 mL) butter

❧ Scrub the potatoes well. Cook them in boiling water. Drain and dry them over low heat. Allow them to cool, then refrigerate for at least 1 to 2 hours.

❧ Peel the potatoes and grate them into long strips using the largest holes on the grater.

❧ Heat the peanut oil to 400°F (200°C). Place the grated potatoes in a frying basket, and immerse them in the hot fat until golden brown and crisp. Drain on paper towels and salt to taste.

❧ Fry the onion in the butter. Add the fried potatoes and mix well.

❧ As a variation, serve with a bowl of grated cheese.

Crispy Potato Cakes

Crispy Potato Cakes

2 potatoes per person
½ cup (125 mL) bacon fat
salt and pepper to taste

❧ Peel the potatoes and slice them into rounds as thinly as possible.

❧ Soak the slices for 2 hours in ice water. Drain and dry the slices well.

❧ Heat the bacon fat in a large skillet which has a tight-fitting lid. Arrange half the sliced potatoes in the hot fat. Season with salt and pepper. Add the rest of the potatoes, and salt and pepper again. Cover and cook over low heat for about 20 minutes, or until the potatoes in the middle yield to the point of a knife. The bottom should be crusty and golden brown. Slide the potatoes out of the pan with a large spatula, oil the skillet with a little oil, and flip the potatoes over into the pan with the uncooked side down. Cook until the bottom is golden brown.

❧ To serve, slide the golden brown potato pancake onto a

Herb-stuffed Potatoes

large heated platter. Sprinkle with parsley or chives or fried onions.

SKILLET-ROASTED POTATOES

This method produces lovely brown potatoes resembling the kind cooked in the roasting pan with a roast of veal or beef.

⁂ If possible, use small potatoes.

⁂ Blanch the potatoes for 3 to 4 minutes in boiling water.

⁂ Heat 2 to 3 tbsp (30 to 45 mL) shortening, oil or butter in a cast-iron or enameled skillet. Arrange the potatoes side by side in the hot fat. Brown them over low heat, turning occasionally, until they are evenly browned on all sides.

⁂ Cover the pan and continue cooking over low heat for about another 10 minutes. Shake the skillet a few times, but do not remove the cover.

⁂ Serve as soon as the potatoes are tender.

PERFECT HASH-BROWNED POTATOES

I have prepared hash browns in many ways in my years of cooking, but they are never as good as when I make them with sour cream. In the summer, I like to serve them completely covered with chopped fresh chives and basil fresh from the garden.

6 large potatoes
2 tbsp (30 mL) butter
or bacon fat
1 tsp (5 mL) salt
¼ tsp (1 mL) pepper
1 tbsp (15 mL) melted butter
4 tbsp (60 mL) sour cream
chives or parsley to taste

⁂ Bake the potatoes the day before and refrigerate them in their skins. The next day, peel the potatoes and grate them using the medium-size holes of the grater. Heat the bacon fat or butter (or a mixture of both) in a heavy skillet. Sprinkle the potatoes lightly over the pan, but be sure not to pack them down. Top with the salt, pepper and the melted butter. Cook gently over low heat until the potatoes are browned on the bottom but do not stick to the skillet; this should take about 20 minutes. Check the progress by lifting the edge gently with a spatula. When the bottom is nicely browned, use the spatula to separate the potatoes into manageable sections, and flip each section over. Brown the second side over low heat. When done, place half the cooked potatoes on a heated serving dish. Spread with a layer of sour cream and cover with the remaining potatoes. Sprinkle to taste with chives or parsley.

HERB-STUFFED POTATOES

4 baking potatoes
3 tbsp (45 mL) butter
2 tbsp (30 mL) sour cream
pinch of thyme
pinch of savory
parsley and chives to taste
salt and pepper to taste

⁂ Bake the potatoes. As soon as the potatoes are cooked, cut them in two lengthwise and scoop out the flesh into a bowl. Reserve the potato skins.

ᕙ Heat the remaining ingredients, but do not let the mixture boil. Add this mixture to the potato flesh and mash until creamy and fluffy.

ᕙ Stuff the potato mixture into the reserved potato skins. Sprinkle with paprika or grated cheese, if desired.

ᕙ Reheat in a 400°F (200°C) oven for 10 to 15 minutes.

BAKED POTATOES

ᕙ Select large baking potatoes of equal size and wash, scrub and dry them.

ᕙ Rub each potato with some fat or butter, then roll it lightly in coarse salt.

ᕙ This procedure produces a tender skin on the baked potato. If you prefer a crisp potato skin, omit the fat and salt. Instead, slash the skin of each potato in 5 or 6 places.

ᕙ Bake in a 425°F (220°C) oven for 40 to 60 minutes, depending on the size of the potatoes. A few minutes before the end of the cooking time, stab each potato with a sharp knife to release the steam; this prevents the flesh from being soggy.

ᕙ Baked potatoes must be served as soon as the are cooked, because they quickly lose their flavor if allowed to sit.

POTATOES BAKED IN FOIL

ᕙ Scrub each potato. Rub each one with butter or fat and slit the skin in a few places with a knife.

ᕙ Seal each potato well in a square of aluminum foil. Bake in a 425°F (220°C) oven for 50 to 80 minutes, depending on the size of the potatoes. Potatoes baked this way can sit 10 to 15 minutes before serving without ill effect.

ᕙ This method of baking produces a moister baked potato with a unique flavor.

MASHED POTATOES

ᕙ Making the perfect bowl of mashed potatoes takes a certain amount of skill. The basic instructions I'm giving you will set you on the right path. But because every type of potato cooks a bit differently and absorbs a different quantity of liquid, your success will depend to a degree on your own cooking experience.

ᕙ Always start with mature or winter potatoes, preferably large or medium-size. Peel the potatoes and, if necessary, cut them into equal-size pieces. Boil them over medium heat, taking care not to overcook them. Drain off the liquid and dry the potatoes for a few moments over high heat, shaking the pan once or twice so they don't stick.

ᕙ Mash the potatoes with a masher, food mill, or potato ricer, or beat them at medium speed with an electric mixer. Add a small quantity of butter, along with salt, pepper and parsley, chives or savory to taste. Stir in 1 cup (250 mL) sour cream for every 8 to 10 potatoes. Beat vigorously until the potatoes are fluffy

and smooth. (You can replace the sour cream with ordinary cream or milk, but the purée will not be as tasty or creamy.)

ᕙ Serve without delay as mashed potatoes do not reheat well. If you really must keep them warm until serving time, set the covered casserole of mashed potatoes in a heated electric frying pan containing 1 cup (250 mL) of water.

POTATOES LOULOU

6 to 8 potatoes
2 tbsp (30 mL) butter
2 tbsp (30 mL) olive oil
1½ tsp (7 mL) grated lemon zest
1 tbsp (15 mL) chopped parsley
1 tbsp (15 mL) chopped chives
pinch of nutmeg
3 tbsp (45 mL) lemon juice
salt and pepper to taste

ᕙ Clean the potatoes and boil them whole, according to the procedure on page 448. Peel them and place them in a serving dish.

ᕙ Melt the butter in a skillet, being careful not to let it brown. Add the remaining ingredients and mix well.

ᕙ Pour the hot butter mixture over the potatoes and serve immediately.

POTATOES WITH TARRAGON

3 potatoes, diced
½ cup (125 mL) cream
½ cup (125 mL) milk
1 tbsp (15 mL) butter
1 tsp (5 mL) tarragon
salt and pepper to taste

🍃 Place the diced potatoes in the upper part of a double boiler. Add the remaining ingredients.

🍃 Cover and simmer over boiling water for 1 hour, or until the potatoes are tender and have absorbed the liquid.

POTATOES PROVENÇALE

1 28-oz. (800-mL) can tomatoes
1 onion, finely chopped
1 tbsp (15 mL) sugar
½ tsp (5 mL) savory or basil
1 tsp (5 mL) salt
1 tbsp (15 mL) catsup
4 to 5 cups (1 to 1.2 L) thinly sliced raw potatoes
¼ cup (50 mL) breadcrumbs
1 tbsp (15 mL) butter

🍃 Pour the tomatoes into a bowl. Add the onion, sugar, savory or basil, salt and catsup. Stir to mix.

🍃 Pour the tomato mixture over the sliced potatoes and mix well.

🍃 Pour the mixture into a buttered baking dish. Top with the breadcrumbs and dot with butter. Cook in a 375°F (190°C) oven for 1 hour.

POTATOES FRIQUET

4 to 6 potatoes
4 tbsp (60 mL) olive oil
1 tsp (5 mL) butter
1 onion, chopped
1 tsp (5 mL) water
2 tsp (10 mL) chopped parsley

🍃 Wash and peel the potatoes, then cut them into large dice.

🍃 Heat the oil in a large skillet. Add the potatoes. Cook over medium heat, stirring often, until the potatoes are golden brown and tender (about 35 minutes).

Remove the potatoes and keep them warm.

🍃 Melt the butter in the skillet and add the onion, water and parsley. Cook until lightly browned.

🍃 Pour this sauce over the cooked potatoes. Stir well and serve very hot.

POTATOES WITH PEAS

1 potato per person
3 tbsp (45 mL) butter
3 tbsp (45 mL) flour
2 cups (500 mL) milk
½ cup (125 mL) cream
1 small package frozen peas
1 tsp (5 mL) salt
pinch of thyme
2 tbsp (30 mL) butter

🍃 Boil the potatoes. (This can be done the day before.) Refrigerate the cooked potatoes until cold. Peel them and cut them into 1-inch (2-cm) cubes.

🍃 Make a white sauce with the 3 tbsp (45 mL) of butter, the flour, the milk and the cream. When the sauce is smooth and creamy, stir in the diced potatoes. Add the peas, the salt, the thyme and the rest of the butter. Simmer over low heat for about 15 to 20 minutes, until the potatoes are nice and hot and the peas are cooked.

🍃 Canned green peas can be used in this recipe, but frozen peas give much more color to the final dish.

Potatoes Provençale

CRISPY POTATO SKINS

This is an economical but tasty little recipe that's just perfect for last-minute cocktails.

🍂 Scrub some potatoes well and peel them thickly to produce large pieces of potato skin.

🍂 Butter or grease each piece of peel with bacon or other fat. Salt and pepper lightly.

🍂 Arrange the peels in one layer on a cookie sheet. Bake in a 375°F (190°C) oven for 30 to 40 minutes.

Potatoes Boulangère

SCALLOPED POTATOES

4 medium potatoes, peeled
2 to 4 tbsp (30 to 60 mL) butter
3 tbsp (45 mL) flour
salt and pepper to taste
3 cups (750 mL) milk

🍂 Thinly slice the potatoes.

🍂 Butter a baking dish and arrange half the potato slices in it. Salt, pepper and sprinkle with half the flour. Add the rest of the potatoes, then salt and pepper again and sprinkle with the rest of the flour. Top with the remaining butter.

🍂 Pour the milk over the mixture. Cover and bake in a 375°F (190°C) oven for 25 minutes. Remove the cover and bake another 20 to 25 minutes.

🍂 You can vary the recipe by adding 2 tbsp (30 mL) thinly sliced onion or ½ cup (125 mL) minced chives or ½ tsp (2 mL) savory.

🍂 The potatoes can be served au gratin by sprinkling the top with 1 cup (250 mL) grated cheese and dotting with a few dabs of butter just before the end of the cooking period.

GOLDEN POTATO CASSEROLE

2 tbsp (30 mL) butter
2 tbsp (30 mL) flour
2 cups (500 mL) milk
½ tsp (2 mL) salt
¼ tsp (1 mL) pepper
3 cups (750 mL) grated raw potatoes
1 green onion, chopped
butter

🍂 Make a white sauce with the butter, flour, milk, salt and pepper.

🍂 Add the grated raw potatoes and the green onion to the sauce. Blend well.

🍂 Pour the mixture into a buttered baking dish. Place a few dots of butter on top. Bake in a 300°F (150°C) oven for 3 to 4 hours or until the top is caramel-colored and very shiny.

POTATOES BOULANGÈRE

4 potatoes
4 onions
3 tbsp (45 mL) peanut oil
salt and pepper to taste
1 cup (250 mL) consommé

🍂 Scrub, peel and thinly slice the potatoes and the onions.

🍂 Heat the oil in a skillet. Fry the onions until golden brown.

❦ TECHNIQUE ❦

POTATOES BOULANGÈRE

1   Fry the onions in the oil until golden.

2   Add the potatoes and mix well.

3   Place the mixture in a baking dish. Season with salt and pepper.

4   Add the consommé.

Add the potatoes and mix well. Salt and pepper to taste and place the potato mixture in a baking dish. Add the consommé. Cover and bake for 1 hour in a 375°F (190°C) oven.

Irish Boxty

When I was a girl, I had an Irish nanny. She couldn't say a word of French, but she would make Boxty almost every day while she sang a ditty to me. To this day, as far as I'm concerned no other dish is as Irish as this.

Good boxty cannot be made with young potatoes; try to use old, large, mealy potatoes. Originally these cakes were cooked on an ungreased griddle, but I have found they turn out tastier and lighter when cooked in the oven. Boxty are a perfect accompaniment to a roast and gravy. You can prepare the boxty in advance and reheat them in a 325°F (160°C) oven while you make the gravy.

2 large potatoes
2 cups (500 mL) mashed potatoes
1 tsp (5 mL) salt
1 tsp (5 mL) baking soda
¼ to ½ cup (50 to 125 mL) all-purpose flour

Peel and grate the potatoes with a fine or medium grater over a bowl of cold water. Let them soak in the water while you prepare the mashed potatoes.

To make 2 cups (500 mL) of mashed potatoes, boil 6 small or 4 medium peeled potatoes. When cooked, drain off the water and place the pan back on the burner over low heat until the potatoes are dry. Mash them, but do not add butter or milk.

Remove the grated potatoes from the bowl. Pour off the soaking water, but reserve the thick layer of potato starch at the bottom of the bowl; add this potato starch to the mashed potatoes. Squeeze the grated potatoes in a cloth until well dried, then add to the mashed potatoes. Add the salt and baking soda mixed with ¼ cup (50 mL) of the flour. Stir all together, adding just enough flour to make a dough that can be rolled out.

Roll out the potato dough on a floured surface, making a circle ½ in. (1 cm) thick. Cut into 4 triangles or into round cakes using a large cookie cutter. Place the boxty on a greased baking sheet. Bake in a 325°F (160°C) oven for 30 to 45 minutes or until the boxty are golden brown.

Potato Cakes

4 large potatoes
1 egg, lightly beaten
1 cup (250 mL) all-purpose flour
salt and nutmeg to taste
½ cup (125 mL) breadcrumbs
2 tbsp (30 mL) butter

Boil the potatoes in their skins. When cooked, drain and peel them. Mash until smooth.

Beat in the egg, flour, salt and nutmeg. Turn the mixture onto a lightly-floured surface. Knead until the dough is smooth. Pat out to ½-in. (1-cm) thickness and cut into rounds with a cookie cutter. Dredge each cake in the breadcrumbs.

Melt the butter in a heavy skillet. Cook the cakes over medium heat until golden-brown on both sides.

Potato Cakes

[455]

❦ TECHNIQUE ❦

POTATO CAKES

1 Peel and mash the cooked potatoes.

2 Beat in the egg, flour, salt and nutmeg.

3 Knead the dough and pat it out. Cut the cakes with a cookie cutter.

4 Dredge each cake in the breadcrumbs.

IRISH POTATO CAKES

This old-fashioned recipe does double duty. You can serve these cakes plain as a "vegetable serving" with a main course. Or serve them for dessert, hot, lightly buttered and topped with honey, brown sugar or marmalade.

1 cup (250 mL) grated
raw potatoes
2 tsp (10 mL) lemon juice
1 cup (250 mL) mashed cooked
potatoes
1 cup (250 mL) flour
1 tsp (5 mL) salt
2 tsp (10 mL) baking powder
1 egg, lightly beaten
1 cup (250 mL) sour milk
or buttermilk
¼ cup (50 mL) melted butter

🍃 Combine the lemon juice with the grated raw potatoes. Place the mixture in a piece of cheesecloth and squeeze hard to squeeze out as much liquid as possible.

🍃 Mix together the cooked mashed potatoes and the flour. Add the grated potatoes, salt, baking powder, egg and sour milk. Beat together until well blended and smooth.

🍃 Heat a cast-iron skillet, greased with some of the melted butter. Drop the potato mixture 1 tbsp (15 mL) at a time onto the hot skillet, leaving space between each cake.

🍃 Cook over medium heat for 3 minutes on each side.

POTATO FRICASSÉE

½ cup (125 mL) fat of your
choice
4 onions, thinly sliced into rings
6 raw potatoes, peeled and diced
½ cup (125 mL) chopped
celery leaves
2 tbsp (30 mL) chopped parsley
1 tsp (5 mL) savory
salt and pepper to taste
hot water

🍃 Melt the fat in a skillet. Add the onions and cook them over high heat, stirring constantly, until golden. Add the remaining ingredients except the hot water.

🍃 Stir until well mixed and add just enough hot water to cover. Bring to a boil. Cover and simmer for 30 minutes or until the potatoes are tender. Remove the cover and crush a few of the potatoes with a fork to thicken the sauce.

🍃 Adjust the seasoning and serve.

SKEWERED POTATOES

🍃 Scrub some medium-size potatoes. Rub each one with soft butter and roll it in coarse salt. Thread the potatoes on skewers. Bake for 20 to 35 minutes, depending on the size of the potatoes. They will be crisp and delicious as long as they are served immediately. If you want potatoes with tender skins, omit the salt and wrap the potatoes in

a double thickness of aluminum foil, then cook for 40 minutes.

COOKING POTATOES ON THE BARBECUE

POTATOES GRILLED IN BACON
🍃 Peel medium-size potatoes. Wrap each one in a slice of bacon or in a piece of salt pork sliced as thin as possible. Slide the potatoes onto a metal skewer and cook over the coals for 20 to 35 minutes, depending on the size. Turn from time to time. Serve immediately.

FROZEN FRENCH-FRIED POTATOES
🍃 Empty the contents of a package of frozen potatoes into a large metal sieve. Shake the potatoes over the hot coals until piping hot. Salt and serve.

POTATOES BARBECUED IN FOIL
🍃 Scrub medium-size potatoes. Rub each with soft butter and sprinkle lightly with salt. Wrap individually in a double thickness of aluminum foil. Cook for 1 hour on the barbecue grill, turning frequently.

POTATOES FRIED WITH BACON
🍃 Fry some bacon slices in a cast-iron skillet set on the barbecue grill. Peel 4 or 5 large potatoes. Slice them as thin as possible. Remove the bacon from the skillet. Place the potatoes in the bacon fat. Salt and pepper, and if you wish, add 1 chopped onion. Cook the potatoes over the coals,

Duchess Potatoes

Heat the oil or fat in a 9-in. (23-cm) skillet. Add the potato mixture and cook over medium heat, stirring often, until the potatoes are browned. Once the potatoes start to brown, stir almost constantly until the potatoes are cooked to your taste. Serve.

ROAST POTATOES

Potatoes cooked right in the pan drippings alongside the roast have an incomparable flavor.

Peel small or medium-size potatoes. Place them in a bowl and cover with boiling water for 3 or 4 minutes. Drain and dry the potatoes, then arrange them around a roast of beef or chicken about 40 to 50 minutes before the end of the roasting period.

Turn the potatoes once or twice in the pan drippings to brown on all sides.

turning frequently, until tender and browned. Add the bacon cut into small pieces. Cover and keep warm on the side of the grill until ready to serve.

DUCHESS POTATOES

4 to 6 potatoes
3 tbsp (45 mL) butter
2 egg yolks
2 tbsp (30 mL) cream
1 tsp (5 mL) salt
pinch of nutmeg
pepper to taste

Boil the peeled potatoes, drain off the cooking water and dry them for a few seconds over high heat.

Add the butter to the potatoes, then mash them well. Beat in the egg yolks, cream, salt, nutmeg

and pepper. Beat until creamy and smooth.

Turn the mixture into a baking dish. Bake in a 400°F (200°C) oven for 10 to 15 minutes or until the top is lightly browned.

NEW BRUNSWICK HASH-BROWNED POTATOES

3 cups (750 mL) cooked potatoes
1 chopped onion
3 tbsp (45 mL) flour
¼ cup (50 mL) milk
1 tsp (5 mL) salt
¼ tsp (1 mL) pepper
3 tbsp (45 mL) peanut oil
or bacon fat

Cut the potatoes into dice. Mix them with the onion, flour, milk, salt and pepper.

POTATOES CHANTILLY

Here's a sophisticated way to prepare instant potatoes. It's perfect served with roast chicken or veal.

6 servings instant mashed potatoes
¼ cup (50 mL) melted butter
salt and pepper to taste
¼ cup (50 mL) whipping cream
⅓ cup (75 mL) grated mild Cheddar cheese

Prepare the potatoes according to the package directions, but omit the butter. When ready, add the melted butter, salt and pepper. Whip the cream. Spoon the potatoes into an 8-cup (2 L) casserole, Cover with the whipped cream and sprinkle the grated cheese on top. Bake for 10 minutes in a 450°F (230°C) oven. Serve as soon as ready.

POTATOES LYONNAISE

5 potatoes, unpeeled
5 tbsp (75 mL) butter
or half butter, half oil
1 cup (250 mL) chopped onion
1 tsp (5 mL) salt
pinch of pepper
chopped parsley

🐦 Scrub the potatoes and boil them in their skins. Drain, then peel and cut in ¼-in (0.5 cm) slices.

🐦 Melt 2 tbsp (30 mL) of the butter in a heavy skillet. Add the onion and cook until golden over medium heat. Remove the onions from the pan and add the rest of the butter. Add the potatoes and brown them over medium heat. Stir in the onions, salt and pepper and heat together for 3 minutes over low heat. Sprinkle with parsley and serve.

POTATO PUDDING

This is a very practical recipe, as few potato dishes lend themselves to freezing. Freeze the cooked puddings right in the muffin tins in which they were baked. When frozen solid, remove the individual puddings from the molds and store

them in a freezer bag or similar air-tight container. This dish goes extremely well with steak and barbecued chicken.

12 medium potatoes
2 medium onions, grated
4 eggs, well beaten
1 cup (250 mL) flour
1 tbsp (15 mL) salt
½ tsp (2 mL) pepper
½ (2 mL) savory
1 tsp (5 mL) baking powder
8 tbsp (120 mL) melted bacon fat

🐦 Peel the potatoes. Grate them into a bowl of cold water to prevent discoloration. Drain the potatoes, squeezing out as much liquid as possible. Add the onions and the eggs. Beat together until well mixed.

🐦 Combine the flour, salt, pepper, savory and baking powder.

Add to the potatoes and mix well. Stir in the melted bacon fat. Spoon the mixture into greased medium-size muffin pans. Bake in a 375°F (190°C) oven for 1 hour or until the tops are brown and crispy.

🐦 Let the cooked puddings cool for 30 minutes on a cake rack, then run a knife around the edge of each mold to loosen the pudding. Remove from the muffin tin and serve hot.

🐦 To freeze: freeze the puddings in the muffin molds. Then remove from the molds and store in a freezer bag.

🐦 This recipe makes 16 servings. The puddings will keep 2 to 3 months in the freezer.

🐦 To serve: reheat the puddings, wrapped individually in foil, for 20 to 25 minutes in the oven preheated to 350°F (180°C).

Potatoes Lyonnaise

POTATOES AU GRATIN

This dish is similar to scalloped potatoes but is prepared the French way. It is made starting with cooked potatoes and is easily reheated. I think this is the perfect potato dish to serve with baked ham.

8 medium potatoes
2 tbsp (30 mL) butter
1 large onion, chopped
2 tbsp (30 mL) flour
½ cup (125 mL) consommé
2 cups (500 mL) light cream
or milk
salt and pepper to taste
½ cup (125 mL) grated Cheddar
or Parmesan cheese
¼ cup (50 mL) fine breadcrumbs
1 tsp (5 mL) butter

🌢 Scrub the potatoes but do not peel them. Boil them until tender.

🌢 Peel the potatoes and slice them into moderately thin rounds.

🌢 Melt the butter in a skillet. Add the onion and cook until lightly browned. Add the flour. Stir until well mixed.

🌢 Add the consommé and the cream or milk, all at once. Cook, stirring, until the mixture is smooth and creamy. Season to taste with salt and pepper.

🌢 Butter an 8-cup (2-L) casserole. Fill with alternating rows of potatoes, sauce and cheese. The top layer should be sauce. Mix the remaining cheese with the breadcrumbs and sprinkle on top of the sauce. Dot with the butter. Bake in a 350°F (180°C) oven until the top is golden-brown.

POTATO PANCAKES

3 potatoes
2 eggs, beaten
1 small onion, grated
1 tbsp (15 mL) flour
1 soda cracker, crushed
salt and pepper to taste
4 tbsp (60 mL) butter

🌢 Wash and peel the potatoes. Grate them into a bowl of cold water; this will prevent the grated potatoes from discoloring. Drain well, then squeeze them dry in a cloth.

🌢 In a bowl, combine the potatoes with the eggs, onion, flour, cracker-crumbs, salt and pepper. Mix well.

🌢 Melt the butter in a skillet. Drop the potato mixture by large spoonfuls into the butter. Flatten the cakes gently with the back of a spoon. Brown for 4 minutes on each side, turning only once. Serve.

SUMMER POTATO SALAD

I like to use fresh herbs from my garden to flavor this light, tasty salad. When available, I use very small new potatoes left whole instead of diced potatoes.

6 medium potatoes or 4 cups
(1 L) small new potatoes
3 green onions, finely chopped
3 tbsp (45 mL) chopped parsley,
chervil and tarragon or chopped
fresh parsley

Potato Pancakes

2 tbsp (30 mL) cider vinegar
6 tbsp (90 mL) olive oil
4 tbsp (60 mL) warm water
salt and pepper to taste

❧ Boil the potatoes in their skins, being careful not to overcook them. Drain the potatoes, then dry them over low heat. Peel while they are still hot. Cut large potatoes into dice. Leave small new potatoes whole. Place them in a bowl. Add the green onions and herbs.

❧ In a jar, combine the vinegar, oil, warm water, salt and pepper. Shake well until mixed.

❧ Pour this dressing over the potato mixture. Toss lightly. Correct the seasonings. Turn the mixture into a wooden salad bowl. Cover and let marinate 2 to 4 hours at room temperature; if you refrigerate it, the potatoes will harden and the flavor will suffer.

NEW POTATO SALAD

12 to 15 small new potatoes
3 egg yolks
3 tbsp (45 mL), cider vinegar
or wine vinegar
2 tbsp (30 mL) butter
1 tsp (5 mL) sugar
salt and pepper to taste
⅓ cup (75 mL) green onions, chopped
⅔ cup (150 mL) celery, diced
½ cup (125 mL) whipping cream
½ cup (125 mL) mayonnaise
chopped fresh parsley to taste

❧ Scrub the potatoes and cook them. Drain off the water and dry the potatoes by shaking the pan over medium heat for a few seconds. Peel them and cut each into 2 or 3 pieces.

❧ Place the egg yolks and vinegar in a saucepan and beat together with a hand beater to blend well. Cook over very low heat until slightly thickened, but do not let boil. Remove the mixture from the burner and let cool.

❧ Cream the butter together with the sugar, salt and pepper. Stir in the green onions and celery. Add this mixture to the egg mixture and stir until creamy.

❧ Whip the cream and fold in the mayonnaise. Fold the whip cream mixture into the egg mixture. Adjust the seasonings.

❧ Make alternate layers of the potatoes and the whipped cream dressing in a glass salad bowl. Do not stir. Top with a layer of dressing and sprinkle with chopped fresh parsley or paprika. This salad should be served warm, not chilled.

AMERICAN POTATO SALAD

6 to 8 medium potatoes
2 tbsp (30 mL) olive oil
2½ tbsp (40 mL) cider vinegar
1 tbsp (15 mL) chopped parsley
1 small onion, chopped
¼ tsp (1 mL) finely ground pepper

¾ cup (175 mL) celery, diced
1 tsp (5 mL) salt
½ tsp (2 mL) fennel seed
¾ cup (175 mL) mayonnaise

❧ Boil the potatoes in their skins until just tender; do not overcook. Drain off the water and dry the potatoes over medium heat. Let the potatoes cool. Peel and dice them.

❧ Combine the remaining ingredients in a large salad bowl.

❧ Add the diced potatoes. Toss together and serve.

HOT POTATO AND BACON SALAD

4 to 6 potatoes
2 hard-cooked eggs, grated
4 slices bacon
1 onion, minced
2 to 4 tbsp (30 to 60 mL) vinegar
salt and pepper to taste

❧ Scrub the potatoes and boil them in their skins. Drain and peel them, then cut them into cubes while they are still hot.

❧ Add the grated hard-cooked eggs to the potatoes.

❧ Fry the bacon, cut in pieces. Pour the bacon and bacon grease over the potatoes. The bacon grease replaces oil in this recipe. Stir in the minced onion. Gradually add the vinegar, until the salad suits your taste. Add salt and pepper. Serve warm.

French Potato Salad

mixture, beating constantly. Continue cooking over low heat for 5 minutes, stirring often. Remove from the heat as soon as the mixture thickens. Add the celery seeds and sour cream. Mix well and refrigerate until ready to serve.

SALAD:
6 to 8 cooked potatoes, diced or sliced
2 tbsp (30 mL) olive oil
2½ tbsp (40 mL) cider vinegar
1 tbsp (15 mL) chopped fresh parsley
2 tbsp (30 mL) minced onion

🌢 Mix all the ingredients together. Add just enough of the dressing to coat the potatoes well. Serve garnished with watercress.

BUTTERY POTATO SALAD

🌢 Do not refrigerate this salad, as the butter will congeal with the cold and change the flavor.

6 to 8 potatoes
salt and pepper to taste
3 green onions, chopped
4 tbsp (60 mL) butter
3 tbsp (45 mL) malt
or wine vinegar

🌢 Scrub the potatoes and boil them in their skins. Peel the potatoes while still hot and cut them into cubes. Salt and pepper to taste. Add the green onions and mix together with a fork so as not to crush the potatoes.
🌢 Melt the butter. Add the vinegar. Heat for a few seconds and pour over the warm potatoes. Mix well and serve immediately.

FRENCH POTATO SALAD

DRESSING:
1 tbsp (15 mL) flour
1 tbsp (15 mL) sugar
1½ tsp (7 mL) salt
½ tsp (2 mL) dry mustard
2 tbsp (30 mL) olive oil
½ cup (125 mL) water
3 tbsp (45 mL) cider vinegar
1 egg, lightly beaten
½ tsp (2 mL) celery seeds
¼ cup (50 mL) sour cream

🌢 Mix the flour, sugar, salt, mustard, oil and water in the top part of a double boiler. Cook over boiling water until smooth and creamy, stirring often.
🌢 In a small bowl, beat together the egg and vinegar. Gradually add the egg mixture to the flour

DELUXE POTATO SALAD

12 medium potatoes
1 to 2 tbsp (15 to 30 ml) oil
1 egg yolk
3 tbsp (45 mL) hot vinegar
1 tbsp (15 mL) butter
1 tbsp (15 mL) sugar
1 tsp (5 mL) salt
⅓ cup (75 mL) minced onions
⅔ cup (150 mL) diced celery,
½ cup (125 mL) whipping cream
½ cup (125 mL) mayonnaise

🌢 Scrub the potatoes and boil them in their skins just until tender. Do not overcook. Peel the potatoes and cut them into slices while still hot.
🌢 Bathe the cubed potatoes with

❦ TECHNIQUE ❦

FRENCH POTATO SALAD

1 Mix the flour, sugar, salt, mustard, oil and water in the top part of a double boiler.

2 Gradually add the egg mixture to the flour mixture.

3 Combine the potatoes, oil, vinegar, parsley and onion in a bowl.

4 Add enough dressing to coat the potatoes well.

1 to 2 tbsp (15 to 30 mL) oil. Cover them with wax paper, then keep them in refrigerator.

⁊ Beat the egg yolk in a saucepan. Add the vinegar and mix. Cook over low heat, stirring constantly. Remove from the heat as soon as the mixture thickens and chill.

⁊ Cream the butter, then stir in the sugar, salt, onions and celery. Add this mixture to the egg mixture. Whip the cream and fold it into the egg mixture. Add the mayonnaise. Refrigerate the sauce in a covered bowl. (This part of the procedure can be prepared in advance.)

⁊ When you are ready to serve the potato salad, combine the potatoes with the dressing.

QUICK HOT POTATO SALAD

6 slices bacon, diced
4 medium raw potatoes, diced
1 onion, thinly sliced
2 to 3 tbsp (30 to 45 mL) sugar
2 tsp (10 mL) salt
¼ tsp (1 mL) pepper
1 tsp (5 mL) mustard
⅓ cup (75 mL) cider vinegar
2 tbsp (30 mL) water
2 tbsp (30 mL) chopped parsley

⁊ Remove the rack from the pressure-cooker and fry the bacon slices in it. Add the diced potatoes and the onion. Combine the sugar, salt, pepper, mustard, vinegar, water and parsley, and add the mixture to the potatoes.

⁊ Close the pressure-cooker cover. Cook the potatoes for 5 minutes under pressure, then quickly cool the cooker.

⁊ Turn the salad onto a warm platter and serve immediately.

DRIED LEGUMES

All dried legumes, with the exception of split peas, yellow peas and black-eyed peas, must be soaked before cooking. Lentils are better if soaked first, but they do not require it. The process of soaking and cooking will double the volume of some dried legumes; lentils will expand even more. Dried legumes should always be cooked in the water in which they were soaked, in order to preserve nutrients. If you want, you can add flavor to the legumes by adding herbs, spices or onions to the cooking water. Bring the water to a boil, then let the legumes simmer gently; do not stir too often or you may crush the legumes.

⁊ On average, legumes need 12 hours of soaking (or overnight) and 2 to 2½ hours of cooking. However, you can reduce the soaking time by bringing the legumes to a boil for 2 minutes, then removing them from the heat and letting them soak for 1 hour in the same water; the legumes can then be cooked as normally.

⁊ Count on about 1½ cups (375 mL) of dried legumes to produce 6 servings. Soak in 3 or 4 times more water than the beans.

LAC SAINT JEAN GOURGANES
Québec's famous gourgane is actually a type of broad bean or horse bean, both of which were native to Persia and Africa. The best variety of gourganes comes from the Lac Saint Jean region of Québec.

⁊ You can prepare a tasty and very traditional Québec dish by shelling the beans, cooking them in boiling water with salt and savory, then draining them and topping them with fried onions and small slices of fried salt pork before serving.

⁊ You can substitute broad beans, horse beans or fava beans, if necessary, as the flavor is very similar.

LENTILS
Lentils originated in Central Asia but are now widely available. They are a very good source of protein—½ cup (125 mL) of dried lentils is equivalent to ¼ lb (125 g) of meat.

STEWED LENTILS

1 lb (500 g) dried green or brown lentils
1 large onion
2 whole cloves
1 carrot, in chunks
1 clove garlic, minced
½ tsp (2 mL) savory
½ tsp (2 mL) basil
salt and pepper to taste

🍃 Place the lentils in a saucepan, cover them with cold water and slowly bring to a boil. Skim off any foam or skin that forms on the surface.

🍃 Add the onion studded with the whole cloves, the carrot, garlic, savory and basil. Season with salt and pepper.

🍃 Cover and let simmer for 1 to 1½ hours or until the lentils are tender.

SAVORY LENTILS

🍃 Follow the recipe for stewed lentils, but add a piece of salt pork or a ham bone to the mixture after skimming the foam from the surface.

🍃 Stewed lentils and savory lentils are usually served in place of a starchy vegetable.

FRUITY PORK AND LENTIL STEW

1½ cups (375 mL) dried brown lentils
1¾ lbs (800 g) shoulder of pork
1 onion, chopped
2 cloves garlic, chopped
4 tomatoes, peeled and chopped
4 cups (1 L) water
3 tsp (15 mL) salt
¼ tsp (1 mL) pepper
1 tsp (5 mL) coriander seeds, crushed
2 bananas, peeled and cut into 1-in. (2-cm) pieces
6 slices fresh pineapple

🍃 Cut the pork into small pieces and put it in a casserole or large heavy saucepan. Add just enough

Lentil Salad

cold water to cover the pork. Simmer uncovered for about 1 hour or until the water is evaporated and the pork is starting to brown.

🍃 Add the onion and garlic. Brown over medium heat. Add the tomatoes and simmer, uncovered, over low heat until the meat is tender and the liquid thickens to a sauce-like consistency.

🍃 In the meantime, cook the lentils in 4 cups (1 L) of water for 40 to 50 minutes. Do not drain. Add the lentils to the pork along with the salt, pepper and crushed coriander seeds. Simmer for 30 minutes or until the lentils are tender and the mixture has the desired consistency. Stir occasionally.

🍃 Five minutes before serving, add the pieces of banana and fresh pineapple. Simmer just long enough to warm the fruit through, then serve.

LENTIL SALAD

1½ cups (375 mL) dried lentils
3 cups (750 mL) cold water
1 tsp (5 mL) salt
½ tsp (2 mL) savory
1 cup (250 mL) diced celery
1 onion, chopped
¼ cup (50 mL) chutney
or chili sauce
½ cup (125 mL) herbed salad dressing

🍃 Soak the lentils in the cold water for 4 to 8 hours. Cook them in the soaking water along with the salt and savory until they are cooked but still shapely. Drain the lentils and allow to cool to room temperature.

🍃 Combine the remaining ingredients and add to the cooled lentils. Let marinate for 2 to

3 hours before serving. Serve sprinkled with chopped fresh parsley or chives.

CHILLED LENTILS BOMBAY

1½ cups (375 mL) dried lentils
3 cups (750 mL) cold water
4 onions, chopped
4 tbsp (60 mL) butter
2 tbsp (30 mL) curry powder
2 cups (500 mL) consommé
2 tsp (10 mL) salt
½ tsp (2 mL) pepper
1 tbsp (15 mL) lemon juice
½ cup (125 mL) sour cream

🍃 Soak the lentils overnight in the cold water. The next day, cook them in the soaking water until they are cooked but still firm and shapely. Drain them well.

🍃 Sauté the onions in the butter. Add the curry powder and simmer over low heat for 20 minutes, stirring often. Add the consommé, salt, pepper and lentils. Cover and simmer over very low heat for 2 hours. The lentils should remain whole and the liquid should thicken to a sauce-like consistency. Chill the mixture in the refrigerator.

🍃 Just before serving, stir in the lemon juice and the sour cream. Toss gently with a fork. If you prefer to serve this dish hot, replace the sour cream with 1 tbsp (15 mL) of butter.

QUÉBEC BAKED BEANS

4 cups (1 L) white or navy beans
12 cups (3 L) cold water
½ to 1 lb (250 to 500 g) salt pork, thinly sliced
1 large onion
dry mustard
½ to 1 cup (125 to 250 mL) molasses
1 tbsp (15 mL) coarse salt

🍃 Sort and wash the beans. Soak them for 12 hours in the cold water. Do not drain.

🍃 Bring the beans to a boil and simmer for 30 minutes.

🍃 Line the bottom of a bean pot with some of the fat from the salt pork. Add the beans and their soaking water. Dredge the onion in the dry mustard and bury it in the center of the beans. Pour the molasses over the bean mixture and top generously with slices of salt pork. Add just enough hot water to cover the beans. Add the salt and cover.

🍃 Bake in a 375°F (190°C) oven for 4 to 6 hours. One hour before the end of the cooking time, uncover the pot and if the beans look dry, add a little water.

OLD-FASHIONED BAKED BEANS

4 cups (1 L) small white beans
1 to 1½ lbs (500 to 750 g) salt pork
1 large red onion
1 tsp (5 mL) dry mustard

2 cups (500 mL) brown sugar
½ to ⅔ cup (125 to 150 mL) molasses
1 tsp (5 mL) savory
1 tsp (5 mL) coarse salt
hot water

🍃 Sort and wash the beans. Soak them for 12 hours or overnight in 12 cups (3 L) cold water. Do not drain.

🍃 Place the beans and their soaking water in a soup kettle. Bring slowly to a boil and then simmer for 1 to 1½ hours or until the skins burst when you blow on a spoonful of the beans.

🍃 Rub an earthenware casserole or bean pot with a piece of salt pork. Pour in the beans and the liquid. Dredge the onion in the dry mustard and bury it in the center of the beans. Slash the piece of salt pork and place it on top of the beans.

🍃 Combine the brown sugar, molasses, savory and salt. Pour over the beans and mix gently. Add just enough hot water to cover the beans. Cover and bake in a 300°F (150°C) oven for 8 hours. One hour before the end of the cooking period, remove the cover and, if the beans look dry, add a little water.

BAKED BEANS WITH APPLE SUGAR

1 recipe of *Québec Baked Beans*
4 unpeeled apples, cored
1 cup (250 mL) maple sugar, grated

½ cup (125 mL) butter
½ cup (125 mL) rum

🍃 Before putting the baked beans in the oven, arrange the four cored apples on top as close to each other as possible.

🍃 Cream together the maple sugar and the butter. Put 1 tsp (5 mL) of this mixture in each apple, then sprinkle the rest over the top of the beans. The sugar mixture will act as the "lid" for the pot. Add a little hot water if the beans dry out during baking.

🍃 When ready to serve, pour the rum slowly over the baked apples.

CANADIAN BAKED BEANS

2 cups (500 mL) white or navy beans
¼ pound (125 g) salt pork, diced
3 tbsp (45 mL) brown sugar
3 tbsp (45 mL) molasses
1 tsp (5 mL) salt
½ tsp (2 mL) dry mustard
1 medium onion, whole or diced
2 tbsp (30 mL) catsup
water

🍃 Soak the beans for 12 hours, then drain. Preheat a pressure-cooker, with the rack removed, then sauté the salt pork in it. Add the beans, brown sugar, molasses, salt, mustard, onion, catsup and just enough water to cover the beans.

🍃 Close the cover securely and adjust the pressure gauge. Cook for 15 minutes. Let the pressure drop on its own. Let the pot cool 20 to 40 minutes before opening it.

BEAN SALAD

1½ cups (375 mL) dried small white beans or flageolets
8 cups (2 L) cold water
½ tsp (2 mL) basil
½ tsp (2 mL) thyme
2 tsp (10 mL) coarse salt
¼ tsp (1 mL) pepper
1 bouquet garni*
3 tbsp (45 mL) olive oil
3 tbsp (45 mL) lemon juice
1 onion, chopped
¼ cup (50 mL) chopped fresh parsley (reserve the stems)

🍃 Sort and wash the beans and soak them in the cold water for 12 hours. Place the beans in a soup kettle with their soaking water. Add the basil, thyme, salt, pepper and the bouquet garni. Simmer for about 2 hours or until the beans are tender. Drain the beans well and refrigerate them until chilled.

🍃 Combine the remaining ingredients, then stir the mixture into the beans about 1 hour before serving time. Adjust the seasonings.

* To make a bouquet garni: tie in a square of cheesecloth 2 bay leaves, the leaves from 3 stalks of celery, the reserved parsley stems and 2 or 3 garlic cloves.

RED BEANS WITH CHEESE

2 cups (500 mL) red or kidney beans
2 cups (500 mL) tomatoes
½ tsp (2 mL) marjoram
1 tsp (5 mL) prepared mustard
2 tsp (10 mL) salt
¼ tsp (1 mL) pepper
6 slices bacon

Bean Salad

1 large onion, chopped
1 cup (250 mL) grated aged Cheddar
1 tbsp (15 mL) butter

🍃 Sort the beans and soak them in 8 cups (2 L) of cold water for 3 to 6 hours. Place them in a soup kettle with their soaking water, and bring to a boil. Simmer 1 to 1½ hours or until the beans are tender. Drain, reserving the cooking water.

🍃 Stir in the tomatoes, marjoram, mustard, salt and pepper.

🍃 Fry the bacon. Brown the chopped onion in the bacon fat and add the bacon, fat and onions to the beans. Cover and let simmer for 1 hour. If more liquid is required add some of the reserved cooking water.

🍃 When ready to serve, add the grated cheese and the butter. Stir and serve immediately.

LIMA BEANS PAYSANNE

1 cup (250 mL) dried lima beans
4 cups (1 L) water
2 tsp (10 mL) salt
3 tbsp (45 mL) butter
¾ cup (175 mL) chopped parsley
6 or 7 green onions, chopped
½ tsp (2 mL) basil
½ tsp (2 mL) pepper
1 large tomato, diced

🍃 Bring the water to a boil. Add the washed lima beans, cover and simmer 1½ to 2 hours over low heat. Add 1 tsp (5 mL) of the salt after the first hour of cooking. Drain, reserving the cooking liquid to make a soup, if you wish.

🍃 Melt the butter. Add the parsley, green onions, basil, the remaining salt and pepper. Simmer for a few minutes. Add the cooked beans. Stir gently with a fork until very hot. Stir in the diced tomato and serve.

LIMA BEAN SALAD

2 cups (500 mL) dried baby lima beans
1 onion, chopped
1 cup (250 mL) sour cream
2 tbsp (30 mL) sugar
2 tbsp (30 mL) cider vinegar
1 tsp (5 mL) prepared horseradish
2 tsp (10 mL) salt
¼ tsp (1 mL) pepper
¼ cup (50 mL) chopped parsley

🍃 Cook the lima beans in 8 cups (2 L) water following the directions given for *Lima Beans Paysanne*. Drain the beans and chill in the refrigerator.

🍃 Combine the remaining ingredients to make the dressing. Stir the dressing gently into the chilled beans just before serving.

WHITE BEANS BRETONNE

In Brittany, this is the classic accompaniment for roast lamb. It reheats very well.

1 lb (500 g) white beans
8 cups (2 L) cold water
5 sprigs parsley
leaves from 3 celery stalks
3 cloves garlic, whole
2 tsp (10 mL) basil

Lima Bean Salad

1 onion, cut in half
1 tsp (5 mL) thyme
1 tbsp (15 mL) salt
pepper to taste
3 large onions, chopped
2 cloves garlic, minced
4 tbsp (60 mL) butter
2 tbsp (30 mL) flour
1½ cups (375 mL) consommé
¼ cup (50 mL) tomato paste
salt and pepper

❧ Sort and wash the beans and soak them for 12 hours in the cold water.

❧ Place the parsley, celery leaves, 3 whole garlic cloves and basil in a piece of cheesecloth and tie it closed. Place the beans and their soaking water in a large pot. Add the wrapped herbs (bouquet garni), the onion cut in two, the thyme, 1 tbsp (15 mL) salt and some pepper to taste. Cover and let simmer for 1 to 1½ hours or until the beans are tender. Do not overcook.

❧ Meanwhile, prepare the sauce. Sauté the chopped onions and the garlic in the butter. Add the flour and blend well. Stir in the consommé and the tomato paste. Cook over low heat, stirring constantly, until the sauce is smooth. Salt and pepper to taste.

❧ Drain the beans, reserving 1 cup (250 mL) of the cooking liquid. Remove the bouquet garni from the cooked beans. Combine the beans with the sauce. Cover and simmer for 1 hour. If the sauce becomes too thick, add a little of the reserved cooking liquid.

PREPARING RICE

METHOD 1
Pour 2 cups (500 mL) water and 1 tsp (5 mL) salt in a large pot with a tight-fitting lid. Bring the water to a boil.

❧ Stir in 1 cup (250 mL) rice. Bring to a boil again.

❧ Cover and let simmer for 14 minutes over low heat. If you like, quickly rinse the rice with hot water before serving.

METHOD 2
Add 1 cup (250 mL) rice to 4 cups (1 L) water in a large pot. Bring to a rolling boil. Add ½ tsp (2 mL) salt. Stir.

❧ Cook, uncovered, over medium heat for 10 to 14 minutes. Drain and serve.

METHOD FOR
ULTRA-TENDER RICE
Follow *Method 2*, but add ⅓ cup (75 mL) cold water as soon as the rice starts to boil. Continue cooking over medium heat, but add 4 to 5 minutes to the cooking time.

RICE PILAF

❧ Melt 2 tbsp (30 mL) butter in a casserole. Add 1 finely chopped medium onion and sauté until limp but not browned, about 10 minutes.

❧ Add 1 cup (250 mL) raw rice. Stir gently over medium heat until the grains are very lightly browned. Stir in 4 cups (1 L) consommé or water. Season to taste. Cover. Bake

in a 400°F (200°C) oven for 2[ ] 30 minutes, without stirring, u[ ] the rice is tender.

VEGETARIAN RICE

1 tbsp (15 mL) butter
1 to 2 cups (250 to 500 mL) rice, cooked
½ pound (250 g) cottage cheese
1 cup (250 mL) sour cream
4 green onions, finely chopped
chopped parsley to taste
salt and pepper to taste

❧ Melt the butter in a heavy saucepan or casserole. Add the cooked rice and the rest of the ingredients.

❧ Stir gently but thoroughly with a fork. Cover. Cook over very low heat about 15 minutes or until the mixture is heated through, stirring once or twice during the cooking period.

CHINESE FRIED RICE

3 tbsp (45 mL) vegetable oil
1 egg
½ cup (125 mL) sliced mushrooms, fresh or canned
2 to 3 cups (500 to 750 mL) cooked rice
¼ cup (50 mL) chopped green onions
¼ cup (50 mL) chopped parsley
2 tbsp (30 mL) soy sauce

❧ Heat the oil in a skillet. Break the egg into the oil and break the yolk. Stir it very gently with a

Curried Rice

fork, but do not scramble it; it should resemble an omelette in texture.

🍃 When the egg is nearly firm, cut it into thin strips and remove the skillet from the heat.

🍃 Add the mushrooms, cooked rice, green onions, parsley and soy sauce. Stir together gently with a fork.

🍃 Heat over low heat and serve at once.

RICE AMANDINE

2 cups (500 mL) rice
3 green onions, chopped
chopped parsley to taste
3 tbsp (45 mL) butter
¼ pound (125 g) salted almonds

🍃 Cook the rice using *Method 1*.

🍃 Rinse the rice rapidly under hot water. Return the rice to the pot, then add the green onions, butter and parsley. Cover and heat over very low heat for 10 to 12 minutes.

🍃 When ready to serve, arrange the rice in a serving dish and sprinkle it with the salted almonds.

RICE AU GRATIN

2 tbsp (30 mL) butter
2 tbsp (30 mL) flour
2 cups (500 mL) milk
3 cups (750 mL) cooked rice
½ cup (125 mL) grated cheese
salt to taste
breadcrumbs
butter

🍃 Make a white sauce with the butter, flour and milk.

🍃 Add the rice to the sauce. Stir in the ½ cup (125 mL) grated cheese. Salt to taste.

🍃 Turn the mixture into a buttered baking dish, sprinkle with breadcrumbs and dot with butter. Top with more grated cheese, if desired. Bake in a 400°F (200°C) oven for 20 minutes.

CURRIED RICE

4 tbsp (60 mL) butter
1 medium onion, sliced thin
1 clove garlic, minced
1 tbsp (15 mL) curry powder
1 cup (250 mL) uncooked rice
2 cups (500 mL) consommé
salt and pepper to taste

🍃 Melt the butter in a skillet. Add the onion and garlic. Cover and let simmer for 10 minutes or until the onion is soft.

🍃 Add the curry powder. Blend well and continue cooking for 1 minute. Add the rice. Stir to coat each grain with the curried butter. Stir in the consommé. Salt and pepper to taste.

🍃 Cover and cook over low heat for 30 minutes, or until the rice is cooked to taste.

CINNAMON RICE

In France, hot cooked grains are often eaten as a light meal in the morning or the evening.

2 cups (500 mL) cooked rice
½ cup (125 mL) milk or cream
¼ to ½ cup (50 to 125 mL) brown or white sugar
2 tbsp (30 mL) butter
¼ tsp (1 mL) cinnamon or nutmeg

❧ TECHNIQUE ❧

CURRIED RICE

1 Add the onion and the garlic to the melted butter. Cover and simmer.

2 Add the curry powder, blend well and cook 1 minute.

3 Add the rice and stir.

4 Stir in the consommé. Season with salt and pepper.

Rice Milanese

🍃 Mix the rice, milk and sugar in a pot. Cover and cook over low heat for about 10 minutes. Stir gently with a fork. When the rice is hot, add the butter and cinnamon or nutmeg. Stir once again with a fork and serve.

PINK PILAF

This is simply long-grain rice cooked in chicken broth and tinted with tomato paste, but it looks very festive and tastes very good!

4 tbsp (60 mL) butter
3 cups (750 mL) long-grain rice
2 medium onions, finely chopped
6 cups (1.5 mL) chicken stock
4 tbsp (60 mL) tomato paste
2 tsp (10 mL) salt

🍃 Melt the butter in a casserole dish (with a lid) or a medium size, heavy saucepan. Add the rice and the onions, and cook over high heat, stirring constantly, until the grains are golden. Add the chicken stock (you can substitute 5 chicken bouillon cubes and water, if you wish). Stir in the tomato paste. Stir until the mixture starts to boil and the tomato paste is well blended in. Add the salt.

🍃 Cover the pan, reduce the heat to low and simmer the rice for 30 minutes, without stirring or lifting the lid. Just before serving, toss the rice gently with a fork.

RICE MILANESE

4 tbsp (60 mL) butter
1 medium onion, chopped
1½ cups (375 mL) uncooked rice
5 cups (1.2 L) consommé
½ tsp (2 mL) salt
3 tbsp (45 mL) consommé
saffron to taste
3 to 5 tbsp (45 to 75 mL) butter
½ cup (125 mL) grated cheese

🍃 Melt the 4 tbsp (60 mL) butter in a heavy saucepan. Add the chopped onion. Cook over medium heat until limp, but not browned. Add the rice and cook, stirring from time to time, until the grains are golden.

🍃 Add the 5 cups (1.2 L) consommé and the salt. Stir to blend thoroughly and cook over low heat for 20 to 25 minutes or until the rice is tender and the liquid is completely absorbed.

🍃 When the rice is cooked, combine the saffron with 3 tbsp (45 mL) consommé. Add the saffron mixture to the rice along with the 4 to 5 tbsp (60 to 75 mL) butter. Stir gently with a fork until well blended. Adjust the seasonings. Serve on a heated serving dish. Sprinkle with the grated cheese.

RICE RING

1 cup (250 mL) uncooked rice
3 tbsp (45 mL) butter
1½ cups (375 mL) chicken stock (cubes or canned)
½ tsp (2 mL) salt
2 carrots, grated
½ clove garlic, minced
4 green onions, thinly sliced
3 stalks celery with leaves, finely chopped
½ cup (125 mL) chopped parsley

In a saucepan, sauté the rice in 1 tbsp (15 mL) of the butter, stirring constantly, for 5 minutes or until the rice is lightly browned. Add the chicken stock and the salt and simmer, uncovered, until the rice is tender and most of the stock is absorbed (about 20 to 25 minutes).

Melt the remaining butter in a skillet. Add the rest of the ingredients. Cook, stirring, for 5 minutes over medium heat.

Add the cooked rice to the vegetable mixture and continue cooking, stirring, until the liquid is absorbed.

Pat the rice mixture into a well-buttered ring mold. Bake for 30 minutes in a 350°F (180°C) oven. Unmold. If you like, garnish with vegetables.

RICE STUFFING

This recipe makes 5 cups (1.2 L) of stuffing and can be used to stuff chicken, turkey or duck.

¼ lb (125 g) sausages
1 tbsp (15 mL) butter
¼ cup (50 mL) chopped onions
¼ lb (125 g) mushrooms, sliced
3 cups (750 mL) cooked rice
1 cup (250 mL) diced celery
¼ cup (50 mL) chopped celery leaves
2 tsp (10 mL) salt
¼ tsp (1 mL) thyme or sage
1 cup (250 mL) cold water
1 egg, beaten

Cut the sausages into 1-in. (2-cm) lengths. Cook the sausage pieces in a skillet until browned. Add the butter, onions and mushrooms. Fry the mixture for about

3 minutes, then remove from the heat.

Add the remaining ingredients. Mix well. Season to taste.

RICE SALAD

2 to 3 cups (500 to 750 mL) cooked rice
2 carrots, peeled and grated
¼ cup (50 mL) finely chopped green onions
¼ cup (50 mL) chopped parsley
¼ cup (50 mL) finely chopped celery with leaves
vinaigrette to taste

Place the rice in a salad bowl.

Add the rest of the ingredients. Mix thoroughly but gently with a fork. Serve.

FRENCH RICE SALAD

3 cups (750 mL) cooked rice
¼ cup (50 mL) olive oil
3 tbsp (45 mL) vinegar
1 tsp (5 mL) salt
¼ tsp (1 mL) pepper
1 cup (250 mL) diced cheese
12 radishes, thinly sliced
2 tbsp (30 mL) chopped walnuts
3 tbsp (45 mL) chopped parsley

Reheat the cooked rice. Add the oil, vinegar, salt and pepper. Mix together gently with 2 forks. Let stand for 1 hour at room temperature.

Add the remaining ingredients, toss and correct the seasonings. Serve on a bed of lettuce.

WILD RICE

Wild rice grows in Western Canada, Wisconsin and in Minnesota. Properly speaking, wild rice is not rice; it is the seed of an aquatic plant which flourishes in shallow water.

French Rice Salad

ఈ Wild rice triples in volume with cooking. It is difficult to set an exact cooking time for wild rice because it varies in size, thickness and hardness, depending on where it was harvested. But be careful to avoid over-cooking it.

ఈ Because wild rice is so expensive, you can cook it with an equal quantity of brown rice. The brown rice will take on the luxurious flavor of the wild rice.

ఈ Wild rice is a wonderful accompaniment for wild game, venison, duck, beef Bourguignonne and other similarly flavorful dishes. It is also very good in casseroles—combined with cheese or chicken livers, for example.

ఈ Wild rice can be cooked using a variety of methods.

METHOD 1
Wash the rice several times in cold water. Bring to a boil 4 cups (1 L) water. Add 1 tsp (5 mL) salt and 1 cup (250 mL) wild rice. Cover and simmer for 20 to 30 minutes. Simmered gently, wild rice will keep its nutty flavor.

METHOD 2
Wash the rice several times in cold water. Place it in a heavy saucepan. Cover the rice with boiling water. Put a lid on the pan and let it stand for 20 minutes. Add 1 tsp (5 mL) salt and cover once again with boiling water (a good part of the earlier water will already have been absorbed by the rice). Cover and let soak for another 20 minutes. Again, add just enough boiling water to cover the rice. Cover and let simmer for 15 minutes over low heat or until all the water is absorbed.

METHOD 3
With this method, you can cook the wild rice in advance and reheat it at serving time.

ఈ Pour 1½ cups (375 mL) washed rice into 12 cups (3 L) of boiling water to wish 1½ tbsp (25 mL) salt has been added. Bring the water to a rolling boil and boil for 5 minutes. Drain. Melt 4 tbsp (60 mL) butter in a heavy casserole. Add 3 tbsp (45 mL) grated carrots, 2 diced celery stalks and 1 chopped onion. Cover. Cook over low heat for 5 or 6 minutes or until the vegetables are tender. Add the well-drained wild rice and stir over low heat for 5 minutes. Add 1½ cups (375 mL) consommé, 1 bay leaf, ¼ tsp (1 mL) thyme, ½ tsp (2 mL) salt, and ¼ tsp (1 mL) pepper. Bring to a boil. Cover and bake in a 350°F (180°C) oven for 30 to 35 minutes or until the rice has absorbed all the liquid.

ఈ Before serving, toss the rice with a fork.

WILD RICE WITH MUSHROOMS

1½ to 2 cups (375 to 500 mL) wild rice
2 cans cream of mushroom soup
1 cup (250 mL) milk
½ to 1 lb (250 to 500 g) mushrooms, sliced
½ cup (125 mL) butter
2 tbsp (30 mL) flour
2 tbsp (30 mL) sherry
1 tbsp (15 mL) lemon juice
1 tsp (5 mL) Worcestershire sauce

ఈ Cook the wild rice following the directions in *Method 1* or *2* (see page 474). Butter a ring mold and pat the rice into it with your hands. Place the mold in a pan of hot water, cover and keep in a warm

Wild Rice with Mushrooms

❦ TECHNIQUE ❦

FERGUSON WILD RICE CASSEROLE

1 Brown the onion until tender.

2 Remove the onion from the skillet and add the dry wild rice to the remaining butter. Cook, stirring constantly, until the rice gives off a nutty aroma.

3 Mix the celery, parsley, thyme, carrots and browned onion.

4 Butter a baking dish and fill it with alternate layers of wild rice, vegetables and grated cheese until all the ingredients have been used.

place or in a 200°F (100°C) oven.

☙ In the meantime, heat together the cream of mushroom soup and the milk.

☙ Sauté the mushrooms in the butter for 3 minutes. Add the flour, mix well, then stir in the sherry and lemon juice.

☙ Stir the mushroom mixture into the soup mixture. Cook for a few minutes. Add the Worcestershire sauce. Adjust the seasonings.

☙ To serve, unmold the rice ring and pour the very hot mushroom sauce over the top.

WILD RICE WITH PINE NUTS

2 cups (500 mL) wild rice
4 cups (1 L) chicken stock
1 tsp (5 mL) salt
¼ tsp (1 mL) pepper
½ cup (125 mL) pine nuts
3 tbsp (45 mL) chopped parsley
½ tsp (2 mL) rosemary
3 tbsp (45 mL) grated Parmesan

☙ Soak the rice in cold water for 12 hours. Drain, then rinse it several times.

☙ Place the rice in a casserole dish with the chicken stock, salt and pepper. Bring slowly to a boil.

☙ Add the pine nuts, parsley and rosemary. Cover and bake in a 350°F (180°C) oven for 35 to 40 minutes. When ready to serve sprinkle with the grated Parmesan.

Note: Pine nuts can be purchased in most specialty food stores and natural foods stores.

WILD RICE AMANDINE

2 to 3 cups (500 to 750 mL) wild rice, cooked
½ cup (125 mL) vegetable oil
1 cup (250 mL) slivered blanched almonds
salt to taste
1 clove garlic, minced
1 large onion, chopped
½ green pepper, finely chopped
salt and pepper to taste

☙ Heat the oil, add the almonds and brown them, stirring, until golden. Remove the nuts from the oil, place them on paper towels and salt them lightly.

☙ Add the garlic, onion and green pepper to the oil remaining in the skillet. Cook for 5 to 6 minutes, stirring almost constantly. Add the cooked rice and stir together with a fork over low heat until the rice is heated through. Salt and pepper to taste.

☙ Arrange the rice on a heated serving dish. Sprinkle with the almonds and serve.

WILD RICE CHASSEUR

2 tbsp (30 mL) cognac
1 tbsp (15 mL) curry powder
3 to 5 tbsp (45 to 75 mL) chutney
1 to 2 cups (250 to 500 mL) wild rice, cooked
salt and pepper to taste
¼ cup (50 mL) butter

☙ Mix together the cognac and curry in a cup. Add the chutney.

☙ Warm the rice in the top of a double boiler. Stir in the cognac mixture 5 to 10 minutes before serving time. Salt and pepper to taste, add the butter, then stir with a fork until the butter is melted. Serve.

FERGUSON WILD RICE CASSEROLE

1 cup (250 mL) wild rice
3 tbsp (45 mL) butter
1 small onion, finely chopped
2 stalks celery, diced
½ cup (125 mL) chopped fresh parsley
¼ tsp (1 mL) thyme
3 medium carrots, grated
½ pound (250 g) strong Cheddar, grated
1½ cups (375 mL) chicken stock
2 tbsp (30 mL) butter, diced

☙ Wash the rice under running water. Spread it on a towel to dry for 2 hours.

☙ Melt the 3 tbsp (45 mL) butter in a heavy skillet. Sauté the onion until tender. Remove the onion from the skillet, leaving the butter. Add the dry wild rice to the same skillet. Cook, stirring constantly, until the rice gives off a nutty aroma.

☙ Combine the celery, parsley, thyme, carrots and sautéed onions. Butter a baking dish, and fill it with alternate layers of wild rice, vegetables and grated cheese until all the ingredients have been used. Cover with the chicken stock. Dot with the butter.

☙ Cover and bake in a 350°F (180°C) oven for 1 hour.

CHEESE

CHEESE

Cheese is as ancient as civilization itself. Aristotle, the great Greek philosopher, wrote a description of the process of cheese-making in the fourth century B.C.

ৰ Cheese is extremely nutritious; it is an important source of protein, vitamins and minerals, especially calcium. Cheese also enlivens ordinary dishes, making them more delicious as well as more nutritious. Cheese is versatile: it can be served as an appetizer before the main course, as a garnish for soups and salads or as a dessert. It can also be served in various types of sauces.

ৰ The texture and flavor differ considerably from one variety of cheese to another. There are creamy cheeses such as Brie, Camembert or Bel Paese. There are firm cheeses such as Gouda, Caerphilly and Cheddar. There are dry cheeses such as Parmesan and there are soft, fresh cheeses such as cottage cheese and cream cheese. In flavor, some prefer the mild cheeses (Edam and Munster, for example) to the strong cheeses (Oka and Liederkranz). For a pungent flavor, there are the goat's milk cheeses or the blue cheeses. In other words, there is a cheese for every taste preference.

ৰ To discover the cheeses that will delight you, be adventuresome! Experiment by seeking out and tasting different cheeses. Try a mild cheese today and a creamy one tomorrow. Use a new cheese in your recipe for cheese sauce. Visit the ethnic groceries in your community and try a cheese that is typical to that ethnic cuisine. You'll get to know your cheeses and discover the most delicious ones to serve your guests.

ৰ It is important to serve cheese at room temperature. Keep cheese in the refrigerator and take it out 2 to 3 hours before serving. Cheese served at room temperature will reveal its fullest flavor and its natural texture.

ৰ Never cook or melt cheese over high heat; the cheese will become rubbery and tough. All grated, diced and sliced cheeses must be cooked over low heat or in a warm—not hot—oven.

SOME FAVORITE CHEESES

BANON
A tasty goat's milk cheese that is usually wrapped in grape leaves. A specialty of Marseille.

BEL PAESE
An Italian cheese that is mellow, creamy and fine. Delicious with desserts, it may also be served with jams or fresh fruits.

BLARNEY
An Irish cheese that is similar to a very young and mild Cheddar. It is an ideal sandwich cheese.

BLEU DE BRESSE
This mellow and creamy blue cheese is a specialty of Lyons, France.

BRIE
The king of French cheeses, Brie is creamy and slightly salty. Some aficionados prefer Brie de Melun, others will eat nothing but Brie de Meaux. A Brie is an excellent dessert cheese, especially when it is truly ripe.

Camembert and Bel Paese

CAERPHILLY
A Welsh cheese that is mild and easily digestible. It has a texture similar to that of Cheddar and is excellent for cooking.

CAMEMBERT
Another famous French cheese. It is similar to Brie though somewhat creamier and saltier. Its distinctive but not strong flavor makes it an excellent dessert cheese.

CANTAL
A cheese that is similar in texture and color to mild Cheddar but that has a creamier flavor.

CARRÉ DE L'EST
The Alsatian Camembert.

CHAVIGNOL
OR CROTTIN DE CHAVIGNOL
A delicious goat's milk cheese.

CHEDDAR
One of North America's most popular and versatile cheeses. It

comes in four flavors (extra-sharp, sharp, medium or mild) and a choice of colors (ranging from creamy-white to orange). This nutritious cheese is excellent for cooking and keeps well.

CHESHIRE

An English cheese that looks very much like Cheddar but that has a zesty flavor all its own: well worth trying!

DANISH BLUE

This somewhat mild blue cheese is made from cow's milk (not sheep's milk like Roquefort). It is oily and tasty because it is made from rich cream, wich gives it a creamy consistency.

DUNLOP

A Scottish cheese that is similar in taste to Cheddar but that is slightly creamier.

EDAM

A mild and soft Dutch cheese made from partly skimmed milk. It usually has a yellow-red color. Because of its delicious flavor, it is excellent for cooking.

EMMENTHAL

Considered the finest and most delicate of the Swiss cheeses. It is ideal for cooking and a favorite among cheese lovers.

ÉPOISSES

Named after the village on the Côte d'Or where it is made. It has the same texture as Port Salut but because it contains almost no salt its flavor is less distinctive.

ESROM

A Danish cheese with a texture similar to those of Oka and Port Salut. It is very mild but it has a distinctive flavor; it goes particularly well with pears or crackers.

FETA

A white Greek cheese made from sheep's milk and preserved in brine. It has a fine flavor reminiscent of a slightly salted and hardened cottage cheese. One way to enjoy its flavor is to add a small quantity to cottage cheese, and it is very tasty in cooked dishes.

FONTINA

A pale yellow and rather mild cheese made from sheep's milk. It is favored among Italians for fondues.

FYNBO

A cheese similar to Gouda that is produced in Denmark and Finland. It is an excellent cheese for cooking and ideal for sandwiches.

Emmenthal

GJETÖST

This caramel-colored Norwegian cheese is made from both cow's milk (90%) and goat's milk (10%). Its taste may seem unusual at first. This cheese is delicious served on crackers with butter and honey. Be sure to slice it very thin.

DOUBLE GLOUCESTER

This English cheese, similar to Cheddar, has a distinctive brown crust formed by brushing the cheese with dark ale during its maturation.

GORGONZOLA

A delicious Italian blue cheese that is cream, and a bit salty. One of my personal favorites.

GOUDA

A mild cheese from southern Holland, Gouda is similar to Edam but has a more pronounced flavor. It keeps well and is used in the preparation of various cooked dishes.

GRUYÈRE

This cheese is made in the Fribourg Canton of Switzerland. Though similar to Emmenthal, it contains more salt and fat. It is an excellent cooking cheese and is also ideal for sandwiches. Uncut, it keeps for a very long time.

LANCASHIRE

An English cheese, superb in fondue, Welsh Rarebit or other cooked dishes with a cheese base. Its flavor is lighter than that of Cheddar.

LEYDEN

A Dutch cheese flavored with caraway seeds, which give it a distinctive flavor. Leyden is creamier and lighter than Gouda.

LIMBURGER

A strong, creamy German cheese, similar to Pont-l'Évêque. Do not use it in cooking.

MOZZARELLA

This Italian cheese is very mild. Excellent for cooking, it has become the standard cheese garnish for pizza.

MUNSTER

A delicious, zesty cheese from the Vosges Mountains. Munster is creamy, or perhaps runny, and comes plain or cumin-scented. It is especially tasty when accompanied by beer and black bread.

NÖKKELÖST

Nökkelöst, similar to Gjetöst, is deliciously flavored with caraway seeds.

OKA

Originally produced in Oka, Québec, by the Trappist monks. It is similar to the French cheese Port Salut. Oka is delicious at any time but especially when served at the end of a meal, perhaps with an apple.

PARMESAN

The cornerstone of Italian cuisine. Grated Parmesan is a favorite with pasta and eggplant. Fresh Parmesan has a texture similar to that of Cheddar, but it tastes completely different.

PETIT SUISSE

A delicious cheese that is enriched with cream. It is delightful when served with sugar or with grated maple sugar and strawberries.

PONT L'ÉVEQUE

A cheese from Normandy that is strong and creamy. Perfect with cider or apples.

REBLOCHON

A Savoyard version of Port Salut but slightly milder.

ROMANO

An Italian cheese used in the same manner as Parmesan,

Bleu de Bresse

although it has a stronger flavor.

ROQUEFORT

A popular French cheese made from ewe's milk. It has a strong flavor.

SAMSOE

A Danish cheese often called "the Danish Swiss" because of its nutty flavor and its texture.

STILTON

An English blue cheese with a refined, mild flavor. It is excellent with port.

TILSIT

This cheese has a texture similar to that of Port Salut and an agreeable, somewhat sharp flavor.

TOMME AU MARC

A French cheese that is white, solid and rather waxy. It contains almost no salt and is quite mild.

WENSLEYDALE

A delicious, slightly creamy cheese that is similar to Stilton but not a blue-mold cheese. It keeps very well.

WENSLEYDALE BLUE

An English cheese that is more mellow in flavor than Stilton.

❧ This is by no means a complete list of the cheeses produced around the world. I have named only the most popular cheeses, those that are found in most cheese shops in North America. A complete list would have named several hundred cheeses!

HINTS ON SERVING CHEESE

Cheese is at its best when served at room temperature. Store cheese in its original wrapping—or in any waterproof wrapping—in the refrigerator. Remove it 2 to 3 hours before you plan to serve it. I believe that cheese attains its full flavor only after sitting at least 3 hours at room temperature. The exceptions to this rule are cream cheese and cottage cheese, which may be taken from the refrigerator and served directly.

❧ Eating cheese with a strong-flavored bread will mask its flavor. Rather than rye or onion bread, or a bread flavored with aromatic seeds such as anise, serve the cheese with crusty French or Italian bread, with dry Scandinavian flatbread or with one of the many varieties of unsalted biscuits.

❧ Choose your cheese with care. You will develop a true appreciation for cheese if you select from among the best cheeses and experiment with your preferences. If your knowledge of cheese is limited, ask for help at a local cheese store. You will probably be invited to sample some of the cheeses! But, in the end, the only way to select cheese is according to your taste. You are the best judge.

☙ Here is a brief discussion of the most popular cheeses—those you are likely to find in your local cheese store and in most supermarkets.Remember that though the imported cheeses are wonderful, there are many fine local cheeses that deserve to be included on any cheese platter.

FRESH MILD CHEESES

These cheeses, which are all variations of cream cheese and cottage cheese, are very mild. Since they are similar in flavor, there is no need to serve more than two of them at a sitting. It goes without saying that those who do not like strong cheeses will appreciate the taste of these.

MOZZARELLA

A tender, delicate and mild cheese.

PETIT SUISSE

Mild and creamy, this cheese is particularly delicious when accompanied with French bread and sprinkled with coarse salt or freshly ground pepper.

SAINT FLORENTIN AND BOURSAULT

These imported soft cheeses are not as easy to find as Mozzarella and Petit Suisse. They are rich, creamy and very popular.

MILD AND RICH CHEESES

The many cheeses in this category owe their great popularity to the fact that they are always delicious and light.

BEL PAESE

A mellow cheese with a very distinctive and pleasant flavor.

EDAM AND GOUDA

Creamy, mild and pleasant, these two cheeses are great favorites. They are the same except that Edam is made from partly skimmed milk and Gouda is made from whole milk: thus they differ in fat content. (In general, the more fat a cheese contains, the softer it is.) Edam has a red wax coating, while Gouda has a yellow coating.

ESROM, FYNBO, DANBO AND SAMSOE

These Danish cow's milk cheeses are very pleasant and widely appreciated.

EMMENTHAL AND GRUYÈRE

These quality cheeses are favorites among cheese lovers. No cheese platter is complete without one of these cheeses, and they can always be enjoyed at wine and cheese parties.

CHEDDARS

CANADIAN OR VERMONT CHEDDAR

A close relative of English Cheddar. The best Cheddars are made in 5 lb (2.3 kg) cheese wheels and are perfectly ripened. The color of Cheddar ranges from creamy white to bright orange. There are four different types of Cheddar: mild, medium, sharp and extra-sharp.

CHESHIRE

This is the oldest among English Cheddars. It has a delicious taste similar to that of salted buttermilk, and it is crumbly without being dry. A cheshire should occupy a place of honor on every cheese tray.

GLOUCESTER

Another type of English Cheddar,

Cheddar

it is rarely served although delicious.

CAERPHILLY

My favorite medium Cheddar. This magnificent cheese, with its firm but slightly grainy texture, is delicious served on crackers and sprinkled with freshly ground pepper.

SCOTTISH DUNLOP

When well ripened, this cheese has a rich flavor—it is slightly piquant without being bitter. Bite into a piece of Dunlop and you'll be reminded of the taste of a rich and refreshing glass of milk.

DERBY

Though less spectacular than Dunlop, this English cheese is mild and tasty.

GREEK KASSERIE

A strong, white sheep's milk cheese. In flavor it falls halfway between Cheddar and Parmesan. Kasserie can be purchased in cheese shops and in Greek and Polish grocery stores.

CAMEMBERT AND BRIE

These two cheeses are by far the most popular of the imported cheeses. The many brands of Camembert are all different in flavor, and there is no comparison between a Camembert made in France and those made here. Care is needed when buying either of these cheeses; you must examine the texture and appearance of the cheese in order to find one that is perfectly ripe.

 Imported Camembert and Brie are very good in the period October to June and at their best between January and April. During the summer, you are advised to buy a locally made Camembert. Always look for a Camembert that is soft to the touch and slightly rounded. If it appears too small to fill its box, do not buy it: the Camembert will be less creamy than it should be, and its rind will be dry.

 There is no more renowned cheese than Brie, and for good reason. This superb cheese, which when whole is a large circle and which is usually sold in wedges, is at the top of every cheese connoisseur's list. I assure you that a good Brie is well worth searching for. Be careful, however; the only cheeses worthy of the Brie name are those made in France. The best Brie of all is Brie de Meaux.

MONASTERY CHEESES

PORT SALUT

This cheese, which is made in Trappist monasteries, has a pale yellow color and a soft creamy texture. It is strong but pleasant in flavor.

SAINT PAULIN

A cheese very similar to Port Salut but less delicate.

OKA

One of the best of the Port Salut type, this cheese was first made by the Trappist monks at Oka, Québec. It is world famous.

TOMME DE SAVOIE

A delicious cheese. In flavor, it falls halfway between Munster and Port Salut.

Oka

WHAT TO SERVE WITH CHEESE

Strong cheeses may be served with drinks and foods that are equally strong in flavor. On the other hand, by serving these cheeses with beer or a light wine and bread and butter, the distinctive flavor of the cheese will be highlighted. It's a matter of taste.

 Cheese lovers always ask if butter should be served with cheese. In my opinion, sweet butter goes well with a strong, salty cheese like Roquefort. However, I serve rich, soft cheeses without butter. Once again, you decide what you prefer.

 Are bread and butter the only foods that go with cheese? Not at all. Apples, pears and all the juicy fruits are delicious with Cheddar as are any of the crunchy vegetables such as watercress, celery, cucumber and carrots.

 When serving cheese, set out some of the above fruits or vegetables as well as an ample supply of French bread or assorted crackers and a choice of sweet or salted butter. Place a few well-sharpened knives by each cheese platter and invite those present to begin the cheese tasting.

FONDUES

 There are several types of fondues. Typically, they are served using the following ustensils:

 An earthenware fondue dish (a heavy casserole with a long handle), or an enamel saucepan, placed over an alcohol burner or on a hot plate heated to 250°F (120°C)

 Long fondue forks, preferably with wooden handles

 A basket for the bread cubes

 Small plates, 4 to 6 in. (10 to 15 cm) in diameter

SWISS FONDUE

1 clove garlic
1 cup (250 mL) light dry wine
2 cups (500 mL) grated Gruyère
1½ tbsp (25 mL) flour
pinch of nutmeg
pinch of salt
1 to 3 tbsp (15 to 45 mL) kirsch

❧ Peel the clove of garlic and cut it in half. Rub the fondue dish with the garlic halves. Pour in the wine and heat it slowly.

❧ Mix the Gruyère and the flour. Stir the hot wine with a fork. Add the cheese to the wine by the handful, stirring constantly. Cook the mixture over low heat, stirring constantly, until it becomes smooth and creamy.

❧ If desired, add a pinch of nutmeg and salt. Add the kirsch, to taste.

❧ Serve the fondue with small cubes of fresh bread. The cubes are speared with a fondue fork and then dipped in the hot cheese. Place the fondue dish in the middle of the table.

PIEDMONT FONDUE

¾ lb (375 g) Fontina
or mild Cheddar
milk
2 tbsp (30 mL) butter
6 egg yolks, lightly beaten
¼ tsp (1 mL) pepper
1 Italian white truffle, thinly sliced (optional)

❧ Dice the cheese and place it in a bowl. Add just enough milk to cover the cheese, then refrigerate the mixture for 6 to 12 hours.

❧ Place the undrained cheese, 1 tbsp (15 mL) of the butter, the egg yolks and the pepper in the top of a double boiler. Stir the cheese with a wooden spoon until it starts to melt. At this point, beat the cheese with a wire whisk or a hand beater. As soon as the mixture is smooth and creamy, remove it from the heat. Add the thinly sliced truffle and the remaining 1 tbsp (15 mL) of butter to the fondue. Stir until well mixed.

❧ Serve the fondue immediately in small heated bowls or pour it over buttered toast.

ENGLISH GOLDEN BUCK

½ lb (250 g) Cheddar
2 tbsp (30 mL) butter
¼ cup (50 mL) brown ale
or porter
1 tsp (5 mL) Worcestershire sauce
1 tsp (5 mL) lemon juice
4 eggs, beaten
¼ tsp (1 mL) pepper
6 slices toast

❧ Dice the cheese and place it in a cast-iron saucepan along with the butter and the ale. Cook over low heat, stirring constantly, until the cheese melts.

❧ Gradually add the Worcestershire sauce, the lemon juice and the beaten eggs, stirring constantly. Cook until the mixture is creamy and smooth. Add the pepper. Pour it over toast and serve immediately.

WELSH RAREBIT

3 tbsp (45 mL) butter
1 lb (500 g) grated sharp Cheddar
pinch of pepper
½ tsp (2 mL) dry mustard
1 cup (250 mL) beer
2 eggs, beaten

Swiss Fondue

🍂 Melt the butter in a cast-iron saucepan. Add the Cheddar, the pepper and the dry mustard. Cook the mixture over low heat, stirring constantly, until the cheese melts.

🍂 Add the beer and keep stirring until the mixture is well blended.

🍂 Add the eggs gradually, stirring all the while and without letting the mixture boil. Serve it on toasted bread along with sliced tomatoes.

FONDUE CASSEROLE

2 cups (500 mL) milk
2 cups (500 mL) breadcrumbs
1 tsp (5 mL) salt
¼ tsp (1 mL) pepper
½ tsp (2 mL) dry mustard
½ lb (250 g) grated cheese
4 egg yolks
4 egg whites

🍂 Heat the milk, add the breadcrumbs, the salt, the pepper, the mustard and the grated cheese. Cook over low heat for 5 minutes, stirring constantly.

🍂 Beat the egg yolks then place them in a large bowl. Add the cheese mixture and beat until well blended. Let cool for 20 minutes.

🍂 Beat the egg whites until stiff and carefully fold them into the cheese mixture. Pour into a large greased baking dish and bake the casserole in a 350°F (180°C) oven for 30 minutes. Serve immediately.

MEXICAN FONDUE

2 tbsp (30 mL) olive oil
1 green pepper, minced
1 onion, minced
1 tbsp (15 mL) flour
½ cup (125 mL) milk
¾ lb (375 g) grated mild cheese
1 cup (250 mL) canned tomatoes
½ tsp (2 mL) sugar
2 red peppers, chopped
3 tbsp (45 mL) chopped black olives
¾ tsp (3 mL) salt
pinch of cayenne pepper
3 egg yolks, beaten

🍂 Heat the oil. Add the green pepper and the onion. Let brown for 10 minutes over medium heat. Add the flour and mix well. Remove the saucepan from the heat.

🍂 Add the milk. Mix well and return the pan to the heat. Mix until the sauce becomes creamy. Add the grated cheese and stir for 2 minutes.

🍂 Drain the canned tomatoes and pour them into the sauce, then add the sugar. Cook for 10 minutes over very low heat, stirring frequently.

🍂 Add the red peppers, the black olives, the salt and the cayenne pepper to the cheese mixture. Cook for a few seconds, then gradually add the egg yolks. Blend well. Serve immediately either Mexican style, with small bowls of steamed rice, or with crusty bread cubes.

AMERICAN FONDUE

2 tbsp (30 mL) butter
2 tbsp (30 mL) flour
1 cup (250 mL) milk
¼ tsp (1 mL) salt
pinch of pepper
2 egg yolks, beaten
1 lb (500 g) grated cheese of your choice

Welsh Rarebit

🐚 Melt the butter. Add the flour and mix well. Add the milk and cook, stirring constantly, until the sauce is white and creamy. Add the salt and the pepper.

🐚 Add a few spoonfuls of the hot sauce to the beaten yolks. Mix well and add the yolks to the rest of the sauce.

🐚 Add the grated cheese. Cook over low heat, stirring constantly, until the cheese melts. Serve with bread cubes, as you would a Swiss fondue.

SWISS CHEESE AND WHITE WINE CASSEROLE

6 slices bread
6 tsp (30 mL) butter
1 clove garlic, minced
6 eggs
½ cup (125 mL) whipping cream
½ lb (250 g) Gruyère or Edam, grated
½ cup (125 mL) white wine
½ cup (125 mL) consommé
¼ tsp (1 mL) dry mustard
pinch of rosemary
or ¼ tsp (1 mL) basil
2 coriander seeds, crushed
½ tsp (2 mL) salt

🐚 Remove the crusts from the bread. Mix the butter and the garlic. Spread each slice of bread generously with the butter and garlic mixture. Place in a casserole, buttered side down.

🐚 Beat the eggs. Add the cream, the grated cheese, the wine, the

American Fondue

consommé, the mustard, the rosemary or basil, the coriander and the salt and beat well. Pour the mixture over the bread.

🐚 Bake in a 350°F (180°C) oven for 30 to 40 minutes, or until the casserole is puffy and golden brown. Serve immediately.

CHEDDAR CASSEROLE

6 slices white bread
1½ cups (375 mL) diced Cheddar
¼ tsp (1 mL) salt
pinch of pepper
¼ tsp (1 mL) sage or marjoram
2 eggs, lightly beaten
1½ cups (375 mL) milk

🐚 Butter the slices of bread, leaving the crusts on. Cut each slice into quarters. Place the bread in a baking dish so that the pieces

overlap each other.

🐚 Sprinkle the cheese over the bread. Mix together the eggs, the salt, the pepper, the sage or marjoram and the milk. Pour over the bread and cheese. Bake in a 325°F (160°C) oven for 30 to 40 minutes.

BACON QUICHE LORRAINE

pie dough of your choice
8 slices of bacon
¼ lb (125 g) Gruyère
4 eggs
1½ cups (375 mL) whipping cream
pinch of nutmeg
2 tbsp (30 mL) butter

🐚 Line a 9-in. (23-cm) pie plate with the dough.

Cheddar Pâté

mushrooms, sliced thin
1 cup (250 mL) whipping cream
½ tsp (2 mL) basil
salt and pepper to taste
3 eggs, lightly beaten
1 cup (250 mL) grated cheese

❧ Line a 9-in. (23-cm) pie plate with the dough.
❧ Heat the butter until it turns a nutty brown color. Add the thinly sliced mushrooms and cook, stirring vigorously, for 3 or 4 seconds.
❧ Mix the cream with the basil, the salt, the pepper and the eggs. Add the grated cheese.
❧ Place the mushrooms in the bottom of the pie plate and pour the cheese mixture over them. Bake in a 375°F (190°C) oven for 40 minutes, or until the blade of a knife inserted in the center of the quiche comes out clean. Serve hot or cold.

QUICHE VAUDOISE

pie dough of your choice
2 tbsp (30 mL) flour
½ lb (250 g) grated Gruyère
or Cheddar
4 eggs, beaten
1 cup (250 mL) whipping cream
1 tsp (5 mL) salt
pinch of pepper

❧ Line a 9-in.(23-cm) pie plate with the dough.
❧ Sprinkle the flour onto the grated cheese. Mix well and pour into the pie plate.
❧ In a bowl, mix together the rest of the ingredients. Beat the mixture well and pour it over the

❧ Cut the bacon slices in half and slice the cheese into thin strips. Place the bacon and the cheese in alternating strips around the inside of the pie plate.
❧ Beat the eggs with the cream and the nutmeg. Pour the mixture over the cheese and bacon. In a skillet, heat the butter until it turns a nutty brown. Sprinkle the cheese, the bacon and the cream mixture with the browned butter.
❧ Bake the quiche in a 375°F (190°C) oven for 35 minutes, or until it is set. The quiche is cooked when the blade of a knife inserted in its center comes out clean.

CHEDDAR PÂTÉ

1½ lbs (750 g) medium Cheddar
¾ tsp (3 mL) dry mustard
⅓ cup (75 mL) chopped parsley

¼ cup (50 mL) chopped green onion
¼ cup (50 mL) soft butter
¼ cup (50 mL) catsup
⅓ cup (75 mL) dry sherry
few drops of Tabasco sauce

❧ Grate the cheese and put it in a blender jar. Add the rest of the ingredients in the order given. Blend well, until the mixture becomes smooth.
❧ Cover the jar and let the mixture stand until you are ready to serve it.

CHEESE AND MUSHROOM QUICHE

pie dough of your choice
1 tbsp (15 cm) butter
1 cup (250 mL) fresh

❦ TECHNIQUE ❦

CHEDDAR PÂTÉ

1 Gather the ingredients.

2 Put grated cheese in the blender jar. Add the mustard, the parsley, the green onions and the butter.

3 Add catsup, the sherry and a few drops of Tabasco sauce.

4 Mix until the mixture becomes smooth.

Bake the quiche in a 375°F (190°C) oven for 40 minutes. The quiche is done when the blade of a knife inserted in its center comes out clean.

FRUIT AND COTTAGE CHEESE RING

Here's a new twist to the fruit and cottage cheese salad. The recipe for the cream dressing that accompanies the fruit is one of my favorites. Any combination of fruits may be used, but I prefer cantaloupe balls and fresh strawberries or raspberries. When you are ready to serve the salad, place a small bowl of the cream sauce in the middle of the cheese ring.

2 envelopes unflavored gelatin
¼ cup (50 mL) apple juice
1 cup (250 mL) light cream
4 cups (1 L) cottage cheese
1 cup (250 mL) whipping cream
salt to taste
fresh fruit of your choice

Soak the gelatin in the apple juice for 5 minutes. In the meantime, heat the cream. Add the gelatin and stir until it has completely dissolved. Cool the mixture, then fold in the cottage cheese. Whip the cream and fold it into the mixture. Add salt to taste. Pour into an oiled ring mold and refrigerate until the mixture becomes firm. Unmold and serve the salad surrounded by the fresh fruits of your choice.

CREAM SAUCE:
1 tbsp (15 mL) dry mustard
1 tsp (5 mL) salt
2 tsp (10 mL) flour
1½ tsp (7 mL) sugar
pinch of cayenne or a few drops of Tabasco sauce
⅓ cup (75 mL) vinegar
1 egg yolk
1 tbsp (15 mL) butter
1 cup (250 mL) whipping cream (well whipped) or sour cream

In the top of a double boiler, mix together all the dry ingredients. Add the vinegar, the egg yolk and the butter and stir.

Cook the mixture over hot water, stirring frequently, until it thickens. Pour it into a bowl. Place a sheet of waxed paper over the sauce (so that a film will not form) and place the bowl in the refrigerator. Just before serving, fold in the whipped cream or sour cream.

COTTAGE CHEESE LOAF

This is a light dish that contains no meat but is nonetheless very nourishing. I like to serve it hot with tomato sauce or cold with mayonnaise and a green salad.

3 tbsp (45 mL) butter
or vegetable oil
1 large onion, chopped fine
½ cup (125 mL) finely diced celery
2 carrots, peeled and grated
2 cups (500 mL) small-curd cottage cheese
2 cups (500 mL) fresh bread, cut into cubes
juice of 1 lemon
grated zest of ½ lemon
1 tsp (5 mL) salt
½ tsp (2 mL) pepper
¼ tsp (1 mL) basil or savory
2 eggs, well beaten

Quiche Vaudoise

🍂 Melt the butter or heat the vegetable oil. Add the onion and cook, stirring vigorously, for 1 or 2 minutes over high heat. Reduce the heat. Add the celery and the carrots. Stir together for about 1 minute. Pour the vegetables into a bowl. Add the rest of the ingredients and mix thoroughly.

🍂 Pour the mixture into a well-buttered loaf pan and bake it in a 350°F (180°C) for 35 to 40 minutes. Serve it with:

SUMMERTIME TOMATO SAUCE:
2½ cups (625 mL) tomato juice
½ tsp (2 mL) sugar
1 onion sliced in two
1 bay leaf
½ tsp (2 mL) basil or savory
4 parsley sprigs
4 cloves
⅓ cup (75 mL) butter
4 tbsp (60 mL) flour
juice of 1 lemon

🍂 In a saucepan, mix together 1½ cups (375 mL) of the tomato juice, the sugar, the onion, the bay leaf, the basil or savory, the parsley sprigs and the cloves.

🍂 Melt the butter. Add the flour and blend. Remove from the heat. Add the remaining 1 cup (250 mL) of cold tomato juice and stir. Pour the hot tomato mixture through a sieve, then cook it over medium heat until it is creamy and smooth. Taste for seasoning. When you are ready to serve it, add the juice of 1 lemon.

Puffed Cheese Biscuits

PUFFED CHEESE BISCUITS

BISCUITS:
½ lb (250 g) butter
2 cups (500 mL) flour
½ lb (250 g) grated cheese
½ tsp (2 mL) salt
1 tbsp (15 mL) ice water

🍂 Place the butter, the flour, the grated cheese and the salt in a bowl. Stir the mixture with a fork until it is well blended. Stir in the ice water. Shape the mixture into a ball (add a few more drops of ice water if necessary) and wrap the ball in wax paper. Refrigerate for 1 to 2 hours.

🍂 Roll the pastry as thin as possible. Cut it into 3-in. (8-cm) circles. Place the circles on an ungreased baking sheet, then brush each one with a bit of egg white. Bake for 10 minutes in a 350°F (180°C) oven, or until the biscuits are lightly browned. Let them cool on a cake rack.

TOPPING:
3 egg yolks
1½ cups (375 mL) whipping cream
pinch salt and pepper
3 tbsp (45 mL) butter
4 tbsp (60 mL) grated cheese

🍂 Beat the egg yolks with the cream, the salt and the pepper. Cook in the top of a double boiler, stirring constantly, until the cream thickens. Remove the mixture from the heat. Cover and refrigerate it until well chilled.

🍃Cream the butter and the cheese. Fold into the chilled cream, then put the mixture back in the refrigerator. To serve, place a spoonful of the cheese topping on a biscuit and cover it with another biscuit.

HOT BISCUITS WITH COTTAGE CHEESE

What delicious morsels these are, especially when served with stew or roast chicken! Cut them in two and spread them with whipped butter scented with chives or basil. At tea time, serve them with butter and honey rather than the herbs. These Dutch biscuits, with their old-fashioned flavor and texture, freeze very well.

3 cups (750 mL) flour
1 tsp (5 mL) salt
2 tsp (10 mL) sugar
4 tsp (20 mL) baking powder
½ tsp (2 mL) baking soda
½ tsp (2 mL) cream of tartar
4 tbsp (60 mL) butter
2 eggs
1½ cups (375 mL) small-curd cottage cheese.

🍃In a large bowl, sift together the dry ingredients. Add the butter and mix with your fingers, breaking the butter into pea-size pieces. Beat the eggs and add them to the flour mixture. Add the cottage cheese. Stir just enough to mix the ingredients.

🍃Pour the contents of the bowl onto a board dusted with flour. Knead the dough until it can be rolled, then roll it to a thickness of between ½ in. and 1 in. (1 cm and 2.5 cm). Cut the dough into diamond-shape pieces (don't

waste any of it) and place the pieces on a buttered cookie sheet. Bake in a 425°F (220°C) oven for 10 to 13 minutes, or until the biscuits turn golden brown.

CHEESE SHORTBREAD

These shortbread biscuits keep well if left in a cool spot in an airtight metal container.

1¼ cups (300 mL) flour
½ tsp (2 mL) salt
pinch of pepper
pinch of nutmeg
¼ lb (125 g) butter
¼ lb (125 g) grated Gruyère
2 eggs, beaten

🍃Sift the dry ingredients. Using two knives, cut the butter until it is in pea-size pieces. Add the grated cheese and the beaten eggs. Mix until the dough can be formed into a ball; if necessary, add 1 or 2 tsp (5 or 10 mL) of cold water. Wrap the dough and refrigerate if for 2 hours.

🍃Roll the dough to a thickness of ¼ in. (0.5 cm). Cut it into circles or squares, as you please. Place the pieces on a buttered cookie sheet, then bake them in a 375°F (190°C) oven for 10 to 12 minutes.

FONTAINEBLEAU

Here is a recipe for a very light home-made cheese. It unmolds easily and makes an elegant dessert, especially when served with strawberries (better yet, with wild strawberries) and sugar. If you prefer, simply serve it with grated maple sugar or cinnamon sugar.

4 tbsp (60 mL) whipping cream
2 lb (1 kg) cream cheese
2 tbsp (30 mL) icing sugar

🍃Whip the cream, then add the other ingredients to the cream. Beat with a hand beater until the mixture becomes smooth.

🍃Line a small bread basket or ring mold with cheesecloth. Pour the cheese mixture into the mold, then place the mold over a slightly smaller bowl so that the cheese mixture can drain without resting in the whey that collects in the bowl. Refrigerate for 12 to 14 hours, time enough for the whey to drain.

COLD CHEESE MOUSSE

¼ cup (50 mL) butter
½ cup (125 mL) flour
1¼ cups (300 mL) milk
2 envelopes unflavored gelatin
½ cup (125 mL) consommé
4 egg yolks
⅔ cup (150 mL) Gruyère, grated
1 green onion, minced
1 tsp (5 mL) dry mustard
salt and pepper to taste
4 egg whites
¼ cup (50 mL) whipping cream
¼ cup (50 mL) minced chives

🍃Make a white sauce with the butter, the flour and the milk.

🍃Soak the gelatin in the cold consommé for 5 minutes. Add this to the hot white sauce and stir until the gelatin is completely melted.

🍃Beat the egg yolks. Add the Gruyère, the green onion, the mustard, the salt and the pepper.

Add this mixture gradually to the hot sauce, stirring constantly, until the cheese melts. Let the mixture cool for about 25 minutes.

🐚 Beat the egg whites until stiff. Whip the cream, then add it and the egg whites to the cooled white sauce.

🐚 Oil a mold and sprinkle it with the chives. Pour the mousse into the mold. Refrigerate it for 3 to 12 hours. Unmold the mousse before serving it.

CHEESE FLAN

3 eggs
2½ cups (625 mL) light cream
1¾ cups (425 mL) grated
Gruyère
1¾ cups (425 mL) grated
Parmesan
6 slices cooked bacon
pinch of salt

🐚 Beat the eggs in a bowl. Add the cream and both of the cheeses. Mix well.

🐚 Cut the cooked bacon into small pieces and stir them into the cheese mixture. Add a pinch of salt.

🐚 Pour the mixture into an 8-cup (2-L) baking dish and cook it for 40 minutes in a 350°F (180°C) oven.

VAUDOISE CHEESE PUFFS

6 slices white bread
½ cup (125 mL) consommé
or white wine
4 tbsp (60 mL) melted butter

¼ cup (50 mL) flour
1 cup (250 mL) milk
½ cup (125 mL) grated cheese
pinch of nutmeg
salt and pepper to taste
2 egg yolks, beaten

🐚 Soak the slices of bread in the wine or the consommé. Place them carefully into a well-greased pie plate. Pour 2 tbsp (30 mL) of the melted butter on top.

🐚 Add the flour to the remaining butter and mix well. Add the milk and cook, stirring constantly, until the sauce becomes creamy. Add the cheese and the nutmeg, then season to taste with salt and pepper.

🐚 Remove the pan from the heat. Add the egg yolks, stirring vigorously. Pour the sauce over the bread, then bake the casserole for 30 minutes in a 375°F (190°C) oven.

SEPTEMBER CHEESE SOUFFLÉ

8 large firm tomatoes
salt
2 tbsp (30 mL) flour
¼ cup (50 mL) light cream
2 tbsp (30 mL) butter, melted
4 egg yolks, beaten
½ tsp (2 mL) salt
¼ tsp (1 mL) pepper
¾ cup (175 mL) grated Gruyère
or Parmesan
4 egg whites

🐚 Cut a 1-in. (2-cm) thick slice off the top of each tomato. Remove the pulp. Sprinkle the interior of the tomatoes with salt and turn them upside down to drain for about 15 minutes.

🐚 Mix the flour and the cream in a saucepan and stir until smooth. Add the butter, the egg yolks, the salt and the pepper and stir well.

Vaudoise Cheese Puffs

❦ TECHNIQUE ❦

VAUDOISE CHEESE PUFFS

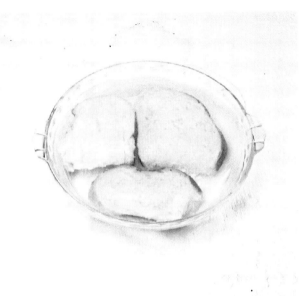

1 Soak the slices of bread in the white wine or the consommé.

2 Place the bread in a greased pie plate. Pour 2 tbsp (30 mL) of melted butter on the bread.

3 Add the egg yolks to the sauce.

4 Pour the sauce over the bread.

Cook over low heat until the mixture thickens, stirring constantly. Add the cheese and stir until the cheese melts completely. Remove the mixture from the heat and let it cool for 15 minutes.

Beat the egg whites until stiff, then carefully fold them into the cheese mixture.

Spoon the mixture into the tomatoes, filling them to about three quarters full. Place the tomatoes on a buttered baking sheet. Bake 25 minutes in 350°F (180°C) oven. Serve immediately.

MILANESE SOUFFLÉ

4 egg yolks
½ cup (125 mL) sour cream
¼ cup (50 mL) flour
¼ cup (50 mL) grated Parmesan
½ tsp (2 mL) salt
¼ tsp (1 mL) pepper
4 egg whites
2 tbsp (30 mL) breadcrumbs
2 tbsp (30 mL) grated Parmesan

Beat the egg yolks in a bowl. Add the sour cream and continue beating until the mixture is smooth.

In another bowl, mix the flour, the Parmesan, the salt and the pepper.

Gradually add the yolk mixture to the Parmesan mixture, stirring constantly.

Beat the egg whites until stiff, then carefully fold them into the mixture.

Butter the top of a double boiler and sprinkle the breadcrumbs evenly into it. Pour in the soufflé mixture. Cover and cook the soufflé for 50 minutes.

When done, run a knife around the edge of the soufflé and carefully unmold it onto a warmed serving plate. Sprinkle Parmesan on top, then serve.

CHEDDAR SOUFFLÉ

2 tbsp (30 mL) butter
2 tbsp (30 mL) flour
⅔ cup (150 mL) milk
½ tsp (2 mL) salt
1 tsp (5 mL) dry mustard
3 egg yolks, lightly beaten
1 cup (250 mL) grated Cheddar
3 egg whites
6 to 8 thin slices of Cheddar

Prepare a smooth and creamy white sauce with the butter, the flour and the milk. Add the salt, the mustard and the egg yolks and mix well.

Add the Cheddar. Cook the mixture over low heat, stirring constantly, until the cheese is completely melted. Set it aside to cool for 15 minutes.

Beat the egg whites until stiff, then carefully fold them into the cheese mixture.

Line an 8-in. (20-cm) soufflé mold with a strip of paper. Butter the mold and sprinkle it with flour, then pour in the mixture. Decorate the top with the **slices** of Cheddar. Bake for 35 minutes in an 375°F (190°C) oven.

CHEESE RICE CASSEROLE

3 tbsp (45 mL) shortening
½ cup (125 mL) chopped onion

½ tsp (2 mL) salt
pinch of pepper
pinch of sage
1 tbsp (15 mL) flour
¾ cup (175 mL) milk
1½ cups (375 mL) grated cheese
3 cups (750 mL) cooked rice

Melt the shortening. Add the onion, the salt, the pepper and the sage. Fry until the onions are golden brown. Add the flour and mix well. Add the milk. Cook over medium heat, stirring constantly, until the sauce thickens.

Remove from the heat. Add the cheese and stir until it melts. Using a fork, stir in the cooked rice. Pour the mixture into greased casserole and bake it in a 350°F (180°C) oven for 30 minutes.

POLISH PIROGHI

In Poland, Christmas Eve is the most important event of the Christmas season, for on that evening the "Wilia" takes place. This is a joyful family celebration, and members of the family who cannot be present are sorely missed. The supper has a number of fixed courses—seven, nine or eleven—and under no circumstances may there be an odd number of people at the table. The heartiest cheers are reserved for the piroghi course. Piroghi can be served in many ways—here is one simple and easy preparation—but it is especially tasty when served as a sweet dish, accompanied by sour cream flavored with cinnamon and sugar.

2 cups (500 mL) cottage cheese
1 tbsp (15 mL) soft butter
4 egg yolks
½ tsp (2 mL) salt

2 tbsp (30 mL) sugar
½ cup (125 mL) flour
4 egg whites

☛ Force the cheese through a coarse sieve. Add the soft butter, the egg yolks, the salt, the sugar and the flour. Beat thoroughly.

☛ Beat the egg whites until stiff and fold them into the egg-yolk mixture.

☛ Pour the mixture onto a floured board. Using your hands, roll it into a long, narrow strip. Flatten the roll a bit, then cut it diagonally to form pieces that are 2 in. (5 cm) long.

☛ Fill a large saucepan with water and add 1 tbsp (15 cm) of salt. Bring the water to a boil. Place a few of the piroghi in the water at a time. Boil, uncovered, for 10 to 12 minutes. Remove the piroghi from the water with a perforated ladle, then place them on a warm platter. Keep hot.

☛ When you have cooked all the piroghi, drain them well. Serve with your choice of a garnish, perhaps *Breadcrumb Sauce*.

BREADCRUMB SAUCE

☛ Melt 3 tbsp (45 mL) of butter and cook until golden brown. Add 2 tbsp (30 mL) of coarse breadcrumbs. Cook the mixture over medium heat for another 2 to 3 minutes, or just until the crumbs turn golden brown. Pour the sauce over the piroghi.

FRUIT

FRESH FRUIT

At the height of the summer season, we are blessed with an abundance of locally grown fresh fruit. Freezing it, or preserving it in some other way, provides a pleasant reminder of summer's bounty during the winter months.

❧ Fruit is an important part of a balanced diet and should be eaten every day. It can be served for breakfast, as a snack or as an accompaniment to the main course of a meal. It is delicious fresh, cooked or preserved. It can be used in appetizers and salads, and to make delicious jams and jellies. It can also be stored in the freezer to brighten our tables in winter.

❧ Fruit is not only nutritious and delicious, but is also pleasing to the eye. What could be more attractive than textured oranges or the smooth, polished shapes of apples in a dessert bowl? Or the contrasting colors of red and green grapes on a cheese platter?

❧ But first, it's important to know how to recognize fruit when it is at its best, and then to prepare it so that it retains as much of its freshness as possible. The following are some points to remember when preparing fresh fruit.

❧ The heaviest citrus fruits are the juiciest. Limes should be bright green and should be kept in the refrigerator, as should grapefruit. Grapefruit can be sweetened with rum or kirsch. Oranges can be found on the shelves year-round. Florida oranges are particularly tasty. They can be flavored with Cointreau or curaçao.

❧ Always chill cherries, grapes, apples, pears and peaches before serving, but only for a short time.

❧ Berries, such as raspberries, strawberries, blackberries, blueberries and red currants, should be placed on sheets of wax paper and refrigerated. Rinse them under cold running water, remove the stems if necessary and sprinkle them with sugar before serving at room temperature. Strawberries and raspberries can be flavored with orange liqueur or cognac.

❧ Never soak fresh fruit.

❧ Always cook the pits of apricots, peaches and nectarines with the fruit. They add extra flavor.

❧ Bananas and apricots are at their best when ripe. Use bananas sparingly in salads as their strong taste tends to overpower the other ingredients.

❧ Lemon juice prevents bananas, apples and some other fruits from turning brown.

❧ Red apples, peeled and diced, are a nice garnish for fruit salads. Some apples, like the Delicious, do not turn brown, but McIntoshes sprinkled with lemon juice can be used in their place.

❧ In a fruit salad, large cherries should be pitted but wild cherries can be left whole.

❧ All types of grapes are good in salads but seedless green grapes are preferable.

❧ If you wish to add red plums to your fruit salad, add them at the last minute as their color tends to stain lighter colored fruit.

❧ Canned peaches will keep their shape, but nothing equals the taste of fresh peaches. If you are adding them to a fruit salad, peel and pit them.

❧ All varieties of melon—watermelon, honeydew, cantaloupe, casaba—are excellent in fruit salads. Cut them into cubes or slices, or shape them with a melon baller, and sprinkle with lemon or lime juice, fresh mint or grated ginger.

❧ Never peel pears before cooking or canning them or they will lose their taste. In salads, peel them and cut them into strips or cubes, and sprinkle them with lemon. Canned Bartlett pears are very popular but, as with peaches, nothing equals the taste of the fresh fruit.

❧ Pineapples can be bought year-round. Choose a heavy pineapple with no signs of rotting at the base or around the eyes. When ripe, pineapples give off a slight scent and the leaves are easily pulled out. Store pineapples in the refrigerator. To prepare, remove a slice from the top. Hold the pineapple upright and peel it following its natural curves, from top to bottom. Remove the eyes with the tip of a knife and slice it, or cut it into cubes if it is to be used in a fruit salad. It can also be grated. Sprinkled with kirsch or maraschino liqueur, pineapple is a classic dessert.

❧ Of course, we mustn't forget the rarer tropical fruit that can now be found on the shelves year-round. Kiwis, mangoes, guavas, pomegranates, papayas, kumquats and persimmons are all just as tasty as the better-known fruits and are a welcome addition to fresh fruit salads.

❧ Fruits contain natural sugars. If one adds as little water as possible when cooking fruits, they will retain their natural sugar and there will be little need to add refined sugar or honey. Should it become necessary to add sugar at all, add it at the end of the cooking period.

FRESH FRUIT COMBINATIONS

❧ Bananas—oranges—pineapple—apricots—raspberries

❧ Grapefruit—grapes—strawberries—cherries—apricots

❧ Oranges—bananas—grapefruit—strawberries—pineapple—cooked rhubarb

❧ Pineapple—oranges—peaches—pears—plums—strawberries—raspberries

❧ Bananas—cherries—strawberries—grapes—raspberries

❧ Peaches—apricots—cherries—strawberries—raspberries—bananas

FRUIT SALADS

There are any number of ways to create a fruit salad.

FRESH FRUIT SALAD WITH MAPLE SYRUP

Pour maple syrup into a bowl and add the juice and zest of ½ lemon or ½ orange. Add any combination of fresh fruits, cut into cubes. Mix well. Sprinkle with chopped fresh mint and serve at room temperature or after having chilled for a few hours.

Fresh Fruit Salad

FRESH FRUIT MEDLEY

Combine several types of fresh fruit, in equal amounts, and sweeten with brown sugar or syrup. Sprinkle with the juice of 1 lemon and let stand at room temperature or in the refrigerator for several hours.

FLAVORED FRUITS

Prepare as for *Fresh Fruit Medley*, but replace the lemon juice with kirsch, cognac or red or white wine.

FRUIT CUP

Flavor the fruit with cognac, but let it soak in champagne. Chill for 6 hours and serve in champagne glasses.

FROZEN FRUIT SALAD

3 large ripe peaches
4 bananas

juice of 1 lemon
2 tbsp (30 mL) sugar
½ cup (125 mL) maraschino cherries, chopped
2 tbsp (30 mL) maraschino cherry juice
1 cup (250 mL) cream, whipped

❧ Peel the peaches and the bananas and cut them into large chunks. Place in a bowl with the lemon juice and the sugar. Mash the fruits and stir until well blended. Add the cherries and the juice. Fold in the cream. Pour into a rectangular container. Cover tightly and freeze.

❧ When the salad is frozen, cut it into slices and serve on a bed of lettuce.

HONEYED FRUIT SALAD

1 cup (250 mL) grapes
1 orange

Cantaloupe Salad

PEAR SALAD

fresh or canned pears
herbed cream cheese
honey French dressing
lettuce

❧ If you are using fresh pears, peel and halve them, remove the core and brush with lemon juice to prevent discoloration. Refrigerate canned pears for 2 to 3 hours before using. Drain well on absorbent paper.

❧ Place 2 pear halves on each plate. Fill each half with cream cheese and drizzle with 1 tbsp (15 mL) French dressing. Serve on a bed of lettuce.

1 banana
juice of 1 lemon
1 pear or peach
1 apple
3 tbsp (45 mL) honey
lettuce
zest of ½ lemon

❧ Wash the grapes and dry them with a cloth. Peel the orange and divide it into sections. Peel and slice the banana. Roll the slices in 1 tsp (5 mL) of the lemon juice to prevent discoloration. Peel and slice the pear or peach. Cut the unpeeled apple into very thin slices.

❧ Mix together the rest of the lemon juice and the honey. Roll the prepared fruits in this mixture with a fork, taking care not to break them.

❧ Arrange the fruits on a bed of lettuce. Pour the juice and honey mixture over the fruits. Garnish with the lemon zest.

CANTALOUPE SALAD

1 head lettuce
1 cantaloupe
1 avocado
lemon French dressing

❧ Wash the lettuce. Wrap the leaves in a cloth and refrigerate until ready to serve.

❧ Peel the cantaloupe and scoop out the seeds. Cut the fruit into thin crescent-shaped slices. Peel the avocado and remove the pit. Cut into thin slices.

❧ To serve, place the lettuce on a serving dish. Arrange the cantaloupe and avocado slices on the bed of lettuce, alternating the orange cantaloupe with the light green avocado. Serve with French dressing on the side.

FRUITS BELLE AURORE

1 tbsp (15 mL) butter
1 tbsp (15 mL) flour
1 cup (250 mL) table cream
½ cup (125 mL) sugar
½ tsp (2 mL) fruit extract
2 to 3 cups (500 to 750 mL) fresh or canned fruits
fresh mint leaves, chopped

❧ Melt the butter in a saucepan and add the flour. Remove the saucepan from the heat, then add the cream. Return to heat and stir until the sauce is smooth. Add the sugar and fruit extract. Stir until the sugar is entirely dissolved.

❧ Pour this hot sauce over your favorite fruit mixture. Sprinkle lightly with the fresh mint. Serve chilled.

QUICK DESSERTS

Here are some suggestions for tasty fruit desserts that can be prepared in a few minutes.

QUICK APPLE DESSERTS

🍂 Cook peeled and quartered apples in cranberry, raspberry or orange juice.

🍂 Add orange or lemon zest to fresh applesauce to give it a nice, fresh taste.

🍂 Melt 1 tbsp (15 mL) butter in a saucepan and add peeled, quartered apples. Sprinkle the apples with cinnamon and brown sugar or maple sugar. Stir to blend well. Cover and cook for 20 minutes over low heat, stirring once or twice. Serve hot or cold.

QUICK STRAWBERRY DESSERTS

🍂 Serve fresh strawberries with brown sugar or maple sugar and sour cream.

🍂 Cream ¼ lb (125 g) butter with 1 cup (250 mL) confectioner's sugar and 1 cup (250 mL) crushed fresh strawberries. Add ¼ cup (50 mL) slivered blanched almonds. Serve this mixture with hot crepes.

🍂 Bring 3 cups (750 mL) strawberries or other berries and ½ cup (125 mL) sugar to a boil. Remove from heat and add the juice of ½ lemon. Butter 8 to 10 slices of bread. Place the bread slices and fruit mixture in alternate layers on a serving platter. Cover and refrigerate for 4 to 8 hours before serving.

STRAWBERRY AND RHUBARB COMPOTE

2 lbs (1 kg) rhubarb
½ cup (125 mL) orange juice
¾ cup (175 mL) sugar
2 cups (500 mL) fresh strawberries
or 1 package frozen strawberries
whipped cream, ice cream
or sour cream

🍂 Cut the rhubarb into 2-in. (5-cm) pieces. In a saucepan, bring the orange juice and the sugar to a boil. Stir until the sugar is dissolved. Add the rhubarb. Simmer over low heat for 5 to 8 minutes. Remove from heat and add the fresh strawberries (cleaned and halved) or the unthawed frozen strawberries. Serve cold with a bowl of whipped cream, ice cream or sour cream.

FOUR-FRUIT COMPOTE

4 peaches
4 blue or red plums
4 apricots
4 pears
1 cup (250 mL) sugar
½ cup (125 mL) water
½ tsp (2 mL) coriander seeds
or 3 whole cloves
juice of 1 lemon

🍂 Wash and dry the fruit. Prepare a syrup by boiling the sugar, water and coriander seeds or whole cloves together for 5 minutes. Place the peaches in the boiling syrup and let simmer for 10 minutes.

🍂 Remove the peaches from the syrup, peel them and place them in a dish. Peel the pears, cut them in half or leave them whole. Cook

Strawberry and Rhubarb Compote

[499]

them in the syrup for 10 minutes. When they are done, remove them and place them with the peaches.

۶ Add the unpeeled apricots and plums to the syrup and cook until the plum skins break. Add to the other fruit.

۶ Pour the lemon juice over the cooked fruit. Stir until the fruit is well coated with the lemon juice. Boil the syrup for a few minutes and pour over the fruit mixture.

۶ To freeze, place the mixture in one or several containers. Pour the syrup on top. Cover and freeze. Allow to thaw at room temperature before serving.

APPLESAUCE WITH CROUTONS

2 cups (500 mL) apple juice
4 to 6 apples

2 tbsp (30 mL) butter
¾ cup (175 mL) bread cubes
½ tsp (2 mL) cinnamon
3 coriander seeds, crushed
¼ to ½ cup (50 to 125 mL) sugar
1 tbsp (15 mL) butter

۶ Bring the apple juice to a boil. Peel the apples and cut them into thin slices. Add them to the apple juice. Cover and simmer over low heat for 20 minutes.

۶ Mash the cooked apples with a wire whisk or a wooden spoon.

۶ Melt the 2 tbsp (30 mL) butter in a skillet. Add the bread cubes and brown over low heat, stirring constantly. Add the cinnamon and the crushed coriander seeds. Mix thoroughly.

۶ Remove the applesauce from the heat. Sweeten to taste, gradually adding the sugar and stirring constantly. Add the remaining

1 tbsp (15 mL) butter and the hot croutons. Stir until the butter is melted. Serve hot or warm.

DRIED FRUIT COMPOTE

۶ Dried fruit compote is a mixture of dried fruit, such as prunes, figs, raisins and currants, and almonds or hazelnuts. It can be served as a snack or a dessert and can be prepared in 15 minutes. It can be stored for more than 1 month in the refrigerator. The following is a recipe for a basic dried fruit compote.

1½ lbs (750 g) dried fruit
3½ cups (875 mL) water
2 oranges
pinch of ground allspice
¼ cup (50 mL) honey
2 tbsp (30 mL) sugar
2 tbsp (30 mL) brandy
(optional)
pinch of ground ginger
2 tbsp (30 mL) sugar
½ cup (125 mL) blanched almonds
2 tbsp (30 mL) honey

۶ Simmer the dried fruits in 3½ cups (875 mL) water.

۶ Drain and reserve the cooking liquid. Add the juice and grated zest of 2 oranges, along with the allspice, honey and sugar, to the liquid. Bring to a boil and simmer until a rich syrup is formed.

Fruit Betty

🌿 Add the fruit, and brandy if desired. Chill.

🌿 Mix the ginger, 2 tbsp (30 mL) sugar and ½ cup (125 mL) blanched almonds. Spread the mixture in a roasting pan and pour 2 tbsp (30 mL) honey over the top. Bake in a 300°F (150°C) oven until the almonds are golden brown. Add this mixture to the fruit mixture.

🌿 This recipe yields 8 to 10 servings.

FRUIT BETTY

1½ cups (375 mL) stale bread cubes
2 tbsp (30 mL) butter
½ cup (125 mL) maple syrup or honey
2 cups (500 mL) thinly sliced peeled apples or peaches
table cream

🌿 Brown the bread cubes in the butter over low heat, stirring often. Add the syrup or honey and the fruits. Mix well, cover and cook for approximately 6 to 8 minutes over low heat. Serve hot or cold, with cream.

APPLE DELIGHT

6 medium apples
4 tbsp (60 mL) melted butter
3 eggs
3 tbsp (45 mL) flour
3 tbsp (45 mL) sugar
zest of 1 lemon, grated
pinch of salt
2 cups (500 mL) milk
superfine sugar

Apple Crisp

🌿 Peel and quarter the apples. Place them in a saucepan with the melted butter and cook for 10 minutes, stirring often.

🌿 Beat together the eggs, flour, sugar, grated lemon zest, salt and milk. Add the apples.

🌿 Turn into a buttered, ovenproof glass dish and bake in a 400°F (200°C) oven for 20 minutes. Sprinkle with superfine sugar and broil until mixture resembles caramel. Watch closely to prevent the sugar from burning.

APPLE CRISP

4 cups (1 L) sliced apples
⅓ cup (75 mL) sugar
2 tbsp (30 mL) flour

½ tsp (2 mL) cinnamon
1 tbsp (15 mL) margarine or butter
2 tbsp (30 mL) lemon juice

TOPPING:
¾ cup (175 mL) brown sugar
¾ cup (175 mL) sifted flour
⅓ cup (75 mL) butter or margarine
pinch of salt
¾ cup (175 mL) chopped nuts

🌿 Place the apples in a well greased baking dish. Mix together the sugar, flour, cinnamon and margarine or butter; spread this mixture over the apples. Pour the lemon juice over the top.

🌿 To prepare the topping, mix together the brown sugar, flour,

❧ TECHNIQUE ❧

APPLE CRISP

1 Place the apples in a well greased baking dish.

2 Mix together the sugar, flour, cinnamon and margarine or butter.

3 Spread this mixture over the apples. Pour the lemon juice on top.

4 Spread the topping mixture over the apples.

butter or margarine, salt and nuts. Spread over the apples and bake in a 325°F (160°C) oven for 1 hour.

APPLE FLOATING ISLANDS

2 cups (500 mL) water
¾ cup (175 mL) sugar
6 apples, peeled
2 stiffly beaten egg whites
3 tbsp (45 mL) sugar
2 egg yolks
2 tbsp (30 mL) sugar
1 cup (250 mL) milk

🍎 Mix together the water and the sugar and boil for 10 minutes. Add the peeled apples. Cover and cook over medium heat until the apples are tender.

🍎 Carefully remove the apples from the syrup and place in a baking dish. Boil the syrup until thick. Pour over the apples and let cool.

🍎 Prepare a meringue with the egg whites and 3 tbsp (45 mL) sugar. Spread over the cooled apples and bake in a 350°F (180°C) oven until golden brown.

🍎 Beat the egg yolks with 2 tbsp (30 mL) sugar and the milk. Cook, without boiling, until the mixture has the consistency of light cream.

🍎 To serve, pour the egg yolk mixture around the meringued apples.

APPLE FLOATING ISLANDS À LA FRANÇAISE

6 large baking apples
¼ cup (50 mL) water
¾ cup (175 mL) sugar
4 egg whites
1 tsp (5 mL) orange-blossom water
2 cups (500 mL) custard, chilled
½ cup (125 mL) gooseberry jam

🍎 Core the apples and place them, unpeeled, in a baking dish with ¼ cup (50 mL) water. Cover and bake in a 400°F (200°C) oven until tender.

🍎 When the apples are sufficiently cooled, force them through a sieve and add the sugar. Beat until the sugar is completely dissolved.

🍎 Beat the egg whites with the orange-blossom water until stiff. Slowly fold into the apple mixture, stirring until light and fluffy.

🍎 Turn the chilled custard into a bowl (see *Custards and Dessert Creams*, page 570). Carefully pour the apple mixture on top. Garnish with gooseberry jam.

ENGLISH APPLE BLACK CAPS

6 large apples
juice and zest of 1 lemon
2 tbsp (30 mL) orange-blossom water
1 cup (250 mL) superfine sugar

🍎 Halve and core the unpeeled apples. Place them, cut side down, in a medium-size baking dish.

🍎 Mix together the lemon juice and zest and the orange-blossom water. Pour over the apples. Sprinkle with ¾ cup (175 mL) sugar. Bake in a 400°F (200°C) oven for 30 minutes. Sprinkle with the remaining sugar and serve.

QUÉBEC APPLE DESSERT

2 medium apples
½ cup (125 mL) walnuts, chopped
1 egg
1 cup (250 mL) sugar
2 tbsp (30 mL) all-purpose flour
1 tsp (5 mL) baking powder
pinch of salt
ice cream

🍎 Peel and core the apples and cut them into thin slices. Place the walnuts in a bowl. Beat the egg and the sugar until fluffy. Add to the apples along with the walnuts.

🍎 Sift together the flour, baking powder and salt. Add to the egg mixture. Stir to blend.

🍎 Turn into a buttered baking dish. Bake in a 350°F (180°C) oven for 25 minutes, or until a crisp golden crust forms on top. Serve warm with ice cream.

Normandy Apples

NORMANDY APPLES

5 apples
¾ cup (175 mL) sugar
⅓ cup (75 mL) water
juice of 1 lemon
zest of 1 lemon, grated
2 tbsp (30 mL) apricot, peach
or plum preserve
2 tbsp (30 mL) sherry

🐟 Choose apples of the same size. Peel and quarter them. Place in a buttered saucepan and cover with a syrup prepared with the sugar, water, lemon juice and lemon zest. Poach the apples in the syrup.

🐟 When the apples are cooked, drain them and place them in a bowl. Add the apricot, peach or plum preserve to the syrup, along with the sherry. Heat until the sauce thickens. Pour over the apples. Serve chilled.

APPLE PUDDING

2 cups (500 mL) milk
⅓ cup (75 mL) cream
½ cup (125 mL) semolina
3 tbsp (45 mL) butter
4 medium apples, peeled
and cubed
½ cup (125 mL) sugar
or brown sugar
½ tsp (2 mL) cinnamon
2 eggs, beaten
½ cup (125 mL) sugar
½ tsp (2 mL) salt
1 tsp (5 mL) butter

🐟 Bring the milk and cream to a boil. Add the semolina, stirring constantly. Simmer for 5 minutes.

🐟 Melt the butter in a saucepan and add the apples, ½ cup sugar or brown sugar and cinnamon. Stir and cook over low heat for

5 minutes. Turn into a baking dish.

🐟 Remove the semolina from the heat. Add the eggs, stirring vigorously, then add the sugar, salt and butter. Blend thoroughly and pour over the apples. Bake in a 350°F (180°C) oven for 20 minutes. Serve hot or cold.

SNOW-CAPPED APPLES

Apples topped with meringue! This light dessert takes on a festive air when served with whipped cream or ice cream.

6 to 8 apples
¼ cup (50 mL) butter
½ cup (125 mL) sugar
¼ cup (50 mL) brown sugar
1 tsp (5 mL) vanilla
or 1 tbsp (15 mL) Irish whiskey
3 egg whites
2 tsp (10 mL) cold water
⅓ cup (75 mL) sugar
1 tsp (5 mL) sugar

🐟 Peel and slice the apples. Melt the butter in a saucepan. Add ½ cup sugar and ¼ cup brown sugar and stir until the butter is melted. Add the apples and stir until well blended. Cook over medium heat, uncovered, for 10 minutes. Cover and simmer for 20 minutes over low heat. Remove from the heat and mash the apples with a fork. Add the vanilla or Irish whiskey.

🐟 Turn into an 8-in. (20-cm) baking dish.

🐟 Make a meringue by beating together the egg whites and the water until the mixture is stiff.

Add ⅓ cup sugar, 1 tbsp (15 mL) at a time, beating well after each addition. Spread over the apples. Sprinkle the meringue with 1 tsp (5 mL) sugar. Bake in a 350°F (180°C) oven for 30 to 35 minutes.

🍂 Do not refrigerate. Serve hot or at room temperature.

APPLE MOUSSE

8 apple(s), peeled and quartered
½ cup (125 mL) water
or apple juice
2 cloves
¾ cup (175 mL) sugar
3 egg whites
pinch of cream of tartar
2 tbsp (30 mL) sugar
rum

🍂 Place the apples, ½ cup (125 mL) water or apple juice and cloves in a saucepan. Cook over medium heat, stirring often, until the apples are cooked. Remove from heat. Pour ¾ cup (175 mL) sugar over the apple mixture and beat vigorously until the sugar is dissolved and the apples are puréed. Allow the mixture to cool and remove the cloves. This recipe makes 3 cups (750 mL) applesauce.

🍂 With a hand beater, beat the egg whites together with the cream of tartar and 2 tbsp (30 mL) sugar. Fold into the applesauce along with the rum. Turn into a bowl and refrigerate.

🍂 If you make this recipe with ready-made applesauce, count 1 egg white per 1 cup (250 mL) applesauce.

APPLE HEDGEHOG

8 medium apples
1 cup (250 mL) light brown sugar or maple sugar
3 cups (750 mL) water
zest of ½ lemon, grated
1 egg white
2 tbsp (30 mL) sugar
10 blanched almonds

🍂 Peel and core 6 of the apples. Bring 1 cup (250 mL) brown sugar or maple sugar and 3 cups (750 mL) water to a boil. Add the apples and cook until they are tender. Remove the apples from the syrup and arrange on a serving platter.

🍂 Peel, core and slice the 2 remaining apples. Add them to the syrup, along with the lemon zest. Cook until very tender, stirring often. Beat until fluffy. Pour over the cooked apples. Allow to cool until lukewarm.

🍂 Beat the egg white with 2 tbsp (30 mL) sugar until stiff and spread over the applesauce. Sliver the almonds and sprinkle over the meringue. Store in a cool place for 2 to 3 hours before serving.

PEACH COBBLER

2 cups (500 mL) fresh peaches and ½ cup (125 mL) sugar
or 10 oz (285 mL) frozen peaches
1 egg, beaten
2 eggs, separated
1 tbsp (15 mL) superfine sugar
1 tbsp (15 mL) cornstarch
½ tsp (2 mL) almond extract

🍂 Peel and slice the peaches. Add the sugar and the beaten egg. (If you are using frozen peaches, allow them to thaw before mixing

Apple Mousse

them with the beaten egg, but do not add sugar as they are already very sweet.) Turn the fruit mixture into a well-greased baking dish.

❧ Beat the egg yolks until they are pale yellow and add the sugar and the cornstarch. Continue beating until the mixture is very light and fluffy. (It is easier to obtain this consistency with a hand beater.) Add the almond extract and fold in the stiffly beaten egg whites.

❧ Pour this light batter over the peaches and bake in a 400°F (200°C) oven for 30 minutes. Serve hot or cold with a light custard (see *Custards and Dessert Creams*, page 570).

ROMANOFF PEACHES

6 egg yolks
1 cup (250 mL) sugar

¾ cup (175 mL) orange juice
¾ cup (175 mL) sherry
1 cup (250 mL) whipping cream
2½ lbs (1.2 kg) fresh peaches
juice of 1 lemon
strawberries or cherries
superfine sugar

❧ Beat the egg yolks until they are very light; add the sugar and continue beating until light and fluffy.

❧ Add the orange juice and the sherry. Cook in a double boiler, over very hot (but not boiling) water, stirring constantly until smooth and thick. Cool and refrigerate.

❧ Whip the cream and fold into the cooled mixture.

❧ A few minutes before serving, peel the peaches and dip them in lemon juice to prevent discoloration. Slice the peaches and fold into the cream mixture. Turn into a bowl and garnish with strawberries or cherries and superfine sugar.

BORDELAISE PEACHES

8 peaches
sugar
3 cups (750 mL) red wine
¼ cup (50 mL) sugar
1 small cinnamon stick
brioches

❧ Peel and halve the peaches and remove the pits. Sprinkle the peach halves with sugar and let them stand for 1 hour.

❧ Mix together the red wine, ¼ cup (50 mL) sugar and cinnamon and bring to a boil. Poach the peach halves in the wine mixture. When the peaches are cooked, place them in a glass bowl.

❧ Reduce the cooking liquid over high heat and pour it over the peaches.

❧ Serve chilled with slices of brioches sprinkled with sugar and lightly browned in the oven.

❧ Melons, pineapple, pears and apples are also delicious when prepared this way.

RASPBERRY PEACHES

6 ripe peaches, peeled
1 cup (250 mL) fresh
or frozen raspberries
¼ cup (50 mL) grape jelly
¼ cup (50 mL) sugar
1 tsp (5 mL) cornstarch
2 tbsp (30 mL) lemon
or orange juice

Romanoff Peaches

❦ TECHNIQUE ❦

ROMANOFF PEACHES

1   Beat the egg yolks until very light.

2   Add the sugar and continue beating.

3   Add the orange juice and the sherry.

4   Cook in a double boiler.

Peaches with Rice

Peel and halve the peaches. Place each half on an individual plate or place them all in a large bowl.

🌿 Mash the fresh or frozen raspberries with a fork. Place them in a saucepan. Add the grape jelly and the sugar. Bring to a boil. Thicken with 1 tsp (5 mL) cornstarch blended with the lemon or orange juice.

🌿 Force the sauce through a sieve and pour it over the peaches. Serve cold.

PEACHES WITH RICE

½ cup (125 mL) rice
2 cups (500 mL) milk
½ cup (125 mL) sugar
vanilla
2 egg yolks
6 peaches
maraschino cherries

🌿 Cook the rice, milk and sugar in the top of a double boiler. When the rice is cooked (which should take about 40 to 60 minutes) and all the milk has been absorbed, flavor with vanilla and add the well-beaten egg yolks.

🌿 Poach the peaches and arrange on a ring of the vanilla rice mixture. Garnish with maraschino cherries and their juice.

🌿 Apricots can be prepared in the same way.

FRESH PEACH COCKTAIL

2½ cups (625 mL) diced, peeled fresh peaches
1 tbsp (15 mL) lemon juice
2 to 4 tbsp (30 to 60 mL) sugar
chilled ginger ale
fresh mint

🌿 Combine the peaches and the lemon juice. Add sugar to taste. Turn the mixture into fruit cocktail glasses. Top with ginger ale. Garnish each cocktail with a sprig of mint. Serve chilled.

POACHED PEACHES

3 large firm ripe peaches
1 cup (250 mL) water
1 cup (250 mL) brown sugar
1 stick cinnamon

🌿 Halve the unpeeled peaches and remove the pits. Mix together the water and the sugar in a saucepan and boil for 5 minutes. Add the cinnamon stick and the peach halves. Poach, uncovered, over low heat for 15 minutes. Remove the peaches from the syrup and place on a serving dish. Remove any skin remaining on the peaches or in the syrup. Boil the syrup for 5 to 8 minutes longer. Remove from the heat. Add the lemon juice to the peaches. Stir and add the syrup.

🌿 The peaches can be replaced with pears or apples. This dish freezes very well.

BRANDIED PEACHES

3 cups (750 mL) sugar
1 cup (250 mL) water
8 cups (2 L) peaches, peeled and halved
¾ cup (175 mL) cognac

🌿 Mix the water and sugar in a saucepan. Bring to a boil over low heat, stirring constantly, until the sugar is dissolved. Then simmer for 10 minutes.

Add the peach halves to the syrup. Simmer for 10 minutes, or until the peaches are tender. Remove from the heat.

Sterilize four 2-cup (500-mL) jars. Place 1 tbsp (15 mL) cognac in each jar. Fill to the half-way mark with peaches. Add another 1 tbsp (15 mL) cognac to each jar. Fill the jars with the remaining peaches and pour another 1 tbsp (15 mL) cognac into each jar. Cover with the hot syrup. Seal.

Pears Boulogne

Use fresh pears to make this beautiful dessert. Place on a glass or crystal serving plate to highlight the color.

8 pears
6 oz (175 mL) frozen orange
or pineapple juice
½ cup (125 mL) sugar
½ cup (125 mL) water
¼ tsp (1 mL) red food coloring
1 package frozen raspberries

Peel the pears and leave them whole. As soon as each pear is peeled, place it in a bowl of cold water.

Mix together the frozen orange or pineapple juice, sugar and water and bring to a boil. Then add the red food coloring and stir until well blended. Add the pears, lower the heat and simmer, uncovered, for 30 minutes, turning often. Remove the pears from the syrup with a slotted spoon. Arrange on a serving plate.

Boil the syrup over high heat for 8 to 12 minutes or until thick.

Add the frozen raspberries to the hot syrup. Bring slowly to a rolling boil. Allow to boil for 5 minutes. Force the sauce through a sieve and pour over the pears. Cover and refrigerate for 12 hours. The pears can be served as they are or with *Crème Chantilly* (see garnish for *Gâteau Saint Honoré*, page 556).

Pears with Sponge Cake

4 fresh pears
½ cup (125 mL) water
1 cup (250 mL) sugar
custard flavored with vanilla
or rum
2 round sponge cakes
applesauce

Peel and halve the pears. In a saucepan, mix together the water and sugar and bring to a boil. Add the pear halves to the syrup.

Cover and simmer over low heat for 15 to 20 minutes. The fruit should be tender but should not break.

Prepare the vanilla- or rum-flavored custard (see *Custards and Dessert Creams*, page 570).

Take one of the sponge cakes and spread the applesauce thickly over it. Top with the second cake.

Place the filled cake on a large round plate. Cover with the poached pear halves and pour the cooled custard over the whole.

Caramel Oranges

zest of 3 oranges
6 oranges
1 cup (250 mL) sugar
1½ cups (375 mL) water,
apple juice or orange juice

Finely grate the zest of 3 oranges. Peel the 6 oranges.

Pears Boulogne

🐦Caramelize the sugar. Add the water, the apple juice or the orange juice. Place the oranges in the syrup. Cover and simmer for 40 minutes. Remove the oranges from the syrup. Add the grated zest. Boil vigorously until the syrup is thick.

🐦Pour over the oranges and serve chilled.

SUMMER RHUBARB

4 cups (1 L) rhubarb
1½ cups (375 mL) water
¼ tsp (1 mL) baking soda
½ to ¾ cup (125 to 175 mL) sugar

🐦Remove the leaves and tips from the rhubarb. Peel and cut into 1-in. (2-cm) cubes. Prepare enough to yield 4 cups (1 L).

🐦Place the rhubarb in a saucepan with 1½ cups (375 mL)

water and ¼ tsp (1 mL) baking soda. Cover and bring to a boil over medium heat. When the mixture is boiling, stir and cook about 5 minutes longer. Remove from the heat and add the sugar.

🐦Rhubarb cooked in this manner is much easier to digest. It is never tart, so does not require much sugar.

BAKED WINTER RHUBARB

½ to 1 cup (125 to 250 mL) sugar
1 tsp (5 mL) lemon zest
pinch of cinnamon
2 cups (500 mL) rhubarb
lemon juice

🐦Wash young rhubarb but do not peel it. Remove the leaves and cut the rhubarb into 2-in. (5-cm) pieces.

🐦Blend together the sugar,

lemon zest and cinnamon. Place the rhubarb in a baking dish, sprinkling each layer with the sugar mixture and lemon juice. Let stand for 2 hours. Bake in a 300°F (150°C) oven, covered, for 1 hour.

STEWED WINTER RHUBARB

2 cups (500 mL) rhubarb
2 tbsp (30 mL) water
1 cup (250 mL) honey or sugar
cinnamon, nutmeg, lemon zest or orange zest
dried currants (optional)
candied ginger (optional)
pineapple cubes (optional)
maple sugar (optional)

🐦Wash the rhubarb and cut it into pieces.

🐦Place the rhubarb pieces in an enameled cast-iron saucepan or a glass saucepan. Add the water. Cover and cook over low heat for 20 minutes. Stir twice as it cooks. Add the honey or sugar. Stir until well blended.

🐦Flavor with the cinnamon, nutmeg and lemon or orange zest. Add some dried currants, candied ginger or a mixture of equal amounts of pineapple cubes and maple sugar, if desired.

BANANAS AU GRATIN

3 to 5 bananas, not too ripe
¼ tsp (1 mL) salt
½ cup (125 mL) toasted, soft breadcrumbs

Sautéed Bananas

3 tbsp (45 mL) butter, cut in small pieces
½ cup (125 mL) brown sugar
¼ tsp (1 mL) cinnamon

🍌 Peel and slice the bananas. Sprinkle with salt.
🍌 Combine the toasted breadcrumbs, butter, brown sugar and cinnamon. Sprinkle the bananas with this mixture. Bake in a 350°F (180°C) oven for approximately 15 minutes.

SAUTÉED BANANAS

6 bananas, not too ripe
juice of 1 lemon
3 tbsp (45 mL) butter
3 tbsp (45 mL) brown sugar
3 tsp (15 mL) rum
ice cream or whipped cream (optional)

🍌 Peel the bananas, soak them in the lemon juice and cut them in four. Place them in a bowl. Turn the brown sugar into an attractive bowl and pour the rum into a glass pitcher. Place the bananas, brown sugar and rum on a tray.
🍌 At the table, melt the butter in a chafing dish. Add the brown sugar and the rum. Stir to blend well. Place the bananas in this syrup. Cover and simmer for 3 to 4 minutes. The bananas can be served as they are or garnished with ice cream or whipped cream.

PRUNES WITH RED WINE

2 cups (500 mL) hot water
1 lb (500 g) prunes
1 cup (250 mL) sugar

Cherries Jubilee

zest of 1 lemon, grated
1 cinnamon stick
4 tbsp (60 mL) butter
2 cups (500 mL) red wine

🍒 Pour the hot water over the prunes. Cover them and leave to soak overnight.
🍒 Turn the water and the prunes into a saucepan and then add the sugar, lemon zest, cinnamon stick and butter. Bring to a boil, then allow to simmer over low heat until the prunes are tender. Boil vigorously until all the liquid has been absorbed. Add the wine. Heat, but do not boil. Serve hot or cold.

CHERRIES JUBILEE

2 cups (500 mL) fresh strawberries
1½ tbsp (25 mL) sugar
3 cups (750 mL) vanilla ice cream

1 can pitted Bing cherries
⅓ cup (75 mL) black currant jelly
¼ cup (50 mL) cognac

🍒 Two hours before serving, wash the strawberries, remove the stems and sprinkle with sugar. Refrigerate.
🍒 Wrap individual scoops of ice cream in aluminum foil and place them in the freezer.
🍒 To serve, mash the sweetened strawberries. Add the drained cherries.
🍒 In a chafing dish or an electric skillet, melt the black currant jelly, stirring constantly. Add the fruits and continue heating until the mixture is simmering.
🍒 Pour the cognac in the center of the fruits. Do not stir as this will prevent the cognac from flaming. Heat for a few seconds, then flame by placing a lighted match just above the cognac.

While the cherries are flaming, pour them over the ice cream and serve immediately.

GRAPEFRUIT HALVES

When selecting grapefruit, choose the heaviest ones as they are the juiciest.

Before preparing the grapefruit, leave them at room temperature overnight. Cut them in half and run the tip of a sharp knife around each section, without piercing the thin membrane.

Sprinkle immediately with superfine sugar. Place the grapefruit halves on a tray. Cover them with plastic wrap and leave them at room temperature until ready to serve.

For a slightly different taste, replace the sugar with maple syrup or honey.

GRAPE HEDGEHOG

1 medium eggplant
or 1 large grapefruit
green grapes
Swiss cheese
colored cocktail picks

Spear one grape and one cheese cube with each pick. Stick the garnished picks all over the eggplant or grapefruit. Serve.

The picks may be prepared ahead of time, covered and refrigerated. All that is left to do is to insert them into the eggplant or grapefruit when ready to serve.

Place the garnished eggplant or grapefruit on a bed of fir branches. The color combination is quite attractive and livens up the table.

CHESTNUTS

There are three ways to prepare chestnuts for cooking.

Slit the shell on the flat side of each chestnut with the tip of a sharp knife. Place in a saucepan of boiling water and boil for 5 minutes. Drain, remove the shells as well as the inner brown skins covering the chestnuts. The chestnuts are then ready to be cooked.

Make two crosscut gashes on the pointed side of the chestnuts with the tip of a sharp knife. Place the chestnuts in a pie plate. Add ¼ cup (125 ml) water for each pound (500 g) of chestnuts. Bake in a preheated 500°F (260°C) oven for 10 minutes. Remove the shells and the inner brown skins. The chestnuts are then ready to be cooked.

Make two crosscut gashes on the pointed end of the chestnuts with the tip of a sharp knife. Place the chestnuts in a cast-iron skillet and brown over low heat, stirring often, for approximately 15 minutes or until they are easy to hull. The chestnuts are then ready to be cooked.

BUTTERED CHESTNUTS

Prepare the chestnuts. Place in a saucepan of boiling water with a pinch of sugar. Cook for 30 minutes or until tender. Drain. Melt 3 tbsp (45 ml) of butter in a saucepan until golden brown. Add the chestnuts and stir until they are well coated with butter. Sprinkle with parsley and serve.

PURÉED CHESTNUTS

2 lbs (1 kg) chestnuts
3 cups (750 ml) consommé
1 tsp (5 ml) sugar
1 clove garlic, minced
salt and pepper to taste
4 tbsp (60 ml) butter
cream, to taste

Prepare the chestnuts according to one of the methods described above. Bring the consommé to a boil. Add the sugar, garlic, salt and pepper. Add the whole or chopped chestnuts. Cook for approximately 30 minutes or until the chestnuts are tender. Drain.

Mash the chestnuts. Add the butter and cream and beat until the puree is light and fluffy. Serve.

PASTRY AND PIES

PIES

EVERYBODY LOVES A PIE

Pastry making is a subject that is both fascinating and frustrating. It is fascinating when you can turn out wonderful, flaky pastry blindfolded, and to such marvelously gifted cooks I say, "Don't follow my rules and advice—just do it your own way." To those of you who find pastry making frustrating, remember to follow these basic rules each and every time you make pastry:

- Use shortening that is as cold and as firm as possible.
- Cut the shortening into the flour only until the pieces are the size of large garden peas.
- Use very cold water so that it will not soften the shortening.
- Use low-gluten flour, known commercially as pastry flour. Pastry made with it is less elastic.
- Bake the pastry in a preheated, hot oven.

ABOUT PIE PASTRY

There are 2 basic kinds of pie pastry: dense-textured pastry and light, multilayered puff pastry. Each is characterized by the type of fat used and by the method used to work the fat into the dry ingredients.

- Dense-textured pastry is made using cold vegetable fat or vegetable oil that is mixed with the dry ingredients using the fingers. It is used for meat pies and as pie shells for certain types of filling.
- Semi-puff pastry is made with hard, cold lard that is cut into the sifted dry ingredients using a pas-try cutter or 2 knives. French puff pastry—the most difficult kind to knead and to preserve—is made exclusively with butter.

- The pieces of cold, firm shortening, which will be mashed into layers when the crust is rolled, prevent the flour in one layer of the crust from sticking to the flour in other layers of the crust. This is what creates the flakiness. If the shortening is warm or soft before the dough is made, or if it becomes warm when mixed with the palms of the hands or when warm water is added, or if the oven temperature is low, you will not have a flaky crust.

- If your pastry starts to crumble and break when you take it out of the oven, you have used too much shortening in relation to the quantity of flour.

- Some pie doughs can be made lighter by adding lemon juice or vinegar. The acidity will break down the gluten in the flour.

MAKING PIE DOUGH

Have all the utensils and ingredients you need close at hand.

- Measure the pastry flour in the sifter, then sift with the salt. If you are a novice pastry-maker and worry that your pastry will be tough, you can add a pinch of baking powder to the dry ingredients—¼ tsp (1 mL) of baking powder per cup (250 mL) of flour is all that is needed.

- Measure the chilled shortening. Cut it into the dry ingredients using a pastry cutter or 2 knives (or knead with the fingers for dense-textured dough).

- Sprinkle the mixture with the ice water and mix it lightly with a fork. Add just enough water so that the dough is moist and elastic but does not stick to the bowl (too much liquid will toughen the dough). Mix briskly with a fork; avoid stirring too much.

- Divide the dough and roll out immediately on a lightly floured board. If you've added too much water and find that your dough is sticky, cover it with wax paper and refrigerate it until the dough is easier to knead (adding flour will not correct the problem).

- Pie doughs wrapped in wax paper will keep in the refrigerator.

ROLLING OUT PIE DOUGH

Here are a few tips on how to roll out the dough properly. Once you have the knack, your pastry will always come out light and flaky.

- Cut the dough, as needed, for a 1- or 2-crust pie. (You might want to cook an extra pie shell and perhaps tart shells at the same time as the pie, to save time.) Be sure to roll out the dough just once; re-rolling is bad for pastry.

- Place the slab of dough in the center of a lightly floured board or pastry cloth. Pat it down a little with the rolling pin. If the edges break, work them together with your fingers.

- Start rolling. Place the rolling pin across the center of the dough; roll the pin outward to the edge of the dough. Place the pin across the center of the dough again; this time roll toward you, again to the edge of the dough. Do this 2 or 3 times. Then turn

❦ TECHNIQUE ❦

NEW-METHOD PIE CRUST

1 Sift the flour and the salt into a bowl.

2 Add ½ cup (125 mL) of the sifted flour to the ice water and mix until smooth.

3 Cut the shortening into the rest of the sifted flour, working only until the pieces of shortening are the size of large garden peas.

4 Add the flour and water mixture.

the dough or work sideways. Always begin at the center, moving once to the right, once to the left.

🕭 Roll until the dough is ⅛ in. (0.3 cm) thick. (This applies to most pie doughs.)

🕭 Roll the circle of dough until it is large enough to line the pie plate and extend over the rim.

LINING A PIE PLATE

The dough should be rolled in a circle large enough to line the bottom and sides of the pie plate without stretching the dough. Stretched dough will shrink during baking.

🕭 Fold the rolled dough lightly in half, then fold into quarters.

🕭 Place this triangle on the pie plate in such a way that the bottom quarter is in the position in which it will remain.

🕭 Open one fold and ease the dough into the pie plate so that it covers half the plate—do this in such a way that you force the air out of that part of the plate ahead of the dough. (Air left under the dough will expand in the heat of the oven, raising the pastry and causing blisters to form.)

🕭 Open the other fold and ease the dough down into the plate, again expelling the air.

🕭 Gently press the dough onto the side of the plate, moving from the bottom upward, forcing out as much air as possible.

🕭 Use a knife or scissors to trim the dough around the pie plate.

MAKING PIE AND TART SHELLS

There are 2 ways of making pie and tart shells.

🕭 The first way is to roll out the dough to a thickness of ⅙ or ⅛ in. (0.4 or 0.3 cm) and stretch it into the pie or tart pan. Press the dough lightly to expel the air. Trim the edge and pierce the dough with a fork. Bake at whatever oven temperature is indicated for the particular dough you are using. Cool.

🕭 The other way is to roll out the dough to a thickness of ⅙ or ⅛ in. (0.4 or 0.3 cm) and line the pie or tart pan without stretching the dough. Trim and flute the edge. In the case of pie shells, the edge should be lightly dampened with cold water and rimmed with a ½-in. (1-cm) strip of dough before fluting. Fill the shell with dried beans to prevent shrinkage. Sear at whatever oven temperature is indicated for the kind of dough you are using. Remove the beans with a fork. Return the shell to the oven and continue baking until it is golden brown. (Keep the beans in a jar and cover with cheesecloth for later use.)

🕭 To make tart shells, cut small circles from the sheet of dough using a side plate or a saucer.

🕭 Many kinds of pie call for the shell to be baked before it is filled.

🕭 Pie fillings such as cream or lemon filling can be cooked before they are turned into the shell, or they can be raw, as in the case of sweetened fresh-fruit fillings. No matter what the filling, make sure it is lukewarm or cold before you fill the pie shell and always cool the pastry before you fill it.

🕭 If you use canned filling, use only a small amount of the juice and thicken it with tapioca or cornstarch, or a combination of both. Flour can be used as thickening, but the filling will not be as clear or as bright in color as those made with cornstarch or tapioca.

MAKING THE TOP CRUST

Whatever filling you are using, never place hot filling on top of dough. Cool it first.

🕭 To cover the filling, roll out the dough until the circle is slightly larger than your pie plate. Fold the sheet of rolled dough over double and slash it or cut designs in the center so that the steam that rises from the filling as it cooks can escape.

🕭 Rub the edge of the bottom crust with a little cold water, milk or egg yolk. Place the top layer of dough over half of the filling, then open it and ease it down over the other half of the surface.

🕭 Press around the edge to seal the 2 layers of dough. Trim the edge. Crimp the border to your liking.

BAKING PIES

The general rule for pies is to bake at a high temperature. There are many variations, but the following rules apply to most pies.

🕭 Filled pies should be baked for 8 to 10 minutes in a preheated 450°F (230°C) oven, the time varying with the size and depth of the pie. This high temperature will set the dough and prevent many a wet bottom crust.

❦ TECHNIQUE ❦

HOT-WATER PIE CRUST

1 Add the boiling water to the shortening.

2 For richer dough, beat in an egg.

3 Sift together the flour, the baking powder and the salt.

4 Add the shortening to the dry ingredients and mix until smooth.

[517]

Before the high heat has time to penetrate the filling, reduce the oven to 375°F (190°C) for most raw fruit fillings; delicate fillings with eggs and cream will require a 325°F (160°C) oven. Although the temperature requirements of pies can vary a great deal, the dough must be seared in the first 5 to 10 minutes of baking.

Most pie and tart shells require a preheated 450°F (230°C) oven; since they are not filled, the baking time is greatly reduced.

GLAZING PIE CRUST

WITH EGG WHITE

When ready to place the pie in the oven, brush the top crust with a slightly beaten egg white, using a small brush or the fingertips. When the crust is well coated with egg white, sprinkle it with sugar—the coarser the sugar, the glossier the glaze.

WITH UNSWEETENED EVAPORATED MILK

Brush the top crust with undiluted evaporated milk. Sprinkle it with sugar.

WITH CREAM, ICE WATER OR VEGETABLE OIL

Brush the top crust with the liquid of your choice. The richer the cream, the more the crust will brown. Vegetable oil is usually used for meat pies.

WITH BUTTER, MARGARINE OR SHORTENING

Brushing the top crust with a spoonful of melted butter, margarine or shortening will not only help the crust brown evenly but

also make it richer. Such a glaze is particularly suitable for fruit pie fillings, since they tend to moisten the crust.

FREEZING PASTRY AND PIES

Both pastry and crumb crusts can be frozen either baked or unbaked.

Unbaked dough: roll the dough to the appropriate size and shape it. Cut a piece of cardboard to the same size and cover it with foil. Place a layer of dough flat on the cardboard, top with 2 layers of freezer paper, then with another layer of dough. Repeat until there are several layers. Put the stack in a plastic bag, twist the bag to expel as much air as possible and close the bag with a twist tie. Storage time: 2 months.

To use, remove one piece of dough from the plastic bag. Place wax paper both on top and underneath it to prevent moisture from condensing on the dough during thawing. Thaw at room temperature for 10 to 15 minutes and treat as freshly made dough.

To serve: bake in a very hot oven (475°F or 240°C) for 8 to 10 minutes.

Baked shell: bake the shell in a very hot oven (475°F or 240°C) for 8 to 10 minutes. Cool. Set it in a rigid container to prevent crushing and wrap with aluminum foil or freezer wrap. Storage time: 4 to 6 months.

To serve: heat in a 325°F (160°C) oven for 5 to 8 minutes.

Pies can be frozen before or after baking, although fruit pies frozen unbaked will have a fresher fruit taste and crisper crust.

Unbaked: when using fresh peaches, apricots or raw apples, sprinkle them to prevent darkening with 1 tbsp (15 mL) lemon juice. Coat sweet cherries and berries with sugar and flour before adding them to the pie.

Freeze the pie and then wrap it in aluminum foil. Put the pie in a plastic bag or in freezer wrap, then seal, label, date and freeze it. Storage time: 2 to 3 months.

Baked: remove a double-crust pie from the oven when the crust is just golden; it will brown more when reheated. Cool and freeze it unwrapped, making sure that the pie is level in the freezer. Package the frozen pie as you would an unbaked pie and return it to the freezer. Recommended storage time: 4 to 6 months.

You may want to save freezer space and freeze the filling only. To use, place the semi-thawed filling in the shell when you are ready to bake the pie.

NEW-METHOD PIE CRUST

3¼ cups (800 mL) pastry flour
1 tsp (5 mL) salt
⅓ cup (75 mL) ice water
1 cup (250 mL) cold shortening

Preheat the oven to 450°F (230°C).

Sift and measure the flour. Add the salt, then sift the flour and the salt into a bowl.

❧ TECHNIQUE ❧

SEMI-PUFF PASTRY

1 Sift the flour with the salt and the sugar.

2 Cut the shortening into the flour.

3 Add the ice water and mix with 2 knives.

4 Place the butter in the center of the dough.

❧ Mix together the ice water and ½ cup (125 mL) of the sifted flour; mix until smooth.

❧ Cut the shortening into the rest of the sifted flour, working only until the pieces of shortening are the size of large garden peas. Add the flour and water mixture. Stir lightly until the dough clears the sides of the bowl.

❧ Roll out and fit into a pie plate. Bake until golden.

CORN OIL PIE CRUST

2¼ cups (550 mL) flour, sifted
1 tsp (5 mL) salt
9 tbsp (135 mL) corn oil
¼ cup (50 mL) + 1½ tsp (7 mL) cold milk

❧ Sift the flour and the salt into a bowl. Add the oil to the milk but do not stir the mixture. Pour it all at once into the dry ingredients and stir lightly with a fork until the dough is well blended.

❧ With the hands, form the dough into a smooth ball and divide it in 2.

❧ Place each piece of dough between 2 sheets of wax paper cut 12 in. (30 cm) square. Flatten the dough lightly with a rolling pin. Roll out first one piece of dough then the other until it reaches the edges of the wax paper. Lift the top sheet of wax paper—if the dough breaks, patch it up. Turn the dough upside-down and carefully remove the bottom sheet of wax paper. (To prevent the wax paper from slipping, roll the dough on a damp surface.)

❧ Fit the bottom layer of dough into a pie plate. Fill. Then place the other layer of dough over the filling. Bake according to whatever pie recipe you are following.

❧ This dough should be used immediately.

HOT-WATER PIE CRUST

Pie crust made by the hot-water, or beaten, method can be delicious and crisp, but it will never be flaky. It is often used for meat pies.

¼ cup (50 mL) boiling water
½ cup (125 mL) shortening
1½ cups (375 mL) pastry flour
½ tsp (2 mL) salt
½ tsp (2 mL) baking powder

❧ Bring the water to a boil. Add the water to the shortening, stirring the mixture until smooth.

❧ Sift and measure the flour. Add the salt and the baking powder to the flour and sift together the dry ingredients.

❧ Add the shortening to the dry ingredients. Mix until the dough is smooth. Cover and refrigerate for 1 hour.

❧ Roll out and use this dough as you would any other.

❧ For a richer dough, beat an egg into the water and shortening mixture.

PUFF PASTRY

¼ lb (125 g) sweet butter
¾ cup (175 mL) sifted flour
¼ tsp (1 mL) salt
¼ cup (50 mL) ice water

❧ Quarter 1 lb (500 g) of butter lengthwise. (Use 1 quarter for 1 puff-pastry recipe.) Divide the ¼-lb (125-g) piece of butter into 3 pieces. Wrap these pieces together in wax paper and refrigerate.

❧ Mix the flour with the salt and the ice water but do not form a ball. Turn the mixture onto a pastry board and knead it with the fingers of one hand while pressing the dough with the palm of the other hand. (This way you will be able to use all of the flour and form a ball with the dough; at this stage the dough can be kneaded as much as necessary.)

❧ On a floured pastry board, roll the dough into a rectangle measuring 11 x 6 in. (28 x 15 cm). The corners should be as sharp as possible. Use the palm of the hand to even out the sides. The dough will be somewhat difficult to work with, but it can shaped.

❧ Place the 3 pieces of butter at one end of the dough, placing the first piece about 1½ in. (4 cm) from the edge. Fold the dough double, to cover the butter. Pinch together the 3 open sides to ½ in. (1 cm) from the edge to prevent the butter from seeping out.

❧ Wrap the dough in aluminum foil. Refrigerate for 30 minutes.

❧ Place the chilled dough on a lightly floured pastry board, with the pinched end to your left, the folded end to your right. Flatten out the butter with a rolling pin.

❧ Roll the dough in both directions, turning the slab over frequently, until you have an 18- x 6-in. (45- x 15-cm) rectangle. The corners should be as sharp as pos-

SHORTBREAD PASTRY

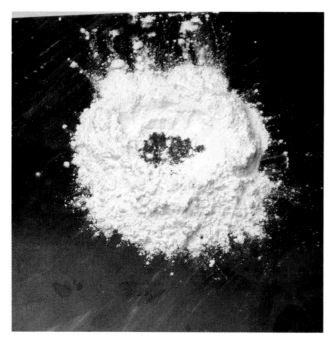

1 Heap the flour onto the middle of a pastry board and form a well.

2 Place the sugar, the egg yolks, the butter and the water in the well.

3 Mix the ingredients.

4 Knead the pastry.

sible, and the dough should be of even thickness throughout. If the butter is not cold enough, and therefore seeps through, flour it lightly with the fingertips.

🙟 Fold the dough over to form a 6-in. (15-cm) square.

🙟 Cover and refrigerate for 30 minutes.

🙟 Roll out the dough again to form a 18- x 6-in. (45- x 15-cm) rectangle, and fold it once more into a 6-in. (15-cm) square. Repeat this procedure 3 times, refrigerating the dough for 30 minutes between each additional rolling of the dough.

SEMI-PUFF PASTRY

4 cups (1 L) all-purpose flour
1 tsp (5 mL) salt
1 tsp (5 mL) sugar
1 lb (500 g) cold shortening
¾ to 1 cup (175 to 250 mL) ice water
¼ lb (125 g) butter, flattened in a square

🙟 Sift together into a bowl the flour, salt and sugar. Using a pastry cutter, cut in the cold shortening, working only until the mixture is coarse. Pour in the ice water and blend the mixture with 2 knives until the dough clears the bowl.

🙟 For this pastry to turn out well, measure the water carefully and add only as much as is needed to make the dough workable. Too much water will make the dough sticky, hard to roll out and tough when cooked. In general, use 4 to 6 tbsp (60 to 90 mL) water for 1 cup (250 mL) of flour.

🙟 Turn the dough onto a pastry board; working with your fingers, knead it for a few minutes and shape it into a ball. Flatten the dough lightly with a rolling pin and roll it into a square.

🙟 Place the butter in the center of the dough then, working with your fingers, flatten the butter into the dough. Fold the dough on 3 sides, like an envelope, sealing the edges so that the butter does not leak out. Roll out. Fold into 3 once more. Roll out again and fold over.

🙟 Wrap and refrigerate for 6 to 24 hours. This dough keeps well; in fact, letting it rest a while will make it lighter.

SHORTBREAD PASTRY

2 cups (500 mL) pastry flour, sifted
5 tbsp (75 mL) sugar
4 egg yolks
½ cup (125 mL) butter, not too cold, cut into pieces
1 tbsp (15 mL) ice water

🙟 Heap the flour onto the middle of a pastry board. In the center of the flour, form a well large enough to contain your hand.

🙟 Place the sugar, the egg yolks, the butter and the ice water in the well.

🙟 Sprinkle a little of the flour over the egg yolks and start mixing with your hand, working in the center of the circle and, little by little, mixing in the surrounding flour.

🙟 When all of the ingredients are mixed, knead the dough by forming it into a ball and pushing it away from you firmly with the palms of the hands. Bring the dough back and knead again until all the ingredients are blended. Form a ball of the dough and knead it until it is smooth and round. Wrap it in wax paper and refrigerate for 1 to 3 hours.

🙟 If the dough is too hard to roll, let it stand at room temperature for 30 to 50 minutes. Roll with a lightly floured rolling pin in short, rotating motions, working up and down on the dough. Roll ¼ in. (0.5 cm) thick.

🙟 Without stretching the dough, place it in a pie plate. Trim it by running the rolling pin along the edge.

🙟 Cover the dough with aluminum foil and fill the foil with rice.

🙟 Bake in a preheated 350°F (170°C) oven for about 10 minutes. Once the edges are browned, the dough will rise no further. Carefully remove the aluminum foil and rice, and bake the shell another 10 minutes or until the dough is well browned.

🙟 Cool it on a cake rack before unmolding. Then fill the shell.

FRENCH-STYLE SWEET TART SHELLS

2½ cups (625 mL) pastry flour
⅔ cup (150 mL) superfine sugar
½ tsp (2 mL) salt
1 cup (250 mL) cold butter
2 eggs
1 tsp (5 mL) grated lemon zest

🙟 Heat the oven to 375°F (190°C).

🙟 Sift and measure the flour.

Add the sugar and the salt and sift the dry ingredients together in a bowl. Cut the butter into the dry ingredients, working until the mixture has the consistency of fine breadcrumbs.

🍂 Beat the eggs, then add the grated zest. Add the eggs and lemon zest to the flour mixture. Mix the dough with a fork until smooth and shape it into a ball.

🍂 Wrap and refrigerate the dough until it is firm enough to roll.

🍂 On a lightly floured pastry board, roll out the dough until it is 1/6 to 1/8 in. (0.4 to 0.3 cm) thick. Cut circles in the dough and lay them in a tart pan.

CRUMB-CRUST PIE SHELLS

🍂 See the chart below for quantities.

🍂 Soften the butter.

🍂 Place the biscuits or cereal between two sheets of wax paper. Crush with a rolling pin. Measure.

🍂 Add the sugar and butter to the crumbs and mix, reserving 3 tbsp (45 mL) of the mixture to sprinkle on top of the filling. With the fingers, press the mixture onto the bottom and sides of a pie plate.

🍂 Bake in a preheated 375°F (190°C) oven for 8 minutes. Cool the shell before filling it.

NO-BAKE SPICY CRUMB-CRUST PIE SHELL

1⅓ cups (325 mL) crumbs
⅓ cup (75 mL) brown sugar
⅓ cup (75 mL) melted butter
½ tsp (2 mL) cinnamon
or nutmeg

🍂 Use graham crackers or vanilla or chocolate wafers. Crush them with a rolling pin to make 1⅓ cups (325 mL) of crumbs. Add the remainder of the ingredients and mix well.

🍂 Press into the bottom and sides of a 9-in. (23-cm) pie plate. Refrigerate the shell before filling it.

🍂 If desired, reserve ¼ cup (50 mL) of the mixture to sprinkle over the filling.

BLENDER LEMON MERINGUE PIE

1 single-crust baked pie shell

FILLING:
3 egg yolks
¾ cup (175 mL) sugar
2 tbsp (30 mL) cornstarch
pinch of salt
1½ cups (375 mL) milk
1½ lemons, peeled and halved
2 in. (5 cm) lemon zest

MERINGUE:
3 egg whites
6 tbsp (90 mL) sugar

🍂 Prepare a single-crust baked pie shell.

🍂 To make the filling, place all the ingredients in a blender jar in the order given. Cover and blend at high speed for 1 minute.

🍂 Turn the mixture into a saucepan and cook over very low heat, stirring almost constantly,

CRUMB-CRUST PIE SHELLS

	BUTTER	COOKIE CRUMBS	SUGAR
Graham crackers (about 16)	¼ cup (50 mL)	1⅓ cup (325 mL)	¼ cup (50 mL)
Vanilla wafers (about 24)	¼ cup (50 mL)	1⅓ cup (325 mL)	None
Chocolate wafers (about 18)	3 tbsp (45 mL)	1⅓ cup (325 mL)	None
Ginger snaps (20 2-in. or 5-cm cookies)	6 tbsp (90 mL)	1⅓ cup (325 mL)	None
Corn flakes (about 3 cups or 750 mL)	¼ cup (50 mL)	1⅓ cup (325 mL)	2 tbsp (30 mL)

Lemon Pie with Nutmeg

until the mixture is creamy. Cool and use to fill the baked pie shell.

• To make the meringue, beat the 3 egg whites until stiff. Gradually mix in the 6 tbsp (90 mL) sugar. Spread the meringue over the lemon filling, covering it entirely.

• Bake in a 400°F (200°C) oven for 7 to 8 minutes or until golden.

LEMON PIE WITH NUTMEG

PASTRY:
1 unbaked pie shell
½ tsp (2 mL) grated nutmeg

FILLING:
1 cup (250 mL) sugar
4 tbsp (60 mL) flour
pinch of salt
½ cup (125 mL) water
3 egg yolks, beaten
1 cup (250 mL) water

2 tbsp (30 mL) butter
juice and zest of 1 lemon

MERINGUE:
3 egg whites, stiffly beaten
6 tbsp (90 mL) sugar
nutmeg

• Roll out the dough and place it in a pie plate. Sprinkle the bottom of the pie shell with the grated nutmeg, pressing it in with the fingertips. Brush the dough with a little milk.

• Bake in a 450°F (230°C) oven for 10 minutes. Reduce heat to 400°F (200°C) and bake it for another 6 to 7 minutes. Cool.

• To make the filling, mix together in a bowl the sugar, flour, salt and ½ cup (125 mL) of water. Add the beaten egg yolks and the remaining 1 cup (250 mL) of water. Cook the mixture in a double boiler until thick. Remove from the heat, then add the but-

ter, the lemon juice and the zest. Cool.

• Turn the cooled filling into the baked, cooled pie shell.

• To make the meringue, beat the egg whites until stiff and mix in the 6 tbsp (90 mL) of sugar. Spread the meringue evenly over the pie and sprinkle it with nutmeg.

• Brown in a 375°F (190°C) oven.

• Let the pie cool thoroughly before serving it.

ORANGE MERINGUE PIE

3 egg yolks
½ cup (125 mL) sugar
3 tbsp (45 mL) flour
1 cup (250 mL) orange juice
juice of 1 lemon
1 baked pie shell

• Beat the egg yolks with the sugar and the flour. Add the orange juice and the lemon juice. Cook over low heat, stirring constantly, until the mixture is smooth and creamy. Cool.

• Turn the cooled orange filling into the baked pie shell.

• Cover with *3-Egg Meringue* (see page 534). Bake the meringue until it is golden brown.

• Serve the pie cold.

GRATED APPLE PIE

CRUST:
1 cup (250 mL) flour
½ tsp (2 mL) baking powder
pinch of salt
¼ cup (50 mL) butter

2 tbsp (30 mL) sugar
1 egg
½ tsp (2 mL) vanilla

FILLING:
4 large apples, peeled and pared
2 tbsp (30 mL) lemon zest
2 tbsp (30 mL) lemon juice
1 cup (250 mL) sugar
1 egg

🍂 Sift together in a bowl the flour, baking powder and salt. Using 2 knives, cut in the butter until it has the consistency of fine breadcrumbs.

🍂 With a fork, beat together the 2 tbsp (30 mL) sugar, 1 egg and the vanilla. Stir this into the flour and butter mixture. Using your fingers, press the mixture onto the bottom and sides of an 8- or 9-in. (20- or 23-cm) pie plate.

🍂 To make the filling, grate the pared apples. To the apples add the lemon zest, the lemon juice, the 1 cup (250 mL) sugar and the egg. Beat until well mixed.

🍂 Lightly brush the bottom of the pie crust with soft butter. Turn the apple mixture into the shell. Bake for 50 to 60 minutes in a 350°F (180°C) oven.

🍂 Serve the pie hot or cold.

FAVORITE APPLE PIE

pie dough of your choice
peeled apples
1 tbsp (15 mL) butter, diced
½ tsp (2 mL) cinnamon
½ tsp (2 mL) nutmeg
zest of ½ lemon, grated
pinch of salt
¾ cup (175 mL) maple sugar

or brown sugar
juice 1 lemon
cheese

🍂 Roll out the bottom crust and line a pie plate with it.

🍂 Slice the peeled apples directly over the dough, piling them quite high in the center. Dot them with the diced butter.

🍂 Mix together the cinnamon, nutmeg, grated lemon zest, salt and maple sugar or brown sugar. Sprinkle this mixture over the apples. Pour the lemon juice on top.

🍂 Roll out the second crust and cover the filling with it. To prevent the juice from spilling over in the oven, dip a 1-in. (2-cm) strip of cotton in milk and place it around the edge of the dough. (Or place a band of aluminum foil around the edge of the pie.)

🍂 Bake in a 425°F (220°C) oven for 15 minutes. Reduce the heat to 325°F (160°C) and bake for 50 minutes longer.

🍂 This pie is delicious served with wedges of Cheddar or some other cheese.

DUTCH APPLE PIE

pie dough of your choice
6 to 8 apples, peeled and sliced
½ cup (125 mL) sugar
1 tbsp (15 mL) cornstarch
¼ tsp (1 mL) nutmeg
¼ tsp (1 mL) cinnamon
⅔ cup (150 mL) 10% cream
1 tbsp (15 mL) diced butter

🍂 Roll out the dough and press into a 9-in. (23-cm) pie plate. Fill it with the sliced apples.

🍂 Mix together the sugar, cornstarch, nutmeg and cinnamon. Sprinkle the mixture over the apples and mix lightly. Pour the cream over the filling and dot it

Favorite Apple Pie

with the diced butter.

🍂 Bake in a 375°F (190°C) oven for 30 to 45 minutes or until the apples are tender.

SCOTTISH APPLE PIE

pie dough of your choice
6 to 8 apples
¾ cup (175 mL) brown sugar
¼ cup (50 mL) hot water
1 egg, well beaten
¾ cup (175 mL) graham cracker crumbs
¼ cup (50 mL) pastry flour
1 tsp (5 mL) cinnamon
¼ tsp (1 mL) nutmeg
pinch of ginger
4 tbsp (60 mL) shortening or butter, softened

🍂 Roll out the dough and line a 9-in. (23-cm) pie plate.

🍂 Peel and core the apples and cut them into 8 sections length-wise. Place in an attractive pattern in the unbaked pie shell.

🍂 Mix together the brown sugar and the hot water then add the well-beaten egg. Place this mixture over the apples.

🍂 Mix together the graham cracker crumbs, flour, spices and shortening or softened butter. Sprinkle the mixture over the apples and brown sugar.

🍂 Bake the pie in a 450°F (230°C) oven until it starts to brown, in approximately 20 minutes. Reduce the heat to 325°F (160°C) and bake it for 20 minutes longer.

🍂 Serve the pie warm, with or without cheese.

DEEP-DISH APPLE PIE WITH FARINA

1¼ cups (300 mL) sugar
1 cup (250 mL) water
1 lemon, thinly sliced
4 tbsp (60 mL) farina
1 tsp (5 mL) nutmeg
5 to 8 apples, peeled and sliced
3 tbsp (45 mL) butter
pie dough of your choice
1 tbsp (15 mL) sugar

🍂 Mix the sugar and the water. Cook the mixture until it has the consistency of a light syrup. Add the sliced lemon and simmer for 10 minutes. Add the farina and the nutmeg, stirring the mixture constantly; add the apples.

🍂 Cook this mixture for 5 minutes over low heat, stirring frequently. Add the butter and stir. Turn the filling into a pudding dish.

🍂 Roll out the dough and place it over the apple filling. Sprinkle the dough with 1 tbsp (15 mL) of sugar.

🍂 Bake the pie in a 450°F (230°C) oven for 25 to 30 minutes, or until it is golden brown.

CHANTILLY STRAWBERRY PIE

1 baked, shortbread pie shell (see page 522)
2 cups (500 mL) strawberries
1 cup (250 mL) whipping cream
1 tbsp (15 mL) icing sugar
1 tsp (5 mL) vanilla

🍂 Unmold the baked, cooled pie crust.

🍂 Hull the strawberries and wipe them clean with a damp cloth. Set them on paper towels and let them dry thoroughly.

Scottish Apple Pie

▰ When you are ready to serve the pie, whip the cream and add the sugar and vanilla. Turn the cream mixture into the pie shell.

▰ Arrange the strawberries attractively in the whipped cream. Sprinkle them generously with the icing sugar and serve the pie.

ENGLISH STRAWBERRY PIE

French-Style Sweet Tart **dough (page 522)**
4 cups (1 L) strawberries
3 tbsp (45 mL) cornstarch
½ cup (125 mL) sugar
1 tbsp (15 mL) lemon juice
1 cup (250 mL) whipping cream
¼ cup (50 mL) sugar
1 tbsp (15 mL) vanilla

▰ Roll out the dough and line a 9-in. (23-cm) pie plate. Bake and cool the pie shell.

▰ Wash and hull the strawberries. Set aside 2 cups (500 mL) of the nicest strawberries. Mash the remaining 2 cups (500 mL). Add the cornstarch, ½ cup (125 mL) of sugar and lemon juice.

▰ Cook the mixture over low heat, stirring constantly, until it is smooth and creamy. Cool.

▰ Fill the cooled pie shell with the 2 cups (500 mL) of whole strawberries and top them with the cooked strawberries. Refrigerate.

▰ When ready to serve the pie, whip the cream and add the sugar and the vanilla. Spread the whipped cream over the filling.

Chantilly Strawberry Pie

MOTHER'S BLUEBERRY PIE

pie dough of your choice
4 cups (1 L) blueberries
¼ cup (50 mL) water
⅔ cup (150 mL) sugar
2 tbsp (30 mL) cornstarch
2 tbsp (30 mL) cold water

▰ Line a 9-in. (23-cm) pie plate with the pie dough of your choice. Bake the shell in a 400°F (200°C) oven. Unmold and cool it.

▰ Wash and clean the blueberries. Cook ¾ cup (175 mL) of the blueberries in ¼ cup (50 mL) of water until they are tender. Force the blueberries through a sieve or put them through a food mill to mash them thoroughly.

▰ Place the blueberry purée in a saucepan. Add the sugar and the cornstarch blended with the 2 tbsp (30 mL) of cold water.

Cook the sauce over medium heat, stirring constantly, until it is transparent and smooth.

▰ Pour the sauce, while very hot, over the remaining blueberries. Mix well. Cover and refrigerate the filling until you are ready to serve the pie.

▰ Then, turn the blueberry cream into the cooked, cooled pie shell. If desired, garnish the pie with sweetened whipped cream.

DE LUXE APRICOT PIE

1 4-oz (125-g) package cream cheese
1 cup (250 mL) sour cream
1 baked puff-pastry
or semi-puff pastry
pie shell (pages 520, 522)
1 can peeled apricot halves

Apple and Cherry Pie

DRIED PEACH OR APRICOT PIE

½ lb (250 g) dried peaches
or apricots
1 slice lemon
¾ cup (175 mL) sugar
2 tbsp (30 mL) cornstarch
or flour
¼ cup (50 mL) cold water
or orange juice
1 unbaked pie shell

❧ Thoroughly wash the peaches or apricots. Cover them with boiling water and let stand for 2 hours.
❧ Bring the fruit to a boil; cover and simmer for 20 minutes. Add lemon to taste. Drain, reserving the liquid. Add the sugar to 1½ cups (375 mL) of the liquid, pour over the fruit and cook for another 3 minutes. Blend the cornstarch or flour with the cold water or orange juice to thicken the fruit mixture.
❧ Turn the fruit into the unbaked pie shell and place strips of pastry in a crisscross pattern across the top.
❧ Bake in a 450°F (230°C) oven until the crust is golden brown.

½ cup (125 mL) sugar
1 tsp (5 mL) cinnamon
or rose water

❧ Mix the cream cheese and the sour cream until the mixture is light and fluffy. Refrigerate.
❧ Half an hour before serving, fill the pie shell with the cheese mixture. Garnish it with the apricot halves, which must be well drained, and sprinkle with the sugar mixed with the cinnamon or the rose water (available at any pharmacy). Refrigerate the pie until you are ready to serve it.
❧ Any canned fruit or previously poached fresh fruit may be substituted for the apricots.

APPLE AND CHERRY PIE

pie dough of your choice
1 tbsp (15 mL) butter, melted

3 unpeeled apples, grated
1 cup (250 mL) canned cherries, drained
½ cup (125 mL) sugar
1 tsp (5 mL) nutmeg
1 tsp (5 mL) butter, diced

❧ Roll out half the dough, line a pie plate with it and brush the surface with the melted butter. Roll out and set aside the top crust.
❧ Fill the unbaked shell with the grated, unpeeled apples. Cover the apples with the well-drained cherries then sprinkle the fruit with the sugar and the nutmeg. Dot with the butter.
❧ Cover the filling with the remaining dough and bake in a 400°F (200°C) oven for 40 minutes.

FRESH PEACH PIE PRALINE

pie dough of your choice
4 cups (1 L) fresh peaches, peeled and sliced
¾ cup (175 mL) sugar
1½ tsp (7 mL) cornstarch
2 tsp (10 mL) lemon juice
¼ tsp (1 mL) almond extract

¼ cup (50 mL) all-purpose flour
⅓ cup (75 mL) brown sugar
½ cup (125 mL) walnuts, chopped
3 tbsp (45 mL) butter

🍂 Roll out the dough and line a 9-in. (23-cm) pie plate.

🍂 Mix together in a bowl the peaches, sugar, cornstarch, lemon juice and almond extract.

🍂 In another bowl, mix together the flour, brown sugar and chopped walnuts. Add the butter and blend with a fork until the mixture is crumbly.

🍂 Sprinkle ⅓ of the walnut mixture into the pie shell. Turn the peach mixture into the shell and top with the remaining walnut mixture.

🍂 Bake in a 425°F (220°C) oven for 45 minutes.

GLAZED PEACH PIE

2 cups (500 mL) water
¾ cup (175 mL) sugar
½ tsp (2 mL) vanilla
6 fresh peaches, peeled
½ cup (125 mL) peach, apricot or strawberry jam
1 baked shortbread pie shell (page 522)
6 tbsp (90 mL) apricot jam
1 tbsp (15 mL) cold water
¼ cup (50 mL) slivered almonds

🍂 Bring the water to boil in a skillet. Add the sugar and vanilla. Boil for 5 minutes. Add the peeled peach halves and poach them over medium heat for 15 minutes. Set the peaches aside to cool.

🍂 Spread the ½ cup (125 mL) jam of your choice over the unmolded pie shell. Cover the jam with the cooled peach halves.

🍂 Heat the 6 tbsp (90 mL) of apricot jam and the cold water. Brush the peaches with this syrup and, cool the pie thoroughly. Sprinkle the fruit with the almonds and serve.

RHUBARB PIE

pie dough of your choice
1 cup (250 mL) sugar
1 tsp (5 mL) orange zest, grated
1 tbsp (15 mL) flour
2 tbsp (30 mL) farina
½ tsp (2 mL) salt
3 cups (750 mL) diced raw rhubarb
1 tbsp (15 mL) lemon juice
2 tbsp (30 mL) melted butter

🍂 Roll out half of the dough and line a pie plate with it. Roll out the top crust and set it aside.

🍂 Mix together all the other ingredients, then turn the rhubarb mixture into the pie shell. Cover with the top crust.

🍂 Bake the pie in a 400°F (200°C) oven for 40 minutes.

PINK SPRING PIE

2½ cups (625 mL) diced fresh rhubarb
¾ cup (175 mL) sugar
2½ tbsp (40 mL) farina
1 tsp (5 mL) lemon juice
1 tsp (5 mL) grated lemon zest
pinch of nutmeg
pinch of salt
2 to 3 cups (500 to 750 mL) strawberries
1 tbsp (15 mL) butter
dough for 1 single-crust pie

🍂 Mix together the diced rhubarb, sugar, farina, lemon juice, grated lemon zest, nutmeg and salt. Let

Pink Spring Pie

the mixture stand for 15 minutes. Add the cleaned whole strawberries and mix with care.

🍃 Pour this fruit filling into a baking dish. Dot it with butter and top with the pastry dough.

🍃 Bake in a 400°F (200°C) oven for 30 minutes or until the crust is golden brown.

AMERICAN PUMPKIN PIE

pie dough of your choice
⅔ cup (150 mL) brown sugar
1 tsp (5 mL) cinnamon
¾ tsp (3 mL) ginger
½ tsp (2 mL) salt
½ tsp (2 mL) orange zest
2 eggs
¼ cup (50 mL) water
1¼ cups (300 mL) fresh
or canned pumpkin
1 cup (250 mL) milk
⅓ cup (75 mL) strained orange juice
¼ tsp (1 mL) vanilla
3 tbsp (45 mL) unblanched almonds, slivered

🍃 Roll out the dough and line a 9-in. (23-cm) pie plate.

🍃 Mix together in a bowl the brown sugar, cinnamon, ginger, salt and orange zest. Beat the eggs lightly and add them to the sugar mixture. Stir well. Stir in the water, pumpkin, milk, orange juice and vanilla.

🍃 Pour the filling into the prepared pie shell. Sprinkle it with the slivered almonds.

🍃 Bake the pie in a 450°F (230°C)

oven for 10 minutes. Reduce the heat to 325°F (160°C) and continue baking for approximately 45 minutes more or until the filling is set (when the blade of a knife inserted in the center comes out clean).

🍃 Garnish with a crown of whipped cream.

ICE CREAM PIE

18 chocolate wafers
½ cup (125 mL) melted butter
2 squares (1 oz or 30 g each) unsweetened chocolate
½ cup (125 mL) sugar
⅔ cup (150 mL) evaporated milk
1 tbsp (15 mL) butter
4 cups (1 L) coffee ice cream

🍃 Crush the wafers with a rolling pin. Mix the fine crumbs with the ½ cup (125 mL) of melted butter. Pat the crumb mixture evenly into a 9-in. (23-cm) pie plate and refrigerate the crust until it is firm.

🍃 Melt the chocolate in a double boiler, along with the sugar, evaporated milk and the butter. Stir the mixture until it is smooth, then set it aside to cool.

🍃 Fill the wafer crust with the slightly softened coffee ice cream, pour the chocolate sauce on top and freeze the pie until it is set.

🍃 To store, wrap the pie in a double thickness of aluminium foil or freezer paper. It will keep for 6 to 8 weeks.

ICE CREAM PIE WITH CHOCOLATE CRUST

2 squares unsweetened chocolate
2 tbsp (30 mL) butter
2 tbsp (30 mL) light cream
⅔ cup (150 mL) icing sugar
1½ cups 375 mL) grated coconut
4 cups (1 L) ice cream of your choice

🍃 Melt the chocolate and the butter in the top of a double boiler.

🍃 When the chocolate is melted, add the cream, icing sugar and coconut. Mix to blend.

🍃 Pat the chocolate mixture evenly into a buttered 8-in. (20-cm) pie plate. Refrigerate for 2 to 4 hours or until the crust is set.

🍃 Remove the pie crust from the refrigerator 20 minutes before serving. Unmold the crust and fill it with scoops of ice cream.

CHOCOLATE MOUSSE PIE

1 chocolate-wafer pie shell (see *Ice Cream Pie*, above)
1 6-oz (175-g) package chocolate chips
1 whole egg
2 egg yolks
1 tsp (5 mL) rum
2 egg whites
1 cup (250 mL) whipping cream

🍃 Press the chocolate-wafer mixture onto the bottom and sides of a 9-in. (23-cm) pie plate. Bake and cool the shell.

🍃 Melt the chocolate chips over hot (not boiling) water. When the chocolate has melted, remove it from the heat and add the whole egg and the 2 egg yolks, one at a time, beating vigorously after each addition. Add the rum.

෧ Beat the 2 egg whites until stiff. Then whip the cream. Add both the beaten egg whites and the whipped cream to the chocolate mixture. Blend well.

෧ Turn into the baked, cooled pie shell. Refrigerate the pie for 1 hour before serving.

෧ If desired, garnish the pie with whipped cream or ice cream.

SUGAR PIE

pie dough of your choice
½ tsp (2 mL) baking soda
½ cup (375 mL) maple syrup
1 cup (250 mL) all-purpose flour
1 cup (250 mL) brown sugar
½ cup (125 mL) butter

෧ Roll out the dough and line a 9-in. (23-cm) pie plate.

෧ Stir the baking soda into the maple syrup and mix until the baking soda has dissolved. Pour the syrup into the unbaked pie shell.

෧ Using your fingers, mix together the flour, the brown sugar and the butter, working until the mixture is crumbly.

෧ Pour this mixture over the maple syrup.

෧ Bake the pie in a 350°F (180°C) oven for 30 minutes. The filling sometimes runs over, so you might want to place a sheet of aluminum foil on the bottom of the oven to protect it.

Chocolate Mousse Pie

MAPLE SYRUP PIE

pie dough of your choice
1 cup (250 mL) maple syrup
½ cup (125 mL) water
3 tbsp (45 mL) cornstarch
2 tbsp (30 mL) cold water
2 tbsp (30 mL) butter
¼ cup (50 mL) chopped nuts

෧ Roll out the dough and line a pie plate with it.

෧ Boil the maple syrup and the ½ cup (125 mL) water for 5 minutes. Blend the cornstarch with the 2 tbsp (30 mL) cold water, then add this to the syrup.

෧ Cook, stirring constantly, until the mixture is transparent and smooth. Add the butter and the chopped nuts. Let cool.

෧ Turn the cooled mixture into an unbaked pie shell. Cover with more dough.

෧ Bake in a 400°F (200°C) oven for 25 to 30 minutes.

MAPLE AND NUT PIE

pie dough of your choice
4 eggs, beaten
3 tbsp (45 mL) melted butter
1⅓ cups (325 mL) maple syrup
1⅓ cups (325 mL) brown sugar, well packed
pinch of salt
3 tbsp (45 mL) all-purpose flour
1 tsp (5 mL) vanilla
1½ cups (375 mL) whole nuts

෧ Line 2 9-in. (23-cm) pie plates with the dough and bake the shells in a 375°F (190°C) oven for 20 to 25 minutes. Cool and refrigerate the shells until you are ready to prepare the pies.

❧ Beat the eggs until light and fluffy. Add the melted butter, maple syrup, brown sugar and salt. Blend thoroughly.

❧ Sift the flour over the egg mixture. Add the vanilla and beat the mixture with a hand beater until it is smooth. Add the nuts.

❧ Divide the filling into the 2 pie shells. Bake the pies until a knife inserted in the center comes out clean.

❧ Black or ordinary walnuts are particularly good in this pie.

PECAN PIE

pie dough of your choice
¼ cup (50 mL) butter
1¼ cups (300 mL) brown sugar
pinch of salt
¾ cup (175 mL) corn syrup
3 eggs, well beaten
1 cup (250 mL) pecans
1 tsp (5 mL) vanilla

❧ Roll out the dough and line an 8-in. (20-cm) pie plate.

❧ Cream the butter. Gradually add the brown sugar and the salt, while beating. Add the corn syrup, beaten eggs, nuts and vanilla. Mix well.

❧ Turn the mixture into the prepared pie shell.

❧ Bake in a 350°F (180°C) oven for 40 to 50 minutes or until the blade of a knife inserted in the center comes out clean.

❧ Cool and serve.

FLUFFY CREAM CHEESE PIE

1 crumb-crust pie shell (page 523)
12 oz (350 g) cream cheese
2 tbsp (30 mL) butter
½ cup (125 mL) sugar
1 egg, well beaten
2 tbsp (30 mL) flour
⅔ cup (150 mL) milk
¼ cup (50 mL) fresh lemon juice
2 tbsp (30 mL) grated lemon zest

❧ Press the crumb mixture along the bottom and sides of a 9-in. (23-cm) pie plate, saving ¼ cup (50 mL) of the crumbs to be used as a garnish. Bake and cool the pie shell.

❧ Beat the cream cheese and the butter together until light and fluffy. Add the sugar and the beaten egg. Mix well, then add the flour and the milk. Stir until the mixture is smooth. Add the lemon juice and the grated lemon zest.

❧ Pour the filling into the cooled pie shell. Sprinkle the top with the reserved crumbs.

❧ Bake in a 350°F (180°C) oven for 35 minutes.

❧ Refrigerate for 4 to 5 hours before serving.

NEW YORK CHEESE PIE

1 crumb-crust pie shell (page 523)
12 to 14 oz (350 to 400 g) cream cheese
2 whole eggs
1 cup (250 mL) sugar
1 tsp (5 mL) grated lemon zest
2 tbsp (30 mL) cognac
2 cups (500 mL) sour cream
2 tsp (10 mL) vanilla
8 tsp (40 mL) sugar

❧ Press the crumb mixture along the bottom and sides of a 9-in. (23-cm) pie plate. Bake and cool the shell.

❧ Beat the cream cheese, eggs, sugar, grated lemon zest and cognac until very light and fluffy.

❧ Turn into the baked and cooled pie shell and bake in a 300°F (150°C) oven for 30 minutes. The filling will be not quite firm so refrigerate the pie until it is firm.

❧ Meanwhile, mix the sour cream, the vanilla and the 8 tsp (40 mL) of sugar. Spread this mixture over the chilled pie.

❧ Bake in a 250°F (120°C) oven for 10 minutes. Refrigerate the pie for 12 to 24 hours before serving it.

STRAWBERRY CHIFFON PIE

1 tbsp (15 mL) unflavored gelatin
¼ cup (50 mL) cold water
3 egg yolks
¼ cup (50 mL) sugar
½ tsp (2 mL) salt
2 tsp (10 mL) lemon juice
2 cups (500 mL) mashed strawberries (fresh or frozen)

3 egg whites
½ tsp (2 mL) cream of tartar
½ cup (125 mL) sugar
1 baked pie shell

🥄 Soak the gelatin in the cold water for 5 minutes.

🥄 Beat the egg yolks in the top of a double boiler. Add the ¼ cup (50 mL) of sugar, the salt and the lemon juice. Mix well. Place over boiling water and cook, stirring frequently, until the mixture is smooth and creamy. Add the gelatin and the mashed strawberries. Beat vigorously for 1 minute.

🥄 Remove from the heat and refrigerate the mixture until it is half set.

🥄 Beat the egg whites with the cream of tartar until they are stiff. Gradually add the ½ cup (125 mL) sugar, while still beating.

🥄 Fold the beaten egg whites into the strawberry mixture, stirring to blend thoroughly. Turn the filling into the baked pie shell.

🥄 Refrigerate the pie for 2 to 4 hours.

🥄 If desired, garnish with sweetened whipped cream flavored with vanilla.

MAPLE CHIFFON PIE

1 tbsp (15 mL) unflavored gelatin
2 tbsp (30 mL) cold water
½ cup (125 mL) milk
½ cup (125 mL) maple syrup
¼ tsp (1 mL) salt
2 egg yolks, well beaten

1½ cups (375 mL) whipping cream
1 tsp (5 mL) vanilla
2 egg whites, stiffly beaten
1 baked pie shell

🥄 Soak the gelatin in the cold water.

🥄 Heat the milk, the maple syrup and the salt in the top of a double boiler. Slowly add the well-beaten egg yolks. Add the gelatin and stir to dissolve. Cool the mixture.

🥄 Whip the cream and flavor it with the vanilla. Set aside half the whipped cream. Fold the other half, with the stiffly beaten egg whites, into the cooled custard.

🥄 Turn the filling into the baked pie shell; top with the remaining whipped cream. Refrigerate the pie until it is well chilled.

LEMON CHIFFON PIE

1 crumb-crust pie shell
(page 523)
1 tbsp (15 mL) unflavored gelatin
¼ cup (50 mL) cold water
4 egg yolks
pinch of salt
½ cup (125 mL) sugar
½ cup (125 mL) lemon juice
2 tbsp (30 mL) grated lemon zest
4 egg whites
½ cup (125 mL) sugar

🥄 Press the crumb mixture onto the bottom and sides of a pie plate.

🥄 Soak the gelatin in the cold water.

🥄 In the top of a double boiler, mix together the egg yolks, salt,

New York Cheese Pie

[533]

Lemon Chiffon Pie

½ cup (125 mL) of sugar, lemon juice and grated lemon zest. Cook until the mixture has the consistency of a light custard. Remove it from the heat and add the gelatin. Stir together and refrigerate.

🐚 Beat the egg whites with the other ½ cup (125 mL) of sugar until stiff.

🐚 When the custard mixture is half set, fold in the beaten egg whites.

🐚 Turn the filling into the pie shell and refrigerate the pie for 2 to 4 hours before serving.

2-EGG MERINGUE

This recipe makes crisp, fluffy meringue for an 8-in. (20-cm) pie. For a larger pie, use 3-Egg Meringue.

2 egg whites
pinch of salt

4 tbsp (60 mL) sugar
few drops of vanilla or other flavoring

🐚 Beat the egg whites with the salt until light and fluffy. Add the sugar gradually, beating until stiff peaks form in the egg whites and the sugar is dissolved. Add the flavoring.

🐚 Spread the meringue over the pie or tart right to the edge of the crust.

🐚 Bake the meringue in a 300°F (150°C) oven until it is golden brown. The baking time will vary according to the amount of steam rising from the pie filling used.

3-EGG MERINGUE

3 egg whites
¼ tsp (1 mL) cream of tartar
6 tbsp (90 mL) sugar

🐚 Remove the eggs from the refrigerator a few hours before using, as egg whites at room temperature will have more volume when beaten.

🐚 Separate the eggs. Place the whites in a medium bowl and add the cream of tartar. Beat with a metal whisk or hand beater until soft peaks form.

🐚 Gradually add the sugar, 1 tbsp (15 mL) at a time, beating well after each addition. Beat until very stiff peaks form and the sugar is dissolved.

🐚 Spread the meringue over the pie right to the edge of the crust.

🐚 Bake in a 300°F (150°C) oven until golden brown.

🐚 This recipe yields enough for a 9- or 10-in. (23- or 25-cm) pie.

NO-BAKE MERINGUE

⅓ cup (75 mL) corn syrup
1 egg white
½ tsp (2 mL) vanilla
¼ tsp (1 mL) salt

🐚 Bring the corn syrup to a boil.

🐚 Beat the egg white in a small bowl until soft peaks form.

🐚 Slowly add the boiling corn syrup to the egg white, beating constantly until the egg white forms stiff peaks. Add the vanilla and the salt.

🐚 Spread the meringue over the of a cooled pie filling.

🐚 If desired, garnish with grated coconut.

MONIQUE'S LEMON MERINGUE PIE

MERINGUE:
4 egg whites (½ cup or 125 mL)
¼ tsp (1 mL) salt
1 tsp (5 mL) vinegar
1 cup (250 mL) sugar

FILLING:
4 egg yolks
⅔ cup (150 mL) sugar
2 tsp (10 mL) grated lemon zest
⅓ cup (75 mL) lemon juice

To make the meringue, beat the egg whites until fluffy. Add the salt and the vinegar and beat until stiff. Add the sugar, 1 tbsp (15 mL) at a time, beating vigorously after each addition.

Butter an 8-in. (20-cm) pie plate. Fill it with the beaten egg whites, lightly hollowing out the center.

Bake the meringue in a 275°F (140°C) oven for 1 hour and 15 minutes. Cool.

To make the filling, beat the egg yolks until thick and lemon-colored. While continuing to beat, gradually add the sugar, the grated lemon zest and the lemon juice.

Cook the mixture in a double boiler until thickened (approximately 5 minutes), stirring constantly.

Place on top of the cooled meringue.

WESTERN SOUR CREAM PIE

pie dough of your choice
1 tbsp (15 mL) all-purpose flour
1 cup (250 mL) dark brown sugar
¼ tsp (1 mL) salt
1 cup (250 mL) sour cream
2 eggs, separated
1 tsp (5 mL) vanilla
1 tbsp (15 mL) melted butter
pinch of salt
4 tbsp (60 mL) sugar

Roll out the dough and line a 9-in. (23-cm) pie plate. Brush the dough with a little soft butter. Refrigerate for 40 minutes.

Mix together the flour, brown sugar, salt, sour cream, egg yolks, vanilla and melted butter. Blend thoroughly with a hand beater. Turn into the chilled pie shell.

Bake in a 450°F (230°C) oven for 10 minutes, then reduce the heat to 350°F (180°C) and bake the pie for another 45 minutes. Cool it on a cake rack.

Beat the 2 egg whites until stiff, gradually adding the pinch of salt and the 4 tbsp (60 mL) of sugar. Spread the meringue over the warm pie and brown it in a 400°F (200°C) oven.

AMERICAN MINCEMEAT

1 cup (250 mL) dried peaches
1 cup (250 mL) dried apricots
zest and juice of 3 oranges
4 apples, peeled and grated
1 cup (250 mL) suet, chopped
1 cup (250 mL) raisins
½ cup (125 mL) candied citron
1 cup (250 mL) grated carrot
2 tbsp (30 mL) cinnamon
1 tsp (5 mL) allspice
½ tsp (2 mL) mace
1 tsp (5 mL) ginger
1 tsp (5 mL) ground cloves
2 cups (500 mL) molasses
¾ cup (175 mL) brown sugar
1 cup (250 mL) cider or red wine

With a pair of scissors, cut the dried peaches and apricots into small pieces. Soak for 30 minutes in a bowl of hot water. Drain.

Place the fruits and all the remaining ingredients in a large bowl. Mix well.

Pour the mincemeat into sterilized jars and seal the jars. Let stand for 10 to 15 days in a cool place.

ENGLISH MINCEMEAT

6 large apples
1 lb (500 g) mixed candied peel
1 lb (500 g) suet, chopped
1 lb (500 g) currants
1 lb (500 g) raisins
1 lb (500 g) brown sugar
¾ cup (175 mL) chopped walnuts
zest and juice of 2 lemons
1 tsp (5 mL) nutmeg
½ tsp (2 mL) cinnamon
½ tsp (2 mL) allspice
½ tsp (2 mL) salt
½ cup (125 mL) brandy or rum

Peel, core and grate the apples. If desired, chop the candied peel to make it finer.

🍂 Mix all the ingredients in a large bowl and stir for 10 minutes.

🍂 Pour the mincemeat into sterilized jars and seal the jars. Let stand 3 to 5 weeks in a cool place.

DEVONSHIRE MINCEMEAT PIE

pie dough of your choice
2 cups (500 mL) mincemeat (see above)
2 beaten eggs
2 cups (500 mL) sour cream
2 tbsp (30 mL) sugar
1 tsp (5 mL) vanilla

🍂 Roll out the dough and line a 9-in. (23-cm) pie plate. Fill the pie shell with the mincemeat.

🍂 Bake in a 425°F (220°C) oven for 20 minutes.

🍂 Mix together the eggs, sour cream, sugar and vanilla. Spread the mixture over the partially cooked mincemeat.

🍂 Bake for another 8 minutes. Cool.

🍂 Refrigerate the pie for 1 hour and serve.

FESTIVE MINCEMEAT PIE

pie dough of your choice
2 cups (500 mL) mincemeat of your choice (see above)
2 apples, unpeeled
¾ cup (175 mL) raisins
½ cup (125 mL) cognac
1 tbsp (15 mL) butter, diced

🍂 Roll out half the dough and line a 9-in. (23-cm) pie plate with it. Roll out and set aside the top crust.

🍂 Place the mincemeat in a bowl. Grate the apples directly over the mincemeat, using a medium grater. Add the raisins and half the cognac.

🍂 Turn the mincemeat into the shell. Dot with the diced butter and pour the remaining cognac over the mincemeat. Cover with the top crust.

🍂 Bake in a 375°F (190°C) oven for 40 minutes. Serve hot or cold.

ENGLISH ROYAL MINCE TARTS

As the saying goes: "Eat 12 mince pies between Christmas and New Year's Day if you want 12 lucky months to follow." A pleasant task . . . unless you count calories as well as pies.

pie dough of your choice

FILLING:
4 tbsp (60 mL) melted butter
⅓ cup (75 mL) sugar
4 egg yolks
juice and grated zest of 1 lemon
2 cups (500 mL) mincemeat

MERINGUE:
4 egg whites
½ cup (125 mL) sugar

🍂 Roll out the dough until it is ⅟₁₆ to ⅛ in. (0.4 to 0.3 cm) thick. Cut into circles of about 2 in. (5 cm) in diameter and line a 12-tart pan.

🍂 To make the filling, blend the melted butter, sugar, egg yolks, lemon juice and grated lemon zest in a bowl. When light and creamy, blend in the mincemeat.

🍂 Fill the tarts ¾ full. Bake, uncovered, in a 350°F (180°C) oven for 25 to 30 minutes.

🍂 To make the meringue, beat the 4 egg whites until stiff. Add the sugar gradually, beating vigorously after each addition.

🍂 Spread the meringue over the filled, baked tarts.

🍂 Return the tarts to the oven and bake them until the meringue is golden brown. Serve warm.

QUÉBEC MOLASSES PIE

½ cup (125 mL) flour
1 cup (250 mL) molasses
1 cup (250 mL) water
½ cup (125 mL) raisins
½ tbsp (7 mL) butter
1 baked pie shell

🍂 Blend together in a saucepan the flour, molasses and water. Cook, stirring constantly, until the mixture is smooth and has the consistency of heavy cream. Add the raisins. When the mixture becomes transparent, add the butter; it will make the filling creamier.

🍂 Turn the filling into the baked pie shell.

🍂 Serve the pie cold. Garnish it with nuts or whipped cream, or, if desired, flavor the filling with a few drops of almond or bitter almond extract.

Butter Tarts

3 tbsp (45 mL) butter
1 cup (250 mL) brown sugar
1 egg
½ tsp (2 mL) salt
¼ cup (50 mL) seedless raisins
¼ cup (50 mL) chopped walnuts
½ tsp (2 mL) vanilla
unbaked tart shells

❧ In a bowl, cream the butter then gradually add the brown sugar, creaming the mixture until it is light. Beat the egg and pour it slowly into the creamed mixture, stirring as you pour. Stir in the raisins, walnuts and vanilla.

❧ Place a spoonful of the mixture in each tart shell.

❧ Bake for 8 minutes in a hot oven (set according to the directions for the pastry recipe you are using). Reduce the heat to 375°F (190°C) and bake until the filling has set and the crust is browned, about 10 to 12 minutes.

French-Style Strawberry Tarts

Puff Pastry (page 520)

Custard:
2 tbsp (30 mL) sugar
1 egg yolk
⅓ cup (75 mL) milk
2 tbsp (30 mL) butter
¼ tsp (1 mL) almond extract

Glaze:
4 cups (1 L) strawberries
¾ cup (175 mL) water

zest of 1 orange, grated
2 tbsp (30 mL) lemon juice
¾ cup (175 mL) sugar

❧ Roll out the pastry and cut it into circles large enough to completely cover the raised molds on an inverted muffin pan.

❧ Bake in a 375°F (190°C) oven for 10 to 15 minutes, or until the pastry is lightly browned. Unmold the tart shells and cool them on a cake rack.

❧ To make the custard, blend together the sugar and the egg yolk. Add the milk. Cook over low heat, stirring constantly, until light and creamy. Do not boil the mixture or it will curdle.

❧ Remove the custard from the heat. Add the butter and the almond extract. Stir to blend.

❧ Cover and refrigerate the custard until it is time to fill the tart shells. The custard will thicken as it cools.

❧ To make the glaze, wash and clean the strawberries. Set aside the larger ones and force the smaller strawberries through a sieve, adding the water a little at a time.

❧ Place this purée in a saucepan together with the grated orange zest, the lemon juice and the sugar. Bring to a boil and boil for approximately 10 minutes, or until the syrup thickens.

❧ To serve the tarts, place a spoonful of the custard in the bottom of each tart shell, arrange 3 to 5 strawberries in each shell and pour a little syrup over the strawberries as a glaze. Serve immediately.

French-Style Strawberry Tarts

[537]

Key Lime Pie

KEY LIME PIE

1 envelope unflavored gelatin
¼ cup (50 mL) cold water
4 eggs, separated
1 cup (250 mL) sugar
⅓ cup (75 mL) fresh lime juice
½ tsp (2 mL) salt
2 tsp (10 mL) grated lime peel
green food coloring
baked 9-in. (23-cm) pie shell

✿ Sprinkle the gelatin over the cold water. Let it soak for 5 minutes.

✿ In the top of a double boiler, beat the egg yolks until light. Add ½ cup (125 mL) of the sugar, the fresh lime juice and the salt. Cook the mixture over hot water until it is slightly thickened, stirring constantly. Add the grated lime peel and the gelatin and stir until the gelatin is dissolved.

✿ Remove the filling from the heat. Add just enough of the food coloring to make the filling a pale green. Cool.

✿ Beat the egg whites until stiff. Gradually add the remaining ½ cup (125 mL) of sugar and beat the whites until thick. Fold them into the cooled lime mixture.

✿ Turn the filling into the baked pie shell. Chill until firm. Garnish the pie with fresh mint leaves.

BERRY TARTS

✿ Cut out aluminum-foil circles of approximately 3 in. (7 cm) in diameter, using a saucer as a guide.

✿ Place the circles one on top of the other on a square piece of foil, separating each with a square piece of white paper.

✿ Use the same saucer to cut circles of pastry dough.

✿ Place each pastry circle on a foil circle. Prick the dough with a fork. With the fingers, push up the edges of the foil to form a shell. The foil will hold the pastry in place.

✿ Bake in a 450°F (230°C) oven for 10 to 15 minutes.

✿ Fill the cooled tart shells with a few spoonfuls of vanilla custard (see page 571). Top with fresh strawberries or any other berries that have been soaked in a syrup so that they will stay fresh and glossy.

A WORD ABOUT JUICY PIES

When fitting the dough for the bottom crust into the pie plate, leave an overlap of ¾ in. (2 cm) around the edge of the plate. After turning the fruit filling into the shell and covering it with the top pastry, moisten the overlap and fold it over the top dough. Press together and crimp. This will prevent the juice from overflowing.

✿ For very juicy pies, fashion 2 funnels out of stiff paper. Through slits in the top dough, insert the narrow ends of the funnels into the filling. The juices will rise through the funnels during baking but will sink back into the filling when the pie is removed from the oven.

✿ Attractive porcelain funnels in the shape of blackbirds, designed for just this purpose, are available in some shops.

✿ In the case of very juicy fruits, brush the bottom crust with egg white or soft butter and sprinkle this with a little sugar and flour mixed together.

CAKES

ABOUT CAKES

Important dates and events in our lives seem to be highlighted with a special cake: Christmas and Easter, as well as christenings, birthdays and weddings, to name but a few of those occasions.

❧ Cakes come in a wide variety of forms and flavors, but basically they fall into 2 categories —sponge cakes and butter cakes.

❧ The family of sponge cakes consists of yellow sponge cakes, white sponge or angel cakes and mock sponge cakes.

❧ Butter cakes—of which there are a great many—include all cakes made with leavening such as baking powder and a high percentage of shortening beaten with the sugar.

❧ It is not easy to make a cake. It takes a natural sense of taste and texture combined with a definite skill. But I am confident that if you study the basic rules that follow you will become an expert cake maker.

MAKING CAKES WITH YOUR BLENDER

You can use your blender to make almost any kind of cake if you follow these basic procedures:

❧ Sift together into a bowl all the dry ingredients in the ingredients list;

❧ Put all the liquid ingredients in your blender container, along with any ingredients that will dissolve in the liquid, such as sugar;

❧ Cover the blender container and proceed as described in the following recipe. Once you have

practiced with this basic cake recipe, you can adapt these 3 simple steps to your own favorite cakes.

❧ Sift into a bowl:

2¼ cups (550 mL) flour
1 tbsp (15 mL) baking powder
1 tsp (5 mL) salt

❧ Place in the blender container:

1 cup (250 mL) milk
2 eggs
½ cup (125 mL) vegetable shortening or soft butter
1¼ cups (300 mL) finely granulated sugar
1 tsp (5 mL) grated lemon or orange zest or 1 tsp (5 mL) vanilla

❧ Cover the blender and blend at high speed for 1 minute. Pour the liquid ingredients over the dry ingredients. Mix well.

❧ Turn into 2 greased 8-in. (20-cm) round cake pans and bake 25 to 35 minutes in a 375°F (190°C) oven.

❧ For chocolate cake, sift with the dry ingredients ¼ tsp (1 ml) baking soda and ½ cup (125 ml) cocoa.

SPONGE CAKES AND ANGEL FOOD CAKES

Sponge cakes and angel food cakes are sometimes called foam cakes because the leavening action depends entirely on eggs.

❧ The true sponge cake, or Génoise, is the yellow sponge cake, because its only leavening

agent is whole eggs—which is also, of course, how it gets its color. Some sponge cakes contain no liquid other than that supplied by the eggs; others call for a small amount of liquid. But sponge cakes contain no butter or fat (other than that found in the egg yolks).

❧ Angel food cake is similar to sponge cake. The only difference is that angel food cake is made with only the whites of eggs; as a result, it is pure white under its delicately golden surface.

❧ Mock sponge cakes can be either yellow and white. They tend to be more economical than the true sponges because they call for fewer eggs. However, they include a little baking powder and some liquid to make up for the reduced egg content.

INGREDIENTS FOR SPONGE AND ANGEL FOOD CAKES

Delicacy and tenderness are the trademarks of a perfect sponge or angel food cake, so use only pastry flour or soft-wheat flour.

❧ Eggs are the basic ingredient in sponge cakes—they provide much of the food value, the flavor and the richness. But their most important contribution is as a leavening agent. To do their job, a great deal of air must be beaten into the eggs; always beat the white and yolks separately.

❧ Cream of tartar beaten in with the egg whites strengthens the cell walls of the tiny individual bubbles and helps to make the cake light and airy. Add it part way through the beating process.

🍃 Lemon juice or vinegar is often substituted for cream of tartar, but in this case it is beaten into the yolk-sugar mixture.

🍃 Use a fine granulated sugar for all sponge and angel food cakes. It is usually beaten into the eggs, but in mock sponges it is sometimes dissolved in hot liquid.

🍃 Only mock sponge cakes will call for shortening or butter, and always in very small quantities. It is usually added in melted or liquid form.

🍃 Mock sponge cakes may be made with a small quantity of hot or cold milk, hot or cold water, or fruit juice.

🍃 Salt is used in sponge cakes, as it is in all other cakes, to bring out the flavor.

🍃 Sponge cakes can be flavored with a wide range of flavorings —including extracts, liqueurs and alcohols.

HOW TO MAKE A SPONGE CAKE

If you want to turn out a perfect sponge cake, follow the instructions carefully. Practice with the following recipe, then adapt it for other sponge cakes.

BASIC YELLOW SPONGE CAKE

1 cup (250 mL) sifted pastry flour
½ tsp (2 mL) salt
5 egg yolks
5 tbsp (75 mL) cold water
¾ cup (200 mL) fine sugar
5 egg whites
1 tsp (5 mL) cream of tartar
¼ cup (50 mL) fine sugar
1 tsp (5 mL) vanilla
1 tsp (5 mL) almond extract

Basic Yellow Sponge Cake

🍃 Remove the eggs from the refrigerator at least 1 hour ahead of time; eggs at room temperature will beat up fluffier.

🍃 Preheat the oven to 325°F (160°C).

🍃 Select the pan. Preferably, this cake should be made in an 8½-in. (21-cm) tube pan with straight sides; the funnel in the center will let the heat penetrate the batter more evenly. But if you want, you can bake it in two 8-in. (20-cm) square cake pans or one rectangular shallow pan, then ice between the squares or layer fruit between them.

🍃 Do not grease the pan. The delicate batter will be better able to climb and cling to the sides of an ungreased pan, particularly in the case of a deep tube pan.

🍃 Assemble all your utensils and bowls.

🍃 Measure out the sifted pastry flour, then add the salt and sift together 3 times.

🍃 Separate the eggs and put the whites aside. In a large bowl, thoroughly beat the yolks until they are thick and lemon colored. Gradually add the cold water, beating all the time. (This is also when you would add any other liquid called for, unless the liquid is lemon juice or vinegar, which must be added after the egg yolks have been mixed with the sugar.)

🍃 Gradually add the first quantity of sugar, beating after each addition. If you use a rotary beater, place the bowl on a folded tea towel to prevent it from skidding; if you use an electric mixer, set it at medium. Beat until the sugar is dissolved and the mixture is very smooth, about 10 minutes.

🍃 Beat the egg whites until frothy, then add the cream of tartar. Beat until just stiff—the egg whites should be glossy on the surface, not dry.

🍃 To the egg whites, gradually add the remaining ¼ cup (50 mL) sugar, beating it in to make a meringue.

🍃 Sift the flour mixture a little at a time over the egg-yolk mixture, folding in lightly after each addition. Add the vanilla and almond extracts.

🍃 Fold in the meringue, working as lightly as possible, until it is completely incorporated.

🍃 Turn the batter into the ungreased 8½-in. (21-cm) tube pan. Cut through the batter with a knife 5 to 6 times in order to break any large bubbles that might have formed.

🍃 Bake in a preheated 325°F (160°C) for 1 hour.

🍃 The critical moment in your cake's preparation is the cooling procedure. In an area that is free of drafts, invert the baked cake, still in its pan. Support the pan on 3 small cups or bowls of equal height and leave the cake suspended until it is completely cooled. This will keep all the delicate air-filled cells extended until "set." If the cake is turned right-side up before it is cooled, the cells will not be able to support their own weight. The cake will settle in the pan and will not be as spongy.

🍃 Loosen the cooled cake from the sides of the pan with a narrow-bladed flexible knife or spatula and gently slide it onto a wire rack or a plate. Store it in a tin with a tight-fitting lid overnight; true sponge cakes are better the

day after they are made—softer yet still spongy.

HOW TO MAKE AN ANGEL FOOD CAKE

Remove the eggs from the refrigerator at least 1 hour ahead of time; eggs beaten at room temperature will beat up fuller.

🍃 Preheat the oven to 300°F (150°C). Angel cakes require lower temperatures than sponge cakes. My favorite angel food cake recipe, included later in this chapter, starts in a cold oven.

🍃 You should use an 8½-in. (21-cm) tube pan; for the same reasons as discussed in *Basic Yellow Sponge Cake*, do not grease the pan.

🍃 Sift the pastry flour first, then measure out the required amount. Always sift the flour the number of times called for in the recipe.

🍃 Sift the icing sugar, if called for, to remove any lumps.

🍃 Separate enough eggs to make the required amount of egg white. (The yolks will keep several days for another use if covered with water and refrigerated.)

🍃 Add the salt to the egg whites and beat them until frothy; then sprinkle in the cream of tartar and beat the mixture until it is stiff but still glossy on the surface, not dry.

🍃 Add the sugar, a few spoonfuls at a time, beating it into the egg whites after each addition. At this point, you should have a large bowl full of snowy meringue.

🍃 Sift the flour over the meringue little by little. Fold in each addition lightly, until no flour is visible. Do not yield to the

temptation to play with the mixture. Fold only until you are sure the flour has been completely combined.

🍃 Gently fold in the flavorings.

🍃 Turn the batter into the ungreased pan and bake according to the recipe instructions.

🍃 Invert to cool according to the instructions for *Basic Yellow Sponge Cake* (see above).

🍃 Remove the cooled cake from the pan and store overnight in a container with a tight-fitting lid.

MAKING A MOCK SPONGE CAKE

Once you understand the basic principles that go into a successful mock sponge cake, you will be able to apply them to many different recipes in this chapter. So I am simply going to explain the basic procedures.

🍃 Even though the number of eggs is greatly reduced in a mock sponge recipe (which explains why you need another leavening agent such as baking powder), the eggs still play a very important role. And the beating process is particularly important.

🍃 Normally, the whole eggs or egg yolks are beaten together with the sugar. It is very important to beat the eggs until they are as light and fluffy as possible. Then, and only then, you should gradually beat in the sugar, and beat it in very thoroughly. The success or failure of the cake can depend on this step. The recipe may call for the egg and sugar mixture to be beaten for up to 10 minutes; in this case, a great deal of air will be incorporated into the mixture and the sugar will be just about dissolved. I advise you not to skip this step.

🙠 You must also treat the egg whites carefully. If the recipe calls for the whites to be beaten separately, beat them till they are stiff and glossy, but never so much that they appear dry or dull looking.

🙠 The sugar must also be added carefully. Sprinkle it gradually over the beaten egg whites and beat well after each addition; beat until stiff peaks form.

🙠 The egg whites must then be folded gently but thoroughly into the other ingredients, so that no trace of egg white is visible.

🙠 To cool the baked cake, follow the same instructions as for *Basic Yellow Sponge Cake* (page 541) unless the directions specify otherwise. Loosen the cooled cake and gently slide it from the pan onto a cake rack or a flat plate.

🙠 Like the true sponges, mock sponge cakes are more tender the day after they are made, if stored overnight in a container with a tight-fitting lid.

MAKING A BUTTER CAKE

Butter cakes are those cakes that contain a fair amount of shortening or butter.

🙠 Most often butter is used, because it gives a wonderful flavor. A high-grade white shortening will make a light, fine-textured cake. Or butter and shortening may be used in combination.

🙠 Vegetable oil is sometimes used as well in butter cakes.

🙠 Most of the cakes we eat and serve are variations on the basic butter cake. It is by far the most versatile kind of cake—and certainly the most popular. But to make a really good one, you must use high quality ingredients, a reliable recipe, exact measurements, an oven with accurate temperature settings, appropriate cake pans . . . and you must understand the role and characteristics of your ingredients.

BUTTER CAKE INGREDIENTS

FLOUR

Flour gives a batter its body. Soft-wheat flour or pastry flour is preferable, because its low gluten content produces a more tender and delicate cake, but all-purpose flour can also be used.

LEAVENING

Butter cakes are leavened by either baking powder or baking soda. Baking powder creates gas when it comes into contact with moisture, and this process is speeded up when the baking powder is exposed to heat. Keep your baking powder dry by closing the tin tightly.

🙠 These leavenings are chemical ingredients and work with scientific precision. Measure exactly.

EGGS

Eggs act as a leavening agent, cutting down on the amount of baking powder required. The more eggs a recipe calls for, the smaller the amount of other leavening it will require. Eggs greatly enrich a cake, not only in flavor and texture, but also, of course, nutritionally.

🙠 Eggs also determine to a great extent the type of crumb a cake will have. Yolks will make it smooth and velvety. Egg whites will make it light and spongy. The

Angel Food Cake

two work together in most batters. The number of eggs and how they are incorporated into the other ingredients have a great deal to do with establishing the character of a butter cake.

SHORTENING

The special role of the fat in a cake is to make it tender. But fats can carry a cake up or down the flavor scale in an unmistakable way. The fat you use will do one of 3 things:

🍂 Improve the flavor of the cake, particularly if butter is part (usually it is half) or all of the fat used.

🍂 Remain completely neutral and let the other ingredients provide the taste; shortenings do this.

🍂 A nut butter (such as peanut butter) can provide part of the fat, at the same time adding its own distinct flavor.

🍂 If the recipe calls for all butter, you can substitute half butter, half shortening without seriously affecting the flavor.

SWEETENER

Finely granulated white sugar is the best choice for most baking purposes.

🍂 Brown sugar is not as heavy as white, so an equal quantity will have slightly less sweetening power. Use a little more brown sugar if you want to replace the white sugar in a given recipe.

🍂 Because brown sugar contains a touch of acid, if it is combined with other ingredients that have a degree of acidity (raisins and some other fruits, spices, chocolate) the build-up of acid can be

put to work with the right amount of baking soda to leaven the mixture.

🍂 Corn syrup, used alone or in combination with sugar, acts as more than merely a sweetener: it makes a cake spongy and porous—a pleasant change from the fine crumb that we are used to. It will also keep a cake moist, adding to the keeping quality.

🍂 Corn syrup does not contain the sweetening power of an equal measure of sugar, so it is a good idea for the inexperienced cook to use only authentic corn syrup recipes. Experiment carefully.

🍂 The special flavor of molasses is a must for certain cakes and cookies. Because of its acidity, a recipe that calls for molasses will almost certainly require baking soda as well; the combination plays the role of the leavening agent in many recipes. Molasses is also a source of iron and calcium.

🍂 Liquid honey provides flavor and much sweetening power, and honey is more easily substituted for part of the sugar in recipes than are corn syrup and molasses. In terms of sweetness, honey and sugar can be interchanged in equal measure, but a little less liquid will be needed when honey is used.

🍂 However, unless you are used to cooking with honey, it is a good idea to stick to the exact recipe until you are familiar with how the cake should turn out.

🍂 White honeys such as clover or apple blossom honey will add a delicate flavor to your cakes. Brown honeys such as buckwheat

will add a pronounced flavor that may not be desirable in some cakes.

LIQUID

In a butter cake, milk is usually the required liquid. Sweet milk is the rule (with baking powder as the leavening), but sometimes sour milk will be called for (in which case baking soda will also be required, either alone or with baking powder).

🍂 Cream, either sweet or sour, will sometimes be called for, providing some or all of the fat required in the recipe.

🍂 Fruit juices, mashed fruit, jams, etc., may provide the liquid in specific cake recipes.

SALT

Salt is an important factor in bringing out the flavors of the other ingredients. Without salt, the most delectable mixture imaginable would be in danger of tasting flat. It is generally added along with the flour.

FLAVORINGS

Fruits, fruit juices, grated citrus zest, nutmeg, various syrups, chocolate, spices, molasses . . . these and other ingredients will give a distinctive flavor to cakes.

OTHER INGREDIENTS

Many ingredients find their way into cake batters, and they play a very important part in giving a cake its special character.

🍂 Dried fruits, candied peel, glacé fruits and fruits in syrup can be used to garnish a light batter delicately or they can provide the bulk of the cake. You may also use nuts, coconuts, and prepared cereals to add texture and flavor.

HOW TO MAKE A BUTTER CAKE

Remove the eggs, milk, shortening, etc., from the refrigerator 1 hour ahead of time.

🍂 Preheat the oven far enough in advance that it is the correct temperature when the cake goes into the oven. It is important that the heat be just right for this kind of batter. An oven that is too hot will cause the cake to rise to a peak in the center, crack on the surface and have a tough crust. If the temperature is too low, on the other hand, the cake will be heavy.

🍂 If the recipe calls for a baking pan lined with wax paper, trace the bottom of the pan onto a piece of wax paper and use scissors to cut just inside the line. Place the paper in the pan and brush the sides of the pan and the paper with melted butter or shortening.

🍂 Organize all your utensils and bowls before you start.

🍂 Sift out an approximate amount of pastry flour or all-purpose flour, then measure out the sifted flour (never the reverse).

🍂 Measure, mix and sift together the dry ingredients as indicated in the recipe.

🍂 Measure the butter or shortening by the tablespoon into a large mixing bowl. You can use a wooden spoon or an electric mixer to cream the fat, which means beating it until it is fluffy.

🍂 Gradually blend in the sugar and continue to cream the mixture (a combination of beating the mixture and working it

Some cake ingredients

against the side of the bowl with the wooden spoon) until the batter is light and fluffy and the sugar has just about dissolved. This thorough creaming will give your cake a fine texture, so don't spare the extra work at this point.

🍂 Beat the eggs until very light, then add them to the creamed mixture, a little at a time, beating well after each addition.

🍂 Measure the principal liquid. Add to it any liquid flavoring.

🍂 Fold about ⅓ of the dry ingredients into the fat-sugar-egg mixture; add about ½ of the liquid and combine lightly. Continue in this way, usually adding the dry ingredients in 3 parts and the liquid in 2 parts. Always start and end with dry ingredients. Combine the mixture lightly but well after each dry or liquid addition. Do not beat unless the recipe indicates it.

🍂 Turn the batter into the pre-

pared pan (or layer-cake pans). Draw it well to the sides and corners with a rubber spatula or a spoon. For a square or loaf-shaped plain butter cake, lift the pan about 2 in. (5 cm) off the table and let it drop 3 or 4 times; this will eliminate the larger air bubbles, which, when they expand in the oven, would result in large air-holes in the cake. (Do not do this if the batter contains fruits or nuts, however, because it will make them sink to the bottom; and avoid doing so with a rich pound cake or sponge cake—with little or no other leavening, these depend on the air in the batter to make them light.)

🍂 Bake until the cake just pulls away from the sides of the pan and a light touch in the center with a fingertip leaves no dent.

🍂 Remove from the oven and let stand for 10 minutes on a cake rack.

[545]

New-Method White Cake

⇘ Bake and unmold according to the instructions for making a butter cake.

NEW-METHOD WHITE CAKE

2½ cups (625 mL) pastry flour
1 cup (250 mL) fine granulated sugar
1 tbsp (15 mL) baking powder
1 tsp (5 mL) salt
1 cup (250 mL) soft shortening or butter
1 tsp (5 mL) vanilla
1 ⅔ cups (400 mL) milk
⅓ cup (75 mL) milk
2 eggs

⇘ Preheat the oven to 350°F (180°C). Grease and line with wax paper 2 8-in. (20-cm) round pans or 1, 9- x 13-in. (23- x 33-cm) rectangular pan.

⇘ Sift together in a bowl the pastry flour, sugar, baking powder and salt. Place the shortening, vanilla and the 1⅔ cups (400 mL) milk on top of the flour mixture. Beat with a wooden spoon for 2 minutes or 300 strokes.

⇘ Add the remaining ⅓ cup (75 mL) milk and the eggs. Beat for another 2 minutes or 300 strokes. Turn the batter into the prepared pans. Bake round cakes for 35 minutes, the rectangular cake for 45 minutes. Cool for 10 minutes before unmolding.

NEW-METHOD WALNUT CAKE

3 cups (750 mL) pastry flour
1 tbsp (15 mL) baking powder

⇘ Loosen the cake around the sides with a sharp knife; place a wire rack over the pan and invert the rack and the pan; if the cake doesn't settle onto the rack, shake the pan gently. If it sticks, place a cold, damp cloth over the bottom of the pan for a few moments. Peel off any wax paper.

⇘ Cool the cake on the rack away from drafts—any sudden change of temperature might make the cake shrink.

⇘ Once cooled, the cake can be filled and frosted as desired. Otherwise, store it in a cake box so that it doesn't dry out.

BUTTER CAKE MADE WITH EGG WHITES

Follow the instructions for making a basic butter cake (see above) just until it is time for the eggs to be added to the batter.

⇘ Then follow these steps:

⇘ Separate the eggs. Beat the yolks until light and add them to the creamed butter and sugar mixture. Beat until well blended.

⇘ Gradually add the sifted dry ingredients, alternating with the liquid ingredients. If the recipe calls for fruit or nuts, add these, as well as any flavoring extracts, as soon as the batter is well mixed.

⇘ Finally, fold in the stiffly-beaten egg whites, as follows:

⇘ Turn the beaten egg whites onto the batter. Using the side of a wooden spoon or a rubber spatula, cut into the batter, going straight to the bottom of the bowl. Turn the spoon over and bring it back towards the side of the bowl then back to the top, letting some of the batter fall onto the egg whites. Repeat this process, cutting into the batter with the whites until they are evenly distributed throughout the batter.

❦ TECHNIQUE ❦

NEW-METHOD WHITE CAKE

1 Sift the flour together with the sugar, baking powder and salt.

2 Add the shortening, vanilla and milk. Beat for 2 minutes.

3 Add the rest of the milk and the eggs.

4 Beat another 2 minutes.

1½ tsp (7 mL) salt
1 cup (250 mL) sugar
1¾ cup (425 mL) soft shortening
or margarine
4 eggs, unbeaten
¾ cup (175 mL) milk
2 tsp (10 mL) vanilla
1 cup (250 mL) walnuts,
chopped fine

🍂 Preheat the oven to 375°F (190°C). Grease a 9-in. (23-cm) tube pan and line it with wax paper.

🍂 Sift together into the bowl of an electric mixer the pastry flour, baking powder, salt and sugar. Add the shortening or margarine and 2 of the eggs. Pour the milk mixed with the vanilla on top. Beat for 2 minutes at medium speed. Clean the sides of the bowl with a rubber spatula.

🍂 Stop the mixer and add the 2 remaining eggs. Beat for 2 more minutes at medium speed.

🍂 Add the chopped walnuts and beat for 1 minute.

🍂 Turn the batter into the prepared pan and bake for 1 hour or until a toothpick inserted in the center comes out clean. Cool 10 minutes before removing from the pan. Unmold on a cake rack. Cool.

NEW-METHOD CHOCOLATE CAKE

2 cups (500 mL) pastry flour
1¾ cups (425 mL) fine
granulated sugar
¾ cup (175 mL) cocoa
1¼ tsp (5 mL) baking soda
¾ tsp (3 mL) baking powder
1 tsp (5 mL) salt
¾ cup (175 mL) shortening
¾ cup (175 mL) milk
1 tsp (5 mL) vanilla
½ cup (125 mL) milk
3 eggs

🍂 Preheat the oven to 350°F (180°C). Grease and line with wax paper 2 9-in. (23-cm) round cake pans.

🍂 Sift together into the bowl of an electric mixer the pastry flour, sugar, cocoa, baking soda, baking powder and salt. Add the shortening and the ¾ cup (175 mL) milk mixed with the vanilla. Beat at medium speed for 2½ minutes. Scrape down the sides of the bowl with a rubber spatula as necessary.

🍂 Add the ½ cup (125 mL) milk and the eggs. Beat for another 2½ minutes. Turn the batter into the prepared pans and bake for 35 minutes. Cool for 10 minutes before unmolding. Unmold onto a cake rack and peel off the wax paper.

SOUR CREAM COFFEE CAKE

This prize recipe from a contest that I once judged is light and tasty, and it is not difficult to make. I usually make 3 at a time, one right after the other; having all the ingredients handy makes it easy to do this, and it yields better results than just tripling the recipe. Serve for breakfast, brunch or lunch, or have it at teatime.

½ cup (125 mL) soft butter
1 cup (250 mL) sugar
2 eggs
1 tsp (5 mL) baking soda
1 cup (250 mL) sour cream
1½ cups (375 mL) all-purpose flour
1½ tsp (7 mL) baking powder
pinch of salt
1 tsp (5 mL) vanilla
¼ cup (50 mL) sugar

New-Method Chocolate Cake

1 tbsp (15 mL) cinnamon
2 tbsp (30 mL) finely chopped walnuts

❧ Cream the butter and the 1 cup (250 mL) sugar until creamy and light. Add the eggs, one at a time, beating well after each addition. If using an electric mixer, beat the butter, sugar and eggs together for 10 minutes.

❧ Stir the baking soda into the sour cream. Gradually beat this into the egg mixture.

❧ Stir together in a bowl the flour, baking powder and salt. Add to the egg mixture along with the vanilla. Stir until well mixed.

❧ Mix together the ¼ cup (50 mL) sugar, the cinnamon and the chopped walnuts.

❧ Turn ½ the batter into well-buttered 8- x 8-in. (20- x 20-cm) pan. Sprinkle with ½ the sugar-cinnamon-walnut mixture. Place the rest of the batter on top and sprinkle with the rest of the cinnamon mixture.

❧ Bake in a preheated 350°F (180°C) oven for 40 to 50 minutes. Let cool.

❧ Yield: 12 2-in. (5-cm) squares.

SOUR CREAM CHOCOLATE CAKE

1 cup (250 mL) boiling water
2 squares (2 oz or 60 g) unsweetened chocolate
2 cups (500 mL) all-purpose flour
¼ tsp (1 mL) salt
1 tsp (5 mL) baking soda
1 tbsp (15 mL) grated lemon zest
½ cup (125 mL) butter
1 tsp (5 mL) vanilla

Sour Cream Cake

1¾ cups (425 mL) well-packed brown sugar
2 eggs
½ cup (125 mL) sour cream

❧ Preheat the oven to 325°F (160°C). Grease a 9- x 5-in. (23- x 12-cm) loaf pan.

❧ Pour the boiling water over the chocolate in a small bowl and stir until the chocolate is melted. Let cool.

❧ Sift together the flour, salt and baking soda. Add the grated lemon zest.

❧ Cream the butter together with the vanilla until light and fluffy, by hand or using an electric mixer. Add the brown sugar and beat until smooth and creamy. Add the unbeaten eggs one at a time, beating vigorously after each addition. Fold in the flour mixture alternately with the sour cream. When well mixed, beat in the chocolate liquid. Mix well.

❧ Pour the batter into the prepared pan and bake for 50 to 60 minutes or until done.

❧ Cool for 5 minutes on a cake rack before unmolding. Unmold onto the rack and let cool completely.

SOUR CREAM CAKE

2¾ cups (675 mL) pastry flour
3 tsp (15 mL) baking powder
1 tsp (5 mL) baking soda
¾ tsp (3 mL) salt
¾ cup (175 mL) butter
1 tsp (5 mL) vanilla
1½ cups (375 mL) sugar
grated zest of 1 orange
4 egg whites
1 cup (250 mL) sour cream
½ cup (125 mL) milk

❧ Preheat the oven to 350°F (180°C). Grease and flour 3 8-in. (20-cm) round cake pans.

Pain de Savoie

🍃 Sift together several times the flour, baking powder, baking soda and salt.

🍃 Cream together the butter and vanilla until light, by hand or with an electric mixer.

🍃 Gradually add 1 cup (250 mL) of the sugar and continue to stir until the mixture is smooth. Fold in the orange zest.

🍃 In another bowl, beat the egg whites until stiff. Gradually beat in the remaining ½ cup (125 mL) sugar. Continue beating until smooth and glossy and stiff peaks form.

🍃 Combine the sour cream with the milk.

🍃 Stir ¼ of the dry ingredients into the butter mixture, then mix in ⅓ of the sour cream mixture. Repeat in the same proportions until both mixtures have been completely added. Mix rapidly but do not beat.

🍃 Add the egg whites, gently folding them in just until the whites are no longer visible.

🍃 Turn into the prepared pans and bake for 25 minutes or until done.

AMERICAN SPONGE CAKE

1¼ cups (300 mL) pastry flour
1¼ cups (300 mL) fine granulated sugar
¼ tsp (1 mL) salt
6 eggs
2 tbsp (30 mL) lemon juice
2 tbsp (30 mL) cold water
1 tsp (5 mL) vanilla
1¼ tsp (6 mL) ground mace
½ tsp (2 mL) cream of tartar

🍃 Preheat the oven to 350°F (180°C). Select a 10-in. (25-cm) tube pan.

🍃 Sift together the flour, 1 cup (250 mL) sugar and salt.

🍃 Separate the eggs. Beat the yolks and combine them with the lemon juice, water, vanilla and mace. Add the dry ingredients. Beat at high speed with an electric mixer for at least 5 minutes.

🍃 Wash the beaters and beat the egg whites until foamy. Sprinkle with the cream of tartar and keep beating until moist glossy peaks form when the beater is lifted out. Gradually add the remaining ¼ cup (50 mL) sugar, 2 tbsp (30 mL) at a time; beat until the meringue is smooth and stiff peaks form.

🍃 Pour the yolk and flour mixture over the meringue; carefully fold it in until the mixture is homogeneous.

🍃 Turn the batter into the tube pan and bake for 40 to 50 minutes, or until the top springs back when pressed lightly with a finger.

🍃 Invert the cake on a rack, let it cool for at least 1 hour, then free it from the mold with a flexible fine-bladed knife and tap on the bottom to unmold the cake.

PAIN DE SAVOIE

1 cup (250 mL) fine granulated sugar
¼ cup (50 mL) water
3 egg whites
¼ tsp (1 mL) salt
1 tsp (5 mL) vanilla or
1 tsp (5 mL) lemon extract
3 egg yolks
1 cup (250 mL) pastry flour
1 tsp (5 mL) baking powder

❦ TECHNIQUE ❦

PAIN DE SAVOIE

1 Boil the sugar and the water together to make a medium syrup (180°F or 80°C on a candy thermometer).

2 Pour the syrup over the beaten egg whites.

3 Fold the beaten egg yolks into the egg white mixture.

4 Sift the flour and the baking powder together and add to the egg mixture.

❧ Place the sugar and water in a saucepan. Boil until the sugar is dissolved and the syrup is medium thick (180°F or 80°C on a candy thermometer).

❧ Beat the egg whites with the salt until they form moist glossy peaks when the beater is lifted out. Pour the hot syrup over the egg whites, beating constantly with an electric mixer or a hand beater or 2 forks.

❧ When all the syrup has been added, the texture should resemble marshmallow. Slowly add the vanilla or lemon extract, while stirring.

❧ Beat the egg yolks until light and fluffy; fold them into the egg white mixture.

❧ Sift the flour and baking powder together 3 times. Fold this mixture into the egg whites, 1 tbsp (30 mL) at a time. (To do this properly, sprinkle the flour mixture over the egg mixture and stir with a spoon around the edge of the bowl, lifting the mixture to cover the flour; 2 or 3 turns should incorporate each spoonful of flour.)

❧ Turn the batter into an ungreased 10-in. (25-cm) tube pan. Bake in a preheated 350°F (180°C) oven for 30 minutes; reduce the heat to 325°F (160°C) and bake for another 30 minutes or until done. You can tell the cake is done if a metal skewer inserted in the cake comes out clean.

❧ Invert the cake on top of 3 cups in such a way that there is a space of at least 3 in. (8 cm) between the mold and the countertop. Let cool completely before unmolding according to the instructions for *Basic Yellow Sponge Cake* (see page 541).

JELLY ROLL

4 egg whites
¼ cup (50 mL) sugar
4 egg yolks
½ cup (125 mL) sugar
2 tbsp (30 mL) lemon juice
1 tbsp (15 mL) grated lemon zest
1 cup (250 mL) sifted pastry flour
¼ tsp (1 mL) salt
jelly or jam

❧ Preheat the oven to 350°F (180°C). Grease an 11- x 6-in. (28- x 15-cm) jelly roll pan.

❧ Beat the egg whites until they stand in foamy peaks. Add the ¼ cup (50 mL) sugar and beat until stiff peaks form.

❧ Beat the egg yolks until frothy. Add the remaining ½ cup (125 mL) sugar and beat until pale yellow and thick. Add the lemon juice and the grated zest. Fold the egg yolk mixture into the beaten egg whites.

❧ Sift together the flour and salt. Fold the dry ingredients carefully into the egg mixture.

❧ Spread the batter in the greased jelly-roll pan and bake for 15 minutes.

❧ Turn the pan upside-down over a clean tea towel. Roll up the cake inside the cloth and let cool on a cake rack.

❧ Unroll when cooled and spread with jam or jelly. Roll again and sprinkle the top with fine sugar.

CHOCOLATE MINT ROLL

CHOCOLATE CAKE:
6 eggs
½ cup plus 2 tbsp (155 mL) sugar
6 tbsp (90 mL) cocoa
1 tsp (5 mL) vanilla
¼ tsp (1 mL) almond extract

❧ Preheat the oven to 350°F (180°C). Grease a 15- x 10-in. (38- x 25-cm) jelly-roll pan. Line with wax paper and grease the paper.

❧ Separate the eggs. Beat the yolks with an electric mixer until thick and creamy, which will take at least 10 minutes. Add the sugar gradually and continue to beat until the mixture is perfectly smooth. Beat in the cocoa, vanilla, and almond extract thoroughly.

❧ Beat the egg whites until they stand in foamy peaks. Fold the whites gently into the cocoa mixture.

❧ Spread the mixture in the prepared pan and bake for 25 minutes or until the cake pulls away from the sides of the pan. Unmold and roll following the recipe for *Jelly Roll*.

❧ No flour is needed for this recipe.

CHOCOLATE-MINT FILLING:
½ cup (125 mL) sugar
¼ cup (50 mL) cocoa
pinch of salt
½ tsp (2 mL) vanilla
¼ tsp (1 mL) mint extract (optional)
1½ cups (375 mL) whipping cream

🍂 Stir all the ingredients together in a bowl, but do not beat. Refrigerate for several hours.

🍂 When well chilled, whip the mixture until it will hold a shape. Use ¾ of the mixture to fill the roll and spread the remainder over the top.

French Sponge Cake

5 whole eggs
1 cup (250 mL) fine granulated sugar
½ tsp (2 mL) salt
1 tsp (5 mL) vanilla
1 cup (250 mL) all-purpose flour, sifted 3 times

🍂 Grease well 2 8-in. (20-cm) round cake pans. Line the bottoms with wax paper.

🍂 Beat the eggs with an electric mixer until light and fluffy. Gradually add the sugar, beating continuously. Beat in the salt and the vanilla. Beat the mixture for 5 minutes until thick and lemon colored.

🍂 Sprinkle in the flour, 2 tbsp (30 mL) at a time. Mix very gently but thoroughly after each addition. Since there is no leavening agent in this cake other than the eggs, they must be handled very gently to keep them light.

🍂 Turn the batter into the prepared cake pans and bake in a preheated 350°F (180°C) oven for 25 to 30 minutes.

🍂 Cool the pans on a cake rack for 5 minutes before unmolding the cakes. Ice and fill with the icing and filling of your choice.

French Sponge Cake (Génoise)

🍂 This cake is ideal for making petits fours, in which case you should bake it in square pans.

Mocha Cake

2 8-in. (20-cm) Génoises
1 cup (250 mL) sugar
½ cup (125 mL) water
4 egg yolks
1 tsp (5 mL) instant coffee
or 1 tsp (5 mL) coffee extract
1 cup (250 mL) soft sweet butter

🍂 To make the Génoises, follow the instructions in the previous recipe.

🍂 Boil the sugar and the water together to make a medium syrup (it should read 180°F or 80°C on a candy thermometer).

🍂 Beat the egg yolks until light in color. Then gradually pour the hot syrup over the egg yolks, beating constantly, until the mixture has

the consistency of whipped cream.

🍂 Stir in the instant coffee powder or coffee extract. Cover and refrigerate until the mixture is well chilled.

🍂 Cream the butter and gradually beat it into the chilled cream mixture. Beat until smooth and creamy.

🍂 Split the 2 cooled layer cakes to make 4 layers. Spread the mocha butter over each layer, then on the top and sides. Decorate the sides with slivered toasted almonds, if desired.

🍂 Refrigerate until ready to serve.

Christmas Yule Log

So that the Yule Log will have a chance to mellow, make it 24 hours in advance. Then carefully slip it into a plastic refrigerator bag and secure the open end. Refrigerate until serving time.

MOCHA FILLING:
¾ cup (175 mL) sweet butter
¾ cup (175 mL) sifted icing sugar
2 egg yolks
1 tsp (5 mL) instant coffee
1 tbsp (15 mL) hot water

CHOCOLATE ROLL:
2 squares (2 oz or 60 g) unsweetened chocolate
1 tsp (5 mL) allspice
¼ tsp (1 mL) cinnamon
4 eggs
¾ cup (175 mL) sifted icing sugar
1 tsp (5 mL) vanilla extract
½ tsp (2 mL) almond extract
⅓ cup (75 mL) sifted pastry flour
½ tsp (2 mL) baking powder
¼ tsp (1 mL) salt

CHOCOLATE GLAZE:
1 square (1 oz or 30 g) unsweetened chocolate
1 square (1 oz or 30 g) sweet cooking chocolate

1 tsp (5 mL) honey
2 tbsp (30 mL) butter

🍂 To prepare the mocha filling, cream the butter until soft. Add the sifted icing sugar gradually, continuing to beat until the mixture is very smooth. Beat in the egg yolks. Dissolve the instant coffee in the hot water and add it to the filling mixture; beat vigorously until firm but spreadable. Set aside.

🍂 To prepare the chocolate roll, preheat the oven to 425°F (220°C). Butter a 15- x 10-in. (38- x 25-cm) jelly-roll pan. Cover the bottom of the pan with wax paper and grease the paper generously.

🍂 Melt the chocolate over hot water in a double boiler. Stir in the allspice and the cinnamon.

🍂 Separate the eggs. Add a pinch of salt to the whites and beat them until they stand in foamy peaks. Gradually sprinkle in the sifted icing sugar and fold it in gently until all the dry patches are absorbed.

🍂 Beat the egg yolks until thick and light in color, using an electric mixer or a hand beater. It will take about 10 minutes. Stir in the vanilla and almond extracts.

🍂 Sift the flour, baking powder and salt together 3 times into a large mixing bowl.

🍂 Pour the egg yolk mixture on top of the flour mixture and fold it in gently until well blended. Gently fold in the egg white mixture. Add the cooled chocolate-spice mixture and fold it in gently.

🍂 Turn the batter into the prepared pan and bake for 15 minutes in the preheated oven.

🍂 Invert the pan over a tea towel sprinkled lightly with icing sugar and let the cake cool until it is lukewarm. Lift off the pan and peel away the wax paper.

🍂 Trim off all crisp cake edges.

🍂 Spread the cake with the prepared mocha filling. Roll the cake neatly and wrap it in wax paper. Refrigerate until chilled.

🍂 To prepare the chocolate glaze, melt the 2 kinds of chocolate over hot water in the top of a double boiler. Stir in the honey and the butter until the butter is melted. Cool slightly and spoon a thin coating of glaze over the chocolate roll.

🍂 Decorate the top of the roll with slivered sweet and unsweetened chocolate and with silver dragées.

Gâteau Saint Honoré

❧ TECHNIQUE ❧

GÂTEAU SAINT HONORÉ

1 Bring the water and the butter to boil in a saucepan.

2 Add the flour and the salt all at once.

3 Cook while stirring vigorously.

4 The paste should pull away from the sides of the saucepan. Remove from the heat and add the eggs, one at a time, beating vigorously after each addition.

GÂTEAU SAINT HONORÉ

CAKE:
1 cup (250 mL) all-purpose flour
¼ cup (50 mL) sugar
¼ cup (50 mL) butter
1 egg yolk
¼ tsp (1 mL) almond extract

CREAM-PUFF PASTRY:
½ cup (125 mL) water
¼ cup (50 mL) butter
½ cup (125 mL) all-purpose flour
pinch of salt
2 eggs

CUSTARD FILLING:
1½ tbsp (25 mL) cornstarch
¼ tsp (1 mL) salt
5 tbsp (75 mL) sugar
1 ½ cups (375 mL) milk
2 eggs
¼ tsp (1 mL) almond extract

GLAZE:
¼ cup (50 mL) brown sugar
¼ cup (50 mL) corn syrup

GARNISH:
1 cup (250 mL) whipping cream
2 tbsp (30 mL) icing sugar
¼ tsp (1 mL) almond extract
finely chopped pistachio nuts

&♣ Using an 8-in. (20-cm) cake pan as a pattern for the cake base, draw a circle on a baking sheet.

&♣ Sift together the flour and the sugar. Cut in the butter with a pastry blender or 2 knives until the mixture is fine and mealy.

&♣ Beat together lightly the egg yolk and the almond extract. Add this to the flour mixture and knead together with the fingertips until the dough holds together well.

&♣ Pat this mixture into the circle on the baking sheet. Set aside.

&♣ To prepare the cream puff pastry, preheat the oven to 375°F (190°C) and grease a second baking sheet.

&♣ Place the water and the butter in a saucepan and bring to a boil. Add the flour and the salt all at once and cook, stirring vigorously, until the paste pulls away from the sides of the saucepan. Remove from the heat.

&♣ Add the eggs to the paste mixture one at a time, beating vigorously after each addition.

&♣ Drop 20 walnut-sized balls of the paste onto the greased baking sheet. Spread the remaining paste evenly over the circle of cake batter.

&♣ Bake both the cake base and the pastry balls for 25 to 30 minutes in the same oven.

&♣ Meanwhile, make the custard filling.

&♣ To prepare the custard filling, mix together in a saucepan the cornstarch, salt and sugar. Slowly stir in the milk and cook over very low heat, stirring constantly, until the mixture starts to bubble.

&♣ Separate the eggs and beat the yolks slightly.

&♣ Add the hot-milk mixture to the beaten yolks very gradually, stirring constantly.

&♣ Return the mixture to the saucepan and cook over very low heat, still stirring, until the custard has thickened. Flavor with the almond extract and refrigerate.

&♣ Shortly before assembling the cake, beat the egg whites until stiff and gently fold them into the cold custard.

&♣ To assemble the cake, make a slit in the bottom of each of the small puff pastry balls and stuff it with some of the custard filling, using a small spoon. Reserve the remaining custard to decorate the cake.

&♣ To prepare the glaze, place together in a saucepan the ¼ cup (50 mL) brown sugar and ¼ cup (50 mL) dark corn syrup. Cook until the sugar is dissolved and the mixture bubbles.

&♣ Use this hot glaze to baste the top of each cream puff and the edge of the baked cake circle.

&♣ Arrange 15 of the little cream puffs around the edge of the cake. Glaze the bottoms of the remaining 5 and place them in a circle in the middle of the cake.

&♣ Spoon the leftover custard filling between the cream puffs at the edge and those in the center.

&♣ To decorate the cake, beat the whipping cream until firm. Carefully mix in the icing sugar and the almond extract. This mixture is called Crème Chantilly. Spoon the mixture over the custard, taking care not to cover up the little cream puffs. Garnish with a sprinkling of the finely chopped pistachio nuts.

MOTHER'S FRUIT CAKE

2 cups (500 mL) currants
2 cups (500 mL) seedless raisins
1 cup (250 mL) mixed candied peel
¼ cup (50 mL) rum or orange juice
2 cups (500 mL) butter

2 cups (500 mL) sugar
6 eggs, well beaten
2 cups (500 mL) molasses
7 cups (1.8 L) all-purpose flour
1 tsp (5 mL) baking powder
1 tsp (5 mL) nutmeg
1 tbsp (15 mL) cinnamon
1 tbsp (15 mL) ground cloves

❧ Place in a large bowl the currants, raisins, mixed candied peel and rum or orange juice. Cover and let marinate for 12 hours, stirring 2 or 3 times.

❧ Cream the butter together with the sugar until very light. Beat the eggs separately, then beat them into the sugar mixture a little at a time, stirring well after each addition. Beat in the molasses.

❧ Sift together the flour, baking powder, nutmeg, cinnamon and cloves.

❧ Add ½ of the flour mixture to the creamed butter mixture. Mix well. Add the rest of the flour mixture alternately with the marinated fruit mixture. Stir until thoroughly blended.

❧ Turn the batter into a greased fruit cake pan lined with brown paper. Make sure you use an unsalted butter or grease. Fill the molds only ¾ full.

❧ Bake in a 250°F (120°C) oven for 3 hours or until a toothpick inserted in the center comes out clean.

❧ Cool the cake on a cake rack before unmolding. Wrap the cake well in a double layer of wax paper and a layer of aluminum foil and store in a cool place.

❧ Yield: a 6-lb (3-kg) fruit cake.

BASIC RULES FOR MAKING FRUIT CAKE

No matter what sort of fruit cake you prefer, you'll have perfect results every time if you follow these basic rules:

❧ Fruit cake made with butter will keep moist longer, crumble less when cut, and have a softer crust.

❧ Do not replace the brown paper with wax paper when lining the mold.

❧ Once the mold is filled, tap it lightly on the countertop a couple of times to settle the mixture.

❧ Cool the cake completely in its pan on a rack before unmolding and removing the paper.

❧ To keep the cake for months, moisten a generous length of cheesecloth in brandy, whisky or fresh lemon juice and wrap it snugly around the cake several times. Wrap in foil and store in an airtight container in a cool place. Do not refrigerate.

BLUEBERRY CAKE

¾ cup (175 mL) sugar
¼ cup (50 mL) shortening
1 egg
½ cup (125 mL) milk
2 cups (500 mL) all-purpose flour
½ tsp (2 mL) salt
2 tsp (10 mL) baking powder
½ tsp (2 mL) nutmeg or ginger
2 cups (500 mL) blueberries

TOPPING:
½ cup (125 mL) sugar
⅓ cup (75 mL) all-purpose flour
½ tsp (2 mL) cinnamon
¼ cup (50 mL) soft butter

❧ Place the sugar, shortening and egg in a bowl and mix well. Add the milk and stir.

❧ Sift the flour together with the salt, the baking powder and the nutmeg or ginger. Add this to the

Blueberry Cake

sugar mixture and stir just enough to mix.

🍂 Spread the mixture in a greased 8- x 8-in. (20- x 20-cm) pan. Spread the blueberries over the batter.

🍂 To make the topping, in a bowl, mix the sugar, flour, cinnamon and butter. Sprinkle this mixture over the blueberries in the pan and bake in a 375°F (190°C) oven for 40 to 50 minutes. Serve hot or warm with whipped cream.

MOTHER'S BANANA CAKE

½ cup (125 mL) butter
1 cup (250 mL) sugar
2 eggs
1 tsp (5 mL) vanilla
2 cups (500 mL) sifted
all-purpose flour
¾ tsp (3 mL) baking soda
½ tsp (2 mL) baking powder
½ tsp (2 mL) salt
¼ tsp (1 mL) nutmeg
¼ cup (50 mL) milk
1 tsp (5 mL) vinegar
½ cup (125 mL) mashed bananas

🍂 Preheat the oven to 375°F (190°C). Grease and lightly flour 2, 8-in. (20-cm) round cake pans.

🍂 Beat together the butter, sugar, eggs and vanilla until light and creamy.

🍂 Sift the flour together with the baking soda, baking powder, salt and nutmeg.

🍂 Stir together the milk and the vinegar. Add the mashed bananas.

🍂 Add the dry ingredients to the egg mixture alternately with the banana mixture. Stir until well mixed. Turn the batter into the prepared pans and bake for 25 to 30 minutes. Let stand 5 minutes before unmolding. Then cool on a cake rack.

DATE CAKE

1 cup (250 mL) pitted dates
1 cup (250 mL) hot water
1 ½ cups (375 mL) sifted pastry
flour
1 tsp (5 mL) baking powder
¼ tsp (1 mL) salt
¼ cup (50 mL) butter
or margarine
¾ cup (175 mL) sugar
1 egg
¾ tsp (3 mL) baking soda

TOPPING:
5 tbsp (75 mL) butter
3 tbsp (45 mL) cream
½ cup (125 mL) brown sugar,
firmly packed
¾ cup (175 mL) chopped walnuts

🍂 Boil the dates in the water until the mixture forms a thick paste, stirring frequently. Let cool.

🍂 Preheat the oven to 325°F (160°C). Grease an 8-in. (20-cm) square cake pan and line the bottom with wax paper.

🍂 Sift together the flour, baking powder and salt.

🍂 Cream the butter or margarine until soft. Gradually beat in the sugar until the mixture is as smooth as possible. Add the unbeaten egg and beat vigorously.

🍂 Mix the baking soda with the cooked, cooled date mixture.

🍂 Stir the date mixture into the egg mixture, alternating with the dry ingredients. Turn into the prepared pan and bake for 45 minutes or until done. Meanwhile, make the topping.

🍂 To prepare the topping, mix the topping ingredients together in a saucepan and boil the mixture for 3 minutes.

🍂 While still warm, spread evenly over the top of the baked cake.

🍂 Slide the cake under the broiler, 4 in. (10 cm) from the broiler element, and broil for 2 minutes, or until the top is golden brown. Let the cake cool in the pan on a wire rack.

OLD-FASHIONED DATE CAKE

1½ cups (375 mL) pitted dates
1½ cups (375 mL) chopped
walnuts
1½ cups (375 mL) seedless
raisins
5 eggs
1 cup (250 mL) sugar
⅓ cup (75 mL) all-purpose flour
1½ tsp (7 mL) baking powder
¼ tsp (1 mL) salt
1½ tsp (7 mL) vanilla
1 tsp (5 mL) cinnamon
juice of 1 lemon
1 cup (250 mL) icing sugar

🍂 Preheat the oven to 350°F (180°C). Grease and line with wax paper a 12- x 7½-in. (30- x 19-cm) cake pan.

🍂 Chop the dates and walnuts coarsely and mix them together

with the raisins.

🍂Separate the eggs. Beat the yolks together with the sugar until thick and lemon colored.

🍂Sift together twice the flour, baking powder and salt. Fold the dry ingredients gently into the egg yolk mixture. Add the vanilla and the cinnamon. Fold in the dates, raisins and nuts.

🍂Beat the egg whites until stiff but not dry and fold them gently into the batter, lifting from the bottom of the mixture until it is light, foamy and well mixed.

🍂Turn the batter into the prepared pan and bake for 1 hour and 15 minutes or until a toothpick inserted in the center comes out clean. Let the cake cool in the pan on a cake rack and unmold it.

🍂Mix together the icing sugar and lemon juice. Glaze the cake, letting the clear glaze run down the sides.

Cherry Cake with Farina

CHERRY CAKE WITH FARINA

2 cups (500 mL) canned pitted cherries, undrained
½ cup (125 mL) sugar
¼ tsp (1 mL) cinnamon
2 egg whites
½ cup (125 mL) sugar
2 egg yolks
½ tsp (2 mL) salt
⅔ cup (150 mL) uncooked farina

🍂Mix the cherries, the first ½ cup (125 mL) of sugar and the cinnamon. Spread the mixture in the bottom of a round cake pan.

🍂Beat the egg whites until stiff. Add the other ½ cup (125 mL)

sugar less 2 tbsp (30 mL) and beat the mixture into a meringue.

🍂Beat the yolks with the remaining 2 tbsp (30 mL) sugar. Add the salt and the uncooked farina. Fold in the beaten egg whites.

🍂Spread this mixture evenly over the cherries.

🍂Bake in a 350°F (180°C) oven for 40 minutes. To unmold, run a knife around the pan.

🍂Serve plain or with cream.

WESTERN BUCKWHEAT CAKE

1 cup (250 mL) buckwheat flour
1 cup (250 mL) all-purpose flour
1¼ tsp (6 mL) baking powder
½ tsp (2 mL) salt
¼ tsp (1 mL) cinnamon
or nutmeg
½ cup (125 mL) butter
1 cup (250 mL) sugar

2 eggs
1 tbsp (15 mL) grated orange zest
⅔ cup (150 mL) milk

🍂Preheat the oven to 350°F (180°C). Grease an 8- x 8-in. (20- x 20-cm) cake pan. Flour lightly.

🍂Sift together the buckwheat flour, the all-purpose flour, the baking powder, the salt and the cinnamon or nutmeg.

🍂Cream the butter. Gradually add the sugar, beating constantly. Add the eggs one at a time, beating well after each addition. Add the grated orange zest.

🍂Add the sifted dry ingredients to the creamed mixture alternately with the milk. Stir until smooth.

🍂Turn the batter into the prepared pan. Bake for 45 minutes or until well done.

Strawberry Meringue Cake

ANGEL FOOD CAKE

1 cup (250 mL) egg whites
(8 to 10)
pinch of salt
1 tsp (5 mL) cream of tartar
1 cup (250 mL) sifted pastry
flour
1½ cups (375 mL) finely
granulated sugar
1 tsp (5 mL) almond extract
1 tsp (5 mL) vanilla

❧ Add the salt to the egg whites and beat until foamy. Add the cream of tartar and beat until firm. Then add the sugar, 2 tbsp (30 mL) at a time, beating well after each addition.

❧ Sift the flour gradually over the egg whites, folding in gently after each addition. Add the almond and vanilla and fold in gently.

❧ Turn the batter into an ungreased 10- x 5-in. (25- x 12 cm) tube pan and place in an unheat-ed oven. Set the temperature at 300°F (150°C) and bake for about 50 minutes.

❧ Invert on top of 3 cups, let cool for 1 to 2 hours and unmold following the instructions for *Basic Yellow Sponge Cake* (see page 541).

STRAWBERRY MERINGUE CAKE

¼ cup (50 mL) butter
½ cup (125 mL) sugar
2 egg yolks
1¾ cups (425 mL) sifted pastry
flour
2 tsp (10 mL) baking powder
½ cup (125 mL) milk
3 tbsp (45 mL) whipping cream
¼ tsp (1 mL) almond extract
¼ tsp (1 mL) vanilla extract
2 egg whites
½ cup (125 mL) sugar
fresh strawberries, sliced and
sweetened

❧ Preheat the oven to 350°F (180°C). Grease a 12- x 8-in. (30- x 20-cm) baking pan. Flour lightly.

❧ Cream together the butter and the first ½ cup (125 mL) sugar. Add the egg yolks and beat until creamy, smooth and very light.

❧ Sift together the flour and the baking powder. Add to the creamed mixture alternately with the milk, cream and the almond and vanilla extracts. Stir until well blended.

❧ Turn the batter into the pre-pared pan.

❧ Beat the egg whites until firm. Add the remaining ½ cup (125 mL) sugar and beat until stiff. Spread this meringue over the batter in the pan.

❧ Bake 40 minutes.

❧ Cool in the pan on a cake rack. To serve, cut into squares and top with a generous helping of straw-berries (or with other fresh fruit of your choice).

QUÉBEC MAPLE SYRUP TOURLOUCHE

1 cup (250 mL) maple syrup
1 tbsp (15 mL) butter
3 tbsp (45 mL) maple sugar or
granulated sugar
1 egg
1 cup (125 mL) whole wheat
flour
2 tsp (10 mL) baking powder
¼ tsp (1 mL) salt
½ tsp (2 mL) nutmeg
½ cup (250 mL) milk
1 tsp (5 mL) vanilla
¼ cup (50 mL) chopped walnuts

❧ Boil the maple syrup for 3 min-utes. Pour it into a buttered 8- x

8-in. (20- x 20-cm) cake pan.

🍂 Cream the butter together with the maple or granulated sugar and the egg until smooth and creamy.

🍂 Sift the whole-wheat flour together with the baking powder, salt and nutmeg.

🍂 Add to the creamed mixture alternating with the milk and vanilla. Stir until well blended.

🍂 Pour the batter over the hot syrup in the baking pan. Cover and bake in a 400°F (200°C) oven for 25 minutes. It is important that the cake pan be well covered (foil can be used) for the whole baking period.

🍂 Unmold on a platter and sprinkle with the chopped nuts.

🍂 If desired, serve with whipped cream. Serve hot or warm.

MAPLE SYRUP CAKE

½ cup (125 mL) butter
⅓ cup (75 mL) finely granulated sugar
2 eggs, beaten
1 cup (250 mL) maple syrup
2 ½ cups (625 mL) sifted pastry flour
¾ tsp (3 mL) baking soda
2 tsp (10 mL) baking powder
¼ tsp (1 mL) ground ginger
½ cup (125 mL) hot water

🍂 Preheat the oven to 375°F (190°C). Grease an 8- x 8-in. (20- x 20-cm) cake pan.

🍂 Cream together the butter, sugar and beaten eggs. Add the maple syrup and beat until smooth and creamy.

🍂 Sift together the flour, baking soda, baking powder and ginger. Add to the creamed mixture alternately with the hot water.

🍂 Turn the batter into the prepared pan and bake for 35 minutes.

DE LUXE UPSIDE-DOWN CAKE

½ cup (125 mL) butter
2 cups (500 mL) dark brown sugar
1 tbsp (15 mL) water
fruit of your choice (canned or fresh)
¼ cup (50 mL) pecans
½ cup (125 mL) butter
1 cup (250 mL) finely granulated sugar
3 eggs
2½ cups (625 mL) sifted pastry flour
4 tsp (20 mL) baking powder
½ tsp (2 mL) salt
¾ cup (175 mL) milk
2 tsp (10 mL) vanilla

🍂 Melt the first ½ cup (125 mL) butter in a 13- x 10-in. (32- x 25-cm) cake pan.

🍂 Spread the brown sugar over the butter. Add the water and stir, over low heat, until the sugar is melted. In this syrup, place well-drained pineapple slices or peach or pear halves, peeled, sliced apples or a similar fruit of your choice. Sprinkle with the pecans.

🍂 To prepare the cake batter, cream together the other ½ cup (125 mL) butter and the fine sugar. Add the eggs, one at a time, beating well after each addition. Beat together until creamy and smooth.

🍂 Sift together the flour, baking powder and salt. Add to the creamed mixture alternately with the milk and vanilla. Pour the cake batter over the fruit.

🍂 Bake in a preheated 375°F (190°C) oven for 45 minutes.

🍂 Invert on a plate immediately and let stand 5 minutes before lifting the pan so that the fruit will have a chance to settle.

CHIFFON CUPCAKES

These light, delicate cupcakes do not need icing and are delicious when they soak up the apricot jam. They will stay fresh for a week, if kept in a cake tin, and will also freeze well.

1 cup (250 mL) fine granulated sugar
6 egg whites
¼ tsp (1 mL) cream of tartar
6 egg yolks
¼ tsp (1 mL) grated lemon zest
1 tbsp (15 mL) lemon juice
pinch of mace or nutmeg
1 cup (250 mL) all-purpose flour
¼ tsp (1 mL) salt
3 tbsp (45 mL) apricot jam
icing sugar or coconut

🍂 Measure out ½ cup (125 mL) of the sugar.

🍂 Beat the egg whites and cream of tartar together until foamy. Sprinkle 2 tbsp (30 mL) of the sugar on top. Using a hand beater or an electric mixer at medium speed, beat until the sugar is dissolved, about 1 minute. Repeat this process until the ½ cup (125 mL) sugar has been used up. Continue to beat until the meringue forms stiff, glossy peaks.

❦ TECHNIQUE ❦

RUM CAKE

1 Cream the butter. Add the sugar and continue beating.

2 Add the grated orange and lemon zests. Add the eggs, one at a time, beating well after each addition.

3 Add part of the flour mixture.

4 Add part of the sour milk.

🍃 Beat the egg yolks in a second bowl. Add the remaining ½ cup (125 mL) sugar, the lemon zest, the lemon juice and the mace or nutmeg, and beat with a hand beater until thick and light in color.

🍃 Sift together the flour and the salt. Fold by hand into the egg-yolk mixture until well blended.

🍃 Fold the flour and egg-yolk mixture into the beaten egg whites very gently, using a rubber spatula, until the mixture is thoroughly blended and there are no streaks of egg white.

🍃 Line a 12-cup muffin pan with paper cupcake liners and spoon the batter into each, filling only ⅔ full.

🍃 Bake in a preheated 350°F (180°C) oven for 12 to 15 minutes.

🍃 Cool slightly. Remove the cups from the pan and cool completely on a wire cake rack.

🍃 To serve, brush the tops with hot apricot jam and sprinkle with icing sugar or coconut.

RUM CAKE

1 cup (250 mL) butter or margarine
2 cups (500 mL) finely granulated sugar
grated zest of 2 oranges
grated zest of 1 lemon
2 eggs
2 ½ cups (625 mL) all-purpose flour
2 tsp (10 mL) baking powder
½ tsp (2 mL) baking soda
½ tsp (2 mL) salt
1 cup (250 mL) sour milk
1 cup (250 mL) walnuts,
chopped fine
juice of 2 oranges
juice of 1 lemon
4 tbsp (60 mL) rum

🍃 Preheat the oven to 350°F (180°C). Grease a 9-or 10-in. (23- or 25-cm) tube pan.

🍃 Cream the butter or margarine. Gradually add 1 cup (250 mL) of the sugar, beating constantly. When light and creamy, add the grated orange and lemon zests. Add the eggs, one at a time, beating well after each addition.

🍃 Sift together the flour, baking powder, baking soda and salt. Add the dry ingredients to the creamed mixture alternately with the sour milk. Fold in the chopped nuts.

🍃 Turn the batter into the prepared pan and bake for 1 hour or until a toothpick inserted in the cake comes out clean.

🍃 Meanwhile, place in a saucepan the orange and lemon juice, the rum and the remaining 1 cup (250 mL) sugar. Bring to a boil while stirring.

🍃 Pour this hot syrup over the cake as soon as it is taken out of the oven. Place the pan on a cake rack to cool before unmolding.

🍃 Serve garnished with sweetened whipped cream flavored with rum, or use a custard sauce (see custard filling for *Gâteau Saint Honoré*, page 556) flavored with rum.

CHOCOLATE BROWNIES

⅔ cup (150 mL) cocoa powder
6 tbsp (90 mL) butter
3 eggs
1 cup (250 mL) sugar
½ cup (125 mL) pastry flour
¼ tsp (1 mL) salt
½ tsp (2 mL) cinnamon
½ cup (125 mL) chopped walnuts
1 tsp (5 mL) vanilla

Rum Cake

ICING:

2 tbsp (30 mL) cocoa
2 tbsp (30 mL) butter
2 tbsp (30 mL) cream
1 cup (250 mL) icing sugar

🍃 Blend the cocoa and the butter over hot water in a double boiler just until the butter is melted. Remove from the heat and let cool slightly.

🍃 Beat the eggs until light in color. Gradually add the sugar, beating until smooth and thick. Add the cocoa and butter mixture and mix well.

🍃 Sift together the flour, salt and cinnamon and add this to the cocoa mixture; when well mixed, fold in the walnuts and the vanilla.

🍃 Bake in a greased 8- x 8-in. (20- x 20-cm) baking pan in a 400°F (200°C) oven for 15 minutes.

🍃 Ice while still hot, then let cool and cut into squares.

🍃 To prepare the icing, blend together over low heat the cocoa, butter and cream until the butter is melted. Remove from the heat, and beat in the icing sugar until smooth and creamy.

FUDGE CAKE SQUARES

This delicious, quick and easy recipe is always a favorite. The cake can be cut into neat little squares or dainty fingers.

2 eggs
1½ cups (375 mL) firmly-packed dark brown sugar
2 squares (2 oz or 60 g) unsweetened chocolate, melted
½ tsp (2 mL) almond extract
2 cups (500 mL) all-purpose flour
1 tsp (5 mL) baking soda
½ tsp (2 mL) salt
¼ cup (50 mL) cider vinegar
¾ cup (175 mL) milk

1 tsp (5 mL) vanilla
½ cup (125 mL) soft butter

🍃 Grease and flour an 13- x 9- x 2-in. (33- x 23- x 5-cm) pan.

🍃 Make sure all the ingredients are at room temperature.

🍃 Combine in a large mixing bowl the eggs, brown sugar, melted chocolate and almond extract. Beat for 3 minutes by hand or 1 minute using an electric mixer.

🍃 Sift together the flour, baking soda and salt.

🍃 Combine the vinegar, milk and vanilla.

🍃 To the chocolate mixture, add the dry ingredients, ½ the milk mixture and the soft butter. Beat for 3 minutes by hand or 1 minute using an electric mixer. Add the remainder of the milk mixture and beat for another few minutes.

🍃 Turn the batter into the prepared pan. Bake the cake in a preheated 350°F (180°C) oven for 45 to 50 minutes or until done. Let cool.

🍃 Sprinkle with icing sugar and cut into squares or fingers.

HONEY-CHOCOLATE BROWNIES

½ cup (125 mL) all-purpose flour
½ tsp (2 mL) baking powder
¼ (1 mL) salt
7 oz (220 g) semi-sweet chocolate
⅓ cup (75 mL) butter
2 eggs
6 tbsp (90 mL) honey
1 tbsp (15 mL) rum

🍃 Sift together the flour, baking powder and salt.

Fudge Cake Squares

🍂 Melt the chocolate and the butter over low heat. Let cool. Add the unbeaten eggs, one at a time, beating well after each addition. Add the honey and rum and mix well. Add the sifted dry ingredients.

🍂 Turn the batter into a buttered 8- x 8-in. (20- x 20-cm) pan and bake in a 350°F (180°C) oven for 35 minutes.

NEW YORK CHEESECAKE

CRUST:

1 cup (250 mL) all-purpose flour
¼ cup (50 mL) sugar
1 tsp (5 mL) grated lemon zest
½ tsp (2 mL) vanilla
1 egg yolk
½ cup (125 mL) butter

CHEESE FILLING:

2½ lbs (1.2 kg) cream cheese
1¾ cups (425 mL) sugar
3 tbsp (45 mL) flour
1½ tsp (7 mL) grated orange zest
1½ tsp (7 mL) grated lemon zest
¼ tsp (1 mL) vanilla
5 eggs
2 egg yolks
¼ cup (50 mL) whipping cream

🍂 To prepare the crust, mix together in a bowl the flour, sugar, lemon zest and vanilla. Make a well in the center and add the unbeaten egg yolk and the butter. Work the mixture together with your hands until it forms a ball.

🍂 Wrap the dough in wax paper and refrigerate for at least an hour.

🍂 When the pastry is thoroughly chilled, separate and oil thorough-

Honey-Chocolate Brownies

ly the bottom and sides of a 9-in. (23-cm) spring-form pan. Preheat the oven to 400°F (200°C).

🍂 Cut off about ¼ of the dough. Using a rolling pin, roll the piece of dough directly onto the bottom of the spring-form pan to a thickness of ⅛ in. (0.3 cm). Trim the edges.

🍂 Bake this crust for 10 minutes or until golden. Cool.

🍂 Divide the remaining dough into 3 pieces. On a lightly floured board, roll out each piece with the palms of your hands into a long narrow strip ⅛ in. (0.3 cm) thick. Fit the 3 strips one on top of the other around the inside of the sides of the spring-form pan, pressing the joining edges of dough together to seal any gaps. The strips should cover ¾ up the sides of the pan. Trim the top edge of the dough neatly.

🍂 Refrigerate until the filling is ready.

🍂 To prepare the cheese filling, mix together in a large bowl the cream cheese, sugar, flour, grated orange and lemon zests and the vanilla. Beat together until smooth, using an electric beater. Add the 5 whole eggs and the 2 egg yolks one at a time, stirring lightly after each addition. Gently stir in the whipping cream.

🍂 Re-assemble the pastry-lined sides and bottom of the spring-form pan. Fill with the cheese mixture.

🍂 Bake the cheesecake for 10 minutes in a preheated 550°F (290°C) oven, then reduce the heat to 200°F (100°C) and bake for 1 more hour.

🍂 Remove from the oven and let cool completely on a wire cake rack.

🍂 Carefully release and remove the sides of the pan. Serve the cheesecake without removing the bottom of the pan.

De Luxe Cream Cheesecake

Beat the egg whites with the remaining ½ cup (125 mL) sugar.

🍃 To the cottage cheese mixture, add the whipped cream, the lemon zest and juice, the almond extract and the beaten egg whites. Stir to blend.

🍃 Turn into the prepared pan. Refrigerate for 4 to 8 hours before serving. If desired, top with fresh fruit for a simply wonderful dessert.

DE LUXE CREAM CHEESECAKE

GRAHAM CRACKER CRUST:
1½ cups (375 mL) Graham cracker crumbs
4 tbsp (60 mL) melted butter
1 tsp (5 mL) cinnamon

FILLING:
1 lb (500 g) cream cheese
1 cup (250 mL) sugar
¼ cup (50 mL) all-purpose flour
5 egg yolks
2 tbsp (30 mL) lemon juice
grated zest 1 lemon
2 cups (500 mL) sour cream
5 egg whites

🍃 To prepare the crust, mix the Graham cracker crumbs with the melted butter and cinnamon. Use to line the bottom and sides of a 10-in. (25-cm) spring-form pan. Refrigerate until ready to use.

🍃 To prepare the cheese filling, beat together the cream cheese and the sugar until very light. Add the flour and the unbeaten egg yolks all at once. Beat until smooth and creamy. Add the lemon juice and the grated lemon zest. Beat in the sour cream. Beat

NO-BAKE CHEESECAKE

GRAHAM CRACKER CRUST:
2 cups (500 mL) Graham cracker crumbs
½ cup (125 mL) light brown sugar or maple sugar
6 tbsp (90 mL) melted butter
½ tsp (2 mL) salt

FILLING:
3 eggs, separated
½ cup (125 mL) milk
1 cup (250 mL) sugar
2 envelopes unflavored gelatin
½ cup (125 mL) cold water
3 cups (750 mL) cottage cheese
1 cup (250 mL) whipping cream
zest and juice of 1 lemon
1 tsp (5 mL) almond extract

🍃 To prepare the Graham cracker crust, mix together all the ingredients and press the mixture onto the bottom and sides of an 8-in. (20-cm) spring-form pan or a 9- x 9-in. (23- x 23-cm) cake pan or a loaf pan. (If using a pan without removable sides, line it with wax paper with the paper overhanging the pan so that the cake can be removed easily at serving time.)

🍃 Refrigerate the crust unbaked.

🍃 To prepare the filling, in the top of a double boiler, beat together the egg yolks, the milk and ½ cup (125 mL) of the sugar. Cook over boiling water, stirring frequently, until thick and creamy.

🍃 Meanwhile, soak the gelatin in the cold water for 5 minutes. Add to the egg-yolk mixture and stir until the gelatin is dissolved. Let cool.

🍃 Press the cottage cheese through a sieve or beat it in with an electric mixer for 30 seconds until it is more or less smooth. Stir in the egg-yolk and gelatin mixture.

🍃 Whip the cream until firm.

10 minutes with an electric mixer until the mixture is smooth and light.

ᔧ Beat the egg whites until stiff. Fold them carefully into the cheese mixture.

ᔧ Turn the cheese filling into the prepared pan. Bake in a 350°F (180°C) oven for 1 hour. Turn off the heat and leave the cake in the oven for 1 more hour. Open the oven door and leave the cake in the open oven for 1 more hour. (The cake is in the oven for 3 hours in total.)

ᔧ Remove from the oven and let it cool completely.

ᔧ Unmold by releasing and carefully removing the sides of the spring-form pan.

FRUIT TOPPING

When fresh fruit is in season, you can prepare a delicious topping for this cheesecake using blueberries, strawberries or raspberries.

ᔧ To prepare the fruit topping, place 2 cups (500 mL) fresh berries in a saucepan along with 1 cup (250 mL) of apple juice and ½ cup (125 mL) sugar. Bring to a boil.

ᔧ Dissolve 1½ tbsp (25 mL) cornstarch in 1 tbsp (15 mL) water. Add it to the fruit and stir constantly until the mixture is thick and transparent. Let cool.

ᔧ Top the cake with the fruit mixture.

SAVARIN CAKE

CAKE:

1 tsp (5 mL) sugar
¼ tsp (1 mL) ground ginger
½ cup (125 mL) warm water

2 packages active dry yeast
4 cups (1 L) all-purpose flour
6 whole eggs, well beaten
⅔ cup (150 mL) melted butter
¼ cup (50 mL) sugar
1 tsp (5 mL) salt
⅔ cup (150 mL) currants

RUM SYRUP:

1 ½ cups (375 mL) sugar
2 cups (500 mL) water
4 slices lemon, unpeeled
4 slices orange, unpeeled
½ to 1 cup (125 to 250 mL) rum

APRICOT GLAZE:

⅓ cup (75 mL) apricot jam
1 tbsp (15 mL) lemon juice

ᔧ To prepare the cake, stir the 1 tsp (5 mL) sugar and the ginger into the warm water until dissolved. Add the yeast and let stand for 10 minutes. Stir well.

ᔧ Sift the flour into a large mixing bowl. Add the yeast and mix (it will be a dry mixture). Cover and let stand for 5 minutes.

ᔧ Add the well-beaten eggs and beat for 5 minutes with a wooden spoon. Cover and let stand for 30 minutes.

ᔧ Add the melted butter in 4 parts, beating well after each addition. The butter will tend to ooze out of the dough, but this is normal. Add the sugar, salt and currants. Beat for 5 minutes with a wooden spoon, or until the batter is smooth and elastic.

ᔧ Grease a 10-in. (25-cm) tube pan. Place the dough in the pan. Even out the top with a greased spatula.

ᔧ Cover the pan and let the dough rise in a warm place until triple in bulk. The dough should come to almost the top of the

tube pan.

ᔧ Bake in a preheated 375°F (190°C) oven for 40 to 45 minutes.

ᔧ Unmold the cake onto a cake rack. When the cake has cooled somewhat, arrange it on a serving dish and nap it with the rum syrup.

RUM SYRUP

ᔧ Bring the sugar and water to a boil. Add the lemon and orange slices, then cover and let simmer for 15 minutes.

ᔧ Let the syrup cool and stir in the rum.

ᔧ Slowly pour the syrup over the cake. Cool for 2 hours, spooning the syrup over the cake as often as possible.

APRICOT GLAZE

ᔧ Mix the apricot jam with the lemon juice. Heat slightly and pass through a fine sieve.

ᔧ When ready to serve, cover the cake with the apricot glaze.

CREAM PUFF SHELLS

½ cup (125 mL) water
¼ cup (50 mL) shortening
½ cup (125 mL) pastry flour
2 eggs

ᔧ Bring the water and shortening to a boil. Add the sifted pastry flour all at once, stirring until the mixture clears the sides of the pan and forms a ball.

ᔧ Remove from the heat. Let cool, then add the eggs, one at a time, beating well after each addition. Continue beating until the mixture is smooth and satiny.

ᔧ Drop 6 rounded tablespoons of

dough onto a greased baking sheet 3 in. (7 cm) apart.

🍂 Bake the puffs in a preheated 450°F (230°C) oven for 15 minutes. Reduce the heat to 350°F (180°C) and bake for another 30 to 35 minutes.

🍂 Let the puff shells cool at room temperature in an area free of drafts.

🍂 Cut the cream puffs open and fill with either sweetened whipped cream flavored with vanilla, or with a custard filling (see the recipe for custard filling for *Gâteau Saint Honoré*, page 556).

RUM BABAS

BABAS:

1 tsp (5 mL) sugar
¼ cup (50 mL) warm water
1 package active dry yeast
¼ cup (50 mL) warm milk
2 cups (500 mL) all-purpose flour
4 eggs, lightly beaten
½ tsp (2 mL) salt
1 tbsp (15 mL) sugar
⅔ cup (150 mL) soft sweet butter
1 tbsp (15 mL) currants (optional)

SYRUP:

1 cup (250 mL) sugar
1 ½ (375 mL) cups water
½ cup (125 mL) rum

🍂 To prepare the babas, stir the 1 tsp (5 mL) sugar into the warm water until dissolved. Add the yeast and let stand for 10 minutes. Add the warm milk. Stir well.

🍂 Sift the flour into the center of a large mixing bowl. Make a well in the middle of the flour and pour in the eggs and the well-stirred yeast. Gradually blend the flour in with the eggs and the yeast mixture by working with the fingertips until everything is well mixed. Knead in the bowl for 2 minutes, adding a little more flour if necessary to make a workable mixture.

🍂 Cover and let rise in a warm place until double in bulk.

🍂 Punch down the dough. Add the salt and the 1 tbsp (15 mL) sugar and mix well. Blend in the butter and the currants. Knead by hand for another 3 to 4 minutes.

🍂 Half-fill greased baba molds or muffin pans with the dough.

🍂 Cover and let rise in a warm place until double in bulk.

🍂 Bake in a preheated 450°F (230°C) oven for 10 minutes, then reduce the heat to 350°F (180°C) and bake for another 20 to 30 minutes, depending on the size of the molds.

🍂 Unmold and the babas and dredge them in the syrup while still hot.

🍂 To prepare the syrup, boil the sugar and water for about 5 minutes or until a light syrup has formed (218°F or 103°C on a candy thermometer). Remove from the heat.

🍂 Cool slightly and add the rum.

🍂 Roll the hot babas in the hot syrup until they are well soaked. Let them cool on a cake rack placed on wax paper.

MEXICAN BUNUELOS

Bunuelos are big, crispy fried cakes eaten at Christmas Eve supper in Mexico. They are served plain or with cinnamon syrup or, sometimes, honey. But no matter how they are served, bunuelos are puffy, brown, crisp and just delicious.

2 to 3 cups (500 to 750 mL) all-purpose flour
1 tsp (5 mL) sugar
1 tsp (5 mL) baking powder
1 tsp (5 mL) salt
2 eggs
½ cup (125 mL) milk
4 tbsp (60 mL) melted butter

🍂 Sift 2 cups (500 mL) of the flour. Measure it out and sift it again together with the sugar, baking powder and salt. Reserve the third cup (250 mL) of flour for later.

🍂 Beat the eggs until very light. Add the milk.

🍂 Beat the egg and milk mixture into the dry ingredients and mix thoroughly. If using an electric mixer, set at medium speed for 3 minutes. Add the melted butter and beat for another 2 minutes.

🍂 Spread the third cup (250 mL) of flour on a pastry board. Turn the dough onto the board and knead it until smooth, picking up just enough of the extra flour to make a soft dough.

🍂 Divide the dough into 1 ½-in. (4-cm) balls. Brush the balls with melted shortening and place them on a piece of wax paper. Cover with another piece of wax paper and let stand for 20 to 30 minutes.

🍂 Flatten each ball with the floured palm of the hand.

🍂 Deep-fry the cakes in fat until they are puffy and golden brown. Fry only as many at one time as will float in the fat without crowding. When they are evenly golden brown, lift them out with a slotted spoon and drain on a paper towel.

🍂 When cooled, sprinkle with icing sugar.

DESSERTS, SAUCES AND FROSTINGS

CUSTARDS AND DESSERT CREAMS

For a light and delicious dessert that may be eaten hot or cold, there is nothing better than a good custard.

🍂 The basic ingredients of a custard are eggs, milk and sugar. The proportions in which these ingredients are used determines whether the custard is firm or cream-like. The size of the eggs also has an effect on the custard's consistency.

🍂 The best custards are made with egg yolks, but whole eggs can be used rather than the yolks only; the trick is to strain the custard after adding the beaten eggs to the milk.

MAKING CUSTARDS

The number of eggs used depends on the type of custard desired.

🍂 As a general rule, for a baked custard use 3 whole eggs (or 2 whole eggs and 2 yolks, or 6 yolks) for every 2 cups (500 mL) of milk or cream.

🍂 For a custard of medium consistency cooked in a saucepan, use 6 egg yolks (or 3 whole eggs and 2 yolks, or 4 egg yolks and 2 whole eggs, or 2 egg yolks and 2 tbsp (30 mL) of cornstarch) for every 2 cups (500 mL) of milk.

🍂 Do not overbake a custard or a dessert with a custard base. If left in the oven too long, it will become watery. Bake in a 300°F (150°C) oven for 40 minutes, if small custard cups are used, or for 60 minutes if a large dish is used. A meat thermometer may also be used to test if the custard is cooked; the custard will be ready when the thermometer indicates 175°F (80°C). Never let the internal temperature rise above 190°F (88°C).

🍂 To reduce the cooking time, heat the milk before adding the other ingredients.

🍂 If you prefer a custard that is golden brown on top, use well-beaten eggs.

🍂 To ensure that the custard remains whole when it is turned out of the mold, beat the eggs lightly.

🍂 For a fluffy custard, use the whole egg. Beat the egg whites until stiff, sweeten them with 2 tbsp (30 mL) of sugar and fold them into the custard.

🍂 When using custard as a filling in tarts, always heat the milk before mixing it with the eggs; this will prevent the bottom crust of the tarts from becoming moist.

🍂 Custards cooked in a saucepan must never boil. Set the heat on low and stir constantly while cooking the custard. It will be done when it coats the spoon. Remove the custard from the heat and pour it through a fine sieve.

🍂 For a caramel custard, replace the sugar with ¼ cup (50 mL) of molasses.

🍂 For a fruit custard, cover the bottom of the dish with sliced fruit that has been sweetened to taste. Pour the very hot custard over the fruit. Cover and refrigerate.

🍂 For a more nutritious custard, add 4 to 8 tbsp (60 to 120 mL) of wheat germ.

🍂 For a rich custard, replace all or part of the milk with light or rich cream.

MAKING DESSERT CREAMS

Use a saucepan or casserole that has a thick base, so that the heat is evenly distributed during the cooking. Pastry creams and almond creams contain flour and are boiled in order to thicken them; a regular custard does not contain flour and is never boiled.

🍂 Begin by boiling the milk. Add any flavoring that the recipe calls for. Once the milk has boiled, take it off the heat, cover and let it stand for 15 minutes in a warm place.

🍂 While the milk is standing, beat the egg yolks or the whole eggs together with the sugar, the flour and the salt. Continue beating until the mixture is very light and fluffy. When making almond cream, add the powdered almonds at this stage.

🍂 Add the egg mixture to the warm milk, a little at a time, stirring constantly. Return the saucepan to the heat and cook, stirring all the time, until the cream thickens.

🍂 When preparing pastry cream and almond cream, add the butter and stir until it melts.

🍂 To prevent a skin from forming on a pastry cream or almond cream, place a knob of butter on the tip of a sharp knife and brush it over the surface of the warm mixture.

PRESSURE-COOKER CUSTARD

2 cups (500 mL) milk
2 whole eggs
⅓ cup (75 mL) sugar
¼ tsp (1 mL) salt
½ tsp (2 mL) vanilla

🐚 Heat the milk. Beat the eggs lightly with the sugar and the salt. Slowly add the hot milk, beating constantly. Add the vanilla. Pour the mixture into custard cups and cover the cups with foil or with several layers of waxed paper, well secured. Place the cups on a rack in the pressure-cooker. Add ½ cup (125 mL) of water to the bottom of the pot.

🐚 Secure the cover and cook the custard 3 minutes at 15 pounds pressure. Reduce the pressure quickly under cold, running water. Refrigerate the custard.

CHOCOLATE CUSTARD
Heat the milk with 3 tbsp (45 mL) of cocoa. Proceed as above.

COCONUT CUSTARD
Sprinkle 1 tbsp (15 mL) of coconut on top of the custard cups before cooking.

COFFEE CUSTARD
Add 2 tbsp (30 mL) of instant coffee to the milk.

BAKED VANILLA CUSTARD

2 whole eggs or 3 egg yolks
2 tbsp (30 mL) white, maple or brown sugar
1 cup (250 mL) cold milk

Pressure-Cooker Custard

¼ tsp (1 mL) vanilla
pinch of nutmeg

🐚 Lightly beat the whole eggs or egg yolks.

🐚 Dissolve the white, maple or brown sugar in the cold milk. Add the eggs, the vanilla and the nutmeg.

🐚 Pour the mixture into custard cups and place them in a pan half-filled with hot water. Bake the custard in a 350°F (180°C) oven for 30 to 40 minutes, or until a knife inserted in the center comes out clean.

🐚 Be careful to set the oven as indicated and to cook the custard only until it is done. If overcooked, the custard will become watery.

QUICK CUSTARD

¼ cup (50 mL) sugar or molasses
½ cup (125 mL) powdered skim milk

pinch of salt
½ cup (125 mL) milk
2 whole eggs
4 egg yolks
1½ cups (375 mL) milk

🐚 Mix together the sugar, the powdered milk and the salt in a saucepan. Add the ½ cup (125 mL) of milk, the whole eggs and the egg yolks and beat until smooth. Add the 1½ cups (375 mL) of milk and stir to blend.

🐚 Cook for 4 to 5 minutes, stirring constantly. The custard will be cooked when it reaches a temperature of 175°F (80°C) on a meat thermometer.

🐚 Refrigerate the custard. If desired, flavor it with vanilla, almond extract, rose water or orange blossom water.

[571]

BAKED COFFEE CUSTARD

2 tsp (10 mL) instant coffee and
1 cup (250 mL) boiling water
or 1 cup (250 mL) strong coffee
1 cup (250 mL) light cream
4 tbsp (60 mL) sugar
pinch of salt
2 or 3 whole eggs

🍃 Instant coffee is perfect for this recipe. Dissolve 2 heaping tsp (10 mL) in the boiling water to make strong coffee.

🍃 Beat the eggs lightly.

🍃 Heat the coffee with the cream, the sugar and the salt. Pour slowly over the eggs.

🍃 Mix thoroughly. Turn into a buttered mold, then place the mold in a pan of hot water. Bake in a 325°F (160°C) oven for 50 minutes. Serve the custard cold.

MAPLE CUSTARD

3 eggs
¼ cup (50 mL) sugar
¼ tsp (1 mL) salt
2 cups (500 mL) scalded milk
½ tsp (2 mL) vanilla
nutmeg
½ cup (125 mL) maple sugar
½ cup (125 mL) brown sugar
1 tbsp (15 mL) flour
½ cup (125 mL) water
1 tsp (5 mL) butter
¼ tsp (1 mL) maple extract

🍃 Beat the eggs. Mix together with the sugar and the salt. Add the scalded milk and the vanilla.

🍃 Pour the mixture into buttered custard cups and sprinkle the custard lightly with nutmeg. Place the cups in a pan of hot water and bake the custard in a 325°F (160°C) oven for 30 to 40 minutes.

🍃 The custard may be served hot or cold with maple sauce prepared as follows:

🍃 Mix together and cook the maple sugar, the brown sugar, the flour, the water, the butter and the maple extract until the sauce is smooth. Taste and, if desired, add more maple extract. Serve the sauce warm.

ALMOND CREAM

Almond cream is similar to pastry cream but it calls for more flour and butter and the addition of powdered almonds or pulverized macaroons. This delicious filling can be flavored with vanilla, lemon or orange.

2½ cups (625 mL) hot milk
flavoring to taste
1 egg
4 egg yolks
½ cup (125 mL) sugar
½ cup (125 mL) flour
2 tbsp (30 mL) powdered almonds or pulverized macaroons
4 tbsp (60 mL) butter

🍃 Scald the milk, add the flavoring, cover and set aside.

🍃 Beat the whole egg and the egg yolks until light. Add the sugar and the flour and beat again, then add the powdered almonds or macaroons.

🍃 Gradually add the egg mixture to the warm milk, stirring constantly. Return the saucepan to the heat and bring the mixture to a simmer, stirring all the while. Cook until the mixture thickens, remove it from the heat and stir in the butter, mixing until it melts. Let cool. (See also the general directions on page 570.)

Almond Cream

❧ TECHNIQUE ❧

ALMOND CREAM

1   Put the eggs in a bowl.

2   Add the sugar, the flour, and the powdered almonds.

3   Mix well with an electric beater.

4   Gradually add the hot milk, stirring constantly.

BLENDER CHOCOLATE CREAM

2 eggs
1 cup (250 mL) sugar
6 tbsp (90 mL) cold water
2½ 1-oz (30-g) squares
unsweetened chocolate
¾ cup (175 mL) butter
1 tsp (5mL) vanilla

❧ Place the eggs in the blender jar. Cover and blend 30 seconds at high speed.
❧ Boil the sugar and water mixture until it makes a thin syrup, or until a few drops in cold water make a soft ball.
❧ Blend the eggs at high speed for another second. With the blender still on high, raise the stopper and slowly pour in the boiling syrup. Blend until the syrup is totally absorbed.

❧ Cut the chocolate into small pieces and add to the blender mixture with the butter and the vanilla. Cover and blend for 50 to 60 seconds. Allow to stand for 1 hour in the refrigerator.
❧ This cream is also perfect when used to fill and ice cakes.

PASTRY CREAM

Pastry cream is used as a filling in pastries such as éclairs and cream puffs, as well as in other desserts. It can be flavored with vanilla, lemon, coffee or chocolate, according to how you plan to use it.

2½ cups (625 mL) boiled milk
flavoring to taste
5 egg yolks or 4 whole eggs
¾ cup (175 mL) sugar
2 tbsp (30 mL) flour
pinch of salt
1 tsp (5 mL) butter

❧ Follow the method outlined on page 570. See also page 603 for the recipe for *Vanilla Pastry Cream.*

QUÉBEC CRÈME BRULÉE

2 cups (500 mL) milk
3 tbsp (45 mL) cornstarch
¾ cup (175 mL) molasses
1 tsp (5 mL) almond extract

❧ Mix the milk and the cornstarch.
❧ Heat the molasses until it starts to caramelize. Pour the molasses into the milk and cook the mixture until it becomes smooth. Flavor with the almond extract.
❧ Pour into a mold and cool. Serve this dessert cream very cold. If desired, garnish with chopped nuts.

CRÈME CARAMEL

⅜ cup (85 mL) brown sugar
3 tbsp (45 mL) butter
1 cup (250 mL) milk
2 tbsp (30 mL) cornstarch
2 tbsp (30 mL) cold milk
1 cup (250 mL) firmly packed brown sugar
¼ lb (125 g) butter
½ cup (125 mL) whipping cream

❧ Cook the ⅜ cup (85 mL) brown sugar and the butter in a heavy-bottomed saucepan for 2 minutes. Add the milk and cook the mixture over low heat until the sugar dissolves.
❧ Mix the cornstarch with the cold milk. Add to the first mix-

Crème Caramel

❦ TECHNIQUE ❦

CRÈME CARAMEL

1 Cook the brown sugar and the butter.

2 Add the milk and cook over low heat.

3 Add the cornstarch mixed with the milk.

4 Make a caramel sauce by mixing together and cooking the brown sugar, the butter and the cream.

Pompadour Cream

SPANISH CREAM

½ tbsp (25 mL) gelatin
¼ cup (50 mL) cold water
3 egg yolks
¼ tsp (1 mL) salt
2¾ cups (675 mL) milk
½ tsp (2 mL) vanilla
3 egg whites
⅓ cup (75 mL) sugar

❧ Soak the gelatin in cold water.

❧ In a double boiler, cook the egg yolks, the salt and the milk until the mixture thickens slightly. Add the gelatin and allow to melt. When cool, flavor the mixture with the vanilla.

❧ Beat the egg whites until stiff, gradually adding the sugar. Fold the egg whites into the first mixture when it starts to thicken. Pour the cream into a mold and place it in the refrigerator to set.

ture and cook until the custard coats a spoon. Pour the custard into a mold and let it cool.

❧ Serve with a caramel sauce prepared as follows:

❧ In a heavy saucepan, simmer the 1 cup (250 mL) brown sugar, the butter and the cream for 10 minutes, stirring occasionally.

SAINT ISIDORE MAPLE SYRUP CREAM

¾ cup (175 mL) maple syrup
2 tbsp (30 mL) butter
½ cup (125 mL) water
2 eggs, separated
2 tbsp (30 mL) cornstarch
2 cups (500 mL) milk or cream
¼ tsp (1 mL) salt
1 tsp (5 mL) vanilla

❧ In a heavy saucepan, cook the maple syrup and the butter until

the syrup is very thick and bubbly. It must caramelize without burning. Add the water all at once. The syrup will harden, so bring it to simmering point and cook it a few minutes longer to soften it. Boil fast for 3 minutes and let the syrup cool.

❧ Place the egg yolks in the top of a double boiler and beat them lightly. Add the maple syrup mixture, the cornstarch blended with ¼ cup (50 mL) of the milk or cream and the salt. Mix thoroughly. Add the rest of the milk or cream and the vanilla and stir constantly until the mixture thickens. Remove it from the heat and let it cool, stirring often.

❧ Beat the egg whites until stiff and fold them into the mixture. Turn the cream into a crystal dish and refrigerate it until set. Garnish with whipped cream if desired.

SWEDISH CREAM WITH STRAWBERRIES

This is a traditional Swedish dessert that never fails to please. Other fruits may also be used, either fresh or frozen. This wonderful and smooth cream will keep for a week in the refrigerator, so you might want to prepare it well in advance.

2 envelopes unflavored gelatin
½ cup (125 mL) light cream
1½ cups (375 mL) whipping cream
1 cup (250 mL) sugar
2 cups (500 mL) sour cream
4 cups (1 L) fresh strawberries
½ cup (125 mL) sugar
1 tsp (5 mL) vanilla

❧ Sprinkle the gelatin over the light cream and let it stand for 5 minutes.

❧ In a saucepan, mix together the whipping cream and the sugar, then add the gelatin and cream mixture. Simmer over low heat until the sugar dissolves. Pour the mixture into a bowl and refrigerate. When the mixture has thickened slightly, and has the texture of egg whites, fold in the sour cream.

❧ Pour the dessert cream into a crystal dish, cover and refrigerate until ready to serve.

❧ A few hours before serving, wash and slice the fresh strawberries. Add the sugar and the vanilla and stir gently, taking care not to bruise the fruit. Arrange the strawberries in a serving dish and serve them as a garnish to the cream.

CHESTNUT CREAM LYONNAISE

60 chestnuts
½ cup (125 mL) sweet butter
1 cup (250 mL) superfine sugar
1 to 2 tsp (5 to 10 mL) vanilla
3 eggs, separated

❧ Using the point of a vegetable knife, make incisions in the rounded end of each chestnut. Place the chestnuts in a saucepan and cover them with cold water. Bring to a boil and boil for 15 minutes. Remove the saucepan from the heat.

❧ Keeping the chestnuts in the warm water (so that they do not cool), remove the peel and the brown skin from each nut. Put the chestnuts through a food mill.

❧ Add the softened butter, the

sugar, the vanilla and the egg yolks to the chestnuts. Beat the egg whites until stiff and fold them into the chestnut mixture. Turn into a buttered dish.

❧ Place the dish in a pan containing 3 in. (8 cm) of hot water and bake the cream in a 325°F (160°C) oven for 1 hour.

❧ Serve hot or cold. If desired, serve this cream with a maple syrup sauce prepared as follows:

❧ Heat together 1 cup (250 mL) of maple syrup, 1 tbsp (15 mL) of butter and 1 tbsp (15 mL) of cognac.

POMPADOUR CREAM

½ cup (125 mL) sugar
2 tbsp (30 mL) flour
2 egg yolks, beaten
1 whole egg
2 cups (500 mL) milk
½ tsp (2 mL) vanilla
2 egg whites, beaten
½ cup (125 mL) confectioner's sugar
1-oz (30-g) square chocolate, melted
vanilla
pinch of salt

❧ Mix together the sugar, the flour, the beaten egg yolks and the whole egg. Warm the milk and flavor it with vanilla. Gradually add this to the first mixture, stirring constantly. Cook in a double boiler until the mixture thickens.

❧ Pour the cream into individual cups and let it cool.

❧ Cover with a mousse prepared as follows:

❧ Beat the egg whites until they form peaks, then add the confectioner's sugar. Mix thoroughly

and carefully fold in the melted chocolate, the vanilla and the salt. Place a spoonful of the mousse on top of each cup of cream.

❧ Serve chilled.

CHOCOLATE FLAN DE NEVERS

FILLING:
1¼ cups (300 mL) milk
4 tbsp (60 mL) sugar
6 egg yolks
8 oz (250 g) imported chocolate
1 cup (250 mL) sweet butter
30 ladyfingers or almond macaroons

PASTRY CREAM:
3 cups (750 mL) light cream
3 egg yolks
⅔ cup (150 mL) sugar
pinch of salt
1 tsp (5 mL) vanilla
or 2 tbsp (30 mL) rum

❧ To make the filling, heat the milk. Place the sugar and the egg yolks in the top of a double boiler. Mix well. Stir in the warm milk and cook the mixture over boiling water, stirring frequently. When it is thick and creamy, take the mixture off the heat and press it through a fine sieve. Allow to cool.

❧ Melt the chocolate in the top of the double boiler. Add the butter and beat until well mixed. Pour the melted chocolate into the first mixture. Beat this with an electric mixer until it is smooth.

❧ Dip the ladyfingers or the macaroons into water flavored with vanilla or rum. Use them to line the bottom and the sides of a mold.

❧ Using a spoon, spread the chocolate mixture over the biscuits. Cover the chocolate with another layer of biscuits, then cover the dish with a sheet of aluminum paper. Put it in the refrigerator for 8 to 24 hours.

❧ Unmold the flan and spread it with chilled pastry cream made with the cream, egg yolks, sugar, salt and flavoring. (Follow the method outlined on page 570.)

ORANGE VELVET CREAM

½ cup (125 mL) milk
1 tbsp (15 mL) gelatin
½ cup (125 mL) sugar
1 egg, beaten
½ cup (125 mL) cream
½ cup (125 mL) orange juice
1 tsp (5 mL) lemon juice
orange sections

❧ Pour the milk into a saucepan. Add the gelatin, the sugar, the beaten egg and the cream. Cook, stirring until the gelatin dissolves and the mixture thickens. Do not let it boil.

❧ Turn the mixture into a mold and let it cool slightly. Stir in the orange juice and the lemon juice. Refrigerate the cream until it is firm and very cold.

❧ Serve with orange sections rolled in confectioners' sugar.

CARAMEL CREAM

¾ cup (175 mL) sugar
3 cups (750 mL) light cream
2 tbsp (30 mL) gelatin
¼ cup (50 mL) cold water
1 tsp (5 mL) vanilla

❧ Heat the sugar until it starts to caramelize. Add the cream and stir until the sugar is completely dissolved and the mixture is smooth.

❧ Soften the gelatin in the cold water. Add the warm sugar mixture and stir until the gelatin is completely dissolved. Stir in the vanilla.

❧ Pour the mixture into a mold and refrigerate. Serve cold.

DE LUXE CHOCOLATE MOUSSE

½ lb (250 g) sweet chocolate
¼ cup (50 mL) hot water
1 tbsp (15 mL) instant coffee
5 egg yolks
2 tbsp (30 mL) cognac
or Cointreau
5 egg whites

❧ Place the chocolate, the hot water and the coffee in the top of a double boiler. Melt the chocolate over hot—not boiling—water. When the chocolate melts, give it a stir and set it aside to cool.

❧ Beat the egg yolks until very light, then stir in the cognac or the Cointreau. Add this to the chocolate and mix thoroughly.

❧ Beat the egg whites until stiff, then fold them into the chocolate mixture. Stir gently until no trace of egg white remains.

❧ Turn the mousse into individual molds. Chill for 12 hours before serving.

PARISIAN CHOCOLATE MOUSSE

½ lb (250 g) semi-sweet chocolate
½ cup (125 mL) sugar
¼ cup (50 mL) water

De Luxe Chocolate Mousse

❦ TECHNIQUE ❦

DE LUXE CHOCOLATE MOUSSE

1 Place the chocolate, the hot water and the coffee in the top of a double boiler.

2 Add the cognac or Cointreau to the egg yolks and beat until light.

3 Add to the chocolate mixture and mix thoroughly.

4 Beat the egg whites until stiff and fold them into the chocolate mixture.

[579]

Strawberry Bavarian Cream

5 egg yolks
1 tsp (5 mL) vanilla
5 egg whites, stiffly beaten

🐸 Place the chocolate, the sugar and the water in the top of a double boiler over boiling water. Stir the mixture until it is light and smooth.

🐸 Beat the egg yolks until fluffy. Stir them into the chocolate mixture. Add the vanilla and stir for a few minutes. Remove the mixture from the heat and allow to cool.

🐸 Beat the egg whites until stiff and fold them into the cooled chocolate mixture.

🐸 Refrigerate the mousse for 6 to 8 hours before serving. As it is very rich, this mousse is usually served in small portions, in individual dessert cups.

FRENCH CHESTNUT MOUSSE

⅔ cup (150 mL) sugar
¼ cup (50 mL) water
6 egg yolks
2 cups (500 mL) whipping cream
1 cup (250 mL) chestnuts in syrup
1 tsp (5 mL) cognac

🐸 Place the sugar and water in a saucepan. Boil the syrup for 5 minutes.

🐸 Beat the egg yolks until they are light and fluffy. Pour the hot syrup slowly over the yolks, stirring lightly. Cook the mixture in a double boiler until it has the consistency of custard. Remove it from the heat and beat until the mixture is lukewarm. Using an electric mixer makes this rather lengthy operation easier.

🐸 Chop the chestnuts into small pieces. Add the chestnuts, the cognac and the whipped cream to the warm mousse. Mix the mousse well, then cover and refrigerate until it has set.

STRAWBERRY BAVARIAN CREAM

1 box frozen strawberries
¼ cup (50 mL) cold milk
2 envelopes unflavored gelatin
¼ cup (50 mL) sugar
2 egg yolks
1 cup (250 mL) crushed ice
1 cup (250 mL) whipping cream

🐸 Thaw the strawberries. Pour ½ cup (125 mL) of the juice into a saucepan and bring it to a boil.

🐸 Put the cold milk, the gelatin, the sugar and the hot juice in the jar of a blender. Cover and blend at high speed for 40 seconds. Add the egg yolks and the strawberries. Cover and blend for another 5 seconds.

🐸 Add the cream and the crushed ice. Cover and blend for 20 seconds, or until the mixture thickens. Pour it into an oiled mold.

🐸 Refrigerate the cream for 30 to 60 minutes, or until it sets. Unmold the cream just before you wish to serve it.

FRENCH BAVARIAN CREAM

1 cup (250 mL) milk
1 tbsp (15 mL) gelatin
2 tbsp (30 mL) water
½ cup (125 mL) sugar
1 tsp (5 mL) vanilla
1 cup (250 mL) whipping cream

🍃 Heat the milk, then soften the gelatin in the water. Add the gelatin, the sugar and the vanilla to the milk and stir to dissolve both the sugar and the gelatin.

🍃 Chill the mixture. When it is half set, whip the cream. Add it to the half-set mixture, beating until thoroughly blended. Turn the mixture into a mold and chill for approximately 6 to 8 hours, or until set.

German Bavarian Cream

1½ tbsp (25 mL) gelatin
2 tbsp (30 mL) cold water
1 cup (250 mL) whipping cream
¼ cup (50 mL) sugar
1 tsp (5 mL) vanilla

🍃 Soak the gelatin in cold water until soft; then heat the gelatin in a double boiler until it dissolves.

🍃 Whip the cream. Pour the gelatin over the whipped cream, stirring constantly. Add the sugar and the vanilla.

🍃 Turn the cream mixture into a mold and refrigerate for 3 to 5 hours, or until it sets.

Cold Chocolate Soufflé

4 whole eggs
3 egg yolks
6 tbsp (90 mL) sugar
1½ tbsp (25 mL) unflavored gelatin
4 tbsp (60 mL) cold water
2 tsp (10 mL) lemon juice
5 oz (150 g) sweet chocolate
3 tbsp (45 mL) cold coffee

2 tbsp (30 mL) cognac
2 tsp (10 mL) vanilla
2 cups (500 mL) whipping cream
1 tsp (5 mL) cognac
confectioner's sugar
cocoa

🍃 Beat together the whole eggs, the egg yolks and the sugar until the mixture is light and fluffy.

🍃 Soak the gelatin in the cold water and the lemon juice for 5 minutes. Heat the mixture in a double boiler to dissolve the gelatin.

🍃 Chop the chocolate into small pieces. Heat the chocolate, the cold coffee and the 2 tbsp (30 mL) cognac in a small saucepan, stirring until the chocolate melts.

🍃 Slowly pour the gelatin into the egg mixture, stirring constantly. Add the chocolate cream and the vanilla, still stirring.

🍃 Whip the cream and add half of it to the chocolate mixture. Place a paper collar around an 8-in (20-cm) soufflé dish. Grease the dish and pour in the soufflé mixture. Cover it with the remaining whipped cream, sweetened to taste with confectioner's sugar and flavored with the rest of the cognac.

🍃 Refrigerate for 2 to 4 hours. Before serving, carefully remove the paper collar and sprinkle the soufflé with a little cocoa.

Cold Lemon Soufflé

1 envelope unflavored gelatin
¼ cup (50 mL) cold water
4 eggs
1 tsp (5 mL) lemon zest
½ cup (125 mL) lemon juice
½ cup (125 mL) sugar
½ tsp (2 mL) salt
1 tsp (5 mL) vanilla
½ cup (125 mL) sugar
1 cup (250 mL) whipping cream

Cold Chocolate Soufflé

[581]

🍂 Soak the gelatin in the cold water for 5 minutes.

🍂 Separate the eggs. Mix together the egg yolks, the lemon zest and juice, ½ cup (125 mL) sugar and the salt. Cook in a double boiler, stirring almost constantly, until very light and creamy.

🍂 Remove from the heat and add the gelatin and the vanilla. Allow to cool.

🍂 Beat the egg whites. Add the other ½ cup (125 mL) of sugar and continue beating until the egg whites are stiff.

🍂 Whip the cream and pour it over the beaten egg whites. Fold this into the gelatin mixture. Pour into a soufflé dish and refrigerate until ready to serve.

COLD ORANGE SOUFFLÉ

4 whole eggs

Cold Orange Soufflé

3 egg yolks
6 tbsp (90 mL) sugar
1½ tbsp (25 mL) unflavored gelatin
3 tbsp (45 mL) cold water
2 tsp (10 mL) lemon juice
2 large oranges
2 cups (500 mL) whipping cream
½ cup (125 mL) black-currant jelly

🍂 Place the whole eggs, the egg yolks and the sugar in a bowl and beat until very fluffy.

🍂 Soak the gelatin in the cold water and lemon juice for 5 minutes, then heat the mixture in a double boiler until the gelatin dissolves. Pour it slowly into the egg mixture, stirring constantly.

🍂 Add the juice and the zest from one of the oranges. Whip the cream and fold it into the mixture.

🍂 Place a paper collar around an 8-inch (20-cm) soufflé dish.

Grease the dish well. Pour in the soufflé mixture and refrigerate for 2 hours. Remove the soufflé from the refrigerator and garnish it with sections of the second orange.

🍂 Heat the jelly over low heat until it melts. Pour it over the soufflé and the orange garnish.

🍂 Return the soufflé to the refrigerator and chill until ready to serve. Just before serving, carefully remove the paper collar.

COLD STRAWBERRY SOUFFLÉ

1 envelope unflavored gelatin
¼ cup (50 mL) cold water
1 box frozen strawberries
4 eggs
½ cup (125 mL) sugar
½ tsp (2 mL) salt
½ cup (125 mL) sugar
1 cup (250 mL) whipping cream

🍂 Soak the gelatin in the cold water for 5 minutes.

🍂 Thaw the strawberries and put them through a sieve to make a purée. Separate the eggs. Mix together the egg yolks, ½ cup (125 mL) of the sugar and the salt. Cook in a double boiler, stirring almost constantly, until very light and creamy.

🍂 Remove the mixture from the heat and add the gelatin. Allow to cool and then add the puréed strawberries.

🍂 Beat the egg whites. Add the second ½ cup (125 mL) of sugar and continue beating until the egg whites are stiff.

🍂 Whip the cream and pour it over the beaten egg whites. Fold

❦ TECHNIQUE ❦

COLD ORANGE SOUFFLÉ

1 With an electric mixer, beat together the whole eggs, the egg yolks and the sugar until very fluffy.

2 Pour the dissolved gelatin slowly into the egg mixture, stirring constantly.

3 Add the juice and zest of one orange. Fold the whipped cream into the mixture.

4 Place a paper collar around a soufflé dish. Grease well and pour in the mixture.

this into the strawberry mixture. Pour into a soufflé dish and refrigerate until ready to serve.

SWEET CHOCOLATE SOUFFLÉ

4 tbsp (60 mL) butter
3 tbsp (45 mL) flour
6 oz (175 g) sweet chocolate
1½ cups (375 mL) whipping cream
¼ tsp (1 mL) vanilla
4 eggs
4 tbsp (60 mL) sugar
2 egg whites
pinch of salt
confectioner's sugar

&◆ Melt the butter and add the flour. Remove the mixture from the heat and blend thoroughly.

&◆ Cut the chocolate into small pieces. In a saucepan, add the chocolate to the whipping cream and stir over low heat until the chocolate melts. Pour the chocolate over the butter and flour mixture and cook this over low heat until it thickens. Do not let the mixture boil. Remove it from the heat and add the vanilla. Allow to cool, stirring occasionally. Cover.

&◆ Separate the eggs. Beat the egg yolks with the sugar until very light. Add to the chocolate mixture and stir well.

&◆ Beat 6 egg whites with the salt until stiff. Carefully fold them into the chocolate mixture.

&◆ Put a collar on an 8-in. (20-cm) soufflé dish and grease the dish. Sprinkle it with sugar, then pour in the mixture. Place the dish in a pan of hot water. Bake for 30 min-

utes at 350°F (180°C). Then increase the temperature to 375°F (190°C) and bake 15 minutes longer.

&◆ Sprinkle the soufflé with confectioner's sugar and serve it with a chocolate sauce (see pages 602 and 605).

COLD COFFEE SOUFFLÉ

4 whole eggs
3 egg yolks
¼ cup (50 mL) sugar
pinch of cinnamon
1½ tbsp (25 mL) gelatin
4 tbsp (60 mL) cold, strong coffee
1 cup (250 mL) whipping cream
confectioner's sugar
1 tsp (5 mL) instant coffee
toasted almonds, finely chopped

&◆ Place the whole eggs, the egg yolks, the sugar and the cinnamon in a bowl and beat until fluffy.

&◆ Soak the gelatin in the cold coffee for 5 minutes. Heat the mixture in a double boiler over boiling water until the gelatin dissolves. Pour it slowly into the egg mixture, stirring constantly.

&◆ Whip half the cream and fold it into the egg mixture. Pour into an 8-in. (20-cm) soufflé dish. Refrigerate for 2 to 4 hours.

&◆ When ready to serve the soufflé, whip the remaining cream. Sweeten it with confectioner's sugar and flavor it with 1 tsp (5 mL) of powdered instant coffee. Spread the whipped cream on the top of the soufflé and sprinkle it with the toasted almonds.

COLD MOCHA SOUFFLÉ

1 envelope unflavored gelatin
¼ cup (50 mL) cold water
2 tsp (10 mL) instant coffee
½ cup (125 mL) cold water
4 eggs
½ cup (125 mL) sugar
½ tsp (2 mL) salt
2 1-oz (30-g) squares unsweetened chocolate
1 tsp (5 mL) vanilla
½ cup (125 mL) sugar
1 cup (250 mL) whipping cream

&◆ Soak the gelatin in the ¼ cup (50 mL) of cold water for 5 minutes.

&◆ Dissolve the instant coffee in the ½ cup (125 mL) of cold water. Separate the eggs. Mix together the egg yolks, the coffee, ½ cup (125 mL) of the sugar and the salt. Add the chocolate and cook the mixture in the top of a double boiler, stirring almost constantly, until it is very light and creamy.

&◆ Remove from the heat. Add the gelatin and the vanilla. Allow to cool.

&◆ Beat the egg whites lightly. Add the remaining ½ cup (125 mL) of sugar and beat until stiff.

&◆ Whip the cream, pour it over the beaten egg whites and fold this into the coffee mixture. Pour the soufflé mixture into a dish and refrigerate until ready to serve.

MOCHA SOUFFLÉ

3 tbsp (45 mL) butter
2 tbsp (30 mL) flour
¼ tsp (1 mL) salt

¾ cup (175 mL) strong coffee
¼ cup (50 mL) light cream
½ cup (125 mL) sugar
3 eggs
1 tsp (5 mL) vanilla

🍂 Melt the butter and add the flour, the salt, the coffee, the cream and the sugar. Cook until the mixture thickens.

🍂 Separate the eggs. Beat the egg yolks until light. Pour the coffee mixture over the egg yolks and stir until well blended. Allow to cool, then add the vanilla.

🍂 Beat the egg whites until stiff and fold them into the coffee mixture. Pour the soufflé into individual molds. Place the molds in a pan of hot water and cook in a 325°F (160°C) oven for about 25 minutes.

LIQUEUR SOUFFLÉ

½ cup (125 mL) milk
½ cup (125 mL) sugar
6 tbsp (90 mL) flour
½ cup (125 mL) light cream
1 tbsp (15 mL) butter
3 eggs
4 tbsp (60 mL) confectioner's sugar
¼ cup (50 mL) liqueur such as cognac or Cointreau
2 egg whites
toasted almonds, finely chopped

🍂 Mix together the milk and the sugar until the sugar dissolves. Blend the flour and the cream to make a smooth paste; add it to the milk. Stir the mixture over low heat until it thickens, but do not let it boil. Remove from the heat

and add the butter, a little at a time, stirring after each addition.

🍂 Separate the eggs. Beat the egg yolks with the confectioner's sugar until the mixture is very light. Add the liqueur gradually and stir well. Add the egg yolks to the flour and butter mixture and mix thoroughly.

🍂 Beat 5 egg whites until stiff and fold them carefully into the soufflé mixture.

🍂 Place a collar on an 8-in. (20-cm) soufflé dish and grease well. Sprinkle the dish with granulated sugar and pour in the soufflé. Place the dish in a pan of hot water and bake in a 375°F (190°C) oven for 40 to 45 minutes.

🍂 Serve with a sauce prepared with equal portions of sweet butter and liqueur (the same as used to flavor the soufflé) and with a dish of chopped toasted almonds.

MAPLE SYRUP SOUFFLÉ

1 cup (250 mL) maple syrup
4 egg whites
½ cup (125 mL) confectioner's sugar
2 tsp (10 mL) baking powder
½ cup (125 mL) maple syrup
1 tbsp (15 mL) butter
3 tbsp (45 mL) cognac

🍂 Boil the cup (250 mL) maple syrup until it is reduced to ¾ cup (175 mL). Allow to cool.

🍂 Beat the egg whites until stiff. Add the confectioner's sugar sifted with the baking powder. Fold into the cooled syrup.

🍂 Place a paper collar on an 8-in. (20-cm) soufflé dish. Pour the ½ cup (125 mL) of maple syrup in the bottom of the dish. Dice the butter and add it and the cognac

Liqueur Soufflé

to the maple syrup. Pour the soufflé mixture on top. Place the dish in a pan of hot water. Bake the soufflé in a 300°F (150°C) oven for 1 hour.

☙ Serve with a maple sauce or a sauce of melted butter and cognac heated together.

SPRING SOUFFLÉ

1 cup (250 mL) maple syrup
4 egg whites
½ cup (125 mL) confectioner's sugar
2 tsp (10 mL) baking powder

☙ Boil the cup of maple syrup until it is reduced to ¾ cup (175 mL). Allow to cool.

☙ Beat the egg whites until stiff. Add the sugar and the baking powder. Fold in the cooled syrup.

☙ Pour the mixture into an ungreased soufflé dish or other mold. Place it in a pan containing 2 in. (5 cm) hot water and bake the soufflé in a 300°F (150°C) oven for 1 hour. Serve immediately.

GARNISHED SOUFFLÉ

8 tbsp (135 mL) sugar
8 eggs
1 tsp (5 mL) vanilla
1¼ cups (300 mL) whipping cream
¼ tsp (1 mL) salt
2 tbsp (30 mL) flour
3 tbsp (45 mL) butter
6 ladyfingers
¼ cup (50 mL) cognac
½ cup (125 mL) candied fruit
confectioner's sugar

☙ Separate the eggs. Beat the 8 tbsp (135 mL) of sugar and the egg yolks. Add the vanilla. Beat until the egg yolks are pale yellow in color and light in texture. Add the cream, a little at a time.

☙ Cook the mixture in the top of a double boiler, over low heat, until it coats the back of a metal spoon. Remove the mixture from the heat and refrigerate it until thoroughly chilled.

☙ Beat the egg whites with the salt until stiff. Sift the flour over the egg whites and fold it in carefully. Then fold the egg white mixture into the cooled yolks.

☙ Place a collar around an 8-in. (20-cm) soufflé dish and butter the dish generously. Sprinkle it with white sugar. Soak the ladyfingers in the cognac and place them, upright, all around the dish, leaving spaces between them. Chop the candied fruit and soak the pieces in the remaining cognac. Place them here and there between the ladyfingers. Pour the remaining cognac into the soufflé dish, then top it with the soufflé mixture. Sprinkle with confectioner's sugar.

☙ Place the dish in a pan of hot water and bake the soufflé in a 325°F (160°C) oven for 45 to 55 minutes.

☙ Serve with a cognac-flavored cream sauce.

APRICOT SOUFFLÉ

2 tbsp (30 mL) butter
3 tbsp (45 mL) flour
¾ cup (175 mL) milk
2 tsp (10 mL) lemon juice
½ cup (125 mL) apricot jam
4 eggs
4 tbsp (60 mL) sugar
1 egg white
confectioner's sugar

☙ Prepare a white sauce with the butter, the flour and the milk. Be careful not to let the mixture boil. As soon as it reaches the creamy stage, remove the sauce from the heat.

☙ Add the lemon juice and the apricot jam to the sauce. Separate the eggs. Add the egg yolks, one by one, beating hard after each addition. Add the sugar and beat until it dissolves.

☙ Beat 5 egg whites until stiff and fold them into the first mixture.

☙ Place a collar around an 8-in. (20-cm) soufflé dish and butter the dish. Sprinkle it with confectioner's sugar, then pour in the soufflé mixture. Bake in a 350°F (180°C) oven for 30 minutes.

☙ Dust the soufflé with confectioner's sugar and serve it immediately.

BLUEBERRY SOUFFLÉ

2 cups (500 mL) blueberries, fresh or frozen
1 cup (250 mL) sugar
3 tbsp (45 mL) water
1 tbsp (15 mL) cognac
2 tsp (10 mL) grated lemon zest
6 egg whites
2 tbsp (30 mL) ground blanched almonds
sour cream or whipping cream

☙ Wash and dry the berries, then press them through a sieve. Set the purée aside.

🍂Boil the sugar and the water together in a saucepan until it forms a thread when tipped from a spoon.

🍂Add the blueberry pulp and mix well. Set aside to cool for 30 minutes.

🍂Add the cognac and the lemon zest and stir well.

🍂Beat the egg whites until stiff. Fold them into the berry mixture, working carefully.

🍂Place a paper collar on an 8-in. (20-cm) soufflé dish. Butter the dish and sprinkle it with sugar.

🍂Pour the soufflé mixture into the dish and dust it with the ground almonds. Bake in a 375°F (190°C) oven for 30 minutes. Serve with sour cream or whipped cream.

Apple Soufflé

APPLE SOUFFLÉ

4 eggs
⅔ cup (150 mL) brown sugar
1½ cups (375 mL) applesauce
2 tbsp (30 mL) cognac
1 tbsp (15 mL) grated orange zest
2 tbsp (30 mL) sugar

🍂Separate the eggs. Beat the egg yolks in a bowl until they are pale yellow. Add the brown sugar and beat the mixture until is well blended.

🍂Drain the applesauce of all its juice. Add the cognac, the orange zest and the sugar to the applesauce. Add this mixture to the beaten egg yolks and stir well.

🍂Beat the egg whites until stiff. Fold them into the apple mixture, working carefully.

🍂Place a paper collar on an 8-in. (20-cm) soufflé dish. Butter the dish and sprinkle it with sugar. Pour in the mixture and bake in a 350°F (180°C) oven for 30 minutes.

COFFEE CHARLOTTE RUSSE

¼ cup (50 mL) sugar
1 envelope unflavored gelatin
pinch of salt
2 tbsp (30 mL) instant coffee
1¼ cups (300 mL) milk
2 eggs
½ tsp (2 mL) vanilla
¼ cup (50 mL) sugar
1 cup (250 mL) whipping cream
8 to 12 ladyfingers

🍂Mix together ¼ cup (50 mL) of the sugar, the gelatin, the salt and the instant coffee in the top of a double boiler. Separate the eggs.

Beat the milk with the egg yolks and add this to the gelatin mixture. Cook over boiling water, stirring constantly, for approximately 5 minutes, or until the gelatin dissolves. Remove from the heat and add the vanilla. Refrigerate the mixture until it is half-set.

🍂Beat the egg whites, add the remaining ¼ cup (50 mL) of sugar and continue beating until stiff peaks form.

🍂Fold the half-set coffee mixture into the egg whites. Whip the cream and add it, stirring gently until well blended.

🍂Line individual molds or a large crystal bowl with the ladyfingers. Pour in the cream and refrigerate for 4 to 12 hours before serving.

Zabaglione

ture until the sugar dissolves. Place over hot—not boiling—water in the bottom of the double boiler and cook, beating constantly, until the mixture begins to hold its shape.

🍂 Gradually add the marsala, beating the mixture until it resembles a heavy cream. This may take a good 10 minutes.

🍂 To serve the zabaglione hot, turn it into a crystal dish or into champagne glasses.

🍂 To serve it cold, turn the mixture into a dish and place it in the refrigerator. When thoroughly chilled, beat the egg whites until they are stiff and add them. The zagablione will resemble a light mousse. Pour it into a crystal dish or into individual cups and serve.

APPLE CHARLOTTE

8 to 12 apples
3 tbsp (45 mL) butter
zest of ½ a lemon, grated
1 tbsp (15 mL) water
1 tbsp (15 mL) apricot jelly
8 to 12 bread slices

🍂 Peel, core and chop the apples. Place the apples in a saucepan with the butter, the lemon zest and the water. Cover and simmer the mixture for 15 minutes, or until the apples are tender. Sweeten to taste, then add the apricot jelly. Purée the mixture by putting it through a sieve.

🍂 Remove the crusts from the bread. Cut some slices in rounds, others in l-in. (2-cm) strips. Soak the rounds, one at a time, in melted butter and place them on the bottom of a charlotte dish (a round, shallow mold with straight sides) or any large mold. Arrange the rounds attractively. Soak the l-in. (2-cm) strips of bread in the melted butter and line them along the sides of the mold. Fill the prepared mold with the cooked apples.

🍂 Cover with a piece of buttered paper and bake in a 350°F (180°C) oven for 40 minutes. When cooked, turn the charlotte upside down on a platter and leave it to stand in its mold. Carefully remove the mold after about 15 minutes.

ZABAGLIONE

8 eggs
1 cup (250 mL) sugar
1 cup (250 mL) marsala

🍂 Separate the eggs. Place the egg yolks and the sugar in the top of a double boiler. Beat the mix-

CARAMELIZED EGG SNOW

4 eggs
½ cup (125 mL) sugar
¼ cup (50 mL) sugar
2 cups (500 mL) milk
vanilla or nutmeg
½ cup (125 mL) sugar
2 tbsp (30 mL) water

🍂 Beat the egg yolks with the ½ cup (125 mL) of sugar until fluffy.

🍂 Beat the egg whites until soft peaks form. Add the ¼ cup (50 mL) of sugar and beat until stiff.

🍂 Heat the milk in a large saucepan. Drop the beaten egg whites into the hot milk a spoonful at a time. When the ball of egg white is well puffed, turn it quickly to cook the other side.

This will take about 1 minute. Remove the cooked ball, using a perforated ladle, and place it on a hot platter. Cook the rest of the egg white in this manner.

❧ Add the egg and sugar mixture to the milk in the saucepan. Cook, stirring quickly, until you have a lovely golden custard. (Do not boil the mixture.) Flavor the custard to taste with vanilla or nutmeg.

❧ Pour the custard over the egg whites. Cook together the remaining ½ cup (125 mL) of sugar and the 2 tbsp (30 mL) of water to make a golden caramel syrup.

❧ Using a fork, drip the caramel in long threads over the egg snow. Chill and serve.

CROQUEMBOUCHE

In France, this is a special Christmas dessert. It is very decorative yet simple to make if you use a packaged mix for the little cream puffs.

24 2-in. (5-cm) cream puffs
pie dough
2 cups (500 mL) whipping cream
½ tsp (2 mL) almond essence
¼ cup (50 mL) red and green candied cherries, finely chopped
1 cup (250 mL) water
1½ cups (375 mL) sugar

❧ Make the little puffs according to directions on the package. Roll the pie dough to form a circle 9 in. (23 cm) in diameter and about ¼ in. (0.6 cm) thick. Place it on a cookie sheet and bake it.

❧ Whip the cream and sweeten to taste. Add the almond extract and the finely chopped cherries. Fill each puff with the cream and

cherry mixture.

❧ Place the baked pastry circle on an attractive serving plate.

❧ In a saucepan, boil the water and the sugar to make a dark caramel syrup.

❧ Using a fork, quickly dip each filled puff into the hot syrup and arrange the puffs around the edge of the pastry circle, syrup uppermost. Then make a second, inner ring of the puffs.

❧ Using a fork, drip the caramel syrup back and forth over the cream puffs until the coating looks like a fine cobweb.

❧ Place the dessert in the refrigerator until you are ready to serve it.

ENGLISH TRIFLE

2 cups (500 mL) whipping cream
4 egg yolks
½ cup (125 mL) brown sugar
1 tbsp (15 mL) flour
pinch of salt
½ tsp (2 mL) vanilla
¼ tsp (1 mL) almond extract
¼ cup (50 mL) sherry
10 ladyfingers or 10 dry sponge-cake fingers
⅓ cup (75 mL) strawberry or raspberry jam
½ cup (125 mL) almonds, slivered

❧ Heat the cream in the top of a double boiler, over boiling water.

❧ Beat the egg yolks together with the brown sugar, the flour and the salt. Pour the mixture over the warm cream, stirring constantly. Cook this in the double boiler, stirring often, until it is light and creamy. Remove from the heat and add the vanilla and the almond extract. Refrigerate the cream until it is well chilled.

❧ Place the sherry in a deep plate and soak the ladyfingers or sponge-cake fingers in it. Butter a large mold and place the soaked biscuits around the sides and bottom of the dish.

Caramelized Egg Snow

🌿 Brush the biscuits with the jam and sprinkle them with some of the almonds.

🌿 Pour the cooled cream carefully into the mold. Cover and refrigerate for 12 hours. Garnish the trifle with whipped cream and the rest of the slivered almonds.

TIPSY PARSON

This delicious trifle dates back to the early Victorian era. It is still a Christmas specialty in many homes in England.

6 egg yolks
4 cups (1 L) light cream or milk
½ cup (125 mL) sugar
pinch of salt
2 tsp (10 mL) vanilla
1 10-in. (25-cm) round angel food or sponge cake
1 cup (250 mL) blanched almonds, slivered
1 cup (250 mL) dry sherry
2 cups (500 mL) currant jelly
2 cups (500 mL) whipping cream
2 tbsp (30 mL) confectioner's sugar
maraschino cherries, halved

CUSTARD FILLING
Beat the egg yolks lightly in the top of a double boiler. Scald the cream or milk and add it to the egg yolks with the sugar and salt. Cook over boiling water, stirring frequently, until the sauce coats the spoon. This will take about 30 minutes. Stir in the vanilla. Cover and refrigerate the custard for 12 hours.

PREPARING THE TRIFLE
Use a commercially prepared cake or bake a cake following the recipes on pages 540–542. Cut the cake horizontally into 6 thin slices. Place the bottom slice in a large, round crystal bowl about 2 in. (5 cm) high. Sprinkle some of the slivered almonds over the cake, then douse it with some of the sherry and dab the currant jelly here and there. Spoon a generous amount of the cold custard on top and spread it around the cake. Cover with another slice of cake and repeat the process until all the cake, custard, almonds, sherry and jelly have been used.

🌿 Beat the whipping cream until it is thick and sweeten it with the confectioner's sugar. Decorate the trifle with large cream rosettes and swirls, and the halved cherries. Refrigerate the trifle for 6 to 8 hours before serving.

PINEAPPLE ICEBOX CAKE

This dessert keeps well overnight in the refrigerator, so prepare it the day before a dinner party or other occasion. Then simply add the garnish of your choice before serving it.

2 eggs
1 19-oz (540-mL) can crushed pineapple
1 cup (250 mL) sugar
juice of ½ lemon
juice of ½ orange
½ cup (125 mL) water
3 tbsp (45 mL) cornstarch
10 to 14 ladyfingers

🌿 Drain the pineapple and set aside 3 tbsp (45 mL) of the juice. Separate the eggs and reserve the whites.

🌿 In the top of a double boiler, mix the drained pineapple, the sugar, the lemon and orange juice, the water and the egg yolks. Blend the cornstarch with the 3 tbsp (45 mL) of pineapple juice and add this to the first mixture. Cook over boiling water, stirring often, until the mixture is thick and creamy. Cool well.

🌿 Beat the egg whites and fold them into the pineapple mixture.

🌿 Butter a 9-in. (23-cm) spring-form pan and line the sides and bottom with ladyfingers. Fill the lined mold with the pineapple mixture. Refrigerate the cake for at least 12 hours.

🌿 Just before serving, remove the cake from the spring-form pan. Top it with sweetened whipped cream or balls of ice cream or grated sweet chocolate.

GATEAU DE NEVERS

1 cup (250 mL) sugar
1 cup (250 mL) milk
½ lb (250 g) macaroons, very dry
4 sugar cubes
½ cup (125 mL) rum
3 eggs

🌿 Melt the sugar in a small saucepan, over low heat, until it turns into a golden syrup. Pour the syrup into a metal or glass charlotte mold and tilt the dish to coat its entire inside surface with the syrup. (Be careful, the syrup will be very hot.) The syrup will harden as it touches the cold sides of the mold.

🌿 Boil the milk. Crush the macaroons and add them, with the sugar and the rum, to the hot milk. Mix to blend into a very light paste. Separate the eggs. Beat the egg yolks until light and fluffy and add them to the macaroon mixture.

❧ Beat the egg whites until stiff. Fold them into the yolk mixture. Pour this into the caramel-coated mold. Place the mold in a saucepan containing a few inches of hot water. Cover and cook for 1 hour. If necessary, add more boiling water during the cooking process. Remove the mold from the heat and cover and refrigerate it for 12 hours.

❧ To serve, unmold the cake onto a large plate; it will be covered in a golden caramel.

ICE CREAM CAKE

1 sponge or angel food cake
2 cups (500 mL) ice cream of your choice
¼ cup (50 mL) orange juice
or 3 tbsp (45 mL) rum or cognac
2 cups (500 mL) whipping cream
2 tbsp (30 mL) confectioner's sugar
1 tsp (5 mL) vanilla

❧ Buy a cake or prepare one, using one of the recipes on pages 540–542. Cut a 4- or 5-in. (10- to 13-cm) circle from the center of the cake. Place the cake on a large platter. Cut a thin horizontal layer from the circle you've just removed and place it in the hole in the cake.

❧ Soften the ice cream a little and use it to fill the hole in the cake. Pour the orange juice, rum or cognac on the cake around the ice cream. Cover the ice cream

Baked Alaska

with the remaining round of cake.
❧ Whip the cream, sweeten it with confectioner's sugar and stir in the vanilla. Using a spatula, frost the cake with this cream. Freeze the cake until the frosting is well set. To store it, remove the cake from the plate, wrap it in a double thickness of waxed paper and freeze until ready to use.

BAKED ALASKA

1 8-in. (20-cm) round sponge cake
4 cups (1 L) ice cream
4 cups (1 L) strawberry or raspberry sherbet
8 egg whites
1 cup (250 mL) sugar

❧ Cut a piece of brown paper in a circle at least ½ in. (1 cm) larger than the cake. Place it on a 14- x 10-in. (25- x 14-cm) baking sheet. Place the cake in the center of the

paper and set it in the freezer or refrigerator to chill thoroughly.
❧ Line a round bowl with foil or wax paper. With a wooden spoon, press the slightly softened ice cream along the bottom and sides of the bowl, to line it. Fill with the sherbet. Cover with wax paper and, using the palms of your hands, press the mixture down evenly. Freeze.
❧ When the ice cream has hardened, prepare the meringue: beat the egg whites until stiff and add the sugar, 2 tbsp (30 mL) at a time, beating hard after each addition.
❧ Unmold the ice cream directly over the center of the cake. Remove the paper. Now spread the meringue completely over the ice cream and cake. The meringue should be at least 1 in. (2.5 cm) thick. Return the cake to the refrigerator until you are almost ready to serve it.

[591]

Blueberry Pudding

🍃 Fifteen minutes before serving time, heat the oven to 500°F (260°C). Remove the Alaska from the refrigerator and bake it for 4 or 5 minutes, or until the meringue browns lightly.

🍃 While the Alaska is in the oven, place a silver platter in the freezer to chill. Using two spatulas, slip the Alaska onto the very cold platter. Serve immediately.

🍃 To make individual portions, use 6 small sponge cakes and hollow the center of each. Fill with 1 tbsp (15 mL) crushed pineapple. Garnish with a large scoop of strawberry ice cream. Top with a meringue prepared with 6 egg whites and ¾ cup (175 mL) sugar. Bake in a 500°F (260°C) oven for 4 or 5 minutes.

🍃 Turn the Alaskas onto chilled plates and serve them immediately.

BLUEBERRY PUDDING

¼ cup (50 mL) butter
1 cup (250 mL) sugar
1 egg, beaten
1 cup (250 mL) milk
juice of 1 orange
2½ cups (625 mL) all-purpose flour
1 tbsp (15 mL) baking powder
¼ tsp (1 mL) nutmeg or allspice
1½ cups (375 mL) blueberries
2 tbsp (30 mL) all-purpose flour
2 tbsp (30 mL) sugar

🍃 Beat together the butter and the sugar until the mixture is light and creamy. Add the beaten egg and continue beating until perfectly blended.

🍃 Mix together the milk and the orange juice.

🍃 Sift together the flour, the baking powder and the nutmeg or allspice.

🍃 Sprinkle the blueberries with the 2 tbsp (30 mL) of flour and stir lightly with a fork.

🍃 Add the flour to the creamed mixture, alternating with the milk and orange juice mixture. Beat until well blended.

🍃 Fold in the blueberries.

🍃 Pour the batter, spoonful by spoonful, into a greased 9- x 9-in. (23- x 23-cm) pan. Sprinkle it with 2 tbsp (30 mL) of sugar and bake in a 375°F (190°C) oven for 40 minutes.

HAWAIIAN PUDDING

2 cups (500 mL) cottage cheese
1 cup (250 mL) sugar
2 tbsp (30 mL) flour
4 eggs
1 16-oz (450-g) can crushed pineapple, drained
1¼ cups (300 mL) yogurt
1 tsp (5 mL) grated lemon zest

🍃 Mix the cottage cheese and the sugar, then add the flour. Separate the eggs. Beat the egg yolks and add them to the cottage cheese mixture, beating all the time. Add the well-drained pineapple, the yogurt and the lemon zest. Mix thoroughly. Beat the egg whites until stiff and gently fold into the pineapple mixture.

🍃 Pour the pudding into a baking dish. Set it in shallow pan of water and bake in a 375°F (190°C) oven for about 40 minutes, or until the top is golden and the custard has set. Let it cool and then refrigerate.

🍃 Serve the pudding as is or garnish it with whipped cream, ice cream or sweetened strawberries.

COCOA PUDDING

3 cups (750 mL) milk
½ cup (125 mL) cream
⅓ cup (75 mL) cocoa
½ cup (125 mL) sugar
¼ cup (50 mL) farina
2 eggs
3 tbsp (45 mL) butter
½ cup (125 mL) sugar

🍃 Boil the milk together with the cream. Mix together the cocoa, the ½ cup (125 mL) sugar and the farina. Add the cocoa mixture to the boiling milk, stirring constantly, and cook over very low heat for 9 minutes.

🍃 Beat the eggs. Pour the hot cocoa mixture over the beaten eggs, stirring as you pour. Add the butter and stir until it melts.

🍃 Melt the other ½ cup (125 mL) of sugar over low heat until it turns light brown. Quickly pour the syrup into the mold, turning it so that the syrup coats the bottom and sides. Then pour the cocoa mixture into the mold. Cover it and refrigerate for 12 to 24 hours. To serve, unmold the pudding and serve it with caramel sauce (see *Crème Caramel* page 574) or with whipped cream.

HOT CARAMEL PUDDING

2 tbsp (30 mL) shortening or butter
¼ cup (50 mL) corn syrup
1 egg
1 cup (250 mL) all-purpose flour
¾ tsp (3 mL) baking powder
¼ tsp (1 mL) salt
¼ cup (50 mL) milk
1 tsp (5 mL) vanilla
¼ tsp (1 mL) nutmeg
1 cup (250 mL) brown sugar
1½ cups (375 mL) sour cream

🍃 Cream together the butter or shortening, the corn syrup and the egg until the mixture is light and foamy.

🍃 Sift together the flour, the baking powder and the salt.

🍃 Add the flour mixture to the creamed mixture, alternating with the ¼ cup (50 mL) of milk. Add the vanilla and the nutmeg. Mix well.

🍃 Place this stiff batter in a buttered pudding dish.

🍃 Stir the brown sugar into the sour cream. Pour over the batter. Bake in a 350°F (180°C) oven for 55 minutes.

APPLE DUMPLINGS

1 cup (250 mL) flour
¼ tsp (1 mL) salt
2 tsp (10 mL) baking powder
2 tbsp (30 mL) shortening
⅓ cup (75 mL) milk
1 egg
peeled apples
sugar
nutmeg or cinnamon
1 cup (250 mL) water
½ cup (125 mL) sugar
1 tbsp (15 mL) butter
pinch of cinnamon

🍃 Sift together the flour, the salt and the baking powder. Cut the shortening into the sifted flour. Beat the milk together with the egg and add to the first mixture to make a soft dough.

🍃 Roll the dough ¼ in. (0.6 cm) thick. Cut it into squares and cover each square with slices of

Apple Dumplings

Old-fashioned Apple Pudding

peeled apple, sugar and a little nutmeg or cinnamon. Fold the dough over the apples.

🍂 Place the apple squares in a baking dish. Bake in a 425°F (220°C) oven for 15 minutes.

🍂 Prepare a syrup by heating together the water, the sugar, the butter and the cinnamon.

🍂 Remove the pan from the oven and pour the syrup over the dumplings. Return the dumplings to the oven and bake for 20 minutes longer.

OLD-FASHIONED APPLE PUDDING

3 tbsp (45 mL) butter
1 cup (250 mL) sugar or maple sugar
2 eggs, beaten
½ tsp (2 mL) nutmeg
½ tsp (2 mL) cinnamon
½ tsp (2 mL) salt

1 tsp (5 mL) baking soda
1 cup (250 mL) all-purpose flour
3 cups (750 mL) unpeeled apples, chopped
¼ cup (50 mL) nuts, chopped
1 tsp (5 mL) grated lemon zest

🍂 Cream together the butter, the sugar and the beaten eggs.

🍂 Sift together the dry ingredients. Add them to the cream mixture, then stir in the chopped apples, the nuts and the lemon zest, stirring constantly.

🍂 Turn into a buttered 8- x 8- x 2-in. (20- x 20- x 5-cm) pan. Bake in a 350°F (180°C) oven for 40 to 45 minutes. Serve hot or cold.

VERMONT RHUBARB COBBLER

1½ cups (375 mL) sugar
1 cup (250 mL) apple juice
½ cup (125 mL) water

2 cups (500 mL) rhubarb, chopped
2 cups (500 mL) strawberries, sliced
1 tsp (5 mL) vanilla
1 cup (250 mL) all-purpose flour
2 tbsp (30 mL) sugar
1½ tsp (7 mL) baking powder
½ tsp (2 mL) mace
¼ cup (50 mL) butter
¼ cup (50 mL) milk or cream

🍂 Bring to a boil the sugar, the apple juice and the water. Stir to dissolve the sugar. Remove from the heat and add the rhubarb, the strawberries and the vanilla. Mix thoroughly and pour into a baking dish.

🍂 To prepare the batter, sift together the flour, the sugar, the baking powder and the mace. Cut in the butter, then add the milk or cream. Stir to mix thoroughly, then drop the batter by spoonfuls over the fruit mixture. Sprinkle with sugar and a little nutmeg and brush with melted butter. Bake in a 450°F (230°C) oven for 20 to 25 minutes.

DATE PUDDING

½ cup (125 mL) sugar
1 cup (250 mL) flour
2 tsp (10 mL) baking powder
½ cup (125 mL) milk
½ tsp (2 mL) salt
1 cup (250 mL) dates or raisins
½ cup (125 mL) water
1 cup (250 mL) brown sugar
1 tbsp (15 mL) butter

🍂 Mix together the sugar, the flour, the baking powder, the milk, the salt and the chopped

❧ TECHNIQUE ❧

OLD-FASHIONED APPLE PUDDING

1 Cream together the butter, the sugar and the eggs.

2 Sift together the dry ingredients.

3 Add the sifted ingredients to the butter mixture.

4 Stir in the apples, the nuts and the grated lemon rind.

dates or raisins. Stir well, then place the dough in a buttered baking dish.

🍴 Make a syrup by placing the water, the brown sugar and the butter in a saucepan. Cook just long enough to melt the sugar.

🍴 Pour the syrup over the dough and bake the pudding in a 400°F (200°C) oven for 30 minutes.

PLUM PUDDING

Here are a few basic rules for making plum pudding, that traditional dessert served at Christmas in homes throughout the English-speaking world.

🍴 Grind the beef suet finely.

🍴 Mix the flour with the suet. For every 4 cups (1 L) of flour or breadcrumbs used, you'll need ½ lb (250 g) suet.

🍴 Replace some of the flour with breadcrumbs; they make the pudding lighter. The more bread used, the lighter the pudding.

🍴 Next, add the remaining dry ingredients. Don't forget the pinch of salt.

🍴 Always add the eggs, the liquids and the essence or flavoring to the batter before adding the fruit.

🍴 Beat the eggs until they are light and frothy before adding them to the batter.

🍴 Measure the quantities carefully; too much fat or liquid can ruin the texture of the pudding.

🍴 Use less liquid if you want a lighter pudding.

🍴 Grease the mold well and pour in the batter. Fill the mold about three-quarters full.

🍴 To steam the pudding, cover the mold with wax paper or aluminum foil and attach the cover securely with string. Place the mold in a large saucepan with a tightly-fitting lid.

🍴 Place a folded newspaper on the bottom of the saucepan to keep the mold from rattling.

🍴 Add water to the saucepan, keeping the water level considerably lower than the rim of the pudding mold. If more water is needed part way through the cooking process, add boiling water. Cover tightly.

🍴 Set the heat so that the water simmers, rather than boils, around the mold. Simmering over low heat results in a lighter pudding.

🍴 Steam for the length of time recommended in the recipe, usually from 5 to 6 hours.

🍴 Do not open the pudding until the cooking period is over, or the pudding will be heavy.

ENGLISH PLUM PUDDING

1½ lb (750 g) seedless raisins
2 oz (60 g) diced mixed peel
1 cup (250 mL) fresh orange juice, cognac or red wine
1 cup (250 mL) finely chopped suet
1½ cups (375 mL) fine breadcrumbs
1 cup (250 mL) all-purpose flour
1 tsp (5 mL) cinnamon
½ tsp (2 mL) ground allspice
½ tsp (2 mL) ground cloves
1 tsp (5 mL) salt
½ cup (125 mL) sugar
3 eggs
1 cup (250 mL) molasses
3 tart apples
zest of 1 lemon, grated
1 cup (250 mL) chopped almonds or walnuts

🍴 Soak the seedless raisins and mixed peel overnight in the orange juice, cognac or red wine.

🍴 Mix together the beef suet and the breadcrumbs. Sift together the flour, the cinnamon, the allspice, the cloves, the salt and the sugar. Add to the bread and suet mixture.

🍴 Beat the eggs. Mix the eggs, the molasses and any liquid drained from the raisins and mixed peel and add this to the dry mixture. Stir well. Grate the unpeeled apples and the lemon zest and add to the soaked fruit with the chopped almonds or walnuts, stirring well. Add the fruit to the first mixture and stir until the batter is smooth. Pour the batter into a mold. Follow the preceding directions and steam the pudding for 6 hours. Serve hot.

🍴 This pudding is at its best when stored in the refrigerator for 2 to 4 weeks before serving. If the pudding has been refrigerated, steam it for an additional 2 hours and serve it piping hot.

BREAD AND BUTTER PUDDING

⅓ cup (75 mL) sugar
½ cup (125 mL) powdered skim milk
pinch of salt
½ cup (125 mL) milk
2 whole eggs or 4 egg yolks
1 tsp (5 mL) vanilla

2½ cups (625 mL) milk
peanut butter (optional)
6 slices bread, buttered
raisins
nutmeg, cinnamon or cardamon

🍃 Mix together the sugar, the powdered milk, the salt, the ½ cup (125 mL) of milk, the whole eggs or yolks and the vanilla. Beat until smooth. Then add the 2½ cups (625 mL) of milk.

🍃 If desired, spread peanut butter on the buttered slices of bread. Arrange the bread in overlapping circles in a baking dish, sprinkling each layer with raisins and with nutmeg, cinnamon or cardamon. Pour the milk and egg mixture over the top.

🍃 Bake in a 325°F (160°C) oven for 50 to 60 minutes, or until the custard is firm. A thermometer inserted in the pudding should indicate 175°F (80°C).

VARIATION

🍃 Simply pour the milk mixture over 4 to 5 cups (1 L) of diced, dried bread and bake as directed.

LAC SAINT JEAN BREAD PUDDING

¾ cup (175 mL) butter
4 cups (1 L) bread
1 tsp (5 mL) cinnamon
¼ cup (50 mL) sugar
2 cups (500 mL) fresh or frozen blueberries
2 tbsp (30 mL) lemon juice
½ cup (125 mL) dark brown sugar

🍃 Melt the butter.
🍃 Cube the bread and place it in

Bread and Butter Pudding

a bowl. Add the cinnamon and the sugar and mix well. Pour the butter over the mixture and stir with a fork until the bread is well coated.

🍃 Mix the blueberries with the lemon juice and the brown sugar.

🍃 Arrange alternating layers of the blueberries and bread in a pudding dish. Bake the pudding in a 350°F (180°C) oven for 20 to 30 minutes. Serve hot or cold.

CARAMEL BREAD PUDDING

5 cups (1.2 L) milk or half milk, half cream
10 slices dry bread
¾ cup (175 mL) brown sugar or maple sugar
3 tbsp (45 mL) butter
4 eggs
1 cup (250 mL) sugar
whipping cream (optional)

🍃 Heat the milk or cream and milk mixture.

🍃 Cube the bread and place it in a bowl. Add the brown sugar or maple sugar, the butter and the warm milk. Let stand for 5 minutes.

🍃 Beat the eggs until very light. Then beat the bread mixture until it is very creamy. Add the beaten eggs to the bread mixture.

🍃 Grease a large metal mold or two 9- x 5- x 3-in. (23- x 13- x 8-cm) bread pans.

🍃 Cook the 1 cup (250 mL) of sugar in the mold over medium heat until it melts and forms a caramel that coats the sides.

🍃 Pour the bread mixture into the mold. Place the mold in a pan containing 1 in. (2 cm) of hot water. Bake in a 325°F (160°C) oven for 1½ hours, or until the blade of a knife inserted in the center of the pudding comes out clean.

[597]

❧ Cool the pudding for 2 to 3 hours at room temperature. Run a knife around the mold to loosen the pudding and unmold it. The pudding will be surrounded by a lovely golden sauce. If desired, garnish it with whipped cream.

BAKED CARAMEL PUDDING

2 tbsp (30 mL) butter
or shortening
¼ cup (50 mL) corn syrup
1 egg
1 cup (250 mL) bread flour
¾ tsp (3 mL) baking powder
¼ tsp (1 mL) salt
¼ cup (50 mL) milk
1 tsp (5 mL) vanilla
¼ tsp (1 mL) nutmeg
1 cup (250 mL) brown sugar
3 tbsp (45 mL) cornstarch

1 cup (250 mL) fresh or sour cream
1 cup (250 mL) milk

❧ Cream the butter or shortening. Add the corn syrup and the unbeaten egg. Beat well. Sift together the flour, the baking powder and the salt. Add the dry ingredients to the first mixture, alternating with the milk. Flavor the batter with the vanilla and the nutmeg. Pour the batter into a buttered baking dish.

❧ To make the caramel topping, mix together in a bowl the 1 cup (250 mL) of brown sugar, the cornstarch, the fresh or sour cream and the 1 cup (250 mL) of milk and pour over the pudding. Bake in a 375°F (190°C) oven for 55 minutes.

RICE PUDDING

1 cup (250 mL) rice
4 cups (1 L) water

De Luxe Rice Pudding

2 eggs
¼ cup (50 mL) sugar
2 cups (500 mL) milk
pinch of salt
½ tsp (2 mL) vanilla
¼ to ½ cup (50 to 125 mL)
raisins (optional)
nutmeg

❧ Boil the rice in the water for 15 minutes. Drain the rice and rinse it under cold water.

❧ Beat the eggs. Blend the eggs with the sugar, the milk, the salt and the vanilla. Mix well. Add raisins, to taste. Add the mixture to the cooked rice and stir well.

❧ Pour into a pudding dish and sprinkle with nutmeg. Place the dish in a pan of hot water and bake in a 400°F (200°C) oven for 20 minutes, or until the blade of a knife inserted in the center comes out clean.

BAKED RICE AND MILK PUDDING

6 tbsp (90 mL) long-grain rice
4 cups (1 L) cold milk
¼ tsp (1 mL) salt
3 tbsp (45 mL) sugar
nutmeg or cinnamon

❧ Place the rice, the milk, the salt and the sugar in a well-greased baking dish. Sprinkle the mixture with grated nutmeg or with a little cinnamon.

❧ Bake in a 300°F (150°C) oven for 1½ hours. (Long, slow baking results in a creamy rice pudding.) Stir well 2 or 3 times during the first ½ **hour** of cooking to remove the film that forms on the surface. Serve hot or cold.

DE LUXE RICE PUDDING

½ cup (125 mL) long-grain rice
2 cups (500 mL) light cream
2 cups (500 mL) milk
¾ cup (175 mL) sugar
¼ tsp (1 mL) salt
4 egg yolks
2 tsp (10 mL) vanilla
½ cup (125 mL) water
½ cup (125 mL) seedless raisins
nutmeg to taste
1 cup (250 mL) whipping cream

🍃 Place the rice, the cream, the milk, the sugar and the salt in the top of a double boiler. Cover and cook over boiling water for 1 to 1½ hours, or until the rice is tender. Stir occasionally while cooking.

🍃 Beat the egg yolks with the vanilla and add the yolks slowly to the hot rice, beating constantly with a fork. Pour the mixture into a pudding dish. Cover the pudding and refrigerate it until cooled.

🍃 Bring the ½ cup (125 mL) water to a boil in a small saucepan. Add the raisins. Remove the pan from the heat and allow the raisins to soak for 1 hour.

🍃 Drain the raisins well, then stir them into the cold rice. Add nutmeg to taste. Whip the cream and fold it into the rice. Pour the rice mixture into a dish. Cover and refrigerate until ready to serve.

🍃 If desired, serve the pudding with a chocolate sauce (see pages 602 and 605) or with fresh or frozen strawberries.

BIGARADE RICE PUDDING

2 cups (500 mL) milk
zest of ½ orange, grated
1 cinnamon stick
2 whole cloves
2 cups (500 mL) rice, cooked
3 eggs
½ cup (125 mL) brown
or white sugar
1 tsp (5 mL) vanilla
cinnamon or nutmeg

🍃 Place the milk, the grated orange zest, the cinnamon and the cloves in a saucepan. Simmer over low heat for 15 minutes.

🍃 Add the rice to the milk and heat the mixture until it is thoroughly warmed.

🍃 Beat the eggs with the sugar and the vanilla. Pour the eggs slowly over the rice, stirring constantly with a fork. Cook the mixture gently until it has the consistency of a light custard. Make sure it does not boil. Pour into a bowl and sprinkle with a little cinnamon or nutmeg. Serve the pudding either warm or cold.

ROYAL RICE PUDDING

1 cup (250 mL) seedless raisins
3 cups (750 mL) milk
1¼ cups (300 mL) rice, cooked
¼ tsp (1 mL) nutmeg
½ tsp (2 mL) salt
1 tbsp (15 mL) grated lemon zest
1 tsp (5 mL) almond extract
3 eggs

6 tbsp (90 mL) brown sugar
6 tbsp (90 mL) sugar
pinch of salt
cherry or raspberry jelly

🍃 Heat the raisins with the milk for 10 to 15 minutes. Add the rice, the nutmeg, the salt, the lemon zest and the almond extract. Separate the eggs. Beat the egg yolks together with the brown sugar and add to the rice mixture.

🍃 Pour into a buttered baking dish. Place the dish in a pan of hot water and bake it in a 350°F (180°C) oven for 1 hour. Refrigerate for about 12 hours.

🍃 To serve, prepare a meringue by beating the 3 egg whites until peaks form and then folding in the sugar and salt. Spread the meringue over the chilled pudding. Bake in a 400°F (200°C) oven for 10 minutes. Garnish to taste with cherry or raspberry jelly.

MOLDED RICE PUDDING

1 cup (250 mL) long-grain rice
½ cup (125 mL) milk
½ cup (125 mL) water
1 tbsp (15 mL) unflavored gelatin
¼ cup (50 mL) water
½ cup (125 mL) sugar
1 tsp (5 mL) vanilla
1 cup (250 mL) whipping cream
crushed pineapple (optional)

🍃 Rinse the rice under cold water and cook it in a double boiler with the milk and ½ cup (125 mL) of water for 1 hour, or until the rice is tender.

Lemon Cups

5 tbsp (75 mL) lemon juice
zest of 1 lemon, grated
3 eggs
1½ cups (375 mL) hot milk

🍃 Mix together the sugar, the flour, the salt, the melted butter, the lemon juice and the grated lemon zest. Separate the eggs. Beat the egg yolks until foamy. Add the hot milk.

🍃 Pour the egg and milk mixture over the flour and stir until the batter is smooth. Beat the egg whites until stiff and fold them into the lemon batter.

🍃 Pour into individual buttered molds and bake in a 325°F (160°C) oven for 45 minutes.

🍃 Soak the gelatin for 5 minutes in the ¼ cup (50 mL) of water. Add to the cooked rice together with the sugar and the vanilla. Mix thoroughly and cool.

🍃 Whip the cream and fold it into the rice. Pour the mixture into an oiled mold. Cover the pudding and refrigerate for 24 hours.

🍃 To serve, unmold the pudding and garnish it with well-drained crushed pineapple or whipped cream.

TAPIOCA PUDDING

½ cup (125 mL) tapioca
3 cups (750 mL) milk
¼ tsp (1 mL) salt
1 egg
⅓ cup (75 mL) sugar
1 tsp (5 mL) vanilla

🍃 Cook the tapioca, the milk and the salt in the top of a double boiler until the tapioca becomes transparent. (This will take from ¾ to 1¼ hours.) Separate the egg. Beat the egg yolk together with the sugar and add this to the tapioca mixture. Cook for 5 minutes, then remove the saucepan from the heat.

🍃 Beat the egg white until stiff and fold it into the tapioca mixture. Flavor with the vanilla.

🍃 This pudding may be eaten hot or cold.

LEMON CUPS

1 cup (250 mL) sugar
¼ cup (50 mL) flour
pinch of salt
2 tbsp (30 mL) butter, melted

DESSERT SYRUPS

Some of the preceding recipes recommend that the dish be served with a syrup. Here are several easy dessert syrups; all can be served cold, but they are at their best when served warm.

🍃 Pure maple syrup makes a delicious topping for custards and puddings.

🍃 Mix half honey and half water.

🍃 Mix 1 cup (250 mL) of sugar with ½ cup (125 mL) of water.

🍃 Mix ½ cup (125 mL) of brown sugar with ½ cup (125 mL) of water.

🍃 To make a syrup from currants or other berries, mix the desired fruit jam or jelly with a small amount of sugar and water and cook over low heat for 10 minutes. Use ¼ cup (50 mL) of water or orange juice to 1 cup (250 mL) of the jam or jelly.

FRENCH DRESSING FOR FRUIT SALAD

¼ cup (50 mL) lemon juice
½ cup (125 mL) salad oil
¼ cup (50 mL) juice from maraschino cherries
1 to 2 tbsp (15 to 30 mL) sugar
½ tsp (2 mL) salt
½ tsp (2 mL) paprika

&❧ Measure all the ingredients and place them in a glass bottle or jar. Close tightly and shake the bottle vigorously. Place it in a cool place for several hours. Shake before using.

HONEY DRESSING FOR FRUIT SALAD

1 tbsp (15 mL) lemon juice
3 tsp (45 mL) honey
1 cup (250 mL) whipping cream
pinch of salt

&❧ Mix together the lemon juice and the honey.
&❧ Whip the cream and gradually add it to the honey mixture. Stir in the salt. Serve.

CREAM SAUCE FOR FRUIT SALAD

⅔ cup (150 mL) cream cheese
¼ cup (50 mL) light cream
1 cup (250 mL) grapefruit juice
1 tsp (5 mL) lemon juice

&❧ Mix together the cream cheese, the light cream and the grapefruit juice. Beat thoroughly. Add the lemon juice and beat the mixture well. Serve.

SWEET EGG SAUCE

2 tbsp (30 mL) sugar
1 egg yolk
½ cup (125 mL) whipping cream
2 tbsp (30 mL) butter
1 tsp (5 mL) vanilla

&❧ Beat the sugar and the egg yolk until foamy and pale yellow in color. Add the whipping cream. Cook the mixture over medium heat, stirring all the while, until it thickens slightly. Do not let it boil. Take it off the heat and let it cool slightly.
&❧ Cream the butter with the vanilla extract. Add to the sauce. Stir until the butter is melted. Serve the sauce hot or cold.

BUTTER SAUCE

¼ cup (50 mL) butter
2 tbsp (30 mL) flour
2 tbsp (30 mL) sugar
1 cup (250 mL) apple or orange juice
pinch of cinnamon

&❧ Melt the butter in a saucepan and add the flour. Mix well. Remove the pan from the heat and add the sugar and the apple or orange juice.
&❧ Place the saucepan back on the burner. Add the cinnamon and cook the mixture, stirring constantly, until the sauce is smooth and creamy. If desired, add more sugar.

BUTTERSCOTCH SAUCE

½ cup (125 mL) corn syrup
½ cup (125 mL) brown sugar
½ cup (125 mL) light cream
3 tbsp (45 mL) butter

Caramel Sauce

🍃 Bring all the ingredients to a boil over low heat, stirring often. Boil for 2 minutes, stirring constantly. This sauce will thicken as it cools.

CARAMEL SAUCE

1 cup (250 mL) brown sugar
2 tbsp (30 mL) flour
pinch of salt
½ cup (125 mL) milk
½ cup (125 mL) water
1 tsp (5 mL) vanilla
pinch of nutmeg or cinnamon
2 tbsp (30 mL) butter

🍃 Put all the ingredients, except the butter, in a blender jar in the order given. Cover and blend 1 minute at high speed.
🍃 Pour the mixture into a saucepan and add the butter. Cook over medium heat, stirring constantly, for about 2 minutes, or until the sauce is creamy. Serve hot or cold over pudding, ice cream or cake.

HARD SAUCE

🍃 Cream ¼ lb (125 g) of sweet butter until it resembles whipped cream. (Thoroughly creaming the butter is the secret behind perfect hard sauce.) Gradually beat in 1 cup (250 mL) of confectioner's sugar, a spoonful at a time, beating after each addition. Beat until the mixture is smooth. Slowly add 3 tbsp (45 mL) of rum or cognac or 1 tbsp (15 mL) of vanilla or lemon juice. Beat thoroughly. Heap the sauce into a silver or glass bowl.

QUÉBEC PEANUT BUTTER SAUCE

1 cup (250 mL) maple syrup
½ cup (125 mL) peanut butter

🍃 Gradually add the maple syrup to the peanut butter. Mix thoroughly and serve.

CHOCOLATE SAUCE

½ cup (125 mL) water
1 cup (250 mL) corn syrup
⅔ cup (150 mL) cocoa
pinch of salt
2 tbsp (30 mL) butter
1 tsp (5 mL) vanilla

🍃 Bring the water, the corn syrup, the cocoa and the salt to a boil over low heat, stirring often. Boil for 2 minutes.
🍃 Remove from the heat. Add the butter and the vanilla. Stir and allow to cool.

UNCOOKED CHOCOLATE SAUCE

2 1-oz (30-g) squares unsweetened chocolate
or 1 cup (250 mL) chocolate chips
6 tbsp (90 mL) milk, cream or coffee
½ cup (125 mL) sugar
½ tsp (2 mL) vanilla
pinch of salt

🍃 Cut the chocolate squares into small pieces. Place the chocolate in a blender jar. Heat the milk, cream or coffee and add it along with the other ingredients. Cover and blend for 1 minute. Store in the refrigerator.

HONEY SAUCE

½ cup (125 mL) honey
¼ cup (50 mL) whipping cream

Chocolate Sauce

zest of 1 orange or lemon
1 tbsp (15 mL) butter

🍮 Heat the honey with the cream and the orange or lemon zest for 5 minutes. Remove from the heat.

🍮 Add the butter and stir until it melts. This sauce may be used hot or cold.

Vanilla Sauce

2 cups (500 mL) light cream
¼ cup (50 mL) white or brown sugar
pinch of salt
3 egg yolks
1 tsp (5 mL) vanilla

🍮 Scald the cream, then add the white or brown sugar and the salt. Stir until the sugar dissolves.

🍮 Beat the egg yolks. Add them to the scalded sauce, stirring constantly. Make sure the mixture does not boil. Cook over low heat, stirring constantly, until the mixture is light and creamy. Stir in the vanilla. Serve this sauce chilled.

Vanilla Mousseline Sauce

🍮 Follow the directions for *Vanilla Sauce* above. Beat 3 egg whites until stiff. Fold the beaten whites into the vanilla sauce. Serve cold.

Mousseline Sauce

1 whole egg
3 egg yolks

5 tbsp (75 mL) sugar
¼ to ½ cup (50 to 125 mL) Cointreau or other liqueur
pinch of salt

🍮 Place all the ingredients in the top of a double boiler. Make sure that the water does not touch the top section of the double boiler. Simmer the water. Do not let it boil.

🍮 Beat the ingredients thoroughly until you have a mixture that is hot and light and that holds its shape. Serve immediately.

Vanilla Pastry Cream

1½ cups (375 mL) milk
2 egg yolks
1½ tbsp (25 mL) of cornstarch
¼ tsp (1 mL) salt
5 tbsp (75 mL) sugar
1 tsp (5 mL) vanilla

🍮 Heat the milk. Beat the egg yolks lightly. Mix together the cornstarch, the salt and the sugar and pour over the beaten egg yolks. Stir in the scalded milk.

🍮 Cook the mixture in a double boiler or over very low heat. Stir constantly until the cream is thick and smooth. Cool and flavor with the vanilla.

VARIATION

🍮 To obtain a coffee-flavored pastry cream, follow the above instructions but substitute ½ cup (125 mL) of very strong coffee and 1 cup (250 mL) of whipping cream for the milk. See also the recipe for *Pastry Cream* on page 574.

Italian White Wine Sauce

3 egg yolks
1 cup (250 mL) white wine
1 tsp (5 mL) cinnamon
small piece of lemon zest
½ tsp (2 mL) lemon juice

🍮 Place the egg yolks and the white wine in the top of a double boiler. Add the cinnamon, the lemon zest and the lemon juice.

🍮 Cook the mixture, beating continuously, until it is thick and fluffy. Make sure that the boiling water does not touch the top section of the double boiler. Serve the sauce immediately.

English Whiskey Sauce

¼ cup (50 mL) soft butter
2 cups (500 mL) brown sugar
1 cup (250 mL) light cream
1 egg
pinch of nutmeg
¼ cup (50 mL) whiskey

🍮 Place the butter and the brown sugar in the top of a double boiler. Beat the mixture continuously until it becomes thick and creamy.

🍮 Add the cream, the egg and the nutmeg. Continue beating until the mixture is very light.

🍮 Place over hot water in the bottom section of the double boiler and cook until the mixture thickens, stirring occasionally. Make sure the water does not boil.

❧ Remove from the heat. Gradually add the whiskey, stirring constantly. Serve hot or cold.

SHERRY SAUCE

⅓ cup (75 mL) sugar
1 cup (250 mL) sherry
1 tbsp (15 mL) lemon juice
3 eggs

❧ Heat the sugar, the sherry and the lemon juice in the top of a double boiler. Cook, stirring often, until the sugar dissolves.

❧ Separate the eggs. Add the egg yolks and beat until the mixture is light and creamy. Remove the pan from the heat.

❧ Beat the egg whites until stiff. Carefully fold them into the sauce and then beat the sauce until it is fluffy.

APRICOT SAUCE

1 cup (250 mL) whipping cream
¼ cup (50 mL) confectioner's sugar
1 tbsp (15 mL) vanilla
½ cup (125 mL) apricot jam
juice of ½ lemon

❧ Whip the cream. Gradually add the sugar and the vanilla, mixing well.

❧ Fold the apricot jam and lemon juice into the cream mixture. Refrigerate the sauce until you are ready to serve it.

LEMON SAUCE

¾ cup (175 mL) sugar
3 tbsp (45 mL) flour

3 egg yolks
¾ cup (175 mL) cold water
2 tbsp (30 mL) butter
¾ cup (175 mL) lemon juice
zest of 1 lemon
1 tsp (5 mL) orange zest

❧ In the top of a double boiler, mix together the sugar, the flour and the egg yolks. Add the cold water and cook the mixture over boiling water, stirring often, until it thickens.

❧ Remove the double boiler from the heat, but leave the top section of the pot over the hot water. Add the butter, a small piece at a time, stirring well after each addition. Add the remaining ingredients and mix well.

❧ This sauce may be served hot or cold.

VARIATION
1 cup (250 mL) sugar
½ cup (125 mL) butter
1 egg, lightly beaten
juice and zest of 2 lemons
½ cup (125 mL) boiling water

❧ Place all the ingredients in the top section of a double boiler and cook until the mixture thickens, stirring constantly. Serve this sauce hot or cold.

QUÉBEC-STYLE LEMON SAUCE

1 cup (250 mL) brown sugar
1 cup (250 mL) water
1 lemon, sliced
1 tsp (5 mL) cornstarch
2 tbsp (30 mL) cold water

❧ Boil the brown sugar with the water and very thin slices of the

unpeeled lemon for 10 minutes.

❧ Thicken this sauce with the cornstarch blended with the 2 tbsp (30 mL) of cold water.

❧ Leave the lemon slices in the sauce when serving it.

LEMON MOUSSE SAUCE

5 tbsp (75 mL) sifted pastry flour
1 cup (250 mL) sugar
1 egg
⅓ cup (75 mL) lemon juice
⅔ cup (150 mL) water
2 tsp (10 mL) butter
1 tsp (5 mL) grated lemon zest
¼ cup (50 mL) whipping cream
¾ cup (175 mL) whipping cream

❧ Mix the flour and the sugar in the top of a double boiler. Beat the egg and add to the flour and sugar along with the lemon juice, the water and the butter. Stir well. Cook the mixture over boiling water, stirring often, until it is creamy and smooth. Cool.

❧ Stir the grated lemon zest into the cooled mixture. Whip the ¼ cup (50 mL) of whipping cream and fold it into the mixture. Use half of this mousse between two layers of sponge cake.

❧ Whip the remaining ¾ cup (175 mL) of cream and add it to the rest of the lemon mousse. Stir well. Serve this sauce with the cake.

HOT ORANGE SAUCE

zest of 1 orange
1 cup (250 mL) water
2 tsp (10 mL) cornstarch

¼ cup (50 mL) orange juice
⅓ cup (75 mL) maple syrup

🖎 Remove the white membrane from the orange zest. Cut the zest into very thin slivers. Place them in a saucepan with the water and simmer for 15 minutes. Pour off the liquid and measure it; you will need ⅔ cup (150 mL), so add more water if necessary to make this amount. Return the liquid to the pot.

🖎 Blend the cornstarch and the orange juice and add to the zest. Stir in the maple syrup. Bring the mixture slowly to a boil and cook for 5 minutes, stirring constantly. Serve the sauce hot or warm.

Chocolate Sauce

CHOCOLATE SAUCE

4 oz (125 g) sweet chocolate
½ oz (15 g) unsweetened chocolate
3 tbsp (45 mL) cold coffee
1 cup (250 mL) light cream
1 tsp (5 mL) vanilla
1 tsp (5 mL) cornstarch
2 egg yolks
½ cup (125 mL) whipping cream

🖎 Cut all the chocolate into small pieces and place in the top of a double boiler. Add the coffee. Melt the chocolate over boiling water.

🖎 Heat the cream and the vanilla over low heat for 10 minutes, stirring almost constantly.

🖎 Blend together the cornstarch and the egg yolks. Add the hot cream and then the melted chocolate, stirring constantly.

🖎 Cook the mixture in the dou-ble boiler, stirring often, until it is creamy and thick. Remove from the heat. Whip the cream and fold it into the sauce.

🖎 If you prefer to serve this sauce cold, chill the chocolate mixture before folding in the whipped cream.

MAPLE CREAM FOR CRÊPES

1 cup (250 mL) maple syrup
½ cup (125 mL) water
1 tbsp (15 mL) cornstarch
¾ tsp (4 mL) cold water
1 tbsp (15 mL) butter
¼ cup (50 mL) maple syrup

🖎 Boil the maple syrup and the water for 2 minutes. Add the cornstarch to the cold water and blend well. Add to the syrup. Stir until the sauce turns transparent, then add the butter. Remove from the heat and allow to cool.

🖎 Place a spoonful of the sauce on each crêpe. Roll the crêpes and place them side by side in a baking dish. This can be done several hours ahead of the meal. Keep the filled crêpes in the refrigerator until almost ready to serve.

🖎 To serve, dot the crêpes with butter and pour the ¼ cup (50 mL) of maple syrup over them. Cover the dish and heat the crêpes in a 375°F (190°C) oven for 20 minutes.

🖎 This recipe yields enough filling for 8 crêpes.

MAPLE BUTTER MAISON

¼ cup (50 mL) maple syrup
¼ cup (50 mL) whipping cream
1 cup (250 mL) honey

❧ Place all the ingredients in a blender jar. Cover and blend for 30 to 40 seconds. Do not overbeat or the mixture will curdle. Pour the maple butter into a clean glass jar, cover and refrigerate until firm and creamy.

QUICK CAKE ICING

2 cups (500 mL) confectioner's sugar
1 tsp (5 mL) instant coffee
2 tbsp (30 mL) hot water
3 tbsp (45 mL) cocoa
1 cup (250 mL) confectioner's sugar
1 tsp (5 mL) vanilla
¼ tsp (1 mL) salt
¼ cup (50 mL) butter
1 egg yolk

❧ Place 2 cups (500 mL) of the confectioner's sugar in a bowl.
❧ Place the remaining 1 cup (250 mL) of confectioner's sugar

and the rest of the ingredients in a blender jar. Blend for 40 seconds at high speed.
❧ Pour the blended mixture over the confectioner's sugar in the bowl and stir until the icing is creamy and smooth.
❧ This recipe yields enough to cover the tops and sides of 2 8-in. (20-cm) round sponge cakes.

FROSTING FOR PETITS FOURS

2 cups (500 mL) sugar
pinch of cream of tartar
1 cup (250 mL) hot water
1 to 1½ cups (250 to 375 mL) confectioner's sugar, sifted

❧ Bring to a boil the sugar, the cream of tartar and the hot water. Boil until you have a thin syrup that registers 226°F (108°C) on a candy thermometer.

Chocolate Whipped-Cream Frosting

❧ Cool the syrup to approximately 100°F (40°C), then slowly add enough confectioner's sugar to make an icing that can be poured on the cakes and still adhere to them. (It is important to stir the confectioner's sugar into the syrup, not the other way around.)
❧ Place a piece of wax paper on a counter or table. Set a cake rack over the paper. Lay the petits fours on the rack and pour the frosting over them. The wax paper will catch the excess, which you can then reheat and use.

ROYAL FROSTING

1½ cups (375 mL) confectioner's sugar
1 egg white
pinch of salt
1 tsp (5 mL) lemon juice
food coloring

❧ Place the confectioner's sugar, the egg white, the salt and the lemon juice in a bowl. Beat the mixture until it is very thick—until stiff peaks form when the beater is slowly raised. It is sometimes necessary to add a little more confectioner's sugar or egg white to obtain the desired consistency.
❧ To tint the icing, add a few drops of the desired color and beat the frosting with a wooden spoon. It will harden very quickly, so use the frosting immediately. If this is not possible, cover the frosting with a damp cloth. Beat it again with a wooden spoon when you are ready to use it.
❧ This frosting is perfect for decorating birthday and wedding

cakes. Apply it with a piping nozzle to form rosettes and other decorative elements.

BUTTER FROSTING

²/₃ cup (150 mL) sugar
½ cup (125 mL) water
1 tbsp (15 mL) corn syrup
3 egg whites
⅓ cup (75 mL) sugar
1 cup (250 mL) sweet butter

🍂 Place the ²/₃ cup (150 mL) of sugar, the water and the corn syrup in a saucepan. Stir over low heat until the sugar dissolves. Boil over medium heat until the syrup registers 238°F (114°C) on a candy thermometer or until it forms a soft ball when a little is dropped into cold water.

🍂 Beat the egg whites lightly, then gradually add the ⅓ cup (75mL) of sugar. Continue beating the mixture until it is very stiff.

🍂 Pour the boiling syrup slowly over the beaten egg whites, stirring constantly. Continue beating until the frosting is very smooth and thick. Allow to cool.

🍂 Cream the butter until very light and fold it into the cooled mixture. Flavor to taste.

🍂 This recipe yields 2 cups (500 mL) of butter frosting.

RUM AND NUT FROSTING

2 cups (500 mL) butter frosting
1 cup (250 mL) walnuts, finely chopped
3 tbsp (45 mL) rum

🍂 Prepare 2 cups (500 mL) butter frosting as indicated above.

🍂 Add the rum and the nuts and stir well.

ALMOND PASTE FILLING

½ cup (125 mL) butter
2 eggs
1 cup (250 mL) almond paste
1 tsp (5 mL) lemon zest
2 tsp (10 mL) flour

🍂 Cream the butter. Beat the eggs. Mash the almond paste and stir it into the butter, alternating with the beaten eggs. Beat the mixture until it is smooth.

🍂 Add the lemon zest and the flour. Stir and use.

RUM FROSTING

2 cups (500 mL) confectioner's sugar
3 tbsp (45 mL) soft butter
3 tbsp (45 mL) whipping cream
1 tbsp (15 mL) rum

🍂 Beat together the confectioner's sugar, the butter and the cream until the mixture resembles a thick smooth cream.

🍂 Add the rum and beat for 1 minute.

🍂 To vary the flavor, just add a different extract or liquor. If the frosting is too thin, do not add more confectioner's sugar; put the frosting in the refrigerator and let it harden to the desired consistency.

AMERICAN CHOCOLATE FILLING

1 egg yolk
¼ cup (50 mL) sugar
2 tbsp (30 mL) all-purpose flour
1 cup (250 mL) milk
pinch of salt
6 oz (175 g) chocolate chips

🍂 Place the egg yolk, the sugar, the flour, the milk and the salt in a saucepan. Mix thoroughly and cook the mixture over medium heat, stirring constantly, until it is smooth and creamy. Remove from the heat.

🍂 Add the chocolate. Allow to stand for 15 minutes, then stir thoroughly until the melted chocolate is well blended.

VIENNESE CHOCOLATE FILLING

4 1-oz (30-g) squares unsweetened chocolate
½ cup (125 mL) sugar
4 tbsp (60 mL) hot water
¾ cup (175 mL) boiling water
½ cup (125 mL) light cream
½ cup (125 mL) sugar
1 egg white
1 tsp (5 mL) vanilla

🍂 Grate the chocolate and mix it with the ½ cup (125 mL) of sugar. Place the mixture in a small saucepan with the 4 tbsp (60 mL) of hot water. Stir over low heat until the sugar and chocolate melt.

Lemon and Orange Icing

BITTERSWEET CHOCOLATE FROSTING

5 1-oz (30-g) squares
unsweetened chocolate
1 tbsp (15 mL) water
pinch of salt
1 can sweetened condensed milk

❧ Melt the chocolate in the top of a double boiler over hot—not boiling—water. Add the water and the salt. Stir until the chocolate is smooth.

❧ Add the condensed milk and stir thoroughly until the mixture is completely blended. Cook for 7 or 8 minutes over the hot water. Place the frosting in the refrigerator. When cool, it is ready to be used.

❧ Add the ¾ cup (175 mL) boiling water, the cream and the remaining ½ cup (125 mL) of sugar. Cook, stirring constantly, until the sugar melts and the mixture starts to boil.

❧ Beat the egg white lightly. Add the vanilla and the beaten egg white to the chocolate mixture. Cook without boiling until the filling is thick enough to spread with a knife. Cool and use.

CHOCOLATE WHIPPED-CREAM FROSTING

1 cup (250 mL) whipping cream
¼ cup (50 mL) superfine sugar
2 tbsp (30 mL) cocoa
½ tsp (2 mL) vanilla

❧ Mix all the ingredients in a bowl. Refrigerate for 2 to 7 hours.

❧ When you are ready to use the frosting, beat it thoroughly until it is thick enough to stand in peaks.

❧ Use to garnish and frost light cakes such as sponge cake or angel food cake.

CHOCOLATE VELVET FROSTING

¾ cup (175 mL) evaporated milk
6 oz (175 g) chocolate chips
½ cup (125 mL) confectioner's sugar

❧ Combine the evaporated milk and the chocolate chips in a saucepan. Cook over very low heat, stirring often, until the mixture comes to a boil. Boil gently for 2 to 3 minutes, or until the mixture thickens slightly.

❧ Remove from the heat. Cool the mixture, stirring occasionally, then add the confectioner's sugar. Beat vigorously, then use.

SACHER CHOCOLATE FROSTING

4 1-oz (30-g) squares sweet chocolate
¼ cup (50 mL) water
½ cup (125 mL) sugar
3 tbsp (45 mL) water
1 tsp (5 mL) butter
2 tbsp (30 mL) whipping cream

❧ Cut the chocolate into small pieces and place them in a saucepan. Add the ¼ cup (50 mL) of water and cook over very low heat until the chocolate melts.

❧ Prepare a syrup by heating the sugar and the 3 tbsp (45 mL) of water. Add the melted chocolate and stir until the mixture reaches a hard boil. Add the butter and cream. Reduce the heat and boil

for 2 minutes more. Allow to cool.
🍂 Beat the icing until it is creamy and smooth, then spread it on the cake of your choice.

COCOA ICING

2 tbsp (30 mL) butter
2 tbsp (30 mL) cocoa
2 tbsp (30 mL) whipping cream
1 cup (250 mL) confectioner's sugar

🍂 Melt the butter in a double boiler over hot water. Add the cocoa and cream and stir well.
🍂 Remove the double boiler from the heat but leave the top section over the hot water. Add the confectioner's sugar. Beat the icing until it is smooth and creamy.
🍂 This icing is used as a light topping for brownies and cookies. When it cools, it is like a light fudge.

COCOA BUTTER FROSTING

1 cup (250 mL) cocoa
½ cup (125 mL) butter
1 lb (500 g) confectioner's sugar, sifted
½ cup (125 mL) milk
1 tsp (5 mL) vanilla

🍂 Place the cocoa and the butter in the small bowl of an electric mixer. Cream until light. Gradually add the confectioner's sugar, alternating it with the milk and vanilla. Beat the mixture until it is smooth and creamy.
🍂 This recipe yields enough to frost 2 8-in. (20-cm) round cakes.

MOCHA ICING

3 egg yolks
1 cup (250 mL) sugar
½ tsp (2 mL) cream of tartar
½ cup (125 mL) water
8 oz (250 g) sweet chocolate
4 tbsp (60 mL) strong coffee
2 tbsp (30 mL) rum
pinch of salt
½ lb (250 g) sweet butter
½ lb (250 g) shortening

🍂 Beat the egg yolks until they are a pale yellow in color and very light and fluffy in consistency.
🍂 Place the sugar, the cream of tartar and the water in a small saucepan and cook over medium heat, stirring constantly, until the sugar dissolves. Boil the syrup, without stirring, until it thickens slightly. Remove the pan from the heat.
🍂 Slowly pour the hot syrup over the egg yolks, stirring the mixture until it thickens. Allow to cool.
🍂 Place the chocolate and the coffee in a saucepan. Heat on low until the chocolate melts. Remove the pan from the heat and add the rum and the salt. Stir well and set the mixture aside to cool.
🍂 While the chocolate is cooling, add the butter and shortening, a spoonful at a time, to the egg mixture. Using an electric mixer, beat until the mixture is creamy and smooth. Pour in the melted chocolate and mix well.
🍂 The darker and finer the chocolate used in this recipe, the better the icing. It yields enough to ice one cake 10 in. (25 cm) in diameter and 3 to 4 in. (8 to 10 cm) high.

AMERICAN MOCHA ICING

½ cup (125 mL) soft butter
1 lb (500 g) confectioner's sugar, sifted
2 tsp (10 mL) instant coffee
2 1-oz (30-g) squares unsweetened chocolate
¼ cup (50 mL) milk
1 tbsp (15 mL) vanilla

🍂 Cream the butter until light and smooth. Gradually add the remaining ingredients in the order given. Beat until very smooth and creamy.
🍂 This recipe is sufficient to fill and frost a round layer cake 8 in. (20 cm) in diameter.

LEMON AND ORANGE ICING

zest of ½ orange
zest of 1 lemon
2 tbsp (30 mL) orange juice
2 tbsp (30 mL) lemon juice
3 tbsp (45 mL) soft butter
1 egg yolk
pinch of salt
3 cups (750 mL) confectioner's sugar

🍂 Remove as much of the white membrane as possible from the orange and lemon peels. Place them in the jar of a blender along with the orange and lemon juice, the soft butter, the egg yolk and the salt. Cover and blend for 1½ minutes at high speed.
🍂 Sift the confectioner's sugar in a bowl. Pour the blended mixture on top and mix well. If the icing

seems too thin, do not add more confectioner's sugar; instead refrigerate the icing until it reaches the desired consistency.

APRICOT JAM FILLING

2 tbsp (30 mL) flour
⅓ cup (75 mL) orange juice or sherry
⅔ cup (150 mL) apricot jam
juice 1 lemon
zest of ½ lemon
3 egg yolks

🍂 Blend together the flour and orange juice or sherry in a small saucepan. Add the apricot jam, the lemon juice and the zest. Cook the mixture over low heat, stirring almost constantly, until it is smooth and creamy.

🍂 Beat the egg yolks, then add a few spoonfuls of hot cream to them. Mix well. Add the rest of the hot cream to the egg yolks,

stirring constantly. Cook the cream for 1 minute, stirring all the time. Make sure the mixture does not boil. Set it aside to cool and then use it as desired.

HONEY LEMON FILLING

¼ cup (50 mL) sugar
2 tbsp (30 mL) flour
¼ cup (50 mL) lemon juice
½ cup (125 mL) honey
zest of 1 lemon
1 egg, lightly beaten
1 tbsp (15 mL) butter

🍂 Mix all the ingredients together in the top of a double boiler.

🍂 Cook over boiling water, stirring often, until the mixture is light and creamy. Set the filling aside and allow to cool before using.

🍂 This cream can also be used to ice certain cakes.

APPLE TOPPING

3 apples
juice and zest of 1 lemon
¾ cup (175 mL) sugar
1 tbsp (15 mL) flour
3 tbsp (45 mL) water
2 egg yolks
2 tbsp (30 mL) butter
½ tsp (2 mL) vanilla

🍂 Peel and core the apples and grate them coarsely.

🍂 In a saucepan, mix together the grated apples, the lemon juice, the zest and the sugar. Cook, uncovered, over medium heat until the mixture reaches the boiling point.

🍂 Blend the flour and the water and add this to the boiling apples. Stir until the mixture thickens. Beat the egg yolks. Add a few spoonfuls of the hot apple mixture to the yolks and pour this into the rest of the apple mixture. Stir for a few moments, then remove from the heat. Add the butter and the vanilla. Stir until the butter melts.

🍂 Set the topping aside to cool, then use as desired. It is particularly good with gingerbread.

ICE CREAMS AND SHERBETS

ABOUT ICE CREAM

Because sugar causes ice cream to granulate, it is advisable to use superfine sugar and to use as little of it as possible. Honey and corn syrup are also recommended as they cause very little granulation.

🍧 A small quantity of unflavored gelatin added to the mixture makes a smoother-textured ice cream.

🍧 For fluffy, creamy ice cream, beat the mixture 2 or 3 times before letting it set completely. Begin beating the ice cream once it starts to set along the edges of the container.

🍧 Turn the temperature control in the refrigerator to the coldest setting at least 30 minutes before pouring the ice cream into the container. When the ice cream has been beaten and is well set, turn the temperature control back to its original setting.

🍧 If whipped cream is used, it should be whipped lightly. Otherwise it takes on a cheesy texture when frozen. Ice cream requires at least 3 hours to freeze.

🍧 Nothing equals a blender for beating ice creams, sherbets or ices. It makes the mixture light and fluffy and produces a smoother, more velvety cream once it is frozen.

🍧 A manual or electric ice-cream maker is commonly used to make sherbets and ice creams. Ice cream made in an ice-cream maker requires 6 to 8 hours to freeze.

🍧 Avoid filling the container completely as ice cream increases in volume when frozen.

🍧 Let the ice cream set for 1 hour before serving.

🍧 Ice cream can be kept up to 3 weeks in a commercial container without losing any of its original texture. To store longer than 6 weeks, wrap the container in freezer paper. If the container is not full, fill the empty space with a layer of crumpled plastic wrap.

VANILLA ICE CREAM

1 tsp (5 mL) unflavored gelatin
1 tbsp (15 mL) cold water
1 cup (250 mL) milk or cream
³/₈ cup (85 mL) superfine sugar
1½ tsp (7 mL) cornstarch
pinch of salt
1 egg lightly beaten
1 tsp (5 mL) vanilla
1 cup (250 mL) whipping cream

🍧 Soak the gelatin in the cold water for 5 minutes. Scald the milk or cream. Mix together the sugar and cornstarch. Add a little hot milk; stir and pour into the remaining hot milk. Cook over low heat, stirring constantly, until the mixture begins to thicken.

🍧 Add the salt and beaten egg, stirring vigorously. Remove from the heat, add the gelatin and stir until dissolved. Allow the mixture to cool.

🍧 When the mixture is completely cooled, beat in the vanilla and cream. Place the mixture in the freezer. Beat 2 or 3 times before the ice cream is completely set.

🍧 If you wish, substitute 1 tbsp (15 mL) instant coffee for the vanilla.

OLD-FASHIONED ICE CREAM

½ vanilla bean
½ cup (125 mL) milk
5 egg yolks
1½ cups (375 mL) superfine sugar
4 cups (1 L) whipping cream

🍧 Cut the vanilla bean in half. Using the blade of a small knife, scrape the seeds into a bowl. Add the seeds and the bean to the milk. Simmer over very low heat for 10 minutes.

🍧 Beat the yolks until foamy. Add the sugar and continue beating until light and lemon colored. Add the whipping cream to the eggs and beat for a few minutes. Remove the vanilla bean.

🍧 Pour the mixture into an ice-cream maker. Churn until the ice cream is well set.

🍧 Cover and let stand 1 hour.

PHILADELPHIA ICE CREAM

6 egg yolks
1½ cups (375 mL) sugar
4 cups (1 L) whipping cream
2 tbsp (30 mL) vanilla
or coffee extract

🍃 Beat the egg yolks until light and foamy. Add the sugar and beat until it is dissolved.

🍃 Add the cream and the vanilla or coffee extract to the eggs. Beat with a hand beater until well blended.

🍃 Transfer the mixture to the ice-cream maker and freeze according to the manufacturer's instructions.

STRAWBERRY ICE CREAM
Add 1 tbsp (15 mL) vanilla extract and 1 package frozen strawberries with the cream.

UNSWEETENED EVAPORATED MILK ICE CREAM

½ cup (125 mL) sugar
2 tbsp (30 mL) cornstarch
½ tsp (2 mL) salt
1 egg
1 can unsweetened evaporated milk
1½ tsp (7 mL) vanilla
1 cup (250 mL) whipping cream

🍃 Place the sugar, cornstarch, salt and egg in the top of a double boiler. Mix well.

🍃 When thoroughly blended, gradually add the evaporated milk and vanilla. Cook in the top of a double boiler over boiling water, stirring constantly, until the mixture thickens slightly (approximately 8 to 10 minutes).

🍃 Remove from the heat. Cool to room temperature. Then freeze.

🍃 While the mixture chills, whip the cream. Pour the chilled mix-

Old-Fashioned Ice Cream

ture into a bowl and beat it with an electric mixer. With the mixer running, beat in the whipped cream.

🍃 Return the mixture to the freezer and freeze until set.

COFFEE ICE CREAM
Mix the sugar with 2 tbsp (30 mL) instant coffee powder. Prepare the ice cream as indicated in the basic recipe.

COCOA ICE CREAM
Mix the sugar with ½ cup (125 mL) cocoa and 3 tbsp (45 mL) cold water. Prepare the ice cream as indicated in the basic recipe.

CHOCOLATE ICE CREAM
Add 2 or 3 1-oz. (30-g) squares unsweetened chocolate, when incorporating the evaporated milk. Prepare the ice cream as indicated in the basic recipe.

MARSHMALLOW ICE CREAM

¾ cup (175 mL) milk
24 large marshmallows
½ cup (125 mL) strong coffee
pinch of salt
1 cup (250 mL) whipping cream
2 tsp (10 mL) vanilla

🍃 Place the milk and marshmallows in the top of a double boiler. Heat over boiling water until the marshmallows melt.

🍃 Add the coffee and salt. Blend well and remove from the heat. Cool until slightly thickened.

🍃 Whip the cream and add it to the cooled mixture. Add the vanilla and blend thoroughly. Place the mixture in the freezer

Strawberry Ice Cream

and freeze until the ice cream is set.

VARIATIONS

🍂 This ice cream lends itself to many variations. Simply replace the coffee with one of the following: ½ cup (125 mL) orange juice, ¼ cup (50 mL) lemon juice and ¼ cup (50 mL) water; ½ cup (125 mL) milk and 2 tbsp (30 mL) rum or cognac; or ½ cup (125 mL) milk and 1 tbsp (15 mL) of your favorite flavoring.

GELATIN ICE CREAM

1½ cups (375 mL) boiling water
1 package strawberry, raspberry, cherry or orange gelatin, to taste
1 cup (250 mL) whipping cream

🍂 Pour the boiling water over the gelatin. Stir until dissolved. Refrigerate until the mixture resembles thick unbeaten egg whites.

🍂 Beat the gelatin until very fluffy. Whip the cream, add it to the gelatin and blend well.

🍂 Place the mixture in the freezer. Freeze until the ice cream is set.

STRAWBERRY ICE CREAM

4 cups (1 L) vanilla ice cream
2 packages frozen strawberries
1 cup (250 mL) whipping cream
1 tsp (5 mL) vanilla
2 egg yolks
½ cup (125 mL) sugar

🍂 Let the ice cream soften and thaw the strawberries. Combine in a bowl and blend thoroughly.

🍂 Whip the cream and add the vanilla. In a separate bowl, cream the egg yolks and the sugar until the mixture is light and the sugar is almost dissolved.

🍂 Add the whipped cream and egg mixture to the ice cream. Stir until well blended and pour into a mold. Freeze until well set. Stir once or twice with a spoon during the first hour of freezing.

RUM AND RAISIN ICE CREAM

½ cup (125 mL) seedless raisins
3 tbsp (45 mL) rum
2 egg yolks
½ cup (125 mL) sugar
pinch of salt
1 cup (250 mL) light cream
1 cup (250 mL) whipping cream
1½ tsp (7 mL) vanilla

🍂 Soak the raisins in the rum for 12 hours. Set aside.

🍂 Beat the egg yolks until foamy and lemon colored. Add the sugar and continue beating until the sugar is dissolved. Add the salt and light cream to the egg yolks. Beat for a few minutes.

🍂 Whip the cream and fold it into the mixture, along with the vanilla. Place the mixture in the freezer and freeze until set.

🍂 Turn the ice cream into a bowl and beat until it takes on the appearance of a chilled cream. Fold in the rum-soaked raisins.

Return to the freezer until the ice cream is firmly set.

COFFEE-RUM ICE CREAM

2 cups (500 mL) milk
½ cup (125 mL) confectioner's sugar
1½ tbsp (25 mL) flour
½ tsp (2 mL) salt
2 eggs, well beaten
1 tsp (5 mL) unflavored gelatin
1 tbsp (15 mL) cold water
2 cups (500 mL) whipping cream
2 tbsp (30 mL) rum
3 tbsp (45 mL) instant coffee

🍃 Scald the milk. In a bowl, combine the confectioner's sugar and flour and add ½ cup (125 mL) scalded milk. Blend thoroughly and pour the mixture into the rest of the milk. Stirring constantly, heat the mixture until it begins to thicken. Remove from the heat. While beating, add the salt and eggs.

🍃 Soak the gelatin in cold water for 5 minutes. Add it to the hot mixture and stir until the gelatin is dissolved. Cool.

🍃 Whip the cream and add the rum and coffee. Beat for a few seconds to blend. Fold the whipped cream into the cooled gelatin mixture. Place it in the freezer and freeze until it is partially set. Then pour it into a bowl and beat it until fluffy. Return to the freezer and freeze until set.

HONEY ICE CREAM

2 cups (500 mL) whipping cream
½ cup (125 mL) clear honey
zest of 1 orange and 1 lemon
pinch of salt
½ tsp (2 mL) almond extract
½ cup (125 mL) toasted almonds, slivered

🍃 Whip the cream until thickened but not stiff. Gradually add the honey, beating constantly, until the mixture is smooth. Add the orange and lemon zest, salt and almond extract.

🍃 If possible, freeze this mixture in an ice-cream maker. Otherwise place it in the freezer. Sprinkle it with almonds and freeze until set.

FRESH PEACH ICE CREAM

2 lb (1 kg) ripe peaches
juice of 1 lemon
1½ cups (375 mL) sugar
2 eggs
2 tbsp (30 mL) confectioner's sugar
1 cup (250 mL) whipping cream

🍃 Scald the peaches and peel them. Set aside 2 peaches for the garnish: slice them, sprinkle them with sugar and place them in a glass jar. Refrigerate until ready to use.

🍃 Place the rest of the peaches and the lemon juice in a bowl. Crush the peaches with a pestle. Add the sugar and mix well.

🍃 Separate the egg yolks from the whites. Beat the whites with the

Fresh Peach Ice Cream

[615]

confectioner's sugar until they form stiff peaks. Beat the yolks lightly and fold them into the whites. Whip the cream and fold it into the eggs. Then carefully add the crushed peaches.

🌰 Place the mixture in the freezer and freeze until the ice cream begins to set along the edges of the container. Transfer the ice cream to a bowl and beat it until fluffy. Return it to the freezer and freeze until set. Unmold and garnish with the reserved peaches.

CHESTNUT ICE CREAM

½ cup (125 mL) seedless raisins
3 tbsp (45 mL) rum
5 egg yolks
1 cup (250 mL) sugar
1 tbsp (15 mL) unflavored gelatin

4 cups (1 L) light cream
¼ cup (50 mL) pineapple juice
1½ cups (375 mL) sweetened chestnut purée
½ tsp (2 mL) salt
½ cup (125 mL) candied fruit, finely chopped
½ cup (125 mL) grated sweet chocolate

🌰 Soak the raisins in the rum for 2 hours. Set aside.

🌰 Cream the egg yolks and the sugar until light and lemon colored.

🌰 Soak the gelatin in 2 tbsp (30 mL) cold water for 5 minutes. Heat the cream and stir in the gelatin until it dissolves. Pour over the egg yolks and mix thoroughly. Cook over very low heat, stirring constantly, until the cream thickens slightly. Do not boil. Refrigerate until chilled.

🌰 Mix together the pineapple juice and chestnut purée. Add to

the cooled cream along with the salt, candied fruit, raisins and grated chocolate. Mix together. If possible, place the mixture in an ice-cream maker and churn until set. Otherwise, pour the mixture into a soufflé dish and freeze until the ice cream is set. Stir 2 or 3 times during the first hours of freezing. Serve with a dollop of whipped cream.

FROZEN CHESTNUT CUPS

4 cups (1 L) vanilla ice cream
½ cup (125 mL) chestnuts in syrup
¼ cup (50 mL) toasted almonds, slivered
¾ cup (175 mL) candied cherries, chopped
¼ cup (50 mL) cognac

🌰 Soften the ice cream. Cut the chestnuts into small pieces and combine them with the almonds, chopped cherries and cognac. Stir and spoon the mixture evenly into glass dessert dishes.

🌰 Garnish each dish of ice cream with crushed macaroons. Cover with a layer of aluminum foil and freeze until set.

ICE CREAM PRALINE

1 tbsp (15 mL) butter
2 tbsp (30 mL) brown sugar
¼ cup (50 mL) chopped nuts
¼ cup (50 mL) cereal, crushed
½ cup (125 mL) sugar
½ tsp (2 mL) salt
1⅓ cups (325 mL) milk

De Luxe Chocolate Ice Cream

2 eggs
1 cup (250 mL) whipping cream
1 tsp (5 mL) vanilla

❧ To make the praline, melt the butter in a skillet and add the brown sugar, nuts and cereal. Stir over low heat and blend until smooth. Spread the praline on a large plate to cool. When cool, break into small pieces.

❧ Blend the sugar with the salt and milk, until the sugar is dissolved.

❧ Beat the egg whites and the egg yolks separately.

❧ Whip the cream. Add the beaten egg whites and yolks, sweetened milk, vanilla and small pieces of praline. Blend together and place the mixture in the freezer. When the mixture begins to set along the edges of the container, pour it into a bowl and beat it until fluffy. Return it to the freezer and freeze until set.

De Luxe Chocolate Ice Cream

1 cup (250 mL) corn syrup
3 egg yolks, well beaten
3 1-oz (30-g) squares unsweetened chocolate
2 cups (500 mL) whipping cream
3 egg whites
1 cup (250 mL) confectioner's sugar

❧ Bring the corn syrup to a boil. Pour it slowly over the beaten egg yolks, stirring constantly. Cool.

❧ Melt the chocolate squares in a double boiler over hot, not boiling, water. Cool.

❧ Whip the cream and beat the egg whites until stiff.

❧ Add the melted chocolate, whipped cream, beaten egg whites and sugar to the egg yolks. Mix until the sugar is dissolved.

❧ Place the mixture in the freezer. Freeze until the ice cream is set.

Praline Bombe

3 egg yolks
½ cup (125 mL) sugar
pinch of cream of tartar
¼ cup (50 mL) cold water
2 tbsp (30 mL) instant coffee
2 tbsp (30 mL) boiling water
4 cups (1 L) whipping cream
½ cup (125 mL) sugar
pinch of cream of tartar
½ cup (125 mL) almonds
3 tbsp (45 mL) rum

❧ Using an electric mixer, beat the egg yolks until light and foamy.

❧ In a saucepan, combine the sugar, cream of tartar and water. Stir, over medium heat, until the sugar is dissolved. Cook until a soft ball forms when tested in cold water. Slowly pour the hot syrup into the egg yolks, stirring constantly. Beat until the mixture is warm and thick.

❧ Dissolve the coffee in boiling water and whip the cream until firm. Add the coffee and the whipped cream to the egg yolk mixture.

❧ To prepare the praline, place the sugar, cream of tartar and almonds in a cast-iron skillet. Cook over low heat, stirring with a metal spoon, until the sugar turns into a brown syrup. Pour onto a buttered baking sheet. Cool. Break the praline into pieces and pulverize. Add to the cream mixture along with the rum.

❧ Coat the inside of a deep bowl with sweet almond oil. Pour in the rum-cream mixture. Cover and wrap the bowl in a sheet of aluminum foil or wax paper to make it airtight. Freeze 5 to 6 hours.

❧ To unmold, surround the bowl with a towel soaked in boiling water. Remove the cover and unmold on a serving dish.

❧ To prepare a larger quantity, use 6 or 7 cups (1.5 L) cream. The other ingredients remain the same.

Garnished Bombe

❧ Choose an ice cream and a sherbet that will go well together. Prepare each one according to the recipe.

❧ Place a mold in the refrigerator and chill it before filling it with ice cream. Freeze the ice cream until it is partially set.

❧ Scoop out some of the ice cream from the center of the mold and fill it with sherbet. Cover the sherbet with a layer of ice cream. Return the ice cream to the freezer.

MOCHA BOMBE

12 oz. (375 g) sweet chocolate
3 tbsp (45 mL) very strong coffee
3 cups (750 mL) whipping cream
¾ cup (175 mL) superfine sugar
pinch of salt

🍃 Cut the chocolate into pieces. Place it in a saucepan over low heat and add the coffee. Stir well once the chocolate is melted. Cool.

🍃 Whip the cream and add the sugar and salt. Mix thoroughly. Carefully fold in the cooled chocolate.

🍃 Pour into a deep bowl that has been lightly coated with sweet almond oil. Cover and wrap the bowl in a sheet of aluminum foil or wax paper.

🍃 Place in the freezer for 2 to 3 hours.

🍃 To serve, unmold on a serving dish and garnish with chocolate or rum sauce, or whipped cream flavored with cognac (see pages 602 and 605).

MAPLE MOUSSE

1 cup (250 mL) maple syrup
3 egg yolks, lightly beaten
½ cup (125 mL) chopped nuts
2 cups (500 mL) whipping cream
3 egg whites

🍃 Combine the maple syrup and egg yolks. Cook in the top of a double boiler, stirring constantly, until slightly thickened. Cool and stir in the nuts.

🍃 Whip the cream and beat the egg whites until stiff. Fold into the cooled cream.

🍃 Place in the freezer and freeze until set. Stir 4 or 5 times during freezing.

EGG-WHITE MOUSSE

½ cup (125 mL) brown or white sugar
¼ cup (50 mL) water, orange juice, coffee or apple juice
4 egg whites
pinch of salt
½ cup (125 mL) sugar
1 tsp (5 mL) vanilla or 1 tbsp (15 mL) liqueur, cognac or rum

🍃 In a skillet, combine the brown or white sugar and the water, orange juice, coffee or apple juice. Cook over medium heat until the syrup caramelizes.

🍃 Beat the egg whites with the salt. Add the rest of the sugar and beat until stiff. Then pour the caramel slowly into the beaten eggs, beating constantly with an electric mixer.

🍃 Once the syrup has been added and the mousse is firm and smooth, flavor it with vanilla or your favorite liqueur, cognac or rum. Pour it into a dish, cover and freeze for 12 hours.

LEMON PARFAIT

3 egg yolks
¼ cup (50 mL) sugar
¾ tsp (3 mL) lemon zest, grated
4 tbsp (60 mL) lemon juice
pinch of salt
½ cup (125 mL) whipping cream
3 egg whites
¼ cup (50 mL) sugar

🍃 Beat the egg yolks. Add the sugar gradually, until the mixture is thick and lemon colored. Add the lemon zest, lemon juice and salt.

🍃 Whip the cream and fold it into the egg yolk mixture. Beat the egg whites until they stand in soft peaks. Gradually add the sugar and continue beating until they stand in stiff peaks. Fold in the egg yolks. Place in the freezer.

STRAWBERRY PARFAIT

2 cups (500 mL) fresh strawberries
12 large marshmallows
¾ cup (175 mL) sugar
1 tsp (5 mL) lemon juice
2 cups (500 mL) whipping cream
1 tbsp (15 mL) vanilla

🍃 Clean the strawberries and place them in a saucepan. Add the marshmallows, sugar and lemon juice. Simmer for 10 minutes over very low heat, stirring occasionally. Remove from the heat and cool.

🍃 Whip the cream, add the vanilla and fold it into the cooled strawberry mixture. Place the mixture in the freezer and freeze until half set. Transfer the mixture to a bowl, beat until fluffy and return to the freezer until the parfait is completely set.

Caramel Parfait

1 cup (250 mL) brown sugar
3 tbsp (45 mL) butter
¾ cup (175 mL) light cream
1 cup (250 mL) whipping cream
4 cups (1 L) vanilla ice cream
½ cup (125 mL) toasted
almonds, slivered

🍃 Place the sugar and butter in a small cast-iron skillet. Cook over moderate heat, stirring constantly, until the sugar is dissolved. Simmer slowly for approximately 2 minutes, stirring to prevent from burning. Reduce the heat.

🍃 In a separate saucepan, heat the light cream and add it gradually to the sugar mixture, stirring constantly. Cook and stir until thoroughly blended. Simmer slowly for approximately 8 minutes, stirring often. Cool, then beat with a hand beater until smooth and golden brown.

🍃 Whip the cream until it begins to thicken. Gradually add ⅓ cup (75 mL) caramel sauce, beating constantly until firm. Set aside the rest of the sauce.

🍃 Place a spoonful of the reserved caramel sauce at the bottom of 6 parfait glasses. Add a spoonful of the whipped cream mixture, then a scoop of vanilla ice cream. Sprinkle with the slivered almonds. Pack tightly. Repeat each layer until the glasses are full.

🍃 The caramel sauce may be prepared in advance and refrigerated. Beat well before use.

SHERBETS

Sherbets are ices made with fruit and flavored with lemon, various extracts or liqueur. They are frozen in a freezer or in an ice-cream maker.

🍃 If made in the freezer, the sherbet should be stirred often: first when it begins to set, then every half-hour until it is completely set.

🍃 Sherbets contain neither milk nor eggs.

Basic Sherbet

2 cups (500 mL) sugar
4 cups (1 L) water
1 tbsp (15 mL) lemon zest
1 cup (250 mL) lemon juice

🍃 Bring the sugar and water to a boil and simmer for 5 minutes.

Cool. Add the lemon zest and juice and freeze.

Raspberry Sherbet

1 package frozen raspberries
¾ cup (175 mL) sugar
1½ tsp (7 mL) unflavored gelatin
½ cup (125 mL) water
2 tbsp (30 mL) lemon juice
2 egg whites

🍃 Combine the raspberries and sugar in a saucepan. Cook over very low heat until the sugar is dissolved. Put the raspberries through a fine sieve to remove the seeds.

🍃 Soak the gelatin in cold water for 5 minutes. Add to the hot raspberries and stir until the gelatin is dissolved. Add the lemon juice. Place the mixture in the freezer and freeze until it begins to set.

Raspberry Sherbet

🐚 Turn the mixture into a bowl and beat until fluffy. Beat the egg whites until stiff and add them to the sherbet. Return to the freezer. Freeze until set.

QUICK PINEAPPLE SHERBET

1 cup (250 mL) fresh pineapple
3 oranges, peeled and quartered
½ cup (125 mL) heavy cream
or condensed milk
juice of ½ lemon
3 tbsp (45 mL) sugar
1 cup (250 mL) crushed ice

🐚 In a blender jar, combine the pineapple, oranges, cream or condensed milk, lemon juice and sugar. Cover and blend 1 minute. Add the ice and blend until light and fluffy. The more ice that is used, the thicker the sherbet.

Serve at once.

🐚 If you use cream, add 6 tbsp (90 mL) sugar.

🐚 The pineapple can be replaced with any other fruit, as long as the quantity used remains the same.

FRUIT SHERBET

1 cup (250 mL) sugar
2 cups (500 mL) water
2 cups (500 mL) puréed fruit (apricots, peaches, strawberries, pineapple)
juice of ½ lemon or orange,
or ¼ cup (50 mL) liqueur,
or 2 tsp (10 mL) extract

Bring the sugar and water to a boil. Boil hard for 5 minutes. Cool. Add the fruit purée and lemon or orange juice, liqueur or extract. Freeze.

STRAWBERRY SHERBET

¾ cup (175 mL) sugar
2 cups (500 mL) water
¼ cup (50 mL) honey
or corn syrup
1 cup (250 mL) fresh strawberries, crushed
1 tbsp (15 mL) lemon juice

🐚 In a saucepan, combine the sugar, water, honey or corn syrup and boil for 10 minutes. Cool, then add the crushed strawberries and lemon juice.

🐚 Place the mixture in the freezer. Stir every 10 minutes until the mixture begins to set along the edges of the container. Serve immediately, as this sherbet melts very quickly.

COOKIES AND SQUARES

COOKIES

BASIC METHOD

A few hours before mixing the cookie dough, take the butter, the margarine or the shortening out of the refrigerator and let it stand at room temperature; it will be easier to work with when soft. Cookies made with butter have a more delicate flavor than those made with shortening or margarine.

🐟 Approximately 15 minutes before baking, heat the oven to the temperature called for in the recipe.

🐟 Assemble all the utensils and ingredients required for the recipe.

🐟 Grease the cookie sheets or pans with shortening. It is advisable to have two cookie sheets on hand, so that you can fill one while the other is in the oven. Scrape off any baked-on dough or crumbs from the cookie sheet and grease it again before baking another batch of cookies. It is not always necessary to grease the cookie sheets before baking, as some recipes indicate.

🐟 Cream the butter, margarine or shortening until fluffy; then, add the sugar, one spoonful at a time, beating constantly. If you are using an electric mixer, set it at medium speed.

🐟 As a rule of thumb: the finer the sugar used, the crisper the cookie.

🐟 Beat the eggs lightly and add them to the butter and sugar mixture. If a liquid is called for, add the eggs all at once; if no liquid is called for, add the eggs to the mixture gradually, alternating them with the dry ingredients. Add the desired flavoring to the liquid or the eggs.

🐟 Sift together the dry ingredients and add them to the mixture a little at a time, alternately with the liquid or eggs. After each addition of the dry ingredients, beat the mixture vigorously.

🐟 Drop the batter onto the prepared cookie sheet, one spoonful at a time, or roll and cut the cookies. Some recipes require that the dough be refrigerated before it is rolled and cut.

🐟 Bake as directed, keeping a close eye on the baking time. This often varies with the thickness of the dough, the size of the cookies and the amount of fat used, so the time indicated in the recipe should serve as a guideline rather than a precise indication of how long to bake the cookies. Be careful not to overbake the cookies or they will become hard and dry.

🐟 Thin, crisp cookies are usually done when lightly browned. To check drop cookies for doneness, press the center with your finger. If the impression disappears, the cookies are done. Some ovens bake unevenly; in such a case, rotate the cookie sheet midway through the allotted baking time.

🐟 As soon as the cookies are done, remove them from the cookie sheet using a spatula. Let them cool on a cake rack in a single layer. Do not stack the cookies, as they will stick to one another.

🐟 Crisp cookies should be stored in a tin or metal container with a loose-fitting lid. Place a sheet of wax paper between the layers. Soft cookies, on the other hand, should be stored in a metal container with a tight-fitting lid.

🐟 Once you understand this basic method, you will produce delicious cookies every time. With experience, you can vary a recipe according to your preference: adding a little less flour than is called for in the recipe, for instance, will produce a crisper cookie. Adding more flour makes a thicker cookie. But, be careful, too much flour makes a cookie that is hard and tough.

MAKING BLENDER COOKIES

Here is a basic recipe for mixing cookie batter with a blender. You may want to use this method to adapt some of your favorite cookie recipes.

🐟 Sift in a bowl:

2⅓ cups (575 mL) all-purpose flour
2 tsp (10 mL) baking powder
1 tsp (5 mL) salt
½ tsp (2 mL) sugar
½ tsp (2 mL) nutmeg
or cinnamon

🐟 Place in the blender jar:

2 eggs
⅔ cup (150 mL) soft butter
or shortening
1 cup (250 mL) sugar
⅔ cup (150 mL) cream
or sour milk
¼ cup (50 mL) nuts or raisins

🐟 Cover and blend 1 minute at high speed. Pour the mixture over the sifted dry ingredients. Mix well. Drop the batter 1 spoonful at a time on a greased cookie sheet.

🍂 Bake in a 400°F (200°C) oven for 8 to 12 minutes. Set the cookies on a cake rack to cool.

NOVA SCOTIA SCONES

1 cup (250 mL) milk
1 cup (250 mL) cold water
1 tbsp (15 mL) sugar
¼ tsp (1 mL) ginger
1 package active dry yeast
2 tbsp (30 mL) sugar
2 tbsp (30 mL) lard or shortening
2 tsp (10 mL) salt
2¼ cups (550 mL) all-purpose flour
2 to 3 cups (500 to 750 mL) all-purpose flour

🍂 Bring the milk to a boil. Remove it from the heat and add the cold water.

🍂 In a bowl, pour ¼ cup (50 mL) of the milk and water mixture. Add 1 tbsp (15 mL) of sugar, as well as the ginger, and stir until the sugar dissolves. Sprinkle the yeast over the mixture and let it stand for 10 minutes. Do not stir.

🍂 To the rest of the milk and water, add the 2 tbsp (30 mL) of sugar, the lard or shortening and the salt. Beat for a few minutes. Stir the yeast and add it to the milk mixture. Sift in 2¼ cups (550 mL) of flour. Beat vigorously about 3 minutes. If you are using an electric mixer, beat the mixture at medium speed.

🍂 Add 2 to 3 cups (500 to 750 mL) of flour, just enough to knead the dough. Knead until the dough no longer sticks to your hands.

Rolled Cookies

🍂 Cover the dough and let it rise until it doubles in size.

🍂 Punch it down and divide it into 2 balls. Shape each ball into a 2-in. (5-cm) cylinder by rolling it on the table.

🍂 Cut each roll into 1-in. (2-cm) slices. Place the slices on a greased cookie sheet. Cover and let rise until they double in size. Bake in a 400°F (200°C) oven for 15 to 20 minutes. (The scones will not brown thoroughly.) To serve, split them in two while still hot, butter them and serve with jam.

ROLLED COOKIES

1 cup (250 mL) butter
½ cup (125 mL) sugar
1 egg
2 to 3 cups (500 to 750 mL) pastry flour
½ tsp (2 mL) baking soda or powder
½ tsp (2 mL) salt
¼ tsp (1 mL) almond extract
1 tsp (5 mL) vanilla

🍂 Follow the first 8 steps of the *Basic Method* on page 622.

🍂 Add the flour, using just enough for the dough to stick together. These cookies will be easier to shape and crisper if less flour is used and if the dough is refrigerated 24 hours before it is rolled. Wrap the dough in wax paper before chilling it.

🍂 Divide the dough into quarters or halves and roll out only one portion at a time. Dust the rolling pin and the table with as little flour as possible. Begin rolling the dough in the center, working your way toward the edges.

🍂 Roll the dough very thin for crisp cookies, a little thicker for soft cookies.

Orange Cookies

Using a cookie cutter, cut as many cookies from each rolling as possible. Avoid excessive reworking of the dough as it will make the cookies dry. Dip the cookie cutter into flour before using.

Bake in a 425°F (220°C) oven for 5 to 6 minutes, or until the cookies are lightly browned.

This basic recipe yields about 8 dozen 1½-in. (1-cm) cookies.

LEMON COOKIES

Replace the vanilla with 1 tsp (5 mL) of lemon juice and add 2 tsp (10 mL) of lemon zest. Beat the juice and zest with the egg.

NUT COOKIES

At the end, add 1 cup (250 mL) of finely chopped nuts to the dough.

CHOCOLATE COOKIES

Melt 2 squares unsweetened chocolate over low heat and add to the butter and sugar mixture.

Bake in a 350°F (180°C) oven for 10 minutes.

ANISE COOKIES

Substitute 1 tbsp (15 mL) of anise for the vanilla.

COCOA COOKIES

Add 4 tbsp (60 mL) of cocoa to the creamed butter. Omit the almond extract.

SPICE COOKIES

Sift 1 tsp (5 mL) of ginger and 1 tsp (5 mL) cinnamon together with the dry ingredients.

ORANGE COOKIES

½ cup (125 mL) butter
1 cup (250 mL) sugar
zest of 1 orange
1 egg, beaten
½ cup (125 mL) orange juice
3 cups (750 mL) pastry flour
1 tsp (5 mL) baking powder

Cream the butter and gradually add the sugar, the orange zest, the beaten egg and the orange juice. Beat until light and fluffy.

Add the sifted dry ingredients. Stir the dough and refrigerate it for 1 hour.

Roll the dough and cut it into the desired shapes. Sprinkle with orange-flavored sugar.

Bake in a 350°F (180°C) oven for 15 to 20 minutes.

This recipe yields soft cookies. For crisp cookies, use ¼ cup (50 mL) of orange juice rather than ½ cup (125 mL).

To prepare orange-flavored sugar, add the zest of half an orange to 4 tbsp (60 mL) of sugar. Beat with a spoon until the sugar turns pale yellow.

PINK SUGAR COOKIES

½ cup (125 mL) butter
½ cup (125 mL) lard
1 cup (250 mL) sugar
1 cup (250 mL) sour cream
3 egg yolks, beaten
1½ tsp (7 mL) vanilla
3 cups (750 mL) all-purpose flour
1 tsp (5 mL) salt
1 tsp (5 mL) baking powder
½ tsp (2 mL) soda
pink sugar

Mix the ingredients following the first 8 steps of the *Basic Method* on page 622.

Cover the dough and refrigerate for 2 to 3 hours. Roll the

dough as thin as possible and cut it into the desired shapes with a 2½-in. (6-cm) fluted cookie cutter. Place the cookies on a buttered cookie sheet. Sprinkle them with pink sugar to taste.

🍧 To prepare pink sugar: add a few drops of red food coloring to ½ cup (125 mL) of sugar. Stir until the desired shade of pink is obtained. Add a few more drops of food coloring, if necessary.

🍧 Bake the cookies in a 375°F (190°C) oven for 10 to 15 minutes.

GINGER SNAPS

½ cup (125 mL) butter
½ cup (125 mL) lard
1 cup (250 mL) sugar
2 eggs, lightly beaten
½ cup (125 mL) molasses
4½ cups (1.1 L) pastry flour
3 tsp (15 mL) ground ginger
1 tsp (5 mL) salt
1 tsp (5 mL) baking soda

🍧 Cream the butter and the lard. Gradually add the sugar, the beaten eggs and the molasses, stirring constantly.

🍧 Fold in the sifted dry ingredients. Mix well. Wrap the dough in wax paper and refrigerate it for 12 hours.

🍧 Roll the dough as thin as possible. Cut the cookies with a round cookie cutter and sprinkle them with sugar.

🍧 Bake in a 400°F (200°C) oven for 15 to 20 minutes.

OLD-FASHIONED LEMON COOKIES

1 cup (250 mL) butter
2 cups (500 mL) sugar
2 eggs
1 cup (250 mL) milk
3 tbsp (45 mL) lemon juice
1 tbsp (15 mL) lemon zest
4 to 5 cups (1 to 1.2 L) all-purpose flour
1 tsp (5 mL) salt
1 tsp (5 mL) baking soda

🍧 Cream the butter until it has the consistency of whipped cream. Gradually add the sugar, beating vigorously. Beat the eggs and add them, mixing lightly.

🍧 Add the lemon zest and juice to the milk. Sift together the flour, the salt and the baking soda. To the creamed mixture, gradually add the sifted dry ingredients alternately with the milk. Add just enough flour to obtain a light dough. Refrigerate it for 4 hours.

🍧 Roll the dough as thin as possible. Cut it with a round cutter. Place the cookies on a lightly greased cookie sheet and bake them in a 375°F (190°C) oven for 5 to 8 minutes.

SCOTTISH SHORTBREAD COOKIES

1 cup (250 mL) butter
1 cup (250 mL) superfine sugar
2½ cups (625 mL) flour

🍧 Cream the butter until light and fluffy. Add the sugar and

blend thoroughly. Fold in the flour and knead the dough on a floured surface until it no longer sticks to your fingers.

🍧 Roll the dough ¼ in. (6 cm) thick. Cut it into the desired shapes and bake the cookies in a 275°F (140°C) oven for 50 minutes, until they are lightly browned.

GRANNY'S COOKIES

¾ cup (175 mL) shortening
¾ cup (175 mL) sugar
1 egg, beaten
1 cup (250 mL) molasses
4 cups (1 L) flour
1 tsp (5 mL) salt
2 tsp (10 mL) ginger
1 tsp (5 mL) baking soda

🍧 Cream the shortening. Add the sugar, the beaten egg and the molasses. Mix until light and fluffy.

🍧 Sift the flour together with the salt, the ginger and the baking soda. Gradually add the dry ingredients to the creamed shortening and sugar, using only as much flour as is needed to make the dough easy to roll.

🍧 Roll out the dough and divide it in half. Cut one half with a round cookie cutter and the other with a doughnut cutter. Bake the cookies in a 350°F (180°C) oven for 10 to 12 minutes. Top a round cookie with the filling and cover it with a cutout cookie.

🍧 The filling is prepared as follows:

1 tbsp (15 mL) butter
½ cup (125 mL) confectioners' sugar

¼ tsp (1 mL) ginger
pinch of salt
1 tbsp (15 mL) boiling water
1½ cups (375 mL) confectioners'
sugar

📛 Cream the butter and add the confectioners' sugar, the ginger, the salt and the boiling water. When the mixture is creamy, add the rest of the confectioners' sugar. Add more boiling water, as needed, to make the filling very light and fluffy.

SOUR CREAM COOKIES

½ lb (250 g) butter
2 cups (500 mL) pastry flour
1 tsp (5 mL) baking powder
¼ tsp (1 mL) salt
1 egg yolk
½ cup (125 mL) sour cream
4 tbsp (60 mL) sugar
jam of your choice

📛 Cream the butter. Using a fork, add the sifted flour, the baking powder and the salt. Stir in the egg yolk, the sour cream and the sugar. Blend thoroughly and refrigerate the dough for a few hours.

📛 Roll out the dough and divide it in two. Cut one half with a round cookie cutter and the other half with a doughnut cutter. Top the round cookie with a cutout cookie and fill the hole with jam.

📛 Place the cookies on a buttered cookie sheet and bake them in a 350°F (180°C) oven for approximately 15 minutes.

SQUARES AND BARS

There are three types of squares or bar cookies:

📛 Those mixed in a single operation, also called "simple cookies."

📛 Those with a crisp or rich cookie base garnished with a cream or other mixture, also called "rich cookies."

📛 Those with a filling placed between two layers of dough, also called "filled bars."

SIMPLE BARS

½ cup (125 mL) shortening
or butter
1 cup (250 mL) sugar
2 eggs
1 tsp (5 mL) flavoring to taste
½ cup (125 mL) raisins
½ to ¾ cup (125 to 175 mL)
chopped nuts
1 tsp (5 mL) cinnamon
pinch of ground cloves
2 cups (500 mL) pastry flour
1½ tsp (7 mL) baking soda
1½ cups (375 mL) applesauce

📛 In a bowl, combine the shortening or butter, the sugar, the eggs and the flavoring. Beat the mixture until it is light and fluffy.

📛 Add the raisins and nuts. Sift the dry ingredients together. Gradually add the dry ingredients to the creamed mixture alternately with the apple sauce.

📛 Pour the batter into a greased 9- x 13- x 2-in. (23- x 33- x 5-cm) or 8- x 8- x 2-in. (20- x 20- x 5-cm) pan; the larger the pan, the thinner the cookie. Bake in a 350°F (180°C) oven for approximately 30 minutes. Even though a slight impression will remain in it when pressed, the batter will be baked.

Scottish Shortbread Cookies

❧ Place the pan on a cake rack and let the cookie partially cool. Cut it into 1½- x 2-in. (4- x 5-cm) bars and roll each bar in confectioners' sugar.

BANANA BARS

Replace the apple sauce with an equal amount of ripe, mashed bananas.

FIG BARS

Replace the raisins with 1 cup (250 mL) dried figs, cut into small pieces. Omit the ground clove and add ½ tsp (2 mL) of nutmeg instead.

BROWN SUGAR BARS

Substitute brown sugar for the white sugar. Use only butter and flavor it with ½ tsp (2 mL) of almond extract.

PUMPKIN BARS

Replace the raisins with dates and the apple sauce with an equal amount of puréed pumpkin.

FILLED BARS

DOUGH:
½ cup (125 mL) shortening
1 cup (250 mL) brown sugar
1½ cup (375 mL) all-purpose flour
½ tsp (2 mL) salt
1 tsp (5 mL) baking soda
1¾ cups (425 mL) rolled oats

FILLING:
1 lb (500 g) pitted dates
1 cup (250 mL) brown sugar
1 cup (250 mL) water
1 tbsp (15 mL) butter
½ tsp (2 mL) cinnamon
zest of 1 lemon

❧ Cream the shortening. Gradually add the brown sugar, stirring constantly. Add the remaining ingredients and mix thoroughly. The dough will be rather thick.

❧ Prepare the filling. Place all the ingredients in a saucepan and cook, stirring often, over medium heat until creamy.

❧ Pour half the dough in a greased 8- x 8- x 2-in (20- x 20- x 5-cm) or 9- x 13- x 2-in. (23- x 33- x 5-cm) pan.

❧ Spread the filling on the dough and top it with the remaining dough. Bake in a 350°F (180°C) oven for 40 minutes. Do not unmold; cool the pan on a cake rack. When completely cool, cut into bars.

RICH BARS

BASE:
5 tbsp (75 mL) butter
1 tbsp (15 mL) sugar
pinch of salt
¾ cup (175 mL) pastry flour
1 tbsp (15 mL) milk

TOPPING:
1 beaten egg
½ cup (125 mL) brown sugar
¾ cup (175 mL) chopped nuts
1 tbsp (15 mL) all-purpose flour
¼ tsp (1 mL) baking powder
½ tsp (2 mL) flavoring to taste
pinch of salt

❧ Mix the ingredients to form a heavy dough. Spread the dough with your hands on the bottom of an ungreased 8- x 8- x 2-in. (20- x 20- x 5-cm) or 9- x 13- x 2-in. (23- x 33- x 5-cm) pan, depending on whether you want thin or thick cookies. Spread the dough out evenly with your fingers.

❧ Bake in a 350°F (180°C) oven for 10 to 12 minutes, or until the edges are lightly browned.

❧ If desired, spread the cooked dough with jam or thinly sliced or grated fruit. You'll need ½ to 1 cup (125 to 250 mL) of either. Cool the bars before spreading them with jam or fruit.

❧ Prepare the topping while the dough is baking. Beat the egg and add the brown sugar. Add the remaining ingredients, stirring constantly. Beat for 1 or 2 minutes and then spread over the baked dough.

❧ Bake in a 350°F (180°C) oven for 18 to 22 minutes. Do not unmold; cool on a cake rack. When completely cool, cut it into bars.

Lemon Squares

DELICIOUS JAM SQUARES

BASE:
¾ cup (175 mL) pastry flour
1 tbsp (15 mL) superfine sugar
pinch of salt
5 tbsp (75 mL) butter
1 tbsp (15 mL) milk

TOPPING:
jam of your choice
1 egg, beaten until foamy
½ cup (125 mL) brown sugar
¾ cup (175 mL) finely chopped almonds
1 tbsp (15 mL) flour
¼ tsp (1 mL) baking powder
½ tsp (2 mL) almond extract
pinch of salt

🍂 Sift the flour together with the other dry ingredients. Add the butter, pour in the milk and mix well.

🍂 Spread the dough on a greased baking sheet. Bake in a 350°F (180°C) oven until lightly browned.

🍂 Remove from the oven and cover the cookie base with a thin layer of jam.

🍂 Mix the ingredients for the topping and spread them over the jam.

🍂 Return the sheet to the oven and continue baking at 350°F (180°C) for 15 to 20 minutes, or until the top is golden brown. Remove from the oven and cut into squares.

LEMON SQUARES

BASE:
½ cup (125 mL) butter
or shortening
2 tsp (10 mL) lemon zest
½ cup (125 mL) confectioners' sugar, sifted

2 egg yolks, beaten
1 cup (250 mL) all-purpose flour

TOPPING:
2 egg whites
½ cup (125 mL) sugar
½ cup (125 mL) chopped nuts
1 tbsp (15 mL) lemon juice

🍂 Cream the butter or shortening and add the lemon zest. Gradually add the confectioners' sugar, beating vigorously after each addition. Beat in the egg yolks and mix thoroughly. Add the flour, beating vigorously after each addition.

🍂 Spread the dough on the bottom of a well-greased 9- x 13- x 2-in. (23-x 33 x 5-cm) pan. Bake in a 350°F (180°C) oven for 10 minutes. Unmold onto a cake rack.

🍂 While the dough is baking, beat the egg whites until soft peaks form. Gradually add the sugar and continue beating until the mixture stands in peaks. Fold in the nuts and the lemon juice.

🍂 Spread the meringue over the baked dough and return the pan to the oven on the cake rack.

🍂 Bake for 25 minutes or until the meringue is golden brown. Let cool, then cut the cookie into 2-in. (5-cm) squares.

BROWNIES

2 squares unsweetened chocolate
¼ cup (50 mL) butter
1 cup (250 mL) sugar
2 eggs, beaten
1 cup (250 mL) all-purpose flour
1 tsp (5 mL) baking soda

½ tsp (2 mL) salt
1 cup (250 mL) chopped nuts
1 tsp (5 mL) vanilla

🐾 Melt the chocolate with the butter over low heat. Pour the mixture into a bowl and add the remaining ingredients. Mix well. Pour the batter into a greased 8- x 8- x 2-in. (20- x 20- x 5-cm) pan.
🐾 Bake in a 350°F (180°C) oven for 30 minutes.

VARIATION
🐾 Add 1 cup pitted dates cut into small pieces.

MOLDED COOKIES

ABOUT MOLDED COOKIES
🐾 Molded and drop cookies are not only the most popular cookies around but also the quickest and easiest to make. The dough is usually rather thick and therefore very easy to mold. It can be prepared following the *Basic Method* on page 622.
🐾 Molded cookies can be shaped any way you like: form them into small balls, bars or crescents; shape them into small rings or flatten them with a fork dipped in cold water or with the bottom of a glass.
🐾 Lightly flour your hands to prevent the dough from sticking to your hands when rolled.
🐾 Roll the balls or bars in sugar to give them a crackled or glazed appearance.
🐾 To bake, place the cookies on an ungreased cookie sheet, 1½ to 2 in. (4 to 5 cm) apart. Most molded cookies are baked in a preheated 350°F (180°C) oven for 10 to 15 minutes. Remove them at once from the cookie sheet and cool them on a cake rack.

FINE BUTTER COOKIES

1 cup (250 mL) soft butter
¼ cup (50 mL) sugar
2 tsp (10 mL) vanilla
2 cups (500 mL) all-purpose flour
1 cup (250 mL) finely chopped blanched almonds

🐾 Mix the ingredients following the *Basic Method* on page 622. Shape the dough into little balls. Roll the balls in sugar. Do not flatten them.
🐾 Bake the cookies in a 300°F (150°C) oven for 15 minutes.

CHOCOLATE-NUT COOKIES

½ cup (125 mL) shortening
1⅔ (400 mL) cups sugar
1 tsp (5 mL) vanilla
2 eggs, unbeaten
2 squares unsweetened chocolate, melted
2 cups (500 mL) pastry flour
2 tsp (10 mL) baking powder
⅓ cup (75 mL) milk
½ cup (125 mL) chopped nuts
confectioners' sugar

🐾 Mix the ingredients following the *Basic Method* on page 622. Molded cookies made of chocolate are easier to shape when the dough is refrigerated for 2 hours before use.
🐾 Shape the dough into small balls, then roll each one in confectioners' sugar until very white.
🐾 Bake in a 350°F (180°C) oven for 15 to 18 minutes.

VARIATION
🐾 Replace the chopped nuts with an equal amount of chocolate chips.

FRUIT COOKIES

1 tbsp (15 mL) butter
¾ cup (175 mL) sugar
2 eggs
1 cup (250 mL) chopped dates
1 cup (250 mL) chopped nuts
½ tsp (2 mL) vanilla
10 red and green cherries, halved
pinch of salt
grated coconut

🐾 Cream the butter and add all the other ingredients to it. When adding the coconut, use only as much as is required to make the dough easy to shape into little balls.
🐾 Bake the cookies on a greased cookie sheet in a 350°F (180°C) oven for approximately 20 minutes.

ALMOND CRESCENTS

½ lb (250 g) butter
½ cup (125 mL) sugar
1⅔ cups (400 mL) pastry flour
¼ tsp (1 mL) salt
⅔ cup (150 mL) finely chopped almonds
½ tsp (2 mL) almond extract

🍂 Cream the butter with the sugar. Sift the flour with the salt and add to the creamed butter mixture. Add the almonds and the almond extract and blend thoroughly. Shape the dough into crescents and place them on an ungreased cookie sheet.

🍂 Bake in a 350°F (180°C) oven for approximately 10 minutes, until golden brown. Cool the cookies, then dip them in confectioners' sugar.

ALMOND COOKIES

½ cup (125 mL) butter
½ cup (125 mL) shortening
½ cup (125 mL) sugar
½ cup (125 mL) brown sugar
1 egg, beaten
¼ tsp (1 mL) almond extract
2 cups (500 mL) all-purpose flour
1 tsp (5 mL) baking soda
¼ tsp (1 mL) cream of tartar
¾ cup (175 mL) chopped almonds

🍂 Cream the butter and the shortening, then add the sugar and the brown sugar. Add the beaten egg, the almond extract and the sifted dry ingredients. Stir in the almonds.

🍂 Shape the batter into little balls. Stuff each one with a small piece of almond.

🍂 Bake the cookies in a 350°F (180°C) oven for 10 minutes.

DROP COOKIES

1 cup (250 mL) shortening
⅔ cup (150 mL) butter
2 cups (500 mL) light brown sugar
3 eggs, beaten
3¼ cups (800 mL) all-purpose flour
2 tsp (10 mL) baking powder
½ tsp (2 mL) baking soda
½ tsp (2 mL) salt
1 tsp (5 mL) cinnamon
½ cup (125 mL) milk
1 tsp (5 mL) vanilla

🍂 In a bowl, combine the shortening, the butter, the brown sugar and the beaten eggs. Beat by hand, or with an electric mixer set at medium speed, until light and creamy.

🍂 Sift together the flour, the baking powder, the baking soda, the salt and the cinnamon. Mix the milk and the vanilla in a separate bowl.

🍂 Gradually add the dry ingredients alternately with the milk and the vanilla to the creamed butter mixture. Blend thoroughly.

🍂 Drop 1 teaspoonful (5 mL) of dough at a time on a greased cookie sheet, leaving 1 in. (2 cm) between the cookies.

🍂 Bake the cookies in a 350°F (180°C) oven for 12 to 15 minutes. Remove them from the sheet as soon as they are done and let them cool on a cake rack.

Almond Cookies

FRUIT COOKIES

To the creamed mixture, add ⅓ cup (75 mL) chopped dates and ½ cup (125 mL) finely chopped nuts.

RAISIN COOKIES

Add ¾ cup (175 mL) raisins and ¼ tsp (1 mL) ground cloves to the dry ingredients.

COCONUT COOKIES

the creamed mixture, add 1 cup (250 mL) of grated coconut and 2 tbsp (30 mL) of orange zest. Substitute ¼ cup (50 mL) of orange juice and ¼ cup (50 mL) of milk for the ½ cup (125 mL) of milk.

DANISH COOKIES

To the creamed mixture, add ½ tsp (2 mL) of crushed cardamon seeds, ½ cup (125 mL) of currants and the zest of 1 lemon.
☙ This cookie dough keeps very well in the refrigerator, in a bowl covered with waxed paper. If the dough is too stiff to work with when it first comes out of the refrigerator, let it sit at room temperature for 1 hour.

SPICE COOKIES

2¾ cups (675 mL) pastry flour
½ tsp (2 mL) salt
½ tsp (2 mL) baking soda
1½ tsp (7 mL) baking powder
½ tsp (2 mL) nutmeg
pinch of ground cloves

Spice Cookies

⅔ cup (150 mL) sugar
½ cup (125 mL) butter
1 egg
1 cup (250 mL) sour cream

☙ Sift together in a bowl the flour, the salt, the baking soda, the baking powder, the nutmeg, the cloves and the sugar. Add the butter to the dry ingredients and cut it with two knives until it is coarse and crumbly.
☙ Beat the egg with the sour cream and add the mixture to the dry ingredients. Blend thoroughly. Cover and refrigerate the dough for 2 to 3 hours.
☙ Drop 1 teaspoonful (5 mL) of dough at a time onto a greased cookie sheet. Sprinkle with sugar.
☙ Bake the cookies in a 350°F (180°C) oven for 15 minutes.

OATMEAL MACAROONS

4 tbsp (60 mL) butter
1 cup (250 mL) rolled oats
½ cup (125 mL) plus 2 tbsp (15 mL) brown sugar
½ tsp (2 mL) baking powder
¼ tsp (1 mL) salt
¼ cup (50 mL) pastry flour
1 egg
½ tsp (2 mL) vanilla
¼ cup (50 mL) chopped nuts

☙ Melt 4 tbsp (60 mL) of butter in a skillet. Add the rolled oats and brown them 4 to 5 minutes, stirring often. Remove them from the heat and cool.

❧ Add the remaining ingredients to the cooled oatmeal, mixing well after each addition.

❧ Bake as directed in the basic recipe for *Drop Cookies*, page 630.

ALMOND MACAROONS

1 cup (250 mL) almonds, unblanched
1 cup (250 mL) sugar
2 or 3 egg whites
½ tsp (2 mL) almond extract
½ tsp (2 mL) vanilla

❧ Grind the almonds and mix them with ⅔ cup (150 mL) of sugar. Gradually add the egg whites, mixing thoroughly until the dough has the consistency of mashed potatoes. Beat another 3 minutes. Add the almond and vanilla extracts.

❧ Drop 1 teaspoonful (5 mL) of dough at a time on a greased and floured cookie sheet. Sprinkle the macaroons with the remaining sugar. Press a half almond in the center of each cookie.

❧ Bake the macaroons in a 400°F (200°C) oven for 15 minutes, or until the tops begin to crack and the macaroons are golden brown.

PINEAPPLE COOKIES

2 cups (500 mL) all-purpose flour
1½ tsp (7 mL) baking powder
¼ tsp (1 mL) baking soda
1 tsp (5 mL) salt
⅔ cup (150 mL) shortening
1¼ cups (300 mL) brown sugar, well packed
2 eggs
¾ cup (175 mL) canned pineapple, cubed and drained
1 tsp (5 mL) vanilla

❧ Sift together the flour, the baking powder, the baking soda and the salt.

❧ Cream the shortening, add the brown sugar gradually and beat the mixture until it is light. Add the eggs one by one, beating after each addition. Add the pineapple and the vanilla. Gradually add the dry ingredients, beating well after each addition.

❧ Drop 1 teaspoonful (5 mL) of dough at a time on an ungreased cookie sheet.

❧ Bake the cookies in a 400°F (200°C) oven for approximately 10 minutes.

CATS' TONGUES

¾ cup (175 mL) shortening
⅔ cup (150 mL) sugar
2 eggs
½ tsp (2 mL) salt
1 tsp (5 mL) vanilla
1½ cups (375 mL) pastry flour, sifted

❧ Cream the shortening and gradually add the sugar. Beat the eggs and add them to the creamed shortening together with the salt and the vanilla. Stir in the sifted flour.

❧ Fill the slots of a lightly greased ladyfinger pan or drop the dough by teaspoonful (5 mL) on a greased cookie sheet, as you would other drop cookies.

❧ Bake the cookies in a 375°F (190°C) oven until they are lightly browned.

BUTTER CATS' TONGUES

½ cup (125 mL) butter
½ cup (125 mL) sugar
3 egg whites
1 cup (250 mL) all-purpose flour
pinch of salt
½ tsp (2 mL) vanilla

❧ Cream the butter and the sugar. Add the unbeaten egg whites, one by one, beating hard after each addition. Stir in the flour, the salt and the vanilla.

❧ Grease and flour 2 cookie sheets. Heat the oven to 340°F (170°C). Drop the dough by small spoonfuls on the cookie sheet, shaping the cookies lengthwise like ladyfingers. Allow 1 in. (2 cm) of space between each cookie. Or use a ladyfinger pan.

❧ Bake the cookies approximately 7 minutes, or until the edges are browned and the center is almost white. Remove them from the cookie sheet immediately.

LEMON CAT'S TONGUES
Add 2 tsp (10 mL) of lemon zest and 1 tbsp (15 mL) of lemon juice to the butter.

CRISP COOKIES

⅓ cup (75 mL) shortening
½ cup (125 mL) sugar
1 egg, beaten
1 cup (250 mL) pastry flour
1 tsp (5 mL) baking powder
¼ tsp (1 mL) salt
½ tsp (2 mL) cinnamon
½ cup (125 mL) raisins
⅓ cup (75 mL) chopped nuts

ᨠ Cream the shortening. Add the sugar and the beaten egg. Sift the dry ingredients and add them to the mixture. Stir in the raisins and the nuts. Blend well.

ᨠ Drop the dough by teaspoonful (5 mL) on a greased cookie sheet.

ᨠ Bake the cookies in a 350°F (180°C) oven for 10 minutes.

SCOTTISH COOKIES

1 egg
½ cup (125 mL) superfine sugar
1 cup (250 mL) rolled oats
1 tbsp (15 mL) melted butter
½ tsp (2 mL) salt
½ tsp (2 mL) vanilla

ᨠ Beat the egg until foamy and gradually add the sugar, beating the mixture until it is light and fluffy. Add the remaining ingredients.

ᨠ Drop the batter by spoonful on a buttered cookie sheet.

ᨠ Bake the cookies in a 325°F (160°C) oven for 15 minutes. Remove them from the cookie sheet immediately.

Crisp Cookies

FLORENTINES

½ cup (125 mL) sugar
⅓ cup (75 mL) whipping cream
⅓ cup (75 mL) honey
2 tbsp (30 mL) butter
¼ cup (50 mL) candied orange peel
1½ cups (375 mL) blanched almonds
3 tbsp (45 mL) all-purpose flour

ᨠ In an enameled cast-iron saucepan, combine the sugar, the cream, the honey and the butter. Stir the mixture over low heat until the sugar has dissolved. Continue cooking over high heat until a few drops of the syrup form a soft ball in cold water, or until the syrup reaches 230°F (115°C) on a candy thermometer. Cool.

ᨠ To the syrup add the finely chopped candied orange peel, the thinly sliced blanched almonds and the flour. Mix thoroughly. Drop the dough by spoonful on a well-greased cookie sheet. Shape it into balls, allowing 2 in. (5 cm) between each. Flatten the balls with a fork dipped in milk.

ᨠ Bake 8 to 10 minutes, or until the cookies are lightly browned. As soon as the Florentines are done, give them a perfectly round shape by cutting them with a 3-in. (8-cm) cookie cutter.

ᨠ Allow the cookies to cool on a cake rack and prepare the chocolate icing, as follows.

CHOCOLATE ICING:

8 ounces (250 g) semi-sweet chocolate
1 tbsp (15 mL) shortening

🍃 Melt the semi-sweet chocolate in the top part of a double boiler, then add the shortening. Use immediately, brushing the icing over each cookie. Make grooves in the icing with the tines of a fork and refrigerate the cookies just long enough for the chocolate to harden.

DANISH WREATHS

These delicious cookies are traditionally served at Christmas time in Denmark. Rich and golden, they are quick and easy to make.

⅔ cup (150 mL) butter
⅓ cup (75 mL) sugar
2 tbsp (30 mL) cognac
¼ tsp (1 mL) salt
1½ cups (375 mL) all-purpose flour
2 tbsp (30 mL) sugar
1 tsp (5 mL) freshly grated nutmeg

🍃 Cream the butter until it is soft and fluffy. Blend in the ⅓ cup (75 mL) of sugar, 1 teaspoonful (5 mL) at a time. Stir in the cognac.

🍃 Combine the salt and the flour. Gradually add the dry ingredients to the butter mixture, stirring well after each addition.

Once the dough is well mixed, shape it into a ball and refrigerate it for 30 minutes.

🍃 Shape the dough into 1-in. (2-cm) balls. Flatten them and cut them into ½-in. (1-cm) strips. Make small wreaths with the strips, crossing the tips as you would a braid. Combine the 2 tbsp (30 mL) sugar and the grated nutmeg; dust some over each wreath. Or sprinkle some decorative candy or colored sugar over the cookies.

🍃 Place the cookies on a lightly greased cookie sheet. Bake them at 400°F (200°C) for 8 to 10 minutes, or until lightly browned.

SWEDISH BEEHIVE COOKIES

These delicious Christmas cookies, which are rolled in nuts, look like small beehives; hence, their name.

1 cup (250 mL) sweet butter or margarine
2 egg yolks, beaten
½ cup (125 mL) brown sugar
1 tsp (5 mL) vanilla
2 cups (500 mL) all-purpose flour
1 egg white
1 cup (250 mL) finely chopped hazelnuts or walnuts
red and green candied cherries

🍃 Cream the butter until it is light and fluffy. Add the beaten egg yolks, the brown sugar and the vanilla. Beat the mixture until creamy. Gradually add the flour, stirring constantly. Mix the dough with your hands, if necessary.

🍃 Form the dough into 1-in. (2-cm) balls. Beat the egg white lightly and dip the balls first in it, then in the chopped nuts. Place them on a lightly greased cookie sheet, about 3 in. (8 cm) apart. Make a small depression in the middle of each ball.

🍃 Bake them in a 350°F (180°C) oven for 10 minutes. Remove the cookies from the oven and press the centers down again. Return them to the oven for another 5 minutes. Place the cookies on a cake rack and fill the indentations with the chopped cherries. Let cool.

SWEDISH CHRISTMAS COOKIES

1 cup (250 mL) butter
⅔ cup (150 mL) brown sugar
⅓ cup (75 mL) corn syrup
⅔ cup (150 mL) honey
1 tsp (5 mL) lemon zest
1 tsp (5 mL) rum
4½ cups (1.1 L) all-purpose flour
1 tsp (5 mL) salt
1 tsp (5 mL) baking soda
1 tsp (5 mL) ginger
½ tsp (2 mL) ground cloves
1 tsp (5 mL) cinnamon

🍃 Cream the butter and the brown sugar until the mixture is light. Add the corn syrup, the honey, the lemon zest and the rum. Beat for 5 minutes with an electric mixer at medium speed.

🍃 Sift together the remaining ingredients. Add just enough flour to the creamed mixture to

Ladyfingers

LADYFINGERS

3 eggs, separated
⅓ cup (75 mL) sugar
1 tsp (5 mL) vanilla
pinch of salt
3 tbsp (45 mL) hot water
½ cup (125 mL) pastry flour
1½ tsp (7 mL) baking powder

⬥ Beat the egg whites until stiff, then gradually add the sugar, stirring constantly.

⬥ Beat the yolks until foamy and carefully fold them into the whites, together with the vanilla, the salt and the hot water. Blend well and add the sifted flour and baking powder.

⬥ Line a cookie sheet with brown paper. From the tip of a spoon, drop the batter in 2½-in. (6-cm) strips on the brown paper, allowing for expansion space between each cookie, or use a ladyfinger pan. Sprinkle the cookies with confectioners' sugar and bake them at 350°F (180°C) for 8 minutes, or until the cookies are lightly browned. They should still be soft when they are taken out of the oven. Remove them from the pan before they are completely cooled. It is sometimes necessary to place the paper on a damp cloth to remove the cookies.

⬥ This recipe yields about 1½ dozen ladyfingers.

obtain a soft dough. Cover the dough and refrigerate it for 8 to 12 hours, until it is firm enough to roll.

⬥ Roll the dough as thin as possible. Cut it into various shapes (for example, stars, angels, Christmas trees, Santa Clauses) with cookie cutters. Place the cookies on a greased and floured cookie sheet.

⬥ Bake the cookies in a 350°F (180°C) oven for 8 to 10 minutes.

NUT CRISPIES

½ cup (125 mL) butter
⅓ cup (75 mL) sugar
pinch of salt
1 tsp (5 mL) vanilla
1½ cups (375 mL) walnuts

⬥ No flour is called for in this recipe; it is replaced with nuts. So make sure that the nuts are chopped very fine.

⬥ Cream the butter and the sugar. Add the salt and the vanilla, and stir in the chopped walnuts. Shape into rolls 1 in. (2 cm) in diameter. Wrap each roll in wax paper and refrigerate for 12 to 24 hours.

⬥ Cut each roll into thin slices. Bake the cookies on an ungreased cookie sheet in a 350°F (180°C) oven for 6 to 8 minutes. The cookies are done when they turn golden brown. Watch them carefully because they scorch easily.

⬥ Cool the cookies on paper towels, to absorb excess fat.

[635]

❦ TECHNIQUE ❦

LADYFINGERS

1 Beat the egg whites until stiff.

3 Beat the egg yolks and add them to the whites, then add the vanilla, the salt and the hot water.

2 Gradually add the sugar, stirring constantly.

4 Add the sifted flour and the baking powder.

BREADS, DOUGHNUTS, MUFFINS AND PANCAKES

MAKING BREAD

Bread making is both a science and an art, for you are dealing with ingredients such as yeast and flour, with factors such as temperature and humidity, and with yourself. If you do not succeed in making beautiful, fragrant and perfect bread the first few times you try (and you might), do try again. Your bread making will improve with practice, and once you have the knack you never lose it.

❧ It helps, however, to understand not only the steps in making bread but also the role of the ingredients.

FLOUR

The flour should be hard-wheat flour or all-purpose flour. Both are high in gluten, which is necessary to develop a high degree of elasticity, and the success of a yeast dough depends on this. Bread made with soft-wheat flour (such as pastry flour) will not rise as high or hold its shape as well. To make bread with graham flour, whole-wheat flour or rye flour, replace half the white flour in the basic recipe for white bread with one of these. Use brown sugar instead of white sugar.

YEAST

There are many types of yeast, but the easiest type to handle is active dry yeast, which is available in envelopes or in bulk. It is a dehydrated product that must be reconstituted before use. Follow the package directions (usually to dissolve 1 tsp or 5 mL of yeast in ½ cup or 125 mL of warm water). Let the yeast stand for 10 minutes and give it a good stir before combining it with other ingredients. The recipes in this section are for traditional yeast. Do not substitute quick-rising yeast.

❧ Because yeast is actually a plant, it must be treated gently. Too much heat will kill it, and it stops growing if it is too cold. So it is important to dissolve the yeast in warm water, between 80°F and 85°F (27°C and 29°C) and to let the dough rise at the proper temperature.

SUGAR

Sugar furthers the growth of the yeast, and helps to produce rich, brown, crusty bread. But too much sugar will somewhat retard the action of the yeast, so always measure accurately. Substitute brown sugar, honey or molasses if you wish.

SALT

Salt brings out the flavor of the bread but retards the growth of the yeast. It should not be added to the bread until the yeast has had a chance to grow strong on the sugar and starch.

FAT

You can use butter, margarine, shortening or vegetable oil to give texture and flavor. Since fat can retard yeast development, add it only after you have added some of the flour.

LIQUID

The liquid plays a very important role in bread making. You can use water, milk, potato water, cream, or fruit or vegetable juices, although the first two are the most common. Dry skim milk can be added for enrichment.

❧ Whichever liquid you choose, remember that it must be lukewarm or it will destroy the action of the yeast. All other ingredients should be at room temperature.

GINGER

The addition of ¼ tsp (1 mL) ground ginger to the yeast is a trick I learned from my grandmother. It is a yeast improver that makes the yeast more active and gives the bread an extra fine flavor.

MIXING BREAD DOUGH

Combine the ingredients in the order given in the recipe. Never add the flour all at once. Flours can differ in absorption depending on the brand or the weather. So add a little over half the quantity called for, beat it in well, then gradually add the remainder until the dough clears the sides of the bowl and can be turned out of the bowl easily (leaving the sides of the bowl relatively clean and dry).

HOW TO KNEAD

Turn the dough out onto a floured surface and sprinkle a ring of flour around the ball of dough. As you knead, work in some of the flour until the dough has a perfect texture.

❧ To "knead thoroughly" does not mean a few punches and pats. It means lifting the dough with the fingers spread underneath to support it, folding the dough over and pushing down hard with the heels of the hands; then turning the dough and repeating the lifting, folding and pushing process until the dough feels right. With practice, you will know how much kneading is sufficient. The dough should be full and rounded, smooth, satiny and tightly stretched. It takes from 10 to 18 minutes.

HOW DOUGH RISES
Put the ball of dough in a lightly greased bowl twice its size. Grease the top of the ball lightly with a film of oil. Cover with a clean dish towel. Let rise in a warm, draft-free place, between 75°F (24°C) and 85°F (29°C), until the dough is double in bulk. The time will vary with temperature, ingredients, etc. To test, poke two fingers into the dough; the holes should remain when the fingers are withdrawn.

🍂 When the dough is double in bulk, punch it down by pressing in the middle with your fist. Then pull the edges into the middle and turn the dough out onto a lightly floured surface.

HOW TO SHAPE LOAVES
Form the dough into a smooth, round ball. With a sharp knife, cut into portions, one for each loaf desired. Grease the appropriate number of loaf pans.

🍂 Flatten each piece of dough into a rectangle about 9 in. (23 cm) long, 7 in. (18 cm) wide and 1 in. (2 cm) thick. The width should be almost the length of the loaf pan.

🍂 Fold each end of the oblong to the center, overlapping the ends slightly. Press each fold down firmly. Pinch the center overlap,

then the ends, to seal the dough.

🍂 Place the loaf, with the sealed edges down, in a loaf pan. Brush the top with melted fat or oil. Cover again with a cloth and let rise in a warm place. The loaf is ready for baking if a slight impression remains when you press the dough lightly with a finger.

🍂 Always place the bread on the middle rack of the oven. Leave a space between each pan and make sure they are not touching the sides of the oven.

BREAD-MAKING TIPS
Bread made with molasses or honey will brown more quickly, so watch it carefully and turn the heat down a little if necessary.

🍂 Bread doughs containing nuts, jams, candied peel, etc., take longer to rise than plain dough.

🍂 If the bread has a coarse texture, it's probably because of insufficient kneading, too much flour, or too long a rising after being shaped.

🍂 If the crust is too thick it is because of too slow cooking or too much sugar.

🍂 Do not cover the bread while it is cooling unless you want a soft crust. Grease the loaves as soon as they come out of the oven.

🍂 For crusty bread, brush the top of the dough with cold water before putting it in the oven and place a pan half-filled with cold water in the bottom of the oven during baking.

🍂 Properly cooled bread freezes well if wrapped airtight in plastic or aluminum foil; it will keep its freshness for many weeks. Unwrap and thaw or heat the

frozen bread in a 400°F (200°C) oven, or thaw at room temperature.

🍂 To freshen dried-out bread, moisten it lightly with cold water or place it in a moistened paper bag. Heat in a 375°F (190°C) oven until the bread or paper bag is dry.

🍂 Never store dried-out bread with fresh, as the dry bread will absorb the moisture from the fresh bread.

PERFECT WHITE BREAD

½ cup (125 mL) warm water
1 tsp (5 mL) sugar
¼ tsp (1 mL) ground ginger
2 packages active dry yeast
⅓ cup (75 mL) sugar
2½ cups (625 mL) warm water
4 cups (1 L) flour
¾ cup (175 mL) skim milk powder
3 cups (750 mL) warm water
5 tsp (25 mL) salt
½ cup (125 mL) soft shortening
6 to 8 cups (1.5 to 2 L) flour
2 cups (500 mL) flour
for kneading

🍂 In a small bowl, combine the warm water, sugar, ginger and yeast and let stand in a warm place until bubbling nicely, about 10 minutes.

🍂 In a large bowl, beat together the ⅓ cup (75 mL) sugar, the 2½ cups (625 mL) warm water, the 4 cups (1 L) flour and the skim milk powder.

🍂 Stir the yeast mixture well and beat it into the flour mixture until smooth.

🍂 Cover the bowl and let stand in a warm place until the sponge is

Cinnamon Roll Raisin Bread

well risen and bubbly.

🍂 Add the 3 cups (750 mL) warm water, the salt and the shortening. Beat well.

🍂 Gradually stir in 6 to 8 cups (1.5 to 2 L) flour, mixing until the dough clears the bowl. Spread the remaining 2 cups (500 mL) flour on the work surface, turn out the dough and knead it well, using a little additional flour if necessary to make it smooth and satiny.

🍂 Return the dough to the bowl, dust the top with flour, cover with a damp cloth and let rise in a warm place for about 30 minutes.

🍂 Turn out. Knead thoroughly, using just enough flour to keep the dough from sticking.

🍂 Divide into even portions and shape into loaves. Place in greased pans. Brush the tops of the loaves with soft shortening and allow to rise again until double in bulk.

🍂 Bake in a preheated 425°F (220°C) oven for 20 minutes,

then reduce the heat to 350°F (180°C) and bake for another 25 minutes.

🍂 If a very soft crust is desired, brush the tops of the loaves with melted shortening or butter as soon as they are removed from the oven; allow the loaves to stand for about 5 minutes before removing them from the pans.

WHOLE-WHEAT BREAD

½ cup (125 mL) warm water
1 tsp (5 mL) sugar
¼ tsp (1 mL) ground ginger
2 packages active dry yeast
1 cup (250 mL) warm water
5 tbsp (75 mL) molasses or honey
2 cups (500 mL) whole-wheat flour
½ cup (125 mL) dry skim milk powder
¾ cup (175 mL) warm water

1½ tsp (7 mL) salt
3 tbsp (45 mL) melted butter
3 to 4 cups (750 ml to 1 L) whole-wheat flour

🍂 Combine the ½ cup (125 mL) warm water, sugar and ginger in a small bowl. Stir well until the sugar is dissolved. Sprinkle in the yeast and let stand in a warm place for 10 minutes.

🍂 In a large bowl, stir together the 1 cup (250 mL) warm water, the molasses or honey, the 2 cups (500 mL) whole-wheat flour and the skim milk powder. Beat in the well-stirred yeast mixture. Cover and let rise in a warm place until light and foamy.

🍂 Add the ¾ cup (175 mL) warm water, the salt, the melted butter and 3 cups (750 mL) of the whole-wheat flour. Stir until the dough clears the bowl.

🍂 Spread the remaining 1 cup (250 mL) flour on the table, turn the dough out on it and knead until it is smooth and stiff. (This is a coarse-textured bread and stiffness is necessary.) Return to the greased bowl and oil the top. Cover and let rise in a warm place until double in bulk.

🍂 Punch down the dough. Divide it in half and shape into two loaves. Place them in greased pans. Brush the tops with melted butter. Cover and let rise until doubled in bulk. Bake in a 350°F (180°C) oven for 45 minutes.

CRUSTY ROLLS

1 cup (250 mL) boiling water
2 tbsp (30 mL) butter
1 tbsp (15 mL) sugar

1 tsp (5 mL) salt
2 tsp (10 mL) sugar
½ cup (125 mL) warm water
2 packages active dry yeast
5 cups (1.2 L) all-purpose flour
2 egg whites, stiffly beaten

🐌 Mix together the boiling water, the butter, the 1 tbsp (15 mL) sugar and the salt. Stir well and let cool.

🐌 Stir the 2 tsp (10 mL) sugar into the warm water until dissolved. Add the yeast and let stand 10 minutes. Stir well and add to the cooled boiling water mixture.

🐌 Add 1 cup (250 mL) of the flour and beat until smooth. Fold in the beaten egg whites and keep adding the remaining flour and beating it in until the dough pulls away from the sides of the bowl.

🐌 Turn the ball onto a floured surface. Knead until it is smooth and elastic. Place the dough in a greased bowl and oil the top. Cover and let rise in a warm place until double in bulk.

🐌 Punch down the dough, turn it out onto a floured surface and knead for 2 minutes. Divide the dough in half and shape each half into a round ball. Cover and let stand for 10 minutes.

🐌 Roll each ball into a cylinder 27 in. (70 cm) long. Cut crosswise into 9 equal pieces. Press down on both cut ends of each section with your fingers and roll lightly back and forth until a point is formed at both ends.

🐌 Place each roll on a greased baking sheet. Cover and let rise in a warm place until double in bulk. With scissors, make two small diagonal cuts in the top of each roll.

🐌 Bake in a 450°F (230°C) oven for 20 minutes.

🐌 For very crusty rolls, place a pan of lightly salted water in the bottom of the oven during the baking.

CINNAMON ROLL RAISIN BREAD

1 tbsp (15 mL) sugar
¼ tsp (1 mL) ground ginger
¼ cup (50 mL) warm water
1 package active dry yeast
¾ cup (175 mL) scalded milk
⅓ cup (75 mL) soft butter
½ cup (125 mL) sugar
1 egg, lightly beaten
3½ cups (875 mL) all-purpose flour
1 tsp (5 mL) salt
1½ cups (375 mL) seedless raisins
2 tbsp (30 mL) melted butter
2 tbsp (30 mL) brown sugar
2 tsp (10 mL) cinnamon
¼ tsp (1 mL) nutmeg

🐌 Stir the 1 tbsp (15 mL) sugar and the ground ginger into the warm water until dissolved. Stir in the yeast. Let stand 10 minutes. Stir well.

🐌 To the scalded milk add the ⅓ cup (75 mL) soft butter and the ½ cup (125 mL) sugar. Stir until the butter is melted. Cool. Add the yeast mixture and the beaten egg. Blend well.

🐌 Sift together the flour and the salt. Add half the flour mixture to the yeast and milk mixture. Beat vigorously until smooth. Cover with a clean cloth and let rise in a warm place, away from drafts, until double in bulk.

🐌 Stir in the rest of the flour and salt mixture. Turn the dough onto a floured surface, fold in the raisins and knead until the dough is smooth and elastic and the raisins are evenly distributed. Place in a greased bowl and oil the top of the dough. Let rise in a warm place until doubled in bulk.

🐌 Punch down the dough and roll it out on a lightly floured board into an 18- x 7-in. (46- x 18-cm) rectangle. Brush the top of the rectangle with the melted butter and sprinkle with the brown sugar, cinnamon and nutmeg mixed together. Roll up tight like a jelly roll, starting to roll from one of the narrow ends.

🐌 Place in a greased 9- x 5- x 3-in. (23- x 13- x 8-cm) bread pan. Cover and let rise in a warm place until double in bulk.

🐌 Bake in a 350°F (180°C) oven for 45 to 50 minutes.

DANISH ALMOND BRAID

1 large potato, peeled and sliced
1 cup (250 mL) water
2 tbsp (30 mL) sugar
2 packages active dry yeast
3 tbsp (45 mL) corn syrup
⅓ cup (75 mL) scalded milk
3 tbsp (45 mL) soft butter
1 egg, well beaten
½ tsp (2 mL) salt
pinch of baking soda
3 to 5 cups (750 mL to 1.2 L) all-purpose flour
1 to 2 cups (250 to 500 mL) almond paste

🐌 Boil the sliced potato in the 1 cup (250 mL) water. Mash the cooked potato in its cooking water. Cool.

🍂 Stir the sugar into the warm mashed potato until dissolved. Add the yeast. Let stand 10 minutes and then stir well.

🍂 In a large bowl, place the corn syrup, the cooled scalded milk, the butter, the well-beaten egg, the yeast mixture and the baking soda sifted together with the salt and 3 cups (750 mL) of the flour. Beat until well blended and smooth.

🍂 Turn the dough onto a floured surface and start kneading while gradually adding the rest of the flour. Knead until smooth and elastic. Place the dough in a bowl, cover with a clean dish towel and let rise in a warm, draft-free place until double in bulk.

🍂 Punch down the dough. Knead it for 1 minute. Cut the dough into 3 equal pieces. Roll each piece into a rectangle about ¼-in. (0.6-cm) thick and cover each rectangle with a layer of almond paste. Roll each rectangle like a jelly roll, starting at the long edge, then braid the three long rolls together. Press the edges to seal.

🍂 Place the braid on a greased baking sheet, cover it with a cloth and let rise until double in bulk.

🍂 Bake in a 350°F (180°C) oven for 40 to 50 minutes.

GINGERBREAD

1 cup (250 mL) molasses
½ cup (125 mL) butter
2⅓ cups (575 mL) all-purpose flour
pinch of salt

¾ tsp (3 mL) baking soda
1 tsp (5 mL) ground ginger
1 tsp (5 mL) ground cinnamon
¼ tsp (1 mL) ground cloves
1 cup (250 mL) sour cream
2 eggs, lightly beaten

🍂 Preheat the oven to 350°F (180°C). Grease a 9-in. (23-cm) square baking pan.

🍂 Heat the molasses and butter together to the boiling point. Remove from the heat, pour into a mixing bowl and let cool.

🍂 Sift the flour together with the salt, baking soda, ginger, cinnamon and cloves.

🍂 Stir the sour cream and the lightly beaten eggs into the molasses mixture. Then stir in the flour mixture.

🍂 Turn the batter into the prepared pan and bake in a 350°F (180°C) oven for 35 to 40 minutes, or until a toothpick inserted in the center comes out clean.

🍂 Remove the cake from the pan and cut it into squares. Serve warm with whipped cream.

HONEY SPICE CAKE

1 cup (250 mL) sugar
¾ cup (175 mL) clear honey
2½ tsp (12 mL) baking soda
¼ tsp (1 mL) salt
1¼ cups (300 mL) boiling water
1 tsp (5 mL) tea leaves or 1 tea bag
3 tbsp (45 mL) rum
1 tsp (5 mL) anise seed
2 tsp (10 mL) cinnamon
4 cups (1 L) all-purpose flour

🍂 Preheat the oven to 450°F (230°C). Grease or butter generously a 10-in. (25-cm) tube pan.

🍂 Place in a bowl the sugar, honey, baking soda and salt.

🍂 Pour boiling water over the tea, let stand 5 minutes and pour the brew (without the tea leaves) over the sugar mixture. Stir until the sugar is melted. Add the rum, anise seed and cinnamon.

🍂 Sift the flour and gradually add it to the liquid mixture, stirring constantly. Continue stirring until smooth.

🍂 Turn the batter into the prepared pan. Bake for 10 minutes at 450°F (230°C), then reduce the heat to 350°F (180°C) and bake for 1 hour. Cool for 10 minutes, then unmold onto a cake rack to cool.

🍂 When the cake is completely cooled, wrap it in wax paper and keep it in a metal cake tin with a lid. This spice cake will keep for 2 to 3 months. It is delicious sliced thin and served with butter or honey butter.

OLD-FASHIONED HOT GINGERBREAD

½ cup (125 mL) sugar
½ cup (125 mL) molasses
¼ cup (50 mL) melted butter or bacon fat
2¼ cups (550 mL) all-purpose flour
⅞ cup (220 mL) hot water (measure 1 cup minus 2 tbsp)
½ to 1 tsp (2 to 5 mL) ginger
1 tsp (5 mL) baking soda

🍂 Mix together in a bowl the sugar, the molasses and the melted butter or bacon fat. Add the flour and mix together until thoroughly combined.

🍂 Mix together the hot water,

ginger and baking soda. Add all at once to the flour mixture. Mix just enough to blend.

🍂 Turn the batter into a well-buttered 8- x 8- x 2-in. (20- x 20- x 5-cm) square pan. Bake in a preheated 350°F (180°C) oven for 30 to 35 minutes or until a toothpick inserted in the center comes out clean.

🍂 If you use an ovenproof glass dish you will not have to unmold the cake to serve it.

🍂 Cut the gingerbread into squares and serve hot.

FRENCH BRIOCHES

1 tbsp (15 mL) sugar
¼ tsp (1 mL) ground ginger
¼ cup (50 mL) warm water
1 package active dry yeast
½ cup (125 mL) soft, sweet butter
⅓ cup (75 mL) sugar
1 tsp (5 mL) salt
½ cup (125 mL) scalded milk
3½ cups (875 mL) sifted all-purpose flour
3 eggs
1 egg white
2 tsp (10 mL) sugar

🍂 Stir the 1 tbsp (15 mL) sugar and the ginger into the warm water until dissolved. Sprinkle in the yeast and let stand for 10 minutes.

🍂 In a large bowl, beat the butter with an electric mixer at high speed until creamy white. Gradually add the ⅓ cup (75 mL) sugar and the salt. When the mixture is well creamed, turn the mixer speed to slow and gradually add the hot milk and 1½ cups (375 mL) of the flour. When well

combined, add the eggs one at a time, beating a few seconds after each addition.

🍂 Work in the remaining flour using a wooden spoon or your hands. Knead the dough for 5 minutes. Place the dough in a bowl, cover, and let rise in a warm place until double in bulk.

🍂 Beat down the dough using a wooden spoon. Cover the dough again and refrigerate it for 12 hours.

🍂 The next day, you must work quickly to finish the bread so that the dough remains cold.

🍂 Turn the dough out onto a lightly floured board and knead it vigorously. Divide the dough into 4 equal pieces. Cut 3 of these balls into 4 pieces each, and shape the pieces into balls; you should have 12 (plus 1 larger ball).

🍂 Put each of the 12 balls into a greased brioche mold. You can substitute any 3½-in. (9-cm) round molds. Make a dent in the

top of each ball with the tips of your fingers and moisten the balls slightly with a little water.

🍂 Divide the remaining piece of dough into 12. Shape into small round balls and place a ball in each of the 12 dents.

🍂 Cover and let rise in a warm place for about 1 hour or until doubled in bulk. Beat the egg white lightly with 2 tsp (10 mL) sugar. Baste the top of each brioche with this mixture.

🍂 Bake in a 375°F (190°C) oven for 15 to 20 minutes or until golden brown. Unmold immediately. Let cool on a cake rack.

PECAN ROLLS

PASTRY:
1 cup (250 mL) scalded milk
⅓ cup (75 mL) sugar
1½ tsp (7 mL) salt
2 tsp (10 mL) sugar

Pecan Rolls

[643]

¼ tsp (1 mL) ground ginger

½ cup (125 mL) warm water

2 packages active dry yeast

2 eggs, unbeaten

5 cups (1.2 L) sifted all-purpose flour

½ cup (125 mL) melted butter

FILLING:

2 tbsp (30 mL) soft butter

½ cup (125 mL) well-packed brown sugar

¼ tsp (1 mL) cinnamon

¼ to ½ cup (50 to 125 mL) coarsely chopped pecans

TOPPING:

¼ cup (50 mL) melted butter

¼ cup (50 mL) corn syrup

¼ cup (50 mL) brown sugar

¼ cup (50 mL) whole pecans

🍃 To scald the milk, heat it just until bubbles start to form around the edge. Add the ⅓ cup (75 mL) sugar and the salt. Stir well and let cool.

🍃 Stir the 2 tsp (10 mL) sugar and the ginger into the warm water until dissolved. Add the yeast and let stand for 10 minutes. Stir well.

🍃 Add the yeast mixture to the cooled milk and mix well. Add the eggs one at a time, beating well after each addition. Add 2 cups (500 mL) of the flour along with the melted butter. Beat vigorously until well blended. Add the rest of the flour less 2 tbsp (30 mL). Mix well.

🍃 Sprinkle the reserved 2 tbsp (30 mL) flour on a pastry board. Place the dough on the board, cover it with a cloth and let stand for 10 minutes. Knead the dough

lightly. Place it in a greased bowl, cover with a cloth and let rise in a warm place, free of drafts, for about 1 hour, or until the dough has doubled in bulk.

🍃 Punch the dough down. Cover again with the cloth and let rise again, for about 45 minutes or until the dough has doubled in bulk. Punch down the dough and turn it out onto the floured pastry board. Divide the dough into two equal pieces. Roll out each piece into a 10- x 15-in. (25- x 40-cm) rectangle.

🍃 To make the filling, spread each dough rectangle with the butter. Combine the brown sugar with the cinnamon and sprinkle it over the butter. Cover with the coarsely chopped pecans. Roll the dough jelly-roll fashion, starting from the long side. Pinch each end of the roll to seal. Cut each roll into 15 slices.

🍃 Grease two 7- x 11- x 1½-in. (18- x 28- x 3-cm) pans or use muffin tins.

🍃 To make the topping, pour equal amounts of the melted butter into each pan. Mix together the corn syrup and brown sugar and divide it equally between the pans. Sprinkle the bottom of each pan with the whole pecans.

🍃 Arrange the dough slices on top, leaving a 1-in. (2.5 cm) space between them. Cover and let rise in a warm, draft-free place for about 45 minutes or until doubled in bulk.

🍃 Bake in a preheated 350°F (180°C) oven for 30 minutes. When done, turn the pans upside-down onto a sheet of wax paper placed on a cake rack.

Leave the pans in place for 2 minutes, then carefully lift them off. Let the rolls cool on the cake rack.

🍃 Yield: about 30 pecan rolls.

LUSSE KATTER

This rich, sweet bun shaped like the letter X is a traditional start to Saint Lucia's day in Sweden.

DOUGH:

1 egg

⅔ cup (150 mL) sugar

¼ cup (50 mL) warm water

1 package active dry yeast

1 tsp (5 mL) salt

1 tsp (5 mL) crushed cardamon seeds or a pinch of saffron

2 cups (500 mL) scalded milk

6 to 8 cups (1.5 to 2 L) all-purpose flour

¼ cup (50 mL) melted butter

raisins

GLAZE:

½ cup (125 mL) strong coffee

4 tbsp (60 mL) sugar

🍃 Dissolve 1 tsp (5 mL) of the ⅔ cup (150 mL) sugar in the warm water; sprinkle the yeast on the water and let stand for about 10 minutes, or until the mixture starts to foam.

🍃 Meanwhile, break the egg into a large bowl. Add the remaining sugar. Beat the egg and sugar until well blended.

🍃 Add the salt and the cardamon or saffron to the scalded milk and let it cool to lukewarm.

🍃 Stir the yeast mixture well. Add it to the egg mixture, along with the lukewarm milk mixture. Slowly beat in 4 cups (1 L) of the flour, 1 cup (250 mL) at a time, beating well after each addition. If you have a mixer with a dough hook, by all means use it.

❧ When the batter is smooth and elastic, stir in the melted butter, and gradually add the remaining flour, just enough to make a soft but workable dough. Turn the dough onto a floured board and knead it until smooth, which should take about 10 minutes. (If you have a dough hook, beat the dough with it for 5 minutes only).

❧ Place the dough in a greased bowl. Cover it with a cloth and let it rise in a warm place until double in bulk, about 1 to 1½ hours. Punch the dough down, cover again, and let rise a second time until double in bulk, about 1 more hour. Punch down the dough again.

❧ To shape the buns, pinch off pieces of the dough about the size of small oranges and roll into strands about 6 in. (15 cm) long and 1 in. (2 cm) in diameter. Slice each strand in half lengthwise starting from each end, leaving a ½-in. (1-cm) piece in the center uncut. Spread the arms apart at right angles so that each bit is shaped like an X. Stud a raisin in each corner.

❧ Arrange the buns on a lightly greased baking sheet and let rise for about 20 minutes or until the buns are puffy, but not doubled in volume.

❧ Bake in a preheated 375°F (190°C) oven for 20 to 25 minutes or until golden brown.

❧ To prepare the glaze, bring the coffee to a boil with the sugar, stirring until the sugar is dis-solved. Boil for 1 minute. Remove from the heat. Brush the buns with this mixture while they are still hot.

ABOUT QUICK BREADS

In the large family of quick breads—which includes not only breads but muffins, pancakes, waffles and doughnuts—the quick-rising action of baking powder usually takes the place of yeast. However, some old-fashioned recipes use baking soda combined with an acidic liquid such as sour milk to create the leavening action.

❧ These quick breads can be classified according to the consistency of the batter, which depends on the proportion of flour in comparison to liquid.

❧ Pour batter is so named because it is thin enough to be poured; it is used for pancakes, waffles, popovers, Yorkshire pudding, etc.

❧ Drop batter is soft enough to drop from a spoon and is the consistency required for muffins, quick breads, dumplings, etc.

❧ Soft dough contains enough flour to be worked and cut into various shapes, such as hot biscuits, scones, shortcakes, etc.

❧ Some types of this family of doughs can be baked in the oven, hot biscuits, quick breads and muffins, for example. Always pre-heat the oven when baking these. Doughnuts and fritters are deep-fried and dumplings are steamed.

❧ Whatever type of dough or method of cooking used, these recipes have several things in common: they are fast and easy to prepare, and they are usually better served hot or warm.

❧ To give an old-fashioned flavor to any quick bread, add ½ tsp (2 mL) of baking soda for each 2 tsp (10 mL) of baking powder called for in the recipe.

PREPARING QUICK BREAD BATTERS

Sift all the dry ingredients together into a large bowl.

❧ Measure out the required fat or shortening when it is firm and cold, then cut it into the dry ingredients with a knife or wire pastry blender. Work with a quick, chopping motion until the mixture is uniformly mealy.

❧ Add any coarse-grained cereals, sugar, raisins, candied peels or nuts and mix well.

❧ There are two ways of adding the liquid: either make a well in the middle of the dough and pour in the liquid all at once; then stir quickly, just enough to blend. Or sprinkle the liquid over the dry ingredients; then mix lightly with a fork. In either case, you should work the dough as little as possible—over-working will make a tough, chewy product. Muffin batters do not need to be smooth; stop beating while the batter is still somewhat lumpy.

❧ Quick breads should be cooked as soon as they are mixed, unless the recipe directs otherwise.

❧ Quick breads are easy to reheat. Simply enclose them in aluminum foil or a paper bag and place in a 450°F (230°C) oven for a few minutes.

QUICK FRUIT AND NUT BREAD

2½ cups (625 mL) pastry flour
5 tsp (25 mL) baking powder
¾ tsp (3 mL) salt
½ cup (125 mL) sugar
½ cup (125 mL) seedless raisins
¼ cup (50 mL) chopped mixed candied peel
¼ cup (50 mL) chopped nuts
2 eggs
½ cup (125 mL) milk
¼ tsp (1 mL) almond extract
1 tsp (5 mL) grated lemon zest
8 tbsp (120 mL) melted shortening

❧ Preheat the oven to 350°F (180°C). Grease an 8½- x 4½-in. (22- x 12-cm) bread pan. Sprinkle it lightly with flour.

❧ Sift together the flour, baking powder and salt. Sift a second time into a bowl. Add the sugar, raisins, mixed peel and nuts. Mix.

❧ Beat the eggs and stir in the milk, almond extract, grated lemon zest and melted shortening.

❧ Make a well in the middle of the dry ingredients and add the egg and milk mixture all at once. Stir until mixed.

❧ Pour into the prepared pan. Bake about 1 hour.

QUICK MAPLE SUGAR BREAD

1 cup (250 mL) all-purpose flour
2 cups (500 mL) whole-wheat flour
½ cup (125 mL) grated maple sugar
2 cups (500 mL) sour milk
1½ tsp (7 mL) baking soda
1 tsp (5 mL) salt

❧ Sift the flour into a bowl. Stir in the whole-wheat flour and the maple sugar.

❧ Combine the milk with the baking soda and the salt. Pour, all at once, over the dry ingredients. Stir just enough to blend.

❧ Turn the batter into a greased loaf pan. Bake in a preheated 350°F (180°C) oven for 1 hour.

❧ Serve this bread hot with butter, maple syrup and some crisp-fried morsels of salt pork.

QUICK RAISIN BREAD

3 cups (750 mL) all-purpose flour
½ cup (125 mL) powdered milk
½ cup (125 mL) sugar
1 tsp (5 mL) salt
3 tsp (15 mL) baking powder
4 tbsp (60 mL) butter
1½ cups (375 mL) water
3 eggs, well beaten
1 cup (250 mL) seedless raisins
½ cup (125 mL) all-purpose flour
1 tbsp (15 mL) caraway seeds
2 tbsp (30 mL) evaporated milk

❧ Sift together into a large bowl the flour, powdered milk, sugar, salt and baking powder. Add the butter and work the mixture together with your fingertips until mealy and well combined.

❧ Beat together the water and the eggs. Add all at once to the dry ingredients. Stir until blended.

❧ Stir together the raisins, the ½ cup (125 mL) flour and the caraway seeds. Fold this mixture into the batter.

❧ Turn the batter into 2 greased loaf pans. Let stand for 20 min-

Quick Fruit and Nut Bread

❦ TECHNIQUE ❦

QUICK FRUIT AND NUT BREAD

1 Sift together the flour, baking powder and salt. Sift again into a bowl.

2 Add the sugar, raisins, mixed peel and nuts.

3 Beat the eggs and stir in the milk, almond extract, grated lemon zest and melted shortening.

4 Make a well in the dry ingredients and add the liquid mixture all at once.

utes, then bake in a preheated 350°F (180°C) oven for 50 to 60 minutes.

&⬥ Brush the crust with the evaporated milk 15 minutes before the end of the baking period. Brush once more 5 minutes before the end of baking.

&⬥ Let the pans stand 5 minutes before unmolding the loaves. Unmold them on a cake rack and allow to cool.

&⬥ Wrap in aluminum foil and let stand for 24 hours before serving.

&⬥ This bread makes wonderful toast.

QUICK RYE BREAD

2 cups (500 mL) all-purpose flour
1 cup (250 mL) rye flour
1 tsp (5 mL) salt
1 tbsp (15 mL) baking powder
1 tsp (5 mL) instant coffee
1 cup (250 mL) chopped walnuts
¼ tsp (1 mL) baking soda
½ cup (125 mL) molasses
2 eggs, well beaten
¾ cup (175 mL) evaporated milk

&⬥ Sift together into a bowl the all-purpose flour, rye flour, salt, baking powder and instant coffee. Add the walnuts and mix until the nuts are well coated with flour.

&⬥ Combine the baking soda with the molasses. Beat the eggs together with the evaporated milk. Pour the molasses mixture and the egg and milk mixture over the dry ingredients all at once. Stir just enough to blend.

&⬥ Turn the batter into a greased and floured loaf pan. Make a small depression in the top.

&⬥ Let the loaf stand for 15 minutes. Bake in a preheated 350°F (180°C) oven for 1 hour.

&⬥ Brush the top with evaporated milk 5 minutes before the end of the baking period and a second time just before removing the loaf from the oven.

&⬥ Unmold the loaf onto a cake rack. Wrap the loaf in aluminum foil and let stand for 24 hours before serving.

&⬥ This loaf keeps very well.

QUICK ORANGE BREAD

4 cups (1 L) all-purpose flour
5 tsp (25 mL) baking powder
½ tsp (2 mL) salt
2 cups (500 mL) milk
3 eggs
1 tbsp (15 mL) melted butter
juice and grated zest of 1 orange
1 cup (250 mL) mixed candied peel
4 tbsp (60 mL) sugar
2 tbsp (30 mL) grated orange zest

&⬥ Sift together the flour, baking powder and salt.

&⬥ Stir together the milk, eggs, melted butter, orange juice and orange zest. Beat together vigorously. Add this mixture all at once to the dry ingredients. Add the mixed peel. Stir just enough to blend.

&⬥ Turn the batter into 2 small greased loaf pans.

&⬥ Combine the sugar with the 2 tbsp (30 mL) grated orange zest. Sprinkle on top of the loaves. Bake in a preheated 375°F (190°C) oven for 1 hour.

QUICK BANANA BREAD

¼ (50 mL) cup shortening
½ (125 mL) cup sugar
1 egg, beaten
1 cup (250 mL) whole bran
1½ cups (375 mL) mashed bananas
2 tbsp (30 mL) water
1½ cups (375 mL) all-purpose flour
1 tsp (5 mL) salt
2 tsp (10 mL) baking powder
½ tsp (2 mL) baking soda
1 tsp (5 mL) vanilla
½ cup (125 mL) chopped walnuts

&⬥ Cream the shortening, adding the sugar gradually. Add the beaten egg and the bran. Mix thoroughly.

&⬥ Combine the mashed bananas with the water.

&⬥ Sift together the flour, salt, baking powder and baking soda. Add the flour mixture to the creamed mixture alternately with the bananas. Add the vanilla and walnut pieces and mix well.

&⬥ Turn into a greased 8- x 8-in. (20- x 20-cm) cake pan. Top with the walnuts.

&⬥ Bake in a preheated 350°F (180°C) oven for 1 hour.

BASIC BAKING POWDER BISCUITS

2 cups (500 mL) pastry flour
4 tsp (20 mL) baking powder
½ tsp (2 mL) salt
3 tbsp (45 mL) vegetable shortening
⅔ cup (150 mL) milk

❧ Sift into a bowl the flour, baking powder and salt. Add the vegetable shortening and cut it in until the mixture is mealy.

❧ Make a well in the center and pour in the milk all at once. Stir rapidly just until all the ingredients are mixed. If the dough seems too dry, add a little more milk; if it seems too moist, add a little more flour. The perfect texture is a soft but not sticky dough that pulls away fairly freely from the sides of the bowl.

❧ Turn the dough onto a lightly floured pastry board and knead very lightly 5 to 10 times.

❧ Gently pat out the dough until it is ½ to ¾ in. (1 to 2 cm) thick. Cut out the biscuits with a floured cookie cutter (cut straight down without turning the cookie cutter).

❧ Place the biscuits on an ungreased baking sheet and bake in a preheated 450°F (230°C) oven for 12 to 15 minutes.

❧ Yield: 8 small biscuits, each 2½ in. (6 cm).

BACON BISCUITS

Fry 6 strips of bacon and drain them on a paper towel. Crumble the bacon and add to the dry ingredients along with the shortening.

CHEESE BISCUITS

To the dry ingredients add ¾ cup (175 mL) grated cheese of your choice (strong or medium Canadian Cheddar is my favorite).

HERB BISCUITS

To the dry ingredients add ¼ cup (50 mL) chopped parsley

Quick Banana Bread

or chives, or 1 tsp (5 mL) basil or marjoram, or ¼ tsp (1 mL) thyme or savory.

NUT BISCUITS

To the dry ingredients add ½ cup (125 mL) finely chopped nuts of your choice.

CURRIED BISCUITS

To the dry ingredients add ½ to 1 tsp (2 to 5 mL) curry, or to taste.

ONION BISCUITS

Fry ¼ cup (50 mL) finely chopped onion in 2 tbsp (30 mL) butter until golden. Add the onions to the dry ingredients along with the milk.

DROP BAKING POWDER BISCUITS

Use 1 cup (250 mL) milk instead of the ⅔ cup (150 mL) called for in the basic recipe. Do not knead or roll out the dough.

❧ Drop the dough by large spoonfuls onto a lightly greased baking sheet. Bake in a preheated 450°F (230°C) oven for 10 minutes, or until golden brown.

ORANGE BAKING POWDER BISCUITS

1 recipe *Basic Baking Powder Biscuits*
2 tbsp (30 mL) melted butter

FILLING:
¼ cup (50 mL) sugar
¼ cup (50 mL) brown sugar
¼ cup (50 mL) chopped nuts
2 tbsp (30 mL) grated orange zest
2 tbsp (30 mL) honey

❧ Roll the dough out into a 12- x 18-in. (30- x 45-cm) rectangle. Brush the top of the dough with the melted butter.

❧ To make the filling, heat the filling ingredients in a saucepan

Blueberry Hot Bread

over low heat until the sugars start to melt. Spread the filling mixture on the buttered dough. Roll the dough up like a jelly roll, starting on the longer side. Cut into 18 slices about 1 in. (2 cm) thick.

❧ Butter 18 muffin molds measuring 3 in. (7 cm) in diameter. Place a roll in each muffin mold, cut side up. Butter the top of each roll with some of the remaining melted butter.

❧ Bake in a preheated 425°F (220°C) oven for 15 minutes. Unmold immediately and serve hot.

STRAWBERRY SHORTCAKE

2¼ cups (550 mL) all-purpose flour
4 tsp (20 mL) baking powder
2 tbsp (30 mL) sugar
½ tsp (2 mL) salt
⅓ cup (75 mL) vegetable shortening
1 egg, lightly beaten
⅔ cup (150 mL) milk
1 to 3 cups (250 to 750 mL) strawberries (or other fruit)
whipped cream

❧ Grease and flour an 8-in. (20-cm) round cake pan.

❧ Sift together into a bowl the flour, baking powder, sugar and salt. Add the shortening and cut it in with a knife or pastry blender until the mixture is mealy.

❧ Beat together the egg and the milk. Add all at once to the flour mixture. Mix rapidly just until blended. Knead the dough lightly and pat it into the prepared pan.

❧ Bake in a preheated 425°F (220°C) oven for 15 to 20 minutes and then let stand for 5 minutes before unmolding. Unmold and split the cake into two layers with a long, sharp knife. Spread each cut side generously with soft butter. Place the bottom half on a large serving plate, buttered side up. Top with 1 cup (250 mL) sweetened sliced fresh or frozen strawberries. Top the fruit with whipped cream, to taste. Place the other cake half on top, buttered side down, and garnish with more strawberries and whipped cream.

❧ To make perfect shortcake, be ready to spread on the butter, sweetened fruit and whipped cream as soon as the cake is unmolded. Serve immediately.

BLUEBERRY HOT BREAD

BASE:
¼ cup (50 mL) shortening or butter
¾ cup (175 mL) sugar
2 eggs
½ cup (125 mL) milk
2 cups (500 mL) all-purpose flour
2 tsp (10 mL) baking powder
½ tsp (2 mL) salt
½ tsp (2 mL) nutmeg or ginger
2 cups (500 mL) blueberries, fresh, frozen or canned

TOPPING:
½ cup (125 mL) sugar
⅓ cup (75 mL) all-purpose flour
½ tsp (2 mL) cinnamon
¼ cup (50 mL) soft butter

❧ To prepare the base, cream the ¼ cup (50 mL) shortening or butter with the ¾ cup (175 mL) sugar and the eggs. Add the milk. Beat well.

❧ Sift together the flour, the baking powder, the salt and the nutmeg or ginger. Add to the creamed mixture and stir just enough to blend.

🍂 Pat the mixture into a greased 8- x 8-in. (20- x 20-cm) pan. Spread the blueberries on top.

🍂 To prepare the topping, stir together the ½ cup (125 mL) sugar, the ⅓ cup (75 mL) flour, the cinnamon and the ¼ cup (50 mL) soft butter. Sprinkle this mixture on top of the blueberries.

🍂 Bake in a preheated 375°F (190°C) oven for 25 to 35 minutes.

🍂 Serve hot or warm with sour cream or fresh cream.

HOT CORNBREAD

1 egg
½ tsp (2 mL) salt
2 tbsp (30 mL) sugar
1 cup (250 mL) buttermilk
or sour milk
½ cup (125 mL) all-purpose flour
½ tsp (2 mL) baking powder
1 cup (250 mL) yellow corn meal
⅓ cup (75 mL) melted butter
½ tsp (2 mL) baking soda
3 tbsp (45 mL) cold water

🍂 Break the egg into a mixing bowl. Add the salt and the sugar. Beat well together. Add the sour milk or buttermilk and mix.

🍂 Mix the flour with the baking powder and add to the liquid mixture. Then add the corn meal, just enough to make a medium-thick batter.

🍂 Melt the butter in the cake pan you plan to use; this also greases the pan. Beat the melted butter into the batter until well mixed. Stir in the baking soda mixed with the cold water. The batter will be rather thin.

🍂 Bake in a 450°F (230°C) oven for 15 to 20 minutes. Serve hot.

SCOTTISH SCONES

2 cups (500 mL) all-purpose flour
2 tsp (10 mL) baking powder
½ tsp (2 mL) salt
2 tsp (10 mL) sugar
4 tbsp (60 mL) butter
1 egg, beaten
½ cup (125 mL) light cream

🍂 Sift together into a bowl the flour, baking powder, salt and sugar. Add the butter and cut it into the flour mixture until the mixture is uniform and mealy. Beat together the egg and the cream and add it all at once to the flour mixture. Blend just enough to mix.

🍂 Turn the dough out onto a floured board. Knead lightly for a few seconds. Roll out to a thickness of ½ in. (1 cm). Cut the dough into equal-size triangles. Place the scones on an ungreased baking sheet and bake in a preheated 450°F (230°C) oven for 15 minutes.

BLENDER BUCKWHEAT PANCAKES

1½ cups (375 mL) buckwheat flour
1 tbsp (15 mL) baking powder
½ tsp (2 mL) baking soda
½ tsp (2 mL) salt
½ cup (125 mL) whole-wheat flour

2 cups (500 mL) sour milk
or buttermilk
2 tbsp (30 mL) molasses
1 egg
3 tbsp (45 mL) soft butter
1 tbsp (15 mL) brown sugar

🍂 Sift into a bowl the buckwheat flour, baking powder, baking soda and salt. Mix in the whole-wheat flour.

🍂 Put the remaining ingredients in the blender container. Cover and blend for 1 minute at high speed. Pour the mixture all at once over the dry ingredients and mix just until blended. Do not overbeat. Let the batter rest for 3 hours, if possible.

🍂 Pour the batter by large spoonfuls onto a heated, lightly greased griddle or skillet. The pan should be just hot enough that a few drops of water sprinkled on the surface will sputter and dance.

🍂 When bubbles appear on the upper surface, but before they break, lift the edges of the pancake gently with a spatula to check if the bottom is cooked. When done, turn the pancake and cook the second side; watch carefully, as the second side will not take as long to cook. Serve the pancakes at once.

🍂 If you do not have sour milk or buttermilk, replace it with ½ cup (125 mL) water, ½ cup (125 mL) powdered milk and 1 tsp (5 mL) vinegar.

BASIC MUFFINS

2 cups (500 mL) all-purpose flour
2 tbsp (30 mL) sugar
½ tsp (2 mL) salt

1 tbsp (15 mL) baking powder
1 egg, well beaten
1 cup (250 mL) milk
4 tbsp (60 mL) melted butter

᷍ Preheat the oven to 400°F (200°C). Grease the muffin tins.

᷍ Sift together into a bowl the flour, sugar, salt and baking powder.

᷍ Mix together the beaten egg and the milk. Add all at once to the dry ingredients. Stir just until blended; the muffins will be more tender if the batter is somewhat lumpy. Gently stir in the cooled melted butter.

᷍ Use 2 teaspoons to pick up the dough, disturbing it as little as possible. Fill each muffin cup ⅔ full. Place the muffins in the preheated oven immediately. Bake 20 to 25 minutes at 400°F (200°C). Unmold and serve hot with butter and jam or honey.

᷍ To make sweeter muffins, use 4 tbsp (60 mL) sugar instead of 2 tbsp (30 mL). For very sweet muffins, use ½ cup (125 mL) sugar.

APPLE MUFFINS

Prepare a very sweet muffin batter following the basic recipe; add 1 tsp (5 mL) ground cinnamon to the dry ingredients; add 1 cup (250 mL) peeled or unpeeled apples, chopped or grated, to the batter along with the melted butter.

BLUEBERRY MUFFINS

Prepare a sweet muffin batter, and fold in 1 cup (250 mL) cleaned blueberries along with the melted butter.

BROWN SUGAR MUFFINS

Replace the 2 tbsp (30 mL) sugar in the basic muffin recipe with ¾ cup (175 mL) brown sugar.

JAM MUFFINS

Prepare a basic muffin batter and spoon it into muffin pans; top each muffin with 1 tsp (5 mL) jam of your choice before baking.

PEANUT BUTTER MUFFINS

Prepare a basic muffin batter; add ¼ cup (50 mL) peanut butter to the milk and egg mixture; reduce the melted butter to 2 tbsp (30 mL).

SOUR CREAM MUFFINS

Prepare a sweet muffin batter following the basic recipe; add ½ tsp (2 mL) baking soda to the dry ingredients; replace the 1 cup (250 mL) milk with an equal quantity of sour cream.

MOLASSES MUFFINS

1 cup (250 mL) all-purpose flour
½ tsp (2 mL) baking soda
½ tsp (2 mL) salt
1 egg, beaten
¼ cup (50 mL) melted butter
½ cup (125 mL) molasses
½ cup (125 mL) sour milk
1 tsp (5 mL) grated lemon zest
1 tsp (5 mL) vanilla

᷍ Sift the flour together with the baking soda and salt.

᷍ Beat together the egg, melted butter, molasses, sour milk, orange zest and vanilla. Add this mixture all at once to the dry ingredients. Beat just until the ingredients are blended but still lumpy.

᷍ Spoon the mixture into greased muffin tins, filling each mold ⅔

Molasses Muffins

full. Bake in a preheated 350°F (180°C) oven for 30 minutes, or until done.

LAC SAINT JEAN DUMPLINGS

2 cups (500 mL) all-purpose flour
½ tsp (2 mL) salt
1 tbsp (15 mL) baking powder
½ tsp (2 mL) baking soda
3 tbsp (45 mL) shortening or lard
1 cup (250 mL) sour milk
or buttermilk

❧ Sift together into a bowl the flour, salt, baking powder and baking soda. Add the shortening or lard, cutting it in with two knifes or a pastry blender until the mixture is mealy and uniform in texture.

❧ Add the sour milk or buttermilk all at once. Stir quickly with a fork just until the mixture forms a ball. Turn the dough out onto a floured board, and knead lightly with the fingertips for about 30 seconds only.

❧ Roll the dough out ¾ in. (2 cm) thick. Cut it into squares or rounds. Cook using one of the following methods.

COOKING METHOD
❧ To make dumplings to serve with a main course, cook them in either beef stock or chicken stock, or in a basic brown sauce.

❧ For dessert dumplings, cook them in boiling maple syrup or molasses mixed with an equal quantity of water. They are also delicious cooked in a fruit sauce: bring to a boil 2 cups (500 mL)

water and 1 cup (250 mL) sugar; add 2 cups (500 mL) berries (blueberries, raspberries, etc.) and simmer for 5 minutes before adding the dumplings.

❧ Whatever liquid is used to cook the dumplings, the method is the same. When the liquid is boiling hot, drop in the dumplings. Do not overcrowd them as they will swell quite a bit; I usually cook 4 or 5 at a time. Cover the saucepan and boil for 12 minutes without lifting the lid. Remove the dumplings with a slotted spoon and keep them warm while cooking the remaining dumplings. By the time the dumplings are cooked, the liquid will be thickened. Serve this sauce over the dumplings.

DUMPLINGS IN CARAMEL SAUCE

CARAMEL SAUCE:
1½ cups (375 mL) sugar
2 cups (500 mL) boiling water
2 tsp (10 mL) vanilla
2 tbsp (30 mL) butter

DUMPLING BATTER:
2 cups (500 mL) pastry flour
½ cup (125 mL) sugar
1½ tsp (7 mL) baking powder
½ tsp (2 mL) salt
½ cup (125 mL) milk
1 tbsp (15 mL) melted butter

❧ To prepare the sauce, place the sugar in a heavy saucepan or enameled skillet and cook over medium heat, stirring lightly, until it is melted and caramelized to a golden brown. Remove from

heat and add the boiling water, being careful as it may spatter. Return to heat and simmer for a few minutes (be careful the mixture doesn't boil over). Remove from the heat and add the vanilla and the butter.

❧ To make the dumplings, sift together into a bowl the pastry flour, sugar, baking powder and salt. Add the milk and melted butter. Stir quickly; the dough should be slightly lumpy. Drop by spoonfuls into the boiling syrup. Cover and cook for 15 minutes over medium heat, without lifting the lid from the pan. Serve hot with ice cream.

BLUEBERRY DUMPLINGS

4 cups (1 L) blueberries, cleaned
¾ cup (175 mL) sugar
¾ cup (175 mL) brown sugar
¼ tsp (1 mL) ginger
¼ tsp (1 mL) cinnamon
1 cup (250 mL) water
2 cups (500 mL) pastry flour
1 tbsp (15 mL) baking powder
½ tsp (2 mL) salt
2 tsp (10 mL) shortening
or butter
⅔ cup (150 mL) warm milk

❧ Combine the blueberries, sugar, brown sugar, ginger, cinnamon and water in a saucepan and boil for 3 minutes.

❧ Sift together the flour, baking powder and salt. Add the shortening or butter and cut it into the flour until the mixture is mealy. Gradually stir in the warm milk.

❧ Drop the dough by small

spoonfuls into the boiling blueberry syrup, leaving spaces between the dumplings for swelling. Cover the saucepan and cook for 15 minutes without lifting the lid.

❧ To serve, pour the blueberry syrup over the dumplings.

DUMPLINGS IN MAPLE SYRUP

2 cups (500 mL) water
1¼ cups (300 mL) maple syrup
1½ cups (375 mL) sifted pastry flour or 1¼ cups (300 mL) sifted all-purpose flour
1 tbsp (15 mL) baking powder
1 tbsp (15 mL) sugar
½ tsp (2 mL) salt
¼ cup (50 mL) cold butter
½ cup (125 mL) milk
chopped nuts

❧ Pour the water and the maple syrup into a large saucepan. Simmer, covered, while preparing the batter.

❧ Sift together into a bowl the pastry flour or all-purpose flour, baking powder, sugar and salt. Add the very cold butter and cut it in with 2 knives until the mixture is very fine.

❧ Make a well in the dry ingredients; pour in the milk all at once and mix lightly. Fold in the chopped nuts.

❧ Drop the dough by large spoonfuls into the boiling syrup. Cover and boil over low heat, without lifting the lid, for 15 minutes. Serve very hot.

QUÉBEC JAM DUMPLINGS

3 cups (750 mL) all-purpose flour
4 tsp (20 mL) baking powder
1 tsp (5 mL) salt
2 eggs
1 cup (250 mL) milk
1 tbsp (15 mL) melted butter
jam of your choice
2 cups (500 mL) apple juice

❧ Sift together in a bowl the flour, baking powder and salt.

❧ Combine the eggs and the milk. Add the egg mixture all at once to the dry ingredients. Stir just enough to blend. Add the melted butter.

❧ Turn the dough out onto a floured board and roll out to a thickness of ¼ in. (0.5 cm). Cut into 1-in. (2.5-cm) squares.

❧ Butter a pudding dish or enameled cast-iron skillet generously. Arrange half the squares of dough in the bottom of the pan. Spread each square thickly with jam. Top with another layer of dough squares and spread them with more jam.

❧ Bring the apple juice to a boil and pour it over the dumplings.

❧ Cover the pan and bake in a preheated 350°F (180°C) oven for 50 to 60 minutes. If you prefer a brown, crispy crust, do not cover the pan during the baking period.

ABOUT WAFFLES

Waffle batter resembles pancake and crêpe batter, but is thicker.

Waffles are cooked in a special electric appliance. It is important to read the manufacturer's instructions before using any waffle iron. Most have an automatic control that will make waffle making easier.

❧ Unless the manufacturer's instructions indicate otherwise, a waffle iron should be greased lightly with unsalted fat such as sweet butter, corn oil, etc., before being used for the first waffle. There is no need to grease it between subsequent waffles as waffle batter contains enough fat to prevent sticking.

❧ Be sure the waffle iron is hot enough before you add the batter. If it has no thermostat, check the temperature by sprinkling a few drops of water on the grill; if the drops sizzle and evaporate quickly, the heat is high enough.

❧ Pour the batter starting in the middle of the hot waffle iron and let it spread until it covers most of the iron. Close the iron and cook until no more steam comes out. Use a fork to lift out the cooked waffle.

❧ Leftover waffle batter will keep for 2 to 3 days if it is sealed in a glass jar. It must be well beaten before being used.

WAFFLES

2 cups (500 mL) all-purpose flour
1 tbsp (15 mL) baking powder
½ tsp (2 mL) salt
2 eggs, separated
1¼ cups (300 mL) milk
6 tbsp (90 mL) melted shortening

ᔰ Sift together into a bowl the flour, baking powder and salt.

ᔰ Beat the egg yolks together with the milk. Add this mixture to the dry ingredients and mix.

ᔰ Add the melted shortening, mix well, then fold in the stiffly beaten egg whites. Cook as indicated in the basic instructions.

BANANA WAFFLES

Before folding in the egg whites, add 1½ cups (375 mL) peeled and thinly sliced bananas.

COCOA WAFFLES

Replace 3 tbsp (45 mL) of the flour with 3 tbsp (45 mL) cocoa powder.

NUT WAFFLES

Add 1 cup (250 mL) finely chopped nuts to the batter before folding in the egg whites.

MOLASSES WAFFLES

⅓ cup (75 mL) butter
1 cup (250 mL) molasses
2 eggs, separated
2 cups (500 mL) all-purpose flour
½ tsp (2 mL) baking soda
2 tbsp (30 mL) baking powder
2 tsp (10 mL) cinnamon
1 tsp (5 mL) ground ginger
½ tsp (2 mL) salt
½ cup (125 mL) sour milk

ᔰ Cream together the butter and molasses. Add the egg yolks, one at a time, beating vigorously after each addition.

ᔰ Sift together the flour, baking soda, baking powder, cinnamon, ginger and salt.

ᔰ Add the flour in stages to the

Waffles

butter and molasses mixture, alternating with the sour milk. Beat until the batter is smooth.

ᔰ Beat the egg whites until stiff and fold them gently into the batter. Cook in a waffle iron following the general instructions for waffles.

ᔰ Serve with butter and apple-sauce or powdered sugar.

FRENCH WAFFLES

¾ cup (175 mL) sweet butter
1 cup (250 mL) sugar
4 eggs, separated
1½ cups (375 mL) all-purpose flour
⅓ cup (75 mL) milk
1 tsp (5 mL) vanilla

ᔰ Cream the butter. Add the sugar little by little. Beat until the mixture is light and fluffy.

ᔰ Add the egg yolks, one at a time, beating vigorously after each addition.

ᔰ Add the flour alternately with the milk and the vanilla, and beat until the batter is very light.

ᔰ Beat the egg whites until stiff and fold them into the batter. Cook in a hot waffle iron following the general instructions.

ᔰ These French waffles are very light and crisp. Serve them for dessert with ice cream, fresh fruit compote or chocolate cream.

PERFECT PANCAKES

ᔰ Pancake recipes vary greatly, depending not only on regional custom and family tradition, but also on whether you are making everyday pancakes or gourmet treats. But no matter what the

Crêpes Suzette

recipe or type, a pancake must always be light, thoroughly cooked and neither moist nor greasy.

⋙ The lightness comes with just the right batter; the cooking know-how is acquired through care and practice.

⋙ A pancake won't be greasy if you use the exact amount of fat called for in the recipe—on the skillet as well as in the batter. The skillet or griddle should have a heavy bottom with good heat distribution, and it must be greased with just enough unsalted fat, such as vegetable shortening, margarine, meat fat or oil. The best way to grease the skillet is to use a wad of cotton tied to a stick and dipped in the fat. Then baste the bottom and sides of the skillet lightly. With this method, the fat will be spread evenly.

⋙ Pancakes should be cooked over medium heat and care

should be taken to ensure that the pan is centered on the burner so that the bottom of the skillet is evenly heated. It is normal for the first 1 or 2 pancakes in the batch to stick to the bottom, but if they still stick after number 5 or 6, the heat is too high.

FRENCH CRÊPES

1 cup (250 mL) all-purpose flour
¼ tsp (1 mL) salt
1 tbsp (15 mL) sugar
2 large or 3 small eggs
1½ cups (375 mL) milk
1 tsp (5 mL) cognac or vanilla
1 tbsp (15 mL) melted butter

⋙ Sift together into a bowl the flour, salt and sugar. Make a well in the dry ingredients and break an egg into it. Beat the egg with a wooden spoon, incorporating the flour little by little; continue in

this manner with the remaining eggs until they are well blended with the flour.

⋙ Add the milk little by little, beating with a wire whisk or hand beater until the batter is smooth. Add the brandy or vanilla and the melted butter. Let the batter stand at room temperature for 1 hour.

⋙ To cook the crêpes, heat a skillet or crêpe pan and brush it with melted fat or butter.

⋙ Pour in just enough batter to cover the bottom of the pan, tilting the pan back and forth to spread the batter evenly.

⋙ When the bottom has browned slightly, turn the crêpe by lifting one corner with a knife and turning it with your fingers. Continue cooking until the second side is golden.

⋙ When cooked, slip it onto a warm plate and keep it warm until all the crêpes are cooked.

⋙ Fill the crêpes as desired or simply fold them in four and serve them with butter and syrup.

CRÊPES SUZETTE

CRÊPE BATTER:
2½ tbsp (40 mL) finely granulated sugar
4 tbsp (60 mL) all-purpose flour
3 eggs
½ cup (125 mL) milk
½ tsp (2 mL) salt
1 tbsp (15 mL) vanilla

SAUCE:
4 tbsp (60 mL) butter
2 tbsp (30 mL) sugar

2 tbsp (30 mL) rum
zest of 1 orange, finely grated, or
2 tbsp (30 mL) Curaçao
¼ cup (50 mL) fine sugar
2 tbsp (30 mL) cognac
2 tbsp (30 mL) Grand Marnier

⁀ To prepare the crêpes, mix together the sugar and flour. In a second bowl, beat the eggs and add the milk, salt and vanilla. Add the dry ingredients to the liquid mixture and blend well with a wire whisk or hand beater.

⁀ Heat a 6-in. (15-cm) crêpe pan and brush the bottom with butter. Pour about 1½ tbsp (25 mL) of the batter into the hot pan. Lift the pan and tilt back and forth to spread the batter evenly over the bottom. Cook the crêpe over medium heat until the bottom is lightly browned, then turn it over by lifting one corner with a knife and grasping it with your fingers. Cook for a few seconds on the second side.

⁀ Stack each crêpe as soon as it is cooked on a large plate set over a pan of hot water; this will keep the crêpes soft and warm. When they are all cooked, cover them with a clean cloth or a bowl.

⁀ To prepare the sauce, melt the butter in a heavy skillet or an electric skillet set at 400°F (200°C). Add the 2 tbsp (30 mL) sugar, stirring to dissolve, and cook until it is lightly caramelized. Stir in the rum and the orange zest or Curaçao.

⁀ Fold each crêpe in four and arrange them, one by one, in the butter mixture. Sprinkle with the ¼ cup (50 mL) sugar.

⁀ Sprinkle a little sugar over the bottom of the skillet to caramelize while the crêpes are warming. Then add the cognac and the Grand Marnier.

⁀ Heat for a few seconds, then flame the crêpes, stirring until the flame dies down. You may add more cognac, to taste. Serve 3 crêpes to each person.

ORANGE CRÊPES

These crêpes may be cooked several hours in advance and kept at room temperature. Reheat them in the sauce when ready to serve.

CRÊPE BATTER:

1 cup (250 mL) pastry flour
¼ cup (50 mL) fine sugar
½ tsp (2 mL) salt
1 cup (250 mL) milk
1 tsp (5 mL) grated orange zest
2 eggs, well beaten

ORANGE SAUCE:

4 tbsp (60 mL) butter
½ cup (125 mL) icing sugar
4 tbsp (60 mL) grated orange zest
½ cup (125 mL) orange juice
2 tbsp (30 mL) cognac

⁀ To prepare the crêpes, sift together the flour, sugar and salt. Add the milk, grated orange zest and well-beaten eggs. Beat until the batter is very light.

⁀ Heat a crêpe pan or small skillet and brush it with melted butter. Pour in just enough batter to cover the bottom, swirling the batter to cover the pan evenly. Cook until the bottom is golden, then lift the edge with a knife and grasp with your fingers to turn the crêpe. Cook the second side.

⁀ To prepare the sauce, cream the butter, then gradually beat in the icing sugar. When well mixed, add the orange zest and the juice. Bring the mixture to a boil, then add the cognac, to taste.

⁀ To serve, roll the crêpes like jelly rolls. Arrange the rolls in the orange sauce and warm them over low heat, basting the crêpes with sauce until they are well coated and very warm.

FRUIT CRÊPES

⁀ To make these the easy way, use a prepared pancake mix —either buttermilk, buckwheat or plain—but add about ½ cup (125 mL) more liquid than the instructions call for. The result will be light, fluffy pancakes, so much nicer than the thick, heavy type.

⁀ If you have an electric skillet, you can prepare the crêpes right on the table; arrange the pan with a jug of prepared batter and the fruits, syrup and butter nearby. (The batter can be mixed the night before and refrigerated, covered, until ready to use.) This way you can serve the pancakes freshly made and piping hot. A warmer filled with crispy broiled bacon can complete the picture.

⁀ For the fruit, use sweetened fresh blueberries or sliced strawberries. Or use thawed frozen berries, drained well. You will need ⅔ to 1 cup (150 to 250 mL) berries for every 3 cups (750 mL) of batter.

🍃 Once the crêpes are cooked, lay a spoonful or two of fruit down the center of each and roll them.

🍃 Use the drained syrup from the frozen berries to make a syrup. Boil it for 10 minutes with an equal quantity of sugar and the juice of 1 lemon; or serve the crêpes with maple syrup.

CANADIAN BUCKWHEAT BLINI

1¼ cups (300 mL) milk
1 tsp (5 mL) sugar
½ cup (125 mL) warm water
1 package active dry yeast
2 cups (500 mL) buckwheat flour
4 eggs, separated
1 tsp (5 mL) salt
1 tbsp (15 mL) sugar
2 tsp (10 mL) soft butter
or margarine

🍃 Heat the milk to just below the boiling point, then let it cool. Stir the 1 tsp (5 mL) sugar into the warm water until dissolved. Add the yeast and let stand for 10 minutes. Stir well.

🍃 Add the yeast mixture to the lukewarm milk. Beat in 1 cup (250 mL) of the buckwheat flour. When well blended, cover the bowl with a cloth and let the batter rise in a warm place, free of drafts, until the mixture is spongy. Beat down the mixture with a wooden spoon.

🍃 Beat the egg yolks until they are thick and lemon colored. Add the salt and the 1 tbsp (15 mL) sugar. Mix well, then add the yolk mixture to the sponge mixture.

Beat until well mixed, then add the soft butter or margarine. Stir in the rest of the buckwheat flour.

🍃 Beat the egg whites until stiff. Fold them gently into the batter.

🍃 Cover and let the batter rise in a warm place, free of drafts, for about 25 minutes or until double in bulk.

🍃 Heat and lightly grease a griddle or cast-iron skillet with vegetable shortening or margarine. Drop the dough by spoonfuls onto the skillet. Each cooked blini should measure about 3 in. (8 cm) in diameter. Cook until small bubbles form on the top surface, then turn each crêpe and cook on the other side.

🍃 Serve hot, Russian-style, with caviar and sour cream, or Prairies-style with soft or melted butter and molasses.

MUSHROOM CRÊPES

½ lb (250 g) fresh mushrooms
3 tbsp (45 mL) butter
salt and pepper to taste
pinch of tarragon
2 cups (500 mL) crêpe batter
(your choice)
3 tbsp (45 mL) butter
2 tbsp (30 mL) fresh lemon juice

🍃 Slice the mushroom stems and caps very thinly. Heat the 3 tbsp (45 mL) butter and brown the mushrooms in it for 2 minutes over high heat, stirring constantly. Remove the mushrooms from the heat and add the salt, pepper and tarragon.

🍃 Prepare a pancake batter of your choice. Stir in the cooked mushrooms. Cook small crêpes in a lightly buttered skillet or crêpe pan.

🍃 Heat the 3 tbsp (45 mL) butter with the lemon juice. Serve this lemon butter with the crêpes. If you prefer, these crêpes can be sprinkled with Parmesan cheese and browned under the broiler for a few seconds before serving with the lemon butter.

DOUGHNUTS

If you want to turn out light, non-greasy doughnuts every time, follow some basic rules.

🍃 Once you have creamed the butter or shortening, cream in the sugar one spoonful at a time, beating vigorously after each addition. This process of dissolving the sugar completely is essential in order to produce a tender and evenly-browned doughnut.

🍃 Never add the total amount of flour all at once; the dough must be as soft as possible. The best way to proceed is to divide the total flour called for into three. Add the first and second quantity all at once, beating each addition in well. Add the third quantity gradually, beating thoroughly to incorporate each bit, and stopping as soon as the dough is barely firm enough to handle.

🍃 The dough will be much easier to work with if you refrigerate it for 4 to 12 hours before rolling it out. Even a very soft dough is very easy to roll when chilled.

🍩 Roll the dough and cut the doughnuts, then let them stand on a lightly floured surface for 15 minutes before cooking them. This makes for lighter doughnuts.

🍩 The fat should be heated to between 360°F and 375°F (180°C and 190°C), measured accurately on a deep-frying thermometer. If the fat is too hot, the doughnuts will be half-cooked in the center. If it is not hot enough, the doughnuts will be soggy and greasy.

🍩 If you do not have a thermometer, here is an easy way to test the temperature of the fat: drop a piece of dough into the hot fat—it should sink to the bottom of the saucepan and then rise almost immediately; if it remains on the bottom too long, the fat is not yet hot enough.

🍩 It is a good idea to cook only a few doughnuts at a time. If too many are added at once, the temperature of the fat will drop and the doughnuts will tend to absorb the fat and become greasy.

🍩 Properly cooked doughnuts should not start to turn golden until they have been in the hot fat for about 3 minutes. If they brown more quickly, you will know that the fat is too hot.

🍩 Turn the doughnuts only once during cooking, at the moment they rise to the surface.

🍩 You will recognize a perfect doughnut by the fact that it is light, non-greasy, almost double its original size, round, and a nice golden color.

Mushroom Crêpes

PLAIN DOUGHNUTS

3 tbsp (45 mL) butter
1 cup (250 mL) sugar
2 eggs, beaten
3¾ cups (925 mL) all-purpose flour
4 tsp (20 mL) baking powder
½ tsp (2 mL) salt
¾ cup (175 mL) milk
1 tsp (5 mL) vanilla

🍩 Cream the butter and add the sugar, a spoonful at a time, alternating with a spoonful of beaten egg. Beat until the sugar mixture is light and creamy.

🍩 Sift the flour together with the baking powder and the salt. Divide into 3 portions.

🍩 Combine the milk with the vanilla. Beat it into the creamed ingredients alternately with the sifted dry ingredients, using no more flour than is necessary to make a soft dough.

🍩 Cover and refrigerate the dough for 4 to 12 hours.

🍩 Divide the dough into 3 balls. Roll out 1 ball at a time, keeping the rest of the dough in the refrigerator while you work.

🍩 Roll the dough ⅓ in. (0.8 cm) thick on a lightly floured surface. Cut with a doughnut cutter or 2 cookie cutters of different sizes. Let the doughnuts stand for 15 minutes before cooking them.

🍩 Heat the fat of your choice to between 360° and 375°F (180° to 190°C). You will need at least 3 in. (8 cm) of hot fat in the pot or deep fryer.

🍂 Drop the doughnuts, one by one, into the hot fat. Do not crowd them.

🍂 When each doughnut is cooked, place it on a paper towel to absorb any excess fat.

🍂 When the doughnuts have cooled, roll them in fine sugar or icing sugar.

ORANGE DOUGHNUTS

Add 1 tsp (5 mL) mace to the dry ingredients and 1 tbsp (15 mL) grated orange zest to the milk.

SOUR MILK DOUGHNUTS

Reduce the amount of baking powder to 2 tsp (10 mL) instead of the 4 tsp (20 mL) called for in the basic recipe; add ½ tsp (2 mL) baking soda. Replace the fresh milk with sour milk. Flavor with ¾ tsp (3 mL) nutmeg.

SPICE DOUGHNUTS

Add ½ tsp (2 mL) nutmeg and ¼ tsp (1 mL) cinnamon to the dry ingredients.

DOUGHNUTS IN HONEY SYRUP

DOUGH:
3 eggs
1 cup (250 mL) sugar
2 tbsp (30 mL) soft butter
3¾ cups (925 mL) all-purpose flour
2 tsp (10 mL) baking powder
1 tsp (5 mL) baking soda
1 tsp (5 mL) salt
¾ tsp (3 mL) nutmeg or mace
⅔ cup (150 mL) sour milk or buttermilk

HONEY SYRUP:
1 cup (250 mL) sugar
1 cup (250 mL) honey
1 cup (250 mL) water
1 tsp (5 mL) lemon juice

🍂 To prepare the doughnut dough, use an electric mixer at high speed to beat together the eggs and sugar in a large bowl until the mixture is light and fluffy. Add the butter and beat for a few more minutes.

🍂 In the meantime, sift the flour together with the baking powder, baking soda, salt and nutmeg or mace.

🍂 Lower the speed of the mixer and add the milk bit by bit to the sugar mixture. Then, still at low speed, gradually add the flour mixture and beat long enough to blend thoroughly. The dough will be quite soft.

🍂 Cover the bowl and refrigerate for 3 to 12 hours.

🍂 To prepare the honey syrup, in a saucepan, boil the sugar with the honey and the water for approximately 5 minutes, scraping the side of the pan from time to time so the sugar does not crystallize around the edge. Cover the pan for the first 2 minutes of cooking.

🍂 Remove from heat, add the lemon juice, stir for 1 second and place the saucepan in a larger pan of boiling water.

🍂 Dip the warm doughnuts in the hot syrup. Spread brown or wax paper on the table, place a cake rack on top and put the doughnuts on the rack to drain and cool.

FRUIT FRITTERS

1½ cups (375 mL) all-purpose flour
2 tbsp (30 mL) sugar
½ cup (125 mL) warm water
2 tbsp (30 mL) melted butter
¼ cup (50 mL) cognac
pinch of salt
2 eggs, separated

🍂 Mix together the flour and sugar, then add the warm water and the melted butter little by little until the dough is smooth and thick (you may need to use a little less or a little more water than called for in the recipe).

🍂 Add the cognac, the salt and the beaten egg yolks. The batter should now have the consistency of heavy cream.

🍂 Beat the egg whites until stiff and fold them into the batter.

🍂 Peel and slice or cube fresh fruit of your choice, or use well-drained canned fruit. Stir the fruit into the batter until each piece is well-coated.

🍂 Drop spoonfuls of the fruit mixture into deep fat heated to 375°F (190°C) and cook until the fritters are golden brown. Serve hot with maple syrup or melted butter, honey and lemon juice.

VEGETABLE FRITTERS

2 eggs, separated
⅔ cup (150 mL) milk
1 tbsp (15 mL) lemon juice

1 tbsp (15 mL) melted butter
1 cup (250 mL) all-purpose flour
½ tsp (2 mL) salt

❧ Beat the egg yolks until light and foamy. Add the milk, lemon juice and melted butter. Mix well.

❧ Sift the flour and salt into the egg mixture and stir just enough to mix.

❧ Beat the egg whites until firm and fold them into the batter.

❧ This batter can be used for fruit or vegetable fritters. Dip pieces of the food of your choice in the batter and drop carefully into deep fat heated to 375°F (190°C).

Choux Paste Fritters

BANANA FRITTERS

4 bananas
¼ cup (50 mL) icing sugar
2 tbsp (30 mL) rum or lemon juice
fritter batter

❧ Peel the bananas. Cut them in two lengthwise, then cut each half in two. Place in a dish and sprinkle with the icing sugar and the rum or lemon juice. Cover and let stand for 30 minutes, turning the bananas several times to coat them well.

❧ Dip each piece of banana in batter and deep-fry until golden brown in fat heated to 375°F (190°C).

CHOUX PASTE FRITTERS

1 cup (250 mL) water
½ cup (125 mL) butter
½ tsp (2 mL) salt
1 tsp (5 mL) sugar
1 cup (250 mL) all-purpose flour
4 whole eggs
2 egg whites, stiffly beaten
vanilla, lemon juice, and brandy or rum

❧ Bring the water to a boil in a saucepan, together with the butter, salt and sugar. When the butter is melted and the water is boiling vigorously, remove from the heat.

❧ Add the flour all at once and stir vigorously until the mixture forms a ball. Return to low heat and stir for another 1 or 2 minutes.

❧ Remove from the heat and add the eggs, one at a time, beating well after each addition. Flavor to taste with vanilla, lemon juice and rum or brandy. Fold in the stiffly beaten egg whites.

❧ Heat deep fat to 375°F (190°C).

❧ Fill a tablespoon with some of the dough; with a knife, cut the lump of dough in half and slip it into the hot fat. Then slide in the other half. Continue in this manner until all the dough has been used. Cook in batches rather than crowd the pan.

❧ Serve hot, sprinkled with icing sugar or with a French custard.

❦ TECHNIQUE ❦

CHOUX PASTE FRITTERS

1 Bring the water to a boil together with the butter, salt and sugar.

2 Remove from the heat, then add the flour all at once and beat vigorously. Return to low heat and stir for 1 or 2 minutes.

3 Remove from the heat, then add the eggs, one at a time, beating vigorously after each addition.

4 Fold in the stiffly beaten egg whites.

PICKLES AND RELISHES

TIPS FOR MAKING PICKLES AND RELISHES

UTENSILS

Store the salt for pickles in a stoneware jar or a waxed wooden tub.

❧ Use saucepans made from glass, stainless steel or enameled cast-iron when cooking pickles.

❧ Stir with stainless steel or wooden spoons.

❧ Store in glass jars, preferably those with fitted glass lids.

❧ Weigh the salt carefully on a kitchen scale in order to ensure a successful brine.

INGREDIENTS

Select top-quality vegetables. Cucumbers and tomatoes should be used as soon as possible after they have been picked. Fruit should be just ripe.

❧ Wash the fruit and vegetables with care. Always cut food into pieces of the same size so that the liquid used in the pickling process can permeate them evenly.

❧ Use vinegar of the highest quality. Wine vinegar is the best as it does not deteriorate. The acid content should be from 4 to 6 percent—most of the bottled vinegars on the market are of this strength, but read the label to be sure. Because of its special flavor, cider vinegar is ideally suited to most pickles, but white vinegar should be used with such vegetables as cauliflower and onions to preserve their natural light color.

❧ Unless a recipe states otherwise, it is best to use whole spices. Place them in a cheesecloth bag if they are to be cooked with the fruit or vegetables. (The bag should be large enough to let the pickling liquid flow freely through the spices.) Remove the bag before packing the pickles in jars.

❧ Use soft water, if possible, especially for long-process pickles—the minerals in hard water will interfere with the curing process. If the water is very hard, boil it, let it cool and strain it through several thicknesses of fine linen.

❧ Brine is made from water and coarse salt. (Many shops sell special pickling salt.) Add the required amount of salt to enough water to cover the vegetables to be pickled. One way of ensuring a perfect brine is to drop an egg into the solution: if it rises to the surface, the proportions are correct.

❧ Brine renders vegetables porous, enabling them to absorb the sugar, vinegar and seasonings more easily.

❧ Always cover the vegetables soaking in brine with a plate. Place a heavy weight on top. Allow to stand for 24 hours in a cool place. Drain well before proceeding.

❧ The usual proportions for brine are 1 tsp (5 mL) salt to every 4 cups (1 L) water for vegetables and 2 tsp (10 mL) salt to every 4 cups (1 L) water for meat.

❧ Certain vegetables, such as corn, cauliflower and green peas, should not be left to soak in brine. The brine for these vegetables is also different: use ½ cup (125 mL) coarse salt to every 8 cups (2 L) water.

❧ Cauliflower will change color if the acidity of the vinegar is lower than 4 to 6 percent. It will also change color if the brine is too weak or if it is made with fine salt or hard water. If the brine is made with fine salt, the vinegar may turn milky. This occurs when the salt combines with the starch from certain vegetables.

❧ Catsup may turn sour if the tomatoes used are not ripe enough or if the recipe does not contain enough salt or vinegar.

❧ For every 10 lbs (4.5 kg) tomatoes, add 2 tbsp (30 mL) salt, 1 cup (250 mL) vinegar and ½ cup (125 mL) sugar. The tomato pulp can be boiled with 2 or 3 onions and 3 or 4 green peppers before the spices, salt and vinegar are added.

CANNING

FRUITS: STERILIZING

Foods for canning can be sterilized in the oven rather than in boiling water, but this will take longer and is effective only in the case of fruits.

❧ To use this method, first close the jars tightly, then open them ¼ in. (0.6 cm). Place them in a dish 3 in. (8 cm) deep, leaving a space of 2 in. (5 cm) between each jar. Add hot water and place the dish in the center of a 275°F (140°C) oven. Do not vary the oven temperature or the sterilization times required.

❧ The following times apply to sterilizing 4-cup (1-L) or 2-cup (500-mL) canning jars:

❧ Small fruits: boiling water, 20 minutes; oven, 68 minutes
❧ Peaches: boiling water, 25 minutes; oven, 1 hour
❧ Rhubarb: boiling water, 16 minutes; oven, 50 minutes
❧ Apples: boiling water, 20 minutes; oven, 1 hour

ENGLISH CHUTNEY

24 ripe tomatoes, peeled and sliced
4 green peppers, diced
12 peaches, peeled and sliced
4 onions, peeled and sliced
½ lb (250 g) seedless raisins
1 cup (250 mL) ginger in syrup
4 cups (1 L) brown sugar
1 tbsp (15 mL) coarse salt

❧ Mix all the ingredients together in a saucepan. Bring to a boil and cook slowly, stirring frequently, for approximately 3 hours or until the chutney is thick.
❧ Turn the chutney into sterilized jars. Seal.

GOOSEBERRY CHUTNEY

2 lbs (1 kg) green gooseberries
1 lb (500 g) red onions
1 package raisins
1 cup (250 mL) dark brown sugar
1 tbsp (15 mL) dry mustard
1 tbsp (15 mL) ginger

English Chutney

2 tbsp (30 mL) coarse salt
¼ tsp (1 mL) cayenne
1 tsp (5 mL) turmeric
2 cups (500 mL) cider vinegar

❧ Wash and clean the gooseberries. Peel and slice the onions. Chop the gooseberries, onions and raisins in a food processor. Place in a saucepan with any juice that might have accumulated.
❧ Add the brown sugar, dry mustard, ginger, coarse salt, cayenne and turmeric. Mix well, then add the vinegar. Bring to a boil over low heat. Simmer for 45 minutes or until the mixture thickens.
❧ Force through a fine sieve, pressing with the back of a wooden spoon.
❧ Turn the chutney into sterilized jars. Seal.

DAMSON CHUTNEY

6 lbs (2.5 kg) damson plums
2 lbs (1 kg) yellow onions
4 lbs (2 kg) apples
3 cups (750 mL) white vinegar
2 lbs (1 kg) sugar
2 lbs (1 kg) dark brown sugar
1 tbsp (15 mL) ground allspice
1 tbsp (15 mL) ground cloves
1 tbsp (15 mL) ginger
3 tbsp (45 mL) coarse salt
1 tsp (5 mL) cayenne

❧ Wash, halve and pit the plums. Peel the onions and cut them into thin slices. Peel, core and grate the apples.
❧ Place the plums, onions and apples in a saucepan along with the vinegar. Bring to a boil, stirring constantly.
❧ Add the remaining ingredients.

Return to a boil, then simmer, uncovered, for 1½ hours.

🍃 Turn the chutney into sterilized jars. Seal.

APRICOT CHUTNEY

2 lbs (1 kg) dried apricots
1½ lbs (750 g) brown sugar
2 tsp (10 mL) coriander
2 onions
5 cloves garlic, minced
2 tbsp (30 mL) coarse salt
2 tsp (10 mL) grated fresh ginger
1 cup (250 mL) sultana raisins
2 cups (500 mL) cider vinegar
or white wine

🍃 Soak the apricots in cold water for 8 hours. Drain well. Cut the onions in thin rings.

🍃 Place the apricots in an enameled cast-iron saucepan along with the remaining ingredients. Mix well.

🍃 Cook over low heat, stirring frequently, until the mixture is the consistency of jam—about 40 to 60 minutes.

🍃 Turn the chutney into sterilized jars. Seal.

CANTALOUPE CHUTNEY

1 large cantaloupe, not too ripe
4 green peppers
5 cups (1.2 L) cider vinegar
1 lb (500 g) light brown sugar
1 tbsp (15 mL) whole allspice
1 tsp (5 mL) cayenne
2 tbsp (30 mL) coarse salt

2 cups (500 mL) raisins
½ lb (250 g) dried apricots
½ lb (250 g) candied ginger
3 cloves garlic, minced

🍃 Peel the cantaloupe and remove the seeds and fiber. Cut the fruit into 1-in. (2-cm) cubes.

🍃 Clean and chop the green peppers.

🍃 Add the brown sugar to 4 cups (1 L) of the vinegar and bring to a boil. Place the whole allspice in a cheesecloth bag and add to the syrup along with the cayenne and the coarse salt. Boil for 15 minutes.

🍃 Add the green peppers, raisins, quartered apricots, ginger and garlic. Boil for 30 minutes.

🍃 Add the cantaloupe and boil for 15 minutes. Add the remaining cup of vinegar and continue cooking for another 30 minutes, making sure the mixture does not stick.

🍃 Turn the chutney into sterilized jars.

PINEAPPLE CHUTNEY

1 3-lb (1.5-kg) pineapple
3 cups (750 mL) cider vinegar
3 cups (750 mL) sugar
1½ tsp (7 mL) crushed hot red pepper
3 cloves garlic, minced
2 tbsp (30 mL) grated gingerroot
1 tbsp (15 mL) coarse salt
½ lb (250 g) raisins
½ lb (250 g) blanched almonds

🍃 Peel and dice the pineapple.

🍃 Make a syrup with the cider vinegar and the sugar. Add the pineapple and the remaining ingredients. Mix well.

🍃 Simmer, stirring frequently, for 2 hours or until the mixture is thickened.

🍃 Turn the chutney into sterilized jars. Seal.

DATE CHUTNEY

2 lbs (1 kg) pitted dates
1 lb (500 g) onions, peeled and quartered
1½ tbsp (25 mL) allspice
1 tsp (5 mL) peppercorns
2 tbsp (30 mL) mustard seed
1 tsp (5 mL) ground ginger
½ tsp (2 mL) cayenne
2 tbsp (30 mL) coarse salt
2 cups (500 mL) cider vinegar
2 cups (500 mL) sugar

🍃 Chop up the dates and the onions. Place in an enameled cast-iron saucepan.

🍃 Put the allspice, peppercorns, mustard seed, ground ginger, cayenne and coarse salt in a cheesecloth bag and tie securely. Add to the dates along with 1 cup (250 mL) of the vinegar. Simmer, stirring frequently, until the mixture is thickened.

🍃 Place the sugar in a pie plate and heat in a 300°F (150°C) oven for 20 minutes.

🍃 Add the heated sugar to the dates along with the remaining 1 cup (250 mL) vinegar. Cook until the mixture is thickened again, stirring frequently to prevent it from sticking to the bottom of the pot. Remove the bag of spices.

🍃 Turn the chutney into sterilized jars. Seal.

SUMMER FRUIT RELISH

4 ripe tomatoes
1 onion
4 pears
4 peaches
1 green pepper
½ cup (125 mL) sugar
1½ cups (375 mL) cider vinegar
2 tsp (10 mL) salt
¼ tsp (1 mL) cayenne
pinch of ground cinnamon
pinch of ground cloves

🍃 Wash and peel the tomatoes and the onion. Core the pears and remove the stones from the peaches. Seed the green pepper and remove the fiber.

🍃 Put the fruits through the medium blade of a food processor.

🍃 Add the tomatoes, onion, pears, peaches and green pepper to the remaining ingredients. Bring to a boil, then simmer, stirring frequently, for 1½ hours or until the relish is thick.

🍃 Turn the relish into heated jars. Seal.

CANTALOUPE RELISH

5 cantaloupes, not too ripe
4 cups (1 L) cold water
¼ cup (50 mL) coarse salt

7 cups (1.8 L) sugar
2 cups (500 mL) white vinegar
2 whole cloves
1 cinnamon stick

🍃 Cut the cantaloupes into 8 sections. Remove the seeds and the fiber. Peel thinly so that the fruit retains a little of the green flesh found just under the skin. Cut each section into triangular pieces.

🍃 Prepare a brine with the water and the coarse salt. Pour over the cantaloupe. Let stand for 2 hours. Drain and then rinse thoroughly under running cold water.

🍃 Place the cantaloupe in a large saucepan and cover with cold water. Bring to a boil, then simmer for approximately 15 minutes or until the cantaloupe is tender but not too soft. Drain.

🍃 Prepare a syrup with the sugar, vinegar, cloves and cinnamon.

Bring to a vigorous boil and pour over the cantaloupe. Let stand overnight.

🍃 The following day, bring the mixture to a boil again.

🍃 Remove from the heat. Turn the chutney into sterilized jars and seal.

PICKLED PEARS

juice of 1 lemon
4 cups (1 L) cold water
7 or 8 small pears (1½ to 2 lbs or 750 g to 1 kg)
4 cups (1 L) sugar
2 cups (500 mL) cider vinegar
2 cinnamon sticks
2 tbsp (30 mL) whole cloves

🍃 Add the lemon juice to the cold water.

🍃 Wash the pears and peel them as closely as possible. As soon as

Pickled Pears

each pear is peeled, drop it into the cold water and lemon juice.

🍂 Halve each pear lengthwise and remove the core. Return to the acidulated water.

🍂 Prepare a syrup with the sugar, vinegar, cinnamon sticks and whole cloves. Bring to a boil and cook for 20 minutes. (This amount of syrup is sufficient for 12 cups or 3 L of pear preserve.)

🍂 Sterilize the jars and place them close at hand.

🍂 Add the pears to the boiling syrup.

🍂 Simmer 5 to 10 minutes or until the pears are tender.

🍂 Remove the pears from the syrup and pack into the sterilized jars. Cover with the syrup to ½ in. (1 cm) of the brim. Place a cinnamon stick in each jar. Before closing each one, run the blade of a knife around the inside to remove air bubbles. Wipe the jar clean. Seal.

🍂 Turn each jar upside-down on a folded cloth and leave to cool.

SPICED PLUMS

4 lbs (2 kg) plums
2 lbs (1 kg) sugar
2 cups (500 mL) vinegar
3 cinnamon sticks
6 whole cloves
½ tsp (2 mL) salt

🍂 Wash, halve and pit the plums.

🍂 In a large saucepan, mix together the remaining ingredients and bring to a boil. Reduce

the heat and cook gently for 3 minutes.

🍂 Add the plums and continue to cook gently for about 5 minutes.

🍂 Place in 4-cup (1-L) jars.

🍂 Bring the syrup to a boil once again and pour over the fruit, filling each jar almost to the brim. Seal.

PICKLED CRAB APPLES

🍂 To yield 4 cups (1 L) of the preserve, you will need 2 lbs (900 g) crab apples.

🍂 Wash the crab apples, but do not peel them or remove the stems.

🍂 Follow the recipe for *Pickled Pears* (see previous page), but add an extra 1 tsp (5 mL) cloves to the syrup.

🍂 Place in sterilized jars, following the same procedure as for pickled pears.

PEARS PICKLED IN PORT WINE

1 cup (250 mL) honey
¾ cup (175 mL) wine vinegar
10 cloves
1 cinnamon stick
¾ cup (175 mL) port
8 to 10 small pears

🍂 Bring to a boil the honey, vinegar, cloves and cinnamon. Boil for

5 minutes. Remove from the heat and add the port.

🍂 Halve the pears lengthwise and core them.

🍂 Add the pears to the syrup. Bring to a boil and simmer for 15 minutes or until the pears are tender.

🍂 Pack in jars and seal.

🍂 Store in a cool place.

PICKLED APRICOTS

🍂 To yield 4 cups (1 L) of preserve, you will need 26 apricots (2 lbs or 900 g).

🍂 Wipe the apricots with a damp cloth. Halve but do not peel them.

🍂 Follow the recipe for *Pickled Pears* (see previous page).

PICKLED PEACHES

🍂 To yield 4 cups (1 L) of preserve, you will need 6 small peaches (1½ lbs or 750 g).

🍂 An easy way of peeling peaches is to drop them into boiling water and let them stand for 1 minute. Drain them and put them in cold water; the skins should then slide off easily.

🍂 To prevent the peaches turning brown once they are peeled, place them in a solution made from 2 tsp (10 mL) salt in 4 cups (1 L) cold water. Rinse before using them.

🍂 Proceed according to the recipe for *Pickled Pears* (see previous page).

PICKLED PUMPKIN

6 lbs (3 kg) pumpkin
5 lbs (2.5 kg) sugar
2 cups (500 mL) white vinegar
2 tbsp (30 mL) whole cloves
6 cinnamon sticks

➣ Peel the pumpkin and remove the seeds and fiber from the center. Cut into thin slices. Cover with the sugar and let stand overnight.

➣ The next day, add the vinegar, cloves and cinnamon to the pumpkin and cook over medium heat for 1 to 1¼ hours or until the mixture is thickened.

➣ Turn the pumpkin into 6 sterilized 2-cup (500-mL) jars and pour any remaining syrup on top. Seal.

CAULIFLOWER AND ONION PICKLES

4 medium-size heads of cauliflower
1 cup (250 mL) coarse salt
16 cups (4 L) small, white pickling onions
4 cups (1 L) cold water
¼ cup (50 mL) pickling spices
2 cups (500 mL) sugar
8 cups (2 L) white vinegar

➣ Wash the cauliflower and separate into small florets. Sprinkle with ½ cup (125 mL) of the coarse salt. Cover with a cloth and let stand for 12 hours. Drain and rinse thoroughly under running cold water.

➣ Pour boiling water over the pickling onions. Let stand for

Cauliflower and Onion Pickles

2 minutes. Drain and cover with cold water so they will be easy to peel.

➣ Make a brine with 4 cups (1 L) cold water and the remaining ½ cup (125 mL) coarse salt. Add the onions and soak for 12 hours. Drain and rinse thoroughly under running cold water.

➣ Put the pickling spices in a cheesecloth bag.

➣ Place the bag of spices, vinegar and sugar in a saucepan and bring to a boil over low heat, stirring continuously. Add the onions and cauliflower. Return to the boil.

➣ Remove the vegetables from the heat, turn into heated sterilized jars and seal while hot.

PEPPER AND TOMATO RELISH

12 green peppers
12 red peppers
12 onions
12 green tomatoes
3 cups (750 mL) white vinegar
3 cups (750 mL) sugar
3 tbsp (45 mL) coarse salt

➣ Wash the peppers and cut in half lengthwise. Remove the seeds and the fiber. Peel the onions. Wash, core and quarter the green tomatoes.

➣ Pour enough boiling water over the mixed peppers and onions to completely cover. Let stand for 5 minutes. Drain. Add the quartered tomatoes.

➣ Chop the peppers, onions and tomatoes in a food processor.

➣ Bring the vinegar, sugar and salt to a boil. Add the vegetables and boil for 10 minutes or until thickened.

➣ Turn the relish into heated jars and seal.

Cucumber Relish

GREEN TOMATO RELISH

7½ lbs (3.5 kg) green tomatoes
½ cup (125 mL) coarse salt
5 yellow onions
2 cups (500 mL) sugar
2 cups (500 mL) white vinegar
1 tbsp (15 mL) mustard seed
1 tsp (5 mL) celery seed
1 tsp (5 mL) peppercorns
1 tsp (5 mL) ginger
1 tsp (5 mL) turmeric
1 tsp (5 mL) salt

🍂 Wash and chop the tomatoes. Slice the onions and separate into rings. Mix the tomatoes and onions together and sprinkle with the ½ cup (125 mL) coarse salt. Let stand for 1 hour. Rinse under running cold water and drain well.

🍂 Meanwhile, place the rest of the ingredients in a saucepan along with the 1 tsp (5 mL) salt. Cook over low heat until the sugar is dissolved. Add the drained tomatoes and onions. Bring to a boil and immediately remove from the heat.

🍂 Place the vegetables in sterilized jars and cover with the hot syrup. Run the blade of a knife around the inside of each jar to remove any air bubbles. Seal.

YELLOW CUCUMBER PICKLES

12 large yellow cucumbers
½ cup (125 mL) coarse salt
16 cups (4 L) cold water
4 cups (1 L) vinegar
2 lbs (1 kg) sugar
3 tbsp (45 mL) pickling spices

🍂 Peel the cucumbers and cut in half lengthwise. Remove the seeds and the soft pulp. Then cut each half into 4 fingers.

🍂 Prepare a brine with the coarse salt and the cold water. Soak the cucumbers in the brine for 2 days. Drain thoroughly.

🍂 Prepare a syrup with the vinegar and the sugar. Place the pickling spices in a cheesecloth bag and add to the mixture. When the syrup reaches a hard boil, add the well-drained cucumber fingers and cook over medium heat for 1 hour or until transparent.

🍂 Pack the cucumbers side by side lengthwise in sterilized 2-cup (500-mL) jars. Cover with boiling syrup. Seal.

CUCUMBER RELISH

6 large cucumbers
4 large onions
¼ cup (50 mL) coarse salt
2 cups (500 mL) vinegar
¾ cup (175 mL) sugar
1 tsp (5 mL) celery seed
1 tsp (5 mL) mustard seed

🍂 Wash the cucumbers (do not peel) and cut into thin slices. Peel the onions. Cut into thin slices and then break the slices into rings.

🍂 Place the cucumbers and onions in a large earthenware or glass bowl. Do not use a metal container. Sprinkle with the coarse salt. Mix together and let stand for 2 hours.

🍂 Heat the vinegar with the sugar, celery seed and mustard seed. Boil for 3 minutes.

🍂 Rinse the vegetables under running cold water and drain them well.

🍂 Tightly pack the cucumbers and onions into 2-cup (500-mL) jars. Cover with the hot vinegar. Seal.

🍂 Store in a cold place.

CRUNCHY CUCUMBERS

8 medium cucumbers
2 tbsp (30 mL) salt
6 medium onions
4 cups (1 L) vinegar
1 tsp (5 mL) dry mustard
2 tsp (10 mL) mustard seed
2 tsp (10 mL) celery seed
½ tsp (2 mL) turmeric
2 cups (500 mL) sugar

🍂 Wash the cucumbers and cut into thin slices. There should be 16 cups (4 L). Cover with the salt and crushed ice. Let stand for approximately 3 hours, then drain well.

🍂 Peel the onions and cut into very thin slices. Add to the cucumbers with the remaining ingredients and bring just to the boil. Remove from the heat.

🍂 Place the vegetables in 6 or 7 sterilized jars and fill almost to the brim with the vinegar mixture. Seal well.

OLD-FASHIONED SWEET PICKLES

16 cups (4 L) cucumbers, unpeeled, cut into 1-in. (2.5-cm) lengths

1½ cups (375 mL) salt
16 cups (4 L) water
9 cups (2.5 L) cider vinegar
5 cups (1.2 L) sugar
3 cups (750 mL) water
2 tbsp (30 mL) pickling spices

🍂 Place the pieces of cucumber in an earthenware dish. Dissolve the salt in the 16 cups (4 L) water and pour the brine over the cucumber. Place a weighted plate over the cucumber pieces so that they remain immersed. Soak for 36 hours, then drain.

🍂 Pour 4 cups (1 L) of the vinegar over the cucumbers and add enough water to cover. Bring to a boil, then simmer for 10 minutes. Drain.

🍂 Place the pickling spices in a cheesecloth bag.

🍂 Mix 2 cups (500 mL) of the sugar with the 3 cups (750 mL) water and the remaining vinegar. Add the bag of spices. Bring to a boil and then simmer for 10 minutes. Remove the spices.

🍂 Pour the spiced vinegar over the cucumbers. Let stand for 24 hours.

🍂 Drain the liquid into a saucepan, add the remaining sugar and bring to a boil. Pour over the cucumbers and let stand another 24 hours.

🍂 Pack the cucumbers in heated jars.

🍂 Bring the syrup to a boil and pour boiling hot over the cucumbers to cover. Seal.

SWEET PICKLES

12 whole allspice
12 peppercorns
3 cinnamon sticks
1 piece ginger root
24 whole cloves
10 cups (2.5 L) vinegar
4 cups (1 L) water
2 cups (500 mL) brown sugar
100 small gherkins

🍂 Place the spices in a cheesecloth bag.

🍂 Mix together the vinegar, water and brown sugar. Add the gherkins and the bag of spices.

🍂 Bring to a boil over medium heat. Reduce the heat and simmer for 3 hours or until the liquid resembles a light syrup. Remove the spices.

🍂 Put the gherkins in sterilized jars and cover them with the boiling syrup. Seal.

🍂 Store in a dark place for 3 weeks before using.

JIFFY SWEET PICKLES

8 cups (2 L) small gherkins
8 cups (2 L) water
½ cup (125 mL) coarse salt
6 cups (1.5 L) brown sugar
4 cups (1 L) cider vinegar
1 tbsp (15 mL) whole cloves
½ tbsp (7 mL) celery seeds
½ tbsp (7 mL) mustard seeds
1 stick cinnamon
bay leaves
hot pepper (optional)

❧Wash the gherkins and soak overnight in a brine made with the water and the salt.

❧The next day, drain the gherkins. Rinse them under running hot water and drain again.

❧Place the spices in a cheese-cloth bag.

❧Bring the cider vinegar and brown sugar to a boil in a large saucepan. Add the gherkins and the bag of spices. Remove from the heat and let the gherkins cool in the syrup.

❧Remove the bag of spices and turn the pickles into 1-cup (250-mL) jars. Add 1 bay leaf to each jar. If desired, add a hot pepper as well.

❧Bring the syrup to a boil and use it to fill the jars to the brim. Seal.

DILL PICKLES

100 small gherkins
16 cups (4 L) cold water
1½ cups (375 mL) coarse salt
40 cups (10 L) water
4 cups (1 L) white vinegar
2 cups (500 mL) coarse salt
sprigs fresh dill
1 cup (250 mL) mustard seed (optional)
1 cup (250mL) grated horseradish, (optional)

❧Wash the gherkins and soak for 12 hours in a solution made from the 16 cups (4 L) cold water and the 1½ cups (375 mL) coarse salt.

❧Bring to a boil the 40 cups (10 L) water, the vinegar and the 2 cups (500 mL) coarse salt. Boil for 10 minutes. Let stand for 12 hours and then drain well.

❧Pack the well-drained pickles in glass jars with a few sprigs of dill. Fill the jars with the water-vinegar mixture.

❧Run the blade of a knife around the inside of the jars to remove any air bubbles. Seal.

❧If desired, add 1 cup (250 mL) mustard seed and 1 cup (250 mL) grated horseradish to the vinegar.

MUSTARD PICKLES

2 stalks celery
16 cups (4 L) gherkins
1 large cauliflower
4 green peppers
2 red peppers
12 cups (3 L) pickling onions
2 cups (500 mL) coarse salt
¾ cup (175 mL) dry mustard
2 tbsp (30 mL) turmeric
2 tbsp (30 mL) curry
4 cups (1 L) sugar
1 cup (250 mL) all-purpose flour
12 cups (3 L) cider vinegar

❧Cut the celery in 1-in. (2-cm) lengths. Wash and clean the gherkins. Cut the cauliflower into florets. Dice the peppers after removing the seeds and the fiber. Peel the pickling onions.

❧Mix the vegetables with the coarse salt. Let stand 12 hours, then drain thoroughly.

❧Cook the remaining ingredients over medium heat, stirring constantly, until smooth and creamy. Add the vegetables and return to boiling point. Do not allow the mixture to boil or the vegetables will soften.

❧Turn the pickles into sterilized jars. Seal.

Pickled Onions

PICKLED ONIONS

12 cups (3 L) small white onions
½ cup (125 mL) salt
4 cups (1 L) water
1 small hot chili pepper, finely chopped
½ tsp (2 mL) peppercorns
4 1-in. (2.5-cm) pieces ginger root
1 cup (250 mL) sugar
6 cups (1.5 L) white vinegar

🍃 Use tiny white "silver skin" onions for pickling. Peel them in cold water or plunge them first into boiling water for 30 seconds. Drain them, cover with cold water and peel. Once they are peeled, put them in iced water to prevent discoloration and keep them firm.

🍃 Drain the onions. Then cover them with cold water and drain them again.

🍃 Dissolve the salt in 4 cups (1 L) water in an enameled saucepan or a glass bowl. Add the onions and enough water to cover. Allow to stand overnight. Rinse under running cold water and drain.

🍃 Boil enough water to cover the onions. Add the onions and continue boiling for 1 minute. Drain.

🍃 Spoon the onions into heated sterilized jars, adding the chili pepper, peppercorns and ginger root at intervals.

🍃 Bring the vinegar and sugar to a boil in an enameled or glass saucepan. Pour over the onions to ½ in. (2 cm) from the top of each jar.

🍃 Cover the jars and place on a rack in a deep saucepan or steamer. Half fill with boiling water. Boil for 15 minutes.

🍃 Remove the jars and seal tightly.

ONIONS IN VINEGAR

3 cups (750 mL) vinegar
1 tbsp (15 mL) peppercorns
1 tbsp (15 mL) coarse salt
2 to 3 lbs (1 to 1.5 kg) small onions

🍃 Mix together the first 3 ingredients. Bring to a boil. Skim. Simmer for 10 minutes.

🍃 Add the peeled onions and boil for 5 minutes.

🍃 Place the onions in sterilized jars. Cool the vinegar and pour it over the onions.

🍃 Let stand for 1 month before using.

PICKLED MUSHROOMS

2 lbs (1 kg) mushrooms
1 cup (250 mL) cider vinegar
½ tsp (2 mL) tarragon
1 tbsp (15 mL) sugar
1 tsp (5 mL) salt

🍃 Slice the mushrooms and place them in 4 cups (1 L) water to which 1 tbsp (15 mL) salt has been added.

🍃 Sterilize 4 1-cup (250-mL) jars.

🍃 Bring to a boil the vinegar, tarragon, sugar and salt. Drain the mushrooms thoroughly and add half of them to the vinegar mixture. Reduce the heat and simmer for 3 minutes. Place the remaining mushrooms in the boiling liquid, then allow them to cool.

🍃 Drain the mushrooms and turn them into the sterilized jars.

🍃 Reheat the vinegar mixture and pour it over the mushrooms. Seal.

🍃 Let stand for 1 month before using.

PICKLED CAULIFLOWER

2 heads of cauliflower
coarse salt
1½ tsp (7 mL) peppercorns
1½ tsp (7 mL) whole allspice
½ stick cinnamon
4 cups (1 L) white vinegar

🍃 Separate the cauliflower into florets. Spread out on a large platter and sprinkle with coarse salt. Let stand for 2 days.

🍃 Add the spices to the vinegar and boil for 15 minutes.

🍃 Drain the cauliflower florets and place them in jars. Cover with the hot vinegar.

🍃 Spread a cloth over the jars. Cool before sealing.

Pickled Wax Beans

PICKLED WAX BEANS

2 lbs (1 kg) fresh wax beans
1 cup (250 mL) white vinegar
½ cup (125 mL) sugar
1 tsp (5 mL) celery seed
pinch of ginger
1 tbsp (15 mL) coarse salt
1 tsp (5 mL) savory

➳ Clean the beans and cut on the bias into 1-in. (2-cm) lengths. Scald and boil for 5 minutes. Drain. Reserve the water.

➳ Add the vinegar, sugar, celery seed, ginger, salt and savory to the reserved cooking water. Bring to a boil. Add the cooked beans and return to a boil. Remove from the heat.

➳ Turn the beans into sterilized jars and cover with the liquid. Seal.

SPANISH-STYLE RELISH

8 medium green tomatoes
3 sweet red peppers
3 green peppers
½ small head cabbage
3 large onions
2 tsp (10 mL) coarse salt
¾ cup (175 mL) sugar
¾ cup (175 mL) vinegar
2 tsp (10 mL) mustard seed
¼ tsp (1 mL) turmeric

➳ Chop the tomatoes. There should be 4 cups (1 L). Remove the seeds and the fibers from the red and green peppers. Chop up the peppers, the cabbage and the onions. Mix together, sprinkle with the salt and let stand overnight.

➳ The next day, drain the vegetables and mix with the remaining ingredients. Bring to a boil and cook over high heat for 20 minutes.

➳ Turn the relish into 5 sterilized 2-cup (500-mL) jars. Seal.

CORN RELISH

24 cobs of corn
1 head celery
4 large onions
2 green peppers
2 red peppers
3 cups (750 mL) brown sugar
3 cups (750 mL) white vinegar
1 cup (250 mL) prepared mustard
2½ tbsp (40 mL) dry mustard
2 tbsp (30 mL) all-purpose flour
1 tbsp (15 mL) coarse salt

➳ Cut the kernels from the uncooked cobs of corn with a sharp knife. Remove the leaves from the celery and wash and dice the stalks. Cut the onions into thin slices. Dice the peppers.

➳ Place the vegetables in a large saucepan. Add the rest of the ingredients and mix well.

➳ Bring to a boil. Cover and simmer for 1½ hours or until the relish is of the desired consistency.

➳ Place the relish in heated sterilized jars while still hot. Seal.

BEET AND CABBAGE RELISH

4 cups (1 L) shredded cabbage
4 cups (1 L) beets, cooked and grated

2 cups (500 mL) sugar
1 cup (250 mL) fresh
horseradish, peeled and grated
1 tbsp (15 mL) salt
1 tsp (5 mL) pepper
white vinegar

❧ Mix together the shredded cabbage and grated beets. Add the sugar and mix.

❧ Add the horseradish, salt and pepper. Mix thoroughly. Pour in enough vinegar to cover. Stir.

❧ Let stand for 1 hour and then stir again.

❧ Turn into small sterilized jars. Seal.

❧ This relish requires no cooking and will keep well.

GREEN AND RED PEPPER RELISH

12 green peppers
12 red peppers
3 onions
2 cups (500 mL) sugar
1 tbsp (15 mL) salt
white vinegar

❧ Wash the peppers and peel the onions. Chop in a food processor. Drop into boiling water and allow to stand for 10 minutes. Drain well.

❧ Add the sugar and the salt. Cover with the vinegar and simmer for 20 minutes.

❧ Place the relish in jars.

APPLE CATSUP

2 lbs (1 kg) tomatoes
2 lbs (1 kg) apples, unpeeled
4 medium onions, peeled

3 cups (750 mL) sugar
2 cups (500 mL) white vinegar
2 tsp (10 mL) salt
2 tbsp (30 mL) pickling spices

❧ Chop the tomatoes, apples and onions in a food processor.

❧ Place the chopped tomatoes, apples and onions in a saucepan and add the sugar, vinegar and salt. Put the pickling spices in a cheesecloth bag and add this to the mixture.

❧ Cook, uncovered, over medium heat, stirring frequently, for 1 hour or until thickened. Remove the bag of spices.

❧ Turn the catsup into sterilized jars. Seal.

GREEN CATSUP

10 lbs (5 kg) green tomatoes
½ cup (125 mL) coarse salt
4 large red onions, sliced

1 head celery, diced
3 cups (750 mL) green cabbage, finely shredded
3 cups (750 mL) white vinegar
2 to 3 cups (500 to 750 mL) sugar
1 tbsp (15 mL) pepper
1 tbsp (15 mL) ground ginger
1 tbsp (15 mL) ground cloves
1 tbsp (15 mL) cinnamon
1 tbsp (15 mL) whole allspice
½ tsp (2 mL) cayenne

❧ Wash and slice the green tomatoes. Place in a glass or earthenware bowl and sprinkle with coarse salt. Let stand at room temperature overnight.

❧ The following day, place the tomatoes in a sieve and let drain for 2 to 3 hours.

❧ Place the drained tomatoes in a large saucepan with the onions, celery and cabbage and all the remaining ingredients.

Green and Red Pepper Relish

❧ Bring to a rapid boil, stirring well. Boil vigorously for 30 to 60 minutes or until the mixture has reached the desired consistency.

❧ Turn the catsup into sterilized jars while still hot. Seal.

SWEET RED PEPPER RELISH

12 large red peppers
1 tbsp (15 mL) coarse salt
1 lemon
1½ cups (375 mL) cider vinegar
½ cup (125 mL) water
3 cups (750 mL) sugar

❧ Clean the red peppers and chop in a food processor. Sprinkle with the coarse salt and let stand for 3 to 4 hours.

❧ Cut the unpeeled lemon into quarters. Drain the peppers. Add the vinegar, water and lemon. Cook over low heat for 30 minutes.

❧ Remove the lemon and add the sugar. Cook over low heat, stirring occasionally, for 1 hour or until

the mixture has the consistency of thick marmalade.

❧ Turn into heated sterilized jars and seal with paraffin.

CHILI SAUCE

12 medium tomatoes
4 green peppers
2 large onions
4 apples
2 cups (500 mL) light brown sugar
2 cups (500 mL) cider vinegar
2 tbsp (30 mL) coarse salt
1 tsp (5 mL) dry mustard
1 tsp (5 mL) celery seed
½ tsp (2 mL) ground cloves
½ tsp (2 mL) whole allspice
1 tbsp (15 mL) cinnamon
¼ tsp (1 mL) pepper
½ tsp (2 mL) cayenne

❧ Peel the tomatoes by placing them in boiling water for 1 minute. Then drop them into cold water—the skins should slide off easily. Chop the tomatoes and the onions. Seed and chop the green peppers. Peel and dice the apples.

❧ Place all the ingredients in a large saucepan and cook over medium heat, stirring frequently with a wooden spoon, for 2 hours or until thickened.

❧ Place the chili sauce in sterilized jars and seal.

❧ Makes about 8 cups (2 L).

PICKLED EGGS

1 tsp (5 mL) whole cloves
½ tsp (2 mL) celery seed
1 tsp (5 mL) peppercorns
3 cups (750 mL) white vinegar
1½ cups (375 mL) water
1½ tsp (7 mL) salt
12 hard-cooked eggs

❧ Put the whole cloves, celery seed and peppercorns in a cheesecloth bag.

❧ Bring the vinegar, water and salt to a boil. Add the bag of spices. Simmer for 10 minutes and then cool.

❧ Peel the eggs and place them in a large glass jar. Add the cooled vinegar mixture.

❧ Cover and refrigerate.

JAMS, JELLIES AND MARMALADES

MAKING JAM

Jam is made with fruit pulp and sugar; because jam does not require the separation of the juice from the fruit, it is easier to make than jelly. Even though jam making is rather simple, the final results will be better if you follow some basic steps.

Your jam will have the best flavor and color if you use perfectly ripened and unblemished fruit The jam should also be made as soon as possible after the fruit is picked. Older fruit requires a longer cooking time, which results in loss of flavor and color.

The fruit should be thoroughly and gently washed just before the jam is made.

It is better to warm the sugar before adding it to the hot fruit so that the cooking process is not interrupted, thus producing a superior flavor. The easiest way to heat the sugar is to place the necessary quantity into 2 or 3 pie plates and place them in a preheated 200°F (100°C) oven for about 20 minutes. Then add the hot sugar directly to the fruit.

Do not boil the fruit until the sugar is added and is completely dissolved.

Take care to use the exact amount of sugar called for. Too much sugar will produce sugar crystals in the finished jam. Always stir the jam gently, especially after the sugar has dissolved.

If the jam cooks too long, it will darken and lose much of its flavor.

To check whether the jam is cooked, drop a spoonful onto a saucer that has been chilled in the refrigerator. Let the jam cool for a few seconds, then poke it in the center with your fingertip; if the surface wrinkles or puckers and breaks, the jam is done.

Skim the scum off the surface only at the end of the cooking process.

Pour the hot jam into hot, dry, sterilized jars. (Cold or wet jars have a tendency to crack.) An easy way to sterilize them is to run them through the dishwasher.

To prevent fruit pieces such as cherries or strawberries from floating to the top of the jars, let the jam cool for 20 or 30 minutes before bottling; stir it just before you pour it in the jars.

Fill jars to within about ¼ in. (1 cm) of the top. Wash off any jam dripped on the lip or exterior of the filled jars. Top the jam with a layer of melted paraffin wax while the jam is still warm. This will help prevent spoilage.

Seal and label the jars, and store them in a cool dark place.

Wonderful jam can be made using the natural pectin in some fruit. For example, apples, black currants, gooseberries and damson plums are high in pectin, but cherries, strawberries and raspberries contain relatively little. Ripe fruit contains less natural pectin than under-ripe fruit.

If you want to make a jam from a fruit that is low in pectin, without using store-bought pectin, replace some of the water called for with the juice of a fruit high in pectin. Or you can add a small amount of lemon juice.

TIPS FOR SUCCESSFUL JAM

To prevent crystallization:

Avoid using more sugar than called for in the recipe.

Do not boil the jam until the sugar is completely dissolved.

Do not stir too much once the sugar is dissolved.

Do not wait too long before sealing the jars.

Do not reduce the cooking time.

To prevent the formation of mold:

Do not reduce the cooking time.

Do not reduce the required amount of sugar.

Do not store the jars of jam in a warm or damp location.

MAKING JELLY

Jelly is made with the juice extracted from fruit. To preserve the maximum flavor of the fruit, add as little water as possible to it. The juice from naturally juicy fruits such as berries and grapes is extracted by a different method than is the juice from less juicy fruits such as apples and pears.

JUICY FRUITS
Put the cleaned fruits into a glass or china bowl and crush them with a spoon. Cover the bowl and place it in a pan of boiling water. Allow the water to simmer below the bowl of fruit for about 1 hour to draw the juice out.

You can also place the covered bowl and the ban of boiling water in a 200°F (100°C) oven for 1 hour.

⚜ To extract the juice from a small quantity of fruit (1 to 3 cups or 250 to 750 mL) crush the fruit in the top of a double boiler (not aluminum), and follow the first procedure.

LESS JUICY FRUITS

⚜ Put the washed, cored and cut fruit into a large, heavy pan and add enough cold water to nearly cover. (The fruit should not be floating in water.) Simmer until the fruit is soft, mashing it with a spoon.

EXTRACTING THE JUICE

Pour the simmered fruits and their liquid into a jelly bag or several layers of cheesecloth and hang the bag over a bowl for several hours to allow the juice to drip. It will take from 6 to 12 hours. Do not squeeze the bag, or the jelly will be cloudy.

⚜ Measure the juice accurately. You will need ¾ to 1 cup (175 to 250 ml) of sugar for each cup (250 mL) of extracted juice. (Black currant and red currant jelly may require slightly more sugar.)

⚜ Heat the juice in a heavy non-aluminum pan. Heat the sugar in the oven as described in the jam-making section. Add the sugar little by little and stir after each addition, until the sugar is completely dissolved.

⚜ Bring the liquid to a rapid boil and cook, uncovered, for about 3 minutes for juicy fruit, and 5 to 10 minutes for less juicy fruit.

⚜ To test if the jelly is ready to set, use the saucer method (see previous page) as for jam. When the jelly mixture tests done, skim the top and ladle it into warm, dry, sterilized jars. It is essential to work quickly since the jelly will tend to stick to the sides of the pot. Follow the procedure for sealing and storing jam.

⚜ It is impossible to give precise cooking times for jellies and jams, as it depends on the natural moisture content of the fruit.

QUANTITY OF SUGAR TO USE WITH COMBINED FRUIT JUICES

ACIDIC FRUITS		NON-ACIDIC FRUITS		SUGAR
Apples	½	Raspberries	½	⅔
Apples	⅓	Rhubarb	⅓	⅔
Apples	½	Cherries	½	⅔
Apples	½	Peaches	½	1
Apples	⅔	Quinces	⅓	¾
Apples	⅔	Cranberries	⅓	¾
Apples	½	Strawberries	½	1
Red currants	⅓	Raspberries	⅓	1
Limes	⅓	Pears	⅔	1
Lemons	¼	Peaches or pears	¾	1

HOMEMADE PECTIN

⚜ Choose apples that are still green or slightly under-ripe. Wash them thoroughly and remove any bruises. Cut them into quarters, but do not core or peel. Put the apple pieces into a large, heavy pot with enough water to half cover them. Bring to a boil, cover, and then simmer until the apples are tender.

⚜ Hang the fruit and liquid in a jelly bag or cheesecloth for 12 hours. Squeeze the cloth to extract the maximum amount of juice possible.

⚜ Put the apple pulp left in the cloth back into the pot and half cover it with water. Bring to a rolling boil for about 5 to 8 minutes, stirring constantly. Hang the pulp and liquid in a jelly bag for 4 to 5 hours. Add the resulting liquid to the first batch of juice.

⚜ This homemade apple pectin is ready to use in the following proportions: 1 cup (250 mL) pectin for each 1 lb (500 g) of sugar. Add the pectin after the sugar has dissolved.

⚜ To store homemade pectin, put it into jars and sterilize them in a bain-marie for 40 minutes. Seal with wax and store in a cool dry place.

⚜ Pectins can be made from red or black currants, from green or red gooseberries, or from ripe plums or green crabapples, using the same procedure.

⚜ For example, you can make raspberry-apple jelly without commercial pectin by using 2 cups (500 mL) apple juice, 2 cups (500 mL) raspberry juice and 2⅔ cups (650 mL) sugar.

Raspberry Jam

4 cups (1 L) into the pan with the berries. Stir in the sugar, cover the pot and let sit for 12 hours.

🍃 Bring the fruit mixture to a rapid boil. Add the lemon zest, lemon juice and baking soda. Continue to boil, stirring frequently, until the jam has the required consistency.

🍃 Skim, pour into warm sterilized jars and seal with paraffin.

24-HOUR STRAWBERRY JAM

4 cups (1 L) strawberries, hulled
5 cups (1.2 L) sugar
3 tbsp (45 mL) fresh lemon juice

🍃 In a large, heavy pot mix 1 cup (250 mL) of strawberries and the same quantity of sugar. Repeat the additions until all the strawberries and sugar are mixed. Slowly bring the mixture to the boil and simmer for 9 minutes, stirring as little and as gently as possible.

🍃 Remove from the heat and stir in the lemon juice. Pour the mixture into a non-metallic bowl, cover and let sit overnight.

🍃 The next day, return the jam to the pot, bring to a rapid boil over high heat, then simmer for 9 minutes over low heat. Remove from the heat and remove the scum. Let cool slightly in the pot, then pour into warm sterilized jars. Seal.

OLD-FASHIONED STRAWBERRY JAM

5 cups (1.2 L) strawberries
5 cups (1.2 L) sugar
½ cup (125 mL) fresh lemon juice

🍃 Wash, drain and hull the strawberries.

🍃 Divide the sugar between 2 pie plates and warm it in the oven at 325°F (160°C) for 15 to 20 minutes.

🍃 Put the strawberries into a large pot. Crush them slightly with a fork or a potato masher to release some of the juice. Cook for 10 minutes over low heat, stirring occasionally.

🍃 Pour the warmed sugar on the strawberries. Add the lemon juice. Bring to a boil, stirring from time to time. Cook at a gentle boil over medium heat, stirring gently, for about 8 minutes, or until the jam tests set. Remove from the heat, remove the scum and pour into warm sterilized jars. Seal.

STRAWBERRY RHUBARB JAM

4 cups (1 L) strawberries, washed and hulled
4 cups (1 L) rhubarb
6 cups (1.5 L) sugar
1 tsp (5 mL) grated lemon zest
1 tbsp (15 mL) lemon juice
pinch of baking soda

🍃 Crush the strawberries with a potato masher and measure 4 cups (1 L) into a large, heavy non-aluminum pot, preferably enameled. Wash the rhubarb but do not remove the skin if the rhubarb is fairly young. Cut the rhubarb into cubes and measure

RASPBERRY JAM

4 cups (1 L) raspberries
¼ cup (50 mL) water
sugar

❧ Wash and crush the raspberries. Add the water and cook in a heavy pan over medium heat.

❧ If you wish, pass the cooked fruit through a sieve to remove the seeds.

❧ Measure the fruit and add ¾ cup (175 mL) sugar for each cup (250 mL) of fruit. Cook over medium heat for 15 to 25 minutes, or until the jam reaches the desired consistency. Pour into warm sterilized jars and seal.

DAMSON PLUM JAM

8 cups (2 L) damson plums
6 cups (1.5 L) sugar
grated zest of ½ orange
juice of 1 orange
1 cup (250 mL) seedless raisins

❧ Wash the plums and cut them in half. Remove the pits before measuring the amount needed in the recipe.

❧ Put the prepared plums and the sugar in a saucepan and cook over medium heat, stirring often, until the juice gels when a few drops are dropped onto a chilled saucer.

❧ Add the grated orange rind, orange juice and raisins. Simmer for 10 minutes. Remove the scum if necessary. Stir, then pour the jam into warm sterilized jars and seal.

QUICK PEACH AND PINEAPPLE JAM

5 cups (1.2 L) sliced peeled peaches
1 19-oz (540 mL) can crushed pineapple

3 cups (750 mL) sugar
¼ cup (50 mL) chopped walnuts

❧ In a large, heavy saucepan, mix the peaches, pineapple and sugar. Cook, stirring, over medium heat until the sugar is dissolved. Simmer uncovered, stirring from time to time, for about 1 hour.

❧ Meanwhile heat the oven to 350°F (180°C). Boil the walnuts in water for about 15 minutes. Drain. Spread the nuts on a cookie sheet and roast them in the oven for about 15 minutes, turning occasionally. Cool, then chop roughly.

❧ Remove the fruit mixture from the heat and stir in the walnuts. Skim. Put the jam into warm sterilized jars and seal.

PEACH AND PEAR JAM

6 cups (1.5 L) sliced peaches
2 peach stones

12 maraschino cherries, sliced
2 tbsp (30 mL) cherry juice
1½ cups (375 mL) ripe pears, diced
1 tbsp (15 mL) grated orange zest
1 tbsp (15 mL) lemon juice
5 cups (1.2 L) sugar

❧ Blanch, peel and chop the peaches. Crack the 2 peach stones and add the seeds to the peaches. Add the sliced cherries with their juice. Wash, but do not peel, the pears. Dice the flesh and add it to the other fruit. Add the orange zest and lemon juice. Mix well.

❧ Stir in the sugar and let sit for 3 hours.

❧ Bring the jam to a boil and simmer gently until it reaches the setting point. Remove the scum, pour into warm sterilized jars and seal.

Peach and Pear Jam

[681]

Spiced Concord Grape Jelly

3 lbs (1.5 kg) Concord grapes
1 tsp (5 mL) ground cloves (optional)
1 tsp (5 mL) ground cinnamon (optional)
½ cup (125 mL) cider vinegar
8 cups (2 L) sugar
½ cup (125 mL) commercial pectin or apple pectin

❧ Detach the grapes from their stems and wash them. Put the grapes in a large pot with the spices and the cider vinegar. Cook over medium heat, crushing the grapes while they are heating to release the juices.

❧ Once the grapes are crushed, boil the mixture for 5 to 8 minutes only. Long cooking will impair the flavor, color and setting.

❧ Put the grapes and juice in a moistened jelly bag or cheesecloth and allow to drip into a bowl for 12 hours. This should produce about 4 cups (1 L) of grape juice.

❧ Heat the juice to a full boil and add the warmed sugar. Cook over low heat, stirring constantly, until the sugar is completely dissolved. Bring to a boil.

❧ Add the pectin. Boil for exactly 30 seconds, stirring constantly. Skim, then pour into hot sterilized jars and seal.

Fresh Mint Jelly

10 to 15 fresh mint sprigs
green or yellow food coloring (if desired)

❧ Proceed as for apple jelly (see below). Once the sugar has completely dissolved, add the washed mint sprigs to the mixture and continue cooking.

❧ Remove the mint once the jelly has reached the set point. Add food coloring if you wish. Place 1 or 2 fresh mint leaves in the bottom of each jar then top with jelly. Seal.

Apple Jelly

❧ Wash the apples and cut them into quarters without peeling them. Do not remove the seeds or the core.

❧ Put the apples into a large, heavy saucepan. Add 1 cup (250 mL) of water for every 3 cups (750 mL) of apples. Cover, bring to the boil and simmer for 30 minutes.

❧ Put the cooked apples and liquid into a jelly bag or cheesecloth and allow to drip into a bowl for 6 to 12 hours.

❧ Measure the juice into a large pot and heat it. Measure out 1 cup (250 mL) of sugar for each cup (250 mL) of juice. Heat the sugar in the oven. Add the sugar to the juice a little at a time, stirring to dissolve it completely. Boil rapidly for 5 to 10 minutes.

❧ After the first 3 minutes, and regularly thereafter, use the saucer test to check whether the jelly is ready to set; there is a great variability in the pectin content of apples. Pour into warm sterilized jars and seal.

Seville Orange Marmalade

12 Seville oranges
cold water
sugar

Apple Jelly

Wash the oranges and cut them in quarters. Remove the seeds. Cut each quarter into small thin slices using a very sharp knife. Weigh the oranges and put them in a large bowl.

Add 6 cups (1.5 L) of water for each 1 lb (500 g) of prepared fruit. Put the seeds into a small piece of cheesecloth and secure it with a thread. Add to the oranges. Cover the bowl and let sit for 24 hours.

After the soaking period, put the mixture in a large, heavy pot and simmer until the rinds have softened; this will take from 3 to 4 hours. Remove the bag of seeds, squeezing well over the orange mixture to remove all the pectin. Put the mixture into a covered bowl and let sit for 12 hours.

The next day, weigh the mixture and add 1 lb (500 g) sugar for every 1 lb (500 g) of fruit. Bring slowly to a boil, stirring constantly to dissolve the sugar thoroughly. Boil until the desired consistency is reached and the liquid gels. Pour into warm sterilized jars and seal.

ENGLISH MARMALADE

8 Seville bitter oranges
3 regular oranges
2 lemons
18 cups (4.5 L) cold water
8 lbs (3.6 kg) sugar

Wash the oranges and lemons. Cut each in half and extract the juice. Put the seeds into a small piece of cheesecloth and tie securely with thread to make a

Orange Marmalade

small bag.

Cut the pulp and rind into small pieces, or chop in a food processor. Put the juice, the bag of seeds, the rind and the pulp into a large bowl. Add the cold water. Cover and let soak for 24 hours.

Put the contents of the bowl in a large, heavy pot and boil for 2 hours, or until the liquid is reduced by half.

Warm the sugar in a 200°F (100°C) oven. Remove the bag containing the citrus seeds, squeezing it well to extract all the pectin. Add the heated sugar to the reduced mixture. Bring slowly to a boil, stirring constantly, making sure that the sugar is thoroughly dissolved before the mixture boils. Boil for approximately 30 minutes, or until the desired consistency is reached. Pour the marmalade into warm sterilized jars and seal.

ORANGE MARMALADE

Cut 6 oranges in half and extract the juice.

Place the seeds in a small bowl, cover them with a little hot water and let soak for 12 hours.

Scrape off the pith or the white membrane from the rind of the oranges and cut the rind into thin slices. Put the rind into a bowl. Add the juice and measure the mixture. Add 1 cup (250 mL) water for each 1 cup (250 mL) of juice with rind. Cover and let soak for 12 hours.

The following day, add a little of the juice mixture to the bowl containing the orange seeds, then pour the diluted liquid (which is full of pectin) back into the juice mixture. Discard the orange seeds.

Bring the juice mixture to a

boil, then simmer uncovered for 2 hours. Measure the mixture accurately, then add an equal quantity of sugar to the quantity of juice.

☙ Boil for 15 minutes, or until a candy thermometer registers 220°F (105°C), or the saucer test indicates a set. Pour into hot sterilized jars and seal.

STRAWBERRY MARMALADE

2 oranges
2 lemons
½ cup (125 mL) water
½ tbsp (2 mL) baking soda
4 cups (1 L) strawberries
7 cups (1.8 L) sugar
½ bottle of commercial pectin

☙ Peel the oranges and lemons. Scrape off the white membrane or pith and slice the rind into fine strips with a sharp knife. Simmer the rind in the water with the baking soda for 10 minutes. Add the juice and pulp of the oranges and lemons and simmer for another 20 minutes.

☙ Wash, hull and crush the strawberries. Add to the orange and lemon mixture. Add the sugar, allowing it to dissolve thoroughly before bringing the mixture to a full boil. Boil for 5 minutes.

☙ Remove from the heat and add the pectin. Let stand for 5 minutes, then skim. Pour into warm sterilized jars. Cover with paraffin before the marmalade cools and seal.

RHUBARB MARMALADE

6 cups (1.5 L) rhubarb
rind and juice of 2 oranges
juice of 2 lemons
rind of 1 lemon
5 cups (1.2 L) sugar
½ tsp (2 mL) salt

☙ Wash the rhubarb, peel if it is tough, and cut into ½-in. (1-cm) pieces.

☙ Put the rhubarb into a stainless steel or enameled pan and add the rest of the ingredients.

☙ Bring to a boil and simmer until the desired consistency is reached and the marmalade will set. Pour into warm sterilized jars and seal.

PINEAPPLE MARMALADE

1 orange
1 grapefruit
1 lemon
1½ cups (375 mL) water
¼ tsp (1 mL) baking soda
1 pineapple
9 cups (2.3 L) sugar
1 bottle commercial pectin

☙ Wash the orange, grapefruit and lemon. Peel the fruit and scrape off the white membranous pith. Cut the peels into fine slivers with a sharp knife. Put the slivers of peel into a pot with the water and the baking soda. Bring to a boil, cover and simmer for 10 minutes.

☙ Remove the pulp from the fruits, working over a bowl to ensure that the juice is not lost. Add the pulp and the juice to the rind, cover and let simmer for another 20 minutes.

☙ Peel the pineapple and grate it into a bowl. Add the simmered citrus fruits and measure the mixture.

☙ Add 1¾ cups (425 mL) of sugar for each 1 cup (250 mL) of mixed fruit and stir well. Return mixture to the pot and bring to a boil. Boil, uncovered, for 10 minutes.

☙ Remove from the heat and add the pectin. Stir gently for 5 minutes, then skim. Pour the marmalade into warm sterilized jars and seal.

GINGERED PEARS

25 firm pears
¾ cup (175 mL) fresh lemon juice
6 cups (1.5 L) sugar
⅓ cup (75 mL) grated fresh ginger
⅓ cup (75 mL) lemon zest

☙ Wash and peel the pears. Cut them in half, remove the cores and put them in a large, heavy pot with 2 cups (500 mL) of water and the lemon juice. Bring to a boil and simmer, uncovered, for 30 to 40 minutes, or until the pears are tender.

☙ Add the sugar, grated ginger and the lemon zest cut into thin shreds. Simmer for another 10 to 15 minutes, stirring from time to time, until the mixture thickens.

☙ Pour into hot sterilized jars and seal.

CANDIES AND CONFECTIONS

CANDIES AND CONFECTIONS

Today, both children and adults alike usually head for the corner store when they want a piece of candy. The days when candy was available only on special occasions are long forgotten. But the satisfaction and pleasure of preparing and serving delicious confections need not be a thing of the past.

The following sweet tidbits make wonderful desserts—especially when served with coffee —and perfect gifts. Children love to get involved in preparing them and will readily take up the wooden spoon to beat the fudge when your arm tires.

Candy making is an activity for a cool, dry day, which is one reason why many candies are associated with the Christmas season.

Cook the syrup to the stage recommended in the recipe, testing it with a candy thermometer (the temperatures corresponding to each stage are provided in the table above). Do not plunge the thermometer directly into the boiling syrup or it might crack; heat the thermometer first in hot water.

Another way to check if the syrup is ready is to test it in cold water. Pour several drops of the syrup into cold water. The different stages of doneness are listed in the above chart.

CHOCOLATE FOR COATING

There are three types of chocolate you can use for coating:

CANDY THERMOMETER TEMPERATURES

STAGE OF COOKING	TEMPERATURE	
Thread	215°F	101°C
Large-thread	225°F	103°C
Soft-ball	230°F to 240°F	109°C to 116°C
Hard-ball	250°F to 260°F	120°C to 126°C
Soft-crack	270°F to 290°F	129°C to 145°C
Hard-crack	300°F	150°C

semi-sweet chocolate, made specially for dipping

milk chocolate

homemade semi-sweet chocolate, which can be made by mixing equal amounts of unsweetened and milk chocolate.

MELTING CHOCOLATE

Cut your favorite chocolate into small pieces and place the pieces in a small, round-bottom bowl. In general, 1 lb (500 g) of chocolate is used at a time.

Place the bowl in the top of a double boiler over boiling water. Beat the chocolate until it is partly melted. Remove the bowl from the double boiler and continue beating with a fork until the chocolate is entirely melted. Note that milk chocolate is heavier than semi-sweet chocolate.

If you want the chocolate to adhere properly to candies, keep it at a constant temperature, between 83°F and 84°F (28°C and 29°C). One way to do so is to place the chocolate in a heavy bowl and set the bowl in hot water at 85°F (30°C). When working with chocolate, it is best to keep the workroom cool, at a temperature of about 65°F (18°C). The chocolate will cool almost instantly at this temperature and take on a smooth, glossy appearance.

COATING CANDIES WITH CHOCOLATE

Have on hand a large 2-tine fork or a special candy-dipping fork, which can be purchased at a pastry specialty shop.

Drop the candies one at a time in the chocolate. Lift them out, making sure to keep the candies between the tines of the fork. Tap the fork several times against the sides of the bowl to drain off any excess chocolate. Place the candies on a baking sheet lined with wax paper. A thin thread of chocolate will form between the fork and the candy. Twist it quickly to give the top of the candy a more attractive appearance.

When the chocolate has hardened, place the candies in a metal box, a sheet of wax paper between each layer. Store in a cool place.

MOCHA NUT ROLL

1 cup (250 mL) brown sugar
⅓ cup (75 mL) unsweetened evaporated milk
2 tbsp (30 mL) corn syrup
1 6-oz (175-g) package of chocolate chips

1 tsp (5 mL) instant coffee
2 tsp (10 mL) vanilla
1 cup (250 mL) chopped walnuts

✍ Place the brown sugar, the evaporated milk and the corn syrup in a saucepan. Bring the mixture to a boil over medium heat, stirring constantly. Boil for 2 minutes and remove from the heat. Add the chocolate, the instant coffee and the vanilla. Stir until the chocolate is melted. Cool.

✍ Continue stirring until the mixture is thick and smooth. Add the nuts and mix well. Divide the mixture into two equal portions and shape each into a 10-in. (25-cm) roll. Wrap the rolls in wax paper and refrigerate them for 3 to 4 hours.

✍ Before serving, slice each roll into 20 pieces.

QUICK FUDGE

✍ Prepare *Chocolate Sauce* (see page 602) and add 3 to 4 cups (750 ml to 1 L) of confectioners' sugar. Beat until the mixture is smooth and creamy. Pour the chocolate fudge into a buttered pan and refrigerate it for 30 to 60 minutes. Cut the fudge into squares and serve. If you wish, add chopped walnuts to the mixture before pouring it into the pan.

CHOCOLATE FUDGE

4 tbsp (60 mL) cocoa
1 cup (250 mL) sugar
1 cup (250 mL) firmly packed

Chocolate Fudge

brown sugar
pinch of salt
1 cup (250 mL) light cream
1 tbsp (15 mL) corn syrup
1 tbsp (15 mL) butter
½ tsp (2 mL) vanilla
or 1 tsp (5 mL) rum
or orange zest

✍ In a saucepan, combine the cocoa, the white and brown sugar and the salt. Add the cream, the corn syrup and the butter. Bring the mixture to a boil over medium heat, stirring constantly. Continue boiling until the thermometer reaches 234°F (112°C) or until a few drops form a soft ball in cold water. Remove the mixture from the heat and add the vanilla, the rum or the orange zest.

✍ To make smooth, velvety fudge, place the saucepan in cold water and let the chocolate mixture stand at least 4 minutes without stirring it. Remove the saucepan from the cold water and beat the mixture about 5 minutes, until it thickens and loses its gloss.

✍ Spread the fudge evenly in a buttered pan.

RAISIN-NUT FUDGE
Chop until fine 1 cup (250 g) of seedless raisins or ½ cup (125 mL) of nuts and sprinkle them over the fudge before adding the vanilla. When cool, stir the fudge until it is creamy.

MARSHMALLOW FUDGE
Using scissors dipped in hot water, cut 8 or 10 marshmallows in half. Dip the cut sides of the marshmallows into shredded coconut and place them in a buttered pan. Pour the fudge over the marshmallows.

❦ TECHNIQUE ❦

CREAM TRUFFLES

1 Place the chocolate and the cream over hot water in the top of a double boiler.

2 Melt the chocolate over very low heat.

3 Add the egg yolks, one at a time, beating hard after each addition.

4 Roll the truffles in cocoa.

ORANGE FUDGE

Grate the zest of 1 orange. Cut the pulp of the orange into very small pieces and place the pieces in a small sieve; press them to drain as much of the juice as possible. Add the pieces of orange to the fudge when it is ready to be stirred. Pour the fudge into a buttered pan and sprinkle it with grated orange zest.

MOCHA FUDGE

Add 1 tbsp (15 mL) of instant coffee to the dry ingredients. Proceed as you would in the master recipe.

CREAM TRUFFLES

These truffles are a chocolate-lover's dream.

½ lb (250 g) Swiss or French chocolate, cut into squares
2 tbsp (30 mL) whipping cream
3 egg yolks
1 tbsp (15 mL) sweet butter

❧ Place the chocolate and the cream in the top of a double boiler, over hot—not boiling—water. Melt the chocolate over very low heat. This is important as truffles are more velvety when they are cooked slowly.

❧ Remove the melted chocolate from the heat. Add the egg yolks, one at a time, beating hard after each addition. Add the butter. Return the mixture to the double boiler and cook it over low heat for 15 to 20 minutes, stirring several times.

❧ Pour the mixture into a pan. Cover and refrigerate it for 24 hours. If you wish, add ½ to

¾ cup (125 to 175 mL) slivered almonds to the mixture before refrigerating it.

❧ Oil your hands, then shape the chocolate mixture into small balls, or truffles. Roll them in sweetened cocoa or in chocolate pastilles or shot. Store the truffles in the refrigerator until you are ready to serve them.

CREAM CARAMELS

---

2 cups (500 mL) sugar
1 cup (250 mL) corn syrup
2 cups (500 mL) light cream
⅓ cup (75 mL) butter
½ tsp (2 mL) salt
1 tsp (5 mL) vanilla
½ cup (125 mL) chopped nuts (optional)

❧ Combine the sugar, the corn syrup and 1 cup (250 mL) of the cream in a large saucepan and cook for approximately 10 min-

utes. Heat the rest of the cream and add it gradually to the sugar mixture. Cook for approximately 5 minutes over medium heat, until the candy thermometer reaches 230°F (110°C).

❧ Cut the butter into small pieces and gradually add them to the caramel mixture. Reduce the heat and continue cooking until the candy thermometer reaches 242°F (117°C), for a soft caramel, or 246°F (119°C), for a harder caramel. Toward the end of the cooking, you may find it necessary to give the mixture the occasional stir; if so, stir only from the bottom of the pan.

❧ Remove the pan from the heat. Add the salt and the vanilla, stirring slowly and with only a few strokes. Let the mixture stand for 10 minutes. Add the nuts and pour the mixture into a buttered 8- x 8- x 2-in. (20- x 20- x 5-cm) pan. Place the pan on a cake rack

Cream Truffles

in a cool place and let the caramel harden.

❧ Unmold the caramel. Wipe the bottom with a clean cloth and cut the caramel into squares with a sharp knife. Wrap the caramels individually in paper.

❧ To make chocolate caramel, follow the above recipe, adding 2 squares of unsweetened chocolate, cut into small pieces, when the caramel is removed from the heat. Stir carefully until the chocolate is melted.

CARAMEL POPCORN

1 cup (250 mL) molasses
1 cup (250 mL) corn syrup
1 tsp (5 mL) vinegar
3 tbsp (45 mL) butter
½ tsp (2 mL) salt
3 cups (750 mL) popcorn

❧ In a saucepan, combine the molasses, the corn syrup and the vinegar. Bring the mixture to a boil and cook until the "hard-ball" stage (when a drop of the syrup forms a hard ball in cold water).

❧ Add the butter and the salt, then pour the mixture over the popcorn. Stir the popcorn gently with a buttered wooden spoon. Butter your hands and shape the popcorn into balls. Work quickly.

MAPLE SUGAR

❧ Boil some maple syrup until it reaches 240°F (115°C) on a candy thermometer, or until it forms soft balls when tested in cold water. Cool the syrup as rapidly as possible by placing the saucepan in a bowl of iced water. When the syrup is lukewarm, stir vigorously with a wooden spoon, until it begins to granulate and change color slightly. Pour it at once into a pan rinsed in cold water. Let it set in a cold place. Unmold the maple sugar as soon as it has hardened.

MAPLE BUTTER

❧ Maple butter is prepared in the same way as maple sugar. Add 1 tbsp (15 mL) of butter and 1 tbsp (15 mL) of cream for every 4 cups (1 L) of syrup. Cook until the syrup reaches 236°F (113°C) on a candy thermometer, or until a few drops form a soft ball in cold water.

CREAMY MAPLE BUTTER

1 cup (250 mL) brown sugar
3 cups (750 mL) maple syrup
1 cup (250 mL) cream or milk
½ cup (125 mL) corn syrup
4 tbsp (60 mL) butter

❧ Combine the brown sugar, the maple syrup, the cream or milk and the corn syrup in a saucepan and slowly bring the mixture to a boil. Continue boiling over medium heat for 20 to 30 minutes, stirring constantly. Cool for 20 minutes. Add the butter and stir until the maple butter is creamy.

❧ Store the maple butter in a sealed glass container in the refrigerator.

MAPLE SYRUP FONDANT

2 cups (500 mL) maple syrup
pecans or walnuts

Maple Syrup Fondant

❧ TECHNIQUE ❧

MAPLE SYRUP FONDANT

1   Bring the syrup to a boil over medium heat.

2   Start working the warm syrup with a wooden spoon, lifting and folding it from the edges to the center.

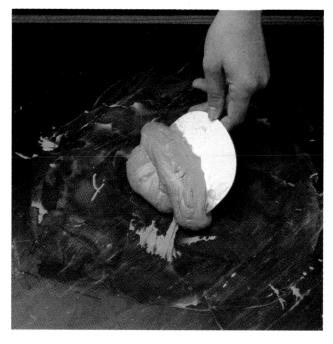

3   Shape the syrup into a ball.

4   Garnish each piece of fondant with half a pecan.

Honey Taffy

≥▲ Bring the maple syrup to a boil over medium heat. Turn up the heat and cook it until it reaches 235°F (113°C), or until a few drops of the syrup form a soft ball in cold water. Remove the saucepan from the heat.

≥▲ When the syrup stops boiling, pour it into a large pan. The syrup should not be more than ½ in. (1 cm) thick.

≥▲ When the syrup is lukewarm, work it with a wooden spoon by repeatedly lifting and folding it from the edges to the center. When the syrup loses its transparency and becomes opaque and creamy, shape it into a ball on the table and knead it like bread dough until the fondant becomes smooth and soft. Shape it into a ball and place it in a bowl. Cover the fondant and let it stand for 12 hours.

≥▲ Shape the fondant into 36 small oval pieces. Press half a pecan or walnut into each piece, then let the pieces dry for 4 hours on a cake rack.

MOLASSES TAFFY

2 cups (500 mL) brown sugar
½ cup (125 mL) water
1 tbsp (15 mL) corn syrup
1 cup (250 mL) molasses
⅓ cup (75 mL) butter

≥▲ Combine the brown sugar, the water, the corn syrup, the molasses and the butter in a large saucepan. Blend well and cook until the mixture reaches 260°F (127°C) on a candy thermometer, or to the hard-ball stage when a few drops of the syrup are tested in cold water. Flavor with vanilla or almond extract.

≥▲ Pour the taffy into a buttered square pan and let it cool. To shape it into bite-size pieces, pull the taffy, cut it and wrap each piece separately.

HONEY TAFFY

2 cups (500 mL) sugar
2 cups (500 mL) honey
⅔ cup (150 mL) water
2 tbsp (30 mL) vinegar
pinch of salt

≥▲ Combine the sugar, the honey, the water and the vinegar in a saucepan and boil over low heat, until the syrup reaches 288°F (142°C) on a candy thermometer or until it separates into hard, flexible threads when dropped into cold water. Stir as little as possible.

≥▲ Add a pinch of salt. Pour the mixture into a buttered pan and allow it to cool. Gather up the mass with your hands and pull the taffy until it becomes almost white. (As you pull the taffy, dip your hands in cold water from time to time). Cut the taffy into 1-in. (2.5-cm) pieces.

CRACKERJACK

1 cup (250 mL) sugar
¼ cup (50 mL) corn syrup
½ cup (125 mL) hot water
2 tbsp (30 mL) butter
¾ tsp (3 mL) salt
2½ tbsp (40 mL) molasses
¾ cup (175 mL) peanuts
6 to 7 cups (1.5 L) popcorn

Combine the sugar, the corn syrup and the hot water in an 8-cup (2-L) saucepan. Cook the syrup over medium heat until it reaches 260°F (127°C) on a candy thermometer.

Reduce the heat and add the butter, the salt and the molasses. Cook to 290°F (143°C), or until the syrup is golden. Stir it once or twice during cooking.

Add the peanuts to the syrup and stir until the nuts are well coated. Cook the mixture until the peanuts are golden brown. Place the popcorn in a large bowl and pour the mixture over it. Stir rapidly with 2 forks. Pour the popcorn mixture over a greased surface, spreading it as much as possible. Allow it to cool, then break it into small pieces.

PEANUT BRITTLE

½ cup (125 mL) corn syrup
2 cups (500 mL) sugar
⅓ cup (75 mL) water
3 tbsp (45 mL) butter
pinch of salt
1 cup (250 mL) unsalted peanuts
1 tsp (5 mL) vanilla

Combine the corn syrup, the sugar, the water, the butter and the salt in a saucepan and cook the mixture over medium heat, stirring constantly, until the sugar is dissolved.

Add the peanuts. Cook the mixture until it reaches 300°F (150°C) on a candy thermometer, or until a few drops of the syrup separate into hard, brittle threads in cold water. Remove the mix-

ture from the heat and add the vanilla. Pour it onto a buttered baking sheet, allow it to cool, then break the peanut brittle into pieces.

Blanched almonds may be substituted for the peanuts.

ENGLISH TOFFEE

2¼ cups (550 mL) sugar
1 tsp (5 mL) cornstarch
¾ cup (175 mL) corn syrup
2 tbsp (30 mL) butter
1 cup (250 mL) water
1 tsp (5 mL) salt
vanilla, mint or almond extract, orange or lemon zest, or rum

Combine all the ingredients, except the flavoring, in a large saucepan and stir the mixture until well blended. Cook, stirring occasionally, until the syrup reaches 250°F (120°C) on a candy thermometer or until a hard ball forms when a few drops of the syrup are tested in cold water. Add the flavoring of your choice.

Pour a few drops of oil onto a marble slab, a porcelain-topped table or a baking sheet, spreading the oil with your fingertips. Pour the cooked toffee over this surface and let it harden for 15 to 20 minutes.

Using a wide spatula, lift the toffee and work it up into a compact mass, folding it over repeatedly. Start pulling the toffee immediately or it will stick; pull with one hand and fold the toffee over with the other. Repeat the motion as rhythmically as possible. Have someone else wipe the

oil from the table and sprinkle it lightly with cornstarch. Continue pulling the toffee until it hardens sufficiently.

Form the toffee into a cone. Roll the pointed end of the cone into a long, thin rope with one hand and, with the other hand, cut the toffee into 1½-in. (4-cm) pieces using scissors sprinkled with cornstarch. Form and cut additional cones until all the toffee has been cut. Wrap the pieces individually in wax paper.

BUTTERSCOTCH

2 cups (500 mL) sugar
⅔ cup (150 mL) corn syrup
¼ cup (50 mL) water
¼ cup (50 mL) light cream
¼ cup (50 mL) butter

Combine the sugar, the corn syrup, the water and the cream in a saucepan. Bring the mixture to a boil over medium heat, stirring constantly. Cook, stirring occasionally, until the syrup reaches 260°F (127°C) on a candy thermometer, or until a few drops of the syrup from a hard ball in cold water.

Add the butter and cook to 280°F (137°C), or until the syrup separates into hard, flexible threads when tested in cold water (soft-crack stage).

Pour the syrup into a buttered 8- x 8- x 2-in. (20- x 20- x 5-cm) pan. Cool slightly and, with the tip of a knife, mark squares in the caramel. When it is hard, break off the pieces.

GLAZING FRUITS AND NUTS

GLAZING SYRUP:
2 cups (500 mL) sugar
⅔ cup (150 mL) water
1 tsp (5 mL) lemon juice
¼ tsp (1 mL) cream of tartar

In the top of a double boiler, stir together the sugar and the water, over low heat, until dissolved. Bring the syrup to a boil. Add the lemon juice and the cream of tartar. Using a damp cloth rolled around a fork, remove any crystallized sugar that may have formed on the sides of the double boiler.

Continue cooking, without stirring, until the syrup reaches 300°F (150°C) on a candy thermometer, or a few drops if it separate into hard, brittle threads in cold water (hard-crack stage).

Dip nuts or pieces of fruit into the syrup with a fork, letting the excess syrup drain into the double boiler. Place the pieces on a well-oiled cookie sheet. Cool them until the glaze hardens.

GLAZED NUTS
Refrigerate pecans, walnuts or Brazil nuts for 1 hour. Dip them in the glazing syrup and let cool.

GLAZED ALMONDS
Color some almond paste red and green and mold 1 tsp (5 mL) at a time it into oval pieces. Press half an almond in the center of each piece. Refrigerate the almonds for 1 hour. Coat them with glazing syrup and let them cool.

GLAZED STRAWBERRIES
Choose very firm strawberries with green stems. Refrigerate them for 1 hour. Dip each strawberry in the glazing syrup up to the stem. Let cool.

GLAZED PRUNES
Stuff pitted prunes with a piece of candied ginger or a Brazil nut. Refrigerate the prunes for 1 hour. Dip the chilled fruits in the glazing syrup and let cool.

GLAZED GRAPES
With scissors, cut grapes from the cluster, keeping the stems as long as possible. Refrigerate the grapes for 1 hour. Dip each grape in the glazing syrup, holding it by the stem. Let cool.

GLAZED ORANGES OR MANDARINE ORANGES
Peel the oranges and separate them into sections, being careful not to break the membranes. Remove all the white skin which adheres to the pulp. Place the orange sections on a cake rack and let them stand in a cool place for 2 to 3 hours, so that they will dry. Dip each section in glazing syrup. Be careful not to pierce the fruit. Cool.

BEVERAGES

WINE

Wine is one of the most ancient and noble beverages known to the world. For many, no fine meal is complete without wine, and preferably a wine with every course. On the other hand. wine is the perfect accompaniment to a simple meal of bread and cheese.

SERVING WINE

When several wines are served during the course of a meal, it is recommended that they follow a traditional "chain of command": lighter wines are served before more robust ones, white wines before red and younger wines before an older wine.

❧ Classic wine service involves the presentation of 3 different wines: a white wine is served with fish or appetizers, a red with meat or cheese and a sweet dessert wine or a sparkling white wine is served with dessert.

❧ Wine labels usually supply a certain amount of information about the wine—its age, grape type and degree of sweetness. But you may need to know more about the vocabulary of wine in order to understand the label. The following short list of terms will introduce you to the specialized language of the wine lover.

ACIDIC:

All wines contain acids, both fixed and volatile. A lack of acid creates a dull, tasteless wine. On the other hand, an acidic wine has a piquant flavor. Too much acid gives wine an unpleasant taste.

AFTERTASTE:

The lingering taste after the wine has been swallowed.

AROMA:

The characteristic fragrance of the grapes in new wine.

BODY:

The sensation of the wine's weight on the palate, which depends on its alcohol and fruit glycerin content. Grapes high in sugar make full-bodied wines.

BOUQUET:

The perfume of the wine as the esters evaporate. You can bring out the bouquet in a glass of wine by swirling the wine delicately in the glass before sipping it.

CORKY:

A wine that has been spoiled by a diseased or faulty cork.

DRY:

White wines that are low in sugar and certain reds that lack body and are not mellow are called dry.

FRESH:

A wine that pleases the palate because of its slightly acidic flavor.

FRUITY:

Describes a wine that tastes like fresh grapes.

GENEROUS:

An alternate term to describe a "full-bodied" wine.

GREEN:

A very young wine that still possesses some degree of acidity and harshness.

HARD:

A wine that is too acidic.

HEADY:

A wine with a high alcohol content.

HOT OR STRONG:

Describes a wine which contains a lot of alcohol.

LIGHT OR DELICATE:

A wine with a low alcohol content.

PASSÉ:

Wine that has lost its flavor because of bad storage conditions or prolonged storage.

PETILLANT:

Denotes a wine that prickles on the tongue.

RACÉ:

A very well-balanced wine that possesses all the characteristics of its type. This term is only applied to truly great wines.

ROBUST:

A term used to describe wines that are full-bodied and have a pronounced aroma.

SEDIMENT:

Solid matter composed of grape particles, tannins and yeast that precipitate in wines aged in the bottle.

SILKY:

Used especially to describe white wines that are both mellow and sweet.

WEAK:

A wine that is too light and lacks personality.

WELL-BALANCED:

A wine in which all the elements are in perfect proportion to one another.

HOW TO STORE AND SERVE WINE

The deterioration of wine is due primarily to its exposure to air, light and temperature extremes. Wines must be stored very carefully. The place where you store your wine, whether a wine cellar or pantry, should meet the following conditions to maintain the quality of wine:

🌢 A constant temperature of about 54°F (12°C) is ideal. Constant humidity of about 75% will prevent the corks from drying out.

🌢 Wine should be kept in almost total darkness and be protected from vibrations.

🌢 Since wine breathes, it is imperative that you do not store it with anything that may stimulate fermentation such as beer, cider, vegetables or fruits. Wine can also absorb the smell of chemicals or heating oil, thus destroying its taste.

🌢 Bottles of wine should be stored on their sides so that the corks remain moist.

🌢 If you end up with a partially full bottle of wine at the end of a meal, decant the wine into a smaller bottle or jar just large enough to hold the wine and close the jar tightly. This will allow you to preserve the wine's quality for several days.

🌢 Red bordeaux should be served at a temperature of 65°F (18°C). Burgundies and Côtes-du-Rhône are better served a little cooler, at about 60°F (16°C). Beaujolais should be served even cooler, at 58°F (14°C).

🌢 To chill a white wine, plunge the bottle up to its neck into a

Red wine

mixture of water and ice. The best drinking temperature for whites is between 46°F and 53°F (8°C to 12°C). The great Chardonnays are better served at 58°F to 60°F (14°F to 16°C).

🌢 Never add ice cubes to wine. Never keep a bottle of wine in the refrigerator for more than 1 hour.

🌢 Like wines, ports and sherries should always be stored in a cool place. And never put wine near a source of heat.

🌢 White ports, sherries and Madeiras are served cold, whereas red ports, Tarragona wines and sweet dessert wines can be served either cold or at room temperature, depending on your preference.

🌢 Champagnes and sparkling wines are stored on their sides in a cool place to keep the corks moist and are always served chilled. If the bottles are left standing in a vertical position for

as little as 24 hours, the corks can dry out and the gas content may escape. And champagne or any sparkling wine without bubbles is a wasted wine!

🌢 The fermentation of red wines sometimes produces, as a by-product, a sediment called "lees" that includes grape particles, tartrates, tannins and dead yeast cells. Usually wines are decanted in the vineyard to remove this sediment—a delicate operation. If you find that you must decant a bottle of wine due to a great quantity of sediment, carefully uncork the wine with the bottle still in the horizontal storage position. Place a light behind the neck of the bottle and pour the contents slowly into a carafe; stop decanting before any particles of sediment pass through the neck of the bottle. (It is simpler and less risky to place the bottle on the table a few hours before serving it so that there is plenty of time for any sediment to sink to the bottom of the bottle.)

🍷 Corkscrews that operate with a lever take less effort to use than those without levers. Wine baskets that hold the selected wine in a nearly horizontal position during the course of the meal make it easier to pour.

CORKS

In order to avoid breaking the cork when you open a bottle of wine, be sure to insert the corkscrew right in the center of the cork. If the bottle has been stored upright so long that its cork has become hard and dry, place the bottle on its side for a few hours to moisten it; it will be much easier to remove the cork.

🍷 Sometimes the cork shows evidence of discoloration or of mold growing between the bottleneck and the cork; these symptoms are the result of moisture being present in the cork during the corking operation. They do not alter the quality of the wine in any way.

FRENCH WINES

BORDEAUX WINES

Bordeaux wines are produced in a number of wine regions, including Médoc, Graves, Sauternes, Entre-Deux-Mers, Saint-Émilion, Pomerol, Blayais, Bourgeais, Fronsac and les Côtes. Let's look at the major regions in a little more detail.

🍷 The region of Médoc produces only red wines, many of them regarded as noble. The major grape used is the Cabernet Sauvignon, which produces a wine with plenty of body and finesse. Four Médoc vineyards have premier cru status:

Château Lafite-Rothschild
Château Latour
Château Margaux
Château Mouton-Rothschild

🍷 The Graves region also produces wines based on the Cabernet Sauvignon grape, with structure and finesse. Graves is also famous for its white wines, based on the White Sauvignon grape.

🍷 The great Graves red and white wines are:

Château Haut-Brion (red)
Château La Mission-Haut-Brion (whites and reds)
Château Haut-Bailly (red)

🍷 The wines of Sauterne are sweet and fragrant whites. The most famous and sumptuous is indisputably Château d'Yquem, which is produced in the area of Barsac.

🍷 The Entre-Deux-Mers region produces fresh and fruity white wines which are wonderful accompaniments to fish and seafood. The region also produces red wines which are usually sold under the appellation of Bordeaux or Bordeaux supérieur.

🍷 The red wines of Saint-Émilion are richer and softer in taste than the Médoc wines. This is because the Merlot grapes dominate the Cabernet Sauvignon grapes in the blend. Some of the most famous of these wines are from Château Ausone and Château Cheval-Blanc.

🍷 Pomerol wines are equally fleshy and rich; the most renowned is Château Pétrus.

BURGUNDY WINES

Burgundy wines hail from five large regions: Chablis, Côte d'Or (comprised of the Côte de Nuits and the Côte de Beaune), Côte Chalonnaise, Beaujolais and Mâcon.

🍷 Chablis produces white wines with green undertones—they are invariably fruity, fresh and light. Chablis wines are classified as Chablis Grand Cru, Chablis Premier Cru, Chablis and Petit Chablis.

🍷 The Côte d'Or includes Côte de Nuits, which produces almost exclusively full-bodied and robust wines based on the Pinot Noir grape. Among the ones that have earned world-wide reputations are:

Romanée-Conti
Clos-Vougeot
Chambertin
Richebourg
Musigny
Bonnes-Marres

🍷 Côte de Beaune, also in the Côte d'Or, produces both great red wines and white wines. The reds have charm and finesse and are less powerful than the Côtes de Nuits. The whites are exquisitely rich and dry. Look for:

Corton-Charlemagne
Montrachet
Meursault

Among the reds, look for:

Corton
Pommard

Volnay
Chassagne-Montrachet
Beaune
Aloxe-Corton

🍂 The Côte Chalonnaise produces both red and white wines,
but none are grand cru. You will
not find bottles marked appellation Côte Chalonnaise, but if you
are interested in trying wines
from the area, look for:

Rully (reds and whites)
Montagny (whites)
Givry (reds and whites)
Mercurey (reds and whites)

🍂 The Mâcon region produces
predominantly white wines; they
are dry, fruity and very agreeable
to drink. The region also turns
out good red and rosé table wines.
The most famous white Mâcon is
undoubtedly Pouilly-Fuissé.
Other appellations to watch for
are Mâcon and Mâcon supérieur
for red, white and rosé wines.
Mâcon-Villages and Chardonnay-
Mâcon produce only white wines.
🍂 The Beaujolais area produces
some exquisite wines, usually red
wines, possessing a wide range of
tastes from full-bodied to light. In
fact, these wines have such a
great variety of tastes that their
selection remains a question of
personal taste. Most of them are
best drunk rather young. The best
wines from the region are labeled
Beaujolais-Villages. Other names
to look for include:

Saint Amour
Juliénas
Chénas
Moulin-à-Vent

Fleurie
Chiroubles
Morgon
Brouilly
Côte-de-Brouilly

WINES OF THE LOIRE VALLEY

Although it produces a few excellent red wines, the Loire Valley is
best known for its fine white and
rosé wines.
🍂 The Loire is made up of three
major regions—Nantais, Anjou,
and Touraine—as well as a number of smaller regions including
Berry, Nivernais, Orléans and
Haut-Poitou.
🍂 The best known Loire wine is
certainly Muscadet, from the
Nantais area, a light, fresh, slightly acidic wine with a unique bouquet and a color that is almost
golden. It does not keep well, so it
should be consumed young.

🍂 The Anjou region produces a
wide variety of wines: sweet,
semi-dry and dry white wines,
sparkling wines, and reds and
rosés. The rosés from Anjou are
particularly popular—they are
light, fruity, and well balanced.
They differ from other rosés in
that they are equally good as
apéritifs or as wines with meals.
🍂 Saumur, in the Anjou region,
produces dry, nerveux and light
white wines as well as reputable
semi-sparkling wines.
🍂 The region of Touraine also
produces reds, whites, and rosés,
with some great white wines such
as Vouvray and Montlouis. Some
of the reds, including Chinon and
de Bourgueil, are also very good.

ALSATIAN WINES

The best known and best loved
wines of Alsace are its whites,
which are dry, fresh and nerveux.
But although its red wines are rare

White wine

in number, they are also excellent. Wines from Alsace are named for the type of grape they contain. Among these "noble grapes" are:

RIESLING:
King of the Alsatian wines, it is rich in bouquet and alcohol, elegant and racé;

TRAMINER:
A wine with a very pronounced bouquet, it is smooth and low in acid;

TOKAY D'ALSACE:
Not to be confused with the Hungarian Tokay; this is a rich, flavorful full-bodied wine;

SYLVANER:
A green, semi-sparkling and fresh wine.

❧ The wines of Alsace that are derived from several types of grapes are called "Zwicker"; if they are made from noble grapes, they are called "Edelzwicker." These two words, which are calling cards for the wines of Alsace, are always found printed near the name of the wine.

CÔTES DU RHÔNE WINES
The Rhone Valley produces a number of good red wines, some of which rival the Burgundies and Bordeaux. Red wines from the Rhone are the deepest in color, fullest in body and most powerful in alcohol. The whites are sophisticated and rich in flavor.

❧ The best known Rhône wines are:

CHATEAUNEUF-DU-PAPE:
A ruby red, rich, fine, generous and very full-bodied wine

TAVEL:
A rosé, aromatic and generous wine

HERMITAGE:
The whites are elegant and racé; the red is rich and powerful.

CHAMPAGNE
To really appreciate champagne, it's important to understand the way in which it is made.

❧ As soon as they are picked, the grapes are pressed using special fast-action presses which produce a clear white juice even from dark grapes. The "must" (freshly pressed juice) is put in barrels for a first fermentation.

❧ The following spring, the blending of the cuvée takes place; the vintner selects and combines wines from the first fermentation, mixing wines made from dark and light grapes, from different vineyards, and sometimes from different years. (The vintage marked on the bottle indicates the year of harvest of the grape which predominates in the blend.) Once these wines have been "married together," a small amount of sugar called "liqueur de tirage" is added, and the blend is ready to be fermented in the bottle.

❧ In the deep cool caves of the Champagne region, the wines undergo a second fermentation, which lasts three months; the carbonic gas that is unable to escape causes the effervescence. The fermentation process produces a sediment, and the bottles are rotated daily so that this sediment gathers in the neck of the bottle. The sediment is removed during the final stage of preparation, known as clearing; then the bottles are topped up with a mixture of crystallized sugar and old wine. The quantity added determines whether the final champagne is sweet, semi-sweet, dry or extra-dry.

❧ The wines of Champagne are sold under the names of the great families or companies that own the vineyards. These famous names have becomes marks of excellence all over the world, and names that champagne lovers can depend on.

❧ A champagne produced from white grapes only is allowed to carry the appellation "blanc de blancs."

❧ Still white wines from the champagne region are called Couteaux Champenois.

❧ The red wines of the Champagne region are never bubbly. The best known are Bouzy, d'Ambonnay and Damery.

WINES OF THE WORLD

Although France is the birthplace of the great wine tradition, a number of other countries also produce excellent wines.

❧ In Europe, Italy produces a huge quantity of good red, white and rosé wines. Germany and Switzerland both produce excellent white wines based on grapes unique to their areas. Spain and

Portugal also share the fine wine tradition.

🍂 The United States produces some excellent wines. California vineyards rely especially on Cabernet Sauvignon, Chardonnay and Zinfandel grapes. Some very good wines are made in Oregon based on Pinot Noir grapes. And Canada has a small but growing wine industry, with some prize-winning efforts being produced in Ontario and British Columbia.

🍂 Some of the best South American wines come from Chili and Argentina.

🍂 Finally, Australia produces an impressive range of wines, some of which rival the finest European wines in quality.

WINE AND CHEESE

Wine, exquisite in its own right, often suggests the cheese that will taste best with it. Gruyère cheese, for example, is truly delicious if it is accompanied with a light white wine. On the other hand, a strong-flavored Roquefort cheese goes well with a robust Burgundy or a full-bodied Bordeaux.

🍂 At a wine and cheese party where many varieties of cheeses are served, the best rule is to begin with a light, dry white wine to drink with the light, creamy and mild cheeses. Select from cream cheese, Baron, Brick, Colby, Emmenthal and Ricotta, for example.

🍂 Serve a more robust wine such as Burgundy to accompany cheeses that have a strong and definite character—strong Cheddars, Anfrom, goat cheese and blue cheeses.

WINE SUGGESTIONS

DRY WHITE WINE

France:	Bordeaux, Muscadet, Gros Plant, Graves, Gaillac, Beaujolais, Alsacian Rieslings, Bourgogne Aligoté, Pouilly-Fumé, Saint-Véran, Sancerre, Chablis.
Italy:	Orvieto, Soave, Franscati, Est-Est-Est, Torgiano, Lacrima Christi.
Portugal:	Vinho Verde, Bucellas.
Germany:	Kabinett de la Moselle, Rheingau.

LIGHT RED WINES

France:	Côtes du Ventoux, Saumur, Mâcon, Bordeaux, Beaujolais, Brouilly, Médoc, Bourgueil, Haut-Médoc, Saint-Émilion, Pauillac, Moulis, Fronsac.
Italy:	Chianti, Valpolicella, Bardolino, Chianti Classico, Reserva, Barbera d'Alba, Dolcetto d'Alba, Vino Nobile de Montepulciano.
Spain:	Rioja.
Portugal:	Dâo.

ROBUST RED WINES

France:	Corbières, Fitou, Minervois, Côtes-du-Rhône, Crozes-Hermitage, Gigondas, Moulin-à-Vent, Madiran, Châteauneuf-du-Pape, Hermitage, Hautes-Côtes de Nuits, Mercurey.
Italy:	Barbera d'Asti, Sangiovese de Romagna, Nebbiolo D'Alba, Barbaresco, Barolo, Amarone.
Spain:	Rioja.
Portugal:	Dâo, Garrafeira.

🍂 Cheeses that are neither particularly mild nor strong (such as Oka, Brie, Camembert, Edam, Gouda, Saint André) are good with a light red wine.

🍂 Of course, it is not necessary to serve three types of wine. A well-chilled Alsatian or Rhine wine can be served with almost any type of cheese. A Chianti or a Valpolicella can also be served with a variety of cheeses. When you make your selection, be as flexible as you wish, since any wine you prefer still remains the best one to serve.

APÉRITIFS

Apéritifs are generally served in the late afternoon. They are light and tasty beverages. Their name comes from the Latin *aperire* meaning to open, that is, to build up an appetite.

🍂 Cocktails and whiskey are not truly apéritifs although they are sometimes served as such.

🍂 Some of the most popular apéritifs are:

French vermouth (dry)
Italian vermouth (sweet)
Madeira
Marsala
Dubonnet
Amer Picon
Pernod
Cinzano
Punt e Mes
Ouzo (Greek)

🍂 There are many more, just as there are also many brand names for each type. Clearly, there is a lot of room for exploration by apéritif lovers!

HOW TO SERVE AN APÉRITIF

🍂 Refrigerate apéritif or port glasses a few hours before using them. If this is not possible, fill the glasses with ice cubes for a few minutes. Discard the ice and pour about 3 oz (85 mL) of the apéritif of your choice into the chilled glass. Serve.

🍂 Apéritif on ice: put 2 to 4 ice cubes in an old-fashioned glass before adding the apéritif of your choice. Add a piece of lemon zest, if you like.

GRENADINE PICON

🍂 Pour over ice cubes 2 oz (60 mL) of Amer Picon and 4 drops of grenadine. Top off with carbonated water.

VERMOUTH CASSIS

🍂 In a large glass put 2 ice cubes, 3 oz (85 mL) of vermouth and 1 tbsp (15 mL) of crème de cassis. Add a little carbonated water and a piece of lemon zest.

ORANGE SAINT RAPHAEL

🍂 Place in a cocktail shaker 2 oz (60 mL) Saint Raphael and 1 oz (30 mL) of orange juice. Fill with crushed ice. Shake and serve with an orange slice.

LIQUEURS

Liqueurs come in a variety of flavors, each with its own distinct aroma. They are derived from fruits, flowers, herbs, aromatic seeds and spices. Liqueurs are usually served as digestives after large meals.

🍂 Ice cream covered with the appropriate liqueur becomes a delicious dessert. An ordinary cake can be transformed into a delightful treat when you pour a bit of liqueur over it. And a fruit salad garnished with liqueur makes a quick and elegant dessert.

🍂 Liqueurs are served in small liqueur glasses. But good brandies and cognacs should ideally be served in snifters, so that the heat of the hands warms the alcohol and releases the bouquet.

🍂 If you want to use a liqueur for cooking purposes, you should make sure you are familiar with its basic flavoring ingredient so you can successfully pair it with the right kind of food. You could, for example, use brandy to flavor an apricot soufflé, but an apricot liqueur would enhance the taste much better; and an orange liqueur will do wonders for a fruit salad.

THE FIVE IMPORTANT LIQUEUR GROUPS

LIQUEURS FLAVORED
WITH FRUITS AND FLOWERS

Apricot
Apricot brandy
Apricot liqueur
Apry Marie Brizard

Black Currant
Crème de cassis

Cherry
Cherry brandy
Cherry liqueur
Cherry Heering (Danish)

Orange
Cointreau
Curaçao
Grand Marnier
Triple Sec

Peach
Peach brandy
Peach liqueur

Grenadine
Grenadine syrup (non alcoholic)

Sloe (blackthorn)
Sloe gin

LIQUEURS FLAVORED
WITH SEEDS, PODS AND HERBS

Almonds
Almond cream
Orgeat (non alcoholic)

Anise
Absinthe
Anisette
Ouzo
Pernod
Ricard

Caraway Seeds
Kummel

Cocoa Bean
Crème de cacao

Coffee
Crème de café
Kahlua (Mexico)

Vanilla Bean
Crème de vanille

Mint
Crème de menthe
(white or green)
Frappé mint

FRUIT-BASED EAUX-DE-VIE
AND BRANDIES

Apple
Calvados
Apple brandy

Cherry
Kirsch

Grape
Armagnac

Liqueur Frappé

Brandy
Cognac
Grappa (Italian)
Marc de Bourgogne
Metaxa (Greek)

Plum
Mirabelle
Dolfis
Quetsch (Alsatian)

LIQUEUR FRAPPÉ

Crème de menthe, Bénédictine, Cointreau or any other liqueur of your choice
crushed ice
small straws

❧ Fill a frappé glass with as much crushed ice as possible. Pour 1 to 2 oz (30 to 60 mL) of liqueur over the ice. Stick 2 small straws in the ice and serve.

HOT CHRISTMAS PUNCH

1 orange
12 whole cloves
2 bottles light red wine
1 lemon, unpeeled, thinly sliced
1 cinnamon stick
½ cup (125 mL) seedless raisins
½ cup (125 mL) sugar
½ cup (125 mL) brandy

❧ Preheat the oven to 400°F (200°C). Wash the orange. With the tip of a sharp knife make diamond-shaped incisions in the skin. Stick a clove in each diamond. Place the orange on a pie plate. Bake 30 minutes in the hot oven.
❧ In the meantime, pour into a large saucepan the wine, lemon, cinnamon stick, seedless raisins and ¼ cup (50 mL) sugar. Add the baked orange. Simmer,

French Punch

the *Colonial Wassail Bowl* recipe (see page 707) and place them in the punch bowl.

❧ Place all the remaining ingredients in a large soup kettle. Bring to a boil and pour over the apples through a fine sieve. Serve hot.

❧ Serves 50.

FRENCH PUNCH

zest of 1 lemon
1 cup (250 mL) sugar
1 cup (250 mL) water
½ cup (125 mL) Cointreau
or another liqueur of your choice
juice of 2 lemons
juice of 2 oranges
ice
2 bottles Burgundy

❧ Bring to a boil the water, sugar and lemon zest. Boil for 3 minutes. Let cool.

❧ Add Cointreau, lemon juice and orange juice to the cooled syrup. Strain through a very fine sieve. Refrigerate.

❧ When you are ready to serve the punch, pour the juice mixture into a punch bowl. Put a large block of ice in the middle of the punch bowl and pour in the red wine.

❧ Yields 14 to 18 punch cups.

uncovered, for 20 minutes. Do not boil. Stir several times. Remove the cinnamon stick and pour into a punch bowl.

❧ Mix the remaining sugar with the brandy in a small saucepan. Warm and then light with a match. Pour into the punch while still aflame.

❧ Yields 12 servings.

CHRISTMAS PUNCH

4 cups (1 L) sweet cider
2 cups (500 mL) pineapple juice
2 cups (500 mL) orange juice
¼ cup (50 mL) lemon juice
1 cup (250 mL) cranberry jelly
pinch of ground cloves
1 banana
1 small pineapple
ice cubes

❧ Mix together the sweet cider, pineapple juice, orange juice and lemon juice. Heat the cranberry jelly over low heat until syrupy. Add the ground cloves. Mix to blend.

❧ Slice the peeled banana into the bottom of a punch bowl. Peel the pineapple and cut into small cubes; place over the banana. Pour the cranberry syrup over the fruits and mix thoroughly.

❧ To serve, pour the cider mixture into the punch bowl and add plenty of ice.

HOT CIDER PUNCH

8 baked apples
48 cups (12 L) good sweet cider
6 cinnamon sticks
4 tsp (20 mL) cloves
1 tsp (5 mL) grated nutmeg
1½ cups (375 mL) sugar

❧ To bake the apples, follow the instructions for baked apples in

RUM PUNCH

6 lemons
3 cups (750 mL) hot strong tea
1 cup (250 mL) sugar
3 cups (750 mL) rum
2 tbsp (30 mL) brandy
ice cubes

Slice the zest off the lemons as thinly as possible and place the zests in a punch bowl. Pour hot tea over the lemon zests and let stand for 1 hour.

Squeeze the juice from the lemons and add to the sugar. Let stand 1 hour, stirring occasionally to dissolve the sugar.

To serve, mix together the tea, lemon syrup, rum and brandy. Add ice cubes and serve.

Yields 8 to 10 punch cups.

CHAMPAGNE PUNCH

ice cubes
1 bottle champagne
¼ cup (50 mL) cognac or brandy
1 tbsp (15 mL) Cointreau
2 tsp (10 mL) sugar syrup
½ cup (125 mL) pineapple chunks, fresh
½ peeled orange, thinly sliced

About an hour before serving, fill the punch bowl with ice cubes.

Mix all the ingredients just before serving.

Throw out the ice. Pour the mixture into the cold punch bowl. Float some attractive rose blossoms in the punch bowl. Serve the punch immediately.

ROYAL PUNCH

1 block ice
2 bottles Champagne
1 cup (250 mL) orange juice
1 cup (250 mL) lemon juice
¼ cup (50 mL) Curaçao
or Cointreau
1 tbsp (15 mL) Angostura bitters

1 large bottle soda water
diced fresh pineapple

Just before serving, put a block of ice in the punch bowl. Never use ice cubes for this punch.

Pour the ingredients over the ice in the order indicated in the ingredient list. Garnish with pineapple cubes and serve immediately.

PEACH AND WINE PUNCH

6 fresh peaches or 1 box frozen peaches
¼ cup (50 mL) honey
1 cup (250 mL) brandy
ice
2 bottles Sauterne or rosé
1 bottle sparkling wine

Peel and slice the fresh peaches or thaw out the frozen peaches. Add the honey and brandy to the peaches. Cover and let marinate for 1 hour.

When ready to serve, place the peaches in a punch bowl. Put a large cube of ice in the middle of the bowl and pour the Sauterne over the ice. Blend thoroughly and pour the sparkling wine over all.

Yields 14 to 18 punch cups.

REIMS PUNCH

2 cups (500 mL) fresh grated pineapple
¼ cup (50 mL) sugar
⅓ cup (75 mL) brandy
1 block ice
1 cup (250 mL) orange juice
2 bottles champagne

Grate the pineapple and mix it with the sugar and the brandy. Stir until the sugar dissolves. Cover the pineapple mixture and refrigerate for 12 hours.

Peach and Wine Punch

Put a block of ice in the punch bowl. Add the orange juice to the pineapple mixture. Pour this mixture over the ice. Add the champagne and serve immediately.

WEDDING PUNCH

2 bottles champagne
1 bottle Sauterne
1 large bottle soda water
ice cubes
¼ cup (50 mL) cognac
or brandy
¼ cup (50 mL) Cointreau
¼ cup (50 mL) sugar syrup
or maple syrup
1 cup (250 mL) thinly sliced
strawberries
fresh mint leaves

Refrigerate the champagne, Sauterne and soda water for 12 hours.

To serve, place the ice in a punch bowl. Mix together the brandy, Cointreau and sugar syrup or maple syrup. Pour the mixture over the ice and stir.

Add the champagne, Sauterne and soda water. Garnish with strawberries and mint leaves. Serve.

This recipe yields 36 punch cups.

STRAWBERRY PUNCH

2 cups (500 mL) fresh strawberries or 1 box frozen strawberries
½ cup (125 mL) sugar
1 bottle white wine
1 cup (250 mL) sugar
¾ cup (175 mL) water
2 bottles Alsatian
or Swiss white wine
3 cups (750 mL) water

Clean the strawberries, slice thin and sprinkle with sugar. If you use frozen strawberries, thaw them and omit ½ cup (125 mL) of the sugar called for in the recipe. Add the white wine to the strawberries. Cover and refrigerate for 12 hours.

Prepare a sugar syrup with the ¾ cup (175 mL) water and 1 cup (250 mL) sugar. Refrigerate.

To serve, add the 3 cups (750 mL) water and Alsatian or Swiss wine to the strawberries. Mix well and sweeten to taste with the sugar syrup.

This punch may be prepared in advance, but it must be refrigerated.

The sugar syrup keeps for a very long period in a tightly corked bottle.

ENGLISH BISHOP

1 orange
whole cloves
½ cup (125 mL) brown sugar
1 bottle port
⅓ cup (75 mL) cognac or brandy

Wash the orange and stud it all over with whole cloves. Sprinkle the brown sugar over the orange. Place in a pie plate. Bake in a 375°F (190°C) oven for 30 to 40 minutes or until the brown sugar caramelizes.

Pour the port into a glass or non-aluminum saucepan. Cut the orange into quarters and add to the port. Simmer the port, without letting it boil, for 20 minutes.

Remove from the heat and add the brandy. Serve this drink hot in china cups.

Yields 6 to 8 cups (1.5 to 2 L).

Strawberry Punch

COLONIAL WASSAIL BOWL

6 medium baked apples
½ tsp (2 mL) whole cardamom seeds
½ tsp (2 mL) whole cloves
½ nutmeg
2 ginger roots
1 tsp (5 mL) coriander seeds
1 cup (250 mL) water
2 bottles port
1 bottle light beer
½ cup (125 mL) sugar
4 egg yolks, beaten
4 egg whites, beaten stiff

🍂 To bake the apples, remove the core from each apple. Place in a cake pan with 1 tbsp (15 mL) sugar and 1 tsp (5 mL) butter in each apple. Bake in a 500°F (260°C) oven for 30 to 40 minutes or until the apples are well browned.

🍂 In a saucepan put the cardamom, cloves, nutmeg, ginger, coriander seeds and water. Bring to a boil. Cover and simmer for 30 minutes. Strain through a very fine sieve.

🍂 Put the port, sugar, simmered spice liquid and beer into a large saucepan. Simmer until the sugar is melted, stirring constantly.

🍂 Add a little of the hot liquid to the beaten egg yolks. Mix well, then pour the egg yolk mixture into the hot liquid while beating constantly. Remove from the heat.

🍂 Add the stiffly beaten egg whites and stir again briskly until very frothy.

🍂 To serve, place an apple in each mug and fill with the hot wine mixture. Serve with a spoon with which to eat the apple.

ENGLISH WASSAIL BOWL

½ tsp (2 mL) ground ginger
½ tsp (2 mL) ground nutmeg
¼ tsp (1 mL) cinnamon
1 cup (250 mL) sugar cubes
2 lemons
6 cups (1.5 L) ale
3 cups (750 mL) dry sherry
6 small baked apples

🍂 Mix the spices together. Rub the sugar cubes over the lemons until they turn yellow.

🍂 Place the spices, lemon-flavored sugar and 2 cups (500 mL) ale in a saucepan. Boil for 1 minute, stirring constantly in order to dissolve the sugar cubes.

🍂 Add the remaining ale and sherry. Bring to a boil and remove immediately from the heat.

🍂 To bake the apples, remove the core from each apple. Place in a cake pan with 1 tbsp (15 mL) sugar and 1 tsp (5 mL) butter in each apple. Bake in a 500°F (260°C) oven for 30 to 40 minutes or until the apples are well browned. Place the apples in the punch bowl and pour the boiling liquid on top.

CHRISTMAS EGGNOG

12 egg yolks
1½ cups (375 mL) finely granulated sugar
4 cups (1 L) milk
4 cups (1 L) whipping cream
40 oz (1.2 L) whiskey
26 oz (750 mL) cognac or brandy
12 egg whites
2 tbsp (30 mL) rum
freshly grated nutmeg

🍂 Beat the yolks together with the sugar until they become very light in color.

🍂 Place a punch bowl on a bed of crushed ice. Pour in the yolk mixture and add the milk. Mix well.

🍂 Whip the cream and stir it into the milk mixture. Slowly add the whiskey and brandy, stirring continuously.

🍂 Beat the egg whites until stiff and add them to the mixture. Pour some rum over the surface and sprinkle with nutmeg.

🍂 Yields 50 servings but can easily be reduced by ½ or by ¼.

🍂 For eggnog with rum, replace the whiskey with an equal quantity of white rum.

SWEDISH GLOGG

For many, there is nothing like a bottle of cold bubbly champagne to celebrate Christmas, but for the Swedes hot potent glogg is the drink of choice. According to tradition, Swedish women were not allowed to sneak a sip of glogg until someone had toasted "skol!"

26 oz (750 mL) aquavit or vodka
¼ cup (50 mL) seedless raisins
¼ cup (50 mL) blanched almonds
seeds from 5 cardamom pods
4 whole cloves
1 4-in. (10-cm) cinnamon stick
zest of 4 oranges
⅔ cup (150 mL) sugar

Whiskey or Brandy Fizz

🍂 Pour the aquavit or vodka into a large non-aluminum saucepan. Add the remaining ingredients except for the blanched almonds. Stir until the sugar is well dissolved, then let the mixture stand for 4 to 6 hours.

🍂 To serve, warm up the glogg but be careful not to let it boil. Pour the glogg into a punch bowl and serve it in punch cups with a raisin and an almond at the bottom of each cup.

🍂 A beautiful Swedish custom is to darken the room and to ignite the glogg. When the fire dies down, put the lights back on and "skol!" until the bowl is empty.

SCANDINAVIAN GLOGG

⅓ cup (75 mL) blanched almonds
½ cup (125 mL) raisins
5 cloves
3 sticks cinnamon
10 cardamom seeds
1 bottle sherry
1 bottle port
½ cup (125 mL) sugar cubes
2 cups (500 mL) cognac

🍂 One week before serving this punch, put the almonds, raisins, cloves, cinnamon sticks and cardamom seeds in a saucepan along with just enough port to cover everything. Bring to a boil over low heat. As soon as the mixture starts to boil, remove it from the heat. Pour into a bottle.

🍂 Cover securely and store in a cool place.

🍂 To make the glogg, strain the spiced port through a fine sieve. Add the remaining port and sherry. Pour into a heat-proof bowl and place on a hot plate. Heat until the mixture boils.

🍂 Place the sugar cubes in a small strainer held over the bowl and soak them with the cognac. Light the cognac and continue pouring it. Drop the remaining sugar into the punch. Stir the mixture lightly until the flames die out. Serve hot, along with a few raisins and an almond in each glass.

COCKTAILS

Traditionally, cocktails were made with distilled spirits (rum, gin, vodka or whiskey), but nowadays they are made with a variety of bases. Like an apéritif, a cocktail is a pleasant prelude to dinner. Next time you have guests over, plan on serving cocktails and offer a couple of suggestions from among the following. Even their names are alluring.

CUBA LIBRE

juice of ½ lime
3 ice cubes
¼ cup (50 mL) rum (preferably white)
cola

🍂 Squeeze the lime juice into a large glass, then throw in the peel. Add the ice and rum and fill the glass with cola. Stir and serve.

SIDECAR

lemon juice
Cointreau
brandy
ice cubes

🍂 Fill a cocktail shaker with equal parts of lemon juice, Cointreau and brandy. Add ice. Shake briskly and serve.

RUM COLLINS

juice of 1 lemon
1 tsp (5 mL) sugar syrup
⅓ cup (75 mL) rum
5 drops Angostura bitters
carbonated mineral water

&• Place the ingredients in a cocktail shaker half-filled with crushed ice. Shake briskly. Pour into a tall glass and fill with carbonated water.
&• To make a Tom Collins, replace the rum with an equal amount of gin.

DRY MARTINI

⅔ gin
⅓ dry vermouth

&• Place the ingredients in a cocktail shaker. Add the ice. Shake briskly and pour into a cocktail glass. Serve with an olive or small onion spiked on a cocktail pick. Twist a piece of lemon zest and drop it into the glass.

MANHATTAN

⅔ whisky
⅓ dry vermouth
3 drops Angostura bitters

&• Fill a very large glass with the ice and pour the ingredients on top. Stir well with a large spoon. Pour into cocktail glasses and serve.

BLACK VELVET

&• Fill a tall glass with equal parts of chilled stout and iced champagne.

WHISKEY OR BRANDY FIZZ

ice
3 tbsp (45 mL) lemon or lime juice
1 tsp (5 mL) sugar syrup
3 tbsp (45 mL) whisky or brandy
soda water

&• Half fill a cocktail shaker with ice. Add the lime or lemon juice, sugar and whisky or brandy. Shake briskly.
&• Pour into a tall glass and fill with carbonated water. Stir with a spoon and serve.

BLACK STRIPE

⅓ cup (75 mL) rum
1 tsp (5 mL) molasses
1 tsp (5 mL) lemon juice
very hot tea
lemon zest

&• Warm a mug by dipping it into hot water.
&• Pour in the rum, molasses and lemon juice. Fill the mug with hot tea. Top with a small piece of lemon zest and serve.

PORT OR SHERRY FLIP

crushed ice
⅓ cup (75 mL) port or sherry

2 tbsp (30 mL) strong coffee, cold
1 tbsp (15 mL) cream
1 egg

&• Half fill a cocktail shaker with crushed ice. Pour the port or sherry, coffee and cream over the ice.
&• Break the egg and add it to the cocktail shaker. Cover and shake briskly until perfectly blended. Pour into an old-fashioned glass.

PLANTER'S PUNCH

ice cubes
2 tsp (10 mL) sugar
juice of 1 lime
2 drops Angostura bitters
½ cup (125 mL) rum
few drops grenadine
or maple syrup
crushed ice
soda water
orange slices, unpeeled
pineapple cubes

&• Fill a cocktail shaker with ice cubes. Add all the ingredients up to and including the rum in the given order.
&• Cover and shake briskly for a few seconds. Pour the desired quantity into large glasses filled with crushed ice. Fill with soda water. Garnish with slices of unpeeled orange and pineapple cubes.

WHISKEY SOUR

ice cubes
¼ cup (50 mL) whiskey
juice of ½ lemon
1 to 2 tsp (5 to 10 mL) sugar
or sugar syrup
orange slice or cherry

❧ Place 8 to 10 ice cubes in a cocktail shaker. Add the remaining ingredients, except the orange slice or cherry. Shake briskly for 1 minute.

❧ Pour into a well-chilled whiskey sour glass. Garnish with an orange slice or a cherry.

TOMATO JUICE SURPRISE

1 cucumber
5 to 6 cups (1.2 to 1.5 L) tomato juice
1 tsp (5 mL) sugar
salt and pepper to taste
juice of ½ lemon
1 tbsp (15 mL) Worcestershire sauce
½ cup (125 mL) gin or vodka
ice cubes

❧ Peel and finely grate 1 medium cucumber. Add the tomato juice, sugar, salt and pepper. Refrigerate

a few hours or overnight. When ready to serve, add the juice of ½ lemon, the Worcestershire sauce and ½ cup (125 mL) alcohol. Serve this drink chilled or unchilled in cocktail glasses over ice cubes. It's so refreshing!

SCREWDRIVER

⅓ cup (75 mL) vodka
1 cup (250 mL) (350 mL) orange juice
ice cubes

❧ Add the vodka to the orange juice. Add ice cubes to taste and serve.

ALEXANDER

2 tbsp (30 mL) gin
1 tbsp (15 mL) cream
1 tbsp (15 mL) crème de cacao
crushed ice

❧ Place all the ingredients in a cocktail shaker. Add crushed ice and shake briskly.

❧ Substitute brandy for the gin to make a Brandy Alexander.

BAMBOO

3 tbsp (45 mL) sherry
3 tbsp (45 mL) dry vermouth
few drops Angostura bitters
crushed ice

❧ Place the ingredients in a cocktail shaker with some crushed ice. Shake briskly and serve in a cocktail glass.

BLOODY MARY

⅓ cup (75 mL) vodka
⅔ cup (150 mL) tomato juice
1 tbsp (15 mL) lemon juice
1 drop Tabasco
few drops Worcestershire sauce
crushed ice

❧ Place all the ingredients in a cocktail shaker.

❧ Add crushed ice to taste. Cover and shake well. Pour into chilled glasses.

SUGAR SYRUP

1 lb (500 g) sugar
4 cups (1 L) cold water
2 cups (500 mL) cold water

❧ Place the sugar in a bowl with the 4 cups (1 L) of water. Stir often to dissolve the sugar without heating; this procedure will make a perfect syrup. As the sugar dissolves, add 2 more cups

Bloody Mary

(500 mL) cold water. When the sugar is completely dissolved, pour into bottles. Cover securely and refrigerate. This syrup will keep very well as long as it is refrigerated, and is a handy addition to any home bar as a sweetener for a wide range of beverages.

SHANDY GAFF

❧ Fill a tall glass with equal parts of chilled beer or ale and chilled ginger beer. Stir just enough to blend the two liquids. Serve.

NON-ALCOHOLIC DRINKS

Fresh Mint Punch

Sometimes you may prefer to serve only non-alcoholic beverages, although on most occasions providing guests with a choice of alcoholic or non-alcoholic beverages is appreciated. Here are several delightful non-alcoholic punches and syrups.

FRUIT JUICE PUNCH

⅓ cup (75 mL) strong tea, hot
1 cup (250 mL) sugar
¾ cup (175 mL) orange
or grape juice
½ cup (125 mL) lemon juice
2 cups (500 mL) ginger ale
2 cups (500 mL) soda water

❧ Prepare tea with 1 tbsp (15 mL) tea or 3 tea bags over which you pour ½ cup (125 mL) boiling water. Let steep for 5 minutes then pour over the sugar. Stir until the sugar is dissolved.

❧ Pour the tea syrup into a large jug, then add the orange juice and lemon juice. Add ice cubes to the mixture, or put it in the refrigerator.

❧ When ready to serve, add the ginger ale and soda water. Garnish to taste with orange slices cut in quarters.

FLORIDA PUNCH

3 cups (750 mL) tea
1½ cups (375 mL) sugar
3 cups (750 mL) grapefruit juice
3 cups (750 mL) orange juice
1½ cups (375 mL) lemon juice
8 cups (2 L) chilled ginger ale
ice cubes (optional)
2 limes, unpeeled, thinly sliced

❧ Heat the tea with the sugar. Boil for 3 minutes. Cool thoroughly.

❧ To the cooled mixture, add the grapefruit juice, orange juice and lemon juice. Refrigerate until ready to serve.

❧ To serve, pour the mixture into a punch bowl, then add the chilled ginger ale. Add ice and garnish with lime slices floating on top.

FRESH MINT PUNCH

2 cups (500 mL) sugar
2 cups (500 mL) water
1 cup (250 mL) fresh mint
2 cups (500 mL) lemon juice
¼ tsp (1 mL) salt
green food coloring
4 cups (1 L) ginger ale

❧ Bring the sugar, water and fresh mint to a boil. Simmer for 5 to 8 minutes. Cool and strain the liquid through a fine sieve.

❧ Add the lemon juice, salt and

Blueberry Punch

some food coloring, if desired. When ready to serve, add the ginger ale.

❧ Garnish with small fresh mint leaves.

YULETIDE PUNCH

2 cans frozen concentrated lemonade
2 cans frozen concentrated limeade
3 cups (750 mL) fresh grapefruit juice
2 cans pineapple juice
12 cups (3 L) ginger ale
4 cups (1 L) weak tea, cold
12 cups (3 L) crushed ice

❧ Mix together the lemonade and limeade, grapefruit and pineapple juices in a punch bowl.
❧ When ready to serve, add the ginger ale and cold tea. Stir thoroughly.

❧ If you wish, float a wreath of holly on the punch and decorate it with green and red candied cherries.

❧ This recipe makes 50 servings.

GRAPE JUICE PUNCH

1 cup (250 mL) orange juice
½ cup (125 mL) lemon juice
2 cups (500 mL) grape juice
2 cups (500 mL) water
4 tbsp (60 mL) liquid honey

❧ Mix all the ingredients together, then put into bottles. Cap and refrigerate for 24 hours. Serve.

MARTHA'S FINNISH SUMMER PUNCH

Prepare everything the day before, then refrigerate. When your guests arrive, all you have to do is add the soda water and the ice cubes.

1 small pineapple
2 cups (500 mL) fresh raspberries
or 2 cups (500 mL) bottled cherry or raspberry juice
2 unpeeled lemons, sliced paper thin
1 orange, peeled and sliced
1 large bottle soda water
ice cubes

❧ Peel the pineapple and cut it into small dice.
❧ Heat the cleaned raspberries, crushing them as they cook in order to extract the juice. Simmer about 5 to 8 minutes. Press the raspberries through a sieve while hot. Measure the juice, then add water until you have obtained 2 cups (500 mL) of liquid.
❧ Add the pineapple to the raspberry liquid (or to the bottled cherry or raspberry juice). Mix together, then add the lemon and orange slices. Mix again, then refrigerate 12 to 24 hours. To serve, pour the mixture into a punch bowl. Add 12 to 24 ice cubes and then pour the soda water into the bowl. Serve in punch cups, making sure that there is a bit of fruit in each cup.

BLUEBERRY PUNCH

1 cup (250 mL) blueberries
1 cup (250 mL) honey
1½ cups (375 mL) orange juice
½ cup (125 mL) lemon juice
2 cups (500 mL) strong tea
2 cups (500 mL) ginger ale
crushed ice

❧ Place the blueberries and honey in a bowl, then lightly crush the blueberries with a fork.

Add the orange juice, lemon juice and tea. Mix together well. Refrigerate for 3 to 4 hours.

🍂 When ready to serve, add the ginger ale and the ice. You can also, if you like, pour the blueberry mixture through a fine sieve before adding the ice.

RASPBERRY VINEGAR

2 pints (1 L) fresh raspberries or 2 boxes frozen raspberries
½ cup (125 mL) cider vinegar
¾ cup (175 mL) sugar
soda water

🍂 Mix together the raspberries and the vinegar. Cover and refrigerate for 24 hours.

🍂 Press the raspberries firmly through a sieve to extract the greatest quantity of juice.

🍂 Add the sugar to the juice and heat until the sugar dissolves, then refrigerate the mixture.

🍂 To serve, fill ⅓ of a glass with crushed ice, then pour in the raspberry vinegar until the glass is about ⅔ full (or even a bit more), then add soda water until the glass is filled.

🍂 The mixture can be kept from 3 to 4 weeks in sterilized containers in the refrigerator.

TROPICAL JULEP

If you choose not to serve alcohol, try this refreshing fruit drink, which is delicious sipped leisurely before dining.

3 to 6 large sprigs of fresh mint
2 cups (500 mL) white grape juice
juice of 1 lemon or 2 limes
juice of 1 grapefruit
1 cup (250 mL) grated fresh pineapple
pinch of salt
2 cups (500 mL) ginger ale

🍂 Place the mint in the bottom of a pitcher. Gently crush with a wooden spoon, until you can smell the fresh perfume of the mint. Add the grape juice, lemon or lime juice and the grapefruit juice. Stir until well blended, then cover and refrigerate. Also refrigerate the grated fresh pineapple in a covered bowl, as well as the ginger ale.

🍂 When ready to serve, place 4 or 5 cubes of ice in some tall glasses. Divide the pineapple equally into each glass, then do the same with the refrigerated juice. Fill each glass with ginger ale. Add some sugar if you like the drink sweeter.

LEMONADE, LIMEADE OR ORANGEADE

Wash a lemon or a lime. Remove a small slice from each end. Cut in quarters and place in the blender without peeling. Cover the blender. Blend at high speed for 40 seconds. Stop the blender, add 3 or 4 ice cubes, then blend at low speed. Add 2 cups (500 mL) of water and sugar to taste. Serve.

🍂 Orangeade is prepared in the same way. However, the orange must be peeled, and you must remove as much of the white pith as possible as it will make the drink bitter.

STRAWBERRY LEMONADE

1 box frozen strawberries
¼ cup (50 mL) lemon juice
¼ cup (50 mL) sugar
2 cups (500 mL) water
8 to 10 ice cubes

🍂 Let the strawberries thaw, then put them in the blender jar.

🍂 Add the rest of the ingredients, then cover and blend for 50 to 60 seconds.

APPLE LEMONADE

6 cups (1.5 L) unsweetened apple juice
1 to 1¼ cups (250 mL to 300 mL) unstrained lemon juice
¼ cup (50 mL) liquid honey
sprigs of fresh mint
ice cubes

🍂 Mix the apple juice, lemon juice and honey together well. Place in a glass pitcher, then add the sprigs of mint and the ice cubes. Stir a second or two.

VICTORIAN GRAPE COOLER

1 cup (250 mL) honey
3 cups (750 mL) water
2 cups (500 mL) grape juice
2 cups (500 mL) orange juice, fresh or frozen
1 cup (250 mL) lemon juice, fresh or frozen

🍂 Place the water and honey in a saucepan and boil for 5 minutes. Cool, then add the grape juice, orange juice and lemon juice. Pour over ice in a large pitcher or in a tall glass.

FLAVORED TOMATO JUICE

🍃 Place in the blender jar 1 can of tomato juice, then add one of the following ingredients or combinations:

½ cup (125 mL) diced celery;
4 slices peeled cucumber, 1 slice onion;
½ cup (125 mL) sliced carrots, salt;
6 sprigs parsley, 1 green onion, pinch of salt and a bit of sugar;
pinch of basil or tarragon;
1 tbsp (15 mL) chives;
1 slice lemon or lime.

🍃 Cover and blend for 20 seconds, then serve over ice.

CELERY COCKTAIL

2 lemons, peeled
½ cup (125 mL) sugar
1 cup (250 mL) green celery leaves, well packed
4 to 5 cups (1 to 1.2 L) water
5 or 6 ice cubes

🍃 Place all the ingredients in the blender jar. Cover and blend for 1 minute at high speed. Strain through a sieve and serve.

FROSTED GRAPEFRUIT DRINK

4 cups (1 L) grapefruit juice
fresh mint
lemon slices

🍃 Pour half of the grapefruit juice into an ice cube tray, then place in the freezer.

🍃 To serve, fill 4 to 6 glasses with the grapefruit ice cubes. Pour the remaining juice over the cubes. Garnish each glass with a lemon slice and a few mint leaves.

CAT'S PAW

🍃 Pour cold ginger ale in a glass. Add a few drops of grenadine syrup, a piece of lemon zest and a slice of orange. Serve.

GREEN CATERPILLAR

🍃 Pour soda water or tonic water over ice cubes slowly, so that it remains bubbly. Then add 2 slices of unpeeled cucumber or 2 leaves of borage (if you have some growing in your garden), or simply a long thin slice of cucumber peel. That's all there is to it!

SUMMER COOLER

🍃 Fill a tall glass with crushed ice, pour the juice of 1 lime or ½ lemon on top, then fill the glass with carbonated mineral water.

ENGLISH PUB SPECIAL

🍃 Place a glass in a freezer for 1 hour, then put in it several dashes of Angostura bitters, crushed ice, a piece of lemon zest, and fill the glass with bitter lemon.

PAPAYA DELIGHT

🍃 Peel and core a papaya, then cut it into pieces and add it to a glass of low-calorie ginger ale.

🍃 If you have a blender, beat the papaya for 2 seconds. Or crush the papaya and beat it with an electric mixer until it is smooth. Pour the fruit over crushed ice in white wine glasses. Top each glass with 3 slices of fresh lime. Fill the glass with ginger ale.

LEMON-LIME COOLER

🍃 This is as simple as can be. Put the juice of 1 lime and ½ a lemon, 2 tsp (10 mL) sugar and 1 cup (250 mL) crushed ice in a cocktail shaker. Cover and shake well for 1 minute. Pour into a very large glass. Fill with ice-cold ginger ale or bitter lemon.

MILK SHAKES

🍃 Put 3 or 4 ice cubes in the blender jar. Cover and slowly blend until the ice is crushed. Turn off the blender and add 2 cups (500 mL) of water. Cover and blend at high speed. Without stopping the blender, remove the feeder plug and add 4 to 6 tbsp (60 to 90 mL) of powdered milk, another 1 cup (250 mL) of water and an egg. Flavor with one of the following combinations:

1 tbsp (15 mL) strawberry jam or sugar, to taste;
1 tbsp (15 mL) cocoa powder, ½

banana and sugar to taste;
1 tbsp (15 mL) instant coffee
and sugar to taste;
1 peeled and pitted peach and
sugar to taste;
½ cup (125 mL) fresh berries
(strawberries, raspberries or blueberries) and sugar to taste.

❧ Blend for 1 second and serve.

MILK PUNCH

1 whole egg
2 egg yolks
3 tbsp (45 mL) honey
pinch of salt
2 cups (500 mL) milk
2 egg whites
2 tbsp (30 mL) honey
ground cinnamon

❧ Beat together the whole egg,
egg yolks and first quantity of
honey. When light and fluffy, add
the milk and stir vigorously.
Refrigerate for 12 hours.
❧ Beat the egg whites stiff with
the salt and second quantity of
honey. When firm and smooth,
fold the egg whites lightly into
the first mixture, so that small
blobs of egg white float on top of
the punch. Sprinkle with cinnamon to taste and serve.

ORANGE MILK

zest of 1 orange
2 cups (500 mL) boiling milk
2 tbsp (30 mL) sugar

❧ Wash and peel the orange as
thinly as possible, so that the
white pith is eliminated. Place
the zest in the blender jar.

❧ Pour scalded milk over the
fruit, then add sugar. Mix well.
Cover and chill. Serve very cold.

TEN A.M. REVIVAL

*A Prince Edward Island potato
grower gave me this recipe, which
he said he had been using for 32
summers. He used whole milk into
which he stirred 1 cup (250 mL)
powdered skim milk. Prepare this
beverage at breakfast time, then
refrigerate. Serve quite cold
instead of tea or coffee, along with
an oatmeal cookie.*

4 cups (1 L) milk
1 tbsp (15 mL) honey
1 tsp (5 mL) anise seeds

❧ Bring the milk of your choice
to a boil with the honey and anise
seed. Strain or not, depending on
whether you like to munch the
seeds (which are very good).
❧ Serve hot when the weather is
cold. Serve cold when the day is
hot and humid.

RED BUTTERMILK

*If you have a blender, it will take
just 2 seconds to prepare this
creamy delicious buttermilk. But
its great taste will not be dimin-
ished if you make it the old-fashioned way.*

1 medium banana
1 tsp (5 mL) bottled lemon juice
½ cup (125 mL) fresh
raspberries
6 tbsp (90 mL) clear honey
or sugar
6 cups (1.5 L) cold buttermilk

❧ Peel and mash the bananas.
Add the lemon juice and stir
together. Press the raspberries
through a sieve, over the bananas.
Add the honey or sugar. Mix
everything together. Stir into a
pitcher of the cold buttermilk.

Hot Chocolate with Honey

[715]

HOT CHOCOLATE WITH HONEY

2 squares unsweetened chocolate
1 cup (250 mL) water
¼ cup (50 mL) honey
pinch of salt
3 cups (750 mL) milk

❧ Place the chocolate and the water in a small saucepan. Stirring frequently, cook the mixture over low heat until the chocolate is melted. Add the honey and salt and boil for 3 minutes, stirring constantly.

❧ Add the milk gradually, then heat slowly. Beat for a few moments with a hand beater until the chocolate is foamy. Serve.

CHOCOLATE MILK

❧ *Chocolate Sauce* (see recipe on page 602) can be used to make a truly delicious chocolate milk. Put 1 tbsp (15 mL) of the sauce in a glass. Fill the glass with milk, stir and serve.

❧ To prepare this drink in a blender with powdered milk, put 1 tbsp (15 mL) of chocolate sauce, 2 tbsp (30 mL) powdered milk and 2 cups (500 mL) water into the jar. Cover, then blend for 2 seconds at slow speed. Serve.

CHOCOLATE SYRUP

1¼ cups (300 mL) cocoa powder
1 cup (250 mL) sugar
½ tsp (2 mL) salt
pinch of allspice
pinch of cinnamon
1½ cups (375 mL) boiling water
½ cup (125 mL) honey
2 tsp (10 mL) vanilla

❧ Place the cocoa, sugar, salt, allspice and cinnamon in a saucepan. Mix together, then add the boiling water. Boil the mixture for 5 minutes while stirring almost non-stop. Remove from the heat and let cool.

❧ Add the honey and the vanilla. Pour the mixture into a jar. Cover and refrigerate. This recipe makes 2¼ cups (550 mL) of chocolate syrup.

❧ To serve, heat ¼ cup (50 mL) of chocolate syrup with 2 cups (500 mL) of milk. Beat the mixture for a few moments with a hand beater, then serve. To serve the cocoa cold, all you have to do is add the same quantity of syrup to very cold milk and beat together until you get a perfect blend.

Viennese Hot Chocolate

VIENNESE HOT CHOCOLATE

2 squares unsweetened chocolate
1 cup (250 mL) water
3 tbsp (45 mL) sugar
pinch of salt
3 cups (750 mL) milk
whipping cream

❧ Put the chocolate and water in a saucepan. Over low heat, stir often until the chocolate is melted. Add the sugar and salt to the chocolate. Bring to a boil, then let simmer for 3 minutes.

❧ Add the milk gradually and heat. When you are ready to serve, beat with a hand beater so that the chocolate becomes foamy. Pour into cups and top with whipped cream.

HOT MOCHA CHOCOLATE

❧ Follow the same procedure as for *Viennese Hot Chocolate*, but substitute 1 cup (250 mL) of strong coffee for the 1 cup (250 mL) of water.

ORANGE HOT CHOCOLATE

❧ Add to *Viennese Hot Chocolate* 1 tbsp (15 mL) grated orange zest along with the sugar.

MINTED HOT CHOCOLATE

❧ Add to *Viennese Hot Chocolate* 1 to 2 tbsp (15 to 30 mL) minced fresh mint along with the sugar.

FRENCH CHOCOLATE

1 cup (250 mL) sugar
¾ cup (175 mL) cocoa powder
1 cup (250 mL) water
1 cup (250 mL) whipping cream
hot or cold milk

❧ Mix together the sugar and cocoa. Add the water. Mix well and cook the mixture over low heat, stirring often, to make a fairly thick syrup; this will take approximately 8 to 10 minutes. Refrigerate.
❧ Whip the cream, then add it to the cooled chocolate mixture.

French Chocolate

Mix together well. Pour into a glass jar, cover and refrigerate.
❧ To serve, place 3 or 4 tbsp (45 to 60 mL) of the chocolate in a cup or glass, then fill the cup or glass with cold or hot milk. Mix well and serve.

INFUSIONS AND DECOCTIONS

Tender plants and flowers are usually used as infusions. The plants or flowers are placed in boiling water, then the saucepan or kettle is removed immediately from the heat and the infusion is left to steep for a few minutes before serving.
❧ Unlike infusions, decoctions are simmered for 5 to 10 minutes in the boiling water in order to extract the flavor and ingredients. Decocting is generally used for tougher plants, barks and roots.
❧ Whichever method you use, the leaves, flowers, bark and roots of plants produce light, tasty beverages that have also earned reputations as universal remedies.

MINT
Hot, it activates digestion; chilled, it soothes and calms the stomach. It has a light flavor and it leaves an impression of freshness. Treat as an infusion.

VERVAIN
It has a slightly acidic taste. It stimulates the digestion and increases the appetite. Treat as an infusion.

CHAMOMILE
If you do not care for its bittersweet taste, drink it with some honey or with a slice of lemon. It calms the stomach. Treat as an infusion.

[717]

STAR ANISE

Most effective against stomach and intestinal gas. Delicious and refreshing taste. Treat as an infusion.

ROSEMARY

Only 1 tsp (5 mL) per cup (250 mL) is all that is needed for an infusion; excellent for liver ailments, especially if taken very hot. Sweeten with honey.

RUSSIAN TEA

1¼ ounces (35 g) cinnamon sticks
1¼ ounces (35 g) whole cloves
zest of 1 lemon
zest of 1 orange
¾ cup (175 mL) honey
2 cups (500 mL) cold water
⅓ cup (75 mL) black tea leaves
20 cups (5 L) boiling water
juice of 3 oranges
juice of 6 lemons

Place the cinnamon, cloves, orange zest, lemon zest, honey and cold water in a saucepan. Boil for 10 minutes, then cover. Remove from the heat and let stand for 1 hour, then strain the liquid through a very fine sieve.

Put the tea leaves in the boiling water, then cover and let stand 5 minutes over very low heat. The tea must not boil.

Add to the tea the orange juice and lemon juice, along with the liquid from the strained spices. Serve very hot, with some honey or sugar on the side.

This recipe makes 45 cups.

FRUIT TEA

ice cubes
6 lemon slices, unpeeled
6 orange slices, unpeeled
4 cups (1 L) strong tea, cold
1 bunch fresh mint
honey or sugar to taste

Fill 6 large glasses with ice cubes. Place in each glass a slice of orange and a slice of lemon. Fill the glass with cold tea.

Garnish each glass with a sprig of mint. Serve the honey or sugar on the side.

MINT TEA

2 cups (500 mL) boiling water
1 bunch fresh mint leaves or 4 tbsp (60 mL) dried mint
4 cups (1 L) cold water
1 lemon, unpeeled, thinly sliced
sugar

Pour boiling water over the mint. Cover and steep for 30 minutes in the top of a double boiler over hot water.

Strain out the mint leaves, then add the cold water and lemon slices to the liquid. Pour into large glasses filled with ice. Sweeten to taste.

IRISH COFFEE

This delicious hot drink, taken in little sips through the thick whipped cream, delights its many admirers. What could be more appropriate for a toast at Saint Patrick's Day parties than Irish coffee!

3 to 5 tbsp (45 to 75 mL) Irish whiskey per serving
1 to 2 tsp (5 to 10 mL) sugar per serving
strong coffee
whipped cream

Warm large coffee cups or mugs in hot water.

Pour whisky into each cup according to the desired strength.

Fill each cup or mug with coffee. Drop a large spoonful of whipped cream into each cup. Do not stir. Do not change the order of the ingredients.

CAFÉ BRULOT

¾ cup (175 mL) cognac or brandy
6 sugar cubes
1 cinnamon stick
6 whole cloves
zest of 1 orange, thinly sliced
zest of 1 lemon, thinly sliced
2 to 3 cups (500 to 750 mL) hot black coffee

Place the brandy, sugar, cinnamon, cloves, and orange and lemon zests in a chafing dish. Heat slowly, while stirring, just long enough to warm up the brandy, but do not let it boil.

Light the hot brandy mixture, let flame a few seconds, then start pouring the very hot strong coffee over the flaming brandy. Use a ladle to pour the mixture into coffee cups as soon as the flame dies down. Serve.

INDEX

Page numbers in *italics* indicate recipe pictures. Page numbers in **bold** indicate general techniques for specific foods and step-by-step technique illustrations for individual recipes. Recipe titles appear in *italics*.

A

Green Cabbage with Apples,
394–395
Jelly, 682
with Meat dishes
   Apple-stuffed Loin of Pork, 242
   Chicken de la Vallée d'Auge,
    288–289
   Normandy-Style Roast Loin of
    Pork, 239–240
   Pheasant Normandy, 322–324,
    323
   Seafood Salad, 133
Muffins, 652
Old-fashioned Green Tomatoes, 421
Pickled Crab Apples, 668
Salads
   Apple and Cabbage Salad, 393
   Autumn Salad, 387–388
   Seafood Salad, 133
   Spanish Salad, 388
Sweet and Sour Cabbage, 395
Apricots:
Chutney, 666
Four-Fruit Compote, 499–500
Glaze *(Savarin Cake),* 567
Jam Filling, 610
Pickled Apricots, 668
Pies
   Deluxe Apricot Pie, 527–528
   Dried Peach or Apricot Pie, 528
Sauce, 604
Soufflé, 586
Armenian Lamb Casserole, 229
Armenian Lamb Stew, 229–231, **230**
Armenian-Style Green Beans, 415
Aromatic Salt, 44
Aromatic Seeds, 38
Artichokes, **407**
Eggs and Artichokes Italian Style, 82
Florentine, 407–408
Greek-Style Artichokes, 408
Parisian-Style Artichokes, 407
Asparagus, **408–409**
au Gratin, 408, 409
Cream of Asparagus Soup, 112
Flemish-Style Asparagus, 410
Milanaise, 409
Parisian-Style Asparagus, 410
Polish-Style Asparagus, 409–410
Aspics:
Basic Aspic, 88
Cucumber, 88
Egg, 89

Meat, 89
Seafood, 88
Tomato, 88, 89
Atlantic Fish Cakes, 136
Aurore Sauce, 48
Australian Filet of Venison, 332–333
Authentic Lobster Newburg, 148–150,
149
Autumn Salad, 387–388
Avocados:
Cantaloupe Salad, 498
Salad, 388–389
with Seafood
   Seafood Avocado, 151
   Shrimp Stuffed with Avocado,
    152
Bacon:
Bacon, Chicken-Liver, and
Mushroom Sandwich, 377
Biscuits, 649
and Eggs, 365
Eggs in a Nest, 368–369
Potatoes with Smoked Pork, 271
Quiche Lorraine, 485–486
Rabbit with Bacon, 318, 320
Spit-roasted Bacon, 271
Baked Alaska, 591–592
Baked beans:
with Apple Sugar, 466–467
Canadian Baked Beans, 467
Old-fashioned Baked Beans, 466
Québec Baked Beans, 466
Baking powder biscuits. *See* Biscuits
Bananas:
au Gratin, 510–511
Banana Bars, 627
Fritters, 661
Mother's Banana Cake, 558
Quick Banana Bread, 648, 649
Sautéed Bananas, 510, 511
Waffles, 655
Barbecued dishes, **28–29**
Beef
   Barbecued Steak, 165–166
Chicken
   Barbecued Half Chicken, 279
   Broiled Chicken in Barbecue
    Sauce, 280
   Lemon Barbecued Chicken, 279
   Oven Barbecued Chicken,
    279–280
Corn, 411

Duck
Barbecued Duck, 313
Fish, **124**
Barbecued Fish Steaks, 132
Trout Barbecued in Bacon, 143
Kebabs, **222–223**
Lamb
Barbecued Lamb Chops, 226
Barbecued Leg of Lamb,
  220–222, **221**
Barbecued Shoulder of Lamb
  en Papillote, 228
Kebabs, **222–223**
  Barbecued Ground-Lamb
   Kebabs, 224
  Lamb Kebabs, 223
  Persian Kebabs, 224
  Shish Kebabs, 223
Sardinian Shoulder of Lamb,
  227
Pork
Barbecued Baby Spareribs, 249
Pressure-Cooker Barbecued
  Spareribs, 249
Potatoes, 457–458
Sauces
Barbecue Sauce, 64
Barbecue sauce, 280
Barbecue Sauce for Chicken, 64
Barbecue Sauce for Sausages, 65
Fast and Easy Barbecue Sauce,
  66
Lemon Barbecue Sauce, 64–65
Smoky Barbecue Sauce, 64
Tomato Barbecue Sauce, 65
Vermont Barbecue Sauce, 65–66
Wine Barbecue Sauce, 65
Barley:
Old Fashioned Barley Soup, 105
Bars and Squares, 626–627
See also Cookies
Banana Bars, 627
Brown Sugar Bars, 627
Brownies, 628–629
Brownies
Brownies, 628–629
Chocolate Brownies, 563–564
Fudge Cake Squares, 564
Honey-Chocolate Brownies,
  564–565
Delicious Jam Squares, 628
Fig Bars, 627
Filled Bars, 627

Page numbers in *italics* indicate recipe pictures. Page numbers in **bold** indicate general technique

[720]

fic foods and step-by-step technique illustrations for individual recipes. Recipe titles appear in *italics.*

Page numbers in *italics* indicate recipe pictures. Page numbers in **bold** indicate general technique

ic foods and step-by-step technique illustrations for individual recipes. Recipe titles appear in *italics*.

Page numbers in *italics* indicate recipe pictures. Page numbers in **bold** indicate general techniqu ic foods and step-by-step technique illustrations for individual recipes. Recipe titles appear in *italics*.

Page numbers in *italics* indicate recipe pictures. Page numbers in **bold** indicate general technique

fic foods and step-by-step technique illustrations for individual recipes. Recipe titles appear in *italics*.

Page numbers in *italics* indicate recipe pictures. Page numbers in **bold** indicate general technique

fic foods and step-by-step technique illustrations for individual recipes. Recipe titles appear in *italics*.

Page numbers in *italics* indicate recipe pictures. Page numbers in **bold** indicate general techniques

fic foods and step-by-step technique illustrations for individual recipes. Recipe titles appear in *italics*.

G

Page numbers in *italics* indicate recipe pictures. Page numbers in **bold** indicate general techniques fo

H

fic foods and step-by-step technique illustrations for individual recipes. Recipe titles appear in *italics*.

Page numbers in *italics* indicate recipe pictures. Page numbers in **bold** indicate general technique

...fic foods and step-by-step technique illustrations for individual recipes. Recipe titles appear in *italics.*

Page numbers in *italics* indicate recipe pictures. Page numbers in **bold** indicate general techniques

Page numbers in *italics* indicate recipe pictures. Page numbers in **bold** indicate general technique.

N

O

cific foods and step-by-step technique illustrations for individual recipes. Recipe titles appear in *italics*.

Page numbers in *italics* indicate recipe pictures. Page numbers in **bold** indicate general techniques

ific foods and step-by-step technique illustrations for individual recipes. Recipe titles appear in *italics*.

Page numbers in *italics* indicate recipe pictures. Page numbers in **bold** indicate general techniques

ific foods and step-by-step technique illustrations for individual recipes. Recipe titles appear in *italics*.

Q

Page numbers in *italics* indicate recipe pictures. Page numbers in **bold** indicate general techniques

...ific foods and step-by-step technique illustrations for individual recipes. Recipe titles appear in *italics*.

Page numbers in *italics* indicate recipe pictures. Page numbers in **bold** indicate general techniques

ific foods and step-by-step technique illustrations for individual recipes. Recipe titles appear in *italics*.

Page numbers in *italics* indicate recipe pictures. Page numbers in **bold** indicate general technique.

cific foods and step-by-step technique illustrations for individual recipes. Recipe titles appear in *italics*.

Page numbers in *italics* indicate recipe pictures. Page numbers in **bold** indicate general techniques

cific foods and step-by-step technique illustrations for individual recipes. Recipe titles appear in *italics.*

Page numbers in *italics* indicate recipe pictures. Page numbers in **bold** indicate general techniques

cific foods and step-by-step technique illustrations for individual recipes. Recipe titles appear in *italics.*